1001 ALBUMS
YOU MUST HEAR BEFORE YOU DIE

GENERAL EDITOR ROBERT DIMERY

PREFACE BY MICHAEL LYDON

A Quintessence Book

Published by Cassell Illustrated
a division of Octopus Publishing Group Limited
2–4 Heron Quays, London E14 4JP
A Hachette Livre UK company

A CIP catalogue record for this book is available from the British Library.

ISBN-13: 9781844036240
QUIN.KALB3

This book was designed and produced by
Quintessence
226 City Road
London EC1V 2TT

First edition published 2005
This edition published 2008

Update Editor   Philip Hall

Assistant Editors   Chris Bryans, Marianne Canty,
                        Jenny Doubt, Bruno MacDonald,
                        Frank Ritter, Chris Shade, Rod Stanley,
                        Victoria Wiggins, David Hutter
Design   Jon Wainright

Editorial Director Jane Laing
Publisher   Tristan de Lancey

Originated in Singapore by Pica Digital Pte Ltd.
Printed in China by SNP Leefung Printers Ltd.

1001 ALBUMS
YOU MUST HEAR BEFORE YOU DIE

Contents

Preface

By Michael Lydon, Founding Editor of *Rolling Stone*

Red-letter dates in the history of recorded sound:

1877   Thomas Edison, looking for a way to record telephone messages, invents the "phonograph" and predicts correctly that soon every home will have one.

1925   Records become electric, with microphones used for recording and loudspeakers for playback.

1948   Ampex introduces editable magnetic tape recording. First big customer: Bing Crosby.

Which is where I come in, a kid in Boston, Massachusetts, as the 1950s began. We had a Victrola phonograph in the living room and, in a cabinet beneath, thick, black, shellac records so fragile I was not allowed to touch them until I was older. Mom and Dad bought a few records of single hit songs, but mostly we had "record albums" that looked like photo albums: paper sleeves bound between cardboard covers that held three, four, or more discs. Turning over or changing these every four minutes, we heard Beethoven symphonies, *Peter And The Wolf*, and *Porgy And Bess*.

Then, overnight it seemed, everything changed. Single discs became little with a big hole in the middle, spinning at 45 revolutions per minute. Albums became light and unbreakable 33⅓ rpm long-playing (LP) discs that sounded much better, lasted 20 minutes each side, and came tucked inside classy covers that had photos and liner notes that you could study as you listened. *Benny Goodman At Carnegie Hall*, *My Fair Lady*, and *Errol Garner's Concert By The Sea*—these early LP albums burned their way into my youthful soul.

At first, pop albums were mostly no more than collections of hit singles, but jazz and rock 'n' roll musicians loved the rich possibilities offered by the LP's length and "high fidelity" sound. Just as composers had once created sustained statements in the form of symphonies, they began to use LPs to issue personal musical manifestos. Frank Sinatra's *In The Wee Small Hours* (1955) and Ray Charles' *Genius Hits The Road* (1960) stand as early examples of what we later called "concept albums."

With the new decade, *Billboard* reported that durable LPs had outpaced disposable 45s, 6 million to 4.5 million sold—in the United

States, that is. In the UK, it took a further eight years for LP sales to surpass sales of singles and EPs (extended play discs with four or five songs). The output of many Sixties pop stars grew in a classic curve from hit-single beginnings to "album artist" maturity. Their audience followed suit, graduating from singles to LPs, which became loved and treasured possessions to be carefully boxed and carried from home to college to first apartment. Whether *Disraeli Gears* or *Aretha: Lady Soul*, albums became mind-opening milestones in millions of lives: we were what we listened to. We followed the tumultuous cultural debates of the 1960s through albums—Bob Dylan answering The Beatles' sumptuous *Sergeant Pepper* . . . with his acerbic *John Wesley Harding*, The Rolling Stones renouncing the psychedelic excesses of *Their Satanic Majesties Request* with the back-to-basics *Beggars Banquet*. If you still fail to understand album mania, read Nick Hornby's highly entertaining novel *High Fidelity* (or see the movie), and you will.

Occasionally, when one LP could not hold enough music, artists issued "double albums"—some pompous monstrosities, others popular masterpieces such as Dylan's *Blonde On Blonde* and The Who's *Tommy*. Single or double, the classic LP album ruled the roost for 30 years, long enough to transmit progressive rock, punk, disco, and early rap to the world. Then, in 1985, a revolutionary new format arrived: the digital compact disc. CDs played for an hour or more, had a brilliant, hiss-less, scratch-free sound, and never wore out. Yet CDs had two drawbacks. First, being much smaller than LPs, their photo-and-notes packaging had less graphic impact; and second, just as guitarists preferred tube over transistor amps, discerning audiophiles preferred the warmer sound of LPs—which captured an "analog" of the music's sound wave in its vinyl grooves—to the cooler sound of CDs that "digitized" sound into long strings of computer code imprinted on shiny glass.

The vinyl Luddites howled in vain. CDs, their sound rapidly improving, began outselling LPs in 1988, and by the mid-1990s LPs had virtually disappeared from the new record market, although countless great LPs were subsequently reissued on CD, often with bonus tracks. Music lovers everywhere came to agree that a CD could be an album—a new kind of album, perhaps, but a similarly pleasing medium for meaningful musical statements. (Indeed, the uninterrupted play that CDs allowed meant that some LPs worked better in this format—think of Marvin Gaye's *What's Going On*, heard best as a continuous song suite.) On the other hand, CDs posed a challenge to the traditional album concept. Since CDs contain music as digital information, their music comes to consumers in computer-friendly form. Personal computers, ubiquitous by 2000, allowed digitized music to travel the world via the Internet, and listeners began grabbing music they loved song-by-song, downloading tunes from legal and illegal websites, then burning them on their own CDs and sharing them with friends. These trends (still changing as I write) have cut into the album's traditional dominance over singles. But unsigned bands still yearn to make album deals, and most fans still feel that to get the real work of art, they have to own and hold the actual CD made and sold by their favorite band.

The record album, now half a century old, has long since established itself as a major object and experience of popular culture. If singles are like magazines and TV shows, albums are like books and movies. They carry a certain weight and influence: *The Godfather*, *Thriller*, and *Bridget Jones's Diary* all touched countless lives. For musicians, making an album poses the same kind of challenge that faces writers and film directors; it demands the same reach for excellence, and excites the same ambitions for riches and renown. Although often collaborative, albums tend to have one auteur in charge—by no means always the lead singer or player— and (usually, even today) a producer working behind the board. Like books and movies, albums can come in familiar forms, sit comfortably in well-known genres, and still surprise us with fresh content and original styles. When an album, by hook, crook, or musical magic, strikes a responsive chord, its music pours through an interlinked media network to a wide world of listeners, starting new fashions in clothing and slang, and turning onetime hipsters into fuddy-duddies who hate the new sound that has got all the kids dancing.

On first listening, albums unfold as books and movies unfold, each track (or chapter or scene) carrying us further into unknown territory, past terrifying peaks and pools of calm. Over weeks and months we explore the album, hearing new beauties with each replay. That, indeed, may be the biggest difference between how we experience books and movies and albums: even if we love a book or movie, we are unlikely to read or see it more than three or four times. Albums stay with us for months, often years. We hear them hundreds if not thousands of times, though seldom at full attention; we absorb their licks and hooks by osmosis until we find ourselves singing and air-guitaring along with the music, even when we are only hearing it in our heads.

The love that people have for their vinyl treasures and stacks of CDs is in itself strong proof that albums can be worthy works of art. As a college kid surviving on summer jobs and scholarships, I spent hours flipping through bins of LPs trying to decide which was worth my precious $2.99. Who was this Bob Dylan who wrote nutty poems for his liner notes? In the New Year of 1968, in the bare attic office of the brand-new *Rolling Stone*, we listened to *Magical Mystery Tour* (released as an album in the United States), "All You Need Is Love" resounding in our heads. Later that same year, we lined up in San Francisco at Tower Records (just opened) to buy the "White Album." Right after Ray Charles died, I heard his last album, *Genius Loves Company*, and burst into tears.

We dance, drive, argue, laugh, and make love to albums; their music enters our lives, our souls. Some we may later find juvenile, but maybe we were juvenile back then too. Whether it is an Eddie Cochran, Fats Domino, James Brown, David Bowie, Led Zep, Funkadelic, or Nine Inch Nails album does not matter. "Different strokes for different folks," as Sly Stone sang on one album back in 1973.

It is time to close the preface and open the book. I know you will discover dozens of your favorites within this great galaxy of albums, and I hope that while flipping through its pages you will be inspired to seek out dozens more soon-to-be favorites that, without *1001 Albums You Must Hear Before You Die*, you might never have heard.

Michael Lydon

New York

Introduction

By Robert Dimery, General Editor

Albums provide the soundtrack to our lives—and the more obsessive music fans among us would not have it any other way. Moreover, as a skim through *1001 Albums You Must Hear Before You Die* reveals, albums also track the breathtakingly swift rise and fall of musical tastes in the past half-century.

The scope of this book affords the reader the chance to re-examine accepted critical assessment of the musical high and low points during those 50 years. The 1970s are frequently dismissed as a badly dressed poor relation of the vibrant '60s, but how could any decade that gave rise to heavy metal, glam, reggae, disco, punk, new wave, post-punk, and Marvin Gaye's *What's Going On* get such a bad press? What is more, some years, such as 1967, are absurdly overburdened with classic album releases.

Of course, the overall choice of albums featured here is highly subjective. As editor, I take a lot of the responsibility for compiling the list, although the energetic input of Project Director Tristan de Lancey cannot be praised highly enough. And many of the writers you are about to read provided invaluable help and advice too, steering us clear of the rocks of mediocrity and toward the straits of the sublime.

Some of you may question that there are multiple entries for a number of artists. To my mind, an uncommonly gifted songwriter such as Joni Mitchell, Elvis Costello, or Nick Cave easily warrants such attention, in order to convey some idea of the breadth and development of his or her work. You may also find that the same artist inspires very different views in our writers. This strikes me as an excellent thing—we are aiming for informed, articulate individual opinions here, not bland consistency.

In this book you will also find a tremendous amount of fascinating trivia about the genesis of these records. Which album's release was delayed as a mark of respect after President John F. Kennedy was assassinated? What inspired Paul Simon's "Mother And Child Reunion?" Which vegetable does Paul McCartney "play" on The Super Furry Animals' *Rings Around The World*? Read on and find out.

One of the best things about putting together this survey was that it threw up a whole heap of surprises. The 1950s may have marked the dawn of rock 'n' roll but, in terms of high-quality, consistent LPs, the jazz of that period beats the early rockers hands down. (Honorable exceptions include

Little Richard and Fats Domino—each of their albums discussed here is a joy from start to finish.) Likewise, disco outsold punk by a mile in the singles charts, but aside from a handful of artists (the sublime Chic, Michael Jackson's wonderful *Off The Wall*), disco artists did not cut many classic albums.

"What about *Saturday Night Fever*?", you may ask. Well, you won't find compilations or soundtracks by "various artists" in this book, although we have made room for soundtracks that consist entirely of original material composed by a particular artist. Otherwise, we would not have been able to tell you about *Superfly*, *Shaft*, or *Purple Rain*—three milestones in pop and some of the best work by Curtis Mayfield, Isaac Hayes, and Prince respectively.

The release details (label, date, track listing, and so on) relate to the album as it was first released, in the artist's country of origin. Thus, for any Beatles album featured herein, the track running order given is that of the UK (Parlophone) release, and not that of its U.S. (Capitol) equivalent.

We have also taken the step of excluding any bonus tracks from the track listings, as these were not part of the original package. The key tracks, in the writer's opinion, are marked by a ▶, and if a particularly strong track was later added to a reissue of the album, thereby making it an even more mouthwatering prospect, we have usually alluded to it. ("Teenage Kicks" was not included on the first version of The Undertones' debut, for example, but not to mention it at all would have been churlish in the extreme.)

Wherever possible, we have also mentioned who was behind the art direction for the album sleeves. You will notice that certain names crop up again and again, visionaries responsible for some of the most iconic covers in popular music. Then again, if you look back to the 1950s, art directors were very often unsung heroes, members of a record company's art department who neither expected nor received credit.

Finally, we have striven to ensure that all the albums listed in this book are currently available to buy. In some cases, the recommended album has been reissued on CD together with another album by the same artist.

I hope you find that the cross-section of artists and genres contained herein makes for a stimulating introduction to some of the greatest albums released over the past 50 years. I have learned an astonishing amount myself in the months it has taken to bring this book to fruition— and one thing above all: music is one thing you can never overdose on.

Contributors

Manish Agarwal (MA) has written for the TV and music sections of London's *Time Out*, and for the *Times, Sunday Times, Kerrang!, Mojo, Q* and independent music magazines.

Leanne Alberghini (LA) has written for *X-Press* magazine in Perth, and most recently in Melbourne for *Inpress* magazine.

Theunis Bates (TB) is urban editor at worldpop.com and contributor to *Touch* magazine. He also reports on popular music for *Time*.

Mark Bennett (MBe) lives in London. He has written about music for Guinness and the BBC. He likes Kraftwerk, reading old copies of *Look-In*, and having his dinner.

Mark Blacklock (MBl) was music editor of *Bizarre* magazine during the 1990s and has contributed to the *Guardian*, the *Telegraph*, and numerous magazines. He has once put legendary theatre maverick Ken Campbell on a bill with Skam Records weirdoes Wevie Stonder.

Keeley Bolger (KBo) is a freelance journalist who has written for Channel 4, BBC, Holy Moly and *The Sun*.

Mary Boukouvalas (MBo) is a photo-journalist from Melbourne, Australia. She is a writer and photographer for Melbourne's *Beat* magazine and the Canada-based website blistering.com.

James Bradley (JB) is a Belfast-Born, London-based vinyl junkie who worked on the *Book of British Hit Singles & Albums* for seven years, and now works in Business Affairs for a major record label.

Chris Bryans (CB) contributes to *Record Collector* magazine. Obviously, this leaves him open to accusations of being an anorak. His specialist area is punk, so he decorated said garment with safety pins in a bid to preserve his street credibility.

Kenneth Burns (KB) lives in Madison, Wisconsin, USA, where he is an editor and writer at the weekly newspaper *Isthmus*. Having grown up in Nashville, he also writes and sings country music, naturally.

Garth Cartwright (GC) is the New Zealand-born, London-based author of *Princes Amongst Men: Journeys With Gypsy Musicians*. He has written for the *Guardian, FRoots, Uncut*, and *Songlines*.

Stevie Chick (SC) has contributed to *Melody Maker, Mojo, Kerrang!*, London's *Evening Standard, The Times, Sleazenation, NME*, and *The Stranger*. He also started *Careless Talk Costs Lives* and co-edits *Loose Lips Sink Ships*.

Jason Chow (JC) writes for the *National Post* in Toronto, Canada, and is a member of a local band The Good Soldiers. Their first album will be released in 2006.

Karen Conrad (KC) has contributed to *Guitar, Beat*, the *Age*, the *Herald Sun*, and numerous Australian music magazines. She is currently completing a book of intimate celebrity interviews.

David Crawford (DC) spent his formative years hanging around record shops. He has written for *Screen International, Televisual, Radio Times*, and the Press Association.

Stephen Dalton (SD) writes about music and film for the *Times, Uncut, NME, The Scotsman* and other publications. He does not live in London, has never written a book, and does not have an amusing fount of anecdotes about sipping cocktails in exotic locations with Bono and Madonna.

Jamie Dickson (JDi) has been a music writer with the *Daily Telegraph* in London since 1999. Before that he studied rock and pop at Leeds University, and he has been a gigging musician since his early teens.

Robert Dimery (RD) is a freelance writer and editor and has worked on a variety of books, including Tony Wilson's *24 Hour Party People, Pump Up The Volume: A History Of House*, and *Breaking Into Heaven: The Rise And Fall Of The Stone Roses*. He has also contributed to books on classic albums and classic singles, and has worked for a variety of magazines, including London's *Time Out* and *Vogue*.

John Doran (JDo) has been a journalist for eight years, during which he has written for magazines such as *Loaded, Marie Claire*, and *Later*. He was the launch associate editor of *Bang* and has written for *Playlouder, Disorder, Bullitt, Metal Hammer, Classic Rock, Plan B*, and *Rip & Burn*. His work as a court reporter and news and features writer has appeared in many UK national papers.

George Durbalau (GD) is editor-in-chief of *Sunete*, Romania's most important music magazine. Prior to this, he was editor at *Mixexpress* magazine, and a DJ at Radio Special where he hosted several daily rock shows.

Daryl Easlea (DE) is former deputy editor of *Record Collector*. His work has also been published in *Mojo, Mojo Collections*, various *Q* and *Mojo* specials, *Uncut*, the *Guardian*, the *Independent*, the *Glasgow Herald*, *The Encyclopaedia of Popular Music*, and the bbc.co.uk website. He also compiles and annotates CDs, DJs, broadcasts, and was born to dance. He is author of *Everybody Dance: Chic & The Politics Of Disco*.

Patrick Emery (PE) writes for the Melbourne weekly *Beat* magazine. He is also a regular contributor to the Sydney garage punk webzine I94Bar.com and FasterLouder.com.au.

Ross Fortune (RF) is former music editor of London's *Time Out*, where he worked for some ten years. He is now based in Austin, Texas.

Will Fulford-Jones (WF-J) spends his days editing travel guides for London's *Time Out*, and his evenings writing about music.

Andrew Gilbert (AG) is a freelance writer who reports on jazz and Brazilian, West African and Afro-Caribbean music for the *San Francisco Chronicle*, the *Boston Globe*, the *San Jose Mercury News*, the *Contra Costa Times*, and the *San Diego Union Tribune*. He also managed the Jazz Bakery in Los Angeles in the mid 1990s.

Jaime Gonzalo (JG) began his writing career with the Spanish rock underground press in the 1970s. Today he is co-editor of the leading Spanish rock monthly *Ruta 66*, established in 1985.

Lino Portela Gutiérrez (LPG) works for *Rolling Stone*, Spain, and contributes to *Tentaciones*, a music supplement for *El Pais*. He has also worked for the Spanish music TV station 40TV and Antena3 Televisión.

Jim Harrington (JiH) is the pop music and jazz critic for the *Oakland Tribune* and ANG Newspapers chain. His work has appeared in such publications as *Rolling Stone*, *Razor Magazine*, and in U.S. newspapers.

Jon Harrington (JoH) is a staff writer at MTV. He also contributes regularly to *Mojo*.

Sophie Harris (SH) writes for *Mojo* and London's *Time Out*, as well as pirate music mag *Loose Lips Sink Ships*. She presents a guide to the greatest singles ever made on BBC 6 Music, and broadcasts on the BBC World Service, LBC, and Radio 5.

Michael Heatley (MH) edited the *History of Rock* partwork. Since then he has written over 100 sport, music, and TV books, edited *Record Buyer* music magazine, written numerous sleeve notes, and contributed to *Record Collector*, *Classic Rock*, *Guitar*, *Music Week*, and *Radio Times*. He edited the acclaimed *Virgin Rock Encyclopedia* and, in late 2004, made the best-seller charts with *John Peel: A Life In Music*.

Alexandra Heller-Nicholas (AH-N) edits *Fiend Magazine*, Australia's largest dark alternative music and culture magazine. While she specializes in goth, industrial, and electronic music, her tastes are wide and varied. She also contributes regularly to Melbourne's *Beat* magazine.

Claire Hughes (CH) is a freelance music and travel writer for London's *Time Out*, *Dazed & Confused*, *DJ Magazine*, and other publications. She is the author of *Waking Up In Chicago*, a music-based travel guide to the city (Sanctuary).

Tom Hughes (TH) is a writer and sub-editor who has worked for several publications in the UK, including *Select*, the *Independent*, *NME*, and currently the *Guardian*, as well as contributing to several websites and student magazines.

David Hutcheon (DH) is a regular music contributor for the *Sunday Times*, *Mojo*, and London's *Time Out*.

Seth Jacobson (SJac) writes on music and popular culture for the *Daily Mirror*, and *Jack*, *Sleazenation*, and *Dazed & Confused* magazines, and he also dabbles in the weirder side of life for *Bizarre* magazine.

James Jam (JJ) contributes to *NME* and enjoys gushing emotively about skratty lo-fi punk rock in his irregularly produced fanzine *Boyeater*. He is also researching his first book, a trashy, sensationalist, tell-all tale of the Sunderland punk rock scene.

Tim Jones (TJ) has worked for *Record Collector* since 1998. As well as writing sleevenotes for the likes of Universal and Warner Bros., he has published several books on subjects including the SAS.

Ignacio Julià (IJ) has been co-editor-in-chief since 1985 of the now classic *Ruta 66*. Among his dozen books on rock music are titles on The Velvet Underground and Sonic Youth. He is now producing for the local BTV station.

Stan Jarin (SJar) has spent a lifetime building up a considerable body of musical history knowledge which he finds rather difficult to weave naturally into dinner party conversation. In 2004, Ramblin' Jack Elliott stayed with the Jarins for almost one month.

Luke Jolly (LJ) abandoned a medical course way back in 1994 to indulge in years of aural abuse in smoke-filled music venues. Since the early 2000s, his work has been published on brownnoiseunit.com and in *Beat*, *Mix Down*, *The Brag*, and *The Echo*.

Yoshi Kato (YK) resides in the San Francisco Bay Area. He currently contributes to the *San Jose Mercury News*, *Contra Costa Times* and *Downbeat*, and has also written for *Vibe*.

Emily Kelly (EK) graduated in Media before writing for various publications, both online and in print. Currently, she dedicates much time and considerable energy to writing for Melbourne's *Beat*.

Jake Kennedy (JK) is the reviews editor at *Record Collector* magazine. He has published sleevenotes for countless funk albums and is a correspondent for *NME* and the BBC. He is writing a study of *Unknown Pleasures* by Joy Division.

Miles Keylock (MK) writes on music and culture in South Africa. He has written for *SL Magazine*, *Black Business Quarterly*, and *GQ South Africa* magazine. He also reviews for *Cape Times* and *Mail & Guardian*.

Johnny Law (JLa) worked as a singles buyer in an Edinburgh record shop until Take That drove him out. Johnny currently manages Channel 4's TV listings and edits the C4 press website.

John Lewis (JLe) is assistant music editor of London's *Time Out* and has also written about music for *Mojo*, the London *Evening Standard*, *Straight No Chaser*, *Wax*, and *BBC Music*. He has compiled several albums.

Christoph Lindemann (CL) is a writer and editor at *Musikexpress*, Germany's biggest music journal, and he has worked for *Rolling Stone*, Germany, and *Primetime Live* at ABC News in New York. In 2000 he also contributed to *Made In Germany: The Hundred Best German Records*.

Pat Long (PL) lives in London and is reviews editor of *NME* magazine. Some say he spends too much money on records, but he would argue it's not nearly enough.

Michael Lydon (ML) has written about pop music since 1964 and was a founding editor of *Rolling Stone*. He has profiled Lennon and McCartney and has toured with The Rolling Stones, B.B. King, Johnny Cash, and many others. His books include *Rock Folk*, *Boogie Lightning*, *Ray Charles: Man And Music*, and *Flashbacks*. Michael is a regular "talking head" on TV and radio, and is also a singer/songwriter.

Bruno MacDonald (BM) has worked on *The Rough Guide To Rock*, *British Hit Singles*, *Rockopedia*, and the *MusicMaster* range. He edited *Pink Floyd: Through The Eyes Of . . .* and contributed to publications including *Record Collector* and *Q*. He lives in London and loves cats and Kiss.

Ali MacQueen (AMa) lives in London and has been a freelance writer for three years. He edits the singles and independent albums section for *Record Collector*, and contributes to *Front* and *Clash* magazines.

Joel McIver (JM) is production editor at *Record Collector* and contributes to several other magazines as well as compiling albums, writing liner notes, and appearing on TV and radio. His most recent book, *Justice For All: The Truth About Metallica*, was hailed as the ultimate book about the band.

Kylie McLaughlin (KM) has contributed to several Australian magazines, including *Rip It Up*, *dB*, and *Revolver*. She currently lives in Melbourne where she works as an online editor and freelancer for *Beat* magazine.

Craig McLean (CM) is a Scottish writer drawn to London by the bright lights of Britpop in 1995. Formerly deputy editor of *The Face*, he is currently a freelancer for the *Daily Telegraph*, the *Independent*, and the *Observer*, as well as *Word*, *GQ*, and *Vogue*. His writing on music and pop culture has appeared in *Composite* (Japan), *Adbusters* (Canada), and *Spin* (US).

Malik Meer (MMe) has written for the *Guardian*, *Time*, *Muzik*, *The Face*, *Mixmag*, and *Smash Hits*. He is currently assistant editor of *NME*.

Alexander Milas (AMi) is a staff writer for *Kerrang!* magazine, where he is frequently found commandeering the office stereo with death metal classics.

Mark Morris (MMo) has been writing about pop, movies, and TV since 1992 for a variety of newspapers and magazines, including *Select*, *Q*, *Neon*, *The Face*, the *Guardian*, and the *Observer*.

Rob Morton (RM) reviews popular music for the *New York Sun*. He has also directed numerous short films and written three feature-length screenplays.

David Nichols (DN) has been writing for music magazines since he was 17. He has written a book on The Go-Betweens and is a historian and university lecturer.

Sarah Norman (SN) is a music journalist, with a degree in music. She contributes regularly to Melbourne magazines *Beat* and *Forte* and the Sydney publication *The Brag*. Sarah is also music editor of the Monash University publication *Lot's Wife*.

Peter Notari (PN) began his career as the London correspondent for *Wan2*, Hungary's biggest music magazine. He has gone on to start ParaRadio, Hungary's first Internet radio station, co-found X-Peripheria, the biggest annual experimental electronic music festival in Hungary.

Matthew Oshinsky (MO) is deputy sports editor at the *New York Sun*, where he arrived after a stint at *CMJ New Music Monthly*. He has also been published by Harvard University Press.

Andy Pemberton (APe) is a New York-based freelance writer who writes for *GQ*, *Details*, the *Observer*, *Q*, *Word*, *Elle*, and *Radar*. He is also a regular on VH1. He was editor-in-chief of *Blender*, the award-winning US music monthly. Before moving to New York, he was the editor of *Q*.

Andy Pickering (APi) began his writing career in New Zealand with local music magazine *Rip It Up*, before going on to co-found *Remix* magazine in late 1997. He has been editor there ever since, and has written countless features and reviews.

Liam Pieper (LP) has written for *Beat* and *Groove* magazines, as well as the literary journals *Going Down Swinging* and *Total Cardboard*. He edits a youth publication called *Voiceworks*, which specializes in publishing emerging writers.

Alex Rayner (ARa) was *Ministry*'s music editor until 2001, when he joined *The Face*'s editorial team. Now deputy editor at *Dazed & Confused*, Alex has also written for *NME*, *Word*, and the *Independent*.

Craig Reece (CR) is a DJ and promoter from Glasgow, Scotland. He has previously written for the *Independent*, *NME*, *Scotland On Sunday*, and *The List*, and helps to run the Glasgow International Jazz Festival.

Max Reinhardt (MR) enjoys a varied freelance career as club DJ, music writer, CD compiler, BBC broadcaster, and musical director for Oily Cart. As a musician he plays all over Europe, and programmes international music festivals in London. He's a columnist for *Straight No Chaser*, writes reviews and features for *Songlines* and *FRoots*, and produced the book *Celebrating Sanctuary . . . Interviews With Refugee Artists In The UK*.

Andy Robbins (ARo) currently works as a reporter and feature writer for various newspapers in the UK and contributes to *Platform*, *Drowned In Sound*, *Do Something Pretty*, and *Rock City*.

Gerard Sampaio (GSa) is a journalist and film-maker living in Glasgow. He writes for AOL (UK) and the *Herald* newspaper and has previously worked on *The Guinness Book Of British Hit Singles*.

Tim Scott (TSc) was first introduced to American hardcore punk at 14, while skateboarding up and down his friend's driveway. Since then he has written for numerous punk rock publications, including *Maximum Rock And Roll*, *Beat*, *Kerrang!*, *Screaming Bloody Mess*, and innumerable punk fanzines.

Chris Shade (CSh) is a London-based writer, musician, and designer. He has contributed to various journals, notably *The Face* and *Shoreditch Twat*. He is currently recording with the band Volunteer.

Tim Sheridan (TSh) has written for such publications as *Mojo*, the *All Music Guide*, *Raygun*, *Downbeat*, *Launch*, *Paste*, and *Entertainment Weekly*. He also served as head writer for Steven Tyler of Aerosmith for two tours of America, writing Mr. Tyler's speech for AC/DC's induction into the Rock & Roll Hall of Fame.

Martin Sinnock (MS) is a broadcaster and writer, specializing in the music of the Democratic Republic of Congo (formerly Zaïre). He has been a columnist for LA magazine *The Beat* since 1996, is a reviewer for *Songlines* magazine, and presents *The Rough Guide Radio Show*, as well as *Viva La Musica — The African & Global Beat*, on totallyradio.com.

Rod Stanley (RS) started a music website purely to get into clubs for free. He writes for the *Times*, *Dazed & Confused*, *The Face*, *Muzik*, *Record Collector*, *Seven*, *Sleazenation*, *The Idler*, *Ammo City*, and *Tank*.

Paul Stokes (PS) has written for *Q*, *Mojo*, *Dazed & Confused*, and *Select*. He joined *NME* as deputy news editor in 2005. When not writing, he DJs at the club Brilliant Maniac in London's Soho.

Claire Stuchbery (CSt) works primarily for Melbourne's *Beat* magazine. She is also a presenter for a radio programme of unsigned artists called *No Frills* on PBS FM, organizing live gigs via the show.

Louise Sugrue (LS) has written for *Record Collector*, *OK!* magazine, *RSA Journal*, the *Daily Telegraph*, and the Press Association.

Giancarlo Susanna (GSu) is an Italian critic who writes both for music magazines (*Rockerilla*, *Audio Review*) and a daily paper (*L'Unità*). He has penned biographies of Neil Young, Jeff Buckley, REM, and Coldplay.

Kate Taylor (KT) joined Melbourne's *Beat* magazine in 2004, where she has become a regular contributor.

Gareth Thompson (GT) has worked for *Music Week*, *Video Week*, *Which Compact Disc?*, *Sounds*, and *Kerrang!* He was also the contributing editor to fanzine *Overall There Is A Smell Of Fried Onions*. He has also written a novel for young adults, *The Great Harlequin Grim*.

Arnar Eggert Thoroddsen (AET) is from Iceland, where he has written for various underground music magazines. Since 2000 he has written on pop culture for Iceland's biggest paper, *Morgunbladid*.

Andrew Tijs (AT) is a Melbourne native who for the last seven years has been reporting on local and international music, film, comedy, theatre, books, and also the occasional rodeo. He contributes to *Beat* magazine, as well as almost every street press in Australia, and also contributes investigative articles on the seamier side of the record industry to the national music magazine *Mess + Noise*.

John Tobler (JT) has been writing about popular music since 1969, for such varied publications as *ZigZag*, *Let It Rock*, *Melody Maker*, *NME*, *Sounds*, *Record Mirror*, *FRoots*, *Music Week*, *Billboard*, and *Country Music People*. He is the author of over 20 published books on rock music, including *ABBA Gold*, *25 Years Of Rock*, *The Record Producers*, and *The Guitar Greats*, as well as biographies of Elton John, Elvis Presley, The Beach Boys, The Doors, among others.

Jesse "Chuy" Varela (JCV) is the music director at KCSM FM 91, a US regional jazz station, where he presents *The Latin Jazz Show* on Sundays. Before this, he was the music director at KPFA in Berkeley for 3 years and was a freelancer with NPR. He writes on music for the *San Francisco Chronicle*, the *Latin Beat Magazine*, the *Jazz Times*, and the *Eastbay Express*. He has recently finished translations for Ry Cooder's latest project for Nonesuch.

Peter Watts (PW) is a regular contributor to *Time Out* London and *Uncut* magazines.

Burhan Wazir (BW) is the deputy features editor at the *Times* in the UK. During his career in journalism he has covered a wide range of issues, including domestic news, foreign affairs, war reporting, and music. He recently covered the second Gulf War.

Jaime Welton (JW) is a copy editor and freelance writer. He has had many articles published in weekly papers in the Bay Area, including *The Metro*, *South Valley Times*, and *Almaden Valley Times*. He has written record reviews for the magazine *Frontera*. He currently lives in San José with his partner, their two kids, and their CD collection.

Lois Wilson (LW) is a freelance writer whose first home is *Mojo* magazine. She is currently their soul columnist, edits their Book and DVD sections and also contributes reviews and features on a monthly basis. She also writes for *Record Collector* and has been published in the *Times* and *Sunday Times*. She has compiled several CD collections related to the soul and reggae fields and regularly writes sleevenotes for record companies. Lois has also been a pundit on VH-1 discussing women in rock.

Agnieszka Wojtowicz-Jach (AW-J) is a former promotion manager for Warner Music Poland and special project/dance labels manager for EMI Poland. She now works in PR & media communication, and is a freelance journalist.

Michael Woodsworth (MW) grew up in Montréal, where he participated in the city's late-1990s underground music scene. After moving to New York in 2001, he reported neighborhood stories for the *Daily News* and later became sports editor of the *Sun*, the city's newest daily paper.

Daniel Zugna (DZ) is a freelance writer based in Melbourne. He is the new releases columnist for the streetpress magazine *Beat*, and has made extensive contributions to a variety of independent music websites.

Album Index

- **Castro becomes Cuba's president**

- **Hawaii becomes 50th U.S. state**

- **Hitler officially declared dead**

- **First satellite launched**

- **Hula hoop invented**

1950s

Frank Sinatra | **In The Wee Small Hours** (1955)

Label | Capitol
Producer | Voyle Gilmore
Art Direction | Tommy Steele
Nationality | USA
Running Time | 50:25

In the early 1950s, Frank Sinatra was washed up—unable even to land a regular nightclub gig, much less a record contract. His savior arrived just in time. Alan Livingston, then VP of A&R at Capitol Records and a confirmed Sinatra fan, signed him to a seven-year deal on March 14, 1953, against the advice of every colleague whose opinion he sought.

Sinatra's Oscar-winning turn in *From Here To Eternity* the same year showed Livingston's prescience. It also signaled the singer's second chance, which he grabbed with *Songs For Young Lovers* and *Swing Easy*. Both are fine sets, but they are most notable because they introduced Sinatra—initially against his wishes—to a young arranger named Nelson Riddle.

In The Wee Small Hours arrived not long after Sinatra's relationship with Ava Gardner collapsed, and it is this split that defines perhaps the all-time greatest break-up album. The wisecracking, finger-snapping Sinatra of popular legend is absent; this is a man alone. Record store clerks who filed Sinatra under easy listening had surely never heard the barfly confessional of "Can't We Be Friends?" much less the pleading take on Cole Porter's "What Is This Thing Called Love." Duke Ellington's "Mood Indigo," meanwhile, never sounded bluer.

Riddle frames this melancholy in wondrously delicate arrangements on what, in hindsight, is the first record where the pair really clicked. Others would follow, though in a new and then-exotic format. Initially issued as two 10-inch discs, *In The Wee Small Hours* was soon reissued in 12-inch format, inadvertently ushering in the album era. **WF-J**

Track Listing

01	**In The Wee Small Hours Of The Morning** (Hilliard·Mann)	3:00
▶ 02	**Mood Indigo** (Bigard·Ellington·Mills)	3:30
03	**Glad To Be Unhappy** (Hart·Rodgers)	2:35
04	**I Get Along Without You Very Well** (Carmichael)	3:42
05	**Deep In A Dream** (De Lange·Van Heusen)	2:49
06	**I See Your Face Before Me** (Dietz·Schwartz)	3:24
07	**Can't We Be Friends?** (James·Swift)	2:48
08	**When Your Lover Has Gone** (Swan)	3:10
▶ 09	**What Is This Thing Called Love** (Porter)	2:35
10	**Last Night When We Were Young** (Arlen·Harburg)	3:17
▶ 11	**I'll Be Around** (Wilder)	2:59
12	**Ill Wind** (Arlen·Koehler)	3:46
13	**It Never Entered My Mind** (Hart·Rodgers)	2:42
14	**Dancing On The Ceiling** (Hart·Rodgers)	2:57
15	**I'll Never Be The Same** (Kahn·Malneck)	3:05
16	**This Love Of Mine** (Parker·Sanicola·Sinatra)	3:33

Elvis Presley | Elvis Presley (1956)

Label | RCA
Producer | Uncredited
Art Direction | William V. Robertson
Nationality | USA
Running Time | 28:42

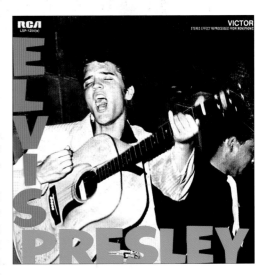

This is not the holy grail. Indeed, when heard through twenty-first century ears, long since attuned to the art and technicalities of the album, Elvis Presley's first LP is a frustratingly inconsistent record.

The collection was pieced together from several sessions: seven tracks were cut in early 1956, just prior to the album's March 13 release, but five were virtual leftovers from Sam Phillips' Sun Records in 1954 and 1955, recorded before RCA bought out his contract. The overwrought vocal on the Sun take of "I'll Never Let You Go (Little Darlin')" verges on self-parody; the irony is that Elvis had no public self-image to mock at that point. And here's a curiosity: though every CD reissue includes "Heartbreak Hotel"—the track which propelled the 21-year-old from Memphis notoriety to global fame in mere weeks—the original release did not.

Yet there is magic here, and plenty of it; certainly, revolutions have sprung from less. The white-boy gospel of "I'm Counting On You" and the jittery rumble through Ray Charles'"I Got A Woman" are an early one-two punch; near the end sits the definitively lonesome version of "Blue Moon." But the key cut is the most stunning "Trying To Get To You," which pitches Presley halfway between country boy and torch singer. It is a landmark recording.

And, for that matter, a landmark cover. Believed to have been shot by photographer William V. "Red" Robertson on July 31, 1955 at a concert in Tampa, Florida, it is among the most iconic Elvis shots ever snapped. The Clash agreed, subverting the design for the sleeve of 1979's *London Calling*. **WF-J**

"Man, I was tame compared to what they do now."

Elvis Presley, 1972

Track Listing

01	**Blue Suede Shoes** (Perkins)		2:00
▶ 02	**I'm Counting On You** (Robertson)		2:25
▶ 03	**I Got A Woman** (Charles)		2:25
04	**One-Sided Love Affair** (Campbell)		2:11
05	**I Love You Because** (Payne)		2:43
06	**Just Because** (Robin·B. Shelton·J. Shelton)		2:34
07	**Tutti Frutti** (LaBostrie·Penniman)		1:59
▶ 08	**Trying To Get To You** (McCoy·Singleton)		2:31
09	**I'm Gonna Sit Right Down (And Cry Over You)** (Biggs·Thomas)		2:01
10	**I'll Never Let You Go (Little Darlin')** (Wakely)		2:24
▶ 11	**Blue Moon** (Hart·Rodgers)		2:40
12	**Money Honey** (Stone)		2:36

The Louvin Brothers | Tragic Songs Of Life (1956)

Label | Capitol
Producer | Ken Nelson
Art Direction | Uncredited
Nationality | USA
Running Time | 35:58

You don't have to be mad, murderous, drunken, driven, lonesome, ornery, or blue to sing country music ... but it sure helps. Ira Louvin wasn't all of the above, but he was something. Emerging in the 1940s, Charlie and Ira Louvin slotted neatly into the country music tradition of close-harmony brother duet singing—following in the footsteps of The Delmore Brothers and acting as an early template for The Everly Brothers. This, their first full album, remains one of country's essential bedrock releases. Charlie's baritone and Ira's pure high tenor trade and fuse with lilting style and beauteous grace. It is gospel-fired bluegrass shot straight from the heart.

The artwork most commonly associated with the record features Charlie and Ira superimposed over a distraught blonde clutching a crumpled letter, dime store novel style. This illustration was added for later reissues, and it romanticizes the truth. In fact, for Ira and Charlie these songs of sin and weakness, tragedy and temptation were all too real. There was nothing at all knowing or kitsch about them.

Still, it was Ira's self-destructive bent that lent them their knife-sharp edge. Charlie was stable but Ira was a drinker, a womanizer, and prone to flying into violent rages. By 1963 Charlie had had enough and quit to go solo. Ira had survived much—including being shot by his third wife, Faye—but in 1965 he was killed (with his latest bride) in a car crash in Missouri.

Gram Parsons would later be responsible for a renewal of interest in the brothers' music, and since then the Louvin legend has continued to deepen and grow over the decades. **RF**

"That word broadminded is spelled S.I.N..."

The Louvin Brothers, 1952

Track Listing		
▶ 01 **Kentucky** (Davis)		2:39
02 **I'll Be All Smiles Tonight** (Carter)		3:14
03 **Let Her Go God Bless Her** (Trad.)		2:55
04 **What Is Home Without Love** (Trad.)		3:00
05 **A Tiny Broken Heart** (Hill·C. Louvin·I. Louvin)		2:34
06 **In The Pines** (Riggs)		3:15
▶ 07 **Alabama** (Hill·C. Louvin·I. Louvin)		2:43
▶ 08 **Katie Dear** (Bolick)		2:34
09 **My Brother's Will** (Nelson)		3:16
▶ 10 **Knoxville Girl** (Trad.)		3:49
11 **Take The News To Mother** (Callahan·Caloway)		2:48
12 **Mary Of The Wild Moor** (Turner)		3:11

Louis Prima | The Wildest! (1956)

Label | Capitol
Producer | Voyle Gilmore
Art Direction | Uncredited
Nationality | USA
Running Time | 32:00

A popular nightclub singer/trumpeter in the 1930s and '40s, initially in his native New Orleans and then in New York, Prima found work had dried up by 1954. With new wife and stage partner Keely Smith in tow—he a rugged 43, she a whitewashed 22—he called in a favor and landed a gig in the lounge of the Sahara, Las Vegas, hiring young New Orleans saxophonist Sam Butera to drill the band. Success came immediately; this sparkling half-hour, cut live in the studio in April 1956, iced the cake.

Jazz hounds often dismiss Prima as just an Italianate Louis Armstrong impersonator, perhaps because of the three Satchmo hits here: "You Rascal You," and a medley joining a restrained "Basin Street Blues" to a non-soporific "When It's Sleepy Time Down South." But that is to miss the point: this is simply irrepressible music that more than matches its glorious cover shot. Prima is joyous, rumbustious, and irresistible, making even the band chuckle on "Oh Marie," with Smith in contrast, a delightfully straight-laced foil. Butera and pals, meanwhile, set them up with some of the fizziest jump-jive ever recorded. The sound has been imitated often, not least when Brian Setzer's cover of "Jump, Jive, An' Wail" helmed a GAP® commercial. Butera, whose arrangement it appropriated, grumbled that he was paid three pairs of pants for the privilege.

Prima died in 1978, but his legacy lives on through daughter Lena, herself seen recently performing at the Sahara, and through his later turn as a regal, jive-talking orangutan in *The Jungle Book*. Truly, the man was the king of the swingers. **WF-J**

> "I've had hit records, but I never liked 'em ... But this is it."
>
> Louis Prima, 1956

Track Listing

▶	01	**Medley: Just A Gigolo—I Ain't Got Nobody** (Brammier•Caesar•Casucci•Graham•Williams)	4:42
	02	**(Nothing's Too Good) For My Baby** (Budston•Falcon)	2:36
	03	**The Lip** (Klages•Knight)	2:15
	04	**Body And Soul** (Eyton•Green•Heyman•Sour)	3:22
▶	05	**Oh Marie** (Dicapua, arr. Prima)	2:25
	06	**Medley: Basin Street Blues — When It's Sleepy Time Down South** (L. Rene•O. Rene•Williams)	4:12
▶	07	**Jump, Jive, An' Wail** (Prima)	3:28
▶	08	**Buona Sera** (De Rose•Sigman)	2:58
	09	**Night Train** (Forrest)	2:46
	10	**(I'll Be Glad When You're Dead) You Rascal You** (Theard)	3:13

Fats Domino | This Is Fats (1956)

Label | Imperial
Producer | Dave Bartholomew
Art Direction | Uncredited
Nationality | USA
Running Time | 27:11

Six years before Bill Haley recorded "Rock Around The Clock," 21-year-old Antoine "Fats" Domino wrote the blueprint for early rock 'n' roll with 1949's "The Fat Man." From that million-selling debut single, the New Orleans-born vocalist/pianist would produce more hits than any other 1950s-era rocker besides Elvis Presley, including a staggering run of 39 straight singles that charted between 1954 and 1962.

While selling some 65 million records in the decade, Domino was arguably the man most responsible for bridging the gap between R&B and rock—although Little Richard might dispute that claim. What is beyond debate is the influence of the singer's 1950s work, which has run and spread through popular music and influenced everyone from Pat Boone to The Beatles.

This Is Fats, the singer's third full-length album on Imperial, was released at the height of Domino's career and remains the most powerful portrait of his artistry thanks to such boogie-woogie beasts as "Blue Monday" and "Honey Chile" and such mournful masterpieces as "So Long" and "Poor, Poor Me."

Triumphant opener "Blueberry Hill" had been a hit for Glenn Miller in 1940, but despite its characteristic charm and warmth, the track proved surprisingly difficult to record. No one could find the sheet music that day in the studio and Domino kept forgetting his lines. No complete take was ever recorded and the studio had to splice the song together out of aborted efforts. The resulting single would top the U.S. R&B charts and hit No. 2 on the pop charts—the highest Domino would ever reach in pop. **JiH**

> ## "My biggest ambition is to keep the Ten Commandments."

Fats Domino, 2002

Track Listing		
▶ 01 **Blueberry Hill** (Lewis·Rose·Stock)		2:21
▶ 02 **Honey Chile** (Bartholomew·Domino)		1:48
03 **What's The Reason (I'm Not Pleasing You?)**		
(Grier·Hatch·Poe·Tomlin)		2:03
▶ 04 **Blue Monday** (Bartholomew·Domino)		2:18
▶ 05 **So Long** (Bartholomew·Domino)		2:13
06 **La–La** (Bartholomew·Domino)		2:15
07 **Troubles Of My Own** (Bartholomew·Domino)		2:15
08 **You Done Me Wrong** (Domino)		2:05
09 **Reelin' And Rockin'** (Domino·Young)		2:20
10 **The Fat Man's Hop** (Domino·Young)		2:26
11 **Poor, Poor Me** (Domino)		2:11
12 **Trust In Me** (Domino·Jarrett)		2:50

Duke Ellington
Ellington At Newport 1956 (1956)

Label | Columbia
Producer | George Avakian
Art Direction | Uncredited
Nationality | USA
Running Time | 44:00

After a spell in the doldrums when swing bands went out of fashion, Duke Ellington's performance at the Newport Jazz Festival on July 7, 1956, heralded a dramatic resurgence in his popularity. The irony is that the record rushed out by Columbia to capitalize on the concert was not really recorded at Newport at all.

Informed that the concert recording was flawed, Columbia executives sent Ellington into a New York studio to re-record the set on the Monday after the gig. The resulting album is a patched-together fusion of live recordings, studio retakes, and canned applause. It became the biggest selling record of Duke's career.

However, a brilliant 1999 reissue finally set the record straight. The original release is included, but thanks to a complicated piece of post-production work using the original masters and a long-lost radio recording, it also presents the actual concert in full, and at last offers insight as to why the show was received so rapturously. The three-part Newport Jazz Festival Suite—so new, says Ellington, "We haven't even had time to title it yet"— offers some typically squealing trumpet work by Cat Anderson. But the concert's reputation, and that of the album, rests on the fizzing blues of "Diminuendo And Crescendo In Blue," and specifically on tenor saxophonist Paul Gonsalves' staggering, reputation-making 27-chorus turn in the spotlight, among the most famous solos in jazz history. **WF-J**

Frank Sinatra
Songs For Swingin' Lovers! (1956)

Label | Capitol
Producer | Voyle Gilmore
Art Direction | Uncredited
Nationality | USA
Running Time | 45:00

By the mid-1950s, Frank Sinatra was back on top of both his game and the charts, bringing the lie to F. Scott Fitzgerald's credo that "There are no second acts in American lives." Regrouping with Nelson Riddle late in 1955, Sinatra mapped out a record with a very different flavor.

What emerged from these sessions, held a month after Sinatra's 40th birthday, was day following night. Next to In The Wee Small Hours' scotch-soaked, 2 a.m. atmospherics, the euphoric Songs For Swingin' Lovers! is a sunny summer afternoon walk in the park, positively skipping with joie de vivre. Sinatra never sounded more at ease, breezing giddily around "You Make Me Feel So Young," delivering "How About You?" as though it is one long marriage proposal, and practically winking his way through "Makin' Whoopee." But it would all be wasted without Riddle's glorious scoring. Legend has it that his unsurpassable arrangement for "I've Got You Under My Skin," hurriedly completed the night before the session, was greeted with spontaneous applause by the musicians who played it on January 12, 1956.

The resulting album is the closest any artist has come to defining the Great American Songbook. However, keen-eyed students of pop music may also notice the symmetry in the 15-cut, 45-minute track listing. Truly, the art of the three-minute pop song begins and ends here. **WF-J**

The Crickets
The "Chirping" Crickets (1957)

Label | Brunswick
Producer | Norman Petty
Art Direction | Uncredited
Nationality | USA
Running Time | 25:59

Surprising to note that this milestone in rock history lasts well under half an hour. But it demonstrates the virtue of brevity—a dozen great songs, many of which are familiar to any pop musicologist, and none of which lasts anywhere near the magic three minutes.

Buddy Holly formed the band with schoolfriend drummer Jerry Allison. The Crickets' mix of rockabilly, blues, R&B, and keen pop sensibility found them in the vanguard of the first flush of rock 'n' roll. This debut album (the only LP to feature Holly released during his lifetime) includes their first three classic hit singles (and the B-sides) as well as two songs that were part-written by Roy Orbison. Numerous aspiring guitarists have striven to duplicate the guitar intro to "That'll Be The Day," a song that Holly titled after an expression used by John Wayne in the 1956 movie *The Searchers*.

Holly's pioneering singer-songwriting skills were to be immensely influential, notably on the songwriting partnerships at the heart of The Beatles and The Rolling Stones. The apparent shortage of songwriting credits for Holly here is explained by the fact that, as a composer, he was often billed as Charles Hardin—his real name was Charles Hardin Holley.

Note also the cover versions of songs written by Chuck Willis and Lloyd Price; whatever accusations have been made posthumously about Holly being racist are debatable. **JT**

Count Basie
The Atomic Mr. Basie (1957)

Label | Roulette
Producer | Teddy Reig
Art Direction | Uncredited
Nationality | USA
Running Time | 39:30

By 1957, the halcyon days of Bill Basie's seminal 1930s group were two decades behind; indeed, changing fashions had forced him to drop his big band for a spell in the early 1950s. Happily, it was the last time he would be without one. All Basie needed, it turned out, was a little fresh blood, which he found in the veins of young arranger Neal Hefti. Just five years after his first job with the band, Hefti was asked to score the whole of Basie's first record for Roulette.

"I have never bragged on anything," the ever-modest Basie wrote in his autobiography, "but [the *Atomic Basie*] band . . . was one I could have bragged on." He's not wrong. Powered by saxophonist Eddie "Lockjaw" Davis and an all-star trumpet section led by Thad Jones, the 12-strong brass section alternate fire ("Whirly-Bird") and ice (the slinky "After Supper") to effervescent effect on Hefti's 11 compositions. But, as always with Basie, the rhythm section is the key: bassist Eddie Jones, drummer Sonny Payne, guitarist Freddie Green, and Basie himself, playing piano with typical economy, bring a swing even to the tender "Li'l Darlin'."

It was Basie's last great record. By the mid-1960s, he had slipped comfortably into his position as one of jazz's most likeable elder statesmen, a role he would hold until his death in 1984. Hefti, meanwhile, largely ditched the serious jazz in favor of Hollywood, finding fame for his themes to *Batman* and *The Odd Couple*. **WF-J**

Thelonious Monk | Brilliant Corners (1957)

Label | Riverside
Producer | Orrin Keepnews
Art Direction | Paul Bacon
Nationality | USA
Running Time | 43:08

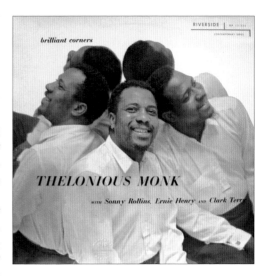

Given his status as one of the most widely revered composers of the twentieth century, to say nothing of his pervasive influence as a pianist, it is difficult to comprehend the marginal position of Thelonious Sphere Monk in 1957.

While he had played a key role in the creation of bebop at the Harlem nightspot Minton's in the mid-1940s and contributed several standards to the jazz canon, a bogus drug conviction that kept him out of Manhattan jazz clubs, along with a disinterested record label, served to sideline Monk throughout the 1950s. It was only when Orrin Keepnews—the guiding spirit behind the indie jazz label Riverside—managed to sign Monk that he started gaining due recognition.

Keepnews reintroduced Monk to the jazz public with two trio sessions, the first exploring Ellington and the second pop standards. *Brilliant Corners* marked Monk's return as a composer of the first order, with a quintet featuring rising tenor sax star Sonny Rollins, the tragically short-lived altoist Ernie Henry, bassist Oscar Pettiford, and drummer Max Roach (trumpeter Clark Terry and bassist Paul Chambers replace Henry and Pettiford on "Bemsha"). The jaw-dropping title track is the reason for the personnel change, as its difficulty meant that there was not one complete take after some 25 attempts.

The tension is palpable on the recording, even though Keepnews spliced together pieces, resulting in Monk's first mid-career masterpiece. Other highlights are the tender melody "Pannonica," written for Monk's friend and patron, Baroness "Nica" Koenigswarter, and Monk's solo version of "I Surrender Dear." **AG**

> ## "I wasn't trying to create something that would be hard to play. I just composed music that fit with how I was thinking. I knew musicians would dig it, because it sounded good."
>
> Thelonious Monk, 1965

Track Listing		
▶ 01 **Brilliant Corners** (Monk)		7:47
02 **Ba-Lue Bolivar Ba-Lues-Are** (Monk)		13:21
▶ 03 **Pannonica** (Monk)		8:52
04 **I Surrender Dear** (Barris·Clifford)		5:27
05 **Bemsha Swing** (Best·Monk)		7:41

Sabu | Palo Congo (1957)

Label | Blue Note
Producer | Alfred Lion
Art Direction | Reid Miles
Nationality | USA
Running Time | 40:52

Chano Pozo nailed the Afro-Cuban conga drum into jazz playing with Dizzy Gillespie's orchestra in the late 1940s. In doing so, he opened a door for such talented percussionists as Louis "Sabu" Martinez, who replaced him in Diz's band following Pozo's death in 1948.

Equipped with a powerful spirit and slap, Sabu triumphed as a session sideman for Blue Note Records, working on Art Blakey's *Orgy In Rhythm* and *Holiday For Skins* among others. As a leader on *Palo Congo*, he served up a variety of beats, drawing on his mixed Spanish/African/West Indian heritage.

Engineered by Rudy Van Gelder, the recording captures the fury of the Cuban rumba and son styles in a studio performance. Martinez hosted a band that included Ray Romero, who played with Miguelito Valdes, and the tres (a Cuban folk guitar with three doubled-up strings) of the prolific Arsenio Rodriguez, a pillar of modern salsa. Musicians chosen largely from the band of Arsenio Rodriguez interact with Sabu in warm, non-distorted analog. The recording is mono, but its judicious balance allows drums, voices, and acoustic bass to emerge individually.

Sabu's singing opens "El Cumbanchero," by Rafael Hernandez, with its infectious melody. The genius of Arsenio permeates through "Rhapsodia Del Maravilloso" where he introduces variations on "El Manisero." The tone of his tres guitar has a soulful, funky timbre.

Sabu himself delivers tough-fisted solos on *Palo Congo*, while interweaving Santeria prayers into an album that illuminates his roots as a native New Yorker living in El Barrio of Spanish Harlem. **JCV**

"First I played on tin cans in backyards. Then when I was 11 years old I joined a trio and got a job on 125th playing for 25¢ every third night."

Sabu Martinez, 1968

Track Listing		
▶ 01 El Cumbanchero (Hernandez)		5:38
▶ 02 Billumba–Palo Congo (Martinez)		6:06
03 Choferito–Plena (Rios)		4:02
04 Asabache (Martinez)		4:22
05 Simba (Martinez)		5:55
▶ 06 Rhapsodia Del Maravilloso (Martinez)		4:39
07 Aggo Elegua (Martinez)		4:28
▶ 08 Tribilin Cantore (Martinez)		5:19

Miles Davis | Birth Of The Cool (1957)

Label | Capitol
Producer | Pete Rugolo
Art Direction | Uncredited
Nationality | USA
Running Time | 37:56

The year 1949: stepping out from under the wing of Charlie "Bird" Parker and Dizzy Gillespie, a 24-year-old Miles Davis realizes he is wasting time attempting to replicate the dizzying harmonic flights of his bebop mentors. His solution: collect a hip young cast of New York City sidemen and set about de- and reconstructing bebop's vocabulary into a fresh improvisational space. And space, for Miles, is *the* pivotal creative place on this, his first session as a leader.

Threading his muted trumpet tones through urbane orchestral arrangements from the likes of Gil Evans, Gerry Mulligan, and John Lewis, Miles shapes a harmonic "cool" jazz signature that owes as much to European classical music as the "hot" jazz of bebop or ragtime. His vibrato-less horn solo on the opening "Move" sets the pace for a series of impressionist tone poems that offer an understated corollary to bebop's chord-obsessed excess. But this is a cool that still swings: witness Miles trading licks with Lee Konitz's airy alto saxophone on "Jeru."

Photographer Aram Avakian captures precisely this interplay between controlled detachment and focused emotional power in his iconic album cover shot. Critics too identified the album's "quietly audacious" attitude— the public however, disagreed. "Cool" was overlooked until its resurrection in the West Coast revisionism of Mulligan's mid-1950s groups. And Miles? Well, he would ease his cool into the cinema on Louis Malle's *L'Ascenseur Pour L'Echafaud* (1957), distilling it into his masterpiece *Kind Of Blue* (1959) and a career-spanning penchant for collaboration and idiomatic renovation. **MK**

"I always had a curiosity about trying new things in music."

Miles Davis, 1962

Track Listing

▶ 01	**Move** (Best)	2:33
▶ 02	**Jeru** (Mulligan)	3:13
03	**Moon Dreams** (MacGregor•Mercer)	3:19
▶ 04	**Venus De Milo** (Mulligan)	3:13
▶ 05	**Budo** (Davis•Powell)	2:34
06	**Deception** (Davis)	2:49
07	**God Child** (Wallington)	3:11
▶ 08	**Boplicity** (Henry)	3:00
09	**Rocker** (Mulligan)	3:06
10	**Israel** (Carisi)	2:18
11	**Rouge** (Lewis)	3:15
12	**Darn That Dream** (DeLange•Van Heusen)	3:25

Machito | **Kenya** (1957)

Label | Roulette Jazz
Producer | Ralph Seijo
Art Direction | Uncredited
Nationality | USA
Running Time | 35:46

In the 1940s, Machito and his orchestra brewed a hot cup of mambo-mania, blending Afro-Cuban beats with American jazz. Frontman Frank Grillo, a.k.a. Machito, sang and shook maracas, while musical director Mario Bauza guided the cross-pollination of early big band sounds into afrocubano musical frameworks.

Bauza had long dreamed of creating a Latin big band that fused the fire of early Cuban orchestras he heard growing up in Havana with the hipness of Duke Ellington, whom he saw in Harlem. (Landing in Harlem aged 19, Bauza had played sax and trumpet in the bands of Chick Webb, Don Redman, and Cab Calloway.)

Bold original compositions and arrangements by Bauza and René Hernandez, who plays piano here, Chano Pozo, and AK Salim (a noted jazz composer and arranger) define this underrated gem. Special guests Cannonball Adderley, Doc Cheatham, and Joe Newman bring strong voices as improvisers, riffing neatly in short but sweet choruses.

Opening cut "Wild Jungle" establishes the unbridled prominence enjoyed by the drummers. José Mangual (bongo), Uba Nieto (timbales), Candido Camero (conga), and Carlos "Patato" Valdes (conga) propel the pieces. "Holiday" and "Blues À La Machito" fuse blues and swing with exceptional cohesion and interplay from the orchestra. "Tin Tin Deo" is a stirring rendering of the Pozo Latin jazz standard.

The Machito Orchestra had set the guideposts for what Latin jazz could be. The all-instrumental *Kenya*, their most African-inspired album, marks a pinnacle of their sterling musicality. **JCV**

> ## "If you've got rhythm, you have everything. Without rhythm you have nothing."
>
> Mario Bauza, 1992

Track Listing

▶	01	**Wild Jungle** (Bauza·Hernandez)	2:46
	02	**Congo Mulence** (Salim)	2:55
▶	03	**Kenya** (Bauza·Hernandez)	3:26
	04	**Oyeme** (Salim)	3:11
▶	05	**Holiday** (Bauza·Hernandez)	2:46
▶	06	**Cannonology** (Salim)	2:29
	07	**Frenzy** (Bauza·Hernandez)	2:40
▶	08	**Blues À La Machito** (Salim)	3:01
	09	**Conversation** (Bauza·Hernandez)	2:55
▶	10	**Tin Tin Deo** (Pozo)	2:55
▶	11	**Minor Rama** (Salim)	3:01
	12	**Tururato** (Salim)	3:10

Little Richard
Here's Little Richard (1957)

Label | Specialty
Producer | Bumps Blackwell
Art Direction | Thadd Roark
Nationality | USA
Running Time | 27:31

"A-wop-bop-a-loo-bop-a-lop-bam-boom—tutti frutti, oh rootie!!" In the summer of 1955, rock 'n' roll was busting out all over, with Fats Domino, Ray Charles, Chuck Berry, and Bo Diddly all scoring hits within weeks of each other. Keen to ride the rock 'n' roll wave, Art Rupe of Specialty Records told his top talent scout, Bumps Blackwell, to find him a Ray Charles-alike. Sensibly, Bumps went south, and at the legendary Dew Drop Inn in New Orleans he found a flamboyant (and openly gay) jump blues singer and pianist named Little Richard Penniman. By September, Bumps had coaxed Richard into Cosimo Matassa's little J&M studio, and on a one-track quarter-inch Ampex they made history.

"Over the top" does not begin to describe the shameless, nearly insane energy recorded by Richard, Bumps, Cosimo, and New Orleans' funkiest session men. "Tutti Frutti" started climbing the charts in October, with "Long Tall Sally," "Slippin' and Slidin'," "Ready Teddy," and "Jenny Jenny" following in 1956. This manic procession was collected on *Here's Little Richard*, featuring an unforgettable photo of Richard in action.

A flat-out classic, *Here's Little Richard* is the artist's highest charting LP. It may prove hard to find on vinyl, but the tracks are collected on many CDs—checking for the Specialty name should ensure that the copies are originals and not the inferior covers that Richard made for many other labels. *Here's Little Richard* is rock 'n' roll's stem cells—from this album (and half a dozen others in this book) the whole genre grew. **ML**

"On stage I'd do anything."

Little Richard, 1980s

	Track Listing	
▶ 01	**Tutti Frutti** (LaBostrie·Lubin·Penniman)	2:24
02	**True Fine Mama** (Penniman)	2:41
03	**Can't Believe You Wanna Leave** (Price)	2:23
▶ 04	**Ready Teddy** (Blackwell·Marascalco)	2:07
05	**Baby** (Penniman)	2:03
▶ 06	**Slippin' And Slidin'** (Bocage·Collins)	2:38
▶ 07	**Long Tall Sally** (Blackwell·Marascalco·Penniman)	2:07
08	**Miss Ann** (Johnson·Penniman)	2:15
09	**Oh Why?** (Scott)	2:06
▶ 10	**Rip It Up** (Blackwell·Marascalco)	2:22
▶ 11	**Jenny Jenny** (Johnson·Penniman)	2:00
12	**She's Got It** (Marascalco·Penniman)	2:25

Tito Puente And His Orchestra
Dance Mania, Vol. 1 (1958)

Label | BMG
Producer | Uncredited
Art Direction | Uncredited
Nationality | USA
Running Time | 38:41

When Tito Puente passed away in the year 2000, at the age of 77, he was known to younger generations as the author of the Santana-covered classic rock/R&B radio staple "Oye Como Va" and also for appearing on a season-ending cliffhanger episode of animated pop culture touchstone *The Simpsons*. But prior to that, the timbales master-bandleader-composer enjoyed life as the King of Mambo. And *Dance Mania*, his best-selling album—and his first devoted wholly to dance music—shows why.

Puente had already been leading a big band for more than a decade before going into a New York City studio to record *Dance Mania*. Hipsters had long known of the Puerto Rican-American's danceable synthesis of Afro-Cuban rhythms, jazz principles, and the musical traditions of his ancestry. Now the rest of the world was beginning to catch on.

Dance Mania also marked the recorded debut of Puente Orchestra vocalist Santitod Colón, whose engaging voice could fire up or seduce an audience. "El Cayuco," the opening track, urbanely slithers through the uptown streets with a tightly orchestrated syncopation propelled by Puente's hypnotic timbales work and spot-on unified horn blasts and lines. Puente brings out his tuned percussion skills on a couple of other standout and stylistically diverse tracks: the instrumental "Hong Kong Mambo" has his slick marimba playing at its fun, cosmopolitan core, while on the regal "Estoy Siempre Junto A Tí" he frames the entire piece with his fluid, often sustained vibraphone flows. **YK**

Track Listing

▶	01	**El Cayuco (Son Montuno)** (Puente)	2:33
	02	**Complicación** (Aguabella)	3:18
▶	03	**3–D Mambo (Mambo Jazz Instrumental)** (Santos)	2:23
	04	**Llegó Mijän (Son Montuno)** (Puente)	3:10
	05	**Cuando Te Vea (Guaguanco)** (Puente)	4:10
▶	06	**Hong Kong Mambo** (Puente)	3:42
	07	**Mambo Gozón** (Puente)	2:44
	08	**Mi Chiquita Quierre Bembé (Cha Cha Cha Bembé)** (Puente)	3:55
▶	09	**Varsity Drag (Mambo Jazz International)** (Brown • DeSylva • Henderson)	2:48
▶	10	**Estoy Siempre Junto A Tí (Bolero)** (Delgado)	3:10
	11	**Agua Limpia Todo (Guaguancó)** (Aguabella)	2:55
	12	**Sacu Tu Mujer (Guaracha)** (Puente)	3:02

Billie Holiday | Lady In Satin (1958)

Label | Columbia
Producer | Irving Townsend
Art Direction | Uncredited
Nationality | USA
Running Time | 39:10

Is *Lady In Satin* merely a voyeuristic portrait of an artist in decline or actually a seminal slice of soul baring from one of jazz's most gifted interpreters of song? Granted, the vivacious "Lady Day" siren call of her 1930s Verve recordings is long gone, now replaced by the ravaged, bittersweet rasp of a singer struggling with a serious heroin habit. With Holiday now sounding more like a 70-year-old than a 40-something starlet making a comeback, arranger Ray Ellis was initially less than happy with her faltering timbre.

Yet by consistently stripping down standards like "You Don't Know What Love Is" and "Glad To Be Unhappy" to their emotional core, Holiday channels her junkie pride into some of the most naked blues ever recorded. These are torch songs unlike anything jazz had heard before: love as distraction, despair, resignation, and above all else, brutal honesty. Unsurprisingly, this was Holiday's own favorite recording and it also proved a myth-making final will and testament.

While Ellis' "satin" string arrangements seem eager to airbrush out Holiday's vocal scars, they actually result in accentuating her singular ability to swing no matter how corny her accompaniment. When she stretches her syllables out into a blistered sigh on "I'm A Fool To Want You," it is as though she is lost in her own imaginary blues frequencies. Granted, there is a grim fascination about the album that is as mesmerizing and harrowing as watching a heroin addict shoot up. But without *Lady In Satin* there would simply have been no divas like Nina Simone or Janis Joplin crying their hearts out so uncompromisingly in the decades to come. **MK**

> ## "I have to change a tune to my own way of doing it."

Billie Holiday, 1939

Track Listing

▶	01	**I'm A Fool To Want You** (Herron • Sinatra • Wolf)	3:23
	02	**For Heaven's Sake** (Bretton • Edwards • Meyer)	3:26
▶	03	**You Don't Know What Love Is** (Depaul • Raye)	3:48
▶	04	**I Get Along Without You Very Well** (Carmichael)	2:59
	05	**For All We Know** (Coots • Lewis)	2:53
	06	**Violets For Your Furs** (Adair • Dennis)	3:24
▶	07	**You've Changed** (Carey • Fisher)	3:17
	08	**It's Easy To Remember** (Hart • Rodgers)	4:01
	09	**But Beautiful** (Burke • Van Heusen)	4:29
▶	10	**Glad To Be Unhappy** (Hart • Rodgers)	4:07
▶	11	**I'll Be Around** (Wilder)	3:23

Jack Elliott
Jack Takes The Floor (1958)

Label | Topic
Producer | Bill Leader • Dick Swettenham
Art Direction | Uncredited
Nationality | USA
Running Time | 31:45

In the engine of modern music, this is one of the spark plugs. *Jack Elliott Takes The Floor* (later released as *Muleskinner*) was recorded off the cuff at London's Topic Records. Jack talks us into each song with wry, leisurely intros that are worth the price of admission alone. His guitar technique was an education to the hard-strumming "folk singers" of the time, but also impacted on later popular music.

The album pulls together a pantheon of previously little-known sources—including Jesse Fuller, Reverend Gary Davis, field hollers, and prison blues—and is remarkably hard edged. The raw, unadorned beauty of "Dink's Song" and "Black Baby" remain spine-chilling highlights. "Mule Skinner's Blues" and "San Francisco Bay Blues" became hallmarks of Elliott's work.

Jack played frequently with Woodie Guthrie in the 1950s. Having settled in New York in 1961, he met a kid in Guthrie's hospital room who was soon to have a poster out announcing his own first NYC gig: "Son of Jack Elliott—Bob Dylan." In *Chronicles*, Dylan describes first hearing . . . *Takes The Floor*: "I felt like I'd been cast into sudden hell . . . His voice leaps all over the room . . . and he plays the guitar effortlessly in a fluid flat-picking perfected style…"

Paul McCartney, Mick Jagger, and Keith Richards have all also acknowledged Jack's influence. Little wonder: this release is still as engaging as it was in 1958. **SJar**

Sarah Vaughan
Sarah Vaughan At Mister Kelly's (1958)

Label | EmArcy
Producer | Bob Shad
Art Direction | Uncredited
Nationality | USA
Running Time | 37:00

Sarah Vaughan was already one of jazz's most beloved divas when she opened a week-long run at the Chicago nightspot Mister Kelly's in the summer of 1957. While Ella Fitzgerald swung harder and Billie Holiday got deeper into a lyric, no jazz vocalist has ever come close to matching Vaughan's flawless delivery and sumptuous sound. A virtuoso with complete control of pitch, timbre, and dynamics, Vaughan used her rich contralto voice like a horn, embellishing melodies with the imaginative leaps and compositional structure of the most profound instrumental improvisers.

Known as "Sassy" for her earthy irreverence, Vaughan was a key, though often uncredited, participant in the formation of bebop. She was best in small group settings, and she never had a better band than the trio she brought into Mister Kelly's, with the underrated pianist Jimmy Jones, bass monster Richard Davis, and seminal modern jazz drummer Roy Haynes, whose idiosyncratic fills and lightning reflexes made him a perfect foil for Vaughan.

The 1991 EmArcy CD *Sarah Vaughan At Mister Kelly's* is a good argument for reissues, containing twice the music of the original album. She is ineffable on "September In The Rain," and sensually assured on "Honeysuckle Rose." When she forgets the lyric to "How High The Moon," she proceeds with aplomb, offering some impromptu props to Ella Fitzgerald. **AG**

Ella Fitzgerald
Sings The Gershwin Song Book (1959)

Label | Verve
Producer | Norman Granz
Art Direction | Bernard Buffet
Nationality | USA
Running Time | 194:10

Ray Charles
The Genius Of Ray Charles (1959)

Label | Atlantic
Producer | Nesuhi Ertegun
Art Direction | Marvin Israel
Nationality | USA
Running Time | 37:58

Norman Granz took 28-year-old Ella Fitzgerald under his wing in 1946, enlisting the singer to take part in his *Jazz At The Philharmonic* all-star concert series. However, it was not until Granz signed Fitzgerald to his new Verve label, and set her working on a series of albums, each devoted to the works of the great American songwriters—Richard Rodgers and Duke Ellington among them—that her reputation became unassailable.

While a little of Cole Porter's archness was lost in Fitzgerald's translation, and not every Rodgers and Hart song proved worthy of her attention, Fitzgerald's easygoing voice and George Gershwin's unmatchable melodies were made for each other. A tender "Oh, Lady, Be Good!" is a revelation next to the more familiar uptempo scat masterclass she delivered at shows for decades; a slumbersome "Embraceable You" is just as warm. But it is the uptempo numbers that really dazzle. The gentle, effortless swing Fitzgerald brought to everything she sung finds its *métier* on the likes of "Clap Yo' Hands," "Bidin' My Time," and a delicious "'S Wonderful"; the relish with which Fitzgerald delivers Ira Gershwin's silly sarsaparilla/"sasparella" couplet on "Let's Call The Whole Thing Off" is priceless. Riddle, at the peak of his powers after several sessions with Frank Sinatra, is inspired throughout. It is the best of the *Song Book* albums, and the definitive collection of the works of perhaps the definitive American songwriters. **WF-J**

During the 1950s, Ray Charles had trouble sitting down at his piano without pioneering a new style of American music. Though he had introduced himself to the mainstream (i.e. white people) with his 1959 crossover smash "What'd I Say," Charles was a veteran of the gas-and-go chitlin circuit, having developed along the way a revolutionary fusion of blues, jazz, R&B, and gospel. By his third proper LP, the suitably anointed genius had the blueprints for soul music at his fingertips.

Categories seemed futile, though, when Charles entered the studio late in 1959. At his essence, he was a romancer of the senses. *Genius…* comes on strong with a ravishing set of six big-band-flavored jazz numbers, highlighted by the swanky horns and walking bass lines of "Let The Good Times Roll" and "Alexander's Rag Time Band." With arrangements by Quincy Jones and accompaniment from members of the Count Basie and Duke Ellington bands, Charles was helming the most richly crafted popular music of the era.

For the second side, Charles turned in a more seductive direction and arrived at a roster of ballads backed by massive, swooning string sections and a chorus of what sounds like flirtatious mermaids. His tuneful command of standards like "Just For A Thrill" and "Come Rain Or Come Shine" was truly astounding for a man still in his twenties, and signaled both his eagerness and ability to transcend genres at will. **MO**

Miles Davis | Kind Of Blue (1959)

Label | Columbia
Producer | Irving Townsend
Art Direction | Jay Maisel
Nationality | USA
Running Time | 45:52

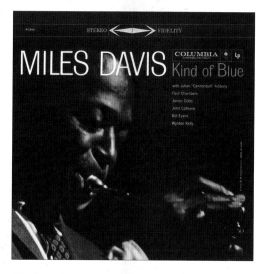

Sometimes an album's hype becomes all too stifling. Easy epithets such as "classic," "groundbreaking," and "milestone" are all too lazily tossed around, and in their midst we lose sight of the original material's worth. Thankfully, *Kind Of Blue* comes with no such critical health warning—it is a genre-defining moment in twentieth-century music, period.

Since 1955, Davis had played with saxophonist John Coltrane, and the following years saw Davis' group honing their sound before arriving at *Kind Of Blue*.

Recorded at Columbia's 30th Street Studio in New York, the five tracks were laid in nine hours over two sessions, a time frame all the more remarkable for the band having never encountered the pieces before—this was a ploy Davis frequently used, feeling that individual artists would consequently focus more on their performances. Davis also only relied on brief preparations, but managed to lead his players in a scintillating display of spontaneity.

From mid-tempo opener "So What," the album swings through a wide range of styles; the haunting "Blue In Green," with Bill Evans's subdued piano accompanying Davis' mournful trumpet; and the languid Hispanic influences of "Flamenco Sketches." The band's tightness is reflected in the six takes needed to record five tracks—yep, only "Sketches ..." required a second run-through.

The album was showered with plaudits from its release. But even Miles was not flawless. Three tracks were recorded in the wrong key (later to be tidied up on re-releases). Like you noticed. **SJac**

> "I don't pay no attention to what critics say about me, the good or the bad. The toughest critic I got is myself ...and I'm too vain to play anything I think is bad."
>
> Miles Davis, 1962

Track Listing

	#	Track		Time
▶	01	**So What**	(Davis)	9:25
	02	**Freddie Freeloader**	(Davis)	9:49
	03	**Blue In Green**	(Davis)	5:37
	04	**All Blues**	(Davis)	11:35
▶	05	**Flamenco Sketches**	(Davis)	9:26

Marty Robbins
Gunfighter Ballads And Trail Songs (1959)

Label | CBS
Producer | Don Law
Art Direction | Howard Fritzson
Nationality | USA
Running Time | 35:53

Martin Robinson often claimed that his childhood was unhappy. One positive he did take from his upbringing, however, was a love of the West. He was raised in the dusty Arizona town of Glendale, stealing off to catch the latest Gene Autry film when he was not working as a horse breaker with his brother. After several mainstream hits during the 1950s (including "Singing The Blues," simultaneously taken to No. 1 by Guy Mitchell), the renamed Robbins turned to his Western heritage for this mold-breaking, trend-setting record.

Recorded in a single day with a well-drilled yet understated band, *Gunfighter Ballads And Trail Songs* was a homage to the Old West. Some cuts were traditional story-songs, most notably "Billy The Kid" and "The Strawberry Roan." What set the record apart was the quartet of Robbins-penned songs, delivered in his unmistakably tender croon. "Big Iron" is a wonderfully evocative piece of widescreen Western myth-spinning, informed by tales told to the young Robbins by his Texas ranger grandfather. "El Paso" worked the theme into a first-person narrative, Robbins telling of how he shot cold a stranger for the love of a mysterious Mexican girl. The recording won the first Grammy awarded to a country song; the LP from which it came set the template for the countless country concept albums that followed.

Robbins went on to further successes: in the charts, sure, but also as an actor, TV host, writer (he penned a novel, *The Small Man*), and stock-car racing driver. **WF-J**

"I despise honest labor."

Marty Robbins, 1982

Track Listing		
▶ 01 **Big Iron** (Robbins)		4:03
02 **Cool Water** (Nolan)		3:16
03 **Billy The Kid** (Trad., arr. Robbins)		2:25
04 **A Hundred And Sixty Acres** (Kapp)		1:47
05 **They're Hanging Me Tonight** (Lowe·Wolpert)		3:11
▶ 06 **The Strawberry Roan** (Trad.)		3:30
▶ 07 **El Paso** (Robbins)		4:26
08 **In The Valley** (Robbins)		1:53
09 **The Master's Call** (Robbins)		3:13
10 **Running Gun** (J. Glaser·T. Glaser)		2:17
11 **The Little Green Valley** (Robinson)		2:32
12 **Utah Carol** (Trad.)		3:18

The Dave Brubeck Quartet
Time Out (1959)

Label | Columbia
Producer | Teo Macero
Art Direction | Uncredited
Nationality | USA
Running Time | 38:21

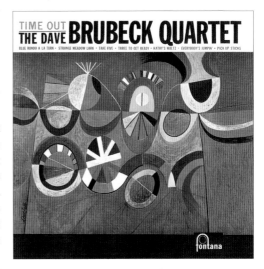

A hit was the last thing that pianist Dave Brubeck expected when he went into the studio in 1959 with a sheaf of odd-metered music. The bespectacled pianist had already built up an enviable empire of fans through his pioneering concerts at college campuses. A cheerfully experimental player who never let his popularity interfere with his muse, Brubeck recorded one of the most popular jazz albums of all time with material that was unlikely fare, to say the least.

The tune "Take Five," conceived in the previously swing-proof time signature of 5/4, finds the pianist maintaining a steady, percussive vamp while altoist Paul Desmond weaves a sinuous line. In many ways, Brubeck is not the star of the proceedings. It is often forgotten that it was Desmond, whose dry-martini sound played such an important role in the quartet's success, who wrote the enduring hit. Just as important is Joe Morello's supremely confident drum work and Eugene Wright's rock-solid bass playing, which turn such tricky material as the 9/8 "Blue Rondo À La Turk" and "Three To Get Ready," which vacillates between 3/4 and 4/4 time, into enduring jazz staples. Remember, this was the era when John Coltrane, Cecil Taylor, and Ornette Coleman were blazing free-jazz trails.

In the self-defeating logic of jazz critics, the often maligned Brubeck lost even more stature with the crossover success of *Time Out*. But the album continues to sell well to this day, and, despite its pervasive use in advertisements, is a captivating achievement. **AG**

> "I look forward to the day I've recorded everything I've written, but I don't think that day's going to happen."
>
> Dave Brubeck, 2002

Track Listing

▶	01	**Blue Rondo À La Turk** (Brubeck)	6:44
	02	**Strange Meadow Lark** (Brubeck)	7:22
▶	03	**Take Five** (Desmond)	5:24
	04	**Three To Get Ready** (Brubeck)	5:24
	05	**Kathy's Waltz** (Brubeck)	4:48
	06	**Everybody's Jumpin'** (Brubeck)	4:23
	07	**Pick Up Sticks** (Brubeck)	4:16

- **Armstrong walks on Moon**

- **Contraceptive pill on sale**

- **Gagarin first man in space**

- **Kennedy assassinated**

- **Cuban missile crisis**

1960s

Joan Baez | Joan Baez (1960)

Label | Vanguard
Producer | Maynard Solomon
Art Direction | Jules Halfant
Nationality | USA
Running Time | 46:07

Joan Baez

After playing to coffee houses around Boston in the late 1950s, Joan Baez's break came with the 1959 Newport Folk Festival, where the pretty girl with the angelic voice astounded the crowd. And despite the seeming absence of the trademark ideological stance she later became known for, even in the early days politics mattered—Baez opted for a record deal with small label Vanguard, impressed by their decision to release material by folk act The Weavers despite many of the members being accused of being Communists.

The decision certainly paid off, for both Baez and Vanguard—her self-titled debut is still one of the highest selling solo female folk albums of all time—and saw her receive the first of her six gold records (a success even more impressive considering that this was a time when the singles charts governed supreme). She released 17 records through Vanguard, and while she later was to become known as "Queen" to Bob Dylan's "King Of Folk Music" (Dylan was in awe of Baez at first), her name was not connected with Dylan's until her third album, on which she first began performing contemporary material.

The debut album from the 20-year-old consisted of traditional songs, including several ballads, from England and America—particular highlights being "Wildwood Flower" and "House Of The Rising Sun," which showcase Baez's vibrant, clear voice. Although her place at the forefront of the protest movement was still around the corner, Baez's strength, compassion, and courage were apparent on this initial release, which did much to revitalize folk music for a new generation. **AH-N**

"My devotion to ... social change ... will go on until I fall into the grave."

Joan Baez, 1993

Track Listing		
▶ 01	Silver Dagger (Trad.)	3:42
02	Fare Thee Well (10,000 Miles) (Gude)	3:18
▶ 03	House Of The Rising Sun (Trad.)	2:54
04	All My Trails (Public Domain)	4:36
▶ 05	Wildwood Flowers (Trad.)	2:34
06	Donna Donna (Secunda·Zeitlin)	3:12
▶ 07	John Riley (Belmonte·Gibson)	3:51
08	Rake And Rambling Boy (Public Domain)	1:57
09	Little Moses (Trad.)	3:27
▶ 10	Mary Hamilton (Trad.)	5:54
11	Henry Martin (Trad.)	4:11
12	El Preson Numero Nueve (Public Domain)	2:47

Elvis Presley | Elvis Is Back! (1960)

Label | RCA
Producer | Chet Atkins • Steve Sholes
Art Direction | Uncredited
Nationality | USA
Running Time | 31:54

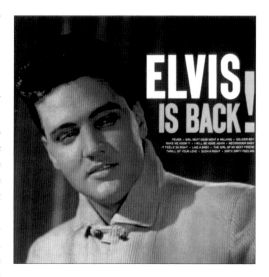

Starved of material for nearly two years, RCA were desperate to record Elvis the moment he left the army; Presley's manager wanted to keep them hungry, so he retained the upper hand in negotiations. It proved to be one of the rare occasions on which the colonel did not get his way.

Gathering the cream of musicians from Elvis' pre-draft days meant that the King felt at home immediately. That said, the first two cuts they attempted, "Make Me Know It" and "Soldier Boy," took forever to get right. But then two sides of a single were cut very quickly ("Stuck On You" was to be in stores within days), and the band sensed the years fall away.

The final pair of songs combined to catapult Elvis right back to his roots after 24 long months. "A Mess Of The Blues" (a non-album track) and "It Feels So Right" are pulsating, sexy teases—the sound of a man who had not been getting any for too long.

Two weeks later, the team reconvened under strict instructions to lay down eight songs—no more—a contractual obligation that would complete the LP. But this was to be a night in which the Memphis Flash came to the fore, as excited and as exciting as he had been for, and since his first Sun sessions. The more they played the looser they got, the rowdier they became. They did pop ("The Girl Of My Best Friend"), they tackled opera ("It's Now Or Never"), they did torch ("Fever" and "Are You Lonesome Tonight"), and then they got lewd ("Such A Night," "Like A Baby," and "Reconsider Baby"). Twelve tracks; it would be nine years before Elvis got so much freedom again. **DH**

"I don't know anything about music. In my line you don't have to."

Elvis Presley, c.1960

Track Listing

01	Make Me Know It	(Blackwell)	2:00
▶ 02	Fever	(Cooley • Davenport)	3:33
03	The Girl Of My Best Friend	(Bobrick • Ross)	2:23
04	I Will Be Home Again	(Benjamin • Leveen • Singer)	2:34
▶ 05	Dirty, Dirty Feeling	(Leiber • Stoller)	1:34
06	The Thrill Of Your Love	(Kesler)	3:01
07	Soldier Boy	(Jones • Williams)	3:06
▶ 08	Such A Night	(Chase)	3:00
▶ 09	It Feels So Right	(Weisman • Wise)	2:10
10	Girl Next Door Went A'Walking	(Rise • Wayne)	2:13
▶ 11	Like A Baby	(Stone)	2:40
▶ 12	Reconsider Baby	(Fulsom)	3:40

Miriam Makeba | Miriam Makeba (1960)

Label | RCA Victor
Producer | Harry Belafonte
Art Direction | Uncredited
Nationality | South Africa
Running Time | 34:42

Traditional Xhosa wedding songs swing into airy African jazz moods, mellifluous Indonesian lullabies, and infectious Calypso romps—myriad influences and styles working to enormous effect. Recorded a year after the international hit musical *King Kong* (1959), which provided many black South African musicians with the opportunity to escape apartheid, Makeba's debut album paints a compelling portrait of the artist in exile.

Building on the rapturous reception she received performing at New York's Village Vanguard, *Miriam Makeba* showcases a 28-year-old singer stepping confidently onto the world stage. To Western ears, much of the album's magic lies in the "exotic" timbres of her Xhosa vocal "clicks" on Afro-pop breezes like the "Click Song" and the melodic lilt of "Mbube" (featuring The Chad Mitchell Trio). *Time Magazine* immediately tuned into this marriage of authentic African sounds and polished Western pop, hailing Makeba as "the most exciting new singing talent to appear in many years." Yet the album failed to translate critical plaudits into sales, and her record label declined to renew her contract. Granted, novelty pop ditties ("The Naughty Little Flea") and folk standards ("House Of The Rising Sun") were tailor made for crossover success, but earthy ballads like "Umhome" remained too quintessentially African for mainstream audiences to fully appreciate.

Less roots-driven offerings would soon reward Makeba with "Mama Afrika" status as the continent's premier diva, but here, it is the sound of a South African émigrée channeling her yearning for her homeland through an exiled lens that most captivates. **MK**

"My life has been like a yo-yo."

Miriam Makeba, 2000

Track Listing

01	**The Retreat Song** (Makeba)		2:34
02	**Suliram** (Trad. Indonesian lullaby)		2:45
▶ 03	**The Click Song** (Makeba · Khoza · Majola · Mdedle · Mogosti)		2:09
▶ 04	**Umhome** (Makeba)		1:16
05	**Olilili** (Silinga)		2:31
▶ 06	**Lakutshn, Ilanga** (Dvashe · Glazer)		2:07
▶ 07	**Mbube** (Linda)		3:17
▶ 08	**The Naughty Little Flea** (Thomas)		3:45
09	**Where Does It Lead** (Davis)		2:29
10	**Nomeva** (Makeba)		2:37
▶ 11	**House Of The Rising Sun** (Lopez)		1:57
12	**Saduva** (Makeba)		2:30
13	**One More Dance** (Carter)		2:40
14	**Iya Guduza** (Makeba)		2:05

The Everly Brothers
A Date With The Everly Brothers (1960)

Label | Warner Bros.
Producer | Don Everly
Art Direction | Uncredited
Nationality | USA
Running Time | 27:53

They had label problems, management woes, marital difficulties, and drug troubles, and Elvis was back from the army to reclaim his throne—the brothers responded to this challenge in 1960, creating their finest body of work. Their first LP for their new label, *It's Everly Time*, had been recorded over two weeks in March and issued in April, becoming a Top Ten hit on both sides of the Atlantic. They had also taped a couple of songs, "Cathy's Clown" and "Always It's You," that were held back for single release. When it rocketed to No. 1, the boys were back in the studio to get a second LP ready.

It would have been reasonable to expect the cupboard to have been bare, and the first tracks recorded, "Lucille" and "Baby What Do You Want Me To Do," suggest that material was in short supply. But the radical reinterpretations showed the Everly harmonies could refresh the most familiar songs. In addition, the brothers' favorite songwriters, the husband-and-wife team Boudleaux and Felice Bryant, offered five songs, so Don and Phil, who had hardly contributed to the previous album, were under pressure to put pen to paper. Within two weeks, they had a dozen paradigm Everly songs ("Love Hurts," "Made To Love," "Stick With Me Baby") that would have kept the singles chart busy for months. Had they waited until the end of the year, it would have been even better: "Temptation," "Ebony Eyes," and "Walk Right Back" had then been recorded. **DH**

Jimmy Smith
Back At The Chicken Shack (1960)

Label | Blue Note
Producer | Alfred Lion
Art Direction | Reid Miles
Nationality | USA
Running Time | 43:49

Redolent of church pews and skating rinks, the organ was once relegated to hip-free zones, a square cousin to the autoharp and accordion. And then along came Jimmy Smith, who turned his attention to the instrument in 1954 just as the Hammond company was unveiling its relatively compact new B3 model.

Smith transformed the organ's lamentable image with his soulful synthesis of bebop, blues, and gospel, creating a powerfully grooving new sound. He spawned a new style of music—soul jazz—and a host of disciples who took up the Hammond B3 and formed combos.

Back At The Chicken Shack is arguably Smith's greatest album, relentlessly grooving, harmonically sophisticated, and earthy as the Delta mud. Recorded on April 25, 1960, it put saxophonist Stanley Turrentine on the map, but the contributions of the elegantly economical guitarist Kenny Burrell and irresistibly funky drummer Donald Bailey are just as crucial.

Whether distilling a hoary standard such as "When I Grow Too Old To Dream" down to its essential notes or surging through "Minor Chant," the quartet sounds ready for a rumble. Almost as arresting as the music is the album's cover. Instead of Reid Miles' typically moody Blue Note character studies set in his trademark uncluttered esthetic, *Back At The Chicken Shack* features a playful shot of Smith in a bright red shirt, seated in front of said shack with a hound dog at his feet. **AG**

Muddy Waters
Muddy Waters
At Newport (1960)

Label | Chess
Producer | Uncredited
Art Direction | Uncredited
Nationality | USA
Running Time | 32:38

Bill Evans
Sunday At The
Village Vanguard (1961)

Label | Riverside
Producer | Orrin Keepnews
Art Direction | Ken Deardoff
Nationality | USA
Running Time | 68:09

Muddy Waters spent most of the 1950s on the R&B charts with hits like "Rollin' and Tumblin'" and "Louisiana Blues," but it was not until 1960 that he introduced himself—and live blues—to the white mainstream audience. After seeing his sales begin to dip toward the twilight of the 1950s, Chess Records decided to market its greatest talent as an album-based performer, and subsequently brought a tape recorder to Muddy's performance at the 1960 Newport Jazz Festival.

When he took the stage that afternoon, Waters was about as unfamiliar with his white audience as they were with his countrified brand of Chicago boogie. The walloping refrain of "Hoochie Coochie Man" and unvarnished wail of "Baby Please Don't Go" were a stark departure from Dizzie Gillespie's chilled trumpet. But by the close of the set, Muddy's powerful baritone, James Cotton's crying harmonica, and Otis Spann's barroom piano had the hip kids dancing in the aisles on the show-stopping "Got My Mojo Working."

If this album simply represented the moment when live blues invited itself into suburban homes, it would still be remembered. If it were only the album that acquainted the likes of Jimmy Page and Eric Clapton with America's urban sound, it would be a landmark. But after 45 years of consistent sales, *Muddy Waters At Newport* is, at its essence, a testament to the magnetism and soulfulness of raw blues at its best. **MO**

One of the most widely influential pianists of the 1960s and '70s, Bill Evans was a seminal force in jazz who seemed to emerge as a fully formed artist in the late 1950s. A ravishingly lyrical player of tremendous harmonic sophistication, he attained a unique, bell-like tone from the piano, which made his long, flowing lines glow with a blue-flame luminescence.

He had already made a huge impact through his work as a sideman with George Russell, Lee Konitz, Jimmy Giuffre, Charles Mingus, and most famously Miles Davis, contributing significantly to the trumpeter's groundbreaking album *Kind Of Blue*. Evans left Davis to start his own band in 1959, and he found the perfect collaborators in virtuoso bassist Scott LaFaro and the supremely sensitive drummer Paul Motian. By the time Evans decided to record the trio at the Village Vanguard in June 1961, it had attained a level of communication that verged on the telepathic. The highly interactive approach the trio developed, erasing the boundaries between accompanist and soloist, introduced radical new possibilities for small-group jazz. Each tune bears repeated listening, but "Gloria's Step" is astonishing, while the interplay on "Alice In Wonderland" ranks among jazz's greatest achievements.

Evans died at only 51 after a decades-long struggle with drug addiction. But even if this was his only legacy, his spot in the jazz firmament would be assured. **AG**

Ray Charles | Modern Sounds In Country And Western Music (1962)

Label | ABC-Paramount
Producer | Sid Feller
Art Direction | Flynn • Viceroy
Nationality | USA
Running Time | 39:51

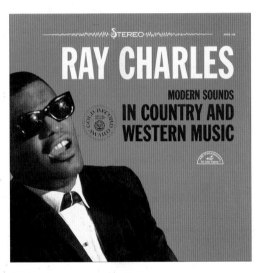

Hard, perhaps, to imagine what a jolt this must have been in 1962: a raw and strung-out black R&B singer tackling Hank Williams and Don Gibson 18 months before Martin Luther King had a dream. But while the record's shock value has grown blurry in the last four decades, the quality of *Modern Sounds In Country And Western Music* is still crystal clear from the first, irresistibly swinging bars of opener "Bye Bye Love."

No record before *Modern Sounds ...*, and only a few that came after it, mixed soul with sentimentality so effectively. Witness the way Charles' heartbroken vocals bounce off the supper-club choir on Gibson's "I Can't Stop Loving You," released only reluctantly as a single—Charles, who made the record against his label's wishes, wanted the album to be treated as a single body of work—but eventually it became a chart-topping million-seller. The ache in his voice is no more restrained on hardy perennial "Born To Lose," but Charles' genius is that he never milks it. He almost whispers his way through Floyd Tillman's "I Love You So Much It Hurts," but treats Eddy Arnold's "Just A Little Lovin'" as a casual come-on, a keyed-in rhythm section adding an acre of sass to what was, in Arnold's hands, little more than a wink across the honky-tonk floor.

Throughout, Marty Paich's string arrangements stay just to the right side of the line that separates sensitive from cloying; there is great big-band scoring from Gil Fuller and, especially, Gerald Wilson. The album spent 14 weeks at the top of the U.S. charts. **WF-J**

" ...if I play it right I just might gain more [fans] than I lose."

Ray Charles, 1962

Track Listing

▶	01	**Bye Bye Love** (B. Bryant • F. Bryant)	2:12
▶	02	**You Don't Know Me** (Arnold • Walker)	3:16
	03	**Half As Much** (Williams)	3:28
	04	**I Love You So Much It Hurts** (Tillman)	3:35
	05	**Just A Little Lovin'** (Arnold • Clements)	3:29
▶	06	**Born To Lose** (Brown • Daffan)	3:18
	07	**Worried Mind** (Daffan • Davis)	2:57
	08	**It Makes No Difference Now** (Davis • Tillman)	3:36
	09	**You Win Again** (Williams)	3:31
	10	**Careless Love** (Handy)	4:01
▶	11	**I Can't Stop Loving You** (Gibson)	4:14
	12	**Hey, Good Lookin'** (Williams)	2:14

Booker T. And The M.G.s | Green Onions (1962)

Label | Stax
Producer | Jim Stewart
Art Direction | Haig Adishian
Nationality | USA
Running Time | 34:55

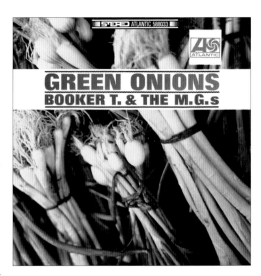

Every few years in the early days of rock an instrumental slipped through the endless ranks of vocal discs and shot to the top—Bill Doggett's "Honky Tonk" in 1956, or The Champs' "Tequila" in 1958, for example. In 1962 it was the turn of "Green Onions," an insinuating organ-guitar blues album that reinvented Jimmy Smith's organ jazz for the pop market, highlighted by taut snatches of guitar. Booker T. and the M.G.s were the most soulful bar band in the whole world.

The album that followed, fronted by its photo of fresh green onions ready for a Southern stew, featured the hit (an improvised studio jam recorded while the group were waiting to start a recording session) along with grooves like the slow-burning "Behave Yourself" and R&B covers of Ray Charles' "I Got A Woman" and Smokey Robinson's "One Who Really Loves You." Other highlights include dynamic reworkings of pop tunes like Acker Bilk's "Stranger On The Shore" and "Rinky-Dink," and the jazzy "Comin' Home Baby." In time, the Stax sound behind Otis Redding and Carla Thomas became famous and we finally learned who the mysterious M.G.s were: organist Booker T. Jones, guitarist Steve Cropper, bassist Duck Dunn, and drummer Al Jackson—unusually for a black music label, Cropper and Dunn were white.

In 1962, *Green Onions*' short, unadorned tracks sounded ultra cool, Cropper's stinging lines cutting through Booker's mellow chords. *Green Onions* is a truly seminal album: its naive vigor and rock-soul fusion were to inspire The Allman Brothers, Lynyrd Skynyrd, and a generation of Southern blues-rockers. **ML**

"A lot of drummers copy Al Jackson."

Steve Cropper, 1994

Track Listing

▶ 01	Green Onions (Cropper•Jackson•Jones•Steinberg)	2:45
02	Rinky Dink (Clowney•Winley)	2:39
03	I Got A Woman (Charles•Richard)	3:32
04	Mo' Onions (Jones•Cropper•Jackson•Steinberg)	2:50
05	Twist And Shout (Medley•Russell)	2:09
▶ 06	Behave Yourself (Jones•Cropper•Jackson•Steinberg)	3:45
07	Stranger On The Shore (Bilk•Mellin)	2:18
▶ 08	Lonely Avenue (Pomus)	3:25
09	One Who Really Loves You (Robinson)	2:22
10	You Can't Sit Down (Clark•Mann•Muldrow)	2:46
11	A Woman, A Lover, A Friend (Wyche)	3:15
12	Comin' Home Baby (Dorough•Tucker)	3:09

Stan Getz And Charlie Byrd | Jazz Samba (1962)

Label | Verve
Producer | Creed Taylor
Art Direction | Olga Albizu
Nationality | USA
Running Time | 33:08

While it is often credited with sparking the bossa nova craze, *Jazz Samba* didn't introduce Brazil's new sound to the rest of the world. Marcel Camus' hit 1959 film *Black Orpheus* had already intrigued international audiences with its haunting score by Luiz Bonfa and Antonio Carlos Jobim. But when guitarist Charlie Byrd returned from a trip to South America with tapes of the music he heard in Brazil and started passing them around to his friends, he lit a fuse that gently detonated with this captivating collaboration. Stan Getz's lithe, luminous tenor sax sound turned out to be a perfect match for bossa nova's ineffably graceful melodies and swaying rhythmic pulse.

Recorded in a single session in a Washington DC church, the album is a perfect melding of swing and samba, with Getz's velvet tenor flowing seamlessly from one track into another. A jazz star of the late 1940s and early '50s, Getz had struggled with drug problems and only recently returned to the United States after several years in Europe when "Desafinado" turned into a runaway hit. The album's success, and Getz's even more popular bossa nova sessions with Joao and Astrud Gilberto, turned the Brazilian sound into a real commercial force at a time when the initial energy of rock 'n' roll had dissipated into forgettable bubble-gum pop and The Beatles were still playing seedy dives in Hamburg.

The partnership of Byrd and Getz soon ended in acrimony, but their music stands as an island of calm, transcendent beauty in a pop music universe too often ruled by flash and image. **AG**

> " ...the reason why I play now is just to bring music to people who want to hear music. To me that's the ultimate."

Stan Getz, 1950

Track Listing

▶	01	**Desafinado** (Cavanaugh·Hendricks·Jobim·Mendonça)	5:49
	02	**Samba Dees Days** (Byrd)	3:33
	03	**O Pato** (Silva·Teixeira)	2:30
	04	**Samba Triste** (Blanco·Powell)	4:44
▶	05	**Samba De Uma Nota Só** (Jobim·Mendonça)	6:11
	06	**E Luxo Só** (Barroso·Peixoto)	3:41
▶	07	**Bahia** (Barroso)	6:40

Ray Price | Night Life (1962)

Label | Koch
Producer | Frank Jones • Don Law
Art Direction | Uncredited
Nationality | USA
Running Time | 37:36

Ray Price was at a crossroads. In 1952, on the advice of Hank Williams, the Texan had moved to Nashville; with Williams' band he soon carved out a successful career as one of honky-tonk's toughest operators. A decade later, though, country was cleaning itself up. Buck Owens' crisp, Telecaster-heavy sound—tailor-made for AM radio and emanating not from Nashville but from Bakersfield, California—was alerting country music to its commercial possibilities. Changes were afoot.

In the record's spoken introduction, Price describes what will follow as "songs of happiness, sadness, heartbreak." There is a lot of the latter here, however almost none of the former. Don't be fooled by Price's trademark dancefloor shuffle—*Night Life* is Nashville's answer to Sinatra's *In The Wee Small Hours*.

The title track, written by Willie Nelson (who played in Price's band for a time before the pair fell out, apparently when Nelson shot one of Price's roosters), is one of the most covered country songs, but Price owns it, his bluesy vocal both implacable and defiant. The 11 songs that follow keep to the same settings: empty houses, dim-lit barrooms, boulevards of broken dreams. A string section appears on two songs, but the key presence is Buddy Emmons, whose pedal-steel work both keys the record to a honky-tonk sound and swamps it in melancholy.

Price traded in his Nudie suits (the Indian headdresses that paid homage to his nickname, the Cherokee Cowboy) for a dapper lounge look and a chart-topping cover of "Danny Boy." But he never made a better disc than this archetype of closing-time misery. **WF-J**

"If I was a vet I'd be a rich man."

Ray Price, 2002

Track Listing		
▶ 01 **Introduction And Theme/Night Life** (Breeland • Buskirk • Nelson)		6:49
02 **Lonely Street** (Belew • Sowder • Stevenson)		3:02
▶ 03 **The Wild Side Of Life** (Carter • Warren)		3:00
04 **Sittin' And Thinkin'** (Rich)		2:47
▶ 05 **The Twenty-Fourth Hour** (Price)		2:54
06 **A Girl In The Night** (Thompson)		2:49
▶ 07 **Pride** (Stanton • Walker)		2:39
08 **There's No Fool Like A Young Fool** (Thomasson)		2:59
09 **If She Could See Me Now** (Cochran)		2:42
10 **Bright Lights And Blonde Haired Women** (Kirk)		2:26
▶ 11 **Are You Sure** (Emmons • Nelson)		2:24
12 **Let Me Talk To You** (Davis • Dill)		3:05

The Beatles | With The Beatles (1963)

Label | Parlophone
Producer | George Martin
Art Direction | Robert Freeman
Nationality | UK
Running Time | 33:24

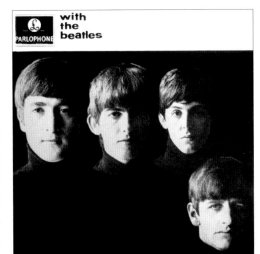

The first-ever million-selling album by a group in Britain, *With The Beatles* cemented The Beatles' unassailable location at the very zenith of the UK hit parade. Recorded over six days between July and October 1963, it is a record that captures their northern soul blazing brightly and assuredly. Although still fundamentally a selection of live favorites and hastily written originals, the album revealed the confidence EMI had in their charges, as it contained no singles—virtually unheard of for that time.

The influence of Motown, in particular, is felt throughout the choice of cover versions. George Harrison and John Lennon's harmonies on The Miracles' "You Really Got A Hold On Me" are arguably the best tribute the group performed on record, and Lennon's tear through Barrett Strong's "Money" provides a showstopping moment. Of the originals, "Little Child" and "It Won't Be Long" continue the frantic rush of the first album, while "All My Loving" is Paul McCartney's first classic. However, a particularly low-key moment steals the show: although absent from any Beatles retrospective, "All I've Got To Do" is one of their most intimate moments—Lennon at his raw and direct best.

Taken by Robert Freeman in Bournemouth's Palace Court Hotel in August 1963, the sleeve photo is arguably the most iconic of The Beatles ever taken, as well as being one of the Sixties' most defining images.

With The Beatles was received rapturously and remains fun and fresh. The sleeve and eight of the tracks became *Meet The Beatles*, their debut album release in America. World domination was but a step away. **DE**

> "Till death do us part."
>
> George Harrison, 1964

Track Listing

▶	01	It Won't Be Long (Lennon·McCartney)	2:11
▶	02	All I've Got To Do (Lennon·McCartney)	2:01
▶	03	All My Loving (Lennon·McCartney)	2:10
	04	Don't Bother Me (Harrison)	2:29
	05	Little Child (Lennon·McCartney)	1:45
	06	Till There Was You (Wilson)	2:14
▶	07	Please Mister Postman (Brianbert·Dobbin·Garman·Garrett)	2:34
	08	Roll Over Beethoven (Berry)	2:44
	09	Hold Me Tight (Lennon·McCartney)	2:29
▶	10	You Really Got A Hold On Me (Robinson)	3:00
	11	I Wanna Be Your Man (Lennon·McCartney)	1:56
	12	Devil In Her Heart (Drapkin)	2:25
	13	Not A Second Time (Lennon·McCartney)	2:05
▶	14	Money (Bradford·Gordy)	2:47

Bob Dylan | The Freewheelin' Bob Dylan (1963)

Label | Columbia
Producer | John Hammond
Art Direction | Uncredited
Nationality | USA
Running Time | 50:04

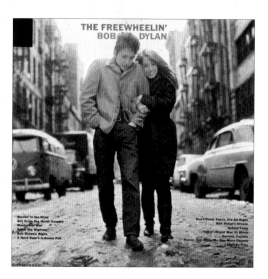

While folk music throughout the 1950s and '60s was often a mainstay of American popular culture, no one quite typified the tensions of the time as well as Bob Dylan. And *The Freewheelin' Bob Dylan* in particular did much to cement his reputation as a singer-songwriter of near-perfect skill, gifted with a poet's eye for detail, narrative, and humor.

The album underlined Dylan's commitment to social change. (Its cover shows Dylan with his then girlfriend, Suze Rotolo, walking in Greenwich Village, where he first drew attention as a folk singer.) A trilogy of songs contained here—"Blowin' In The Wind," "A Hard Rain's A-Gonna Fall," and "Masters Of War"— seemed to encapsulate one generation's desire for change. The three remain, in many respects, Dylan's most enduring songs, covered by artists from all genres, including rap, reggae, and country.

As ever, Dylan went out of his way to defy categorization—setting a pattern for the rest of his career. On songs like "Don't Think Twice, It's All Right" and the sublime "Girl From The North Country," he toyed with tragic love balladry, surrealism, and even comedy. In that respect at least, *The Freewheelin'...* owes much to the body of work that initially inspired him: that of Woody Guthrie. These songs similarly ignore swathes of American society, preferring to identify with the country's downtrodden masses. As such, the album can be viewed as a manifesto.

While Dylan endlessly bemoaned his typecasting as a spokesperson for his era, *The Freewheelin'...* was a rare and timely evocation of his country. **BW**

"I never wanted to be a prophet or a savior."

Bob Dylan, 2004

Track Listing		
▶ 01 Blowin' In The Wind [Dylan]		2:48
02 Girl From The North Country [Dylan]		3:22
▶ 03 Masters Of War [Dylan]		4:34
04 Down The Highway [Dylan]		3:27
05 Bob Dylan's Blues [Dylan]		2:23
▶ 06 A Hard Rain's A-Gonna Fall [Dylan]		6:55
▶ 07 Don't Think Twice, It's All Right [Dylan]		3:40
08 Bob Dylan's Dream [Dylan]		5:03
09 Oxford Town [Dylan]		1:50
10 Talking World War III Blues [Dylan]		6:28
11 Corrina Corrina (Trad., arr. Dylan)		2:44
12 Honey, Just Allow Me One More Chance (Dylan•Thomas)		2:01
▶ 13 I Shall Be Free [Dylan]		4:49

Phil Spector
A Christmas Gift For You (1963)

Label | Philles
Producer | Phil Spector
Art Direction | Uncredited
Nationality | USA
Running Time | 35:11

Sam Cooke
Live At The Harlem Square Club (1963)

Label | RCA
Producer | Uncredited
Art Direction | Uncredited
Nationality | USA
Running Time | 35:65

Phil Spector is arguably the best-known record producer of the rock era, not least because he is more famous than most of the acts he produced. Artistically, this audacious album of seasonal material was his greatest achievement, but commercially, it was disastrous—due to the assassination of President John F. Kennedy the day after it was released in November 1963. Spector withdrew the album immediately as a mark of respect.

The Ronettes, Bob B Soxx and The Blue Jeans, The Crystals, and Darlene Love worked on this project, and it is rumored that it had been designed to give Spector the No. 1 album in a Christmas chart, introduced in 1963.

Most of the material on the album allowed Spector to use his celebrated "Wall Of Sound" technique to transform familiar oldies like "Rudolph," "Frosty," and "Sleigh Ride" into contemporary classics, but he had also written a new song, "Christmas (Baby Please Come Home)," with regular collaborators, Jeff Barry and Ellie Greenwich, and this was given to Darlene Love after an unsuccessful attempt by The Ronettes. The closing track is a soliloquy by Spector himself, wishing listeners a Merry Christmas while the assembled artists sing "Silent Night" behind him.

For many, this album, which has been reissued several times on other labels, remains the greatest seasonal collection ever. Strangely enough, it was recorded during a hot Los Angeles August. **JT**

Confined to mellow politeness on his pop-oriented studio recordings, Sam Cooke revamped himself on stage into a raw R&B singer who oozed sexual cool. *Live At The Harlem Square Club* illustrates this drastic transfiguration more clearly than any other Cooke album—an exorcism drawing a definitive line between the sacred and the profane in his gospel-rooted career.

In 1963 Cooke was a successful black icon, a proven hitmaker, owner of the SAR record label and publishing company (with a new record deal that assured him full artistic control), and a recent Top Thirty *Best Of* compilation that confirmed him as R&B's biggest star. Captured at a working-class club in Miami's ghetto, *Live At the Harlem Square Club* has long been considered one of the best live albums, period—all the more ironic, then, that it remained unreleased for 22 years.

With a joyful radiancy, this posthumous document stands alone in Cooke's output. Backed by the sturdy and sharp pulsation of a band that included sax supremo King Curtis and ace guitarist Cliff White, a freewheeling Cooke delivers sweaty, exhilarating renditions of gems such as "Feel It," "Chain Gang," "Twistin' The Night Away," and "Bring It On Home To Me," mostly picked from his more recent songbook.

Throughout, Cooke is a triumphant showman, brimming with self confidence and delivering a torrid, swaggering performance. **JG**

Charles Mingus
The Black Saint And The Sinner Lady (1963)

Label | Impulse!
Producer | Bob Thiele
Art Direction | Hollis King
Nationality | USA
Running Time | 39:25

James Brown
Live At The Apollo (1963)

Label | King
Producer | James Brown
Art Direction | Dan Quest
Nationality | USA
Running Time | 31:33

Start with the liner notes, which were penned by Charles Mingus' psychologist, and it is clear that this is no typical modern jazz album. Of course, nothing about the virtuoso bassist and composer could be described as typical, but in a discography filled with masterpieces and near masterpieces, this stands out as his most powerfully realized extended work.

From the first chords of "Solo Dancer," underpinned by Don Butterfield's rasping tuba, the music announces itself as a seething psychodrama. Altoist Charlie Mariano attains astonishing heights of lyricism and intensity, while the roaring, growling, plunger-muted trombone of Quentin Jackson, echoed by trumpeters Rolf Ericson and Richard Williams, is startlingly beautiful. There are also quiet moments, in which Jay Berliner's flamenco-influenced guitar engages in a nimble pas de deux with Jaki Byard's quicksilver piano. Holding the music together and driving it forward is Dannie Richmond, the extraordinary drummer who spent some two decades in Mingus' employ.

While clearly inspired by Ellington's orchestral palette, Mingus ventures into far more emotionally combustible territory than the Duke. What is particularly remarkable about *The Black Saint And The Sinner Lady* is that it was recorded just three months after Mingus' most public disaster, the notoriously chaotic Town Hall concert—the bassist obviously didn't let that debacle stop him. **AG**

His nickname, The Hardest Working Man In Show Business, fitted him as snugly as his famously slick stagewear. James Brown's early hits had been driven by his relentless touring regime: by 1962, he was clocking more than 300 dates a year. Noticing the enthusiastic response his shows were getting, he pitched the idea of a live album to label boss Syd Nathan. When Nathan refused, Brown went it alone, spending $5,700 of his own money on taping a session at Harlem's Apollo Theater in October 1962. Nathan reluctantly released it—Brown got his money back, and more besides.

There is no fat here. Brown and musical director Lewis Hamlin had drilled their band to an immaculate, fiery precision; there is barely room for the eight-strong horn section to catch its collective breath. The group belt through four hits in the blink of an eye before an extraordinary, gospel-soaked slow-dance through "Lost Someone." Just as it appears to be lolling toward an explosive climax, Brown roars through a nine-hit medley and leaves the stage to a storming "Night Train." The crowd respond to all this with screaming enthusiasm. Exactly why Nathan felt the need to overdub applause on to the original release is anyone's guess.

Live At The Apollo was a phenomenon, reaching No. 2 on the Billboard charts. Two years later, Brown dropped the funk for the first time, and set about accumulating the music world's greatest collection of sobriquets. **WF-J**

Stan Getz And João Gilberto | Getz / Gilberto (1963)

Label | Verve
Producer | Creed Taylor
Art Direction | Uncredited
Nationality | Brazil • USA
Running Time | 34:02

America's love affair with Latin American dance music is nothing new—throughout the twentieth century the tango, the cha-cha, the rumba, and the mambo had provided the soundtrack to many a U.S. ballroom and jazz club. Philly-born West Coast tenorist Stan Getz recorded *Jazz Samba* in 1962 as an exotic diversion from his lyrical hard bop, distilling the clattering rhythms of the Brazilian samba to a simple, undulating acoustic guitar vamp that became known as bossa nova.

Unwittingly, Getz and Byrd found themselves surfing a huge international wave, their version of "Desafinado" by Brazilian songwriter Antonio Carlos Jobim selling a million copies. Unlike the subsequent bossa nova bandwagon jumpers, Getz's music was not dismissed as "inauthentic" by Brazilians, but reciprocated by bossa pioneers like Baden Powell and Jobim.

Stan Getz was the only gringo on *Getz/Gilberto*, joined by Jobim on piano (he had also played guitar with Getz) and Brazilian drummer Milton Banana. But the true star here was guitarist and singer João Gilberto, the grumpy bossa nova purist whose hesitant vocal drone and gentle guitar vamps had created the genre.

Legend has it that the producer wanted one verse of "Girl From Ipanema" to be sung in English, not Portuguese. João could not speak English, so his young wife Astrud volunteered to sing a take. Of course, her breathy, girlish vocals became one of the defining vocal performances of the century and her two tracks here—including a reading of Gene Lees' lyric to "Corcovado"—are among this album's many highlights. A 1990s reissue added the 45 rpm versions of both songs. **JLe**

> ## "Stan sounds like he's trying to charm every woman on the beach of Ipanema."
>
> Charlie Byrd, 1964

Track Listing

▶	01	The Girl From Ipanema (De Moraes • Gimbel • Jobim)	5:24
▶	02	Doralice (Almeida • Caymmi)	2:46
	03	Para Machuchar Meu Coração (To Hurt My Heart) (Barroso)	5:05
▶	04	Desafinado (Off Key) (Jobim • Mendonça)	4:15
▶	05	Corcovado (Quiet Nights Of Quiet Stars) (Jobim • Lees)	4:16
	06	Só Danço Samba (I Only Dance Samba) (De Moraes • Jobim)	3:45
	07	O Grande Amor (De Moraes • Jobim)	5:27
	08	Vivo Sonhando (Dreamer) (Jobim)	3:04

The Beatles | A Hard Day's Night (1964)

Label | Parlophone
Producer | George Martin
Art Direction | Robert Freeman
Nationality | UK
Running Time | 29:47

Career peaks for most mortals, two chart-topping albums were merely hors d'oeuvres for The Beatles. Just weeks after *Meet The Beatles* and The Beatles' *Second Album* claimed the USA top slot in quick succession, *A Hard Day's Night* followed.

The difference? For the first time on a Beatles album, all tracks are Fabs originals. Though credited to Lennon/McCartney, all bar three are actually by Lennon, although McCartney's "And I Love Her," "Can't Buy Me Love," and "Things We Said Today" prove quality is more than a match for quantity (appropriately, the all-original gambit had been pioneered by Paul's beloved Buddy Holly). The album was however butchered for the U.S., with George Martin-helmed instrumentals replacing "Any Time At All," "Things We Said Today," "When I Get Home," "You Can't Do That," and "I'll Be Back."

From the unmistakable opening clang of Harrison's 12-string Rickenbacker on the title track, the album is a lesson in superlatively simple guitar pop. Aware of his hero Elvis' cinematic shortcomings, Lennon insisted the *Hard Day's Night* film be more than "a fuckin' shitty pop movie," and its accompanying album adheres to similarly strict standards.

True, there are cheery throwaways like "I'm Happy Just To Dance With You" and "Tell Me Why," but they are balanced by the lovely likes of "And I Love Her" and "If I Fell." Meanwhile, rockers like "A Hard Day's Night" and "Any Time At All" had an electrifying effect on would-be guitar heroes The Byrds (and, in due course, baby Byrd Tom Petty)—and will remain influential for as long as young men continue to pick up guitars. **BM**

"We're out!"

Ringo Starr, *A Hard Day's Night*, 1964

Track Listing

▶ 01	A Hard Day's Night (Lennon•McCartney)	2:28
02	I Should Have Known Better (Lennon•McCartney)	2:42
03	If I Fell (Lennon•McCartney)	2:16
04	I'm Happy Just To Dance With You (Lennon•McCartney)	1:59
▶ 05	And I Love Her (Lennon•McCartney)	2:27
06	Tell Me Why (Lennon•McCartney)	2:04
▶ 07	Can't Buy Me Love (Lennon•McCartney)	2:15
08	Anytime At All (Lennon•McCartney)	2:10
09	I'll Cry Instead (Lennon•McCartney)	1:44
10	Things We Said Today (Lennon•McCartney)	2:35
11	When I Get Home (Lennon•McCartney)	2:14
12	You Can't Do That (Lennon•McCartney)	2:33
13	I'll Be Back (Lennon•McCartney)	2:20

Jacques Brel | Olympia 64 (1964)

Label | Barclay
Producer | Jean-Marie Guérin
Art Direction | Uncredited
Nationality | Belgium
Running Time | 47:56

Brel's second album of 1964 was also his second recorded at the Parisian concert hall, a venue that was to Europe what Carnegie Hall or the Royal Albert Hall were in their respective countries: you hadn't made it until you'd played there. By October 16–17, Brel hadn't just made it—as far as the French and the Belgians were concerned, he was king of the world. Unlikely though it might seem, French chanson was even starting to build a hip following in the notoriously resistant Britain and America. (Bob Dylan once described Charles Aznavour as one of the greatest performers he had ever seen.)

Following close behind Brel's 1964 studio LP *Les Bonbons*, *Olympia 64* introduces "Amsterdam," "Mathilde," and "Tango Funèbre," and revives "Au Suivant," all of which would be covered by Scott Walker. It also features "Les Bonbons," "Les Vieux," "Les Toros," and "Les Bigotes" from his previous album, but the repetition simply demonstrates the difference between Brel in person and in the studio. At Olympia, he inhabits the songs, living the stories, throwing himself in from the outset, acting them out. There is no let-up in drama, satire, or passion. He dies many, many times over the course of the 48 minutes; the rest is spent in sick beds, mobile brothels, and bars. In "Les Toros," he becomes a dying bull, staring up at his tormentors, relating it to Waterloo, Verdun, and contemporaneous wars on formerly French territories.

Released as *Music For The Millions* in America and Britain, this album is the reason a Belgian chanson singer is still the coolest rock cult of all time. **DH**

EN EGISTRE MENT PUBLIC

"I will die, loving."

Jacques Brel, 1966

Track Listing

▶ 01	Amsterdam (Brel)	3:20
02	Les Timides (Brel)	3:41
03	Le Dernier Repas (Brel)	3:34
04	Les Jardins Du Casino (Brel·Jouannest)	3:29
05	Les Vieux (Brel·Corti·Jouannest)	4:10
06	Les Toros (Brel·Corti·Jouannest)	2:38
▶ 07	Tango Funèbre (Brel·Jouannest)	3:04
08	Le Plat Pays (Brel)	3:12
09	Les Bonbons (Brel)	3:08
▶ 10	Mathilde (Brel·Jouannest)	2:29
11	Les Bigotes (Brel)	2:43
▶ 12	Les Bourgeois (Brel·Corti)	2:52
13	Jef (Brel)	3:27
▶ 14	Au Suivant (Brel)	2:55
15	Madeleine (Brel·Corti·Jouannest)	3:14

Solomon Burke | Rock 'n Soul (1964)

Label | Atlantic
Producer | Bert Berns
Art Direction | Uncredited
Nationality | USA
Running Time | 34:06

Of all the great songs Philadelphia-born Solomon Burke recorded for the Atlantic label in the years between 1962 and '68, none showcase the sublime talent of the self-ordained "King of Rock 'n' Soul" with the aplomb of those that feature on 1964's *Rock 'n Soul*, Burke's third album for the label.

Previous to his music career, Burke had served as a certified mortician, sometime TV evangelist, and father to 21 children, but on *Rock 'n Soul* he plays the role of lover to sensual perfection. The wistful "If You Need Me," written by contemporary Wilson Pickett, sees Burke howl a gloriously uncouth vocal. It is a demonstration of breathy grace that utilizes every nuance of the man's astonishing voice.

"Cry To Me"—later covered by The Rolling Stones who were huge Solomon fans—calls upon Burke's time as a childhood chapel preacher to deliver a devoutly impassioned sermon. "Just Out Of Reach," however, curiously juxtaposes Burke's velveteen croon with a country and western-infused swing. It is a style atypical of many songs Burke recorded for Atlantic in the 1960s, a decade when, in Burke's opinion, Atlantic was "the greatest rhythm and blues label in the world."

While the record is still officially deleted, repackaged editions of *Rock 'n Soul* have surfaced alongside Burke's Atlantic 1963 release *If You Need Me*. Mastering and presentation of said records leave something to be desired, but the combined collection ably explains the prolific run of greatness Burke enjoyed in the Sixties— though the real meat is in the brilliance packed into 1964's *Rock 'n Soul*. **JJ**

"Once you record a song it becomes a part of your life."

Solomon Burke, 2002

Track Listing	
01 **Goodbye Baby (Baby Goodbye)** (Farrell · Russell)	3:16
▶ 02 **Cry To Me** (Russell)	2:27
03 **Won't You Give Him (One More Chance)** (Martin · Scott)	2:31
▶ 04 **If You Need Me** (Bateman · Pickett · Sanders)	2:29
05 **Hard Ain't It Hard** (Trad., arr. Guthrie)	2:45
06 **Can't Nobody Love You** (Mitchell)	2:30
07 **Just Out Of Reach** (Stewart)	2:46
08 **You're Good For Me** (Covay · Ott)	2:45
09 **You Can't Love Them All** (Leiber · Nugetre · Russell · Stoller)	2:40
10 **Someone To Love Me** (Burke)	2:59
▶ 11 **Beautiful Brown Eyes** (Burke · Russell)	3:42
▶ 12 **He'll Have To Go** (A. Allison · J. Allison)	3:16

Dusty Springfield | A Girl Called Dusty (1964)

Label | Philips
Producer | John Franz
Art Direction | Uncredited
Nationality | UK
Running Time | 28:37

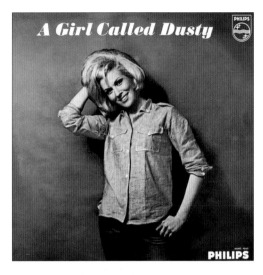

In retrospect, it was clear that from the beginning, Dusty Springfield was something of a musical schizophrenic. Her many hit singles were mostly pop princess stuff ("I Only Want To Be With You," her first UK hit, was the first song to be played on the UK's weekly music show *Top Of The Pops*), but the lady herself was more interested in the soulful sounds of Motown, Atlantic, and Scepter.

The latter was the label that released 40 hits by Dionne Warwick and 25 by The Shirelles, and this delightful album—Dusty's first, and arguably best— has a Motown cover (of the first U.S. Top Thirty hit by The Supremes), a Shirelles cover, and two Warwick covers, as well as more obscure material like Lee Dorsey's "Do-Re-Mi" and Lesley Gore's feminist anthem "You Don't Own Me."

Significantly for a white artist of the time, Dusty's versions of these songs retain the edge and warmth of the originals, and helped to establish her as one of the UK's finest soul singers. (Her respect for black R&B and soul strayed into other areas too—she was deported from South Africa later the same year for playing in front of a nonsegregated audience.)

Few singers conveyed the acute pain of love as convincingly as Dusty Springfield. Even on this debut album she was already laying a claim as a superlative torch singer, with "Anyone Who Had A Heart" and the plaintive "My Colouring Book"—musical territory that she would explore more deeply in later tours de force, such as her version of Jacques Brel's "If You Go Away."

And all this from an ex-convent girl. **JT**

"I was a total, unadulterated, obnoxious idiot ... "

Dusty Springfield, 1995

Track Listing		
▶ 01 **Mama Said** (Denson•Dixon)		2:05
02 **You Don't Own Me** (Madora•White)		2:26
03 **Do Re Mi** (King)		2:20
04 **When The Lovelight Starts Shining Thru His Eyes** (Dozier•B. Holland•E. Holland)		2:53
▶ 05 **My Colouring Book** (Ebb•Kander)		3:01
06 **Mockingbird** (C. Foxx•I. Foxx)		2:33
▶ 07 **Twenty Four Hours From Tulsa** (David•Bacharach)		3:01
08 **Nothing** (Augustus•Elgin•Lewis)		2:07
09 **Anyone Who Had A Heart** (Bacharach•David)		2:52
10 **Will You Love Me Tomorrow?** (Goffin•King)		2:40
▶ 11 **Wishin' And Hopin'** (Bacharach•David)		2:53
12 **Don't You Know** (Charles)		2:39

The Rolling Stones
The Rolling Stones (1964)

Label | Decca
Producer | Andrew Loog Oldham
Art Direction | Uncredited
Nationality | UK
Running Time | 32:59

Forty years young, *The Rolling Stones* is as pivotal a moment as John meeting Paul or Nirvana knocking Michael Jackson off No. 1. Jagger, Richard (as he was credited then), and co. weren't strangers to the studio when they began their debut in January 1964. They'd already scored hits in 1963 with Chuck Berry's "Come On" and Lennon and McCartney's "I Wanna Be Your Man."

Confident songwriters, however, they were not. Judging initial efforts unsuitable for the Stones, Jagger and Richard gave them to Marianne Faithfull and Gene Pitney. Of the album's originals, "Now I've Got A Witness" and "Little By Little" (credited to the collective nom de plume Nanker Phelge) are indebted to, respectively, Marvin Gaye's "Can I Get A Witness" and Jimmy Reed's "Shame, Shame, Shame," while "Tell Me (You're Coming Back)" is almost a Merseybeat pastiche.

But relying on covers did not do Sinatra or Elvis any harm, and the Stones established a reliable template: take a blues tune; make it harder and faster and scarier.

In The Beatles' wake, the result was a smash. In America, London Records added "England's Newest Hit Makers" to a sleeve that, in Britain, boldly bore no information bar the label's logo. London also replaced Bo Diddley's "I Need You Baby (Mona)" with a hit take on Buddy Holly's "Not Fade Away."

The Rolling Stones is not as good as material they would release in ensuing years—or even months. But its arrogant raunchiness had a seismic impact on polite pop then—and continues to echo today. **BM**

"I don't regret nuthin' ..."

Keith Richards, 1980

Track Listing

01	Route 66 (Troup)	2:21
02	I Just Want To Make Love To You (Dixon)	2:18
03	Honest I Do (Reed)	2:10
04	I Need You Baby (Mona) (McDaniel)	3:35
05	Now I've Got A Witness (Like Uncle Phil And Uncle Gene) (Phelge)	2:32
06	Little By Little (Phelge·Spector)	2:40
▶ 07	I'm A King Bee (Moore)	2:37
▶ 08	Carol (Berry)	2:34
09	Tell Me (You're Coming Back) (Jagger·Richard)	4:05
10	Can I Get A Witness (Dozier·B. Holland·E. Holland)	2:56
11	You Can Make It If You Try (Jarrett)	2:02
▶ 12	Walking The Dog (Thomas)	3:09

Buck Owens And His Buckaroos
I've Got A Tiger By The Tail (1965)

Label | Capitol
Producer | Ken Nelson
Art Direction | Uncredited
Nationality | USA
Running Time | 28:19

Country music emerged, before World War II, as a hybrid of styles from the American South. But in the 1950s and '60s, musicians on the West Coast made Bakersfield, CA an important site for a new movement in country—an electrified sound influenced as much by rock as by what was still sometimes referred to as hillbilly music.

One of the brightest luminaries of the Bakersfield scene was Buck Owens, the son of a Texas sharecropper. In 1951, when he was 22, Owens moved to Bakersfield and began honing his sound in honky-tonk bands, the most distinctive component of which would eventually be the guitar playing of Don Rich. Rich famously played a Telecaster, the twangy Fender instrument that has become country music's standard guitar.

Owens was in the middle of a string of No. 1 hits in 1965 when he and his band, the Buckaroos, released *I've Got A Tiger By The Tail*. Produced by Ken Nelson, a Capitol executive who championed Bakersfield music, the album is typical of Owens' sound, with its driving rockabilly beats, Rich's trebly guitar lick, and Owens' plaintive tenor. Legendary Nashville tunesmith Harlan Howard collaborated with Owens on the rollicking title track, and it is one of his most appealing songs, as is "Cryin' Time," which Ray Charles famously covered.

Beginning in 1968, a year-long stint hosting the television show *Hee Haw!* eroded Owens' musical credibility. But in the 1980s, the Bakersfield Sound was revived by Dwight Yoakam, who collaborated with Owens on a remake of "Streets Of Bakersfield." **KB**

"I came from the dirt people."

Buck Owens, 1995

Track Listing

▶ 01 I've Got A Tiger By The Tail (Howard・B. Owens) 2:12
02 Trouble And Me (Howard) 1:54
03 Let The Sad Times Roll On (B. Owens・Simpson) 2:14
▶ 04 Wham Bam (B. Owens・B. Owens・Rich) 2:01
▶ 05 If You Fall Out Of Love With Me (B. Owens・B. Owens) 2:15
06 Fallin' For You (B. Owens・B. Owens・Rich) 2:01
07 We're Gonna Let The Good Times Roll (B. Owens) 2:15
▶ 08 The Band Keeps Playin' On (Simpson) 3:02
09 The Streets Of Laredo (Howard・B. Owens) 2:55
▶ 10 Cryin' Time (B. Owens) 2:30
11 A Maiden's Prayer (Wills) 2:33
12 Memphis (Berry) 2:27

Jerry Lee Lewis
Live At The Star Club, Hamburg (1965)

Label | Philips
Producer | Siegfried E. Loch
Art Direction | Uncredited
Nationality | USA
Running Time | 37:48

Most people would be hard pressed to name four songs made famous by the Killer, but almost everybody knows of the news story that engulfed his 1958 tour of Britain. Fortunately, his marriage to his 13-year-old cousin Myra did not finish Jerry Lee—it just drove him underground, where, away from public gaze, he could record the wildest live album in rock 'n' roll.

When he arrived at the Star Club in April 1964, Lewis had just toured Britain with another group of Liverpudlians, The Nashville Teens, who were booked into a residency in Hamburg, so the American joined them for one night. You can feel the years in the wilderness roll off the 30-year-old veteran from the second he hurtles into "Mean Woman Blues." It is safe to say that his piano stool lay in splinters by the end of the first song. Count-ins? Synchronized endings? Nowhere. The band can barely keep up with Lewis for the first 20 minutes, which include "Mean Woman Blues," "High School Confidential," and perhaps the definitive version of "What'd I Say," which removes any reference to gospel sensuality and replaces it with pure lust. The home straight—"Hound Dog," "Long Tall Sally," and "Whole Lotta Shakin'"—is distilled anarchy.

Supercharged? This is rock as it was always meant to be: faster, more breathless, and more possessed than anything the world would pay money to hear until the arrival of The Ramones. **DH**

The Sonics
Here Are The Sonics (1965)

Label | Etiquette
Producer | Kent Morrill • John Ormsby
Art Direction | John Vlahovich
Nationality | USA
Running Time | 29:20

"The Sonics weren't great musicians," said Buck Ormsby, the guy who signed them to Etiquette Records, "but they had this magic thing." With their 1965 debut album, the Tacoma, WA five-piece managed to distill just about everything that was going on musically at the time—from the "British Invasion" scene championed by The Kinks to the rock 'n' roll sounds of Little Richard—with a ferocious energy and wildness that predates punk by more than a decade.

The idea of a "garage band" was not exactly new before The Sonics. But it was clear from debut single "The Witch" that The Sonics were going to shake things up. Drummer Bob Bennett remembers the engineers fretting over the recording: "One guy says, 'That doesn't even sound like drums,' and the other guy goes, 'Well, what am I going to do—look at this guy!'"

After "The Witch" became the biggest selling single in the Northwest, the band recorded their album at Audio Cuts in Seattle. The songs were recorded live, and it shows—from the rat-a-tat battering of Bennett's drums, to the bloodcurdling screams of frontman Jerry Roslie on standout tracks like the mighty "Pscyho." Little wonder the group's name was inspired by the local Boeing factory and their own jet-like sound.

Despite never breaking nationally, The Sonics scored a run of hits in the Northwest, inspired a legion of bands, and left a dirty great mark on rock 'n' roll. **SH**

Bob Dylan
Bringing It All Back Home (1965)

Label | Columbia
Producer | Tom Wilson
Art Direction | Uncredited
Nationality | USA
Running Time | 47:21

Otis Redding
Otis Blue: Otis Redding Sings Soul (1965)

Label | Stax
Producer | Jim Stewart
Art Direction | Haig Adishian
Nationality | USA
Running Time | 32:54

The year 1965 saw Bob Dylan cutting a swathe through the pop world at such a speed that not even The Beatles could keep up with him. While Britain's best were asking for *Help!*, Dylan was serenading Mr Tambourine Man. It would take a motorcycle accident and a long lay-off before everyone else could catch up.

Enclosed in a sleeve that displayed plentiful signifiers for those who would one day dedicate themselves to Dylanology, the music itself is just as much of a head trip. The first side, the electric half, blows folk music open: "Outlaw Blues" and "On The Road Again" are rambunctious 12-bar blues; "Subterranean Homesick Blues" is a stream of nonsense consciousness based around Chuck Berry's "Too Much Monkey Business"; "She Belongs To Me" and "Love Minus Zero/No Limits" are extraordinarily tender love songs. Flipping the LP over should have pleased the purists, but even solo Dylan and an acoustic guitar was too much for them by this point: what had "Mr. Tambourine Man" or "Gates Of Eden" got to do with the dignity of labor? What did they mean?

Dylan, of course, did not look back. He could not: the words were pouring out too fast. He was about to record two even greater albums, but here you can still feel the excitement of the world being turned on its head, of a cult figure discovering his talent and joyously making the most of it. **DH**

The world of music has thrown up its fair share of cheats, scoundrels, and downright swine, and often seen them prosper in a degree out of proportion to their worth, making the tragedy of Otis Redding's short life especially sharp. Less than three years after this breakthrough record, on December 10, 1967, sweet Otis' plane crashed into Lake Monona, Wisconsin.

As the son of a minister, gospel was in Redding's blood, yet *Otis Blue* encompasses soul, R&B, and pop. Recorded at the legendary Stax studio in Memphis with a team of session musicians that included the classic M.G.s line-up, it boasts a lush sound throughout—all arrangements were mastered by Redding.

The tracks are a mix of originals and covers—two by Redding's mentor Sam Cooke—yet the intensity of emotional delivery is Otis' alone. "Respect" sees a cocksure and punchy Redding, while "Down In The Valley" is fruity and funky in equal measure. There is also a cover of the Stones' "Satisfaction"—ironic, perhaps, considering the group was selling black soul back to the USA—which puts Jagger's vocals to shame.

The album set Redding on the road to crossover fame, the zenith of which was 1967's Monterey Festival, where he wowed a predominantly white audience with numbers such as "Try A Little Tenderness," which he ended with the cruelly fateful words, "I've got to go now, but I don't want to." **SJac**

The Beach Boys | The Beach Boys Today! (1965)

Label | Capitol
Producer | Brian Wilson
Art Direction | Uncredited
Nationality | USA
Running Time | 28:42

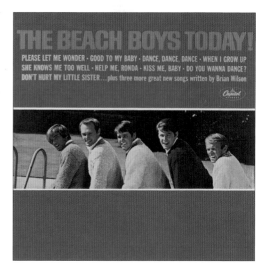

Despite containing what is easily the worst track in this entire book, this is the perfect Beach Boys LP, split evenly between carefree boy-meets-girl pop and dramatic ballads inspired by Phil Spector's girl groups. Even arguing that it is better than *Pet Sounds* is a cinch, with a bit of practice—there is none of the self-pity that weighs heavy on the later album.

Although it was recorded shortly after Brian Wilson had broken down while on tour, exhausted by his relentless schedule, ...*Today!* opens with one of the most exuberant songs the band ever recorded. After a muted first couple of verses of "Do You Wanna Dance?," Brian turns the volume up for the first chorus and the Sixties start swinging. The rest of the side continues the party groove: "When I Grow Up" was the most complex and mature thing Wilson had written to date; "Help Me, Ronda" was an early attempt at what would soon become one of their most celebrated singles (with an extra "h" in the title).

But it is the second side that gets connoisseurs purring. The five ballads are lush, personal, sensitive, and vulnerable love songs, unlike anything else in pop at the time. There are clear blueprints for what would evolve into *Pet Sounds* in "Please Let Me Wonder" and "Kiss Me, Baby," but the latter is every bit as good as "God Only Knows."

For the first time, Brian had overtaken The Beatles and the Stones, catapulting the band into the A-list and beginning a two-year battle for supremacy that would end with another breakdown and the aborted *Smile* sessions. Remember them this way. **DH**

"For months, I plotted and planned ..."

Brian Wilson, 1965

Track Listing

▶	01	Do You Wanna Dance? (Freeman)	2:20
	02	Good To My Baby (B. Wilson)	2:17
	03	Don't Hurt My Little Sister (B. Wilson)	2:08
▶	04	When I Grow Up (B. Wilson)	2:03
	05	Help Me, Ronda (Love • B. Wilson)	3:10
	06	Dance, Dance, Dance (B. Wilson • C. Wilson)	1:59
▶	07	Please Let Me Wonder (Love • B. Wilson)	2:47
▶	08	I'm So Young (Tyrus)	2:32
▶	09	Kiss Me, Baby (Love • B. Wilson)	2:36
	10	She Knows Me Too Well (B. Wilson)	2:30
	11	In The Back Of My Mind (B. Wilson)	2:10
	12	Bull Session With "Big Daddy" (Jardine • Love • B. Wilson • C. Wilson • D. Wilson)	2:10

John Coltrane
A Love Supreme (1965)

Label | Impulse!
Producer | Bob Thiele
Art Direction | George Gray
Nationality | USA
Running Time | 32:59

Coltrane's definitive tone poem *A Love Supreme* was his fifth studio recording for the hip indie jazz label Impulse!, following a spell on the R&B imprint Atlantic. Previous incarnations had seen him zigzag through jazz history—responding to Miles Davis' modal innovations; immersing himself in the "New Thing"; recording a collection of ballads and an unlikely collaboration with crooner Johnny Hartman; assembling a fearsome orchestra for *Africa/Brass*; and even sharing the bill with Duke Ellington.

By 1962, however, Coltrane had developed a brand of modal jazz that invoked Indian and Arabic scales while maintaining an impassioned spiritual focus. As he spoke in tongues on tenor and soprano sax, his now legendary Fab Four rumbled beneath him, playing hard bop that pushed toward India and Africa, toward soul, even toward psychedelia.

A Love Supreme pulls off the rare trick of being utterly uncompromising yet completely accessible. Garrison's insistent four-note bassline that kicks off "Acknowledgement" ("a LOVE su-PREME") serves as a leitmotif, constantly restated, explored, and mutilated, both on tenor sax and with haunted vocals. "Resolution" takes us into Coltrane's more familiar upbeat territory, complete with Jones' flailing drumming (he sounds like he is soloing for the entire song, yet the pulse remains solid) while the album's coda, "Psalm," is an instrumental expression of a prayer.

As a journey through awakening, understanding, and spiritual enlightenment, it is damn near perfect. **JLe**

B.B. King
Live At The Regal (1965)

Label | ABC
Producer | Johnny Pate
Art Direction | Uncredited
Nationality | USA
Running Time | 34:46

It could not have been easy to learn how to play electric guitar growing up in a town with no electricity, but by the time B.B. King reached Chicago via Indianola, or Mississippi, to play the Regal Theater in November of 1964, he had spent 39 years trying. Taking the stage that night with more than 20 charted singles under his wide belt, a notorious Gibson guitar named Lucille strapped on his back, and an army of women dangling from the balconies, one might say he had pulled it off.

Lucille spoke first when the band picked up, introducing herself and her man to the rapturous crowd with two or three dancing riffs over the tight horns and double-time drums. B.B. quickly responded, proclaiming in his signature gallant wail, "Everyday I Have The Blues!" It was an undying conversation that over the previous decade had made them both stars.

King commanded his room like a Delta preacher, inducing moans and whimpers from the congregation, luring each of them into a three-way exchange with him and Lucille. After the opener came the sweltering "Sweet Little Angel" and how "she loves to spread her wings." The shrieks wafted from the floor like fog.

But this was not sex; it was the blues, and B.B. was the one bursting with longing and heartache. Burning renditions of "It's My Own Fault," "How Blue Can You Get," and "You Upset Me Baby," accentuated by King's emotive caresses of Lucille's neck, would become the standard bearer of live blues and help crown the King as the greatest guitarist in the genre's history. **MO**

The Beatles
Rubber Soul (1965)

Label | Parlophone
Producer | George Martin
Art Direction | Robert Freeman
Nationality | UK
Running Time | 35:50

In 1964, American album buyers invited to Meet The Beatles met moptops in suits that may as well have been straitjackets for all the freedom they embodied. Just two years later, fans got closer to meeting the real Beatles—pop stars with imagination to spare. Much later, the band—particularly Lennon—would bare their souls. But this Rubber one is much more rewarding.

The album injected mystique into FabWorld. The psychedelic cover—angled, shot through a fish-eye lens, giving the unsmiling group a distinctly "turned-on" air—even omits the band's name (a first in America).

Of the elliptical lyrics, finest is Lennon's "Norwegian Wood (This Bird Has Flown)"—which, like McCartney's "I'm Looking Through You," alludes to turbulence in his personal life. "Nowhere Man," meanwhile, jettisons romance entirely—a rarity for the group until then.

The soppy "Michelle" makes up in loveliness what it lacks in depth, while "Girl" is deceptively simple ("a good deal more sophisticated than Dylan's 'Just Like a Woman,'" sniffed critic Greil Marcus).

Musically, too, *Rubber Soul* is a step forward. Key elements include the sitar, and fuzz bass on "Think for Yourself"—which, like "The Word," rocks in a way that does not sound outdated.

The biggest indignity in Beatledom is not "Ob-La-Di, Ob-La-Da." It is that *Rubber Soul* is so often overlooked. It contained no hits (the U.S. smash "Nowhere Man" was left off the American version), yet would be the highlight of a lesser band's discography. **BM**

Bert Jansch
Bert Jansch (1965)

Label | Transatlantic
Producer | Bill Leader
Art Direction | Brian Shuel
Nationality | UK
Running Time | 39:25

Bert Jansch began playing his personal mix of folk, blues, and jazz on the folk club scene of the early 1960s, having hitchhiked down from Scotland to London. His eponymous debut album was released in April 1965, on the opening day of the now famous Les Cousins folk club in London's Soho. Performed on borrowed guitars and recorded with portable equipment in freelance producer Bill Leader's flat in Camden Town, it was sold for the modest sum of £100 ($180, and no royalties) to Nat Joseph, founder of Transatlantic Records.

The songs, highlighted by fluid, astonishingly accomplished guitar playing, all bear the stamp of Jansch's strong personality—from easygoing opener "Strolling Down The Highway" to the poignant "Needle Of Death," written about a friend who died from a heroin overdose; from the reflective, spine-tingling "Running From Home" to the riveting guitar showcase "Angie," written by Davy Graham and later covered by Simon And Garfunkel.

With its innovative guitar technique and strong material, the album caused a sensation, and it has remained deeply influential ever since. Many of the songs were covered by other singers of the era, including Donovan, Julie Felix, and Marianne Faithfull, while guitarists including Jimmy Page, Neil Young, Johnny Marr, and Noel Gallagher have acknowledged its impact on them. But its reputation does not rest exclusively on Jansch's musicianship, its beauty lies also in his lyricism. **GSu**

The Byrds | Mr. Tambourine Man (1965)

Label | Columbia
Producer | Terry Melcher
Art Direction | Uncredited
Nationality | USA
Running Time | 30:45

When leader Jim (later Roger) McGuinn's vocals—pitched halfway between John Lennon and Bob Dylan—combined with Gene Clark and David Crosby's beautiful harmonizing and the chiming sound of McGuinn's 12-string Rickenbacker guitar on the single "Mr. Tambourine Man," The Byrds became the first U.S. group to rival the artistic and commercial dominance of The Beatles. They also gave the song's composer Bob Dylan his first international No. 1 hit, inspiring him to go electric and kickstart the folk-rock movement.

The *Mr. Tambourine Man* album, expanded on the sound of the single, containing three more souped-up Dylan covers including sophomore hit single "All I Really Want To Do." It also introduced the extraordinary songwriting talent of Gene Clark. He contributed the quintessential Byrds rocker "I'll Feel A Whole Lot Better" (later covered by Tom Petty), and wrote or co-wrote a further four tracks, including the tender, poetic love odes, "You Won't Have To Cry" and "Here Without You." The Byrds nodded to their folk roots with the sublime "Bells Of Rhymney," which directly inspired The Beatles' "If I Needed Someone." Elsewhere, as a thank you to Byrds champion Jackie De Shannon, they covered her "Don't Doubt Yourself, Babe," adding a Bo Diddley beat, and bizarrely tackled Vera Lynn's WWII anthem "We'll Meet Again" from the *Dr. Strangelove* soundtrack, an early live favorite.

The Byrds' jangling guitars and soothing harmonies have endured, inspiring countless contemporary outfits, The Pretenders, The Smiths, The Stone Roses, R.E.M., and Primal Scream, to name but a few. **JoH**

> ## "Regardless of what Dylan meant, I was turning it into a prayer."
>
> Roger McGuinn, 1998

Track Listing

▶ 01	Mr. Tambourine Man (Dylan)	2:29
▶ 02	I'll Feel A Whole Lot Better (Clark)	2:32
03	Spanish Harlem Incident (Dylan)	1:57
▶ 04	You Won't Have To Cry (Clark·McGuinn)	2:08
▶ 05	Here Without You (Clark)	2:36
06	The Bells Of Rhymney (Davies·Seeger)	3:30
▶ 07	All I Really Want To Do (Dylan)	2:04
08	I Knew I'd Want You (Clark)	2:14
09	It's No Use (Clark·McGuinn)	2:23
10	Don't Doubt Yourself, Babe (De Shannon)	2:54
11	Chimes Of Freedom (Dylan)	3:51
12	We'll Meet Again (Charles·Parker)	2:07

Bob Dylan | Highway 61 Revisited (1965)

Label | Columbia
Producer | Bob Johnston
Art Direction | Uncredited
Nationality | USA
Running Time | 51:34

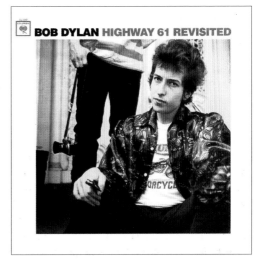

Not since the premiere of Stravinsky's groundbreaking *Rite Of Spring* incited a riot at Paris' Théâtre des Champs-Elysées in 1913 has a musical transformation caused the kind of controversy that resulted when Bob Dylan plugged in on July 25, 1965 at the Newport Folk Festival. But the jeers from folk purists would soon fade amid the cheers Dylan received when he released *Highway 61 Revisited* one month later.

In transforming from acoustic folkie to electrified rocker, a process begun in earnest on side one of 1965's *Bringing It All Back Home*, Dylan rewrote the rulebook for pop music. A hit song, such as the swirling organ-drenched anthem "Like A Rolling Stone," no longer had to adhere to a three-minute limit. (Only two of the album's nine tracks are under four minutes; the mighty closing number, "Desolation Row," runs for more than 11 minutes.)

With such artful, literate songs as "Just Like Tom Thumb's Blues," which obliterated the traditional focus on sing along choruses, *Highway 61 Revisited* was a huge success that established the singer-songwriter as the dominant figure in rock. Dylan's voice, although seldom more earnest or powerful, was not the selling point. It was what he said as opposed to how he said it—another paradigm shift for the genre.

Although debated and critiqued like no pop album ever before, *Highway 61 Revisited* works best when it is enjoyed for itself outside of the classroom. It does not take a literary reference guide to enjoy the pure adrenaline rush of "Tombstone Blues" and "From A Buick 6," which is the likely reason Dylan turned to rock 'n' roll in the first place. **JiH**

"I couldn't go on being the lone folkie out there, you know, strumming 'Blowin' In The Wind' for three hours every night."

Bob Dylan, 1978

Track Listing

▶	01	Like A Rolling Stone (Dylan)	6:13
▶	02	Tombstone Blues (Dylan)	6:00
	03	It Takes A Lot To Laugh, It Takes A Train To Cry (Dylan)	4:09
	04	From A Buick 6 (Dylan)	3:19
▶	05	Ballad Of A Thin Man (Dylan)	5:58
	06	Queen Jane Approximately (Dylan)	5:31
▶	07	Highway 61 Revisited (Dylan)	3:30
▶	08	Just Like Tom Thumb's Blues (Dylan)	5:32
▶	09	Desolation Row (Dylan)	11:22

The Who | My Generation (1965)

Label | Brunswick
Producer | Shel Talmy
Art Direction | Uncredited
Nationality | UK
Running Time | 36:13

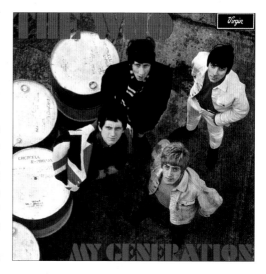

The Who's first album, which nowadays evokes the spirit of a kind of Carnaby-Street-London-that-never-was, is only superficially the sound of mod. In reality, *My Generation* is the desperate sound of a young band confused about their identity, helplessly exploited by senior industry figures, and only sure of one thing: their fearsome energy and their ability to channel it into audience-leveling songs.

Having been through three name changes in just one year, personnel and management shuffles, record label changes, and a failed single (the Pete Meaden-penned "I'm The Face," released in 1964 in an attempt to bracket them into the mod scene), Daltrey, Townshend, Entwistle, and the newly arrived Moon knew that their first album needed to attract attention.

It did. Having secured the production services of Kinks producer Shel Talmy (for whom Townshend had adapted "I Can't Explain," whose chopped chords recall The Kinks' early hits), the band recorded a high-quality clutch of songs. Obvious highlights are "My Generation," in which Daltrey emulates the stutter of a speed user on lines such as the overly quoted but succinct "Hope I die before I get old"; "I Don't Mind," the luxurious vocal harmonies and rolling guitar riff of which were ahead of their time in production terms; and the almost-anthem for a generation, "The Kids Are Alright," in which Townshend addresses (not for the last time) the rigors of youth.

The Who may have evolved into a much more sophisticated beast on later albums, but the rawness of *My Generation* makes it a landmark. **JM**

> ## "We won't let our music stand in the way of our visual act."
>
> Pete Townshend, 1967

Track Listing

01	Out In The Street (Townshend)	2:32
▶ 02	I Don't Mind (Brown)	2:33
03	The Good's Gone (Townshend)	4:00
04	La-La-La-Lies (Townshend)	2:18
05	Much Too Much (Townshend)	2:45
▶ 06	My Generation (Townshend)	3:21
▶ 07	The Kids Are Alright (Townshend)	3:10
08	Please, Please, Please (Brown·Terry)	2:46
09	It's Not True (Townshend)	2:34
10	I'm A Man (McDaniel)	3:23
11	A Legal Matter (Townshend)	2:54
12	The Ox (Entwistle·Hopkins·Moon·Townshend)	3:57

The Beatles | Revolver (1966)

Label | Parlophone
Producer | George Martin
Art Direction | Klaus Voorman
Nationality | UK
Running Time | 34:58

Once The Beatles were fab and gear; now they oozed self-assurance. It is there in the mysterious black-and-white cover, a line drawing-cum-collage created by Klaus Voorman, whom The Beatles knew from their Hamburg days. It is there in the ambiguous title—so much cooler than the mooted *Abracadabra*, *Magic Circles*, and *Beatles On Safari*.

And it is there in 14 unimpeachable tracks. Or 11 if you were American in 1966, since Capitol put "I'm Only Sleeping," "And Your Bird Can Sing," and "Doctor Robert" on *Yesterday and Today*, a hodgepodge of album and single cuts that *Revolver* actually knocked off the top of the Billboard chart (again, very cool).

Revolutionary at the time—"I am sick," declared McCartney, "of doing sounds that people can claim to have heard before"—*Revolver* resounds down the decades. Earth Wind And Fire brought the brassy strut of "Got To Get You Into My Life" into the disco era. The Jam carbon-copied the rifftastic "Taxman" for their UK chart-topping "Start!" And The Chemical Brothers based a career on "Tomorrow Never Knows."

Revolver is cited as the point when The Beatles broke up: they played their last paying gig weeks after its release, Lennon and McCartney were no longer writing together, and Harrison was rumbling with resentment.

The payoff was astonishing, and summed up by its sole single, "Yellow Submarine/Eleanor Rigby": one side a children's song that will outlive us all, the other a string-driven lament that even today sounds nothing at all like pop music—yet is still, like its parent album, simply brilliant. **BM**

"We played it to the Stones ..."

Paul McCartney, 1966

Track Listing		
01 **Taxman** (Harrison)		2:38
▶ 02 **Eleanor Rigby** (Lennon·McCartney)		2:08
03 **I'm Only Sleeping** (Lennon·McCartney)		3:01
04 **Love You To** (Harrison)		3:01
05 **Here, There And Everywhere** (Lennon·McCartney)		2:26
▶ 06 **Yellow Submarine** (Lennon·McCartney)		2:41
07 **She Said She Said** (Lennon·McCartney)		2:37
08 **Good Day Sunshine** (Lennon·McCartney)		2:10
09 **And Your Bird Can Sing** (Lennon·McCartney)		2:01
10 **For No One** (Lennon·McCartney)		2:02
11 **Doctor Robert** (Lennon·McCartney)		2:15
12 **I Want To Tell You** (Harrison)		2:30
13 **Got To Get You Into My Life** (Lennon·McCartney)		2:31
▶ 14 **Tomorrow Never Knows** (Lennon·McCartney)		2:57

The Beach Boys | Pet Sounds (1966)

Label | Capitol
Producer | Brian Wilson
Art Direction | Capitol Photo Studio • George Jerman
Nationality | USA
Running Time | 36:19

If *Rubber Soul* marked a pivotal moment for The Beatles, signaling the psychedelic journey they were to embark on, it also served as a spur to Brian Wilson, the errant genius at the heart of The Beach Boys. Inspired by "every cut [on *Rubber Soul* being] very artistically interesting and stimulating," Wilson headed for the studio to create *Pet Sounds*, an album that matched—and even topped—the Fab Four's effort.

Wilson spent two months in early 1966 writing the album with Tony Asher, an advertising executive who specialized in jingles. The tenor of the album is radically different from previous releases. Gone were the one-dimensional sun 'n' surf anthems; in their stead, a more complex sound emerged, joyous but tinged with deeper, troubled emotions.

Opening with the astonishing "Wouldn't It Be Nice," a rich outpouring of heartfelt emotion backed by gorgeous layers of horns, percussion, and bicycle bells, *Pet Sounds* transcends the genre of pop. Wilson's flair for songwriting, both lyrically and melodically, shines through every song, from "I Just Wasn't Made For These Times" to "Caroline No," his favorite track of the album.

After *Pet Sounds* (the front cover, shot in San Diego Zoo, was a pun on the album being full of Wilson's favorite—or "pet"—sounds) Wilson's slide into madness began. Confused by this new music, many fans shunned the album (ditto Capitol, who failed to promote it). Henceforth, Wilson became obsessed with the quest for the perfect pop album. Meanwhile, in England, The Beatles were rising to the challenge *Pet Sounds* had set with the release of *Sgt. Pepper's* … **SJac**

"I dreamed I had a halo … "

Brian Wilson, 1990

Track Listing

▶ 01	Wouldn't It Be Nice (Wilson•Asher)	2:25
02	You Still Believe In Me (Wilson•Asher)	2:34
03	That's Not Me (Wilson•Asher)	2:30
▶ 04	Don't Talk (Put Your Head On My Shoulders) (Wilson•Asher)	2:54
05	I'm Waiting For The Day (Wilson•Love)	3:06
06	Let's Go Away For A While (Wilson)	2:21
07	Sloop John B (Trad •Arr. Wilson)	3:00
▶ 08	God Only Knows (Wilson•Asher)	2:52
09	I Know There's An Answer (Wilson•Sachen)	3:11
10	Here Today (Wilson•Asher)	2:55
11	I Just Wasn't Made For These Times (Wilson•Asher)	3:15
12	Pet Sounds (Wilson)	2:23
▶ 13	Caroline No (Wilson•Asher)	2:53

Fred Neil
Fred Neil (1966)

Label | Capitol
Producer | Nick Venet
Art Direction | Uncredited
Nationality | USA
Running Time | 37:56

The Byrds
Fifth Dimension (1966)

Label | Columbia
Producer | Jim Dickson • Allen Stanton
Art Direction | Uncredited
Nationality | USA
Running Time | 29:25

Although his own recording career was brief, the late Fred Neil was a key figure in the transition of folk to folk-rock. Born in Florida but based in New York's bohemian Greenwich Village, he made an immediate impact with his 1965 debut *Bleecker & MacDougal*, which featured John Sebastian (The Lovin' Spoonful) on harmonica. Having outraged genre purists by mixing acoustic and electric instrumentation, Neil went a step further with a groundbreaking synthesis of folk, rock, and jazz, bound by hypnotic songs and his low, honey-thick croon.

Essential listening for all singer-songwriters, this album contains no filler. That said, there are two obvious peaks. Understated classic "Everybody's Talkin'" became a global pop smash for the great Harry Nilsson, whose speeded-up version featured in the movie *Midnight Cowboy*. "The Dolphins" insinuates itself with a yearning, elliptical melody, while the lyric conflates philosophy and environmentalism. The track was regularly covered by Tim Buckley; its author donated all royalties to dolphin conservation charities.

Another famous Neil acolyte was Mama Cass Elliott of The Mamas And The Papas, who is rumored to be the "UFO" credited with backing vocals on "Badi-Da." The artist's coffee-black humor surfaces in the funky groove of "That's The Bag I'm In," while the bluesy "Sweet Cocaine" observes without passing judgment. Progressive work-out "Cynicrustpetefredjohn Raga" makes an exotic closer, driven by Cyrus Faryar's "magic bouzouki" and loose ensemble playing. **MA**

It is a curious feature of The Byrds' career that as their popularity waned, and as personality clashes arose, they produced their best work. The pressures of touring, and of being the group's chief songwriter, finally got to Gene Clark, who quit in early 1966. Forced to push their own songwriting skills to offset this crucial loss, David Crosby and Roger McGuinn began to find their own voices.

McGuinn's fascination with things spacey and sci-fi characterizes the title track and the country-esque, whimsical "Mr Spaceman." Crosby's proto-hippy musings in "What's Happening?!?!" are answered by McGuinn's snakey 12-string solos. McGuinn's guitar spits fire on the jazz-raga-rock stunner "I See You" and—famously—on the extraordinary "Eight Miles High." Co-written with the departed Clark, the song is an impressionistic, psychedelic account of the culture shock the group experienced during their ill-fated UK tour in 1965. A heavy diet of Ravi Shankar and John Coltrane on the tour bus inspired McGuinn's freeform solos, grounded by Hillman's rumbling bass and Clarke's fizzing drums. Alas, the word "high" in the title saw the track banned in the U.S., crippling sales. The Byrds' slide from the charts starts here.

Elsewhere, there are nods to the group's folk roots and, uncharacteristically, R&B. This makes for an uneven album, true, and it is not without filler. But come on! The Byrds were now straddling rock 'n' roll, folk, jazz, "raga" rock, and country—and their best was yet to come. **RD**

Bob Dylan
Blonde On Blonde (1966)

Label | Columbia
Producer | Bob Johnston
Art Direction | Uncredited
Nationality | USA
Running Time | 71:00

The Monks
Black Monk Time (1966)

Label | Polydor
Producer | Jimmy Bowien
Art Direction | Uncredited
Nationality | USA
Running Time | 28:01

Bizarrely, in the aftermath of the infamous Manchester Free Trade Hall "electric" concert on May 17, 1966 (erroneously bootlegged as "The Royal Albert Hall Concert"), at least two people claimed the voice that infamously branded Dylan "Judas" was theirs. It seems strange anyone is proud of the attack because, on hindsight, it was horrifically misguided.

If 1965's *Highway 61* was the impressive rock 'n' roll debut, then this album, which followed six months later, was no simple consolidation; it was Dylan providing the new genre with its first masterpiece.

Blonde On Blonde's wild blues establishes a sense of late-night rants, reflections, and desperation. The direct rock 'n' roll songs such as "I Want You" switch in a heartbeat into heartbreaking ballads such as "Visions Of Johanna" or the touching melancholy of "Just Like A Woman," while closer "Sad Eyed Lady Of The Lowlands" is a manifesto for the lovelorn.

Surreal yet perceptive, Dylan's poetic observations suggest that the "voice of a generation" tag is more deserved for charting an age's inner feelings rather than protesting its political beliefs.

This was rock's first double album and its success helped ensure that progression, experimentation, and excitement became key to rock 'n' roll's outlook. Little wonder, then, that the cover photo is blurred. In 1966, Bob Dylan was, in creative terms, moving so fast that the rest of the world was struggling to catch up. In many ways, it never did. **PS**

Recorded in late 1965, The Monks' *Black Monk Time* is one hell of a contender for the "first punk album," and as hollow and silly as such a title might be (after all, punk was a cross-fertilizing, fashion-conscious, countercultural movement and these guys were geopolitical exiles) the group certainly do sound much more normal today than they possibly could have in their milieu.

Though The Monks never played outside Germany (reluctance to undertake a mooted tour of war-torn Vietnam was one of the reasons they broke up; what they really wanted to do was play in their native America), this five piece group, all ex-U.S. servicemen and all dressed for the part (robes and bald heads), have developed a strong and deserved reputation in certain quarters, based almost entirely on this exceptional album (and a short-lived reunion in the 1990s).

Organ and a custom-made electric banjo join traditional rock instruments on this album, all played with precision and in anger. *Black Monk Time* is at turns hilarious, raucous, radical, and exhilarating, with opener "Monk Time" perhaps one of the greatest fanfares to mayhem ever recorded. "I Hate You" would not have been entirely out of place in Sixties cult movie *Bedazzled*. Other tracks, like "Boys Are Boys And Girls Are Choice" and "Drunken Maria," reference a bastardized Teutonic folk music—but is it affectionate, condemnatory, or simply stuff that rubbed off onto these poor deluded soldiers far from home? The sleeve notes, after all, tell us "The Monks believe in nothing"[sic]. **DN**

The Kinks | Face To Face (1966)

Label | Pye
Producer | Shel Talmy
Art Direction | Uncredited
Nationality | UK
Running Time | 38:31

Ray Davies did not like the sleeve of The Kinks' fourth album. "I wanted the cover to be black and strong like the sound of the LP," recalled the north London band's leader, "instead of all those fancy colors."

Face To Face signaled a change of approach for Ray, his guitarist brother Dave, drummer Mick Avory, and bassist Pete Quaife. It was the first time they had spent months on a record, overdubbing tracks over the course of several sessions. It also marked the end for American producer Shel Talmy, whose rough 'n' ready methods did not suit the cleaner arrangements.

"Party Line" kicks things off in familiar rock 'n' roll style, while "Dandy" follows up the Swinging London satire of early hit "Dedicated Follower Of Fashion." Much of the rest is deeper and darker. Ray explores his fragile mental state in the harpsichord-laden "Too Much On My Mind"; UK chart-topper "Sunny Afternoon" floats its world-weary sentiment on a beautifully descending bassline. "House In The Country" and "Most Exclusive Residence For Sale" fit the accepted view of the album as a song cycle about British society. However, the "quintessentially English" cliché underplays the diversity of both the music and lyrics. Chuck Berry homage "Holiday In Waikiki" laments the commercialization of Hawaii. "Fancy" is a droning mood piece inspired by Indian ragas, while "Rainy Day In June" is awash with thunderclaps and mystery.

Face To Face was not a big hit—No. 139 in the U.S. chart, No. 13 in the UK—but it heralded the start of The Kinks' classic period. The fiery chart stars were now a multi-faceted albums act. **MA**

"They must love us, really."

Ray Davies, 1969

Track Listing

▶ 01	Party Line (Davies)	2:35
02	Rosy Won't You Please Come Home (Davies)	2:34
▶ 03	Dandy (Davies)	2:12
▶ 04	Too Much On My Mind (Davies)	2:28
05	Session Man (Davies)	2:14
▶ 06	Rainy Day In June (Davies)	3:10
▶ 07	House In The Country (Davies)	3:03
▶ 08	Holiday In Waikiki (Davies)	2:52
▶ 09	Most Exclusive Residence For Sale (Davies)	2:48
▶ 10	Fancy (Davies)	2:30
11	Little Miss Queen Of Darkness (Davies)	3:16
12	You're Lookin' Fine (Davies)	2:46
▶ 13	Sunny Afternoon (Davies)	3:36
14	I'll Remember (Davies)	2:27

The Mama's And The Papa's
If You Can Believe Your Eyes And Ears (1966)

Label | RCA Victor
Producer | Lou Adler
Art Direction | Uncredited
Nationality | USA
Running Time | 34:10

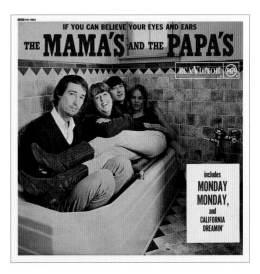

After forming in the Virgin Islands from the remnants of folk-rock groups The Journeymen and The Mugwumps, the quartet of Denny Doherty, Cass Elliott, Michelle Gilliam, and her husband singer/songwriter/guitarist John Phillips moved to Los Angeles in 1965, where their sublime vocal harmonies secured them work with Barry ("Eve Of Destruction") McGuire and his manager, Lou Adler. The group's first hit was the million-selling "California Dreamin'," a wistful paean to the West Coast that highlighted their sumptuous vocals and stellar harmony work, followed by the gold U.S. chart-topping "Monday, Monday."

Both feature on *If You Can Believe . . .* —their debut album—which also topped the U.S. chart and was certified gold. Alongside the big hits were tracks that reflected the quest for personal freedom which characterized the times ("Go Where You Wanna Go"); the closing track, "The In Crowd," is a hugely enjoyable piece of social satire ("If it's square, we ain't there!"), which was later memorably covered by Roxy Music.

John Phillips was undoubtedly the architect behind their sound, although the group's backing musicians included drummer Hal Blaine, Joe Osborn on bass, and Larry Knechtel on keyboards. Phillips' songwriting prowess is demonstrated (he also wrote Scott McKenzie's "San Francisco [Flowers In Your Hair]"), but he brought a fresh approach to cover versions as well—"Do You Wanna Dance," "Spanish Harlem," and "I Call Your Name"—all set sparkling by the group's harmonies. **JT**

"I've never heard anything like this in my life."
Lou Adler, 1966

Track Listing

▶	01	Monday, Monday (J. Phillips)	3:25
▶	02	Straight Shooter (J. Phillips)	2:56
	03	Got A Feelin' (Doherty • J. Phillips)	2:53
	04	I Call Your Name (Lennon • McCartney)	2:36
▶	05	Do You Wanna Dance (Freeman)	2:56
	06	Go Where You Wanna Go (J. Phillips)	2:26
▶	07	California Dreamin' (J. Phillips • M. Phillips)	2:38
▶	08	Spanish Harlem (Leiber • Spector)	3:14
	09	Somebody Groovy (J. Phillips)	3:14
	10	Hey Girl (J. Phillips)	2:22
	11	You Baby (Sloan • Barri)	2:19
	12	The In Crowd (Page)	3:11

Paul Revere And The Raiders
Midnight Ride (1966)

Label | Columbia
Producer | Terry Melcher
Art Direction | Uncredited
Nationality | USA
Running Time | 27:38

Was ever any band more maligned than the Raiders? In the face of an onslaught by a whole host of British beat groups, they stood shoulder to shoulder with The Byrds and The Beach Boys.

In the period that remains the high-water mark of pop music, they scored a succession of hits and played with a unique verve forged through years of gigging at every club that would take them. Their lean punk sound has never dated, and is still every bit as gritty as it was 40 years ago. Yet those who remember them generally recall the Revolutionary War costumes, the clowning and acrobatics, and the fact they were Dick Clark's pet outfit on the daily TV show *Where The Action Is*. Even The Monkees have more cred.

But in 1966, the trademark snarl of lead vocalist Mark Lindsay on "Louie, Go Home" sounded every bit as fierce as that of The Animals' Eric Burdon or Them's Van Morrison, and was a significant influence on The Who's Roger Daltrey. And musically, everything came together perfectly on *Midnight Ride*, on which nine of the tracks are band compositions. The remaining tunes are arguably two of the greatest singles of the 1960s. Barry Mann and Cynthia Weill's "Kicks" is a pounding antidrugs warning that nevertheless treats your brain as if it has been reduced to mush already. Garage classic "I'm Not Your Stepping Stone" (by Tommy Boyce and Bobby Hart) would later be covered by The Monkees, but this version is the one that inspired the Sex Pistols' cover.

Pop-punk just does not get any better. **DH**

> "I wanted the band to be fun ...
> not just a jukebox with legs ... "
>
> Paul Revere, 2004

Track Listing

▶	01	Kicks (Mann • Weill)	2:28
	02	There's Always Tomorrow (Levin • Smith)	2:39
	03	Little Girl In The 4th Row (Lindsay • Revere)	2:58
	04	Ballad Of A Useless Man (Levin)	2:08
▶	05	I'm Not Your Stepping Stone (Boyce • Hart)	2:31
	06	There She Goes (Lindsay • Revere)	1:47
	07	All I Really Need Is You (Lindsay • Revere)	3:27
	08	Get It On (Levin • Volk)	3:12
▶	09	Louie, Go Home (Lindsay • Revere)	2:41
	10	Take A Look At Yourself (Lindsay • Revere)	1:48
	11	Melody For An Unknown Girl (Lindsay • Revere)	1:59

The Mothers Of Invention | Freak Out! (1966)

Label | Verve
Producer | Tom Wilson
Art Direction | Jack Anesh
Nationality | USA
Running Time | 60:05

Frank Zappa's band had been known simply as The Mothers until a nervous MGM realized what the company had on their hands with this cataclysmic debut. On the verge of releasing *Freak Out!*, rock's second double LP (Dylan's *Blonde On Blonde* just pipped it), the label panicked that the implications of the group's controversial monicker might scare off DJs. "As if our name was going to be The Big Problem," Zappa observed dryly in his autobiography.

Coming from the heart of the burgeoning freak culture on the West Coast, and having been signed by producer Tom Wilson, Zappa and his band set out to blow minds with this debut release. What's more, this record was about something. "Each tune had a function within an overall satirical concept," said Zappa.

"Who Are the Brain Police?" sums up that concept neatly: creepy, antiauthoritarian moaning that describes the melting of objects and minds alike. Alongside overtly weird numbers are parodies of bubbly pop, such as the doo-wop pastiche "Go Cry On Somebody Else's Shoulder," juxtaposed with intricately arranged love songs such as "How Could I Be Such A Fool?" Psychedelic guitars and dirty blues riffs start dragging the album deeper as it enters its second half: "Help, I'm A Rock" distills the freak essence and turns everything abstract; "The Return Of The Son Of Monster Magnet," the entirety of side four on the vinyl release, is an experimental and noisy showstopper.

Freak Out! signaled the emergence of a uniquely exciting and challenging composer who made a career out of breaking down boundaries. **MBI**

"I wasn't doing drugs."

Frank Zappa, 1989

Track Listing		
01	Hungry Freaks, Daddy (Zappa)	3:27
02	I Ain't Got No Heart (Zappa)	2:30
▶ 03	Who Are The Brain Police? (Zappa)	3:22
▶ 04	Go Cry On Somebody Else's Shoulder (Zappa)	3:31
05	Motherly Love (Zappa)	2:45
06	How Could I Be Such A Fool? (Zappa)	2:12
▶ 07	Wowie Zowie (Zappa)	2:45
08	You Didn't Try To Call Me (Zappa)	3:17
09	Any Way The Wind Blows (Zappa)	2:52
10	I'm Not Satisfied (Zappa)	2:37
11	You're Probably Wondering Why I'm Here (Zappa)	3:37
12	Trouble Every Day (Zappa)	6:16
▶ 13	Help, I'm A Rock (Zappa)	8:37
▶ 14	The Return of The Son of Monster Magnet (Zappa)	12:17

The Rolling Stones | Aftermath (1966)

Label | Decca
Producer | Andrew Loog Oldham
Art Direction | Sandy Beach
Nationality | UK
Running Time | 53:58

In the 1960s it was simple: Beatles good; Stones bad. By 1965, the Fabs had got deeper but, "Help!" aside, not much darker. The Stones, however, were snarling "Satisfaction" and "She Said Yeah." These appeared on albums, such as the delicious *December's Children*, which were ragbags put out by production line labels and eyes-on-the-prize manager Andrew Loog Oldham.

Aftermath, in contrast, was a proper album, not padded with off-cuts. It saw the Stones stretching out: literally in the case of "Goin' Home," but, more entrancingly, in experimental songs.

"Lady Jane" is most startling: an Elizabethan ballad whose icy delicacy would reverberate through the Stones' later laments. "Under My Thumb" is astonishing both for its imperious sexism and marimba-driven rhythm. "Mother's Little Helper" is a portrait of pill-popping housewives, embellished by sitar—although, like "Out Of Time," "Take It Or Leave It," and "What To Do," it was left off the U.S. release. America did not fare badly, though: it got the brilliant "Paint It Black" instead.

Key to these departures were Jack Nitzsche—an innovative writer, performer, and arranger who had come to the Stones via Phil Spector—and Brian Jones. The latter, recalled Keith, "was so versatile" but had "lost interest in guitar"—hence his sitar and marimba work.

The conventional cuts do not disappoint either; best being the impishly rude "Stupid Girl."

Aftermath was the first Stones album to consist entirely of originals, and hence is their *Hard Day's Night*. The Beatles and the Stones had come of age—and the world was theirs. **BM**

"It's the first time we wrote the whole record ..."

Mick Jagger, 1995

Track Listing

01	Mother's Little Helper	(Jagger·Richard)	2:48
▶ 02	Stupid Girl	(Jagger·Richard)	2:57
▶ 03	Lady Jane	(Jagger·Richard)	3:11
▶ 04	Under My Thumb	(Jagger·Richard)	3:43
05	Doncha Bother Me	(Jagger·Richard)	2:42
06	Goin' Home	(Jagger·Richard)	11:16
07	Flight 505	(Jagger·Richard)	3:29
08	High And Dry	(Jagger·Richard)	3:10
09	Out Of Time	(Jagger·Richard)	5:40
10	It's Not Easy	(Jagger·Richard)	2:57
11	I Am Waiting	(Jagger·Richard)	3:13
12	Take It Or Leave It	(Jagger·Richard)	2:48
13	Think	(Jagger·Richard)	3:10
14	What To Do	(Jagger·Richard)	2:34

Simon And Garfunkel
Parsley, Sage, Rosemary And Thyme (1966)

Label | Columbia
Producer | Bob Johnston
Art Direction | Uncredited
Nationality | USA
Running Time | 28:30

The world was about to fall apart but there was still room for beauty when Paul Simon and Art Garfunkel recorded their first great album, *Parsley, Sage, Rosemary And Thyme*. Indeed, it is the tension between the sense of impending doom and Simon's insistence on emotional connection that makes the album such an enduring work, despite numerous phrases and lines that reveal it as an artifact of the 1960s ("Feelin' Groovy").

Where their previous album, *Sounds Of Silence*, was a rush job driven by the label's desire to capitalize on the hit title track, Simon insisted on total control this time around, which perfectly explains the brilliantly detailed production, achieved with ace engineer Roy Halee. The painstaking work is instantly obvious on opening track "Scarborough Fair/Canticle," an intricate, haunting pop masterpiece that rivals any of Brian Wilson's creations. But Simon is no one-trick pony. The range of material he created for *Parsley, Sage, Rosemary And Thyme* revealed him as one of the era's most gifted songwriters, from Garfunkel's luminous showpiece "For Emily, Whenever I May Find Her" to "Homeward Bound," arguably the greatest song written about a musician's life on the road. The literary ennui of "The Dangling Conversation," is pitch perfect, while the caustic rock of "A Simple Desultory Philippic" still hits home, even if many of its targets no longer inspire scorn.

The final track is a sweet rendition of "Silent Night" over a news broadcast mentioning the death of Lenny Bruce and the escalation of the war in Vietnam. **AG**

Track Listing

▶ 01	Scarborough Fair/Canticle (Garfunkel • Simon)	3:10
02	Patterns (Simon)	2:45
03	Cloudy (Simon)	2:21
▶ 04	Homeward Bound (Simon)	2:29
05	The Big Bright Green Pleasure Machine (Simon)	2:47
06	The 59th Street Bridge Song (Feelin' Groovy) (Simon)	1:53
07	The Dangling Conversation (Simon)	2:37
08	Flowers Never Bend With The Rainfall (Simon)	2:10
09	A Simple Desultory Philippic (Or How I Was Robert McNamara'd Into Submission) (Simon)	2:19
▶ 10	For Emily, Whenever I May Find Her (Simon)	2:05
11	A Poem On The Underground Wall (Simon)	1:52
12	7 O'Clock News/Silent Night (Simon)	2:02

The 13th Floor Elevators | The Psychedelic Sounds Of The 13th Floor Elevators (1966)

Label | International Artists
Producer | Lelan Rogers
Art Direction | John Cleveland
Nationality | USA
Running Time | 35:43

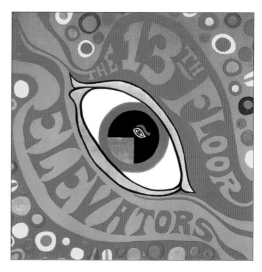

Hailing from Austin, Texas, the Elevators had already played shows in San Francisco, before the psychedelic movement there came to prominence. Thereafter, they had to be threatened with contract suspension to get them to Austin to record what would be the first acid rock album. It sold surprisingly well, due partly to the success of an already released single, the classic garage sneer "You're Gonna Miss Me," which made it to No. 55 on the Billboard charts.

Openly promoting the benefits of hallucinogenics in the album's sleevenotes was never going to endear the band to the authorities; Texan police officers even dismantled the band's gear to search for drugs. "The quest for pure sanity . . . forms the basis of the songs on this album," according to the back cover, but the brand of garage rock and R&B contained here is anything but sane. "Reverberation (Doubt)" and "Tried To Hide" are intense rockers, while "Roller Coaster" and "Fire Engine" have a dark, eerie quality to them. Frontman Roky Erickson yelps and howls like a man possessed while the alien sounds from Tommy Hall's electric jug add to the already gorgeously skewed mood.

The Elevators burnt out quickly, and Erickson has pursued an erratic (though intermittently brilliant) solo career since. But the band's legend lives on, partly through covers by bands such as Spacemen 3 and, most notably, Primal Scream, who memorably reworked "Slip Inside This House" (from the Elevators' sophomore *Easter Everywhere*) on *Screamadelica*. **AET**

"Them doctors and nurses . . . They couldn't hold me in!"

Roky Erickson, 1980

Track Listing		
▶ 01 You're Gonna Miss Me [Erickson]		2:31
▶ 02 Roller Coaster [Erickson·Hall]		5:08
03 Splash 1 [Erickson·Hall]		3:57
▶ 04 Reverberation (Doubt) [Erickson·Hall·Sutherland]		2:51
05 Don't Fall Down [Erickson·Hall]		3:03
▶ 06 Fire Engine [Erickson·Hall·Sutherland]		3:23
07 Thru The Rhythm [Hall·Sutherland]		3:10
08 You Don't Know (How Young You Are) [St. John]		2:59
09 Kingdom Of Heaven [St. John]		3:11
10 Monkey Island [St. John]		2:40
▶ 11 Tried To Hide [Hall·Sutherland]		2:50

John Mayall's Blues Breakers
Blues Breakers With Eric Clapton (1966)

Label | Decca
Producer | Mike Vernon
Art Direction | Decca Publicity Art Department
Nationality | UK
Running Time | 37:06

Around the time that *Blues Breakers With Eric Clapton* was released, graffiti started appearing around London, which stated, simply, "Clapton is God." Anyone who doubts Clapton's credentials as a bluesman should listen to this scorching 1966 recording, which ignited the British scene like a tinderbox.

Clapton had quit the chart-friendly Yardbirds in search of a purist outfit, and in Mayall he found both a bandleader who shared his tastes and a father figure.

In the studio with bassist John McVie and drummer Hughie Flint, the aim was to reproduce the energy of the band's live performances. This can be felt from the first track, a smoldering cover of an Otis Rush song, "All Your Love," which hustles along on its Hammond and splintered guitar lines.

The next track, "Hideaway," is an unforgettable slice of Clapton grandstanding—on this instrumental version of Freddie King's classic, the young guitarist lets rip with everything he has got, delivering a storming performance with zest and assurance. He also shines on "Steppin' Out," a switchblade-sharp boogie.

Mayall's own contribution was no less a part in the album's success. His original songs, such as "Little Girl" and "Key To Love," epitomized the jubilant Sixties but gave little away to populism, remaining squarely within the blues tradition.

The Thames Estuary may have been a thousand miles from the Mississippi Delta, but *Blues Breakers With Eric Clapton* made it seem a whole lot nearer. **JDi**

"I had an accelerator going. I just moved at speed."

Eric Clapton, 1966

Track Listing

▶ 01	All Your Love (Dixon•Rush)	3:35
▶ 02	Hideaway (King•Thompson)	3:14
▶ 03	Little Girl (Mayall)	2:33
04	Another Man (Trad. arr. Mayall)	1:44
05	Double Crossing Time (Clapton•Mayall)	3:00
06	What'd I Say (Charles)	4:26
▶ 07	Key To Love (Mayall)	2:05
08	Parchman Farm (Allison)	2:21
09	Have You Heard (Mayall)	5:54
10	Ramblin' On My Mind (Trad., arr. Johnson)	3:07
▶ 11	Steppin' Out (Frazier)	2:27
12	It Ain't Right (Jacobs)	2:40

The Yardbirds
The Yardbirds (1966)

Label | Columbia
Producer | Various
Art Direction | Chris Dreja
Nationality | UK
Running Time | 33:10

The Yardbirds finally unleashed their first studio LP in August 1966, by which time the band featured the incendiary guitar soloing of Jeff Beck (who replaced Eric Clapton). The album was much delayed by heavy touring of Europe and the U.S. (where The Yardbirds became a primary inspiration to the myriad garage and psychedelic bands springing up) and was eventually written and recorded in just one week at Advision Studios in London.

The Yardbirds (aka *Roger The Engineer*) mixes up supercharged blues, prototype psychedelia, feedback, and Gregorian monk chants to great effect. Anticipating the heavy blues-rock of Cream and Led Zeppelin, the searing "Lost Woman," "The Nazz Are Blue," and "Rack My Mind" reflect the way the band built fiery workouts from traditional blues riffs and licks (Snooky Pryor's "Someone To Love Me," Elmore James's "Dust My Broom," and Slim Harpo's "Baby Scratch My Back" respectively), in the process showcasing Beck's astonishing talent (he makes a sustained one-note solo exciting on "The Nazz Are Blue"). Hit single "Over, Under Sideways, Down" is based around the bassline to "Rock Around The Clock," yet manages to sound positively futuristic with the addition of Beck's winding guitar, the stop-start structure of the song, and the rabble-rousing calls of "Hey!"

Reissues include "Happenings Ten Years Time Ago," a storming rave-up featuring the dream-team of Beck and Jimmy Page, and its B-side "Psycho Daisies." **JoH**

Nina Simone
Wild Is The Wind (1966)

Label | Philips
Producer | Various
Art Direction | Uncredited
Nationality | USA
Running Time | 39:07

Nina Simone could be as bluesy as Billie or as jazzy as Ella. The fact that she was never as consistent as either, stylistically speaking, was a major roadblock in her career, causing many critics to underrate her. But by the mid-1960s, she had proven herself to be equally comfortable in the worlds of jazz, Broadway, gospel, pop, and folk, and produced her share of satisfying, as well as confounding, music everywhere she roamed.

Although culled from studio and live recordings from 1964 to '65, *Wild Is The Wind* is nonetheless the best example of how Simone's eclecticism could gel into a cohesive musical statement. The album shows staggering range, the 11 hitherto unreleased tracks taking the listener on a zigzagging, yet always convincing, ride through styles and emotions.

Simone is at her most joyous with the rowdy juke-joint opener "I Love Your Lovin' Ways," which makes the somber follow up, "Four Women," an even more devastatingly effective turn. The song, which tells of the hardships of four black women, simmers with the type of barely subdued rage that would color much of the songwriter's later, more politically oriented, material.

"Why Keep On Breaking My Heart" and "Either Way I Lose" seem targeted at satisfying the mainstream pop audience that had made her version of Gershwin's "I Loves You, Porgy" a major hit in 1959. The tour-de-force title track, which clocks in at nearly seven minutes, is a wonderfully indulgent love song that stands among Simone's finest works. **JiH**

Astrud Gilberto
Beach Samba (1967)

Label | Verve
Producer | Creed Taylor
Art Direction | David Krieger
Nationality | Brazil
Running Time | 38:58

Nico
Chelsea Girl (1967)

Label | Polydor
Producer | Tom Wilson
Art Direction | Uncredited
Nationality | Germany
Running Time | 45:36

Who can resist an album that opens with "Stay . . . and we'll make sex with music," Astrud Gilberto's invitation on the opening track of her 1967 *Beach Samba* album?

The one-time wife of João Gilberto, Astrud had whimpered her way onto the pop charts singing the English lyric on Stan Getz's recording "The Girl From Ipanema." Despite range limitation, she developed her accented articulations into a sensual delivery, working at her new-found craft between 1963 and '67 and maturing into a stylist with an original vocal identity.

Working with producer Creed Taylor and arrangers Eumir Deodato and Don Sebesky, Astrud's repertoire on *Beach Samba* is a mixture of Brazilian tunes translated into English alongside American folk pop filtered through bossa nova or samba.

"Stay" was written by Gayle Caldwell, who also provided big hit "Cycles" for Frank Sinatra, and arranged by Deodato; the presence of flautist Hubert Laws on this and other pieces here adds sparkle to the orchestrations. Tim Hardin's "Misty Roses" is a Sebesky masterpiece with French horns, strings, and harp.

Throughout, Astrud surfs the wave nicely. She is so cool on Deodato's "Canoeiro" with its contagious, wordless melody, while "You Didn't Have To Be So Nice" is a cute duet with her then six-year-old son Marcello.

No rough edges here, just smooth easy-listening music with Astrud starring in *Beach Samba*, an album that shows the indelible mark she made worldwide as the singing Brazilian girl-next-door. **JCV**

Famous for her work with The Velvet Underground and infamous for her list of lovers (including Jim Morrison, Iggy Pop, and Brian Jones), Nico finally went solo with 1967's *Chelsea Girl* (*Chelsea Girls* was the name of a Warhol film in which she had appeared). The material came from some of the finest songwriters of the era, including Bob Dylan, Tim Hardin, an unknown Jackson Browne (then a teenager and Nico's boyfriend), and The Velvet Underground's Lou Reed, Sterling Morrison, and John Cale. (The three Velvets also provide backing here.) But though the material is not self-composed (save for one co-write), *Chelsea Girl* provides ample confirmation of Nico's originality and potential.

Her magical vocals are austere yet mesmerizing; the sparse, folksy instrumentation includes flute, electric viola, marimba, guitar, cello, and harmonium. The tracks have a haunting, alluring quality, particularly on the evocatively serene "These Days"/"I'll Keep It With Mine." Elsewhere, the Morrison/Reed title track references the life of the scenesters at Andy Warhol's New York Factory.

The public were unprepared for Nico's experimental art-rock masterpieces and their melancholic ambience, and the album made little impression upon release. But its desolate beauty—and Nico's unique, provocative later work with John Cale—has fascinated subsequent generations: Patti Smith lauded her, Siouxsie Sioux wanted her for a support act, and two *Chelsea Girl* tracks were included on the soundtrack of Wes Anderson's 2001 comedy *The Royal Tenenbaums*. **MBo**

The Beatles
Sgt. Pepper's Lonely Hearts Club Band (1967)

Label | Parlophone
Producer | George Martin
Art Direction | Peter Blake
Nationality | UK
Running Time | 39:50

Warp with us back to 1967, when Fabs fans who had persevered through the feet-finding of *Rubber Soul* and *Revolver* were to be rewarded with a musical funtasia. *Sgt. Pepper* ... spent 15 weeks atop the Billboard chart and was still in the Top Five when *Magical Mystery Tour* hit No. 1 six months later.

Why? Because its boundary-pushing was matched by scintillating songwriting. From McCartney's rousing opener (which Jimi Hendrix was playing live two days after its release), through Lennon's kaleidoscopic "Lucy In The Sky With Diamonds," to the duo's astonishing "A Day In The Life," every one is a gem.

Despite the omission of "Strawberry Fields Forever" —the queasy single that bridged the gap from *Revolver* to *Sgt. Pepper* ... —the album embodied elements of psychedelia: Eastern philosophy (Harrison's "Within You Without You") and druggy allusions (though Lennon denied the LSD connotations of "Lucy," McCartney conceded "Fixing A Hole").

Sgt. Pepper ...'s Pop Art credentials were secured by music's most famous cover. Designer Peter Blake envisaged it as a gift box of goodies but settled for cardboard cutouts tucked into the sleeve (a few famous faces—Jesus, Hitler, Gandhi—did not make the final cut).

The album's impact was unprecedented. U.S. radio played it for days; *Times* critic Kenneth Tynan called it "a decisive moment in the history of Western civilization." That hyperbole is long gone, leaving perfect pop in which ambition and melody twirl together forever. **BM**

Track Listing

▶ 01	Sgt. Pepper's Lonely Hearts Club Band (Lennon·McCartney)	2:02
▶ 02	With A Little Help From My Friends (Lennon·McCartney)	2:44
▶ 03	Lucy In The Sky With Diamonds (Lennon·McCartney)	3:29
04	Getting Better (Lennon·McCartney)	2:48
05	Fixing A Hole (Lennon·McCartney)	2:36
▶ 06	She's Leaving Home (Lennon·McCartney)	3:35
07	Being For The Benefit Of Mr. Kite (Lennon·McCartney)	2:37
08	Within You Without You (Harrison)	5:06
09	When I'm Sixty-Four (Lennon·McCartney)	2:37
10	Lovely Rita (Lennon·McCartney)	2:42
11	Good Morning, Good Morning (Lennon·McCartney)	2:42
12	Sgt. Pepper's Lonely Hearts Club Band (Reprise) (Lennon·McCartney)	1:19
▶ 13	A Day In The Life (Lennon·McCartney)	5:33

Country Joe And The Fish
Electric Music For The Mind And Body (1967)

Label | Vanguard
Producer | Samuel Charters
Art Direction | Uncredited
Nationality | USA
Running Time | 44:03

A left-wing activist before and after a stint in the navy, Joe McDonald arrived in San Francisco as a student but quickly became absorbed into the folk scene and the Instant Action Jug Band (aka Country Joe and the Fish for recording purposes, a name that invoked—to those in the know—Stalin and Mao). It was only in the summer of 1966 that the band started replacing folk instruments with electric guitars, and an EP, the band's second, boosted their profile enough to have them signed to the New York-based folk and classical label Vanguard, which had been watching the transformation of its rival Elektra into a credible rock imprint.

At the time, San Francisco was a hotbed of radical students, fueled by LSD and politics. Musically, psychedelia was in its early stages, with few bands aware of the possibilities 1967 would bring. The Fish's LP opened the doors to everything that would follow in the next two years—even if their label insisted on the absence of the band's most popular live song, "I Feel Like I'm Fixin' To Die Rag."

Laced through with acid wit and acid grooves, *Electric Music* is one of the most cohesive artifacts of the Summer of Love and the hippie generation; the guitars alternate between soothing and brain-busting; the lyrics contain satirical attacks on Lyndon Johnson ("Superbird") and uncompromising drug epics ("Bass Strings"); it is either blues, folk, or rock, to suit all tastes. And in its wake, the mood of the country, its young people, and its music all changed. No mean feat. **DH**

"Music was of a different proportion then."

Barry "The Fish" Melton, 2004

Track Listing		
01 **Flying High** (McDonald)		2:41
▶ 02 **Not So Sweet Martha Lorraine** (McDonald)		4:24
03 **Death Sound Blues** (McDonald)		4:26
04 **Porpoise Mouth** (McDonald)		2:51
▶ 05 **Section 43** (McDonald)		7:26
▶ 06 **Superbird** (McDonald)		2:07
07 **Sad And Lonely Times** (McDonald)		2:26
08 **Love** (McDonald·Melton·Cohen Barthol·Gunning·Hirsch)		2:24
▶ 09 **Bass Strings** (McDonald)		5:03
10 **The Masked Marauder** (McDonald)		3:12
▶ 11 **Grace** (McDonald)		7:03

Buffalo Springfield
Buffalo Springfield Again (1967)

Label | Atco
Producer | Buffalo Springfield • Jack Nitzsche
Art Direction | Loring Eutemey
Nationality | USA
Running Time | 33:10

Buffalo Springfield (the name was borrowed from that of a steamroller resurfacing a road in L.A.) was simply too full of singer/songwriters to survive. They rose to fame with a 1967 U.S. Top Ten single, "For What It's Worth"—Stephen Stills' beautifully understated snapshot of the turbulent times. But by the time this second LP appeared, Stills and Young were competing fiercely for time and space, edging out the less competitive Furay.

By now the Springfield was less a group than a collection of individuals, each of whom concentrated on their own songs—with the exception of "Good Time Boy," written by Furay as a vehicle for drummer Dewey Martin to sing. Several tracks provided clues to future musical directions: "Expecting To Fly" and "Broken Arrow" feature ambitiously orchestrated soundscapes by Young and Jack Nitzsche, who later worked with the singer on several solo projects, including *Harvest*. Elsewhere, "Everydays," the standout "Bluebird," and particularly "Rock And Roll Woman" are typical of the later Stills approach—powerful vocals over a rich blend of bright, clear acoustic and tough electric guitars. The blending of the Springfield's folk-rock and country roots with a harder rock sound would be a major influence on the next generation of West Coast rock groups, most obviously The Eagles.

The rear of the album sleeve features a thank-you list to "friends, enemies and people we don't know from Adam." First name on the list? Hank B. Marvin, lead guitarist of British Instrumental group, The Shadows. **JT**

> ## "I think we're one of the most popular, mysterious American bands."
> Richie Furay, 1997

Track Listing

▶ 01	Mr. Soul (Young)	2:35
02	A Child's Claim To Fame (Furay)	2:09
▶ 03	Everydays (Stills)	2:38
▶ 04	Expecting To Fly (Young)	3:39
▶ 05	Bluebird (Stills)	4:28
06	Hung Upside Down (Stills)	3:24
07	Sad Memory (Furay)	3:00
08	Good Time Boy (Furay)	2:11
▶ 09	Rock And Roll Woman (Stills)	2:44
▶ 10	Broken Arrow (Young)	6:13

Captain Beefheart And His Magic Band
Safe As Milk (1967)

Label | Buddah
Producer | Bob Krasnow • Richard Perry
Art Direction | Tom Wilkes
Nationality | USA
Running Time | 35:40

After a stint with A&M, Beefheart signed with Bob Krasnow's Buddah label, taking all the "negative" songs A&M co-owner Jerry Moss had refused to release.

Maybe the square look Cap and his crew portray on the cover does not seem as revolutionary today, but in 1965 and '66, while British R&B was the underground trend in the States and The Beatles and Tamla ruled the airwaves, *Safe As Milk* was a hipsters' must.

Against all odds, the combination of Krasnow and Perry's straight pop production and the humungous vision of the inimitable Beefheart cooked up a storm. The Captain still had one eye on commercial success and commissioned bassist and professional songwriter Herb Bermann to polish some tunes, while Ry Cooder, then a member of might-have-beens The Rising Sons, provided arrangement and trademark slide guitar. Jazz vibraphonist Milt Jackson and future Magic Band pillars Alex St. Clair and John French rounded off the core of this blend of Delta blues, jazz, pyschedelia, R&B, and traditional mid-1960s U.S. folk rock.

Marvels abound, from the childlike wonder of "Yellow Brick Road" to the sneering "Dropout Boogie." "I'm Glad" is pure soul, "Autumn's Child" an ambitious acid symphony, and "Electricity" a Theremin-led, ratchety classic. And throughout, Beefheart's worn, bluesy voice—a Howlin' Wolf recanting surrealistic poetry.

The resulting album is a well-balanced, even radio-friendly hybrid that also hints at what was just around the bend—*Trout Mask Replica*. **JG**

> ## "I'm not a rock star. I'm a soft person. I'm not a rock."
>
> **Captain Beefheart, 1971**

Track Listing

	01	Sure 'Nuff 'N Yes, I Do (Bermann•Van Vliet)	2:10
▶	02	Zig Zag Wanderer (Bermann•Van Vliet)	2:35
	03	Call On Me (Van Vliet)	3:10
▶	04	Dropout Boogie (Bermann•Van Vliet)	2:20
	05	I'm Glad (Van Vliet)	3:22
▶	06	Electricity (Bermann•Van Vliet)	3:00
	07	Yellow Brick Road (Bermann•Van Vliet)	2:50
	08	Abba Zaba (Van Vliet)	3:35
	09	Plastic Factory (Bermann•Handley•Van Vliet)	3:00
	10	Where There's Woman (Bermann•Van Vliet)	2:05
	11	Grown So Ugly (Williams)	2:22
▶	12	Autumn's Child (Bermann•Van Vliet)	4:35

Moby Grape
Moby Grape (1967)

Label | Columbia
Producer | David Rubinson
Art Direction | Uncredited
Nationality | USA
Running Time | 33:11

Record company arrogance, rock 'n' roll shenanigans, and sheer bad luck saw Moby Grape's star rise and fall within a year. But their debut album was a cracker.

A veteran of Jefferson Airplane (his "My Best Friend" features on *Surrealistic Pillow*), Skip Spence and ex-Airplane manager Matthew Katz set about corraling a new group of musicians around Spence's maverick genius. The four they found (guitarists Jerry Miller and Peter Lewis, drummer Don Stevenson, and bassist Bob Mosley) were each capable songwriters and gifted harmony singers, and the mouthwatering package were soon causing a stir in San Francisco.

Their eponymous debut (made for $11,000) looked set to launch the Grape as the United States' next big thing. Opener "Hey Grandma" bursts with ebullient harmonies and shrill guitars. Lewis' pounding "Fall On You" features a hectoring vocal, fluid guitar solo, and driving drums. From the sweet, Spanish-style acoustic of "8.05" to the effusive "Come In The Morning" and Spence's psyche-stunner "Omaha"—the songs are crisp, confident, and infused with joy. How could they fail?

Well, for starters, Columbia released five of the tracks as singles simultaneously—killing their chances of any chart action. Then three band members were arrested for marijuana possession and liaising with underage girls. And Stevenson was clearly giving the camera the finger on the cover (Columbia caught on, and the offending digit was subsequently airbrushed out). But forget all that—this is one of 'Frisco's finest. **RD**

Love
Da Capo (1967)

Label | Elektra
Producer | Paul Rothchild
Art Direction | William S. Harvey
Nationality | USA
Running Time | 36:16

When Elektra founder Jac Holzman went to see Love play in Los Angeles, he arrived early enough to catch the opening act, The Doors. That one event probably sealed Love's fate as a cult—rather than mainstream—attraction, although 40 years on, Love's leader, Arthur Lee, has never been more popular and tours more than the original Love ever did.

This was the group's second album, and the use of a single track lasting the entire second side of the LP was regarded as audacious at the time. "Revelation," which was apparently originally titled "John Lee Hooker," lasts somewhat longer than all the other tracks combined, and is frankly only worth listening to once.

However, the first six tracks are more than adequate compensation, making a perfect suite. Particular highlights include the exhilarating, tempo-shifting "Stephanie Knows Who," "Orange Skies" by the late Bryan Maclean (once a roadie for The Byrds, but here more Broadway theater than Hollywood Boulevard), and the crunching "Seven And Seven Is." The latter took more than 50 takes to complete, with both Lee and "Snoopy" Pfisterer taking turns at the drums because the part was so energetic, and provided Love with a U.S. hit single. It is followed by the gentle acoustic guitar intro to "The Castle," a track that later became the signature tune for a TV travel show.

The contrast between the subtle beauty of the first half and the excesses of "Revelation" make this one of the most schizophrenic albums ever released. **JT**

The Beau Brummels
Triangle (1967)

Label | Warner Bros.
Producer | Lenny Waronker
Art Direction | Ed Thrasher
Nationality | USA
Running Time | 26:08

The Monkees
Headquarters (1967)

Label | RCA Victor
Producer | Douglas Farthing Hatlelid
Art Direction | Uncredited
Nationality | UK • USA
Running Time | 36:14

San Francisco's Beau Brummels are most famous for 1963's British Invasion-aping folk-rock hit "Laugh Laugh" (which won them a cameo on an episode of *The Flintstones*, appearing as The Beau Brummelstones). But their fourth album is a genuine lost classic—a mix of folk rock and haunting country that still stands up when played alongside their bigger-selling contemporaries.

The Brummels' preceding record, *Beau Brummels '66*, consisted entirely of faintly lackluster cover versions, instigating drummer John Peterson's departure for Harper's Bizarre. The remaining members were freed from touring commitments by guitarist Ron Elliott's recurring diabetes and opted instead to concentrate on exploring new studio technology. To this end they were aided by producer Lenny Waronker, then establishing himself at Warner Bros. and advocating maximum artistic control for the label's bands.

The result was their strongest album. Elliott's songwriting had matured beyond the confines of two-minute chart fodder, while Sal Valentino's vocals had begun to take on a rootsy, nasal edge that contrasted wonderfully with the eerie arrangements, which included strings, accordion, and harpsichord (the latter played on "Magic Hollow" by Brian Wilson collaborator Van Dyke Parks). Elliott saw it as "sort of a mood swing into the world that was around us at the time . . . the music became very ethereal, mystic and mysterious." Despite rave reviews, however, *Triangle* peaked at a disappointing No. 197 on the U.S. Billboard chart. **PL**

The Monkees, the first band manufactured for a TV show, had had enough of being mocked by the hippies for being puppets: they wanted to be an actual rock band. They sacked musical supervisor Dan Kirshner and took charge. "This is all ours," they proclaim on the sleeve, which also carefully lists all the instruments they play on the album.

The reinvention was not total: The Monkees wrote seven of the songs (eight really: the royalties for "No Time" were given to a friend), and two of those are just skits. Tommy Boyce and Bobby Hart, who wrote "(Theme from) The Monkees," still contribute three songs. But the genius of *Headquarters* is in its balance: the love-beads mood of "For Pete's Sake" comes in an urgent pop-sized burst, rather than meandering in the manner that was already setting in for proper hippy bands. Mike Nesmith's terrific "You Just May Be The One" tips a nod to The Who and country rock all at once, while "Forget That Girl" is the band's most beautifully subtle song. There was even some controversy: Mickey Dolenz's "Randy Scouse Git"—jaunty verses and brilliant, deranged, shouted choruses—became "Alternate Title" for the UK because its original name was deemed offensive. As a single, it still made No. 2 in the UK charts.

Headquarters sold well, seeming to have proved the band right. But at this point, the "did they/didn't they" argument mattered a whole lot less than the fact that as automatons and as autonomous beings alike, The Monkees were a great band with great tunes. **MMo**

Tim Buckley | Goodbye And Hello (1967)

Label | Elektra
Producer | Jerry Yester
Art Direction | William S. Harvey • Guy Webster
Nationality | USA
Running Time | 42:41

goodbye and

Tim Buckley's second LP should have made him a star. The 20-year-old troubadour was already a face in L.A., thanks to his eponymous 1966 debut—an accomplished set of post-Dylan love songs that showcased his rich tenor and emotive phrasing. He was now eager to break out of the folk-rock scene.

Influenced by The Beatles' *Sgt. Pepper, Goodbye And Hello* is a masterpiece of baroque psychedelia. A heavy, explosion-strafed atmosphere pervades Vietnam commentary "No Man Can Find The War," one of five co-writes with schoolfriend Larry Beckett. The shimmering "Hallucinations" and circus-themed "Carnival Song" are similarly evocative, while the title track flits between two contrasting melodies and has a medieval feel.

These soundscapes are balanced by the feverish "Pleasant Street," soaring ballad "Once I Was," and plaintive closer "Morning Glory" (which was covered by Linda Ronstadt, retitled "Hobo"). "I Never Asked To Be Your Mountain" is a tumultuous, self-justifying address to Tim's estranged wife Mary and son Jeff—who later performed it at a tribute concert to Tim in 1991.

Elektra were so pleased with *Goodbye And Hello* that they paid for expensive gatefold packaging; Buckley was in high spirits for the cover shoot, squinting with a bottle cap in his eye. Reviews were positive, but the album peaked at No. 171 on the U.S. chart. Buckley responded with the jazz-influenced *Happy Sad*, then the avant-garde *Lorca* and *Starsailor*. He died in June 1975, aged 28, from an accidental heroin overdose. *Goodbye And Hello* is a cornerstone of his legend: a lush, accessible work by an enduringly complex artist. **MA**

"You can daydream with music ... it takes you away and creates a new world."

Tim Buckley, 1968

Track Listing

01	No Man Can Find The War	(Beckett • Buckley)	2:58
02	Carnival Song	(Buckley)	3:10
▶ 03	Pleasant Street	(Buckley)	5:15
▶ 04	Hallucinations	(Beckett • Buckley)	4:55
▶ 05	I Never Asked To Be Your Mountain	(Buckley)	6:02
▶ 06	Once I Was	(Buckley)	3:22
07	Phantasmagoria In Two	(Buckley)	3:29
08	Knight-Errant	(Beckett • Buckley)	2:00
▶ 09	Goodbye And Hello	(Beckett • Buckley)	8:38
▶ 10	Morning Glory	(Beckett • Buckley)	2:52

Love | Forever Changes (1967)

Label | Elektra
Producer | Arthur Lee • Bruce Botnick
Art Direction | William S. Harvey • Bob Pepper
Nationality | USA
Running Time | 42:52

In 1967, Love were the hippest band in Los Angeles after The Byrds. The latter's hit-making phase was coming to an end, however, but Love were ill-equipped to take their place: they were ethnically mixed, with two black front men playing music unlikely to appeal to a black audience; songs stretched out for entire LP sides; and their drug use had spiraled. By the summer of 1967, The Doors and Jimi Hendrix were stealing the kudos. So Love went back to basics, dreaming up an album that would be all about songs.

When Bruce Botnick arrived to produce the album, he found a band in such a bad way that he immediately hired session musicians. Two tracks, "The Daily Planet" and "Andmoreagain," were recorded in a single day, then the band took time off to get their act together again and practice the next batch of tunes. Henceforth, each date in the studio would involve dedicated work on a couple of tunes, after which the band would disappear to learn the next few songs.

It took four months to get everything down on tape, but the results were unlike anything heard before. Acid rock could never be played by acoustic guitars and a symphony orchestra—could it? Too different for the West Coast, the LP failed even to equal the modest chart placings of its two predecessors in the United States; reminiscent of the playful, folky moods of The Beatles, Small Faces, and Donovan (though closer listening would reveal the turmoil within the band and L.A. during the Summer of Love), it entered the Top 30 in Britain. By then, however, the band was splintering up, never to regain its momentum. **DH**

> "When I did that album, I thought I was going to die."

Arthur Lee, 2001

Track Listing

▶ 01	Alone Again Or (Maclean)	3:17
02	A House Is Not A Motel (Lee)	3:31
▶ 03	Andmoreagain (Lee)	3:18
04	The Daily Planet (Lee)	3:30
05	Old Man (Maclean)	3:02
06	The Red Telephone (Lee)	4:46
▶ 07	Maybe The People Would Be The Times Or Between Clark And Hilldale (Lee)	3:34
08	Live And Let Live (Lee)	5:26
09	The Good Humor Man He Sees Everything Like This (Lee)	3:08
10	Bummer In The Summer (Lee)	2:24
▶ 11	You Set The Scene (Lee)	6:56

Cream | Disraeli Gears (1967)

Label | Polydor
Producer | Felix Pappalardi
Art Direction | Martin Sharp
Nationality | UK
Running Time | 33:30

Updating the avid experimentalism of their debut album, 1966's *Fresh Cream*, by infusing it with the psychedelic tricks of the trade prevalent in 1967—the newly refined guitar wah-wah and distortion among them—the jazz-blues-rock trio Cream hit their artistic peak with *Disraeli Gears*. Labeled the first supergroup due to the dazzling skills of guitarist Eric Clapton, bassist/vocalist Jack Bruce, and drummer Peter "Ginger" Baker, with this album Cream opened the doors to many future musical genres, including jazz fusion and —some say—progressive rock.

The album's iconic dayglo-collage sleeve was the perfect accompaniment to the barrage of avant-garde music it contained, starting with the remarkable, sparse "Strange Brew," in which Bruce's banshee-like vocals overlay Clapton's jerky, almost funk guitar pattern with ethereal economy. It gets better and better: "Sunshine Of Your Love" (which, along with "White Room," remains Cream's best known song) was an inspiration to Clapton's only serious contemporary rival, Jimi Hendrix, who turned it into an on-stage guitar storm. "Tales Of Brave Ulysses" is a fiery poem drenched in Clapton's lacerating, bluesy guitar, while the traditional "Mother's Lament" is a direct nod to the musicians' influences.

It was primarily as a live act that Cream ("The Cream" as they were originally known) made their enduring reputation—and with good reason: on stage they played as if possessed by Robert Johnson and Charlie Parker. *Disraeli Gears* remains the best they got on record, despite the strengths of their other albums. It is still a vital snapshot of a unique era. **JM**

> "My focus is always on 'Is this good enough?' Not 'Will it sell?' Always 'Is this good enough?'"
> Eric Clapton, 2001

Track Listing

▶	01	Strange Brew (Clapton·Collins·Pappalardi)	2:50
▶	02	Sunshine Of Your Love (Brown·Bruce·Clapton)	4:13
	03	World Of Pain (Collins·Pappalardi)	3:05
	04	Dance The Night Away (Brown·Bruce)	3:36
	05	Blue Condition (Baker)	3:32
▶	06	Tales Of Brave Ulysses (Clapton·Sharp)	2:49
▶	07	Swlabr (Brown·Bruce)	2:34
	08	We're Going Wrong (Bruce)	3:29
	09	Outside Woman Blues (Reynolds)	2:27
	10	Take It Back (Brown, Bruce)	3:08
	10	Mother's Lament (Trad.)	1:47

Pink Floyd | The Piper At The Gates Of Dawn (1967)

Label | Columbia
Producer | Norman Smith
Art Direction | Syd Barrett
Nationality | UK
Running Time | 41:52

As the house band at the UFO Club in the mid-1960s, Pink Floyd launched a psychedelic musical revolution in London rivaling that which The Grateful Dead created in San Francisco. Despite the deceiving moniker—stolen from bluesmen Pink Anderson and Floyd Council—Pink Floyd were not a group of shabby hippies expanding on black music, but a band of fashionably dressed architecture and art students searching for their own sound. *The Piper At The Gates Of Dawn* achieved that goal with spellbinding results.

The album's success stemmed from how well the band balanced the sonic exploration of their live show with the songcraft behind early hits "Arnold Layne" and "See Emily Play." Nobody wrote better psychedelic singles than Syd Barrett. Even "Astronomy Domine" orbited a very familiar pop structure. However, the songwriter was clearly fighting for control of the music, as well as his mind, as bassist Roger Waters, pianist Richard Wright and drummer Nick Mason pushed for further space travel. This tension bred the effectiveness of the baroque "Matilda Mother" and the jazzy "Pow R Toc H." The album's centerpiece is the 10-minute rocket-ride "Interstellar Overdrive," which features the best non-David Gilmore guitar work of the band's career.

The group were soon to lose Barrett to a mental breakdown and gain Gilmore's epic guitar leads. Waters became the creative force and fueled a fascination with conceptual song cycles. Pink Floyd would reach greater heights, notably on *Dark Side Of The Moon*, but with *The Piper . . .* they managed to capture the essence of 1960s psychedelia perfectly. **JiH**

"I don't think I'm easy to talk about. I've got a very irregular head."

Syd Barrett, 1971

Track Listing		
▶ 01 Astronomy Domine (Barrett)		4:12
02 Lucifer Sam (Barret)		3:07
▶ 03 Matilda Mother (Barrett)		3:08
04 Flaming (Barrett)		2:46
▶ 05 Pow R Toc H (Barrett·Mason·Waters·Wright)		4:26
06 Take Up Thy Stethoscope And Walk (Waters)		3:05
▶ 07 Interstellar Overdrive (Barrett·Mason·Waters·Wright)		9:41
08 The Gnome (Barrett)		2:13
09 Chapter 24 (Barrett)		3:42
10 The Scarecrow (Barrett)		2:11
11 Bike (Barrett)		3:21

The Who | **The Who Sell Out** (1967)

Label | Track
Producer | Kit Lambert
Art Direction | David King • Roger Law
Nationality | UK
Running Time | 39:26

THE WHO SELL OUT

Replacing the stale smell of excess with the sweet smell of success, Peter Townshend, who, like nine out of ten stars, needs it. Face the music with 'Odorono,' the all-day deodorant that turns perspiration into inspiration.

THE WHO SELL OUT

This way to a cowboy's breakfast. Daltrey rides again. Thinks: "Thanks to Heinz Baked Beans everyday is a super day." Those who know how many beans make five get Heinz beans inside and outside at every opportunity. Get saucy.

A pop-art masterpiece, *The Who Sell Out* boasts a levity that would later desert London's volatile mod icons. David Montgomery's hilarious cover portraits unveiled the concept. Guitarist and bandleader Pete Townshend holds a ridiculously outsized tube of Odorono—the deodorant "that turns perspiration into inspiration." Singer Roger Daltrey sits in a bathtub filled with baked beans, cradling an enormous can of Heinz (the UK's premier beans manufacturer). On the reverse, drummer Keith Moon uses Medac spot cream, while it is claimed that bassist John Entwistle "was a nine and a half stone weakling until Charles Atlas made a man of him at nine and three-quarter stone."

The Who Sell Out was the quartet's satirical take on the relationship between music and advertising. Townshend devised the album as a faux pirate radio broadcast, interspersing regular tracks with fake commercials. These jingles still retain a charm, though time ran out before the idea was fully realized.

The songs are sensational. A gift from future Thunderclap Newman star Speedy Keen, "Armenia City In The Sky" strikes a dizzying accord between rock and psychedelia. "I Can See For Miles" was The Who's biggest U.S. hit: a tempo-shifting storm of dilated harmonies and tightly wound axe, driven by Moon at his most dynamic. There is a lightness of touch elsewhere. "Mary Anne With The Shaky Hand" jangles like The Byrds; Daltrey is camp and elliptical on "Tattoo"; "Our Love Was" and "I Can't Reach You" are blissfully melodic. Finally, nautical mini-opera "Rael" points the way to Tommy and superstardom. **MA**

> ## "The effect pop has on society is incredible. It's a power thing."

Pete Townshend, 1968

Track Listing

▶	01	Armenia City In The Sky (Keen)	3:48
	02	Heinz Baked Beans (Entwistle)	1:00
▶	03	Mary Anne With The Shaky Hand (Townshend)	2:28
	04	Odorono (Townshend)	2:34
▶	05	Tattoo (Townshend)	2:51
▶	06	Our Love Was (Townshend)	3:23
▶	07	I Can See For Miles (Townshend)	4:44
▶	08	I Can't Reach You (Townshend)	3:03
	09	Medac (Entwistle)	0:57
	10	Relax (Townshend)	2:41
	11	Silas Stingy (Entwistle)	3:07
	12	Sunrise (Townshend)	3:06
▶	13	Rael (Townshend)	5:44

The Velvet Underground
The Velvet Underground And Nico (1967)

Label | Verve
Producer | Andy Warhol • Tom Wilson
Art Direction | Andy Warhol
Nationality | USA
Running Time | 48:34

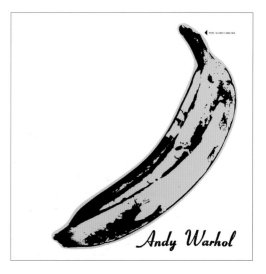

As a dark counterpoint to Sixties West Coast optimism, *The Velvet Underground & Nico* has few peers.

The sound is scratchy, lo-fi—hardly surprising, as it was mostly recorded in one eight-hour session in New York for about $2,000. Lou Reed's streetwise lyrics introduced a disturbing demi-monde to rock 'n' roll: "Venus In Furs"—a sensual paean to S&M, John Cale's droning viola alternately stroking and snapping, like a whip. "Heroin"—a disarmingly amoral take on the drug, the music alternately soothing and head-splittingly chaotic. Yet the Velvets could also make beguilingly pretty music—witness the music-box tinkle of "Sunday Morning." "All Tomorrow's Parties" was Andy Warhol's favorite Velvets song, a snapshot of the beautiful people and losers at Warhol's Factory warehouse in New York.

Its straight talk about sex and drugs got the album banned on New York radio; stations elsewhere in the United States simply ignored it. Critics hated it, many feeling that it was simply an elaborate put-on by Warhol (he supplied the iconic peel-off banana cover); *Rolling Stone* did not even review it. And hardly anyone bought the album at the time. But as Brian Eno once commented, everyone who did formed a band. New wave acts such as Joy Division, Talking Heads, and Television owed much to the Velvets' edgy minimalism; Lou Reed's sneer inspired a host of punk vocalists, while the band's feedback-riven excesses were revisited by bands such as The Jesus and Mary Chain, who also stole the band's black-leather-and-shades look. **RD**

"Those songs are still so good."

Sterling Morrison, 1970

Track Listing

01	Sunday Morning (Cale·Reed)	2:54
02	I'm Waiting For The Man (Reed)	4:37
03	Femme Fatale (Reed)	2:37
04	Venus In Furs (Reed)	5:10
05	Run Run Run (Reed)	4:20
06	All Tomorrow's Parties (Reed)	5:58
07	Heroin (Reed)	7:10
08	There She Goes Again (Reed)	2:38
09	I'll Be Your Mirror (Reed)	2:12
10	The Black Angel's Death Song (Cale·Reed)	3:12
11	European Son (Cale·Morrison·Reed·Tucker)	7:46

Francis Albert Sinatra & Antonio Carlos Jobim
Francis Albert Sinatra & Antonio Carlos Jobim (1967)

Label | Reprise
Producer | Sonny Burke
Art Direction | Ed Thrasher
Nationality | USA
Running Time | 28:34

His years at Capitol Records, from 1954 to 1961, are regarded as the zenith of Frank Sinatra's career. Yet although the 1960s found the singer growing audibly complacent, there are joys in the recordings he made for Reprise, the artist-friendly label he founded in '61. The two albums he made with Count Basie are both treats, for example, but it is this unlikely little record, easily the gentlest of his career, which best shows that when he chose his material wisely, Sinatra remained a peerless interpreter of the popular song.

The fad for bossa nova had evaporated; what had previously been exotic in the hands of Stan Getz and (particularly) the voice of Astrud Gilberto had long since become cliché. But Sinatra was unconcerned by fashion; his only worry, in fact, was the lack of adequate translations available of Jobim's songs, hence the presence of three American standards next to the seven Jobim cuts.

Those who have prosecuted Sinatra for singing marginally flat have often used this set as Exhibit A. But the flaws in his voice on tender cuts such as "Dindi" are, if not deliberate, then deliberately exposed: Sinatra may have done weary and blue throughout his life, but he never sounded this vulnerable. And although he decided only relatively late to invite Jobim to join him, the album is a true collaboration. Claus Ogerman's featherlight orchestra is the first thing you notice, but the heartbeat of the record is provided by Jobim's flexible yet steady guitar. **WF-J**

Track Listing

01	The Girl From Ipanema (Gãrota De Ipanema) (De Moraes・Gimbel・Jobim)	3:14
▶ 02	Dindi (De Oliveira・Gilbert・Jobim)	3:29
03	Change Partners (Berlin)	2:40
▶ 04	Quiet Nights Of Quiet Stars (Corcovado) (Jobim・Lees)	2:44
05	Meditation (Meditacáo) (Gimbel・Jobim・Mendonca)	2:52
06	If You Never Come To Me (De Oliveira・Gilbert・Jobim)	2:08
▶ 07	How Insensitive (Insensatez) (De Moraes・Gimbel・Jobim)	3:16
08	I Concentrate On You (Porter)	2:36
▶ 09	Baubles, Bangles And Beads (Borodine・Forrest・Wright)	2:31
10	Once I Loved (O Amor En Paz) (De Moraes・Gimbel・Jobim)	2:35

The Doors | The Doors (1967)

Label | Elektra
Producer | Paul A. Rothchild
Art Direction | William S. Harvey
Nationality | USA
Running Time | 43:25

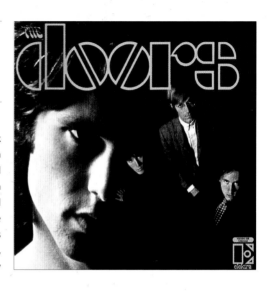

The Doors' profound influence on the evolution of rock music in the late Sixties is attributable not only to Jim Morrison's compelling voice, dark poetry, and personal charisma but also to the assured interaction between Ray Manzarek's keyboards, Robby Krieger's guitar, and John Densmore's drums. Morrison's was the face of the group (quite literally on the cover, Guy Webster's photograph reducing the other Doors to mere satellites), but this album's impact is down to the dynamic interplay between all four musicians.

The Doors drew on a rich range of genres—including rock, blues, jazz, and flamenco—for their sound. Opener "Break On Through" is a passionate call-to-arms for the psychedelic generation, while the hypnotic "Soul Kitchen" demonstrates the subtle shifts in dynamics that were to become a characteristic of the group. "The Crystal Ship" showcases Morrison as crooner (Sinatra was one of his heroes) against some spellbinding keyboard work from Manzarek. Indeed, so firmly do The Doors assert their musical authority that adaptations of Brecht/Weill's "Alabama Song" and blues track "Back Door Man" sound like originals.

The two longest tracks did most to establish the band (and to help drive the album to No. 2 in America). The much-covered "Light My Fire" (a U.S. No. 1, in edited form) is a glorious jazz-influenced paean to sexual desire. But it is with "The End" that The Doors' ethos is most fully realized—an 11-minute-plus Oedipal epic of lust and death, in which the group provide a stunning polymorphous foil to Morrison's captivating narration.

Rock theater starts here. **GSu**

Track Listing

▶ 01	Break On Through (To The Other Side) (Densmore•Krieger•Manzarek•Morrison)	2:25
02	Soul Kitchen (Densmore•Krieger•Manzarek•Morrison)	3:30
03	The Crystal Ship (Densmore•Krieger•Manzarek•Morrison)	2:30
04	Twentieth Century Fox (Densmore•Krieger•Manzarek•Morrison)	2:30
05	Alabama Song (Whisky Bar) (Weill•Brecht)	3:16
▶ 06	Light My Fire (Densmore•Krieger•Manzarek•Morrison)	6:50
07	Back Door Man (Dixon•Burnett)	3:30
08	I Looked At You (Densmore•Krieger•Manzarek•Morrison)	2:18
09	End Of The Night (Densmore•Krieger•Manzarek•Morrison)	2:49
10	Take It As It Comes (Densmore•Krieger•Manzarek•Morrison)	2:13
▶ 11	The End (Densmore•Krieger•Manzarek•Morrison)	11:35

The Byrds | Younger Than Yesterday (1967)

Label | Columbia
Producer | Gary Usher
Art Direction | Uncredited
Nationality | USA
Running Time | 28:27

The Byrds' fourth album saw the group expanding on the eclecticism of 1966's *5D (Fifth Dimension)*. Opener "So You Want To Be A Rock 'n' Roll Star" (a U.S. Top 30 hit) satirized teenybop faves such as The Monkees, who had achieved massive success without playing on their own records (though only McGuinn had actually played on The Byrds' chart-topping "Mr. Tambourine Man"). The track featured a memorable trumpet part by Hugh Masekela, the first brass to grace their music.

"CTA–102" saw The Byrds experimenting with studio trickery to produce sci-fi sound effects. The group's first serious inroads into country music came with Hillman's "Time Between" (featuring future Byrd Clarence White) and "The Girl With No Name." David Crosby contributed the sparkling "Renaissance Fair," inspired by a medieval festival held by an L.A. radio station, and the timeless "Everybody's Been Burned." The latter ranks among the finest of all Byrds tracks, Crosby's crystal-clear, heartfelt vocal complemented by Hillman's fluid bassline and a wonderfully understated McGuinn guitar solo. Crosby's "Mind Gardens" is less successful, a piece of psychedelic philosophizing complete with Shakespearean references. The group returned to safer ground with another Dylan cover, the poignant "My Back Pages," which inspired the album's title and features another classy McGuinn solo. (The CD re-release adds "Lady Friend"—a scorching, brass-dominated track, Crosby's only Byrds A-side—and the lilting "It Happens Each Day," unfinished at the time.)

Hindsight reveals the album to be one of The Byrds' best—ambitiously wide-ranging, beautifully performed, and featuring some of their most lasting work. **RD**

> **"This is my favorite Byrds album of all … we did really good work on that record."**
>
> David Crosby, 1998

Track Listing

▶	01	So You Want To Be A Rock 'N' Roll Star (Hillman·McGuinn)	2:05
	02	Have You Seen Her Face (Hillman)	2:40
▶	03	CTA—102 (Hippard·McGuinn)	2:28
	04	Renaissance Fair (Crosby·McGuinn)	1:51
	05	Time Between (Hillman)	1:53
▶	06	Everybody's Been Burned (Crosby)	3:05
▶	07	Thoughts And Words (Hillman)	2:56
	08	Mind Gardens (Crosby)	3:46
▶	09	My Back Pages (Dylan)	3:08
	10	The Girl With No Name (Hillman)	1:50
	12	Why (Crosby·McGuinn)	2:45

The Young Rascals | Groovin' (1967)

Label | Atlantic
Producer | Tom Dowd • Arif Mardin • The Young Rascals
Art Direction | Uncredited
Nationality | USA
Running Time | 34:44

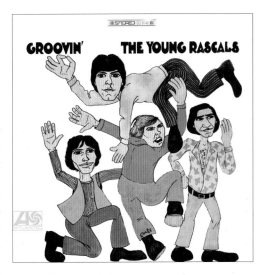

The Young Rascals are remembered primarily as one of the relatively few mid-Sixties white groups to whip up an exhilarating brew of soulful R&B and rock 'n' roll that could stand comparison with their African-American peers. (Significantly, the band were Atlantic's first rock signing.) By mid-1965 they were supporting The Beatles at Shea Stadium. But they are remembered for their string of hit singles rather than their albums, which are dismissed as patchy.

Groovin' is powerful evidence for the defense. Its origins lay in the eponymous, summer-flavored single, providing the group's only major UK hit (No. 8), and encouraged Atlantic Records to splash out on the accompanying album. In fact, the title track acts rather like a surface shine that blinds us to the other precious pieces of pop music offered.

The Rascals' most important album grabs you from the start, switching from garage thrash into psychedelia-tinged experimentation (which the band explored further on later albums), jazz (drummer Dino Danelli had worked with Lionel Hampton), and even gospel. Take the fuzz-tone guitar riffs on "Find Somebody," the melancholic, Beatles-like pop jewel "I Don't Love You Anymore," or the punk precursor "You Better Run" (a U.S. No. 20 in July '66). Pop gem "How Can I Be Sure" provided a U.S. No. 4 hit (and gave David Cassidy a UK chart-topper in 1972). The record brims with intelligent arrangements, blending deep soulfulness with raw, loose guitar, introspective lyrics, and unexpected touches such as the Latino "Sueño."

The result? A U.S. No. 4 and triumphant sales. **GD**

> ## "The group had a fan club before anybody heard a note of their music."
>
> Sid Bernstein (ex-manager), 1997

Track Listing

▶	01	A Girl Like You (Brigati•Cavaliere)	2:53
▶	02	Find Somebody (Brigati•Cavaliere)	3:49
	03	I'm So Happy Now (Cornish)	2:50
	04	Sueño (Brigati•Cavaliere)	2:49
▶	05	How Can I Be Sure (Brigati•Cavaliere)	2:56
	06	Groovin' (Brigati•Cavaliere)	2:34
	07	If You Knew (Brigati•Cavaliere)	3:04
▶	08	I Don't Love You Anymore (Cornish)	3:10
▶	09	You Better Run (Brigati•Cavaliere)	2:28
	10	A Place In The Sun (Miller•Wells)	4:52
	11	It's Love (Brigati•Cavaliere)	3:19

Jefferson Airplane
Surrealistic Pillow (1967)

Label | RCA
Producer | Rick Jarrard
Art Direction | Uncredited
Nationality | USA
Running Time | 33:40

The Kinks
Something Else By The Kinks (1967)

Label | Pye
Producer | Ray Davies • Shel Talmy
Art Direction | Pye Records Studios
Nationality | UK
Running Time | 36:26

Just as The Beach Boys gave listeners a glimpse of southern California surf culture in the early 1960s, Jefferson Airplane's *Surrealistic Pillow* painted a musical picture of the free-thinking Summer of Love in San Francisco Bay. The group's sophomore album was the first to feature vocalist-keyboardist-songwriter Grace Slick, who contributed the album's twin powerhouses—the hard-rocking "Someone To Love" (a U.S. No. 5) and the acid-bolero "White Rabbit."

Like fellow San Franciscans The Grateful Dead, Jefferson Airplane combined the folk esthetic and some of its form with a determinedly electric approach. The lilting "My Best Friend" suggests the open-range sound of the American West while still maintaining a distinctly (West) coastal breeziness. "3/5 Of A Mile In 10 Seconds" espouses expansion of consciousness in a classic blues-rock form. Elsewhere, "DCBA–25" combines the open sound of proto-country-rock with the economical but snappy drumming of the first wave of British rock and the most haunting overtones of psychedelia—and all in a neat two-and-a-half-minute package. "White Rabbit" has lived on as a stone-cold classic, its *Alice In Wonderland* imagery, a seductive beat, and Slick's strident vocals merging perfectly to create a most concise epic—one of a select handful of hallucinogenically influenced tracks that does not overstay its welcome. **YK**

Although it contained some of The Kinks' finest material, including two UK Top Ten hits—Ray Davies' masterpiece "Waterloo Sunset" and Dave Davies' elegiac "Death Of A Clown"—*Something Else By The Kinks* was their worst selling LP to date, only reaching No. 35 in the British charts in October 1967.

Its gentle, plaintive vignettes and bittersweet, subtle melodies—Ray sang of "Afternoon Tea," cigarettes ("Harry Rag"), and mourning the "End Of The Season"—were a precursor to the following year's *The Kinks Are The Village Green Preservation Society*, which shared its very English, nostalgic vision. Unfortunately, it was out of step with the time: flamboyant new psychedelic acts such as The Jimi Hendrix Experience and Cream were on the rise, and The Beatles had just unleashed their tour de force concept LP, *Sgt. Pepper's Lonely Hearts Club Band*. The result: The Kinks' opus seemed old fashioned and inconsequential.

In fact, it is the musical understatement and Davies' charming, melancholy lyrics about everyday life that make the album treasured today. Songwriting highlights include: "Two Sisters," an allegory for the Davies brothers (Ray as Priscilla suffering "the drudgery of being wed," Dave the free and single Sybilla); "David Watts," a homoerotic tale of schoolboy admiration; and "Waterloo Sunset," a peerless homage to London that represents the pinnacle of Ray Davies' talent. **JoH**

Donovan
Sunshine Superman (1967)

Label | Pye
Producer | Mickie Most
Art Direction | Dick Smith
Nationality | UK
Running Time | 49:26

Framed in fruity shades of raspberry red, lime green, and orange, a doe-eyed Leitch sports a paisley Oxford shirt and a mightily wavy head of hair on the cover—part teen idol, part pop guru. Having already established himself as a folk troubadour, Leitch was marching toward an innocent brand of psychedelic pop with *Sunshine Superman*. The title track was a groovy Top Two hit single on both sides of the Atlantic, while the lengthy "Legend Of A Girl Child Linda" nicely spotlights Leitch's calm voice amid a chamber-folk instrumentation of wind and stringed instruments and arpeggiated acoustic guitar.

"Three Kingfishers" and "Ferris Wheel" feature amplified sitar and follow through on the declaration on the album's back cover: "dedicated to the bearer of the eastern gift." Side two opens with the delicious basement rock of "Season Of The Witch," a most understated classic with mesmerizing scratchy guitar and a captivatingly phrased vocal (the track provided an appropriately dark accompaniment to the closing credits of Gus Van Sant's 1995 movie *To Die For*). "Bert's Blues" closes the album on a Western classical note, with sweet strings and hefty harpsichord supporting Leitch's everyman royalty vocals. (The U.S. track listing differs slightly.) True, not all the tracks here reach such distinct heights. But even *Superman* has to come back to earth every so often. **YK**

Merle Haggard
I'm A Lonesome Fugitive (1967)

Label | Capitol
Producer | Ken Nelson
Art Direction | Uncredited
Nationality | USA
Running Time | 28:14

Merle Haggard and Johnny Cash both learned the value of prison at around the same time. For Cash, it was the release of the two prison albums that made him one of the biggest-selling artists in America; for Haggard, a former convict who saw Cash play San Quentin in 1958, it was the discovery that a country singer with a criminal record was an attractive commercial proposition.

Between 1967 and 1974 Haggard (then married to the ex-wife of fellow Bakersfield legend Buck Owens) released a string of excellent albums on Capitol that allowed the singer to ruminate upon his past—*I'm A Lonesome Fugitive*'s title track was his first country No. 1, and became an unofficial anthem for this part of his career. The album was a big hit—a blend of love songs and prison ballads, delivered in Haggard's direct and witty way, and kickstarting a welcome period of acclaim.

A superb songwriter, guitarist, and lyricist, Haggard mixed Hank Williams and Lefty Frizzell with Frank Sinatra, and was backed by a band, The Strangers, who could play a blend of country, swing, blues, soul, pop, and "country jazz." His outlaw outlook gave Haggard considerable counterculture appeal (despite hippie-baiting smash "Okie From Muskogee"): The Grateful Dead sang his songs, The Byrds covered "Life In Prison" on *Sweetheart Of The Rodeo*, and in 1973 Haggard agreed to produce Gram Parsons' next album, a plan curtailed by Parsons' early death. **PW**

The Jimi Hendrix Experience
Are You Experienced (1967)

Label | Reprise
Producer | Chas Chandler
Art Direction | Bruce Fleming
Nationality | UK • USA
Running Time | 40:07

An aura surrounds James Marshall Hendrix to this day. His almost supernatural gifts with electric guitar, and deft control over effects, remain unsurpassed; his playing represents a seismic shift in the use of the instrument at a time when musicians like Eric Clapton were at their height. His fusion of psychedelia, blues, and funk, his authorship of great songs, his emergence as the pre-eminent black musician in the world of white rock, his addled dandyism, all stunned the Sixties rock aristocracy.

Hardly surprising, then, that *Are You Experienced* is one of the greatest debuts ever. On the repackaged and remastered 1997 CD version, produced under the aegis of original engineer Eddie Kramer, the three singles (jagged acid classic "Purple Haze," "Hey Joe"—his first hit, a UK No. 6—and the tender "The Wind Cries Mary"), plus their B-sides, are included. All are slices of rock history that are undiminished in their power to excite and transport.

But there was no filler on the original. The frenetic "Manic Depression" elevates the depths of despair, as does "I Don't Live Today," both presaging Jimi's comet-like trajectory. Extended tour de force "Third Stone From The Sun" features distorted vocals and psychedelic jangling. "Are You Experienced" poses a quintessentially hippy question to a backdrop of reversed drums and whiplash bursts of guitar. "Red House" reveals Jimi's ability to play stunning blues, and his thorough understanding of the form.

Essential. **MBI**

> ## "Let me live my life the way I want to."
>
> Jimi Hendrix, 1967

Track Listing

▶	01	Foxy Lady (Hendrix)	3:19
▶	02	Manic Depression (Hendrix)	3:42
▶	03	Red House (Hendrix)	3:44
	04	Can You See Me (Hendrix)	2:33
	05	Love Or Confusion (Hendrix)	3:12
	06	I Don't Live Today (Hendrix)	3:55
	07	May This Be Love (Hendrix)	3:11
▶	08	Fire (Hendrix)	2:45
▶	09	Third Stone From The Sun (Hendrix)	6:44
	10	Remember (Hendrix)	2:48
▶	11	Are You Experienced (Hendrix)	4:14

The Electric Prunes
I Had Too Much To Dream (Last Night) (1967)

Label | Reprise
Producer | David Hassinger
Art Direction | Ed Thrasher
Nationality | USA
Running Time | 29:15

The story of The Electric Prunes is the classic tale of a group plucked from obscurity. A group of friends from Taft High School in Los Angeles were practicing in a garage one day, when a passing real estate agent heard them and was inspired to introduce the group to her friend, RCA studio engineer Dave Hassinger.

Hassinger believed the group had talent, but lacked songwriting ability, and so brought in professional songwriters Annette Tucker and Nancie Mantz. This pair had originally penned the LP's title track as a slow piano ballad, but the group's interpretation, inspired by the hippy scene of the day, was a fuzz- and reverb-soaked trip into the fantastical. Double-tracked vocals and echoes added to its soaring sound and led to the track's release as a single (it reached No. 11 in the U.S. charts). This swiftly led to the recording of an album (mostly of Mantz/Tucker material) with the Reprise label.

Their follow-up single "Get Me To The World On Time" was a similarly lush psychedelic affair, but failed to re-create the commercial success of their debut.

The album sold well on both sides of the Atlantic, certainly equaling sales of contemporaries such as Jefferson Airplane and so, at least at the start, the Prunes were viewed as the frontrunners of the burgeoning West Coast psychedelic scene. Years later, the large number of copies of their album that became cheaply available in second-hand markets in the States led to them becoming a huge influence on garage punk bands of the 1970s such as the MC5 and The Stooges. **CR**

Track Listing

▶ 01	I Had Too Much To Dream (Last Night) (Mantz•Tucker)	2:55
02	Bangles (Walsh)	2:27
03	Onie (Mantz•Tucker)	2:43
▶ 04	Are You Lovin' Me More (But Enjoying It Less) (Mantz•Tucker)	2:21
05	Train For Tomorrow (Lowe•Ritter•Spagnola•Tulin•Williams)	3:00
06	Sold To The Highest Bidder (Mantz•Tucker)	2:16
▶ 07	Get Me To The World On Time (Mantz•Tucker)	2:30
08	About A Quarter To Nine (Dubin•Warren)	2:07
09	The King Is In The Counting House (Mantz•Tucker)	2:00
10	Luvin' (Lowe•Tulin)	2:03
11	Try Me On For Size (Jones•Tucker)	2:19
12	The Toonerville Trolley (Mantz•Tucker)	2:34

Loretta Lynn | Don't Come Home A Drinkin' (With Lovin' On Your Mind) (1967)

Label | Decca
Producer | Owen Bradley
Art Direction | Uncredited
Nationality | USA
Running Time | 30:14

Thanks in no small part to the biopic *Coal Miner's Daughter*, the arc of Loretta Lynn's singing career is well known. It resembles that of many country stars—she emerged from a desperately poor childhood to become wealthy and internationally famous. However, unlike many country singers, men and women alike, Lynn wrote her own material, and beginning in the mid-1960s, she composed outspoken songs about the frustrations of womanhood that, in their frequently humorous way, anticipated feminism.

In 1967, Lynn was 32, and had been recording with Nashville's Decca label for five years, where she had charted with innocuous fare such as "Blue Kentucky Girl." But starting with 1966's "You Ain't Woman Enough (To Take My Man)," Lynn began to write songs of great honesty and courage, perhaps none as courageous as the title track from her 1967 release *Don't Come Home A Drinkin'*. The song, which starts the album, has a bouncy tempo and cheerful steel guitar riffs that belie the dark subject matter. For in her alto twang, Lynn is singing about what has, in recent years, come to be known as acquaintance rape—"You come in a-kissin' on me, it happens every time/No don't come home a-drinkin' with lovin' on your mind." Her frankness here is matched only by that of her superb 1974 hit "The Pill."

Elsewhere there are other terrific songs of her own ("Get What 'Cha Got and Go"), and versions of country standards ("I Really Don't Want to Know"), but the title cut alone sends this record into the stratosphere. **KB**

Track Listing

▶	01	Don't Come Home A 'Drinkin' (With Lovin' On Your Mind) (Lynn•Wills)	2:06
	02	I Really Don't Want To Know (Barnes•Robertson)	2:56
	03	Tomorrow Never Comes (Bond•Tubb)	2:42
	04	There Goes My Everything (Frazier)	2:46
▶	05	The Shoe Goes On The Other Foot Tonight (Mize)	4:20
	06	Saint To A Sinner (Perry)	2:27
	07	The Devil Gets His Dues (Statler)	2:14
	08	I Can't Keep Away From You (Statler)	2:00
▶	09	I'm Living In Two Worlds (Crutchfield)	2:42
▶	10	Get What 'Cha Got And Go (Lynn•L. Williams•R. Williams)	2:00
	11	Making Plans (Morrison•Russell)	2:00
▶	12	I Got Caught (Lynn)	2:01

Shivkumar Sharma / Brijbushan Kabra / Hariprasad Chaurasia | Call Of The Valley (1967)

Label | EMI Hemisphere
Producer | G.N. Joshi
Art Direction | Uncredited
Nationality | India
Running Time | 39:06

A key recording in introducing Indian music to Western audiences, *Call Of The Valley* was namechecked by George Harrison, Paul McCartney, Bob Dylan, David Crosby, and Roger McGuinn. Doubtless it rubbed spines with Grateful Dead albums in many a hippy record collection for years on end.

Call Of The Valley is a satisfying introduction to Indian classical music, partly because it uses instruments common to both Indian and Western music—the flute and the acoustic guitar. The song cycle was conceived as a suite, in which the instruments (also including the Kashmiri santoor and the tabla) are used to tell the story of a day in the life of a Kashmiri shepherd, and features ragas associated with various times of the day.

All instruments seem to be playing independently—as is usually the case in much Indian music—but all interlock perfectly. Brijbushan Kabra's finger-picked guitar melodies are a feast of pitch-bending slides and slurs, often sounding like a sitar. Shivkumar Sharma's santoor (a trapezoid-shaped hammered dulcimer common in Persian music) lends a dramatic quality. But the star here is Hariprasad Chaurasia's bansuri flute, floating high over the other instruments like a bird over the Kashmiri valley, sighing, quivering, slowly ascending before swooping from a great height.

Exquisitely recorded in Bombay's EMI India studios, the album galvanized Indian music, influencing dozens of ECM albums and proving that psychedelic rock had created an audience for Indian music in the West. **JLe**

> "I had been trying for years to get the santoor respected as a classical—and not just a folk —instrument. I achieved that with this album."
>
> Shivkumar Sharma, *c.* 2003

Track Listing

01	Ahir Bhairav/Nat Bhairav	(Chaurasia•Sharma)	12:35
▶ 02	Rag Piloo	(Chaurasia•Sharma)	7:58
▶ 03	Bhoop Ghara–Dadra	(Chaurasia•Sharma)	6:16
▶ 04	Rag Des	(Chaurasia•Sharma)	6:09
05	Rag Pahadi	(Chaurasia•Sharma)	6:48

The Velvet Underground
White Light / White Heat (1967)

Label | Verve
Producer | Tom Wilson
Art Direction | Andy Warhol
Nationality | UK • USA
Running Time | 38:55

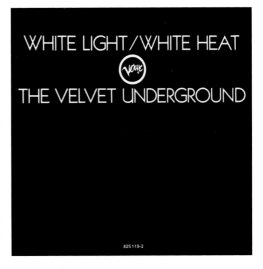

By the end of 1967, The Velvet Underground's celebrity benefactor Andy Warhol was losing interest, prompting singer/lyricist Lou Reed to call on Boston businessman Steve Sesnick. The new manager urged Reed to pursue a more commercial agenda—to the displeasure of bassist/organist John Cale.

Side one of their second LP is notable for its perverse subject matter, with the tunefully distorted title track advocating amphetamine use. "The Gift" tells the tragicomic tale of Waldo Jeffers, who is so afraid that his college girlfriend will be unfaithful that he mails himself to her. Cale handles the narration, his amiable Welsh accent appearing in one speaker while the other carries a midtempo R&B groove laced with electric guitar curlicues. "Lady Godiva's Operation" puts a queasy medical spin on the medieval legend, voices jumping out of the psych-noir mix to artful effect.

Side two is pure onslaught. "I Heard Her Call My Name" sees Cale, guitarist Sterling Morrison, and drummer Mo Tucker hammer out a speedy rhythmic base while lead axeman Reed unleashes squalling free-jazz runs. "Sister Ray" is the big bang of noise-rock: 17 minutes of sex, drugs, and guns carried along on tidal waves of serrated feedback, discordant keys, and primal garage pounding.

White Light/White Heat shifted even fewer copies than their debut, peaking at No. 199 on the Billboard chart. However, in terms of over-amped attitude and raw exhilaration, there is nothing quite like it. **MA**

> "I always believed that I had something important to say and I said it ... My God is rock 'n' roll."
>
> Lou Reed, 1998

Track Listing

▶	01	White Light/White Heat (Reed)	2:44
▶	02	The Gift (Cale • Morrison • Reed • Tucker)	8:14
	03	Lady Godiva's Operation (Reed)	4:52
	04	Here She Comes Now (Cale • Morrison • Reed • Tucker)	2:00
▶	05	I Heard Her Call My Name (Reed)	4:05
▶	06	Sister Ray (Cale • Morrison • Reed • Tucker)	17:00

The Jimi Hendrix Experience
Axis: Bold As Love (1967)

Label | Reprise
Producer | Chas Chandler
Art Direction | Ed Thrasher
Nationality | UK • USA
Running Time | 38:49

With the possible exception of Cream, The Jimi Hendrix Experience was debatably the world's finest ever power trio. While this and their reputation for dazzling musicianship and improvisation secured them huge acclaim, the constant pressure to tour and record that hung over them after the impact of their debut record, *Are You Experienced*, meant that *Axis: Bold As Love* was rushed rather than solid. Nonetheless, there is no arguing—even after almost four decades—with the brash, scintillating songs, the grasp that Jimi and his cohorts had on the studio technology at their disposal, and the lyrical beauty of Hendrix's guitar playing.

The spiraling melodies of "Spanish Castle Magic," the stop-start command of "If 6 Was 9," the sweet balladry of "Castles Made Of Sand" and the simplicity of bassist Noel Redding's "She's So Fine" are all high points—but the most lasting song for many is the awe-inspiring "Little Wing." With its perfect blend of lead and rhythm guitar (the song's introductory phrases blurred the line forever between the two), the tune is a pure, simple thing of beauty, and has been covered since by artists as diverse as Sting and Metallica.

In true 1967 style, the production on *Axis* is superb. Jimi never sounded as vulnerable and accessible, vocally and instrumentally, while the analog thud of Mitch Mitchell and the solid basslines of Redding were the ultimate rhythm section of the day—with a nod, of course, to Jack Bruce and Ginger Baker, their only rivals in so many respects. **JM**

"I wanted to be listened to."

Jimi Hendrix, 1970

Track Listing

#	Title		Time
01	EXP	(Hendrix)	1:55
02	Up From The Skies	(Hendrix)	2:55
▶ 03	Spanish Castle Magic	(Hendrix)	3:00
04	Wait Until Tomorrow	(Hendrix)	3:00
05	Ain't No Telling	(Hendrix)	1:46
▶ 06	Little Wing	(Hendrix)	2:24
▶ 07	If 6 Was 9	(Hendrix)	5:32
08	You Got Me Floatin'	(Hendrix)	2:45
▶ 09	Castles Made Of Sand	(Hendrix)	2:46
10	She's So Fine	(Redding)	2:37
11	One Rainy Wish	(Hendrix)	3:40
12	Little Miss Lover	(Hendrix)	2:20
13	Bold As Love	(Hendrix)	4:09

Aretha Franklin
I Never Loved A Man The Way I Love You (1967)

Label | Atlantic
Producer | Jerry Wexler
Art Direction | Uncredited
Nationality | USA
Running Time | 32:51

Anybody could tell you Aretha was the queen of soul, although her accession was hardly obstacle-free. Before signing to Atlantic in 1966, Franklin had spent six years—and nine albums—with Columbia, who curbed her innate soulfulness and turned her into a singer of supper-club standards.

Freed from these shackles by Atlantic's Jerry Wexler, Franklin traveled to Fame Studio in Muscle Shoals, Alabama, in February 1967. Problems developed when Aretha's husband and manager, Ted White, fell out with one of the members of the all-white session band with only one and a half songs recorded. Production was swiftly relocated to Atlantic's New York studios.

Accompanying herself on piano and writing four album tracks, Franklin bucked the trend of soul artists being written and arranged for by studios. Aretha's piano playing was compared to Ray Charles, and was the base around which all the tracks were built.

The album opens with a cover of Otis Redding's "Respect," which is subverted into a feminist anthem. Sam Cooke's civil rights classic "A Change Is Gonna Come" is similarly refocused—the struggle becoming that of Franklin. "Dr. Feelgood" is startlingly confident, infused with a sexuality rarely heard before in a black female artist.

Released from Columbia's constraints, Aretha soon became soul royalty by her powerful expression of sentiment as much as by sentiment itself. You cannot but be moved by this extraordinary album. **SJac**

Track Listing

▶ 01	Respect (Redding)	2:27
02	Drown In My Own Tears (Glover)	4:07
▶ 03	I Never Loved A Man (The Way I Love You) (Shannon)	2:51
04	Soul Serenade (Ousley•Dixon)	2:39
05	Don't Let Me Lose This Dream (A. Franklin•White)	2:23
06	Baby, Baby, Baby (A. Franklin•C. Franklin)	2:54
07	Dr. Feelgood (Love Is A Serious Business) (A. Franklin•White)	3:23
08	Good Times (Cooke)	2:10
09	Do Right Woman—Do Right Man (Penn•Moman)	3:16
10	Save Me (Ousley•A. Franklin•C. Franklin)	2:21
▶ 11	A Change Is Gonna Come (Cooke)	4:20

The Rolling Stones | Beggars Banquet (1968)

Label | Decca
Producer | Jimmy Miller
Art Direction | Tom Wilkes
Nationality | UK
Running Time | 39:43

The previous two years had not been kind to the Stones. Mick Jagger and Keith Richard had been busted at Keith's Sussex home, resulting in an infamous court case. Drug abuse and repeated busts had turned Brian Jones, the band's erstwhile leader, into a shadow of the multi-talented musician he had once been. And they had lost their way during psychedelia, producing 1967's aimless *Their Satanic Majesty's Request*.

From such chaos came *Beggars Banquet*. Abandoning psychedelic studio trickery, the Stones embraced their blues and country roots to produce an acoustic guitar-driven classic that also hinted at the darker path their music would shortly take. "Street Fighting Man" embraced the zeitgeist of 1968, a nod to student protests and civil disorder. The epic "Sympathy For The Devil" set an infamous lyric (based in part on the plot of Mikhail Bulgakov's classic novel *The Master and Margarita*) to a relentless samba beat. Jones was noticeable by his absence, though his slide guitar on "No Expectations" was a reminder of past glories.

The cover took the form of a simple invitation to the eponymous banquet, though the white gatefold sleeve unfortunately mirrored that of The Beatles' magnum opus *The Beatles* (aka *The White Album*), released a few weeks earlier. It did not matter. The public bought it in droves on both sides of the Atlantic.

The dark country blues of *Beggars Banquet* became a trademark, one that The Rolling Stones explored to mesmerizing effect on the three albums that followed. The next four years, up to 1972's *Exile On Main St.*, still stands as their golden age. **RD**

"It was a magical time, because I actually managed to turn my little juvenile fantasies into a way of life."

Keith Richards, 1987

Track Listing		
01 Sympathy For The Devil (Jagger•Richard)		6:18
02 No Expectations (Jagger•Richard)		3:56
03 Dear Doctor (Jagger•Richard)		3:22
04 Parachute Woman (Jagger•Richard)		2:20
05 Jigsaw Puzzle (Jagger•Richard)		6:06
06 Street Fighting Man (Jagger•Richard)		3:16
07 Prodigal Son (Rev. Wilkins•T. Wilkins)		2:52
08 Stray Cat Blues (Jagger•Richard)		4:37
09 Factory Girl (Jagger•Richard)		2:09
10 Salt Of The Earth (Jagger•Richard)		4:47

Traffic | Traffic (1968)

Label | Island
Producer | Jimmy Miller
Art Direction | Jim Capaldi
Nationality | UK
Running Time | 40:42

By 1968, British rock music was over the first thrill of copying rhythm and blues from America. Now, instead of pure imitation, UK musicians sought to reconcile their own musical heritage with these imported sounds.

Traffic pulled this off with style. Of course, it helped that they boasted one of the most gifted interpreters of American music around—Steve Winwood, formerly of The Spencer Davis Group, not only played Hammond with formidable verve, but was also the vocal and instrumental powerhouse of the band.

The opening track shows how Traffic blended the two traditions with humor and elan—"You Can All Join In," by guitarist Dave Mason, is an off-kilter hoedown, but with a hint of Merrie Olde England. While the lead guitar pulls off country bends, the lyrics proclaim the brotherhood of man with cheery alehouse bonhomie.

"Pearly Queen," Winwood's first song on the album, stands firmly on American soil. A sleazy tale of debauched romance, it sets the tone for blue-eyed soul in late-Sixties London. The band thump down to earth with the Dylan-esque lament of "Feelin' Alright," while "Vagabond Virgin" combines pastoral woodwind with a little-girl-lost morality tale of dubious charm.

The album also visits exotic climes with "40,000 Headmen," a feverish, tropical blues, laced with smoky bamboo-flute refrains, while the loaded honky-tonk of "Means To An End" reveals the debt owed to Traffic by retro-stylists such as Paul Weller.

The cover of Traffic's self-titled second album features photography by Gered Mankowitz, already renowned for his iconic images of Jimi Hendrix and The Stones. **JDi**

"We never announced we were splitting up. We just have long gaps between albums."

Steve Winwood, 1994

Track Listing	
▶ 01 You Can All Join In (Mason)	3:38
▶ 02 Pearly Queen (Capaldi·Winwood)	4:19
03 Don't Be Sad (Mason)	3:23
04 Who Knows What Tomorrow May Bring (Capaldi·Winwood·Wood)	3:13
▶ 05 Feelin' Alright (Mason)	4:19
06 Vagabond Virgin (Capaldi·Mason)	5:22
▶ 07 (Roamin Thro' The Gloamin With) 40,000 Headmen (Capaldi·Winwood)	3:14
08 Cryin' To Be Heard (Mason)	5:32
09 No Time To Live (Capaldi·Winwood)	5:02
▶ 10 Means To An End (Capaldi·Winwood)	2:40

The Incredible String Band | The Hangman's Beautiful Daughter (1968)

Label | Elektra
Producer | Joe Boyd
Art Direction | Osiris
Nationality | UK
Running Time | 48:51

This acid folk marvel represents a potent seed of the current "world music" movement, and a time capsule for the UK rural hippy lifestyle between 1966 and '73. The colorful rural idyll suggested by the cover artwork (ISB duo Mike Heron and Robin Williamson with assorted group members and the children of a friend) certainly inspired many to try communal country living.

Plucked by producer Joe Boyd from the Glasgow folk scene, The Incredibles had established themselves as one of the hippest acts on the UK's rapidly evolving underground scene with 1967's *The 5,000 Spirits*. Their songwriting skills and apparent ability to play any instrument picked up on the hippy trails to Morocco (gimbri, oud, sitar etc.) and captivated the likes of McCartney, Dylan, Plant, and Winwood. Jagger and Richard even sent a Bentley round, in an unsuccessful attempt to sign them to their label over a superstar tea.

The huge buzz culminated in *The Hangman's . . . ,* released in spring 1968 and a UK No. 5, which revealed a sustained grandeur of vision, lyrics, and musicality that the group were never to approach again. Recorded at Sound Techniques using a then revolutionary eight-track machine, they overdubbed the unique sonic vision of their colorful dreams, a tapestry woven solely from acoustic instruments and sounds. Each track is closer to a suite than a song, as Celtic folk, rock 'n' roll, gospel, plainsong harmonies, near qwaali moments, and North African and Indian sonics all drift effortlessly before the ears. **MR**

> "The hangman is the past 20 years of our lives and the beautiful daughter is now."
>
> Mike Heron, 1968

Track Listing

▶ 01	Koeeoaddi There (Williamson)	4:41
02	The Minotaur's Song (Williamson)	3:18
▶ 03	Witches Hat (Williamson)	2:30
▶ 04	A Very Cellular Song (Heron)	12:55
▶ 05	Mercy I Cry City (Heron)	2:40
▶ 06	Waltz Of The New Moon (Williamson)	5:01
07	The Water Song (Williamson)	2:47
08	Three Is A Green Crown (Williamson)	7:40
09	Swift As The Wind (Heron)	4:50
10	Nightfall (Williamson)	2:29

The Kinks | The Kinks Are The Village Green Preservation Society (1968)

Label | Pye
Producer | Ray Davies
Art Direction | John Prosser • Barrie Wentzell
Nationality | UK
Running Time | 38:46

Coming to it now, when *The Village Green Preservation Society* is universally hailed as a pop masterpiece and one of The Kinks' finest albums, it is hard to imagine the lukewarm non-reception it received upon release in 1968. Sure, it might have sounded naive up against Hendrix, The Rolling Stones, and the war in Vietnam—but the songs!

After years of churning out hit singles, Ray Davies was stressed out and eager for a change of pace. So he turned inward to idealized memories of his youth for inspiration. The result was an album of timeless pop songs about pastures, photo albums, and first kisses.

Title track "The Village Green Preservation Society" starts things off with a whimsical ode to Donald Duck and strawberry jam. "Do You Remember Walter," with its chugging piano and snare-drum snap, captures the album's subtext of wistful nostalgia as Davies reminisces about sneaking cigarettes and dreaming big dreams with an old school chum. Imagining Walter now, Davies sings, "I bet you're fat and married and you're always home in bed by half-past eight."

Other highlights include insanely catchy pop gems like "Picture Book" and "Animal Farm" or the sublime beauty of "Big Sky" and "Sitting By The Riverside." Even the bizarre hobbit-on-helium chorus of "Phenomenal Cat" sounds—well—phenomenal.

Fans will want to check out the recent three-CD deluxe edition of this essential album from Sanctuary Records, which features a truckload of rarities. **RM**

Track Listing

▶ 01	The Village Green Preservation Society (Davies)	2:45
▶ 02	Do You Remember Walter (Davies)	2:23
▶ 03	Picture Book (Davies)	2:34
04	Johnny Thunder (Davies)	2:28
05	Last Of The Steam-Powered Trains (Davies)	4:03
▶ 06	Big Sky (Davies)	2:49
07	Sitting By The Riverside (Davies)	2:21
▶ 08	Animal Farm (Davies)	2:57
▶ 09	Village Green (Davies)	2:08
10	Starstruck (Davies)	2:18
11	Phenomenal Cat (Davies)	2:34
12	All Of My Friends Were There (Davies)	2:23
13	Wicked Annabella (Davies)	2:40
14	Monica (Davies)	2:13
15	People Take Pictures Of Each Other (Davies)	2:10

Ravi Shankar | The Sounds Of India (1968)

Label | Columbia
Producer | Uncredited
Art Direction | Uncredited
Nationality | India
Running Time | 53:40

Anybody who has ever made a mix tape or CD for a friend, family member, or potential sweetheart is familiar with the two main motivations for doing so—to educate and, in the case of prospective romantic partner, to court.

Ravi Shankar's *The Sounds Of India* was the ultimate mix compilation for classical Indian music, in that it was accessible, gloriously played, and inherently well informed. At a time when tracking down global musical styles took some effort, Shankar was the perfect musical ambassador, one who was already familiar to legions of listeners as both an elder friend and informal musical teacher to The Beatles (George Harrison once called him "the godfather of world music").

Listening to *The Sounds Of India* is like attending an educational concert by the master himself. The liner notes are reminiscent of programs at classical concerts, with composer and Indian music expert Alan Hovhaness providing explanations of core forms, themes, structures, and motifs, even going to the lengths of including musical notation.

Shankar himself offers a four-minute-plus recorded introduction at the beginning of the album during which he explains, in a gentle speaking voice, the basic principles of his music and demonstrates aspects of the music that the listener should be aware of. From there, he and tabla player Chatur Lal and tamboura player N.C. Mullick perform four ragas (melodic motifs with built-in scale structures), with Shankar providing a brief spoken explanatory introduction to each. In all, an excellent way into Shankar's music. **YK**

> **"I'm always hungry, always unhappy because I know I haven't reached. I'm still trying and the more I try the more I find that there is nothing to be proud of."**
>
> Ravi Shankar, 1999

Track Listing	
01 **An Introduction To Indian Music** (Shankar)	4:13
02 **Dádrá** (Shankar)	10:30
▶ 03 **Máru-Bihág** (Shankar)	11:44
▶ 04 **Bhimpalási** (Shankar)	12:13
05 **Sindhi-Bhairavi** (Shankar)	15:00

Os Mutantes | Os Mutantes (1968)

Label | Polydor
Producer | Manoel Barenbein
Art Direction | Pebroy
Nationality | Brazil
Running Time | 35:59

To the rest of the world Brazil meant soccer, beautiful bodies, and bossa nova. The phrase "repressive military dictatorship" featured in few guides. The arrival of envelope-pushing hippies in the summer of 1967 brought the counterculture into focus, with devastating results. Led by young songwriters such as Gilberto Gil and Caetano Veloso, the "tropicalistas" took what they heard from London and San Francisco and moved it on. The right hated the hair, morality, and drugs; the left despised their corruption of pure Brazilian music.

Into this maelstrom floated Os Mutantes—Rita Lee and the three Baptista brothers (only two of whom appeared on stage). You want to talk weird? Two minutes into the opening track, "Panis Et Circenses," your record player slows down and stops. Just as you get up to find out what has happened, it bursts back into life. And once you have sat back down, the band stops and has a coffee break. No, really.

The sunkissed "A Minha Menina" follows, the distorted guitars and electronic effects all handmade by the third Baptista brother. It sounds like the perfect posing pop for Copacabana, but the hippies were being physically attacked from all sides. In 1968 the Brazilian government abolished all human rights; Gil and Veloso would be exiled; tropicalia withered away. The Mutantes, clearly incapable of leading any revolution, played on, actually growing in popularity in the early Seventies. Remember them for the simple nuttiness of "Bat Macumba" (the samba "Tomorrow Never Knows") and "Baby" (an erotic "Eleanor Rigby") and stay away from the brown acid. Okay? **DH**

"We've heard it all and we've used it all."

Rita Lee, 1972

Track Listing

▶ 01	Panis Et Circenses (Gil•Veloso)	3:38
▶ 02	A Minha Menina (Ben)	4:41
03	O Relógio (A. Baptista•S. Baptista•Lee)	3:29
04	Adeus Maria Fulô (Sivuca•Teixeira)	3:04
▶ 05	Baby (Veloso)	2:59
06	Senhor F (A. Baptista•S. Baptista•Lee)	2:33
▶ 07	Bat Macumba (Gil•Veloso)	3:08
08	Le Premier Bonheur Du Jour (Gerald•Renard)	3:37
09	Trem Fantasma (A. Baptista•S. Baptista•Lee•Veloso)	3:16
10	Tempo No Tempo (Once Was A Time I Thought) (A. Baptista•S. Baptista•Lee•Philips)	1:47
11	Ave Genghis Khan (A. Baptista•Dias•Lee)	3:47

The Jimi Hendrix Experience
Electric Ladyland (1968)

Label | Reprise
Producer | Jimi Hendrix
Art Direction | Ed Thrasher
Nationality | UK • USA
Running Time | 75:47

As both studio technology and guitar effects improved and expanded in the last years of the 1960s, so did the sounds recorded by The Jimi Hendrix Experience—and Jimi's best-known album, *Electric Ladyland* (known for its notorious, unprecedented gatefold sleeve, which depicted a bevy of naked females), took full advantage of the new science of rock. Although the musicians' playing and the structures of the songs became more dissolved, freer now from the parameters of the soul and R&B traditions in which Experience had honed their craft, Hendrix maintained a relatively tight ship despite the flurry of LSD and other narcotics that surrounded them. Indeed, *Electric Ladyland* is indebted both to pop and to blues, with the razor-sharp radio stalwart "Crosstown Traffic," the perfect Hendrix single, and his cover of Earl King's "Come On," as honed a blues workout as he had ever attempted.

The political fire and acidic experimentation of *Electric Ladyland* are not simply what make the record so immensely influential, however. Jimi's take on Bob Dylan's vitriolic "All Along The Watchtower" led Dylan himself to remark: "It's not a wonder to me that Jimi recorded my songs, but rather that he recorded so few of them, because they were all his." But then, the sprawling, 15-minute "Voodoo Chile" and the tighter, poppier "Voodoo Child (Slight Return)" alone would have made this record a classic anyway. **JM**

Leonard Cohen
The Songs Of Leonard Cohen (1968)

Label | Columbia
Producer | John Simon
Art Direction | Machine
Nationality | Canada
Running Time | 38:05

The art of the singer/songwriter changed forever when Canadian writer Leonard Cohen released his debut. The year 1968 saw this poet laureate of angst marry his verse to minor chords and reinvent melancholy. The cover shows a grave Cohen in his early thirties; a reflection of the minimalist esthetic of the music. The songs feature little more than Cohen's voice and guitar, forcing the focus on his wordplay and bittersweet delivery.

Tracks such as "Teachers" and "So Long, Marianne" paint such a poignant picture of heartbreak and loneliness that the listener feels the pain acutely, while "Suzanne" is packed with religious symbolism and sentiment (the success of Judy Collins' cover of the song had convinced Cohen to try his hand at performing).

Despite its sparse production, the album was a hit. In its second year it sold more than 100,000 copies, the greatest commercial success Cohen enjoyed until his renaissance in the late Eighties.

While subsequent albums were not as well received as this one, the legacy of Cohen's debut lived on. The Sisters Of Mercy named themselves after one of his most enduring songs from this album, while "Suzanne" was parodied by Randy Newman (on *12 Songs*) and reworked by R.E.M. (as "Hope" on *Up*). Other artists, notably Jeff Buckley, have been influenced and inspired by Cohen, helping direct new generations of music lovers back to *The Songs of Leonard Cohen*. **LP**

Johnny Cash
Johnny Cash
At Folsom Prison (1968)

Label | Columbia
Producer | Bob Johnston
Art Direction | Jim Marshall
Nationality | USA
Running Time | 44:49

Cometh the hour, cometh the Man In Black. The year 1968 was a momentous one for Johnny Cash, marking the end of wilderness years during which his music was shunned by the country establishment and his personal problems came to a head. He had met June Carter, scion of one of country's great families, whom he married that year and who helped him conquer his amphetamine addiction, and in January he recorded *At Folsom Prison*, which became his first hit album in five years.

Cash's performance in front of 2,000 inmates (and a sizable contingent of heavily armed guards) at the rough California jail crackles with tension. Kicking off with "Folsom Prison Blues"—his 1956 hit that held understandable relevance to his audience—Cash sets himself at one with the cranked crowd, almost to the exclusion of the custodians in the room. When he defiantly howls "Well I laughed in [the sheriff's] face and I spit in his eye" to roars of approval, the line is almost crossed during "25 Minutes To Go."

But the tracks were well chosen by the authorities, for his tales in *Folsom* speak of redemption grasped through hard-learned lessons of loss—the laments of the dying ex-con in "Give My Love To Rose"—or the electrifying "Greystone Chapel," a paean to Folsom's church written by then inmate Glen Sherley, whom Cash acknowledges before launching into this closer.

The sound of a man back on top of his game. **SJac**

Laura Nyro
Eli And The Thirteenth Confession (1968)

Label | Columbia
Producer | Charlie Calello • Laura Nyro
Art Direction | Bob Cato
Nationality | USA
Running Time | 46:15

Considering her "idiosyncratic" performance at the 1967 Monterey Pop Festival (she was booed off stage after a soul-style revue), and her underachievement in the sales charts, singer-songwriter Laura Nyro is all too frequently passed over as an original artist of worth. *Eli And The Thirteenth Confession* deserves better.

Recorded under the aegis of David Geffen, these piano-based songs are introspective, sensual, and poetic offerings, embracing an eclectic combination of blue-eyed soul, jazz (Nyro's father had been a jazz trumpeter), folk music, and gospel. Her openness to experimentation saw Nyro incorporate unexpected tempo shifts, something that irked contemporary critics. But whether it is the bohemian life depicted in her swinging "Sweet Blindness," the wandering and sunny soul-wrapped melody of "Stoned Soul Picnic," or the sad and lingering blues of "Woman's Blues," Nyro's intense, unconventional songwriting—and striking delivery, ranging from whispering to strident within a phrase—touches both the head and the heart.

The album barely hit the Top 200, but though Nyro herself remained a stranger to chart success, well-known acts such as Fifth Dimension and Three Dog Night made the big time with cover versions of tracks herein. This album was to be Nyro's spiritual legacy to many female musicians who became icons after her, including Janis Ian, Phoebe Snow, and Tori Amos. **GD**

Aretha Franklin | Aretha: Lady Soul (1968)

Label | Atlantic
Producer | Jerry Wexler
Art Direction | Loring Eutemey
Nationality | USA
Running Time | 28:39

The daughter of gospel singer C. L. Franklin, she sure had pedigree. But it was not until signing to Atlantic Records, 12 years into her recording career, that Aretha Franklin was crowned Lady Soul. Previous employers Columbia had her singing bland pop, but Atlantic producer Jerry Wexler matched her force-of-nature voice to Memphis' Muscle Shoals Sound Rhythm Section, and Aretha's rapturous soul was set free.

Lady Soul was their third album together, and their best. Aretha had gained confidence from the Atlantic debut I Never Loved A Man The Way I Love You, while its more eclectic follow up, Aretha Arrives, highlighted the strengths and limits of her talent. Lady Soul played to those strengths by showcasing Aretha's twin passions of R&B—Don Covay's bad-ass anthem "Chain Of Fools," and "Since You've Been Gone," Franklin's backing singers The Sweet Inspirations conducting a fiercely vocal sortie against the titular absentee boyfriend—and gospel (an orchestrated take on Curtis Mayfield's "People Get Ready," arranged by Arif Martin).

While Eric Clapton's solo on the molten blues "Good To Me As I Am To You" acknowledged contemporary goings on in rock 'n' roll, Lady Soul covers the masters (Mayfield, James Brown, Ray Charles) with flair and authority. "A Natural Woman" is the standout; the Muscle Shoals musicians' pilgrimage to Atlantic studios in New York for these sessions mirrors Aretha's own artistic journey, infusing the beautifully crafted song by Brill Building writers Carole King and Gerry Goffin with the honesty and passion she acquired in Memphis, and finding her true voice in the process. **SC**

> "When I went to Atlantic, they ...let me do my thing. The hits started coming ..."

Aretha Franklin, 1989

Track Listing

▶ 01	Chain Of Fools (Covay)	2:45
02	Money Won't Change You (Brown•Jones)	2:02
▶ 03	People Get Ready (Mayfield)	3:35
04	Niki Hoeky (L. Vegas•P. Vegas)	2:33
▶ 05	(You Make Me Feel Like) A Natural Woman (Goffin•King•Wexler)	2:37
▶ 06	Since You've Been Gone (Sweet Sweet Baby) (A. Franklin•White)	2:16
07	Good To Me As I Am To You (A. Franklin)	3:25
08	Come Back Baby (Charles)	2:29
09	Groovin' (Brigati•Cavaliere)	2:45
10	Ain't No Way (A. Franklin•C. Franklin)	4:12

Blue Cheer | Vincebus Eruptum (1968)

Label | Polygram
Producer | Eric Albronda • Abe "Voco" Kesh
Art Direction | Uncredited
Nationality | USA
Running Time | 32:06

This is where things get really heavy. Named after a type of LSD that was itself christened after a washing powder, this impossibly powerful San Francisco power trio upped the ante for noisy rock 'n' roll with their debut album, paving the way for everything from the Stooges to Zeppelin, from heavy metal to experimental rock. Sure, there was the primal thud of countless garage bands throughout the 1960s, but none had the foundation-shaking bottom end or howling, feedback-ridden intensity of Blue Cheer. Not for nothing did they have the epithet "louder than God."

The first time Blue Cheer tried to record *Vincebus Eruptum*, they blew up the soundboard. Gotta love that. But, with appropriate precautions in place, they laid down the LP that was the best of their career by far. It consists of four originals and two covers: a blistering, bludgeoning, dirtying-up of Eddie Cochran's "Summertime Blues" (outdoing The Who's mighty and meaty version by some way) and blues standard "Rock Me Baby." The former was a Top Twenty hit in the U.S., surprising perhaps for a band intent on pushing the boundaries of volume and not all that concerned with musicianship. They were hardly the sharpest players around, but there is something admirable and punkily hypnotic in the clearly ad-libbed squall of solos and barely controlled all-out noise, or in Dickie Peterson's hot-headed hollering as the band literally rattle through "Parchment Farm."

A high-watermark of heavy music's early days: from the beautiful purple-and-silver sleeve to the crazy, brilliant "one louder" spirit of it all. **TH**

> "Rock 'n' roll … is 10 percent technique and 90 percent attitude. If you deliver one note with the right attitude, it will do more than 60 notes with no attitude."
>
> Dickie Peterson, 2005

Track Listing

▶	01	Summertime Blues (Capehert • Cochran)	3:47
	02	Rock Me Baby (Josea • King)	4:22
	03	Doctor Please (Peterson)	7:53
▶	04	Out Of Focus (Peterson)	3:58
▶	05	Parchment Farm (Allison)	5:49
	06	Second Time Around (Peterson)	6:17

The Byrds | The Notorious Byrd Brothers (1968)

Label | Columbia
Producer | Gary Usher
Art Direction | Uncredited
Nationality | USA
Running Time | 28:25

The sleeve of their fifth LP indicated that The Byrds were undergoing changes. Guitarist David Crosby had left the LA group in acrimony, which is why only bassist Chris Hillman, bandleader Roger McGuinn, and drummer Michael Clarke are pictured.

Despite this turmoil, the album turned out to be a celestial synthesis of melody and experimentation, including innovative electronic textures. "Artificial Energy" employs a blaze of trumpets to simulate the buzz of amphetamines; the song's euphoria is undercut by its lyric, particularly the jarring last line. This dramatic opener melts into a pedal steel-tinged version of Gerry Goffin and Carole King's "Goin' Back," its nostalgia gaining poignancy in the light of Vietnam. The war provides further context for Crosby's ethereal "Draft Morning" and the twangy "Wasn't Born To Follow," another Goffin/King cover, which only underlines the fact that The Byrds pioneered both folk-rock and psychedelia.

Side two flows like aural nectar, encompassing cosmic Americana ("Change Is Now," "Old John Robertson"), utopian reveries ("Tribal Gathering," "Dolphin's Smile"), and Moog-driven futurism ("Space Odyssey"). The CD reissue features several out-takes, notably Crosby's ménage-à-trois ballad "Triad."

Although it only reached No. 47 on the Billboard chart, *The Notorious Byrd Brothers* now sounds like one of the last great artifacts of Sixties pop, a unified studio statement in the mold of *Sgt. Pepper* . . . The Byrds, meanwhile, went on to recruit Southern maverick Gram Parsons, relocate to Nashville, and cut the country-rock classic *Sweetheart Of The Rodeo*. **MA**

"I've talked to more people over the years who've said that's their favorite Byrds album."

Chris Hillman, 2003

Track Listing		
▶ 01 Artificial Energy (Clarke·Hillman·McGuinn)	2.18
▶ 02 Goin' Back (Goffin·King)	3.26
03 Natural Harmony (Hillman)	2.11
▶ 04 Draft Morning (Crosby·Hillman·McGuinn)	2.42
▶ 05 Wasn't Born To Follow (Goffin·King)	2.04
06 Get To You (Hillman·McGuinn)	2.39
▶ 07 Change Is Now (Hillman·McGuinn)	3.21
08 Old John Robertson (Hillman·McGuinn)	1.49
▶ 09 Tribal Gathering (Crosby·Hillman)	2.03
10 Dolphin's Smile (Crosby·Hillman·McGuinn)	2.00
11 Space Odyssey (Hippard·McGuinn)	3.52

Big Brother And The Holding Company
Cheap Thrills (1968)

Label | Columbia
Producer | John Simon
Art Direction | Robert Crumb
Nationality | USA
Running Time | 36:54

Cheap Thrills' critical reputation rests on the theatrical grandeur of Janis Joplin's raw, visceral vocals. Blending traditions and influences through a hippy Haight haze, Joplin's performances here transcended contemporary discussions about whether a white Texan female could sing the blues. If you can wring more emotion out of these songs, it ain't gonna happen on this planet.

After the group's Monterey Pop Festival appearance in 1967, *Cheap Thrills* was eagerly anticipated. It swiftly topped the U.S. charts and stayed there for eight weeks, going gold in the process; the single "Piece Of My Heart" made U.S. No. 12. Joplin's singing makes the album timeless (her scorching reading of Willie Mae Thornton's "Ball And Chain" had been one of the Monterey highlights; film footage showed Mama Cass watching in awe). There are plentiful reminders of late-Sixties Haight-Ashbury, though. Its strengths can be seen in the iconic strip-cartoon cover art by Robert Crumb, which blew the photo of Joplin onto the back cover, and also in the exuberance with which the band adopt a range of black music styles—notably doo-wop, soul, and blues. The limitations of genre are also clear: the sometimes leaden quality of the band's solos and rhythms restrain them from taking off with Joplin; it's her pleading, ecstatic, mighty voice that stays with you.

Given this fact, it is not surprising that she quit Big Brother (along with guitarist Sam Andrew) while the album still topped the charts—sadly, she never found another musical context that really nurtured her. **MR**

> "What we're trying to do in our music is just get back to old-time havin' a good time, jumpin', gettin' stoned."
>
> Janis Joplin, 1968

Track Listing

01	Combination Of The Two	(Andrew)	5:47
02	I Need A Man To Love	(Andrew·Joplin)	4:53
▶ 03	Summertime	(G. Gershwin·I. Gershwin)	3:58
▶ 04	Piece Of My Heart	(Berns·Ragonov)	4:13
05	Turtle Blues	(Joplin)	4:21
06	Oh, Sweet Mary	(Albin·Joplin)	4:14
▶ 07	Ball And Chain	(Thornton)	9:28

The United States Of America
The United States Of America (1968)

Label | Columbia
Producer | David Rubinson
Art Direction | Eric Schou
Nationality | USA
Running Time | 37:07

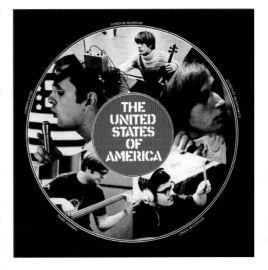

A registered Communist starts a band called The United States Of America and lands a major label record deal before playing a single live gig? Only in the Sixties.

After studying with avant-garde legend John Cage in New York City, composer Joseph Byrd moved to Los Angeles in 1967 and decided to form a psychedelic rock band. His first recruit was ex-girlfriend Dorothy Moskowitz, whose icy vocals formed the perfect complement for the trippy sonic experiments Byrd had in mind. The band recorded only one self-titled album before dissolving, but it was a memorable one.

"The American Metaphysical Circus" begins the album with a lilting calliope tune upon which Byrd heaps one patriotic marching band tune after another. Just when the whole insane cacophony is on the verge of collapse, in comes Moskowitz—transmitting from a sinking submarine. "Cloud Song" features delicate plucked bass and an ever-haunting melody. Like an LSD flashback, the final minutes of closing track "The American Way Of Love" features snippets of all the preceding songs flowing in and out of consciousness.

The United States Of America sold poorly upon release, thanks to Columbia's near total lack of faith. As Byrd puts it, "There was scant enthusiasm from the executives for a band whose name they hated, whose music they didn't understand, and whose politics they thought treasonous." But over the years, the group has developed a devoted cult following and influenced numerous modern bands, most notably Broadcast. **RM**

"Joe had vision."

Dorothy Moskowitz, c.2000

Track Listing

▶ 01	The American Metaphysical Circus (Byrd)	4:55
02	Hard Coming Love (Byrd•Moskowitz)	4:43
▶ 03	Cloud Song (Byrd•Moskowitz)	3:18
04	The Garden Of Earthly Delights (Byrd•Moskowitz)	2:39
05	I Won't Leave My Wooden Wife For You, Sugar (Byrd•Moskowitz)	3:52
06	Where Is Yesterday (Bogas•Marron•Moskowitz)	3:07
07	Coming Down (Byrd•Moskowitz)	2:40
▶ 08	Love Song For The Dead Ché (Byrd)	3:25
09	Stranded In Time (Bogas•Marron)	1:50
▶ 10	The American Way Of Love (Byrd•Forbes•Marron•Moskowitz•Woodson)	6:38

Dr. John, The Night Tripper | *Gris-Gris* (1968)

Label | Atlantic
Producer | Harold Battiste
Art Direction | Marvin Israel
Nationality | USA
Running Time | 33:12

We can thank Sonny and Cher for this landmark in New Orleans funk. While filming a TV special in the autumn of 1967, the pair bequeathed some of the studio time they had block-booked at Gold Star in L.A. to one of their session musicians—Malcolm Robert Rebennack, a journeyman piano and guitar player from New Orleans. Rebennack was toying with a project based around a real-life voodoo preacher called Dr. John Creaux. He had approached the singer Ronnie Baron to play the Dr. John role, but Baron's manager warned him to "Stay away from that voodoo stuff." After much persuasion from his percussionist, Richard "Didimus" Washington, Rebennack reluctantly took on the role himself, fronting a band of fellow New Orleans natives exiled in L.A.

Gris-Gris presented a New Orleans that had largely been absent from the city's recordings. It was the sound of the marching bands, of the Creole, of the feral chants wailed out by voodoo preachers, and the clattering polyrhythms of its Latin inhabitants. But this sonic chaos was refracted through the prism of pure, primal R&B. "Walk On Gilded Splinters," all rasping distorted vocals, clattering mandolins, and echo-laden drums, sets the tone, a crepuscular groove that spawned a hundred samples; "Mama Roux" is an elastic funk track that influenced Sly Stone, with Rebennack playing a propulsive bassline on the Hammond organ pedals.

Later projects would see the good Doctor exploring solo stride piano, Southern roots music, heavy-duty funk with The Meters, and even performing Southern-fried readings of Duke Ellington and Ray Charles. But *Gris-Gris* remains his definitive release. **JLe**

> "You had New Orleans street rhythms and church stuff, but it was mixed up with Cuban, Brazilian, Ethiopian beats, all sorts of weird shit."
>
> Dr. John, 2002

Track Listing

▶ 01	Gris-Gris Gumbo Ya Ya (Creaux)	5:36
02	Danse Kalinda Ba Boom (Battiste•Creaux)	3:44
▶ 03	Mama Roux (Dr. John•Hill)	2:59
04	Danse Fambeaux (Creaux)	4:56
05	Croker Courtbullion (Battiste)	6:00
06	Jump Sturdy (Rebennack)	2:20
▶ 07	I Walk On Gilded Splinters (Dr. John)	7:37

Iron Butterfly | In-A-Gadda-Da-Vida (1968)

Label | Atco
Producer | Jim Hilton
Art Direction | Loring Eutemey
Nationality | USA
Running Time | 36:00

Iron Butterfly's sophomore effort was the first album to be certified platinum, for sales of more than one million copies. Although the psychedelic tunes on side one are enjoyable enough, the record's success was entirely due to its title track, an unprecedented epic that took up all of side two.

Formed in San Diego in 1966, Iron Butterfly blended hard rock with ornate, acid-friendly textures. They cut their debut LP as a quintet, but by the time the aptly titled *Heavy* was released, three members had left. Singing keyboardist Doug Ingle and drummer Ron Bushy opted to carry on, recruiting teenage guitarist Erik Brann and bass player Lee Dorman. Late one night, Bushy came home from his job as a pizza chef to find that Ingle, the son of a church organist, had sunk a bellyful of red wine and composed a new song. Too drunk to speak properly, Ingle slurred the title, which Bushy wrote down phonetically. And so it was that "In The Garden Of Eden" became known as "In-A-Gadda-Da-Vida."

Originally a ballad, the band developed the track on the road, eventually recording a lysergic leviathan of droning guitar, mystical organ, and exploratory drum solo. "In-A-Gadda-Da-Vida" was a huge hit with the nascent FM radio format; a Top 30 single edit emphasised the song's proto-metal riff and enigmatic vocals, while the full-length version gave DJs time to go to the bathroom. It has been covered by thrash titans Slayer, sampled by hip-hop star Nas, and was performed as a hymn in the classic episode of *The Simpsons* where Bart sells his soul to Milhouse. **MA**

"In the late Sixties it wasn't really a social convenience to be going around—especially the Midwest—with hair down to your tailbone. It was interesting."

Doug Ingle, 2002

Track Listing

01	Most Anything You Want (Ingle)	3:41
02	Flowers And Beads (Ingle)	3:09
03	My Mirage (Ingle)	4:51
04	Termination (Brann–Dorman)	2:50
05	Are You Happy (Ingle)	4:25
▶ 06	In-A-Gadda-Da-Vida (Ingle)	17:05

The Pretty Things | S.F. Sorrow (1968)

Label | EMI
Producer | Norman Smith
Art Direction | Phil May
Nationality | UK
Running Time | 37:54

The Pretty Things came to prominence in the early 1960s by boiling up Bo Diddley-inspired R&B; their initial sound, captured on early singles like "Road Runner," was even raunchier, though far less popular, than what The Rolling Stones were offering. Inspired by the thriving psychedelic scene, the group entered a transitional stage with 1967's introspective *Emotions*, an unremarkable effort but one that set the stage for their greatest achievement.

Recorded during a druggy stay at Abbey Road during the Summer of Love, *S.F. Sorrow* was a daring project that provided the blueprint for all future rock operas. Pete Townshend cites *S.F. Sorrow* as a major influence behind 1969's *Tommy*—which is putting it mildly, given the similarities between the two.

Utilizing tricks learned from working on *Sgt. Pepper…*, Norman Smith helped bring vocalist Phil May's story of Sebastian F. Sorrow to life through a kaleidoscope of vocal collages, Middle Eastern instrumentation, and fuzzy guitar. The sounds range from the breathtaking a cappella intro of "Bracelets Of Fingers" and the graceful sitar on "Death" to the lush vocal harmonies of "The Journey" and the dense guitar of "Old Man Song."

Although expertly executed, *S.F. Sorrow* was greeted with indifference outside the United Kingdom (in the United States, its late release led many to believe the band was simply cashing in on the success of *Tommy*). The fact is, fans might never have gotten to hear *Tommy*, scale Pink Floyd's *The Wall*, or even mosh along with Green Day's *American Idiot* if The Pretty Things had not come of age first with *S.F. Sorrow*. **JiH**

"An unequaled masterpiece."

Mike Stax, 1988

Track Listing

▶	01	S.F. Sorrow Is Born (May·Taylor·Waller)	3:12
▶	02	Bracelets Of Fingers (May·Taylor·Waller)	3:41
▶	03	She Says Good Morning (Alder·May·Taylor·Waller)	3:23
	04	Private Sorrow (May·Povey·Taylor·Waller)	3:51
	05	Balloon Burning (May·Povey·Taylor·Waller)	3:51
	06	Death (Alder·May·Povey·Taylor·Waller)	3:05
	07	Baron Saturday (May·Taylor·Waller)	4:01
▶	08	The Journey (Alder·May·Taylor·Waller)	2:46
▶	09	I See You (May·Taylor·Waller)	3:56
	10	Well Of Destiny (Alder·May·Povey·Smith·Taylor·Waller)	1:46
	11	Trust (May·Taylor·Waller)	2:49
▶	12	Old Man Song (Alder·May·Povey·Taylor·Waller)	3:09
	13	Loneliest Person (Alder·May·Taylor·Waller)	1:29

Simon And Garfunkel | Bookends (1968)

Label | Columbia
Producer | Art Garfunkel • Roy Halee • Paul Simon
Art Direction | Uncredited
Nationality | USA
Running Time | 28:55

BOOKENDS/SIMON & GARFUNKEL

"They're very American college student and college students can identify with them," Lillian Roxon wrote of Simon and Garfunkel in her 1971 *Rock Encyclopedia*. Certainly, the tasteful black and white sleeve of *Bookends*, their penultimate (and most intellectual) album, gave the duo the look of serious young scholars.

"Mrs. Robinson," the standout track from the movie *The Graduate* was radically rewritten and re-recorded; the duo were to win a Grammy for it the following year. (Simon had originally intended it as a song about Eleanor Roosevelt, but adapted it at *Graduate* director Mike Nichols' insistence.) Joe Di Maggio was the only one who did not "get it," and once publicly attacked Simon for a perceived slur in the song.

"Mrs. Robinson" was not the only instant classic on show, though. "America" was a splendid vignette of a road trip by young lovers; both intimate and epic in scale, it traces an inner journey from naive optimism to more mature understanding. Folk-rocker "Hazy Shade Of Winter," featuring a fizzing riff and a world-weary lyric, had given the duo a U.S. Top Twenty hit in 1966.

"Fakin' It" has a guest interpolation from Beverley Kutner (soon to become Beverley Martyn) in which she addresses Simon in his "former life" as Mr. Leitch—a namecheck for folkie Donovan. Garfunkel's sound collage, "Voices Of Old People," adds perfect depth to Simon's stark and ghostly songs on side one—between the "Bookends." Side two is more fun—particularly the surreal "Punky's Dilemma"—while "At The Zoo"—both singalong children's song and allegorical satire on the human condition—makes an adroit closer. **DN**

> **"Paul is a very creative artist but I'm more that thorough, meticulous, disciplined nut."**
> Art Garfunkel, 1990

Track Listing

01	Bookends Theme (Simon)	0:32
02	Save The Life Of My Child (Simon)	2:49
03	America (Simon)	3:34
▶ 04	Overs (Simon)	2:14
05	Voices Of Old People (Garfunkel)	2:00
06	Old Friends (Simon)	2:36
07	Bookends (Simon)	1:16
▶ 07	Fakin' It (Simon)	3:14
▶ 08	Punky's Dilemma (Simon)	2:10
▶ 09	Mrs. Robinson (Simon)	4:02
10	A Hazy Shade Of Winter (Simon)	2:17
11	At The Zoo (Simon)	2:11

The Small Faces | Ogden's Nut Gone Flake (1968)

Label | Immediate
Producer | Ronnie Lane • Steve Marriott
Art Direction | Ronnie Lane
Nationality | UK
Running Time | 38:27

Although it missed the Summer of Love by 12 months, the mod quartet's third and final LP is the quintessential slice of British psychedelia. While the San Francisco groups had a political slant, the Brits preferred something more frivolous—a good trip guaranteed for all. It wasn't the Vietnam War that Steve Marriott attacked, but his neighbors' complaints about the noise he made. Half of the first side is full-on psychedelic rock (the title track, "Afterglow," and "Song Of A Baker"); the other three tracks are London music hall put through the lysergic blender.

The second side, however, is what makes the music on this album so memorable. Concepts then being all the rage, the band came up with Happiness Stan, who goes in search of the dark side of the moon, a journey that brings him into contact with talking flies and a hermit called Mad John and ends in a dance party. It is linked by a narrative by the comedian Stanley Unwin, whose bizarre language is a typically British take on the beat slang of hipsters such as Lord Buckley. It is so close to making perfect sense that you understand every word, but it is also laugh-out-loud funny. Unfortunately, this "mini-opera" style made live performances almost impossible, and Steve Marriott split in frustration. While the rest of the band found greater fame with Rod Stewart as The Faces, there will always be a sense of missed opportunity.

And the sleeve? An award-winning masterpiece: a circular pastiche of a tobacco tin, which folds out to offer you cigarette papers and a psychedelic collage. What were they implying? **DH**

"Well produced with menacing sounds throughout."

Record Mirror, 1968

Track Listing	
01 Ogden's Nut Gone Flake (Jones • Lane • Marriott • McLagan)	2:29
02 Afterglow (Of Your Love) (Lane • Marriott)	3:31
03 Long Agos And Worlds Apart (McLagan)	2:34
04 Rene (Lane • Marriott)	4:31
05 Song Of A Baker (Lane • Marriott)	3:18
06 Lazy Sunday (Lane • Marriott)	3:06
07 Happiness Stan (Lane • Marriott)	2:36
08 Rollin' Over (Lane • Marriott)	2:49
09 Hungry Intruder (Lane • Marriott • McLagan)	2:15
10 The Journey (Jones • Lane • Marriott • McLagan)	4:13
11 Mad John (Lane • Marriott)	2:46
12 Happy Days Toy Town (Lane • Marriott)	4:19

The Band | Music From Big Pink (1968)

Label | Capitol
Producer | John Simon
Art Direction | Milton Glaser
Nationality | Canada • USA
Running Time | 42:00

In 1968, The Band—Bob Dylan's back-up musicians—were ready to make musical history without their star vocalist. This, their debut album, still sounds bracingly fresh more than three decades after it was recorded.

Though created by four Canadians and an Arkansas farm boy, *Music From Big Pink* is an enduring piece of Americana, an epoch-marking event that seemed to synthesize a century of American culture.

Famously named after the house in Woodstock, New York, where the quintet had holed up with Dylan in the mid-1960s, *Music From Big Pink* detonated in the middle of the psychedelic era, offering concise, finely etched portraits as an alternative to the sprawling, abstract canvas of acid rock. Working with producer/sideman John Simon, the quintet delved deeply into the American soil for their sound and themes, using organ, fiddles, and mandolins in place of effects-laden electric guitars. The album captures The Band as a band, before guitarist Robbie Robertson became its driving creative force. Dylan also features prominently, penning the classic plea "I Shall Be Released" and collaborating with pianist Richard Manuel on the wrenching opening track, "Tears Of Rage," and bassist Richard Danko on the vengeful "This Wheel's On Fire" (a tune that was revamped as the theme for UK sitcom *Absolutely Fabulous*).

Robertson's genius is already fully evident on "Caledonia Mission" and especially "The Weight," used so effectively the following year in Peter Fonda's hit film *Easy Rider*. Recognized as a classic even before it hit the stores, *Music From Big Pink* inspired Eric Clapton to disband the supergroup Cream and search for a new sound. **AG**

"It was like a clubhouse. We'd go every day ... Bob [Dylan] ... really liked the vibe."

Robbie Robertson, 2003

Track Listing

▶	01	Tears Of Rage (Dylan•Manuel)	5:24
	02	To Kingdom Come (Robertson)	3:22
	03	In A Station (Manuel)	3:34
	04	Caledonia Mission (Robertson)	3:00
▶	05	The Weight (Robertson)	4:38
	06	We Can Talk (Manuel)	3:06
	07	Long Black Veil (Dill•Wilkin)	3:06
▶	08	Chest Fever (Robertson)	5:18
	09	Lonesome Suzie (Manuel)	4:04
▶	10	This Wheel's On Fire (Danko•Dylan)	3:14
▶	11	I Shall Be Released (Dylan)	3:14

Jeff Beck
Truth (1968)

Label | Columbia
Producer | Mickie Most
Art Direction | Uncredited
Nationality | UK
Running Time | 40:50

Jeff Beck—the best, yet the least productive, guitar hero—had gone solo after leaving The Yardbirds, and somehow found himself working with pop producer Mickie Most. On the perennially popular hit single, "Hi Ho Silver Lining," Most insisted that Beck sing, dismissing the vocalist in The Jeff Beck Group—Rod Stewart. For the album, Stewart got his chance.

"Morning Dew" may be better than the Tim Rose hit version; "You Shook Me" was recorded shortly afterwards by Led Zeppelin, whose leader, Jimmy Page, had been Beck's colleague in The Yardbirds. ("My heart just sank when I heard 'You Shook Me,'" Beck later reflected.) "Shapes Of Things" had been a UK Top Three/U.S. Top Twenty hit for The Yardbirds, but neither Beck nor Most thought it worth reprising, while two of bluesman Willie Dixon's songs were given a good but respectful kicking.

"Greensleeves" was played on Mickie Most's guitar, "Ol' Man River" (from the musical *Showboat*) shows Rod Stewart at his best. "Beck's Bolero" credits "You know who" as the drummer (it was, in fact, Keith Moon—rumored at the time to be joining Beck, Page, and others in a supergroup) rather than Mickey Waller, while the bass player is Rod's chum, Ron Wood.

Truth was a U.S. Top 20 album, and charted there for eight months, yet unaccountably never charted in Beck's homeland. Later Beck albums have won Grammy awards, but this is his best ever—not least because its sleeve features a Magritte painting. **JT**

Caetano Veloso
Caetano Veloso (1968)

Label | Philips
Producer | Caetano Veloso
Art Direction | Uncredited
Nationality | Brazil
Running Time | 34:54

Try to explain Caetano Veloso to an Anglo-American audience and you end up constructing some fabulous hybrid of Brian Wilson, Stevie Wonder, Bob Dylan, Syd Barrett, John Lennon, and Bob Marley. The English-speaking pop world does not really have a Caetano Veloso, which is probably why the likes of Beck, Kurt Cobain, and David Byrne have worshipped him. Androgynous, profoundly intellectual, yet gloriously irreverent, he performs to packed soccer stadiums while playing unashamedly highbrow music.

This self-titled debut was a key text in the formation of tropicalia, a slyly seditious pop art movement of late-1960s Brazil. Veloso unwittingly unified a mix of leftish poets, painters, dramatists, and film-makers with his defiantly Brazilian response to the "neo-rock" of The Beatles. It is bossa nova played by psychedelic rockers and orchestrated by classical composers, complicated by horn arrangements and baroque vocal harmonies. The music is stunning—the wobbly psychedelic rock of "Clarice," the haunting, complex chord changes of "Clara," the jaunty Che Guevara tribute "Soy Loco Por Tí, América"—but even those who do not speak a word of Portuguese may be intrigued by Veloso's "concrete poetry" lyrics.

Brazil's teenagers loved it; the military dictatorship of the time did not. Within two years Veloso was forced out of Brazil into exile in London, something that only confirmed his legendary status and propagated a remarkable career. **JLe**

Scott Walker
Scott 2 (1968)

Label | Philips
Producer | John Franz • Peter J. Olliff
Art Direction | Uncredited
Nationality | USA
Running Time | 43:47

"Putting me in front of a camera," Scott Walker once mused, "is like taking a hermit who has lived in a cave and suddenly standing him in Trafalgar Square." However, it was not only Walker's profound aversion to attention that led him to leave The Walker Brothers in 1967. He had, he believed, richer records in him than the Spectoresque ballads (all covers) with which the band he led had peppered the British charts since 1965.

Ravishing orchestral arrangements drew the public to *Scott*, his 1967 solo debut, although those who listened closely to the jumble of covers and originals found a headily introspective record. *Scott 2* continued the theme with a similar mix of material, to greater effect. The straighter covers, among them a bleak reading of Bacharach and David's "Windows Of The World," kept Walker Brothers fans happy, but the real gems lie elsewhere: in the trio of Jacques Brel songs, led by galloping opener "Jackie," and the quartet of pieces written by Walker himself. The singer's decision to credit his songs to "S Engel," his real surname, lent credence to the suspicion that cuts like the haunting "Plastic Palace People" were autobiographical.

Scott 2 was Walker's most commercially successful solo album, but also the point at which he started to lose his public. Following the more cohesive but less consistent *Scott 3* came *Scott 4*, a dense collection of self-penned material. It failed to chart, leading Walker into a creative decline not fully broken until 1995's overwhelming *Tilt*. **WF-J**

The Zombies
Odessey & Oracle (1968)

Label | CBS
Producer | The Zombies
Art Direction | Terry Quirk
Nationality | UK
Running Time | 33:31

A landmark British album, *Odessey & Oracle*'s lush, baroque-sounding chamber pop steadily wins new fans every year—yet it sold minimally on its release and was made by a band so disillusioned with the music business that they split up soon afterwards.

Formed in the small town of St Albans in 1963, The Zombies' debut, the sublime "She's Not There," was a No. 2 hit in America, but succeeding singles were less commercially successful. After three years of near-constant touring, the group resolved to split up in late 1966. Bassist Chris White persuaded his bandmates to record a final album—this foreknowledge of their split meant that they were freed from commercial pressures and able to make the record that they wanted.

What they wanted was spectacular. Recorded at Abbey Road Studios immediately after The Beatles had finished *Sgt. Pepper…*, the band's first cohesive album —rather than just a ragbag of singles and cover versions—indulges keyboardist Argent's love of jazz but retains the band's woozy soft-pop on their most daring arrangements yet.

White's flatmate Terry Quirk was commissioned to paint the sleeve art, but misspelt the word "Odyssey." The band decided to leave it as it was, and split with little fanfare soon after. CBS Producer Al Kooper later heard the album on a trip to Britain and persuaded the label to release closing track "Time Of The Season" as a single in 1969. It sold two million copies worldwide, ironically becoming the biggest hit of their career. **PL**

Van Morrison | Astral Weeks (1968)

Label | Warner Bros.
Producer | Lewis Merenstein
Art Direction | Ed Thrasher
Nationality | UK
Running Time | 46:50

By the time the 23-year-old Van Morrison came to record *Astral Weeks*, there was not much for the young Ulsterman to prove. He had already had hit singles on both sides of the Atlantic with "Gloria" and "Brown-Eyed Girl," so when he hooked up in New York City with a core of talented jazz stalwarts, the world knew to expect something special.

Morrison had always had a yen for jazz—despite having been pigeonholed first as a folk artist, then as a bluesman—and on *Astral Weeks* he gave full reign to those sensibilities, finding in the genre the perfect foil to his fugue-like lyrics. The album was cut in an extraordinary two days, with Morrison giving the musicians minimal direction and letting on little about the lyrics and their meaning, instead scatting off the band's largely improvised instrumentals.

Lyrically, Morrison had never been so oblique and poetic before. "Madame George" is a heartfelt flight of fantasy set in his native Belfast about a seasoned drag artist, which is painted in the smudged pastels of a recollected dream, while "Sweet Thing" is an electrifying love song that sets off the hair on your neck from the first strum of an acoustic guitar.

To their credit, the artist-friendly Warner Bros. recognized that in Morrison they had an artist more suited to albums than the sure-fire single hitmaker they perhaps assumed they were taking on, and took the poor commercial reaction to *Astral Weeks* in their stride. Critics then and since recognized the genius in Morrison's startling solo effort, and *Astral Weeks* regularly troubles the upper reaches of best-album polls. **SJac**

> "I was really pretty happy with the album. I thought it was closer to the type of music I wanted to put out. And still is, actually."
>
> Van Morrison, 1972

Track Listing

01	Astral Weeks (Morrison)	7:00
02	Beside You (Morrison)	5:10
▶ 03	Sweet Thing (Morrison)	4:10
04	Cyprus Avenue (Morrison)	6:50
▶ 05	The Way Young Lovers Do (Morrison)	3:10
▶ 06	Madame George (Morrison)	9:25
07	Ballerina (Morrison)	7:00
08	Slim Slow Slider (Morrison)	3:20

The Byrds | Sweetheart Of The Rodeo (1968)

Label | Columbia
Producer | Gary Usher
Art Direction | Butler Advertising • Geller
Nationality | USA
Running Time | 31:52

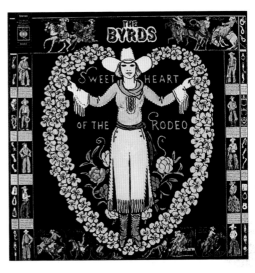

In March 1968, when The Byrds entered Columbia Records' Nashville studio to record their sixth album, only two original members remained: Roger McGuinn and Chris Hillman. McGuinn had envisaged this project as a double LP that told the story of American popular music from traditional country, through rock, to futuristic Moog-powered electronica. New recruit Gram Parsons—who had played country with his International Submarine Band on *Safe At Home* for Lee Hazlewood's LHI Records—persuaded him to stop at country.

Along with ISB's Bob Buchanan, Parsons co-wrote *Sweetheart…*'s standout—the yearning, steel guitar-laden ballad of lost innocence, "Hickory Wind." He also sang lead on it, authored the only other original song, "One Hundred Years From Now," and suggested four of the nine cover versions. Parsons would have completely dominated the LP if it had not been for Hazlewood, who claimed he was still under contract to him and threatened to sue. Consequently, Parsons' vocal was wiped from versions of William Bell's "You Don't Miss Your Water" and The Louvin Brothers' "The Christian Life." The sole nods to The Byrds' past were covers of Dylan's "You Ain't Going Nowhere" and "Nothing Was Delivered," culled from *Basement Tapes*.

The Byrds' audience was used to groundbreaking experimentation from the band, but balked at the album's adoption of a genre they associated with conservative rednecks. A relative failure on release, it has since been resurrected as a pioneering text in country rock, exerting a powerful influence on bands as diverse as The Eagles and Wilco. **JoH**

> "We got into the whole country thing—playing poker, drinking whiskey, wearing cowboy hats."
>
> Roger McGuinn, 2003

Track Listing

▶ 01	You Ain't Going Nowhere (Dylan)	2:33
02	I Am A Pilgrim (Trad., arr. Hillman • McGuinn)	3:39
▶ 03	The Christian Life (C. Louvin • I. Louvin)	2:30
04	You Don't Miss Your Water (Bell)	3:48
▶ 05	You're Still On My Mind (McDaniel)	2:25
06	Pretty Boy Floyd (Guthrie)	2:34
▶ 07	Hickory Wind (Buchanan • Parsons)	3:31
▶ 08	One Hundred Years From Now (Parsons)	2:40
09	Blue Canadian Rockies (Walker)	2:02
10	Life In Prison (Haggard • Sanders)	2:46
▶ 11	Nothing Was Delivered (Dylan)	3:24

The Beatles
The Beatles (a.k.a. The White Album) (1968)

Label | Parlophone
Producer | George Martin
Art Direction | Richard Hamilton
Nationality | UK
Running Time | 93:43

The Mothers Of Invention
We're Only In It For The Money (1968)

Label | Verve
Producer | Frank Zappa
Art Direction | Cal Schenkel
Nationality | USA
Running Time | 39:04

The Beatles officially broke up in 1970, but the Fab Four had stopped functioning as a true band years previously. The process started as early as *Rubber Soul* and picked up steam as John, Paul, George, and Ringo were pulled in different directions by creative differences, religious philosophies, drugs, and, most famously, the presence of Yoko Ono. Amid band squabbling, The Beatles produced *The Beatles*, an epic masterpiece that equals *Sgt. Pepper . . .* , though its artistic success stems more from the talents and personalities of the band members than from collaboration.

The album starts with a roar, and a screech of airplane tires, as The Beatles tweak the Beach Boys formula on the rocking "Back In The USSR." It mixes peerless acoustic-driven ballads such as "Dear Prudence" and "Mother Nature's Son" with comical tales like "Ob-La-Di, Ob-La-Da" and "Rocky Raccoon." Lennon and McCartney—by now mostly a songwriting team in name only—produced some of their most lasting work with "Blackbird" and "Revolution 1," while Lennon's surreal "Happiness Is A Warm Gun" is a mini song suite in itself. However, it is Harrison's "While My Guitar Gently Weeps" that truly stands out.

A mishmash, then. One that sold two million copies during its first week in the United States alone. **JiH**

One of the most influential albums of the second half of the twentieth century, Zappa's fourth album with The Mothers confirmed his status as a visionary genius.

From the start it was extraordinary—courageously alienated from its time and beloved by first-generation dope-smoking hippies—even while it ripped apart their lifestyle and its totems with a savage wit and vitality. Check "Who Needs The Peace Corps?" or "Flower Punk"—to the tune of "Hey Joe" at double tempo. Gaze at its artwork—an all-dragged-up surreal mockery of *Sgt. Pepper . . .* , considered rock's holy grail. And consider its confrontational title, just as musicians were being lauded as visionaries, philosophers, and saints.

But the album is also a hauntingly prescient attack on conservative mores, lifestyle, and nihilistic politics in the United States. Its tightly interconnecting and seductively catchy songs, featuring Zappa on lead vocals, weave a cogent analysis of a society that breeds imperialist warmongering, addiction, and personal and family breakdown—see the chirpily belligerent "Mother People." (Zappa's swipes at U.S. über-authoritarianism started to look like prescience with the killing of two anti-war student demonstrators at Kent State University in 1970.) All of which places it toward the top of the "best concept album ever" chart. **MR**

Neil Young With Crazy Horse
Everybody Knows This Is Nowhere (1969)

Label | Reprise
Producer | David Briggs • Neil Young
Art Direction | Ed Thrasher
Nationality | USA
Running Time | 40:29

Recorded in a fortnight, and released only four months after his eponymous debut, *Everybody Knows This Is Nowhere* united Young with a ragged LA pickup band he renamed Crazy Horse, and saw production duties assumed by David Briggs, who had assisted Jack Nitzsche on the overdub-heavy *Neil Young*. By contrast, *Everybody Knows ...* embraced Briggs' great love of live recording, a method that perfectly suited Young and Crazy Horse's spontaneous, raw, epic country-rock.

Their crunch was never better displayed than on "Cinnamon Girl"—overloaded guitars bruising modal harmonies from the speakers. Elsewhere, Young essays a frayed Americana on the loping "The Losing End" and "Round And Round." Bobby Notkoff's gothic fiddle on "Running Dry" is bewitching.

But the standouts are the two loose, elongated jams, bleak murder ballad "Down By The River" and the elliptical "Cowgirl In The Sand." Here, the sparse songs lend copious space for Young and Danny Whitten's eerie guitar duels, jagged, edgy bursts of noise (in relief to the bluesy ejaculations of their contemporaries) that lucidly evoke the songs' chilling, troubled essences.

These songs would remain on Young and Crazy Horse's setlists for decades, beyond Young's canonization as the Grandfather of Grunge. **SC**

Captain Beefheart And His Magic Band
Trout Mask Replica (1969)

Label | Straight
Producer | Frank Zappa
Art Direction | Cal Schenkel
Nationality | USA
Running Time | 77:38

After the experimentalism of the hippy movement, the avant-garde's influence on rock blossomed with the likes of Captain Beefheart And His Magic Band, and Frank Zappa and the Mothers Of Invention. With Beefheart's old high-school friend Zappa on production duties, *Trout Mask Replica* fused blues, country, free jazz, and southern boogie into an opus that would go on to become one of the most influential albums of the Seventies and beyond.

The double album's 28 tracks are generally seen as too testing for most, with the freewheeling approach to composition and lyrics bewildering the casual listener. However, Zappa's tight control behind the desk helps form an abstract canvas for the Captain's flights of lyrical fantasy, with "Moonlight In Vermont," "Neon Meate Dream Of A Octafish," and "Old Fart At Play" among the most memorable.

Beefheart did not use headphones when recording his vocals for the album—the result was that he sang in time to the reverberations in the studio, which added another element of complexity to their already heady brew. *Trout Mask Replica* went on to be influential far beyond the success the Magic Band enjoyed at the time, with prog, punk, and new wave all taking cues from this late Sixties masterpiece. **CR**

Creedence Clearwater Revival
Bayou Country (1969)

Label | Fantasy
Producer | John Fogerty
Art Direction | Basul Parik
Nationality | USA
Running Time | 34:05

Before national service claimed vocalist John Fogerty and drummer Doug Clifford, the group that became Creedence Clearwater Revival recorded as the Brit-sounding pre-psychedelic bands The Visions and The Golliwogs. National service completed, the group changed its name, abandoned its British pretensions, and released its eponymous debut album in 1968.

Years of touring had made them a mouthwatering live prospect. Clearly motivated by the primal sound of 1950s rock 'n' roll, Creedence served up an irresistible slice of pure, Southern-style rock, a back-to-basics approach that mirrored the way The Band and Dylan had turned their back on psychedelia's excesses.

Bayou Country, Creedence's second album, included their first big hit in the million-selling "Proud Mary," a paean to the majesty of a Mississippi paddle steamer written by Fogerty—the group's lead vocalist, lead guitarist, songwriter, arranger, and producer. Fogerty did so much to perpetuate a myth of the Deep South in Creedence's output, but he was Californian by birth.

Other highlights include the rocking cover of a Little Richard classic, as well as the swampy "Born On The Bayou," bluesy "Graveyard Train," and "Keep On Chooglin'," in which John Fogerty was able to stretch out instrumentally in a nigh-on eight-minute groove.

This hit set the pattern for a further eight gold or platinum U.S. Top Ten singles in the next two and a half years. And in 1971, an NME poll rated the band the world's top group—above The Beatles. **JT**

> "Creedence Clearwater Revival was probably the greatest American singles band."
>
> Dave Marsh, 1979

Track Listing

01 Born On The Bayou (Fogerty)		5:15
▶ 02 Bootleg (Fogerty)		3:01
03 Graveyard Train (Fogerty)		8:37
▶ 04 Good Golly Miss Molly (Blackwell · Marascalo)		2:44
▶ 05 Penthouse Pauper (Fogerty)		3:40
06 Proud Mary (Fogerty)		3:08
07 Keep On Chooglin' (Fogerty)		7:40

Crosby, Stills And Nash
Crosby, Stills And Nash (1969)

Label | Atlantic
Producer | David Crosby • Graham Nash • Stephen Stills
Art Direction | Gary Burden
Nationality | UK • USA
Running Time | 40:52

Hailed by the music press of the day as the ultimate supergroup, the trio of singer/songwriters David Crosby, Stephen Stills, and Graham Nash were under pressure to deliver with their debut album. All three were known for their immaculate grasp of close vocal harmonies, their guitar skills, and their ways with a winning folk/pop melody. Fortunately, they matched up to the standards expected of them with aplomb, dishing up a collection of expertly arranged, performed, and produced songs that hinted at a whole world of influences.

Stills' fantastic opener, "Suite: Judy Blue Eyes" is an almost symphonic work for vocals and guitar, with the occasional Eastern melody and that rollercoaster rush at the end—a career highlight for all three performers. But subtler, more introspective joys are to be found in the trancelike, almost soporific "Guinevere"—the deep vocal lines are spine-chilling—the spiraling, upbeat "Marrakesh Express," and the era-statement of "Long Time Gone," later covered by acid-jazzers Galliano.

The album's textured production perfectly suits the simmering vocal harmonies, and is to this day one of the more convincing arguments for old-fashioned vinyl and the analog mixing desk.

It would all go downhill from here, unfortunately. Despite their often-inspired work with Neil Young in the following decade, they would never quite shake off the "disillusioned hippies with too much money and drug problems" aura. But this first, excellent three-quarters of an hour of wistful exuberance remains a landmark. **JM**

> ## "I don't have control over what comes out of my pen."
>
> David Crosby, 2004

Track Listing

▶ 01	Suite: Judy Blue Eyes (Stills)	7:25
02	Marrakesh Express (Nash)	2:39
▶ 03	Guinevere (Crosby)	4:40
04	You Don't Have To Cry (Stills)	2:45
05	Pre-Road Downs (Nash)	3:01
06	Wooden Ships (Crosby • Stills)	5:29
07	Lady Of The Island (Nash)	2:39
08	Helplessly Hoping (Stills)	2:41
▶ 09	Long Time Gone (Crosby)	4:17
10	49 Bye-Byes (Stills)	5:16

Blood, Sweat, And Tears
Blood, Sweat, And Tears (1969)

Label | Columbia
Producer | James William Guercio
Art Direction | John Berg
Nationality | USA
Running Time | 45:26

He was a singer at 15 (in two-hit-wonders The Royal Teens), then a Brill Building songsmith and the organist on "Like A Rolling Stone," but Al Kooper always wanted his own band. He got it in 1967 when, with guitarist Steve Katz, he left Blues Project with the aim of fusing their fiery blues-rock with jazz under the banner of Blood, Sweat, And Tears. Kooper quit after the well-received *Child Is Father To The Man*, but Katz and pals decided to carry on without their driving force, hiring Canadian singer David Clayton-Thomas to replace him. Good move. A poppy reworking of Kooper's ideas, *Blood, Sweat And Tears* hit No. 1 and scooped the Grammy for Album Of The Year.

Even by 1960s standards, the album is too big for its boots, bookended by two psychedelic rewrites of the first of Satie's *Trois Gymnopédies* and centered on an indulgent 12-minute jazz-rock jam. Still, there is plenty that works: horn-heavy covers of Traffic's "Smiling Phases" and Laura Nyro's "And When I Die" are well judged, as is the reading of Brenda Holloway's "You've Made Me So Very Happy." Taking on Billie Holiday's "God Bless The Child" is risky, but the convincing Clayton-Thomas is up to the task.

Their success proved short-lived. After a Nixon-funded tour of Europe and a Las Vegas cabaret run, Blood, Sweat, and Tears' credibility was shot. Kooper's thoughts on the matter are aired in his outlandishly entertaining autobiography, *Backstage Passes And Backstabbing Bastards*. **WF-J**

> "I came from ... rock 'n' roll into a world of Julliard graduates."
>
> David Clayton-Thomas, 1999

Track Listing

01	**Variations On A Theme By Erik Satie (1st And 2nd Movements)** (arr. Halligan)	2:28
02	**Smiling Phases** (Capaldi·Winwood·Wood)	5:08
03	**Sometimes In Winter** (Katz)	3:07
04	**More And More** (Juan·Vee)	3:03
05	**And When I Die** (Nyro)	4:03
▶ 06	**God Bless The Child** (Herzog Jr · Holiday)	5:52
▶ 07	**Spinning Wheel** (Thomas)	4:06
▶ 08	**You've Made Me So Very Happy** (Gordy·B. Holloway·P. Holloway·Wilson)	4:16
09	**Blues—Part II** (Blood, Sweat And Tears)	11:43
10	**Variation On A Theme By Erik Satie (1st Movement)** (arr. Halligan)	1:40

Flying Burrito Brothers
The Gilded Palace Of Sin (1969)

Label | A&M
Producer | The Burritos • Henry Lewy • Larry Marks
Art Direction | Tom Wilkes
Nationality | USA
Running Time | 37:02

Following their acrimonious departure from The Byrds during 1968, Chris Hillman and Gram Parsons formed The Flying Burrito Brothers, along with steel guitar maestro "Sneaky" Pete Kleinow and bass player Chris Ethridge. The songwriting partnership of the hugely experienced Hillman and the visionary Parsons produced a perfect blueprint for country-rock—a genre in which the Burritos were pioneers.

Partly to attract the rock audience, the group sported snazzy clothes designed by Nudie's Rodeo Tailors in Hollywood. On the sleeve, Parsons wears a jacket motif of cannabis plants. He wanted to be noticed. He should not have worried: the music was good enough on its own. "Wheels," "Christine's Tune" (aka "Devil In Disguise"), and "Sin City" have become country-rock standards, as have the two "Hot Burrito" tracks, while the two "outside tracks" (both part written by Dan Penn) are standards. A gifted vocalist, Parsons sang of heartbreak with an aching country catch in his voice, while Hillman supplied strong harmonies.

Of course, with such a self-indulgent, if talented and charismatic, character at its heart, the band's chances of long-term survival were minimal. After this LP, Ethridge left and Bernie Leadon joined, providing a direct link to The Eagles, the ultimate country-rock act.

In the late Sixties, with the gulf between country and rock fans still wide, *The Gilded Palace Of Sin* bombed. Posterity has restored it to its rightful place as a groundbreaking gem. **JT**

"Gram Parsons was like the white country Jimi Hendrix."

Terry Melcher, 1991

Track Listing

▶	01	Christine's Tune (Hillman•Parsons)	3:02
▶	02	Sin City (Hillman•Parsons)	4:10
	03	Do Right Woman (Moman•Penn)	3:56
▶	04	Dark End Of The Street (Oldham•Penn)	3:55
	05	My Uncle (Hillman•Parsons)	2:36
▶	06	Wheels (Hillman•Parsons)	3:02
	07	Juanita (Hillman•Parsons)	2:28
	08	Hot Burrito No.1 (Ethridge•Parsons)	3:37
	09	Hot Burrito No.2 (Ethridge•Parsons)	3:15
	10	Do You Know How It Feels (Goldberg•Parsons)	2:06
	11	Hippie Boy (Hillman•Parsons)	4:55

Johnny Cash | Johnny Cash At San Quentin (1969)

Label | Columbia
Producer | Bob Johnston
Art Direction | Henry Fox
Nationality | USA
Running Time | 36:47

Following the success of *At Folsom Prison*, Johnny Cash arrived at San Quentin in February 1969 accompanied by a Columbia recording team and a British television crew. This was Cash's fourth visit to the prison (Merle Haggard witnessed one early gig as a convict) but the first without Luther Perkins, his guitarist since their Sun days, who had died a few months before.

Cash's set at Folsom Prison featured a barrage of songs about death, prison, and murder, but at San Quentin the material was less bleakly violent, perhaps mirroring the taming of his own wild ways. However, it did contain the first airing of one new song, "San Quentin," and Cash's uncompromising delivery of this powerful condemnation of prisons in general and San Quentin in particular almost provoked an audience riot (producer Bob Johnston apparently "enhanced" the audience noise at a studio in London, but the tension in the air is unmistakable); this reaction so impressed Cash, he promptly sang it again.

Otherwise, the album is a combination of spirituals ("Peace In The Valley"), wild rockabilly ("Big River"), and novelty ("A Boy Named Sue"). The latter reached No. 2 in the U.S. charts, Cash's biggest hit. The album itself reached No. 1, and by the end of the year Cash was hosting his own prime-time network TV show, the antiauthoritarian prison albums having proved popular with anti-war West Coast liberals as well as the country-loving crowd that formed Cash's typical audience. The album is now only available in its extended version, but that is no bad thing: every extra track adds to a remarkable experience. **PW**

> "I had that audience where all I had to do was say, 'Take over!' and they would have."

Johnny Cash, 1988

Track Listing

▶ 01	Wanted Man (Dylan)	3:24
▶ 02	Wreck Of The Old 97 (Trad., arr. Blake•Cash•Johnson)	2:05
03	I Walk The Line (Cash)	3:29
04	Darling Companion (Cash)	3:21
▶ 05	Starkville City Jail (Cash)	6:15
▶ 06	San Quentin (Cash)	4:07
▶ 07	San Quentin (Cash)	3:13
▶ 08	A Boy Named Sue (Silverstein)	3:59
09	Peace In The Valley (Dorsey)	2:30
▶ 10	Folsom Prison Blues (Cash)	4:24

Creedence Clearwater Revival | Green River (1969)

Label | Fantasy
Producer | John Fogerty
Art Direction | Uncredited
Nationality | USA
Running Time | 29:20

Creedence's self-titled 1968 debut album demonstrated a band who could mix up blues and rock 'n' roll to create a fresh, soulful sound. Follow-up *Bayou Country* had "Proud Mary," their first huge international hit. With *Green River*, however, Creedence defined their vision and sound— clipped, clean, and direct.

Creedence were from the San Francisco area, but eschewed the drug-influenced, psychedelic jams popularized by many Haight-Ashbury bands—and in doing so, found themselves hailed by critics and listeners alike as the saviors of American rock 'n' roll. *Green River* opens with the title track—a Fogerty ode to the magical South, it chugs along on a twangy groove while John sings of returning to a place where girls dance barefoot and the bullfrogs call your name. "Wrote A Song For Everyone" provides a rare glimpse into Fogerty's personal life as he focuses on marital problems. "Bad Moon Rising" was Creedence's biggest hit and—after "Proud Mary"—is their most famous song. Over a funky, almost rockabilly rhythm, drummer Doug Clifford, bassist Stu Cook, and guitarist Tom Fogerty power away while John sings of ominous events on the horizon—with the Vietnam War at its height and the Nixon administration newly installed, that rang all too true. "Lodi" is a chugging ballad about the life of struggling musicians. The rest of the album consists of tough, blues-flavored rockers.

Creedence would go on to even greater artistic and commercial heights on the albums *Willie And The Poorboys* and *Cosmo's Factory,* but *Green River* was the first sustained demonstration of what would become their trademark clean-but-gutsy sound. **GC**

"My favorite album is *Green River.*'Bad Moon Rising.' 'Green River.' That's the soul of where I live musically."

John Fogerty, 1997

Track Listing

▶	01	**Green River** (Fogerty)	2:36
	02	**Commotion** (Fogerty)	2:44
	03	**Tombstone Shadow** (Fogerty)	3:39
▶	04	**Wrote A Song For Everyone** (Fogerty)	4:57
▶	05	**Bad Moon Rising** (Fogerty)	2:21
▶	06	**Lodi** (Fogerty)	3:13
	07	**Cross-Tie Walker** (Fogerty)	3:20
	08	**Sinister Purpose** (Fogerty)	3:22
	09	**Night Time Is The Right Time** (Herman)	3:08

The Beatles
Abbey Road (1969)

Label | Apple
Producer | George Martin
Art Direction | Iain MacMillan
Nationality | UK
Running Time | 47:36

Often neglected in Beatles all-time best album polls in favor of the more technicolor *Sgt. Pepper . . .* and the darker, less orthodox *Revolver*, The Beatles' last-recorded album (*Let It Be* was merely the last to see the light of day) is a shimmering, never-predictable array of songs and song fragments. It is as progressive as anything the quartet ever recorded, and stuffed full of emotional twists and turns, thanks to their chaotic final years together now coming to a messy close.

Despite their fundamental differences at this stage, McCartney and Lennon were still capable of writing searing material. George Harrison, for so long lumped in with Ringo Starr as a Fabs also-ran compared to the other two stellar members, had become a serious songwriter, contributing the awe-inspiring "Something" and "Here Comes The Sun," probably the sweetest song John and Paul never wrote.

But the vitriol, ecstasy, and social commentary of Lennon and McCartney is what makes *Abbey Road* an essential, and they came through with a vengeance. There is the sexual swamp-rock of "Come Together," the psychedelic monster "I Want You (She's So Heavy)" (highlighted by McCartney's nimble bass-playing) and, of course, that unique side-two song suite, loved and loathed by Beatles-heads in equal measure. "Sun King" is a musical dose of LSD; "Golden Slumbers" is the band at their most nursery-rhyme-epic; and "The End" is a prophetic dose of virtuosity on which everyone takes a solo—even Ringo. **JM**

The Who
Tommy (1969)

Label | Track
Producer | Kit Lambert
Art Direction | Mike McInnerney
Nationality | UK
Running Time | 75:03

Endlessly labeled a rock opera, equally often dubbed a load of self-indulgent high-school conceptualism, the expansive, naive *Tommy* has all the attributes of a classic but all the flaws of a Frankenstein monster. Ostensibly the story of a deaf, dumb, and blind child who is born into a dysfunctional family (he is terrorized by a cousin and uncle), is enlightened through pinball and music, and becomes a messianic icon in true late-Sixties style, the album is more accurately a journey through Pete Townshend's actual and imagined early life.

Musically, it is a cross between sort-of-mod anthems and uniquely Who-style dextrous rock, with the career-best of "Pinball Wizard," "I'm Free," and "We're Not Gonna Take It"—remarkable high points. Ambitious concept-supporting compositions such as "1921," "Underture," and "Smash The Mirror" are solid rather than essential—and the album could probably have had 15 minutes shaved off its hour and a quarter and no one would have complained—but most listeners accepted that this was the price of epicdom, and took it all in.

While the total meaning of it all has never really been fully explained, *Tommy* is as culturally influential as it is musically diverse. The album took the high-blown concepts of the previous year's obvious inspiration, *Sgt. Pepper . . . ,* developed them with a touch of street cool absent from that album, and inspired the full-on prog rock of later works such as Pink Floyd's *Dark Side Of The Moon*. For that—even if it is a rocky ride at times—we should be grateful. **JM**

Miles Davis
In A Silent Way (1969)

Label | Columbia
Producer | Teo Macero
Art Direction | Uncredited
Nationality | USA
Running Time | 37:55

In A Silent Way is not an album for the traditional jazz fan, the rock listener, or the devotee of fusion-lite. However, it is determinedly a record for anyone who likes their music to stretch out unhurriedly; who enjoys the touch of an artist sensitive enough to let empty silences speak as loudly as the music; and who relishes the unalloyed freedom of musicians allowed to move freely through sounds without restriction.

Made up of two extended songs, each just under 20 minutes in length, *In A Silent Way* (rarely has an album title been so apt) is a record that could only have been made at the tail-end of the 1960s, and by a musician who had almost exhausted the possibilities of the first, enormously influential half of his career. High points of the A-side include the keyboard mastery of Herbie Hancock and Chick Corea, the dreamy soprano sax of Wayne Shorter, and the incredible atmospherics of Joe Zawinul. Meanwhile, flip the record and the oceans of silence between Miles' gorgeous, always-understated melodies and John McLaughlin's apparently infinite guitar solo are nothing short of genius.

In A Silent Way sits between Miles' early, sometimes over-enthusiastic forays into the electric medium and the full-on jazz-rock roar that he and his supremely talented band would record in the following decade— and is the stepping stone to the genre's high point, Davis' own *Bitches Brew*. Older jazz fans deplored it all; the younger generation adored it. Three decades later, its triumph is both acknowledged and complete. **JM**

The Bee Gees
Odessa (1969)

Label | Polydor
Producer | Robert Stigwood
Art Direction | Uncredited
Nationality | Australia • UK
Running Time | 63:36

For their seventh original album in four years The Bee Gees retreated to Atlantic Studios in New York with a vague idea of a conceptual double album based on the mythical loss of *HMS Veronica* in 1899. It was August 1968, and the group had already shed an important member—guitarist Vince Melouney—en route to losing Robin Gibb and then experiencing a two-year split.

While the title track—and arguably some of the other songs with a focus on the nineteenth century, such as the celebratory "Edison"—might have fitted the concept, nonsense like the parody country rock "Marley Purt Drive" bears as much connection to mysterious Crimean shipwrecks as a rock 'n' roll show at Redcliffe Speedway. "Melody Fair" is Sixties sexism at its worst, but is redeemed by a marvelous tune and classic Gibb harmonizing. "You'll Never See My Face Again" is delightfully goth, but the best track here is the majestic, solemn and witty "I Laugh in Your Face"; which typifies the grandeur of most of the whole enterprise.

Odessa was originally produced in a lavish flock sleeve with gold lettering, yet the flock caused a major allergic reaction among workers during production, and as a result—and possibly due to flagging album sales—the album was reissued in a cardboard sleeve. In recent years, Barry Gibb has dismissed *Odessa* as a confused attempt by a disintegrating and exhausted band to live up to their record company's desire that they do something "meaningful," yet it remains the most enduring of their 1960s work. **DN**

The Pentangle | Basket Of Light (1969)

Label | Transatlantic
Producer | Shel Talmy
Art Direction | Diogenic Attempts
Nationality | UK
Running Time | 41:04

In 1967, established UK folk guitar heroes Bert Jansch and John Renbourn moved on from their collaborative album, *Bert And John*, to form a new band, The Pentangle. The rhythm section—Danny Thompson (bass) and Terry Cox (drums)—came from Alexis Korner's Blues Incorporated, while vocalist Jacqui McShee was a well-known figure on the folk club circuit. The new quintet would embrace not only folk and traditional ballads but also blues, jazz, and original songs.

Basket Of Light is the quintet's most important album, both in terms of quality and commercial success. "Light Flight" may not be the Pentangle fans' favorite song, but in the UK the BBC used it as the theme tune for their TV series *Take Three Girls* and the track soared to No.5 in the UK singles chart (though it's not a straightforward tune and the time signature varies between 5/8, 7/8, and 6/4 in the middle).

Elsewhere on the album are songs that rank among the best that Pentangle recorded: "Once I Had A Sweetheart," with sitar by Renbourn; "Train Song"; "Hunting Song," with Cox on glockenspiel; "House Carpenter"; and "Sally Go Round The Roses," a cover of the song written in 1963 by American producer Abner Spector (unrelated to the more famous Phil) for The Jaynetts.

Lavishly attired in a gatefold sleeve featuring a picture of the band playing a concert at London's Royal Albert Hall, *Basket Of Light* made Top Five in the UK album charts, stayed in the Top Ten for a month, and became one of the best-selling records in the history of the legendary Transatlantic Records. **GSu**

"Donovan used to play exactly like Bert."

John Renbourn, 1970

Track Listing

▶ 01 **Light Flight**
(Cox・Jansch・McShee・Renbourn・Thompson) 3:19

02 **Once I Had A Sweetheart**
(Cox・Jansch・McShee・Renbourn・Thompson) 4:43

03 **Springtime Promises**
(Cox・Jansch・McShee・Renbourn・Thompson) 4:10

04 **Lyke-Wake Dirge**
(Cox・Jansch・McShee・Renbourn・Thompson) 3:36

05 **Train Song**
(Cox・Jansch・McShee・Renbourn・Thompson) 4:48

06 **Hunting Song**
(Cox・Jansch・McShee・Renbourn・Thompson) 6:44

▶ 07 **Sally Go Round The Roses** (Spector) 3:41

08 **The Cuckoo**
(Cox・Jansch・McShee・Renbourn・Thompson) 4:31

09 **House Carpenter**
(Cox・Jansch・McShee・Renbourn・Thompson) 5:32

The Rolling Stones | Let It Bleed (1969)

Label | Decca
Producer | Jimmy Miller
Art Direction | Robert Brownjohn • Victor Kahn
Nationality | UK
Running Time | 43:26

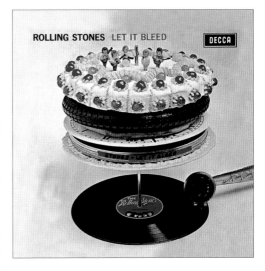

"That is the one I'd rescue from the fire," enthused Sheryl Crow. Easier to go to Best Buy, surely, but the sentiment is indisputable. Some Stones records are Important and Interesting but Not Actually Very Good, but some are full of top tunes that anyone with ears should enjoy—and this is one of the best.

In fact, it is the filling in a triple-decker sandwich. *Beggar's Banquet*, *Let It Bleed*, and *Sticky Fingers* were cherry-picked from recordings made from 1968 to 1970 —the original plan being to issue both *Sticky Fingers* and a follow-up in 1969.

Contractual complications canned that. Instead, *Let It Bleed* became a blood-soaked bookend to the decade, its apocalyptic tone set by "Gimme Shelter" (the Stones documentary of the same name captures the stabbing of a fan at a 1969 gig at Altamont Speedway).

The contrast with old rivals The Beatles could not be sharper: *Let It Be* consists of bored blues and syrupy strings; *Let It Bleed* has (as one critic complained) "sleazy sex, sadomasochism, hard drugs, and gratuitous violence." Those ingredients make even the non-rocking "Country Honk," "Let It Bleed," and "Love In Vain" irresistible.

But it rocks hard too. Hard to believe the murderous "Midnight Rambler" and thrillingly taut "Monkey Man" were written on a relaxing holiday in Italy. Then there is "You Can't Always Get What You Want," which grows from a hymn to a howl.

Notoriously dismissive of his own work, Mick Jagger concedes *Let It Bleed* is "a good record. I'd put it as one of my favorites." The old tart is right on the money. **BM**

"It's a very rough, very violent era. The Vietnam War. Violence on the screens, pillage and burning."

Mick Jagger, 1995

Track Listing		
▶ 01	Gimme Shelter (Jagger•Richard)	4:40
02	Love In Vain (Johnson)	4:26
03	Country Honk (Jagger•Richard)	3:12
04	Live With Me (Jagger•Richard)	3:40
05	Let It Bleed (Jagger•Richard)	5:37
06	Midnight Rambler (Jagger•Richard)	7:00
07	You Got The Silver (Jagger•Richard)	2:59
▶ 08	Monkey Man (Jagger•Richard)	4:19
▶ 09	You Can't Always Get What You Want (Jagger•Richard)	7:33

Nick Drake | Five Leaves Left (1969)

Label | Hannibal
Producer | Joe Boyd
Art Direction | Cally
Nationality | UK
Running Time | 41:41

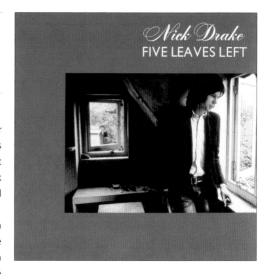

Although the cult of Nick Drake, like those of later luminaries such as Marc Bolan and Kurt Cobain, has elevated him beyond his music to an entirely different level, the work of this most understated of British folk artists remains essential listening for anyone interested in finding out what the Sixties were actually about.

Drake's debut album, *Five Leaves Left*, was a remarkable work: stuffed with complex, introspective music but leavened with arrangements and production straight off the pop shelf. Thanks to his formidable troupe of co-conspirators, which included the two folk Thompsons (Fairport Convention's Richard and Pentangle's Danny) as well as string maestro Robert Kirby, the record is full of glittering, warm sounds that have not aged a jot in the interim. Although his later work would be both more experimental and more accessible, *Five Leaves Left* remains the place to begin for any Drake investigation.

Start with the phenomenal "River Man," whose weary, questioning lyrics lie beautifully on Nick's exquisitely soft tenor voice, and where his grasp of the acoustic guitar pitches him between folk and psychedelia. The surging strings of "Way To Blue" are equally inspiring, as is the heart-rending, once-heard-never-forgotten semi-Eastern cello melody of "Cello Song." But it is an inspired journey, with barely a skippable track.

Drake would go on to more popular levels during his lifetime, but he rarely excelled himself more than on this first album—and while his early death was certainly tragic, the music he left behind will undoubtedly ensure him a degree of immortality. **JM**

> ## "If I could find making music a fairly natural connection with something else, then I might move on to something else."

Nick Drake, 1971

Track Listing

01 Time Has Told Me (Drake)		4:28
▶ 02 River Man (Drake)		4:22
03 Three Hours (Drake)		6:15
04 Way To Blue (Drake)		3:11
05 Day Is Done (Drake)		2:29
▶ 06 Cello Song (Drake)		4:47
07 The Thoughts Of Mary Jane (Drake)		3:22
08 Man In A Shed (Drake)		3:55
09 Fruit Tree (Drake)		4:49
10 Saturday Sun (Drake)		4:03

Dusty Springfield **Dusty In Memphis** (1969)

Label | Philips
Producer | Tom Dowd • Arif Mardin • Jerry Wexler
Art Direction | Haig Adishian
Nationality | UK
Running Time | 33:31

The writing was on the wall by 1968. Pop had turned into rock and solo female vocalists were finding hits hard to come by. Dusty was no exception: her last significant hits on either side of the Atlantic had been in the summer of 1966. Nevertheless, Ahmet Ertegun, the visionary head of Atlantic Records, figured she was still as fine an interpretative singer as Aretha Franklin, and wanted to get her in a studio with the same band that had turned Franklin, Wilson Pickett, and The Box Tops into hot acts.

When Dusty arrived in Memphis, however, she was horrified by the material she was offered (classy adult ballads rather than gritty funk), and demanded that everything be worked out before recording, with her voice added to final mixes (the musicians and producers wanted something spontaneous, Dusty singing with only a rhythm track). The singer lost her nerve and fought with everybody, accusing the producers of being prima donnas; ashtrays were thrown and sessions canceled. Dusty fled back to New York to record in a (slightly) better atmosphere.

The results, though, could hardly have been improved upon. For all Springfield's tantrums, the material is top notch, by excellent composers at the top of their game. The arrangements are incredible, the vocals imperious. The first single, "Son Of A Preacher Man," returned her to the Top Ten.

It took Dusty a year before she could listen to the album. Record buyers were not even that forgiving: despite rave reviews, *Dusty In Memphis* bombed, registering only a lowly No. 99 (in the U.S.). Her career never recovered. **DH**

" I was destined to become a librarian."

Dusty Springfield, 1995

Track Listing

▶	01	Just A Little Lovin' (Mann•Weil)	2:18
	02	So Much Love (Goffin•King)	3:31
▶	03	Son Of A Preacher Man (Hurley•Wilkins)	2:29
	04	I Don't Want To Hear It Anymore (Newman)	3:11
▶	05	Don't Forget About Me (Goffin•King)	2:52
▶	06	Breakfast In Bed (Fritts•Hinton)	2:57
	07	Just One Smile (Newman)	2:42
	08	The Windmills Of Your Mind (A. Bergman•M. Bergman•Legrand)	3:51
	09	In The Land Of Make Believe (Bacharach•David)	2:32
▶	10	No Easy Way Down (Goffin•King)	3:11
	11	I Can't Make It Alone (Goffin•King)	3:57

Elvis Presley | From Elvis In Memphis (1969)

Label | RCA
Producer | Chips Moman
Art Direction | Jacqueline Murphy
Nationality | USA
Running Time | 37:08

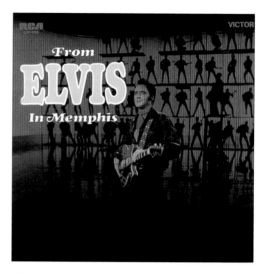

Elvis Presley spent much of the 1960s concentrating on starring in increasingly awful films. His comeback began with a 1968 TV special in which he concentrated on the R&B numbers of his youth.

Inspired by the experience, Elvis relocated to his home town of Memphis—then a red-hot musical metropolis issuing forth regular soul and pop hits—and booked sessions at American Sound Studios. ASS was run by top producer Chips Moman and employed a crew of legendary session musicians (among them Dan Penn, Tommy Cogbill, and Reggie Young). Elvis had not recorded in Memphis for 14 years but the sessions, with their easy-going Southern humor and the warm local ambience, meant he enjoyed himself immensely.

Along with covers of songs Elvis wanted to record, Moman fed him songs that he, as a publisher and producer, had procured. There was soul singer Jerry Butler's recent hit "Only The Strong Survive" and Hank Snow's "I'm Moving On," a country gem that Elvis and the band morph into a funky workout. "In The Ghetto" was procured especially for Elvis and as the album's major hit single, would help re-establish him as a contemporary talent. "Long Black Limousine" features a soulful vocal full of sorrow and anger, while Burt Bacharach's "Any Day Now" is a stone-cold classic ballad. ("Suspicious Minds"—recorded at the Memphis sessions but not included on the album—returned Elvis to No.1 in late 1969.)

An America unhinged by war and assassinations wanted Elvis back as its rock icon: the Memphis sessions established his relevance again. **GC**

"It's very hard to live up to an image."

Elvis Presley, 1972

Track Listing

01	Wearin' That Loved On Look	(Frazier•Owens)	2:49
▶ 02	Only The Strong Survive	(Butler•Gamble•Huff)	2:44
03	I'll Hold You In My Heart	(Arnold•Dilbeck•Horton)	4:34
▶ 04	Long Black Limousine	(George•Stovall)	3:44
05	It Keeps Right On A-Hurtin'	(Tillotson)	2:39
06	I'm Movin' On	(Snow)	2:55
07	Power Of My Love	(Baum•Giant•Kaye)	2:40
08	Gentle On My Mind	(Hartford)	3:25
09	After Loving You	(Lantz•Miller)	3:09
10	True Love Travels On A Gravel Road	(Frazier•Owens)	2:41
▶ 11	Any Day Now	(Bacharach•Hilliard)	3:03
▶ 12	In The Ghetto	(Davis)	2:45

The Velvet Underground
The Velvet Underground (1969)

Label | MGM
Producer | The Velvet Underground
Art Direction | Dick Smith
Nationality | USA
Running Time | 43:59

In contrast to their groundbreaking debut album and the self-destructive rush of sophomore release *White Light/White Heat*, The Velvet Underground's self-titled third record was created in a comparatively relaxed atmosphere. There were fewer extremes in the lyrics or the band's sound—in part due to John Cale having left the band, but also because their usual equipment had been stolen at the airport on their way to the L.A. studios where it was recorded.

From the sublime introduction ("Candy Says," about transvestite Candy Darling, sung by Cale's replacement Doug Yule) to its unforgettable final scene ("After Hours," featuring the childlike voice of drummer Maureen Tucker), *The Velvet Underground* saw Lou Reed graduate from druggy street poet to articulate songwriter, excelling himself in songs like the exquisite confessional "Pale Blue Eyes," the redemptive "I'm Set Free," and the literary experiment "The Murder Mystery." Rockers "What Goes On" and "Beginning To See The Light" showed the fire was still burning inside. But the album's understated peak is the slow, sexy "Some Kinda Love," with Reed and guitarist Sterling Morrison trading infectious licks.

The Velvets were no longer such a weird creature, as their conservative appearance on the cover indicates. (The shot was taken by Billy Linich, aka Billy Name, at Andy Warhol's Factory.) They had been boosted up to the MGM label, but the record company promoted the album poorly and it was lost to the general public. **IJ**

"The songs are all very quiet and it's kind of insane. I like the album."

Sterling Morrison, 1983

Track Listing		
▶ 01 Candy Says (Reed)		4:04
▶ 02 What Goes On (Reed)		4:55
▶ 03 Some Kinda Love (Reed)		4:03
▶ 04 Pale Blue Eyes (Reed)		5:41
05 Jesus (Reed)		3:24
▶ 06 Beginning To See The Light (Reed)		4:41
▶ 07 I'm Set Free (Reed)		4:04
08 That's The Story Of My Life (Reed)		2:04
09 The Murder Mystery (Reed)		8:56
▶ 10 After Hours (Reed)		2:07

Quicksilver Messenger Service
Happy Trails (1969)

Label | Capitol
Producer | Uncredited
Art Direction | George Hunter
Nationality | USA
Running Time | 50:08

Unlike most hippie bands from San Francisco's Haight-Ashbury scene, Quicksilver Messenger Service were able to transfer their wide-eyed on-stage sonic exploration to the studio—witness their masterful self-titled debut of 1968. Yet the band would really wave the freak flag with their next release, *Happy Trails*, a mostly live set recorded at both Fillmore East and West.

The opening track, a side-long workout of Bo Diddley's "Who Do You Love," remains one of the most vibrant psychedelic jams ever put to wax. Broken into six parts, with the central four each showcasing a different band member, the "Who Do You Love" suite conveys what it must have been like to be munching an apple, drinking spiked Kool-Aid, and dancing until 4 a.m. at one of Bill Graham's colorful parties.

The group keeps right on grooving with Diddley on "Mona," a cohesive, yet appropriately loose collaboration that delivers some of the most blistering fretwork of John Cipollina's impressive career. "Calvary" is a haunting mix of styles that builds to a glorious conclusion over 13 minutes. The record closes with the short farewell "Happy Trails" (TV cowboy Roy Rogers' signature tune), the tone of which is emulated perfectly by George Hunter's period cover painting.

Happy Trails bettered the band in sales and reached the Top 30 in the United States. The album remains the clearest snapshot of the band at the height of their improvisational powers, and its influence can still be heard in the jam-band music of today. **JiH**

> ## "I have no qualms about taking anything from any kind of music."
>
> John Cipollina, 1989

Track Listing

▶	01	Who Do You Love Part 1 (McDaniels)	3:32
▶	02	When You Love (Duncan)	5:14
▶	03	Where You Love (Elmore)	6:07
▶	04	How You Love (Cipollina)	2:45
▶	05	Which Do You Love (Freiberg)	4:38
▶	06	Who Do You Love Part 2 (McDaniels)	3:01
	07	Mona (McDaniels)	7:01
	08	Maiden Of The Cancer Moon (Duncan)	3:01
	09	Calvary (Duncan)	13:21
	10	Happy Trails (Evans)	1:28

Led Zeppelin | Led Zeppelin (1969)

Label | Atlantic
Producer | Jimmy Page
Art Direction | George Hardie
Nationality | UK
Running Time | 44:46

Even at the beginning of their careers, the approach of the world's most famous and influential heavy-blues-folk-rock act was identifiable and unique. Grasping the fearsome riffage of pioneers such as Cream and updating it to a new and awe-inspiring brand of rock, Led Zeppelin both advanced the boundaries of music on their debut album of 1969 and paid homage to their inspirations from the folk, blues, and R&B fields.

While Jimmy Page's alarmingly nifty guitar playing on covers of Willie Dixon's "You Shook Me" and "I Can't Quit You Baby" express a rock-solid grip on the band's roots, the future of 1970s rock was already mapped out in career-best songs such as "Dazed And Confused" (check out the super-fat descending bassline) and "Communication Breakdown" (listen out for the clean, almost Pete Townshend-like riff). The earth-shaking, overdriven sound of bassist extraordinaire John Paul Jones on anthemic tunes such as "Good Times, Bad Times" was only equaled in contemporary low-end terms by John Entwistle and perhaps Roger Glover, while the now-legendary John "Bonzo" Bonham—whose frantic, famously "tight but loose" playing made Zep's big songs still bigger—was a law unto himself.

Led Zeppelin was far more than the sum of their parts. The whimsical, often naive but much-idolized lyrics and genre-defining vocal style of Robert Plant were better used on later Led Zeppelin albums, perhaps, and in 1969 the musicians had yet to really hit their stride. But the benchmark set by this multilayered, full-range dynamic album makes it an object of deserved worship. **JM**

> ## "We went in and recorded exactly where we were at that point in time."
>
> Jimmy Page, 1999

Track Listing

01	Good Times, Bad Times (Bonham·Jones·Page)	2:47
▶ 02	Babe I'm Gonna Leave You (Bennett·Bredon·Darling)	6:41
03	You Shook Me (Dixon·Lenoir)	6:27
▶ 04	Dazed And Confused (Page)	6:26
05	Your Time Is Gonna Come (Jones·Page)	4:34
06	Black Mountain Side (Page)	2:12
▶ 07	Communication Breakdown (Bonham·Jones·Page)	2:29
08	I Can't Quit You Baby (Dixon)	4:42
09	How Many More Times (Bonham·Jones·Page)	8:28

The Band
The Band (1969)

Label | Capitol
Producer | The Band • John Simon
Art Direction | Bob Cato
Nationality | Canada • USA
Running Time | 43:54

In 1969, with America politically divided, culturally riven, and inextricably mired in Vietnam, the once glorious Sixties were stumbling to an end. Dylan had closed the door and pulled down the shades on a generation looking to him for answers. Drugs were getting heavier and psychedelia had turned flaccid. It was into this environment that the most influential band of the time unleashed their masterpiece.

Built upon Robbie Robertson's extraordinary cycle of songs inspired by the American South, *The Band* is an album with a hefty contemporary resonance rooted in the hurt and pride of the nation's past (it was nearly called "America"). Intriguingly—coming from four Canadians and a Southern boy from Arkansas—it is a heritage they both absorbed and memorably defined.

Recorded (mostly) in a house rented from Sammy Davis Jr., high up in the Hollywood hills, these recordings are the culmination of all their rockabilly years on the road, their time spent with Dylan, and their Woodstock sojourn. From barrelhouse piano to ragtime soul, there is a grainy texture to the sound and a rolling flow to the rhythm. Levon Helm, Richard Manuel, and Rick Danko's interlinking vocals seamlessly switch and trade to ghostly, ethereal effect.

The Band had many highs, but their second album is their most haunting, poetic, and their most beautifully realized. On the cover they look like a raggedy bunch of frontiersmen or a glowering gang of outlaws—which (in both cases) they were. **RF**

Led Zeppelin
Led Zeppelin II (1969)

Label | Atlantic
Producer | Jimmy Page
Art Direction | David Juniper
Nationality | UK
Running Time | 41:21

Led Zeppelin's second album is all the more remarkable for the lack of time its creators had to perfect it— *Led Zeppelin II* was laid down in brief breaks between shows, while they were on tour in America. In some ways, it is obvious how the rushed schedule made the album better: the songs "Whole Lotta Love," "The Lemon Song," and "Bring It On Home" are all based on vintage blues standards and retain a rawness that might have been polished with the luxury of time and budget.

Even more impressively, the band manage to retain plenty of subtlety despite the live bludgeoning they engaged in every night: newbies to Led Zep should listen to "Ramble On," a beautiful, multilayered acoustic ballad with a weighty chorus that epitomizes the band's primary strengths—riffing heaviness and fragile economy. "Thank You" is another expertly executed acoustic workout, but *Led Zeppelin II* remains a superb album, its greatest asset the huge sounds emitted by Jimmy Page, John Paul Jones, and John Bonham.

"Whole Lotta Love" in particular has stood the test of time, employed as the long-running theme tune to the perennial British TV music show *Top Of The Pops* and a stalwart on any rock lover's playlist. In fact, songs such as this one have entered and re-entered the rock canon so many times that they have passed the point of cliché and become enshrined as items of musical vocabulary. All of which makes it even more awe-inspiring that Led Zep's second album is so full of light and shade. Its place on this list is well deserved. **JM**

MC5
Kick Out The Jams (1969)

Label | Elektra
Producer | Bruce Botnik • Jac Holzman
Art Direction | William S. Harvey
Nationality | USA
Running Time | 36:17

The Temptations
Cloud Nine (1969)

Label | Motown
Producer | Norman Whitfield
Art Direction | Ken Kim
Nationality | USA
Running Time | 34:41

Rolling Stone cover stars The Motor City Five lived as renegades from the cops in their own hippy commune, toting mean, psychedelicized R&B and an ethos of dope, guns, and sex in the streets. *Kick Out The Jams* was a typical night of revolutionary rock 'n' roll from these ass-kicking provocateurs, spanning white noise, "liquid frenzy," and cosmic jazz. Recorded at their regular haunt, the Grande Hotel Ballroom in Detroit, *Kick Out The Jams* ran through their setlist with clumsy abandon; guitars sprinted out of tune, ragged vocals overlapped, songs collapsed into feedback—a glorious chaos.

Punches are emphatically not pulled. The title track opens with an invitation to "Kick out the Jams, motherfuckers!" From the apache-whooping drone-rock of "Rocket Reducer," through the politicized blues "Motor City's Burning," to their freakout Sun Ra tribute, "Starship," the ambience is one of flammable protest.

It was a controversial album. Legendary rock hack Lester Bangs slated it as "ridiculous, overbearing, pretentious," and at a party almost convinced guitarist Wayne Kramer of this. When Hudson's record store chain refused to stock the "obscene" album, the band ran adverts reading "Fuck Hudson's!"; Elektra released an edited version of the album, and soon dropped them.

This was not the end for the MC5—though it was the beginning of the end. *Kick Out The Jams* remains their definitive statement, however; an album where you can smell the pepper spray, feel the heat from burning flags, sense the revolution raging. **SC**

When the producer Norman Whitfield teamed up with The Temptations in the late 1960s, they were already on a roll, for the quintet had notched up several U.S. hits. But Whitfield—who had a proven track record himself, having penned "I Heard It Through The Grapevine" among others—relished the challenge.

When their lead singer David Ruffin left in 1968, Whitfield grabbed his chance, giving both the band—Melvin Franklin, Otis Williams, Eddie Kendricks, Paul Williams, and Ruffin's replacement Dennis Edwards—and the label a makeover. Escaping the label's formulaic pounding four-four beat, Whitfield knowingly referenced the West Coast, with liberated lyrics and exhilarating musical exploration, proving he and the group could easily adapt to the changing times.

The album's foundations were laid in the Motown Producers' Workshop at Hitsville, Detroit. Central was that title cut, which landed the label its first Grammy and introduced a fresh new Motown sound. Funk Brother Dennis Coffey created the track's distinctive guitar intro: "It was my first session with Motown and it was then that I introduced them to the wah-wah. I started throwing a few licks around and within a week I was in the studio recording with them on *Cloud Nine*."

Other LP stand-outs include the atmospheric, peerless vocal showcase, "Run Away Child, Running Wild." The album left Berry Gordy scratching his head, but the likes of Funkadelic, Curtis Mayfield, Isaac Hayes, and Barry White all took serious note. **LW**

Sly And The Family Stone | Stand! (1969)

Label | Epic
Producer | Sly Stone
Art Direction | Uncredited
Nationality | USA
Running Time | 41:40

Few records captured the optimism of the late 1960s better than Sly And The Family Stone's fourth LP. Formed by singer and multi-instrumentalist Sly Stone in San Francisco, the racially mixed, bi-gender septet broke new ground with their colorful blend of funk, pop, rock, and psychedelia. In 1968 they scored a Top Ten U.S. hit with the effervescent "Dance To The Music," but *Stand!* was the first time their leader's kaleidoscopic approach sustained a full-length statement.

The album was trailed by No. 1 smash "Everyday People," an evergreen ode to tolerance that married the accessibility of a nursery rhyme to iconic phrases such as "Different strokes for different folks." "I Want To Take You Higher" became one of Woodstock's festival's signature anthems, uniting gospel fervor, blues guitar, and punchy, levitational horns. Its four-to-the-floor beat was a clear precursor to disco, and a similar rhythm features in the coda to the title track—a sublime, rainbow-hued message of pride. "Sing A Simple Song" filters its sunny sentiment through communal vocals and harmonious organ, while "Don't Call Me Nigger, Whitey" experiments with wah-wah mic effects to create a darker urban vibe.

Stand! spent more than 100 weeks on the Billboard chart, peaking at No. 13. 1970's *Greatest Hits* collection went to No. 2, while 1971's *There's A Riot Goin' On* actually made the top spot. Sly Stone paved the way for the socio-political tone of 1970s soul, not to mention Miles Davis' electric jazz-fusion. His genre-bending vision continues to inspire contemporary stars such as Prince, OutKast, and the Red Hot Chili Peppers. **MA**

> "We all bought motorcycles together, bought dogs together, bought T-Bird cars together. We did a lot of stuff together."
>
> Larry Graham, 1997

Track Listing

▶ 01	Stand! (Stewart)	3:08
▶ 02	Don't Call Me Nigger, Whitey (Stewart)	5:59
▶ 03	I Want To Take You Higher (Stewart)	5:22
04	Somebody's Watching You (Stewart)	3:29
▶ 05	Sing A Simple Song (Stewart)	3:55
▶ 06	Everyday People (Stewart)	2:20
07	Sex Machine (Stewart)	13:48
08	You Can Make It If You Try (Stewart)	3:39

Tim Buckley | Happy Sad (1969)

Label | Elektra
Producer | Zal Yanovsky • Jerry Yester
Art Direction | William S. Harvey
Nationality | USA
Running Time | 44:43

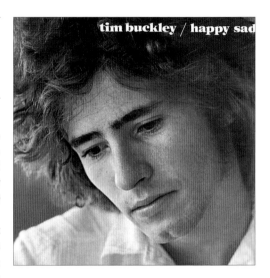

Tim Buckley died of a heroin overdose at the age of 28, leaving behind nine albums of charismatic songwriting. Some were abstract commercial failures, like the vilified *Lorca*, but all were charged with an instinctive musicality that struck at the heart. "It's not two minutes and 50 seconds of rock 'em, sock 'em," he once said.

A meditation on love and memory that evokes lost highways and midnight encounters, *Happy Sad* is Buckley at his best—the unvarnished romantic with a poet's eye. With the loose, melodic guitar of Lee Underwood and John Miller's forceful acoustic bass behind him, Buckley embarks on "Strange Feelin'," a lonesome blues that nods to Miles Davis. Beginning almost discordantly, Buckley's tenor soon harmonizes the jostling elements into a rolling, jazz-slanted refrain.

"Buzzin' Fly," which became (to his irritation) Buckley's most requested live tune, is more conventional, its breezy folksiness inviting parallels with Fred Neil, who wrote "Everybody's Talkin'" for the film *Midnight Cowboy*. More representative of Buckley's mature style is the wave-swept suite "Love From Room 109 ..." Alive with the texture and scent of a remembered affair, it meanders from sunlit motel rooms to cello-racked introspection and back.

He pursues a darker vein with "Dream Letter," a moving Celtic lament, while "Gypsy Woman" displays the side of his music that irritated critics—a mojo-rousing jam with atonal undercurrents that is memorable for the awesome range of Buckley's voice. "Sing A Song For You" brings the album to a close on surer footing—a simple, devotional song of understated beauty. **JDi**

> "I haven't deliberately avoided fame. It's just that I'm too odd for the white middle-class. But ... there's nobody like me so they've got to keep me around."

Tim Buckley, 1972

Track Listing		
01 **Strange Feelin'** (Buckley)		7:40
▶ 02 **Buzzin' Fly** (Buckley)		6:04
▶ 03 **Love From Room 109 At The Islander** **(On Pacific Coast Highway)** (Buckley)		10:49
04 **Dream Letter** (Buckley)		5:12
05 **Gypsy Woman** (Buckley)		12:19
▶ 06 **Sing A Song For You** (Buckley)		2:39

Chicago | Chicago Transit Authority (1969)

Label | Columbia
Producer | James William Guercio
Art Direction | Maria Villar
Nationality | USA
Running Time | 76:30

Before legal action from the city's transport company resulted in the renaming of the band to Chicago, the band played across the United States as Chicago Transit Authority. Their specialty was fusing blues, jazz, and rock into a distinctive high-octane mix, and their debut required a double album of studio-recorded and live material to communicate this to the masses.

With a core rock quartet of Terry Kath (lead guitar/vocals), Robert Lamm (keyboards/vocals), Peter Cetera (bass/vocals), and Danny Seraphine on drums, along with the trio of Lee Loughnane (trumpet/vocals), James Pankow (trombone), and Walter Parazaider (woodwind/vocals), the group were able to craft both energized pop and leftfield rock concurrently.

The single releases from the album of "Does Anybody Really Know What Time It Is?," "Questions 67 And 68," and their cover of The Spencer Davis Group's "I'm A Man" were all enormously popular, while the avant-garde was also catered for with the experimentation of "Liberation," "Free Form Guitar," and the politically charged "Prologue" and "Someday." Indeed, these last two tracks had been recorded at the previous year's Democratic Party Conference in Chicago.

The extended version of "I'm A Man," with its lengthy percussion breakdown, was also employed to great effect by the groundbreaking New York DJ Francis Grasso, who was the first person to develop beat-mixing. Splicing together the drum break from this track and the erotic moans from Led Zeppelin's "Whole Lotta Love," he drove crowds wild and invented disco in the process. **CR**

"We enjoy making people happy with our music."

James Pankow, 1969

Track Listing

01	Introduction (Kath)	6:35
▶ 02	Does Anybody Really Know What Time It Is? (Lamm)	4:36
▶ 03	Beginnings (Lamm)	7:54
▶ 04	Questions 67 And 68 (Lamm)	5:02
05	Listen (Lamm)	3:21
06	Poem 58 (Lamm)	8:37
▶ 07	Free Form Guitar (Kath)	6:47
08	South California Purples (Lamm)	6:11
▶ 09	I'm A Man (Miller·Winwood)	7:39
▶ 10	Prologue (August 29, 1968) (Guercio)	0:57
11	Someday (August 29, 1968) (Lamm·Pankow)	4:13
▶ 12	Liberation (Pankow)	14:38

Fairport Convention
Unhalfbricking (1969)

Label | Island
Producer | Joe Boyd • Simon Nicol
Art Direction | Diogenic Attempts
Nationality | UK
Running Time | 39:45

Unhalfbricking was Fairport Convention's third LP and featured the legendary Richard Thompson on guitar, the now sadly deceased Sandy Denny as vocalist, Ashley Hutchings, the "John Mayall of UK folk rock," on bass, Simon Nicol, the longest serving Fairporter on guitar, and Martin Lamble on drums (who tragically died in a traffic accident before the album's release).

This album preceded *Liege & Lief*, the first Fairport LP to feature mostly traditional folk songs and, in many ways, *Unhalfbricking* was a transitional album. Bob Dylan was strongly represented. His "If You Gotta Go, Go Now" was translated into French—Fairport were well educated—and the result became a UK Top 30 hit single. They adopted an invigorating Cajun style on this and "Million Dollar Bash" (at the time an unreleased Dylan *Basement Tapes* composition). Denny's "Who Knows Where The Time Goes," surely her best known composition, was later covered by Judy Collins.

The longest track is the traditional song "A Sailor's Life," which Denny had been performing for some time in folk clubs. This jaw-dropping epic was recorded in a single take, and saw folk fiddler Dave Swarbrick duel at length with Thompson's guitar.

The enigmatic picture on the sleeve shows Sandy Denny's parents outside their garden—it is at once very English and slightly unsettling (the group are visible through the fence). And the odd title? A word Denny coined in the course of a word game the band were playing on the road. **JT**

The Youngbloods
Elephant Mountain (1969)

Label | RCA
Producer | Bob Cullen • Charles E. Daniels
Art Direction | Uncredited
Nationality | USA
Running Time | 39:07

Native New Yorkers, The Youngbloods were drawn to L.A. after their single "Get Together" became a local West Coast smash. Finding the lifestyle and attitude more in tune with their own, they based themselves in Inverness, California, flying down to L.A. for recording sessions that resulted in this album—though original guitarist Jerry Corbitt soon tired of the journeying (among other things) and quit, leaving the band as a trio. The band still had talent aplenty, however—notably multitalented Lowell "Banana" Levinger, who plays most instruments here, and Jesse Colin Young's mellifluous tenor.

The group's previous two albums had presented them as purveyors of the same sunny folk rock and bluesy pop as the Lovin' Spoonful. But their interest in jazz and dynamic subtleties marked them out from their new West Coast neighbors ("we were able to engage an audience without being real powerful, loud and crunchy, like Blue Cheer and that type of scene," Levinger observed in 2003).

Elephant Mountain makes its star appearance here on account of a slew of great songs (mostly by Young): "Quicksand," a mellow, melodious hymn featuring a string section; "Darkness, Darkness," a dark and desperate folky ballad featuring a gritty guitar solo; "Sunlight," a Latin excursion highlighted by a tender vocal; "Ride The Wind," a jazzy, earthy track of almost seven minutes' length; and the swinging instrumental "On Sir Francis Drake," highlighted by Levinger's electric piano. **GD**

Isaac Hayes
Hot Buttered Soul (1969)

Label | Stax
Producer | Al Bell • Allen Jones • Marvell Thomas
Art Direction | Honeya Thompson
Nationality | USA
Running Time | 45:23

Hot Buttered Soul was an early blueprint for how soul would exist in the Seventies—with its earthier forms marking a counterpoint to the newer, stone-cold funk rhythms of James Brown et al. The three-and-a-half-minute pop formula is abandoned in favor of two songs per LP side, while the opener is a mighty 12-minute cover of the staple "Walk On By," which, despite being written as a sorrowful ballad, oozes sex from every pore. In fact, this album, more than any before it, is a blatant attempt to produce "make-out" music—a style that would be copied through the 1970s and '80s to lesser effect by artists such as Barry White.

Hayes' backing band The Bar-Kays are the unspoken stars, providing groove after fluid groove for generations of hip hop and house producers to come. But the crowning moment is the cover of Jimmy Webb's "By The Time I Get To Phoenix," which features a breathtakingly audacious nine-minute spoken introduction, or "rap," in which Hayes paints the background story to the song's narrator—the song starts to climax after the quarter of an hour mark.

In recent years, Hayes' depiction of himself as sex god has been opened up to gentle ridicule (not least by himself as the voice of Chef in *South Park*). It is hard to imagine today just how important the sleeve art was at the time, with his shaven head, sunglasses indoors, and weighty gold chain on bare chest indicators of a raw, black sexuality unfettered by concerns of a mainstream (that is, white) audience. **JDo**

The Grateful Dead
Live / Dead (1969)

Label | Warner Bros.
Producer | Betty Cantor • Bob Matthews
Art Direction | Ed Thrasher
Nationality | USA
Running Time | 75:07

The Grateful Dead's first three studio albums never quite managed to capture what the kids were experiencing at places like the Fillmore West. Thankfully, the band was able to extend a proper invitation for the rest of the world to "get on the bus" with *Live/Dead*.

The concert album represented a watershed moment in pop history, especially for those who had not spent time in Haight-Ashbury or on Carnaby Street. *Live/Dead* contained just seven songs on two albums, compared to the 30 tracks that made up The Beatles' double-disc *White Album*. The tracks were culled from live performances in San Francisco during roughly the same time the group was recording *Aoxomoxoa*.

"Dark Star," the all-time favorite tune among Dead-Heads, was set to wax for the first time here and it has seldom been played better. The music swirls, bubbles, and seemingly loses direction countless times before erupting in Coltrane-worthy epiphanies. The Grateful Dead flesh out the skeleton version of "St. Stephen" found on *Aoxomoxoa* and then dive straight into an epic rendition of "The Eleven."

While many critics view the twin releases from 1970, *Workingman's Dead* and *American Beauty*, as the Dead's peak recordings, this first live album may well rank as the band's most influential work. Released well before tape-trading was common practice, *Live/Dead* would fully illustrate the power of long, improvised music and provide the blueprint for Phish and other jam bands to follow well into the twenty-first century. **JiH**

The Kinks | Arthur—Or The Decline And Fall Of The British Empire (1969)

Label | Pye
Producer | Ray Davies
Art Direction | The Kinks • Bob Lawrie
Nationality | UK
Running Time | 47:43

Much closer to the classic "concept album" than *Village Green*—from which some of its themes sprang—many could justifiably argue that Ray Davies' "opera" *Arthur…* is also a better album both in quality of composition and performance. *Arthur…* has so many high points it seems churlish to argue about its lows (which for some involves the simplistic satire of "She Bought a Hat Like Princess Marina"—but then, other diehard Kinks fans consider that the best song on the album!).

Arthur… is a soundtrack to an ill-fated British TV project on which Davies collaborated with dramatist and screenwriter Julian Mitchell. It's also a soundtrack to the dying days of the British Empire and its people. Arthur is an English everyman of the twentieth century, participating in gruesome wars and contributing a brother and a son to England's glorious dead. Now, he's about to lose another son, Derek, to Australia's "ten pound pom" post-war immigration program. Is he happy? Sometimes, The Kinks think he is—he's got his house, Shangri-La, and his generally cozy life. Sometimes they think he's an automaton without a clue.

Funny, concise, and infectious, Davies uses his unique music-hall calypso approach to great effect here. The best tracks are surely the thumping and bitter "Victoria" —covered by The Fall—and the bumptious "Shangri-La"—covered by Versus—as well as the hilarious and vigorous "Australia" and the sensational "Drivin'," both of which really ought to be covered if they haven't been already. It's a classic from beginning to end. **DN**

"Be like me and be unhappy."

Ray Davies, 1969

Track Listing

▶ 01	Victoria (Davies)	3:25
02	Yes Sir, No Sir (Davies)	3:42
03	Some Mother's Son (Davies)	3:22
04	Drivin' (Davies)	3:15
05	Brainwashed (Davies)	2:30
▶ 06	Australia (Davies)	6:40
▶ 07	Shangri-La (Davies)	5:17
08	Mr. Churchill Says (Davies)	4:40
09	She Bought A Hat Like Princess Marina (Davies)	3:05
10	Young And Innocent Days (Davies)	3:20
11	Nothing To Say (Davies)	3:07
12	Arthur (Davies)	5:20

King Crimson | In The Court Of The Crimson King (1969)

Label | Island
Producer | King Crimson
Art Direction | Uncredited
Nationality | UK
Running Time | 44:01

A vehicle for left-field guitar hero Robert Fripp, King Crimson are one of the major progressive rock acts, surviving countless personnel changes since their formation nearly four decades ago. The other original members were singer/bassist Greg Lake, drummer Michael Giles, lyricist Peter Sinfield, and keyboard/vibes/woodwind player Ian McDonald. This lineup only recorded one LP, but it remains their best-known work.

From the scary cover painting—best appreciated on gatefold vinyl—to the portentous lyrics, *In The Court Of The Crimson King* is a heavy-duty album. "21st Century Schizoid Man" sets the tone. It's perhaps the first alternative anthem, featuring a gargantuan main riff, squalling sax, and apocalyptic visions.

There's yet more doom in "Epitaph," a beautifully resigned ballad that finds Lake's plaintive voice supported by a rich array of textures. "Moonchild" is a spooky pastoral love song stretched out to epic length by an improvised ambient-jazz interlude, while the title track melds folky arabesques, bombastic drum rolls, and baroque flute to conjure its medieval scenario.

In The Court Of The Crimson King peaked at UK No. 5 and U.S. No. 28. Other landmarks include the colorful follow-up *In The Wake Of Poseidon*, 1973's electrifying freakout *Larks' Tongues In Aspic* and 1981's funky, Talking Heads-influenced *Discipline*. The band are revered by contemporary neo-prog stars Tool and The Mars Volta, while the ever-versatile Fripp has played on several iconic records by David Bowie and Brian Eno. **MA**

> "The band was never promoted. It was totally by word of mouth. It spread like smallpox!"
>
> Greg Lake, 2001

Track Listing

▶	01	21st Century Schizoid Man (Fripp•Giles•Lake•McDonald•Sinfield)	7:21
	02	I Talk To The Wind (McDonald•Sinfield)	6:08
▶	03	Epitaph (Fripp•Giles•Lake•McDonald•Sinfield)	8:52
▶	04	Moonchild (Fripp•Giles•Lake•McDonald•Sinfield)	12:15
▶	05	The Court Of The Crimson King (McDonald•Sinfield)	9:25

Leonard Cohen | Songs From A Room (1969)

Label | Columbia
Producer | Bob Johnston
Art Direction | Uncredited
Nationality | Canada
Running Time | 33:51

Columbia's A&R department probably did not expect Leonard Cohen to be very popular when they signed him, but after his 1968 debut album *The Songs Of Leonard Cohen* sold more than 100,000 copies, this unlikely star was firmly on the map. A world apart from the musicians filling the label's roster, he was in his mid-thirties at the time of his first success, having spent more than a decade writing poetry and novels.

For his sophomore effort, *Songs From A Room*, Cohen retreated further into the world of melancholia that characterized his work. Whereas his previous album had contained highlight tracks such as "Suzanne" (originally a 1966 hit for folkie Judy Collins) and "So Long Marianne," his second album was more low key.

Instead, Cohen crafted a collection of narrative efforts that enhanced his claims to be a troubadour to rival Bob Dylan. Throughout the ten tracks, he ruminates on the nature of friendship and more intimate relationships—"The Partisan," a song written during World War II, dissects the patriot's connection with his country, while "The Butcher" examines the relationship between father and son.

There is also a fair degree of ennui of a romantic nature. "Tonight will be fine," the Canadian crooner sings on the chorus of the closing track, though he has to add the rejoinder:"for a while." Nancy, a former muse, comes off no better on "Seems So Long Ago, Nancy," wherein her alleged promiscuity is bandied about.

While not a commercial success—a pattern largely unbroken until *I'm Your Man*—this lackadaisical triumph is an inspiration to the misanthrope in us all. **SJac**

> "Songwriting is basically like a courting process, like hunting women. Most of the time it's a hassle."

Leonard Cohen, 1972

Track Listing		
▶ 01 Bird On The Wire (Cohen)		3:23
▶ 02 Story Of Isaac (Cohen)		3:31
03 A Bunch Of Lonesome Heroes (Cohen)		3:10
04 The Partisan (Marly·Zaret)		3:20
▶ 05 Seems So Long Ago, Nancy (Cohen)		3:35
06 The Old Revolution (Cohen)		3:42
07 The Butcher (Cohen)		3:11
08 You Know Who I Am (Cohen)		3:24
▶ 09 Lady Midnight (Cohen)		2:50
10 Tonight Will Be Fine (Cohen)		3:45

Fairport Convention
Liege And Lief (1969)

Label | Island
Producer | Joe Boyd
Art Direction | R. Nicol • Fairport
Nationality | UK
Running Time | 41:01

Scott Walker
Scott 4 (1969)

Label | Philips
Producer | John Franz
Art Direction | John Constable
Nationality | USA
Running Time | 32:36

Fairport's second album, *Unhalfbricking* (1969), with singer Sandy Denny, Richard Thompson (lead guitar), Ashley "Tyger" Hutchings (bass), Simon Nicol (guitar), and Martin Lamble (drums), included an overwhelming reworking of the traditional song "A Sailor's Life" that effectively became the manifesto of English folk-rock. Tragedy then struck when the band's van overturned, killing Lamble and a young friend of Fairport, Jeannie Franklyn. Reeling from the disaster, the survivors regrouped with drummer Dave Mattacks and the folk circuit star Dave Swarbrick (violin and mandolin) for recording sessions at a country house in Hampshire, England. *Liege And Lief* was the result.

If *Unhalfbricking* had troubled the folk purists but delighted the growing folk-rock audience, *Liege And Lief* stirred further controversy—not least within the band itself. Building on "A Sailor's Life," Fairport were now singing and playing traditional dances and ballads with electric instruments—notably on the legendary version of the murder ballad "Matty Groves" featuring Richard Thompson's superlative guitar work. They were also writing quality original songs too, such as "Farewell, Farewell" and "Crazy Man Michael." However, Hutchings' insistence on traditional material over originals irked Sandy Denny—the most beautiful voice in contemporary British rock, and much admired by Led Zeppelin among others. Both she and Hutchings parted from Fairport Convention soon after *Liege and Lief*, leaving a unique legacy. **GSu**

After his fourth solo album was a commercial failure, the naturally shy Scott Walker gave up writing for much of the next decade and became a virtual recluse. A shame, because *Scott 4* is a breathtaking album, Walker's first entirely self-composed work. The orchestral bombast that characterized his previous solo albums is stripped back, its sparse feel perfectly complementing his rich baritone. Opener "The Seventh Seal" marries Ennio Morricone-influenced orchestral textures to a narrative based on the film of the same name by Ingmar Bergman, Walker the Europhile's favorite director.

"The Old Man's Back Again" sees Walker, an avowed socialist, warning of the spectre of Stalinism in the Eastern bloc, following Russia's 1968 invasion of Czechoslovakia—over a funky bassline. The rousing "Get Behind Me" and the passionate "Duchess" explore Walker's growing interest in soul and country music respectively, while his emotional vocal conveys haunting vulnerability on "The World's Strongest Man." "Hero Of The War" cynically and intelligently parodies the growth of militarism. "Boy Child" is a meditation on innocence set to a spine-tingling arrangement.

The record elicited mixed and confused reactions on release and was deleted just weeks later. Yet it was to receive critical re-evaluation thanks to its influence on the likes of David Bowie, Nick Cave, Mark Almond, and The Divine Comedy's Neil Hannon. Now rightfully reissued, its lush textures and extraordinary breadth of scope will astound many generations to come. **CSh**

The Stooges
The Stooges (1969)

Label | Elektra
Producer | John Cale
Art Direction | William S. Harvey
Nationality | USA
Running Time | 34:33

A town with a proud musical heritage, by the late 1960s Detroit was synonymous with the sweet soul pioneered by Berry Gordy's Motown label. This all changed in 1969 with The Stooges' eponymous debut album, a corrosive swell of skirling guitars and primeval howls from frontman Iggy Stooge (as he was then known).

The Stooges were picked up by Elektra as an afterthought—A&R man Danny Fields came to sign garage-rockers MC5, but was so impressed by The Stooges' live performances that he took a chance on them as well. In June 1969 the band headed to New York to produce their debut with John Cale (ex-Velvet Underground). The only problem was a lack of songs. Despite their live heroics, the band only had three songs ready, so label boss Jac Holzman sent them to a hotel room with a two-day ultimatum to fill out the album.

What the band emerged with was a collection of brilliant curios, which were neither full-on garage rock, nor out-and-out dirge. Cale introduced restraint to songs such as "1969," which threatens to explode but is shepherded away from wig-out territory, and to "I Wanna Be Your Dog," where the powerful guitar assault is kept firmly on a leash. Cale also plays viola on "We Will Fall," a ten-minute slab of druggy stupor straight from the Velvets' canon, for Iggy's unmistakable voice.

The album became iconic, as Iggy metamorphosed from Stooge to Pop, and although laughingly referred to by Fields as a "commercial curio," it helped lay the ground for the coming punk explosion. **SJac**

Alexander Spence
Oar (1969)

Label | Columbia
Producer | Alexander Spence
Art Direction | Lloyd Ziff
Nationality | USA
Running Time | 44:03

By 1968, Alexander "Skip" Spence's mental stability was wavering. After he used an axe to try and break into the hotel room of fellow Moby Grape band members Don Stevenson and Jerry Miller, Spence was committed to Bellevue mental hospital for six months.

Following his release, he took a $1,000 advance from Columbia, bought a motorcycle, and rode it down to Nashville, where he set about recording the songs that he had written in Bellevue. There is nothing else quite like them in rock.

Oar was recorded at low volume; the sound is intimate—and all the more unsettling for it. The music has an improvised quality, and the accompaniment—all by Spence—is sparse. Opener "Little Hands" seems to grow in energy as it continues, driven by big-top-style drum rolls. "Cripple Creek," "Weighted Down (The Prison Song)," and "Broken Heart" are ghostly country music, graced by Spence's deep, somnolent baritone.

Off-kilter humor and wordplay emerge in flashes. There are darker waters here, though. "Books Of Moses" sets a resonant, bluesy guitar and rich vocals against rumbles of thunder and a persistent, metallic hammering. The vocal on "Diana" is fragility itself, while "War In Peace," with its splintered guitar, cymbal washes, and almost wordless singing is more an eerie collection of aural textures than a song. Closer "Grey/Afro" threatens to break down completely, the drums busy but anarchic. Yet, like the rest of this album, the track is also beguilingly mesmeric. **RD**

Frank Zappa | Hot Rats (1969)

Label | Bizarre/Reprise
Producer | Frank Zappa
Art Direction | Cal Schenkel
Nationality | USA
Running Time | 47:05

By 1969 Zappa was a frustrated man. His records with the Mothers Of Invention did not sell well and paying his group a salary all year round had left a big dent in his pocket. After witnessing jazz legend Duke Ellington begging his record label for a ten-dollar advance, Zappa broke up the band.

He retreated into the studio to record *Hot Rats* with a new group of musicians—including Ian Underwood, who had first appeared on *Uncle Meat* and whose technical ability Zappa could rely upon; old friend Don "Captain Beefheart" Van Vliet; and violinists Don "Sugarcane" Harris and Jean-Luc Ponty.

An entirely instrumental album, apart from Beefheart's vocal on "Willie the Pimp," *Hot Rats* is all about virtuoso playing, and is heavily jazz influenced. "Peaches En Regalia" has become a staple of Zappa compilations and was a live favorite for the next 20 years, quirky and uplifting, sax, organs, and Zappa on octave bass. By contrast, "Willie The Pimp" digs a rough blues mine while Beefheart growls, before Zappa's seven-minute guitar solo blows your head off. "Son Of Mr. Green Genes" expands on the blueprint of "Green Genes" from *Uncle Meat*, with jazzoid jamming. "Little Umbrellas" is a more laidback affair, plinky and odd, while "The Gumbo Variations" is a monster blues jam, on which Underwood, Zappa, and Harris all let rip.

It gave him a No. 9 UK hit (U.S. No. 173), and provided rock with one of its most famous covers: Christine Frka, a member of Zappa-approved groupies GTOs (Girls Together Outrageously), lurking in the empty lilypond of a Beverly Hills mansion. **MBI**

> "The very idea! An instrumental album, except for one vocal cut—and that had to feature Captain Beefheart! ...Why are you wasting America's precious time with this, you asshole!"
>
> Frank Zappa, 1989

Track Listing		
▶ 01 Peaches En Regalia (Zappa)		3:37
▶ 02 Willie The Pimp (Zappa)		9:16
03 Son Of Mr Green Genes (Zappa)		8:58
04 Little Umbrellas (Zappa)		3:04
▶ 05 The Gumbo Variations (Zappa)		16:55
06 It Must Be A Camel (Zappa)		5:15

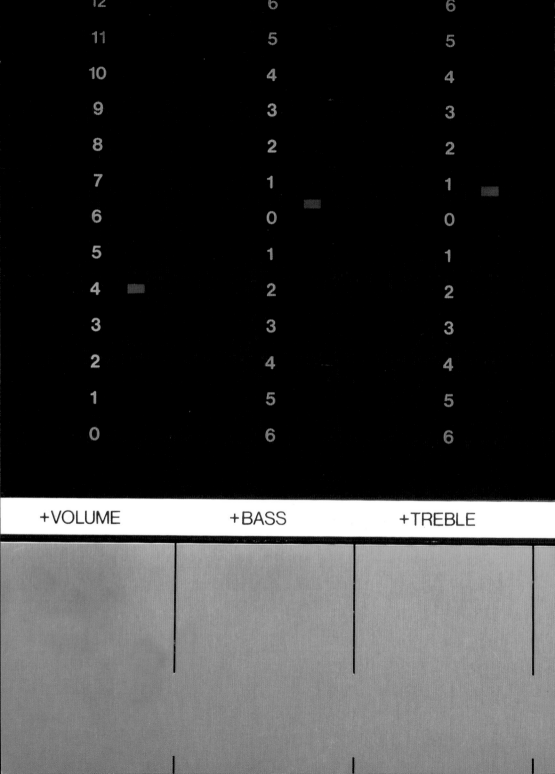

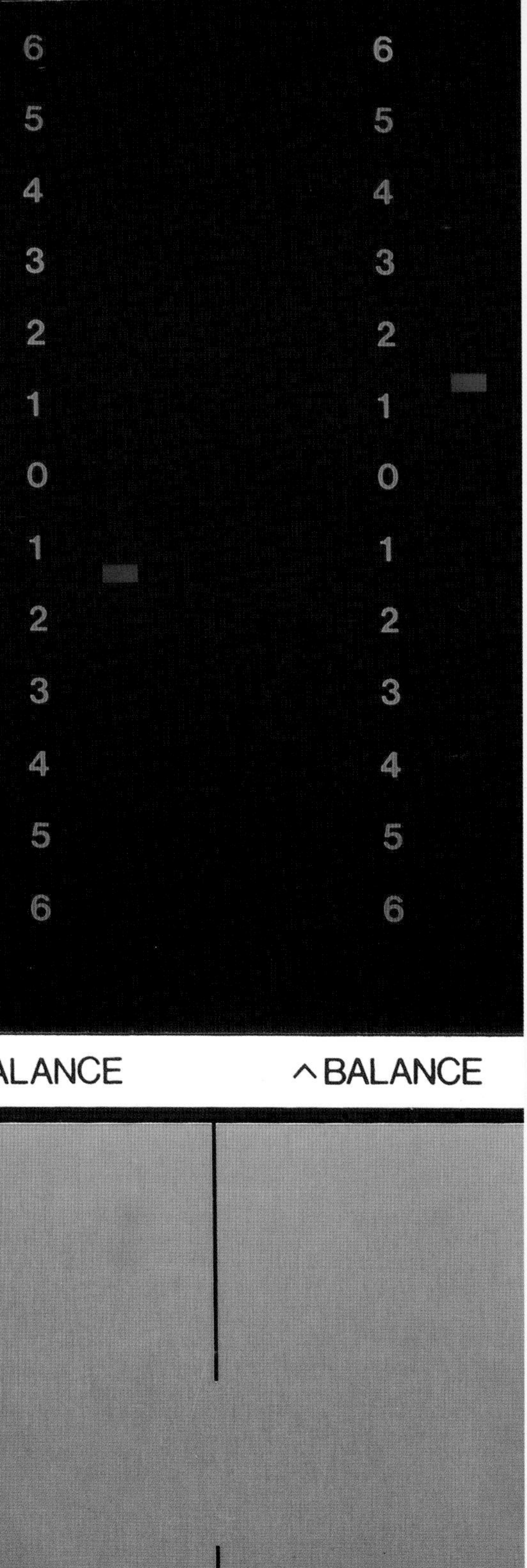

6   6

5   5   • U.S. combat troops leave Vietnam

4   4   • Nixon resigns over Watergate

3   3   • First test-tube baby born

2   2   • Rubik's Cube invented

1   1   • First email sent

0   0

1   1

2   2

3   3

4   4

5   5

6   6

LANCE   ∧BALANCE

1970s

Creedence Clearwater Revival
Cosmo's Factory (1970)

Label | Fantasy
Producer | John Fogerty
Art Direction | Bob Fogerty
Nationality | USA
Running Time | 42:40

Creedence Clearwater Revival released six essential albums in just two and a half years, all bashed out quick, nothing fancy, just pure and catchy, pop-styled rock 'n' roll. This was their fifth, and it topped the U.S. album charts for nine consecutive weeks.

It is quintessential Creedence. A glorious distillation of their distinctive, Southern-styled mix of choogling swamp boogie and prime, blistering pop. Eschewing the druggy psychedelic excesses of many of their San Francisco peers, the album includes both sides of their three recent hit singles, to which they added covers of songs made famous by Elvis Presley, Roy Orbison, and Bo Diddley—plus a stubbornly groovesome, extended jam of "I Heard It Through The Grapevine." Elsewhere, "Travelin' Band" tips its hat to Little Richard, while Vietnam was the darker source of inspiration for "Who'll Stop The Rain" and "Run Through The Jungle."

John Fogerty, the man with the grittiest, growliest voice in rock 'n' roll, once again dominates: he writes, he produces, and he sings, as well as playing guitar, saxophone, and keyboards. But within the rest of the band, simmering resentments were beginning to boil. This was to be their last major success. The cover shot was taken in their warehouse/office/rehearsal room (at 1230 Fifth Street, Berkeley), a place they had dubbed "Cosmo's Factory." John's brother Tom (who later quit, foreshadowing the end for the band) lies back, resting his feet on a sign that reads, "Lean, clean, and bluesy." A simple recipe for such enduring greatness. **RF**

"It may actually be our best record."

John Fogerty, 1997

Track Listing	
01 **Ramble Tamble** (Fogerty)	7:10
02 **Before You Accuse Me** (McDaniels)	3:26
03 **Travelin' Band** (Fogerty)	2:09
04 **Ooby Dooby** (Moore · Penner)	2:07
▶ 05 **Lookin' Out My Back Door** (Fogerty)	2:33
▶ 06 **Run Through The Jungle** (Fogerty)	3:07
▶ 07 **Up Around The Bend** (Fogerty)	2:42
08 **My Baby Left Me** (Crudup)	2:19
▶ 09 **Who'll Stop The Rain** (Fogerty)	2:29
10 **I Heard It Through The Grapevine** (Strong · Whitfield)	11:04
▶ 11 **Long As I Can See The Light** (Fogerty)	3:34

Derek And The Dominos
Layla And Other Assorted Love Songs (1970)

Label | Polydor
Producer | Tom Dowd • The Dominos
Art Direction | Frandsen de Schonberg
Nationality | UK • USA
Running Time | 76:58

An almost fictitious group ended up making a double vinyl album that, though it bombed at the time, has since been re-evaluated as a rock classic thanks to its title track's single success. The Derek in question was Eric Clapton who, after stints with The Yardbirds, John Mayall's Bluesbreakers, Cream, and (briefly) Blind Faith, recruited a band and created this, his first solo gem.

Behind said Derek, the Dominos featured three Americans: keyboardist Bobby Whitlock, bassist Carl Radle, and drummer Jim Gordon, all ex-members of Delaney and Bonnie and Friends, a loose-knit aggregation with which Clapton had guested. Most of the songs here resulted from a series of relaxed, informal jams, and all concerned play with refreshing economy.

Clapton's masterstroke was recruiting Duane Allman as a guest player: Allman's slide guitar on the title track screamed like a train coming off the rails over one of rock's most memorable riffs. Even hard-bitten producer Tom Dowd was impressed. "When I finished," he revealed, "I walked out of the studio and said, 'That's the best goddamn record I've made in ten years.'" Having peaked at No. 7 first time out, "Layla" climbed three places higher when reissued exactly ten years on.

That song of unrequited love was inspired by Patti Boyd, the wife of Clapton's best friend, George Harrison. Clapton channeled his frustrated passion into all the music on the album, offering energetic reworkings of blues classics by artists from Big Bill Broonzy to Hendrix that are now classics in their own right. **MH**

Track Listing

	01	**I Looked Away** (Clapton • Whitlock)	3:06
▶	02	**Bell Bottom Blues** (Clapton)	5:03
	03	**Keep On Growing** (Clapton • Whitlock)	6:22
	04	**Nobody Knows You When You're Down And Out** (Clapton • Whitlock)	4:59
	05	**I Am Yours** (Clapton • Nizami)	3:34
	06	**Anyday** (Clapton • Whitlock)	6:37
	07	**Key To The Highway** (Broonzy • Segar)	9:40
	08	**Tell The Truth** (Clapton • Whitlock)	6:40
	09	**Why Does Love Got To Be So Sad?** (Clapton • Whitlock)	4:43
	10	**Have You Ever Loved A Woman** (Myers)	6:55
▶	11	**Little Wing** (Hendrix)	5:34
	12	**It's Too Late** (Willis)	3:51
▶	13	**Layla** (Clapton • Gordon)	7:05
▶	14	**Thorn Tree In The Garden** (Whitlock)	2:49

Miles Davis | Bitches Brew (1970)

Label | Columbia
Producer | Teo Macero
Art Direction | Uncredited
Nationality | USA
Running Time | 93:54

Recording sessions for *Bitches Brew* began at 8 a.m. on August 18, 1969, a few hours after Jimi Hendrix had demolished "The Star Spangled Banner" at Woodstock, and it is Hendrix's incendiary voice that haunts this double album. Miles wanted to re-create the loose-limbed jam sessions of *Electric Ladyland* but, like the most interesting homages, *Bitches Brew* sounds nothing like its source. Nor does it resemble the "jazz-rock" that it pioneered. The backbeats are relatively orthodox—whipcrack rimshots, rumbling kick drums, and rubbery basslines borrowed from Sly and the Family Stone. Everything else is from another planet.

The sheer density of the music is often symphonic. At some points there are three keyboards—Chick Corea, Larry Young, and Joe Zawinul—all playing clashing, dissonant chord clusters. There are two bassists—Ron Carter and Dave Holland—set against the serpentine baritone voicings of Benny Maupin's bass clarinet. Up to three kit drummers and another three percussionists lay down hypnotic grooves that would hook in the Grateful Dead fans.

Soaring over the top is the quiet storm of Miles' Harmon-muted horn, Wayne Shorter's granite-hard soprano sax, and the finely controlled chaos of John McLaughlin's guitar. All improvised freely, borrowing from modal jazz, free improv, and Indo-Arabic themes.

Bitches Brew sold half a million copies within a year and made Miles "relevant" in a way that he had not been in more than a decade. He had reclaimed his crown as the king of jazz, something he retained until his death 20 years later. **JLe**

> "In high school I was best in music class on the trumpet, but the prizes went to the boys with blue eyes. I made up my mind to outdo anybody white on my horn."
>
> **Miles Davis, 1962**

Track Listing

	01	**Pharaoh's Dance** (Zawinul)	20:05
	02	**Bitches Brew** (Davis)	26:58
	03	**Spanish Key** (Davis)	17:32
	04	**John McLaughlin** (Davis)	4:22
▶	05	**Miles Runs The Voodoo Down** (Davis)	14:01
▶	06	**Sanctuary** (Shorter)	10:56

Spirit | Twelve Dreams Of Dr. Sardonicus (1970)

Label | Epic
Producer | David Briggs
Art Direction | John Locke • Bruce McCauley
Nationality | USA
Running Time | 38:50

By 1970 southern California's Spirit had recorded three innovative LPs, but their synthesis of rock, classical, and jazz had thus far awoken little interest. Powerful West Coast impresario Lou Adler, who had signed the band to his label Ode in 1968, abandoned them. To top it all, a split had arisen in the camp, between Spirit's main creative forces—guitar whiz Randy California (who had played with and learned from Jimi Hendrix when both were in the Blue Flames) and singer Jay Ferguson. California championed experiment; Ferguson was after straightforward commerciality.

Feelings could not have been worse when Spirit recorded *Twelve Dreams Of Dr. Sardonicus*. Luckily, David Briggs, who worked with Neil Young, managed to harness all the animosity into Spirit's masterwork. The album was enriched by meaty horn arrangements ("Morning Will Come"), imaginative vocal harmonies ("Nothin' To Hide"), and a structured approach to psychedelic studio trickery such as stereo panning and tapes run backward. The band experimented with the then new Moog on "Love Has Found A Way" and "Space Child" and unveiled perfect rock singles in "Mr. Skin" and the funky "Animal Zoo"— still light years ahead of their time. It also spawned a classic FM single, the acoustic treat "Nature's Way."

After a New Year's Eve concert at Fillmore East that year, the band split; the album finally went platinum five years later, a belated reward for the superb job done by Briggs and Spirit's original line-up. Oh, and "Dr. Sardonicus?" It is the nickname Spirit coined for the mixing desk at the studio. **JG**

"Spirit will eventually get into a total environmental field."

Ed Cassidy, 1971

Track Listing

01	**Prelude—Nothin' To Hide** (California)	3:41
▶ 02	**Nature's Way** (California)	2:30
▶ 03	**Animal Zoo** (Ferguson)	3:20
04	**Love Has Found A Way** (California • Locke)	2:42
05	**Why Can't I Be Free** (California)	1:03
▶ 06	**Mr. Skin** (Ferguson)	3:50
▶ 07	**Space Child** (Locke)	3:26
08	**When I Touch You** (Ferguson)	5:35
09	**Street Worm** (Ferguson)	3:40
▶ 10	**Life Has Just Begun** (California)	3:22
11	**Morning Will Come** (California)	2:58
12	**Soldier** (California)	2:43

Black Sabbath
Black Sabbath (1970)

Label | Warner Bros.
Producer | Various
Art Direction | Uncredited
Nationality | UK
Running Time | 40:16

On this list for its enormous influence rather than its scintillating musical qualities, Black Sabbath's debut album is as weighty in reputation as it is in sonic depth. With its opening, eponymous song routinely hailed as the unholy-trinity anthem ("Black Sabbath" on *Black Sabbath* by Black Sabbath) that kickstarted heavy metal, the dark, dark sleeve art and the sludgy production seeping all over the basic, bludgeoning songs, the record still sounds supremely evil today. In reality, as Messrs. Osbourne, Iommi, Butler, and Ward have explained on many occasions, the album sounds grim because they recorded it in two days with a tiny budget—and what is more, recorded it as a live band, volume peaks and all. Guitarist Tony Iommi, his fretting fingers infamously disfigured in an industrial accident, tuned his guitar down half a step to E flat and in doing so accentuated the song's crushing sound even further. The then-scary, now-laughable lyrics dealing with death and darkness only added to the brew.

While the two extended song suites keep the album from sounding mundane—and prove that the musicians had what it took to be inventive—it is the individual songs that reveal most to the listener. Where "Black Sabbath" is all about grime and graveyard dirt, "N.I.B." has stood the test of time and remains a Sabbath live staple for its subtler qualities.

Drink it all in, the gloomy atmosphere and the dark introspection: this is, after all, the world's first heavy metal record. **JM**

The Doors
Morrison Hotel (1970)

Label | Elektra
Producer | Paul A. Rothchild
Art Direction | Gary Burden
Nationality | USA
Running Time | 37:24

Generally referred to as *Morrison Hotel*, although its title according to the U.S. chart "bible" is *Morrison Hotel/Hard Rock Café*, this was the fifth album by The Doors in three years. (Keyboardist Ray Manzarek had spotted the hotel in downtown L.A. during a drive around town with his wife.) The group was under pressure because vocalist and USP Jim Morrison was due in court to answer obscenity charges. Indeed, they had recorded several shows that could become a live album if Morrison received a jail term, but the U.S. legal system was so slow that there was time for this new studio release.

The album's predecessor, *The Soft Parade*, had been regarded as disappointingly unchallenging. Perhaps as a result, this was a muscular R&B-inspired offering, betraying the group's roots. The chugging, ballsy "Roadhouse Blues" makes most immediate impact, featuring hitmaker Lonnie Mack on bass and The Lovin' Spoonful's John Sebastian ("G Puglese") on harmonica. (It was subsequently covered by acts as diverse as Blue Öyster Cult and Frankie Goes To Hollywood.) The twitchy funk of "Peace Frog" echoes the social unrest of the time, and namedrops New Haven, where Morrison had once been arrested onstage. The clattering, keyboard driven "You Make Me Real" features Morrison at his bawling best; elsewhere, he croons smoothly through "Blue Sunday," the sinuous "The Spy," and "Indian Summer," a beautiful ballad whose undulating bassline recalls Doors magnum opus "The End." The Doors were back on course again. **JT**

The Carpenters
Close To You (1970)

Label | A&M
Producer | Jack Daugherty
Art Direction | Tom Wilkes
Nationality | USA
Running Time | 36:75

Pop culture's romantic view of early 1970s U.S. teen culture is of radicalized, long-haired youths listening to The Stooges and fighting the Nixon administration. In reality, most looked like, and listened to, The Carpenters.

Close To You was The Carpenters' second album, but the first to be a hit. Their recording of the Bacharach/David song "(They Long To Be) Close To You" had topped the U.S. charts for four weeks, going on to become a huge international success. *Close To You* was assembled quickly thereafter, drawing largely on songs that Karen (vocals and drums) and Richard (piano) had played in clubs and cocktail bars over the previous four years. Karen's assured, bell-like voice invests covers of classics by Tim Hardin and Bacharach/David with a timeless innocence, complemented by her brother's clean, inventive arrangements. "We've Only Just Begun," another pop gem, soared to No. 2 Stateside (bizarrely, this wide-eyed love song was originally written for a bank's TV ad). The album spent more than a year in the U.S. charts; Carpenter-mania was born.

The Carpenters' albums have always sold well, putting them in the exclusive club of artists who have sold more than 100 million units. Beneath the pop sheen though, melancholy pervades much of their work (made all the more poignant by Karen Carpenter's death in 1983, from a heart attack brought on by years of anorexia). Critics tended to ignore The Carpenters. Not that this mattered. Their fans were not the types who bothered with the fashion-oriented music press. **GC**

Stephen Stills
Stephen Stills (1970)

Label | Atlantic
Producer | Bill Halverson • Stephen Stills
Art Direction | Gary Burden
Nationality | USA
Running Time | 38:19

He had nothing to prove, but did it anyway. A superstar of late Sixties California soft rock, Stills was already familiar with success by the time his first solo album came out. While in Buffalo Springfield he wrote the classic counterculture anthem "For What is Worth"; by 1970 he was a million-seller. At 25, the Texas-born musician had enjoyed a golden age few could touch.

However, critics underrated Stills in comparison with comrades Neil Young, David Crosby, and David Nash. With this album, he shut them all up.

Backed by an all-star lineup—including Jimi Hendrix (to whom the album is dedicated), Eric Clapton, Booker T., Crosby, Rita Coolidge, Nash, John Sebastian, and Cass Elliot—Stills' raspy voice and strumming guitar injects the standard singer-songwriter formula with his idiosyncratic combination of grit and melancholy. The album fuses CSN&Y high harmonies ("Do for The Others"), gospel-soaked R&B in the Leon Russell/Joe Cocker school (the splendorous "Church"), Latin rhythms (the passionately driven single "Love The One You're With," a radio favorite), folk blues (electric in "Go Back Home," acoustic in the live track "Black Queen"), and hard rock (funky, driven "Old Times Good Times"). A reflective quality is never far below the surface, though.

Ten superb songs sketch a soulful journey through a deeply personal Ecclesiastes of love, and the lack of it. With his debut album, Stephen Stills manages to imprint his own strong and lyrical signature on a vibrant mosaic of American music. **JG**

John Lennon
John Lennon / Plastic Ono Band (1970)

Label | Apple
Producer | John Lennon • Yoko Ono • Phil Spector
Art Direction | Dan Richter
Nationality | UK
Running Time | 39:41

Free, or so he thought, of The Beatles, John Lennon headed for New York with Yoko Ono to participate in primal scream therapy. Forced to leave the country before any progress was made, they ended up back at home in Britain, where Lennon started writing songs that would close the curtain not only on the 1960s but also on his past, all 30 years of it. For John, this was not just 1970, this was Year Zero.

So "Mother" begins with the sound of a church bell and continues with the son saying goodbye. "Hold On" bids farewell to what had been the womb of his band, with Lennon now out in the world with only Ono for support. And "I Found Out" simply underlines the fact that he no longer believes in 1960s idealism ("I seen through religion from Jesus to Paul"). If your favorite Beatles songs were "You've Got To Hide Your Love Away" or "Help!," you would probably find this the most appealing solo Fab album.

Among the self-analysis, two songs stand out as coming from a place The Beatles could never have approached. "Working Class Hero," with its Class-A swearing, and "God," which renounces as many of the past 30 years' cultural landmarks (Hitler, Kennedy, yoga, even Beatles) as could fit in four minutes. It closes with the final farewell: "I was the walrus but now I'm John." The dream, in the form of everything The Beatles had represented, was over, and once he had got it off his chest, you felt happy for him. Now he would start writing pop songs again, wouldn't he? **DH**

"He was up and happy ... but very emotional, crying a lot."

Klaus Voorman, 2000

Track Listing

▶ 01 **Mother** (Lennon)		5:36
02 **Hold On** (Lennon)		1:53
▶ 03 **I Found Out** (Lennon)		3:37
▶ 04 **Working Class Hero** (Lennon)		3:50
▶ 05 **Isolation** (Lennon)		2:53
06 **Remember** (Lennon)		4:36
07 **Love** (Lennon)		3:24
08 **Well, Well, Well** (Lennon)		5:59
09 **Look At Me** (Lennon)		2:54
▶ 10 **God** (Lennon)		4:10
11 **My Mummy's Dead** (Lennon)		0:49

Crosby, Stills, Nash, And Young
Déjà Vu (1970)

Label | Atlantic
Producer | Crosby, Stills, Nash, And Young
Art Direction | Gary Burden
Nationality | Canada • USA
Running Time | 35:34

For their sophomore release, David Crosby (ex-Byrds), Stephen Stills (ex-Buffalo Springfield), and Graham Nash (ex-Hollies) called on the help of fellow Buffalo Springfield alumnus Neil Young, who had just released *After The Gold Rush*, one of his best loved works.

The album took nearly 800 hours to record, and circumstances were less than auspicious. Crosby's girlfriend Christine Hinton had died in a car accident in September 1969—he remained grief-stricken and took solace in heroin; cocaine and booze abounded during recording; the four musicians squabbled—the moody Young was often absent—and Nash was forced to play peacemaker. Somehow they created a masterpiece, one that encapsulates the spirit of American West Coast culture in the early Seventies.

"Carry On"—like "Suite: Judy Blues" from CSN's 1969 debut—is a shape-shifting beauty featuring spine-tingling harmonies, and is surely one of the best songs to cure a Sunday morning hangover. "Our House" and "Teach Your Children" demonstrate Nash's gift for simple, catchy melody. "Almost Cut My Hair" is Crosby at his most antiauthoritarian, delivering a throaty vocal at odds with his trademark pure harmonies. The majestic, spare "Helpless" reflects Young's response to the wide open spaces of his Canadian homeland, while "Country Girl" is a stunning piece with an ambitious arrangement.

With peerless vocals, dynamic musicianship, and top-notch songwriting, little wonder the album catapulted to No. 1 in the United States. **LPG**

> ## "We used to believe we could change the world."
>
> Graham Nash, 2002

Track Listing

▶ 01	**Carry On** (Stills)	4:25
02	**Teach Your Children** (Nash)	2:53
▶ 03	**Almost Cut My Hair** (Crosby)	4:25
▶ 04	**Helpless** (Young)	3:30
05	**Woodstock** (Mitchell)	3:52
06	**Déjà Vu** (Crosby)	4:10
07	**Our House** (Nash)	2:59
08	**4+20** (Stills)	1:55
▶ 09	**Country Girl** (Young)	5:05
	a) **Whiskey Boot Hill**	
	b) **Down, Down, Down**	
	c) **Country Girl (I Think You Are Pretty)**	
10	**Everybody I Love You** (Stills·Young)	2:20

Black Sabbath | Paranoid (1970)

Label | Vertigo
Producer | Rodger Bain
Art Direction | Keef
Nationality | UK
Running Time | 42:13

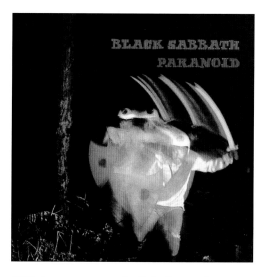

Black Sabbath had already raised eyebrows in their native England with their self-titled debut: a seismic re-routing of the blues that, along with the first two Led Zeppelin classics, helped give birth to a new form of rock 'n' roll: heavy metal.

In terms of songwriting, the Birmingham quartet's second LP was a quantum leap. Leviathan protest number "War Pigs" is one of the all-time great intros, capturing the embittered mood of Western youth as the U.S. government fought its bloody campaign in Vietnam. All the Sabbath trademarks are here: Ozzy Osbourne's eerie, ominous wail; supple, tempo-shifting dynamics from drummer Bill Ward and bassist/lyricist Geezer Butler; and, most recognizably, the hulking presence of guitar hero and lord of the riff, Tony Iommi.

The iconic title track comes next, a proto-punk blast of alienation that remains Black Sabbath's signature anthem—Ozzy and Iommi even performed it at Queen Elizabeth II's Golden Jubilee celebrations in London in 2002. Ghostly ballad "Planet Caravan" displays an oft-overlooked tender side, while lumbering sci-fi drama "Iron Man" seems to anticipate the entire grunge movement. The final four tracks are less well known, but just as imposing. Heroin nightmare "Hand Of Doom" is especially apt, helping consolidate Sabbath's position as the darkest force in Seventies music.

Paranoid broke them in America, reaching No. 12 on the U.S. chart. Its songs have been covered by acts as diverse as Pantera and The Cardigans; its influence on the heavier end of the rock spectrum, from Nirvana to Queens Of The Stone Age, is incalculable. **MA**

> "This country is frightening for the younger generation because it's at war."
>
> Ozzy Osbourne, 1972

Track Listing

▶	01	**War Pigs** (Butler·Iommi·Osbourne·Ward)	8:49
▶	02	**Paranoid** (Butler·Iommi·Osbourne·Ward)	2:45
▶	03	**Planet Caravan** (Butler·Iommi·Osbourne·Ward)	4:26
▶	04	**Iron Man** (Butler·Iommi·Osbourne·Ward)	5:47
	05	**Electric Funeral** (Butler·Iommi·Osbourne·Ward)	4:46
▶	06	**Hand Of Doom** (Butler·Iommi·Osbourne·Ward)	7:06
	07	**Rat Salad** (Butler·Iommi·Osbourne·Ward)	2:27
	08	**Fairies Wear Boots** (Butler·Iommi·Osbourne·Ward)	6:07

Neil Young
After The Gold Rush (1970)

Label | Reprise
Producer | David Briggs • Neil Young
Art Direction | Gary Burden
Nationality | Canada
Running Time | 33:41

Led Zeppelin
Led Zeppelin III (1970)

Label | Atlantic
Producer | Jimmy Page
Art Direction | Zacron
Nationality | UK
Running Time | 43:01

A starkly poignant record, *After The Gold Rush* contains some of Neil Young's most love-lorn lyrics. The cover photograph sums up the album's sentiment—a solarized photograph of the glowering singer-songwriter walking in a near-deserted street.

Young's latest songs—he had, until recently, been hard at work on the Crosby, Stills, Nash, & Young album, *Déjà Vu*—indicate a more introspective approach. Songs like "Tell Me Why," "Only Love Can Break Your Heart," and "Don't Let It Bring You Down" all go some way to solidify his reputation as a hopeless romantic. The energy and fire of his electric guitar playing emerges only twice, notably on the corrosive (and controversial) "Southern Man."

In patenting the late night feel of the record, *After The Gold Rush* was recorded with Young's latest find—a young singer-songwriter and multi-instrumentalist named Nils Lofgren, whose guitar playing and piano work would elevate this collection of songs to among the finest ever written by Neil Young. The beautifully evocative title track, for instance, a near-mystical eulogy to a vanished and fast vanishing America, has now become a cornerstone of Young's live set.

The record would pave the way, two years later, for *Harvest*, regarded by many as one of the most influential country-rock albums ever produced. Until then, though, *After The Gold Rush*, an altogether more sanguine collection of songs, would remain the highpoint of Young's career. **BW**

The third Led Zeppelin album entered the UK chart at the top, a week after starting its four-week run atop the U.S. chart, and was certified triple platinum. The inventive cover artwork housed a picture-packed wheel, which could be turned to present different images through cut-away windows in the outer sleeve.

The thunderous "Immigrant Song" became the group's second U.S. Top 20 single, but was not released as a single in the UK, where the group did not release any singles before 1997. The first side of the album delivered the expected high-octane hard rock, but the striking flip-side was acoustic led, Page and Plant having been particularly inspired by the music of folk artists Bert Jansch, John Fahey, and Davy Graham. "Gallows Pole" features pretty banjo playing alongside John Bonham's thumping drums, while "Bron-Y-Aur Stomp" is highlighted by flights of nifty acoustic guitar picking. (The track is named after a cottage in North Wales owned by friends of Plant's parents, where Page and Plant worked on some of the album's material.)

Six of the tracks were recorded with a mobile studio in the grounds of a country house in Hampshire, including "Tangerine," its eloquent 12-string passages an early blueprint for "Stairway To Heaven," though the West Coast harmonies and country licks were atypical of Zep. "Hats Off To (Roy) Harper," dominated by shimmering slide guitar, is Page's tribute to the veteran English folk singer. *Led Zeppelin III* showed us a band as capable of subtlety as of heavy metal thunder. **JT**

Deep Purple
In Rock (1970)

Label | Harvest
Producer | Deep Purple
Art Direction | Edwards Coletta
Nationality | UK
Running Time | 41:46

Van Morrison
Moondance (1970)

Label | Warner Bros.
Producer | Van Morrison
Art Direction | Bob Cato
Nationality | UK
Running Time | 39:14

A hard rock milestone, Purple's fifth set appeared as another Middle Eastern war loomed in mid-1970. It was an apt climate to unleash what *Rolling Stone* summarized as "a dynamic, frenzied work, sounding like the MC5"—though there is far more to it than that.

The Mount Rushmoresque-sleeved set was prepped at a hall in west London by Purple's soon-to-be classic *Mark II* lineup: guitarist Ritchie Blackmore, keyboardist Jon Lord, and drummer Ian Paice, with new boys Ian Gillan on vocals and Roger Glover on bass.

The results put the console meters (manned by future Iron Maiden producer Martin Birch) permanently in the red. The material had progressive tendencies; notably "Flight Of The Rat," with Paice's Indian-sounding drums and Lord's Hammond vortices complementing Blackmore's plum riffing. But it is the powerhouses for which *In Rock* is revered: Glover's Hendrix-esque juggernaut "Speed King," with Gillan's wicked laughter and screaming, the wailathon "Hard Lovin' Man," and "Into The Fire," whose fiery riff is almost Sabbath-esque. Then, in "Child In Time"—"The story of a loser," Purple wrote, "It could be you." Its poignant grandiloquence and climactic shrieking (unrelated to Gillan's receipt of in-corridor groupie "relief") epitomize Purple and its times like little else.

Held up while Lord completed his lamentable *Concerto For Group And Orchestra*, the album was cut at three London studios between October and the following April. But it was well worth the wait. **TJ**

Van Morrison's 1968 LP *Astral Weeks* had made him a cult hero. But *Moondance* was his first U.S. Top 30 album, and also his first to go platinum.

Morrison was living in Woodstock's rural paradise when he wrote many of these songs, although he left the area following the influx of people after the celebrated festival. Some of the musicians he assembled for the album remained with him for several years, including guitarist John Platania, horn player Jack Schroer, and Jeff Labes on keyboards.

Moondance showcases Van Morrison as a masterly songwriter and charismatic vocalist. In contrast to the acoustic *Astral Weeks*, the sound is bigger, meatier, with a horn section to add punch; the songs are more tightly structured, less improvisatory. The first side of the LP is almost perfect. "And It Stoned Me" paints a vignette of adolescence with a storyteller's eye for detail, while the smoky, jazz-infused title track remains one of Morrison's best-loved songs. Ethereal sailor's ballad "Into The Mystic" is a moving meditation on the splendor of love; the shivering strings are a wonderfully appropriate complement to his vocals. Elsewhere, a celebratory air, bordering on spiritual joy, haunts many of the tracks—witness the closing trio of "Brand New Day," "Everyone," and "Glad Tidings."

Helen Reddy had a 1971 U.S. hit with "Crazy Love," while Johnny Rivers' version of "Into The Mystic" charted in 1970. Van himself had a U.S. Top Forty hit with "Come Running." His solo career was on the rise. **JT**

The Grateful Dead | American Beauty (1970)

Label | Warner Bros.
Producer | The Grateful Dead • Robin Hurley
Art Direction | Mouse Studios
Nationality | USA
Running Time | 41:23

Although the late 1960s and early '70s saw leaps in studio technology, some groups, such as The Grateful Dead, seemed to revel in their undisciplined approach to recording. But 1970's *Workingman's Dead*—a mature-sounding document that referred to their country/jazz/pop roots—surprised fans. Follow-up *American Beauty*, though, would outlast all their other offerings as the definitive album by the group.

It is a joy to listen to: rich in acoustic instrumentation (including pedal steel guitar and mandolin), well-rounded backing vocals, and a subtle electric presence. *American Beauty* established the group as more than a house band for its charismatic stoner leader, Jerry Garcia. For the first time, the Dead seemed a cohesive unit with a battery of accomplished singer-songwriters, including Phil Lesh and Bob Weir.

Opener "Box Of Rain," penned by Lesh, is the perfect example of the group's new-found enthusiasm for the studio, while Weir delivered one of the record's standout moments on the joyous "Sugar Magnolia." Garcia, though, remains the undisputed heavyweight of the group, delivering an especially strong trilogy of songs to the set: "Candyman," "Ripple," and "Friend Of The Devil," and supplying expressive pedal steel playing. The album's closing track, "Truckin'" would also endure as their anthem for generations of Deadheads.

Expertly played, with some gorgeous harmony singing, this is an intricate album. Its influence has resonated in successive generations of musicans, from the West Coast scene to the recent breed of Liverpudlian acts such as The Coral and The Zutons. **BW**

> "The records are not total indicators, they're just products."

Jerry Garcia, 1972

Track Listing

▶	01	**Box Of Rain** (Hunter•Lesh)	5:16
▶	02	**Friend Of The Devil** (Dawson•Garcia•Hunter)	3:20
▶	03	**Sugar Magnolia** (Hunter•Weir)	3:15
	04	**Operator** (McKernan)	2:21
▶	05	**Candyman** (Garcia•Hunter)	5:12
▶	06	**Ripple** (Garcia•Hunter)	4:10
	07	**Brokedown Palace** (Garcia•Hunter)	4:18
	08	**Till The Morning Comes** (Garcia•Hunter)	3:13
	09	**Attics Of My Life** (Garcia•Hunter)	5:09
▶	10	**Truckin'** (Garcia•Hunter•Lesh•Weir)	5:09

Nick Drake
Bryter Layter (1970)

Label | Island
Producer | Joe Boyd
Art Direction | Nigel Waymouth
Nationality | UK
Running Time | 39:27

Lying at the emotional midway point between his wistful debut *Five Leaves Left* (1969) and the broken, despondent *Pink Moon* (1972), *Bryter Layter* found Nick Drake in fine form, something that his bleak myth now overshadows. This was just his second album, nothing more. Bruised by the indifference that met *Five Leaves Left*, he simply tried again.

On *Five Leaves Left* it was primarily Drake's guitar or Robert Kirby's orchestrations in the foreground; now it was the core of Fairport Convention. Reprising his role on the first album, guitarist Richard Thompson roped in bassist Dave Pegg and drummer Dave Mattacks, while John Cale provided both piano and celeste. Even a saxophone appears on "At The Chime Of A City Clock." While his hushed vocals were a constant factor in all of his albums, this was the closest Drake came to being in a rock band.

The album's relatively playful mood is at odds with legend. The jazzy "Poor Boy" seemed to poke fun at Drake's own melancholy, while it is impossible to detect anything other than sunlight in the opening instrumental "Introduction." Moreover, "Northern Sky" is simply too beautiful to have been written by someone who was indifferent to life. Only the weary "One Of These Things First" and the faintly unsettling "Fly" suggest the slow deterioration of Drake's emotional state.

Bryter Layter documents a time when Drake was disappointed but not yet disheartened by his lack of success. It is an ideal introduction to his music. **MBe**

Ananda Shankar
Ananda Shankar (1970)

Label | Reprise
Producer | Alex Hassilev
Art Direction | Ed Thrasher
Nationality | India
Running Time | 40:35

L.A., 1968, and Jimi Hendrix has been hanging out with a 26-year-old classically trained sitar player called Ananda Shankar. They have been jamming for a few days when Hendrix asks Ananda to make a record with him.

"For three nights I couldn't sleep," said Ananda. "But eventually I decided that it wouldn't be my music. So I made the album alone." The resulting record is the best example of a micro-genre that might be termed "sitar rock"—as purveyed by California-based pandit Harihar Rao, London-based sessionman "Big" Jim Sullivan and the mysterious "Lord Sitar"—where the sitar serves as exotic lead instrument in a bubblegum rock context.

But none were as successful as Ananda Shankar, the nephew of sitar legend Ravi and son of Hindustani dancer Uday Shankar. Ananda's Moog-fried readings of "Jumpin' Jack Flash" and "Light My Fire" still pack out dancefloors today. "Snow Flower" and "Mamata" create ambient pop, while "Metamorphosis" moves into funkier territory. Side two moves the emphasis back toward India with the 13-minute raga-rock epic "Sagar" and the stomping, chant-based "Raghupati."

Subsequent Ananda Shankar recordings, such as 1975's *Streets Of Calcutta* and *Dancing Drums*, would change hands for huge sums of money. Shankar's "rare groove" credentials even led him to be hauled out of retirement to tour and record with Sam Zaman's State Of Bengal. By the time of his untimely death in 2000, Shankar's fusion style had been adopted by a whole generation of British Asians, his reputation assured. **JLe**

The Who
Live At Leeds (1970)

Label | Track
Producer | Jon Astley
Art Direction | Graphreaks
Nationality | UK
Running Time | 37:09

Soft Machine
Third (1970)

Label | CBS
Producer | Soft Machine
Art Direction | John Hays
Nationality | UK
Running Time | 75:21

The legendary power and volume of The Who was always best sampled live. The studio tended to deaden their electricity: they recorded some fabulous singles, but no truly perfect albums; even *Tommy* suffered from pretentious production. *Live At Leeds*, then, is not just possibly the greatest live album of all time; it is almost certainly The Who's finest moment.

The album caught the band soon after touring *Tommy* in its entirety, itching to cut loose. A show at Britain's Leeds University on Valentine's Day 1970 was the location; the band surged at full strength for more than two hours, playing *Tommy*, their classic singles, and a clutch of rock 'n' roll gems along the way. Unrestrained onstage, the power-trio of musicians behind Roger Daltrey swelled to fearsome strength—bassist John Entwistle carrying the melodies, drummer Keith Moon rolling and filling with powerhouse abandon, and Pete Townshend proving himself a pioneer of feedback and dynamics, his terse solos full of ideas and emotion, a truly understated guitarist.

The resulting album arrived later that year, packaged like a faux-bootleg in a shabby cardboard gatefold. Though later expanded on CD (2000's complete two-CD Deluxe Edition is the one to buy), the original six-track vinyl is perfect in itself, especially the devil-driven cover of Mose Allison's "Young Man's Blues," and the sprawling "My Generation," which soon becomes a kaleidoscope of windmill riffage. *Live At Leeds* is as pure as heavy rock gets. **SC**

Recorded over four days, Soft Machine's *Third* shows a major British band at its peak, and at the same time, in complete turmoil. Prog rock would soon be huge and the rest of the group were tired of Robert Wyatt's singing—and he was sick of their intransigent desire to get all serious and jazzy.

"Moon In June" is the last real Wyatt piece for Soft Machine, and it is quite possibly the group's masterpiece, as much as the members other than Wyatt did not really like it (Wyatt is credited with "bass and organ" on the sleeve, despite these being the usual instruments of long-term cohorts Hugh Hopper and Mike Ratledge). The piece blends old Softs tunes with new bridging sections presided over by Wyatt's good-humored self-deprecation; another recording of the song-suite from contemporaneous *Peel Sessions* is even more irreverent, at one point even poking fun at Ratledge. Of the other tracks, Hopper's "Facelift"—featuring the short-lived eight-piece version of the group—is probably the most challenging, intriguing, and amusing. Ratledge's "Slightly All the Time" was credited on the original LP as featuring a 40-second snippet of Hopper's "Noisette"—spot it if you can!

The inner sleeve of the album features a brilliant photograph by Jurgen D. Ensthaler of the core members of this amazingly underrated group, bored and out of alcohol in a hotel room; you can practically smell the antagonism amid the ashy carpet, recently fried sausages, and hair. **DN**

Rod Stewart | Gasoline Alley (1970)

Label | Vertigo
Producer | Lou Reisner • Rod Stewart
Art Direction | Keel
Nationality | UK
Running Time | 42:27

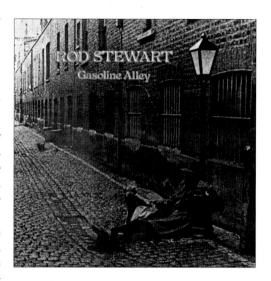

Stewart's underrated sophomore album immediately preceded the mega-selling *Every Picture Tells A Story*. That album included "Maggie May," but otherwise the two offer similar fare—reworkings of folk, R&B, soul, and rock classics, alongside covers of contemporary originals, and utilizing essentially the same musicians.

At the time, Stewart was leading a double life as vocalist and frontman of The Faces and as a solo artist. Regarded by many as the best live band around at the time, The Faces also feature intermittently here—their good-time rock 'n' roll is stamped all over "It's All Over Now"—while Ron Wood is omnipresent.

A large proportion of the album is acoustic, and in "Gasoline Alley" Wood and Stewart conjured an understated classic, a wistful glance back at teenage years highlighted by Stewart's gritty vocal. A host of uncredited instrumentalists—such as the fiddler on the neo-acoustic version of "Cut Across Shorty," and the mandolin player on the title track—imbue the album with a folk feel, though the musicians work up an endearingly slapdash storm on the rockers.

Stewart's tender reading of "Only A Hobo," and the beautifully judged acoustic backing, results in one of the best Dylan covers, and the two originals near the end are smartly executed. Two tracks signposted past involvements—the Elton John cover was good for E.J., though the Small Faces cover was less inspired.

Co-producer Lou Reisner had signed Stewart as a solo act after his heroics in The Jeff Beck Group. Solo stardom would come with the next album, but the groundwork was pretty much laid out with this disk. **JT**

> ## "Rod's understanding of what he was capable of ...was developing fast."
>
> Lloyd Bradley, 1999

Track Listing

▶	01	**Gasoline Alley** (Stewart•Wood)	4:08
▶	02	**It's All Over Now** (B. Womack•S.J. Womack)	6:25
▶	03	**Only A Hobo** (Dylan)	4:22
	04	**My Way Of Giving** (Lane•Marriott)	4:03
▶	05	**Country Comfort** (John•Taupin)	4:45
	06	**Cut Across Shorty** (Walker•Wayne•Wilkin)	6:34
▶	07	**Lady Day** (Stewart)	4:05
	08	**Jo's Lament** (Stewart)	3:31
	09	**I Don't Want To Discuss It** (Beatty•Cooper•Shelby)	4:34

George Harrison
All Things Must Pass (1970)

Label | Apple
Producer | George Harrison • Phil Spector
Art Direction | David Costa • Sian Rance
Nationality | UK
Running Time | 126:25

The partnership of John Lennon and Paul McCartney did not leave much room for George Harrison, though he managed to slip several classics into The Beatles' catalog. But, by the time the group imploded, he had a treasure trove of songs saved up for presentation on *All Things Must Pass*, which ranks among the two or three best albums released by a former Beatle.

Fascinatingly enough, while Phil Spector worked with Lennon creating his stripped-down, emotionally wrought recordings recorded in the early 1970s, he simultaneously continued down the *Abbey Road* path with Harrison's post-Beatles debut, refining his orchestral "wall of sound." Harrison is joined by a stellar cast, including Billy Preston, Phil Collins, Eric Clapton, and the remnants of the Delaney & Bonnie band (drummer Jim Gordon, bassist Carl Radle, and keyboardist Bobby Whitlock), who were coalescing with Clapton as Derek And The Dominos at the time.

Admittedly, the three-album boxed set was padded with an album of mostly forgettable jam sessions, but, with such finely crafted, spiritually charged songs as "Beware Of Darkness," "The Art Of Dying," "What Is Life," and the hit "My Sweet Lord," this album only sounds better with time. Harrison allows himself to enter The Beatles brouhaha with "Wah-Wah," a slashing tune that many interpreted as a slap at Paul McCartney, but most of the album rises far above score settling. **AG**

Simon And Garfunkel
Bridge Over Troubled Water (1970)

Label | Columbia
Producer | Art Garfunkel • Roy Halee • Paul Simon
Art Direction | Tony Lane
Nationality | USA
Running Time | 37:17

Bowing out in 1970, The Beatles left *Let It Be* as a messy legacy. Fellow Sixties stalwarts Simon And Garfunkel exited with more grace and an album with a title track that coincidentally also became a hymnal standard.

Short on stature and style, the duo's greatness was nonetheless secure, thanks to astonishing classics from "The Sound Of Silence" in 1965 to "America" in 1968. A preview of *Bridge . . .* in 1969—the hit "The Boxer"—confirmed once and for all that songwriter Paul Simon had emerged from the shadow of Bob Dylan.

Like Dylan, Simon wrote literate lyrics. But, like Smokey Robinson, he wrote literate lyrics and lovely songs that everyone from children to Aretha Franklin could sing. In a way, the epic title track does *Bridge . . .* an injustice, for it gives no hint of the chirpy likes of "Cecilia" and "El Condor Pasa (If I Could)."

There are delicacies too; deceptively so in the case of "The Only Living Boy In New York" and "So Long, Frank Lloyd Wright." Both were addressed to Simon's soon-to-be ex-partner Art Garfunkel, a former student of architecture (hence Frank Lloyd Wright) who skipped some recording sessions to act in *Catch-22*.

Bridge . . . is easy to adore even if you do not care about squabbling singers or folk music. Take a trip on *. . . Troubled Water* and you will learn why so many get misty-eyed whenever the old sparring partners bury the hatchet long enough to sing together. **BM**

Cat Stevens
Tea For The Tillerman (1970)

Label | Island
Producer | Paul Samwell-Smith
Art Direction | Cat Stevens
Nationality | UK
Running Time | 36:40

Traffic
John Barleycorn Must Die (1970)

Label | Island
Producer | Chris Blackwell • Guy Stevens • Steve Winwood
Art Direction | Mike Sida
Nationality | UK
Running Time | 34:32

London-born Cat Stevens (a.k.a. Steven Georgiou) had scored hits since the late 1960s, but with *Tea For The Tillerman*, his fourth album, he became a global star.

Previous LP *Mona Bone Jakon* (featuring hit single "Lady d'Arbanville") had seen Stevens emerge as one of a new breed of reflective singer-songwriters. For . . . *Tillerman*, he preserved the same core of musicians (Alun Davies, guitar; Harvey Burns, drums; John Ryan, bass) and the producer, maintaining the uncluttered production of *Mona Bone Jakon*.

Apart from Stevens' ear for a great melody, what caught the listener's attention most was the sensibility of his lyrics and his readiness to address pressing issues of his time—notably the search for spiritual direction that underpins "But I Might Die Tonight" and "On The Way To Find Out." "Father And Son" was written at the heels of a massive explosion of youth culture, but the song is all the more poignant for the lack of recrimination between the eponymous pair. (The album's sleeve, painted by Stevens, picks up on the subject of youth and age.) The album's melodic appeal and gentle charm saw sales soar and it garnered a gold disc. Seven years later, Stevens became a Muslim, changed his name to Yusuf Islam, and abandoned the music business to practice the spirituality yearned for in his songs. Since then, his work has rarely approached the tuneful simplicity of this much-loved album. **LP**

Steve Winwood graduated from teenage soul-singing prodigy with The Spencer Davis Group to chart-riding psychedelic single star with Traffic, whose "Hole In My Shoe" was one of the anthems of 1967. After the demise of supergroup Blind Faith, he returned to his former Traffic bandmates Jim Capaldi and Chris Wood. A proposed solo album, to be called *Mad Shadows*, became a comeback vehicle for Traffic, who would continue their merry way through to the mid-1970s.

The reduction of pressure after Blind Faith helped Winwood overcome a writing block. Capaldi, his lyricist of choice, also contributed drums, while Wood brought to the mix his facility on sax and flute, the latter adding a pastoral touch to the title track, an adaptation of a traditional folk song about the evils of alcohol. A scorn for all things commercial was conveyed by the opening 13-minute medley of "Glad," a piano-led instrumental, and "Freedom Rider."

A certain amount of overdubbing was needed to produce the album. Winwood carried the triple load of lead vocals, guitar, and piano, but the inevitably spacey arrangements allowed Winwood and pals to "go places within the music that we had never gone before." It all took place in the cottage at Aston Tirrold where the centerfold picture was taken—the venue where Traffic started a trend among rock groups for "getting it together in the country." **MH**

The Stooges | Fun House (1970)

Label | Elektra
Producer | Don Gallucci
Art Direction | Robert L. Heimall
Nationality | USA
Running Time | 36:28

Following The Stooges' widely panned debut, Elektra assigned them a lowly staff producer for *Fun House*. However, Don Gallucci would prove to be an excellent choice; an experienced session man who had played organ on The Kingsmen's "Louie, Louie," aged 14, he advised The Stooges to capture their infamous live show—a riot of sinful riffage and frontman Iggy Pop's drug-addled misadventures with cream-pies and broken glass—in the studio. The Stooges set up their gear at Elektra like they were playing a club, Iggy prowling as if on a stage. Sessions were bridged by parties at the wild and seedy Tropicana Motel, and the surrounding mania seeped deep into the tracks.

Side one is the "party" side, smoldering metallic guitars growling a mean street-hustler's strut, Iggy slurring slutty tales of hedonism. Side two, however, is the comedown, the songs stretching past the comfort zone, saxophonist Steven Mackay spraying freeform noise, and Iggy sounding like a scared, lost child, warning from bitter experience that "The Fun House will steal your heart away." The album sleeve—Pop writhing in what appears to be the furnace of Hell, which is in fact a scarlet-filtered close-up of his own face— perfectly suits its content.

Fun House's wild abandon and bitter aftertaste ill suited a generation undergoing a collective post-Altamont hangover, and The Stooges soon dissolved. But the album's corrosive psychosis directly influenced Richard Hell, The Birthday Party, and Black Flag, and many other dark-hearted punks have begun their musical careers by aping these brutal licks. **SC**

> " **When I made *Fun House*, back in 1970, nobody wanted to interview me. It was wonderful.**"
>
> Iggy Pop, 1996

Track Listing

▶	01	**Down On The Street** (Alexander·R. Asheton·S. Asheton·Pop)	3:42
▶	02	**Loose** (Alexander·R. Asheton·S. Asheton·Pop)	3:33
▶	03	**T.V. Eye** (Alexander·R. Asheton·S. Asheton·Pop)	4:17
	04	**Dirt** (Alexander·R. Asheton·S. Asheton·Pop)	7:00
	05	**1970** (Alexander·R. Asheton·S. Asheton·Pop)	5:15
▶	06	**Fun House** (Alexander·R. Asheton·S. Asheton·Pop)	7:46
	07	**L.A. Blues** (Alexander·R. Asheton·S. Asheton·Pop)	4:55

James Taylor | Sweet Baby James (1970)

Label | Warner Bros.
Producer | Peter Asher
Art Direction | Ed Thrasher
Nationality | USA
Running Time | 31:58

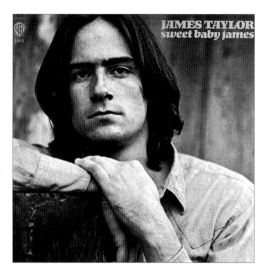

On *Sweet Baby James*, pastoral American beauty is presented within the simple, unaffected frame of James Taylor's songwriting. But when he surveys the inner landscape a different horizon is revealed—one of solitude lit by sparse rays of hope.

Rolling Stone wrote that Taylor's "persistent lonely prairie/lovely Heaven visions . . . work their way up to the intensity of a haiku or the complexity of a parable." The title track is a lullaby of canyons and cowboy blues that draws on country-folk traditions for its plaintive power. Taylor has an honest, low-key vocal delivery that suits his lyrical content and guitar playing perfectly.

His blues efforts, including the gleefully libidinous "Steamroller," are entertaining and ripe with wry humor, though Taylor lacks the raw edge to work well in that idiom. What he does have is a fine grasp of human frailties and a sense of the power of redemption—witness the great "Fire And Rain." Departure haunts the song—departure from people, places, and life itself. An adieu to a dead friend, its cold-light-of-day clarity is a masterpiece of understated regret.

"Blossom" is another standout track, and plays like a folk-inflected "Here Comes The Sun." More emphatically upbeat is the closing track, "Suite For 20G," which begins in familiar Taylor territory, with sunlit lyricism and a neat descending guitar refrain. Halfway through, however, it shifts gear and slides into a high-rolling R&B blow-out, complete with majestic horn section.

Sweet Baby James went on to achieve triple platinum sales, and triumphantly established Taylor as a musical force in the new decade. **JDi**

"We had all the fun. It almost killed us."

James Taylor, 2002

Track Listing

▶	01	**Sweet Baby James** (Taylor)	2:54
	02	**Lo And Behold** (Taylor)	2:37
	03	**Sunny Skies** (Taylor)	2:22
	04	**Steamroller** (Taylor)	2:59
	05	**Country Road** (Taylor)	3:23
	06	**Oh, Susannah** (Foster)	2:01
▶	07	**Fire And Rain** (Taylor)	3:24
	08	**Blossom** (Taylor)	2:14
	09	**Anywhere Like Heaven** (Taylor)	3:28
	10	**Oh, Baby Don't You Loose Your Lip On Me** (Taylor)	1:50
▶	11	**Suite For 20G** (Taylor)	4:46

Paul McCartney | McCartney (1970)

Label | Apple
Producer | Paul McCartney
Art Direction | Linda McCartney • Paul McCartney
Nationality | UK
Running Time | 34:19

Although for years shunned and treated as the devil's plastic, for ostensibly shattering The Beatles' dream, Paul McCartney's first solo album is never less than charming. While Lennon and Harrison were busy making their point and Ringo was busy recording pub singalongs, McCartney released this naive template for his solo career: some blinding songs; some stoned doodles; and some frankly embarrassing tosh.

Recorded during the end of 1969 at home in London's St. John's Wood, *McCartney* feels wistfully undercooked—a deliberate reaction to the smooth veneers of The Beatles' swansong, *Abbey Road*. After all the recent tension of working with the group in the studio, here McCartney worked alone, overdubbing on his Studer four-track recorder with a lone microphone.

The album is full of the touches that both enthrall and infuriate about McCartney. His two Beatles leftovers display these extremes perfectly: whereas "Junk" is wistful, poetic, and vivid, "Teddy Boy" is painfully silly. However, the whole album rests in the shadow of "Maybe I'm Amazed," which arrives late and effortlessly demonstrates just how much an architect of the *Abbey Road* sound he was. A mature, adult love ballad, it is possibly his finest song ever.

Released in April 1970, the album received sniffy reactions from the media, but quickly topped the American charts and reached the runner-up position in the UK. With its symbolic cover and snapshots of his new family, *McCartney* was not so much a willful post-Fab nose-thumbing as a manifesto of his intent and a catalog for his new life. **DE**

"[The tracks] were almost throwaways."

Paul McCartney, 1973

Track Listing

	01	**The Lovely Linda** (McCartney)	0:43
	02	**That Would Be Something** (McCartney)	2:38
	03	**Valentine Day** (McCartney)	1:39
▶	04	**Every Night** (McCartney)	2:31
	04	**Hot As Sun / Glasses** (McCartney)	2:05
▶	05	**Junk** (McCartney)	1:54
	06	**Man We Was Lonely** (McCartney)	2:56
▶	07	**Oo You** (McCartney)	2:48
	08	**Momma Miss America** (McCartney)	4:04
	09	**Teddy Boy** (McCartney)	2:22
	10	**Singalong Junk** (McCartney)	2:34
▶	11	**Maybe I'm Amazed** (McCartney)	3:50
	13	**Kreen–Akrore** (McCartney)	4:15

Santana | Abraxas (1970)

Label | Columbia
Producer | Fred Catero • Santana
Art Direction | MATI
Nationality | Mexico • USA
Running Time | 37:18

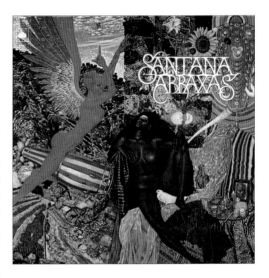

In the summer of 1970, 22-year-old Carlos Santana scored two Top 40 singles on a multiplatinum record, turned in a show-stopping performance before half the world at Woodstock, and earned a growing faction of devotees. Today, debut darlings are encouraged to regurgitate whatever worked the first time, but Carlos subscribed to the San Francisco freak-rock scene, where musicians mined their imaginations and turned whatever they discovered into rock 'n' roll.

Santana did the scene proud, crafting a sophomore record that voyaged beyond rock into jazz and salsa on the beat of a pounding Latin heart. Despite being the face of the band, Carlos and his impeccable guitar were merely components in a supremely gifted outfit, and on *Abraxas*, each member of the band made his presence felt. Gregg Rolie supplied the articulate, seductive organ grooves that made "Black Magic Woman" and "Oye Como Va" instant radio classics, and composed the stomping rockers "Mother's Daughter" and "Hope You're Feeling Better," with Carlos' signature riffs soaring high above. Bassist Dave Brown and drummer Mike Shrieve laid the bedrock of what was quickly becoming one of the tightest rhythm sections known to man, and paved the road for the exuberant timbals and congas of Mike Carabello and Jose Areas.

Upon the release of *Abraxas*, *Rolling Stone* opined that Santana "might do for Latin music what Chuck Berry did for the blues." When the album rode to No. 1 on the back of the tightest grooves the rock establishment had ever heard, it seemed even that prediction was somewhat modest. **MO**

> "Music is the union of two lovers: melody and rhythm. The melody is the woman, and the rhythm is the man."

Carlos Santana, 1994

Track Listing

01	Singing Winds, Crying Beasts (Carabello)		4:48
▶ 02	Black Magic Woman/Gypsy Queen (Green • Szabo)		5:24
▶ 03	Oye Como Va (Puente)		4:19
04	Incident At Neshabur (Gianquinto • Santana)		5:02
05	Se A Cabo (Areas)		2:51
06	Mother's Daughter (Rolie)		4:28
▶ 07	Samba Pa Ti (Santana)		4:47
▶ 08	Hope You're Feeling Better (Rolie)		4:07
09	El Nicoya (Areas)		1:32

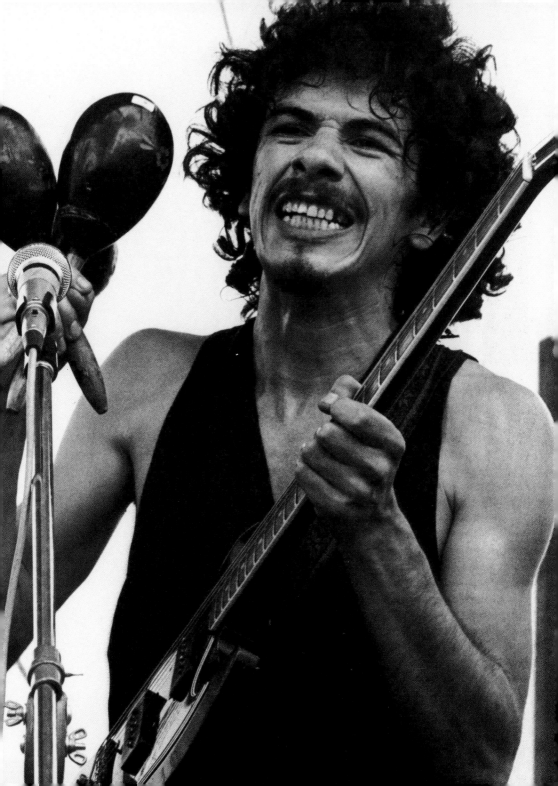

Syd Barrett | The Madcap Laughs (1970)

Label | Harvest
Producer | Various
Art Direction | Hipgnosis
Nationality | UK
Running Time | 37:04

Precisely what does Syd Barrett's legend rest on? Well, for starters, he was the artisan behind Pink Floyd's remarkable debut, *The Piper At The Gates Of Dawn*. And like Kenneth Grahame's book that *Piper*'s title sprang from, Barrett infused his work with charming English whimsy, cosmic paganism, even. Then there is the reclusive painter reputation, and history of LSD mingling with mental illness. For, after his departure from Pink Floyd (for reasons he never openly discussed), Syd's solo career was brief and erratic.

Recorded over a few days, *Madcap* sounds hastily prepared, as implied on the false start to "If It's In You." Indeed, without help from Roger Waters and Dave Gilmour (the latter replaced Syd's Floydian role) it might never have surfaced. Barrett's guitar playing is patchy, and his voice often a tuneless wail. You hear the rustle of lyric sheets being turned mid-song. Yet the album's Eastern-tinged melodies, and eccentric English pop, inspired a host of rock mystics, including Julian Cope.

There are moments of genius, naturally. "Dark Globe," with its fabulous lyric and hammered waltz chords, is gripping. And "Late Night," where gentle percussion checks Barrett's excesses, features lovely slide guitar—played with a cigarette lighter. Elsewhere, there is an eerie setting of excerpts of James Joyce's poetry in "Golden Hair," and the spontaneously catchy "Here I Go."

Depression, schizophrenia, and other forms of mental trauma are forever misunderstood and misdiagnosed. Syd Barrett only gave us a few hours of intensely recorded creativity, but history affords him the contentment of a man who left his mark. **GT**

"It's just writing good songs that matters, really."

Syd Barrett, 1971

Track Listing		
▶ 01 **Terrapin** (Barrett)		5:02
▶ 02 **No Good Trying** (Barrett)		3:22
03 **Love You** (Barrett)		2:25
04 **No Man's Land** (Barrett)		2:59
▶ 05 **Dark Globe** (Barrett)		1:58
06 **Here I Go** (Barrett)		3:09
▶ 07 **Octopus** (Barrett)		3:43
▶ 08 **Golden Hair** (Barrett · Joyce)		1:56
09 **Long Gone** (Barrett)		2:46
10 **She Took A Long Cold Look** (Barrett)		1:55
11 **Feel** (Barrett)		2:17
12 **If It's In You** (Barrett)		2:22
▶ 13 **Late Night** (Barrett)		3:10

Jethro Tull | Aqualung (1971)

Label | Island
Producer | Ian Anderson • Terry Ellis
Art Direction | Burton Silverman
Nationality | UK
Running Time | 44:51

Two classic, Christopher Guest-penned movies come to mind on hearing Jethro Tull's *Aqualung—This Is Spinal Tap* and *A Mighty Wind*. The former is a heavy metal mockumentary; the latter portrays a fictional folk group. From *Aqualung* onward, the Tull often found themselves placed in the ranks of the former genre while drawing their inspiration from the latter.

The title track opens with typical eclecticism. Calmly strummed acoustic guitar and urbane piano are presented in one measure, a frenzied bass guitar and drums-led passage in the next—all topped off by a determined electric guitar solo. "Cross-Eyed Mary" follows in a more traditional setting, with vocalist Ian Anderson's trademark flute playing floating over a pulsing Jeffrey Hammond bassline and the elevated swirls of the David Palmer-arranged orchestra. The song then merges into guitar territory, though the piano, cowbell, and return of Anderson's flute play off the rock power of the core guitar, bass, and drum work.

Aqualung's lyrics fit into an impressively unfolded narrative, which relates partly to the experiences of a down-and-out, and help to match the album's singular sound with a mind-opening message suited to the times. The concept is set with written passages on the album's rear, which present a spin on the first chapter of Genesis. For the *Aqualung* version of the biblical story, man creates God and later *Aqualung* itself.

An intriguing prog-rock-folk musical landmark, then, though its subject matter did not prevent its riff-friendly tracks becoming FM radio favorites—or the album becoming a multimillion seller. **YK**

"We're kind of out there on the periphery of rock music."

Ian Anderson, 2003

Track Listing

▶	01	**Aqualung** (I. Anderson • J. Anderson)	6:31
	02	**Cross–Eyed Mary** (I. Anderson)	4:06
	03	**Cheap Day Return** (I. Anderson)	1:21
	04	**Mother Goose** (I. Anderson)	3:51
	05	**Wond'ring Aloud** (I. Anderson)	1:53
	06	**Up To Me** (I. Anderson)	5:10
▶	07	**My God** (I. Anderson)	7:08
▶	08	**Hymn 43** (I. Anderson)	3:15
	09	**Slipstream** (I. Anderson)	1:12
	10	**Locomotive Breath** (I. Anderson)	4:23
	11	**Wind Up** (I. Anderson)	6:01

David Crosby
If I Could Only Remember My Name (1971)

Label | Atlantic
Producer | David Crosby
Art Direction | Gary Burden
Nationality | USA
Running Time | 37:03

When David Crosby's girlfriend Christine Hinton died in a traffic accident in 1969, the singer was devastated. After barely making it through sessions for Crosby, Stills, Nash, and Young's *Déjà Vu*, Crosby sought an outlet in work for his debut solo album.

Recruiting musicians from his expansive circle of friends, including Jerry Garcia, Joni Mitchell, and Grace Slick, Crosby pieced the album together at a San Francisco studio over three months in 1970. Opener "Music Is Love" (featuring Nash and Young) evolves casually, as if from a jam, its title becoming a mantra. There is grit in Crosby's voice on "Cowboy Movie," another slow-builder that rises to a tussle of scratchy guitars against the drums' laidback slap. "Laughing" is a masterpiece—glistening acoustic guitars, wistful pedal steel, and luminous harmonies. The delicate "Traction In The Rain," provides another highpoint; Crosby delivers a perfectly controlled, crystal-clear vocal.

But what marks this release out from its West Coast peers is the darkness at its heart. The restless "Song With No Words/Tree With No Leaves" features wordless scatting and shifting minor chords. "Orleans" is ripe with melancholy, ending in a scrabble of 12-string harmonics. And then there is the eerie a cappella "I'd Swear There Was Somebody Here"—its unsettling flurries of harmonies all provided by Crosby.

It made No. 12 on both sides of the Atlantic, and went gold in the United States—but that's incidental. This is a unique, and uniquely moving set of songs. **RD**

> ## "I'm about content. My songs are about something."
>
> David Crosby, 2004

Track Listing

▶	01	**Music Is Love** (Crosby·Nash·Young)	3:16
	02	**Cowboy Movie** (Crosby)	8:02
▶	03	**Tamalpais High (At About 3)** (Crosby)	3:28
▶	04	**Laughing** (Crosby)	5:20
	05	**What Are Their Names** (Crosby·Garcia·Lesh·Shrieve·Young)	4:09
▶	06	**Traction In The Rain** (Crosby)	3:40
	07	**Song With No Words (Tree With No Leaves)** (Crosby)	5:53
▶	08	**Orleans** (Trad., arr. Crosby)	1:56
▶	09	**I'd Swear There Was Somebody Here** (Crosby)	1:19

Sly And The Family Stone
There's A Riot Goin' On (1971)

Label | Epic
Producer | Sylvester "Sly Stone" Stewart
Art Direction | John Berg
Nationality | USA
Running Time | 47:38

Sly And The Family Stone's upbeat multiracial rock 'n' soul reflected the optimism of the Civil Rights movement through the 1960s; but as that optimism withered away into bitter radicalism, so Stone underwent a similarly painful spiritual journey. Darkness was no stranger to Sly's Day-Glo fusion-pop; "Hot Fun In The Summertime" slyly sang of the Watts riots. But worsening civil unrest and the carnage of Vietnam, combined with his fragile emotional state and a mess of drugs, prompted him to deliver this haunted State of the Nation address.

This album was the product of endless sessions and overdubs, a coke-wired Stone wearing out the tapes. Rumor has it Miles Davis contributed some trumpet to the album, and live drums struggle for space with primitive drum machines; bass squelches freely about, loose and predatory; wah-wah guitars slash.

The heavyweight funk that dominates the album— hazy, spooked, stoned—lends an extra poignancy to the album's wistful slivers of pop, "Runnin' Away" and "You Caught Me Smilin'"— moments of tenderness, relief from the defeated, angry funk. Previous Sly hits are referenced, pointedly the "'Everyday People' looking forward to a simple beating" on "Time," or a death-rattle crawl through previous hit "Thank You" as a closer.

A painfully accurate diagnosis of America's malaise and Sly's own spiritual disintegration, it alienated much of the fanbase, and signaled Sly's subsequent drug-fueled descent. It remains, however, a starkly brilliant album, a bruised, funky howl of soul under pressure. **SC**

"We will never sell out."

Sly Stone, 1970

Track Listing

▶	01	**Luv 'N' Haight** (Stewart)	4:01
	02	**Just Like A Baby** (Stewart)	5:10
	03	**Poet** (Stewart)	3:00
▶	04	**Family Affair** (Stewart)	3:04
	05	**Africa Talks To You "The Asphalt Jungle" There's A Riot Goin' On** (Stewart)	8:45
	06	**Brave And Strong** (Stewart)	3:28
▶	07	**(You Caught Me) Smilin'** (Stewart)	2:53
▶	08	**Time** (Stewart)	3:01
	09	**Spaced Cowboy** (Stewart)	3:57
▶	10	**Runnin' Away** (Stewart)	2:55
▶	11	**Thank You For Talkin' To Me Africa** (Stewart·Stone)	7:13

Marvin Gaye | What's Going On (1971)

Label | Tamla
Producer | Marvin Gaye
Art Direction | Curtis McNair
Nationality | USA
Running Time | 35:46

How can you be sexy and smile when the weight of the world is on your shoulders? Turn tragedy into triumph? Oh, and revolutionize soul music at the same time? Simple: be Marvin Gaye.

Stricken by the death of his singing partner Tammi Terrell, increasingly ruled by drugs, and desperate to stretch the musical style for which he was famous—short and sweet soul songs—Gaye's salvation lay in his humor and extraordinary talent. Both shine from an album that, in lesser hands, could have easily been a self-righteous drag.

Words cannot do *What's Going On* justice. It ebbs and flows from the ironically uplifting title track, through waves of gospel and jazz (the relaxing kind, not the noise)—then explodes into "Mercy Mercy Me (The Ecology)" and finally closes with the unsettling "Inner City Blues (Make Me Wanna Holler)."

Bar Smokey Robinson, who rates it the greatest album of all time, Motown could not see how a politically charged yet lushly languid suite could translate into hits. Certainly the sentiments were not the saccharine ones of Gaye's Sixties smashes—but today it sounds like a natural evolution from the loving lyrics of "You're All I Need To Get By" and the musical sophistication of "I Heard It Through the Grapevine." Three Top Ten singles and 30 years of strong sales vindicated Gaye's threat to record nothing more for Motown unless it was released.

Let your ears decide. As Gaye wrote, "You don't have to be told how groovy it is, or which tunes you should dig, or how great his or her majesty is …" **BM**

> "We've got to find the Lord … What other weapons have we to fight the forces of hatred and evil?"
>
> Marvin Gaye, 1971

Track Listing

▶	01	**What's Going On** (Benson·Cleveland·Gaye)	3:53
	02	**What's Happening Brother** (Gaye·Nyx)	2:43
	03	**Flyin' High (In The Friendly Sky)** (Gaye·Gordy Gaye·Stover)	3:50
	04	**Save The Children** (Benson·Cleveland·Gaye)	4:03
	05	**God Is Love** (Gaye·Gordy Gaye·Nyx·Stover)	1:42
▶	06	**Mercy Mercy Me (The Ecology)** (Gaye)	3:16
	07	**Right On** (DeRouen·Gaye)	7:32
	08	**Wholy Holy** (Benson·Cleveland·Gaye)	3:08
▶	09	**Inner City Blues (Make Me Wanna Holler)** (Gaye·Nyx)	5:39

Yes
The Yes Album (1971)

Label | Atlantic
Producer | Eddie Offord • Yes
Art Direction | Jon Goodchild
Nationality | UK
Running Time | 40:56

The Bee Gees
Trafalgar (1971)

Label | Polydor
Producer | Robert Stigwood
Art Direction | Nicholas Pocock
Nationality | Australia • UK
Running Time | 44:19

As the Indo–Pakistan war erupted in March 1971, so did Yes' third studio effort. Having ditched guitarist Peter Banks in May 1970, the quintet absorbed Bodast's Steve Howe and decamped to Devon, England. Under pressure from Atlantic for a hit, they spent two months at a farm near Ilfracombe developing a fresh sound. Missing the release date of June 15 (for an album new manager Brian Lane dubbed "Stunt Of The Month"), they rehearsed till they were nearly broke and unveiled their new three-part harmonies—as heard on the heavenly Anderson alto of "Sweet Dreams"—at London's Lyceum in July. Chris Welch of *Melody Maker* attested to their "marvelous music" and, by November, they had added the swirling staccato, battling organ-guitar tour de force of "Yours Is No Disgrace" (Howe's attacking soloing a response to Vietnam) and the sunny a cappella reverie of "I've Seen All Good People."

Assisted by engineer Eddie Offord, the band refined their sound at London's Advision, culminating in the monumental "Starship Trooper." Boasting multiple changes of pace, mood, and style, it showcases joyous vocals, Howe's skittering guitar (highlighted on his pedal steel, Chet Atkins-like, in-concert favorite, "The Clap,") Bruford's precision percussion, Squire's forceful bass thumps, and Kaye's earth-shaking Hammond crescendos. The clipped piano of "Perpetual Change" and the intense "Würm" diversify the tone, but the UK No. 7 set marked Yes' move from psych to prog and stands as a genre benchmark. **TJ**

The Bee Gees had spent some years in the wilderness before *Trafalgar*, but the quality of the album more than made up for the wait. Recorded between January and April 1971, it revealed the Brothers Gibb truly working together in harmony again.

A few things had changed in the re-formed band. They were now much more pedantic about their songwriting credits, and Robin—having proved himself during the two-year split with the magnificent *Robin's Reign*—exercised his right to do nothing but sing, so half the album does not feature him at all.

Bad news first: "Don't Wanna Live Inside Myself" pays too much homage to "While My Guitar Gently Weeps," while Robin's funeral Edwardian parlor song "Dearest" is horrendous. But the rest is pure lush pop brilliance. Maurice's two solo compositions show him finally coming out as a truly great songwriter. "Lion In Winter" is infectiously experimental—much of it is just drums, and the rhythm expands epically at the end. The usual bizarrely maudlin lyrics are in evidence in spades: "Now I feel as good as if I were dead" is a gem, but "Somebody crown the clown with the red balloon" takes the trophy. And the hits kept coming, "How Can You Mend A Broken Heart" providing a U.S. No. 1.

The cover was the usual early 1970s Bee Gee strangeness, the group enacting the death of Nelson in the gatefold, new member Geoff Bridgeford reading a *Beezer* comic. The lads' dad, Hugh, is in the picture because, apparently, he was "just there." **DN**

The Who
Who's Next (1971)

Label | Track
Producer | Glyn Johns • The Who
Art Direction | John Kosh
Nationality | UK
Running Time | 43:21

It is The Who's best-selling album—and, in main man Pete Townshend's view, the finest. But it was born out of a crisis: *Lifehouse*, the follow-up to The Who's conceptual hit *Tommy*, had faltered after months of preparation because no one, bar its author, understood it. Ethan A. Russell's cover photo for *Who's Next* poked fun at *2001: A Space Odyssey*, but served equally well as a comment on the band's own more grandiose ambitions (a rejected cover idea featured Keith Moon in a corset, with a riding crop).

Humiliated, Townshend was persuaded to put the best songs on an album that told no story. Some were hard, such as "Bargain"; some were singalongs, such as "Getting in Tune"; and one—bassist John Entwistle's droll "My Wife"—was nothing to do with *Lifehouse* at all (the woman in question, said Entwistle, took it well: she did not come after him—her lawyers did).

Towering above all the rest were a trio of the finest hard rock anthems that ever erupted. "Baba O'Riley"—its name a conflation of Townshend's guru Meher Baba and avant-garde composer Terry Riley—is a sublime blend of synthesizer and slashing guitar. "Behind Blue Eyes" is poetry with an attitude. And "Won't Get Fooled Again" is simply a monster.

All three were part of The Who's performance at the post-9/11 gig at Madison Square Garden, The Concert for New York. The night's most rapturously received set, it proved that the passing decades had diminished neither the singers nor the songs. **BM**

Carole King
Tapestry (1971)

Label | Ode
Producer | Lou Adler
Art Direction | Roland Young
Nationality | USA
Running Time | 44:09

Having already established herself in pop's pantheon during the 1960s as half of a legendary Brill Building songwriting partnership (with then husband Gerry Goffin), Carole King dramatically reinvented herself as a solo star with this landmark release.

The cover is unapologetically domestic—a blue-jeaned King, needlework in hand, with her cat in the foreground—and its homespun ambience is reflected in the uncluttered production and arrangements of the album. King's unadorned vocals are by turns strident and charged ("I Feel The Earth Move"), wistful ("So Far Away"; "Home Again") and playful ("Smackwater Jack"). Songs such as "Will You Still Love Me Tomorrow?" and "(You Make Me Feel Like) A Natural Woman" had already been "claimed" by The Shirelles and Aretha, respectively. But King's stripped-down versions—particularly of the former, to which she brings an affecting sadness—are worthy reinterpretations.

The sheer quality on offer swiftly reaped results. The achingly honest "It's Too Late" gave King a U.S. No. 1; the album topped the U.S. charts for 15 weeks straight, selling more than 15 million copies worldwide.

There is an unofficial tradition Stateside that freshmen get introduced to Simon And Garfunkel—the duo's literate, often melancholy reflections seem to resonate with undergraduates. In the same spirit, *Tapestry* should be on the curriculum of every first year student, as an example of an artist claiming her own legacy while making the listener feel right at home. **YK**

Isaac Hayes | Shaft (1971)

Label | Stax
Producer | Isaac Hayes
Art Direction | The Graffiteria
Nationality | USA
Running Time | 69:35

Cotton Comes To Harlem was screened first, but Shaft was the undisputed herald of early 1970s blaxploitation cinema. Widely influential at the time, its soundtrack still makes the movie one of the best remembered icons of the era.

Composer, producer, and arranger Isaac Hayes contrived the whole musical plot, his best-known achievement in a career that has seen him co-write 200 hit songs with Dave Porter for Stax Records. Recorded at Stax studios, with The Bar-Kays carving the beat and The Memphis Strings and Horns weaving torrid orchestrations, the Shaft soundtrack is a sophisticated stew of Hayes' vast range of musical knowledge, the Memphis sound from A to Z. The man himself sings and plays vibes, organ, and electric piano.

Things kick off in style with four minutes of arrogant, symphonic soul cushioned with lusty vocal raps, hissing cymbals, and hypnotic chops of wah-wah. The majestic dynamics of "Theme From Shaft" are a paean to Shaft's virility, shaping the mold of all blaxploitation movie scores to come and permeating Barry White's bedroom moaning and Gamble And Huff's Philly Sound. Elsewhere, "Soulsville" is a trademark Hayes down-tempo ballad, while The Bar-Kays stretch "Do Your Thing" into a 20-minute funk epic without dropping the pace once. The remainder of the album is a triumph of mood music and a tribute to Hayes' arrangement skills.

"Theme From Shaft" shot to the top of the U.S. charts, giving Hayes his only No. 1; the double album it was taken from won the Oscar for the best soundtrack, and became Stax's fastest selling album. **JG**

"My music is very honest."

Isaac Hayes, 1995

Track Listing		
▶ 01 **Theme From Shaft** (Hayes)		4:37
02 **Bumpy's Lament** (Hayes)		1:49
▶ 03 **Walk From Regio's** (Hayes)		2:22
04 **Ellie's Love Theme** (Hayes)		3:15
05 **Shaft's Cab Ride** (Hayes)		1:07
06 **Cafe Regio's** (Hayes)		6:09
07 **Early Sunday Morning** (Hayes)		3:47
08 **Be Yourself** (Hayes)		4:27
09 **A Friend's Place** (Hayes)		3:21
10 **Soulsville** (Hayes)		3:47
11 **No Name Bar** (Hayes)		6:09
12 **Bumby's Blues** (Hayes)		4:04
13 **Shaft Strikes Again** (Hayes)		3:04
▶ 14 **Do Your Thing** (Hayes)		19:38
15 **The End Theme** (Hayes)		1:59

The Allman Brothers Band | At Fillmore East (1971)

Label | Capricorn
Producer | Tom Dowd
Art Direction | Jim Marshall
Nationality | USA
Running Time | 76:26

Led by visionary slide guitarist Duane Allman and his singing and organ-playing younger sibling Gregg, The Allman Brothers Band both invented and transcended Southern rock. Based in Macon, Georgia, the original sextet also featured guitarist Dicky Betts, bassist Berry Oakley, and two drummers, Jai Johanny Johanson and Butch Trucks. They were known for extended live jams, evolving a symphonic blend of rock, blues, country, soul, and jazz. When their first two studio albums flopped, a concert disc seemed the obvious answer.

The double LP *At Fillmore East* was assembled by producer Tom Dowd from a pair of March 1971 shows at the New York venue. The record begins with three faithful R&B covers, then takes a turn for the spectacular with side two: a 19-minute, tempo-shifting run through Willie Cobbs' "You Don't Love Me." This is more telepathy than boogie. Give a million bar bands a million gigs and they would never match the fluid interplay of the Allman originals "Hot 'Lanta" and "In Memory Of Elizabeth Reed." A side-long version of "Whipping Post" brings the house down. Simmering with a tension that is almost cinematic, this Southern gothic lament is one of the all-time great roots-rock performances.

At Fillmore East broke the Allmans, reaching No. 13 on the Billboard chart, but it would also prove to be the classic lineup's swansong. On October 29, 1971, 24-year-old Duane was killed in a motorcycle accident on his way to Berry Oakley's house. Tragedy struck again on November 12, 1972, when Oakley died in the same way and at the same age, a mere three blocks from where his mentor had perished. **MA**

> "I just went into a sort of revolt. I said, other people can write songs, and if they can do it, let's see if I can. So I sat down, and started doing it."

Gregg Allman, 1997

Track Listing

01	**Statesboro Blues** (McTell)		4:08
02	**Done Somebody Wrong** (James・Levy・Lewis)		4:05
03	**Stormy Monday** (Walker)		8:31
▶ 04	**You Don't Love Me** (Cobbs)		19:06
▶ 05	**Hot 'Lanta** (D. Allman・G. Allman・Betts Johanson・Oakley・Trucks)		5:10
▶ 06	**In Memory Of Elizabeth Reed** (Betts)		12:46
▶ 07	**Whipping Post** (Allman)		22:40

The Rolling Stones | Sticky Fingers (1971)

Label | Rolling Stones Records
Producer | Jimmy Miller
Art Direction | Craig Braun • Andy Warhol
Nationality | UK
Running Time | 46:06

Sticky Fingers was the first LP released on The Rolling Stones' own label, the first to feature the world famous John Pasche-designed tongue and lips logo, and the first to top both the U.S. and UK album charts.

Its roots were established as early as 1969, when the Stones laid down backing tracks for "Brown Sugar," "Wild Horses," and the rural blues "You Gotta Move" at Muscle Shoals Sound Studios. These set the album's relaxed tone, a blend of blues, country, and Southern-styled soul.

Opener "Brown Sugar" is built around an irresistible guitar riff that led it to become a massive worldwide hit and party anthem, despite extremely controversial lyrical content. "Bitch" meshes Bobby Keyes' sax and Jim Price's trumpet with another pounding guitar riff. The horn section surfaces again on "I Got The Blues" evoking the passion of Otis Redding's Stax label ballads while Billy Preston adds gospel-infused searing organ. The album is full of explicit drug references not least on the Marianne Faithfull co-write "Sister Morphine," a dark tale of addiction. The influence of Keith Richard's buddy Gram Parsons is felt on the album's two country songs—the beguiling ballad "Wild Horses" and the tongue-in-cheek "Dead Flowers."

Guitarist Mick Taylor shines on the Santana-like workout "Can't You Hear Me Knocking." "Moonlight Mile" features a genuinely moving vocal by Jagger backed with lavish strings by Paul Buckmaster.

Andy Warhol's cover of a jeans-clad crotch originally came with a working zipper, sealing the consummate sleazy Stones package. **JoH**

> *"**Sticky Fingers** was the first time we added horns—that was the influence of people like Otis Redding and James Brown."*
>
> Charlie Watts, 2003

Track Listing

▶	01	**Brown Sugar** (Jagger•Richard)	3:49
	02	**Sway** (Jagger•Richard)	3:51
▶	03	**Wild Horses** (Jagger•Richard)	5:42
	04	**Can't You Hear Me Knocking** (Jagger•Richard)	7:14
	05	**You Gotta Move** (Davis•McDowell)	2:32
▶	06	**Bitch** (Jagger•Richard)	3:36
	07	**I Got The Blues** (Jagger•Richard)	3:52
▶	08	**Sister Morphine** (Faithfull•Jagger•Richard)	5:31
▶	09	**Dead Flowers** (Jagger•Richard)	4:03
	10	**Moonlight Mile** (Jagger•Richard)	5:56

John Lennon | Imagine (1971)

Label | Apple
Producer | John Lennon • Yoko Ono • Phil Spector
Art Direction | Yoko Ono
Nationality | UK
Running Time | 39:20

After the primal existential confessions in his solo debut album *Plastic Ono Band*, the ex-Beatle needed a breath of utopia, a pinch of hope. This and the rich musicality of the output provided by a stellar cast—George Harrison, Klaus Voorman, Nicky Hopkins, Jim Keltner, Alan White, King Curtis, and members of Badfinger—made *Imagine* a huge hit that charted at No. 1 on both sides of the Atlantic, just as Lennon and Yoko Ono were moving to the United States.

Produced by Phil Spector at the studio Lennon had built in his English mansion, Tittenhurst, *Imagine* gave us the song for which the world remembers the most interesting personality in The Beatles, a hymn to human trust in a better world in the face of the most despairing reality. It also featured some of the best love songs a man has written to a woman—"Oh My Love" and "Jealous Guy"—and its share of crude rock 'n' roll too, Lennon style, as in the political outcry "Gimme Some Truth" and the infamous McCartney diatribe "How Do You Sleep?"

Some tracks recalled past introspections, such as "Crippled Inside" or "How?," but the newfound center in John's life provided by Yoko—along with Spector's orchestrated but still rough production—made this his most accomplished, balanced solo record.

A self-portrait of a man at the same time sensitive and aggressive, insecure and bold, introspective but socially aware. The title song alone, a work of stunning simplicity (released four years later in the UK, it made No.1—naturally), will undoubtedly keep bringing this evergreen masterpiece to the attention of new generations for years to come. **IJ**

"Well, you make your own dream. That's The Beatles' story, isn't it?"

John Lennon, 1980

Track Listing

▶ 01	**Imagine** (Lennon)	3:04
02	**Crippled Inside** (Lennon)	3:49
▶ 03	**Jealous Guy** (Lennon)	4:15
04	**It's So Hard** (Lennon)	2:26
04	**I Don't Wanna Be A Soldier** (Lennon)	6:08
▶ 06	**Gimme Some Truth** (Lennon)	3:16
▶ 07	**Oh My Love** (Lennon•Ono)	2:45
08	**How Do You Sleep?** (Lennon)	5:36
▶ 09	**How?** (Lennon)	3:42
10	**Oh Yoko!** (Lennon)	4:19

The Beach Boys
Surf's Up (1971)

Label | Brother
Producer | The Beach Boys
Art Direction | Uncredited
Nationality | USA
Running Time | 33:57

Like many Beach Boys albums, *Surf's Up* presents a difficult target to hit squarely, in terms of critical appreciation. Released in 1971, it was the work of a band being pulled apart by internal dissent and the slow eclipse of Brian Wilson's sanity.

The ambiguity starts with the first track. No sooner have you dismissed "Don't Go Near The Water" as ecological hand-wringing, then along comes Carl Wilson's "Long Promised Road," with its determination and choral beauty, halting derision in its tracks. The oceanic mysticism of "Feel Flows" is equally arresting.

There are certainly moments of sublime emotional clarity. The faux-naivety of "Take A Load Off Your Feet" is misconceived, but skip forward to the heartbreakingly nostalgic "Disney Girls (1957)" and you remember how it was to be ten years old. From another band it would be manipulative dross, but The Beach Boys at their best had a matchless gift for tapping into something larger than themselves.

The erratic, half-brilliant course continues throughout. "Student Demonstration Time," a Leiber and Stoller tune given new lyrics by Mike Love, tries to hit a raw nerve with its sneering R&B grind about civil rights, but misses. Likewise, oddity "A Day In The Life Of A Tree"—though prettily melodic—sounds more a product of psychosis than genius.

The star-swept loneliness of "'Til I Die" and the crumbling majesty of the title track gives the album the superb conclusion it deserves. **JDi**

Yes
Fragile (1971)

Label | Atlantic
Producer | Eddie Offord • Yes
Art Direction | Roger Dean
Nationality | UK
Running Time | 39:52

After touring April to December 1971 with the likes of Iron Butterfly, Jon Anderson and Chris Squire sought to develop the band's sound with newfangled synthesizers. Tony Kaye's preference for Hammonds (and arguments with roommate Steve Howe) led to his exit in August, by which time Wakeman had left The Strawbs, bringing Yes a whole new level of virtuosity and showmanship. Drummer Bill Bruford was bewildered by Anderson and Squire's drive to be the world's best band, but sessions above a brothel in London's Shepherds Market were immediately productive (producing four group efforts to complement five solo ones).

Although uncredited on the sleeve due to publishing wrangles, Wakeman contributed on the first day to the sweet surging, rifled keys and guitar of the ecstatic "Roundabout," and the raging-cum-dreamy, soaring-vocal "Heart Of The Sunrise." The visceral jazz-psych storm "South Side Of the Sky" is another epic story-song that emerged during five weeks of rehearsals prior to September at Advision, where Yes played at deafening volume. Engineer Eddie Offord edited hours of recording for a few bars, with fans allowed in 20 at a time to watch. Anderson's lyrical mysticism is to the fore on the chanting "We Have" and Dean's sleeve artwork encapsulates the fractured world at the heart of the album's concept. Critically lauded and Top Ten in the UK and the United States, it signaled, as Jon said, "Yes are a people's band"—albeit people with a love of the music at its most complex. **TJ**

The Doors
L.A. Woman (1971)

Label | Elektra
Producer | Bruce Botnick • The Doors
Art Direction | Carl Cossick
Nationality | USA
Running Time | 48:51

Can
Tago Mago (1971)

Label | United Artists
Producer | Can
Art Direction | Ulli Eichburger
Nationality | Germany • Japan • Poland
Running Time | 73:30

Just when everyone thought the Doors were going to disappear up the dark, claustrophobic tunnel of their own pretension, along came L.A. Woman.

Suddenly, their brooding, lysergic pomp morphed into garrulous comedy and low-key cool. Rolling Stone stated: "The Doors have never been more together, more like the Beach Boys, more like Love." Augmented by bassist Jerry Scheff and Marc Benno on rhythm guitar, their sound became fuller and tighter.

Jim Morrison had transformed from rake-thin acid rock shaman to a figure of boozy, boorish charisma. When he shouts the defiant chorus of "The Changeling," you sense that he has crossed a personal meridian and become a freer, less studied performer.

There is a new playfulness, too. "Love Her Madly," a salute to infatuation, capers with a cops-and-robbers energy, courtesy of Ray Manzarek's spirited keyboard work, while "Hyacinth House" is imbued with silent-movie melodrama. Crowning the album is the burning exuberance of the title track, a supercharged cruise through the City of Angels. Morrison cries triumphantly at the top of the climactic "mojo rising" section, the band's wheels leave the runway, and they really fly.

Contrasting with the boiler-room temperatures of "L.A. Woman" and "Crawling King Snake" are two iced-out downers. "Cars Hiss By My Window" is all cheap-motel languor, while "Riders On The Storm" takes us back to classic Doors territory—a canyon landscape populated by ghosts and peyote visions. **JDi**

After original vocalist Malcolm Mooney departed shortly after the release of Can's debut Monster Movie in 1969, bassist Holger Czukay and drummer Jaki Leibezeit chanced upon Japanese street musician Damo Suzuki performing in Munich and invited him to perform with the band that evening. Suzuki's flexible vocals—ranging from a calm whisper to wild shrieking—caused the 1,500-strong audience to flee the venue.

Tago Mago opens with the gentle eastern melodies of "Paperhouse," the almost alien-sounding "Mushroom," and the explosive, mysterious backward vocals of "Oh Yeah." After this remarkable beginning, the relentless rhythmic groove of "Halleluwah" (sampled by Primal Scream on 1997's "Kowalski") features guitarist Michael Karoli's Teutonic funk licks and Czukay's tape loops alongside blues piano, tortured violins, and industrial noise before blistering into a huge psychedelic climax.

The Aleister Crowley-inspired "Aumgn" takes the experimentation further; a vocal mantra delivered by keyboardist Irmin Schmidt is shrouded with sinister ambience. The closing "Bring Me Coffee Or Tea" is no small comfort after these musical endurance tests.

Alongside groups such as Kraftwerk and Faust, Can's fusion of Stockhausen's early electronic experiments and The Velvet Underground's art rock proved German rock bands were starting to find their own identity without resorting to a pastiche of American or British acts. Even after 30 years Tago Mago sounds refreshingly contemporary and gloriously extreme. **CSh**

Elton John | Madman Across The Water (1971)

Label | DJM
Producer | Gus Dudgeon
Art Direction | David Larkham
Nationality | UK
Running Time | 45:17

Elton John was so dedicated to his art, or so contractually bound, that he released five albums in 18 months from April 1970—although one was a movie soundtrack and another a live effort. *Madman . . .* , which started with two tracks recorded in February 1971 and was completed that August, was his fourth studio album, and included no major hit singles, yet remained in the U.S. chart for almost a year; by contrast, it was one of his least successful in the UK. It was also the first Elton album to feature Scottish guitarist Davey Johnstone (ex-Magna Carta), who became a permanent band member in early 1972, and more than 30 years later, is still in Elton's band (as is drummer Nigel Olsson). Among the session musicians helping out here are Rick Wakeman (keyboards), Herbie Flowers (bass), and Chris Spedding (guitar). Unsurprisingly, given Wakeman's involvement, there is a whiff of prog rock about the proceedings, while Paul Buckmaster's rich string arrangements serve to further expand the sound.

The best songs here are at the start: "Tiny Dancer" was written about Bernie Taupin's first wife, Maxine Feibelman, and both this and another ballad, the lyrically abstruse "Levon," were U.S. Top 40 singles—no mean feat given their uncommercial length.

Taupin has stated that the title track—an unnerving portrait of insanity, hinting at an introspective streak which pervades much of this album—has the dubious distinction of being his most misunderstood lyric. Many people have presumed that it is about the disgraced U.S. president Richard Nixon. While dismissing this idea, Taupin has not provided an alternative explanation. **JT**

> "What that album still reminds me of most is simply ... driving down those freeways in L.A., listening to the car radio."
>
> Bernie Taupin, 1992

Track Listing

▶	01	**Tiny Dancer** (John · Taupin)	6:17
▶	02	**Levon** (John · Taupin)	5:22
	03	**Razor Face** (John · Taupin)	4:44
▶	04	**Madman Across The Water** (John · Taupin)	5:57
	05	**Indian Sunset** (John · Taupin)	6:46
	06	**Holiday Inn** (John · Taupin)	4:16
	07	**Rotten Peaches** (John · Taupin)	4:58
	08	**All The Nasties** (John · Taupin)	5:09
	09	**Goodbye** (John · Taupin)	1:48

Dolly Parton | Coat Of Many Colors (1971)

Label | RCA Victor
Producer | Bob Ferguson
Art Direction | Uncredited
Nationality | USA
Running Time | 27:35

Dolly Parton left her Appalachian mining town for Nashville in 1965. She had a recording contract within two weeks and a hit within two years. By 1970 she had had so many hits RCA released a Best Of album, but it was 1971's *Coat Of Many Colors*, an album of all-original material, that established her as one of country music's most original singers and songwriters.

Opening with the title track, Parton sings of rural poverty not as a tragic experience but as one that bonded the family in love—her coat of rags was sewn by her mother with such deep feeling Dolly felt truly privileged. The album follows this theme, each song reflecting on lived experience and homespun wisdom. Parton's soprano voice breaks into a cracked vibrato when she is impassioned—she is a very convincing singer—and the Nashville session men behind her display a masterful touch, decorating every song with fluid, melodic picking.

Coat Of Many Colors is a model of economy, its ten songs clock in at less than 30 minutes, and the sentiments expressed helped reassure a rural, white, working-class America that found itself increasingly alienated by pop and rock music. The album cover, the kind of simple painting of a young girl popular prior to the photographic era, again reflects Parton's roots. If the public loved Dolly then *Coat Of Many Colors* also won around the critics who realized they were dealing with a seriously talented singer-songwriter.

Parton has subsequently proved herself one of the smartest and most enduring individuals in showbiz. *Coat Of Many Colors* remains her masterpiece. **GC**

> ## "Looking back to the good old days when times were bad."
>
> Dolly Parton, 1973

Track Listing

▶ 01	Coat Of Many Colors (Parton)	3:06
▶ 02	Traveling Man (Parton)	2:42
03	My Blue Tears (Parton)	2:18
04	If I Lose My Mind (Parton·Wagoner)	2:31
▶ 05	The Mystery Of The Mystery (Parton·Wagoner)	2:29
▶ 06	She Never Met A Man She Didn't Like (Parton)	2:43
07	Early Morning Breeze (Parton)	2:56
08	The Way I See You (Parton·Wagoner)	2:48
09	Here I Am (Parton)	3:21
10	A Better Place To Live (Parton)	2:41

Don McLean | American Pie (1971)

Label | EMI
Producer | Ed Freeman
Art Direction | George S. Whiteman
Nationality | USA
Running Time | 36:16

When Buddy Holly died in a plane crash in February 1959, Don McLean was a 13-year-old paperboy. The headlines he read would sow the seed for his greatest song, an eight-and-a-half-minute epic and U.S. chart-topper that, by its timing and oblique references to the likes of Bob Dylan, Mick Jagger, and The Beatles, appears to double as an elegy to the Sixties.

The track has unjustly overshadowed "Vincent," the album's second single, which hit No. 1 in the UK chart in mid-1972. This was also inspired by a legendary figure, Dutch painter Vincent Van Gogh whose inner torment in his search for perfection led him to cut off part of one of his own ears. All songs on the album were penned by McLean except for the traditional "Babylon," whose arrangement is co-credited to McLean and Lee Hays of The Weavers, who taught it to him. Another track, "Crossroads," is an outstandingly constructed—both thematically and musically— song that deserves better than "also-ran" status.

McLean's biggest hit may have been inspired by a rock 'n' roll giant but his background had been in folk, a fact reflected in an acoustic presentation reminiscent of Gordon Lightfoot. ("Everybody Loves Me, Baby," a self-conscious rocker, is the album's weakest track.) He had worked with the legendary Pete Seeger but his debut album (which charted in the wake of *American Pie*) was allegedly rejected by 34 record labels despite containing the classic "And I Love You So." (It has also been reported that he refused to sign away his publishing to prospective labels, so perhaps the last laugh was his after all.) **MH**

"What does 'American Pie' mean? It means I don't have to work if I don't want to."

Don McLean, 1998

Track Listing

▶	01	**American Pie** (McLean)	8:36
	02	**Till Tomorrow** (McLean)	2:15
▶	03	**Vincent** (McLean)	4:03
▶	04	**Crossroads** (McLean)	3:39
	05	**Winter Wood** (McLean)	3:10
	06	**Empty Chairs** (McLean)	3:27
	07	**Everybody Loves Me, Baby** (McLean)	3:36
	08	**Sister Fatima** (McLean)	2:35
	09	**The Grave** (McLean)	3:14
	10	**Babylon** (Trad., arr. Hays·McLean)	1:41

Emerson, Lake, And Palmer | Tarkus (1971)

Label | Island
Producer | Greg Lake
Art Direction | William Neal
Nationality | UK
Running Time | 38:29

As the International War Crimes Conference convened in Oslo in June 1971, so Emerson, Lake, And Palmer unveiled their sophomore album: a comment on the futility of war, the cover sports an armadillo tank.

Keyboardist Keith Emerson, bassist/singer Greg Lake, and drummer Carl Palmer began work in January on a concept devised on tour by Emerson, inspired in part by Argentine composer Alberto Ginastera, and recorded in six days in February.

"Carl was very struck by different time signatures," Emerson told *Contemporary Keyboard*. "He told me that he'd like to do something in 5/4, so I said that I'd keep that in mind and started writing *Tarkus* from there. Greg wasn't too sure about it. It was too weird. But he agreed to try it, and afterwards he loved it."

The opening magnum opus is marked by siren-like keyboard and rattling percussion fusillades between "Tarkus" and three adversaries—the brooding "Stones Of Years," parping "Iconclast," and fractious "Mass"— before defeat by an evil "Manticore" of Persian mythology (cue cathedral organ and phased drums).

These battles are flanked by "Eruption"—Emerson's synths, Hammond and Moog, complemented by Palmer's explosive tub swipes—then the soaring "Battlefield" and dramatic "Aquatarkus." The second half brings light relief with the honky-tonking "Jeremy Bender" and rock 'n' rolling "Are You Ready Eddy?" (for engineer Eddy Offord). "Bitches Crystal" and "Infinite Space" are jauntily jazzy, while "The Only Way"—a Bach-based baroque— questions religion.

This is an album that defines prog grandeur. **TJ**

"The words are about revolution... Where has it got anybody?"

Greg Lake, 1971

Track Listing

▶ 01 **Tarkus:**
    a) **Eruption** (Emerson)
    b) **Stones Of Years** (Emerson·Lake)
    c) **Iconclast** (Emerson)
    d) **Mass** (Emerson·Lake)
    e) **Manticore** (Emerson)
    f) **Battlefield** (Lake)
    g) **Aquatarkus** (Emerson)   20:35

02 **Jeremy Bender** (Emerson·Lake)   1:46

▶ 03 **Bitches Crystal** (Emerson·Lake)   3:55

04 **The Only Way (Hymn)** (Emerson·Lake)   3:48

05 **Infinite Space (Conclusion)** (Emerson·Palmer)   3:18

06 **A Time And A Place** (Emerson·Lake·Palmer)   2:57

07 **Are You Ready Eddy?** (Emerson·Lake·Palmer)   2:10

Led Zeppelin | Led Zeppelin IV (1971)

Label | Atlantic
Producer | Jimmy Page
Art Direction | Graphreaks
Nationality | UK
Running Time | 42:34

Responsible for at least two generations of bedroom air guitarists, Led Zeppelin's ... *IV* practically defined hard rock and heavy metal. It drew on folk music, the blues, rock 'n' roll, and even psychedelia. But make no mistake, ... *IV* was the also sound of a band grooming itself for stadium-level success.

Riff-driven cuts like "Black Dog" and "Rock And Roll" are augmented by more spiritual mediations like "Misty Mountain Hop" and "Going To California." "Stairway To Heaven" revealed the group's increased obsession with the occult, religion, and English mythology (rumors even emerged that playing the track backward would reveal satanic messages). Jimmy Page's performance—especially the two fiery solos on "Stairway To Heaven" (the most played song of all time on U.S. radio)—would influence legions of rock groups to follow, including Aerosmith, Metallica, Guns N' Roses, and Tool.

The album's mystique was increased by its cover, which features no group name or album title (hence its alternative monickers "Four Symbols" and "Zoso," a reference to the runic symbols displayed within).

That said, ... *IV* does suffer, if only occasionally, from overblown pretensions. While its predecessor, the predominantly acoustic ... *III*, was a more humble affair, ... *IV* shows Led Zeppelin at its most majestic and indulgent, and its grandiose sound would leave them open to ridicule. Within five years, heavy rock would be superceded by punk rock, which would sound the death knell for groups like Led Zeppelin. But that was all to come. *Led Zeppelin IV* reveals a group at the height of its powers—and enjoying itself. **BW**

> "If the feel was good and it was a little bit out of tune, flat or sharp, it didn't matter. We'd keep it just for the feel."

Robert Plant, 1983

Track Listing

▶ 01	**Black Dog** (Jones·Page·Plant)	4:57
02	**Rock And Roll** (Bonham·Jones·Page·Plant)	3:40
03	**The Battle Of Evermore** (Page·Plant)	5:52
▶ 04	**Stairway To Heaven** (Page·Plant)	8:03
▶ 05	**Misty Mountain Hop** (Jones·Page·Plant)	4:38
06	**Four Sticks** (Page·Plant)	4:45
▶ 07	**Going To California** (Page·Plant)	3:31
▶ 08	**When The Levee Breaks** (Bonham·Jones·Memphis Minnie·Page·Plant)	7:08

Serge Gainsbourg
Histoire De Melody Nelson (1971)

Label | Philips
Producer | Jean-Claude Vannier
Art Direction | Jean-Yves Billet
Nationality | France
Running Time | 27:57

Rod Stewart
Every Picture Tells A Story (1971)

Label | Mercury
Producer | Rod Stewart
Art Direction | Uncredited
Nationality | UK
Running Time | 40:31

Serge Gainsbourg's Mr. Hyde-style alter ego, Gainsbarre, runs the show on this gloriously seedy concept album exploring the author's fascination with the unattainable teen heroine. Of course, these heroines were not really unattainable for France's famed dirty old man. By this time, the chain-smoking vocalist had already been with the ultimate bombshell, Brigitte Bardot, and the topless charmer clutching a stuffed monkey to her chest on the album cover was Gainsbourg's lover, Jane Birkin.

Gainsbourg was only known outside France for the breathy "Je T'Aime Moi Non Plus" duet with Birkin. Hoping to replicate that success, the singer enlisted Birkin and turned the heat up in a fashion that makes that early hit sound like mere foreplay.

Utterly fixated on the heroine, he leers through the opening cut, "Melody," whispering lines over some of the dirtiest funk of the era. He woos Birkin through softly swelling violins on "Ballade De Melody Nelson," then sounds like he is backed by Sly And The Family Stone on "En Melody," which features Birkin squealing with laughter (allegedly, her brother was tickling her).

The album failed to be a commercial success, even in France, and most early critics dismissed it as self-indulgent. Today, the work is seen as a groundbreaking union of rock band and orchestra style that has immeasurably influenced artists such as Beck, David Holmes, and—most noticeably—Air. **JiH**

The Faces were a quintessential rock 'n' roll band: the brotherly, empathetic flipside to The Rolling Stones' satanic majesty. In husky Rod Stewart they had one of the all-time great British voices, capable of investing myriad song styles—folk, blues, country, soul—with an intuitive warmth. For a few glorious years, Stewart's rootsy solo career coexisted with the group's laddish bonhomie, his bandmates making appearances on *An Old Raincoat Won't Ever Let You Down* (1969) and *Gasoline Alley* (1970). *Every Picture Tells A Story* was the zenith of this fertile period, topping the album charts on both sides of the Atlantic.

The opening title track ingeniously applies acoustic instrumentation to hard rock form, its amusingly crude tale of round-the-world sex whipped to a breathless climax by Mick Waller's caveman drumming. In contrast, "Mandolin Wind" is a breathtakingly tender ballad soaked in pedal steel and pathos, while the similarly furnished "Tomorrow Is A Long Time" places Stewart at the top table of Dylan interpreters.

The gorgeous, organ-driven reading of Tim Hardin's "Reason To Believe" was released as a single, but the big hit—No. 1 in both the U.S. and the UK—proved to be its original B-side, the immortal "Maggie May." Gilded with mandolin and acoustic guitars, this bittersweet coming-of-age saga is swinging yet layered, while Rod's off-the-cuff performance defines him as an artist. **MA**

Emerson, Lake, And Palmer | Pictures At An Exhibition (1971)

Label | Island
Producer | Greg Lake
Art Direction | William Neal
Nationality | UK
Running Time | 53:29

Leonard Cohen Songs Of Love And Hate (1971)

Label | Columbia
Producer | Bob Johnston
Art Direction | John Berg
Nationality | Canada
Running Time | 44:48

Always ones for the big entrance, Emerson, Lake, And Palmer premiered their rocked-up version of Russian composer Modeste Mussorgsky's classical work at 1970's Isle Of Wight Festival, their first proper show together.

William Neal's artwork was a very sedate affair—empty picture frames in a gallery—completely out of scale with the impact of the music. Far more noteworthy was Emerson's work with the Moog synthesizer, an innovation rarely found outside the studio due to its unpredictability and because many bands did not regard it as a "real instrument."

Ironically, the highlight of the record was an original composition from Lake, "The Sage," which had been intended for another record but fitted the mood perfectly. It featured his best ever recorded acoustic guitar playing. By contrast, "The Hut Of Baba Yaga" saw Emerson follow some speedy Hammond organ with a chunky Moog workout. He then switched to boogie-woogie piano for a cover of B. Bumble And The Stingers' 1962 Tchaikovsky pastiche "Nut Rocker," concluding proceedings with a suitably irreverent bang.

Pictures ... was only released in the U.S. after import levels became overwhelming, upon which it went to No. 10 on the Billboard chart. The album gave them their third UK Top Three in a year and a groundbreaker in the mold of Keith Emerson's previous band, The Nice. For better or worse, a trail had been blazed. **MH**

The weak of heart should fear to tread in the Leonard Cohen songbook. That is especially true of *Songs Of Love And Hate*, a sparse and haunting collection of open wounds, lingering contempt, and feverish love that ranks among his most emotionally intense offerings. The line between love and hate has rarely sounded thinner.

The songs unfold like short stories or, frequently, small poems, which makes sense given the author's background. Cohen had already written two novels and was a noted poet long before he became a darling of the folk movement and inked a recording contract. His first two releases on Columbia were greeted with wild critical acclaim and mild commercial success. With his flat monotone delivery and richly literate songs, Cohen was seen as Canada's answer to Bob Dylan. But he clearly showed that he was his own man on this release.

The artist's dramatic blend of folk and pop is perfectly captured here, starting with the twitchy acoustic guitar melding into a softly swelling string arrangement on the heartbreaking "Avalanche" and continuing through the singer's growling choruses pitted against lovely female harmonies on "Diamonds In The Mine." Love is indeed a battlefield and Cohen appropriately dubbed his backing band "The Army." Still, the album's best moments come when Cohen basically walks alone on such mournful numbers as "Last Year's Man" and "Joan of Arc." **JiH**

Joni Mitchell | Blue (1971)

Label | Reprise
Producer | Henry Lewy
Art Direction | Gary Burden
Nationality | Canada
Running Time | 35:41

On 1975's *The Hissing Of Summer Lawns*, Joni Mitchell painted nuanced portraits of suburban America with a cool, objective eye. *Blue*, by contrast, is so raw and personal that it feels like a confession. Mitchell later remarked that she had "absolutely no secrets from the world and couldn't pretend in my life to be strong. Or happy." The result is an album of almost painful beauty.

The cover recalls bebop-era classics with its two-tone portrait of Mitchell, drowned in indigo shadows. The music, however, shows her at her least jazz-inflected, with plain string instruments and bare piano work. Billboard admired her "stronger, surer singing voice," but this scarcely conveys the thrilling sincerity of Mitchell's vocal performance on the album, which went on to sell more than a million copies.

The focus is on relationships—their brittle joys and nerve-flaying failures. "My Old Man" describes the loyalties of a love affair with heartbreaking clarity. Likewise, "A Case Of You" is a sad, generous toast to a love that cannot quite be laid to rest. Only the title track embraces wider concerns in its lament for a once so optimistic but now faltering generation.

Even the two joyful songs, "California" and "Carey," are about departures for warmer climes and nostalgic places. Mitchell does, however, give a foretaste of her skill in drawing characters with "The Last Time I Saw Richard"—an austere portrait of a life in decline.

Although James Taylor and Steven Stills contributed guitar parts, *Blue* is devoid of any presence other than Mitchell's. She stands alone in the cold heart of this utterly compelling work. **JDi**

> "When the spirit of child's play enters into the creative process, it's a wonderful force and something to be nurtured."
>
> Joni Mitchell, 2004

Track Listing

01	**All I Want** (Mitchell)		3:32
▶ 02	**My Old Man** (Mitchell)		3:33
03	**Little Green** (Mitchell)		3:25
04	**Carey** (Mitchell)		3:00
▶ 05	**Blue** (Mitchell)		3:00
▶ 06	**California** (Mitchell)		3:48
07	**This Flight Tonight** (Mitchell)		2:50
08	**River** (Mitchell)		4:00
▶ 09	**A Case Of You** (Mitchell)		4:20
▶ 10	**The Last Time I Saw Richard** (Mitchell)		4:13

Funkadelic | Maggot Brain (1971)

Label | Westbound
Producer | George Clinton
Art Direction | David Krieger
Nationality | USA
Running Time | 36:45

Their first two albums—the blues-influenced warped acid rock of 1970's eponymous debut and the psych-tinged sophomore, *Free Your Mind And Your Ass Will Follow*—introduced The Funk as a way of life, a religion. Their third outing captured the group at the height of their creative and imaginative powers.

First came the packaging; a shrieking woman's head erupts from the soil on the cover, while the sleevenotes quote the Process Church Of The Final Judgment. Then the music—brave and bold, it meshes spine-tingling lyrics ("I have tasted the maggots in the mind of the universe") with an eerie, demented, transcendental score. "Back then people said, 'You just can't do that sorta thing on a record,'" explained frontman George Clinton. "And I was sayin' right back, 'You bet yo' ass I can.'"

Recorded at Universal Studios, Detroit, in the latter parts of 1970 and the beginning of 1971, *Maggot Brain* excelled at gospel-infused, call-and-response ebullience ("Can You Get To That") and pulsating funk rock stomps ("Super Stupid"). It also hit hard with penetrating social commentary—"You And Your Folks, Me And My Folks" overtly attacks racism, "War Of Armageddon" tackles the traumatic fallout of the Vietnam War.

But the real power lies with the title track. Myth has it that Clinton discovered his brother's rotting body and cracked skull, sprawled in a Chicago apartment—hence the "maggot brain." Locking guitarist Eddie Hazel in the studio he demanded, "Play like your mother just died." Hazel did just that providing a spectral, plaintive nine-minute guitar solo that eclipsed everything he and the group did, before or after. **LW**

> "I think I'm lucky to have survived that time. I don't remember a lot about it, but I survived."

George Clinton, 1996

Track Listing

▶	01	**Maggot Brain** (Clinton·Hazel)	10:18
▶	02	**Can You Get To That** (Clinton·Harris)	2:49
	03	**Hit It And Quit It** (Clinton·Nelson·Shila)	3:48
▶	04	**You And Your Folks, Me And My Folks** (Clinton·Jones·Worrell)	3:35
	05	**Super Stupid** (Clinton·Hazel·Nelson·Ross)	3:56
	06	**Back In Our Minds** (Haskins)	2:37
	07	**Wars Of Armageddon** (Clinton·Fulwood·Ross·Worrel)	9:42

Janis Joplin | Pearl (1971)

Label | Columbia
Producer | Paul A. Rothchild
Art Direction | Barry Feinstein
Nationality | USA
Running Time | 34:23

In her too-brief career, Janis Joplin seemed to teeter permanently on the precipice of self-destruction. As with Billie Holiday, it was Joplin's struggle with drug addiction and relationship woes that made her blues sound so convincing. Yet the singer seemed to be in the process of righting her personal ship when she went into the studio to record *Pearl*. Having gone gold with 1968's *Cheap Thrills*, Joplin had left Big Brother and assembled the more versatile Full Tilt Boogie Band; she also seemed ready to settle down and was engaged to be married. Of course, settling down is a relative term. The album's cover showed Joplin with her regular companions—a drink and cigarette.

Pearl is a convincing argument that Joplin might not only have been the premier blues singer of the era, but the premier singer of the day. Starting with the Full Tilt Boogie assault of "Move Over" and continuing with the mournful "Cry Baby," Joplin displays astonishing vocal versatility as she fills her words with tangible drama and passion. Listening to the chops shown on "A Woman Left Lonely," it is hard not to draw comparisons with all-time greats like Bessie Smith. Joplin also knew how to have a good time, witness "Me and Bobby McGee" and "Mercedes Benz."

In retrospect, the most moving number on the album does not feature a single word sung by Joplin. The vocalist was found dead of a heroin overdose in a Hollywood hotel room before she had added her vocals to "Buried Alive In The Blues." Released posthumously, *Pearl* would top the charts and forever secure the singer's legend. **JiH**

> "Don'cha understand? Music is just about feelin' things and havin' a good time! "

Janis Joplin, 1968

Track Listing

▶	01	**Move Over** (Joplin)	3:43
▶	02	**Cry Baby** (Berns·Ragovoy)	3:58
▶	03	**A Woman Left Lonely** (Oldham·Penn)	3:29
	04	**Half Moon** (J. Hall·J. Hall)	3:53
▶	05	**Buried Alive In The Blues** (Gravenites)	2:27
	06	**My Baby** (Ragovoy·Shuman)	3:45
▶	07	**Me And Bobby McGee** (Foster·Kristofferson)	4:31
▶	08	**Mercedes Benz** (Joplin·McClure·Neuwirth)	1:47
	09	**Trust Me** (Womack)	3:17
	10	**Get It While You Can** (Ragovoy·Shuman)	3:33

Fela Ransome-Kuti And The Africa '70 With Ginger Baker | Live! (1971)

Label | Celluloid
Producer | Jeff Jarratt
Art Direction | Uncredited
Nationality | Nigeria • UK
Running Time | 45:19

Fela Kuti returned to Nigeria from America and Europe as if he had discovered tobacco and the potato. He was bringing both funk, or Afrobeat, and newly politicized lyrics. Trouble was, despite the *London Scene* LP (the Africa '70's first album) and singles such as "Lady" and "Buy Africa," their homeland was not ready for them.

Help came in the form of an outsider: James Brown toured West Africa for the first time in December 1971. Now, Nigeria was primed. Shortly after Brown left, Kuti had his first serious hit, "Jeun K'oku." The band changed its name to Africa (or Afrika) '70, moved headquarters to a bigger club, and then traveled to London to record at Abbey Road.

A long-time fan of African music, Ginger Baker moved to Lagos in 1971 with a 16-track studio. He had worked with Kuti in London, co-producing some of the band's earliest recordings, so a collaboration was the obvious next step. Baker takes the place of Tony Allen behind the drum kit on the first track, "Let's Start," a blunt, no-messing order to get the sex underway. But it is on "Ye Ye De Smell" that the former Cream man comes into his own: as Fela begins his piano solo, Allen picks up the baton, then Baker adds fire and flash to the rhythm. By the time Kuti moves onto sax, the track belongs to the drummers. They never yield.

Shortly after, the same principals reconvened to record Baker's *Stratavarious*, itself a landmark LP that increased awareness of the African essence of rock. In the space of six months, Kuti had gone global. **DH**

> "I refuse to live my life in fear
> ...If somebody wants to do
> harm for you, it's better for
> you not to know. So I don't
> think about it. I can say I don't
> care. I'm ready for anything."
>
> Fela Kuti, 1974

Track Listing

▶ 01	**Let's Start** (Kuti)	7:48
02	**Black Man's Cry** (Kuti)	11:36
▶ 03	**Ye Ye De Smell** (Kuti)	13:17
04	**Egbe Mi O (Carry Me I Want To Die)** (Kuti)	12:38

Faces | A Nod Is As Good As A Wink ... To A Blind Horse (1971)

Label | Warner Bros.
Producer | The Faces • Glyn Johns
Art Direction | Uncredited
Nationality | UK
Running Time | 36:03

When Rod Stewart hooked up with the remnants of The Small Faces in 1969 by hanging round their rehearsal rooms with similarly unemployed pal Ron Wood, he was not universally welcomed. Having been ditched by Steve Marriott, en route to supergroup Humble Pie, the three remaining Small Faces were not keen to be anyone else's backing band. Yet overwhelming musical compatibility kept such worries in the background until 1971, when the band's excellent third album coincided with Rod's solo *Every Picture Tells A Story*.

A Nod is As Good As A Wink ... To A Blind Horse had much going for it, not least the songwriting ability of bassist Ronnie Lane. His vignettes of East London life—the likes of "Last Orders Please" and especially "Debris"—were the necessary antidote to the Wood/Stewart laddishness for which the Faces became famed. It can only be a matter of time, for example, before "Stay With Me," still Wood's finest open-tuned moment despite a quarter of a century as a Stone, is resurrected as a theme for a lads' magazine commercial.

It was this tough but tender dichotomy that led John Peel to make them his pre-Undertones favorites. Even a cheery trundle through Chuck Berry's hoary old "Memphis, Tennessee" cannot spoil things.

Sadly for the Faces, the follow-up, *Ooh-La-La*, is best forgotten, and their star waned as Stewart's rose toward the commercial apogee of *Atlantic Crossing* and stadium anthem "Sailing." One thing is for sure—it would never have been given house room here. **MH**

> "Me and Ron had come from the so-called Underground ... The Faces were more pop ... "
>
> Rod Stewart, 1971

Track Listing

	01	**Miss Judy's Farm** (Stewart • Wood)	3:40
▶	02	**You're So Rude** (Lane • McLagan)	3:43
	03	**Love Lives Here** (Lane • Stewart • Wood)	3:06
	04	**Last Orders Please** (Lane)	2:35
▶	05	**Stay With Me** (Stewart • Wood)	4:39
▶	06	**Debris** (Lane)	4:36
	07	**Memphis, Tennessee** (Berry)	5:27
	08	**Too Bad** (Stewart • Wood)	3:13
	09	**That's All You Need** (Stewart • Wood)	5:04

Flamin' Groovies
Teenage Head (1971)

Label | Kama Sutra
Producer | Richard Robinson
Art Direction | Murray Brenman
Nationality | USA
Running Time | 28:23

The Flamin' Groovies arose out of the San Francisco music scene of the mid-1960s, but they never attempted to be part of that city's big psychedelic party. Instead, they concentrated on recreating a raw sound that owed much to 1950s rockabilly alongside a debt to early Beatles and Stones records.

The Groovies' most fertile time was between 1968 and '71, when they were a great garage band and wrote a slew of memorable songs. *Teenage Head* was the last album to be recorded by the original lineup and the tensions between guitarist Cyril Jordan and singer Roy Loney are reflected in the record's tough, rumbling sound. The title song is an anthem of adolescent alienation while "High Flying Baby" rips and snorts. The band handle several blues cuts deftly—Robert Johnson's "32-20" swaggers and struts. (This mix of blues and rock has led some to compare *Teenage Head* favorably with the Stones' *Sticky Fingers*.) The album's moody greaser cover rejects prevailing hippie imagery of the time, and presents the Groovies as a band of outcasts—certainly, they saw themselves as such.

The few reviews *Teenage Head* attracted were good, but the Groovies were out of place in an America obsessed with guitar-soloing rock bands; Roy Loney left, disillusioned, only a few months after the album's release. Cyril Jordan reshaped the band and shifted them to England, where they would have an influence on the burgeoning punk movement before disbanding in 1979. **GC**

Gene Clark
White Light (1971)

Label | A&M
Producer | Jesse Davis
Art Direction | John Dietrich
Nationality | USA
Running Time | 34:58

Following his enjoyable country rock releases with banjo player Doug Dillard, Gene Clark returned to the solo path he had chosen when he left The Byrds in 1966. The result was *White Light*, one of the best albums in the field of American singer-songwriters and folk-rock. That it failed commercially has more to do with Clark's idiosyncrasies and strong character than with flaws in the recording.

Working at his refuge near Mendocino, Northern California, Clark produced a set of songs more intimate and poetically complex than hitherto. A bleakness runs through much of the material here, true, but the songs bear a beauty that matched the cream of his work with The Byrds. With the help of guitarist Jesse Ed Davis, who had been working in Los Angeles with Leon Russell, and a band of musicians including Chris Ethridge (bass), Gary Mallaber (drums), Mike Utley (organ), Ben Sidran (piano), John Selk (guitar), and Bobbye Hall (percussion), he recorded an acoustic masterpiece.

Alongside his original songs—standouts include "With Tomorrow," "Spanish Guitar," "Because Of You," and "White Light"—there is an excellent cover of "Tears Of Rage," written by Bob Dylan and Richard Manuel for The Band's debut *Music From Big Pink*.

For unexplained reasons the album's title, chosen by Clark and A&M, did not appear with his name on the cover, but the stark sleeve is in perfect tune with the album's melancholic atmosphere.

A masterclass for the singer-songwriter. **GSu**

John Prine
John Prine (1971)

Label | Atlantic
Producer | Arif Mardin
Art Direction | Tom Wilkes
Nationality | USA
Running Time | 44:33

For nearly as long as there has been a Dylan, there have been Next Dylans—clever, tuneful singer-songwriters who, some believe, just might replicate the artistic success of the inscrutable Minnesotan. Of course, there can be no Next Dylan, and woe betide the talented young musician charged with being just that. John Prine got stuck with the label early on in his career and that is a testament to his immense talent. But so too is the fact that the label fits him uneasily.

Signed to Atlantic with the help of Kris Kristofferson, the 25-year-old Prine released his country-tinged, eponymous debut in 1971, just as the Vietnam War was peaking. Although it is not explicitly a protest record, unhappiness about the war does emerge, most devastatingly in "Sam Stone," a heart-wrenching ballad on the demise of a morphine-addicted veteran; the song is made sadder still by the plainness of Prine's gravelly baritone. The Southeast Asian conflict also appears, implicitly at least, in "Your Flag Decal Won't Get You Into Heaven Anymore," a cheery novelty tune tinged with bitter irony.

Those two songs represent Prine's most effective songwriting modes—unstintingly bleak and laugh-out-loud funny. You may think "Sam Stone" is the most depressing song you have ever heard, but that is only because you have not yet experienced "Hello In There," a doleful number about old age. Meanwhile, "Spanish Pipedream" playfully exhorts listeners to blow up their television sets. **KB**

Harry Nilsson
Nilsson Schmilsson (1971)

Label | RCA Victor
Producer | Richard Perry
Art Direction | Acy Lehman
Nationality | USA
Running Time | 34:48

With John Lennon and Paul McCartney hailing him as their favorite American artist, Harry Nilsson seemed destined for great things. But Nilsson was a shy, private man who struggled in the limelight, and unfortunately he never quite achieved his full potential.

The album *Nilsson Smilsson* was a pivotal point in his career. Nilsson had decided to team up with British producer Richard Perry for the recording, and Perry unleashed a new, crazily creative side to Nilsson. "Gotta Get Up," a witty tale about needing sleep, immediately strikes a chord with its 1930s ragtime tone, while "Down," with its earth-shattering, bluesy piano ensemble, commands attention. The insanely catchy calypso track "Coconut" was a hit (No. 8 in the U.S., No. 42 in the UK), and featured years later in the Quentin Tarantino movie *Reservoir Dogs.* "Jump Into The Fire" is dirty rock, proving that Nilsson could get down with the best of them.

Oddly, Nilsson's greatest success came from his cover of Badfinger's mesmerising "Without You," which made both U.S. and UK No. 1. His interpretation of this timeless classic whirls the listener on an emotional rollercoaster ride and subsequently earned him a second Grammy Award.

The success of "Without You" led to the album shooting rapidly up the charts in both America and the UK. It spawned three hit singles and went gold before reaching No. 3 on the U.S. Billboard chart, yet somehow Nilsson still remains the unsung hero of the American pop music scene. **KT**

T. Rex | Electric Warrior (1971)

Label | Fly
Producer | Tony Visconti
Art Direction | Hipgnosis
Nationality | UK
Running Time | 36:33

Marc Bolan is one of the most compelling characters in rock history. With his updated Byronic style and delightfully obscure brand of hippy mysticism, he was never less than audacious. While his career featured some maddeningly uneven output (as well as a bestselling book of poetry entitled *The Warlock Of Love*), its pinnacle was *Electric Warrior*. And, like all of his work, it was packed with surprises.

T. Rex had already achieved success in the UK—however, Bolan wanted to reach the unconverted across the Atlantic. Hitting the road with new members Steve Currie on bass, and drummer Bill Legend abetting percussionist Mickey Finn, the band began cutting tracks on the fly in London, New York, and Los Angeles. While singles released at the time hinted at a bolder sound for the group, the full wonder of *Electric Warrior* only became clear on its release.

Its cover art epitomizes the dangerous promise of rock's power, with Bolan wielding an electric weapon before a munitions dump of amplifiers. However, instead of blasting the listener with a metal onslaught when the needle hits the groove, . . . *Warrior* begins with a sultry guitar chug, easy backbeat, and an invitation to croon "beneath the bebop moon" on "Mambo Sun." The wide-eyed acoustic strum of "Cosmic Dancer" follows, with its rich string arrangement. So goes the record, by turns raucously salacious and meditatively romantic. While single "Bang A Gong (Get It On)" would reach the U.S. Top Ten, T. Rex never achieved Bolan's large ambition of international superstardom—at least not in his lifetime. **TSh**

> ## "I just want to make contact with all the kids. That's what it's all about, the contact between me and my audience."
>
> Marc Bolan, 1973

Track Listing

▶	01	**Mambo Sun** (Bolan)	3:38
▶	02	**Cosmic Dancer** (Bolan)	4:26
▶	03	**Jeepster** (Bolan)	4:10
	04	**Monolith** (Bolan)	3:45
	05	**Lean Woman Blues** (Bolan)	3:01
▶	06	**Bang A Gong (Get It On)** (Bolan)	4:24
	07	**Planet Queen** (Bolan)	3:11
▶	08	**The Motivator** (Bolan)	3:57
	09	**Life's A Gas** (Bolan)	2:23
▶	10	**Rip Off** (Bolan)	3:38

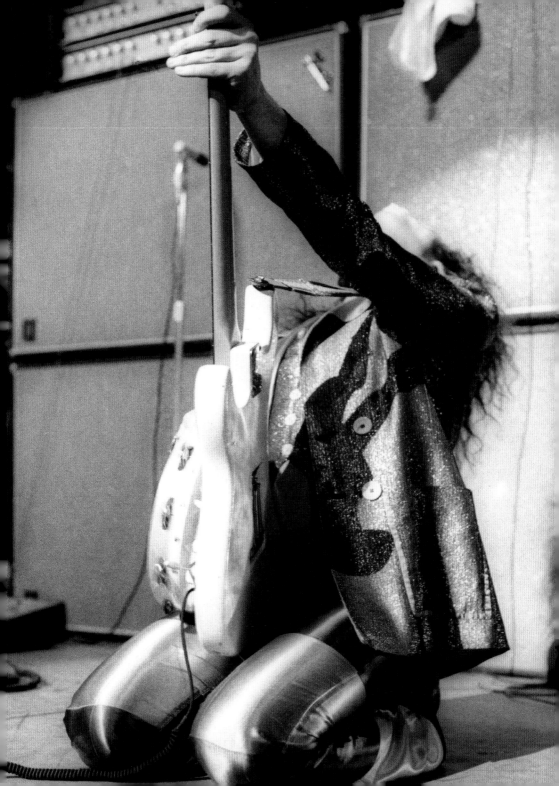

David Bowie | Hunky Dory (1971)

Label | RCA Victor
Producer | David Bowie • Ken Scott
Art Direction | Terry Pastor • George Underwood
Nationality | UK
Running Time | 41:37

A hard-rock concept album about a shaven-headed transvestite failed to make David Bowie a star. So *NME*'s "thinking man's Marc Bolan" followed *The Man Who Sold The World* with a toybox of acoustic oddities, tributes to heroes, and surrealism.

Amazingly, that did not do the trick either and 1969's "Space Oddity" was increasingly looking like a one-hit wonder. So Bowie claimed to be gay, reveled in the ensuing publicity, wrote songs about a spaceman, and became the decade's most influential musician.

At which point, finally, people turned on by *Ziggy Stardust* bought that toybox—*Hunky Dory*. They found an album endearingly affected—I can be Dylan, Lou Reed, and Syd Barrett all at once!—but packed with evidence of a songwriter easing into first gear. It also marks the emergence proper of Camp David, with exquisite gems such as "Queen Bitch." Bowie arrived at the photoshoot for the cover clutching a Marlene Dietrich photobook, and the tinted portrait definitely has something of a faded movie queen about it.

The temporarily calming effect of a wife and baby led to family snapshots like "Kooks," making this Bowie's most human album. But it has harder moments, notably "Andy Warhol" (which appalled its namesake). And for three cuts the album soars. "Quicksand," was inspired by America's "bliss and calamity" but is a beautiful ballad, not a fractured rocker, while "The Bewlay Brothers" is a bewitching portrait of mental illness.

Best of all, "Life on Mars?"—which sprang from Bowie being commissioned to write lyrics for the song that became "My Way"—sounds like nothing on Earth. **BM**

"I'm going to be huge, and it's quite frightening in a way."

David Bowie, 1972

Track Listing

▶	01	**Changes** (Bowie)	3:37
	02	**Oh! You Pretty Things** (Bowie)	3:12
	03	**Eight Line Poem** (Bowie)	2:56
▶	04	**Life On Mars?** (Bowie)	3:54
	05	**Kooks** (Bowie)	2:54
▶	06	**Quicksand** (Bowie)	5:06
	07	**Fill Your Heart** (Rose • Williams)	3:08
	08	**Andy Warhol** (Bowie)	3:57
	09	**Song For Bob Dylan** (Bowie)	4:12
	10	**Queen Bitch** (Bowie)	3:19
▶	11	**The Bewlay Brothers** (Bowie)	5:22

Randy Newman | Sail Away (1972)

Label | Reprise
Producer | Russ Titelman • Lenny Waronker
Art Direction | Mike Salisbury
Nationality | USA
Running Time | 30:14

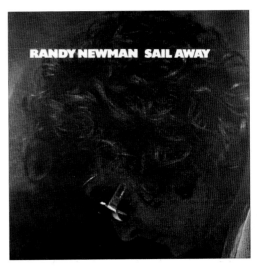

Randy Newman was, and still is, seen as a songwriter first and a performer second. Back in 1972, the 28-year-old's musically old-fashioned but lyrically sharp little Tin Pan Alley-style pieces had been hits for many acts (most famously Three Dog Night's cover of "Mama Told Me Not To Come"), but Newman's own albums had sunk like lead. It was with this immaculate song-cycle that people began to pay attention.

"Simon Smith And His Amazing Dancing Bear" was a jaunty hit in 1967 for Alan Price, but here, with Newman's inimitable wreck of a voice backed only by his precise piano, it's swamped in pathos, the narrator not a winking entertainer but a pitiable fantasist. (For the record, Newman writes the majority of his songs in character.) Several singers have, chillingly, turned the orchestral slave-trader pitch-piece "Sail Away" into an anthem extolling America as the land of the free. Most famously, the pathetic, almost sinister "You Can Leave Your Hat On" was morphed by Joe Cocker and, later, Tom Jones, into a tumescent come-on. No one misinterpreted "Political Science," a richly sarcastic dig at American foreign policy ("They all hate us anyhow/So let's drop the big one now"), which might be why no one has ever covered it.

Newman had his hit in 1977 with the acerbic satire of "Short People," since when he has spent much of his time in the family business. Alfred Newman, his uncle, was the head of music at 20th Century Fox; Newman has received a tidy wage—and 16 Oscar nominations—writing scores for movies both memorable (*Toy Story*) and abysmal (*Three Amigos*). **WF-J**

> ## "It's great to be an American."
>
> Randy Newman, "Sail Away," 1972

Track Listing

▶ 01	**Sail Away** (Newman)	2:56
▶ 02	**Lonely At The Top** (Newman)	2:32
03	**He Gives Us All His Love** (Newman)	1:53
04	**Last Night I Had A Dream** (Newman)	3:01
05	**Simon Smith And The Amazing Dancing Bear** (Newman)	2:00
▶ 06	**Old Man** (Newman)	2:42
▶ 07	**Political Science** (Newman)	2:00
08	**Burn On** (Newman)	2:33
09	**Memo To My Son** (Newman)	1:56
10	**Dayton, Ohio—1903** (Newman)	1:47
▶ 11	**You Can Leave Your Hat On** (Newman)	3:18
▶ 12	**God's Song (That's Why I Love Mankind)** (Newman)	3:36

Deep Purple
Machine Head (1972)

Label | Purple
Producer | Martin Birch
Art Direction | John Coletta • Roger Glover
Nationality | UK
Running Time | 37:25

In April 1972, Vietnam raged and Apollo 16 was on the moon. Even more momentously, Purple unleashed their magnificent seventh album—a UK chart-topper and the pinnacle of their heavy rock prowess.

Part written on the road in summer 1971, *Machine Head* was made in Switzerland for tax purposes. During their three-week stay, Purple witnessed the theater fire during a Frank Zappa gig, which destroyed their studio and inspired "Smoke On The Water." The latter's celebrated riff is just one highlight of a set that delivers, according to *Rolling Stone*, "the rushing, grating crunch of the hard attack."

It was mainly recorded in the corridors of the closed Grand Hotel, using The Rolling Stones' mobile unit. "For playbacks," recalled guitarist Ritchie Blackmore, "I had to go through six doors, down a fire escape and across a courtyard where it was snowing!"

"Highway Star" opens, with pummeling percussion and a pyrotechnic fusillade of keys, guitars, and snarls. The pace slows for "Maybe I'm A Leo," then picks up for the booming "Pictures Of Home." The funky "Never Before" is followed by a triple-whammy: "Smoke On The Water"— an immortal guitar-led anthem that the band first dubbed "Durh! Durh! Durh!"—then the phased-organ and percussion crescendo of "Lazy" and the breakneck "Space Truckin'," replete with vocalist Ian Gillan's howls over all-guns-blazing foundations.

Glover remembered making *Machine Head* as the best of times. It was also the best of albums. **TJ**

Big Star
No. 1 Record (1972)

Label | Ardent
Producer | John Fry
Art Direction | Uncredited
Nationality | USA
Running Time | 39:02

Classicist, romantic, anglophile pop was what doomed Memphis quartet Big Star offered, coining both the power-pop genre and the associated curse of cult obscurity. Big Star were dominated by the songwriting duo of Alex Chilton and Chris Bell; Chilton had topped the charts aged 16, fronting The Box Tops for blue-eyed soul classic "The Letter." Bell fronted Ice Water, who also featured drummer Jody Stephens and bassist Andy Hummell, re-christening themselves Big Star upon Chilton's arrival, after a nearby supermarket.

Recorded in local Ardent studios, the band's swiftly recorded debut betrays not a drip of Southern sweat; in its place remains pristine pop (the nobly heroic "Ballad Of El Goodo"), sunshine harmonies ("When My Baby's Beside Me"), and a most unvarnished and affecting sense of heartbreak and longing, pervading most of the second side and peaking on the distraught "Try Again."

Big Star's eerie and idiosyncratic recreation of a more innocent age of pop was out of time and out of place; Ardent, a subsidiary of Stax, had no idea of how to market these harmonious white boys, and the album stalled. This jolt of failure critically wounded the band, Bell leaving before their second album, *Radio City*, and only haunting their bleak swansong *Sister Lovers* in spirit.

So despite its generous soul, its delight in the details, its effortless melodies, *No. 1 Record* was, in stark terms, anything but. But its influence is deep and wide, felt in bands like R.E.M., Teenage Fanclub, The Posies— in fact, anyone with a sweet, sad song left to sing. **SC**

Black Sabbath
Black Sabbath Vol 4 (1972)

Label | Warner Bros.
Producer | Black Sabbath • Patrick Meehan
Art Direction | The Bloomsbury Group
Nationality | UK
Running Time | 42:46

Long before Black Sabbath broke down as a result of drug-fueled infighting, there was a brief period of drug-fueled sludge-metal genius. The proof— ...Vol 4.

The band have long said the writing and recording of the album coincided with their most hedonistic and substance-heavy period, after their label transplanted the four Brits to California to record the album. The record's original title, Snowblind, was nixed by label execs for its obvious reference to cocaine.

The negative consequences of their decadence would be heard at the end of the decade, when the band descended into Spinal Tap versions of their early selves. But ... Vol 4 was before the burnout and bloat and the songs were still riff-packed, rough, and heavy— or, as Rolling Stone put it, "slabs of liquid metal."

Because of the lack of an anthemic single, ... Vol 4 is often overlooked. There is no track to rival the popularity of "Paranoid" or "Sweat Leaf"; only "Snowblind" gets the odd nod on radio these days. Rather, the album's strengths lie in the songs' confident, heavy crunch and in small touches of experimentation. The band dabble with psychedelic overdubs ("The Straightener"), live strings ("Laguna Sunrise"), and even a mellow side— the slow piano ballad "Changes," which makes for an odd addition to this collection. But unlike the band's later albums, the meat of this record stays true to the band's original dark and heavy roots. It was with Sabbath Bloody Sabbath and all that followed that the Sabs' trademark sound began to slip away from them. **JC**

Steely Dan
Can't Buy A Thrill (1972)

Label | ABC
Producer | Gary Katz
Art Direction | Robert Lockart
Nationality | USA
Running Time | 40:57

In 1972, nobody really knew quite what to make of Steely Dan and their debut album Can't Buy A Thrill, not even founding members Donald Fagen and Walter Becker. However, those that saw them as just another polished West Coast rock outfit were missing the point. Although the album was just the first step of a voyage of musical discovery, there was already plenty to distinguish Steely Dan from the pack.

While the vocal harmonies here are often suggestive of Crosby, Stills, Nash, And Young, the arrangements reach new levels of sophistication. Miles Davis had previously had a go at fusing rock and jazz, but when Fagen's vocals drop in after the exquisite Latin jazz intro to "Do It Again," you know these guys were really on to something. When Denny Dias' electric sitar solo comes in, you know they could really nail it.

Vocalist David Palmer, who did not feature on any later albums, has his finest moments on "Dirty Work" even if he lacks Fagen's snarl and bite. His inclusion was arguably an attempt to make their sound even more radio friendly than it already was. "Reeling In The Years" sounds like a classic hit single after just a few bars. Unforgettable buzzy guitar solos give way to indelible lush choruses propelled by Walter Becker's bass. It's foot-stomping fun but executed with a precision that was to become a Steely Dan trademark.

Billboard were masters of understatement when they said this album would have "good hit possibilities for a group that should be around for some time." **GSa**

Neil Young | Harvest (1972)

Label | Reprise
Producer | Elliott Mazer
Art Direction | Tom Wilkes
Nationality | Canada
Running Time | 37:10

An album that perfectly evoked both the dying optimism of San Francisco's counterculture movement and the burgeoning cynicism of the Watergate generation, *Harvest* stands as a commercial pinnacle of the West Coast country-rock scene, a U.S. and UK No. I. Yet its relevance was almost pre-empted by both The Byrds and Buffalo Springfield.

Harvest, though, undoubtedly augured Young's 1970s creative peak, utilising harmonies by Linda Rondstadt and James Taylor to strike commercial paydirt on the hit single "Heart Of Gold." The song's success would daunt Young for the next three decades, and he has purposely omitted it from live sets since. "This song put me in the middle of the road," he wrote. "Traveling there soon became a bore and I headed for the ditch."

That song aside, *Harvest* contains some of the most arresting imagery of Young's career to date, from the slow-burning scorn of "Alabama," an acerbic denunciation of corruption in America's Southern beltway, to the haunting and personal "The Needle And The Damage Done," and the touching if sentimental "Old Man," written as a homage to the caretaker of Young's ranch. *Harvest* often threatens to descend into country mawkishness, but ultimately shines with its creator's songwriting strengths.

Unsurprisingly, Young would soon retreat from the runaway success of this album. And the majority of his Seventies work would veer toward a more insidious realization of America via explorations in the realm of punk and the blues. *Harvest*, though, stands as the coming-of-age of the Baby Boomer generation. **BW**

> *"Harvest* yielded Young's only Number One hit ... and helped set the stage for the Seventies soft-rock explosion."
>
> *Rolling Stone*, 2003

Track Listing

01	Out On The Weekend	(Young)	4:35
▶ 02	Harvest	(Young)	3:03
03	A Man Needs A Maid	(Young)	4:00
▶ 04	Heart Of Gold	(Young)	3:05
05	Are You Ready For The Country	(Young)	3:21
▶ 06	Old Man	(Young)	3:22
07	There's A World	(Young)	3:00
▶ 08	Alabama	(Young)	4:02
▶ 09	The Needle And The Damage Done	(Young)	2:00
10	Words (Between The Lines Of Age)	(Young)	6:42

Curtis Mayfield | Superfly (1972)

Label | Curtom
Producer | Curtis Mayfield
Art Direction | Glen Christensen
Nationality | USA
Running Time | 36:17

Chicago native Curtis Mayfield became a fixture on the U.S. soul scene in 1961, when his vocal harmony group The Impressions began their run of evergeen chart hits. He embarked on a solo career in 1970, enlivening dance floors everywhere with the euphoric "Move On Up" (from debut LP *Curtis*). The signature sound was lush yet funky, a deftly orchestrated mélange of guitar, fluttering strings, majestic brass, and fluid rhythms. The icing on the cake was his silky falsetto, which often gilded searing commentaries about urban America.

Superfly was Mayfield's only No. 1 album, a soundtrack to the popular blaxploitaton film that neatly denounced the very things the movie was in danger of glorifying. The symphonic, minor-key "Little Child Runnin' Wild" paints a foreboding portrait of inner city life, its dramatic crescendos giving way to "Pusherman." Built around a mesmerizing bassline springloaded with congas, this first-person piece of street-level reportage anticipates gangsta rap; it was sampled by Ice-T on his 1988 song "I'm Your Pusher." The sweeping, Latin-flavored "No Thing On Me (Cocaine Song)" is another powerful anti-drug statement, but the big singles were "Freddie's Dead"—a poignant, flute-driven character sketch that reached No. 4—and the deceptively suave title track (a No. 8).

Mayfield never matched this commercial high, though 1975's *There's No Place Like America Today* is an overlooked gem. Tragedy struck in August 1990, when he was paralyzed from the neck down after a lighting rig fell on him. This gentle giant of twentieth century music died on December 26, 1999, aged 57. **MA**

> ## "It seems as though *Superfly* was really just a prediction of what is actually happening today."
>
> Curtis Mayfield, 1988

Track Listing

▶	01	**Little Child Runnin' Wild** (Mayfield)	5:23
▶	02	**Pusherman** (Mayfield)	4:50
▶	03	**Freddie's Dead** (Mayfield)	5:27
	04	**Junkie Chase** (Mayfield)	1:36
	05	**Give Me Your Love (Love Song)** (Mayfield)	4:14
	06	**Eddie You Should Know Better** (Mayfield)	2:16
▶	07	**No Thing On Me (Cocaine Song)** (Mayfield)	4:53
	08	**Think** (Mayfield)	3:43
▶	09	**Superfly** (Mayfield)	3:55

Slade | Slayed? (1972)

Label | Polydor
Producer | Chas Chandler
Art Direction | Gered Mankowitz
Nationality | UK
Running Time | 34:26

Memorably distinguished by the extraordinary howl and phenomenal sideburns of vocalist Noddy Holder—never forgetting guitarist Dave Hill's pudding bowl haircut and knee-high silver platform boots—this was glam rock at its most earthy and yobbish. David Bowie and Roxy Music aside, it is the songs (mostly singles) of T. Rex and Slade that endure best from this gloriously "crazee" era of British pop. If Bolan had his boogie, Slade had their stomp.

Between 1971 and '76, they enjoyed 17 consecutive UK Top 20 hits (including six No. 1s). Possessed of an irascibly sly and rascally self-effacing humor, this album is Slade at their peak, before the formula started to fade (and that wacky spelling started to pall). In truth, what they did was not revolutionary, or even that new, but they did it so well and with such aplomb that three decades later they are now affectionately ingrained in the fabric of British popular culture. As powerfully evidenced by "Mama Weer All Crazee Now" and "Gudbuy T'Jane," the best pop is often simple, stupid, yet somehow simultaneously sublime. Slade never took themselves too seriously, so they were never unduly concerned by perceived notions of "cool." Frankly, they were beyond that.

Newcomers to the band have a choice between picking up a greatest hits collection (accepting that it will also include a fair sprinkling of lesser later stuff) or this—their best album. It might contain only two of their mighty smash singles, but still it represents a great hefty wodge of pure, prime, shouty, and stamp-along period pop. **RF**

> ## "We never followed what was going on around us but just carried on in our own sweet way and style."
>
> Noddy Holder, 1986

Track Listing

▶ 01	How D'You Ride (Holder•Lea)	3:11
▶ 02	The Whole World's Goin' Crazee (Holder)	3:36
03	Look At Last Nite (Holder•Lea)	3:05
04	I Won't Let It 'Appen Agen (Lea)	3:17
05	Move Over (Joplin)	3:44
▶ 06	Gudbuy T'Jane (Holder•Lea)	3:29
07	Gudbuy Gudbuy (Holder•Lea)	3:29
▶ 08	Mama Weer All Crazee Now (Holder•Lea)	3:44
09	I Don' Mind (Holder•Lea)	3:06
10	Let The Good Times Roll•Feel So Fine (Lee)	3:45

Deep Purple | Made In Japan (1972)

Label | Purple
Producer | Deep Purple
Art Direction | Roger Glover
Nationality | UK
Running Time | 76:17

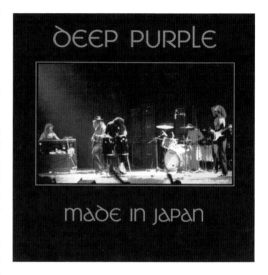

As the United States pummeled North Vietnam to the Paris negotiating table, Deep Purple unleashed an aural cannonade in the shape of their live double album. Having toured America during the summer, they visited Japan, where the local label pressed for a live set to satiate a fan-base that sang along to every word over three August nights in Osaka and Tokyo.

Purple insisted that engineer Martin Birch oversee the recording. Ian Gillan, who had been suffering with a throat ailment, was "ashamed" of his vocals, but his assessment was harsher than his tones. The set was issued without overdubs and demonstrates the raw majesty of Deep Purple at the peak of their powers.

It appeared in the UK partly to stem the bootleg market. Imports sold so well in the United States, it was issued in spring 1973 and hit No. 6, making it their highest-charting album Stateside. By then, *Made In Japan* was confirmed as a classic.

Each track is a massive, melodramatic version of its studio counterpart. "Highway Star" opens with furious keys, guitar, and percussion melding into a sonic storm topped by Ian Gillan's primal screams. His poignant vocal on "Child In Time" provides respite before the swagger of "Smoke On The Water" and "Strange Kind Of Woman." Guitarist Ritchie Blackmore and keyboardist Jon Lord space out on "Lazy" solos, while "The Mule" is a showcase for the virtuosity of Ian Paice.

The behemoth "Space Truckin'"—20 minutes of stratospheric mayhem—rounds out what *Rolling Stone* dubbed "an assured treat . . . Purple's definitive metal monster." Hear hear! **TJ**

"It's the best these numbers have ever been played ..."

Ian Paice, 1998

Track Listing

▶ 01	**Highway Star** (Blackmore·Gillan·Glover·Lord·Paice)	6:42
▶ 02	**Child In Time** (Blackmore·Gillan·Glover·Lord·Paice)	12:18
▶ 03	**Smoke On The Water** (Blackmore·Gillan·Glover·Lord·Paice)	7:37
04	**The Mule (Drum Solo)** (Blackmore·Gillan·Glover·Lord·Paice)	9:28
▶ 05	**Strange Kind Of Woman** (Blackmore·Gillan·Glover·Lord·Paice)	9:52
▶ 06	**Lazy** (Blackmore·Gillan·Glover·Lord·Paice)	10:27
▶ 07	**Space Truckin'** (Blackmore·Gillan·Glover·Lord·Paice)	19:53

Yes | Close To The Edge (1972)

Label | Atlantic
Producer | Eddie Offord • Yes
Art Direction | Roger Dean
Nationality | UK
Running Time | 37:50

This remains the apotheosis of prog rock itself. First, one encounters Roger Dean's enigmatic jacket design, presented in a gatefold format that is ideal for both contemplation and joint-rolling. The track listing is the next hallmark, boasting only three titles, two in four-movement, ersatz-symphonic structure. Pull out the sleeve and Jon Anderson's delightfully obtuse lyrics reveal themselves in all their florid glory.

As ripe as it is for parody on the surface, the music on *Close To The Edge* is a wonder. Whereas Yes had showcased their individual talents on their breakout disc *Fragile* earlier the same year, on *Close To The Edge* they forged a more cohesive whole, striking a balance between esthetics and audacity. Their determinedly eclectic approach had them moving from furious jazz to gothic organ flourish, then on to a driving rock groove—one false move and it would all fall to pieces. However, here was an assemblage of stellar musicians, each of whom sought to stretch the limits of the rock idiom. The melodic, stop-time rhythms of Bill Bruford and Chris Squire were the perfect grounding for Steve Howe's funky, Eastern-tinged guitar lines and Rick Wakeman's rococo keyboard noodling. At the center was Jon Anderson's high-flown tenor. It was something that should not have worked, but it did—beautifully.

The fragile equilibrium of their approach would prove to be too good to last. Bruford quit the band shortly after completing the disc to join King Crimson, and their follow-up, the four-song double album *Tales From Topographic Oceans*, proved to be an over-ambitious attempt to one-up themselves. **TSh**

> "I couldn't understand physically what [Jon Anderson] was saying, he had a very strange accent from the north of England. He speaks in strange sentences that nobody can understand."
>
> Bill Bruford, 1972

Track Listing		
▶ 01 **Close To The Edge** (Anderson • Howe)		18:42
▶ 02 **And You And I**		
(Anderson • Bruford • Howe • Squire • Wakeman)		10:08
03 **Siberian Khatru** (Anderson • Howe • Wakeman)		9:00

Lou Reed | Transformer (1972)

Label | RCA
Producer | David Bowie • Mick Ronson
Art Direction | Mick Rock • Ernst Thormahlen
Nationality | USA
Running Time | 37:00

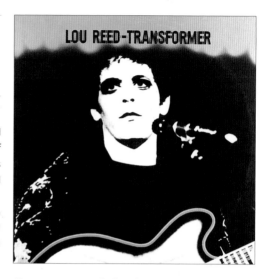

Lou Reed had the credibility and the songs, David Bowie the sound and the media appeal. The meeting of American master and British alumni gave the Seventies one of its most delicious icons, a record that exploited and at the same time defined glam rock.

Reed had left The Velvet Underground in 1970 with the bitter taste of defeat and animosity. New York had been cold and unappreciative; London now seemed where the action was. Reed moved to England and debuted on RCA with a failed self-titled solo album concocted with Velvet's leftovers rehashed by non-empathic studio musicians.

A second chance was offered by Bowie, who had been producing shiny, dramatic recordings with his guitar player Mick Ronson. Both labored to extract from the usually dry poet and musician an exhilarating mix of camp decadence and unforgettable tunes: transatlantic hit "Walk On The Wild Side," "Satellite Of Love," and "Perfect Day." The vocal arrangements are as gorgeous as the guitars were searing; the presence of upright bass and saxophone adding a cabaret ambience; the sexual ambiguity of front and back cover appealing to a teenage audience still discovering the facts of life. It also had rockers to warm up the dancefloor. And, behind it all, the shadow of a never-made Warhol musical populated by adoring transvestites and debauched speed freaks, arty parties, and urban sophistication.

Transformer is Lou Reed's most commercial effort, and its chart history in the UK alone spans three decades. It's also a superficial exception, as proven by the depths of Reed's adventurous career. **IJ**

> ## "You can't fake being gay. That line that everyone's bisexual, I think that's just meaningless."

Lou Reed, 1973

Track Listing

▶	01	**Vicious** (Reed)	2:58
	02	**Andy's Chest** (Reed)	3:20
▶	03	**Perfect Day** (Reed)	3:46
	04	**Hangin' Round** (Reed)	3:35
▶	04	**Walk On The Wild Side** (Reed)	4:14
	06	**Make Up** (Reed)	3:01
▶	07	**Satellite Of Love** (Reed)	3:42
	08	**Wagon Wheel** (Reed)	3:19
	09	**New York Telephone Conversation** (Reed)	1:33
	10	**I'm So Free** (Reed)	3:09
	11	**Goodnight Ladies** (Reed)	4:23

Hugh Masekela
Home Is Where The Music Is (1972)

Label | Blue Thumb Chisa
Producer | Stewart Levine • Caiphus Semenya
Art Direction | Uncredited
Nationality | South Africa
Running Time | 77:53

Milton Nascimento And Lo Borges
Clube Da Esquina (1972)

Label | World Pacific
Producer | Milton Miranda
Art Direction | Uncredited
Nationality | Brazil
Running Time | 63:13

In 1968 the success of his crossover pop hit "Grazing In The Grass" had allowed Hugh Masekela to kickstart his own Chisa Records label, but the times they were a-changing. Jazz just was not hip any more. Trane was dead, Miles wanted to be Jimi Hendrix, and Motown had dropped Masekela's distribution deal. Yes, after more than a decade in exile "Bra Hugh" was getting seriously homesick. He knew he could not go back to apartheid's madness, but ex-wife Miriam Makeba had gone to Guinea and there was this Nigerian saxophone preacher, Fela Kuti who was starting his own African jazz revolution—so maybe *Home Is Where The Music Is*?

Recorded just months before his own departure to Guinea, this album finds Masekela digging into his African jazz heritage. Gone are the patented pop covers, replaced by a pan-African songbook that rejuvenates exiled composer Caiphus Semenya's soul jazz ("Ingoo Pow-Pow") with globe-trotting township bop grooves ("The Big Apple"). Brotherhood of Breath alto saxophone firebrand Dudu Pukwana and powerhouse drummer Nakhaya Ntshoko's mbaqanga-fueled energy provide a delightfully funk-soaked counterfoil for pianist Larry Willis and bassist Eddie Gomez's moody blues.

And Masekela? Well, he lets rip, easing his flugelhorn solo through a rendition of Kippie Moeketsi's "Blues For Huey" that takes the listener straight to the vibrant sheebeen swing of Sophiatown in the Fifties. **MK**

If *Clube Da Esquina* was merely Brazil's answer to *Sgt. Pepper…* it would stand out as a major contribution to international pop music. But this gorgeous collection of songs, originally released as a double LP, also turned Milton Nascimento, Lo Borges, Beto Gueges, and Toninho Horta into successful recording artists in their own right.

While Nascimento—a charismatic performer with a pure, spiritually charged falsetto—is the album's center of gravity, he was not yet a superstar, and … *Esquina* is very much a group effort, co-credited to Borges. Mixing dreamy soundscapes, surreal lyrics, and a remarkably broad range of South American influences, it was a pop landmark that opened creative doors for other artists.

The Corner Club consisted of a group of friends from Belo Horizonte, a city located in the landlocked state of Minas Gerais. They spent six months of 1971 in a rented house on the beach in Piratininga north of Rio, writing songs and sharing their love of The Beatles. Back in the studio, the music took on a lush grandeur with orchestrations by Eumar Deodato and Wagner Tiso. The album produced a number of standards, including "Cravo E Canela" (Clove And Cinnamon) and "Nada Sera Como Antes" (Nothing Will Be Like Before). The Beatles' influence is particularly strong on Lo Borges' exquisitely produced "Mineiro rock" songs such as "O Trem Azul" (The Blue Train) and "Nuvem Cigana" (Gypsy Cloud), shimmering tunes full of wonder and whimsy. **AG**

Todd Rundgren
Something / Anything? (1972)

Label | Bearsville
Producer | Todd Rundgren
Art Direction | Todd Rundgren
Nationality | USA
Running Time | 86:57

A photo on the inside cover art of Todd Rundgren's third post-Nazz LP, *Something/Anything?*, features Rundgren alone in a room packed with equipment, guitar strapped to his shoulder, arms flung wide, and hands flashing victory signs. That about sums up the album.

Rundgren produced *Something/Anything?*, played every instrument, did all the vocals on 19 of the 25 tracks, and wrote all the songs with the exception of the two songs in a medley and "Dust In The Wind." The result is an album that stands as Rundgren's zenith both commercially and critically. "Hello It's Me," one in a series of gorgeous ballads that dot Rundgren's career, is his highest charting single, peaking at No. 5, and the album stayed on the charts for many months. Other songs, the sorrowful and beautiful "It Wouldn't Have Made Any Difference," the hard-rocking "Black Maria," and pop wonders like "Couldn't I Just Tell You," present a mastery of different styles almost unparalleled in popular music. The musicianship, particularly Rundgren's guitar work in songs like "Black Maria," is top-notch.

This is Rundgren's most compelling work. In a career rife with experimentation and littered with confounded audience expectations, it offered no hint that he would turn his back on commercial aspirations in the wake of his newfound success. But *Something/Anything?* was a critical and commercial success that could sustain any artist for a good long while. **JW**

Nitty Gritty Dirt Band
Will The Circle Be Unbroken (1972)

Label | United Artists
Producer | William E. McEuen
Art Direction | William E. McEuen
Nationality | USA
Running Time | 119:30

This momentous album was conceived by NGDB manager, Bill McEuen, who wanted the country-rock band to be taken more seriously by their label. Without asking for a budget, he booked a Nashville studio and invited legendary local luminaries like Roy Acuff, Mother Maybelle Carter, Earl Scruggs, Merle Travis, and Doc Watson, as well as such revered pickers as Vassar Clements on violin and Norman Blake on dobro, to become part of this ambitious project.

The plan worked: this became the band's first gold album, although—curiously—on some tracks, such as "The End Of The World," "Cannonball Rag," "Wabash Cannonball," and others, none of the group members are credited as participating! That said, for anyone interested in great country songs by the likes of Hank Williams, A.P. Carter, Scruggs, and Travis played in authentic bluegrass style, this album can hardly be bettered. The relaxed atmosphere resulted in some superb performances, and consistently high quality. Moreover, the combined talents of the NGDB and their revered guests attracted sales from both old-time country aficionados, and younger country-rock fans.

The Nitty Gritty Dirt Band is still active—four of the members who played on this album feature on their latest (2004) offering. The band has also released two subsequent sequels—*Volume 2* in 1989 and *Volume 3* in 2002, featuring many of the same luminaries. **JT**

Stevie Wonder | Talking Book (1972)

Label | Motown
Producer | Stevie Wonder
Art Direction | Robert Margouleff
Nationality | USA
Running Time | 43:26

Robert Margouleff's iconic photo of Stevie Wonder—clad in an African robe and crouched in clay, deep in thought—spoke of the solitary vision his early 1970s trilogy of masterpieces pursued. But the sleeve (featuring sightless Stevie unusually *sans* sunglasses) also suggested that *Talking Book* was a confessional album about love, and the loss of it, as befits an artist who has just left his mate (singer Syreeta Wright, who wrote lyrics for two downbeat tracks here).

Opener "You Are The Sunshine Of My Life" was upbeat enough, an ecstatic paean to the redemptive powers of love that was, tellingly, written before Wonder's contractual hiatus from Motown (which resulted in these auteurist soul classics). But the paranoid, sludgy funk of "Maybe Your Baby" (played entirely by Stevie, save for a solo from guitarist Ray Parker Jr.) announced the album's true, uncertain tone. The heartbreakingly vulnerable "You And I" pondered the fragility of love over a rapturous soundscape of ghostly piano and Margouleff and Malcolm Cecil's keening synths. And "Superstition," the bad-ass clavinet riff Stevie stole back from Jeff Beck, announced a bruised Stevie's cynical take on free love, set against the meanest funk he ever wrote.

The album ended on a hopeful note absent from *Fulfillingness' First Finale*, two years later. "I Believe" finds Stevie's heart broken, but his belief in love still intact. He would write love songs that charted higher, but never would he deliver so personally felt and so painfully wise a treatise as *Talking Book*. The book was Stevie Wonder's heart, and it was talking truthfully. **SC**

> ## "Here is my music. It is all I have to tell you how I feel."
>
> Stevie Wonder, 1972

Track Listing

▶	01	**You Are The Sunshine Of My Life** (Wonder)	2:59
	02	**Maybe Your Baby** (Wonder)	6:50
▶	03	**You And I (Together We Can Conquer The World)** (Wonder)	4:38
	04	**Tuesday Heartbreak** (Wonder)	3:02
▶	05	**You've Got It Bad Girl** (Wonder·Wright)	4:58
▶	06	**Superstition** (Wonder)	4:26
	07	**Big Brother** (Wonder)	3:33
	08	**Blame It On The Sun** (Wonder·Wright)	3:25
	09	**Lookin' For Another Pure Love** (Wonder·Wright)	4:43
▶	10	**I Believe (When I Fall In Love It Will Be Forever)** (Wonder·Wright)	4:52

Stephen Stills
Manassas (1972)

Label | Atlantic
Producer | Various
Art Direction | Stephen Stills
Nationality | USA
Running Time | 71:58

T. Rex
The Slider (1972)

Label | EMI
Producer | Tony Visconti
Art Direction | Ringo Starr
Nationality | UK
Running Time | 43:35

Knowing that his old friend Chris Hillman was bored with The Flying Burrito Brothers, Stephen Stills recruited him to play on his new solo album, along with Burrito pedal steel guitarist Al Perkins and bluegrass fiddler Byron Berline. Working at the Criteria Studios in Miami, Florida, Stills developed a concept album that would draw on rock, folk, Latin, country, and blues—with the help of Calvin "Fuzzy" Samuels (bass), Dallas Taylor (drums), Paul Harris (keyboards), and Joe Lala (percussion).

The wealth of material and musicianship resulted in an ambitious double album, arguably the greatest release in Stills' career—something zestfully fresh, yet recognizably within rock 'n' roll's grand tradition. What could have been a sprawling set is actually a remarkably cohesive whole. The record divides broadly into four parts, mirroring the four sides of the original vinyl release. "The Raven" covers rock and Latin styles; "The Wilderness" is country and bluegrass, highlighted by beautiful mandolin, violin, and pedal steel playing and exceptional multipart harmonies; "Consider" prioritizes folk and folk-rock; "Rock And Roll Is Here To Stay" is mostly blues and rock, and includes the epic "Treasure," one of the group's standout tracks. (The acoustic solo "Blues Man" is dedicated to Jimi Hendrix, Al "Blind Owl" Wilson, and Duane Allman.)

Stones bassist Bill Wyman helped Stills complete "The Love Gangster," and later revealed to Dallas Taylor that he had wanted to leave The Rolling Stones to join *Manassas*—but nobody ever asked him. **GSu**

Recorded in Paris and Copenhagen with producer Tony Visconti, *The Slider* was released in the summer of 1972 at the peak of T. Rexstasy. Among the charismatic Marc Bolan fans was David Bowie, who dedicated his hit "Lady Stardust" to Marc. *The Slider* was successful on both sides of the Atlantic and marked a breakthrough for glam rock in the United States.

"Telegram Sam" (200,000 copies sold in its first four days) and the ecstatic "Metal Guru"—both UK No. 1s— are gold-plated classics. But there is plenty of quality material elsewhere too: charming, off-kilter ballads ("Mystic Lady," "Ballrooms Of Mars") as well as uptempo rockers ("Rock On," "Main Man"). Bolan proved once again that he was the master of refined, catchy tunes. And of spontaneity too—he lost interest if any track required more than two or three takes, imbuing his best work with a vibrant immediacy. His talents were not confined to composer and bandleader, either. The lyrics are typical of Bolan—dadaistic, witty, perverse, and full of surprising associations and metaphors.

It was not all harmony in the studio, however: producer Visconti has commented that he felt that by this stage the group were definitely working to a formula, while Bolan's ego was starting to become outsized. That said, the magic is still working here.

Bolan died in a car accident in London in 1977, leaving a musical legacy that has influenced a diverse range of musicians, from gothic-rock knights Bauhaus to American hard-rock band Guns N' Roses. **AW-J**

David Ackles
American Gothic (1972)

Label | Elektra
Producer | Bernie Taupin
Art Direction | Michael Ross
Nationality | USA
Running Time | 43:13

David Ackles had been involved in show business since early childhood, when he starred in a number of B-movies. By the late 1960s, however, he was writing songs of stunning beauty and Elektra signed him, initially just as a songwriter. After proving his worth at the company, he was awarded a five-album contract.

His third offering, *American Gothic*, still remains a largely unrecognized work of genius, one of the most unfashionable and uncompromising American albums ever. Ackles paints a colorful and poetic portrait of America, a hauntingly dark piece of theater filtered through a composer's melodic sensibility. Crafted layer upon layer, it reveals itself more as a dramatic work than a conventional rock or pop release, drawing on modern American classical composers such as Charles Ives and Aaron Copland as well as gospel, rock, blues, and soul. Imagine an art-folk album that bridges Woody Guthrie's passionate storytelling and Kurt Weill's orchestrations.

The title track is a sad story depicting an everyday American drama. "Oh, California!" is a jazzy and bohemian vaudeville song that features Ackles' raucous vocals and might easily have served as an inspirational model for such artists as Tom Waits or even Frank Zappa. The album's distinctive sound owes much to Ackles' collaboration with producer Bernie Taupin, Elton John's long-term creative partner.

It did not even reach the U.S. Top 150 at the time of release. But this distinctive, uncategorizable album fully warrants seeking out. **GD**

The Eagles
Eagles (1972)

Label | Asylum
Producer | Glyn Johns
Art Direction | Gary Burden
Nationality | USA
Running Time | 37:28

Although none of the original members of the Eagles were originally from California, the group came to symbolize the West Coast country rock that became hugely popular in the 1970s. Originally members of Linda Ronstadt's backing band, The Eagles' formation as a distinct group coincided with the launch of Asylum Records, and they were one of the first acts signed to the label, along with Ronstadt and Jackson Browne.

Anxious to work with Glyn Johns, the English engineer/producer who had worked with The Who, The Rolling Stones, The Small Faces, Led Zeppelin, and The Steve Miller Band, the group recorded their debut album at Olympic Studios in London, which was where Johns liked to work: "I brought them to England, and we made the album very quickly, in under three weeks," he remembered. "I don't think I'd been as excited since probably Led Zeppelin—they were amazing but they didn't really know what they'd got."

"Take It Easy," "Witchy Woman," and "Peaceful Easy Feeling" were all U.S. Top 30 singles and the album was soon certified gold. Part of its success was down to the quartet's glorious vocal harmonies. Factor in accomplished musicianship (Bernie Leadon's country roots are strongly evident in the banjo and guitar work), and the strength of the songwriting (all of the group contributed original material; lead vocals were also rotated) and it is little wonder that the band soon secured a strong live attraction, and were one of the biggest acts in the world five years later. **JT**

Tim Buckley | Greetings From L.A. (1972)

Label | Warner Bros.
Producer | Jerry Goldstein
Art Direction | Cal Schenkel
Nationality | USA
Running Time | 39:39

After the poorly received *Starsailor*, Buckley waited a while before recording *Greetings From L.A.* Meantime, the 25-year-old began to absorb jazz, funk, and R&B influences. Sidelining his co-writer Larry Beckett, Buckley now began playing with other musicians who could fulfill his new musical vision. Coupled with Buckley's love of blaxploitation movies, this led to a feverish, sexually charged album that was a quantum leap away from his image as a wide-eyed troubadour.

"Move With Me" begins with jaunty pianos and smoky trumpets; Buckley's boisterous vocal work—counterpointed, for the first time in the studio, by female backing singers—revels in the tale of a casual sexual encounter. "Get On Top" offers up orgasmic talking-in-tongues, creaking beds, and choppy jazz riffs, reminiscent of The Doors' *L.A. Woman*. "Sweet Surrender" is highlighted by Jerry Goldstein's production, which sets Buckley's macho, yowling delivery against aching strings that echoes Goldstein's previous work with the group War. "Nighthawkin'" shows Buckley at his lascivious best, riding in a taxi, scoping for women. Swarthy keyboards decorate "Devil Eyes," while the closer "Make It Right" is an unhinged celebration of lust that provides the album with a head-spinning climax.

A postcard of Los Angeles covered in a thick smog decorates the cover; on the reverse, two stamps portray Buckley with a gas mask. "The message the sleeve was intended to impart was that even in this horrific atmosphere, there can still be a lot of musical activity going down," Buckley insisted to *Melody Maker*. The album proved his point in spades. **AMa**

> "I don't need the rock world to be a person or a singer or a musician or to play for people. All I have to do is walk up on a stage and play."
>
> Tim Buckley, 1972

Track Listing

▶	01	**Move With Me** (Buckley•Goldstein)	4:53
▶	02	**Get On Top** (Buckley)	6:33
	03	**Sweet Surrender** (Buckley)	6:47
▶	04	**Nighthawkin'** (Beckett•Buckley)	3:21
▶	05	**Devil Eyes** (Buckley)	6:50
	06	**Hong Kong Bar** (Buckley•Falsia)	7:08
	07	**Make It Right** (Beckett•Buckley•Falsia•Goldstein)	4:07

Nick Drake | Pink Moon (1972)

Label | Island
Producer | John Wood
Art Direction | Michael Trevithick
Nationality | UK
Running Time | 26:30

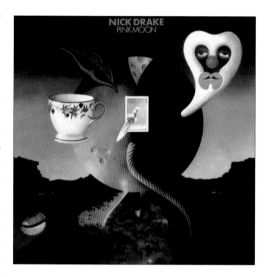

After his glorious second album *Bryter Layter* attracted a paucity of reviews, Nick Drake retreated to his sparsely furnished home in London. *Pink Moon* was to be devoid of the orchestral flourishes that gave *Bryter Layter* and debut *Five Leaves Left* their emotive sway.

REM's Peter Buck once asked producer John Wood how he had achieved the intimacy of the sound on *Pink Moon*. Wood explained that Drake simply sat down in front of a microphone at Sound Techniques studios and played; any atmosphere created came from the unadorned power of Drake's guitar and haunting vocals, filled with tremulous emotion.

The baroque elements of Drake's melodies, intricate guitar plucking, and open tunings create descending chimes on "Parasite" and a plethora of colorful chords on "Pink Moon" (the only song on the album to feature an overdub). Elsewhere, the pastoral elements of "Place To Be" recall the nature imagery common in Drake's work, while "Ride" features breathtakingly swift chord changes. Drake's exceptional guitar-playing talents were still intact, but the stark songs they decorated were bleak, unsettling. An apathetic Drake apparently walked into the record company offices and simply dropped off the master tapes for this final album with one of the secretaries.

"From The Morning" ends things on a rare note of optimism. All the sadder, then, that one of its lines—"and now we rise, and we are everywhere"—was to be inscribed on the gravestone of this enormously talented musician, who died prematurely in 1974 at the age of 26. **AMa**

> ## "A record of quiet desperation, the sound of someone hanging on by their fingernails."
>
> Joe Boyd, 1978

Track Listing

▶	01	**Pink Moon** (Drake)	2.00
	02	**Place To Be** (Drake)	2:39
	03	**Road** (Drake)	1:58
▶	04	**Which Will** (Drake)	2:56
	05	**Horn** (Drake)	1:19
▶	06	**Things Behind The Sun** (Drake)	3:23
	07	**Know** (Drake)	2:23
▶	08	**Parasite** (Drake)	3:30
	09	**Ride** (Drake)	2:57
	10	**Harvest Breed** (Drake)	1:00
▶	11	**From The Morning** (Drake)	2:25

Paul Simon | Paul Simon (1972)

Label | CBS
Producer | Roy Halee • Paul Simon
Art Direction | John Berg • Ron Coro
Nationality | USA
Running Time | 34:03

If Paul Simon was not already sure the game was up, then the recording of "So Long, Frank Lloyd Wright" surely confirmed it. The closing track on side one of *Bridge Over Troubled Water* was sung with inimitable grace by Art Garfunkel, seemingly unaware that Simon had written the song about the dissolution of their friendship. Simon kept "The Only Living Boy In New York" for himself, but the water came from the same well: Simon's sadness at Garfunkel's desire to spend less time on the group and more on his movie career. The album emerged in early 1970, but the partnership did not much outlast the Grammys in March.

With Garfunkel filming *Catch-22* for much of its recording, *Bridge Over Troubled Water* was virtually a Simon solo album in all but name. *Paul Simon* was a very different record, though. There are signs of Simon's magpie enthusiasm for exotic musics: the reggae lilt of "Mother And Child Reunion," featuring an assortment of Jamaican music notables (the title was inspired by a chicken-and-egg dish Simon ate at a Chinese restaurant), and "Hobo's Blues," with Simon playing Django to violinist Stephane Grappelli.

But *Paul Simon* is best approached as one of the best singer-songwriter albums of the Seventies. With the microphone to himself, Simon's in wonderful vocal form, yet his compositional voice is stronger on "Duncan" ("The Boxer" meets "El Condor Pasa"), on the waltzing melancholia of "Congratulations," and on "Everything Put Together Falls Apart," whose flowing yet labyrinthine chord structure is a supreme two-minute masterclass in sophisticated songwriting. **WF-J**

> "It was a chance to back out and gamble a little bit; it's been so long since it was a gamble."
>
> Paul Simon, 1972

Track Listing		
▶ 01	Mother And Child Reunion (Simon)	3:05
02	Duncan (Simon)	4:39
▶ 03	Everything Put Together Falls Apart (Simon)	1:59
04	Run That Body Down (Simon)	3:52
05	Armistice Day (Simon)	3:55
▶ 06	Me And Julio Down By The Schoolyard (Simon)	2:42
07	Peace Like A River (Simon)	3:20
08	Papa Hobo (Simon)	2:34
09	Hobo's Blues (Grappelli•Simon)	1:21
10	Paranoia Blues (Simon)	2:54
▶ 11	Congratulations (Simon)	3:42

Roxy Music | Roxy Music (1972)

Label | Island
Producer | Peter Sinfield
Art Direction | Bryan Ferry
Nationality | UK
Running Time | 43:39

Recorded in 19 days, Roxy Music's debut still stands as one of the most exciting and innovative debuts ever. Leaving Newcastle R&B band Gasboard, vocalist Bryan Ferry and bassist Graham Simpson relocated to London forming Roxy Music with guitarist Phil Manzanera, saxophonist Andy Mackay, drummer Paul Thompson, and synthesizer genius Brian Eno. Roxy's innovative clash of Fifties rock, barking sax, and space-age electronics was inspired by Ferry's interest in Pop Art.

Its lavish gatefold sleeve starred model Kari Ann Muller as a Fifties starlet. Selling steadily on the back of their live reputation, *Roxy Music* stormed the UK Top Ten after the success of debut single, the non-LP "Virginia Plain." Opening with the sound of a cocktail party, "Re-Make/Re-Model," inspired by Derek Boshier's 1962 painting *Re-Think/Re-Entry*, is a glam-rock stomper featuring the bizarre chant of British car registration number "CPL5 93H" alongside Ferry's sophisticated croon.

Eno's re-creation of the sound of a lunar landing acts as a startling backdrop to a combination of modern and classical instruments on "Ladytron." Eno's Moogs and mellotrons fizz against Manzanera's incendiary guitars on "Would You Believe?" and the futurist country of "If There Is Something."

The year's hectic schedule took its toll. Simpson was sacked after falling ill and Ferry was hospitalized after losing his voice. (*NME* showed the singer drinking champagne in his hospital bed wearing "Roxy Music" silk pyjamas.) Despite the inclusion of "Virginia Plain" on the U.S. release, the album flopped, but Roxy Music was a major influence on UK punk and beyond. **CSh**

> "Most of the band have this approach of inspired amateurism, and as long as we ...retain that we'll be all right."
>
> Bryan Ferry, 1972

Track Listing

▶	01	**Re-Make/Re-Model** (Ferry)	5:14
▶	02	**Ladytron** (Ferry)	4:26
▶	03	**If There Is Something** (Ferry)	6:34
	04	**2HB** (Ferry)	5:30
	05	**The Bob (Medley)** (Ferry)	5:48
	06	**Chance Meeting** (Ferry)	3:08
▶	07	**Would You Believe?** (Ferry)	3:53
	08	**Sea Breezes** (Ferry)	7:03
	09	**Bitters End** (Ferry)	2:03

Alice Cooper | School's Out (1972)

Label | Warner Bros.
Producer | Bob Ezrin
Art Direction | Wilkes & Braun Inc.
Nationality | USA
Running Time | 35:57

Arriving in Los Angeles from Tucson, Arizona, the Alice Cooper band swiftly conceived a controversial image and signed with Frank Zappa's Straight label. Two infamous albums of psychedelic pandemonium later, they moved to Detroit, and befriended The Stooges, whose Motor City roar was as vital in their evolution as Bob Ezrin's cinematic sense of production.

When Warner purchased Straight, Cooper's band was urged to make a new record. Two hard-rocking albums and some hit singles with Ezrin later, they had found their sound, and were actively reinforcing their popularity by means of the Grand Guignol antics of their high-camp live shows.

Alice Cooper's mainly visual appeal was fully transferred to vinyl with *School's Out*, the new album preceded by the hit single of the same name. The single was their most popular to date, a graphic riot of stabbing riffs and seditious slogans that became a punk anthem for every dropout teen of the early 1970s. The band—guided by Cooper's vicious voice and guitarist Michael Bruce's badass sense of pop—had worked hard with Ezrin on a concept album that was inspired by *West Side Story*. The imaginative fantasy of juvenile delinquence featured sumptuous scores of big-band jazz arrangements ("Gutter Cat Vs. The Jet," "Grand Finale," "Blue Turk"), an operatic symphony ("My Stars"), a Beatles rip-off ("Alma Mater"), and terrific rockers ("Luney Tune" and "Public Animal No. 9"). An overproduced but perfect teenage epic, Alice Cooper's rock vaudeville was to be the foundation of such acts as Marylin Manson and Turbonegro. **JG**

"We had a sort of sarcastic view of American life."

Michael Bruce, 1996

Track Listing

▶ 01	**School's Out** (Bruce·Buxton·Cooper·Dunaway·Smith)	3:26
02	**Luney Tune** (Cooper·Dunaway)	3:36
▶ 03	**Gutter Cat Vs. The Jets** (Bernstein·Buxton·Dunaway·Sondhelm)	4:39
04	**Street Fight** (Bruce·Buxton·Cooper·Dunaway·Smith)	0:53
05	**Blue Turk** (Bruce·Cooper)	5:29
▶ 06	**My Stars** (Cooper·Ezrin)	5:46
▶ 07	**Public Animal No. 9** (Bruce·Cooper)	3:53
▶ 08	**Alma Mater** (Smith)	3:39
09	**Grande Finale** (Bernstein·Bruce·Buxton Cooper·David·Dunaway·Ezrin·Smith)	4:36

The Temptations | All Directions (1972)

Label | Tamla Motown
Producer | Norman Whitfield
Art Direction | Uncredited
Nationality | USA
Running Time | 33:33

It has been tempting to write off this vocal group at several points in its career, but never more so than in the early 1970s, following the departure of Eddie Kendricks and Paul Williams. Kendricks' absence, in particular, was seen as potentially devastating to the group, as he had sung lead on the 1971 chart topper "Just My Imagination (Running Away With Me)."

Housed in a deceivingly run-of-the mill cover shot of the five Temps hanging out around a tree, the album was an admirably ambitious work that built upon the experimentalism of 1970's *Psychedelic Shack* to further embrace new avenues. Thanks mainly to the nearly 12-minute epic "Papa Was A Rolling Stone," the Temps were able to successfully shed their image as 1960s-style balladeers and latch on to the grittier soul and R&B sounds of the day.

The Temptations immediately wave goodbye to "My Girl"-type material as they convincingly shake down "Funky Music Sho' Nuff Turns Me On," a heavily addictive Earth, Wind, And Fire-style groove, and keep the pace up on the War-like "Run Charlie Run." Following the workout of "Papa ...," the band shows it can still pull the heartstrings on "Love Woke Me Up This Morning" and out-doo-wop the competition with "I Ain't Got Nothing." Things round off with a tuneful and tight treatment of Isaac Hayes' "Do Your Thing."

Led by the savvy production of Norman Whitfield, and bolstered by new band addition, Damon Harris, *All Directions* was an immediate critical and commercial hit that earned three Grammy Awards and solidified its place in the business for the next decade. **JiH**

> **"God creates talented persons every day. It's the makeup of the person's heart and head that makes him an asset."**
>
> Otis Williams, 2002

Track Listing

▶ 01	**Funky Music Sho' Nuff Turns Me On** (Strong·Whitfield)	2:56
▶ 02	**Run Charlie Run** (Foreman·King)	2:59
▶ 03	**Papa Was A Rolling Stone** (Strong·Whitfield)	11:45
▶ 04	**Love Woke Me Up This Morning** (Ashford·Simpson)	2:38
05	**I Ain't Got Nothing** (E. King·M. King)	3:30
06	**The First Time Ever I Saw Your Face** (MacColl)	3:59
07	**Mother Nature** (Fekaris·Zesses)	2:54
▶ 08	**Do Your Thing** (Hayes)	2:52

David Bowie | The Rise And Fall Of Ziggy Stardust And The Spiders From Mars (1972)

Label | RCA
Producer | David Bowie • Ken Scott
Art Direction | Terry Pastor
Nationality | UK
Running Time | 38:29

With *Ziggy . . .* David Bowie abruptly redefined what being a male rock star was all about. The cover depicts Bowie as a skinny, crop-haired androgyne in a rainswept alley (though in the recording studio he was still wearing the fey long locks sported on his previous album, *Hunky Dory*). Clutching an electric guitar, he is an alien beamed down to the drab Earth to bring us rock 'n' roll. (Shot on Heddon Street, London, the photograph was originally black and white but later tinted, giving it an odd Fifties sci-fi cartoon quality.)

Ziggy . . . is the only glam rock album to have stood the test of time. Guitarist Mick Ronson's crunching guitar riffs and soaring solos—heard to spine-tingling effect on "Moonage Daydream,""Suffragette City," and the title track—helped to define the glam sound. Bowie's vocals change with every song—by turns reflective, preening, desperate, and ecstatic. *Ziggy . . .* contains a wealth of sexual ambivalence and space-age imagery, but it is couched in solid songwriting and carefully thought-out arrangements.

It may have sounded like a lightning bolt from the future, but in assuming the role of a troubled rock 'n' roll outsider Bowie immediately clicked with teenagers and critics alike (*Rolling Stone* gave it "at least 99/100"). Britain, and America's East and West coasts, fell deliriously for Ziggy (though he was just too weird for the Midwest)—as did punks and New Romantics later, with whom the character's sexual ambiguity and outrageous appearance struck a chord. **RD**

> " . . . the '70s were the start of the 21st century . . . "

David Bowie, 1982

Track Listing

▶	01 **Five Years** (Bowie)	4:42
	02 **Soul Love** (Bowie)	3:34
	03 **Moonage Daydream** (Bowie)	4:40
▶	04 **Starman** (Bowie)	4:10
	05 **It Ain't Easy** (Davies)	2:58
	06 **Lady Stardust** (Bowie)	3:22
	07 **Star** (Bowie)	2:47
	08 **Hang On To Yourself** (Bowie)	2:40
▶	09 **Ziggy Stardust** (Bowie)	3:13
▶	10 **Suffragette City** (Bowie)	3:25
▶	11 **Rock 'N' Roll Suicide** (Bowie)	2:58

War | The World Is A Ghetto (1972)

Label | United Artists
Producer | Jerry Goldstein
Art Direction | Howard Miller
Nationality | USA
Running Time | 43:49

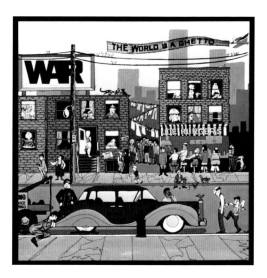

By the early 1970s, urban life in America was a dichotomy of experience, particularly in Los Angeles—the dreams of Hollywood contrasted sharply with the realities of life for growing Latino and African-American populations in the east and south of the city. While such a divergent culture created tension (with the 1965 Watts riots still stinging the collective memory), it also provided a fertile breeding ground for music, informing the growth of adventurous bands such as Sly And The Family Stone and War.

A convergence of jazz, funk, rock, and Latin influences, War had scored a hit with "Spill The Wine," under the sponsorship of former Animals front man Eric Burdon. Continuing as an independent outfit, the seven members of the band showed increasing promise in their first two albums, but *The World Is A Ghetto* realized their full potential. While the title suggested an overt political statement, Howard Miller's cover design captured the album's lighthearted vibe—a Rolls-Royce stuck in the ghetto with a flat tire. Indeed, the Latin-flavored "The Cisco Kid" (a tongue-in-cheek homage to the heroic 1950s movie caballero) and the funky "Where Was You At" are as apolitical as it gets, celebrating life rather than preaching an agenda. Even the lyrics of the title track offer an optimistic message of love emerging from the overpowering city smog.

The remarkably positive reception of the album (it was the best-selling record of 1973) illustrated how well War had captured the urban experience. While they would enjoy success throughout the decade, *Ghetto* remains their most cohesive and satisfying work. **TSh**

> **"The world is still a ghetto. There will always be a reason to play our songs … because *war* is reality."**
>
> Lonnie Jordon, 2000

Track Listing

▶ 01	**The Cisco Kid** (Allen·Brown·Dickerson Jordan·Miller·Oskar·Scott)	4:35
02	**Where Was You At** (Allen·Brown·Dickerson Jordan·Miller·Oskar·Scott)	3:25
▶ 03	**City, Country, City** (Allen·Brown·Dickerson Jordan·Miller·Oskar·Scott)	13:18
04	**Four Cornered Room** (Allen·Brown·Burdon Dickerson·Jordan·Miller·Oskar·Scott)	8:30
▶ 05	**The World Is A Ghetto** (Allen·Brown Dickerson·Jordan·Miller·Oskar·Scott)	10:10
06	**Beetles In The Bog** (Warner)	3:51

Al Green | Let's Stay Together (1972)

Label | Hi
Producer | Willie Mitchell
Art Direction | Marlene Bergman
Nationality | USA
Running Time | 33:38

In 1969, producer Willy Mitchell signed a 23-year-old singer named Al Green to Memphis-based Hi Records. Green was originally from Forrest City, AR, just across the Mississippi River from Memphis, and that year he was performing in the R&B group the Soul Mates, with middling success. Mitchell and Green soon began collaborating on records, and they triumphed with Green's 1972 album release, *Let's Stay Together*, the title track of which sat atop the singles chart for nine weeks.

Mitchell, a bandleader from Ashland, MS, had joined Hi Records in 1959, and there perfected the Hi sound, a dense sonic wash that featured growling organs, and tight horn and string arrangements. Mitchell's production techniques had some of their clearest expression on Green's records, thanks in no small part to Green's voice, a startling and supple instrument capable of leaping, with no advance notice, from a scratchy growl to an aching falsetto.

Let's Stay Together takes remarkable musical risks—the title track, for example, has a melody that ascends and descends unpredictably, in a manner rather unorthodox for a top-selling pop record; meanwhile, another track, "La-La For You," explores a dissonant minor key. Elsewhere, Green takes a pleasant if undistinguished Bee Gees tune, "How Can You Mend A Broken Heart?," and turns it into a devastating lament, epic in its scope. In the mid-1970s, Green began devoting more of his time to preaching. In retrospect, the change seems not altogether surprising—sensuous, soulful and transcendent, *Let's Stay Together* is hearty spiritual food indeed. **KB**

"I've noticed a lot of brawls at my concerts, girls getting overwhelmed ..."

Al Green, 1996

Track Listing

▶	01	**Let's Stay Together** (Green·Jackson·Mitchell)	3:18
▶	02	**La–La For You** (Green·Mitchell)	3:31
	03	**So You're Leaving** (Green)	2:57
▶	04	**What Is This Feeling?** (Green)	3:42
	05	**Old Time Lovin'** (Green)	3:19
▶	06	**I've Never Found A Girl (Who Loves Me Like You Do)** (Floyd·Isbell·Jones)	3:41
	07	**How Can You Mend A Broken Heart?** (B. Gibb·R. Gibb)	6:22
	08	**Judy** (Green)	3:47
	09	**It Ain't No Fun To Me** (Green)	3:23

The Rolling Stones Exile On Main St. (1972)

Label | Rolling Stones Records
Producer | Jimmy Miller
Art Direction | Robert Frank
Nationality | UK
Running Time | 66:25

By 1972, the Stones were outlaws—albeit on the run from the taxman rather than the demons that had been on their tail three years earlier—and a pack you only ran with if you had the strongest constitution. When they arrived at Keef's villa in the South of France, they brought with them only their hardiest compadres, but the 12 months it took to record and then mix *Exile On Main St.* took a toll on all concerned, and eventually on the band. Drugs and booze were a given; the fractious hell of living and working en masse in an unsuitable mansion, once a Nazi headquarters, was their choice. Mick's decision to disappear with Bianca only added to the grumbling.

So, *Exile On Main St.* was Richard's baby, but he could not have made it without the strongest backup the band ever had: Jimmy Miller (production and percussion), Bobby Keys on saxophone, Jim Price on trumpet and trombone, and Nicky Hopkins on piano are everywhere, contributing to a loosely layered sound that hides just as much as it highlights. The noted photojournalist Robert Frank was enlisted to come up with the "And you think we're the freaks?" cover. He then followed them on tour, but when the band saw the footage intended for the *Cocksucker Blues* road movie, they cannily spotted the difference between sexy and sexist and had it shelved.

And the music? The band hated it, but if you like rock, its entire DNA is here, spread over four sides, and better than *The White Album*. Not everything you hear about it is true, but believe the legends. The Stones never rolled this well again. **DH**

Track Listing

▶	01	**Rocks Off** (Jagger·Richard)	4:30
	02	**Rip This Joint** (Jagger·Richard)	2:22
	03	**Shake Your Hips** (Moore)	2:57
	04	**Casino Boogie** (Jagger·Richard)	3:31
▶	05	**Tumbling Dice** (Jagger·Richard	3:42
	06	**Sweet Virginia** (Jagger·Richard)	4:25
	07	**Torn & Frayed** (Jagger·Richard	4:16
	08	**Sweet Black Angel** (Jagger·Richard)	2:52
	09	**Loving Cup** (Jagger·Richard)	4:21
▶	10	**Happy** (Jagger·Richard)	3:02
	11	**Turd On The Run** (Jagger·Richard)	2:34
	12	**Ventilator Blues** (Jagger·Richard·Taylor)	3:24
	13	**I Just Want To See His Face** (Jagger·Richard)	2:51
▶	14	**Let It Loose** (Jagger·Richard)	5:16
	15	**All Down The Line** (Jagger·Richard)	3:47
	16	**Stop Breaking Down** (Trad.)	4:34
▶	17	**Shine A Light** (Jagger·Richard)	4:14
	18	**Soul Survivor** (Jagger·Richard)	3:47

Lynyrd Skynyrd
Pronounced Leh-nerd Skin-nerd (1973)

Label | MCA
Producer | Al Kooper
Art Direction | Emerson-Loew
Nationality | USA
Running Time | 42:58

In 1973, Lynyrd Skynyrd emerged from the Florida swamplands as a stepchild of the new American South, a culture at once repentant and defiant about its tarnished heritage. By the time they recorded their debut album, Skynyrd had honed a dexterous, chicken-fried sound in Dixieland's dives and juke joints, assembling along the way a vicious triple-guitar attack to complement a taut rhythm section and Ronnie Van Zant's remarkably soulful voice. But most important to their product, as well as to the countless bands this album would eventually inspire, were the ambiguities that distinguished the group. They looked like truculent confederates, but their music was haunted by black immigrants. *Pronounced* ... flaunted and defied stereotypes of the Southern man and became the first truly meaningful Southern rock statement.

Part blues, part country, part The Who, it features the finest that rock riffing has to offer on the blistering opener "I Ain't the One" and the cautionary "Poison Whiskey." Where the rival Allman Brothers ventured into jazz and hippie noodling, Skynyrd offered a comparable virtuosity anchored deeper in the blues. The acoustic "Mississippi Kid" is all Delta boogie; "Things Goin' On" reminds us all of the band in our local saloon.

And then there is "Freebird," the breathtaking finale that transformed the group into celebrities and vaulted the album into the charts. Pensive, brash, uplifting, and heartrending, the song offers a nine-minute lesson in rock, complete with the most exhilarating outburst of electric guitar to that point, and maybe since. **MO**

> **"Southern rock's a dead label, a hype thing for the magazines to blow out of proportion. We don't play like the Allmans ..."**
>
> Ronnie Van Zant, 1977

Track Listing		
▶ 01 **I Ain't The One** (Rossington·Van Zant)	3:53
02 **Tuesday's Gone** (Collins·Van Zant)	7:30
03 **Gimme Three Steps** (Collins·Van Zant)	4:27
▶ 04 **Simple Man** (Rossington·Van Zant)	5:56
05 **Things Goin' On** (Rossington·Van Zant)	4:57
▶ 06 **Mississippi Kid** (Burns·Kooper·Van Zant)	3:54
07 **Poison Whiskey** (King·Van Zant)	3:13
▶ 08 **Freebird** (Collins·Van Zant)	9:08

Michael Viner's Incredible Bongo Band
Bongo Rock (1973)

Label | Pride
Producer | Perry Botkin Jr. • Michael Viner
Art Direction | Uncredited
Nationality | Canada • USA
Running Time | 33:17

Bongo Rock. The Story Of The Incredible Bongo Band

The Incredible Bongo Band was assembled from a variety of unknown session musicians to provide chase music for the 1972 MGM B-movie *The Thing With Two Heads*. Michael Viner, head of the short-lived MGM subsidiary label Pride, gathered the musicians together and recorded two tracks—"Bongo Rock" and "Bongolia." MGM decided to release these tracks as a double-sided 45, which went on to sell more than one million copies. An LP was hurriedly recorded to follow up on its success.

Once again, Viner rounded up the session players (whose names have been lost to time—Viner himself cannot recall the lineup), and they recorded the album over a few days in Canada with a variety of players, Viner included, dropping into the sessions.

The album sold in reasonable quantities at the time, but has since grown to legendary status due to its appropriation by subsequent generations. It was the drum breakdowns in the band's cover of The Shadows' hit "Apache" that, when extended with the use of two vinyl copies by New York's DJ Kool Herc, heralded the birth of hip hop. And since then, the track has been sampled by hundreds of artists (beginning with the Sugarhill Gang's track of the same name), as has the LP's title track "Bongo Rock," the result being that the album has become a cult classic and a collector's item.

A followup, *The Return Of The Incredible Bongo Band*, appeared in 1974 but failed to capture the energy or success of the debut, despite guest appearances from the likes of Ringo Starr. **CR**

"They say it's been sampled 200 times over 100 million records, I'm sure we've got paid for only three percent."

Michael Viner, 2004

Track Listing

01	**Let There Be Drums** (Nelson•Podolar)		2:38
▶ 02	**Apache** (Lordan)		4:54
▶ 03	**Bongolia** (Botkin)		2:14
04	**Last Bongo In Belgium** (Botkin•Viner)		6:55
05	**Dueling Bongos** (Botkin•Viner)		2:56
06	**In–A–Gadda–Da–Vida** (Ingle)		7:42
07	**Raunchy '73** (Justis•Manker)		3:23
▶ 08	**Bongo Rock** (Egnoian•Epps)		2:35

David Bowie | Aladdin Sane (1973)

Label | RCA
Producer | David Bowie • Ken Scott
Art Direction | Duffy Design Concepts
Nationality | UK
Running Time | 40:47

The ultimate rock chameleon did not change colors between 1972's groundbreaking *Ziggy Stardust ...* and 1973's *Aladdin Sane* (his breakthrough effort in America). He was still the same glitter-rocking starchild, "making love to his ego" through song.

Written mostly during Bowie's 1972 tour of America, *Aladdin Sane* picks up where *Ziggy* left off to serve as a brutal memoir for one rock Martian's meteoric rise to the top. The tracks ooze desperation and alienation as the central character strives, through a haze of drugs and alcohol, to find some kind of enlightenment and, perhaps, rediscover himself. Admittedly, the theme never gels in Ziggy-like fashion, but the album proved to be a worthy—if more mercurial—follow-up, thanks to such diversely addictive songs as "Panic In Detroit," "Time," and "The Jean Genie."

As with *Ziggy*, guitarist Mick Ronson is as much of a star as Bowie. He slams through Keith Richards-style licks on the stunning opener, "Watch That Man," and makes like Godzilla walking into Suffragette City with the vicious "Panic In Detroit." Producer Ken Scott, who engineered The Beatles' *Magical Mystery Tour* and *White Album*, moves from sleek sophistication on the title track, to raunchy rock with "Cracked Actor."

Mike Garson's distinctive keyboard flurries decorate the spine-tingling closer "Lady Grinning Soul," while Bowie's melodramatic reading of "Time" is the album's one true anthem. The record's one failure comes from the misguided remake of the Stones' "Let's Spend The Night Together," heralding Bowie's disappointing next album, the covers-only collection *Pin-Ups*. **JiH**

> ## "It's the union between the user and the art that creates and finishes the art."
>
> David Bowie, 1999

Track Listing

01	Watch That Man	(Bowie)	4:25
▶ 02	Aladdin Sane	(Bowie)	5:06
03	Drive-In Saturday	(Bowie)	4:29
▶ 04	Panic In Detroit	(Bowie)	4:25
05	Cracked Actor	(Bowie)	2:56
▶ 06	Time	(Bowie)	5:09
07	The Prettiest Star	(Bowie)	3:26
08	Let's Spend The Night Together (Jagger • Richard)		3:03
▶ 09	The Jean Genie	(Bowie)	4:02
10	Lady Grinning Soul	(Bowie)	3:46

King Crimson | Larks' Tongues In Aspic (1973)

Label | Island
Producer | King Crimson
Art Direction | Tantra Designs
Nationality | UK
Running Time | 46:41

Second only to *In The Court Of The Crimson King*, King Crimson's masterpiece, *Larks' Tongues In Aspic* was a fine artistic achievement and a breakthrough in the music of the band. It was recorded in the winter of 1973 by a reshuffled lineup: guitar virtuoso and leader Robert Fripp, ex-Yes drummer Bill Bruford, vocalist and bass player John Wetton (formerly of Family), violinist David Cross, and percussionist Jamie Muir. The bizarre title of this record was provided by the eccentric Muir, who abruptly (and very unexpectedly) vanished for years shortly after the recording of the album. *Larks' Tongues . . .* marked the last appearance of this unpredictable musician in King Crimson.

The music is a remarkable piece of art, from the first sounds of tinkling finger cymbals until the closing dialogues of bass and violin. Spacious and passionate improvisations unequivocally demonstrate the band's exceptional musical abilities. The lyrics, penned by the new lead writer in the band—Richard Palmer-James (Supertramp's first guitarist)—were more down-to-earth than those of previous Crimson records. "Exiles," "Book Of Saturday,""Easy Money," and "The Talking Drum" are all nothing short of exceptional. The dramatic climax, however, belongs to Robert Fripp's heavy guitar riffs in the reprise of the title track.

Larks' Tongues . . . is innovative both rhythmically and sonically, and its compositions revealed new and visionary forms of musical thinking, the cover art also being revolutionary. Although the album was never a smash chart success (U.S. No. 61; UK No. 20), it stands today as one of the pillars of progressive rock. **AW-J**

> **"You know, that was hell, really, to make—because nobody could decide what on earth kind of music we were supposed to be playing anyway."**
>
> Bill Bruford, 1980

Track Listing

▶ 01 **Larks' Tongues In Aspic, Part One**
(Bruford·Cross·Fripp·Muir·Wetton)　　13:36

▶ 02 **Book Of Saturday**
(Fripp·Palmer-James·Wetton)　　2:59

▶ 03 **Exiles** (Cross·Fripp·Palmer-James)　　7:37

▶ 04 **Easy Money** (Fripp·Palmer-James·Wetton)　　7:51

▶ 05 **The Talking Drum**
(Bruford·Cross·Fripp·Muir·Wetton)　　7:28

▶ 06 **Larks' Tongues In Aspic, Part Two** (Fripp)　　7:10

Bob Marley And The Wailers | Catch A Fire (1973)

Label | Island
Producer | Chris Blackwell
Art Direction | Rod Dyer • Bob Weiner
Nationality | Jamaica
Running Time | 35:59

In December 1971, a down-and-out Bob Marley walked into the London offices of Chris Blackwell, founder of Island Records, looking to catch a break. Recognizing a golden opportunity, the Jamaican-born Blackwell fronted Marley and his band, The Wailers, $6,000 to fly home to Jamaica and record an album. Upon receiving the master tapes, Blackwell recruited American session men, overdubbed some catchy rock guitar and keyboard licks, and commissioned a cool Zippo-shaped record jacket. The album generated rave reviews and set the stage for reggae's international ascent.

Not only was this the first reggae album to penetrate the rock market, it was also Marley's key collaboration with fellow Wailers founders Peter Tosh and Bunny Livingston. Backed by the thick, disciplined basslines of Aston Barrett and the squeaky-clean upbeats of Tosh's guitar, the trio laid out the range of their vocal ability, broadcasting their militant message in rich harmony.

Haunting opener, "Concrete Jungle" despairs at the grinding poverty of the urban ghetto; Tosh's forceful "400 Years" and the wailing, menacing "Slave Driver" recall slavery's oppressive historical legacy; "No More Trouble" defiantly delivers a solution: "What we need is love." In between are forays into flirtatious romance—the deliciously upbeat "Stir It Up," with its bouncy, rising bassline and meandering wah-wah solo (courtesy of Blackwell's overdubs) leads into the laid-back "Kinky Reggae," with its funny call and response.

Marley sings lead on all save two of the tracks, but *Catch A Fire* is definitely the work of a band—one bursting with hunger and creative energy. **MW**

> "I don't see I self as being Jamaican. I see I self as a Rasta being Rasta! Soh, Jamaica is Jamaica ... I man a Rasta!"
>
> Bob Marley, 1973

Track Listing

▶	01	Concrete Jungle (Marley)	4:13
	02	Slave Driver (Marley)	2:53
	03	400 Years (Marley • Tosh)	2:45
▶	04	Stop That Train (Tosh)	3:55
	05	Baby We've Got A Date (Marley)	3:57
▶	06	Stir It Up (Marley)	5:32
▶	07	Kinky Reggae (Marley)	3:37
▶	08	No More Trouble (Marley)	3:57
	09	Midnight Ravers (Marley)	5:10

Hawkwind
Space Ritual (1973)

Label | United Artists
Producer | Hawkwind
Art Direction | Barney Bubbles • Pierre
Nationality | UK
Running Time | 115:32

John Cale
Paris 1919 (1973)

Label | Warner Bros.
Producer | Chris Thomas
Art Direction | Mike Salisbury
Nationality | UK
Running Time | 31:30

Featuring the classic lineup of guitarist/vocalist (and founder) Dave Brock, poet Robert Calvert, saxophonist/flautist Nik Turner, bassist Lemmy Kilmister, drummer Simon King, synth player Del Dettmar, and electronics man DikMik, this double live album is Hawkwind's magnum opus and perhaps the ultimate sonic trip.

Devised by Calvert, the urban guerrillas' 1972 tour was a multimedia concept involving naked dancers, cosmic stage design and costume, and a kaleidoscopic lights and lasers show. Songs from the group's second and third LPs, *In Search Of Space* and *Doremi Fasol Latido*, were linked by eerie sound collages and spoken-word pieces. These formed a pseudo-operatic narrative about seven cosmonauts traveling in a state of suspended animation. That said, it is the musical anthems that provide the highlights on disc. "Born To Go" and the pulverizing "Brainstorm" are driven by metronomic bass and marinated in whooshing effects. The phased and confused "Orgone Accumulator" and blissed-out "Space Is Deep" create a more lysergic ambience, while contrasting "Master Of The Universe" is a brain-frying piledriver composed of hypno-metal riff, intergalactic oscillator grooves, and comic book fantasy.

Hawkwind continued to release great records throughout the 1970s, but later decades saw a number of personnel changes and dodgy "official bootlegs" diminish their status (although Brock is still plugging away). Nevertheless, their audiovisual presentation has proved hugely influential. **MA**

It is hard to envision such a European album being produced in L.A., at the appropriately named Sunwest Studios. Maybe that is the reason *Paris 1919* shines with a light that only shimmered through Cale's solo debut *Vintage Violence* (1971).

Of course, producer Chris Thomas is British, but in the studio band are Lowell George and Richard Hayward from Little Feat, champions of Californian Seventies rock. Orchestration features extensively, but this is not a classical work like *The Academy In Peril* (1972). Rather, it is a memorably lush pop album used by the artist to exorcize his past as a sonic experimentalist with LaMonte Young and The Velvet Underground.

The mesmerizing opener "Child's Christmas In Wales" references the most famous poet of Cale's country, Dylan Thomas. "Andalucia" and "Half Past France" are traveling autobiographies, while "Macbeth" is rendered boogie-rock style and "Graham Greene" takes tea with a pinch of reggae. "Hanky Panky Nohow" and "Antarctica Starts Here" both express a bygone sensibility in rock.

The portrait of a convulsive soul in a rare moment of personal balance, and a musical feat he would never revisit, the album still excels as a cohesive, uplifting mixture of nostalgia and surrealism; a wonder of arrangements—credited to Cale, who had arranged the mercurial *The Marble Index* by fellow maverick Nico—and musical genius. Other Cale albums might be closer to the challenging spirit adored by a minority, but none has penetrated pop history like *Paris 1919*. **IJ**

Can
Future Days (1973)

Label | Spoon
Producer | Can
Art Direction | Ingo Trauer
Nationality | Germany • Japan
Running Time | 41:04

Future Days is the sound of Can thinking way outside any "Kings of Krautrock" box. Gone are the space-rock freakouts of *Monster Movie* (1969) and pop-prog experimentalism of *Ege Bamyasi* (1972). Granted, traces of *Tago Mago* (1971) still echo beneath the cartoon reggae funk of the album's solitary single "Moonshake," but this time the Germans also escape the guitar soloing cul-de-sac of British counterparts like Pink Floyd.

On "Spray," they set their sights on discovering their own saucer full of rock secrets in Michael Karoli's sparse guitar drones, Irmin Schmidt's hypnotic keyboard layers, and Damo Suzuki's often incoherent Morse code incantations. Add metronomic master drummer Jaki Liebezeit's cyclical jazz pulse and Czukay's monotonic bass groove, and you have the glue that allows *Future Days* to continually swing out. This is rock for jazz and classical buffs, head music that maps each member's uncharted inner space as much as it does the collective improvisational architectures. By the time "Bel Air" eases its 20-minute drift of ambient guitars, drum loops, bird song samples, eery electronic washes, and breakbeats to a close, Can as a rock band have left the building.

Suzuki certainly did, becoming a Jehovah's Witness. The group he left behind imploded into the ambient global groove of *Soon Over Babaluma* (1974) before ultimately splitting up. Can next reappeared on the global radar when *Future Days* resurfaced in the Nineties as the improvisational blueprint for post-rock stylists like Tortoise. **MK**

Lou Reed
Berlin (1973)

Label | RCA
Producer | Bob Ezrin
Art Direction | Pacific Eye And Ear
Nationality | USA
Running Time | 49:30

After the commercial success of 1972's *Transformer*, critics and fans were hungry for another slice of catchy, sexually ambiguous glam rock. What Reed served up was a lot harder to swallow.

Berlin was Reed's most brutal work to date. Envisaged as a "movie for the ears," the album chronicles the demise of a relationship between two Americans, Caroline and Jim, living in the divided German city. The songs weave through infidelity ("Caroline Says I"), drug abuse ("How Do You Think It Feels"), and violence ("Caroline Says II"), ending with Caroline's suicide ("The Bed"). Chillingly, Jim refuses to mourn his girlfriend's death, and "Sad Song" closes with the unsettling couplet, "I'm gonna stop wastin' my time/Somebody else would have broken both her arms."

Producer Bob Ezrin crafted the perfect widescreen soundtrack to accompany Reed's script. Ezrin recruited an all-star studio band and carefully layered the ten tracks with lush symphonic sweeps. The result was a glorious slab of orchestral rock, wildly different from the stripped-back sound of *Transformer*.

The record buying public was not ready for such an ambitiously bleak project. *Rolling Stone* declared *Berlin* a "disaster" and the album just scraped into the U.S. Top 100. The album may have been a commercial disaster, but its gloomy atmospherics stirred a new generation of musicians. Less than a decade later, Joy Division's Ian Curtis would be praised for creating the sort of dark imagery that had left Reed critically crucified. **TB**

Genesis | Selling England By The Pound (1973)

Label | Charisma
Producer | John Burns • Genesis
Art Direction | Betty Swanwick
Nationality | UK
Running Time | 53:40

GENESIS

SELLING ENGLAND BY THE POUND

Their fifth studio album represented a quantum leap for Genesis in both creative and commercial terms. Many of their fans still consider it their finest achievement both with Peter Gabriel at the helm and beyond.

Although not a concept piece like the follow-up, *The Lamb Lies Down On Broadway*, its lyrics represented a scathing commentary on contemporary Britain, a country suffering industrial strife and economic uncertainty in stark contrast to the color and energy of the 1960s. The tone is set by opener "Dancing With The Moonlit Knight," wherein an unaccompanied Gabriel asks the question: "Can you tell me where my country lies?" From then on, Arthurian legend and medieval minstrelsy combine as the group set commercialism, Americanization, and the erosion of long-standing values firmly in their sights.

Paul Whitehead's surrealistic artwork had adorned studio predecessors *Trespass*, *Nursery Cryme*, and *Foxtrot*. This time the band chose a curious naive painting by Betty Swanwick, the inspiration for "I Know What I Like (In Your Wardrobe)"—a surprise hit that undoubtedly helped *Selling England By The Pound* rise to No. 3 in the UK. "Firth Of Fifth," a masterpiece of prog rock, also deserves a mention. And with "The Battle Of Epping Forest" and "The Cinema Show," both 11-minute-plus epics, this is far from the bite-size Genesis of later years.

Having recently entered the Top Ten for the first time with a live album, Genesis would henceforth be a bankable commodity, even with the departure of figurehead Gabriel and the controversial elevation of Phil Collins from the drum stool. **MH**

> ## "It's just kind of mad, surreal—the whole package always makes me smile, you just can't pin it down."
>
> Steve Hackett, 2004

Track Listing

01	Dancing With The Moonlit Knight	(Genesis)	8:04
▶ 02	I Know What I Like (In Your Wardrobe) (Genesis)		4:07
▶ 03	Firth Of Fifth	(Genesis)	9:37
04	More Fool Me	(Genesis)	3:11
▶ 05	The Battle Of Epping Forest	(Genesis)	11:48
06	After The Ordeal	(Genesis)	4:16
▶ 07	The Cinema Show	(Genesis)	11:05
08	Aisle Of Plenty	(Genesis)	1:32

Marvin Gaye | Let's Get It On (1973)

Label | Motown
Producer | Marvin Gaye • Ed Townsend
Art Direction | Vartan
Nationality | USA
Running Time | 31:36

This is probably the only Motown album to feature a credit for the world-famous modernist poet T.S. Eliot. The author of *The Wasteland*, once said: "Birth and copulation and death, that's all the facts when you get to brass tacks"; a quote that adorns the gatefold sleeve to this seminal album.

And bizarrely, this sentiment fits the nature of this release beautifully. After the furrow-browed social commentary of *What's Going On*, Marv was telling his listeners to get back to the more basic business of, "sex between consenting anybodies." And what a torrid, engorged, breathlessly sweat-slicked beast (with two backs) the music is.

Despite being constantly overshadowed critically and commercially by its predecessor, *Let's Get It On* (a U.S. No. 2) is much more charming, convincing, and, dare it be said, soulful. It made perfect sense that Gaye, whose lyrics and entire live performance were covertly sexually charged earlier in his career, would eventually become entirely overt. The album's title track (which became a No.1 smash) was a fairly obvious way of nailing his colors to the mast. The track, with its musical and lyrical climaxes, became the benchmark of bedroom music until, perhaps, Gaye himself released "Sexual Healing" in 1982. "You Sure Love To Ball," with its panting and barely concealed rutting noises was an erotic tour de force to some, and unbelievably beyond the pale to others. But, like good sex, the album was playful, inventive, sumptuous, and surprising; qualities that other albums have aped since, but not ever come close to surpassing. **JDo**

> "Marvin Gaye is as much a minister as a man in any pulpit."
>
> Rev. Jesse Jackson, 1971

Track Listing

▶	01	**Let's Get It On** (Gaye•Townsend)	4:52
▶	02	**Please Stay (Once You Go Away)** (Gaye•Townsend)	3:28
	03	**If I Should Die Tonight** (Gaye•Townsend)	3:03
	04	**Keep Gettin' It On** (Gaye•Townsend)	3:09
	05	**Come Get To This** (Gaye•Townsend)	2:40
	06	**Distant Lover** (Gaye•Gordy Gaye•Greene)	5:15
▶	07	**You Sure Love To Ball** (Gaye)	4:43
▶	08	**Just To Keep You Satisfied** (Gaye•Stover)	4:26

John Martyn
Solid Air (1973)

Label | Island
Producer | John Martyn • John Wood
Art Direction | Fabio Nicoli
Nationality | UK
Running Time | 32:88

Roxy Music
For Your Pleasure (1973)

Label | Island
Producer | Roxy Music • Chris Thomas
Art Direction | Nicholas de Ville
Nationality | UK
Running Time | 42:16

John Martyn had five albums under his belt by *Solid Air*. Rather than folk or jazz or blues, the album is instead a dusky alchemy of all three and represents a career performance from Martyn, who sings with wonderfully grizzled sincerity on this after-hours classic. Fabio Nicoli's cover art may look like it was lifted from a science textbook, but the music inside is anything but clinical.

Nowhere is this more apparent than on the title track; a slow, hypnotic blues. Written as both warning and homage to singer Nick Drake, who died 18 months after *Solid Air*'s release, Martyn's haunting vocals are backed by elegantly understated double bass and lithe soprano sax, which curl around the song like smoke, as cool vibraphone chords ring long and low beneath.

This sparse but most expressive instrumentation is repeated in "Don't Want To Know," and the two songs set the album's languid, nocturnal tone perfectly. In part this reflects the strength of Martyn's musical partnership with virtuoso bassist Danny Thompson, which is shown in its best light on these tracks. But there is more on offer in *Solid Air* than midnight-hour meditations on the human condition.

The abrasive, wrong-hearted blues of "I'd Rather Be The Devil" sits easily beside the fragile eroticism of "Go Down Easy" and "May You Never"'s sturdy pledge of kinship. Time and again, Martyn's gutsy sincerity knits it all together—and the evident warmth of this album comes from the same source; a charismatic, bull-hearted performance from a musician on sparkling form. **JDi**

Bryan Ferry wanted to be beautiful. Brian Eno wanted to be wild. And, for two albums in the early 1970s, Roxy Music managed to be both. However, it was not without cost. Enraged by Ferry's reluctance to record his songs, Eno called it quits after 1973's *For Your Pleasure* and the band was never the same again.

However, it was exactly that artistic tug-of-war that fueled their great eponymous debut and pushed *…Pleasure* to even greater heights. When a compromise between the two giants was reached, such as on the decadently avant-garde pop single "Do The Strand," the results were glorious. By stark contrast, a track like "In Every Dream Home A Heartache," apparently an ode to an inflatable sex doll, was just plain ponderous. Fortunately, *…Pleasure* features far more of the former.

"Do The Strand" is one of the most uproarious rock numbers Roxy Music ever recorded. Ferry takes over for the haunting goodbye "Beauty Queen" and showcases his raising falsetto on "Strictly Confidential." Eno's robotic keyboards are the perfect counterpoint to Phil Manzanera's soaring guitar in "Editions Of You."

…Pleasure was another Top Ten hit for Roxy Music in the UK and the follow-up, *Stranded*, released at the tail end of 1973, became the band's first No. 1 in its homeland, though Americans did not latch on to Roxy Music until Ferry replaced the artsy experimentation with an equally appealing soul-pop sound, perhaps heard to best effect on 1982's *Avalon*, the group's lone gold record Stateside. **JiH**

Faust
Faust IV (1973)

Label | Virgin
Producer | Uwe Nettelbeck
Art Direction | Uwe Nettelbeck
Nationality | Germany
Running Time | 41:57

In the early Seventies, Germany's progressive scene became known in Europe and the United States as "Krautrock," a faintly pejorative tag coined by the British press after Virgin and United Artists began to license and sign German acts. The genre was established as a profitable trend, but rapidly became associated with acts sadly lacking the European avant-garde sense of rock established by the first wave of Krautrockers.

A left-wing students' commune formed in 1971, their coalescence of San Francisco politics and electro-acoustic sound trips was championed by Uwe Netlebeck, a music journalist who became their producer and mentor. Via Netlebeck, in 1972 Virgin released *The Faust Tapes*, a collection of home recordings. Fifty thousand copies were sold, winning the band underground popularity. A British tour followed, and Faust was signed to record their first British album.

Faust IV opens with the megalithic drone "Krautrock," an adventurous, metronomic, low-fi jam that captures the essence of the band's teutonic romanticism. Other tracks, such as "Just A Second," "Picnic On A Frozen River," and "Giggy Smile" experiment with electronica and musique concrète, jazz and folk in a very evocative way.

Unfortunately, disappointingly poor cover art and the inclusion of dadaist pop oddities such as "Sad Skinhead," "Jennifer," and "It's A Bit Of Pain" (today praised as some of Faust's best lyrical moments) deterred fans of *The Faust Tapes* from buying an album now perceived as a Krautrock classic. **JG**

Herbie Hancock
Headhunters (1973)

Label | CBS
Producer | David Rubinson
Art Direction | Victor Moscoso
Nationality | USA
Running Time | 41:46

After the cryptic electronic jazz of *Sextant*, *Headhunters* saw Herbie Hancock take a more linear funk route. He had been listening to James Brown and Stevie Wonder, and had recorded some unreleased session work with Marvin Gaye, but it was the polyrhythmic funk of Sly And the Family Stone that shaped his next move.

Hancock stripped away the exploratory jazz baggage of his hugely innovative—and hugely unprofitable—*Mwandishi Sextet*, retaining only multi-reedist Benny Maupin from that lineup, and enlisting Paul Jackson to play the role of Sly Stone's finger-popping bassist Larry Graham. It ended up sounding nothing like Sly Stone, but it did invent several genres of music.

Somewhere in the juddering, chromatic bassline of "Chameleon" is the DNA for electronic dance music. Tangled up in Herbie's modal improvisations on the Fender Rhodes are the first rumblings of smooth jazz, while enmeshed in Harvey Mason's crisp, razor-sharp breakbeats is the birth of techno, disco, and drum 'n' bass.

Unlike Hancock's subsequent electric funk outings, *Headhunters* retains a vestigial avant-garde sensibility—the mournful, military two-step of "Vein Melter," the wobbly, mutant funk of "Sly," the beer-bottle hollers of "Watermelon Man" (a rereading of his 1962 R&B hit, here based on an African pygmy chant).

The band would go on to record two much-sampled albums as The Headhunters, and Hancock's subsequent career would contain smatterings of genius, but no one here bettered this seminal jazz-funk masterpiece. **JLe**

Mott The Hoople | Mott (1973)

Label | CBS
Producer | Dan Loggins
Art Direction | Roslav Szaybo
Nationality | UK
Running Time | 43:06

The chemistry between Mott the Hoople singer Ian Hunter and guitarist Mick Ralphs threatened to explode during the recording of 1973's *Mott*, the band's only UK Top Ten album. Hunter had originally joined Ralphs' small-time band, Silence, as a keyboard player, but came to exert a greater grip on both singing and songwriting following their David Bowie-produced hit "All The Young Dudes."

First single "Honaloochie Boogie" saw the band augmented by cello and Andy Mackay's saxophone. (Roxy Music were recording *For Your Pleasure* next door in London's Air Studios at the time, and Mackay was allegedly keen to join Mott.) Opening track "All The Way From Memphis" remains one of Hunter's finest moments and would be edited for single release. Brian May, whose Queen supported Mott round the United States, recalls a performance of said song in said city as "a great moment of reconnection to the original capital city of white rock."

Mott The Hoople had not forgotten their wilder side, even though Bowie had temporarily coached it out of them, and "Violence" would put evidence of their pre-punk rudeness back on vinyl. Ralphs enjoyed his only moment of solo glory with an automotive-based number, "I'm A Cadillac," which segued into the slide-guitar-laced instrumental "El Camino Dolo Roso" (literally "The Road Of Sadness").

Mott was, for Ian Hunter, "the most complete album we did, but it was tinged with tragedy because Ralphs was leaving." He now had the spotlight to himself, but he'd lost his soulmate and would soon seek another in Mick Ronson. He never beat *Mott*, though. **MH**

> "I didn't want Mick to leave … I even offered him half my royalties …"

Ian Hunter, 2002

Track Listing

▶	01	**All The Way From Memphis** (Hunter)	4:58
	02	**Whizz Kid** (Hunter)	3:07
▶	03	**Hymn For The Dudes** (Allen•Hunter)	5:38
	04	**Honaloochie Boogie** (Hunter)	2:42
▶	05	**Violence** (Hunter•Ralphs)	4:48
	06	**Drivin' Sister** (Hunter•Ralphs)	3:51
▶	07	**Ballad Of Mott** (Allen•Griffin•Hunter•Ralphs•Watts)	5:23
	08	**I'm A Cadillac/El Camino Dolo Roso** (Ralphs)	7:48
	09	**I Wish I Was Your Mother** (Hunter)	4:51

Mike Oldfield | Tubular Bells (1973)

Label | Virgin
Producer | Simon Heyworth • Tom Newman • Mike Oldfield
Art Direction | Trevor Key
Nationality | UK
Running Time | 48:56

When fresh-from-the-folk-clubs prodigy Mike Oldfield first presented his epic *Tubular Bells* concept to Virgin label owner Richard Branson, he was slightly intimidated by the social gulf he perceived between the perma-grinning ex-prep school entrepreneur and himself. This fueled a determination that can be heard to this day behind every note of this most misused album, which today finds itself as much the fodder for dinner-table background muzak as it is the hallowed listening material for progressive rock freaks.

Musically, *TB* is a fantastic mish-mash of rock guitar, (both rhythm guitar grind, with all the primitive overdrive the early Seventies could muster, and blues-tinged lead), soupy bass, and a whole slew of instruments centered on the ethereal chime of the bells themselves. Oldfield sits at the hub of the melodic chaos, orchestrating proceedings with a degree of precocious confidence that is surprising, given how little he has chosen to deviate from this route in subsequent decades.

The caveman grunts in "Part 2" may become irritating after a few listens, but the madcap humor Oldfield injects into the project makes such excesses forgivable. Listen out for the fantastically inebriated Bonzo Dog frontman Viv Stanshall, who introduces each instrument as they enter the main theme and the volume spikes that reveal the young Oldfield's inexperience—but also serve to accentuate the organic composition.

Less exciting sequels overlabored the *Tubular Bells* point somewhat, but Oldfield stuck stubbornly to the ambient, experimental template he had pioneered so memorably and the album is still a '70s essential. **JM**

> **"The truth is, I was never completely satisfied with the result, neither with the general sound, nor the performing. I always thought it could be much better."**
>
> Mike Oldfield, 2003

Track Listing

▶	01	**Tubular Bells, Part 1** (Oldfield)	25:36
	02	**Tubular Bells, Part 2** (Oldfield)	23:20

Todd Rundgren
A Wizard, A True Star (1973)

Label | Bearsville
Producer | Todd Rundgren
Art Direction | Arthur Wood
Nationality | USA
Running Time | 47:05

Elton John
Goodbye Yellow Brick Road (1973)

Label | DJM
Producer | Gus Dudgeon
Art Direction | Michael Ross
Nationality | UK
Running Time | 76:20

Todd Rundgren's 1973 was clearly like no one else's. He was riding high on a wave of apparently boundless talent. He had been hoping to follow up *Something/Anything?* with yet another double album, but the oil crisis led to a vinyl shortage. Always one to embrace limitations, Rundgren took on a different project: a 19-to-24 track (depending on how you count) album, which, like all of Rundgren's work, showcased his exceptional abilities as a vocalist and musician, at the same time as it challenged and delighted his audience.

"There are no limitations as to what is sung about or what the music sounds like, or how long it is . . . or whether it is even music at all," he said at the time. So, "When The Shit Hits the Fan" harks back to *Pet Sounds*; "Zen Archer" (a longtime live favorite in the Seventies) is a long, loping foray into cosmic pop, all falsetto and flair. "Rock And Roll Pussy" was, apparently, about John Lennon—famously having his "lost weekend" year in L.A. at the time; the two had a public spat about Rundgren's pronouncements on Lennon's behavior.

Jumping between styles and sounds, the album is hard to digest at first, but Rundgren's great strength is his ability to write incredible songs. The intricacy of the die-cut original sleeve does not translate well to CD: the theme, clearly, is mirrors, and there is a coded message on the front which might merely be the album title in pseudo-runes— but who really knows? **DN**

Three of the first four tracks on this release rank among Elton John's best-loved songs. Apart from "Candle In The Wind," revised from a tribute song for Marilyn Monroe to the funeral theme for Princess Diana, they also include a million-selling U.S. chart-topper in "Bennie And The Jets," which was also the first John/Taupin single to crack the U.S. R&B chart.

Plans for the album, which topped the U.S. chart for eight weeks during a two-year residency, started badly after a studio in Jamaica was found wanting (hence the cod-reggae of "Jamaica Jerk-Off"). Stuck in his hotel room, Elton had nothing else to do but write music for Taupin's lyrics. He wound up with enough songs for a double album (his first), and recorded them at the famous "honky chateau" where his two previous chart-topping albums had been captured.

The duo scored another UK Top 10/U.S. Top 20 single in "Saturday Night . . . ," which Taupin claimed was his attempt to redress the lyrical balance away from his favorite American themes. Other delights include the dynamic instrumental intro on the prog-rock opener. Taupin's lyrics also included possibly the earliest rock song to address lesbianism in "All The Girls Love Alice."

Prog, ballads, straightout rock'n'roll, novelty songs— such diversity, spread over 17 tracks, makes for an inconsistent set. But the highs—particularly that stirring title track—are popcraft at its best. **JT**

Steely Dan
Countdown To Ecstasy (1973)

Label | ABC
Producer | Gary Katz
Art Direction | Dotty of Hollywood
Nationality | USA
Running Time | 41:04

After the million-selling success of their debut album *Can't Buy A Thrill*, Steely Dan had a lineup change, with Donald Fagen taking over vocal duties. It marked the start of the "classic" Dan sound.

With a hit behind them, it was time to expand the scope of the band's material. *Countdown ...* introduces more of the jazz influences and oblique lyrics that define their later work, while the impressionist cover art hints at this bolder agenda.

The opener "Bodhisattva" is a beauty. A satirical blast at karma-conscious California, the song plays like high-IQ rockabilly, the highlight an outrageous lead-guitar duel between Jeff "Skunk" Baxter and New York jazz shredder Denny Dias.

"Your Gold Teeth" employs Dias again but in more tangential style—telling the story of a jaded female grifter who lives off her looks and cunning, the song is like an Elmore Leonard novel in miniature. The verse is given glacial cool by Victor Feldman's vibes and the edgy electric piano of Fagen, while the solo section visits strange psychotropic regions. No such ambiguity haunts "My Old School," their straightahead rock number about collegiate misdeeds, barbed with guitar hooks from "Skunk" Baxter.

Harder in tone than their debut, *Countdown To Ecstasy* presages the themes of their later work with acerbic style. **JDi**

Waylon Jennings
Honky Tonk Heroes (1973)

Label | RCA
Producer | T. Glaser • W. Jennings
Art Direction | Uncredited
Nationality | USA
Running Time | 27:06

In 1958, 21-year-old Waylon Jennings joined Buddy Holly's Crickets as temporary bass player, a gig that ended with Holly's untimely death the following year. Jennings then played music on the West Coast until 1965, when he began working the trenches for RCA in Nashville. However, recording albums in the studio system left him unsatisfied, and in 1973 he took on the mantle of producer for *Honky Tonk Heroes*, one of country music's landmark albums.

For writing duties, Jennings enlisted Billy Joe Shaver, a 34-year-old Texan who was just beginning to make a name as a Nashville songwriter. The collaboration proved to be an inspired one—Shaver wrote or co-wrote all but one of the album's ten tracks, and his bleak parables of lawlessness and wantonness were the perfect match for Jennings' low, weary singing voice.

With Jennings at the helm, the album had a stripped-down sound uncharacteristic of Nashville records at the time—he gave songs languorous tempos, while Ralph Mooney's pedal steel was mournful and evocative. Shaver's lyrics, meanwhile, were simple and forceful, but with careful rhymes and wryly amusing imagery. One of his standout tracks, "Black Rose," runs: "When the devil made that woman, Lord, he threw the pattern away/She was built for speed with the tools you need to make a new fool every day." **KB**

Pink Floyd | The Dark Side Of The Moon (1973)

Label | Harvest
Producer | Pink Floyd
Art Direction | Hipgnosis
Nationality | UK
Running Time | 42:30

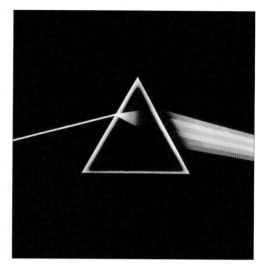

Acid blues guitar solos. Lyrics that tackle woe and warmongering. A spacey title. Issued in 1973 by a group who were individually anonymous yet vastly influential.

This is *Cosmic Slop* by Funkadelic. Nothing to do with *Dark Side of the Moon*, except that both soundtracked a cynical era, when Watergate and the end of the Vietnam War killed off whatever was left of the Sixties spirit after Altamont.

The Floyd's zeitgeisty opus, however, had mundane beginnings. Anxious to shed their psychedelic shackles, the band gathered in drummer Nick Mason's kitchen to compile a shortlist of things that bothered them. Those pressures—time, money, madness, death—were wedded to vaguely funky rockers much like those on *Obscured By Clouds*, then toured for a year as *Eclipse (A Piece For Assorted Lunatics)*. Sprinkled with studio fairydust—gospel vocals, explosive solos, sound effects—*Eclipse* became *Dark Side of the Moon*. A Stateside million-seller on the strength of the band's live reputation, the album went interstellar when parent company Capitol turned "Money" into a rare Floyd hit.

These days it is available in anniversary editions, and has been re-made by reggae mischief-makers (2003's *Dub Side Of The Moon*) and Phish. Opened out, the gatefold cover displays a prism endlessly refracting a beam of light. Evoking both the Floyd's legendary light show and the "vaulting ambition" in the lyrics—it remains one of rock's most iconic images.

With its burden of heritage, you would expect it to be a bore. In fact, it is a tuneful, rousing set of brilliant songs. For Floyd virgins, this is the place to start. **BM**

> "We still had a common goal, which was to become rich and famous."
>
> Roger Waters, 2003

Track Listing		
01	**Speak To Me** (Mason)	1:15
02	**Breathe** (Gilmour·Waters·Wright)	2:18
03	**On The Run** (Gilmour·Waters)	3:33
▶ 04	**Time/Breathe (Reprise)** (Gilmour·Mason·Waters·Wright)	7:07
▶ 05	**The Great Gig In The Sky** (Wright)	4:44
▶ 06	**Money** (Waters)	6:32
07	**Us And Them** (Waters·Wright)	7:41
09	**Any Colour You Like** (Gilmour·Mason·Wright)	3:25
10	**Brain Damage** (Waters)	3:51
11	**Eclipse** (Waters)	2:04

Stevie Wonder | Innervisions (1973)

Label | Motown
Producer | Stevie Wonder
Art Direction | Mathieu Bitton
Nationality | USA
Running Time | 44:12

Innervisions closed a trinity of albums begun with 1972's *Music Of My Mind*, the final fruits of the burst of creativity that followed Wonder's renegotiated creative freedom under Motown. Released barely seven months after *Talking Book*, *Innervisions* was no final scraping of the barrel, however. As Efram Wolff's startling cover painting suggested, this was Wonder's most ambitious, sprawling and, yes, visionary album yet.

Before its release, Wonder took journalists on a blindfolded bus ride across New York City, experiencing urban life like Stevie would, followed by a similarly blindfolded playback of the album. One can only wonder what hearing "Living For The City" must have felt like, an epic aural thriller (complete with dialogue and sound effects) tracing a naive country boy's descent into crime and death in the rotten Big Apple. Politics drove the album: the melancholic "Visions," the righteously funky "Higher Ground" (later butchered by the Chili Peppers), the smouldering "Jesus Children Of America" all spoke of an America fast coming apart at the seams. But Stevie was never preachy: the luscious, celebratory "He's Misstra Know-It-All" was lower-case "p" political, with the deftest of touches. And, as if to prove his versatility, the melodramatic "All In Love Is Fair" was later covered by both Frank Sinatra and Barbra Streisand.

"I felt something was going to happen that would be very, very significant," remembered Wonder later of his prophetic mood at the time. Indeed, a horrific car accident while touring the album—leaving Wonder in a coma and cruelly robbing him of his sense of smell—would signal the beginning of another new chapter. **SC**

> *"**Innervisions** gives my own perspective of what's happening in my world, to my people, to all people."*
>
> Stevie Wonder, 1973

Track Listing

▶ 01	**Too High** (Bollenback • Wonder)	4:36
02	**Visions** (Bollenback • Wonder)	5:23
▶ 03	**Living For The City** (Wonder)	7:21
04	**Golden Lady** (Wonder)	5:00
▶ 05	**Higher Ground** (Wonder)	3:42
06	**Jesus Children Of America** (Wonder)	4:10
07	**All In Love Is fair** (Wonder)	3:41
▶ 08	**Don't You Worry 'Bout A Thing** (Wonder)	4:44
▶ 09	**He's Misstra Know–It–All** (Wonder)	5:35

ZZ Top | Tres Hombres (1973)

Label | London
Producer | Bill Ham
Art Direction | Bill Narum
Nationality | USA
Running Time | 33:26

Tres Hombres marked ZZ Top's elevation into the megaleague as one of the biggest touring acts in the United States. The jury will probably always be out on which was the better of ZZ's two great eras—straight-down-the-line blues rock (1970s) or pumpin' blues disco (1980s and '90s). What is indisputable is that their Texas roots were absolutely inseparable from their down 'n' dirty sound.

Tres Hombres is a showcase of everything that is magnificent about the group—and the inclusion of the huge hit "La Grange" is only part of that story. In fact, "La Grange," based around a riff so simple yet so inspired that you will never forget it, is atypical for its mumbling novelty vocal. "Precious And Grace"—a song about picking up a couple of hitch-hiking women who turn out to be ex-cons—mixes a great Led Zep-styled riff in the verse with a ripsnorting near-psychedelic chorus. The two devices come together seamlessly. "Move Me On Down the Line" is a snappy boogie that sounds indebted to post-Cream Jack Bruce. "Jesus Just Left Chicago" is another gem of a track, fluid and apparently effortless. The incredible "Master of Sparks" concerns a fine Texas tradition, the habit of kickin' your buddies off the back of a speeding pickup just for the heck of it.

The cover of the album—the original vinyl is a gatefold that opens on a garish photograph of the Mexican dish after which the record is named—says it all, really, though the oblique cover shots of the threesome hide the fact that these guys were only in their mid-twenties. **DN**

> ## "Everybody everywhere goes to whores, drinks beer, and drives fast."
>
> Dusty Hill, 1973

Track Listing

01	Waitin' For The Bus (Gibbons·Hill)	2:59
▶ 02	Jesus Just Left Chicago (Beard·Gibbons·Hill)	3:29
03	Beer Drinkers & Hell Raisers (Beard·Gibbons·Hill)	3:23
04	Master Of Sparks (Gibbons)	3:33
05	Hot, Blue, And Righteous (Gibbons)	3:14
▶ 06	Move Me On The Line (Gibbons·Hill)	2:30
▶ 07	Precious And Grace (Beard·Gibbons·Hill)	3:09
▶ 08	La Grange (Beard·Gibbons·Hill)	3:51
09	Shiek (Gibbons·Hill)	4:04
10	Have You Heard? (Gibbons)	3:14

Paul McCartney And Wings
Band On The Run (1973)

Label | Apple
Producer | Paul McCartney
Art Direction | Hipgnosis
Nationality | UK
Running Time | 41:10

Paul McCartney's early solo work did little to suggest he could make timeless music outside The Beatles. He delivered solitary gems—notably "Maybe I'm Amazed" and "Live And Let Die"—but full albums such as 1973's *Red Rose Speedway* were not Beatlesque killer.

Moreover, McCartney, who had recently garnered headlines for a drugs bust, went to work on this album with more than a few feathers missing—drummer Denny Seiwell and guitarist Henry McCullough split a week before the band flew out to record in Lagos, Nigeria. And when they got there, McCartney and wife Linda were robbed at knifepoint. But out of adversity …

McCartney dominated every inch of what was essentially a solo record. *Band On The Run* kicks off with its rollercoaster of a title track—a kind of mini-suite actually, recalling the heavily nuanced arrangements of the side-two *Abbey Road* song cycle. He immediately makes good on that high-flying start with the punchy "Jet" and continues to soar through the sunny "Bluebird," a companion piece of sorts to The Beatles' "Blackbird." The work momentarily stumbles on "Let Me Roll It," a misguided answer to Lennon's scathing "How Do You Sleep?," but again finds focus thanks to solid side-two tracks like "Mamunia" and "No Words."

Six (mainly British) celebs co-starred on the prison break cover, half suggesting a scaled down *Sgt. Pepper* … Fittingly so, as *Band On The Run* also proved a critical and commercial hit, and one that stands as the singer/songwriter/bassist's finest post-Beatle hour. **JiH**

> ## "The more crises you have, the more material you have."
>
> Paul McCartney, 1984

Track Listing

▶	01	**Band On The Run** (L. McCartney • P. McCartney)	5:12
▶	02	**Jet** (L. McCartney • P. McCartney)	4:13
▶	03	**Bluebird** (L. McCartney • P. McCartney)	3:24
	04	**Mrs. Vandebilt** (L. McCartney • P. McCartney)	4:44
	05	**Let Me Roll It** (P. McCartney)	4:52
▶	06	**Mamunia** (L. McCartney • P. McCartney)	4:51
	07	**No Words** (Laine • P. McCartney)	2:33
	08	**Picasso's Last Words (Drink To Me)** (L. McCartney • P. McCartney)	5:52
	09	**Nineteen Hundred And Eighty Five** (L. McCartney • P. McCartney)	5:29

The Sensational Alex Harvey Band
Next ... (1973)

Label | Vertigo
Producer | Phil Wainman
Art Direction | Uncredited
Nationality | UK
Running Time | 35:47

Two years after Glasgow band Tear Gas met Alexander Harvey, fully 16 years their senior, the partnership's second album gave them a career highlight. After a UK tour, supporting Slade forged a gung-ho mentality, they performed "Next" and "Faith Healer" on BBC TV's *Old Grey Whistle Test*, in 1973. The band's mixture of hard rock and theatricality, combined with Harvey's vocals and demonic charisma, made them a powerful draw.

Jacques Brel's title-track tale of depravity could have been tailor-made for Harvey, with its lyrical references to whore-houses and sexually transmitted diseases. "Faith Healer," meanwhile, singlehandedly made them the hit of the 1973 Reading Festival when Harvey's question "Can I lay my hands on you?" was met by a frenzied, arms-aloft response from 30,000 festival-goers. "Everyone went completely wild," guitarist Zal Cleminson confirms. Yet like so many great rock 'n' roll moments, it was born out of pure chance. Bassist Chris Glen: "'Faith Healer' was an accident ... in those days the cassette had to be the same length on each side and we ended up about two minutes short, so we stuck a loop on the front of it!"

With Harvey and keyboardist Hugh McKenna now in songwriting harness, and producer Phil Wainman on board to add vital chart knowhow, the stage was set for further triumphs, but a combination of bad luck, fatigue, and mismanagement—not to mention a "novelty" hit single with "Delilah" that did them more harm than good—all helped slow the band's progress. **MH**

> "Alex proposed we do a tango ["Next"]. We all went okay, it's not exactly what we're used to playing, but we'll have a go."
>
> Chris Glen, 2004

Track Listing		
▶ 01	**Swampsnake** (Harvey•McKenna)	4:52
02	**Gang Bang** (Harvey•McKenna)	4:44
▶ 03	**The Faith Healer** (Harvey•McKenna)	7:11
04	**Giddy-Up-A-Ding-Dong** (Bell•Lattanzi)	3:16
▶ 05	**Next** (Blau•Brel•Shuman)	4:03
▶ 06	**Vambo Marble Eye** (Harvey•McKenna)	4:24
07	**The Last Of The Teenage Idols** (Cleminson•Harvey•McKenna)	7:17

Alice Cooper | Billion Dollar Babies (1973)

Label | Warner Bros.
Producer | Bob Ezrin
Art Direction | Pacific Eye And Ear
Nationality | USA
Running Time | 40:51

When *Billion Dollar Babies* was released, Vincent Furnier—a.k.a. Alice Cooper, the king of shock rock—was still with the original members of the Alice Cooper Band. One album later the band parted, but they left behind this, their most powerful album.

A collaboration with producer Bob Ezrin saw the band embrace a much harder rock style, though now with a smoother polish, and accommodating strings and brass. Recording took place both in the United States (The Cooper Mansion, Connecticut and The Record Plant, New York) and the UK (Morgan Studios, London)—where among the friends who passed by to lend a hand during the sessions were Marc Bolan, Donovan, and The Who's Keith Moon.

The album also marked the commercial explosion of the Alice Cooper phenomenon, and the accompanying tour was to prove one of the biggest money-spinners in rock history. Fake blood, gallows (replaced by a guillotine for this tour), and electric chairs had been the props of Cooper's performances for a while, and now the songs followed suit. The choice cut here is perhaps "I Love The Dead," an unnerving story of necrophilia that helped take the album to No. 1 in both the U.S. and the UK charts. It is in excellent company however, with storming, stadium-friendly fare such as "Elected" (another hit single, and one of three UK Top Tens extracted from the LP) and "No More Mr. Nice Guy" (originally planned for 1971's *Killer*) which became something of a theme song for Cooper. (The original vinyl album was housed in a gatefold sleeve complete with a pullout billion-dollar banknote.) **LPG**

"They are the worst band ever. But they have a sense of humor. They know how to entertain ..."

Frank Sinatra, 1967

Track Listing		
▶ 01 **Hello, Hooray** (Kempf)		4:14
02 **Raped And Freezin'** (Bruce•Cooper)		3:15
▶ 03 **Elected** (Bruce•Buxton•Cooper•Dunaway•Smith)		4:05
04 **Billion Dollar Babies** (Bruce•Cooper•Smith)		3:39
05 **Unfinished Sweet** (Bruce•Cooper•Smith)		6:17
▶ 06 **No More Mr. Nice Guy** (Bruce•Cooper)		3:05
07 **Generation Landslide** (Bruce•Buxton•Cooper•Dunaway•Smith)		4:31
08 **Sick Things** (Bruce•Cooper•Ezrin)		4:18
09 **Mary Ann** (Bruce•Cooper)		2:19
▶ 10 **I Love The Dead** (Cooper•Ezrin)		5:08

Iggy And The Stooges | Raw Power (1973)

Label | Columbia
Producer | Iggy Pop
Art Direction | Mick Rock
Nationality | USA
Running Time | 33:57

The image of a defiant, staring Iggy Pop on *Raw Power*'s cover perfectly encapsulates his response to the trials and tribulations he went through before this album took shape. After an unhappy relationship with their label Elektra, who had mismarketed the band's first two albums and ditched them before their third took shape, Pop had disbanded the Stooges and escaped Detroit to hook up with David Bowie in New York.

At Bowie's suggestion, Iggy and guitarist James Williamson decamped to London to record *Raw Power*. There, Pop re-recruited Ron and Scotty Asheton, the brothers who made up The Stooges' primal rhythm section. The genteel surroundings of "Merrie Olde [England]," as Pop put it, in no way tempered the raucous machismo of *Raw Power*; indeed, the record could not be further from the sexual ambiguity of the glam rock that Bowie and others were touting at the time. Pop's vision for the record was ambitious—initial mixes of "Search And Destroy" featured the sound of a sword fight, while "Penetration" utilized that rock 'n' roll staple, the celeste (a keyboard of orchestral bells)—but the driving guitar of Williamson and the raw stomp of the Ashetons keep the album simple and centered firmly in the belly and the balls.

Columbia hated the album, viewing it as even less accessible than the band's material for Elektra, and charged Bowie with salvaging what he could from the mess. Thankfully, Bowie paid heed to Iggy's vision, and delivered eight tracks that influenced the proto-punks of New York and London and secured Pop's legacy as the movement's godfather. **SJac**

> "We were a rip-snortin', super-heavy, nitro-burnin', fuel-injected rock band that nobody could touch ..."
>
> Iggy Pop, 1997

Track Listing

▶	01	**Search And Destroy** (Pop•Williamson)	3:29
▶	02	**Gimme Danger** (Pop•Williamson)	3:33
	03	**Your Pretty Face Is Going To Hell** (Pop•Williamson)	4:54
	04	**Penetration** (Pop•Williamson)	3:41
▶	05	**Raw Power** (Pop•Williamson)	4:16
	06	**I Need Somebody** (Pop•Williamson)	4:53
	07	**Shake Appeal** (Pop•Williamson)	3:04
	08	**Death Trip** (Pop•Williamson)	6:07

The Isley Brothers | 3 + 3 (1973)

Label | T-Neck
Producer | The Isley Brothers
Art Direction | Ed Lee
Nationality | USA
Running Time | 38:58

Until the album *3 + 3* came out in 1973, people knew The Isley Brothers as a group like The Drifters or The Moonglows: smiling black guys in cool mohair suits. Listeners loved the Isleys' hits—The Beatles covered their "Twist And Shout," and the group had a hit with the gospel-inspired R&B stomper "Shout"—but their work for Motown proved frustratingly inconsistent.

3 + 3 announced their dramatic rebirth, starting with the cover, which showed photos by Don Hunstein of the five brothers, Ronald, O'Kelly, Rudolph, Ernie, and Marvin Isley, plus buddy Chris Jasper, self-confident and decked out in eye-popping threads. (The Isleys originally performed as a trio—the album's title is a reference to the introduction of a younger generation.)

The album proved that the brothers from Teaneck, New Jersey, could play and sing with as much passion and pop appeal as any Seventies act from David Bowie to Al Green. Seventeen-year-old Ernie's long, legato lines on fuzztone Stratocaster® (Hendrix was a direct influence—he had played in the Isleys' backing band in the Sixties) fueled the brothers' move into rock-friendly territory. "That Lady," the opening track, became the big single, but "What It Comes Down To" and the epic "Summer Breeze" linger fondly in the memory. The vocals are light, melodious, and soulful—and, on "Summer Breeze," Ronald's tenor is deliriously ecstatic.

A warm, romantic album, *3 + 3* is filled with danceable grooves (Marvin ranks with the best of funk's bassists), and the overall sound has a light, almost acoustic R&B-folk-rock feel that makes one yearn for the innocent days before disco. **ML**

"We played our own instruments when black groups didn't do that ... the people on the cover made all the sounds on the record."

Ernie Isley, 1973

Track Listing		
▶ 01 **That Lady** (The Isley Brothers)		5:35
▶ 02 **Don't Let Me Be Lonely Tonight** (Taylor)		4:00
03 **If You Were There** (The Isley Brothers)		3:22
04 **You Walk Your Way** (The Isley Brothers)		3:08
▶ 05 **Listen To The Music** (Johnston)		4:07
▶ 06 **What It Comes Down To** (The Isley Brothers)		3:54
07 **Sunshine Go Away Today** (Edwards)		4:23
▶ 08 **Summer Breeze** (Seals·Crofts)		6:12
09 **The Highways Of My Life** (The Isley Brothers)		4:17

New York Dolls | New York Dolls (1973)

Label | Mercury
Producer | Todd Rundgren
Art Direction | Album Graphics Inc.
Nationality | USA
Running Time | 42:14

Pilloried by the press as merely drag impersonators of The Rolling Stones, the New York Dolls were in fact a tight and well-rehearsed band who loved Fifties R&B and Sixties girl groups. In New York they paid their dues at a theater called the Mercer Arts Center, where they were adopted by Andy Warhol's Arts Factory entourage. Convinced they were the next big thing, Marty Thau, who was associated with Aerosmith's management team, struck a record deal. The Dolls' hard-boiled insights into Manhattan's day-to-day decadence and chronicles of underground despair were set to keep The Velvet Underground's flame alive.

Not without some opposition from the Dolls, producer Todd Rundgren transformed the band's basement dynamics with a cinematic sound spectrum. Johnny Thunders' stormy, Chuck Berry-like guitar-playing collided with David Johansen's drunken howl at a wild recording session that yielded an explosive set of songs. The Dolls' streetwise rock 'n' roll majesty (and sharp wit) fueled such gutter classics as "Frankenstein," "Human Being," the joyous romp "Personality Crisis," and "Trash"—articulating cheap romance and urban alienation within a grotesque but beautiful soundscape.

Trailblazers of New York's early Seventies proto-punk scene, the Dolls were in the middle of an acrimonious breakup by 1975, partly brought about by their self-destructive tendencies. Their achievements had not gone unnoticed in London, though—in that same year, Malcolm McLaren (who managed the Dolls briefly toward the end of their career) stole their concept and formed a new band, the Sex Pistols. **JG**

> "We were Dolls 24 hours a day. You couldn't hang up your Dolls suit and go play golf."
>
> Arthur Kane, 1998

Track Listing

▶	01	**Personality Crisis** (Johansen·Thunders)	3:42
	02	**Looking For A Kiss** (Johansen)	3:19
	03	**Vietnamese Baby** (Johansen)	3:30
▶	04	**Lonely Planet Boy** (Johansen)	4:08
	05	**Frankenstein** (Johansen·Sylvain)	5:58
▶	06	**Trash** (Johansen·Sylvain)	3:07
	07	**Bad Girl** (Johansen·Thunders)	3:03
	08	**Subway Train** (Johansen·Thunders)	4:20
	09	**Pills** (McDaniel)	2:48
	10	**Private World** (Johansen·Kane)	3:39
▶	11	**Jet Boy** (Johansen·Thunders)	4:40

Eno | Here Come The Warm Jets (1974)

Label | Island
Producer | Brian Eno
Art Direction | Lorenz Zatecky
Nationality | UK
Running Time | 41:58

Roxy Music simply was not big enough for Bryan Ferry's beauty as well as Brian Eno's experimentation. By 1973's *For Your Pleasure*, both knew it and Eno left the band.

After releasing *No Pussyfooting* with guitarist Robert Fripp, Eno realized his own vision with this solo debut. Despite the cheeky title, *Here Come The Warm Jets* was a masterwork of art-school ambitions and straightforward pop-rock, both echoing his Roxy work and hinting at what he would later accomplish with David Bowie.

Working with Andy Mackay, Phil Manzanera, Fripp, and other sonic explorers, Eno developed a synth-rock sound that would serve as a major inspiration for 1980s new wave artists. ...*Warm Jets* embraced both widely accessible melodies and obscure postmodern punches. A counterpoint to the pretentious art-rock of ELP and Yes, the album comes across foremost as a rock record, sometimes recalling the directness of The Velvet Underground. It is also a guitar record—unfortunately, one that never features Manzanera and Fripp on the same track. Instead, the two fret wizards take turns, with Manzanera going first and delivering razor-sharp rhythms on "Needles In The Camel's Eye," then Fripp upping the ante with "Baby's On Fire." Eno maintains a sense of humor throughout, building "Cindy Tells Me" around classic doo-wop, and nearly poking his tongue through his cheek on "Dead Finks Don't Talk" with his mimicking of an ex-bandmate.

Despite its lack of obvious commerciality, the album was surprisingly successful, cracking the UK's Top 30. Eno would build upon his debut with 1975's far-reaching *Another Green World*. **JiH**

> ## "It's only in the last six years or so that anyone's ever bothered about skill in rock music ..."
>
> Brian Eno, 1974

Track Listing

▶	01	**Needles In The Camel's Eye** (Eno・Manzanera)	3:11
	02	**The Paw Paw Negro Blowtorch** (Eno)	3:04
▶	03	**Baby's On Fire** (Eno)	5:19
	04	**Cindy Tells Me** (Eno・Manzanera)	3:25
▶	05	**Driving Me Backwards** (Eno)	5:12
	06	**On Some Faraway Beach** (Eno)	4:36
	07	**Blank Frank** (Eno・Fripp)	3:37
▶	08	**Dead Finks Don't Talk** (Eno)	4:19
	09	**Some Of Them Are Old** (Eno)	5:11
▶	10	**Here Come The Warm Jets** (Eno)	4:04

Bad Company | Bad Company (1974)

Label | Island
Producer | Bad Company • Terry Thomas
Art Direction | Hipgnosis
Nationality | UK
Running Time | 34:35

As Turkey prepared to invade Cyprus in mid-1974, Led Zeppelin's manager Peter Grant unleashed his own Young Turks: ex-Free men Paul Rodgers (vocals) and Simon Kirke (drums), former Mott The Hoople guitarist Mick Ralphs, and erstwhile King Crimson man Boz Burrell (the sixteenth bassist who auditioned!).

Long before his future employers Queen made a name for themselves, Rodgers was already a rock 'n' roll star (and accordionist), and there was great anticipation about his first, post-Free foray. He did not disappoint.

Rodgers and Ralphs formed Bad Company— christened after a 1972 Western starring Jeff Bridges— after meeting on the road and jamming. They were taken under Zeppelin's wing, signed to their label Swan Song in the United States and—during a lull in Zep's recording schedule—allowed to make *Bad Company* in November 1973 at Ronnie Lane's Headley Grange studio.

The U.S. No. 1 album captures the energy of a coke-fueled high life, built on a Cream and Hendrix template, with added soul and country. It boasts glittering standouts such as the swaggering "Can't Get Enough," the pounding "Movin' On," the pleading "Ready For Love," and ballad "Seagull." *Bad Company* was engineered by Ron Nevison, later an in-demand producer. Kirke was recorded in a hallway, while the title track's vocals were taped at night—for atmosphere—in a nearby field. As Rodgers reminisced, "alcohol and drugs" were the band's true lifeblood, yet *Bad Company* epitomizes good-time blues rock. Steve Clarke of *NME* enthused, "Everything they touch turns to gold." He could have added platinum too. **TJ**

> "I had to fight to get the management and the record company to accept the name 'Bad Company' ..."
>
> Paul Rodgers, 2002

Track Listing

▶	01	**Can't Get Enough Of Your Love** (Ralphs)	4:10
	02	**Rock Steady** (Rodgers)	3:46
	03	**Ready For Love** (Ralphs)	5:00
	04	**Don't Let Me Down** (Ralphs • Rodgers)	4:18
	05	**Bad Company** (Kirke • Rodgers)	4:50
	06	**The Way I Choose** (Rodgers)	5:05
▶	07	**Movin' On** (Ralphs)	3:20
▶	08	**Seagull** (Ralphs • Rodgers)	4:06

Genesis
The Lamb Lies Down On Broadway (1974)

Label | Charisma
Producer | John Burns • Genesis
Art Direction | Hipgnosis
Nationality | UK
Running Time | 92:25

Although 1974 can be seen as the apogee of progressive rock excess, this album is dark and brittle with spare instrumentation. Recorded in rural Wales at a difficult time for Genesis, with Peter Gabriel's vocals captured separately in London's Island Studios, the album actually displays the group at their most bite-sized.

Gabriel was, at that time, being courted as a serious writer and took it upon himself to write a modern-day *Pilgrim's Progress*, which begins with Rael, a leather-clad Puerto Rican street punk, seeing a lamb—wait for it—lying down on Broadway. Whether anyone, Gabriel included, really understood what it was about is open to conjecture, but the double album features some of his most consistent writing and the band's pithiest playing.

"Back In NYC," covered by Jeff Buckley on his final recordings, signposts punk; "In The Cage" is as readily climactic as "Supper's Ready," but in just eight minutes; "Carpet Crawlers" gave the group another anthem; and "The Chamber Of 32 Doors" allows the soul music that Gabriel was steeped in as a teenager to spill over.

With its clean, modern, Hipgnosis cover, the album was finally released to general acclaim at the end of 1974. It is a vocalist's record, which is why the musicians hated it, and Gabriel loved it. Clear that he would never again be allowed quite so much leeway on a Genesis album, at the end of the grueling world tour to support the album, he was gone. **DE**

Shuggie Otis
Inspiration Information (1974)

Label | Epic
Producer | Johnny Otis • Shuggie Otis
Art Direction | T.E. St. John
Nationality | USA
Running Time | 32:07

In spite of a twenty-first-century CD re-release, this timeless musical gem remains a little-known album. But it casts a sublime spell and deserves wider renown as a delicate, spacey, beautiful funk essential.

The year 1965 saw Shuggie, aged 12(!), debut at No. 29 in the U.S. R&B charts, a born-again B. B. King on the fine but filthy "Country Girl." The track was a funky blues classic by his father, legendary R&B star Johnny Otis, writer of classics like "Hound Dog" and "Willy And The Hand Jive." In that deeply fertile musical soil, Shuggie blossomed into a total musical prodigy: guitarist, songwriter, vocalist, arranger, multi-instrumentalist. By the time he was 19, he had played with Frank Zappa and Al Kooper, turned down The Rolling Stones (who asked him to be Mick Taylor's replacement), and created four unique albums, the last of which was *Inspiration…*

It is a delicious ride from the laidback funk of the title track to the outrageously futuristic trip hop of his drum-machine-led excursions "XL-30" and "Pling!" And Shuggie plays everything himself. The re-release even features four breathtaking tracks from *Freedom Flight* (1971), adding psychedelia, funky blues, and an exquisite jazz suite to the soundscape.

The combination of minimal sales, maximal studio time, and the fact that Sly Stone was their big-selling funk star, saw Epic drop Shuggie in 1974. And then the world forgot him—until a new century dawned. **MR**

Stevie Wonder
Fulfillingness' First Finale (1974)

Label | Tamla Motown
Producer | Stevie Wonder
Art Direction | Bob Bleason
Nationality | USA
Running Time | 43:53

Fulfillingness' First Finale marks the last—and most commercially successful—of Stevie's remarkable quartet of albums with synth wizards Robert Margouleff and Malcolm Cecil, the engineers who had assisted his transition from child genius to adult superstar.

Sessions could last three full days, as Stevie multi-tracked his unorthodox, self-taught drumming and Moog-created basslines to conjure compelling grooves. These were the raw material for perfect pop songs, with all the drama and complexity of Schubert lieder.

The songs, recorded after Stevie's near-fatal car crash of August 6, 1973, are more life affirming than 1973's often-angry *Innervisions*. The country ballad "Too Shy To Say" features a Ray Charles-ish vocal, accompanied by gorgeous pedal steel guitar by Sneaky Pete Kleinow of the Flying Burrito Brothers. There is the jittery funk of "Boogie On Reggae Woman," the spooky ballad "Creepin'," and the Brazilian fusion of "Bird Of Beauty."

The neo-gospel epic "They Won't Go When I Go"—with lyrics by Stevie's sister-in-law Yvonne Wright—borrows from Islamic prayer and Gregorian chants, and was later covered by George Michael.

Most memorable of all was the militant "You Haven't Done Nothin'." It revisited the stomping funk-rock of "Superstition" and became Stevie's fourth U.S. No. 1, aided by Motown label-mates The Jackson Five on backing vocals. The album itself also made U.S. No. 1. **JLe**

Eric Clapton
461 Ocean Boulevard (1974)

Label | RSO
Producer | Tom Dowd
Art Direction | Bob Defrin
Nationality | UK
Running Time | 36:46

However unfairly, Eric Clapton's *461 Ocean Boulevard* will always live in the shadow of his success with *Layla And Other Assorted Love Songs* (1970), which set the course of the stellar guitarist's post-Cream career as a mellow-bluesy and occasionally anthemic pop-rocker. Released after endless Layla tours and their live recording, *461 Ocean Boulevard* was inevitably seen as a pleasant but modest continuation of music that was already familiar. Yet this album has a smouldering groove that still burns today.

The cover photos (by David Gahr) and title suggest that Eric and the band—most notably bassist Carl Radle and drummer Jamie Oldaker—alternated making the album in laidback sessions at Miami's Criteria Studios with living together and hanging out by the pool of a big house nearby. Maybe *461 Ocean Boulevard* did not fall into place as easily (there is evidence of painstaking mixing and delicate overdubs), but the musicians' interplay has an easy camaraderie and the tunes and overall sound have a falling-off-a-log naturalness that is still highly appealing. Eric touches his blues and rock bases, dips successfully into reggae with Bob Marley's "I Shot The Sheriff" (a U.S. No. 1), and achieves gospel profundity with the sublime "Give Me Strength." The melodic, yearning "Let It Grow" is another standout track, with sublime chord shifts that echo Led Zeppelin's "Stairway To Heaven." **ML**

Kraftwerk | Autobahn (1974)

Label | EMI
Producer | Ralf Hütter • Florian Schneider
Art Direction | Ralf Hütter • Florian Schneider
Nationality | Germany
Running Time | 42:27

Though it is their fourth album, *Autobahn* is widely considered to be the true beginning of Kraftwerk. Ralf Hütter and Florian Schneider had met in 1968 and formed Kraftwerk and their experimental electronic Kling Klang Studio in early 1970.

After years playing the university, club, and art gallery circuit, where they developed their music, Ralf Hütter and Florian Schneider composed and recorded the symphonic synthesizer title track "Autobahn" together with poet and painter Emil Schult. Inspired by the long road journeys on the German motorway system, the title track marked the band's definitive separation from their "Krautrock" peers.

On *Autobahn*, joined by new percussionists Wolfgang Flür and Karl Bartos, Hütter and Schneider crystallized the pristine sound and deadpan four-man image that would define Kraftwerk. The album contains sublime pieces of wordless and ambient "Electronic-Volks-Musik" in the tracks "Mitternacht," "Morgenspaziergang," and "Kometenmelodie," but it was the symphonic title track that became symbolic of the international breakthrough of Kraftwerk.

A chart success on both sides of the Atlantic, the album became a landmark in avant-garde pop minimalism. As Ralf Hütter commented in 2003: "In *Autobahn* we put car sounds, horns, basic melodies and tuning motors. Adjusting the suspension and tyre pressure, rolling on the asphalt, that gliding sound when the wheels go onto those painted stripes. It's sound poetry, and also very dynamic."

Autobahn is cinema for the ears. **SD**

> "Sometimes I can taste the sounds. There are a lot more feelings than just the feeling going through the ears. The whole body can feel the sounds."
>
> Florian Schneider, 1975

Track Listing

▶	01	**Autobahn** (Hütter•Schneider•Schult)	22:42
	02	**Kometenmelodie 1** (Hütter•Schneider)	6:20
▶	03	**Kometenmelodie 2** (Hütter•Schneider)	5:45
	04	**Mitternacht** (Hütter•Schneider)	3:40
▶	05	**Morgenspaziergang** (Hütter•Schneider)	4:00

Van Morrison | It's Too Late To Stop Now (1974)

Label | Warner Bros.
Producer | Van Morrison • Ted Templeman
Art Direction | Ed Caraeff • David Larkham
Nationality | UK
Running Time | 92:20

After spending much of the earlier 1970s making a series of studio albums, Morrison toured with his ten-piece Caledonia Soul Orchestra. Shows were recorded in both California and London, resulting in this stunning double set, one of the greatest live albums of all time and one acknowledged by Morrison as a career peak.

Guitarist John Platania, horn player Jack Schroer, drummer David Shaw, and keyboardist Jeff Labes are familiar names among Morrison's sidemen. The addition of a string section provided extra magic, especially on "Here Comes The Night," which became an almost entirely different song to Them's 1965 original.

Several tracks are versions of songs associated with Morrison's favorite soul stars—Bobby Bland, Ray Charles, Sam Cooke, and Sonny Boy Williamson. Unsurprisingly, many of the original songs had appeared on Morrison's recent albums (Moondance, His Band And Street Choir, Saint Dominic's Preview, and Hard Nose The Highway), but by all accounts, the reason for the lack of material from Tupelo Honey was that Morrison insisted that this should be a genuinely live album without studio overdubs (hence the omission of the title track from Moondance—the live take included a bum note). The lengthy but wonderful final track here was the only item from Astral Weeks, arguably the album that launched Morrison's career as a truly great solo artist.

The album did not chart in the UK, though it made No. 53 in the United States. Sadly, this Olympian backing group started to disband after Veedon Fleece, Morrison's next studio album, but no one who saw one of these shows will ever be able to forget it. **JT**

Track Listing

01	Ain't Nothin' You Can Do (Malone • Scott)	3:44
▶ 02	Warm Love (Morrison)	3:05
▶ 03	Into The Mystic (Morrison)	4:31
04	These Dreams Of You (Morrison)	3:37
05	I Believe To My Soul (Charles)	4:11
06	I've Been Working (Morrison)	3:55
07	Help Me (Williamson)	3:25
08	Wild Children (Morrison)	5:04
09	Domino (Morrison)	4:47
10	I Just Want To Make Love To You (Dixon)	5:14
11	Bring It On Home To Me (Cooke)	4:40
▶ 12	Saint Dominic's Preview (Morrison)	6:17
13	Take Your Hands Out Of My Pocket (Williamson)	4:04
14	Listen To The Lion (Morrison)	8:41
▶ 15	Here Comes The Night (Berns)	3:14
▶ 16	Gloria (Morrison)	4:19
▶ 17	Caravan (Morrison)	9:16
▶ 18	Cypress Avenue (Morrison)	10:16

Joni Mitchell | Court And Spark (1974)

Label | Asylum
Producer | Uncredited
Art Direction | Anthony Hudson
Nationality | USA
Running Time | 36:52

Ladies Of The Canyon (1970) offered the right-on environmentalism of "Big Yellow Taxi" and "Woodstock," a much-covered paean to the festival (which she did not attend); the painstaking confessional of *Blue* followed. More so than David Crosby (whom she dated) and James Taylor (a guest on *Blue*), Canada-raised, California-based Joni Mitchell was the archetypal early Seventies singer-songwriter, a mascot for lost souls with acoustic guitars and broken hearts. Which made the early 1974 arrival of single "Raised On Robbery," a boogie helmed not by Mitchell's dulcimer but Robbie Robertson's heads-down electric guitar, so unlikely.

The rest of *Court And Spark* is not such a radical departure, but still, the main characteristic it shares with *Ladies Of The Canyon* is that both have Mitchell paintings on the cover. The songs are less intense than on *Blue*; "Free Man In Paris" is a sly tribute to label boss David Geffen, "stoking the starmaker machinery behind the popular song." But the loose, sun-soaked sound is the greatest surprise, from the starry-eyed lap-steel of the title song to the winking silliness—and guest turn from, of all people, stoner comics Cheech and Chong—on "Twisted." Like Steely Dan, with whom the likes of "Car On A Hill" shares a jazzy radio-friendliness, *Court And Spark* could only have come from California.

Any commercial imperative went out of the window with 1975's *The Hissing Of Summer Lawns*, as Mitchell began a retreat into artfulness and, eventually, her acoustic roots. The atrocious *Travelog* (2002), a two-disc indulgence in which she reworked her catalogue with a glutinous orchestra, was a sad valediction. **WF-J**

> "Dylan and Leonard Cohen are my real peers. We're the poets of that generation."
>
> Joni Mitchell, 1995

Track Listing

01	**Court And Spark**	(Mitchell)	2:46
▶ 02	**Help Me**	(Mitchell)	3:22
▶ 03	**Free Man In Paris**	(Mitchell)	3:02
04	**People's Parties**	(Mitchell)	2:20
05	**Same Situation**	(Mitchell)	3:05
▶ 06	**Car On A Hill**	(Mitchell)	2:58
07	**Down To You**	(Mitchell)	5:36
08	**Just Like This Train**	(Mitchell)	4:23
09	**Raised On Robbery**	(Mitchell)	3:05
10	**Trouble Child**	(Mitchell)	3:57
11	**Twisted**	(Grey·Ross)	2:18

Queen | Queen II (1974)

Label | EMI
Producer | Various
Art Direction | Mick Rock • Queen
Nationality | UK
Running Time | 40:28

Queen II was the group's first UK hit album, although its chart entry resulted in Queen's debut album joining it a week later. Their first (eponymous) album had been recorded when Trident Studio, the company that also managed Queen and producer Roy Baker, was empty—in the three hours from 10 a.m. and in the middle of the night. The results were so manifestly worthwhile (especially in the United States, where it made the Top 100) that this second LP, and particularly "The March Of The Black Queen," was allotted "every conceivable musical and production technique," according to Baker.

Perhaps surprisingly, given Queen's standing today as purveyors of expansive, stadium-pleasing anthems, this was a distinctly dark album (sides one and two were dubbed the "white" and "black" sides respectively). They displayed their diversity, with rockers ("Ogre Battle"), ballads ("Nevermore," "White Queen"), and prog-rock excursions with a mythological bent ("The Fairy Feller's Master-Stroke," named after the extraordinary painting by Victorian artist Richard Dadd).

The clincher, the track that propelled Queen into the stratosphere, was the driving "Seven Seas Of Rhye," which, according to Baker, became a UK Top Ten hit primarily because Queen played it on *Top Of The Pops*, then Britain's most influential music TV show. Guitarist Brian May notes: "The whole world happens in the first 20 seconds, and you've almost heard the whole song in that time. Great big swooping things, then the vocal launches straight in." In the United States, without a hit single, the album still managed to give the group their Top 50 debut. **JT**

"We're a very expensive group; we break a lot of rules ... my dear."

Freddie Mercury, 1977

Track Listing

	01	Procession (May)	1:12
▶	02	Father To Son (May)	6:12
	03	White Queen (As It Began) (May)	4:33
	04	Some Day One Day (May)	4:21
	05	The Loser In The End (Taylor)	4:01
	06	Ogre Battle (Mercury)	4:08
	07	The Fairy Feller's Master-Stroke (Mercury)	2:39
	08	Nevermore (Mercury)	1:17
▶	09	The March Of The Black Queen (Mercury)	6:03
	10	Funny How Love Is (Mercury)	3:14
▶	11	Seven Seas Of Rhye (Mercury)	2:48

Roxy Music | Country Life (1974)

Label | Island
Producer | John Punter • Roxy Music
Art Direction | Bryan Ferry
Nationality | UK
Running Time | 41:37

Bryan Ferry met Roxy Music fans Constanze Karoli and Eveline Grunwald in Portugal when he was writing the lyrics for *Country Life* (the band's fourth studio album) and asked them to model for their new album cover. The resulting photograph of the German girls caused a sensation—the flesh on view, combined with the suggestive placement of the girls' fingers, was deemed too risqué by many retailers, leading to less-suggestive artwork in many countries.

It is impossible to tell if the album would have been as successful in America without this controversy. In the UK, however, critical response upon its release was most positive. Roxy Music were previously positioned between glam-oriented art rock and sophisticated, elegant pop. With the departure of Brian Eno after their second album, the band was noticably shifting away from its original concept, but it would still be a while before the adult pop of *Avalon* would eradicate the traces of their past.

While the strongest tracks, "The Thrill Of It All," "Prairie Rose," and "Casanova" were praised at the time, it is curious that the theatrical ballad "Bitter-Sweet" (the German lyrics translated for Ferry by Grunwald and Karoli) was dismissed at the time of the album's release. This, as well as many other Roxy Music tracks, was included in Todd Haynes' 1998 glam-rock movie *Velvet Goldmine*. Re-recorded with Radiohead's Thom Yorke on vocals, this later version of "Bitter-Sweet" not only unearthed a new audience for Roxy Music's earlier work, but also proved that their influence extends far beyond their popular singles. **AH-N**

> ## "There's nothing wrong with being commercial if it's good."
>
> Bryan Ferry, 1972

Track Listing

▶	01	**The Thrill Of It All** (Ferry)	6:24
	02	**Three And Nine** (Ferry•Mackay)	4:04
	03	**All I Want Is You** (Ferry)	2:52
▶	04	**Out Of The Blue** (Ferry•Manzanera)	4:46
	05	**If It Takes All Night** (Ferry)	3:10
▶	06	**Bitter–Sweet** (Ferry•Mackay)	4:50
▶	07	**Triptych** (Ferry)	3:09
▶	08	**Casanova** (Ferry)	3:26
	09	**A Really Good Time** (Ferry)	3:45
▶	10	**Prairie Rose** (Ferry•Manzanera)	5:11

Tangerine Dream | Phaedra (1974)

Label | Virgin
Producer | Edgar Froese
Art Direction | Edgar Froese
Nationality | Germany
Running Time | 37:32

Brian Eno gave ambient music its name, but Tangerine Dream pioneered the sound. The group formed in Berlin in 1967, their leader and only constant being guitarist Edgar Froese. Inspired by surrealism and the dadaist art movement, he had worked with Salvador Dali and opened for Jimi Hendrix. Other players came and went, leading to a German-label debut in 1970. *Electronic Meditation* was one of the earliest examples of Krautrock: a minimalist, experimental work utilizing household objects alongside standard rock instruments.

Synthesizers came to the fore on *Alpha Centauri* (1971)—three years before Kraftwerk fully embraced them—and the classic TD lineup of Froese, Chris Franke, and Peter Baumann was in place for double LP *Zeit*. Influential British DJ John Peel declared 1973's *Atem* to be his album of the year, earning the space-music innovators a major contract with Virgin Records.

Virgin debut *Phaedra* was a commercial and stylistic landmark. The trio used Moog™ and sequencers for the first time, enabling their vast instrumental soundscapes to be composed rather than improvised. The title track is a quasi-symphonic constellation of hypnotic burbling, celestial textures, and pulsating bassline. "Movements Of A Visionary" involves whispers and arpeggiated tone clusters, while "Mysterious Semblance At The Strand Of Nightmares" features luminescent keyboard washes that evoke the ocean as much as the cosmos.

Phaedra cracked the UK Top 20 and made No.196 in America. It remains essential listening for fans of electronic music—a mesmeric precursor to trance, techno, and the dance music of the future. **MA**

> "When *Phaedra* got released, I said, 'In about 10 years' time, everybody will play synthesizers'—the guy ... said 'You're an idiot,' and walked out!"
>
> Edgar Froese, 1997

Track Listing

▶	01	**Phaedra** (Baumann·Franke·Froese)	16:45
▶	02	**Mysterious Semblance At The Strand Of Nightmares** (Froese)	10:35
▶	03	**Movements Of A Visionary** (Baumann·Franke·Froese)	7:55
	04	**Sequent C'** (Baumann)	2:17

Sparks | Kimono My House (1974)

Label | Island
Producer | Muff Winwood
Art Direction | Nicholas Deville
Nationality | UK • USA
Running Time | 35:44

L.A. keyboard-playing lyricist Ron Mael and singing younger brother Russell relocated to London in 1974 following positive reactions to their live shows by the British press. Recruiting a new band through the classifieds, they crashed into the UK Top Ten with the glam-rock operetta "This Town Ain't Big Enough For The Both Of Us," opening with hypnotic keyboards and unsettling vocals to a triumphant tidal wave of gunfire, operatic wailing, and screeching guitars. This led to a memorable appearance on BBC's weekly music show *Top Of The Pops*—Ron glowering at the camera, his "Hitler" mustache emphasizing his deadpan child-scaring demeanor, while Russell danced giddily around him, proudly displaying his bad teeth.

With its kitsch and garish sleeve, featuring cheeky geisha girls, *Kimono* . . . was an instant commercial and critical success. Russell's falsetto on the frenetic bubble-gum romp "Amateur Hour" is a perfect off-kilter complement to Ron's frequently hilarious wordplay, which bizarrely name-checks violinist Yehudi Menuhin. The high-camp dramatics of "Thank God It's Not Christmas" and "Hasta Mañana Monsieur" sound like early Roxy Music directing a Broadway musical. Sparks anticipated new wave with the spiky po-punk of "Talent Is An Asset," while "Equator"'s collision of jazz textures and increasingly demented vocals displays the Maels' more experimental edge.

Three decades on, *Kimono* . . . remains a key album, its influence acknowledged by lifelong fan Morrissey, who invited Sparks to perform the album in its entirety in 2004 at London's Royal Festival Hall. **CSh**

> ## "When you've got a nice ballad, you really gotta try and ruin it."
>
> Russell Mael, 1975

Track Listing

▶	01	**This Town Ain't Big Enough For The Both Of Us** (R. Mael)	3:03
▶	02	**Amateur Hour** (R. Mael)	3:37
	03	**Falling In Love With Myself Again** (R. Mael)	3:02
	04	**Here In Heaven** (R. Mael)	2:45
▶	05	**Thank God It's Not Christmas** (R. Mael)	5:00
	06	**Hasta Mañana, Monsieur** (R. Mael • R. Mael)	3:49
▶	07	**Talent Is An Asset** (R. Mael)	3:14
	08	**Complaints** (R. Mael)	2:50
	09	**In My Family** (R. Mael)	3:46
▶	10	**Equator** (R. Mael)	4:38

Supertramp | Crime Of The Century (1974)

Label | A&M
Producer | Ken Scott
Art Direction | Paul Wakefield
Nationality | UK
Running Time | 43:25

By the time Supertramp convened for their third album, the writing was on the wall. The whole band had quit after 1971's *Indelibly Stamped*, leaving the creative hub of Roger Hodgson and Rick Davies needing to regroup and write a masterpiece to save their A&M recording contract. This was especially important after Dutch millionaire benefactor Stanley Miesegaes also abandoned ship, having written off $90,000 worth of loans. Supertramp had been so broke they had even backed Chuck Berry for cash!

Fortunately the fruits of a mammoth writing session in a Somerset farmhouse from November 1973 to February 1974—*Crime Of the Century*—changed the picture entirely. The tuneful, tightly played songs, pristine clarity of sound (courtesy of Ken Scott, who had worked on Bowie's *Ziggy Stardust*), and myriad imaginative sound effects, helped create an album that *Sounds* magazine likened to "Genesis, The Beach Boys ... a smattering of [Pink] Floyd." The success of intense, keyboard-driven single "Dreamer" helped *Crime ...* pay by sending the album all the way to UK No. 4.

The distinctive cover, designed (but not produced) as a gatefold sleeve, was created by graphic artist Paul Wakefield after exposure to the completed album. Reminiscent of Traffic's *Shootout At The Fantasy Factory*, its "prison bars" have become an iconic image.

Supertramp had arrived in the spotlight long enough before punk to allow them to launch a career, even if post-new wave this was to be sustained mostly abroad. *Crime ...* was its foundation, and provided the backbone to their set for many years. **MH**

> ## "It wasn't originally thought of as anything more than having the songs slightly related for good listening ...it's not like *Tommy*."
>
> Rick Davies, 1986

Track Listing

▶	01	**School** (Davies·Hodgson)	5:35
	02	**Bloody Well Right** (Davies·Hodgson)	4:26
	03	**Hide In Your Shell** (Davies·Hodgson)	6:52
▶	04	**Asylum** (Davies·Hodgson)	6:30
▶	05	**Dreamer** (Davies·Hodgson)	3:30
▶	06	**Rudy** (Davies·Hodgson)	7:07
	07	**If Everyone Was Listening** (Davies·Hodgson)	4:05
▶	08	**Crime Of The Century** (Davies·Hodgson)	5:20

Richard And Linda Thompson
I Want To See The Bright Lights Tonight (1974)

Label | Island
Producer | Richard Thompson • John Wood
Art Direction | Uncredited
Nationality | UK
Running Time | 36:55

Husband-and-wife duos are not usually the stuff of rock 'n' roll legend, but Richard Thompson, the only known Muslim guitar hero, has never played the game by the book. He quit Fairport Convention, the pioneering folk-rock band he had helped found, in 1971; Glaswegian Linda Peters had helped out with backing vocals on his unsuccessful solo debut *Henry The Human Fly*. This duo effort has become a perennial critics' favorite.

Despite insisting "there's always hope in the third verse of my songs," Thompson holds out little here. The album depicts the dark underbelly of British society—the destitute, lawless, homeless, and hopeless. The timing of the album, allegedly due to a vinyl shortage that was a by-product of an oil embargo, chimed in nicely with the three-day week and associated social unrest of the period.

Musicians recruited from Fairport, Sandy Denny's Fotheringay, and Gryphon supply the muscle. Touches like the use of a traditional silver band for the title track adds a quintessential Englishness that a standard horn section could not —perhaps one reason why Thompson has a major cult following Stateside. Elvis Costello has covered the bleak "End Of The Rainbow" but his version lacked the "up" feel of Linda's voice that dragged theirs toward some kind of commerciality.

Journalist and producer Richard Williams described Thompson here as "the Coltrane of the guitar, the folk poet of the rainy streets." Many believe that he has never surpassed this album in either sphere. **MH**

> "I don't find bleak songs particularly depressing."
>
> Richard Thompson, 1996

Track Listing

▶	01	When I Get To The Border (R. Thompson)	3:26
	02	The Calvary Cross (R. Thompson)	3:51
▶	03	Withered And Died (R. Thompson)	3:24
▶	04	I Want To See The Bright Lights Tonight (R. Thompson)	3:07
	05	Down Where The Drunkards Roll (R. Thompson)	4:05
	06	We Sing Hallelujah (R. Thompson)	2:49
	07	Has He Got A Friend For Me (R. Thompson)	3:32
	08	The Little Beggar Girl (R. Thompson)	3:24
▶	09	The End Of The Rainbow (R. Thompson)	3:55
	10	The Great Valerio (R. Thompson)	5:22

Gil Scott-Heron / Brian Jackson
Winter In America (1974)

Label | Strata-East
Producer | Brian Jackson • Gil Scott-Heron
Art Direction | Eugene Coles
Nationality | USA
Running Time | 44:29

Gil Scott-Heron's innovative, thought-provoking mix of poetry and music were to have a great impact on latter-day African-American music. Often called the "Godfather of rap," Scott-Heron spoke openly about the injustices laid upon America's black community, best sampled on the anthem "The Revolution Will Not Be Televised."

It was on *Winter In America* that Scott-Heron's name crept into the public consciousness. This was largely due to his cohort, talented keyboardist Brian Jackson, who aided Scott-Heron in transforming himself from a aggressive, streetwise poet to a musical messenger. *Winter In America* combines razor-sharp criticism with affecting, soulful tunes; Scott-Heron is both tough and tender—but determined in getting his view across.

Songs like "Rivers Of My Father" and "Very Precious Time" have a laidback, spiritual feel to them. They are sung beautifully by Scott-Heron, while Jackson's keyboards are subtle and low key. The duo then offer two groovin' numbers, "Back Home" and "The Bottle." The latter, which addresses the alcoholism that has plagued black communities historically, became an underground hit, and features a memorable contribution from Jackson on flute. "H₂O Gate Blues" is a frigidly humorous and inspired rant against the Nixon administration.

Righteous anger, leavened by wit, intelligence, and beautifully crafted wordplay. Little wonder that Gil Scott-Heron's lyrics were later to have profound effect on socio-conscious rappers such as Public Enemy and Disposable Heroes Of Hiphoprisy. **AET**

"I don't hear any music as a point in time."
Brian Jackson, 2005

Track Listing		
01 Peace Go With You, Brother (As–Salaam–Alaikum) (Jackson•Scott-Heron)		5:27
▶ 02 Rivers Of My Father (Jackson•Scott-Heron)		8:19
03 A Very Precious Time (Jackson•Scott-Heron)		5:17
▶ 04 Back Home (Jackson•Scott-Heron)		2:51
▶ 05 The Bottle (Scott-Heron)		5:14
06 Song For Bobby Smith (Scott-Heron)		4:38
▶ 07 Your Daddy Loves You (Scott-Heron)		3:25
▶ 08 H₂O Gate Blues (Scott-Heron)		8:08
09 Peace Go With You, Brother (Wa–Alaikum–Salaam) (Jackson•Scott-Heron)		1:10

Queen | Sheer Heart Attack (1974)

Label | EMI
Producer | Roy Thomas Baker • Queen
Art Direction | Mick Rock • Queen
Nationality | UK
Running Time | 39:04

After flirtations with funk, opera, and electro, it is easy to forget Queen were a fantastic hard rock band: as heavy as Sabbath, as dense as Zeppelin, as clever as Cream. *Sheer Heart Attack* was their breakthrough on both sides of the Atlantic, courtesy of guitarist Brian May's gothic rock and singer Freddie Mercury's flamboyant pop.

May fell ill when recording began, so the band laid down their parts and left space for his overdubs. These include a spectral assault on the tour-de-force "Brighton Rock," the incendiary live favorite "Now I'm Here," and the proto-thrash "Stone Cold Crazy."

These stand alongside Mercury's delicious "Lily Of The Valley" and May's funereal "Dear Friends." There are also signs of the pastiches that litter their music, like the banjo-driven "Bring Back Leroy Brown."

The centerpiece is Queen's breakthrough single "Killer Queen," a delightfully bitchy rock masterpiece that tells the tale of a high-class call girl; a flamboyant juxtaposition of high and low culture that seemed to define the singer's complex public persona.

With their own Lennon and McCartney in May and Mercury, Queen also had a George Harrison in bassist John Deacon. The Caribbean-tinged "Misfire" was the first of his charming vignettes for the band.

Drummer Roger Taylor contributed too, though his "Sheer Heart Attack" would not surface until 1977's *News Of The World*. "He played it to us [in 1974] but it wasn't quite finished," explained Mercury. And Mick Rock's water-soaked sleeve shot? "God, the agony we went through to have the pictures taken, dear," Mercury told *NME*. "We're still as poncy as ever." **JLe**

"I always knew I was a star."

Freddie Mercury, 1975

Track Listing

▶ 01	**Brighton Rock** (May)	5:08
▶ 02	**Killer Queen** (Mercury)	2:57
03	**Tenement Funster** (Taylor)	2:48
04	**Flick Of The Wrist** (Mercury)	3:46
05	**Lily Of The Valley** (Mercury)	1:43
▶ 06	**Now I'm Here** (May)	4:10
07	**In The Lap Of The Gods** (Mercury)	3:20
08	**Stone Cold Crazy** (Deacon•May•Mercury•Taylor)	2:12
09	**Dear Friends** (May)	1:07
10	**Misfire** (Deacon)	1:50
11	**Bring Back That Leroy Brown** (Mercury)	2:13
12	**She Makes Me (Stormtrooper In Stilettoes)** (May)	4:08
13	**In The Lap Of The Gods ... Revisited** (Mercury)	3:42

10cc | Sheet Music (1974)

Label | UK
Producer | 10cc
Art Direction | Hipgnosis
Nationality | UK
Running Time | 37:32

SHEET MUSIC

Following 10cc's self-titled debut album, *Sheet Music* took a big step toward the sound that would become the group's trademark. The record typifies the eclecticism and breathless invention that characterized 10cc's earlier work—soft and fuzzed art-rock guitars, seamless harmonies, elements of spoof and parody, and shifts between musical genres (often within the same song).

Part of the album's strength lies in the fact that all four musicians (Lol Creme, Kevin Godley, Graham Gouldman, and Eric Stewart) were also songwriters and multi-instrumentalists. (Indeed, Gouldman wrote a string of major hits in the Sixties, including The Yardbirds' "For Your Love" and The Hollies' "Bus Stop.") With lyrics that are never less than sharp, and are frequently sarcastic ("The Worst Band In The World," a satire on musical mediocrity, may be the most ironic song ever), and a host of melodic twists and turns, 10cc created a piece of well-crafted, highly idiosyncratic pop.

The album evinces a passion for polished production, the narratives are bizarrely humorous—"Clockwork Creep" imagines a dialogue between a jumbo jet and a bomb, elsewhere there are references to voodoo—and the band seems just as comfortable with rockers such as "Silly Love" and hit single "The Wall Street Shuffle" (a UK No. 10) as with their bizarre creations of artsy pop and even reggae. On "The Sacro-Iliac," Eric Stewart and Graham Gouldman create a new dance for nondancers, while "Old Wild Men" sees the introduction of Godley and Creme's "Gizmo," which could be placed on the bridge of a guitar to simulate a range of instruments.

In a word, inventive. **GD**

"We were kind of bursting with ideas. Everything we did was right."

Graham Gouldman, 1999

Track Listing

▶	01	**The Wall Street Shuffle** (Gouldman·Stewart)	3:54
▶	02	**The Worst Band In The World** (Creme·Gouldman)	2:49
▶	03	**Hotel** (Creme·Godley)	4:54
	04	**Old Wild Men** (Creme·Godley)	3:21
	05	**Clockwork Creep** (Creme·Godley)	2:46
▶	06	**Silly Love** (Creme·Stewart)	4:01
	07	**Somewhere In Hollywood** (Creme·Godley)	6:39
	08	**Baron Samedi** (Gouldman·Stewart)	3:46
	09	**The Sacro–Iliac** (Godley·Gouldman)	2:33
	10	**Oh Effendi** (Godley·Stewart)	2:49

Neil Young | On The Beach (1974)

Label | Reprise
Producer | David Briggs • Mark Harman • Al Schmitt
Art Direction | Gary Burden
Nationality | Canada
Running Time | 39:17

Even by Neil Young's melancholic standards, *On The Beach* is one bleak trip. An odyssey of regret, disgust, and disappointment, the album marked the end of a love-in. The cover portrays him removed from the coke-addled decay of the West Coast: alone on a gray beach, his back to a pile of California refuse.

"Revolution Blues" takes this alienation to violent extremes. Over ragged minor chords, Young plays a longhaired avenger, gunning down the wealthy hippy residents of L.A.'s Laurel Canyon. The track's Charles Manson allusions shocked his 1974 touring partners Crosby, Stills, and Nash, who pleaded with Young to drop the song.

But wasted West Coast stars were only one of the targets in Young's sniper scope. The gentle "Ambulance Blues" hides an attack on blinkered critics, while "Vampire Blues"—an inspired exercise in John Lee Hooker minimalism—takes a bite out of hangers-on. Even his troubled marriage to actress Carrie Snodgress is dissected in the mournful "Motion Pictures."

Though the lyrics are often bilious, the music is definitely relaxed. "Walk On" grooves past in a toxic fug, staggering at the time to No. 69 on the chart—here Young continues his banter with Lynyrd Skynyrd, who had namechecked him in their "Sweet Home Alabama."

Rolling Stone called it his best since *After the Gold Rush*, but *On The Beach* has unfortunately gone almost unheard by modern audiences. Young himself came to dislike the album's emotional rawness and withheld its release on CD until 2003. **TB**

> "I was pretty down I guess at the time ... I think if everybody looks back at their own lives they'll realize that they went through something like that."
>
> Neil Young, 1985

Track Listing

01	**Walk On** (Young)	2:41
02	**See The Sky About To Rain** (Young)	5:00
▶ 03	**Revolution Blues** (Young)	4:02
04	**For The Turnstiles** (Young)	3:13
▶ 05	**Vampire Blues** (Young)	4:09
06	**On The Beach** (Young)	6:56
▶ 07	**Motion Pictures** (Young)	4:21
▶ 08	**Ambulance Blues** (Young)	8:55

George Jones
The Grand Tour (1974)

Label | Epic
Producer | Billy Sherrill
Art Direction | David Richman
Nationality | USA
Running Time | 28:35

Gene Clark
No Other (1974)

Label | Asylum
Producer | Thomas Jefferson Kaye
Art Direction | John Dietrich
Nationality | USA
Running Time | 44:07

The Grand Tour is one of the main reasons that George Jones has been dubbed the grandfather of country music. This is a glorious and uninterrupted stream of well-crafted jewels. Jones' troubled marriage to fellow country music legend Tammy Wynette was to end in divorce the following year, and their personal problems are a complement to the songs of love and heartbreak.

The strength and polished feel of the album owes much to Jones' collaboration with producer Billy Sherrill. The opening song, "The Grand Tour," is an outstanding example of what a great country song can do: a vibrant string section, warm and colorful guitars, and a vocal outpouring of heartache delivered with incredible feeling by Jones (Wynette's future husband, George Richey, was a co-writer). As far as honky-tonk numbers go, the record parades one extraordinary hit after another, leading with "Pass Me By (If You're Only Passing Through)," an easy-paced love song delivered with The Jordanaires that, once heard, lodges forever in the mind. Then there is "Once You've Had The Best," a ballad that wraps around the heart effortlessly—by comparison, the original version of this song, by Johnny Paycheck, seems only a suggestion as to how the song might sound. (Paycheck and Jones were later to collaborate on 1980's *Double Trouble*.) The high-spirited "The Weatherman" (another Richey co-write) provides an intermission in the rally of slow honky-tonk hymns.

Honest songs, superbly produced and arranged, and sung by one of country music's finest vocalists. **GD**

Immediately—and unfairly—forgotten on its release in 1974, Clark's *No Other* would spend the next 30-odd years reviled as one of the most colossally expensive and equally wasteful records of all time. That reputation however, as proved by its first ever reprinting recently, is a monumental misjudgment. In many respects, *No Other* was, and remains, a stunning addition to the canon of West Coast Seventies' rock.

For *No Other*, Clark would assemble a hothouse of some of the world's leading session musicians—Butch Trucks, Chris Hillman, Danny Kortchmar, Timothy B. Schmidt. Their combined talents, buoyed by Clark's gift for wistful narratives, set the album up as a sprawling and ambitious venture that unites country, rock, jazz, blues, and psychedelia. This hybrid, which his label would later refuse to release, has never sounded so enchanting: the album opener "Life's Greatest Fool" alone gives the lie to the record's critical pasting. Also of note is the title track, which starts as a straightforward post mortem of the West Coast sound but quickly mutates into something far more adventurous featuring a gospel choir and strange voodoo-influenced guitar by Clark himself. "Strength Of Strings," with its slide guitar, is as haunting as anything ever produced by Clark's former group, The Byrds.

Within the context of the L.A. post-Byrds music scene, *No Other* is an influential release. Listeners will recognize a musical deftness that emerged again in the infinitely more successful Fleetwood Mac. **BW**

Steely Dan
Pretzel Logic (1974)

Label | ABC
Producer | Gary Katz
Art Direction | Ed Caraeff
Nationality | USA
Running Time | 33:14

Randy Newman
Good Old Boys (1974)

Label | Reprise
Producer | R. Titelman • L. Waronker
Art Direction | Mike Salisbury
Nationality | USA
Running Time | 36:37

Before Donald Fagen and Walter Becker became the songwriting duo behind Steely Dan, they were tunesmiths with ABC, penning hits for such notables as Barbra Streisand. After carving their own sound with *Can't Buy A Thrill* and taking it further with *Countdown To Ecstasy*, the pair returned to Tin Pan Alley. Using three-minute pop as a framework, they decided to play ironic games with style and genre. The result was the platinum-selling *Pretzel Logic*.

The opening track typifies the album. "Rikki Don't Lose That Number" is an affecting story of unrequited love, which switches between light samba and piano ballad, until Jeff "Skunk" Baxter's beautifully phrased guitar solo shoots a thread of California country rock straight through the middle. Broadly in the same vein, "Any Major Dude Will Tell You" is illuminated by beams of Orange County sunshine.

But the group had not forgotten how to bite, either—"Monkey In Your Soul," which somehow crosses Noël Coward with Stax, is a wonderfully bitchy poison-pen letter, while the wounded petulance of envy is given darkly comic treatment in "Through With Buzz."

The third element of the album is witty pastiche. The defiance of the lonely man is given cop-show dynamism in "Night By Night," while the bungled homicide of "With A Gun" should be made into a Coen Brothers movie. "East St Louis Toodle-Oo" is playtime for the band and notable for introducing pedal steel guitar to the ragtime genre if nothing else. **JDi**

Even today, Randy Newman's *Good Old Boys* is an album you think twice about playing in civilized company. The title track is one of the most startling musical contributions to America's troubled history of race relations. Newman was riding high after the critical success of *Sail Away* when he watched Georgia governor and segregationist Lester Maddox being mocked by a Northern TV audience. Annoyed by what he saw as inverted snobbery, hypocrisy, and liberal smugness, Newman wrote a song about the incident from the perspective of a Southerner. "Rednecks" was the result, a scathing indictment of, well, everything, which features a self-mocking singalong chorus "We're rednecks/we're rednecks/we don't know our ass from a hole in the ground" and frequent use of the word "nigger."

Realizing this would raise hackles, Newman intended to feature the song as part of a contextualizing concept album about a Southern man called "Johnny Cutler's Birthday." This never-released album came out in 2002, and included Newman's own original spoken preamble explaining each track to the producers.

Although the rest never reaches the same level of provocation, it is a beautiful piece of work, possibly Newman's finest. "Louisiana 1927" has a chorus that rolls off the tongue, "Mr President" is a curious contribution to post-Watergate politics, and Newman approvingly describes "Back On My Feet Again" as "a genuinely strange song." From here to Disney soundtracks? It seemed even more unlikely at the time. **PW**

Bob Marley And The Wailers | Natty Dread (1974)

Label | Island
Producer | Chris Blackwell • The Wailers
Art Direction | Tony Wright
Nationality | Jamaica
Running Time | 38:48

This is the album that introduced the world to Bob Marley and his new Wailers. Marley's long-term singing partners Peter Tosh and Bunny Livingston had left the band—a reaction to the stresses of continual touring and the pressures of their burgeoning international stardom—after ten years as the Wailing Wailers (their first Jamaican No. 1 had been 1963's "Simmer Down").

Rumor had it that Marley's sound would now become thinner, his politics blander. *Natty Dread* proved the doubters wrong. It rocks, tune for tune, like no other in his catalog. From his first ululating rebel yell on call to action "Lively Up Yourself," it takes no prisoners and simply overflows with great tunes.

Natty Dread certainly introduced Trenchtown ghetto cool to the well-heeled youth of the world, but the politics of "Them Belly Full," "Rebel Music," "Talkin' Blues" ("Cause I feel like bombing a church, now,/ Now that you know that the preacher is lying"), and "Revolution" sent shivers down the spine of Jamaica's political establishment. A live version of "No Woman, No Cry" would give Marley his first UK Top Ten hit in 1975. (Marley allegedly wrote the song but credited it to Vincent Ford, who ran a kitchen in Kingston and had fed and housed the young Bob in harder times.)

The vital, utterly compelling sound of the album still explodes out of the speakers, propelled by the mighty Barrett brothers' drum and bass, fanned hotter still by New Jerseyite Al Anderson's guitar licks, and crowned by the unsurpassable African vocal revelation that is Bob and the I-Threes (Rita Marley, Marcia Griffiths, and Judy Mowatt). **MR**

> "Me don't dip on the black man's side or the white man's side, me dip on God's side."
>
> Bob Marley, 1977

Track Listing

▶	01 **Lively Up Yourself** (Marley)	5:11
▶	02 **No Woman, No Cry** (Ford)	3:46
▶	03 **Them Belly Full** (Barrett • Cogill)	3:13
▶	04 **Rebel Music (3 O'Clock Road Block)** (Barrett • Peart)	6:45
	05 **So Jah Seh** (Francisco • Marley)	4:28
	06 **Natty Dread** (Cole • Marley)	3:35
▶	07 **Bend Down Low** (Marley)	3:21
▶	08 **Talkin' Blues** (Barrett • Cogill)	4:06
	09 **Revolution** (Marley)	4:23

Robert Wyatt | Rock Bottom (1974)

Label | Virgin
Producer | Nick Mason
Art Direction | Alfreda Benge
Nationality | UK
Running Time | 39:28

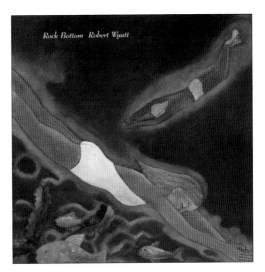

Robert Wyatt's debut album for Virgin was recorded in the aftermath of a tragic event. He had decamped to Venice, while partner Alfreda worked on 1973 horror film *Don't Look Now*, to start working on the material that would make up *Rock Bottom*. Returning to London, he had begun assembling musicians for the project, but on June 1, 1973, a fall from a fourth-storey window resulted in him being paralyzed from the waist down.

Subsequently confined to a wheelchair, Wyatt turned his attention to keyboards and his inventive tabletop percussion. Produced by Pink Floyd's Nick Mason, a close friend, *Rock Bottom* marries Wyatt's haunting love songs with an unpretentious fusion of rock melodies and freeform jazz signatures, and is markedly less political than much of his later work (he later briefly joined the British Communist Party).

The ambient jazz of "Alfie" honors Alfreda, his lover, muse, and *Rock Bottom*'s sleeve designer. "Little Red Riding Hood ..." features beguiling tape loops and jazz trumpeter Mongezi Feza's abrasive squawks. The ethereal joy of "Sea Song" confirmed that Wyatt was not wallowing in self-pity, despite the anguish and vulnerability of his vocal. The "second" "Little Red Robin Hood ..." concludes the album with some Wyatt-penned poetry delivered by absurdist Scots poet Ivor Cutler. Wyatt married Alfreda the day of the album's release, and scored a UK hit two months later with his upbeat rendition of The Monkees' "I'm A Believer."

Rock Bottom still sounds fresh today, while Wyatt remains an underrated treasure, continuing to inspire with his music and unapologetic political stance. **CSh**

> "It was a happy time, really! It was physically difficult, adjusting to wheelchair life, but I remember a great relief and happiness that I was finally getting somewhere."
>
> Robert Wyatt, 1998

Track Listing		
▶ 01 **Sea Song** (Wyatt)		6:30
02 **A Last Straw** (Wyatt)		5:46
▶ 03 **Little Red Riding Hood Hit The Road** (Wyatt)		7:37
04 **Alifib** (Wyatt)		6:56
▶ 05 **Alife** (Wyatt)		6:31
06 **Little Red Robin Hood Hit The Road** (Wyatt)		6:08

Gram Parsons | Grievous Angel (1974)

Label | Warner Bros.
Producer | Gram Parsons
Art Direction | Ginny Winn
Nationality | USA
Running Time | 35:00

With the last album he recorded before his death in 1973—it was released posthumously in 1974—Gram Parsons showed not only that he had he invented country rock, but also that nobody would do it better.

By this point Parsons, Keith Richards' citrus-heir drug-buddy, had assembled the perfect team around him. Emmylou Harris' pure singing is there every time Parsons himself sounds a little ragged, and the band includes several members of Elvis' Vegas band.

Elvis and his drug problems crop up allusively on the lovely "Return Of The Grievous Angel," an epic journey around the United States that, like *The Wizard Of Oz*, concludes that there is no place like home. This is mostly a mournful album, ranging from the gently regretful "Brass Buttons" (about Parsons' mother) to the bitter, compelling "$1,000 Wedding," the one song on the album that would have suited Parsons' friends, The Rolling Stones. In a gesture that has prompted some fans to think that he saw his end coming, the album even includes a faux-live revisiting of one of Parsons' best early songs, "Hickory Wind" (from the Byrds' *Sweetheart Of The Rodeo*). There are some rockier moments— "I Can't Dance" and the frantic "Ooh Las Vegas"—but they do not change the mood.

Much admired by his peers, when they were not fed up with his spoiled-kid ways, Parsons never became a star in his lifetime. But his influence continued to seep through: into rock via the Eagles and the Stones and later Elvis Costello, The Lemonheads, and The Thrills, to name just a few, and back into country via his muse Emmylou Harris. **MMo**

> **"The greatest PR stunt you can perform is dying young, but Gram would be a bit bemused by all this worship stuff."**
>
> Emmylou Harris, 2004

Track Listing

▶	01	**Return Of The Grievous Angel** (Parsons)		4:19
	02	**Hearts On Fire** (Egan·Guidera)		3:50
	03	**I Can't Dance** (Hall)		2:20
▶	04	**Brass Buttons** (Parsons)		3:27
▶	05	**$1,000 Wedding** (Parsons)		5:00
	06	**Medley Live From Northern Quebel**		6:27
		a) Cash On The Barrelhead (C. Louvin·I. Louvin)		
		b) Hickory Wind (Buchanon·Parsons)		
▶	07	**Love Hurts** (Bryant)		3:40
	08	**Ooh Las Vegas** (Grech·Parsons)		3:29
	09	**In My Hour Of Darkness** (Harris·Parsons)		3:42

Eno | Another Green World (1975)

Label | Island
Producer | Rhett Davies • Brian Eno
Art Direction | Tom Phillips
Nationality | UK
Running Time | 40:47

Brian Eno's third solo release was conceived when, immobilized while recovering from a car accident, he discovered the atmospheric properties of music. With a background of two albums on synthesizers with art-glam supremos Roxy Music, a tape-loop collaboration with Robert Fripp, and two solo records of avant pop, he was about to craft the genesis of ambient music.

Despite declaring himself a non-musician, Eno is a cultivated man with an art-school education. Also a respected producer (Talking Heads, Devo, U2) and visual artist, he was well aware of the avant-garde and kept a close eye on the more experimental advances in contemporary music—Krautrock, for example—that he could manipulate to give form to a new esthetic.

In *Another...*, Eno created a beautiful confluence of traditional pop/rock patterns and ambient soundscapes. Naive and minimalistic, the record was at the same time deeply moving and sophisticated, interspersing five highly evocative vocal tracks of alliterative and cryptic poetry among nine imaginative instrumental pieces. "I'll Come Running" and "St. Elmo's Fire" are the best of the vocals, both of them adorned by Robert Fripp's extraordinary lead guitar. John Cale and Phil Collins were also involved, lending a feel of Collins' band Brand X to jazz-rock tracks such as "Zawinul/Lava" and "Sky Saw." But it was Eno's captivating voice and custom-made battery of devices (treated guitars, tape trickery, electronic rhythm generators, and synthesizers) that propelled the album into new musical territory. David Bowie's *Low*, *"Heroes"*, and *Lodger* took inspiration from this masterpiece. **JGi**

"I wanted to make music that had an emotional connection."

Brian Eno, 1999

Track Listing

01	**Sky Saw** (Eno)	3:27
02	**Over Fire Island** (Eno)	1:51
▶ 03	**St. Elmo's Fire** (Eno)	3:02
04	**In Dark Trees** (Eno)	2:30
05	**The Big Ship** (Eno)	3:03
▶ 06	**I'll Come Running** (Eno)	3:50
07	**Another Green World** (Eno)	1:37
▶ 08	**Sombre Reptiles** (Eno)	2:25
09	**Little Fishes** (Eno)	1:30
10	**Golden Hours** (Eno)	4:00
11	**Becalmed** (Eno)	3:57
▶ 12	**Zawinul/Lava** (Eno)	3:00
13	**Everything Merges With The Night** (Eno)	3:59
14	**Spirits Drifting** (Eno)	2:36

The Dictators
Go Girl Crazy! (1975)

Label | Epic
Producer | Murray Krugman • Sandy Pearlman
Art Direction | David Gahr
Nationality | USA
Running Time | 34:48

Neu!
Neu! '75 (1975)

Label | Brain
Producer | Conrad Plank
Art Direction | Neu!
Nationality | Germany
Running Time | 42:07

In 1975, two American kids, Legs McNeil and John Holmstrom, spent their summer listening to *Go Girl Crazy!* by The Dictators. Each night they ended up shouting out every song on the record. Not long after, they founded *Punk* magazine, one of the bibles of the anarchic movement that exploded in the late Seventies.

Like The New York Dolls, The Dictators were punk forerunners. Years before The Ramones, The Dead Boys, and the Sex Pistols were even heard of, Dick Manitoba, an ex-roadie and The Dictators' "secret weapon," was singing about gorging food, drinking beer, going with girls, and watching B-movies. *Go Girl Crazy!* was one of the first punk records, long before that term was coined. But it offered much more: garage sounds, surf (a cover of The Rivieras' "California Sun") and heavy metal—guitarist Ross "the Boss" Funichello was later to form Manowar. The Dictators gained a devoted following, partly through their offbeat sense of humor—witness the striking cover of *Go Girl Crazy!*, with Manitoba posing in a filthy locker room.

The record had all the ingredients for success, but then events took an unfortunate turn. Not long after it was released, Epic ditched them; bad management, badly planned tours, and inter-band bickering had not helped. The album did not attract mass interest until 1977, by which time bands such as The Ramones had minted their own brand of high-energy cartoon punk; The Dictators were sadly relegated to the sidelines. Nevertheless, *Go Girl Crazy!* was there first. **LPG**

One of the archetypal Krautrock bands of the 1970s, Neu!'s negligible commercial success belies the enormous influence the band still has on rock and electronic music. Former Kraftwerk members Michael Rother (guitar, keyboards) and Klaus Dinger (drums) were poles apart: Rother's obsession with drones and gradual timbral changes clashed wonderfully with Dinger's powerful drumming. Their Conny Plank-produced debut *Neu!* would become a touchstone for practically the entire post-punk era, but exposed the gulf between the duo.

The pair made up for a recording budget shortfall on *Neu! 2* (1973) by recycling the two songs they already had ("Super" and "Neuschnee") at different speeds, unwittingly inventing the remix in the process. Then the pair went their separate ways.

After Kraftwerk reaped global success, Rother and Dinger set aside their differences long enough to deliver their masterpiece, *Neu! '75*. Using a combination of synthesizers and drummers Hans Lampe and Thomas Dinger (freeing Klaus Dinger to wreak havoc on all the other instruments), the pair split the album between Rother's beautiful ambient textures ("Seeland" and "Leb' Wohl") and Dinger's proto-punk thrashing ("Hero" and "After Eight"), only joining forces for the opening "Isi" and the definitive Neu! statement, "E-Musik."

Having finally meshed their instruments together to create the perfect motorik machine, they did the only logical thing—split up permanently. **MB**

Led Zeppelin
Physical Graffiti (1975)

Label | Swan Song
Producer | Jimmy Page
Art Direction | Peter Corriston • Mike Doud
Nationality | UK
Running Time | 82:15

While Led Zeppelin could never be blamed for the macho homogeneity of the heavy metal they inspired, *Physical Graffiti* was an album of truly ambitious scope and lusty abandon. The sixth Zeppelin album, and the first on their own Swan Song label, *Physical Graffiti* has a nomadic spirit, consisting of sessions interrupted by a bout of illness on John Paul Jones' part and their inability to find a free studio for any length of time.

Its four sides of vinyl allowed Zep to experiment at length. The innovative die-cut sleeve (each window revealing an image printed on the inner sleeve) housed raw, rootsy rock 'n' roll ("Boogie With Stu"), precious folk miniatures ("Bron-Yr-Aur"), funk-metal ("Trampled Underfoot"), mordant prog ("In The Light"), and giddy pop ("Down By The Seaside").

Inspired by Page and Plant's recent trip to Morocco, the colossal "Kashmir" was a shuddering beast of faux-mysticism and exotica, John Paul Jones' droning synth-strings forming modal melodies as John Bonham pounded away, monolithically. Epic jam "In My Time Of Dying," written as they recorded it, was a blur of Jimmy Page's murderous slide-guitar, the band roaring like a force of nature (a clear influence on The White Stripes). "Ten Years Gone" was the most surprising—a touching, sentimental lament from Robert Plant for the love he left to join the band—Page's closing solo proving how tender Zeppelin could be, when they deigned.

Physical Graffiti is Led Zeppelin's last true peak, and remains a truly dizzying achievement. **SC**

Keith Jarrett
The Köln Concert (1975)

Label | ECM
Producer | John Cale
Art Direction | Barbara Wojirsch
Nationality | USA
Running Time | 66:04

Musical lightning in a bottle, *The Köln Concert* is at once one of the great jazz albums and one of the greatest pieces of extended musical improvisation—of any kind—ever recorded.

As comfortable playing Mozart concertos as jazz-funk workouts with Miles Davis, Keith Jarrett had already established himself as one of the most versatile and creative pianists of his generation by the time he took to the stage at the Köln Opera House on January 24, 1975. On that auspicious night, he cemented his reputation as one of the all-time greats.

The concert was very nearly canceled however, as Jarrett felt ill and the piano he had ordered failed to arrive on time. With the top and bottom ends of the substitute piano far from his satisfaction, he built his improvisation from scratch—around the piano's middle keys.

Unlike many of his contemporaries, Keith Jarrett's spontaneous composition and thrilling performance was drenched in lyricism and had an unusually optimistic streak to its sense of adventure. This exuberance can be heard through his audible groans, whoops, and sighs as he plays; he was as excited to hear this music for the first time as the audience was. *The Köln Concert* is a monument to musical possibility, the sublime sound of a peerless talent playing his music from the inside out. With more than one million copies sold, *The Köln Concert* remains Jarrett's highest selling album. For non-aficionados it is an opportunity to be seduced by a musical form that might otherwise pass them by. **GSa**

Aerosmith | Toys In The Attic (1975)

Label | Columbia
Producer | Jack Douglas
Art Direction | Pacific Eye And Ear
Nationality | USA
Running Time | 37:08

Led Zeppelin and Black Sabbath may have blazed the trail for hard rock, but with their third album, Aerosmith sprang forth as the progenitors of "cock rock"—a subgenre that reveled in sex, drugs, and double-entendre to a level that made Led Zep's "The Lemon Song" sound like something from the church hymnal. It also won the band an international audience.

After several years pounding the circuit as a support act, the Boston-based unit landed a contract with Columbia after playing Max's Kansas City with punk godfathers The New York Dolls. However, their first two albums failed to make an impression as the band struggled to define itself amid unflattering comparisons to The Rolling Stones. With Jack Douglas in charge of console knob-twiddling, they entered the studio for what was now surely their make-or-break effort.

From the outset, it is clear that the band knew what was at stake. With a sizzling hi-hat crash, crunching riff, and growling chant, the title track pounces on the listener with a mixture of imagination and sheer insanity. The more laidback "Uncle Salty" is no less brazen, detailing a sleazy tale of whores, pimps, and dealers. But it is "Walk This Way" and "Sweet Emotion," with their funk-flavored grooves, insistent guitar work, and thinly veiled references to any number of illicit activities, that established the band's modus operandi and cemented their place in rock history. *Toys* ... reached No. 11 in the United States, and even brought about the re-release of "Dream On," a single from their first album that had floundered just two years earlier. The single became their second Top Ten hit. **TSh**

> " ...at heart, we're just a bunch of guys who like to get out, kick ass, and rock 'n' roll live."

Steve Tyler, 2002

Track Listing

▶	01	**Toys In The Attic** (Perry•Tyler)	3:05
	02	**Uncle Salty** (Hamilton•Tyler)	4:10
	03	**Adam's Apple** (Tyler)	4:34
▶	04	**Walk This Way** (Perry•Tyler)	3:40
▶	05	**Big Ten Inch Record** (Weismantel)	2:16
▶	06	**Sweet Emotion** (Hamilton•Tyler)	4:34
	07	**No More No More** (Perry•Tyler)	4:34
	08	**Round And Round** (Tyler•Whitford)	5:03
	09	**You See Me Crying** (Solomon•Tyler)	5:12

David Bowie
Young Americans (1975)

Label | RCA
Producer | Various
Art Direction | Eric Stephen Jacobs
Nationality | UK
Running Time | 40:20

Released in March 1975, *Young Americans* represents the zenith of David Bowie's flat-pack soul period. An often overlooked record, it nestles in the valley between the twin peaks of *Ziggy Stardust* and the "Berlin Trilogy."

While on tour in America in 1974, Bowie was seduced by black American music, and subsequently called his producer, Tony Visconti, to fly over from England and make a quick and dirty soul album. For his backing band, Bowie used a hybrid of his touring players, experienced sessioneers (such as bass legend Willie Weeks), and talented newcomers (guitarist Carlos Alomar and singer Luther Vandross).

Written mainly in the studio, the album shimmers in its limpid exuberance. From the ostensible banality of "Right" to the plaintive cry of "Can You Hear Me," there is much to savor. The powder-white aggression of "Fame"—recorded after the body of the album with Bowie's new best friend, John Lennon—is like a song version of Bowie's BBC documentary, *Cracked Actor*.

The cover art reinforced Bowie's new authenticity and apparent accessibility. Gone was the stylized androgyny; here he was, looking straight at camera, cigarette smoke crumpling skyward, a straight portrait shot suggestive of several decades earlier. Even the album's title clearly pointed to its target audience. Although Bowie has since enjoyed a schizophrenic relationship with the record, and was to spend most of the rest of the 1970s courting the Old World, *Young Americans* made him a superstar in America. **DE**

Burning Spear
Marcus Garvey (1975)

Label | Mango
Producer | Lawrence "Jack Ruby" Lindo
Art Direction | Bloomfield And Travis
Nationality | Jamaica
Running Time | 33:28

Winston Rodney was born in St Ann's Parish, Jamaica, where Marcus Garvey was born in 1887, some 58 years previously. The experience of growing up among the working class in St Ann's (also the birthplace of Bob Marley), would color both men's work. Garvey would champion the "back to Africa" crusade through political activism; Rodney would fight injustice using song.

Marcus Garvey was the third album by Rodney, a.k.a. Burning Spear—a name borrowed from Kenyan rebel leader Jomo Kenyatta—but it translated as one of the most impressive introductions in reggae history. Despite being remixed by the record label for mass (otherwise known as white) consumption, which enraged Rodney, the album was a poignant blend of religious aspirations and cultural concerns that came across as both warning cry and peaceful meditation.

The cover illustration, depicting two angry young black warriors, sets the mood even before Rodney opens with, "Weeping and wailing and moaning/ You've got yourself to blame, I tell you." The political edge grows even sharper on "Slavery Days," as the singer remembers his ancestors' shackles. Burning Spear, the band, was a trio at the time and Rodney's raw emotional delivery was intensified by the sweet sounds of bass-vocalist Rupert Willington and tenor Delroy Hinds on such devotionals as "Jordan River" and "Resting Place." With further help from the Black Disciples, Rodney ensured that future generations would remember both Garvey and Burning Spear. **JiH**

Bruce Springsteen
Born To Run (1975)

Label | Columbia
Producer | Various
Art Direction | John Berg • Andy Engel
Nationality | USA
Running Time | 39:33

Everything you have heard about *Born To Run* is true. It's a wannabe soul singer with pseudo-Spector production. It's constantly threatening to buckle beneath its own self-importance. And it sounds like a template for Bon Jovi. But its exhilarating classics are as sing-a-long-able as "You Give Love A Bad Name."

It could have been a disaster. Determined "to use the studio as a tool and not in an attempt to replicate the sound of when we played," Springsteen envisaged a concept album, with prospective titles including *The Legend of Zero* and *Blind Terry*. Happily, those conceits were abandoned—as were (mostly) the Dylanisms of his earlier albums. The harmonicas of "Thunder Road" have a whiff of Zimmerman, but thereafter it is the tinkling pianos and bells, muscular guitars, and dramatic drums that hallmarked Springsteen's sound. There are also elegant epics—"Backstreets," "Jungleland" —whose intros alone make grown men weep. There is "Born to Run," which still thrills after a thousand listens when Bruce revs onto that highway "jammed with broken heroes." There are subtle delights too: Randy Brecker's trumpet showcase "Meeting Across the River"; the Bo Diddley beat conveying lovesick tension on "She's the One." And, of course, the smiling memoir "Tenth Avenue Freeze-Out."

More classics would come. But this is how it started: a snowballing live reputation and a rising tide of hype met a songwriter who understood sonic sophistication and lyrical simplicity—and the winners were us. **BM**

Emmylou Harris
Pieces Of The Sky (1975)

Label | Reprise
Producer | Brian Ahern
Art Direction | Tom Wilkes
Nationality | USA
Running Time | 37:25

Still recoiling from the death of her friend, duet partner, and mentor, Gram Parsons, Emmylou came under the sensitive control of Brian Ahern, who had enjoyed success with another female vocalist, Anne Murray. Harris has effectively carried the torch for Parsons ever since.

To record this, her first post-Parsons solo album, a large house was rented in Beverly Hills, and Ahern's mobile studio was set up in the yard. Ahern did not want to make a straight country album, and assembled a session band including two members of Elvis' Vegas band—guitar legend James Burton and ex-Cricket Glen D. Hardin as arranger and pianist. He also invited Bernie Leadon of The Eagles, Bill Payne of Little Feat, and Herb Pedersen (ex-Dillards) as harmony vocalist.

Several familiar songs were selected as well as original material such as "Bluebird Wine," by the then unknown Rodney Crowell, and Harris' personal tribute to Parsons, "Boulder To Birmingham." Most of the other songs were well known. Mixing Merle Haggard with The Beatles with The Louvin Brothers was intrepid to say the least, but it sounded fabulous.

It says much for Emmylou that musicians like Burton and Hardin, as well as Crowell, became members of the appropriately named Hot Band, which toured with her for several years. Other notables lending a hand here included Amos Garrett on guitar and fiddlers Richard Greene and Byron Berline. The fifth and tenth tracks were live recordings featuring the bar band she had fronted before catching the ears and eyes of Parsons. **JT**

Dion
Born To Be With You (1975)

Label | Phil Spector Records
Producer | Various
Art Direction | Lockhart
Nationality | USA
Running Time | 35:10

Dion DiMucci and Phil Spector both grew up in the New York Bronx, and both had their first hit in 1958 (Spector with The Teddy Bears). By the 1970s, however, Dion's position in the rock hierarchy had slipped, and Spector was no longer "The Tycoon Of Teen."

In trademark style, Spector included three drummers, umpteen guitarists, three bass players, and a host of horns and strings on *Born To Be With You*—then saw it all dismissed as a dirge by critics. Later, fans as disparate as Pete Townshend and Primal Scream's Bobby Gillespie proclaimed its brilliance. And in retrospect, it is hard to see why these tales of heartbreak and loss— and sheer wonder at the beauty of life—sung with such striking conviction and complemented by majestic arrangements, elicited insults. Nevertheless, Spector initially blocked the release of the album.

Dion claims that his vocal on the epic, country-tinged title track—originally a 1956 U.S. Top Five hit for The Chordettes—was his first attempt (hence, perhaps, the loose, easy delivery), and he was amazed when Spector kept it. "Make The Woman Love Me" (written by the great Mann/Weil team) might have been a UK hit single, had it not been banned by the BBC for mentioning the trade name Levi's; both "Only You Know" and "In And Out Of The Shadows" were co-written with the legendary Gerry Goffin. (Tracks three and six did not originate from the Spector sessions.) **JT**

Joni Mitchell
The Hissing Of Summer Lawns (1975)

Label | Asylum
Producer | Joni Mitchell
Art Direction | Joni Mitchell
Nationality | Canada
Running Time | 42:22

As baffling as it is beautiful, *Summer Lawns* confirmed Mitchell as the "songwriter's songwriter." Fearlessly original, presaging the rock/pop world's fascination for all things jazz and world by a decade, the artist pigeonholed as a confessional folk star dazzled with an eclectic collection of symphonic-style compositions.

Lamenting the spiritual bankruptcy of the U.S. meritocracy, Mitchell's vision has also expanded thematically, turning her usual inward gaze out to the Seventies social-political scene. One of the album's recurring images (and leitmotifs) is the savage earth heart that beats beneath the respectability—for example, the Burundi drums on "The Jungle Line," the African imagery in "Boho Dance," and the album cover, featuring a group of natives carrying a vast snake across stylized suburban lawns.

The songs are stuffed with rich, literary imagery. If "Don't Interrupt The Sorrow" appears impenetrable, you may have not listened to the album in the spirit in which it was conceived—as a whole. Such precocity, however, is rewarded with "Edith" and "Scarlett," in which Mitchell's sublime, arched vocals perfectly match the melody and lyrical sentiment. "Harry's House/ Centerpiece" is also a gem, particularly as it segues into the Johnny Mandel-Jon Hendrick tune. The hymn-like closer "Shadows and Light" was one of her favorites (though 1 of its 26 overdubbed vocals is out of tune). **LS**

Tom Waits
Nighthawks At The Diner (1975)

Label | Asylum
Producer | Bones Howe
Art Direction | Cal Schenkel
Nationality | USA
Running Time | 73:48

Although it could be dismissed as an entertaining conceit, the fake nightclub atmosphere of *Nighthawks...*, possibly captures the appeal of early Waits even better than the two impressive albums (*Closing Time* and *Heart Of Saturday Night*) that preceded it.

At the time, Waits was a singer of lounge-lizard late-night jazz-blues poetry about optimistic bums, restless drinkers, experienced deadbeats, and heartbroken losers. Some found his smudged romanticism a little too earnest or maudlin, but *Nighthawks ...*, recorded with experienced jazz session musicians in a studio occupied by a live audience, allowed Waits to soften the L.A. lowlife-isms with his natural gift for theater.

Playing to the audience with a lyrical, self-deprecating wit and pre-empting his later move into acting, he displays the timing of a standup comedian in a series of long, atmospheric, beguiling monologues ("Nighthawks Postcards" is 11:30 minutes of mood-setting). "She's been married so many times she's got rice marks all over her face," goes one line in "Better Off Without A Wife"; the intro to the same song has Waits talking about taking advantage of himself: "I'm not weird about it or anything, I don't tie myself up first ... " The audience whoops appreciation, Waits gives out a Muttley laugh, the intros segue into the songs, and the listener surrenders to the vibe of contentment and mild inebriation. **PW**

R. D. Burman / Bappi Lahiri | Shalimar / College Girl (1975)

Label | Polygram India
Producer | R.D. Burman • Bappi Lahiri
Art Direction | Uncredited
Nationality | India
Running Time | 72:18

From the infancy of the Indian movie industry, Hindi movies borrowed music from around the world—not only using Indian folk and classical music, but liberally stealing from Italian opera, German polka, Cuban rumba, Brazilian samba, bebop, and early rock 'n' roll.

No one stole quite as creatively and intelligently as Rahul Dev Burman (1939–1994), a music director who dominated Bollywood soundtracks for much of the 1960s and '70s. Like his illustrious father S. D. Burman, R. D. Burman was a jazz fan, but he also borrowed heavily from funk, soul, and psychedelic rock. As the plotlines of mainstream Bollywood movies flirted with racy, youthful themes, R. D. Burman's modish soundtracks cranked up the wah-wah guitars, Motown beats, Latin percussion, and the coquettish vocals of his wife Asha Bhosle.

Shalimar serves as one of his key 1970s recordings, containing the much-sampled wah-wah and chorus pedal riff of "Title Music," the loping deep soul classic "Baby Let's Dance Together," the jaunty "One Two Cha Cha Cha," and the Italianate zither- and string-laden "Romantic Theme." Burman's long-term musical and personal partner Asha Bhosle is also on hand to lend her flirty voice to the epic "Mera Pyar Shalimar."

Shalimar is only available on a CD with the soundtrack to *College Girl*, an equally remarkable score by Bollywood's faintly ridiculous "king of disco," Bappi Lahiri. Western listeners will have fun spotting his sources. **JLe**

Neil Young | Tonight's The Night (1975)

Label | Reprise
Producer | David Briggs • Neil Young
Art Direction | Gary Burden
Nationality | USA
Running Time | 44:52

In 1973, Neil Young should have been the happiest man in California. His last album *Harvest* had topped the charts on both sides of the Atlantic, and critics were calling him the finest singer-songwriter of his generation. But Young was depressed and despondent; in the past year he had lost two close friends—Crazy Horse guitarist Danny Whitten and roadie Bruce Berry—to heroin overdoses, and his commercial success had left him feeling trapped and isolated.

Tonight's The Night was Young's attempt to escape this past. Recorded in a series of late-night, tequila-fueled sessions at L.A.'s SIR studio, the album saw Young reinvent himself as a boozy, barroom troubadour. Gone were the note-perfect country-rockers and gentle folk tracks of *Harvest*; in their place were bluesy musings on fame and death. The album's title track, littered with gutter-sweeping guitar from Nils Lofgren, tackles Bruce Berry's sad and wasted life. "Tired Eyes" invokes Whitten's drug struggles with the world-weary chorus, "He tried to do his best, but he could not." "World On A String," featuring ethereal pedal steel from Ben Keith, is a beautifully cynical rejection of Young's celebrity status. The cover artwork was as confrontational as the music.

Although recorded in 1973, Reprise held *Tonight's The Night* back in the vain hope that Young would record a more commercial album. Finally released in 1975, the album was praised by critics, but failed to match the sales of previous releases. Its true influence would not become apparent until more than a decade later, when grunge and alt.country acts alike would mimic its raw and emotionally apocalyptic sound. **TB**

"I don't think *Tonight's The Night* is a friendly album."

Neil Young, 1975

Track Listing

▶ 01	**Tonight's The Night** (Young)	4:39
02	**Speakin' Out** (Young)	4:56
▶ 03	**World On A String** (Young)	2:27
04	**Borrowed Tune** (Young)	3:26
05	**Come On Baby Let's Go Downtown** (Whitten•Young)	3:35
06	**Mellow My Mind** (Young)	3:07
07	**Roll Another Number (For The Road)** (Young)	3:02
08	**Albuquerque** (Young)	4:02
09	**New Mama** (Young)	2:11
10	**Lookout Joe** (Young)	3:57
▶ 11	**Tired Eyes** (Young)	4:38
12	**Tonight's The Night, Pt. 2** (Young)	4:52

Bob Dylan | Blood On The Tracks (1975)

Label | Columbia
Producer | Bob Dylan
Art Direction | Ron Coro
Nationality | USA
Running Time | 51:53

The wordy whining, the wheezing harmonica—we won't lie to you, they're here. But so too are some of the brightest songs in a career not short of sparklers.

The omens were not brilliant. Dylan spent the early 1970s making scrappy records (*Planet Waves*? Yes, please. *Pat Garrett And Billy The Kid*? No, thanks), leaping from label to label and generally suggesting that he was not adapting too well to the new decade. To complete the chaos, his marriage was unraveling. You could expect only maudlin musings on love lost.

Instead, you get the lovely "Tangled Up In Blue" (even the title is fantastic), the sneering "Idiot Wind" ("You're an eeeediot, babe"), the beautiful "Simple Twist Of Fate," and the breathless "Lily, Rosemary And The Jack Of Hearts," which drags not once in a running time of nearly nine minutes. "Shelter From The Storm" is an expression of gratitude that any world-oppressed, beleaguered male will understand.

The music touches on blues, folk, and proto-Dire Straitisms without dwelling on any style long enough for its appeal to pall. This diversity is due in part to Dylan having revamped the album after a test pressing was issued in November 1974 (making that Christmas the best ever for bootleggers). Unsatisfied with recordings made in New York, he re-cut "Tangled Up In Blue," "You're A Big Girl Now," "Idiot Wind," "Lily, Rosemary And The Jack Of Hearts," and "If You See Her, Say Hello" with musicians in his native Minnesota—resulting in his second consecutive U.S. No. 1.

If you listen to only one Dylan album, or you want something to blame for Dire Straits, this is it. **BM**

"I haven't been able to spend as much time with my wife as I would like to."

Bob Dylan, 1975

Track Listing

▶	01	**Tangled Up In Blue** (Dylan)	5:42
▶	02	**Simple Twist Of Fate** (Dylan)	4:19
	03	**You're A Big Girl Now** (Dylan)	4:36
	04	**Idiot Wind** (Dylan)	7:50
	05	**You're Gonna Make Me Lonesome When You Go** (Dylan)	2:56
	06	**Meet Me In The Morning** (Dylan)	4:22
	07	**Lily, Rosemary And The Jack Of Hearts** (Dylan)	8:54
	08	**If You See Her, Say Hello** (Dylan)	4:49
▶	09	**Shelter From The Storm** (Dylan)	5:03
	10	**Buckets Of Rain** (Dylan)	3:22

Patti Smith | Horses (1975)

Label | Arista
Producer | John Cale
Art Direction | Bob Heimall
Nationality | USA
Running Time | 43:10

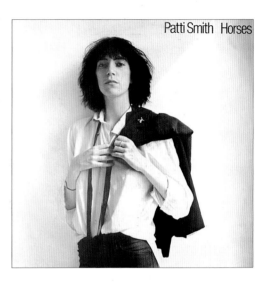

Patti Smith Horses

Horses rewrote the rules for female pop stars and provided a new road map for everyone from Chrissie Hynde and Johnette Napolitano to Courtney Love and Liz Phair. Yet the effect of Patti Smith's debut was not limited to one gender. The vocalist combined the power of the burgeoning NYC punk scene with the adventurous narratives of the San Francisco Beat poets to create a truly unique sound that influenced such artsy acts as the Talking Heads and R.E.M.

Working with producer John Cale, Smith delivered a work so hypnotically raw and achingly personal that its punch has not lessened in 30 years. The album was a completely realized piece of art, starting with the exquisitely honest cover portrait of Smith by Robert Mapplethorpe. *Horses* begins with a total overhaul of Van Morrison's "Gloria" as the singer delivers one of the greatest opening lines in the history of rock—"Jesus died for somebody's sins, but not mine"—and then rides a bouncy merry-go-round of sounds on "Redondo Beach." Smith would begin her career-long exploration of long-form compositions with dramatic results on the nine-minute epics "Birdland" and "Land." Lenny Kaye's urgent guitar work played a big hand in shaping such tracks as "Break It Up." Yet, it was Smith's singular delivery, a combination of Burroughs spoken-word and Lou Reed snarl, that separated "Free Money" and "Kimberly" from everything that had come before—or, really, after.

Horses was championed by critics and became a moderate commercial hit, peaking at No. 47 on the Billboard charts. More significantly, it established Smith as rock's premier punk poet, a title she has yet to lose. **JiH**

> **"I want every night to remember, every night to transport people . . . I feel real honor to have to prove myself."**
>
> Patti Smith, 1975

Track Listing

▶	01	**Gloria** (Morrison·Smith)	5:54
▶	02	**Redondo Beach** (Kaye·Smith·Sohl)	3:24
	03	**Birdland** (Kaye·Kral·Smith·Sohl)	9:16
▶	04	**Free Money** (Kaye·Smith)	3:47
	05	**Kimberly** (Kral·Lanier·Smith)	4:26
	06	**Break It Up** (Smith·Verlaine)	4:05
▶	07	**Land: Horses/Land Of A Thousand Dances La Mer (De)** (Kenner·Smith)	9:36
▶	08	**Elegie** (Lanier·Smith)	2:42

Pink Floyd | Wish You Were Here (1975)

Label | Harvest
Producer | Pink Floyd
Art Direction | Hipgnosis
Nationality | UK
Running Time | 44:19

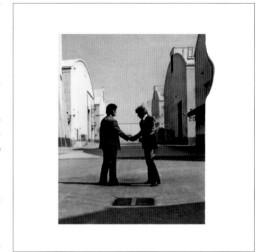

Faced with the enormous task of following up *Dark Side Of The Moon*, Pink Floyd momentarily embraced their old experimental spirit and began to make *Household Objects*, an opus to be recorded entirely with, um, household objects. Touring refocused the group and also began to harden Roger Waters' hatred of the music business as Pink Floyd became a number-crunching, stadium-sized commodity.

Recording for *Wish You Were Here* began at Abbey Road in early 1975. Opening with the multitracked whirr of wineglass rims circled with moistened fingers (the only surviving element of *Household Objects*), "Shine On You Crazy Diamond" is possibly the Floyd's single greatest moment, complete with David Gilmour's album-defining four-note guitar figure. Its nine parts bookend the record, a majestic 25-minute eulogy to departed leader, Syd Barrett. Barrett's unexpected arrival in the studio in June chimed with the thread of quiet desperation that haunted the album; no one recognized the fat, bald man who slipped into in the control room.

"Have A Cigar"—sung by group friend Roy Harper—is one of the best hand-biting songs ever written, and the title track is as bittersweet as the group would ever be. Hipgnosis' artwork reflected the album's isolation and distance; it came shrinkwrapped in black cellophane, with only a sticker indicating the name.

Released in September 1975, to indifferent reviews, the album shot to No. 1 on both sides of the Atlantic, and turned the group into an even bigger number-crunching stadium-sized commodity. **DE**

> "At the beginning of the recording sessions most of us didn't wish we were there at all, we wished we were somewhere else."
>
> Roger Waters, 1993

Track Listing

▶	01	**Shine On You Crazy Diamond (1–5)** (Gilmour·Waters·Wright)	13:38
	02	**Welcome To The Machine** (Waters)	7:31
▶	03	**Have A Cigar** (Waters)	5:24
▶	04	**Wish You Were Here** (Gilmour · Waters)	5:17
▶	05	**Shine On You Crazy Diamond (6–9)** (Gilmour·Waters·Wright)	12:29

Queen | A Night At The Opera (1975)

Label | EMI
Producer | Roy Thomas Baker • Queen
Art Direction | David Costa
Nationality | UK
Running Time | 42:52

Since their 1973 debut, Queen's ambitious template had included bombastic classical references, falsetto freak-outs, and pagan mysticism. But it was on album number four that they melded all these into the epic "Bohemian Rhapsody." The six-minute single was the UK No. 1 for nine weeks and made the U.S. Top Ten.

Drummer Roger Taylor remembers frontman Freddie Mercury playing "Bohemian Rhapsody" to the band at the piano. "And here, darlings, is where the opera section starts," he would say. "Freddie had the bare bones, even the composite harmonies, written on scraps of paper," said Taylor, "So it was quite hard to keep track of what was going on."

Nonetheless, with 180 overdubs and a vocal section that took some 70 hours to record, "Bohemian Rhapsody" came to define the band. Its multilayered harmonies (the distortion that came from endless "track bouncing" contributes to the saturated effect), over-the-top balladry (using the same piano McCartney played on "Hey Jude"), and razor-sharp metal guitar are tied together by Mercury's vision, both Nietzschean and camp.

The album has less overblown gems. Bassist John Deacon's Wurlitzer piano-driven "You're My Best Friend" is perhaps the band's most touching love song. Then there is the mystic "'39," the Arab-tinged "The Prophet's Song," the English music hall of "Lazing On A Sunday Afternoon," and the ballad "Love Of My Life," a live favorite blending Mercury's flamboyant vocals with guitarist Brian May's acoustic flourishes. "*A Night At The Opera* featured every sound from a tuba to a comb," declared Mercury. "Nothing is out of bounds." **JLe**

"It's unheard of to combine opera with a rock theme."

Freddie Mercury, 1977

Track Listing		
01	Death On Two Legs (Dedicated To...) (Mercury)	3:43
02	Lazing On A Sunday Afternoon (Mercury)	1:08
03	I'm In Love With My Car (Taylor)	3:05
▶ 04	You're My Best Friend (Deacon)	2:50
05	'39 (May)	3:25
06	Sweet Lady (May)	4:01
07	Seaside Rendezvous (Mercury)	2:13
08	The Prophet's Song (May)	8:17
▶ 09	Love Of My Life (Mercury)	3:38
10	Good Company (May)	3:26
▶ 11	Bohemian Rhapsody (Mercury)	5:55
12	God Save The Queen (Trad., arr. May)	1:11

Willie Nelson
Red Headed Stranger (1975)

Label | Columbia
Producer | Willie Nelson
Art Direction | Monica White
Nationality | USA
Running Time | 33:20

By 1975, Willie Nelson had released some very fine albums, and he had penned great country songs for other artists, including Patsy Cline's "Crazy" and Faron Young's "Hello Walls." But it was *Red Headed Stranger* that made Nelson a country superstar.

Executives at his new label, Columbia, were understandably nervous about the LP's prospects. At a time when hit country records were lush with strings, the instrumentation of *Stranger* was simple—acoustic guitar, piano, and harmonica. It was also something of a formal experiment, a loose concept album about a lovelorn murderer's adventures. Nelson used the narrative of the Old West to stitch together his own tunes and a handful of covers while, on the back of the sleeve, Monica White drew a series of striking cartoon panels that told the story, sort of.

The suits at Columbia need not have worried. The album sold enormously and yielded his first No. 1 single, a quietly intense version of "Blue Eyes Crying In The Rain," an old Fred Rose song that became one of Nelson's signature tunes. Moreover, *Red Headed Stranger* came out just months before RCA, Nelson's old label, released *Wanted! The Outlaws*, a compilation of music by Nelson, Waylon Jennings, and others that gave its name to an important back-to-basics movement. The significance of Outlaw country remains a subject of debate, but it's certainly the case that with *Red Headed Stranger*, Nelson released an album that shrugged off the strictures of Nashville. It also defined a career. **KB**

Track Listing

▶	01 **Time Of The Preacher** (Nelson)	2:24
▶	02 **I Couldn't Believe It Was True** (Arnold・Fowler)	1:32
	03 **Time Of The Preacher (Theme)** (Nelson)	1:12
	04 **Medley: Blue Rock Montana / Red Headed Stranger** (Lindeman・Nelson・Stutz)	1:32
▶	05 **Blue Eyes Crying In The Rain** (Rose)	2:17
▶	06 **Red Headed Stranger** (Nelson)	3:57
	07 **Time Of The Preacher (Theme)** (Nelson)	0:25
	08 **Just As I Am** (Nelson)	1:45
	09 **Denver** (Nelson)	0:55
	10 **O'er The Waves** (Trad.)	0:48
	11 **Down Yonder** (Gilbert)	1:53
	12 **Can I Sleep In Your Arms?** (Cochran)	5:22
▶	13 **Remember Me** (Tyler)	2:50
	14 **Hands On The Wheel** (Callery)	4:20
	15 **Bandera** (Nelson)	2:18

Earth, Wind, And Fire
That's The Way Of The World (1975)

Label | Columbia
Producer | Charles Stepney • Maurice White
Art Direction | Howard Fritzson
Nationality | USA
Running Time | 38:53

Few remember the movie. Directed by Sig Shore, *That's The Way Of The World* told of a record producer torn between the desire to break a new band and the need to follow orders and cut a blandly commercial hit. Harvey Keitel, fresh from *Alice Doesn't Live Here Anymore*, took the producer's role, while the band were played by a young-ish soul group with a few minor hits under their belts. The movie tanked, but the soundtrack was a blockbuster, singlehandedly lifting Earth, Wind and Fire from relative obscurity to the top of both the U.S. singles and albums charts.

Despite the casting, they were not novices. *That's The Way Of The World* was the group's sixth album (seventh if you include their music for blaxsploitation flick *Sweet Sweetback's Baadasssss Song*); while none had set the charts alight, their preposterously over the top stage shows showed they were not a band short on self-belief. From "Shining Star"'s irresistible groove to the six-minute shuffle of "See The Light," such confidence is writ large all over the music: a glory-be hybrid of soul, disco, funk, and Latin, it is driven by bassist Verdine White but dominated by bandleader Maurice White's sparkling brass and vocal arrangements. The lyrics are frequently facile—"Loving is a blessing/Never let it fade away" is a typical couplet—but the sheer joy with which they are delivered by Philip Bailey is hard to knock. Several terrific albums and a half-dozen huge hits followed, among them "Boogie Wonderland," "After The Love Has Gone," and "Fantasy," but this was their greatest moment. **WF-J**

> "I felt that our music should be more to people than just music to dance to."

Maurice White, 1976

Track Listing

▶	01	**Shining Star** (Bailey•Dunn•M. White)	2:50
▶	02	**That's The Way Of The World** (Stepney•M. White•V. White)	5:46
	03	**Happy Feelin'** (Bailey•Dunn•McKay•M. White•V. White)	3:36
	04	**All About Love** (Dunn•M. White)	6:35
	05	**Yearnin' Learnin'** (Bailey•Stepney•M. White)	3:40
	06	**Reasons** (Bailey•Stepney•M. White)	4:59
▶	07	**Africano** (Dunn•M. White)	5:09
	08	**See The Light** (Angelo•Bailey•Dunn)	6:18

Curtis Mayfield
There's No Place Like America Today (1975)

Label | Curtom
Producer | Curtis Mayfield
Art Direction | Peter Palombi
Nationality | USA
Running Time | 35:47

As a singer, songwriter, social commentator, and musical pioneer, Curtis Mayfield was an original, and one of the twentieth century's most talented popular musicians. His 1972 soundtrack album *Superfly* won Mayfield great acclaim and a wide audience, but by 1975 black American music was becoming very disco-oriented, with most songs simple celebrations of hedonism. Mayfield reacted with *There's No Place Like America Today*, one of the bleakest ever artistic comments on being black in the United States. The cover has a line of black people dwarfed by a huge billboard featuring a smiling white family. Recreated from Margaret Bourke-White's 1937 photograph, it conveys the chasm between the American Dream and street-level reality.

As with Marvin Gaye's epic *What's Goin' On*, Mayfield unflinchingly outlines the dilemmas he sees around him, but gently and resolutely preaches hope. Opener "Billy Jack" chronicles a small-time criminal who ends up murdered; the gospel-esque "When Seasons Change" looks at the despair that underlies so much poverty. "So In Love" is a gorgeous Mayfield love song, while "Jesus" considers the possibility of spiritual redemption. "Blue Monday People" is a plea to love more than money; "Love To The People" delivers an uplifting message about loving your community.

On release, the album proved popular with black Americans but—perhaps unsurprisingly—was ignored by whites. Since then *There's No Place ...* has only taken on a greater resonance. **GC**

> "Most of my songs are songs I'm sure relate to the majority of people's everyday life."
>
> Curtis Mayfield, 1971

Track Listing

▶	01	**Billy Jack** (Mayfield)	6:09
	02	**When Seasons Change** (Mayfield)	5:28
▶	03	**So In Love** (Mayfield)	5:15
	04	**Jesus** (Mayfield)	6:13
	05	**Blue Monday People** (Mayfield)	4:50
▶	06	**Hard Times** (Mayfield)	3:45
▶	07	**Love To The People** (Mayfield)	4:07

Tom Petty And The Heartbreakers
Tom Petty And The Heartbreakers (1976)

Label | Shelter
Producer | Denny Cordell
Art Direction | Ed Caraeff
Nationality | USA
Running Time | 30:25

Prophets without honor in their own country for a long while, *Tom Petty And The Heartbreakers* went Top 20 in Britain and sold well in Germany and France before the group's native United States took any notice. Taking equally from The Byrds (Mike Campbell's classic guitar sound) and Dylan (Petty's rough-hewn delivery; the pair would later team up in The Travelin' Wilburys), the band added a new-wave energy to songs that (with two exceptions) were written in an afternoon and recorded the same evening. "It was very fresh and really exciting, so I wanted the material to be fresh too," Petty recalled. Even chief Byrd Roger McGuinn capitulated, covering the final track "American Girl."

Petty and Shelter Records labelmate Dwight Twilley were both running neck and neck for glory. Both bands combined pop hooks and melodies with guitars a-plenty, but Petty won because he rocked harder. (Twilley here provides backing vocals for "Strangered In The Night.") Indeed, compared with Neil Young sidekick Nils Lofgren, with whom he toured Britain, Petty seemed like a punk. There was also a touch of the swagger of The Rolling Stones and Animals in there, which may well explain why the Brits picked up on them first.

Songs on this album would later be covered by the diverse likes of Lew Lewis ("Hometown Blues") and Suzi Quatro ("Breakdown"), while Petty himself would continue with what he called "the big jangle" until 1985's *Southern Accents*, when he let Eurythmics' Dave Stewart tamper with the formula. **MH**

> "We wanted ... a sensibility that was a mixture of The Rolling Stones and The Byrds."
>
> Tom Petty, 1999

Track Listing

01	**Rockin' Around (With You)** (Campbell·Petty)		2:25
▶ 02	**Breakdown** (Petty)		2:42
03	**Hometown Blues** (Petty)		2:11
04	**The Wild One, Forever** (Petty)		3:00
▶ 05	**Anything That's Rock 'n' Roll** (Petty)		2:23
▶ 06	**Strangered In The Night** (Petty)		3:29
07	**Fooled Again (I Don't Like It)** (Petty)		3:48
08	**Mystery Man** (Petty)		3:01
09	**Luna** (Petty)		3:56
▶ 10	**American Girl** (Petty)		3:30

The Modern Lovers
The Modern Lovers (1976)

Label | Beserkley
Producer | John Cale • Kim Fowley
Art Direction | Uncredited
Nationality | USA
Running Time | 44:05

David Bowie
Station To Station (1976)

Label | RCA
Producer | David Bowie • Harry Maslin
Art Direction | AGI
Nationality | UK
Running Time | 38:08

Bostonian Jonathan Richman had been an avid Velvet Underground fan. Hence the stripped-down sound of his first band, The Modern Lovers, whose original recording lineup featured drummer David Robinson (The Cars), keyboard player Jerry Harrison (Talking Heads), and bassist Ernie Brooks. Live appearances around Boston elicited interest from Warner Bros., who booked the band into a California studio in 1973, for sessions produced first by John Cale then Kim Fowley.

His early work voiced a beautifully contradictory world view: he embraced the "Modern World" but would not dismiss the "Old World"; was attracted to self-destructive girls ("She Cracked," "Hospital") but sang of a new romanticism in the awesome "Girlfriend" and "Someone To Care About," songs that turned their back on the Sixties sexual revolution.

Most of all he had a penchant for modern hymns— to the macho lifestyle of painter Pablo Picasso in a song covered by Cale himself and later Bowie, and to the eternally appealing call of the road on the two-chord classic "Roadrunner," covered by a legion of garage bands since, perhaps most famously the Sex Pistols.

Warner then dropped the band. Three years later, Beserkley released the album, scoring a hit single with "Roadrunner." But Jonathan had split the band by the time the demos were finished, and had a new career in mind: he would downsize his sound to acoustic rock 'n' roll and sing, in his nasal tone, about insects, Martians, and rocking leprechauns. **IJ**

In 1976, David Bowie's personal life was in chaos. His open marriage with Angie Bowie had collapsed and he was trying to cope with cocaine and alcohol addiction. Increasingly paranoid, he had become obsessed with UFOs, occultism, and Adolf Hitler.

With guitarists Carlos Alomar and Earl Slick, and drummer Dennis Davies who had worked on *Young Americans*, work began on the provisionally titled *Thin White Duke*, a soul record "devoid of soul." The opening title track was a brooding, cocaine paranoia epic, influenced by Bowie's interest in the German avant-garde rock of Can, Neu!, and Kraftwerk, and introduced Bowie's Thin White Duke, whose white tuxedo and slicked back hair recalled his character in *The Man Who Fell To Earth,* whom he stars as on the album's sleeve.

Hit single "Golden Years" lifts the numbing intensity with slick funk guitar and its sleazy groove. The theme of paranoia dominated the record, delivered in a cold, clinical croon—most effectively on "TVC 15," where it was beautifully complemented by Davies' acrobatic drumming. By the time we reach the closing track, "Wild Is The Wind," Bowie's voice has transformed, sounding as vulnerable as it is heartbreaking.

The album was a transition both artistically (moving from plastic soul toward electronic minimalism) and personally (inspiring Bowie to clean up his addictions before relocating to Berlin). An inspiration to the British post-punk and New Romantic scenes, it remains one of Bowie's most accomplished and enduring works. **CSh**

Joni Mitchell
Hejira (1976)

Label | Asylum
Producer | Joni Mitchell
Art Direction | Glen Christensen
Nationality | Canada
Running Time | 52:03

In 1974, Joni Mitchell sat at the apex of the pop music universe, adored by most critics and millions of fans for a series of brilliant, often achingly personal albums, a run that culminated that year with the monster hit *Court And Spark*. She then had the nerve to follow her muse into a smoky, jazz-drenched dive, a journey that led to her most supple and graceful album, *Hejira*.

Composed on the road, it is the only Mitchell album on which every tune is written on and for the guitar. The name stems from the prophet Muhammad's journey of exile from Mecca to Medina. In Mitchell's case, *Hejira* traces a cross-country road trip sparked by the end of an affair. The album marks the beginning of the singer/songwriter's profound relationship with the pioneering electric bassist Jaco Pastorius.

While Pastorius' genius fully flowered in the fusion supergroup Weather Report, he never played more beautifully than in the confines of a stripped-down, tightly constructed five-minute Mitchell epic, like the opening track "Coyote." His supple melodic lines serve as a burnished counterpoint to her increasingly rich soprano, reaching a graceful climax on the mysteriously affecting "Amelia," a song that traces an arc of romantic discovery with references to previous tunes "Woodstock," "Both Sides Now," and "Cactus Tree."

Mitchell made more ambitious and popular albums, but, with its vivid imagery, poetic scope, and emotional insight, *Hejira* stands as a perfect melding of instrumental virtuosity and confessional storytelling. **AG**

Boston
Boston (1976)

Label | Epic
Producer | John Boylan • Tom Scholz
Art Direction | Paula Scher
Nationality | USA
Running Time | 37:48

After the celebration of the Bicententennial in the United States, engineer-turned-guitarist Donald "Tom" Scholz and his bandmates unleashed soft rock's ultimate Christmas present in December 1976.

Scholz, recording demos since 1970, borrowed Aerosmith's equipment to cut an album in November 1975. He recorded at studios across Los Angeles, to conform to union regulations requiring approved engineers, yet only one of those tracks made the album. For the rest, Scholz slaved over a hot console at home while his bandmates indulged in Californian excess (hence drummer Sib Hashian's herbal surname).

The set was Scholz's take on the Cream/Zeppelin template and boasts melodic rockers, flashing guitars, powerhouse rhythms, and sweet cascading vocals by Brad Delp. There was not a synth in sight, yet "Foreplay" is as space age as the UFO-inspired sleeve. "There was a rumor that I wrote the entire first album with a computer program," recalled Scholz. "Smokin'" rocks like a juggernaut, while the boisterous "Rock And Roll Band" and engaging "Let Me Take You Home Tonight" are outstanding slices of pristine rock.

Then there is the definitive anthem "More Than A Feeling." Alternately lilting and loud, it sounds like a blueprint for "Smells Like Teen Spirit"—Nirvana even took to vamping it when they played "Teen Spirit" live. The song's enduring popularity helped make *Boston* a multi-platinum monster. Clocking up its 17 millionth sale in 2003, this album cannot be stopped. **TJ**

Eagles | Hotel California (1976)

Label | Asylum
Producer | Bill Szymczyk
Art Direction | Don Henley • Kosh
Nationality | USA
Running Time | 43:28

Released in December 1976, *Hotel California* depicts the emotional burnout of the West Coast scene after peace and love hardened into cynical hedonism. The soundtrack of decadent times, it went on to sell more than 16 million copies. It is a mature work from a band whose reflections on the cost of excess had been formed the hard way—by five years of hit records and touring. As founder member Glenn Frey said, the album "explores the underbelly of success, the darker side of paradise."

Part delirious road trip, part murder ballad, the title track's lilting tempo and stinging guitar lines evoke a place where evil lurks behind potted palms and welcoming smiles; the searing lead duel between Joe Walsh and Don Felder is one of the most memorable in rock. Shifting focus from widescreen excess to close-up portraits of the damage done is one of the album's hallmarks. "Life In The Fast Lane" sends us on a dirty boogie down the freeway with a callous pair of socialites—only to encounter their smoking wreckage in the next track, "Wasted Time," a grandly orchestrated ballad of compromised, disappointed lives.

The band's country roots are present throughout, most notably on "New Kid In Town," where Walsh's electric piano evokes the sleepy sadness of a Mexican cantina amid vocal harmonies as lush as a manicured Hollywood lawn. In many ways *Hotel California* represents everything that punk came to destroy: glassily perfect production, harmonized guitar solos, and "themes." But like many musical styles in their last bloom, West Coast country-rock reached a refinement in *Hotel California* never equaled again. **JDi**

> ## "Man will ultimately destroy heaven if left to his own devices, because he has destroyed every heaven on earth."
>
> Don Henley, 1976

Track Listing

▶	01	**Hotel California** (Felder•Frey•Henley)	6:30
▶	02	**New Kid In Town** (Frey•Henley•Souther)	5:04
▶	03	**Life In The Fast Lane** (Frey•Henley•Walsh)	4:46
▶	04	**Wasted Time** (Frey•Henley)	4:55
	05	**Wasted Time (Reprise)** (Frey•Henley•Norman)	1:22
	06	**Victim Of Love** (Felder•Frey•Henley•Souther)	4:11
	07	**Pretty Maids All In A Row** (Vitale•Walsh)	4:05
	08	**Try And Love Again** (Meisner)	5:10
	09	**The Last Resort** (Frey•Henley)	7:25

Abba | Arrival (1976)

Label | Polydor
Producer | Benny Andersson • Björn Ulvaeus
Art Direction | Ola Lager • Rune Soderqvist
Nationality | Sweden
Running Time | 33:32

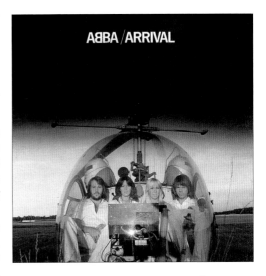

By 1976, Abba had escaped from the deadly stigma that affects the musical credibility of all Eurovision Song Contest winners. Moreover, their string of hits had proved that they had the commercial wherewithal to continue and expand on their musical conquest of Europe and take on the U.S. market.

Arrival was their fourth UK album release, and their second of eight consecutive albums to top the UK chart. The biggest song here is the joyous "Dancing Queen," their fourth UK No. 1 single, and also their only U.S. chart-topper. The quartet, as the only pop musicians invited, had performed the song at a gala held the day before Sweden's King Carl Gustaf's marriage to his wife, Silvia Sommerlath, although contrary to local reports, the song was not composed especially for the royal wedding. Nearly 30 years later, it has become a gay anthem.

The album also included a second UK No. 1 in "Knowing Me, Knowing You"—introducing a quality of reflective melancholy that was increasingly to become part of Abba's work as their career progressed—as well as a UK Top Three single in "Money, Money, Money." True, some particular critics felt that other songs— such as "When I Kissed The Teacher" and particularly "Dum Dum Diddle"—betrayed Abba's Eurovison past a little too clearly. But "That's Me," (the Latin-American flavored B-side of the "Dancing Queen" 45), "Why Did It Have To Be Me" (which the group also recorded, using different lyrics, as "Happy Hawaii"), and the very Celtic-sounding instrumental "Arrival," which was later covered by Mike "Tubular Bells" Oldfield, were all highly respectable—for Eurovision winners. **JT**

> ## "Pop music is a here-today-and-gone-tomorrow thing."
>
> Björn Ulvaeus, 2004

Track Listing

01	**When I Kissed The Teacher** (Andersson • Ulvaeus)	3:03
▶ 02	**Dancing Queen** (Anderson • Andersson • Ulvaeus)	3:52
03	**My Love, My Life** (Anderson • Andersson • Ulvaeus)	3:53
04	**Dum Dum Diddle** (Andersson • Ulvaeus)	2:54
▶ 05	**Knowing Me, Knowing You** (Anderson • Andersson • Ulvaeus)	4:02
▶ 06	**Money, Money, Money** (Andersson • Ulvaeus)	3:07
07	**That's Me** (Anderson • Andersson • Ulvaeus)	3:17
08	**Why Did It Have To Be Me** (Andersson • Ulvaeus)	3:22
09	**Tiger** (Andersson • Ulvaeus)	2:56
▶ 10	**Arrival** (Andersson • Ulvaeus)	3:01

Kiss | Destroyer (1976)

Label | Casablanca
Producer | Bob Ezrin
Art Direction | Dennis Woloch
Nationality | USA
Running Time | 33:03

Flamenco guitar solos and steals from Beethoven are not obvious ingredients for success. Especially not for comic-book rock 'n' rollers famed for "Rock And Roll All Nite." Yet *Destroyer* is the iconic Kiss album.

Alive! (1975) bookended the band's primal phase, leaving them free to experiment. In came producer Bob Ezrin, who had honed his craft with Lou Reed and Alice Cooper. Envisaging Kiss as "a caricature of all the urges of youth," he pushed them to transcend the groin-grinding of their earlier work.

The fruits included enduring anthems, notably "Detroit Rock City" (home of the aforementioned flamenco solo) and "God Of Thunder" (a Paul Stanley song that became Gene Simmons' signature tune). There were oddities too, including the hit ballad "Beth" and "Great Expectations," for which Ezrin raided Beethoven's Pathétique ("I laugh every time I hear it," he confessed to Kisstorian Ken Sharp).

Ezrin commissioned L.A. scenester Kim Fowley's help with the strutting "King Of The Night Time World" and "Do You Love Me?"—and, in a bid to bump up the running time, added sound collages at the start and close. An eerie 86-second coda mixes backward bits of *Destroyer* with a snippet from *Alive!* The package was wrapped in an eye-popping painting by Ken Kelly, cousin of fantasy artist Frank Frazetta; Def Leppard's Joe Elliott said, "I bought it purely for the sleeve."

Fans have debated *Destroyer*'s merits since its release, a fire fueled by the revelation that Ezrin had dumped guitarist Ace Frehley from two cuts. But the band have spent their career trying to match it. **BM**

"I don't know about 'classic.' I don't toss that word around."

Gene Simmons, 2002

Track Listing

▶	01	**Detroit Rock City** (Ezrin·Stanley)	5:18
	02	**King Of The Night Time World** (Anthony·Ezrin·Fowley·Stanley)	3:21
▶	03	**God Of Thunder** (Stanley)	4:17
	04	**Great Expectations** (Ezrin·Simmons)	4:25
	05	**Flaming Youth** (Ezrin·Frehley·Simmons·Stanley)	3:00
	06	**Sweet Pain** (Simmons)	3:22
	07	**Shout It Out Loud** (Ezrin·Simmons·Stanley)	2:50
▶	08	**Beth** (Criss·Ezrin·Penridge)	2:50
	09	**Do You Love Me?** (Ezrin·Fowley·Stanley)	3:40

Rush
2112 (1976)

Label | Mercury
Producer | Terry Brown • Rush
Art Direction | Hugh Syme
Nationality | Canada
Running Time | 38:46

The ambitious *2112* was a milestone in Rush's career, a make-or-break album for the Canadian power trio sometimes dubbed as "the biggest cult band in the world." With this release, the band drastically decided to go ahead with their own thing, no matter what.

Rush nearly folded after *Fly By Night* and *Caress Of Steel* (both 1975), which were poorly received. In the aftermath, drummer/lyricist Neal Peart became deeply affected by the libertarian writings of Ayn Rand. Her philosophy, which emphasizes that the individual should follow his own path, provided the story for the album's epic title track—a 20-minute composition broken down in seven segments. This track tells the tale of a man who leads a revolution through music after rejecting the Priests of Syrinx, a story that mirrored the band's own frustration with the music business.

Rush's trademark sound—prog-meets-heavy rock— comes fully into its own on this record and the magnificent title track has stood the test of time well— a meticulously assembled opus that utilizes classical compositional technique to great effect. Of the other tracks, hard rockers like "A Passage To Bangkok" and "Something For Nothing" are now established classics.

The album was well received by fans at the time, though critics dismissed it as overblown and pretentious. Not that the band cared: since *2112*, they have single-mindedly followed their own path, amassing hordes of devoted fans and staying firmly— and happily—below the critical radar. **AET**

Jorge Ben
Africa / Brasil (1976)

Label | Philips
Producer | Mazola
Art Direction | Jorge Vianna
Nationality | Brazil
Running Time | 41:35

It is impossible to overstate the influence of Jorge Ben on the loosely affiliated international confederation of funk. By the time he created his Rio soul manifesto *Africa/Brasil*, Ben had been a musical force for more than a decade, but the album's samba percussion, R&B horns, sassy background vocals, and hypnotic rhythm guitar distills Ben's hard-grooving essence.

The album opens supremely with the barn-burning "Umbabarauma," which David Byrne used to kick off his popular anthology on *Musica Popular Brasil*. Ben's brilliant combination of Sly Stone and James Brown with the equally deep grooves of samba is best experienced in "Xica Da Silva," while the insanely catchy chorus of his updated version of "Taj Mahal" makes it clear why Rod Stewart ripped it off on his hit "Do Ya Think I'm Sexy."

Ben started his career as a graceful bossa nova player, following in the footsteps of Joao Gilberto. He scored a huge international hit in 1963 with "Mas Que Nada," but his music reached a creative peak in the 1970s, as he fully integrated the influence of American funk and R&B with heavily syncopated Afro-Brazilian percussion. His driving acoustic guitar work, warm, intimate vocals, and production genius resulted in a series of exceptional albums, culminating with *Africa/Brasil*. Though he was not central to the late 1960s Tropicalia movement that brought together Caetano Veloso, Gilberto Gil, Tom Ze, and Gal Costa, Ben's exploration of African themes has served as an inspiration for many Brazilian artists. **AG**

Joan Armatrading
Joan Armatrading (1976)

Label | A&M
Producer | Glyn Johns
Art Direction | Uncredited
Nationality | West Indies/UK
Running Time | 40:32

Citing Joan Armatrading as one of the first black women to venture into the singer/songwriter arena is to do her something of a disservice. While this distinction is valid on one level, it does not begin to acknowledge the full power of her talents, and confines her to far too neat a pigeonhole. After all, anyone who could deliver a piece of work as superbly honest and resonant as her eponymous third release deserves note, regardless of their race or gender.

While her earlier efforts had shown certain promise, Armatrading's songwriting skills came to full flower here, set off by a keen eye for detail, as well as a playful sense of humor. The disc opens with the sweeping strum of "Down To Zero," as the singer chastises a lover for his fickle ways, while at the same time scolding herself for taking him back. Adding a melancholic depth to the track is B. J. Cole's expert lap steel work. Elsewhere, Armatrading shares more "morning after" wisdom on "Water With The Wine," and turns in one of her best vocal performances on "Save Me," exploring the full range of her voice's rich qualities.

Credit for the record's overall strength is also due to producer Glyn Johns, who had worked with such artists as Steve Miller, The Who, and The Rolling Stones. On this album, Armatrading enjoyed excellent support from members of Fairport Convention and The Faces, mixing folksy pop with elements of jazz, reggae, and R&B. The resulting sound is polished and professional, but still allows Armatrading's unique gifts to shine through. **TSh**

Aerosmith
Rocks (1976)

Label | Columbia
Producer | Aerosmith • Jack Douglas
Art Direction | Uncredited
Nationality | USA
Running Time | 34:30

Flushed with the success of *Toys In The Attic*, Aerosmith wasted no time or momentum in returning to the studio to cut what for many is their magnum opus. *Rocks*, recorded partly at their Wherehouse rehearsal space and at the Record Plant in New York, was fueled by the excesses that would prove to be their near-undoing. But with the help of Jack Douglas, the band managed to focus their talents like never before, creating an aptly titled package of gems.

More cohesive than *Toys . . .*, *Rocks* also features a richer, tougher sound—the downright dangerous guitar combination of Joe Perry and Brad Whitford is spurred on by the sleazy rhythm section of Tom Hamilton and Joey Kramer, making tracks like "Rats In The Cellar" and "Back In The Saddle" send sparks.

At the center of it all is Steven Tyler's determined, devilish howl—a vocal style that earned him the moniker "The Demon of Screamin'." On "Get The Lead Out," Tyler requested the support of a singer from the Metropolitan Opera on the refrain (making one wonder what happened to the singer's career after a session that must have shredded a once-fine voice).

The lyrics deal with extremes, whether it is sex ("Back In The Saddle"), drugs ("Combination"), or fame ("A Lick And A Promise")—there is either too much or too little, typically at the same time. The subject matter is fitting for a band whose predilections scared the most drug-addled musicians in the business, leading them to dub Tyler and Perry the Toxic Twins. **TSh**

Parliament | Mothership Connection (1976)

Label | Casablanca
Producer | George Clinton
Art Direction | Gribbitt Management
Nationality | USA
Running Time | 38:17

Inspired by Motown's production line of sound, George Clinton gradually constructed the funk juggernaut that was Parliament-Funkadelic: two groups, several side projects, and more than 50 musicians, including sax star Maceo Parker and bass deity Bootsy Collins.

Mothership Connection—Parliament's third and best album—testifies to the sheer power of their extreme musicianship and innovation. The cover depicts a spreadeagled Clinton in makeup and thigh-length platform boots jumping out of a spaceship, which is as close as a photo can get to describing what is on the album itself. Under Clinton's guidance, Parliament took funk, washed it in acid, dressed it in a camp, sci-fi outfit, and wrapped it in cool. The result is seven tracks of relentlessly perfect R&B, immaculately arranged by Collins, Clinton, trombonist Fred Wesley, and keyboardist Bernie Worrel.

"P-Funk (Wants To Get Funked Up)" heralds what is to come. Clinton speaks smoothly over languid basslines, before kicking into high gear and letting the synths, horns, and harmonies take over. From then on, each track is an explosion of interweaving rhythms and melodies.

Mothership Connection's innovation alone makes it one of the best ever funk albums. A huge success at the time ("Tear The Roof Off The Sucker" was Parliament's biggest hit on the Hot 100), it changed the way people looked at funk and R&B. Decades later, its impact resounded in the work of rappers like Warren G. and Snoop Dogg, and rockers like The Red Hot Chili Peppers and Primus. The P-Funk legacy makes Clinton and Co. one of the most important American acts ever. **LP**

> "Back then when everybody took a lot of acid, you had a choice to go the way that you liked."

George Clinton, 2002

Track Listing

▶ 01	**P-Funk (Wants To Get Funked Up)** (Clinton·Collins·Worrell)	7:41
▶ 02	**Mothership Connection** (Clinton·Collins·Worrell)	6:13
03	**Unfunky UFO** (Clinton·Collins·Snider)	4:23
04	**Supergroovalisticprosifunkstication** (Clinton·Collins·Snider)	5:03
05	**Handcuffs** (Clinton·Goins·McLaughlin)	4:01
▶ 06	**Give Up The Funk (Tear The Roof Off The Sucker)** (Brailey·Clinton·Collins)	5:46
07	**Night Of The Thumpasorus Peoples** (Clinton·Collins·Snider)	5:10

The Penguin Cafe Orchestra
Music From The Penguin Cafe (1976)

Label | Obscure
Producer | Simon Jeffes • Steve Nye
Art Direction | Emily Young
Nationality | UK
Running Time | 45:01

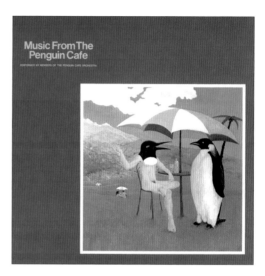

With its surreal cover art and unconventional spin on hallowed musical conventions, *Music From The Penguin Cafe* stands as one of the truly unique works of 1970s pop music. According to the group's founder and driving creative force, the late Simon Jeffes, the idea for his postmodern orchestra came to him in a vision after eating some bad fish in France.

Recorded over three years, the mostly instrumental tunes on *Music . . .* are by turns satirically playful and achingly lovely, employing disparate elements of baroque, jazz, pop, and avant garde. The disc opens with the bright proto-chamber music of "Penguin Cafe Single," a wry reference to their noncommercial approach. Later, they set about deflating the self-important pomp of old-guard Britain with intentionally flat singing on "Coronation." (This record boasts the only vocal performances the band ever attempted, including the one-word lyric on "Milk"). Perhaps not surprisingly, the album was originally released through Brian Eno's Obscure music label.

The music throughout is as challenging as it is rewarding. The album's centerpiece is the gorgeous and emotionally harrowing "The Sound Of Someone You Love Who's Going Away And It Doesn't Matter." Working off a deceptively simple theme, this epic instrumental seems to trace the denouement of a love affair with devastating effectiveness. Such a track is one of the many reasons that the band's first album is still its most adventurous—and satisfying. **TSh**

Track Listing

▶ 01 **Penguin Cafe Single**
(Jeffes•Liebman•Nye•Wright) 6:20

▶ 02 **From The Colonies** (Jeffes) 1:38

03 **In A Sydney Motel** (Jeffes) 2:28

04 **Surface Tension** (Jeffes) 2:22

▶ 05 **Milk** (Jeffes) 2:22

▶ 06 **Coronation** (Jeffes) 1:33

07 **Giles Farnaby's Dream** (Jeffes) 2:19

08 **Pigtail** (Jeffes) 2:44

09 **The Sound Of Somone You Love Who's Going Away And It Doesn't Matter**
(Jeffes•Liebman•Nye•Wright) 11:46

▶ 10 **Hugebaby** (Jeffes•Liebman•Nye•Wright) 4:48

11 **Chartered Flight**
(Jeffes•Liebman•Nye•Wright) 6:41

Jean Michel Jarre
Oxygene (1976)

Label | Disques Motors
Producer | Jean Michel Jarre
Art Direction | Editions Marquet • Michel Granger
Nationality | France
Running Time | 39:39

In November 1976, Jimmy Carter won the U.S. elections, and the son of French film composer Maurice unveiled his third studio offering. While the likes of Tangerine Dream and Kraftwerk blazed the trail, and Vangelis' *Albedo 0.39* was a paean to natural grandeur, *Oxygene* was a template for otherworldly soundscapes, a synth-based parallel universe that inspired the electronica movement and sales of more than ten million copies.

Although it won praise and made UK No. 2, Jarre had to shop around his magnum opus for months before securing a deal with an indie label. Sporting a futurist design (and photos by future wife, actress Charlotte Rampling), it drew on Jarre's group and screen work while offering a new and fresh perspective on the scope of electronic instrumentation—from Farfisa organ to Mellotron® via ARP® synthesizers.

Jarre used his classical grounding to formulate swirling, floating melodies, often in odd sequences, such as 34.5 bars. They range from the eerie (as per the opener) to the ethereal ("Part 2," which unintentionally connotes the space-obsessed times, from *Mars Viking* to *Star Wars*, with a crescendo of throbbing, burbling beats overtaken by cascading synths and laser-burst effects). Following the sea wash of the John Carpenter-esque "Part 3," there is the hypnotic vibrato of "Oxygene Part 4," with its memorable, ice-dance refrain—still a global TV theme staple—and its successor, mixing subterranean atmospheres with Bolero-like Twenties gothicism, before an expressive finale. **TJ**

"You have to be a bloody perfectionist. If you don't, you kill a lot of people. I'm not suggesting that my music will kill, but ... "

Jean Michel Jarre, 2004

Track Listing

▶	01	**Oxygene Part 1** (Jarre)	7:40
▶	02	**Oxygene Part 2** (Jarre)	8:08
	03	**Oxygene Part 3** (Jarre)	2:54
▶	04	**Oxygene Part 4** (Jarre)	4:14
	05	**Oxygene Part 5** (Jarre)	10:23
▶	06	**Oxygene Part 6** (Jarre)	6:20

Ramones | Ramones (1976)

Label | Sire
Producer | Tommy Erdelyi • Craig Leon
Art Direction | Greg Allen • Sevie Bates
Nationality | USA
Running Time | 29:04

From its simple black-and-white cover photo to its quick-fire sonic assaults, the Ramones' debut album is the ultimate punk statement.

Recorded in two days for a meagre $6,000, *Ramones* stripped rock back to its basic elements. There are no guitar solos and no lengthy fantasy epics, in itself a revolutionary declaration in a time of Zeppelin-inspired hard-rock excess. Pushed along by Johnny Ramone's furious four-chord guitar and Tommy's thumping surf drums, all of the tracks clock in under three minutes. And while the songs are short and sharp, the group's love of 1950s drive-through rock and girl-group pop means they are also melodically sweet.

The album's lyrics are very simple, boiled-down declarations of teen lust and need. Joey Ramone yelps about what he wants ("I Wanna Be Your Boyfriend," "Now I Wanna Sniff Some Glue") and what he does not ("I Don't Wanna Walk Around With You"). Only "53rd And 3rd"—a dark narrative based on Dee Dee's experiences as a rent boy—hints at the expression of something more meaningful and deeply felt.

Praised on its release by a small circle of music journalists (*Creem* declared, "If their successors are one-third as good as the Ramones, we'll be fixed for life"), *Ramones* failed to enter either the U.S. Top 100 or the UK Top 40. But the few kids who bought the album took its hyped-up, melodic minimalism as a call to arms. The Sex Pistols, The Clash, and the Buzzcocks all used The Ramones' four-chord blueprint to express their frustration at rock's stale and self-indulgent state. Revolution would never sound so simple again. **TB**

Track Listing

▶	01	**Blitzkrieg Bop** (Ramones)	2:14
	02	**Beat On The Brat** (Ramones)	2:31
▶	03	**Judy Is A Punk** (Ramones)	1:32
	04	**I Wanna Be Your Boyfriend** (Ramones)	2:24
	05	**Chain Saw** (Ramones)	1:56
▶	06	**Now I Wanna Sniff Some Glue** (Ramones)	1:35
▶	07	**I Don't Wanna Go Down To The Basement** (Ramones)	2:38
	08	**Loudmouth** (Ramones)	2:14
	09	**Havana Affair** (Ramones)	1:56
	10	**Listen To My Heart** (Ramones)	1:58
	11	**53rd And 3rd** (Ramones)	2:21
	12	**Let's Dance** (Lee)	1:51
	13	**I Don't Wanna Walk Around With You** (Ramones)	1:42
▶	14	**Today Your Love, Tomorrow The World** (Ramones)	2:12

Fela Kuti And The Afrika '70 | Zombie (1976)

Label | Coconut
Producer | Fela Anikulapo Kuti
Art Direction | Uncredited
Nationality | Nigeria
Running Time | 25:23

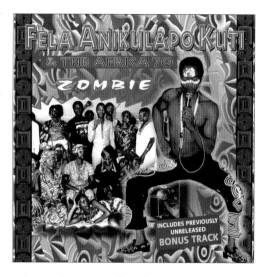

By 1976, Fela Anikulapo Kuti was *the* African superstar, a giant of twentieth-century music at his coruscating, volcanic peak. Over the previous decade, with drummer Tony Allen, his rhythmic guiding light, and his band Afrika '70, Fela had created a whole new school of music—Afrobeat. It fused together the jazz and funk elements of African-American music with West African highlife, Nigerian traditional music, and Yoruba rhythms, and added the fire of a black consciousness-led political vision for Africa—powerful, witty lyrics, and an outrageous lifestyle. His records sold millions throughout Nigeria and West Africa; the superstars of the West (McCartney, Ginger Baker, Stevie Wonder, James Brown, Lester Bowie et al.) rushed to Lagos to dig the sounds and smoke the weed.

Zombie is one of the 18 albums Fela Kuti released in 1976 and 1977. The characteristically epic duration of the title track (too mind-boggling even for FM radio at the time) allows it a long fuse. The unstoppable rhythm guitar riffs are joined by the funky bassline, drums, and an outrageous Fela tenor solo, before the blinding light of a horn chorus and a drum riff you can sing. After five minutes of a deliciously funky horn, Fela sings the ultimate antimilitarist anthem against those who only follow orders: "Zombie no go stop unless you tell him to stop/Zombie no go think unless you tell him to think." The Nigerian military government's response was a cataclysmic army raid, which resulted in the injury and eventual death of Fela's mother and the total razing of his compound, called the Kalakuta Republic, and his club, the Shrine. **MR**

"People are playing more revolutionary music, political music, and they're making people very aware of situations, and whatnot. So then, the struggle is not very dead, getting momentum through music."

Fela Kuti, 1986

Track Listing		
▶ 01	**Zombie** (Kuti)	12:26
▶ 02	**Mister Follow Follow** (Kuti)	12:57

Peter Tosh | Legalize It (1976)

Label | Virgin
Producer | Peter Tosh
Art Direction | Howard Fritzson
Nationality | Jamaica
Running Time | 38:19

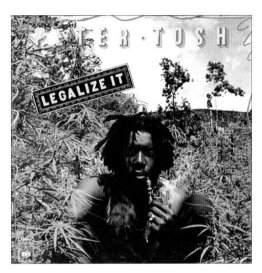

A founder of The Wailers, Peter Tosh had recorded dozens of solo tracks during the band's decade-long rise from the Trenchtown ghetto to stardom, but it was only after fleeing Bob Marley's ever-expanding shadow that he kicked off his career in earnest.

Although his first album, *Legalize It*, featured The Wailers' former supporting cast and Bunny Livingston's distinctive harmonies (Tosh returned the favor on Livingston's solo debut, the roots classic *Blackheart Man*), it showed off Tosh's uniquely forthright sound and versatility as a songwriter. The no-nonsense title track wields a driving bassline and fragmented melody that contrasts with Marley's winding phrasing; the simple refrain—"Legalize it, don't criminalize it"—got the song banned on Jamaican radio. The mystical "Igziabeher (Let Jah Be Praised)" features a rasta prayer of invocation over thunder-and-lightning dub effects.

Tosh also veers from melancholic introspection— from the many-layered "Why Must I Cry," to angry tongue-lashings of his enemies, as in the deceptively pretty "Burial." Another Tosh trademark, brutal irony, comes through on "Whatcha Gonna Do," which uses cheeky synth riffs and a bouncy chorus to tell a parable of a ghetto family destroyed by a marijuana-related arrest. He also rocks on "No Sympathy," highlighted by former Wailer Al Anderson's leering guitar solo.

The album is less politically focused than Tosh's later work, but listeners loved his exuberance—and the cover image of him in a marijuana field. The album charted at No. 54 in the UK, staking Tosh's claim to Marley's place atop reggae's emerging pantheon. **MW**

> "Now, today in this September of 1976, I am a new mon again—as I have jus' recently come to realize it."
>
> Peter Tosh, 1976

Track Listing

▶	01	Legalize It (Tosh)	4:35
▶	02	Burial (Tosh)	3:54
▶	03	Whatcha Gonna Do (Tosh)	2:25
	04	No Sympathy (Tosh)	4:35
▶	05	Why Must I Cry (Marley・Tosh)	3:08
	06	Igziabeher (Let Jah Be Praised) (Tosh)	4:37
	07	Ketchy Shuby (Tosh)	4:53
▶	08	Till Your Well Runs Dry (Livingston・Tosh)	6:09
	09	Brand New Second Hand (Tosh)	4:03

Stevie Wonder
Songs In The Key Of Life (1976)

Label | Tamla Motown
Producer | Stevie Wonder
Art Direction | Motown Graphics Department
Nationality | USA
Running Time | 86:53

On August 15, 1975, Stevie Wonder signed a $13 million contract with Motown, guaranteeing complete artistic freedom. He had stockpiled hundreds of songs, but the ensuing months saw him record 200 more, forcing Motown to clear the decks for the first of two double albums that propelled him from precocious maverick to international megastar (it was one of the first albums to enter the U.S. chart at No. 1).

At times it is close to jazz: "Sir Duke" is a big-band celebration of Duke Ellington, "Contusion" a jazz-rock instrumental in the vein of the Mahavishnu Orchestra. The samba-tinged "As" features Herbie Hancock, the salsa-flavored "Another Star" boasts flautist Bobbi Humphrey and guitarist George Benson, and the blended heavenly "If It's Magic" is a duet with harpist Dorothy Ashby.

New songs constantly delayed the album. "There were times when he'd stay in the studio 48 hours straight," recalled bassist Nathan Watts. "You couldn't even get the cat to stop and eat!" Indeed, the CD's final four tracks initially came as a bonus, 33rpm seven-inch.

Songs… was much lauded, though Robert Christgau of the *Village Voice* thought it riddled with New Age baloney ("Saturn"), didactic lectures ("Black Man"), and soupy sentimentality ("Isn't She Lovely"). Nonetheless, it set the tone for Stevie's Rainbow Coalition politics—the booklet thanks Jesse Jackson and Louis Farrakhan alongside Frank Zappa and Andy Williams. **JLe**

Peter Frampton
Frampton Comes Alive! (1976)

Label | A&M
Producer | Peter Frampton
Art Direction | Roland Young
Nationality | UK
Running Time | 78:06

Peter Frampton's live double epitomizes post-Vietnam, escapist sunshine rock. With an estimated 16 million sales, it is second only to Bruce Springsteen's 1985 blockbuster as history's most successful live set.

Recorded between March and November 1975—principally at Frampton's first headlining gig, at Winterland in San Francisco—the album was summed up by Cameron Crowe in *Rolling Stone* as "much more than a souvenir. It is a testimony to Peter Frampton in his natural habitat." Following a template established by Kiss with their *Alive!*, the album transformed a minor leaguer into a major player. The former member of British rockers The Herd and Humble Pie had made three, moderately successful albums: now he enjoyed ten weeks atop the Billboard chart.

The 14-song selection provides a fine cross-section of his albums and Humble Pie days. Jaunty "Somethin's Happenin'" and insistent "Show Me The Way" lay out his stall of echo-rich vocals, jazzy electric and sweet acoustic guitars, melodious harmonies and—"Ooh baby"—lyrics. The band rock out on the likes of "I Wanna Go To The Sun," but it is the hysteria elicited by the hit anthem "Baby, I Love Your Way" and talkbox-laden "Do You Feel Like We Do" that proves the life-affirming nature of the Frampton sound. The album prompted an invitation to the White House from President Gerald Ford. We are not worthy! **TJ**

Brian Eno
Before And After Science (1977)

Label | Polydor
Producer | Rhett Davies • Brian Eno
Art Direction | Brian Eno
Nationality | UK
Running Time | 39:07

Before And After Science could be Brian Eno's secret masterpiece, yet it remains an uncelebrated album.

Eno built each piece from layer upon layer of performances from the likes of Phil Manzanera, Robert Fripp, Achim Roedelius, and Mobi Moebius of Cluster, and er ... Phil Collins. The results still sound astonishing. "Kurt's Rejoinder" samples dadaist performance artist Kurt Schwitters before samplers were even invented, while "No One Receiving" and the rampaging "King's Lead Hat" (an anagram of Talking Heads, whom Eno was producing at the time) foreshadow the febrile ethnic funk of 1981's collaboration with David Byrne, *My Life In The Bush Of Ghosts*.

Yet this album points to more than one future for Eno. Its introspective second half prefigures much of his 1980s work, particularly the atmospheres of the *Ambient* series. Where the album's earlier tracks were built up from nothing, these seem intent on returning there. Dedicated to Harold Budd, the limpid "Through Hollow Lands" sounds like a premonition of Eno's later albums with the minimalist pianist, while the exquisitely sad Cluster collaboration "By This River" consists of little more than a two-finger piano riff and Eno's resigned vocals. Best of all is "Spider And I," an elegiac synth piece that makes it clear that *Before And After Science* is the end of one way of making music and the beginning of many more. Essential. **MBe**

Kraftwerk
Trans-Europe Express (1977)

Label | EMI
Producer | Ralf Hütter • Florian Schneider
Art Direction | Ralf Hütter • Florian Schneider
Nationality | Germany
Running Time | 42:44

A glistening panorama of elegance and decadence, travel and technology, *Trans-Europe Express* is a streamlined celebration of Europe's romantic past and shimmering future. The gorgeous rolling vistas of "Europe Endless" bookend the album, while Kraftwerk's often overlooked sense of black humor surfaces on "Showroom Dummies," a wry riposte to critics of their emotionless image. There is also a rare diversion into the macabre on the eerie, darkly comic "Hall Of Mirrors."

During this period, Bowie was one of Kraftwerk's army of famous fans, paying homage on his classic Berlin album *Heroes*. Hütter and Schneider returned the favor by namechecking Bowie and Iggy Pop on the title track to *Trans-Europe Express*, a locomotive whose relentless, piston-pumping rhythm mimics the sound of train wheels on metal rails, with a trance-like intensity.

With its innovative use of early sequencer technology, Kraftwerk's sixth album helped shape the musical climate that filled the vacuum after punk rock, alerting a new generation of record buyers to electronic music. "Metal on Metal," the panel-beating sister track and "Trans-Europe Express," later became a key influence on hip hop, electro, and industrial music. Most famously, Afrika Bambaataa sampled these beats and that melody with the electro and dance movement to come on his 1982 hip-hop hit, "Planet Rock." Once again, Kraftwerk sounded effortlessly ahead of their time. **SD**

Billy Joel | The Stranger (1977)

Label | Columbia Records
Producer | Phil Ramone
Art Direction | Jim Houghton
Nationality | USA
Running Time | 45:02

The Stranger was the third album from the 28-year-old Billy Joel, who had just begun making a living from his music, having played in piano bars throughout high school in New York to supplement the income of his single mother. Whilst he had already achieved headline status with 1974's *Streetlife Serenade*, *The Stranger* was Joel's first album to hit number one on the charts and remained Columbia Records' biggest selling album until 1985. It also prompted his biggest tour yet, playing 54 shows in the United States and Europe in the fall of 1977.

The nine-track-long album produced four singles; "Just The Way You Are" that provided his first two Grammy Awards in 1979, "Movin' Out (Anthony's Song)" with its teen rebellion message and car sounds included, the gentler "She's Always A Woman," and the infectious "Only The Good Die Young." Whilst the lyrics are poetic and clever, the album has a youthful appeal and Joel's gift for storytelling is particularly poignant on the astonising "Scenes From An Italian Restaurant."

Musically diverse, Joel's dynamic songwriting is further dramatized in the title track's quiet piano introduction before rocking out in the middle section incorporating a barrage of electric guitars, concluding with the haunting sound of whistling. An amazing 24 people played various parts on the recording. The album is reasonably warm in tone, but slightly eerie in its execution, further exemplified by the stark black-and-white image of a bare-footed, suit-and-tie-wearing Joel, sitting on a bed looking at a mask with boxing gloves hanging in the background. **CSt**

"People tend to define me in terms of my hits and may not know the substantive elements of my composition."

Billy Joel, c.1987

Track Listing

▶	01	Movin' Out (Anthony's Song) (Joel)	3:30
▶	02	The Stranger (Joel)	5:10
	03	Just The Way You Are (Joel)	4:50
▶	04	Scenes From An Italian Restaurant (Joel)	7:37
	05	Vienna (Joel)	3:34
▶	06	Only The Good Die Young (Joel)	3:55
	07	She's Always A Woman (Joel)	3:21
	08	Get It Right The First Time (Joel)	3:57
	09	Everybody Has A Dream (Joel)	9:08

Bob Marley And The Wailers | Exodus (1977)

Label | Island
Producer | Bob Marley And The Wailers
Art Direction | Neville Garrick
Nationality | Jamaica
Running Time | 37:24

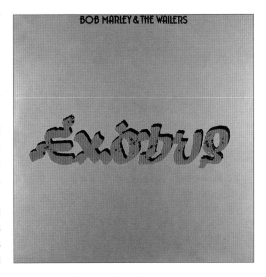

Bob Marley was a man of many faces—a third-world visionary and first-world pop star, a prophet of national revolution and messenger of global peace, a Rastafarian mystic and lascivious lover. *Exodus*, released in 1977, best captured these diverse identities.

Exodus (along with *Kaya*, released the following year) was recorded in London during the mellow months that followed an assassination attempt at Marley's Kingston home. The album shows Marley exploring contemporary musical movements such as funk, dub, and rock, particularly on the heavily political side one, which fades in with the powerful religious groove of "Natural Mystic" and issues an epic trumpet call for audiences to "listen carefully." What follows is worth it: "The Heathen"—a hypnotic battle cry with a substantial sprinkling of psychedelic guitar riffs—and the rousing title track, a call for repatriation marching to a driving dub/disco beat.

Side two, by contrast, is a lush love-fest, featuring the beautifully crafted smash hit "Jamming," a groovy ode to dancing; the sublime "Waiting In Vain," a tender ballad about unrequited love; and the simple yet irrepressible "One Love" and "Three Little Birds," which ostensibly wrote the recipe for the upbeat reggae anthem—ganja-thick bass, palm-tree chords, and a positive chorus—that musicians worldwide have worked in vain to improve upon ever since.

The album reached No. 8 in the UK, and "Exodus" and "Waiting in Vain" also made the Top 40 on the American R&B charts. And in 1999, *Time* magazine named *Exodus* its album of the century. **MW**

> "Rasta don't believe, Rasta know. Yuh see, is when yuh believe, is that mash yuh up."
>
> Bob Marley, 1973

Track Listing

▶ 01	**Natural Mystic** (Marley)	3:28
02	**So Much Things To Say** (Marley)	3:08
03	**Guiltiness** (Marley)	3:19
▶ 04	**The Heathen** (Marley)	2:32
▶ 05	**Exodus** (Marley)	7:39
06	**Jamming** (Marley)	3:31
▶ 07	**Waiting In Vain** (Marley)	4:15
08	**Turn Your Lights Down Low** (Marley)	3:39
▶ 09	**Three Little Birds** (Marley)	2:60
▶ 10	**One Love/People Get Ready** (Marley)	2:53

Electric Light Orchestra
Out Of The Blue (1977)

Label | Jet
Producer | Jeff Lynne
Art Direction | John Kosh • Ria Lewerke
Nationality | UK
Running Time | 70:12

Jeff Lynne is a man with serious ambitions. That much was clear from the start, when he and two other ex-members of pre-ELO psychedelic-pop outfit The Move announced that they would now pick up where The Beatles had left off with "I Am The Walrus." But even by Lynne's standards, *Out Of The Blue* was a daringly ambitious project—a galaxy-spanning double platter that melded spacey art rock, Beatlesque pop, and sleek orchestral arrangements.

Despite its length, . . . *Blue* does not contain much filler. It kicks off with a trio of tunes that rank among ELO's finest—the giddy "Turn To Stone" and "Sweet Talkin' Woman" that bookend the meticulously produced "It's Over," a track that hints at what Lynne would later accomplish with George Harrison. The album draws inspiration from both Berry and Beethoven as it moves through rockers such as "Birmingham Blues" and the symphonic side-long "Concerto For A Rainy Day," which climaxes with "Mr. Blue Sky." The cinematic "Wild West Hero," complete with its McCartney-like refrain, brings the album to a triumphant close.

Released at the height of disco, *Out Of The Blue* was seen by some as a futuristic fish out of water. (The trippy spaceship cover was illustrator Shusei Nagaoka's expansive development of the UFO-shaped logo from the band's previous LP, *A New World Record*.) Nonetheless, it quickly became a platinum-selling hit and launched the band on one of the most ambitious world tours of the 1970s. **JiH**

Weather Report
Heavy Weather (1977)

Label | Columbia
Producer | Jaco Pastorius • Joe Zawinul
Art Direction | Nancy Donald
Nationality | Austria • Peru • USA
Running Time | 37:39

List the key players behind the Seventies jazz-rock fusion movement and it's headed by Joe Zawinul and Wayne Shorter's Weather Report, John McLaughlin's *Mahavishnu Orchestra*, Chick Corea's *Return To Forever*, Herbie Hancock and, of course, Miles Davis' electric bands, in which all these guys had played. But when it comes to chart-topping commercial success for the music, we are talking Weather Report and this album—a jazz record that reached No. 30 on the Billboard pop chart, went gold (500,000 sales), and spawned a hit single, "Birdland," which charted again with versions by Manhattan Transfer (1979) and Quincy Jones (1990). Not just their best seller, *Heavy Weather* was also their critical high-tide mark, hailed as Jazz Album of the Year by virtually every relevant mag, including *Playboy*.

All that cash-register action and acclaim tends to obscure what a triumph this album is: devastatingly brilliantly played, genre-defining compositions with a sound that suggests the production was a meticulous act of love. With their new lineup, Shorter and Zawinul left behind the sparser airy understatement of earlier albums for a funkier kingdom. Virtuoso bassist Jaco Pastorius' innovative stylings do not just occupy *Heavy Weather*'s center stage, but created the template for fretless bass playing into the twenty-first century. Alex Acuña and Manolo Badrena (drums and percussion) propel the band with a fluid Afro-Cuban feel, climaxing on Shorter's tribute to the legendary 1950s Manhattan Latin nightspot, "Palladium." **MR**

Muddy Waters
Hard Again (1977)

Label | Blue Sky
Producer | Johnny Winter
Art Direction | Josh Cheuse
Nationality | USA
Running Time | 45:23

It is ironic that the guitarist responsible for electrifying the blues would never strum a note on his trusty red Fender Telecaster, nicknamed "Hoss," on what is arguably his greatest record.

Having ended a 28-year career with Chess Records, which had initially resulted in such early genre-redefining singles as "Rollin' Stone," but mostly Muddy mediocrity in the 1970s, Waters (then 71) went into the studio with something to prove. He succeeded in creating a work so powerfully raw and undeniably passionate that it sounds as if it is being performed at the fabled blues "crossroads," with both the Devil and Robert Johnson listening from across the street, merely able to shake their heads in admiration.

Bob Margolin, a member of Waters' road band, and producer Johnny Winter juice "I Want To Be Loved" and "Jealous Hearted Man" with sturdy leads that almost perfectly echo the master in his prime. On the soulful "Crosseyed Cat" and "Little Girl," James Cotton provides Waters with the best harmonica accompaniment he has had since, perhaps, the Little Walter days. Yet, it is Waters' singing, which had not sounded this poignant in at least a decade, that manages to breathe new, even greater, life into the old classics "Mannish Boy" and "I Can't Be Satisfied."

Hard Again received uniformly positive reviews, earned Waters his fourth Grammy and, most importantly, perfectly illustrated that nobody gets the blues quite like Muddy Waters. **JiH**

The Stranglers
Rattus Norvegicus (1977)

Label | United Artists
Producer | Martin Rushent
Art Direction | Paul Henry
Nationality | UK
Running Time | 39:47

The Stranglers stood apart from their contemporaries. For a start, they used keyboards. They were also a long time out of short trousers. In drummer Jet Black's case, significantly so. This gave an additional twist to the undoubted anger that surfaced on their debut, originally to be live and titled *Dead On Arrival*. Not for them petulant abstractions about "the system": they already had a wealth of experiences to share.

Observing the punk ethos, *Rattus Norvegicus* was recorded in just six days. But, while the aggression is there, the performance is also very accomplished, resulting in an album where "virtually every track is a little masterpiece," as *NME* testified.

The magazine did have reservations, condemning the lyrics as "grossly sexist." Accusations of misogyny were never far away, a viewpoint that "Sometimes" and "London Lady" did little to allay. Tongue in cheek or guilty as charged? The band defended themselves, saying they were merely commenting.

Musically, the band hit the purplest of purple patches at the midpoint. Following Hugh Cornwell's scabrous vocals in "Hanging Around," J. J. Burnel uses his karate expertise to great effect for the brutal bassline of "Peaches." Then it is full throttle for "(Get A) Grip (On Yourself)" and its exhortation to "strap on your guitar and we'll play some rock 'n' roll."

Controversial, yes, but what else would you expect from an album named after the rodent blamed for spreading the Black Death? **CB**

The Clash | The Clash (1977)

Label | Columbia
Producer | Mickey Foote
Art Direction | Kate Simon
Nationality | UK
Running Time | 35:13

Often taking second place—undeservedly so—to the Sex Pistols, The Clash eschewed the self-destructive ethos and instead opted for edgy political songs, catchy slogans, and clothes from a decorator's van.

The green-black-and-white cover shot of Joe Strummer, Mick Jones, and Paul Simonon was taken in their rehearsal studios in north London and is in keeping with the unadorned music on their 14-track debut, recorded over the course of three weekends in 1977. Bordering on the incoherent, Strummer's sing/shout style fits perfectly with start/stop guitars in songs such as "I'm So Bored With The USA."

Their output was often derided as sloganeering but the lyrics of "Career Opportunities" brilliantly capture the prospect facing the nation's youth: menial work or life on the dole. The Clash's appeal also lay in their ability to absorb other musical genres within their sound. Their cover of Junior Murvin and Lee Perry's "Police And Thieves" sees Simonon's bass stride above the guitars as the drums of Terry Chimes (a.k.a. Tory Crimes) provide a snapping rhythm. It is an arrangement that reoccurs to great effect elsewhere on the album.

Coming from west London, they were right in the middle of a multicultural melting pot. Surrounded by reggae, ska, and rock steady influences, the band had a political and musical vision that reached a good way beyond the myopic outlook of their punk contemporaries.

The Clash's incendiary style and exhortations to action can still be heard today in groups such as The Libertines, whose second (and final) album was produced by Mick Jones. What goes around … **AMa**

> "The Clash was always from the heart."
>
> Joe Strummer, 1988

Track Listing

▶	01	**Janie Jones** (Jones•Strummer)	2:08
	02	**Remote Control** (Jones•Strummer)	3:03
	03	**I'm So Bored With The USA** (Jones•Strummer)	2:24
▶	04	**White Riot** (Jones•Strummer)	1:56
	05	**Hate And War** (Jones•Strummer)	2:06
▶	06	**What's My Name** (Jones•Levine•Strummer)	1:41
	07	**Deny** (Jones•Strummer)	3:06
▶	08	**London's Burning** (Jones•Strummer)	2:12
▶	09	**Career Opportunities** (Jones•Strummer)	1:54
	10	**Cheat** (Jones•Strummer)	2:06
	11	**Protex Blues** (Jones•Strummer)	1:46
▶	12	**Police And Thieves** (Murvin•Perry)	6:03
	13	**48 Hours** (Jones•Strummer)	1:36
	14	**Garageland** (Jones•Strummer)	3:12

David Bowie
Low (1977)

Label | RCA
Producer | David Bowie • Tony Visconti
Art Direction | Steve Shapiro
Nationality | UK
Running Time | 38:50

The first of David Bowie's legendary "Berlin trilogy," *Low*'s troubled atmosphere reflected its creator's own fractured mental state at the time. Things reached a head when Thomas Newton, the stranded alien he had played in *The Man Who Fell To Earth*, met Bowie's own nasty "Thin White Duke" persona and the pop star started spouting nonsense about Nazis. In an effort to reconnect with reality, Bowie shacked up with old pal Iggy Pop in Berlin—then the drug capital of Europe.

However, much of *Low* was conceived at the Château d'Herouville studios in France, where Bowie and producer Tony Visconti coaxed Bowie's R&B-schooled sidemen into replicating the Teutonic perfection of Neu!, Cluster, and Kraftwerk. The result was a side of classic experimental pop—notably the breathtaking "What In The World," single "Sound And Vision," and "A New Career In A New Town."

If fans were bemused by what was a left-turn even by Bowie's standards, heaven knows what they made of the album's second half: four ambient pieces constructed with Brian Eno. A brilliant (mostly) instrumental evocation of Bowie's desolate outlook, these experiments were a bleak keynote for the post-punk era, especially for Joy Division, who were originally known as Warsaw, named after the chilling "Warszawa." Bowie himself now acknowledges *Low* as something of a career high point, an opinion shared by fans who lapped up his one-off live re-creation of the album at London's Royal Festival Hall in 2002. **MBe**

Steely Dan
Aja (1977)

Label | ABC
Producer | Gary Katz
Art Direction | Oz Studios
Nationality | USA
Running Time | 39:28

By 1977, Steely Dan was less a band than a movable feast presided over by founders Donald Fagen and Walter Becker—but what a feast.

As an album, *Aja* has little of *Pretzel Logic*'s playful pastiche, or the cynicism of *The Royal Scam*. Instead, Fagen and Becker crafted a polished, jazz-inflected opus that went on to sell more than five million copies.

"Black Cow" sets the mood—metropolitan and wry, it tells the story of a cheated-on lover who finally loses patience. Victor Feldman's Fender®Rhodes solo is a deft delight, while elegantly syncopated horns ride the bop to the end with impeccable class.

The title track is a different proposition—a tone poem to the mystique of the Orient, which broadens into philosophical reverie, "Aja" is the album's center of gravity. The song builds a delicate, opium-tinged world, then destroys it in Steve Gadd's shattering drum finale, while Wayne Shorter cries murder on tenor sax.

Perhaps such esoteric leanings led *Rolling Stone* to say that the album "exhibits a carefully manipulated isolation from its audience." This is partly true but it is difficult to hear in "Deacon Blues," their swan song for an aging L.A. hipster, as tender as it is bleakly humorous.

There are also two solid party tunes on the album—the irresistibly funky "Peg" (later sampled by De La Soul on "Eye Know") and "Josie," a slick homecoming boogie.

With superlative production and performances from 30 of the best session musicians of the day, *Aja* is a genuine landmark in jazz rock. **JDi**

Wire
Pink Flag (1977)

Label | Harvest
Producer | Mike Thorne
Art Direction | David Dragon
Nationality | UK
Running Time | 35:14

Unashamedly middle-class, and older than most of their contemporaries, ex-art school students Wire nonetheless recorded the most original album of punk's first wave. *Pink Flag* takes punk rock's template to even further extremes. It features 21 songs in 35 minutes; few of the tracks follow traditional verse/chorus patterns, with the band grinding to a halt once they had run out of lyrics or had become tired of repeating a riff or hook. The resulting sound was far colder and more brutal than anything else around at the time, a minimalist approach reflected in the solitary raised pink flag on the album's stark sleeve.

The consciously intellectual lyrics sometimes read like mathematical equations or surrealist poetry. They touch upon politics ("Reuters") and sexual paranoia ("12XU"), while vocalist Colin Newman reserves much of his vitriolic bile for the thrashing rant of "Mr. Suit." The genius "Field Day For The Sundays" deconstructs the mentality of the British press in less than 30 seconds. Despite the title track's avant-garde tendencies and the claustrophobic intensity of "Strange," Wire make their ability to write fantastic pop evident on "Mannequin" and lost single "Ex Lion Tamer."

Pink Flag's lowly sales at the time are inversely proportional to its artistic influence. The immediate post-punk scene embraced its experimental minimalism, while hardcore adopted its savage intensity and brevity. Elastica's borrowing from "Three Girl Rhumba" for 1994's "Connection" confirmed Wire's lasting influence. **CSh**

John Martyn
One World (1977)

Label | Island
Producer | Chris Blackwell
Art Direction | Tony Wright
Nationality | UK
Running Time | 38:44

As the Seventies progressed, John Martyn was becoming increasingly tired. The deaths of his friends Nick Drake and Paul Kossoff had deeply troubled him. His hell-raising drink-and-drugs lifestyle—diametrically opposed to the sweet-voiced cosmic troubadour he portrayed on record—coupled with his general mistrust of the music industry had pushed him to the limit. At the invitation of Island founder Chris Blackwell, Martyn spent some time in Jamaica, where he met legendary producer Lee Perry and jammed on several reggae cuts.

Revitalized after what became a three-year lay-off, Martyn recorded throughout summer 1977. *One World* was made throughout the night at Blackwell's Berkshire retreat, surrounded by friends and family, with engineer Phill Brown setting up microphones outdoors and taping Martyn across a lake, capturing the ambience of the surroundings. Using experienced players such as Steve Winwood and Rico Rodriguez, Martyn sculpted an incredible, ethereal sound, especially on "Small Hours," an eight-minute rumination on life and love. Perry's spirit floats over *One World* as the space of his Black Ark Studio dub sides informs a large proportions of the recording, especially on tracks such as "Smiling Stranger" and "Big Muff."

Although released at the height of the punk movement in the UK, *One World*, with its sleeve depicting the symbols of different cultures captured in a mermaid's wake, is an almost perfect piece of work, a smart album made by one very smart hippie. **DE**

Talking Heads | Talking Heads: 77 (1977)

Label | Sire
Producer | Tony Bongiovi
Art Direction | David Byrne
Nationality | UK • USA
Running Time | 38:37

Formed as The Artistics in New York City by Scottish-born David Byrne alongside Chris Frantz and Tina Weymouth, Talking Heads' live reputation made them one of the most highly touted bands of the CBGB's scene. After being signed by Seymour Stein to his Sire label, they recruited ex-Modern Lovers guitarist Jerry Harrison and commenced work on their classic debut album with Tony Bongiovi, cousin of Jon Bon Jovi.

Preceding single "Love Goes To Building On Fire" aroused concern that the band were compromising their sound to gain commercial acceptance, but *Talking Heads: 77* proved their integrity remained intact. The blistering opener "Uh-Oh, Love Comes To Town," influenced by Byrne's affection for Sixties groups, saw his trademark straining voice set against Frantz and Weymouth's jerky funk rhythms. Bongiovi initially added psychedelic strings to the twisted monologue "Psycho Killer," but the band complained he had made it sound like a novelty record. However tracks such as "New Feeling" and "Don't Worry About The Government," with their distinctive guitar work, sudden tempo changes, and Byrne's intelligent, disconnected, lyrical stanzas, showed Talking Heads had taken elements of punk, funk, and disco and convincingly created a unique sound of their own.

Talking Heads: 77 initially found Top 40 success in Europe. *Rolling Stone* declared them to be the most promising new act of 1977, alongside Peter Gabriel, and this excellent album has continued to influence bands such as Radio 4 and The Rapture, who have kept alive much of Talking Heads' initial creative spirit. **CSh**

> ## "We want to make good music in a song format."
>
> David Byrne, 1977

Track Listing

▶ 01	**Uh–Oh, Love Comes To Town** (Byrne)	2:48
▶ 02	**New Feeling** (Byrne)	3:09
03	**Tentative Decisions** (Byrne)	3:04
04	**Happy Day** (Byrne)	3:55
05	**Who Is It?** (Byrne)	1:41
▶ 06	**No Compassion** (Byrne)	4:47
07	**The Book I Read** (Byrne)	4:06
▶ 08	**Don't Worry About The Government** (Byrne)	3:00
09	**First Week/Last Week ... Carefree** (Byrne)	3:19
▶ 10	**Psycho Killer** (Byrne • Frantz • Harrison • Weymouth)	4:19
11	**Pulled Up** (Byrne)	4:29

Fleetwood Mac | **Rumours** (1977)

Label | Warner Bros.
Producer | Ken Caillat • Richard Dashut • Fleetwood Mac
Art Direction | Desmond Strobel
Nationality | UK • USA
Running Time | 39:55

The Lazarus-like renaissance and transformation of a London-based blues band into the cutting-edge Los Angeles-based world champions of Adult Oriented Rock is one of the greatest stories of rock's rich history.

Drummer Mick Fleetwood and bass player John McVie had been there since the start in 1967, and with McVie's wife, Christine (née Perfect), on keyboards since 1970, had weathered major personnel changes. In 1974, they met singer/songwriter/guitarist Lindsey Buckingham and his girlfriend, vocalist/songwriter Stevie Nicks. This infusion of new blood resulted in an eponymous 1975 album that briefly topped the U.S. chart and included three U.S. Top 20 singles. Its successor, *Rumours*, almost immediately topped the U.S. album chart, where it reigned supreme for 31 weeks, was certified 13 times platinum, and won the 1977 Grammy award for Album Of The Year. The breezy West Coast harmonies, tighter-than-tight musicianship, and hook-laden AOR made for a great combination. The four tracks highlighted right were U.S. Top Ten singles, while "Dreams" was a million-selling U.S. No. 1. For years "The Chain" introduced the BBC's Grand Prix coverage.

Scratch the surface of these smoothly produced gems, however, and there is a darker subtext. Recording took place while the McVies, and Fleetwood, were in the throes of divorce; Buckingham and Nicks were also splitting up (her cold-eyed "Gold Dust Woman" was later covered by Hole). A blizzard of cocaine further racked up the tension. And all this collective trauma provided the album's title—John McVie once observed that the songs sounded like gossip or rumors. **JT**

> **"I think you can smell the people through the songs..."**
>
> Mick Fleetwood, 2003

Track Listing

01	**Second Hand News** (Buckingham)	2:45
▶ 02	**Dreams** (Nicks)	4:17
03	**Never Going Back Again** (Buckingham)	2:14
▶ 04	**Don't Stop** (C. McVie)	3:12
▶ 05	**Go Your Own Way** (Buckingham)	3:39
06	**Songbird** (C. McVie)	3:21
07	**The Chain** (Buckingham • Fleetwood • C. McVie J. McVie • Nicks)	4:30
▶ 08	**You Make Loving Fun** (C. McVie)	3:36
09	**I Don't Want To Know** (Nicks)	3:16
10	**Oh Daddy** (C. McVie)	3:53
11	**Gold Dust Woman** (Nicks)	4:52

David Bowie | "Heroes" (1977)

Label | RCA
Producer | David Bowie • Tony Visconti
Art Direction | Sukita
Nationality | UK
Running Time | 40:21

Riding the wave he had found with *Low*, *"Heroes"*—the second part of the so-called "Berlin trilogy"—saw David Bowie continue his gradual reintroduction to humanity. Fresh from a liberating stint as keyboard player on Iggy Pop's *Idiot* tour, Bowie was now living with Iggy in West Berlin. Relatively drug-free, the pair immersed themselves in seedy Berlin nightlife, miraculously avoiding falling back into old habits.

"Heroes" gives the trilogy its decadent splendor, its dramatic, performance-art-influenced black-and-white cover photograph, and the darkly evocative song titles clearly inspired by Bowie's new home. Where *Low* mapped the internal landscape of Bowie's fractured psyche, *"Heroes,"* like Iggy's *The Idiot* (1977) is all about Berlin, from the denizens of its nightclubs in "Blackout" to the gloomy Turkish immigrant quarter in "Neuköln."

Featuring many of the musicians who had played on *Low* (producer Tony Visconti, collaborator Brian Eno, guitarist Carlos Alomar, and rhythm section George Davis and Dennis Davis) the album was recorded in the summer of 1977 at Hansa Studios, a former Gestapo ballroom near to the Berlin Wall. Eno, Visconti, and Bowie distilled their location's powerful atmosphere in view of the Red Army guards at Checkpoint Charlie.

Like *Low*, *"Heroes"* mixed avant-garde pop songs with ambient instrumentals. Eno's influence is felt on the title track, a Velvets-like stomp taken somewhere different by Fripp's inspired, fluid guitar. Re-contextualized by its performance at 1985's Live Aid concert, the song's current existence as stadium fodder belies the emotional complexity of its parent album. **MBe**

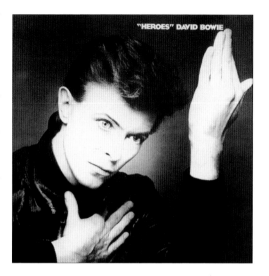

> "It really runs the gamut of emotions, from deep despair through to that upward spiraling of 'V2 Schneider.'"
>
> David Bowie, 1997

Track Listing

▶	01	**Beauty And The Beast** (Bowie)	3:34
	02	**Joe The Lion** (Bowie)	3:06
▶	03	**"Heroes"** (Bowie•Eno)	6:08
▶	04	**Sons Of The Silent Age** (Bowie)	3:17
	05	**Blackout** (Bowie)	3:48
▶	06	**V–2 Schneider** (Bowie)	3:10
▶	07	**Sense Of Doubt** (Bowie)	3:57
▶	08	**Moss Garden** (Bowie•Eno)	5:05
▶	09	**Neuköln** (Bowie•Eno)	4:32
	10	**The Secret Life Of Arabia** (Alomar•Bowie•Eno)	3:44

Dennis Wilson
Pacific Ocean Blue (1977)

Label | Caribou
Producer | Gregg Jakobson
Art Direction | John Berg
Nationality | USA
Running Time | 37:39

Suicide
Suicide (1977)

Label | Red Star
Producer | Craig Leon • Marty Thau
Art Direction | Rob Soares
Nationality | USA
Running Time | 31:51

Dennis Wilson was The Beach Boys' resident drummer, stud, actor, Charles Manson acolyte, and the first to die (drowning after a vodka binge). He also released the only solo album of real note by any Beach Boy.

Recorded over seven years, *Pacific Ocean Blue* offers up a glimpse of L.A. in the Seventies, when being a coke-fueled rock star was truly to live like a god. Reviews of the album were positive and while not a hit—there are no radio-friendly singles on *Pacific Ocean Blue*—it has been long admired. Its multitracked voices, synth washes, bruised melodies, undercurrent of despair, and stoned, late-night ambience make it stand up better today than any Beach Boys album since *Surf's Up.*

The piano motifs and massed voices of stunning opener "River Song" create an epic, gospel-like quality. "Moonshine" is built over a heavy percussion rhythm and offers up rich-white-guy California blues. "Thoughts Of You" is Dennis at his most wistfully reflective; "Time" is complemented by a gorgeously blue trumpet line that recalls Chet Baker, before morphing into a rocker. The title track is a great nature song with Dennis' voice at its most grizzled, while "Farewell My Friend" is an elegiac goodbye. Wilson was addicted to cocaine and alcohol and much of *Pacific Ocean Blue* has a weary, zonked flavor to it, as if he was digging through his messy psyche to truly express the real Dennis.

Gratified by the album's positive response, he set about recording a follow-up to be called *Bamboo* but his wild lifestyle meant it was never to be completed. **GC**

"23 Minutes Over Brussels," included as a bonus on the CD reissue of Suicide's classic, eponymous debut album, gives some indication of the public's reaction to this confrontational duo in their heyday. Recorded on June 16, 1978, when Suicide were supporting Elvis Costello at the L'Ancienne Belgique ballroom, it is the sound of a riotous comedy.

Utilizing a primitive drum machine, Martin Rev's mutant fuzz organ, and Alan Vega's blues holler, Suicide had been performing for six years before unleashing their debut at the height of punk. With their roots in the New York art scene, their provocative name, nihilistic attitude, and the lack of rock 'n' roll accoutrements such as a drummer or guitarist, they often aroused violent reactions in their bewildered audiences.

Arriving in a sleeve full of slash-and-blood imagery, and sounding like a nightmarish netherworld, *Suicide's* technical and musical innovations make it sound almost contemporary today. "Cheree," lifted as a single, is a piece of sweet electronica, while the manic electro-billy of "Ghost Rider" proved to be a massive influence on the likes of Soft Cell and The Sisters of Mercy. Psycho-monologue "Frankie Teardrop" is unnervingly intense and features the most spine-chilling scream committed to vinyl, while the album concludes with the icy mechanized cellos and haunting vocals of "Che."

Suicide's harrowing vision of 1970s America has won praise from acts as diverse as Spiritualized, Nick Cave, and Bruce Springsteen. **CSh**

Iggy Pop
The Idiot (1977)

Label | RCA
Producer | David Bowie
Art Direction | Andrew Kent
Nationality | USA
Running Time | 38:36

In the eight years since The Stooges' debut album exploded into popular consciousness, Iggy Pop had burned brighter and fallen more spectacularly than any other artist of his generation. Sobering up from a self-imposed stint in a mental institution, Detroit's finest was aching for a second chance, but record labels were understandably wary of taking a chance on one of rock's greatest flakes. Enter, his fairy godmother, David Bowie.

Bowie, who had worked with Iggy Pop on 1974's *Raw Power*, pulled together a band and brought Pop to Berlin, where the Thin White Duke was mining a rich seam of inspiration. Out went the wild abandon of The Stooges' raucous guitar and rhythm section, and a more cerebral, subdued sound developed in the songs the pair co-wrote. Keyboards and bass featured heavily, leading Iggy to dub the sound "James Brown meets Kraftwerk."

The lyrics serve as redemption for Pop. Whether it is the wistful odes to his previous drug and sexual excesses on "Funtime," or the almost mawkish recollection of his ex-band buddies during "Dum Dum Boys" and its spoken-word intro ("How about Dave?" / "OD-ed on alcohol …" / "How about James?" / "He's going straight"), you sense *The Idiot* is a step out of Iggy's mental miasma.

But while his anguished howls and sinister baritone suggest a man pained, there is room for play too, as he apes Bowie on "China Girl" (subsequently a hit for the latter), and the anthem of the anti-Studio 54 brigade, "Nightclubbing." If music as rehab was always this successful, the clinics would soon be empty. **SJac**

Peter Gabriel
Peter Gabriel (I) (1977)

Label | Atco
Producer | Bob Ezrin
Art Direction | Hipgnosis
Nationality | UK
Running Time | 42:14

Two years after leaving Genesis in 1975, Peter Gabriel launched his solo career with the eclectic set of nine songs that comprise *Peter Gabriel I*. Free from the tension and constraints which had restricted his creative development, he unleashed an avalanche of bottled-up ideas and flamboyant arrangements.

"Moribund The Burgermeister" lays it on thick right from the outset. Deep jungle drums and warbly synths are just the first ingredients in the song's smorgasbord of prog-rock theatricality. Gabriel sings in a variety of vocal styles, including a rumbling growl as the evil Burgermeister. The song is strange but compelling.

Next up is "Solsbury Hill," Gabriel's first hit, and one of the best and most enduring songs of his long career. Anchored by a bouncy acoustic guitar melody, the song gives a tangible feeling of hope and endless possibility. Its lyrics touch upon Gabriel's liberating departure from Genesis when he sings, "I was feeling part of the scenery/I walked right out of the machinery."

Not surprisingly, all this diversity results in a few less interesting genre exercises, like the Randy Newman-esque barbershop ditty "Excuse Me" or the lengthy blues number "Waiting For The Big One." But the album closes strong with "Here Comes The Flood," a bombastic anthem that Gabriel would rework into an introspective piano ballad. Either way, it is a powerhouse.

This album was just the beginning of Peter Gabriel's legendary success as a solo artist—but all the signs were already in place for great things to come. **RM**

Television | Marquee Moon (1977)

Label | Elektra
Producer | Andy Johns • Tom Verlaine
Art Direction | Robert Mapplethorpe
Nationality | USA
Running Time | 45:48

Television were the least commercially successful major band to come out of the punk scene they helped to create at CBGB's. However, their finest hour, *Marquee Moon*, was as good, if not better, than contemporary seminal works such as Patti Smith's *Horses* (both of the albums sported a Robert Mapplethorpe front cover) and Talking Heads' debut.

After being shopped around to various labels, Television signed with Elektra in 1976 for their debut. The band was operating without original bassist Richard Hell, who left the group to start the Heartbreakers with Johnny Thunders. Bassist Fred Smith was a most fitting replacement, but his greatest contribution was in introducing Tom Verlaine to Andy Johns (Glyn Johns' brother), who knew enough not to tinker with the blurry jazz-punk sound honed at CBGB's.

The result was a guitar album like no other. Turning away from the bluesy sound that had dominated rock guitar since the 1960s, Television created a work that in its own way is every bit as sweeping as Led Zeppelin's finest offerings. Starting with the churning "See No Evil," Verlaine and Richard Lloyd tangle their stinging leads into spiraling celebrations of urban grime and street culture. The 11-minute title track led some to draw comparisons with hippie bands, but there was no flower power—just power—to be found in "Prove It" and "Guiding Light."

Marquee Moon received a lukewarm response from the public but was hailed by critics, including *NME*'s Nick Kent, who enthused that "the songs are some of the greatest ever." **JiH**

> "I'm not aware of drawing on anything. The thing I'm aware of when writing a song is talking to somebody."
>
> Tom Verlaine, 1981

Track Listing

▶	01	**See No Evil** (Verlaine)	3:53
▶	02	**Venus** (Verlaine)	3:51
	03	**Friction** (Verlaine)	4:44
▶	04	**Marquee Moon** (Verlaine)	10:40
	05	**Elevation** (Verlaine)	5:07
	06	**Guiding Light** (Verlaine)	5:35
▶	07	**Prove It** (Verlaine)	5:02
	08	**Torn Curtain** (Verlaine)	6:56

Meat Loaf | Bat Out Of Hell (1977)

Label | Epic
Producer | Todd Rundgren
Art Direction | Richard Corben
Nationality | USA
Running Time | 46:33

The combination of Meat Loaf (real name Marvin Lee Aday), a larger-than-life actor from Texas with an operatic voice, his surreal songwriting friend from New York, Jim Steinman, and producer Todd Rundgren resulted in an album that, despite never topping the UK album chart, resided there on and off for nearly ten years. Using backing musicians such as Roy Bittan and Max Weinberg from Bruce Springsteen's E Street Band plus members of Rundgren's group Utopia, *Bat Out Of Hell* included the three hit singles (highlighted right), which, much like most of the album, were of appropriately epic proportions (the fourth label which had been involved with the project).

Several extraordinary video clips promoted the album, and "Paradise By The Dashboard Light," a story of lust in a car, included a commentary by Phil Rizzuto on events, which he likened to a baseball game. The songs on the album were written by Steinman for his musical *Neverland*, a futuristic rock version of Peter Pan, in which Meat Loaf would play the part of Tinkerbell (when asked, he did not deny it, other than to say the character would be called Tink).

For some, the real stars of this brilliantly over-the-top extravaganza were the songs, the work of Jim Steinman's highly disturbed, but extremely imaginative mind; Steinman later wrote big hit songs for Bonnie Tyler ("Total Eclipse Of The Heart"), Barry Manilow ("Read' Em And Weep") and Celine Dion ("It's All Coming Back To Me Now"), among others. But those tracks have never inspired the affection aroused by this high-camp metal musical extravaganza. **JT**

> "Frenetic hard rock played at breakneck speed by ex-Ted Nugent lead singer Meat Loaf (rock's first 300-pound star since Leslie West)."
>
> John Swenson, 1979

Track Listing

▶	01	Bat Out Of Hell (Steinman)	9:51
▶	02	You Took The Words Right Out Of My Mouth (Hot Summer Night) (Steinman)	5:04
	03	Heaven Can Wait (Steinman)	4:41
	04	All Revved Up With No Place To Go (Steinman)	4:20
▶	05	Two Out Of Three Ain't Bad (Steinman)	5:25
	06	Paradise By The Dashboard Light (Steinman)	8:28
	07	For Crying Out Loud (Steinman)	8:44

Elvis Costello | My Aim Is True (1977)

Label | Stiff
Producer | Nick Lowe
Art Direction | Uncredited
Nationality | UK
Running Time | 32:57

My Aim Is True was recorded, before the recruitment of The Attractions, in six four-hour sessions in an eight-track demo studio in North London Costello now likens to a telephone booth. It says much for the standard of the songwriting that his debut stands up as a classic.

With future Doobie Brother John McFee laying down Byrds-like guitar licks, "Red Shoes" was an obvious single choice. It had been preceded by "Less Than Zero," inspired by British fascist leader Oswald Mosley, and the brilliant (and untypical) ballad "Alison," from whose lyric the album title had come. But it would take "Watching The Detectives" to make the necessary singles-chart mark at the very end of 1977. (Recorded with members of The Rumour, this track was included only on later reissues of the album.)

The overriding emotion of *My Aim Is True* was a lack of satisfaction, openly expressed by "Blame It On Cain" and "Mystery Dance," while "No Dancing" was a second song to equate dancing and sex. Producer Nick Lowe, whom Costello had followed round the country when Lowe was frontman with Brinsley Schwarz, added just enough studio fairydust to make this a "proper" record rather than another set of demos, but there was no doubting songs like "Mystery Dance," with its Jerry Lee Lewis vibe, would add a new dimension live when attacked by The Attractions.

Few of Costello's songs bar "Alison" have been covered, and this No. 14 album (in the UK), which retains its quirkiness today, suggests why. A heady combination of punk and quality songcraft, it remains unique even by Elvis' standards. **MH**

"I just *am* rock 'n' roll ...."

Elvis Costello, 2004

Track Listing		
01 **Welcome To The Working Week** (Costello)		1:23
02 **Miracle Man** (Costello)		3:33
03 **No Dancing** (Costello)		2:43
04 **Blame It On Cain** (Costello)		2:53
▶ 05 **Alison** (Costello)		3:25
06 **Sneaky Feelings** (Costello)		2:12
▶ 07 **(The Angels Wanna Wear My) Red Shoes** (Costello)		2:49
▶ 08 **Less Than Zero** (Costello)		3:18
▶ 09 **Mystery Dance** (Costello)		1:37
10 **Pay It Back** (Costello)		2:36
11 **I'm Not Angry** (Costello)		3:02
12 **Waiting For The End Of The World** (Costello)		3:26

Iggy Pop | Lust For Life (1977)

Label | RCA
Producer | Bewley Brothers
Art Direction | Andrew Kent • Mirage
Nationality | USA
Running Time | 41:00

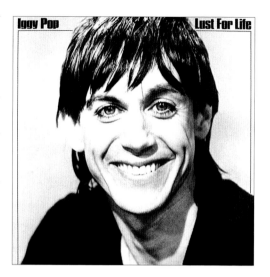

The year 1977 was Iggy Pop's annus mirabilis. He returned from well-documented mental and professional problems to produce two albums that any artist would be happy with over the course of a career, and he also saw punk—the movement he was often hailed as the "godfather" of—come to fruition.

Like *The Idiot*, *Lust For Life* was recorded in Berlin's Hansa Studios, just by the Wall, but where that album had been more contemplative and influenced by producer David Bowie, *Lust . . .* represented a return to the more punchy sound of The Stooges (although Bowie did play piano and contribute vocals). Where the former album had been the sound of a man feeling his way back in music, *Lust For Life* was far more confident.

From the ebullient drum intro of the title track, the songs are driven by the rhythm section of Hunt (drums) and Tony (bass) Sales, the second pair of brothers to fulfill this role for Pop. (The Sales brothers were later to reappear as half of Tin Machine, Bowie's late-Eighties stab at art-house hard rock, of whom the less said the better.) The band seamlessly cover a range of genres from wig-out stomp to bluesy rock.

Lyrically, *Lust For Life* is a revelation, as Pop uses the experience of his troubled years to great effect on "The Passenger," a jaunt through a metropolis of excesses which, while he may not be able to sample them any more himself, are picture-perfectly recalled. He is in even more caustic form with "Success," a tongue-in-cheek poke at his newfound position.

While a generation of young punks paid tribute to his previous work, Pop was moving up a notch. **SJac**

> "When I made *Lust For Life*, I really thought America was gonna rock to this motherfucker."
>
> Iggy Pop, 1999

Track Listing

▶	01	**Lust for Life** (Bowie • Pop)	5:13
	02	**Sixteen** (Pop)	2:26
	03	**Some Weird Sin** (Bowie • Pop)	3:42
▶	04	**The Passenger** (Gardiner • Pop)	4:44
	05	**Tonight** (Bowie • Pop)	3:39
▶	06	**Success** (Bowie • Pop)	4:25
	07	**Turn Blue** (Bowie • Lacey • Peace • Pop)	6:56
	08	**Neighborhood Threat** (Bowie • Gardiner • Pop)	3:25
	09	**Fall In Love With Me** (Bowie • Pop • Sales • Sales)	6:30

Ian Dury | New Boots And Panties!! (1977)

Label | Stiff
Producer | Peter Jenner • Laurie Latham • Rick Walton
Art Direction | Chris Gabrin
Nationality | UK
Running Time | 36:30

In England, punk's first wave was a heady period of one-chord wonders and two-minute heroes. It was a time for great singles, if not always great albums. Notable exceptions included The Clash's first, Elvis Costello's *My Aim Is True*, and this.

New Boots And Panties!! was like nothing else, then or now—a wild and raw, pithy, lewd, funny, cruel, and brilliantly coarse work of not-quite-punk in a sort of twisted British music hall tradition. Dury had a genius for words, cockney rhyming slang picked up or invented: "I had a love affair with Nina in the back of my Cortina/A seasoned up hyena could not have been more obscener/She took me to the cleaners and other misdemeanors/But I got right up between her rum and her Ribena" ("Billericay Dickie"). Most reissues of this album now include the trademark Dury anthem "Sex And Drugs And Rock And Roll."

At 35 Dury fitted in with punk just fine. He took no crap and he had grown up tough. Crippled by polio aged seven, he had no choice. Toward the end of his life, after being diagnosed with cancer ("I mustn't grumble, I've had a good crack"), he devoted much of his time to charitable causes.

The cover photo, incidentally, was taken outside the long-closed Axfords clothing store in Victoria, London. Standing next to Dury is his son Baxter who, at his father's wake in 2000, performed "My Old Man," which was originally written by Dury about his father. Ending with the line, "All the best mate from your son" it was an appropriately poignant moment in memory of a truly unique man. **RF**

> **"I bought a lot of brandy when I was courting Sandy took eight to make her randy."**
>
> Ian Dury, "Billericay Dickie," 1977

Track Listing

▶	01	**Wake Up And Make Love With Me** (Dury•Jankel)	4:19
▶	02	**Sweet Gene Vincent** (Dury•Jankel)	3:31
	03	**I'm Partial To Your Abracadabra** (Dury•Jankel)	3:12
▶	04	**My Old Man** (Dury•Nugent)	3:34
▶	05	**Billericay Dickie** (Dury•Nugent)	4:08
▶	06	**Clevor Trever** (Dury•Jankel)	4:54
	07	**If I Was With A Woman** (Dury•Jankel)	3:20
▶	08	**Blockheads** (Dury•Jankel)	3:27
	09	**Plaistow Patricia** (Dury•Nugent)	4:03
	10	**Blackmail Man** (Dury•Nugent)	2:02

Sex Pistols | Never Mind The Bollocks Here's The Sex Pistols (1977)

Label | Virgin
Producer | Bill Price • Chris Thomas
Art Direction | Jamie Reid
Nationality | UK
Running Time | 38:35

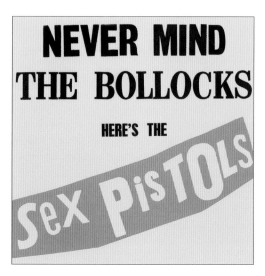

In a decade of social unrest, the grey façade of 1970s Britain was crumbling under high unemployment and apathy. The entire country seemed in a state of cold turkey, the optimism of the 1960s a distant memory. Along came a kick in the balls, literal as well as titular.

As soon as the Pistols played their first gigs, their notoriety was in danger of surpassing the music. This was a feeling intensified by Jamie Reid's luminous cover. With its iconic logo and use of an expletive, stores refused to stock it and a court case came to pass (dismissed after Richard Branson called in a linguistics professor to testify to the non-obscene origins of the word). With style about to overshadow substance, the marching steps that introduce "Holidays In The Sun" were a venomous reminder that beneath the artwork was an album that was about to alter our perception of music, fashion, and generational attitudes.

There is the ferocity of "Bodies," with its abortion-based theme, and Steve Jones' simple but devastatingly effective riff on "Pretty Vacant," which gave hope to useless guitarists everywhere.

"Anarchy In The UK," of course, is the album's most famous rallying cry but "God Save The Queen" matches it all the way as an epicenter of anger. Johnny Rotten bends and sculpts every note into a vituperative, royalty-aimed arrow. Few moments from popular music can ever match Rotten's guttural cry of "no future for you." Years of misery for the nation's youth were encapsulated right there and then. **AMa**

Track Listing

01	**Holidays In The Sun** (Cook•Jones•Rotten•Vicious)	3:20
▶ 02	**Bodies** (Cook•Jones•Rotten•Vicious)	3:02
03	**No Feelings** (Cook•Jones•Rotten•Vicious)	2:49
04	**Liar** (Cook•Jones•Rotten•Vicious)	2:40
▶ 05	**God Save The Queen** (Cook•Jones•Rotten•Vicious)	3:18
▶ 06	**Problems** (Cook•Jones•Rotten•Vicious)	4:10
07	**Seventeen** (Cook•Jones•Rotten•Vicious)	2:02
▶ 08	**Anarchy In The UK** (Cook•Jones•Rotten•Vicious)	3:31
09	**Submission** (Cook•Jones•Rotten•Vicious)	4:12
▶ 10	**Pretty Vacant** (Cook•Jones•Rotten•Vicious)	3:16
11	**New York** (Cook•Jones•Rotten•Vicious)	3:05
▶ 12	**EMI** (Cook•Jones•Rotten•Vicious)	3:10

Pere Ubu | The Modern Dance (1978)

Label | Blank
Producer | Ken Hamann • Pere Ubu
Art Direction | S. W. Taylor
Nationality | USA
Running Time | 36:36

If you found *Trout Mask Replica* a little hard to follow, it'd probably be best to skip this one. Pere Ubu's debut *The Modern Dance* is a daunting, sheer rock face of an album, seemingly well versed in and yet completely at odds with the logic of rock.

Once a sort of punk band—though arguably the link faded after the death of guitarist Peter Laughner—the Cleveland, Ohio-based Ubu stretched rock music to beyond breaking point with a unique configuration of rock riffs, musique concrète, and wayward, unintuitive song structures. Atop this were keyboard player Allen Ravenstine's inspired analog synthesizers and David Thomas' restless vocals.

As has been suggested elsewhere, they were perhaps to American new wave as Joy Division were to the British strain—rooted in rage and frustration but emotionally far more complex. But then, "Non-Alignment Pact" and "Life Stinks" demonstrate a whimsical humor that one doubts Ian Curtis would have thought to set to music.

Released on Mercury offshoot Blank Records in 1978, the album's overwhelming rush of sounds left listeners baffled but amazed. It still does. The breathtaking dynamics of the more conventional songs like "Street Waves" and "Laughing" have echoed through alternative rock ever since. Ravenstine's keyboards are exceptional. Most astonishing, though, is how successfully Ubu weave in expressionist and avant-garde touches without moving away from the "mainstream," which Thomas insists Ubu are. Instead of a guitar solo, "The Modern Dance" features what sounds like a shopping mall break—a really great shopping mall break. **MBe**

Track Listing

▶ 01	**Non–Alignment Pact** (Herman • Kraus Maimone • Ravenstine • Thomas)	3:19
▶ 02	**The Modern Dance** (Herman • Kraus Maimone • Ravenstine • Thomas)	3:30
▶ 03	**Laughing** (Herman • Kraus Maimone • Ravenstine • Thomas)	4:37
04	**Street Waves** (Herman • Kraus Maimone • Ravenstine • Thomas)	3:06
▶ 05	**Chinese Radiation** (Herman • Kraus Maimone • Ravenstine • Thomas)	3:29
▶ 06	**Life Stinks** (Laughner)	1:53
07	**Real World** (Herman • Kraus Maimone • Ravenstine • Thomas)	4:01
08	**Over My Head** (Herman • Kraus Maimone • Ravenstine • Thomas)	3:49
▶ 09	**Sentimental Journey** (Herman • Kraus Maimone • Ravenstine • Thomas)	6:08
10	**Humor Me** (Herman • Kraus Maimone • Ravenstine • Thomas)	2:44

Kraftwerk | The Man-Machine (1978)

Label | EMI
Producer | Ralf Hütter • Florian Schneider
Art Direction | Ralf Hütter • Florian Schneider
Nationality | Germany
Running Time | 36:14

Kraftwerk's living artwork acquired a new conceptual twist with *The Man-Machine*. While the iconic cover referenced Russian Modernist El Lissitzky, the songs addressed an increasingly automated world of urban alienation, space-age engineering, and the vacant glamor of fame.

A futuristic vision of humanity fused with technology informed both the funky title track and "The Robots," another hilarious commentary on the band's android-like image. For the album's launch, the Düsseldorf quartet even replaced themselves with lookalike robots that have since become fixtures of their live shows. The use of synthetic voices would come to dominate Kraftwerk's ever-evolving sound. But *The Man-Machine* also contains some of the band's most timeless compositions. Featuring Ralf Hütter's plaintive vocals, "Neon Lights" is an achingly romantic song while "The Model" is a sardonic satire on the beauty industry, so ahead of its time that it topped the UK charts three years after the album's release. This prophetic snapshot of celebrity culture became one of Kraftwerk's most recognizable calling cards, inspiring generations of artists—from 1980s techno-pop pioneers like the Human League, New Order, Pet Shop Boys, and Depeche Mode to the recent "electroclash" movement.

The achievement of *The Man-Machine* lies not only in its huge influence but also in its economy. Closer inspection of the tracks reveals minute variations in the repetitive percussive motifs and an almost classical interplay of synthesizer parts. With their seventh album, Kraftwerk proved the power of electronic music was not in musical sleight-of-hand but in scientific mastery of Zen-like simplicity. **SD**

> "We find posing very boring. The robots are so much better at it, they have more patience."
>
> Ralf Hütter, 1991

Track Listing

01	**Robots** (Bartos•Hütter•Schneider)		6:12
02	**Spacelab** (Bartos•Hütter)		5:55
▶ 03	**Metropolis** (Bartos•Hütter•Schneider)		6:02
▶ 04	**Model** (Bartos•Hütter•Schneider)		3:42
05	**Neon Lights** (Bartos•Hütter•Schneider)		8:55
▶ 06	**Man Machine** (Bartos•Hütter)		5:28

Blondie | Parallel Lines (1978)

Label | Chrysalis
Producer | Mike Chapman
Art Direction | Ramey Communications
Nationality | USA
Running Time | 41:03

September 1978: Israeli-Egyptian Accords are signed. More importantly, *Parallel Lines* is released! Bleach-blonde bombshell Debbie Harry and her quintet, led by guitarist/boyfriend Chris Stein, hurtled into the pop firmament with their third set. It topped the UK chart, reached No. 6 Stateside and sold by the million.

The sleeve—shot by the Goddard Brothers, from an idea by manager Peter Leeds—aped 1960s simplicity. Harry thought it stank, but its sophistication reflected the band's new sound—which melded their punk roots with Mike Chapman's glam-based commerciality. The producer "conducted us as we played," said Harry. "We weren't prepared for his expertise."

The result was new wave par excellence. Infectious harmonies complement Harry's vocals, by turns raucous and luscious. "Hanging On The Telephone," originally by The Nerves, is 2:22 of electrostatic verve, while "Fade Away (And Radiate)"—replete with Robert Fripp's psychedelic guitar—creates a dreamy canvas. The UK chart-topper "Sunday Girl" adds a layer of ice-cream sweetness and "Pretty Baby" is the cherry on top.

Hit-makers in Europe a year before they were accepted at home, Blondie finally struck the United States with "Heart Of Glass." Chapman took their James Brown-esque original and turned it into disco, much to the chagrin of drummer Clem Burke.

Recorded in a sweltering New York summer, *Parallel Lines* was worth the sweat. Billboard summarized the result as "witty, infectious rock" demonstrating "maturity in delivery, credibility, and vocal power." It remains a classic—much imitated, rarely equaled. **TJ**

"[Albums] were like trips. And I guess we're still tripping."

Debbie Harry, 2003

Track Listing		
▶ 01	**Hanging On The Telephone** (Lee)	2:22
▶ 02	**One Way Or Another** (Harrison·Harry)	3:35
▶ 03	**Picture This** (Destri·Harry·Stein)	2:56
04	**Fade Away (And Radiate)** (Stein)	4:02
05	**Pretty Baby** (Harry·Stein)	3:18
06	**I Know But I Don't Know** (Infante)	3:56
07	**11:59** (Destri)	3:20
08	**Will Anything Happen?** (Lee)	3:00
▶ 09	**Sunday Girl** (Stein)	3:05
▶ 10	**Heart Of Glass** (Harry·Stein)	5:50
11	**I'm Gonna Love You Too** (Mauldin·Petty·Sullivan)	2:06
12	**Just Go Away** (Harry)	3:33

Elis Regina
Vento De Maio (1978)

Label | EMI Hemisphere
Producer | Uncredited
Art Direction | Bill Smith
Nationality | Brazil
Running Time | 48:15

Brazil seems to produce an unending supply of dazzlingly talented female pop singers, but they cannot dissipate the long shadow cast by Elis Regina, whose impact reached far beyond South America.

A star by the age of 20, when she won a talent contest at a major music festival, Regina offered an emotionally extroverted alternative to the cool, minimalist style that came to fore with bossa nova (though some of her best-loved work was on her album of duets with Tom Jobim). Through her job hosting television shows designed to expose new musical talent, and her unerring ear for finding gifted young composers, Regina shepherded two generations of artists into the spotlight. When her life was cut short in 1982 by a drug overdose, she was on the verge of several new projects, including a collaboration with Milton Nascimento.

Vento De Maio (May Wind) captures Regina at the peak of her powers, phrasing with utter precision and rhythmic dexterity. Her voice is lithe and clear, and she sings with absolute control of tone and shading. The album's numerous highlights include her captivating, emotionally raw version of "O Trem Azul" (The Blue Train) and her wistful duet with Nascimento on "O Que Foi Feito Devera" (What Was Really Done). Regina displays her playful side on "Calcanhar De Aquiles" (Achilles Heel). Still, fans of her earlier, lighter work may be put off by the emotional intensity of the album, which also includes some arrangements that do not stand the test of time as well as her impassioned vocals. **AG**

Pere Ubu
Dub Housing (1978)

Label | Chrysalis
Producer | Ken Hamann • Pere Ubu
Art Direction | John Thompson
Nationality | USA
Running Time | 34:17

Having defined their own hard-rock proto-punk style, Pere Ubu had a goldmine they could have tapped for a few more years at least. Instead, brilliantly contrary, they created a whole new sound that, while still distinctively Ubu, showed them to be miles ahead of most of their peers. With its eerie two-color cover (high-rise residential towering over an old industrial building—surely a reference to the album title, if it only made sense!) and song titles that referenced movies, music, and catchphrases of days gone by, this was music of honesty and warmth that was simultaneously creepy and exciting.

The album came cheaply, quickly, and with a lot of spontaneity. Guitarist Tom Herman now says that the group "were just beginning to realize we wouldn't be commercial," but that nevertheless they hoped to herald a time when music would "move away from being product" and back to being expressions of artists' musical and emotional visions. We all remembered the excitement of the period of change from Neil Sedaka, Fabian, etc. to The Beatles, Moby Grape, Hendrix etc."

Every member makes a special contribution here, though it is, of course, David Thomas' unusual and distinctive vocals that stick in so many listeners' minds. On *Dub Housing*, Thomas' own whimsical musings finally grow wings: the rousing "Hey, hey, boozy sailors" refrain of "Caligari's Mirror," "Ubu Dance Party"—one of Thomas' many "walking" songs—and the irresistible flip-flopping of "Navvy." This is the biggest leap the group made, and very satisfying. **DN**

The Only Ones
The Only Ones (1978)

Elvis Costello
This Year's Model (1978)

Label | Columbia
Producer | Robert Ash
Art Direction | Nicolas Marchant
Nationality | UK
Running Time | 33:49

Label | Radar
Producer | Nick Lowe
Art Direction | Barney Bubbles
Nationality | UK
Running Time | 39:20

The London punk explosion of the late 1970s provided the impetus for street urchin poet Peter Perrett to take his dysfunctional pop songs out of the pub-rock ghetto and realign them within the burgeoning new movement.

The Sex Pistols, The Clash, and, in particular the Buzzcocks, were an inspiration, but while their peers tore strips from the rock establishment, The Only Ones recklessly clawed clumps from their heart. Perrett's flair for trembled lyrical gush, bolted onto his band's polished punk finesse, distinguished them in an era when most of their peers were scratching their heads over the whereabouts of the fourth chord.

Preferring flawed romance to fiery nihilism, Perrett peppered this 1978 debut with offerings of paranoid beauty. "Breaking Down" is dank, yet delicately pretty, while the choppy "Language Problem" owes much to the literate sneering of The Kinks' Ray Davies. The album peaks with that preposterously brilliant flourish of broken-hearted pop, "Another Girl, Another Planet," a lovelorn classic to rank with Pete Shelley's best.

It is saddening that The Only Ones failed to quell the inner band tensions that resulted in just three albums to their name and a messy breakup in 1981. Almost two decades of heroin-addicted anonymity followed for Perrett, foggying the productivity of this deeply gifted songwriter. Their legacy however, remains strong— R.E.M. are among those to cover "Another Girl, Another Planet," while Perrett resurfaced in 2004 to perform the hit with The Only Ones-indebted Libertines. **JJ**

When it comes to affairs of the heart, pop music loves black and white. Songs of love's wonders and the misery of rejection are everywhere, but the shades of gray between love and sex are not as popular. For a start, they do not make great choruses.

Not unless you are a self-proclaimed "bug-eyed monster from the Planet Guilt and Revenge"—in which case the heart's ugliness, all the hate and harm, the cruelty and betrayal, are fair game. Thus in 1978, Elvis Costello and his new band The Attractions arrived at London's Eden studios to tear viciously away at the fresh scabs of fractured relationships.

Surrounded by cold swirling organs and the heart-pulpating rhythm section of his new band, *This Year's Model* finds its protagonist at his most scathing. The icily staccato "(I Don't Want To Go To) Chelsea" sees Costello tearing into self-indulgent posers, while the choppy "The Beat" sees him wrestling with the guilt of a meaningless nightclub encounter.

The raging "Lipstick Vogue" is hypnotic, as Pete Thomas' athletic drumming shakes the whole song like a voodoo maraca, while "Pump It Up"'s woozy stomp reflects the desperate and frantic rush of an evening of "assisted insomnia," as Costello euphemistically put it.

Uncompromising and vicious, *This Year's Model* is no meaningless rant. It cuts deeply, and tellingly, straight to the bone. Revenge and guilt might scare off other songwriters, but among the anger and disgust Costello finds his truth. **PS**

The Jam | All Mod Cons (1978)

Label | Polydor
Producer | Vic Coppersmith-Heaven
Art Direction | The Jam • Bill Smith
Nationality | UK
Running Time | 37:28

Signed in February 1977, within 12 months The Jam were washed up. Their second LP, *The Modern World*, had been a disaster, and everybody involved acknowledged that Paul Weller's songwriting muse had disappeared. When their A&R man heard their new recordings, he bluntly told them to scrap it. They did, but the breathing space this created, and the pressure they were now under, forced Weller to take stock—with astonishing results.

The first fruit was a single, a double-A side comprising The Kinks' "David Watts" and a new song, "'A' Bomb In Wardour Street." It was followed by another single, "Down In The Tube Station At Midnight." The transformation was complete: instead of blustering observations and naive politics, Weller's songs were now mini-operas, inspired by The Who's "A Quick One While He's Away." Mindless violence in a punk club, being mugged on the way home: the songwriter and the listener were central to the action.

When the album arrived, the promise was realized. Twelve three-minute vignettes delivered with a crisp, sharp modernist attitude. Get in, do it, get out; no slack, no frills, no pretty stuff. And no sneering: Weller created characters, filled them in, made them breathe, then watched the modern world dump on them. The pop star on his uppers ("To Be Someone"), the aspirational suburban drone ("Mr. Clean"), a Walter Mittyesque dreamer ("Billy Hunt"), the poor sod drowning in consumerism ("In The Crowd"). There is even a tender love song, "English Rose," about which Weller was so embarrassed it was not mentioned on the LP sleeve. Well, he was only 20. **DH**

"The Jam are The Jam and they play Jam music ... "

Paul Weller, 1978

Track Listing

01	All Mod Cons (Weller)	1:15
▶ 02	To Be Someone (Didn't We Have A Nice Time) (Weller)	2:27
03	Mr. Clean (Weller)	3:26
04	David Watts (Davies)	2:56
▶ 05	English Rose (Weller)	2:47
▶ 06	In The Crowd (Weller)	5:36
07	Billy Hunt (Weller)	2:59
▶ 08	It's Too Bad (Weller)	2:34
09	Fly (Weller)	3:18
10	The Place I Love (Weller)	2:52
11	"A" Bomb In Wardour Street (Weller)	2:35
▶ 12	Down In The Tube Station At Midnight (Weller)	4:43

Joe Ely
Honky Tonk Masquerade (1978)

Label | MCA
Producer | Chip Young
Art Direction | Paul Milosevich
Nationality | USA
Running Time | 33:57

When The Clash invited Joe Ely to support them in concert in the late 1970s, few of their fans had any idea why a Texan country singer should be chosen to support the world's hottest rock band. Ely himself must have wondered at times, as punk audiences showered him in spit and beer, yet The Clash knew they were promoting a serious talent—Ely's *Honky Tonk Masquerade* is a country classic: *Rolling Stone* magazine even went so far as to call it one of the finest albums of the 1970s.

Ironically, Ely has never won more than a cult following, despite the excellence of his recordings. Today he is recognized as one of the godfathers of alt. country, yet he deserved a much wider audience. Raised in Lubbock, Texas, Ely formed The Flatlanders with friends Jimmie Dale Gilmore and Butch Hancock. The group loved Hank Williams and Bob Dylan, and set out to create a new form of country music, but Nashville was not ready for them. *Honky Tonk Masquerade*'s tough, soulful songs of love and deception are backed by a hot band and Ely has never sung better, from the classic country melancholy of the title track and the abject loneliness of "Tonight I Think I'm Gonna Go Downtown" to roof-raising rocker "Fingernails." It should have made him famous. Instead, he proved too individual for country radio and too country for rock radio.

Honky Tonk Masquerade gives you homespun, hard-won Texan wisdom and timeless American music. **GC**

The Adverts
Crossing The Red Sea With The Adverts (1978)

Label | Bright
Producer | John Leckie
Art Direction | Nicholas Deville
Nationality | UK
Running Time | 34:48

The Adverts were among the most original of first-wave UK punk bands. They boasted classic punk credentials: discovered playing at Covent Garden's Roxy Club; signed for their debut single to Stiff Records; toured with The Damned; barely competent musicianship; songs stuffed with social anger. Lacking an aggressive image, however, they were also the scene's misfits.

Fronted by singer T. V. Smith and his bass-playing partner Gaye Advert—one of the first female musicians in punk, and something of a pin-up in 1977—the band possessed a dynamic sound that mixed thrashing guitars with melodic, yearning choruses. Producer John Leckie would build on *Crossing*'s sound when later producing The Stone Roses and Radiohead. The Adverts built a considerable following across 1977 and their second single "Gary Gilmore's Eyes" garnered much tabloid outrage and a place in the UK Top Twenty.

Yet Smith did not deal in simple sensationalism, and his songs suggest a rebel with a cause: "No Time To Be 21," "One Chord Wonders," and "Bored Teenagers" all served as anthems for the blank generation.

Perhaps because of the timing—when many taste-setters were decrying punk as dead—*Crossing* . . . was not a success, gaining lukewarm reviews and only briefly entering the UK Top Forty. More than 20 years on it now sounds much fresher, less aggressive, and more soulful than many of its lauded contemporaries. **GC**

Big Star
Third / Sister Lovers (1978)

Label | Rykodisc
Producer | Jim Dickinson
Art Direction | Steven Jurgensmeyer
Nationality | USA
Running Time | 54:35

The hugely influential Big Star's third and final album *Third/Sister Lovers* is often described as stark, bleak, and depressing. Admittedly, the band's upbeat Beatles/Byrds jangle nearly gets smothered by narcoleptic offerings like "Big Black Car" and "Kangaroo," but it works.

Frustrated by years of creative disputes and commercial failure, Alex Chilton and the band sound like they pretty much do not give a damn anymore. The album is part love letter, part kiss-off. They sound looser than ever, but there is an edge of tension and bitter despair that producer Jim Dickinson draws out using just the right amount of echo and feedback.

"Thank You Friends" is a joyous, up-tempo rocker featuring a soaring backing chorus. "Stroke It Noel" sneaks up on you, with its halting melody and lovely string section. "Big Black Car" moves so slow it almost rolls to a stop but the effect is druggy and numbing—unlike "Holocaust," which is so emotionally devastating you may choose to crawl under your bed and never come out.

For years, *Third/Sister Lovers* never saw a proper release. Nobody could agree on the proper track sequence, so various bootleg versions floated around (hence the double title). However, thanks to the power-pop explosion fueled by bands like R.E.M. and The Replacements, the world finally caught up with Big Star. And so, in 1992, Rykodisc released the definitive version of *Third/Sister Lovers*. It is not to be missed. **RM**

The Residents
Duck Stab / Buster And Glen (1978)

Label | Ralph
Producer | The Residents
Art Direction | Pore No Graphics
Nationality | USA
Running Time | 34:46

Atonal honking, nonsense poetry, cartoon voices, and fairground riffs: The Residents possess a singularly unhinged compositional talent that allows them to fuse the weirdest sounds into an even weirder whole. Their members have always protected their identities by appearing in public in disguise, and while they have been tentatively identified, you are going to have to look elsewhere to break that spell. As conceptualists and willful obscurants, they have rarely been bettered.

This compilation of two EPs followed 1974's *Not Available* and 1976's *Third Reich 'n' Roll*, a collection of pop oldies covers released in a controversial Hitler sleeve. *Duck Stab/Buster And Glen* represented the evolution and emergence of their fantastic sonic mondo bizarro from the primordial noise soup of earlier releases. It is a spare sound, with chanting, high-pitched vocals, comedy accents, and effects.

"Constantinople" sets out on this wobbly tack, a repeated call to arms and classically absurd; "Sinister Exaggerator" and "Blue Rosebud" nail the Lewis Carroll vibe—"Your lichen-covered corpuscles are filthy as a fist"—and "Bach Is Dead" picks up the chanting refrain. The *Buster And Glen* side lurches on with the baton: "creaming eyes explode upon an apple pirate toad" gives a flavor of "Birthday Boy," and "Hello Skinny," were it not for its creepy lyrics, would sound like the score for a mystery on the Nile. Grotesque genius. **MBI**

Public Image Ltd. | Public Image (1978)

Label | Virgin
Producer | Public Image Limited
Art Direction | Terry Jones • Dennis Morris • PIL
Nationality | UK
Running Time | 39:55

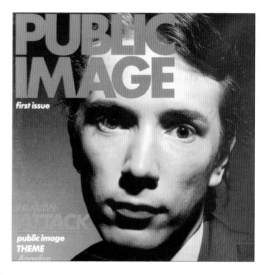

"Do you ever get the feeling you've been cheated?" whined John Lydon in January 1978, a kiss-off to the Sex Pistols. "Hello, Hello, Hello, Hello," he chuckled some months later, announcing the formation of Public Image Ltd. over the motorik drums and rumbling midnight bass of his new band's eponymous debut single. Reeling from the debris of the Pistols, feeling his identity under siege, Lydon fashioned the band as a scarring, honest expression of his deepest thoughts and fears.

But Public Image was more than just the post-Pistols project of punk's totemic figurehead; guitarist Keith Levene (an early Clash sideman), bassist Jah Wobble, and drummer Jim Walker sculpted a noise that pushed the primitivism of punk rock in an experimental direction, pointing new directions. Where "Public Image" seemed anthemic, opener "Theme," was anything but. A pulverizing dirge colored by turbulent hurricanes of distortion, its funereal stomp set the intensity bleeding into the red, Lydon's unearthly howls and screams of "I wish I could die!" illuminating the bleakness of post-punk England, Levene's guitar poisonously eloquent.

Catharsis was key: "Religion" (in two parts) railed at the Catholic Church, over a lascerating rut; "Annalisa" vented less specific frustrations over psychotic garage rock. "Fodderstompf," an extended sham-disco groove with a stinging, satiric chorus of "We only wanted to be loved," ended things on a controversially arch note. But while *Public Image* was certainly a dark, unwelcoming record, the vitality of its candor and its bloody-minded pursuit of a different future made it a highly influential— and still highly unsettling—album. **SC**

> ## "If I'll be destroyed by rock 'n' roll, I will make sure that rock 'n' roll will be destroyed with me."
>
> John Lydon, 1979

Track Listing

▶ 01	**Theme** (Public Image Limited)	9:11
02	**Religion I** (Public Image Limited)	1:26
03	**Religion II** (Public Image Limited)	5:53
▶ 04	**Annalisa** (Public Image Limited)	6:05
▶ 05	**Public Image** (Public Image Limited)	3:02
06	**Low Life** (Public Image Limited)	3:38
07	**Attack** (Public Image Limited)	2:55
08	**Fodderstompf** (Public Image Limited)	7:45

Magazine | Real Life (1978)

Label | Virgin
Producer | John Leckie
Art Direction | Linder
Nationality | UK
Running Time | 41:24

Were Magazine the band that dragged British punk rock into a new thinking dimension? Or were they just a dilution of the original energy into some kind of nerdy "maturity"? As *Real Life* shows, they were a bit of both, except they were only nerdy in the cool sense.

Howard Devoto had left the Buzzcocks in the very capable hands of Pete Shelley and Steve Diggle to create his own group: imagine the anticipation felt by anyone who cared about the future of rock music in June 1978 while putting the needle on track one, side one of *Real Life*.

Consider the various strange feelings they might have had as "Definitive Gaze" went through its paces, alternatively reflective, rambling, rousing—and Dave Formula's rather mellow, yet compelling, synthesizer figure throughout. The fact is, Magazine were not going to make things easy for anyone, though "Recoil" and "Shot By Both Sides" might satisfy the punkers, while "The Light Pours Out Of Me" is simply great pop rock. "Shot . . . " was, of course, based on an old Buzzcocks hook—Devoto thought he had taken it with him when he left but Shelley retained it for "Lipstick"; it works equally well for both songs. Which is not to say that Shelley's ghost haunts the album: tracks like the epic "Burst" (Devoto's only sole composition here) and the early "Motorcade"—co-written with keyboard player Bob Dickinson, who had left the band by this stage to be replaced by Dave Formula—show that Magazine was already developing a signature sound. Devoto's lyrics set a whole new style: jangled, edgy, and pointed. Very clever indeed. **DN**

> "I've always liked to produce records that have a great number of moods."
>
> Howard Devoto, 1978

Track Listing

▶	01	**Definitive Gaze** (Devoto·McGeoch)	4:25
	02	**My Tulpa** (Devoto·McGeoch)	4:47
	03	**Shot By Both Sides** (Devoto·Shelley)	4:01
	04	**Recoil** (Devoto·McGeoch)	2:50
▶	05	**Burst** (Devoto)	5:00
▶	06	**Motorcade** (Devoto·Dickinson)	5:41
	07	**The Great Beautician In The Sky** (Devoto·McGeoch)	4:56
▶	08	**The Light Pours Out Of Me** (Devoto·McGeoch·Shelley)	4:36
	09	**Parade** (Adamson·Devoto·Formula)	5.08

Bruce Springsteen
Darkness On The Edge Of Town (1978)

Label | Columbia
Producer | Jon Landau
Art Direction | Frank Stefanko
Nationality | USA
Running Time | 42:55

Funkadelic
One Nation Under A Groove (1978)

Label | Capitol
Producer | George Clinton
Art Direction | Ed Thrasher
Nationality | USA
Running Time | 52:45

Thanks to a legal dispute with former manager Mike Appel, Springsteen had three years to bask in the stellar success of *Born To Run*, and to contemplate its follow-up. The resulting album, *Darkness On The Edge Of Town*, is a very different beast from its predecessor.

Like Dylan before him, Springsteen withdrew from fame, moving to a farm in New Jersey so he could refocus on "life in the close confines of the small towns I grew up in." He wanted to "write about the stress and tension of my father's and mother's life that came with the difficulties of trying to make ends meet." (The album was originally to be called "American Madness," after a Frank Capra movie about the Depression.) Fatherhood is one of the album's themes ("Adam Raised A Cain"); struggle another ("Streets Of Fire," "Factory"). These are songs about small-town frustration, sometimes sexual ("Candy's Room"), sometimes social ("The Promised Land").

Being Bruce, the angst is tempered with romance, particularly for the road—many songs involve driving, either for escape, for thrills, or both—but musically, this is a much more subdued affair than *Born To Run*. Clarence Clemons' sax is rarely heard. Instead, Springsteen's guitar and Roy Bittan's measured, melancholic piano set the tone.

Uplifting, downbeat, bleak, and mad as hell, *Darkness…*, is a spellbinding B-movie epic to follow the blockbuster of *Born To Run*. **PW**

Funkadelic liberated rock music from the psychedelic bad trip taken by American West Coast bands at the turn of the 1960s and played a major part in transferring black sounds and rhythms to white rock music. The presence of several ex-members of James Brown's backing band, the JBs—including ace bassist and showman extraordinaire Bootsy Collins—was a vital ingredient in the heady Funkadelic brew.

The absurd sense of humor of Funkadelic's leader, George Clinton, manifested itself not only in his colorful, eccentric costumes and circus-like performances but also in the lyrics, track titles, and coherent artistic concept of the band's records. *One Nation …* was released at the time when the two projects led by Clinton—Parliament and Funkadelic, which assembled an almost identical lineup of musicians—merged into one coherent concept band named P-Funk. Members claimed that fans would enjoy transcendental experiences through listening to the music.

One Nation … was a platinum seller. Little wonder: there are pure funk numbers descended from James Brown and Sly Stone ("One Nation," "Grooveallegiance"), Hendrix-like guitars ("Who Says A Funk Band Can't Play Rock?!"), and avant-garde dance beats produced by synthesizers and other electronica. The title track, meanwhile, was a U.S. R&B No. 1 and became one of Funkadelic's biggest anthems. **AW-J**

Throbbing Gristle
D.O.A. Third And Final Report (1978)

Label | Industrial
Producer | Throbbing Gristle
Art Direction | Genesis P-Orridge
Nationality | UK
Running Time | 42:55

D.O.A. . . immediately attracted controversy—as was usually the case with Throbbing Gristle—over its provocative sleeve, featuring a photo Genesis P-Orridge had taken on holiday in Poland of a friend's daughter exposing her underwear whilst playing.

Its arty jokes like speeding up "United" to last a mere 16 seconds, also has some musical moments of splendor. P-Orridge's beautiful "Weeping" is as worthy as anything Jim Morrison or Ian Curtis composed, whilst Chris Carter's "AB/7A" is an excellent Kraftwerk-esque tribute to Abba. The harrowing "Hamburger Lady" utilizes synthesized psychedelic vacuum cleaner noise to create a dark clinical ambience around the story of a burn victim. "Death Threats," taken straight from TG's answering machine, is a fair representation of this notorious quartet's popularity back then. Their live sonic assault is documented by the pummeling "Walls of Sound." Throughout the record the band's lack of technical ability is compensated by their inventive use of electronics, field recording equipment, early computers, and primitive sampling techniques. Despite splitting acrimoniously in 1981, their tremendous influence has encompassed everyone from Depeche Mode and Nine Inch Nails to other electronic innovators such as Carl Craig and Andrew Weatherall, leading to a triumphant live reunion in 2004. Even so, this album can stand alone as a worthy legacy. **CSh**

Thin Lizzy
Live And Dangerous (1978)

Label | Vertigo
Producer | Tony Visconti
Art Direction | Chalkie Davies
Nationality | Ireland • UK • USA
Running Time | 76:36

As Israel pulled out of Lebanon in June 1978, Thin Lizzy pulled out the stops with one of music's greatest live albums. Its airbrushed quality caused critical murmurs; manager Chris O'Donnell claimed the recording was "75 percent live," with overdubs correcting Phil Lynott's overdriven bass and backing vocals from guitarists Scott Gorham and Brian Robertson. Producer Tony Visconti, told BBC Radio 1, "We erased everything except the drums . . . even the audience was done again in a very devious way . . . "Southbound" was recorded at a sound check, and I added a tape loop of an audience."

Fans were not bothered. The result is magical, and Vertigo's fears for a full-price double album were unfounded—it shipped 600,000 in the UK. Nominally recorded in London and Toronto, it is really a best of.

Full-throttle melodic rockers boast some of rock's most memorable riffs and choruses, tempered by moments of poignancy. The opening barrage hurtles from "Jailbreak," through the fiery "Emerald," singalong "Southbound" and definitive "Rosalie," to the delightful "Dancing In The Moonlight."

"Still In Love With You" has lighters swaying; "Cowboy Song" is a fantastic cascading romp, and "Suicide" a glorious story song. Then there are the anthems: "The Boys Are Back In Town" and "The Rocker."

As *NME* marveled, "It's a near perfect statement of intent by the best hard rock band in the world." **TJ**

Talking Heads
More Songs About Buildings And Food (1978)

Label | Sire
Producer | Brian Eno • Talking Heads
Art Direction | David Byrne
Nationality | UK • USA
Running Time | 41:32

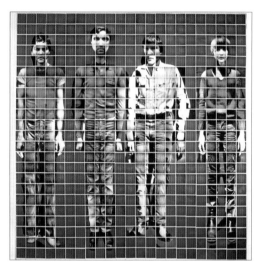

David Byrne and Brian Eno were a match made in art-school heaven. The Talking Heads debut, *Talking Heads: 77*, good as it was, showed the band needed focus and Eno provided that without whitewashing the Heads' wild eclecticism or undermining Byrne's individual voice.

The modernist cover design by Byrne, which shows the four Heads reconstructed on a grid, only hints at the experimental nature of the album. The singer's eccentric, smartly self-conscious lyrics remain at the forefront of "With Our Love" and "The Good Thing," but they have to elbow for space against the increasingly complex rhythm work of bassist Tina Weymouth and drummer Chris Frantz. If . . . *77* was primarily for your head, *More Songs About Buildings And Food* was equally intended for the feet as it boogied through classical minimalism, spacey disco, and African funk.

The frenzy of the band's earlier hit "Psycho Killer" would materialize again with the stunning opener, "Thank You For Sending Me An Angel," and Byrne absolutely twitches with nervous energy on "Artists Only." The tempo drops, and the intensity lifts, for a powerful reading of Al Green's "Take Me To The River," the band's first Top Forty single.

The album was a moderate commercial success. More significantly, it kicked off a four-year association between Eno and the Heads that culminated with 1980's *Remain In Light*. That run stands as the zenith of the band's career and equals the string of albums Eno recorded with David Bowie. **JiH**

"... you could express yourself with very minimal means."

David Byrne, 1997

Track Listing

▶	01	**Thank You For Sending Me An Angel** (Byrne)	2:11
	02	**With Our Love** (Byrne)	3:30
	03	**The Good Thing** (Byrne)	3:03
	04	**Warning Sign** (Byrne • Frantz)	3:55
▶	05	**The Girls Want To Be With The Girls** (Byrne)	2:37
	06	**Found a Job** (Byrne)	5:00
▶	07	**Artists Only** (Byrne • Zieve)	3:34
	08	**I'm Not In Love** (Byrne)	4:33
	09	**Stay Hungry** (Byrne • Frantz)	2:39
▶	10	**Take Me To The River** (Green • Hodges)	5:00
	11	**The Big Country** (Byrne)	5:30

Buzzcocks
Another Music In A Different Kitchen (1978)

Label | United Artists
Producer | Martin Rushent
Art Direction | Malcolm Garrett
Nationality | UK
Running Time | 35:43

Buzzcocks are rightly remembered as the poppiest of the original punk bands. But they were also the most sleekly modernist, and their debut album, from its elegant cover onward, shows a band who had not an ounce of spare fat. It is all speed, noise, and melody, with a healthy sense of adventure and a willingness from the start to move beyond punk's rules on lyrics and sound.

Another Music... is an album made by a band with a phantom fifth member: Howard Devoto had left the band to found Magazine by this point, but three of the songs he co-wrote are here. One area in which the band took punk principles more seriously than some was in their distaste for record company tactics—thus, most of the band's classic singles were left off the album (contrast with *Never Mind The Bollocks...*, which included all the hits). The exception is the wonderful "I Don't Mind," which a sulking band insisted was packaged as "Marketing Ploy."

But *Another Music...* does not need the chart hits, when it has wonders of its own such as "Fast Cars" ("I hate...") and "Sixteen." Pete Shelley's voice floats above the alternately chiming and grinding guitars. The audaciously undogmatic closing move is the seven-minute long "Moving Away From The Pulsebeat."

The unabashedly romantic saved punk from its insistence that love was off the agenda, and his vulnerable boyish Englishness opened doors that many others, from Morrissey and Edwyn Collins to Damon Albarn, would step through. **MMo**

> ## "It was...something you launched yourself into."
>
> Pete Shelley, 1999

Track Listing

▶	01	**Fast Cars** (Devoto·Diggle·Shelley)	2:26
	02	**No Reply** (Shelley)	2:16
	03	**You Tear Me Up** (Devoto·Shelley)	2:28
	04	**Get On Your Own** (Shelley)	2:27
▶	05	**Love Battery** (Devoto·Shelley)	2:09
	06	**Sixteen** (Shelley)	3:38
▶	07	**I Don't Mind** (Shelley)	2:18
	08	**Fiction Romance** (Shelley)	4:28
▶	09	**Autonomy** (Diggle)	3:43
	10	**I Need** (Diggle·Shelley)	2:44
	11	**Moving Away From The Pulsebeat** (Shelley)	7:06

Van Halen | Van Halen (1978)

Label | Warner Bros.
Producer | Ted Templeman
Art Direction | Dave Bhang
Nationality | USA
Running Time | 35:22

History trashed in half an hour? With the skimpiest running time since the Fab Four's first forays, the new Led Zeppelin rewrote the rulebook. Once hard rock lumbered; now it leaped.

Frontman David Lee Roth, bassist Michael Anthony, drummer Alex Van Halen, and his six-string sibling Eddie were found in L.A. in 1976 by Kiss monster Gene Simmons. He put them to work on demos—including songs for his own band's *Love Gun*—and fruitlessly tried to recruit Eddie.

But Kiss, like every other hard rock band, were to be eclipsed by Van Halen—and nothing explains this better than their astonishing debut.

From the car horns that usher in "Runnin' with the Devil" to the pummeling "On Fire," it is an unbeatable blend of sonic swagger and lyrical lust. So what are the highlight tracks? Try "Eruption," an Eddie showcase rated second only to "Stairway To Heaven" by *Guitar World* magazine. Or "You Really Got Me," a Kinks cover acclaimed by Ray Davies as superior to his original version. Or "Ain't Talkin' 'bout Love," sampled by 2 Live Crew and Apollo 440 (while "Jamie's Cryin'" supplied the riff for Tone Loc's 1988 smash "Wild Thing"). Or "Ice Cream Man," written by bluesman John Brim, but with added flair courtesy of Roth.

In 1999, the RIAA certified *Van Halen* diamond, for ten million U.S. sales. Purchasers doubtless included every perpetrator of Eighties "hair metal," but don't damn them. They sinned but, lo, it was great. As Roth put it, "We sold hope and faith and a jubilation right on par with a lot of your favorite religions." **BM**

Track Listing

▶ 01 **Runnin' With The Devil**
(Anthony • Roth • A. Van Halen • E. Van Halen)   3:35

02 **Eruption** (Anthony • Roth • A. Van Halen
E. Van Halen)   1:43

03 **You Really Got Me** (Davies)   2:38

▶ 04 **Ain't Talkin' 'bout Love**
(Anthony • Roth • A. Van Halen • E. Van Halen)   3:50

05 **I'm The One**
(Anthony • Roth • A. Van Halen • E. Van Halen)   3:47

▶ 06 **Jamie's Cryin'**
(Anthony • Roth • A. Van Halen • E. Van Halen)   3:30

07 **Atomic Punk**
(Anthony • Roth • A. Van Halen • E. Van Halen)   3:02

08 **Feel Your Love Tonight**
(Anthony • Roth • A. Van Halen • E. Van Halen)   3:43

09 **Little Dreamer**
(Anthony • Roth • A. Van Halen • E. Van Halen)   3:23

10 **Ice Cream Man** (Brim)   3:20

11 **On Fire**
(Anthony • Roth • A. Van Halen • E. Van Halen)   3:01

Willie Colón And Ruben Bládes | Siembra (1978)

Label | Fania
Producer | Willie Colón
Art Direction | Irene Perlicz
Nationality | USA
Running Time | 42:18

This essential release was the result of a collaboration between salsa titans Willie Colón, a New York City trombonist/bandleader, and Ruben Bládes, a singer/songwriter/actor from Panama. Colón had been a salsa pioneer and his collaborations with Hector Lavoe and Celia Cruz are milestones, but with Bládes he practiced music making with a social conscience.

The themes are wide ranging, from shedding light on street realities to the vanities of the upwardly mobile young Latino. But the album also includes songs to soothe the homesick immigrant soul and to offer uplifting messages of hope for a better future. "Plástico" pulsates with a thumping funk bassline, while "Pedro Navaja," a "Mack The Knife" spinoff, offers straightahead mambo coupled with atmospheric street sounds; both are urban epics. Bládes croons in a rich, resonate tenor, strong and expressive. A storyteller who spontaneously improvises verses, the acclaimed artist is at the top of his game here.

Colón employed a potent band of New York City's finest musicians, and the hook-friendly choruses helped to give this album legs across the Spanish-speaking world. In the late 1970s *Siembra* (meaning "to plant") served as an anthem for a generation of college students, who found inspiration in its positive message of Latino pride. But it also became a soundtrack for struggles of peace and justice to the many countries in Central and Latin America who were enmeshed in civil war and attendant conflicts at the time.

Strong narratives complemented by stellar playing—little wonder this was also salsa's first million seller. **JCV**

> "These songs were telling stories that were familiar to people in Latin America ... everybody identified with these songs."

Ruben Bládes, 1996

Track Listing		
▶ 01 **Plástico** (Blades)		6:37
02 **Buscando Guayaba** (Blades)		5:43
▶ 03 **Pedro Navaja** (Blades)		7:21
04 **Maria Lionza** (Blades)		5:27
05 **Ojos** (Ortiz)		4:50
06 **Dime** (Blades)		6:59
▶ 07 **Siembra** (Blades)		5:21

The Cars | The Cars (1978)

Label | Elektra
Producer | Roy Thomas Baker
Art Direction | Ron Coro
Nationality | USA
Running Time | 35:40

The Cars pulled in at the dawn of that often justifiably maligned genre known as new wave with songwriting acumen, superlative musicianship, and a unique visual "appeal" equaled at the time only by Blondie. With this, their debut LP, they created a gold-plated pop masterpiece dressed up in new wave duds.

The listener, beckoned to on the cover by a deliriously happy model giddily losing control at the wheel of a car (clever, boys), is swept up by the opening mission statement "Good Times Roll"; from there the album hurtles from one new wave gem to the next. Though The Cars would have more chart success with later singles, the track listing on the debut reads like a best-of collection. Radio hits like "My Best Friend's Girl" and "Just What I Needed" sit next to fan favorites like "Bye Bye Love" and "All Mixed Up." Ric Ocasek's songs run the gamut, shifting moods and tempos from the infectious pop of "My Best Friend's Girl" to weirder-sounding ditties like "I'm In Touch With Your World," which employs a variety of sound effects that would be at home in a *Looney Tunes* cartoon, and the 'luded out crawl of "Moving In Stereo." Guitarist Elliot Easton is the unsung hero, littering songs like "Bye Bye Love" with staggeringly good fills. Little wonder that this million-selling album went on to spend 139 weeks on the U.S. Billboard charts.

A superbly stylized mash of influences (from Velvet Underground to David Bowie) filtered through unabashed radio-ready pop, The Cars' debut is an introductory handbook to new wave that sounds great nearly three decades later. **JW**

> ## "I never wanted to really be a musician and I don't care about musicianship that much. I care about style and content."
>
> Ric Ocasek, 1997

Track Listing

▶	01	**Good Times Roll** (Ocasek)	3:44
▶	02	**My Best Friend's Girl** (Ocasek)	3:44
▶	03	**Just What I Needed** (Ocasek)	3:44
	04	**I'm In Touch With Your World** (Ocasek)	3:31
	05	**Don't Cha Stop** (Ocasek)	3:01
▶	06	**You're All I've Got Tonight** (Ocasek)	4:13
▶	07	**Bye Bye Love** (Ocasek)	4:14
▶	08	**Moving In Stereo** (Hawkes·Ocasek)	5:15
	09	**All Mixed Up** (Ocasek)	4:14

Devo | Q: Are We Not Men? A: We Are Devo! (1978)

Label | Warner Bros.
Producer | Brian Eno
Art Direction | Erik Munsön
Nationality | USA
Running Time | 34:23

In 1970s pop music, synthesizers were heard largely on disco records and in the elaborate studio productions of progressive rock acts like Yes. Certainly, they were not a staple of punk performances, although Kraftwerk made expert use of the instruments as they explored punkish themes of alienation in their proto-techno music.

Alienation was the stock in trade of Devo, the Ohio quintet whose explosive, Brian Eno-produced 1978 debut, *Q: Are We Not Men? A: We Are Devo!*, embellished punk's big guitar sound with harsh, metallic synthesizers. To be certain, they made relatively sparing use of them on *Q: Are We Not Men?*, especially compared to the oceans of synths that typified subsequent efforts like 1980's *Freedom Of Choice*.

But Devo's four studio releases between 1978 and 1981 were linked thematically. The group, former art students and deft satirists, cultivated a despairing if vague philosophy—thanks to dubious modern innovations like space exploration and fast food, civilization was not evolving but rather "de-volving" (hence the name). Happily, Devo never let sociological theory get in the way of great music, and little of this ideology is spelled out explicitly on *Q: Are We Not Men?*, a marvelous, rocking set of funny, quirky songs about topics such as mongoloids and paranoia.

Interestingly, the album's most distinctive and famous song is a cover of "Satisfaction." But while the Stones' version is swaggering and sexy, when Devo frontman Mark Mothersbaugh sings, the song becomes an anxious, frenetic cri de coeur about feeling overwhelmed in the face of an oppressive consumer culture. **KB**

" ... Beyond rock 'n' roll."

Mark Mothersbaugh, 1997

Track Listing

▶	01	**Uncontrollable Urge** (M. Mothersbaugh)	3:09
▶	02	**Satisfaction (I Can't Get No)** (Jagger • Richards)	2:38
	03	**Praying Hands** (Casale • M. Mothersbaugh)	2:48
▶	04	**Space Junk** (Casale • M. Mothersbaugh)	2:14
▶	05	**Mongoloid** (Casale)	3:42
▶	06	**Jocko Homo** (M. Mothersbaugh)	3:39
	07	**Too Much Paranoias** (M. Mothersbaugh)	1:55
	08	**Gut Feeling** (Casale • M. Mothersbaugh)	4:54
	09	**Slap Your Mammy** (Casale)	0:51
	10	**Come Back Jonee** (Casale • M. Mothersbaugh)	2:53
	11	**Sloppy (I Saw My Baby Gettin')** (Casale B. Mothersbaugh • M. Mothersbaugh • Jacket)	2:36
	12	**Shrivel Up** (Casale • M. Mothersbaugh)	3:04

Dire Straits | Dire Straits (1978)

Label | Vertigo
Producer | Muff Winwood
Art Direction | Alan Schmidt
Nationality | UK
Running Time | 41:47

Dire Straits, and in particular lead vocalist, lead guitarist, and songwriter Mark Knopfler, an ex-journalist and schoolteacher, were not punks, and the release of this album in 1978, when punk and new wave (and disco, for that matter) were dominating the British media and charts, was brave to say the least.

Owing more to blues-influenced U.S. acts such as J. J. Cale than to the Sex Pistols, the quartet (completed by Knopfler's younger brother, social worker David, on rhythm guitar, sociology undergraduate John Illsley on bass, and Welsh drummer Pick Withers) were initially ignored (with the notable exception of London broadcaster Charlie Gillett, who played them on his local show), and when the first single, "Sultans Of Swing," was released in the UK in early 1978, it made little impression. It was not until Warner Bros., to whom the group were signed in the United States, made this song about a band of elderly musicians into a Top Five hit, that Britain realized its mistake.

Apart from that single, this album provided early examples of Mark Knopfler's storytelling abilities and highly impressive guitar work, with "Down To The Waterline," "In The Gallery" (about England's north-east, where Knopfler grew up), and "Wild West End" (about being in London). The album was finally released in Britain six months after the single, making the Top Five; in the United States it made the Top Three and was certified double platinum.

From those hesitant beginnings, Dire Straits were to go on to become, arguably, the biggest band in the world in the early 1980s. **JT**

> ## "From the start, Dire Straits was a classic case of wrong time, wrong place."
>
> Charlie Gillett, 1996

Track Listing

▶	01	**Down To The Waterline** (Knopfler)	4:02
▶	02	**Water Of Love** (Knopfler)	5:26
	03	**Setting Me Up** (Knopfler)	3:19
▶	04	**Six Blade Knife** (Knopfler)	4:13
	05	**Southbound Again** (Knopfler)	2:59
▶	06	**Sultans Of Swing** (Knopfler)	5:48
	07	**In The Gallery** (Knopfler)	6:16
	08	**Wild West End** (Knopfler)	4:41
	09	**Lions** (Knopfler)	5:03

The Saints
Eternally Yours (1978)

Label | EMI
Producer | Chris Bailey • Ed Kuepper
Art Direction | Cream
Nationality | Australia
Running Time | 35:22

The Saints were fish out of water in 1977 London when they wrote and recorded their second album at Roundhouse and Wessex studios that October.

The great punk wave had swept them all the way from Brisbane to London and they had been signed to EMI on the strength of their punky sound, but they hated the conformist nature and anti-historical approach of the London punks. A lot of this hatred manifests in lyrics that now read like the rantings of a cranky hippie (Chris Bailey rails against corporations, consumerism, television culture: "I ain't no puppet for no capital gain," he claims) but that come out vividly heartfelt and potent on record.

The music—thanks in part to Ivor Kay's empathetic drumming—is fast, furious, and pure gold. Genius moves include the use of a brass section, taking "Know Your Product," for instance, from mere brilliance to another plane entirely. Bailey's caustic vocal interplay with Ed Kuepper in "Private Affair," the breathless and savage "No, Your Product" and, of course, the group's only Top Forty single, "This Perfect Day"—are all examples of the greatness of *Eternally Yours*.

If there are any throwaway tracks, they are the glib "Orstralia" and the comedic "International Robots." Think of them as palate cleansers. The first three Saints records were collected on the 2004 boxed set *All Times Through Paradise*, which includes demo versions, recorded in September 1977, of almost all the songs from *Eternally Yours*. **DN**

Marvin Gaye
Here, My Dear (1978)

Label | Motown
Producer | Delta Ashby • Marvin Gaye
Art Direction | Kosh
Nationality | USA
Running Time | 73:18

From *Rumours* to *Achtung Baby*, magical music has been conjured from rotting relationships, and pain translated into beauty. But nowhere is it more explicitly done than on *Here, My Dear*.

In contempt of court for failing to pay alimony, Gaye agreed to sign over the advance for an album, and part of its earnings, to Anna Gordy—his ex-wife and, inconveniently, the sister of Motown boss Berry Gordy. Grimly fascinated by his own misfortune, Gaye conceived a cycle that documented the disintegration of his marriage. The album's gatefold sleeve opened to reveal love as a Monopoly-esque board game called "Judgment," packed with daggers poised above hearts and similar ill omens.

Here, My Dear retains the smooth, spooky soul of its predecessors *Let's Get It On* and *I Want You*. The three most memorable songs feature early; thereafter, it is a dreamily uneasy ride. "Sweet, quiet, seductive, and," wrote *Village Voice* critic Robert Christgau, "slightly boring." Jamiroquai's Jay Kay describes it as "the same song being subtly changed ten different ways."

At war with his label, his musicians, and his own demons, Gaye knew the album—his last for three years—was doomed. Accordingly, it was received frostily by critics, customers, and—naturally—Anna Gordy. Indeed, it was deleted only a few years after its release. Today, however, it's a rare and compelling example of artistic nakedness that does not make you want to bellow "get over it!" at a sulking singer. **BM**

Willie Nelson
Stardust (1978)

Label | Columbia
Producer | Booker T. Jones
Art Direction | Susanna Clark
Nationality | USA
Running Time | 36:22

Chic
C'est Chic (1978)

Label | Atlantic
Producer | B. Edwards • N. Rodgers
Art Direction | Bob Defrin
Nationality | USA
Running Time | 41:23

After the success of 1975's quietly iconoclastic *The Red Headed Stranger*, Willie Nelson's bosses at Columbia Records were probably inclined to let him try just about anything. Still, the concept of *Stardust* must have made them nervous—why would the honky-tonker release a lavishly produced collection of Tin Pan Alley standards?

But if *Red Headed Stranger* confirmed that Nelson was one of the great country artists of his day, *Stardust* sealed his reputation as one of the best and most distinctive American singers of any day. Often imitated, even mocked, but seldom matched, Nelson's singing was already rather more jazzy than that of his colleagues in Nashville, and *Stardust* let him take on the idiom of jazz singing directly. On the title cut, Nelson sings sometimes a little ahead, sometimes well behind the beat, and plucks notes seemingly from nowhere.

Nelson broke new commercial ground with *Stardust*, which stayed on the U.S. Billboard album chart for two years and, improbably enough, with tunes by pop songsters like Hoagy Carmichael and Irving Berlin on the country charts. If *The Red Headed Stranger* made Nelson a country legend, *Stardust* made him a household name. A movie career followed, as well as more country hits, and Nelson later continued his genre experiments with forays into blues and gospel. But a quarter century later, Nelson was still interpreting and reinterpreting tunes from *Stardust* at his concerts, which affirms that with Willie Nelson, there is no country or pop, just Willie Nelson songs. **KB**

Modern dance music is indebted to Chic. Influenced by Roxy Music and Kiss as much as R&B, Nile Rodgers (guitar), Bernard Edwards (bass), and Tony Thompson (drums) were the disco era's key band: musicians who created a fluid, hypnotic groove that resonates today.

C'est Chic was their second and biggest LP, propelled by two Top Ten U.S. singles. "I Want Your Love" is an elegant study in heartbreak, its four-note signature echoed by horns, bells, strings, and yearning female vocals, while the core trio worked their magic in support. Joel Brodsky's cover portrait may have suggested a bunch of upwardly mobile go-getters, but there was fervent emotion beneath that cool exterior.

Rodgers' clipped, chicken-scratch riffing on euphoric chart-topper "Le Freak" anticipated the post-punk guitar style that hordes continue to pilfer today, while Edwards' chunky bassline was ripe for sampling by the nascent rap scene. The remaining tracks showed an extraordinary range and confidence, encompassing twilight balladry ("At Last I Am Free"), party-hearty exhortations ("Chic Cheer"), cinematic instrumentalism ("Savoir Faire"), and sheer eccentricity ("[Funny] Bone").

Sadly, Chic's next album, the exquisitely melancholy *Risqué*, was their last major success. America's cultural climate had grown hostile, fueled by the poisonous—and implicitly racist—"disco sucks" campaign. Ironically, the same people who staged mass burnings of Chic records would later enjoy disco hits by Queen, The Rolling Stones, Rod Stewart, and The Clash. **MA**

X-Ray Spex | Germ Free Adolescents (1978)

Label | Virgin
Producer | Falcon Stuart
Art Direction | Cooke Key • Trevor Key • Falcon Stuart
Nationality | UK
Running Time | 35:46

When *Germ Free Adolescents* was released in November 1978, X-Ray Spex looked and sounded like a great punk rock group with a distinctive new sound combining elements of Patti Smith and the Pistols and undeniable style—not to mention the not-so-secret weapon of Poly Styrene, aka Marion Elliott. They had already had a minor hit with "Oh Bondage, Up Yours" (included only on reissues of this album), and this release was to spawn four more singles.

However the group's firing of the redoubtable Lora Logic after that single apparently because Styrene did not think two women should be in a band together, and the undeniable influence of Logic on the sax lines of her replacement, Steve "Rudi" Thompson, pointed to trouble brewing. Yet Styrene's lyrics, insisting that people be genuine and candid in a world of unreality, are searingly passionate and convincing.

"Identity" and "I Am A Poseur" are two stand-out tracks, but the whole record is thunderingly radical and real; production is straightforward and merely delivers the sound of a scorching, hectic band unto the listener. In fact, the only dated element of the album is the cover art, showing the group trying to escape from test tubes, and the themes of cold war paranoia, yet overall it remains a truly lovable record.

Styrene was soon to renounce punk altogether—after a religious vision, she made a couple of mellow albums under her own name then retreated into Krishna studies, where ironically she was reacquainted with Logic, another devotee—all of which suggests she genuinely owned the angst expressed herein. **DN**

> "It soon got spoilt by adults, but while it was our thing I had a good time."
>
> Poly Styrene, 2001

Track Listing

▶ 01	**Art–I–Ficial** (Styrene)	3:21
02	**Obsessed With You** (Styrene)	2:26
03	**Warrior In Woolworths** (Styrene)	3:04
04	**Let's Submerge** (Styrene)	3:23
05	**I Can't Do Anything** (Styrene)	2:55
▶ 06	**Identity** (Styrene)	2:22
07	**Genetic Engineering** (Styrene)	2:45
08	**I Live Off You** (Styrene)	2:06
▶ 09	**I Am A Poseur** (Styrene)	2:29
10	**Germ Free Adolescents** (Styrene)	3:09
▶ 11	**Plastic Bag** (Styrene)	4:56
12	**The Day The World Turned Day–Glo** (Styrene)	2:50

Brian Eno | Ambient 1: Music For Airports (1978)

Label | EG
Producer | Brian Eno
Art Direction | Brian Eno
Nationality | UK
Running Time | 48:33

If the first three solo records Brian Eno released in the early 1970s represented a left turn from his work with Roxy Music, then 1975's *Discreet Music* was virtually a lift-off into space. The quartet of drifting, peculiarly hypnotic soundscapes, three of them reinventions of Pachelbel's "Canon In D Major," marked his first forays into what he called ambient music. The idea was a progression of sorts from French composer Erik Satie's creation in 1920 of musique d'ameublement: literally, "furniture music," designed less to be listened to and more to be occasionally overheard. *Discreet Music* was conceived during an extended hospital visit; for its follow-up, Eno produced this set, inspired by a similarly sterile environment.

"It must be as ignorable as it is interesting," wrote Eno on the liner notes to *Ambient 1: Music For Airports*. As a manifesto, it could scarcely have been more fully realized. The four shapeless works drift glacially in and out of focus: a ghostly choir, some muted brass, countless piano teardrops (played on "1/1" by Robert Wyatt). And yet despite the lack of structure, it is never displeasing, due chiefly to its astutely grounded tonality.

Some critics called it boring, missing the point by a mile. Undeterred, Eno followed *Ambient 1: Music For Aiports* with numerous other records of a similar bent, most notably 1982's mysterious, enveloping *Ambient 4: On Land*, and the gorgeously ethereal *Apollo: Atmospheres And Soundtracks* from 1983. However, it is as a producer that he found greater renown: famously working with *Apollo* collaborator Daniel Lanois on U2's *The Joshua Tree*. **WF-J**

> "On the one hand, the music sounds to me very emotional, but the emotions are confused, they're not straightforward: in things that are very up-tempo and frenzied, there's nearly always a melancholy edge."

Brian Eno, 1979

Track Listing		
▶ 01	**1/1** (Davies·Eno·Wyatt)	16:39
02	**2/1** (Eno)	8:25
03	**1/2** (Eno)	11:36
04	**2/2** (Eno)	9:38

Siouxsie And The Banshees | The Scream (1978)

Label | Polydor
Producer | Steve Lillywhite • Siouxsie And The Banshees
Art Direction | Siouxsie And The Banshees
Nationality | UK
Running Time | 38:57

Bridging the gap between punk and goth rock, *The Scream* contains music that combines the DIY ethos of the former with the latter's sense of dark drama.

In the late 1970s, Sioux's sharply cut black hair and pale makeup was rapidly making her a style icon, so it is perhaps surprising that the cover features not her, but eerily beautiful shots of anonymous underwater swimmers. The intended message may have been that this was definitely an all-round quartet collaboration.

On the track "Carcass," the tight interplay between Steve Severin's buoyant bass guitar and Kenny Morris' pounding drum work stand out even more strikingly than Sioux's punchy vocals. This is uncomplicated playing executed smartly and performed with passion. "Helter Skelter," *The Scream*'s sole cover, is given an even more feverish reading than The Beatles' original, while guitarist John McKay's screechy guitar style is on full sonic display on "Metal Postcard (Mittageisen)." The Banshees had already moved on from straightforward punk anger, to deal with more complex areas, such as psychological trauma (on "Suburban Relapse" and "Jigsaw Feeling").

On the final two tracks, McKay breaks out his sax and applies appropriate wails to the Banshee mix. The album closes with the dramatic "Switch," a nearly seven-minute micro-epic that unfolds both lyrically and musically like a compelling novella.

The Scream was a declaration of messy elegance for a band that would further explore both messiness and an elegant darkness throughout its successful and influential career. **YK**

> "Punk nostalgia seems to be every year. I think people keep going back to it because it's a thing that can't be repeated."
>
> Siouxsie Sioux, 2004

Track Listing

01	**Pure** (McKay•Morris•Severin•Sioux)		1:50
02	**Jigsaw Feeling** (McKay•Severin)		4:39
▶ 03	**Overground** (McKay•Severin)		3:50
▶ 04	**Carcass** (Fenton•Severin•Sioux)		3:49
▶ 05	**Helter Skelter** (Lennon•McCartney)		3:46
06	**Mirage** (McKay•Severin)		2:50
07	**Metal Postcard (Mittageisen)** (McKay•Sioux)		4:14
▶ 08	**Nicotine Stain** (Severin•Sioux)		2:58
09	**Suburban Relapse** (McKay•Sioux)		4:12
10	**Switch** (McKay•Sioux)		6:49

AC/DC | Highway To Hell (1979)

Label | Albert Productions
Producer | Robert John Lange
Art Direction | Bob Defrin
Nationality | Australia • UK
Running Time | 41:48

Whilst AC/DC's music could be criticized for its technical simplicity, to this day they remain one of the most influential groups in rock 'n' roll. Their rough, ballsy style epitomizes the very essence of rock. Combined with blues-influenced chord structures and a perfect balance of power and restraint in equal measures, few heavy rock fans can resist their basic, working-class appeal. Based around the strong guitar riffs of brothers Malcolm and Angus Young (the man who earned the respect of the metal fraternity worldwide wearing a school uniform and tie on stage), simplistic drum rhythms, and the tough vocal styling of Bon Scott, AC/DC's music is infectious.

Although the band had moderate success through the Seventies, *Highway To Hell* is heralded as their "breakthrough." Recorded at Roundhouse Studios in London, producer "Mutt" Lange manages to control their brute force with eloquence. *Highway To Hell*, whilst being their first release to achieve platinum status, also became Scott's swansong following his death in 1980.

Living up to its title, the album serves as a celebration of sin (Angus even sports devil horns and a tail on the cover art). Lyrically it is an ode to sex, songs such as "Girl's Got Rhythm" and "Touch Too Much" being particularly frank about the topic. However the title track and "If You Want Blood" move slightly off the subject. Similarly, "Walk All Over You" and "Night Prowler" ease the pace slightly, providing an element of space within the ten tracks. It is not often that every track on an album could stand up as a single, but AC/DC have come pretty close to it with *Highway To Hell*. **CSt**

> "They say to me, 'Are you AC or DC?,' and I say, 'Neither, I'm the lightning flash in the middle.'"
>
> **Bon Scott, 1994**

Track Listing

▶	01	**Highway To Hell** (Scott•A. Young•M. Young)	4:14
▶	02	**Girl's Got Rhythm** (Scott•A. Young•M. Young)	3:23
	03	**Walk All Over You** (Scott•A. Young•M. Young)	5:08
▶	04	**Touch Too Much** (Scott•A. Young•M. Young)	4:24
	05	**Beating Around The Bush** (Scott•A. Young•M. Young)	3:55
	06	**Shot Down In Flames** (Scott•A. Young•M. Young)	3:21
	07	**Get It Hot** (Scott•A. Young•M. Young)	2:24
	08	**If You Want Blood (You've Got It)** (Scott•A. Young•M. Young)	4:32
	09	**Love Hungry Man** (Scott•A. Young•M. Young)	4:14
	10	**Night Prowler** (Scott•A. Young•M. Young)	6:13

Sister Sledge | We Are Family (1979)

Label | Cotillion
Producer | Bernard Edwards • Nile Rodgers
Art Direction | Bob Defrin
Nationality | USA
Running Time | 42:53

With its jubilant bassline, propelling drumbeat, and theme of sisterhood, the title track to this disco-era classic migrated from the nightclubs to the dancefloors of countless wedding receptions. And even to the mammoth speakers of Three Rivers Stadium, when Major League Baseball's yellow-and-black-clad Pittsburg Pirates adopted it as a theme in 1979 for their World Series-winning season.

Like the '79 Pirates, the story of how the *We Are Family* album came to be is one of the right players clicking together at the right time. Guitarist Nile Rodgers and bassist Bernard Edwards were a crack production team that, along with drummer Tony Thompson, formed the heart of the band Chic. Philadelphia siblings Debbie, Kim, Joni, and Kathy Sledge had been on the R&B scene for several years but were still relative unknowns when Atlantic Records match-made them with their labelmates Chic, who had scored a trio of pop hits with discotheque staples "Dance Dance Dance (Yowsah Yowsah Yowsah)," "Everybody Dance," and "Le Freak."

The sisters were given quality songs, with the music placed within a pristine setting courtesy of the core Chic threesome, as well as dazzling horn players such as trumpeter Jon Faddis and saxophonist/flautist Alex Foster, and backing vocals by Luther Vandross and Chic singer Norma Jean Wright. The result? Elegant, string-laden masterpieces such as "He's The Greatest Dancer" and the euphoric "Lost In Music" that stand alongside Chic's own work as perhaps the pinnacle of the disco era. Oh, and multi-platinum sales. **YK**

> " ...with Sister Sledge we ...have complete control on what goes down in the studio from start to finish."
>
> Bernard Edwards, 1979

Track Listing

▶ 01 **He's The Greatest Dancer** (Edwards•Rodgers) 6:15
▶ 02 **Lost In Music** (Edwards•Rodgers) 4:52
▶ 03 **Somebody Loves Me** (Edwards•Rodgers) 4:59
  04 **Thinking Of You** (Edwards•Rodgers) 4:31
▶ 05 **We Are Family** (Edwards•Rodgers) 8:23
  06 **Easier To Love** (Edwards•Rodgers) 5:05
  07 **You're A Friend To Me** (Edwards•Rodgers) 5:31
  08 **One More Time** (Edwards•Rodgers) 3:17

Crusaders
Street Life (1979)

Label | MCA
Producer | Wilton Felder • "Stix" Hooper • Joe Sample
Art Direction | Stuart Kusher
Nationality | USA
Running Time | 39:21

Street Life is like a sporting match that begins with a team's quick offensive onslaught and is won because its defense holds up the rest of the game with a smattering of scoring to back it up. The 11-minute-plus title track that kicks off the six-cut collection is so strong that it could be released as a four-track EP with an instrumental, radio edit, and live version thrown in—and still qualify as a classic.

Pianist-keyboardist Joe Sample, saxophonist Will Felder, and drummer Nesbert "Stix" Hooper were high-school classmates in Houston, Texas, when they started their first group, The Swingsters. Eventually, they became The Jazz Crusaders before dropping the "Jazz" from the name—though not from the sound. With a jazz musician's ear for instrumental accompaniment and a strong feel for the blues, The Crusaders offer up accessible numbers with enough musical nutrition to satisfy both the critic and the dancer in every listener.

Street Life finds the group at the height of its musical strengths at a time when electric jazz (aka jazz fusion) was making way for a proto-acoustic movement—as personified in trumpeter and jazz messenger Wynton Marsalis. The players are in no hurry to prove their chops and instead are satisfied simply to drive the party, whether it is fueled by Randy Crawford's effortlessly joyful vocals on the title track or the cool funkiness of the appropriately named "Carnival Of The Night."

The album went U.S. and UK Top Twenty, and topped the U.S. jazz charts for an unprecedented 20 weeks. **YK**

The Germs
(GI) (1979)

Label | Slash
Producer | Joan Jett
Art Direction | Darby Crash
Nationality | USA
Running Time | 24:33

Sid was self-destructive; Johnny was snotty; Rollins was furious; and Johnny and Dee Dee were cartoon-like. Darby Crash was all of these. A charismatic and confrontational frontman, many took him to be barking mad. Many happened to be right. But his oddball lyrics and unpredictable and incendiary stage shows helped stamp The Germs as one of the most influential punk bands ever.

Released in 1979, *(GI)*—"Germs Incognito"—is a classic that has stood the test of time. Songs such as "Richie Dagger's Crime" and "American Leather" make it one of the best snotty punk albums ever. Like their chaotic live shows, some of the album sounds like it is all over the shop, and the production of Joan Jett—who promised Darby it would sound better than *Never Mind the Bollocks . . .* —makes the record sound a little light. But slickness was never part of The Germs' appeal. Listen to a song such as "Communist Eyes" and you can almost smell the bags of glue and cheap speed that were a big part of their scene in the early 1980s L.A.

As much of a commanding figure as Crash was, The Germs were not just about his self-lacerating hi jinx. Guitarist Pat Smear (who later went on to join Nirvana) co-wrote everything and was responsible for some of the biggest pure punk riffs of the time.

Three years after the band's first live performance (at L.A.'s Whisky in 1977), Crash died of a reportedly self-inflicted drug overdose but his—and *(GI)*'s—legacy in the annals of U.S. hardcore is indisputable. **TSc**

The B-52's
The B-52's (1979)

Label | Warner Bros.
Producer | Chris Blackwell
Art Direction | Sue Ab Surd
Nationality | USA
Running Time | 39:06

There is a scene in Paul Simon's underrated 1980 film *One Trick Pony* in which Simon's character—a former protest singer called Jonah Levy—plays on a bill with The B-52's, whom we see doing "Rock Lobster." The message of this early part of the film is clear: like it or not, The B-52's are the music of the future. And so it came to be.

The Athens, Georgia group's debut album still holds up by dint of the great singles ("Planet Claire" and "Rock Lobster," which is almost musical theater); two marvelously punk pop songs written by guitarist Ricky Wilson with outside help—"52 Girls" and "Hero Worship"; and some general, rave-up fun: "Dance This Mess Around," the cheap eroticism of "Lava," and the ludicrous "There's a Moon in the Sky." By the end of the album, "6060-842" is a strange joke which wears a little thin and a live rendition of Tony Hatch's "Downtown" is almost certainly there because the group ran out of songs and the record company would not accept eight tracks as an album. Perhaps they should have recorded the full "52 Girls" (this version only names 25!).

Fred Schneider, a kind of Groucho Marx meets John Waters, was a bizarre but attractive feature. Cindy Wilson and Kate Pierson looked great without pandering to conventional glamor, played guitars and other instruments, and sang as raucously as they wanted to. The group's retro style and new wave dance sound had an extraordinary influence in the 1980s and continues to be irresistible today. **DN**

Holger Czukay
Movies (1979)

Label | Harvest
Producer | Holger Czukay
Art Direction | Holger Czukay
Nationality | Germany
Running Time | 39:43

Best known as the bassist and producer for visionary German rock pioneers Can, Holger Czukay retreated to his home in Cologne after the band's split in 1978 and found an outlet in playing his bass along with the television, improvising film scores for his amusement.

The roots of his first post-Can solo album, *Movies*, lay in this approach to music-making. Unsurprisingly, the four pieces have a soundtrack-like quality. Combining Czukay's sinuous bass and whispered vocals with washes of synthesizer and lilting African rhythms provided by percussionist Kwaku Baah, *Movies* was also assembled like a film, piecing together different segments of various takes into a unified whole.

The other major influence on Czukay's career was avant-garde composer Karlheinz Stockhausen, under whom Czukay had studied between 1963 and 1968. *Movies* continued Can's work marrying progressive rock to electronic textures and tape loops inspired by Stockhausen's musique concrète techniques. It was also an early experiment in sampling, utilizing media samples accumulated over months of channel surfing and random radio listening. "Persian Love," for example, contains clips of an Iranian singer recorded from the radio that Czukay discovered by chance.

Despite the rather academic aegis under which it was made, *Movies* is a languid and often lighthearted record, typified by the playful "Cool In The Pool." This synthesis of experimental art-rock with frothy pop textures set the tone for Czukay's solo albums. **PL**

Police | Reggatta De Blanc (1979)

Label | A&M
Producer | Nigel Gray • The Police
Art Direction | Michael Ross
Nationality | UK • USA
Running Time | 41:43

The first Police album, *Outlandos D'Amour*, appeared in late 1978 and included three hit singles. But when this second album with a pidgin English title—meaning "white reggae,"—appeared in the autumn, it quickly topped the UK chart, also becoming The Police's second U.S. Top Thirty album of 1979.

The transformation of The Police from ersatz punks in 1977 into perhaps the biggest mainstream rock band in the world by 1983 was remarkable. *Reggatta . . .* supplied their first two UK chart-toppers—"Walking On The Moon" and "Message In A Bottle." ("The Bed's Too Big" was the lead track on the so-called "Six Pack," a specially released collection that also contained the group's previous five A&M hit singles.) Both singles were prime examples of the band's off-kilter brand of new wave, highlighted by Andy Summers' economic but ear-catching riffs and Stewart Copeland's deft drumming. The trio's key member, however, was former Newcastle schoolteacher Gordon Sumner, aka Sting—a world-class lead vocalist and bass player, and commercial songwriter.

Copeland had previously been in the successful Curved Air, and had invited the unknown Sting into The Police, who were managed by Copeland's brother, Miles. Playing on a single by a new group, Strontium 90, Stewart and Sting encountered guitarist Summers, who had played with Zoot Money, Eric Burdon, Kevin Coyne, and Kevin Ayers, among many others.

Despite worldwide success, however, the balance of power in the band always remained delicate. The Police broke up in 1985, and Sting has retained a high profile as a solo artist ever since. **JT**

"Reggae . . . just showed me that you can turn a drumset completely upside down."

Stewart Copeland, 1982

Track Listing

▶	01	**Message In A Bottle** (Sting)	4:50
	02	**Reggatta De Blanc** (Copeland•Sting•Summers)	3:06
	03	**It's Alright For You** (Copeland•Sting)	3:13
	04	**Bring On The Night** (Sting)	4:16
	05	**Deathwish** (Copeland•Sting•Summers)	4:11
▶	06	**Walking On The Moon** (Sting)	5:02
	07	**On Any Other Day** (Copeland)	2:57
▶	08	**The Bed's Too Big Without You** (Sting)	4:25
	09	**Contact** (Copeland)	2:38
	10	**Does Everyone Stare** (Copeland)	3:46
	11	**No Time This Time** (Sting)	3:19

The Fall | Live At The Witch Trials (1979)

Label | Step Forward
Producer | The Fall • Bob Sargeant
Art Direction | Mark E. Smith
Nationality | UK
Running Time | 38:36

One of the most distinctive and influential British bands ever, The Fall formed in 1977, in Manchester, around singer/writer Mark E. Smith. Signing to Miles Copeland's Step Forward label, they debuted with the freakish subject matter of the *Bingo Master's Breakout* EP. This, coupled with a superb live reputation, secured much critical adulation, and airplay support from Radio DJ John Peel, who was to become a lifelong fan.

Despite a fluctuating membership, The Fall recorded and mixed *Live At The Witch Trials*, made up of highlights from their early shows, in just two days. Smith's distinctive accented voice and clever wordplay is complemented by Martin Bramah's abrasive guitar and Yvonne Pawlett's fantastically off-key organ, as well as a powerful rhythm section. "Crap Rap 2" introduces itself with the assertion "We are the Fall, Northern white crap that talks back." "Futures And Pasts" and "Industrial Estate" are ingenious Mancunian takes on the garage rock of The Seeds or The Stooges, full of sarcastic punk invective, while the anti-heroin "No Xmas for John Quays" is an often overlooked classic of the time. The music industry-damning "Music Scene" (complete with studio engineer trying to stop the band during its elongated ending) and "Underground Medicine" showed them overcoming their musical limitations with vibrancy, humor, and intelligence.

The album was an instant success. Documenting the beginnings of what became a unique British institution, it remains compelling listening today and has garnered new generations of admirers after the likes of Pavement and Franz Ferdinand achieved mainstream success with their approximation of The Fall's sound. **CSh**

> "People used to call the Fall a punk band, but we were always outside of that."
>
> Mark E. Smith, 1999

Track Listing

01	**Frightened** (Friel•Smith)		5:02
▶ 02	**Crap Rap 2/Like To Blow** (Bramah•Smith)		2:04
03	**Rebellious Juke Box** (Bramah•Smith)		2:55
▶ 04	**No Xmas For John Quays** (Smith)		4:38
05	**Mother–Sister!** (Baines•Smith)		3:20
▶ 06	**Industrial Estate** (Bramah•Friel•Smith)		1:59
07	**Underground Medicine** (Bramah•Smith)		2:08
08	**Two Steps Back** (Bramah•Smith)		5:03
09	**Live At The Witch Trials** (Smith)		0:51
▶ 10	**Futures And Pasts** (Bramah•Smith)		2:36
▶ 11	**Music Scene** (Bramah•Pawlett•Riley•Smith)		8:00

Talking Heads | Fear Of Music (1979)

Label | Sire
Producer | Brian Eno • Talking Heads
Art Direction | David Byrne • Jerry Harrison
Nationality | USA
Running Time | 40:25

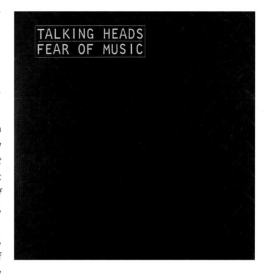

With *Fear Of Music*, Talking Heads drilled deep into a seam of paranoia that their first two albums had only scraped at. *Talking Heads: 77* and *More Songs About Buildings And Food* were offbeat slices of pop that deconstructed life in culture-lite America. On *Fear Of Music*, David Byrne turned his withering gaze inward, and dissected his own anxiety-ridden mind.

This cutting self-analysis is backed by a bleaker, denser sound. Tracks such as "Animals"—a prime cut of psychosis that sees Byrne bark distrust at our furry neighbors—and "Mind"—a funeral song for a dead love affair—build up an atmosphere of menace through simple but skewed funk-driven repetitions.

Brian Eno's hyper-processed production adds to the sense of foreboding. The former Roxy Music star, who had also produced 1978's *More Songs . . .* , piled strange sonic effects onto *Fear Of Music*—a marked departure from the live-in-the-studio sound of the group's first two albums. Riffs are stretched and fragmented on "Electric Guitar," ghostly backing vocals—provided by bassist Tina Weymouth's sisters—float in and out of "Air," and Byrne's visions of mental breakdown on "Memories Can't Wait" are loaded with distortion and waves of echo.

The band's journey to the dark side confused many British fans (*Fear Of Music* only reached No. 29 in the UK chart), but critics and record buyers on the other side of the Atlantic loved the album's experimental sounds. Legendary music hack Lester Bangs declared it "the best Heads' album yet," and *Fear Of Music* charted at No. 21 in the Billboard 100, higher than any previous Talking Heads release. **TB**

> ## "I'm not an entirely comfortable person ... But that isn't necessarily neurotic."

David Byrne, 1979

Track Listing

▶	01	**I Zimbra** (Ball•Byrne•Eno)	3:06
	02	**Mind** (Byrne)	4:12
	03	**Paper** (Byrne)	2:36
	04	**Cities** (Byrne)	4:05
▶	05	**Life During Wartime** (Byrne•Frantz•Harrison•Weymouth)	3:41
	06	**Memories Can't Wait** (Byrne•Harrison)	3:30
▶	07	**Air** (Byrne)	3:33
▶	08	**Heaven** (Byrne•Harrison)	4:01
	09	**Animals** (Byrne)	3:29
	10	**Electric Guitar** (Byrne)	2:59
	11	**Drugs** (Byrne)	5:13

Joy Division | Unknown Pleasures (1979)

Label | Factory
Producer | Martin Hannett
Art Direction | Peter Saville
Nationality | UK
Running Time | 38:21

Following their appearance on 1978's noted *Factory Sample* EP, financed by local television personality Tony Wilson, Joy Division opted to release their landmark debut album on tiny independent Factory too, despite interest from major labels.

Recorded in a week at Stockport's Strawberry Studios, sonic visionary Hannett took the sheet metal guitar of Bernard Dicken (aka Sumner), Peter Hook's unique bass melodies, and Stephen Morris' innovative combination of acoustic and electronic drums and created a muted, unnerving ambience through pioneering use of digital effects, muffled screams, and crashing glass.

Lyricist Ian Curtis documents his experiences as an epileptic in the mutant disco of "She's Lost Control," whilst the sodium-lit "Shadowplay" conjures images of the urban decay and paranoia of late-1970s Manchester. The sparseness of the music perfectly complements his cold baritone, particularly on the majestic death anthem "New Dawn Fades" and the haunting "I Remember Nothing," while the energetic "Interzone" and "Disorder" remind listeners of the band's fierce live reputation.

In the immediate post-punk period of "busy design" and primary colors, the stark textured black sleeve, featuring the radio waves emitted from a dying star, was as groundbreaking as the music contained within, and ushered in a minimalist design revolution.

Unknown Pleasures was a commercial and critical success—though one journalist paid the backhanded compliment of describing the record as perfect listening prior to committing suicide. Twenty-five years later, *Unknown Pleasures* is still compelling listening. **CSh**

> ## "At Factory, no one's restricting us, the music or the artwork."
>
> Ian Curtis, 1979

Track Listing

	01	**Disorder** (Curtis·Hook·Morris·Sumner)	3:36
▶	02	**Day Of The Lords** (Curtis·Hook·Morris·Sumner)	4:43
	03	**Candidate** (Curtis·Hook·Morris·Sumner)	3:00
	04	**Insight** (Curtis·Hook·Morris·Sumner)	4:00
▶	05	**New Dawn Fades** (Curtis·Hook·Morris·Sumner)	4:47
▶	06	**She's Lost Control** (Curtis·Hook·Morris·Sumner)	3:40
▶	07	**Shadowplay** (Curtis·Hook·Morris·Sumner)	3:50
	08	**Wilderness** (Curtis·Hook·Morris·Sumner)	2:35
	09	**Interzone** (Curtis·Hook·Morris·Sumner)	2:10
▶	10	**I Remember Nothing** (Curtis·Hook·Morris·Sumner)	6:00

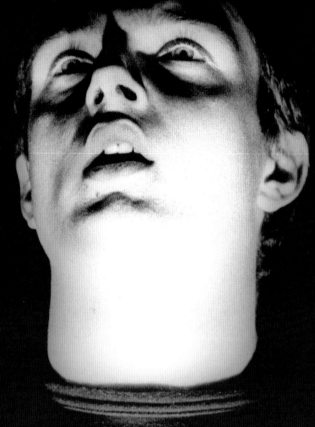

Chic | Risqué (1979)

Label | Atlantic
Producer | B. Edwards • N. Rodgers
Art Direction | Carin Goldberg
Nationality | USA
Running Time | 36:58

Recorded at Kendun Studios, California, The Power Station, and Electric Lady in New York over eight weeks in winter/spring 1979, *Risqué* is Exhibit A in the case against those who suggest that there was little substance to disco music. The album is the acme of Bernard Edwards and Nile Rodgers' creative partnership. Backed by a budget of $160,000, it remains a widescreen record with widescreen ambitions.

With its jet-engine drone and its achingly gorgeous repetition, "Good Times" is Chic's lasting monument to pop, an ironic re-creation of Depression-era standard "Happy Days Are Here Again." Edwards' 20-note bass refrain came to define not only urban music, but hip hop as well, famously sampled by The Sugarhill Gang in "Rapper's Delight." Although it could be argued that the whole album struggles to live up to that track, it is a fantastically dark listen, with only "A Warm Summer Night" and "Will You Cry (When You Hear This Song)" offering respite among the relentless groove.

It was released in August 1979, with a full design concept that looked like something from the Hipgnosis stable, its sepia sleeve sat well alongside the other major Atlantic release of the summer, Led Zeppelin's *In Through The Out Door*. Atlantic even went back to its silver label, a staple of its jazz and R&B roster, as a one-off for the album.

Risqué is a record that dwells on relationships: bleak, unrequited ones, ones tinged with sadism and despair; relationships with the past, and, of course, with the dancefloor. Ornate and detailed, it was soon eclipsed by the "disco sucks" movement. **DE**

"We were talking to people in a time of financial chaos and putting a bright face on it."

Nile Rodgers, 2004

Track Listing

▶	01	**Good Times** (Edwards • Rodgers)	8:09
▶	02	**A Warm Summer Night** (Edwards • Rodgers)	6:11
▶	03	**My Feet Keep Dancing** (Edwards • Rodgers)	6:46
	04	**My Forbidden Lover** (Edwards • Rodgers)	4:42
	05	**Can't Stand To Love You** (Edwards • Rodgers)	2:55
▶	06	**Will You Cry (When You Hear This Song)** (Edwards • Rodgers)	4:05
	07	**What About Me** (Edwards • Rodgers)	4:10

The Undertones | The Undertones (1979)

Label | Sire
Producer | Roger Bechirian
Art Direction | Bush Hollyhead
Nationality | UK
Running Time | 29:09

Some albums reflect their time and place. And some do not. Back in 1979, few thought of Northern Ireland as an idyll. But an album of May that year proved adolescence is the same wherever and whenever you are: girls, the weekend, breathless excitement, big plans. The Undertones' debut album is an unfettered, unalloyed delight.

While much of English punk was plugged into fashion and politics, the Undertones had an absence of artifice—TV appearances wearing parkas and sweaters best left at the back of the wardrobe, and a black-and-white cover featuring the band sat on a wall. With an image of no image, everything was left to the music.

And so, of course, to "Teenage Kicks?" Not so fast. In the kind of contrary move that characterized their career, the track that inspired moist-eyed devotion from the late John Peel was included only on the version released five months after this original.

No matter. That just leaves more room for the irresistible bounce of "Here Comes the Summer," "Jump Boys," and "Jimmy Jimmy" (the band's first Top Twenty UK single). Of their contemporaries, only Blondie and the Buzzcocks could rival John O'Neill's ear for a great tune. And no one at all came close to making the impression of Feargal Sharkey's voice. Part warble, part croon, it has an urgency that dovetails perfectly with the verve of "True Confessions" and "Male Model."

Less than half an hour after "Family Entertainment" kicks things off, it is all over and you are sitting there with a huge grin. Just put it down to the power of perfect pop. **CB**

"It was an extended childhood, being in The Undertones."

Michael Bradley, 1997

Track Listing

▶	01	**Family Entertainment** (D. O'Neill)	2:39
	02	**Girls Don't Like It** (J. O'Neill)	2:17
	03	**Male Model** (Bradley·D. O'Neill·J. O'Neill)	1:55
	04	**I Gotta Getta** (J. O'Neill)	1:54
	05	**Wrong Way** (J. O'Neill)	1:24
▶	06	**Jump Boys** (J. O'Neill)	2:41
▶	07	**Here Comes The Summer** (J. O'Neill)	1:36
	08	**Billy's Third** (Doherty)	1:57
▶	09	**Jimmy Jimmy** (J. O'Neill)	2:43
▶	10	**True Confessions** (Bradley·D. O'Neill·J. O'Neill)	2:23
	11	**Runaround (She's A)** (J. O'Neill)	1:49
	12	**I Know A Girl** (J. O'Neill)	2:37
	13	**Listening In** (Bradley·D. O'Neill·J. O'Neill)	2:25
	14	**Casbah Rock** (J. O'Neill)	0:49

The Clash
London Calling (1979)

Label | CBS
Producer | Guy Stevens
Art Direction | R. Lowry • P. Smith
Nationality | UK
Running Time | 64:59

They may be accused of watering down punk rock with stylistic digressions, and spouting off about politics without really knowing about it, but a quarter of a century after the recording of The Clash's masterpiece *London Calling*, it still stands as the work that offered a vital exit from punk's solipsism.

London Calling was the definitive Clash statement after the punk manifesto of their first album and the States-friendly production of *Give 'Em Enough Rope*. The songwriting partnership of Joe Strummer and Mick Jones now embraced other influences apart from punk and reggae, including rockabilly ("Brand New Cadillac"), pop ("Lost In The Supermarket"), and R&B ("I'm Not Down"), though Simonon provided the dark anthem "Guns Of Brixton." "Spanish Bombs" was a genuinely stirring political hymn, while the loping bassline, slicing guitar, and throat-shredding vocal of the title track gave them their biggest hit single to date.

But what really makes this record gel is Guy Stevens' strong production. A genius entrepreneur in the record industry since the late 1960s, Stevens had fallen out of grace by the mid-'70s, but his gung-ho approach to recording side-stepped the band's intimidating reputation, and he was able to extract the best from them.

The cover knowingly referenced that of Elvis' first album, though Pennie Smith's iconic photo of Simonon on the point of smashing his bass guitar was pure punk. One of those rare records that both defines the time and reveals the creators coming to terms with their art. **IJ**

Japan
Quiet Life (1979)

Label | Hansa
Producer | John Punter
Art Direction | Fin Costello
Nationality | UK
Running Time | 43:28

With the UK unleashing an influential wave of synth-pop acts, Japan's transition from glam rock to trendy arthouse was a revelation. The band's third LP catches the new wave of romanticism perfectly, and exposes David Sylvian as a singer of some stature. Sylvian's voice attains a sultry gravitas here that drew strong comparisons with Bryan Ferry, while the vocalist's hazy pouting on the cover gained him great iconic clout.

With a pair of overlooked recordings under their belt, the band as a whole were eager for attention. The interplay of Richard Barbieri's keyboards and Rob Dean's slinky guitar chords are almost incoherent compared to Mick Karn's throbbing fretless bass. If anyone could remember the instrument sounding this sexy in a while, then they were not letting on. Steve Jansen remains subtle and sympathetic on percussion, while Sylvian's darkly idyllic warblings are a dream.

The opening title track and equally catchy "Fall In Love With Me" seem to set the stage for an album of outrageous commerciality. Yet the doomed autumnal piano on "Despair" really offers a fairer summation of proceedings. Melancholy and meditative, *Quiet Life* presents itself as a challenging listen. A stark rendering of Lou Reed's "All Tomorrow's Parties" fits both snugly and smugly among Sylvian's own compositions. But it is the lengthy workouts on "In Vogue" and "The Other Side Of Life" that indicate the experimental path Sylvian would shortly lead his band along. Back then, though, Japan were pop stars at last. **GT**

Marianne Faithfull
Broken English (1979)

Label | Island
Producer | Mark Miller Mundy
Art Direction | Dennis Morris
Nationality | UK
Running Time | 37:40

She could have played Sid Vicious' mother—literally. Instead, having spent a decade in a dope-addled wilderness, Marianne Faithfull opted not to appear in the Sex Pistols movie *The Great Rock 'n' Roll Swindle*, but to channel her punk-fueled fury into an album.

The energy and directness of punk was sheer inspiration to Faithfull. Musically, *Broken English* owes nothing to her more familiar musical heritage—The Rolling Stones and the pretty ballads that first made her name. There is the electronic throb of "Broken English," the spacey blues of "Brain Drain," and the blue-eyed soul of "Guilt."

"Working Class Hero" is icy yet electric, with imperious vocals that sound more like the sneers of Marie Antoinette than the bitter everyman of Lennon's original. The edgily electronic "The Ballad Of Lucy Jordan" is a mix of melancholy and melody that would be Abba-esque were it not for the ravaged vocals.

But the track for which *Broken English* remains notorious is "Why D'Ya Do It." Based on a poem by playwright Heathcote Williams, it is full of Robert Fripp-ish guitars. The star is Marianne: enraged by her own partner's infidelity, she pitches up vocally between Patti Smith and Grace Jones to snarl lyrics of which "Why'd you spit on my snatch?" is not even the nastiest.

The album kickstarted a recovery that led to masterpieces such as 1987's *Strange Weather*. But not even when she sang with Metallica would Marianne make jaws drop as she did with *Broken English*. **BM**

The Slits
Cut (1979)

Label | Island
Producer | Dennis Bovell
Art Direction | Pennie Smith
Nationality | Germany • UK
Running Time | 31:52

Formed at a Patti Smith show in 1976 by 14-year-old German vocalist Ari Up, The Slits (with their unique thrift-store fashion sense) soon acquired a reputation for being wild and obnoxious. They were invited to support The Clash on their 1977 White Riot tour, but the driver had to be bribed to allow them on the bus. However, despite being part of the Sex Pistols' inner circle, they did not release their debut until 1979.

A fluctuating lineup eventually settled around Ari, guitarist Viv Albertine, bassist Tessa Pollitt, and future Banshees drummer Budgie. By the time of *Cut*'s release, their wall of noise had developed into dub-influenced "jitterpunk," helped by the production skills of Bovell, from groundbreaking British reggae group Matumbi.

The group combined skipping rhythms and discordant harmonies with Ari's Teutonic warble (an obvious influence upon Björk); their lack of musical ability never hinders their inventiveness—witness the rolling piano and varying tempos of "Typical Girls" or the raw skank of "Instant Hit." Male shortcomings are brilliantly addressed on anti-love song "Love Und Romance" and "Ping-Pong Affair"'s twisted funk. Best of all are the anti-consumerism of "Spend, Spend, Spend" and "Shoplifting"'s hilarious "Do a runner" chant.

The album was deservedly greeted with acclaim, though the "urban primitive" imagery of *Cut*'s sleeve, attracted immediate controversy. But The Slits' refusal to compromise their image or stance made them an empowering influence on female musicians. **CSh**

Elvis Costello And The Attractions
Armed Forces (1979)

Label | Demon
Producer | Nick Lowe
Art Direction | Barney Bubbles
Nationality | UK
Running Time | 36:13

Recorded in a frantic six weeks at London's Eden Studios—and originally titled *Emotional Fascism, Armed Forces*—Elvis Costello's third album was a distinct step back from the confrontational music of its predecessor, *This Year's Model*. Its pop arrangements betrayed the hand of classically trained keyboardist Steve Naive (born Steve Nason) who was exerting an increasing influence on proceedings from behind His Master's Voice. First single "Oliver's Army" sold 400,000 copies but could not shift Gloria Gaynor's "I Will Survive" from No. 1: the album performed likewise, reaching No. 2.

The album secreted a three-track live 7" single in an elaborate foldout sleeve. Its tracks included a piano and vocal take on the album's opener, "Accidents Will Happen," that outscored the studio cut in every respect. Another notable highlight was "Green Shirt," "addressed" to BBC TV newsreader Angela Rippon, and allowing Naive full rein to plunder his keyboard armory.

To some, the inclusion of "Sunday's Best," a number written for and rejected by Ian Dury, might have suggested that Costello's songwriting wellspring was drying up. That song was removed on the U.S. album and replaced by a cover of Nick Lowe's "What's So Funny 'Bout Peace Love And Understanding."

There was little doubt when "Two Little Hitlers" faded out with the repeated refrain "I will return" that Costello would make good on his promise, though. He had successfully infiltrated the mainstream: by contrast, his next project would be soul based. **MH**

"Armed Forces is a very modern record of its time ..."

Elvis Costello, 1995

Track Listing		
▶ 01 **Accidents Will Happen** (Costello)		3:00
02 **Senior Service** (Costello)		2.17
▶ 03 **Oliver's Army** (Costello)		2:58
04 **Big Boys** (Costello)		2:54
▶ 05 **Green Shirt** (Costello)		2:42
06 **Party Girl** (Costello)		3:20
07 **Goon Squad** (Costello)		3:14
08 **Busy Bodies** (Costello)		3:33
09 **Sunday's Best** (Costello)		3:22
10 **Moods For Moderns** (Costello)		2:48
11 **Chemistry Class** (Costello)		2:55
▶ 12 **Two Little Hitlers** (Costello)		3:10

Neil Young And Crazy Horse
Rust Never Sleeps (1979)

Label | Reprise
Producer | David Briggs • Tim Mulligan • Neil Young
Art Direction | Uncredited
Nationality | Canada
Running Time | 38:16

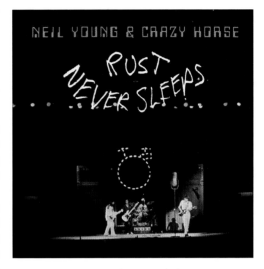

By 1979 Neil Young was celebrating surviving the 1970s with his integrity intact. *Village Voice* magazine even nominated him as "Artist of the Decade," confirming him as one of the few stars of his era, along with Dylan and Van Morrison, to make the successful transition.

Young was forging ahead with his solo career on two fronts. A film entitled *Rust Never Sleeps* premiered in July 1979, comprising concert footage shot the previous year at San Francisco's Cow Palace, but a simultaneously released album of the same title was more interesting. An acoustic side featured Young solo, while an electric side saw him backed by stage band Crazy Horse. The record is bookended by variations on a song, "My My, Hey Hey," which ruminated on the fleeting nature of stardom; it became legendary after Nirvana's Kurt Cobain quoted it in his suicide note.

Acoustic highlights included "Pocahontas," inspired by Sacheen Littlefeather's appearance at the Academy Awards to turn down Marlon Brando's Oscar for his role in *The Godfather*. (Young had explored the destruction of the Native American peoples on Buffalo Springfield's "Broken Arrow.") "Thrasher" was a veiled commentary on his relationship with Crosby, Stills, and Nash.

The four scorching electric numbers on side two, recorded live but with audience sound removed, kicked off with "Powderfinger," a Western tale, and concluded by a second blast of the album's theme song, entitled "Hey Hey, My My (Into The Black)." The sound of an artist refusing to burn out or fade away. **MH**

"There's an edge to real rock 'n' roll, where it's all that matters."

Neil Young, 1979

Track Listing

▶	01	**My My, Hey Hey (Out Of The Blue)** (Blackburn•Young)	3:45
	02	**Thrasher** (Neil Young)	5:38
	03	**Ride My Llama** (Neil Young)	2:29
▶	04	**Pocahontas** (Neil Young)	3:22
	05	**Sail Away** (Neil Young)	3:46
▶	06	**Powderfinger** (Neil Young)	5:30
	07	**Welfare Mothers** (Neil Young)	3:48
	08	**Sedan Delivery** (Neil Young)	4:40
▶	09	**Hey Hey, My My (Into The Black)** (Neil Young)	5:18

Gang Of Four
Entertainment! (1979)

Label | EMI
Producer | Andy Gill • Jon King • Rob Warr
Art Direction | Andy Gill • Jon King
Nationality | UK
Running Time | 45:13

Gang of Four formed in Leeds, England, in 1977, naming themselves after the Chinese political faction associated with Mao Tse-tung's widow. Eyebrows were raised when this avowedly left-wing group signed to EMI, but their uncompromising attitude remained intact.

Entertainment!'s groundbreaking sound is due to the tight funk rhythms laid down by bassist Dave Allen and drummer Hugo Burnham, and Andy Gill's scratchy staccato guitar. The use of space allows Jon King's intelligently delivered vocals to be heard, while the gaps are filled with jagged guitar feedback and melodica.

Defiantly anti-sexist and anti-Fascist, the band were lyrically inspired by the looming specter of Thatcherism and the rise in violence between right- and left-wing factions that they witnessed in their native Yorkshire in the late 1970s. " . . . Tourist" and "Contract" attempt to challenge men and women's traditional roles in society; "Ether"'s Funkadelic-inspired call-and-answer vocals examine the way the media's exposure of British mistreatment of Northern Irish prisoners was obscured by the discovery of North Sea oil. "Damaged Goods" explores the metaphors between sex and consumerism. Most powerful of all is "5:45," with its portrayal of graphic war scenes on prime-time television news.

The music is, however, delivered with wit, anger, and raw energy, and the vocals never descend into mindless ranting. *Entertainment!* is fresh and consistent, the Gang's "Neo-Marxist funk" inspiring groups as disparate as the Red Hot Chili Peppers and The Rapture. **CSh**

Cheap Trick
At Budokan (1979)

Label | Epic
Producer | Cheap Trick • Bruce Dickinson • Jack Douglas
Art Direction | Koh Hasebe
Nationality | USA
Running Time | 42:27

It took a trip across the Pacific for Cheap Trick to become megastars at home. While garnering only moderate success in the United States with its first three records, the quartet managed to generate Beatlemania-type frenzy during its 1978 Japan tour. With the document of that tour, *At Budokan*, the band took the seeds sown on earlier records—the carefully constructed pop melodies, the heavyweight hooks—and watered them with a kinetic stage energy learned from pulling 200 dates annually. In short, Cheap Trick provided a textbook in power-pop, one that continues to influence noise-pop bands today.

The cover, a live shot of vocalist Robin Zander and bassist Tom Petersson, was a smart marketing move, putting the pretty boys in front to attract young female buyers. But it was also deceiving, since it is the talented—though less photogenic—twosome of guitarist Rick Nielsen and drummer Bun E. Carlos that really made this album sail. Nielsen, who wrote or co-wrote nine of the ten tracks, makes each note count with powerfully melodic leads, making "Surrender" and "Big Eyes" still sound urgent today. Carlos punishes his kit on the opener, "Hello There," and then is a model of exacting restraint on the remake of the Fats Domino hit "Ain't That A Shame."

At Budokan remained on the charts for over a year and sold more than three million copies. The group would later achieve success in the studio, quickly releasing the 1979 hit *Dream Police*, but it would never again reach the heights found at Budokan Arena. **JiH**

Fleetwood Mac
Tusk (1979)

Label | Reprise
Producer | Ken Caillat • Richard Dashut • Fleetwood Mac
Art Direction | Vigon Nahas Vigon
Nationality | USA
Running Time | 72:25

Fleetwood Mac were bound to fall from the heights reached on 1977's *Rumours*, which spent a staggering 31 weeks on the top of the charts. But few have "fallen" in such an epic fashion as the Mac did with *Tusk*.

Recorded over a ten-month period, the sprawling two-disc set reached new heights of studio excess and ran up a then-unprecedented one-million-dollar tab. However, the money seems well spent—including whatever it cost to rent out Dodger Stadium and hire the USC marching band to record the title track.

Borrowing equally from both Brians (Eno and Wilson), the album is a dreamy collage that utilizes every bell and whistle then known to man. Lindsey Buckingham, who assumed control of the band with *Rumours*, stays at the forefront here and creates his own sparkling version of *Pet Sounds*.

Rumours boils with tension, stemming mainly from Buckingham's failed relationship with Stevie Nicks, but level-headed professionalism reigns on *Tusk*. It is an older, wiser band that brings a sense of steely detachment, and even acceptance, to poignant tracks like "Angel" and "Save Me A Place." Nicks' breathy alto has never sounded better than on "Sara" and Christine McVie is absolutely haunting on the country-tinged folk rock of "Over & Over."

Tusk could not match *Rumours* in sales, but it did go platinum four months after its release. It was not the expected follow-up, but what else would you expect from the band that told us to "Go Your Own Way?" **JiH**

Pink Floyd
The Wall (1979)

Label | Columbia
Producer | Various
Art Direction | Gerald Scarfe • Roger Waters
Nationality | UK
Running Time | 81:11

Punk could not kill Pink Floyd. Led Zeppelin, Yes, and ELP's days were numbered. Genesis shrank to survive. But the Floyd did whatever the hell they wanted.

Always socially aloof from their contemporaries (except, oddly, The Who), the Floyd now sought to express their alienation from their audience. The result: a concept album about a disillusioned pop star who wigs out and imagines himself a Fascist leader. So far, so *Tommy*, so *Ziggy*. And the central metaphor—bricks—hardly sets the pulse racing.

So the thrill is in the frills: production elaborate even by the Floyd's grandiose standards, Beach Boys soundalikes singing about worms, and unusually concise songs—notably the disco protest "Another Brick In The Wall Pt II" and fan favorite "Comfortably Numb."

A mega-selling sensation to rival *Dark Side Of The Moon*, it spent six months in Billboard's Top Five, topping the chart for 15 weeks. Two decades on—according to chief writer Roger Waters—it still "does anything up to four million each year."

Beloved of Brits such as Noel Gallagher of Oasis and Robbie Williams, *The Wall* also has legions of Stateside disciples. Double albums by The Smashing Pumpkins and Nine Inch Nails would not exist without it; Marilyn Manson's *Antichrist Superstar* is its (conceptual) evil twin.

So entrenched is the album, it can even withstand a disco makeover of "Comfortably Numb" by the Scissor Sisters, and threats of a Broadway adaptation. Hear it now before it is tarnished for ever. **BM**

Public Image Ltd. | Metal Box (1979)

Label | Virgin
Producer | Public Image Limited
Art Direction | Charles Dimont
Nationality | UK
Running Time | 60:30

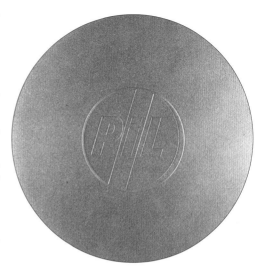

If punk rock had been a violent attempt to usurp the mainstream, post-punk was in many ways a wounded retreat, a cathartic primal scream. Where the Sex Pistols twisted their sickness into a rousing, party-ready rock 'n' roll, Public Image saw Lydon refine his nails-on-a-blackboard whine into an instrument—or perhaps, more accurately, a measurement—of torture. And the Cochran-esque riffs of *Never Mind The Bollocks* gave way to the repetition of Can, the dub understanding of Lee Perry, and new wrinkles of dissonance cooked up by bassist Jah Wobble and genius guitarist Keith Levene.

Following the textured noise of their debut a year earlier, *Metal Box*—so called because initial pressings came as three 45 rpm 12-inches in a utilitarian movie can (it was subsequently reissued as *Second Edition*, with cheaper packaging)—gave Public Image the space to unfurl, to pursue their bad trip to its end. Some tracks ran long, so the quasi-industrial grooves wore themselves into the listener, the claustrophobic walls of noise closing in. Even among this mess of noise, beautifully unusual sounds could be heard—the off-kilter "Careering," the propulsive "Poptones." But *Metal Box* was primarily an album of the ambience suggested by its title: cold, dank, unforgiving, subterranean.

It summed up the mood of the band, falling into deepening addictions, exhausted from chaotic and disastrous touring sorties. It was, in many ways, the sound of a band without a future, though the abrasive textures and powerful sounds they discovered on their way down would influence all manner of experimental music for decades to come. **SC**

"...we can do nothing but benefit your dreary little lives."

John Lydon, 1980

Track Listing

▶ 01	**Albatross** (Public Image Ltd.)	10:34
02	**Memories** (Public Image Ltd.)	5:05
03	**Swan Lake** (Public Image Ltd.)	4:11
▶ 04	**Poptones** (Public Image Ltd.)	7:46
▶ 05	**Careering** (Public Image Ltd.)	4:32
06	**No Birds** (Public Image Ltd.)	4:41
07	**Graveyard** (Public Image Ltd.)	3:07
08	**The Suit** (Public Image Ltd.)	3:29
09	**Bad Baby** (Public Image Ltd.)	4:30
10	**Socialist** (Public Image Ltd.)	3:10
▶ 11	**Chant** (Public Image Ltd.)	5:01
▶ 12	**Radio 4** (Public Image Ltd.)	4:24

Michael Jackson | Off The Wall (1979)

Label | Epic
Producer | Michael Jackson • Quincy Jones
Art Direction | Steve Harvey • Mike Salisbury
Nationality | USA
Running Time | 45:45

Unlike Stevie Wonder, who shifted seamlessly from child phenomenon to adult star, Michael Jackson endured a tricky musical adolescence. By 1979 he had not had a solo hit in seven long years and the 19-year-old was desperate to find a new musical mentor.

While rehearsing for the all-black musical *The Wiz* in 1977, Jackson shyly asked jazz and funk mastermind Quincy Jones if he could recommend a producer. Jones volunteered himself, building a studio band around two of his acts—the Brothers Johnson and Rufus—along with session musicians including Stevie Wonder's keyboard player Greg Philanganes. Together, they created an intricate fusion of razor-sharp disco beats, state-of-the-art funk, heartbreaking ballads, and clean pop hooks that reinvented the sonic vocabulary of R&B.

There are some premier songwriters on board—Paul McCartney, Stevie Wonder, Bacharach's partner Carole Bayer Sager, Brit soul guru Rod Temperton—but the centerpiece of the album is Michael's jittery, frenetic opening track "Don't Stop 'Til You Get Enough." Jackson's falsetto hollers and frisky yelps serve as an obbligato to the lead line, punctuating Ben Wright's thrilling string arrangement and Jerry Hey's tight horn charts. Other tracks replicate this triumphalism, but even schmaltz like "She's Out Of My Life" is so simple and unaffected that you are left weeping with Michael by the song's end.

It sold 12 million copies and Quincy Jones' overhaul established a precedent for other artists seeking to escape the teen band ghetto. But none can match the sheer genius of *Off The Wall*, an album that serves as the Rosetta Stone for all subsequent R&B. **JLe**

> "All my life I wanted to see an entertainer like Michael really do his thing with no limitations..."
>
> Quincy Jones, 1979

Track Listing

▶	01	**Don't Stop 'Til You Get Enough** (Jackson)	6:05
▶	02	**Rock With You** (Temperton)	3:40
	03	**Working Day And Night** (Jackson)	5:14
	04	**Get On The Floor** (Jackson • Johnson)	4:39
	05	**Off The Wall** (Temperton)	4:06
	06	**Girlfriend** (McCartney)	3:05
▶	07	**She's Out Of My Life** (Bahler)	3:38
	08	**I Can't Help It** (Greene • Wonder)	6:06
	09	**It's The Falling In Love** (Foster • Sager)	3:48
	10	**Burn This Disco Out** (Temperton)	5:24

The Damned | Machine Gun Etiquette (1979)

Label | Chiswick
Producer | Roger Armstrong • The Damned
Art Direction | Uncredited
Nationality | UK
Running Time | 36:28

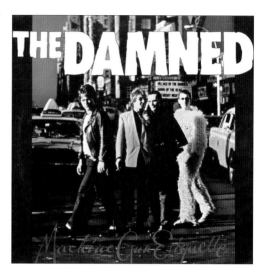

The perpetual adolescence of The Damned on stage masked how they had been growing up in the studio. Their end product in the dying days of the 1970s was an album that punk bands—and The Damned in particular—were not making: complex, contentious, and hugely ambitious. Throw in tunes and velocity and you have Motörhead meets The Beach Boys.

The band's landscape had changed radically since 1976. Captain Sensible had replaced Brian James as lead guitarist and creative hub, shifting the sound from the straightforward rock 'n' roll of their *Damned Damned Damned* debut toward something much more English and eccentric.

The classics fall over themselves in a rush to get to your ears: the thunderously nonsensical "Love Song," the marvelously melancholic "I Just Can't Be Happy Today," "Melody Lee" (a character from the girls' comic *Bunty*), "Antipope" (with lyrics from Sensible's brother Phil), and "Noise, Noise, Noise" (The Clash's Joe Strummer lending vocal assistance). "Smash It Up" (banned by the BBC when it was released as a single) even featured a purely instrumental "Part 1" (very un-punk), a tribute to supporter Marc Bolan.

But it is on "Plan 9 Channel 7"—Dave Vanian's paean to actress Vampira and her role in Ed Wood's trash-classic movie *Plan 9 from Outer Space*—that the album scrapes the sky.

Machine Gun ... showed that The Damned had polish to go with their spit. It was an unlikely transformation, but one that the band were to complete the following year with *The Black Album*. **CB**

"One of those one-off records."

Roger Armstrong, Co-producer, 2004

Track Listing		
▶ 01	**Love Song** (Scabies•Sensible•Vanian•Ward)	2:22
02	**Machine Gun Etiquette** (Scabies•Sensible•Vanian•Ward)	1:49
▶ 03	**I Just Can't Be Happy Today** (Dadomo•Scabies•Sensible•Vanian•Ward)	3:42
04	**Melody Lee** (Scabies•Sensible•Vanian•Ward)	2:07
05	**Antipope** (Burns•Scabies•Sensible•Vanian•Ward)	3:21
06	**These Hands** (Scabies•Sensible•Vanian•Ward)	2:03
07	**Plan 9 Channel 7** (Scabies•Sensible•Vanian•Ward)	5:09
08	**Noise, Noise, Noise** (Scabies•Sensible•Vanian•Ward)	3:10
09	**Looking At You** (MC5)	5:07
10	**Liar** (Scabies•Sensible•Vanian•Ward)	2:44
▶ 11	**Smash It Up (Parts 1 & 2)** (Scabies•Sensible•Vanian•Ward)	4:54

Gary Numan | The Pleasure Principle (1979)

Label | Beggars Banquet
Producer | Gary Numan
Art Direction | Malti Kidia • Steve Webbon
Nationality | UK
Running Time | 41:08

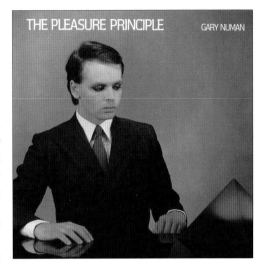

It must have been hard to determine exactly what Gary Numan represented back in 1979. On the cover of *The Pleasure Principle*, he is part androgynous Bowie alien, part Kraftwerk robot, and at least somewhat later Roxy Music Savile Row dandy. Sonically, the album represents musical elements of all those artists.

Gary Numan had already tasted chart success with electro group Tubeway Army, scoring a surprise UK No. 1 with "Are 'Friends' Electric?" and topping the UK chart with its parent album, *Replicas*. On this solo debut Numan employs a quartet of keyboards, bass guitar, drums, and viola. Not unlike Japan's technopop power trio Yellow Magic Orchestra with strings thrown into the mix.

It sounded revolutionary at the time to have the lead (and some rhythm) parts played on electronic keyboards, but Numan's take on electronica did not adhere strictly to the all-machine esthetic popularized by Kraftwerk or Depeche Mode. Rather, the album represented a sophisticated brand of new wave synth-rock driven by his dispassionate vocals and a symphonic wash of early synthesizer sounds, a clear inspiration to later synth-led groups such as The Human League and Soft Cell.

"Cars"—an excursion into paranoia and loneliness driven by one of the most distinctive synth riffs in all electronica—gave Numan a well-deserved UK No.1 single (and U.S. Top Ten) in September 1979. Elsewhere, whether in the economical, well-placed drum fills on "Films" and "Observer" or the precise basslines of "Engineers" and stand-out "Metal," *The Pleasure Principle* manages to sound at once futuristic and oddly timeless in a postmodern world. **YK**

> "When I first started to write songs, it was all for the love of music."
>
> Gary Numan, 2001

Track Listing

	01	**Airplane** (Numan)	3:18
▶	02	**Metal** (Numan)	3:33
	03	**Complex** (Numan)	3:12
▶	04	**Films** (Numan)	4:09
	05	**ME** (Numan)	5:37
	06	**Tracks** (Numan)	2:51
	07	**Observer** (Numan)	2:53
	08	**Conversation** (Numan)	7:36
▶	09	**Cars** (Numan)	3:58
▶	10	**Engineers** (Numan)	4:01

The Specials | Specials (1979)

Label | Two Tone
Producer | Elvis Costello
Art Direction | Chalkie Davies • Carol Starr
Nationality | UK
Running Time | 44:40

Songwriter/keyboardist Jerry Dammers, bassist Sir Horace Gentleman, and guitarist Lynval Golding honed their craft playing a mix of rock and reggae around Coventry, England from 1977 with a variety of personnel and names, including The Jaywalkers, The Hybrids, and The Coventry Automatics. By early 1979, as The Specials or Special AKA—a seven-piece adding Terry Hall (vocals), Roddy Radiation (guitar), John "Brad" Bradbury (drums), and Neville Staple (vocals)—they were fusing the angry intensity of punk with the rhythms of 1960s Jamaican ska music, heard to thrilling effect on debut single "Gangsters."

Adopting an image that referenced the Jamaican rude boys and UK mods that had been ska's original audience, The Specials dressed in tonic suits, button-down shirts, skinny ties, wraparound sunglasses, pork pie hats, and loafers. This striking look was presented in stark monochrome on the cover of their debut LP, released on their own Two Tone Records via Chrysalis.

Reflecting their live set, the album mixed covers—a feisty version of The Maytals' "Monkey Man," a slow skank through Dandy Livingstone's "A Message To You Rudy"—with self-penned material that reflected the turbulent times (mass unemployment, the rise of the UK's fascist National Front). "Doesn't Make It Alright" called for racial unity; Roddy Radiation's "Concrete Jungle" tackled inner-city violence.

With horns added by veteran ska trombonist Rico Rodriguez and production by Elvis Costello emphasizing The Specials' raw energy, the album entered the UK chart at No. 4 and remained in the Top Forty for 45 weeks. **JoH**

Track Listing

▶	01	**A Message To You Rudy** (Thompson)	2:53
	02	**Do The Dog** (The Specials • Thomas)	2:11
	03	**It's Up To You** (Dammers • The Specials)	3:23
▶	04	**Nite Klub** (Dammers • The Specials)	3:24
▶	05	**Doesn't Make It Alright** (Dammers • Goldberg)	3:25
▶	06	**Concrete Jungle** (Radiation)	3:18
	07	**Too Hot** (Campbell)	3:09
▶	08	**Monkey Man** (Hibbert)	2:44
	09	**(Dawning Of A) New Era** (Dammers)	2:26
	10	**Blank Expression** (Dammers • The Specials)	2:44
	11	**Stupid Marriage** (Dammers • Harrison • Staple)	3:50
▶	12	**Too Much Too Young** (Charmers • Dammers)	6:05
	13	**Little Bitch** (Dammers)	2:32
	14	**You're Wondering Now** (Anderson • Dennis)	2:36

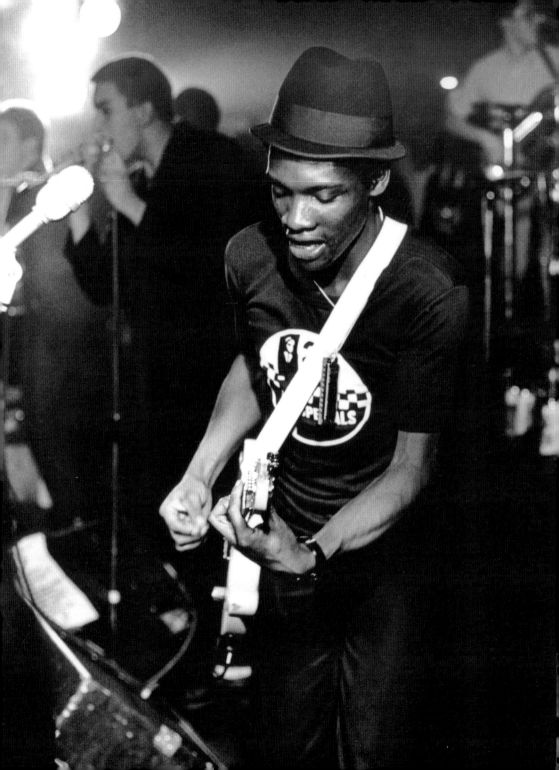

- **Argentina invades Falkland Islands**

- **Cabbage Patch Kids on sale**

- **Berlin Wall demolished**

- **MTV founded**

- **Live Aid**

1980s

Adam And The Ants
Kings Of The Wild Frontier (1980)

Label | CBS
Producer | Chris Hughes
Art Direction | Peter Ashworth
Nationality | UK
Running Time | 46:35

The first incarnation of Adam And The Ants recorded an angular 1979 debut, *Dirk Wears White Sox*, which still holds up as one of the era's great post-punk albums. But Adam was eager to distance himself from punk's drab, anti-pop agenda.

Sex Pistols' svengali Malcolm McLaren had suggested using African rhythms but, when Adam assembled his band of Burundi drummers, McLaren immediately poached them to form Bow Wow Wow. Undeterred, Adam assembled a new band of pirates led by guitarist buddy Marco Pirroni. By the end of 1980, "Dog Eat Dog" and "Antmusic" had stormed the UK singles chart and made him the biggest pop star in Europe.

"We stole what we could, like magpies," says Marco Pirroni. "We used ocarinas, echo chambers, textures from John Barry and Ennio Morricone soundtracks, rockabilly guitar riffs from Duane Eddy and Hank Marvin. We were even twanging rulers on desks and recording the results!" You can also hear even weirder sonic traces— the thundering tom toms of the Glitter Band, the thrilling snare-drum salutes of Loyalist marching bands, the mutant disco of Ze Records, even Aboriginal grunts and stomps borrowed from Rolf Harris.

Artists as diverse as Robbie Williams, Slipknot, Marilyn Manson, Pavement, Blur, Elastica, Suede, and Timbaland have all cited this album. Even Michael Jackson used to phone Adam and ask how he recorded his drum tracks. Not for nothing did Adam call this album "the final nail in the coffin of punk." **JLe**

"Punk is not anarchy ..."

Adam Ant, 1978

Track Listing

▶ 01	**Dog Eat Dog** (Ant·Pirroni)	3:10
▶ 02	**Antmusic** (Ant·Pirroni)	3:37
03	**Los Rancheros** (Ant·Pirroni)	3:30
04	**Feed Me To The Lions** (Ant·Pirroni)	3:20
05	**Press Darlings** (Ant)	3:59
06	**Ants Invasion** (Ant·Pirroni)	3:20
07	**Killer In The Home** (Ant·Pirroni)	4:22
08	**Kings Of The Wild Frontier** (Ant·Pirroni)	3:56
09	**The Magnificent 5** (Ant·Pirroni)	3:07
▶ 10	**Don't Be Square (Be There)** (Ant·Pirroni)	3:32
11	**Jolly Roger** (Ant·Pirroni)	2:11
12	**Physical (You're So)** (Ant)	3:59
13	**The Human Beings** (Ant·Pirroni)	4:32

Dexy's Midnight Runners
Searching For The Young Soul Rebels (1980)

Label | Parlophone
Producer | Pete Wingfield
Art Direction | Peter Barrett
Nationality | UK
Running Time | 39:05

Kevin Rowland and Kevin "Al" Archer, previously of punk act The Killjoys, formed Dexy's Midnight Runners in Birmingham, England, in July 1978, taking their name from Dexedrine—a pep pill favored by Sixties mods.

After Dexy's played several gigs with The Specials— whose audience included many skinheads—Rowland decided that a hard, gang-based look was needed for the post-punk times. The New York stevedores in the movie *On The Waterfront* and the Italian Americans in *Mean Streets* provided the spur for the band's trademark wooly hats, donkey jackets, and leather coats.

Sophomore single "Geno" married Rowland's lyrical tribute to soul singer Geno Washington with Archer's punchy music, including an irresistible brass riff cribbed from Washington and the Ram Jam Band over a solid rhythm section. Dominated by Big Jim Paterson's trombone, Jeff Blythe's saxophone, and Steve Spooner's alto sax, the song became a UK No. 1 and a live favorite.

This inaugural LP proved just as strong, opening with the sound of a radio switching channels before a cry of, "For God's sake burn it down" kicks things off. The track was a reworking of debut single "Dance Stance," Rowland's angry diatribe against anti-Irish jokes. Other album highlights included Rowland and Archer's dual vocal on the defiant "Tell Me When My Light Turns Green," a breakneck cover of Chuck Wood's northern soul favorite "Seven Days Too Long." "There, There, My Dear" (another UK hit) closes proceedings on a high.

Welcome the new soul vision indeed. **JoH**

" ...I couldn't walk down the road if I wore dungarees ..."

Kevin Rowland, *c.* 2000

Track Listing

▶	01	**Burn It Down** (Rowland)	4:21
▶	02	**Tell Me When My Light Turns Green** (Rowland)	3:46
	03	**The Team That Meet In Caffs** (Archer)	4:08
	04	**I'm Just Looking** (Blythe·Rowland·Saunders)	4:41
▶	05	**Geno** (Archer·Rowland)	3:31
▶	06	**Seven Days Too Long** (Bailey·Harell)	2:43
	07	**I Couldn't Help It If I Tried** (Rowland)	4:14
	08	**Thankfully Not Living In Yorkshire It Doesn't Apply** (Rowland·Saunders)	2:59
	09	**Keep It** (Archer·Blythe)	3:59
	10	**Love Part One** (Rowland)	1:12
▶	11	**There, There, My Dear** (Archer·Rowland)	3:31

AC/DC | Back In Black (1980)

Label | ATCO
Producer | Robert John Lange
Art Direction | Bob Defrin
Nationality | Australia · UK
Running Time | 41:31

Album cover that can only be described as (none more) black? Check. Lead singer lost, choked on vomit? Uh-huh. Stone Age perspective on sexual politics reflected in track titles? Yep. You could be forgiven for mistaking AC/DC for Spinal Tap, fulfilling all the requirements for a parody metal act. Where the Aussie rockers swerved the caricature, however, was by producing enjoyably no-nonsense music that seriously rocked.

By the time of original vocalist Bon Scott's February 1980 death, AC/DC had conquered Europe, but the United States were still to be convinced. The group was fiercely ambitious, and recruited singer Brian Johnson on the recommendation of producer Robert Lange.

The only real hint of Tappery comes at the beginning of "Hells Bells," when the ominous tones of a bell being struck give you the fear that the band are about to embark on their personal "Stonehenge," but the entry of the Youngs' guitars signal business as usual.

"Back In Black" and "Have A Drink On Me" paid tribute to Scott, but elsewhere his absence was scarcely noticed, as Johnson's raucous howl fitted seamlessly into the mix.

The bawdy licentiousness of "Let Me Put My Love ..." —"Let me cut your cake with my knife"—also signals that Scott's passing has not enlightened the boys one bit, while their sign-off, "Rock And Roll Ain't Noise Pollution," serves as a one-fingered salute to the band's cultured critics.

AC/DC finally broke the United States with *Back In Black*, notching up a million sales annually over the next five years. They—and all those buyers who boogied to the album—never looked back. **SJac**

> ## "I just want to go further ... "
>
> Angus Young, 1984

Track Listing		
▶ 01 **Hells Bells** (Johnson·A. Young·M.Young)		5:09
02 **Shoot To Thrill** (Johnson·A. Young·M.Young)		5:14
03 **What Do You Do For Money Honey** (Johnson·A. Young·M.Young)		3:33
04 **Givin The Dog A Bone** (Johnson·A. Young·M.Young)		3:30
05 **Let Me Put My Love Into You** (Johnson·A. Young·M.Young)		4:12
▶ 06 **Back In Black** (Johnson·A. Young·M.Young)		4:13
▶ 07 **You Shook Me All Night Long** (Johnson·A. Young·M.Young)		3:28
08 **Have A Drink On Me** (Johnson·A. Young·M. Young)		3:57
09 **Shake A Leg** (Johnson·A. Young·M.Young)		4:03
10 **Rock And Roll Ain't Noise Pollution** (Johnson·A. Young·M.Young)		4:12

The Cramps
Songs The Lord Taught Us (1980)

Label | IRS
Producer | Alex Chilton
Art Direction | Carl Grasso
Nationality | USA
Running Time | 53:32

Dead Kennedys
Fresh Fruit For Rotting Vegetables (1980)

Label | Alternative Tentacles
Producer | East Bay Ray • Norm
Art Direction | Annie Horwood
Nationality | USA
Running Time | 32:57

Songs The Lord Taught Us celebrates the trashiest elements of twentieth-century Americana. The Cramps' debut chewed up rockabilly riffs, punk rebellion, and B-movie imagery, and spat out a gloriously primeval gob of rock 'n' roll noise.

To capture their warped vision, the group headed to the Sam C. Philips Studio in Memphis, where Elvis and Jerry Lee Lewis cut early tracks. The songs sound at once nostalgic and incredibly fresh. "TV Set"—the wickedly funny tale of a girlfriend-slaughtering psycho—rolls along on a surf beat, punctuated by singer Lux Interior's lupine howling and guitarist Poison Ivy's punk noise.

"I Was a Teenage Werewolf" and "The Mad Daddy"— a tribute to rock 'n' roll DJ Pete Myers—sound like transmissions straight from Dracula's lair, thanks to layers of echo piled on by producer Alex Chilton.

Songs The Lord Taught Us should have been a smash. Critics raved, but problems in the band nixed any chance of success. During a 1980 tour of the United States, guitarist Bryan Gregory drove off with a van full of their equipment—sold to fund his growing drug addiction—and was never seen by the band again.

It may have been a flop, but *Songs The Lord Taught Us* exerted a huge influence. It showed groups like The Gun Club and The Birthday Party that they did not have to burn rock's back catalog, just reinvent it in their own twisted way. **TB**

It is no coincidence that Dead Kennedys' debut album came out the same year that Ronald Reagan became American president. Reagan's brand of Far-Right populism tempered with born-again Christianity served as the perfect counterpoise to—and inspiration for—the band's radically political music.

Dead Kennedys initially took inspiration from the original wave of UK punks such as the Sex Pistols, but became disenchanted with their anarchic posturing, so they created their own take on the movement.

Fresh Fruit . . . is an intelligent and humorous album, which satirizes the bleak social landscape of the era. "Holiday In Cambodia" is a searing attack on the nascent yuppies, while "Kill The Poor" is Jonathan Swift's *A Modest Proposal* set to a blistering soundtrack. And to show that his scorn was not reserved for the Far-Right, Biafra cheerfully let rip at Democrat Jerry Brown (dubbing him a "Zen fascist") on "California Uber Alles."

But as much as Dead Kennedys were about Biafra's lyrics, the sharpness and wit of the band's music set them apart from the basic three-chorders of the punk scene. The doom-laden intro to " . . . Cambodia" presages the song's dark sentiments, while "California . . ." opens like a Nuremberg rally on Venice Beach.

Dead Kennedys may have ultimately lost their battle with Reagan and his forces of Right(eousness), but as a call to arms not much beats this album. **SJac**

Peter Gabriel
Peter Gabriel III (a.k.a. Melt) (1980)

Label | Charisma
Producer | Steve Lillywhite
Art Direction | Hipgnosis
Nationality | UK
Running Time | 45:31

The Soft Boys
Underwater Moonlight (1980)

Label | Armageddon
Producer | Pat Collier • Mike Kemp
Art Direction | George Wright
Nationality | UK
Running Time | 35:56

With the psychedelic musings of Genesis and self-conscious eccentricity of albums *I* and *II* behind him, the 29-year-old prog rocker emerges as an avant-garde solo artist, in the mold of Bowie and Eno.

Based in his own studio, and aided by friends including Phil Collins, Robert Fripp, and David Rhodes, Gabriel finally felt free to play with his perennial enthusiasms—world music and technology, notably the Fairlight CMI and drumming machine. Alongside the more traditional guitar-thrashing on "And Through The Wire," Gabriel includes a mix of eerie and ambient sounds never heard before on a rock album—the "gated snares" on "Intruder," or the sampling of South African chants on the rousing beatbox anthem "Biko."

Consistently edgy and impassioned, *Melt* is a perfectly produced collage of warped sonic landscapes, befitting Gabriel's sparse, insular lyrics of alienation, paranoia, and identity.

Indeed, so astonishing was *Melt*, that in the United States, Atlantic dumped Gabriel after executives failed to persuade him to "make it sound like the Doobie Brothers." A decision they came to regret, after Mercury took it on and sold 250,000 copies (far more than Gabriel's two previous releases). In Britain, the album hit No. 1, and the single "Games Without Frontiers," featuring Kate Bush on backing vocals, reached No. 4—Gabriel's highest UK singles placing up to that point. **LS**

Formed in Cambridge in 1976, The Soft Boys fused pop hooks with British folk rock and snotty punk aggression. Lead singer Robyn Hitchcock, guitarist Kimberly Rew, drummer Morris Windsor, and bassist Matthew Seligman never quite fitted in with the music trends of the time, but time has a funny way of catching up when the music is this good.

Underwater Moonlight hits the ground running with "I Wanna Destroy You," a pissed-off anthem featuring swirling guitars and bright vocal harmonies. "Kingdom Of Love" showcases Hitchcock's surreal wit as he compares infatuation with insect eggs hatching under his skin; "Now there's tiny insects showing through/All them tiny insects look like you!" Guitar hooks and crashing drums lead the attack on "Positive Vibrations," but it is the sitar break midway through that sets it apart. And "Queen Of Eyes" is simply an incredibly precise and addictive two minutes of guitar pop.

It would be the last proper Soft Boys album. Hitchcock went on to pursue a prolific solo career with Windsor in his backing band The Egyptians, while Rew went on to form Katrina and the Waves. But The Soft Boys' legacy grew as bands such as R.E.M. and The Replacements cited them as prime influences.

Check out Matador's superb 2001 reissue, featuring nine bonus tracks and a second disc packed with outtakes and rarities—an absolute must for fans. **RM**

The Cure | Seventeen Seconds (1980)

Label | Fiction
Producer | Mike Hedges • Robert Smith
Art Direction | The Cure • Bill Smith
Nationality | UK
Running Time | 35:41

THE CURE
SEVENTEEN SECONDS

The Cure opened the 1980s with the followup to their debut *Three Imaginary Boys*, resulting in what many argue is their finest work to date—a tough call, considering their prolific output.

Seventeen Seconds marks the band's introduction into the wider pop consciousness, providing their first hit—"A Forest," a sparse Cure classic that turns on a sublimely succinct bass riff, which almost made the UK Top 20. The Cure had already made an art form out of dark simplicity—Robert Smith's trademark teased hair, white face, red lipstick, and black clothes are as synonymous with The Cure as his dreamlike lyrics and deadpan vocals.

Like the album's cover art, which is little more than an abstract blur, the bleak, minimalist sound of this *Seventeen Seconds*-era Cure is subtly suggestive. The dark, existential motifs that are so much a part of The Cure became more prevalent (as Douglas Wolk noted in *The Nation* in 2004, Robert Smith "sings 'never' the way Joey Ramone sang 'wanna'—that little word implies an entire philosophy of being"), and introduced an atmosphere of beguiling bleakness, both in brief instrumentals and the more pop-oriented tracks (such as the sharp, hook-laden "Play For Today") that hark back to their earlier work.

Smith is compiling a special 2005 two-disc re-release of *Seventeen Seconds* digitally remastered with a disc of rarities from the same era with a 20-page booklet. Hopefully this will push *Seventeen Seconds* into the limelight—along with albums such as *Pornography* and *Disintegration*—where it belongs. **AHN**

> ## "We've never been part of any movement. We don't follow fashion."
> Robert Smith, 1996

Track Listing

01	**A Reflection** (Gallup•Smith•Tolhurst)	2:09
▶ 02	**Play For Today** (Gallup• Hartley•Smith•Tolhurst)	3:39
03	**Secrets** (Gallup•Smith•Tolhurst)	3:19
04	**In Your House** (Gallup•Smith•Tolhurst)	4:06
05	**Three** (Gallup•Smith•Tolhurst)	2:36
06	**The Final Sound** (Gallup•Smith•Tolhurst)	0:52
▶ 07	**A Forest** (Gallup• Hartley•Smith•Tolhurst)	5:55
▶ 08	**M** (Gallup•Smith•Tolhurst)	3:03
09	**At Night** (Gallup• Hartley•Smith•Tolhurst)	5:54
10	**Seventeen Seconds** (Gallup•Smith•Tolhurst)	4:01

Echo And The Bunnymen | Crocodiles (1980)

Label | Korova
Producer | David Balfe • Ian Broudie • Bill Drummond
Art Direction | Brian Griffin
Nationality | UK
Running Time | 32:34

Heavy with introspective doom and caustically cryptic, *Crocodiles* marked the full-length and major-label debut of the weird and wonderful Echo And The Bunnymen, launching them into the alternative music scene.

Ian McCulloch, Will Sergeant, and Les Pattinson had been together since an alchemical gig at Liverpool venue Eric's in 1978. The "Pictures On My Wall" single, on Bill Drummond's Zoo Records, had received a rapturous reception in the press, while sessions for DJ John Peel and London gigs brought major label attention.

The Bunnymen stood out from the crowd: McCulloch's sonorous voice and cryptic lyrics blended with Sergeant's murky, warped, and chopped guitar to produce music steeped in emotion. Their drum machine (dubbed Echo) had been replaced by Pete de Freitas.

The album was recorded over three weeks in June 1980 at Rockfield Studios in Wales. Tight, jarring, and urgent, with most songs clocking in at less than three minutes, this was basement music, every number a dark gem. Side one worked its way under the skin slowly, led by bass and guitar jangles; "Stars Are Stars" set up a juxtaposition of despair and optimism that would define the Bunnymen sound.

Side two opened with "Rescue"—a song McCulloch regards as a personal triumph—then strode out with the bad acid of "Villiers Terrace," closing with the heady melancholy of "Happy Death Men."

The sleeve, shot in woodland in Southeast England, set the tone for a decade of Bunnymen shoots: mysterious and vainglorious, with McCulloch sporting an overcoat nabbed from The Fall's Mark E. Smith. **MBI**

Track Listing

01	**Going Up**	(de Freitas • McCulloch • Pattinson • Sergeant)	3:57
02	**Stars Are Stars**	(de Freitas • McCulloch • Pattinson • Sergeant)	2:45
▶ 03	**Pride**	(de Freitas • McCulloch • Pattinson • Sergeant)	2:41
04	**Monkeys**	(de Freitas • McCulloch • Pattinson • Sergeant)	2:49
05	**Crocodiles**	(de Freitas • McCulloch • Pattinson • Sergeant)	2:38
▶ 06	**Rescue**	(de Freitas • McCulloch • Pattinson • Sergeant)	4:26
▶ 07	**Villiers Terrace**	(de Freitas • McCulloch • Pattinson • Sergeant)	2:44
08	**Pictures On My Wall**	(de Freitas • McCulloch • Pattinson • Sergeant)	2:52
09	**All That Jazz**	(de Freitas • McCulloch • Pattinson • Sergeant)	2:46
10	**Happy Death Men**	(de Freitas • McCulloch • Pattinson • Sergeant)	4:56

Motörhead | Ace Of Spades (1980)

Label | Bronze
Producer | Vic Maile
Art Direction | Martin Poole
Nationality | UK
Running Time | 36:34

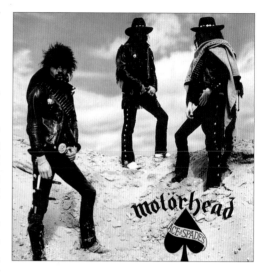

Ace Of Spades entered the chart at No. 4 in early November 1980. It was the product of a six-week session between producer Vic Maile, of Dr. Feelgood fame, and the classic Motörhead lineup: bassist/vocalist Ian "Lemmy" Kilmister, "Fast" Eddie Clarke (guitar), and Phil "Philthy Animal" Taylor (drums).

The 33 UK gigs played in October and November 1980 to promote *Ace Of Spades* would set up the band for 1981's live No. 1 LP *No Sleep 'Til Hammersmith*. "People had been waiting for a live album from us for three years," opined Lemmy, "but I was more pleased when *Ace Of Spades* went in at No. 4, because *No Sleep* … was a one-off."

The title track, "Ace Of Spades," which made UK No. 15 as a single, surely ranks with Pete Townshend's "Hope I die before I get old" as the ultimate rock 'n' roll death wish. "They say that I was born to lose/'Cos gambling's for fools/But that's the way I like it baby/I don't want to live forever." (In 2000, Lemmy, 55 at the time, added a qualification. "I'd like to die the year before forever. To avoid the rush …")

The first, glorious period of Motörhead history, concluded by *Ace Of Spades*, undoubtedly laid the foundations (jackhammer drums, fret-meltingly fast riffage, lethal bass, throat-shredding vocal treatment) for speed-metal practitioners Anthrax and Metallica to build on later in the 1980s. At the time, *Sounds'* Garry Bushell awarded *Ace Of Spades* a full five stars. He explained: "Motörhead are heavy metal in the only meaningful sense of the term—everyone else is just pretending." **MH**

> ## "We didn't become fossilized after that record, you know!"
>
> Lemmy, 2002

Track Listing

▶	01	**Ace Of Spades** (Motörhead)	2:47
	02	**Love Me Like A Reptile** (Motörhead)	3:23
	03	**Shoot You In The Back** (Motörhead)	2:39
	04	**Live To Win** (Motörhead)	3:37
	05	**Fast And Loose** (Motörhead)	3:22
	06	**(We Are) The Road Crew** (Motörhead)	3:12
	07	**Fire, Fire** (Motörhead)	2:42
▶	08	**Jailbait** (Motörhead)	3:33
	09	**Dance** (Motörhead)	2:37
	10	**Bite The Bullet** (Motörhead)	1:38
▶	11	**The Chase Is Better Than The Catch** (Motörhead)	4:17
	12	**The Hammer** (Motörhead)	2:47

Killing Joke
Killing Joke (1980)

Label | EG
Producer | Killing Joke
Art Direction | Mike Coles
Nationality | UK
Running Time | 35:04

Inside the cover of this eponymous, extraordinary debut, a Christ-like figure approaches some children in an urban wasteland. He is making a most un-Christ-like hand gesture. That is the first sign you will be getting anything but a comfortable ride from an album that is the aural equivalent of having thumbs pushed through your eyes while being told the end is nigh.

The combination of Youth, a.k.a. Martin Glover, Kenneth "Geordie" Walker, Jaz Coleman, and Paul Ferguson was awesomely combustible. "Requiem" sets the agenda, with man deemed "cattle for slaughter" by the maniacal Coleman, self-styled seer, thespian, and treader of the fine line between sanity and psychosis. "Wardance" is relentless, intensifying the mood of alienation with Jaz's distorted vocals set against Youth's funk-influenced basslines, Big Paul's tribal beats, and Geordie's effortlessly cool but sustaining guitar.

No one could be sure of anything on this record. There are bludgeoning dance riffs ("Bloodsport"), raid-the-barricades rock ("The Wait"), and spartan soundscapes ("Tomorrow's World" and "SO36"). So confident were the band in their powers that, on the UK release, they could afford to save "Change," the era's finest punk-funk splintering, and the utterly savage "Psyche" for use as B-sides.

One of the decade's most bleakly beautiful releases, embraced by everyone who, the year after the election of Margaret Thatcher as British prime minister, could sense disturbing times ahead. **CB**

Judas Priest
British Steel (1980)

Label | CBS
Producer | Tom Allom
Art Direction | Roslav Szaybo
Nationality | UK
Running Time | 35:51

Judas Priest fans have long debated which is the quintet's best album. Mature headbangers cite 1978's *Stained Class*, which signaled a harder, faster direction for heavy metal. Arena crowds love *Screaming For Vengeance* (1982); others acclaim 1990's *Painkiller* as a thrashing return to form. But *British Steel* is definitive.

The group's sixth studio set was iconic. The cover found its way onto T-shirts, one of which was sported by Pantera's Dimebag Darrell on TV in 1991; impressed, Halford jammed with Pantera on a cover of "Metal Gods."

Though originating in 1973, Priest slotted into the new wave of British heavy metal, alongside Iron Maiden and Def Leppard. Metal appealed to those who craved sounds more streetwise than prog rock, yet were alienated by punk's posturing and anti-musicality.

British Steel embodied this, channeling Halford's scream-to-a-sigh vocals and the guitars of Glenn Tipton and K. K. Downing into lightning strike proto-thrasher "Rapid Fire." The outsiders' clarion call "Breaking The Law" was a future *Beavis And Butthead* anthem, while "United" and "Metal Gods" were indelible stompers, the latter utilizing cutlery and electric cables as percussion.

The album was recorded at John Lennon's former country residence outside London. "It was an enormous rush of excitement being there," Halford told *Blender*, "Because I was a huge Beatles fan."

Party anthem "Living After Midnight" propelled British Steel up the Billboard chart. Eight Top 40 albums—and immortality—beckoned. **MA**

The Circle Jerks
Group Sex (1980)

Label | Frontier
Producer | The Circle Jerks • Cary Markoff
Art Direction | Diane Zincavage
Nationality | USA
Running Time | 15:07

While there were faster, angrier, and more frantic punk bands in the L.A. punk scene of the early 1980s, none could fuse politics and fun as well as The Circle Jerks did on their classic debut *Group Sex*. Named after a nasty frat-house initiation rite, the band formed in 1980 when original Black Flag singer Keith Morris left that band to start his own, along with former Redd Kross guitarist Greg Hetson, Roger Rogerson on bass, and "Lucky" Lehrer on drums. The quartet quickly earned a reputation as beer-swilling wild men who helped define the party punk scene of the time.

Despite its brevity—14 songs in fewer than 15 minutes—*Group Sex* is a raw, witty, and focused document of adolescent frustration that stands alongside Black Flag's *Damaged* and TSOL's debut for all out slam-dancing rage. Morris' snotty, spoken-word-like delivery and Hetson and Lecher's jaw-dropping four-stomp rhythm changes on songs about alienation ("World Up My Ass"), sex ("I Just Want Some Skank"), and drugs ("Wasted") make this a must have for any self-respecting punk rocker, an album that even excited the interest of legendary BBC DJ John Peel.

In later years, Hetson went on to join Bad Religion. The remaining members floundered, even resorting to the gimmick of recording with bland pop singer Debbie Gibson, but still there is no doubting the influence that *Group Sex* has had on a whole new generation of Southern Californian party punk bands such as NOFX and the Vandals. **TSc**

Talking Heads
Remain In Light (1980)

Label | Sire
Producer | Brian Eno
Art Direction | M. & Co.
Nationality | USA
Running Time | 40:02

Originally entitled *Melody Attack*, *Remain In Light* is Talking Heads' greatest statement, the last and most accomplished of the trio of albums they recorded with Brian Eno. Recorded at a fractious point in the Heads' history, it can be viewed as a fight for leader David Byrne's attention between the other group members (Tina Weymouth, Chris Frantz, and Jerry Harrison) and producer and co-writer Eno. This creative tension makes for a continually invigorating listen.

After recording all the basic tracks, the band regrouped in New York in summer 1980 to complete the work. Fighting writer's block, Byrne sculpted the jams—often simple variations on one chord—into recognizable songs. With layer upon layer of vocal, groove, and percussion, the record's intermeshing rhythms still leave the listener breathless, from the African-inspired "The Great Curve" to the Kurtis Blow-influenced, "Crosseyed And Painless." The greatest jam, however, "Weird Guitar Riff Song," became "Once In A Lifetime," with its illusions to the work of Fela Kuti, and Byrne emulating the rapture of preachers.

Released in October 1980, *Remain In Light* ably demonstrated that pop could be both for your head and your feet. The making of the album divided the group smartly into two camps—Eno and Byrne and Weymouth and Frantz—with Harrison playing mediator. Although Eno was to leave the equation, the tension from this record dogged the group and led to their split ten years later. **DE**

Joy Division | Closer (1980)

Label | Factory
Producer | Martin Hannett
Art Direction | Peter Saville
Nationality | UK
Running Time | 44:23

·CLOSER·

After 25 years, it is almost impossible to separate the unsettling atmosphere of Joy Division's music from the disintegration of its singer's personality and sudden death. While their 1979 debut *Unknown Pleasures* peered into a terrifying abyss, it was still just music.

Not so with *Closer*. Compared to its violent, more conventional predecessor, *Closer* is a quantum leap. The songs stray far from the punk-inspired template of the band's early years. Where much of the dank atmosphere of *Unknown Pleasures* came from producer Martin Hannett's revolutionary use of digital effects, here the music itself is alien—from the strange, militaristic rhythms of "Colony" to the hysterical twisted guitars on "Atrocity Exhibition." The addition of synthesizers—notably on "Isolation" and "Heart And Soul"—hints that had the band continued with Curtis, they may still have ended up sounding like New Order.

The ambience Hannett creates here is practically an instrument in itself. While it once provided a dark background for the band's assault, his trademark reverb and delay treatments are now part of the skeletal songs, somehow rendering them all the more stark.

But it is on the final three songs—the desperate "Twenty Four Hours" and the defeated "The Eternal" and "Decades"—where, with hindsight, one can clearly see that the boundary between Curtis' personal torment and his bleak lyrical themes no longer existed. The cover's gravestone design may have been an unfortunate coincidence, as it was decided upon long before Curtis' death, but it is hard not to interpret this grim full stop of an album as anything other than a suicide note. **MB**

> "It's almost as if writing that album contributed to his state: he immersed himself in it, rather than just expressing it."
>
> Tony Wilson, 1994

Track Listing

01	**Atrocity Exhibition**	(Joy Division)	6:05
▶ 02	**Isolation**	(Joy Division)	2:53
03	**Passover**	(Joy Division)	4:46
04	**Colony**	(Joy Division)	3:55
05	**A Means To An End**	(Joy Division)	4:07
▶ 06	**Heart And Soul**	(Joy Division)	5:51
▶ 07	**Twenty Four Hours**	(Joy Division)	4:26
08	**The Eternal**	(Joy Division)	6:07
09	**Decades**	(Joy Division)	6:13

Iron Maiden | Iron Maiden (1980)

Label | EMI
Producer | Will Malone
Art Direction | Cream • Derek Riggs
Nationality | UK
Running Time | 37:41

Iron Maiden's debut remains one of the keystones of heavy rock. Speed, thrash, death, grunge—all owe something to this record's dazzling mesh of punk attitude and metal obsession.

In the early 1980s, UK rock magazine *Sounds* ardently promoted (and christened) the new wave of British heavy metal; among its contenders were Saxon, Samson, Def Leppard, Girlschool, and Angelwitch. As punk struggled to maintain its commercial footing, a band from London's East End emerged who combined the working-class grit of The Stranglers with Black Sabbath's gift for creating stunning riffs.

Iron Maiden were led by bassist Steve Harris, and their cause was championed by charismatic manager Rod "Smallwallet" Smallwood. Constant touring, and a UK hit with the urgent anthem "Running Free," saw their debut album reach No. 4. (Their refusal to mime to the single on BBC TV's weekly music show *Top Of The Pops* saw the band become the first to play live on the program for seven years.) The tough production delivers a live aura, with Paul Di'Anno's raspings adding mystique to Steve Harris' dark lyricism. Guitars are restrained yet gutsy, as Di'Anno's voice wraps closely around complex riffs.

The second Maiden album, *Killers*, offered little more than consolidation, and Di'Anno was replaced by Samson's Bruce Dickinson and his laser precision vocals. Iron Maiden, and their gruesome mascot Eddie (depicted on the cover), hit enormous commercial heights with Dickinson. But the streetwise intensity, created here with Di'Anno, was gone for good. **GT**

> **"All we wanted to do was make records and go out and play. But then when things started really happening ..."**
>
> Steve Harris, 1982

Track Listing

01	**Prowler** (Harris)	3:57
▶ 02	**Remember Tomorrow** (Di'Anno • Harris)	5:28
▶ 03	**Running Free** (Di'Anno • Harris)	3:17
▶ 04	**Phantom Of The Opera** (Harris)	7:09
05	**Transylvania** (Harris)	4:19
06	**Strange World** (Harris)	5:32
▶ 07	**Charlotte The Harlot** (Murray)	4:13
▶ 08	**Iron Maiden** (Harris)	3:46

The Undertones **Hypnotised** (1980)

Label | Sire
Producer | Roger A. Bechirian
Art Direction | M. Bradley • B. Hollyhead • D. O'Neill
Nationality | UK
Running Time | 39:02

With "More Songs About Chocolate And Girls" (the title an oblique nod to Talking Heads), The Undertones were poking fun at themselves just in case anyone thought this remarkable powerpunk group from Derry, Northern Ireland, actually believed all the miraculously good publicity they had been getting.

Recorded in the Netherlands, after their first U.S. tour *Hypnotised* quite possibly exceeds its predecessor in terms of quality, excitement, and that intangible, oblique essence d'Undertone that so many have tried to capture—or even define. Sure, some songs are a little tossed-off, including the rather fumbling (though funny) opener and the light, jaunty "See That Girl." But with material as strong and vibrant as "Whizz Kids," "Girls That Don't Talk," and "Boys Will Be Boys"; the perfect title track (even if you did spend too long thinking Feargal was singing "pinch rub me I'm hypnotized" instead of the more logical "H.Y.P . . . "); and the simply genius "Tearproof," with its joyous instrumental break, all criticisms are neatly knocked into a cocked hat.

Add to that the supreme singles—the saddest pop song ever, "Wednesday Week," with its swooping guitar solo, and the boisterously hilarious "My Perfect Cousin" —and you have an album of higher hook-laden quality than would be found on almost any other group's greatest hits package.

Recent reissues contain one non-LP single, possibly their most wonderful, "You've Got My Number." It is featured, though, with four disposable B-sides, including an extremely inessential, vocalless "Hard Luck." **DN**

Track Listing

01	**More Songs About Chocolate And Girls** (D. O'Neill)	2:43
02	**There Goes Norman** (J. O'Neill)	2:27
▶ 03	**Hypnotised** (Bradley • D. O'Neill)	3:31
04	**See That Girl** (J. O'Neill)	2:24
05	**Whizz Kids** (D. O'Neill)	2:19
06	**Under The Boardwalk** (Resnick • Young)	2:26
07	**The Way Girls Talk** (J. O'Neill • Sharkey)	2:30
08	**Hard Luck** (Bradley • Doherty • D. O'Neill J. O'Neill • Sharkey)	3:41
▶ 09	**My Perfect Cousin** (Bradley • D. O'Neill)	2:36
10	**Boys Will Be Boys** (D. O'Neill • J. O'Neill)	1:27
▶ 11	**Tearproof** (Bradley • J. O'Neill)	2:20
▶ 12	**Wednesday Week** (J. O'Neill)	2:17
13	**Nine Times Out Of Ten** (Doherty • J. O'Neill)	2:37
14	**Girls That Don't Talk** (J. O'Neill)	2:26
15	**What's With Terry?** (D. O'Neill)	3:18

The Jam | Sound Affects (1980)

Label | Polydor
Producer | Vic Coppersmith-Heaven
Art Direction | Bill Smith
Nationality | UK
Running Time | 35:35

The Angry Young Man is a central figure in postwar British culture, from Jimmy Porter in John Osborne's 1956 play *Look Back In Anger* to the punk explosion of the late 1970s.

Few bands explored this with keener insight than The Jam. With a string of ever more confident and potent albums, their chief songwriter and incendiary singer-guitarist Paul Weller became the bard of bile, giving voice to very British frustrations and dreams.

Their previous release, *Setting Sons*, broke the Top Five and spawned two No. 1 singles in the UK, but America still did not pay much attention, underscoring their distinctly British perspective. After emerging from the Townhouse studio with their followup, they drew mild criticism for the obvious references to touchstones of the British pop canon, such as lifting the bassline from The Beatles' "Taxman" for the punchy "Start!" Such complaints, however, misunderstood the incorporation of elements that informed the work's creative milieu (the cover itself apes a vintage BBC sound effects record Weller discovered in the studio). In reality, the album is a work of startling originality.

While not a formal concept album, taken together, the songs form a portrait of the disgruntled yearning that is central to the complaint of the Angry Young Man. From the empty consumerism of "Pretty Green" to the bitter dolor of "Scrape Away," the listener enters a world of failed potential. At the center of it all lies "That's Entertainment!"—with its double-tracked acoustic strum and litany of everyday annoyances, it captures the essence of what made the band so important. **TSh**

> ## "It all ends up that you can't help but be affected by your times."
>
> Paul Weller, 2004

Track Listing

▶	01	**Pretty Green** (Weller)	2:37
▶	02	**Monday** (Weller)	3:02
	03	**But I'm Different Now** (Weller)	1:52
	04	**Set The House Ablaze** (Weller)	5:03
▶	05	**Start!** (Weller)	2:33
▶	06	**That's Entertainment** (Weller)	3:38
	07	**Dream Time** (Weller)	3:54
	08	**Man In The Corner Shop** (Weller)	3:12
	09	**Music For The Last Couple** (Buckler·Foxton·Weller)	3:45
▶	10	**Boy About Town** (Weller)	2:00
	11	**Scrape Away** (Weller)	3:59

Tom Waits | Heartattack And Vine (1980)

Label | Asylum
Producer | Bones Howe
Art Direction | Ron Coro • Norm Ung
Nationality | USA
Running Time | 44:25

In hindsight, the seeds of change were planted here, though no one noticed at the time. *Heartattack And Vine* was Tom Waits' seventh album for Asylum, and he had still not moved beyond cult status, his beatnik barfly image on the edge of wearing out what little welcome it still received. A pity; this is one of the strongest sets of his early period.

Though the record contains a few of the downtrodden piano ballads for which he had become known (spellbinding movie theme "On The Nickel," the elegiac "Ruby's Arms"), *Heartattack And Vine* is more notable for the dirty guitar that anchors roughly half the record and pre-empts his later work. The grimy lead track—which contains the classically Waitsian couplet, "There ain't no devil/That's just God when he's drunk"—is a swampy rumble through the sleazy L.A. that Waits then called home; for "Heartattack," read Hollywood Boulevard, whose junction with Vine Street was then one of the area's seediest corners. "Mr. Siegal" takes a similarly half-cut bluesy tack. The two worlds meet on "Jersey Girl": one of his most affecting love songs, it found a wider audience than Waits ever had or ever will when Bruce Springsteen included a faithful reading of it on his *Live 1975–1985* set.

When *Heartattack And Vine* failed to creep beyond No. 96 in the Billboard charts, Waits lost his deal, but not his inspiration. Following his soundtrack for Francis Ford Coppola's flop *One From The Heart*, the singer reinvented himself with the dark, unhinged cabaret of 1983's *Swordfishtrombones*, the first record in the second phase of a perennially fascinating discography. **WF-J**

> "I used to think I was making movies for the ears—writing them, directing them, releasing them."

Tom Waits, 2004

Track Listing

▶	01	**Heartattack And Vine** (Waits)	4:50
	02	**In Shades** (Waits)	4:25
	03	**Saving All My Love For You** (Waits)	3:41
	04	**Downtown** (Waits)	4:45
▶	05	**Jersey Girl** (Waits)	5:11
	06	**'Til The Money Runs Out** (Waits)	4:25
▶	07	**On The Nickel** (Waits)	6:19
	08	**Mr Siegal** (Waits)	5:14
	09	**Ruby's Arms** (Waits)	5:35

UB40
Signing Off (1980)

Label | Graduate
Producer | Ray Pablo Falconer • UB40
Art Direction | UB40
Nationality | UK
Running Time | 66:28

UB40, who took their name from a British unemployment benefit form, would eventually become the world's greatest reggae cover band. But there was no taste of "Red Red Wine" on the group's smart, deeply moving debut.

Those who know only the aforementioned Neil Diamond song and Elvis Presley's "(I Can't Help) Falling In Love With You" might be surprised to find out that UB40 actually had something to say of their own. And this album says plenty, from its cover that shows a UB40 form to the hymn-like songs that reflect the band's roots in working-class Birmingham.

Formed late in Britain's ska revival, UB40 quickly became a presence in the British Top Ten with the pop-heavy, reggae-influenced protest singles "King," "I Think It's Going To Rain Today," and "The Earth Dies Screaming," the first two of which feature on *Signing Off*.

Vocalist Ali Campbell's lyrics are simmering with rage on the likes of "Burden Of Shame" and "Little By Little," targeted at everyone from governments (for their part in creating world famine) to the band's complacent fellow countrymen (for allowing it to happen). But he delivers the message in a voice so velvety smooth that it makes the most bitter line sound like a lullaby on such memorable tracks as "Tyler" and the Billie Holiday classic "Strange Fruit."

Signing Off proved to be popular in Britain, charting for well over a year. But it would take a subsequent and significant watering down of the message to take the band to international superstardom. **JiH**

The Teardrop Explodes
Kilimanjaro (1980)

Label | Mercury
Producer | Various
Art Direction | Brian Griffin
Nationality | UK
Running Time | 36:93

If Echo And The Bunnymen were Liverpool's Doors, then Julian Cope's Teardrop Explodes were the Scouse Love. They formed in the autumn of 1978, taking their name from a DC comic, but by the time *Kilimanjaro* was released two years later, their reputation had already been made and to some they had passed their peak. This perception was reinforced by the sacking of original guitarist/co-writer Mick Finkler and their signing to Phonogram, a major label, from the local indie Zoo run by Bill Drummond and Teardrops keyboardist Dave Balfe.

The tracks "Treason," "Bouncing Babies," and "Sleeping Gas" had already appeared as Zoo singles, and were re-recorded for the album. Yet only purists would prefer the weedier indie versions, as *Kilimanjaro* displayed all the bounce and pizzazz of *Forever Changes* or *The Notorious Byrd Brothers*. The combination of Balfe's innate pop sensibility and Cope's further-out experimentation combined to make a perfect album that reached No. 24 on the national chart. Yet it would take the non-album single "Reward" (a UK No. 6)—released in February of 1981 and highlighted by the strident brass stabs of Ray Martinez and Hurricane Smith—to truly break the Teardrops.

Record Collector described the original sleeve of *Kilimanjaro* as "one of the worst record sleeves ever," and the album was later (and thankfully!) re-sleeved and reissued with the addition of "Reward"; the music was also remixed. **MH**

The Specials
More Specials (1980)

Label | Two Tone
Producer | J. Dammers • D. Jordan
Art Direction | C. Davies • C. Starr
Nationality | UK
Running Time | 42:33

Steve Winwood
Arc Of A Diver (1980)

Label | Island
Producer | C. Blackwell • S. Winwood
Art Direction | Tony Wright
Nationality | UK
Running Time | 40:01

The runaway success of The Specials' debut LP and UK chart-topping *Too Much Too Young Live* EP caused a craze for all things ska. The Specials' label Two Tone had launched the careers of Madness, The (UK) Beat, and The Selecter, and when The Specials played America in early 1980 their U.S. record company decorated L.A.'s Whiskey A Go-Go in black and white checks in tribute.

By mid-year, the band were exhausted from touring, but needed to record a sophomore long player. A stopgap punk-ska single, the Roddy Radiation-penned "Rat Race," hit the UK Top Five, but Jerry Dammers decided the style was becoming a cliché and that the next Specials album should break new ground.

Side one was varied, featuring energetic ska ("Enjoy Yourself"), reggae (hit single "Do Nothing"), stomping northern soul ("Sock It To Em JB") and "Pearl's Café," a kitsch singalong with the chorus refrain: "It's all a load of bollocks." But it was side two that entered radical territory, drawing on Dammers' love of movie scores and exotica—hence "Stereotypes," which marries Dammers' put-down of a macho drunk driver to a fusion of muzak beats and spaghetti Western themes as Neville Staple toasts about loving his stereo and marijuana. Elsewhere, "International Jet Set" tells of a hellish plane journey ending in disaster—over catchy elevator music.

The eclectic mixture of styles influenced 1990s trip-hop acts such as Portishead and Massive Attack, while the 1990s saw a revival of interest in the easy listening that Dammers drew on for this album. **JH**

After kicking his 1960s-to-'70s band Traffic to the curb, Steve Winwood had floated around guesting with Stomu Yamash'ta, Reebop, Amazing Blondel, and many other low-key labelmates before cutting an excellent, though totally ignored, eponymous solo album. The final track, "Midland Maniac," was entirely self-created and pointed the way to a one-man followup.

The recordings were overdubbed onto a click track, drums last. His lyricist of choice was no longer Jim Capaldi—a writing collaborator from Traffic days who had now emigrated to Brazil—but Will Jennings, an American he had contacted via Van Morrison. George Fleming, nephew of novelist Ian, who was a hunting pal of Winwood's and had never written lyrics before, also penned some material. His second effort, "Dust," a ballad like all Winwood's closing tracks, was particularly splendid, contrasting with the chauvinist sentiments of "Second-Hand Woman." And there was still room for a cameo from Viv Stanshall, former Bonzo Dog frontman, on the lyrics for the title track.

If *Arc Of A Diver* has a fault, it is down to the fact that albums created by individuals alone can tend to be a little sterile—though certainly, given the 1970s technology at his disposal, Winwood did an admirable job in his own Netherturkdonic studios. That said, the audience he sought to reach was not Traffic fans who loved that band's organic feel, but music lovers of a new decade—and the album's U.S. Top Three chart success suggests that he succeeded. **MH**

Pretenders | Pretenders (1980)

Label | Real
Producer | Chris Thomas • Nick Lowe
Art Direction | Kevin Hughes
Nationality | UK • USA
Running Time | 47:11

Punk claimed to trample gender underfoot, but that did not stop Chrissie Hynde's contemporaries in the Pistols/Clash camps calling her a mouthy Yank who would never amount to much. The Ohio native was ideally placed to board the bandwagon, having landed in London and worked for *NME*. But while white riots and anarchy erupted, Hynde remained a hanger-on.

Finally, a put-up-or-shut-up lecture from Lemmy (Motörhead's metal guru) spurred her to recruit bassist Pete Farndon, guitarist James Honeyman-Scott, and drummer Martin Chambers. A cover of The Kinks' "Stop Your Sobbing," produced by Nick Lowe, introduced Hynde's extraordinary, rich voice, but still did not prove she could pen anything other than record reviews.

The album did. On tightly wound tales of lust and loathing, choppy riffs met their match in Hynde's honeyed venom. The first half is vicious, highlights including the exasperated "Baby, fuck off" in "Precious," Honeyman-Scott's tribute to his guitar heroes in the "Tattooed Love Boys" solo, and the baffling "The Wait." "I still don't know the words," admitted Jeff Buckley, 16 years after its release, "But it's cool just to go Merchow, licka-chow, licka-chow herc" (actually "Said the wait child magic child work it on out now").

The second half boasts the hit "Kid," the brooding "Private Life" (promptly co-opted by Grace Jones), the irresistible "Brass In Pocket," and the nervy "Mystery Achievement" that previews 1981's terser *Pretenders II*.

"I thought, Yeah, she's got balls ..." Madonna told *Q*. "It gave me courage, inspiration, to see a woman with that kind of confidence in a man's world." **BM**

> "There was a time when they said, You can't say 'fuck off' on your record."
>
> Chrissie Hynde, 1995

Track Listing

▶	01	**Precious** (Hynde)	3:37
	02	**The Phone Call** (Hynde)	2:30
	03	**Up The Neck** (Hynde)	4:28
	04	**Tattooed Love Boys** (Hynde)	2:58
	05	**Space Invader** (Farndon•Honeyman-Scott)	3:28
	06	**The Wait** (Farndon•Hynde)	3:37
	07	**Stop Your Sobbing** (Davies)	2:39
	08	**Kid** (Hynde)	3:07
▶	09	**Private Life** (Hynde)	6:26
▶	10	**Brass In Pocket** (Honeyman-Scott•Hynde)	3:06
	11	**Lovers Of Today** (Hynde)	5:51
	12	**Mystery Achievement** (Hynde)	5:24

Einstürzende Neubauten
Kollaps (1981)

Label | Zick Zack
Producer | Einstürzende Neubauten
Art Direction | Blixa Bargeld
Nationality | Germany • USA
Running Time | 32:26

Formed in 1980, in Berlin, by vocalist Blixa Bargeld and American-born percussionist Andrew Chudy, Einstürzende Neubauten (German for "Collapsing New Buildings") picked up the gauntlet laid down by fellow sonic terrorists Throbbing Gristle and Faust. They explored their obsession with destruction using scrap materials and power tools alongside Bargeld's heavily distorted guitar; their early recordings were conceived in a service hatch beneath a Berlin Autobahn. Recruiting Stuart "F. M." Einheit from Hamburg band Abwarts, they set out to record "the most unlistenable album ever."

Opening with the sound of a broken record player, the mutant funk of "Tanz Debil" utilizes innovative percussion made from metal pipes. "Steh Auf Berlin"'s devastation of drills, breaking glass over metal sheeting conjures images of some post-apocalyptic street carnival. The nightmarish vision continues with Bargeld's tortured scream interrupting the calm water and plucked guitar of "Negativ Nein" and the cruel machine ambience of "U-Haft Muzak." "Hören Mit Schmerzen" ("Listen With Pain") makes the band's ideology crystal clear. The album's grandest moment, however, is its title track, the slow ominous rhythm and explosive effects painting an horrific vision of the end of the world.

Einstürzende Neubauten's early assaults proved to be a great influence on Depeche Mode circa *Construction Time Again*, and Nine Inch Nails. **CSh**

Siouxsie And The Banshees
Juju (1981)

Label | Polydor
Producer | Nigel Gray • The Banshees
Art Direction | Rob O'Connor
Nationality | UK
Running Time | 41:12

By the time they entered the studio to record their fourth album, Siouxsie And The Banshees had moved from punk to post-punk. Sid Vicious may have been their first drummer and Siouxsie a part of the legendary Bromley Contingent, but by 1981, the days of 20-minute versions of "The Lord's Prayer" were behind them.

London nightclub The Batcave provided a birthplace for the gothic subculture that same year and *Juju* was integral to that scene. With the swirling guitars of John McGeoch added to the tribal rhythms of Steve Severin (bass) and Budgie (drums), the foundations were laid for Siouxsie's relentlessly powerful vocals. Harsh and beautiful, aggressive yet delicate—Siouxsie's voice is almost elemental. "Spellbound" is unremittingly forceful, the music's intense energy complemented by lyrics that laced the band's past punk spirit with a macabre humor. "When your elders forget to say their prayers, take them by the legs and throw them down the stairs."

The dark motifs inspired by the album's cover permeate the album, as do influences by bands such as The Cramps and The Doors. Not that innovation is in any way in short supply—from the psychedelia of "Voodoo Dolly" and the unbridled dynamism of "Monitor" to the slower "Night Shift" and inspirational "Arabian Knights." It is Siouxsie's commanding, demanding vocals and Budgie's fearsomely heavy beats that leave the most lasting impression. **AH-N**

Heaven 17
Penthouse And Pavement (1981)

Label | Virgin
Producer | British Electric Foundation
Art Direction | Ray Smith
Nationality | UK
Running Time | 37:52

After the original Human League's acrimonious split in late 1980, the band's principal musicians Martyn Ware and Ian Craig Marsh formed British Electric Foundation—less a group than a corporate identity similar to John Lydon's concept for Public Image Ltd. They recruited vocalist Glenn Gregory, an old friend from Sheffield arts collective The Meatwhistle, for the BEF offshoot Heaven 17, named after a pop group in Anthony Burgess' novel *A Clockwork Orange*.

The disjointed sequenced rhythms of debut single "(We Don't Need This) Fascist Groove Thang" was received warmly in the press and on the dancefloor, and received much support from DJ John Peel, yet chart success proved elusive after the single was banned by the BBC for implying that recently elected U.S. president Ronald Reagan was a fascist.

Recorded simultaneously at the same studio as The Human League's *Dare*, the album's lyrics and image intelligently parodied the emergence of global corporations. The record's first side is dominated by the title track's Latin funk rhythms and "Play To Win"'s call-and-response routine. Side two is much more avant-garde territory, developing on the earlier electronic innovations of their previous incarnation and fellow Sheffield natives Cabaret Voltaire, most effectively on the post-apocalyptic nightmare "Let's All Make A Bomb." **CSh**

The Go-Gos
Beauty And The Beat (1981)

Label | IRS
Producer | R. Gottehrer • R. Freeman
Art Direction | Various
Nationality | USA
Running Time | 35:31

The Go-Gos were heirs to a girl-group tradition that could be traced to The Shangri-Las in the 1960s, with attitude courtesy of fellow Californians The Runaways.

"It was a Cinderella story," says Belinda Carlisle. "We didn't even know how to play our own instruments when we started. It was just unknown forces that propelled us to a point where we were big stars." Big indeed: *Beauty And The Beat* spent six weeks atop the Billboard chart.

The album is an intoxicating mix of punk attitude and pop sensibility. Richard Gottehrer had experience with both bubblegum (writing "My Boyfriend's Back") and punk (producing Blondie). Greil Marcus described the album as "wonderful... even if you never get below its surface, you still come away satisfied."

The classics "We Got The Beat," "Our Lips Are Sealed" (co-written by Terry Hall of The Specials) and "Can't Stop The World" are built around Charlotte Caffey and Jane Wiedlin's riffs, Gina Schock and Kathy Valentine's rhythms, and Belinda Carlisle's girl-group vocals. "Tonite" and "You Can't Walk in Your Sleep" are distinguished by Caffey's spidery guitar.

The lyrics suggest a band brimming with Californian hedonism. But there was always more to The Go-Gos than their happy-go-lucky image suggested. "This Town," ostensibly an ode to Los Angeles, contains the darker observations that foreshadowed the band's breakup amid drugs and self-destruction. **PE**

Motörhead | No Sleep 'Til Hammersmith (1981)

Label | Bronze
Producer | Vic Maile
Art Direction | Hugh Gilmour
Nationality | UK
Running Time | 40:34

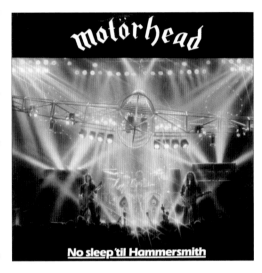

Motörhead's *No Sleep 'Til Hammersmith* is one of the most important live albums in rock history. Its wall of dirty sound was created by only three musicians: singer, bass player, and bandleader Ian "Lemmy" Kilmister (ex-Hawkwind), guitarist "Fast" Eddie Clarke, and drummer Phil "Philthy Animal" Taylor. The London-based trio had made several successful studio albums and were in peak form when they recorded this classic, which took just one week to make its way to the top of the British charts.

The music here is overwhelming, delivered with a hurricane-like power: bass with overdrive distortion that makes it sound like a lead guitar on drugs; mad, thrilling riffs; piercing guitar solos; and a dense rhythm driven by a kit fitted with two bass drums (the Ace of Spades emblazoned on each). Lemmy's lyrics revolve around the lifestyle typically associated with rock 'n' roll, although stories from the Wild West and references to war movies are never far away.

Rooted in the hard-rock traditions of the 1960s and '70s, the music is served up with insane punk-rock energy. Although he once played with The Damned, Lemmy never identified himself with the left-wing punk movement, always stressing that Motörhead was simply a rock 'n' roll band. Lemmy's Nazi insignia and black leather image cast the band as rock's very own Hell's Angels (indeed, "Iron Horse" is a nod to those biker gangs). Witness the dedication on the cover, to "all the people who have traveled with, drunk with, fought with, and screwed with us on the roads of England and Europe for five years." **AW-J**

"Thanks to Smirnoff and Carlsberg without whom lots of this would have been coherent."

Sleevenote on *No Sleep 'Til Hammersmith*, 1980

Track Listing		
▶ 01 **Ace Of Spades** (Clarke·Kilmister·Taylor)		3:01
02 **Stay Clean** (Clarke·Kilmister·Taylor)		2:50
03 **Metropolis** (Clarke·Kilmister·Taylor)		3:31
04 **The Hammer** (Clarke·Kilmister·Taylor)		3:05
05 **Iron Horse** (Brown·Taylor·Tramp)		3:58
06 **No Class** (Clarke·Kilmister·Taylor)		2:34
07 **Overkill** (Clarke·Kilmister·Taylor)		5:13
▶ 08 **(We Are) The Road Crew** (Clarke·Kilmister·Taylor)		3:31
09 **Capricorn** (Clarke·Kilmister·Taylor)		4:40
▶ 10 **Bomber** (Clarke·Kilmister·Taylor)		3:24
▶ 11 **Motorhead** (Kilmister)		4:47

Soft Cell | Non-Stop Erotic Cabaret (1981)

Label | Some Bizzare
Producer | Mike Thorne
Art Direction | Andrew Prewett
Nationality | UK
Running Time | 40:38

By the time of 1983's edgy *The Art Of Falling Apart*, Marc Almond's take on the sex industry had grown dark. But on *Non-Stop Erotic Cabaret*, Almond and fellow art-schooler Dave Ball approached London's twilights and lowlifes with the wide-eyed romanticism of two naifs up from the suburbs for the first time. The title came from a Soho neon sign; the publication Almond furtively hides on the cover is unlikely to be *Melody Maker*. The duo took their roles as ambassadors of sleaze a little too seriously: when a filthy video they had made for the high-camp "Sex Dwarf" was sent to the tabloids, apparently by the starring midget, the furor led to police raids on the Some Bizzare offices.

However, sex is not the sole theme on *Non-Stop Erotic Cabaret*—it is a mix of the credulous and the world-weary that wears its debut-album heart on its sleeve. "Frustration," "Secret Life," and "Chips On My Shoulder" are portrayals of the suburbs in which Almond and Ball had been raised; "Bedsitter" is what happened when they left them behind. But the key cuts are "Youth" and closing torch-song "Say Hello, Wave Goodbye," which set the template for Almond's entire career. And, yes, "Tainted Love": which was actually the group's third single, after dirt-cheap EP *Mutant Moments* and pioneering dance cut "Memorabilia," made No. 1 in a staggering 17 countries.

The band imploded less than two years later, when an on-the-brink Almond reacted to a bad review in *Record Mirror* by storming into its offices and lashing its writer with a bullwhip. His retirement lasted only days, but Soft Cell were through. **WF-J**

> "We wanted the album to be a peep-show of sounds, a glimpse into a seedy world, a soundtrack to a striptease clip joint."
>
> Marc Almond, 1999

Track Listing

01	Frustration	(Almond • Ball)	4:12
▶ 02	Tainted Love	(Cobb)	2:34
03	Seedy Films	(Almond • Ball)	5:05
04	Youth	(Almond • Ball)	3:15
▶ 05	Sex Dwarf	(Almond • Ball)	5:15
06	Entertain Me	(Almond • Ball)	3:35
07	Chips On My Shoulder	(Almond • Ball)	4:05
▶ 08	Bedsitter	(Almond • Ball)	3:36
09	Secret Life	(Almond • Ball)	3:37
▶ 10	Say Hello, Wave Goodbye	(Almond • Ball)	5:24

Orchestral Manoeuvres In The Dark
Architecture And Morality (1981)

Label | Dindisc
Producer | Richard Manwaring • OMD
Art Direction | Peter Saville • Brett Wickens
Nationality | UK
Running Time | 37:02

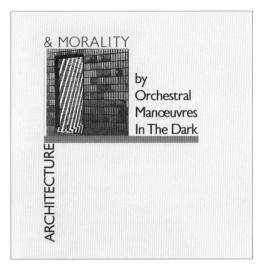

Detractors of the English synth-pop scene of the early 1980s are quick to decry the music as soulless or lacking in warmth, but, in the early part of their career, OMD made pure and yearning pop music with experimental techniques. It is no coincidence that all of the tracks on *Architecture And Morality* (apart from the brilliant ambient wash of "Sealand") are nearly exactly three-and-a-half minutes long. In fact, "She's Leaving" is a knowing nod to the duo's fellow Liverpudlians The Beatles—another band who combined experimentation and pop success, albeit on a much larger scale.

In a stroke of arrogant conceptual genius, they both wrote two separate paeans to the most famous of French Catholic martyrs—both were called "Joan Of Arc" and both were released within months of each other as singles. It was only due to bosses at Virgin panicking that the second single was differentiated by having the moniker "Maid Of Orleans" added in brackets. The group would have to wait another half-decade to hit big in the States, when they benefited greatly from the patronage of teen-flick director John Hughes, but *Architecture And Morality* remains not only their best album but one of the greatest synth-pop albums ever released. **JDo**

"[Synthesizers] are the ideal punk instrument."

Andy McCluskey, 1982

Track Listing

▶	01	**The New Stone Age** (McCluskey)	3:22
▶	02	**She's Leaving** (Humphreys•McCluskey)	3:28
▶	03	**Souvenir** (OMD)	3:34
	04	**Sealand** (Humphreys•McCluskey)	7:47
▶	05	**Joan Of Arc** (McCluskey)	3:46
▶	06	**Joan Of Arc (Maid Of Orleans)** (McCluskey)	4:10
	07	**Architecture And Morality** (Humphreys•McCluskey)	3:43
	08	**Georgia** (Humphreys•McCluskey)	3:24
	09	**The Beginning And The End** (Humphreys•McCluskey)	3:48

Brian Eno And David Byrne
My Life In The Bush Of Ghosts (1981)

Label | Sire
Producer | David Byrne • Brian Eno
Art Direction | Brian Eno • Peter Saville
Nationality | UK • USA
Running Time | 40:06

Permed nerds REO Speedwagon ruled the roost in February 1981. But while their *Hi Infidelity* was No. 1, an album with no hits or arena-friendly choruses stole into Billboard's Top 50.

Its inspiration was 1979's *Movies* by Holger Czukay. But unless you are one of the few people who knows what that sounds like, think of Peter Gabriel's third album, or Eno and Byrne's Talking Heads. In fact, the album was planned as a forerunner to the latter's *Remain In Light*, but legal tangles caused it to be suspended and revamped.

Tribal rhythms, funk, and electronic ambience are embellished with sampled singers, radio broadcasts, and evangelists—notoriously, "The Jezebel Spirit" showcases an exorcist ("Blasphemy is beside the point: Byrne and Eno have trivialized the event," complained *Rolling Stone*).

"America Is Waiting" and "Regiment" are the closest things get to rock as we know it. The rest is sinister ("Mea Culpa"), spooky ("Moonlight In Glory," a sister to "Seen And Not Seen" on *Remain In Light*), or just lovely.

The original album's "Qu'ran" was replaced on some later editions by the "Jezebel" single B-side "Very Very Hungry," to fend off Islamic objections. But *Bush Of Ghosts* remains testament both to Byrne and Eno's foresight (hip-hop sampling and a Western welcoming of world music were years away) and to how extraordinarily attractive music can be when it breaks all the rules. **BM**

> "What we wanted was to create something mysterious."
>
> Brian Eno, 1980

Track Listing

▶	01	**America Is Waiting** (Byrne•Eno•Laswell•Van Tieghem•Wright)	3:37
▶	02	**Mea Culpa** (Byrne•Eno)	3:43
	03	**Regiment** (Byrne•Eno•Jones)	3:57
	04	**Help Me Somebody** (Byrne•Eno)	4:19
▶	05	**The Jezebel Spirit** (Byrne•Eno)	4:57
	06	**Qu'ran** (Byrne•Eno)	3:47
	07	**Moonlight In Glory** (Byrne•Eno)	4:22
	08	**The Carrier** (Byrne•Eno)	3:35
	09	**A Secret Life** (Byrne•Eno)	2:30
	10	**Come With Us** (Byrne•Eno)	2:42
	11	**Mountain Of Needles** (Byrne•Eno)	2:37

Black Flag
Damaged (1981)

Label | SST
Producer | Black Flag • Spot
Art Direction | Ed Colver
Nationality | USA
Running Time | 34:33

Not so much burning but napalming its way onto the often violent California punk scene of the early 1980s, *Damaged* is one of the angriest and most confronting albums ever. It is the definitive U.S. hardcore album.

Although Black Flag had been recording for three years prior to its release, the fact that 20-year-old fan and sometime ice-cream store manager Henry Rollins was now grasping the microphone made the difference. His physical and tenacious presence, backed by the powerful guitar of founder Gregg Ginn, shook the Los Angeles punk community scene with such ferocity that the band were considered by some sections of the L.A. law enforcement as "political terrorists" and were often kept under surveillance. *Damaged* was dangerous music, though leavened with Ginn's humor and Rollins' smarts.

MCA Records refused to release it, stating that it was "immoral," but when Ginn finally released it on his own SST label American punk rock was changed forever. *Damaged* can even be credited with helping to lay the groundwork for the U.S. DIY punk touring circuit that exists today—the band set off on tour with nothing but a van, a map, and a lot of rage.

While the band's earlier albums had a much more 1977-style punk sound, *Damaged* introduced the hardcore/thrash/metal blitz that they were to become famous for. Songs such as "Rise Above," "Six Pack," and standout "Life Of Pain" are short, fast, and punchy odes to teenaged "pissed-offness" that sound as relevant and nasty today as they did back in 1981. **TSc**

X
Wild Gift (1981)

Label | Slash
Producer | Ray Manzarek
Art Direction | E. Cervenka • J. Doe
Nationality | USA
Running Time | 33:40

Los Angeles' X took no chances with their second LP, let alone prisoners. The group teamed up a second time with "fifth X-er" Ray Manzarek who both produced and played keyboards on the album creating a great, dense rock sound that did not downplay their punk credentials at the same time as it harked back to earlier rock eras, thanks particularly to the hotshot Billy Zoom on guitar. This album also included the lolling "White Girl" alongside the almost rockabilly "In This House That I Call Home" and the frantic "When Our Love Passed Out On The Couch."

It bears remembering that *Wild Gift* is the sound of a group kicking against the pricks in the radio, TV, and music industry generally—though an extremely popular live act, signed to Warner Bros., the band's rough edges and look guaranteed that they were not going to get exposure in a mainstream dominated by Seventies dinosaurs (such as Fleetwood Mac, though these days it is hard to appreciate how stark the difference appeared between, say, Christine "Exene" Cervenka and Christine McVie).

The groups own, controversial, response was to become increasingly mainstream in sound and style for albums following *Wild Gift* (and then to break up for a considerable time); this, therefore, is the last real unadulterated original X. This album has been reissued as a package with the debut *Los Angeles*, and more recently as a single disc with extra tracks including various live versions, remixes, and out-takes. **DN**

The Psychedelic Furs
Talk, Talk, Talk (1981)

Label | Columbia
Producer | Steve Lillywhite
Art Direction | Howard Fritzson
Nationality | UK
Running Time | 41:11

One of many bands in the 1980s to successfully bridge the gap between the underground art-rock scene and commercial acclaim were the Psychedelic Furs. Their second album, *Talk, Talk, Talk* is their finest moment. Their influence can be traced across the spectrum, with elements of their approach appearing in everything from Ryan Adams to the vocal style of VNV Nation.

Produced by Steve Lillywhite (U2, Peter Gabriel), the album highlight is "Pretty In Pink," a track that received a second lease of life in 1986 when it featured in John Hughes' movie of the same name. "Pretty In Pink" encapsulates the spirit of the album, with its exploration of the darker side of relationships. "That whole album is anti-relationship and anti the idea of love and very pro-sex-for-sex's-sake," vocalist Richard Butler told Billboard in 1997. This theme continues in "Into You Like A Train," whose meaning seems clear by the title alone (although Butler later said the song was written on the train as he rode to the London studio where *Talk, Talk, Talk* was being recorded).

With John Ashton and Roger Morris providing solid guitar support throughout, *Talk, Talk, Talk* introduces pop elements to the band's traditional high-energy underground rock sound. Joined by Butler's brother Tim on bass, drummer Vince Ely, and most notably Duncan Kilburn's signature saxophone, it is clear why *Talk, Talk, Talk* gave the band their first U.S. chart entry and made them one of the most significant but underrated British rock bands of the 1980s. **AH-N**

The Human League
Dare (1981)

Label | Virgin
Producer | Human League • M. Rushent
Art Direction | Human League
Nationality | UK
Running Time | 39:31

By rights this album should not have been made. The Human League's founder members Martyn Ware and Ian Craig Marsh had left to form Heaven 17. Lead singer Phil Oakey took the brave—some would say foolhardy—move of replacing them with two Sheffield schoolgirls. What chance could you possibly have of making the biggest album in the world?

Dare saw The Human League mix the arty electronica of earlier albums such as *Travelogue* and *Reproduction* with robotic Giorgio Moroder-style dancefloor populism. Backing singers Joanne Catherall and Suzanne Sulley, famously discovered by Oakey in a long-defunct Sheffield club called Crazy Daisies, struck the perfect balance between glamor and ordinariness. But they also helped to refract the avant-garde impulses of Oakey and Phil Adrian Wright through a populist filter. "When we first heard 'Sound Of The Crowd' it was just thump-crash-thump-crash," said Sulley. "But we knew it was a definite hit. You could dance to it."

Yet, for an album that spawned a million drunken disco singalongs in the shape of its international chart topper "Don't You Want Me Baby," there is an air of darkness that haunts *Dare*, be it the spooky reading of Roy Budd's theme for *Get Carter*, the haunting paranoia of "Darkness," or the John Lennon lament of "Seconds." Fittingly, it proved to be the very last album that the legendary music journalist Lester Bangs ever heard—the run-out grooves of side two were playing in his New York apartment as his body was discovered. **JLe**

The Gun Club | Fire Of Love (1981)

Label | Ruby
Producer | Chris D. • Tito Larriva
Art Direction | Chris D.
Nationality | USA
Running Time | 39:35

From out of nowhere, Los Angeles' punk-psychobilly pioneers The Gun Club arrived with a debut album that would outshadow their Californian contemporaries and prove hugely inspirational for The White Stripes and many another twenty-first-century garage band. The sound is paint-peelingly raw, the lyrics often psychotic, and the songs—the songs are some of the best American rock 'n' roll ever recorded.

Originally named Creeping Ritual, Pierce and guitarist Kid Congo Powers formed a band in 1980 to play L.A.'s burgeoning punk scene. Pierce blended a huge array of influences—primarily blues with country and rockabilly touches alongside nods to The Doors and Creedence Clearwater Revival—to create a savage brew. He sang up a storm, whooping, shrieking, and crooning while his songs were steeped in dark Southern lore with references to "hunting niggers" and threatening "I will fuck you 'til you die." Obviously, this could have been hugely offensive, but he sings with such theatrical élan that you know it is an act. Or maybe it isn't.

Anyway, the likes of "Sex Beat," "She's Like Heroin To Me," "For The Love Of Ivy," and "Jack On Fire" rock fiercely and Pierce's readings of country blues standards "Preaching The Blues" and "Cool Drink Of Water" suggest an immersion in the music that way outstrips technique bores like Eric Clapton and Gary Moore.

Released on a tiny independent label with a brutal Haitian zombie cover, *Fire Of Love* generated U.S. and European acclaim and garnered a strong cult following, though subsequent Gun Club releases, while often showcasing fine songs, never matched *Fire Of Love*. **GC**

"We conjured up and released many different malevolent spirits on that one."

Terry Graham, 2001

Track Listing

	#	Track		Time
▶	01	**Sex Beat**	(Pierce)	2:46
▶	02	**Preaching The Blues**	(Son House)	3:57
	03	**Promise Me**	(Pierce)	2:35
▶	04	**She's Like Heroin To Me**	(Pierce)	2:31
	04	**For The Love Of Ivy**	(Pierce • Powers)	5:30
	06	**Fire Spirit**	(Pierce)	2:47
▶	07	**Ghost On The Highway**	(Pierce)	2:42
▶	08	**Jack On Fire**	(Pierce)	4:39
	09	**Black Train**	(Pierce)	2:12
	10	**Cool Drink Of Water**	(Johnson)	6:16
	11	**Good Bye Johnny**	(Pierce)	3:40

Bauhaus | Mask (1981)

Label | Beggars Banquet
Producer | Various
Art Direction | Daniel Ash
Nationality | UK
Running Time | 31:48

Bauhaus may be the ultimate goth band, but their second album, *Mask*, demonstrates that the four-piece British act (comprising Daniel Ash on guitar, Peter Murphy on vocals, and brothers David J. Haskins on bass and Kevin Haskins on drums) were drawing on a broad range of influences.

The sounds were harder edged than those of Bauhaus' debut, but the introduction of more pop-friendly melodies helped to make *Mask* digestible for a mainstream audience (it was a UK Top 40 hit) and showed a clear maturation of their sound. The near-primal rhythms of stop-start opener "Hair Of The Dog," "Kick In The Eye," and "In Fear Of Fear" (which, like "Dancing," features Ash on sax) share a distinctive air of dark theatricality with perhaps the quartet's finest effort, "Of Lilies And Remains," with its darkly humorous spoken-word intro. As a follow-up to their successful debut album *In The Flat Field*, *Mask* was a notable step forward, and confirmation that each musician had the potential for artistic longevity (all members continued successful solo careers after Bauhaus' split in 1983, and have become a familiar name on the reunion circuit).

Bauhaus were always defined by a pervasive theatrical starkness, and *Mask* was no exception—from Daniel Ash's black-and-white cover and the perfect balance of angst and humor in Murphy's eloquent lyrics, to the band's bright-white-lit stage show ("Colored lights are for Christmas trees," they note on their official website). *Mask*-era Bauhaus never needed the trappings of modern rock. One reason why this album still makes for exhilarating listening today. **AH-N**

"We took ourselves very seriously ... "

Peter Murphy, 1995

Track Listing

▶ 01	**Hair Of The Dog** (Ash・D. Haskins・K. Haskins・Murphy)	2:42
02	**The Passion Of Lovers** (Ash・D. Haskins・K. Haskins・Murphy)	3:52
▶ 03	**Of Lilies And Remains** (Ash・D. Haskins・K. Haskins・Murphy)	3:18
04	**Dancing** (Ash・D. Haskins・K. Haskins・Murphy)	4:47
▶ 05	**Kick In The Eye** (Ash・D. Haskins・K. Haskins・Murphy)	3:39
▶ 06	**In Fear Of Fear** (Ash・D. Haskins・K. Haskins・Murphy)	2:58
07	**Muscle In Plastic** (Ash・D. Haskins・K. Haskins・Murphy)	2:51
08	**The Man With X–Ray Eyes** (Ash・D. Haskins・K. Haskins・Murphy)	3:05
09	**Mask** (Ash・D. Haskins・K. Haskins・Murphy)	4:36

Bobby Womack
The Poet (1981)

Label | Beverly Glen
Producer | Tom Cartwright
Art Direction | Ginny Livingston
Nationality | USA
Running Time | 39:37

Tom Tom Club
Tom Tom Club (1981)

Label | Sire
Producer | Chris Frantz • Tina Weymouth
Art Direction | Uncredited
Nationality | USA
Running Time | 36:49

The 1970s did not end at all well for Bobby Womack. After establishing himself as a superstar with such chart-topping hits as "Woman's Gotta Have It" and "Lookin' For A Love" early in the decade, he suffered drug-related problems, the death of his infant son, record-label changes, and a variety of odd career choices (notably his disappointing venture into country music, *BW Goes C&W*).

Leaving Arista for the small independent label Beverly Glen, Womack was in dire need of a comeback —and that is exactly what he found with *The Poet*. The album's cover, which shows Womack looking late-1970s cool in an all-lavender outfit, was the perfect introduction for what remains one of the slickest batch of soul songs of the era.

The deep tenor vocalist sounds as sexy as Wilson Pickett—who recorded several of Womack's tunes—on the celebratory opener "So Many Sides Of You" and then slips on the silk pajamas for some Barry White-worthy action on "Lay Your Lovin' On Me." The slow jam only grows more sensual with "Just My Imagination" and turns into a Sly Stone-style party on the funk-rich "Stand Up." Womack's gospel roots sink deeper as the album draws to a close with the rich "If You Think You're Lonely Now" and "Where Do We Go From Here."

The Poet was a smash that brought Womack back to the top of R&B album charts and yielded three hit singles, the biggest of which—"If You Think You're Lonely Now"—went to No. 3 in the United States. **JiH**

Chris Frantz and Tina Weymouth created the Tom Tom Club in 1981 as a personal creative outlet while working with Talking Heads. Their debut album quietly crept into the collective consciousness and struck a chord. It eventually became one of the earliest influences on the hip-hop movement, and the idea that everyone could be included in their musical "club" caught fire. Their obvious love of the groove and delight in exploring this new territory seduced their listeners.

Chris and Tina had originally hired legendary reggae producer Lee "Scratch" Perry to produce, but he failed to turn up at the recording sessions. Instead, they employed a DIY ethic with the help of a young Jamaican engineer, Steven Stanley, and stunt guitarist Adrian Belew, whose playful guitar riffs combined perfectly with the Tom Tom Club's schoolyard chants.

These tunes have been sampled by just about every hip-hop or rap artist of note, with the occasional diva thrown in to complete the mix—2Pac & Outlawz's "High Speed," Black Eyed Peas' "Who Needs," GrandMaster Flash and the Furious Five's "It's Nasty/Genius Of Love," Mariah Carey's "Fantasy," Ziggy Marley and The Melody Makers' "Tomorrow People," Coolio's "One Mo," and Chicks On Speed's "Wordy Rappinghood" are just a few.

"Wordy Rappinghood" went to the top of the charts in 17 countries, although it was never released as a single in the United States. Other tunes were sampled by L L Cool J on "Hot, Hot, Hot" and by Sean "Puffy" Combs on "Puff Daddy's Groove." **KC**

Rush
Moving Pictures (1981)

Label | Mercury
Producer | Terry Brown • Rush
Art Direction | Hugh Syme
Nationality | Canada
Running Time | 39:44

Abba
The Visitors (1981)

Label | Polydor
Producer | B. Andersson • B. Ulvaeus
Art Direction | Rune Soderqvist
Nationality | Sweden
Running Time | 38:01

A huge concert draw since the mid-1970s, Rush were one of the few progressive-rock acts to successfully respond to new wave. In 1980, the Ontario trio streamlined their sound with seventh studio LP *Permanent Waves*, which reflected influences such as The Police, Talking Heads, and Peter Gabriel's solo work. It featured "Spirit Of Radio," an exuberant blend of pop, metal, and ska which showed that lyricist and drummer Neil Peart could write songs with universal themes.

The band were also experimenting with non-standard instrumentation. High-pitched singer and bassist Geddy Lee was now credited with Mini Moog, Oberheim polyphonic, and Taurus pedal synthesizers. He would multitask onstage, using all his limbs to recreate the record's technological advances. The follow-up was even more accomplished—notwithstanding the lame visual pun uniting its title and cover photo.

Moving Pictures opens with the FM radio staple "Tom Sawyer." This anthemic ode to individualism stacks virtuoso guitarist Alex Lifeson's heavy riffs against a gleaming electronic backdrop, while Peart fires off rapid percussion rolls in support. Lee's melodic vocal illuminates the plea for privacy "Limelight," while "Vital Signs" marries a dramatic refrain to futurist reggae. "The Camera Eye" sees a return to winding epic mode, but with an urban rather than fantasy setting.

Moving Pictures has now been certified quadruple platinum, the biggest selling album of their 30-plus years (and counting) career. **MA**

After longer at the top of the popularity tree than any but the most outstanding talents achieve, Abba—once a happy family of two couples—had become a great songwriting/production team (Benny and Björn) plus two ex-wives (Agnetha and Anni-Frid) who were never the best of friends. Hardly surprising, as this quartet had effectively been in each other's pockets for eight years. After their early years of creating perfect pop swathed in rich harmonies, Abba were maturing—a development reflected in their music and particularly in Björn's lyrics.

"When All Is Said And Done" was written about Benny and Anni-Frid's separation, although the first single, "One Of Us," was a more general reflection on the tribulations of love. Follow-up "Head Over Heels" peaked outside the UK Top 20, however—their crown as pop royalty was slipping.

The title track tackled the concern felt by political activists in Russia, and "Soldiers" was built along similar lines, while "Two For The Price Of One" was an odd fantasy about an advertisement for a lover placed by a girl and her mother.

It would have been unreasonable to expect an album by divorcees to be as joyful and uplifting as an album by two married couples. Still, *The Visitors* became Abba's seventh consecutive UK chart-topper, and remains their most thought-provokingly original album. Subsequently, only Benny and Björn would make major musical headlines—mainly for *Chess*, the musical on which they collaborated with Sir Tim Rice. **JT**

ABC | The Lexicon Of Love (1982)

Label | Neutron
Producer | Trevor Horn
Art Direction | Visible Ink • ABC
Nationality | UK
Running Time | 37:25

Martin Fry's ABC were arty punk funkers from the same Sheffield scene that spawned Cabaret Voltaire and The Human League. Buggles frontman Trevor Horn had just produced a string of saccharine pop singles for Dollar. Their union could have been a disaster. Instead, it became a marriage made in pop heaven.

Horn, the prog-rock fan who had toured with Yes 18 months beforehand, was inducted into ABC's post-punk obsessions—Fry recalls taking him to nightclubs and playing him records by Defunkt and James Chance and the Contortions. Meanwhile, Horn introduced the band to the limitless potential of the studio. "He gave us the keys to the candy store," says Fry. "Trevor would say to us: 'If you want pizza, I'll get you pizza; if you want a string section, I'll get you a string section.'"

Horn and Fry programed the arrangements for each song using a primitive sequencer, a Mini-Moog, and a drum machine. Then the band re-recorded every part, erasing the synth demos as they went along. "It was like tracing," says Horn. "Which meant that we got it really spot on and snappy and in your face."

Punk-funk demos like "Tears Are Not Enough" and "Poison Arrow" are executed with the most razor-sharp musicianship and dressed in Anne Dudley's super-lavish orchestrations. These grandiose settings are constantly undercut by Fry's beautifully bleak lyrics, about the impossibility of love and the illusory nature of beauty.

It is this tension that so perfectly embodies the delicious contradictions of the slick, clever, "new pop" agenda of the early 1980s. The genius of *The Lexicon* ... is to do so without lapsing into smugness or parody. **JLe**

> ## "Most producers look in terms of limitations. Trevor Horn looked in terms of possibilities."

Martin Fry, 2004

Track Listing

01	**Show Me** (Fry•Palmer•Singleton•White)		4:01
▶ 02	**Poison Arrow** (Fry•Lickley•Singleton•White)		3:22
03	**Many Happy Returns** (ABC)		3:57
04	**Tears Are Not Enough** (Fry•Lickley•Singleton•White)		3:28
05	**Valentine's Day** (ABC)		3:40
▶ 06	**The Look Of Love, Pt. 1** (Fry•Palmer•Singleton•White)		3:27
07	**Date Stamp** (ABC)		3:51
▶ 08	**All Of My Heart** (Fry•Lickley•Singleton•White)	5:12
09	**4 Ever 2 Gether** (ABC•Dudley)		5:29
10	**The Look Of Love, Pt. 2** (Fry•Palmer•Singleton•White)		0:58

Prince | 1999 (1982)

Label | Warner Bros.
Producer | Prince
Art Direction | Prince
Nationality | USA
Running Time | 69:27

"Masturbating with a magazine?" Hard to believe that this saucy snippet from *Purple Rain*'s "Darling Nikki" kickstarted the Parental Advisory bandwagon. Where were the moral guardians two years earlier, when Prince was flinging filth like "I sincerely wanna fuck the taste right outta your mouth" (an ad-lib Tina Turner opted to omit when she covered "Let's Pretend We're Married")?

So far, so Prince. No surprise to anyone who had heard 1980's *Dirty Mind*. The real revelation of *1999* was Prince alchemizing his shameless steals from other artists into a template of his own. The mechanical beats and treated voices are not a million miles from Funkadelic's *The Electric Spanking Of War Babies*—but Prince had the songs to match the sonic trickery.

The war is won on what used to be side one. If there is an opening salvo in rock 'n' soul stronger than "1999," "Little Red Corvette," and "Delirious," it is locked in a leopard-guarded filing cabinet.

But let us hotfoot to the hidden treasures. "Automatic" is what Kraftwerk would sound like if they exchanged their bicycles for loveless sex. "Lady Cab Driver" is funk with an itch begging to be scratched (and is that an elephant at 6:44 or is he just pleased to see us?). "Free" is a lighter-waver that pre-dates "Purple Rain." "D.M.S.R." is dance music sex romance, and "International Lover" is splendid silliness writ large.

Janet Jackson's carbon copy *Control* testified to *1999*'s impact—a legacy maintained today by The Neptunes. And, dammit, on the sleeve Prince even manages to make lying naked amid neon lights look cool. Such a talented man. **BM**

> "Whatever you heard 'bout me is true: I change the rules and do what I wanna do."
>
> Prince, 1982

Track Listing

▶	01	**1999** (Prince)	6:15
▶	02	**Little Red Corvette** (Prince)	5:04
	03	**Delirious** (Prince)	4:00
▶	04	**Let's Pretend We're Married** (Prince)	6:15
	05	**D.M.S.R.** (Prince)	8:17
	06	**Automatic** (Prince)	9:29
	07	**Something In The Water (Does Not Compute)** (Prince)	4:02
	08	**Free** (Prince)	5:09
	09	**Lady Cab Driver** (Prince)	8:19
	10	**All The Critics Love U In New York** (Prince)	5:59
	11	**International Lover** (Prince)	6:38

Grandmaster Flash And The Furious Five
The Message (1982)

Label | Sugar Hill
Producer | Sylvia Robinson
Art Direction | Hemu Aggarwal
Nationality | USA
Running Time | 44:00

The debut LP from the first hip-hop crew to make it to vinyl was also the first time the whole group was included in a recording—earlier works had replaced DJ Grandmaster Flash with the Sugar Hill studio. *The Message* is an important milestone in hip-hop's history, displaying the key elements of lyrical delivery with breakbeats garnered from forgotten funk records. "Scorpio" takes its title from the Dennis Coffey original, "It's Nasty" from the Tom Tom Club, while "The Adventures . . . " is an extended turntable workout by Flash, showcasing the dexterity and creativity that gave birth to the genre in the first place. Swathes of "Rapture" from Blondie, Queen's "Another One Bites The Dust," and Chic's "Good Times" are weaved together to create a new dancefloor-centered soundscape—the perfect platform for the lyrical talents of the group's MCs.

However, it was the overt socio-political remit of "The Message" that most captured the imagination of the public at the time. Recalling the poetic verse of Gil Scott-Heron and The Last Poets, the track began the hip-hop tradition of keeping lyrical content centered on "the street," while outlining injustices and the poor living conditions in New York housing projects. This served as a directive that would influence future pioneers such as Public Enemy and KRS One.

The real success of the group, however, was their single releases and it is ultimately these that they will be remembered for. Disagreements over money and royalties eventually led to the group's breakup. **CR**

> "Somebody said we should do a rap record, and we said hell no."
>
> Grandmaster Flash, 1997

Track Listing

01	She's Fresh (Edwards·Knight)	4:57
▶ 02	It's Nasty (Frantz·Weymouth)	4:18
▶ 03	Scorpio (Glover·Morris·Wiggins·Williams)	4:55
04	It's A Shame (Mt. Airy Groove) (Garrett HarmonLloyd·Napoleon·Wonder·Wright)	4:57
05	Dreamin' (Henry)	5:46
06	You Are (Grandmaster Flash)	4:50
▶ 07	The Message (Chase·Fletcher·Glover·Robinson)	7:11
▶ 08	The Adventures Of Grandmaster Flash On The Wheels Of Steel (Chase·Glover·Jackson·Robinson)	7:06

Elvis Costello And The Attractions
Imperial Bedroom (1982)

Label | F-Beat
Producer | Geoff Emerick
Art Direction | Barney Bubbles
Nationality | UK
Running Time | 50:50

Six albums in five years and still the driven and prolific Elvis Costello had barely put a foot wrong. He had emerged from punk snarling, dallied with delusions of Abba, homaged soul, even been to Nashville to record an honest-to-goodness country album. What next?! Well, he enlisted as producer Geoff Emerick (inspired engineer on The Beatles' *Sgt. Pepper* . . .), and together they set to work on what would gradually reveal itself to be a darkly seductive collection of lush and heady pop. That is if anything so shot through with melancholy, guilt, and despair can ever be described as pop.

The Attractions, meanwhile, proved once again that genius does not always need to be a frontman. "Go mad, write a really eccentric arrangement . . ." were the instructions Costello gave to Steve Nieve for " . . . And In Every Home." And boy, did he oblige!

But, was *Imperial Bedroom* Costello's masterpiece— as trumpeted by the U.S. ad campaign? Some critics balked at what they perceived to be overproduced melodrama and sales were disappointing. More than two decades on, the music continues to sparkle and the words still twist like a knife. No, masterpiece does not seem too strong a word. *Imperial Bedroom* remains a boldly compelling and strangely beautiful album, a heart in a jar, a clenched fist in a velvet glove.

Incidentally, the Picasso-esque sleeve art that so savvily defines the sound is credited to "Sal Forlenza, 1942," which was actually a nom de plume of the late great Barney Bubbles. **RF**

Track Listing

▶	01	**Beyond Belief** (Costello)	2:34
	02	**Tears Before Bedtime** (Costello)	3:02
▶	03	**Shabby Doll** (Costello)	4:48
	04	**The Long Honeymoon** (Costello)	4:15
▶	05	**Man Out Of Time** (Costello)	5:27
▶	06	**Almost Blue** (Costello)	2:50
▶	07	**. . . And In Every Home** (Costello)	3:23
	08	**The Loved Ones** (Costello)	2:48
	09	**Human Hands** (Costello)	2:43
	10	**Kid About It** (Costello)	2:45
	11	**Little Savage** (Costello)	2:37
	12	**Boy With A Problem** (Costello·Difford)	2:13
	13	**Pidgin English** (Costello)	3:58
	14	**You Little Fool** (Costello)	3:11
▶	15	**Town Cryer** (Costello)	4:16

The Cure | Pornography (1982)

Label | Fiction
Producer | The Cure • Phil Thornalley
Art Direction | The Cure • Ben Kelly
Nationality | UK
Running Time | 43:20

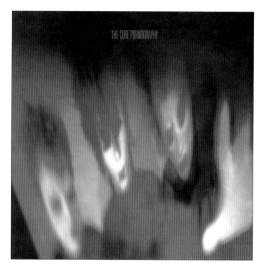

Robert Smith formed The Easy Cure while at secondary school in 1976, shortening the band's name to The Cure soon after. Their first single came out in 1978 on Fiction Records. After a straggling first album, The Cure went on to make some of the best albums of the early 1980s. *Pornography* is probably the best and darkest of all the early Cure records, a dazzling insight into Robert Smith's extraordinary mind.

Based on huge, blasting, repetitive drum and bass patterns, the album's development is organic, a monumental opus of gloom squeezed into 43 minutes. Despite the gloom there is great musicality on offer. Simon Gallup's tuned-down bass coupled with Tolhurst's monotonous drumming and Smith's deadpan voice create the perfect soundtrack for any aspiring goth, while Smith's lyrics descend into a dark abyss on "Siamese Twins," "The Figurehead," and the title track. The opening "One Hundred Years" has one of the album's strongest riffs and remains a live favorite. "The Hanging Garden," a relatively playful number, was the album's only hit (a UK No. 34). The closing track is an experimental sound collage that laments the mess that has been made of the planet. (Co-producer Phil Thornalley would later become The Cure's bassist, and also wrote and produced Natalie Imbruglia's smash hit "Torn.")

The tour following the album's release saw Smith and Gallup coming to blows at the end of the last gig in Strasbourg, France. Eventually, after a short hiatus, The Cure successfully continued as a duo on a more pop-based path, and Smith took to moonlighting with Siouxsie and the Banshees. **PN**

> ## "I thought we should be making music that was on a par with Mahler symphonies, not pop music."
>
> Robert Smith, 2002

Track Listing

▶	01	**One Hundred Years**	(Gallup•Smith•Tolhurst)	6:40
	02	**A Short Term Effect**	(Gallup•Smith•Tolhurst)	4:23
▶	03	**The Hanging Garden**	(Gallup•Smith•Tolhurst)	4:33
	04	**Siamese Twins**	(Gallup•Smith•Tolhurst)	5:30
▶	05	**The Figurehead**	(Gallup•Smith•Tolhurst)	6:15
	06	**A Strange Day**	(Gallup•Smith•Tolhurst)	5:04
	07	**Cold**	(Gallup•Smith•Tolhurst)	4:27
▶	08	**Pornography**	(Gallup•Smith•Tolhurst)	6:28

Kevin Rowland And Dexy's Midnight Runners
Too-Rye-Ay (1982)

Label | Mercury
Producer | Clive Langer • Kevin Rowland • Alan Winstanley
Art Direction | Peter Barrett
Nationality | Ireland • UK
Running Time | 43:34

After the success of *Searching For The Young Soul Rebels*, Kevin Rowland could hardly have foreseen Dexy's next step: most of the band leaving, a label change, and singles "Keep It Part Two," "Plan B," and "Liars A To E" failing to gain significant chart placings. There is not a marketing whiz who could have predicted the band's own plan B: Rowland recruited three violinists who specialized in Irish music.

This new lineup's first single, "The Celtic Soul Brothers," stalled outside the Top 40, and then the band's horn section split, only to return as hired hands (thus, Big Jimmy Patterson, who co-wrote nine of the songs on the album, is absent from the band picture). So when Dexy's played a concert for a national radio station in June, few people in the audience knew what to expect. Dungarees? Unkempt hair? Fiddles and brass jousting for attention? The speech in the middle of "There, There My Dear" in which Rowland announced he was giving up his search for young soul rebels?

"Come On Eileen" was a last roll of the dice. Lacking support, it lingered at the bottom of the chart for weeks, then took off, becoming 1982's biggest selling single in Britain. By the spring of the next year it had reached the top in America—their debut hit there—and Dexy's were trapped in fame of truly global proportions.

In retrospect, *Too-Rye-Ay*, with its fussy production and reliance on reworkings of old songs, is the worst of the three Dexy's albums; but if this is the worst album in your collection, pat yourself on the back. **DH**

"I used to argue with EMI."

Kevin Rowland, 1982

Track Listing		
▶ 01 **The Celtic Soul Brothers** (Billingham•Patterson•Rowland)		3:09
▶ 02 **Let's Make This Precious** (Patterson•Rowland)		4:03
03 **All In All (This One Last Wild Waltz)** (Patterson•Rowland)		4:09
04 **Jackie Wilson Said (I'm In Heaven When You Smile)** (Morrison)		3:04
05 **Old** (Patterson•Rowland)		5:37
06 **Plan B** (Patterson•Rowland)		5:04
07 **I'll Show You** (Patterson•Rowland)		2:40
▶ 08 **Liars A To E** (Patterson•Rowland•Torch)		4:12
▶ 09 **Until I Believe In My Soul** (Patterson•Rowland)		7:01
▶ 10 **Come On Eileen** (Adams•Patterson•Rowland)		4:35

Simple Minds
New Gold Dream (81/82/83/84) (1982)

Label | A&M
Producer | Peter Walsh
Art Direction | Malcolm Garrett
Nationality | UK
Running Time | 46:02

Although Simple Minds had five albums under their belt before *New Gold Dream*, its release marked the breakthrough that would ultimately establish them as one of the big rock names of the late 1980s.

"Glittering Prize" and the album's other big single, "Promised You A Miracle," encapsulate Simple Minds' ability to craft dazzling and sophisticated pop anthems. Combining a warm romanticism with their blend of new wave pop, the album illustrated just how capable and diverse a songwriting unit Simple Minds was.

Jim Kerr's vocals blend seamlessly into the lush sonic landscapes of Michael MacNeil's keyboard and Charlie Burchill's signature guitar work, but it is the diversity of the rhythms that creates the album's solid foundation. At a time when live drums were frequently replaced by programed beats, Simple Minds took the unusual step of using three separate drummers across the nine-track album. Combined with Derek Forbes' bass, the effect provided a relentlessly fresh percussive framework on which Kerr, Burchill, and MacNeil built the delicate, swirling, and vibrant songs.

"Hunter And The Hunted" provides some of the band's densest combinations of atmosphere and melody, and complemented by Kerr's most evocative lyrics the track stands tall as the album's highlight. But the pop-savvy "Promised You A Miracle" and "Glittering Prize," along with third single, "Someone, Somewhere In Summertime," indicate collectively why this was the album that broke Simple Minds in America. **AH-N**

Track Listing

▶ 01 **Someone, Somewhere In Summertime**
(Burchill·Forbes·Kerr·MacNeil)   4:36

02 **Colours Fly And Catherine Wheel**
(Burchill·Forbes·Kerr·MacNeil)   3:49

▶ 03 **Promised You A Miracle**
(Burchill·Forbes·Kerr·MacNeil)   4:28

04 **Big Sleep** (Burchill·Forbes·Kerr·MacNeil)   5:00

05 **Somebody Up There Likes You**
(Burchill·Forbes·Kerr·MacNeil)   5:02

06 **New Gold Dream (81/82/83/84)**
(Burchill·Forbes·Kerr·MacNeil)   5:39

▶ 07 **Glittering Prize**
(Burchill·Forbes·Kerr·MacNeil)   4:33

▶ 08 **Hunter And The Hunted**
(Burchill·Forbes·Kerr·MacNeil)   5:55

09 **King Is White And In The Crowd**
(Burchill·Forbes·Kerr·MacNeil)   7:00

Madness | The Rise And Fall (1982)

Label | Stiff
Producer | Clive Langer • Alan Winstanley
Art Direction | Laurie Lewis
Nationality | UK
Running Time | 45:36

Madness were on a high when they approached their fourth album. With "House Of Fun" and the hits set *Complete Madness* having topped the UK chart, it seemed they could do no wrong. This confidence fueled a rich, dark album—the nuttiness of yore twisted into something slightly macabre, yet still exquisitely pop.

A concept album of sorts, it was planned as a song cycle based on recollections of childhood. This inspired Cathal Smyth's wistful "Our House," which filtered fond memories through their typically wry lens, and won Top Ten success in America.

Other songs painted on a larger but no less personal canvas. The downbeat title track opened the album on a gritty note, frontman Suggs recalling his childhood in rundown Liverpool. Elsewhere, the lyrics tackled sinister underground cartels ("Blue Skinned Beast"), blustering politicians ("Mr Speaker"), and alienated voyeurism ("Primrose Hill"). The hallucinatory whole conjured a vivid portrait of England equal to *The Village Green Preservation Society* by The Kinks.

Like the great British sitcoms that *The Rise And Fall* recalled, Madness' gift was their pathos. "Tomorrow's Just Another Day"—a cry of hopelessness from behind bars—is crushing in its melancholy.

Touches like this gave *The Rise And Fall* a resonance deeper than its pantomime sleeve suggests, and signaled the more serious tone of the remaining albums. Its pervading sense of angst and paranoia, best evinced on the queasily psychedelic tour diary "New Delhi," also signaled the internal friction that would result in Mike Barson's exit during 1983's *Keep Moving*. **SC**

" . . . wacky and cerebral."

Suggs, 1999

Track Listing

	01	**Rise And Fall** (Foreman • McPherson)	3:16
▶	02	**Tomorrow's Just Another Day** (Barson • Smyth)	3:10
	03	**Blue Skinned Beast** (Thompson)	3:22
▶	04	**Primrose Hill** (Foreman • McPherson)	3:36
	05	**Mr. Speaker (Gets The Word)** (Barson • McPherson)	2:59
	06	**Sunday Morning** (Woodgate)	4:01
▶	07	**Our House** (Foreman • Smyth)	3:23
	08	**Tiptoes** (Barson • McPherson)	3:29
	09	**New Delhi** (Barson)	3:40
▶	10	**That Face** (Foreman • McPherson)	3:39
	11	**Calling Cards** (Barson • Foreman • Thompson)	2:19
	12	**Are You Coming (With Me)** (Barson • Thompson)	3:17
	13	**Madness (Is All In The Mind)** (Foreman)	5:25

Donald Fagen
The Nightfly (1982)

Label | Warner Bros.
Producer | Gary Katz
Art Direction | George Delmerico
Nationality | USA
§Running Time | 38:53

"The songs on this album represent certain fantasies that might have been entertained by a young man growing up in the remote suburbs of a north-eastern city during the late fifties and early sixties," wrote Donald Fagen on the sleeve of *The Nightfly*. The coda confirmed what the note implied: "i.e., one of my general height, weight and build."

While Steely Dan wrote, with dry and sardonic detachment, about life in 1970s California, Fagen's first solo record recalled his formative years with little of his trademark archness. The singer spent his childhood in Kendall Park, New Jersey, breaking up his obligatory teen-boy romantic dreamings (detailed on the delightful "Maxine") by listening obsessively to jazz radio beamed into his bedroom from the promised land of New York City. Both the title track ("An independent station/ WJAZ, with jazz and conversation") and the cover shot (the record in the bottom left corner is 1958's *Sonny Rollins And The Contemporary Leaders*) pay a nostalgic tribute to these radio days; rock 'n' roll also gets a nod with a cover of "Ruby Baby," a hit for Dion when Fagen was 15 years old.

There is irony, although it may not be intended. Despite the pre-Beatles themes, *The Nightfly* sounded more modern than any Steely Dan album: produced by Gary Katz and engineered by Roger Nichols, both longtime Dan collaborators, it was the first mainstream album recorded solely on digital equipment, and remains a favorite among audiophiles. **WF-J**

Haircut One Hundred
Pelican West (1982)

Label | Arista
Producer | Bob Sargeant
Art Direction | David Shortt
Nationality | UK
Running Time | 42:21

This was the Haircuts' year and the *Pelican West* album—plus one other single, the exceptional "Nobody's Fool"—makes up the entire oeuvre of the original, brilliant Haircut One Hundred, although the group did produce another LP after Heyward's departure.

The name Haircut One Hundred was obviously a knowing nod to the vagaries of fashion and definitely better than Smakky Robo Dandy, which they were known as in Beckenham, Kent, in the mid-1970s.

Heyward's non-ironic love for pop shows through in every track. The irresistibly plaintive "Love Plus One," the light but funky "Love's Got Me In Triangles" and the atmospheric "Lemon Firebrigade" have instant appeal. "Calling Captain Autumn" and "Surprise Me Again" hint at complexity, but do not deliver it.

The words are another matter: Heyward claimed that he wrote extremely simple lyrics on purpose. On many songs, however, they are indecipherable. "Fantastic Day" seems to be about, erm, having a fantastic day (but only the title leads one to that conclusion). "Love Plus One" makes even less sense—a video the group made at the time in which they dressed as cavemen did not give away too many clues.

The cover shot—of a bunch of happy, generally attractive youngsters lying on autumn leaves, most in chunky sweaters—and some of the cappuccino funk arrangements make *Pelican West* seem a little dated. Get past that and it is a hilarious, clever, intricate, enthusiastic record that retains tons of appeal. **DN**

Kate Bush
The Dreaming (1982)

Label | EMI
Producer | Kate Bush
Art Direction | Bill Clark
Nationality | UK
Running Time | 43:28

Speeding off the rails, some young stars do drugs, or die, or—worse yet—dally with Fred Durst. Four years after her breakthrough at 19 with "Wuthering Heights," the oh-so-English Kate Bush channeled her demons into a brilliantly unsettling album.

The banging, bonkers "Sat In Your Lap"—inspired by Stevie Wonder, apparently—is just the start. Still to come are eerie evocations of war-torn Vietnam ("Pull Out The Pin") and aboriginal Australia ("The Dreaming").

There is also "There Goes A Tenner"—so odd that it is her only single not to chart in the UK—and the unhappy closer, "Get Out Of My House," inspired by intrusive journalists and *The Shining*.

But there is beauty amid the horror. "Suspended In Gaffa" is heartbreaking even if you have no idea what it is about (unobtainable goals, apparently). "Night Of The Swallow" is prettily Irish and "Houdini" arouses empathy with the long-dead (the escapologist is illustrated on the cover, in which Kate passes a key with a kiss).

At the time, *The Dreaming* bombed. "That was my 'She's gone mad' album, my 'She's not commercial any more' album," Kate conceded later. Today, it slots into a lineage of eccentricity from Pink Floyd (Dave Gilmour, an old Bush sponsor, pops up on "Pull Out The Pin") to Tricky (who cites Bush as an influence). And the thunderous drums are dead ringers for those of Nine Inch Nails. "Leave It Open" closes with a line she sang backward (this is Kate Bush, remember). It is "We let the weirdness in." Do yourself a favor and do the same. **BM**

Orange Juice
Rip It Up (1982)

Label | Polydor
Producer | Martin Hayles
Art Direction | Pete Watson
Nationality | UK
Running Time | 42:20

Orange Juice were part of the early 1980s scene that their original label, Postcard, celebrated as "The Sound of Young Scotland." The influential indie band's style was earnest, lovelorn, witty, naive, and soulful, and with this album, they would reach their commercial peak.

In the hands of Martin Hayles, Orange Juice's performance is polished, colorful, and even funky, compared to their relatively lo-fi debut. The album kicks off with a UK Top Ten single, a song that would become Edwyn Collins' calling card. Absorbing white-boy funk while playfully aspiring to Chic, the song even manages to pay homage to the Buzzcocks' debut "Boredom."

Rip It Up sees the whole band engaged in the songwriting process. Zeke Manyika (later of The The) contributes "A Million Pleading Faces," while ex-Josef K. guitarist Malcolm Ross pens "Turn Away," referencing his former band's "Heaven Sent." But it is Collins' songwriting skills that really shine. Two relatively obscure songs from the band's Postcard days are revived; the Velvet Underground-tinged "Louise Louise" and the introspective "Breakfast Time" ("How I wish I was young again," implores a prematurely aged 22-year-old Collins. Minor hit "I Can't Help Myself" is the band's most joyous and exuberant pop confection, while the album's closing "Tenterhook" is a mesmerizing and rueful reflection on lost love.

Collins' frustration with the music industry was soon to see the band fold, but *Rip It Up* showcases Orange Juice at their most dynamic, vibrant, and optimistic. **JLa**

Michael Jackson | Thriller (1982)

Label | Epic
Producer | Quincy Jones
Art Direction | Dick Simmerman
Nationality | USA
Running Time | 42:15

Thriller is surrounded by a cloud of statistics—the biggest album in history, it sold more than 40 million copies on its first release; it shifted a million copies a month in the first half of 1983; of its nine tracks, seven were hit singles.

It does not stand up as well as *Off The Wall* overall, but some of its meticulous fusions of pop, rock, and R&B manage to improve on even that template. Ignore the ridiculously camp title track—a song that drains the life out of the record at the end of side one—and concentrate on the undisputed masterpieces. The funk opener "Wanna Be Startin' Somethin'" serves the same function as *Off The Wall*'s "Don't Stop Till You Get Enough"—a minimal, riff-based framework for Jacko's hyperkinetic hiccups. It also "borrows" rather heavily from Manu Dibango's "Soul Makossa" (Jacko's lawyers made a large out-of-court settlement). Elsewhere you will thrill to the airbrushed funk-rock of "Beat It" (Eddie Van Halen's guitar solo was cut and spliced from 50 different takes); while "Human Nature" is a digital ballad so beautiful that Miles Davis covered it.

But the star turn is "Billie Jean," on which a creepy, electronic bassline gets under your skin while the dubious lyric asks you to side with the paranoid millionaire superstar rather than the impoverished single mother. Like the rest of *Thriller*, it is machine-tooled pop that has been painstakingly crafted by state-of-the-art session men for months, but there is not a note out of place.

Jacko's increasingly freakshow lifestyle should not detract from the brilliance of this album. **JLe**

> " I feel I was chosen as an instrument to just give music and love and harmony to the world."

Michael Jackson, 1993

Track Listing

▶	01	**Wanna Be Startin' Somethin'** (Jackson)	6:02
	02	**Baby Be Mine** (Temperton)	4:20
	03	**The Girl Is Mine** (Jackson)	3:42
	04	**Thriller** (Temperton)	5:57
▶	05	**Beat It** (Jackson)	4:17
▶	06	**Billie Jean** (Jackson)	4:57
▶	07	**Human Nature** (Bettis・Porcaro)	4:05
▶	08	**P.Y.T. (Pretty Young Thing)** (Ingram・Jones)	3:58
	09	**The Lady In My Life** (Temperton)	4:57

The Birthday Party
Junkyard (1982)

Label | 4AD
Producer | Tony Cohen
Art Direction | Ed Roth
Nationality | Australia
Running Time | 39:13

Venom
Black Metal (1982)

Label | Neat
Producer | Keith Nichol • Venom
Art Direction | Richie Nichol • Venom
Nationality | UK
Running Time | 39:20

The Birthday Party relocated to London in 1980, presuming the UK to be dominated by equally uncompromising acts, such as The Fall and The Pop Group. Instead, they were disgusted to find the city in the grip of New Romantic fever. Signed to 4AD, they released *Prayers On Fire* in 1981, and started attracting attention following their unhinged—and often violent—live shows, and support from radio's John Peel for their Goth-baiting single "Release The Bats."

Circumstances surrounding the recording of *Junkyard* were chaotic, to say the least. Tracy Pew was jailed for three months for theft and drunk driving; drummer Phill Calvert was slowly being ousted; and copious amounts of alcohol and narcotics fueled the band's psychotic sleaze blues. The chaos is mirrored in the raw and powerful music, which often sounds as though each member is playing a different song to the others.

Nick Cave's lyrics veer from the casual murderous misogyny of "6" Gold Blade" to the pummeling "Hamlet (Pow, Pow, Pow)"—a recasting of Shakespeare's Danish prince as a Cadillac-driving, gun-toting psychopath. Considering the band's reputation for stealing cars, the Ballard-esque auto-accident monolog "Dead Joe" is perhaps autobiographical. The drag-strip imagery of "Big-Jesus-Trash-Can" is echoed by the mechanical grotesque on the album's sleeve.

This extremely volatile band split explosively just one year later, yet *Junkyard* remains a timeless document of arguably Australia's most original rock band. **CSh**

The second album by Newcastle, England, trio Venom has the rare distinction of giving its name to an entire genre. Black metal, as pioneered by Norwegian acts Mayhem and Emperor, is a cult strain of ultra-thrash characterized by sacrilegious bile and icy noise. The scene came to international prominence in the 1990s when a few of its participants were convicted of murder and church burning. Ironically, the forefathers of this none-more-extreme movement were just having a laugh.

Inspired by Kiss' outré showmanship and punk's DIY attitude, Venom combined sonic primitivism with pseudo-Satanic imagery. The leather-clad, chain-wielding trio lacked the instrumental chops of new wave British heavy metal pioneers Iron Maiden, but they made up for it with imagination and humor. The sleeve of *Black Metal* featured a mock anti-piracy symbol that read: "Home taping is killing music … So are Venom."

Their songs were crudely catchy bursts of speedfreak rhythms and bludgeoning riffs, over which Cronos puked nightmarish scenarios ("Buried Alive," "Raise The Dead"), horror mythology ("Countess Bathory"), and gleeful smut ("Teacher's Pet").

The no-budget production made it sound like they were playing in a dungeon; drummer Abaddon started the title track by chainsawing through a bolted door. *Black Metal* was tongue-in-cheek outrage at its best, annoying critics and parents. Few could have predicted such Grand Guignol absurdity would spawn a genuinely dark subculture. **MA**

Bruce Springsteen
Nebraska (1982)

Label | Columbia
Producer | Bruce Springsteen
Art Direction | Andrea Klein
Nationality | USA
Running Time | 40:51

As a follow-up to his breakthrough album, 1980's boisterous double set *The River*, on the face of it *Nebraska* sounded like career suicide. Yet Springsteen was determined to have his album of home demos released, even though it saw the light of day against the backdrop of the singer falling out with his record label.

Nebraska's 10 songs would mark a distinct departure for the all-American singer/songwriter. The record is a relentlessly bleak and often deeply political portrayal of America's small-town communities, dwellings ridden with unemployment, few chances, and endemic crime. The title track tells the true-life story of mass murderer Charlie Starkweather's killing spree. "State Trooper" narrates the tale of a local policeman forced to confront his errant criminal brother. And "Atlantic City" paints the famous gambling town as a corrupt, seething hell of losers and chancers. Throughout, Springsteen manages to hold the songs together on his own, with riveting narratives.

Nebraska pointed up Springsteen's desire to challenge both himself and his fans, and was a resounding triumph, both artistically and commercially. While its follow-up, *Born In The USA*, would return the singer to familiar stadium rock territory, he would often gravitate back toward the pessimism of *Nebraska*—years later on *Tunnel Of Love* and much later on *Ghost Of Tom Joad*, both predominantly acoustic records. In that sense alone, Springsteen perhaps remains rock's closest link to the legacy of Woody Guthrie. **BW**

Associates
Sulk (1982)

Label | Associates
Producer | Mike Hedges
Art Direction | Ian MacDonald
Nationality | UK
Running Time | 41:52

By covering David Bowie's "Boys Keep Swinging" for their debut single and touring with The Cure, The Associates whetted appetites for their 1982 masterpiece, *Sulk* (debut LP, *The Affectionate Punch*, had been released on Fiction Records in 1980). This was clearly a band working to its own agenda. Was it pop, art rock, or glam rock? In fact, The Associates were a little bit of all these and more besides.

The ten tracks listed here are those of the original UK release. In the United States they appeared in a different order, with extra tracks added—the result was a good album, but quite a different one. The Associates had two major assets in their favor: first, the lovely awkwardness of Billy Mackenzie's voice, and second, the crafted soundscapes developed by multi-instrumentalist Alan Rankine. From the Human League-esque opener "Arrogance Gave Him Up," this is the band's definitive statement. "Party Fears Two" provided a definitive demonstration of the band's intelligent and intuitive songwriting talent and gave them their highest UK chart placing, a No. 9.

The album became one of the most influential albums of 1980s synth pop, containing seeds that would later flower in the work of numerous other bands, including Duran Duran ("Bap De La Bap" could be the father of "Rio"). Just a glimpse at the cover artwork is enough to confirm that The Associates were setting the tone of that exotic, indulgent, and ultimately self-parodying decade. **GD**

Iron Maiden | The Number Of The Beast (1982)

Label | EMI
Producer | Martin Birch
Art Direction | Derek Riggs
Nationality | UK
Running Time | 44:55

Iron Maiden were already established frontrunners of British heavy metal when they released 1981's rapturously received *Killers*. But after singer Paul Di'Anno's self-destructive behavior necessitated his abrupt replacement with Samson frontman Bruce Dickinson in 1982, it seemed likely that *The Number Of The Beast* would be a postscript on the band's success.

Not so. The unrelenting gallop of instant classics such as "Run To The Hills" and the unabashed escapism of the album's title track—spearheaded by Dickinson's soaring, vocal theatrics—would send the album straight to the top of the British charts, breach the U.S. Top 40, and place the band on the brink of global superstardom.

Predictably, some long-time fans would reject Dickinson's presence, one writing in to the UK's *Melody Maker* magazine complaining that it was like hearing his favorite songs played through an air-raid siren. The din of disapproval would soon fade, but the nickname has remained playfully attached to Dickinson since.

The real controversy came when Christian activists in America—already fueled by the bat-biting antics of Ozzy Osbourne and suspicious of the album's title track—mired the band in accusations of Satanism. That the song was in fact inspired by bassist Steve Harris' nightmares and quoted the Book of Revelations did little to calm matters, and Derek Riggs' inimitably demonic cover art did not help. But such passing notoriety would soon be eclipsed by an endless string of globetrotting tours by the band, who—though perhaps unaware of it at the time—had authored one of the greatest heavy metal albums of all time. **AMi**

> "Before I joined I desperately wanted to sing for Iron Maiden, to be part of this huge fire-breathing dragon."
>
> Bruce Dickinson, 1997

Track Listing		
01 **Invaders** (Harris)		3:25
02 **Children Of The Damned** (Harris)		4:35
03 **The Prisoner** (Harris·Smith)		6:04
04 **22 Acacia Avenue** (Harris·Smith)		6:37
▶ 05 **The Number Of The Beast** (Harris)		4:52
▶ 06 **Run To The Hills** (Harris)		3:54
07 **Gangland** (Burr·Harris·Smith)		3:48
08 **Total Eclipse** (Burr·Di'Anno·Harris)		4:26
09 **Hallowed Be Thy Name** (Harris)		7:14

Duran Duran | Rio (1982)

Label | EMI
Producer | Colin Thurston
Art Direction | Malcolm Garrett
Nationality | UK
Running Time | 42:19

Despite popular memory locating new romanticism as a backlash to punk, the most famous band of the genre, Duran Duran, stemmed from John Taylor's declaration that the band was intended to be a combination of the Sex Pistols and Chic. But this band from Birmingham, England, did things, as the song states, their own way.

"Durandemonium" swept the globe with 1982's *Rio* album: it heralded the arrival of the music video revolution. "I think Duran Duran owes its life to MTV," Norman Samnick of MTV's parent company Warner Communications told *Time* magazine in 1983. The flamboyant videos to the title track and "Save A Prayer" (by Russell Mulcahy, who went on to make *Highlander*) portray the band as sophisticated jet setters, lolling around exotic locales with beautiful women—these clips epitomize the 1980s spirit, as does the album's artwork (Patrick Nagel's cover painting captures the decade's graphic style: its Japanese woodblock look typifying a fascination with the exotic).

Rio demonstrates in songs such as "New Religion" and "The Chauffeur" how far John Taylor (bass), Roger Taylor (drums), and Nick Rhodes (keyboards) define the band's sound: glossy, sexy, slick, and infectious. But Simon Le Bon (vocals) and Andy Taylor (guitar) are equally vital to the overall experience—with Le Bon's obscure lyrics and (not always technically sound) vocal delivery augmented by Andy Taylor's guitar giving tracks such as "Hungry Like The Wolf" a rock edge that made them accessible to a mainstream audience. *Rio*-era Duran Duran were matchless in their ability to craft perfect pop that defined a decade. **AH-N**

"We provide a service that helps people get through their lives."

Simon Le Bon, 2004

Track Listing

▶	01	Rio (Le Bon•Rhodes•A. Taylor•J. Taylor•R. Taylor)	5:38
	02	My Own Way (Le Bon•Rhodes•A. Taylor•J. Taylor•R. Taylor)	4:51
	03	Lonely In Your Nightmare (Le Bon•Rhodes•A. Taylor•J. Taylor•R. Taylor)	3:50
▶	04	Hungry Like The Wolf (Le Bon•Rhodes•A. Taylor•J. Taylor•R. Taylor)	3:41
	05	Hold Back The Rain (Le Bon•Rhodes•A. Taylor•J. Taylor•R. Taylor)	3:49
▶	06	New Religion (Le Bon•Rhodes•A. Taylor•J. Taylor•R. Taylor)	5:33
	07	Last Chance On The Stairway (Le Bon•Rhodes•A. Taylor•J. Taylor•R. Taylor)	4:20
▶	08	Save A Prayer (Le Bon•Rhodes•A. Taylor•J. Taylor•R. Taylor)	5:25
▶	09	The Chauffeur (Le Bon•Rhodes•A. Taylor•J. Taylor•R. Taylor)	5:12

Violent Femmes | Violent Femmes (1982)

Label | Slash
Producer | Mark Van Hecke • Violent Femmes
Art Direction | Jeff Price
Nationality | USA
Running Time | 36:14

Violent Femmes' debut album redefined the term slowburner, taking almost eight years to sell the million copies to attain platinum status—without troubling the chroniclers of Billboard's Top 200. Not that label Slash can be too peeved, as they signed the cult Milwaukee three-piece for the princely sum of $0. Welcome to the weird and wonderful world of the Femmes.

As you would imagine of a band "discovered" while busking, the essence of the band's sound was raw and antsy, traits frequently lost in the transition from the stage to the studio. Amazingly, the Femmes retained this freshness, probably due to their lack of sophistication—the trio comprised an acoustic bass, Victor De Lorenzo's legendary drum kit, and a guitar.

Together, the instruments veer from an air of compelling urgency ("Kiss Off") to lovesick languor on "Please Do Not Go," where bassist Brian Ritchie's strings resonate down to the pit of the stomach. The band's principal image as guardians of geek-cool emanates from Gordon Gano's angst-ridden lyrics and delivery so heartfelt it touches on self-parody.

Few outsiders have touched on feelings of persecuted otherness as Gano has, and none with the humor he brings. He impassionedly bemoans his lack of action on "Add It Up"—"Why can't I get just one fuck? I guess it's got something to do with luck"—and manages to switch from spat-out self-examination to hilarious realization in one short, bitter twist.

"Weird kids," both as performers and audience, are rock's mainstay; few have articulated their world view with such brilliance as Violent Femmes. **SJac**

> "What we're saying is, 'Here's romanticism thrown back in your face ... Here's raw emotion. Can you deal with this?'"
>
> Victor De Lorenzo, 1983

Track Listing

	01	Blister In The Sun (Gano)	2:24
	02	Kiss Off (Gano)	2:55
▶	03	Please Do Not Go (Gano)	4:14
	04	Add It Up (Gano)	4:42
	05	Confessions (Gano)	5:31
▶	06	Prove My Love (Gano)	2:38
	07	Promise (Gano)	2:48
	08	To The Kill (Gano)	4:06
▶	09	Gone Daddy Gone (Gano)	3:05
	10	Good Feeling (Gano)	3:51

Malcolm McLaren
Duck Rock (1983)

Label | Charisma
Producer | Trevor Horn
Art Direction | Nick Egan
Nationality | UK
Running Time | 37:09

Malcolm McLaren's spell as Sex Pistols' manager had made him an A-list celebrity in Britain by the early 1980s, and it whetted his appetite for being a pop star himself. Accordingly, he blagged himself a recording contract with Charisma with a vague idea of investigating "folk dances of the world." Recruiting ultra-fashionable New Pop producer Trevor Horn, McLaren embarked on a costly and farcical journey around America and Africa. "It became apparent that he didn't really have a clue what he was doing," says Horn, "which meant that I had a lot of creative input."

The project started in New York, where McLaren was fascinated by the emergent hip-hop phenomena. From there McLaren went on to record NuYorican salsa bands, jug bands in East Tennessee, and township jive troupes from South Africa. In the Bronx, McLaren found two pirate radio DJs—the Supreme Team—who were given acetates of these global recordings to "scratch." These were cobbled into a coherent musical voyage by Horn and narrated by McLaren—who was so musically illiterate that he needed the rhythms physically slapped into him by Horn in the vocal booth.

"Buffalo Gals," while only a minor hit in the United States, was the first big hip-hop hit in Europe, introducing scratching, breakdancing, and hip-hop graffiti to the masses. And, in celebrating the paganistic elements of folk culture (what McLaren described as "the roots of rock 'n' roll"), Duck Rock certainly facilitated the birth of world music as we know it. **JLe**

Def Leppard
Pyromania (1983)

Label | Mercury
Producer | Robert John Lange
Art Direction | Satori
Nationality | UK
Running Time | 44:57

If there is one thing alone that dates Pyromania, it is the front cover. In these post-9/11 times, with incidences of snipers in America, the portrait of gun sights trained on a burning skyscraper would be unthinkable. Yet there the anachronisms end, for Def Leppard's third album still sounds fresh and wild. Even the mighty Guns N' Roses took inspiration from the torn jeans, cute looks, and hooky blockbusters of this Northern English act.

Hailing from Sheffield, a city famed for steelworks and experimental high-rise slums, the Lepps were gazing Stateside from the beginning. One of their earliest songs, "Hello America," was a clear pointer. But the band was soon in a quandary after their first two albums failed to soar. Slave-driving producer Robert John "Mutt" Lange strained each Leppard to the limit, also bringing in backing singers and drum machines. The latter item glossed and commercialized the new pop-oriented approach, though drummer Rick Allen responded by chucking a drumstick so hard it stuck in the studio wall. Guitarist Pete Willis was suffering with alcoholism and was replaced by Girl's Phil Collen.

Lange's painstaking efforts wrapped harmonies over every glissando and grace note. Def Leppard ran up massive debts after months of overtime, but the hard work paid off. In the United States, MTV took the bittersweet "Photograph" and stadium stomper "Rock Of Ages" on heavy rotation. Pyromania sold ten million copies worldwide and the group rapidly became the gods of high-school metal. **GT**

R.E.M.
Murmur (1983)

Label | IRS
Producer | Don Dixon • Mitch Easter
Art Direction | Various
Nationality | USA
Running Time | 44:01

The The
Soul Mining (1983)

Label | Sony
Producer | Matt Johnson
Art Direction | Andy Dog
Nationality | UK
Running Time | 45:27

Dylan Thomas once joked that his early poems were so complex he no longer understood them himself. Michael Stipe was also to confess three years after writing *Murmur*'s anthemic "Pilgrimage" that "It still baffles me." Thus the band's debut, characterized by his hazy mutterings, is aptly titled. But Stipe never aspired to classical poetics. He recognized that implication and cryptic imagery could suggest an awful lot.

In truth, early R.E.M. needed Stipe's mystic warblings to stand them apart. Musically, *Murmur* swerves around Peter Buck's jangly Rickenbacker® chords and Stipe's nagging melodies. Having formed amid the alternative bands of Athens, Georgia, R.E.M. won a following on the college gig and radio circuit. *Murmur* was created in a Carolina gospel studio, with their label demanding the producers deliver a hit. A classical cellist played on "Talk About The Passion"—and was baffled at having no sheet music to work from.

Murmur was a critical sensation. *Rolling Stone* named it Album of the Year, and the LP crept into the U.S. Top Thirty. The band's hefty grassroots following was a factor, and R.E.M. offered homegrown talent with a subtler sound than, say, Hüsker Dü or Green On Red. Even the gothic cover photo takes a rootsy approach, portraying the creepy kudzu vine that proliferates in Georgia, and a rural Athens railway trestle.

The *New York Times* review claimed *Murmur* would "sound as fresh ten years from now as it does today." Make that 20 years, or even 30. **GT**

If any rock artist ever had the tag "miserable bastard" tattooed on his forehead, it is Matt Johnson, the one-man band who has operated as The The since 1980. He denies this, but the downbeat nature of much of his music, including this first release under his The The handle, tends to undermine his protests.

Londoner Johnson's love of music was fostered by growing up in his dad's East End pub where David Essex and Long John Baldry, among others, performed. "I heard it coming upstairs through the dumb waiter. And when the pub was closed my brother and I would play on the equipment we found on the stage." After one album as himself, *Burning Blue Soul* (1981), he adopted a mysterious name, "to create a concept group, inspired by The Plastic Ono Band: a concept group that changed constantly."

The songs combined thought-provoking, intense lyrics, many ("That Sinking Feeling") inspired by the prime minister at the time, Margaret Thatcher, with music that often made use of unusual instrumentation. Lyrically, in one reviewer's words, *Soul Mining* "overflows with ideas, rants, doubts, fears, and more musical experimentation than most bands would dare attempt in a lifetime." Few guest musicians are featured, but Jools Holland's piano solo on "Uncertain Smile" merits special mention.

A 2002 repackage/remaster was superintended by Johnson himself, and *Soul Mining* joins the more commercially successful follow-ups *Infected*, *Mind Bomb*, and *Dusk* in a *London Town* boxed set. **MH**

Tom Waits | Swordfishtrombones (1983)

Label | Island
Producer | Tom Waits
Art Direction | Frank Mulvey
Nationality | USA
Running Time | 41:41

Put simply, Tom Waits' career splits neatly in two—before *Swordfishtrombones* and after. Even Waits himself—a man partial to obfuscation—acknowledges this. This album was Waits moving away from what he would later refer to as "my barfly lounge, pseudo-jazz kind of period," and embracing instead the shock of the new in the shape of Brecht and Weill, Captain Beefheart, and Harry Partch. The meeting of his wife Kathleen Brennan had been the inspiration behind all this.

At odds with the mood of the times, the songs are mostly short, the words imagistic, the sound bent, rusted, twisted, and skewed. His previously signature lush orchestration, saxophone, and plain recorded piano and guitar are here eschewed in favor of a percussive carnival whirl of pump organ, marimba, and buckshot brass. It makes for a wheezing and moaning, clanking and creaking work of darkly cinematic, elegiac, snapshot poise.

"There's a rumblin' groan/down below/there's a big dark town/it's a place I've found/there's a world going on/underground" he barks on the album's opener, sort of catching the fire and setting the tone.

Another track, "Frank's Wild Years," was to take on a life all its own. It formed the basis for Waits' and Brennan's 1986 stage musical of the same name, which in turn spawned a studio album the following year. Indeed, *Swordfishtrombones* was the first part of an unintended Waits trilogy (along with 1985's *Raindogs* and *Franks Wild Years*). An undeniably influential, landmark album, it was Waits' first for Island Records after Warner Bros. had—incredibly—rejected it. **RF**

"I've never liked Chihuahuas."

Tom Waits, 1983

Track Listing

▶ 01	Underground (Waits)	2:01
▶ 02	Shore Leave (Waits)	4:18
03	Dave The Butcher (Waits)	2:20
▶ 04	Johnsburg, Illinois (Waits)	1:33
▶ 05	16 Shells From A Thirty–Ought Six (Waits)	4:33
06	Town With No Cheer (Waits)	4:28
▶ 07	In The Neighborhood (Waits)	3:07
08	Just Another Sucker On The Vine (Waits)	1:46
▶ 09	Frank's Wild Years (Waits)	1:53
10	Swordfishtrombone (Waits)	3:08
11	Down, Down, Down (Waits)	2:16
12	Soldier's Things (Waits)	3:23
13	Gin Soaked Boy (Waits)	2:24
14	Trouble's Braids (Waits)	1:17
15	Rainbirds (Waits)	3:14

The Blue Nile
A Walk Across The Rooftops (1983)

Label | Linn
Producer | Robert Bell • Paul Buchanan
Art Direction | Uncredited
Nationality | UK
Running Time | 38:17

Hanoi Rocks
Back To Mystery City (1983)

Label | Johanna
Producer | D. Buffin Griffin • P. Watts
Art Direction | Kathe Schreyer
Nationality | Finland
Running Time | 44:16

The Blue Nile are a brand you can buy with confidence. All their stuff sounds essentially the same. They rarely tour and average an album every five years, so being a fan requires only patience. And the music is heartbreakingly beautiful, as suited to solitary enjoyment as snuggling with a significant other.

Having convened at Glasgow University at the end of the 1970s, Paul Buchanan, P. J. Moore, and Robert Bell issued the single "I Love This Life" on their own label in 1981, but were later signed by hi-fi manufacturer Linn. The company wanted to show off a recording system—but instead got a masterpiece that made The Blue Nile one of the best loved cult bands, whose admirers include Peter Gabriel, Rickie Lee Jones, and Annie Lennox. *A Walk Across The Rooftops* is recommended here, but *Hats* (1989), *Peace At Last* (1996), and *High* (2004) are magical too.

The sound is a strange sort of electronic soul, topped by the aching voice of Paul Buchanan (think Joe Cocker gargling with sand, not gravel). The songs are spare evocations of small-town life—which, like Bruce Springsteen, make mundane observations of men and women sound tearjerkingly poignant. On the key track—"Tinseltown In The Rain"—Buchanan sings "Do I love you? Yes, I love you—but it's easy come and it's easy go …" and the synths squeak like violins and the guitars tighten like wires. If you are not moved, you may be dead. **BM**

Axl Rose reportedly once said Hanoi Rocks should have been bigger than Guns N' Roses. Inspired by The New York Dolls and Alice Cooper, the band wore wildly theatrical garb, gobbed on tons of makeup, and played loud, abrasive, hook-filled music that was impossible to classify. Their music connected the dots between glitter, punk, and heavy metal and helped set the blueprint for Eighties hair metal.

Mott the Hoople's Dale Buffin Griffin and Pete Watts produced this fourth album and managed to translate the band's dynamic live show and sense of humor in the studio for the first time. The record starts with the tongue-in-cheek "Strange Boys Play Weird Openings," a short acoustic ditty complete with flutes and bird noises. Then, like a flip of a switch, Michael Monroe begins howling against the dueling guitars of Andy McCoy and Nasty Suicide on "Malibu Beach Nightmare" and the party is underway. Nicholas "Razzle" Dingley, a major improvement over former drummer Gyp Casino, is equally colorful and powerful on "Lick Summer Love" and "Tooting Bec Wreck."

The album topped out at No. 87 on the British charts and translated to a three-album deal with CBS. The band seemed ready for superstardom—however, tragedy struck when Razzle was killed in a traffic accident while a passenger in Vince Neil's car in 1984. Hanoi Rocks called it quits one year later. **JiH**

Cyndi Lauper
She's So Unusual (1983)

Label | Portrait
Producer | Rick Chertoff
Art Direction | Janet Perr
Nationality | USA
Running Time | 38:37

Paul Simon
Hearts And Bones (1983)

Label | Warner Bros.
Producer | Paul Simon
Art Direction | Jeffrey Kent Ayeroff
Nationality | USA
Running Time | 40:42

Betty Boop bombshell Cyndi Lauper would have been a breath of fresh air anytime. But in the dark ages of 1983, when Men At Work were the biggest band in the world, she was a helium-voiced hurricane.

The 30-year-old Brooklynite had survived bankruptcy to emerge stronger than steel. On her debut, classics come tumbling one after another. The pounding opener has her backed by The Hooters, remembered for hits such as "Satellite.""Girls Just Wanna Have Fun" was written by unknown Robert Hazard, but a rewrite and epochal video made it Lauper's anthem. "Time After Time" is a delicacy that has been covered nearly 100 times. "She Bop" is a slinky ode to self-gratification that helped kick-start the music censorship debate. And, ahead of Sinéad O'Connor, she took a Prince track (*Dirty Mind*'s "When You Were Mine") and made it better.

In the second half, the collision of Sixties-style bubblegum, new wave, and pop-rock gets added ingredients. There is the elegant "All Through The Night" by Jules Shear and the 1920s curio "He's So Unusual." The latter, originally from the musical *Sweetie*, completes her transformation into a warbling cartoon, a persona that talks all over the punky closer "Yeah Yeah."

For a time Cyndi Lauper and Madonna were rivals. History's decided the outcome, but *She's So Unusual* remains a terrific testament to a time when Lauper coulda been a contender. **BM**

The 1980s did not begin well for Paul Simon. His movie *One Trick Pony* and its soundtrack were critically lambasted, and his acrimonious departure from CBS was succeeded by writer's block. However, therapy drew him back out of his shell, and the songs that followed form the crux of *Hearts And Bones*.

This record was originally intended to be a Simon And Garfunkel album, the duo having reformed in 1981 for a free concert in Central Park (500,000 saw it) and a subsequent tour. However, it did not take long for old wounds to open. The few Garfunkel contributions Simon originally allowed were excised from the album, which eventually emerged as Simon's fifth solo set.

Hearts And Bones is at its best when it shows Simon's age. The singer turned 40 in 1981; "Train In The Distance" (about his first wife), "Song About The Moon" (seemingly written as self-analysis), and "The Late Great Johnny Ace" (a tribute to John Lennon, with strings scored by Philip Glass) are pure reflection. Conversely, the record slips when it dates not Simon but itself: "Allergies" is almost lost beneath the booming drums of sessioneer Steve Gadd. Still, weak moments are few.

Simon may have approached his 40s with equanimity, but the public were not ready. *Hearts And Bones* performed even less well than its predecessor, leading Simon to head to Africa for its followup. *Graceland* fared a little better. **WF-J**

Echo And The Bunnymen | Porcupine (1983)

Label | Korova
Producer | Kingbird
Art Direction | Martyn Atkins
Nationality | UK
Running Time | 44:39

Porcupine split critical and fan opinion. Perhaps, given the troubled birth of the album and the spiky thinking behind it, this was always to be its fate. The Bunnymen had found 1981's *Heaven Up Here* a breeze to write. Their third full-length album, preceded by a period of creative block, was anything but.

Porcupine represented singer Ian McCulloch's most autobiographical writing and repelled many with its sharp quills, including parent company WEA, who deemed it insufficiently commercial. Weirdly, the band—bar guitarist Will Sergeant—agreed and went back to the studio to use the first version as the springboard for a second attempt.

This turmoil goes some way to explaining the power of *Porcupine*. Its first single, "The Back of Love"—alternately breakneck and dreamy—distilled perfectly the feelings of awe and otherness that only Echo and the Bunnymen seemed able to conjure: who else could "break the back of love" in so celebratory a fashion?

Indian violinist Shankar recorded a sitar-led intro and chorus to second single "The Cutter," much to the chagrin of the entire band. Manager Bill Drummond also recorded a trumpet section for a joyously soaring middle eight. Despite their anger, the band conceded it improved the song. "The Cutter" reached No. 8 in the UK in January 1983 (the album peaked at No. 2).

Thereafter, there was no easy listening on *Porcupine*. McCulloch's isolationism and increasingly operatic delivery were little softened by the production and Eastern sounds. Less accessible and more troubled certainly, but repeated listening rewards tenfold. **MB**

Track Listing

▶	01	**The Cutter** (de Freitas·McCulloch·Pattinson·Sergeant)	3:50
▶	02	**The Back Of Love** (de Freitas·McCulloch·Pattinson·Sergeant)	3:13
	03	**My White Devil** (de Freitas·McCulloch·Pattinson·Sergeant)	4:32
	04	**Clay** (de Freitas·McCulloch·Pattinson·Sergeant)	4:07
	05	**Porcupine** (de Freitas·McCulloch·Pattinson·Sergeant)	5:55
	06	**Heads Will Roll** (de Freitas·McCulloch·Pattinson·Sergeant)	3:29
	07	**Ripeness** (de Freitas·McCulloch·Pattinson·Sergeant)	4:50
▶	08	**Higher Hell** (de Freitas·McCulloch·Pattinson·Sergeant)	4:59
	09	**Gods Will Be Gods** (de Freitas·McCulloch·Pattinson·Sergeant)	5:18
	10	**In Bluer Skies** (de Freitas·McCulloch·Pattinson·Sergeant)	4:26

ZZ Top | Eliminator (1983)

Label | Warner Bros.
Producer | Bill Ham
Art Direction | Bob Alford • Tom Hunnicutt
Nationality | USA
Running Time | 45:23

In the beginning there was Donna Summer. She decreed disco, drums, and rock guitars be wedded in holy matrimony and, lo, it was good (or, rather, it was her *Bad Girls*). Later, Eddie Van Halen consummated the union on Michael Jackson's "Beat It" and his own "Jump."

In such company, ZZ Top risked looking like embarrassing uncles. Instead, they conjured an electro-boogie masterpiece that equaled Eddie both in entertainment and sales (ten million and counting).

The Texan trio toyed with new-fangled noise-making on 1981's *El Loco*. Then, on *Eliminator*, they plunged in with such aplomb that drummer Frank Beard was suspected of having been drum-machined off the tracks. In truth, his crisp beats and Dusty Hill's chugging bass are merely supports for the star: guitarist Billy Gibbons—forever wrapping furry licks round the wry lyrics, but never overindulging like lesser soloists.

It is not all a hard-rock hoedown. There is the elegiac "I Need You Tonight" and the slap-happy bass showcase "Thug." But it was "Gimme All Your Lovin'," "Sharp Dressed Man," and "Legs" that sent *Eliminator* into excelsis. Key to their success were Tim Newman's videos, heavily rotated on the fledgling MTV, which made ZZ an amusing anachronism amid cars and girls (note Tom Hunnicutt's iconic cover illustration of a hotrod come to life). "We decided that the girls were a lot better looking than we were," explained Beard, "and that the car was even better looking than we were."

And so it was that the little ol' band from Texas became superstars, *Eliminator* became a classic—and, lo, it was good. **BM**

> ## "ZZ Top will never be considered a punk, new wave, or highly electronic band."
>
> **Billy Gibbons, 1983**

Track Listing

▶	01	**Gimme All Your Lovin'** (Beard•Gibbons•Hill)	4:04
	02	**Got Me Under Pressure** (Beard•Gibbons•Hill)	4:03
▶	03	**Sharp Dressed Man** (Beard•Gibbons•Hill)	4:18
	04	**I Need You Tonight** (Beard•Gibbons•Hill)	6:17
	05	**I Got The Six** (Beard•Gibbons•Hill)	2:56
▶	06	**Legs** (Beard•Gibbons•Hill)	4:34
	07	**Thug** (Beard•Gibbons•Hill)	4:19
	08	**TV Dinners** (Beard•Gibbons•Hill)	3:51
	09	**Dirty Dog** (Beard•Gibbons•Hill)	4:04
	10	**If I Could Only Flag Her Down** (Beard•Gibbons•Hill)	3:41
	11	**Bad Girl** (Beard•Gibbons•Hill)	3:16

Eurythmics
Sweet Dreams (Are Made Of This) (1983)

Label | RCA
Producer | Dave Stewart
Art Direction | Laurence Stevens
Nationality | UK
Running Time | 41:52

By marrying synthesized sounds with strong melodies and powerful vocal delivery, artsy post-punk popsters guitarist Dave Stewart and soulful tenor Annie Lennox effectively ended all the Eighties electro-pop rip-offs.

Although early singles (the Latino "This Is The House" and the jazzy "The Walk") failed to ignite, the stunning title track, with its thumping kick-drum pulse and haunting hook, became a worldwide smash (U.S. No. 1; UK No. 2). The groundbreaking video was crucial to its success. Featuring an androgynous-looking Lennox (resplendent in a severe orange crop and man's suit), amid a field of cows, it was a clear subversion of the sexist, profit-driven culture of the 1980s. The effect was startling, rendering the shy but ballsy singer a cover star (*Newsweek*, *The Face*). The Eurythmics' concern for artistic control was reflected in the album sleeve with its D&A (Dave and Annie) logo.

Apart from its variety of musical styles—from the gutsy Sam and Dave cover "Wrap It Up" to the sublime "This City . . . "—the album is notable for its emotional intensity: the distinctly chilly "Sweet Dreams" was composed after the former lovers had had an argument in the studio and were not talking to one another; while the video accompanying the poignant single about obsession, "Love Is A Stranger," was immediately banned by unsympathetic U.S. censors, who dubbed Lennox a "youth-corrupting transvestite."

By the end of 1983, it was only right that the duo had become international stars. **LS**

"Sometimes I . . . like to make beautiful sublime music."

Annie Lennox, 1990

Track Listing

▶ 01	**Love Is A Stranger** (Lennox•Stewart)	3:45
02	**I've Got An Angel** (Lennox•Stewart)	2:43
03	**Wrap It Up** (Hayes•Porter)	3:22
04	**I Could Give You (A Mirror)** (Lennox•Stewart)	3:49
▶ 05	**The Walk** (Lennox•Stewart)	4:35
▶ 06	**Sweet Dreams (Are Made Of This)** (Lennox•Stewart)	3:35
07	**Jennifer** (Lennox•Stewart)	5:00
08	**This Is The House** (Lennox•Stewart)	4:58
09	**Somebody Told Me** (Lennox•Stewart)	3:28
▶ 10	**This City Never Sleeps** (Lennox•Stewart)	6:37

U2
War (1983)

Label | Island
Producer | Steve Lillywhite • Bill Whelan
Art Direction | Uncredited
Nationality | Ireland
Running Time | 40:03

U2's third album saw the Dublin four-piece articulate their impassioned views on politics and the human condition. With a sound tending more toward garage than high-gloss production, *War* remains one of U2's most sonically raw sets. "Sunday Bloody Sunday" is undoubtedly the album's most vital track: the militaristic rhythms of drummer Larry Mullen Jr. and the steady descending riff of Edge's guitar providing the perfect backdrop for Bono's personal statement against the continuation of the war between the IRA and British authority.

"New Year's Day" is another track with proven shelf-life. Simultaneously deploring stagnancy and reveling in a promise of change, the track declares boldly that despite being torn in two the world may also be "as one." "Surrender" is a softer gem and showcases U2's ability to create stirringly atmospheric music. *War* is also notable for its inclusion of "Seconds"—one of only two U2 tracks ever recorded with the Edge on lead vocals. The hymn-like "40" was used to close U2 shows throughout the 1980s.

War entered the UK charts at No. 1 (U.S. No. 12)—and proved to be their last with Steve Lillywhite at the helm (the producer had also worked on *Boy* and *October*). It is a fine swansong: Lillywhite's treatment of *War*'s material marries undiluted energy to astute studio guidance. Bono's vocals are prominent and demand attention, while Edge's guitar lines are vital but never overpowering. An enduring record. **SN**

The Police
Synchronicity (1983)

Label | A&M
Producer | Hugh Padgham • The Police
Art Direction | Jeffrey Kent Ayeroff
Nationality | UK • USA
Running Time | 44:11

Synchronicity, recorded in the winter of 1982 in London, Montserrat, and Quebec, brought down the final curtain on The Police's stunning career. While the title refers to philosopher Carl Jung's theory of meaningful coincidence, its sleeve shows drummer Stewart Copeland, bassist/singer Sting, and guitarist Andy Summers starkly divided.

Copeland drummed in a dining room connected to the Quebec studio by CCTV, and arguments over his elaborate style led to a meeting where the tapes were nearly scrapped. Nonetheless, the music is among their best, from the loose-limbed "Walking In Your Footsteps" to the eerie "Tea In The Sahara" (inspired by a story in Paul Bowles' *The Sheltering Sky*).

Sting allowed two of his associates' songs on the album: "Mother"—"Which we loved because it was so crazy," he told BBC Radio 1's *Classic Albums*—and "Miss Gradenko" ("I used to enjoy singing Stewart's songs"). Summers also co-wrote the jazzy "Murder By Numbers."

But it is for the haunting "Every Breath You Take" (penned in mere minutes), enticing "Wrapped Around Your Finger," and yearning "King Of Pain" that the album is celebrated. Inspired by the breakdown of Sting's first marriage, all three were U.S. Top Ten hits and made *Synchronicity* the band's biggest seller (eight million in the United States alone).

After a final tour, The Police disbanded. "The band lasted for the right amount of time," declared Sting. "Another album would have been a disaster." **TJ**

Meat Puppets
Meat Puppets II (1983)

Label | SST
Producer | Spot
Art Direction | Curt Kirkwood
Nationality | USA
Running Time | 30:35

Culture Club
Colour By Numbers (1983)

Label | Virgin
Producer | Steve Levine
Art Direction | Assorted Images
Nationality | UK
Running Time | 37:52

Although the Meat Puppets' sophomore effort features three songs covered by Nirvana on their *Unplugged In New York* set, the Phoenix, Arizona trio definitely were not a grunge act. Signed to Black Flag's trailblazing SST label, singer/guitarist Curt Kirkwood, his bass-playing brother Cris, and drummer Derrick Bostrom played a beatific mix of country, punk, and psychedelia. They got hardcore out of their system on 1982's self-titled debut, then set about making an album that more accurately reflected their desert heritage and hippy-era influences.

The original versions of "Plateau," "Oh, Me," and "Lake Of Fire" exude an otherwordly aura that was understandably absent on Nirvana's MTV studio takes. The first is mid-tempo rock at its most hallucinogenic, culminating in a gorgeous, levitational coda. The latter pair's funereal sentiments are offset by surreal imagery and Curt's endearingly reedy warble.

The frontman's supreme guitar playing is revelatory throughout: he is able to switch from blues-searing electricity to acoustic fingerpicking in the blink of a tripped-out eye. Panoramic instrumental "Aurora Borealis" evokes sun-baked vistas filled with cacti and peyote, while lysergic hoedown "Lost" protests against "living Nixon's mess." A folk-art cover painting and inner sleeve cartoons (all by the band) complete this landmark of left-field Americana.

Meat Puppets II received huge critical acclaim—even getting a rave writeup in *Rolling Stone*, as did the following year's *Up On The Sun*. **MA**

Culture Club had already put themselves on the map with 1982's *Kissing To Be Clever* debut album. A trio of singles—the calling card "Do You Want To Hurt Me?," the teen slow-dance favorite "Time (Clock Of The Heart)," and the catchy (though some would say less impressive) "I'll Tumble 4 Ya"—gave the quartet some pop musical substance to back the flashy image it had cultivated—thanks to stylish music videos and the androgynous wardrobe, hairstyles, and makeup of singer Boy George. But some critics still tended to dismiss the group as a victory of style over substance.

Released a year later, *Colour By Numbers* backed up that initial salvo with a quartet of hits. "Karma Chameleon" became the band's anthem (and gave them a U.S. and UK No. 1), while the hip-swaying "Church Of The Poison Mind" highlighted guest Helen Terry's powerful backing vocals. Whereas the debut album had featured reggae and dub elements, *Colour ...* expands on that palette to include torch song, rootsy rock stylings, and even gospel ("Black Money). "It's A Miracle" pairs a hook-friendly verse with an addictive rhythmic arrangement, while "Miss Me Blind" features not one but two economical Roy Hay guitar riffs that could serve as a gateway to the world of classic rock and blues solos.

Admittedly, some momentum is lost in the final third of the album. But the perfectly crafted pop served up elsewhere comfortably justifies *Colour By Numbers'* classic status—and gave them multiplatinum sales in the United States, Canada, Japan, and Australia. **YK**

Frankie Goes To Hollywood
Welcome To The Pleasuredome (1984)

Label | ZTT
Producer | Trevor Horn
Art Direction | Lawrence Cole
Nationality | UK
Running Time | 64:01

WELCOME TO
THE
PLEASUREDOME

Although Liverpool quintet Frankie Goes To Hollywood (named after an American newspaper headline referring to Frank Sinatra) are best remembered for the singles "Relax" and "Two Tribes," listeners who took the time to explore the expansive *Welcome To The Pleasuredome* found that there was more to this unusual bunch of chancers than risqué costumes and Reagan fighting Chernenko. Although . . . *Pleasuredome* included four covers and a clutch of spoken-word/ ambient between-track sections, the record as a whole statement is a powerful one.

Much of this can be attributed to the masterful production of Trevor Horn, who inspired an entire generation of precision-engineered, super-crisp albums in the 1980s: the searing clarity of the background birdsong and jungle noises in the title track, plus the layered beauty of Frankie's version of Bacharach and David's "Do You Know The Way To San Jose?" are still miraculous to the ear. But the thrill of the record is also down to those amazing singles: "Relax," a filthy anthem for a generation; "Two Tribes," the perfect Cold War paean; "The Power Of Love," an exquisite Christmas hit; and "Welcome . . ." itself, an underrated anthem released as Frankie-mania began to subside.

The paranoia, the sexual nastiness (the "Relax" 12-inch single sleeve bore a paragraph mentioning coprophagia), and the sheer, twisted glamor of *Welcome* . . . made it seem, for a brief moment, as if a whole new movement had been spawned. **JM**

Track Listing

	01	The World Is My Oyster (F.G.T.H.)	1:57
▶	02	Welcome To The Pleasuredome (F.G.T.H.)	13:38
▶	03	Relax (F.G.T.H.)	3:56
	04	War (Strong・Whitfield)	6:12
▶	05	Two Tribes (F.G.T.H.)	3:23
	06	Including The Last Voice (F.G.T.H.)	0:35
	07	Ferry Cross The Mersey (Marsden)	1:49
	08	Born To Run (Springsteen)	3:56
	09	San Jose (Bacharach・David)	3:06
	10	Wish The Lads Were Here (F.G.T.H.)	2:48
	11	The Ballad Of 32 (F.G.T.H.)	4:47
	12	Krisco Kisses (F.G.T.H.)	2:57
	13	Black Night White Light (F.G.T.H.)	4:05
	14	The Only Star In Heaven (F.G.T.H.)	4:16
▶	15	The Power Of Love (F.G.T.H.)	5:28
	16	Bang (F.G.T.H.)	1:08

Run-DMC
Run-DMC (1984)

Label | Profile
Producer | Russell Simmons • Larry Smith
Art Direction | Uncredited
Nationality | USA
Running Time | 39:26

It has been a little over two decades since this Hollis trio blew up and paved the way for rap music to follow. This debut is perhaps the most influential rap album of all time, rap music's sermon on the mount.

Although hip hop had been born in the Bronx, NYC, in the late 1970s, Run-DMC steered the genre away from the block-party stylings of The Sugar Hill Gang and Grandmaster Flash to produce a stripped-down, hardcore, rock-influenced sound. The production is hard and minimalist, built on a drum machine, snippets of guitar or sythesizer, and the groundbreaking scratching of Jam Master Jay (Jason Mizell) .

MCs Run (Joseph Simmons) and DMC (Daryl McDaniel) were the first great MC team; their delivery was tough and uncompromising, taunting the listener and the "Sucker MC's" that receive the brunt of their vitriol. Their ability to trade lines and finish each other's rhymes is showcased to great effect here on "Hard Times" and "It's Like That," a confrontational exploration of the problems of urban life, violence, poverty, and lack of education. (A Jason Nevins remix of "It's Like That" would give the group a worldwide hit in 1998, including a UK No. 1.)

The production values, the themes, and above all, the attitude of this trio set a new paradigm for hip hop. This is the infancy of battle rap, and, although Run-DMC drew no gang affiliations, this is also the formative point of the gangsta phenomenon that would change the face of rap again half a decade later. **LP**

> ## "The big labels wouldn't even look at us because they thought Rap wasn't selling nothin'."
>
> Run-DMC, 1998

Track Listing

▶	01	**Hard Times** (McDaniels•Smith•Ward•Waring)	3:53
▶	02	**Rock Box** (McDaniels•Simmons•Smith)	5:28
	03	**Jam–Master Jay** (McDaniels•Mizell•Simmons)	3:21
	04	**Hollis Crew** (McDaniels•Mizell•Simmons)	3:12
▶	05	**Sucker MC's** (McDaniels•Simmons•Smith)	3:15
▶	06	**It's Like That** (McDaniels•Simmons•Smith)	4:45
	07	**Wake Up** (McDaniels•Simmons•Smith)	5:30
	08	**30 Days** (McDaniels•Simmons•Smith)	5:45
	09	**Jay's Game** (McDaniels•Simmons•Smith)	4:17

Sade
Diamond Life (1984)

Label | Epic
Producer | Robin Millar
Art Direction | Graham Smith
Nationality | Nigeria / UK
Running Time | 44:52

It is hard to imagine a softer voice making a bigger impact. In the R&B and soul realms, Sade's sleek, restrained, and sophisticated sound marked a paradigm shift away from the decades-old dominance of Aretha Franklin, Tina Turner, and other blues-and-gospel-drenched singers. Moreover, *Diamond Life*'s inclusion of world beats would spur on countless Top 40 artists to subtle experimentation with Latin, Caribbean, and other exotic sounds.

The album opens with the warm bossa nova of "Smooth Operator"—a huge worldwide hit—then strolls leisurely through the romantic "Your Love Is King" and "Hang On To Your Love." The London-raised vocalist's detached delivery borders on icy at times, but the velvety accompaniment of her band (also known as Sade) turns "I Will Be Your Friend" and "Why Can't We Live Together" into alluring after-hours affairs.

Its appeal cut through class, culture, race, age, and sex. With *Diamond Life*, it became acceptable for a man to buy a romantic album for reasons other than simply to impress a woman. The key that unlocked those doors was Sade's voice. The 25-year-old Nigeria-born singer's mesmerizing mix of smoky blues, steely jazz, and sterling pop simply sounded like no one else.

The album would be an immediate hit in the UK and its 1985 release in the United States garnered similar results. *Diamond Life* would eventually move six million copies and become the bestselling debut by any British female vocalist in history. **JiH**

Cocteau Twins
Treasure (1984)

Label | 4AD
Producer | Cocteau Twins
Art Direction | 23 Envelope
Nationality | UK
Running Time | 41:32

The alluring and mysterious beauty of the Cocteau Twins first unfolded with *Treasure,* their third album. Bassist Simon Raymonde, the band's newest member, was gradually getting more involved with writing, arranging, and producing. Together with guitarist Robin Guthrie and incomparable vocalist Liz Fraser, the trio disappeared into West London's Palladium Studios and emerged with an ethereal masterpiece.

The shimmering lace on the album cover and the song titles taken from beautiful-sounding mythological names are a perfect example of the influential 4AD esthetic. Appropriate then, that the first track should be named after 4AD founder Ivo. With its delicate "peep-bo" vocal intro and squalling guitar wash, "Ivo" kicks off the album on a high note, literally.

Next up is "Lorelei," the album's best song. Leading off with ear-tickling chimes and two-tone, ambulance synths, the song soon erupts into a propulsive beat and a gorgeous vocal performance. Fraser's voice swoops and pants and soars and sighs high above the music. It is hard to believe her ascending, singsong choruses are coming out of the same mouth as the deeper, fluttering vibratos that anchor the song.

"Persephone" lends the album a grungey, industrial feel while "Pandora" slides in with a slightly jazzy touch. "Donimo" ends the album as strongly as it began with its angelic, ambient two-minute intro giving way to one last explosion of drums before quietly fading away. *Treasure* is simply unforgettable. **RM**

Minor Threat
Out Of Step (1984)

Label | Dischord
Producer | Minor Threat
Art Direction | Jeff Nelson
Nationality | USA
Running Time | 23:32

The 50-odd minutes of music that Minor Threat released during their all-too-short reign on the busy Washington D.C. scene of the early 1980s etched their place in hardcore punk history. Just as impressive is the fact that with one anthem, 1981's "Straight Edge," they kick-started (and provided a name for) a worldwide punk rock phenomenon—a lifestyle choice that rallied against the use of drugs, alcohol, and promiscuous sex.

The title track on the follow-up album *Out Of Step* is a short and simple reiteration of the themes found in "Straight Edge," but the record marks a maturation in the sound and songwriting of volatile vocalist Ian McKaye, who along with drummer Jeff Turner founded the seminal D.C. punk label Dischord. Indeed, from the first D chord on the opener "Betray," about punk kids abandoning their beliefs in order to conform, to the ending (featuring strings!) on the hidden track "Cashing In," this is a quantum leap forward. Sure, they were still pissed off, the riffs were still raucous, but the lyrics to songs such as "Sob Story" and "Look Back And Laugh" deal with more personal issues. The addition of a second guitarist (original bassist Brian Baker switched while Steve Hansgen took over bass duties) tightened up the sound and provided greater dynamic variation.

While the growing straight edge movement and McKaye's reputation as a puritanical firebrand divided some sections of the hardcore scene, the band were not afraid to laugh at themselves—"Cashing In" pokes fun at the growing rumors of their zealotry. **TSc**

Van Halen
1984 (1984)

Label | Warner Bros.
Producer | Ted Templeman
Art Direction | P. Angelus • R. Seireeni
Nationality | USA
Running Time | 33:23

1984 is lead singer David Lee Roth's own macho-aggressive vision of early 1980s California—a place where sex is first and foremost, be it legs that make you wanna hump or teachers who seduce their pupils.

So *1984* was not a profound album in terms of its lyrics, but it was revolutionary in its sound. At a time when new wave was the dominant pop genre, the metal band did the unthinkable and fused keyboards into their sound. In hindsight, there had already been hints about the band's future direction: Eddie Van Halen, the band's lead guitarist and musical leader, had made a guest appearance on Michael Jackson's 1983 megahit "Beat It" and, apparently, had pushed for the inclusion of synthesizers on previous albums. He had met resistance then, especially from Roth. But in 1984, the band acquiesced to Eddie's vision and the musical gamble paid off handsomely: album sales of ten million, while "Jump" became an instant camp classic.

"Jump" showcased Eddie's adept keyboard skills, but most of the other tracks—except for the instrumental "1984" and the synth-heavy ballad "I'll Wait"—proved that he had not lost his virtuosity as a guitarist, with his trademark fingertapping, slides, and fancy harmonics. Roth's trademark *joie de vie* is in evidence throughout, an embodiment of the band's boyishness that seems to ooze out of every song—especially on "Panama," a song that is simultaneously about an alluring woman and a fast car. Clownish and ridiculous, but that was exactly the point. **JC**

Prince And The Revolution | Purple Rain (1984)

Label | Warner Bros.
Producer | Prince And The Revolution
Art Direction | Prince
Nationality | USA
Running Time | 43:50

Although he came close with 1987's *Sign O' The Times*, Slave, The Purple One, Squiggle, or the artist originally known as Prince Rogers Nelson never really topped 1984's *Purple Rain*. At a time when planet pop was awaiting the arrival of tomboy Madonna's second album, and Michael Jackson's *Thriller* (released two years previously) was still eating up everything in its wake, early reviews dismissed *Purple Rain* as a soundtrack album lacking obvious hits. "Little Red Corvette," sniffed *Rolling Stone*. Yet the soundtrack to Prince's semi-autobiographical tale (short-ass alienated youth from poor, dysfunctional family takes refuge in his music) proved to be Prince's most complete pop statement. It shifted 14 million units worldwide, spawned five Top Ten singles (including two No. 1 hits) and rocketed him from sexed-up star to icon extraordinaire.

The key to *Purple Rain*'s success was Prince's genre-defying sound. Replacing the sleazy synthesized funk he had become known for was a new rock, pop, and soul hybrid that incorporated screaming guitars over drum machine-driven tracks such as "When Doves Cry" and "Computer Blue." The album's title track—believe it or not—was Prince's attempt at writing a country-rock track à la Bob Seger.

Prince knew he would never cross over globally unless he toned down his lyrics. Typically, though, he could not help himself and with "Darling Nikki" (starring a man-eater who masturbates over magazines) Prince placed himself in the history books once again, becoming almost directly responsible for the arrival of Tipper Gore's parental advisory stickers. **MM**

> ## "I wish people would understand that I always thought I was bad."
>
> **Prince, 1985**

Track Listing

▶	01	**Let's Go Crazy** (Prince)	4:39
	02	**Take Me With U** (Prince)	3:54
	03	**The Beautiful Ones** (Prince)	5:15
	04	**Computer Blue** (Coleman · Melvoin · Nelson · Prince)	3:59
	05	**Darling Nikki** (Prince)	4:15
▶	06	**When Doves Cry** (Prince)	5:52
▶	07	**I Would Die 4 U** (Prince)	2:51
	08	**Baby I'm A Star** (Prince)	4:20
▶	09	**Purple Rain** (Prince)	8:45

The Replacements | Let It Be (1984)

Label | Twin/Tone
Producer | S. Fjelstad • P. Jesperson • P. Westerberg
Art Direction | Bruce Allen
Nationality | USA
Running Time | 33:23

It has been well documented that, depending on what night you saw them, The Replacements could have been the world's best or worst rock band. Their unpredictable and often very drunken antics meant that anything could and often did happen during their live shows. But following a string of scrappy but infectious records The Replacements released the breakthrough *Let It Be*, an album that straddled the band's punk days and the more melodic and sensitive songs that would come to define their later career. Finding itself atop many critics' 1984 polls, *Let It Be*, along with fellow Minneapolins Hüsker Dü's *Zen Arcade*, came to help define "college rock" in the mid-1980s and made them the darlings of the rock underground.

Key to the band's appeal was frontman Paul Westerberg's knack for writing melodies that were bold, reeked of attitude, but remained remarkably accessible. Witness "Unsatisfied," whose shimmering acoustic guitars belie its bitter sentiments, and the solo "Answering Machine," whose rumbling guitars and final repetitive line—"Oh, I hate your answering machine"—closes the album on a powerful note.

While some critics have argued that the more rowdy "Gary's Got A Boner" and "Tommy Gets His Tonsils Out," could be deemed fillers, they are, after all, about erections and tonsils. Indeed, The Replacements were never averse to a joke (or a drink, for that matter): the album title itself pokes fun at The Beatles, while their rollicking if shambolic cover of the Kiss classic "Black Diamond" caused Gene Simmons to storm from a club upon hearing it performed live. **TSc**

"I figure if everybody doesn't get it, that's OK."

Paul Westerberg, 2002

Track Listing		
▶ 01 **I Will Dare** (Westerberg)		3:18
02 **Favorite Thing** (Mars • B. Stinson • T. Stinson • Westerberg)		2:19
03 **We're Comin' Out** (Mars • B. Stinson • T. Stinson • Westerberg)		2:21
04 **Tommy Gets His Tonsils Out** (Mars • B. Stinson • T. Stinson • Westerberg)		1:53
▶ 05 **Androgynous** (Westerberg)		3:11
06 **Black Diamond** (Stanley)		2:40
▶ 07 **Unsatisfied** (Westerberg)		4:01
08 **Seen Your Video** (Westerberg)		3:08
09 **Gary's Got A Boner** (Mars • Nugent • B. Stinson • T. Stinson • Westerberg)		2:28
▶ 10 **Sixteen Blue** (Westerberg)		4:24
▶ 11 **Answering Machine** (Westerberg)		3:40

The Style Council | Café Bleu (1984)

Label | Polydor
Producer | Various
Art Direction | Simon Halfon
Nationality | UK
Running Time | 43:57

The Style Council's first full-length album, *Café Bleu*, like so much of the band's material, is a hit-and-miss affair. But when the album hits, its combination of R&B, jazz, and damn near any other musical style that was floating around Paul Weller's brain at the time of recording is a blissful sound indeed.

The muted tones of the cover art and the band's flair for style all found expression in the music, by turns sophisticated jazz and R&B-tinged pop. The preponderance of instrumentals (perhaps too many) allows Weller and partner Mick Talbot to stretch out, with the title track showcasing some of Weller's best playing and "Mick's Blessings" providing a showcase for Talbot. "My Ever Changing Moods" confirms Weller's ability to pen a flawless pop tune, and his vocal work on the ballad "You're The Best Thing" is a career high point. One of the most breathtaking songs, "The Whole Point Of No Return," balances a scathing Weller attack on upper-class privilege with a beautifully strummed guitar. On "The Paris Match," Everything But The Girl's Tracey Thorn turns in a vocal performance so tearjerkingly beautiful that you almost forgive "A Gospel" the ill-advised rap experiment that comes later.

Café Bleu is a flawed album, too eclectic for its own good, though such a restless appetite for variety warrants applause in itself. The disc was extremely popular in the UK, peaking at No. 5, and in retrospect its influence is obvious on similarly jazz- and R&B-inclined acts of the era, from Everything But The Girl to Swing Out Sister. The selection of gems on this album make it more than worth searching out. **JW**

"I wanted to be Bob Dylan."

Paul Weller, 2004

Track Listing

▶ 01	Mick's Blessings (Talbot)	1:17
▶ 02	The Whole Point Of No Return (Weller)	2:42
03	Me Ship Came In! (Weller)	3:06
▶ 04	Blue Café (Weller)	2:17
▶ 05	The Paris Match (Weller)	4:27
▶ 06	My Ever Changing Moods (Weller)	3:38
07	Dropping Bombs On The White House (Talbot • Weller)	3:14
08	A Gospel (Weller)	4:44
09	Strength Of Your Nature (Weller)	4:21
▶ 10	You're The Best Thing (Weller)	5:40
▶ 11	Here's One That Got Away (Weller)	2:36
12	Headstart For Happiness (Weller)	3:20
13	Council Meetin' (Talbot • Weller)	2:35

Tina Turner | Private Dancer (1984)

Label | Capitol
Producer | Various
Art Direction | Roy Kohara
Nationality | USA
Running Time | 44:09

Private Dancer trumpeted Tina Turner's comeback from her post-Ike withdrawal years. Competing against *Purple Rain* and *Born In The USA*, the album hit Billboard's No. 1, sold ten million copies, and won four Grammies; "Private Dancer," "What's Love Got To Do With It," and "Let's Stay Together" all became monster singles.

The album's recurring themes—"What's love but a second-hand emotion?," "I'm your private dancer, dancer for money"—coupled with the cover photos of Turner's tawny skin and long, shapely legs—were to embody her persona perfectly: a tough, sexy woman schooled in a tough world. Joy, knowledge, and pain color Turner's raw but vulnerable voice; the songs of *Private Dancer* sound like pages torn from the diary of a passionate woman who has suffered hurt and heartbreak but remains defiant. The production may be slick, but this never detracts from the majestic power and presence of Turner's vocals.

"I Can't Stand The Rain" stands out for its drip-drop counterpoint, as does Turner's reworking of "Help!," for its subtle insinuation. Not every song still thrills. The sneering synths on "I Might Have Been Queen" and "Steel Claw" are so aggressively macho that they nearly crush Tina's yearning. Slamming drum-machine beats were still new in 1984 and we barely noticed the straitjacket they put on the beat; today, we do. Yet *Private Dancer* is Turner's triumph, heart-wrenching singing by an artist at the peak of her career. The album had a string of great producers, but when it finishes it is not their backing tracks but Tina Turner's indomitable soul that makes us play it again. **ML**

"Mick Jagger? I just love the way he wiggles his ass!"

Tina Turner, 1969

Track Listing

01	**I Might Have Been Queen**	(Hine·Obstoj·Oran)	4:10
▶ 02	**What's Love Got To Do With It**	(Britten·Lyle)	3:48
03	**Show Some Respect**	(Britten·Shifrin)	3:18
04	**I Can't Stand The Rain** (Bryant·Miller·Peebles)		3:43
▶ 05	**Private Dancer**	(Knopfler)	7:13
▶ 06	**Let's Stay Together** (Green·Jackson·Mitchell)		5:16
▶ 07	**Better Be Good To Me** (Chapman·Chinn·Knight)		5:11
08	**Steel Claw**	(Brady)	3:49
09	**Help!**	(Lennon·McCartney)	4:30
10	**1984**	(Bowie)	3:11

Echo And The Bunnymen
Ocean Rain (1984)

Label | Korova
Producer | "All concerned"
Art Direction | Martyn Atkins
Nationality | UK
Running Time | 36:53

While their peers U2 and Simple Minds were playing stadiums, Echo And The Bunnymen were touring islands off the west coast of Scotland. *Ocean Rain* proves which ultimately was more rewarding.

Epic and romantic, but less cryptic than previous albums, it employed an orchestra to add soaring strings and flourishes. The drumming of Pete de Freitas drew on lighter touches for the first time: brushes and cymbals rather than rolling toms. Ian McCulloch crooned and occasionally stuttered lyrics that shunned self-indulgence in favor of warmth and poetry. The orchestra added more than lush strings: dynamism is the soul of *Ocean Rain*. Its highs and lows are exemplified by "Thorn Of Crowns"—with McCulloch yelping and roaring to a rambunctious backing—and the epic string quartet rock of the title track.

The confidence of *Ocean Rain* means that it stands the test of time better than any other Bunnymen album. "Our definitive statement," said McCulloch. Accordingly, it was their first to crack the U.S. Top 100. "The Killing Moon," the aching and torchlike first single, reappeared on the soundtrack to *Donnie Darko*.

The cover, shot in a watery cavern and bathed in blue, completed a deck of sleeves steeped in the mysteries of nature. For Bill Drummond, their manager, *Ocean Rain* meant the end of the road (the KLF awaited). How could the Bunnymen better this? **MBI**

Minutemen
Double Nickels On The Dime (1984)

Label | SST
Producer | Ethan James
Art Direction | Dirk Vandenberg
Nationality | USA
Running Time | 73:35

Although they shared a label and DIY ethic with Black Flag, the Minutemen did not play bellicose hardcore. Working-class heroes from the California port of San Pedro, D. Boon (guitar/vocals), Mike Watt (bass/vocals), and George Hurley (drums) expressed hyper-articulate leftism via concise nuggets that fused punk, funk, jazz, folk, and Beefheartian skronk. This was their masterpiece: a 45-song, double LP assembled in response to labelmates Hüsker Dü's conceptual *Zen Arcade*.

Sides one, two, and three were labeled "D," "Mike," and "George," according to which member programed them. The fourth, modestly titled "Chaff," featured breathless deconstructions of Van Halen and Steely Dan; they also saluted Creedence Clearwater Revival on Boon's side. Original highlights include Latin-pop protest "Corona," which would later became the theme to TV show *Jackass*, and spoken-word/acoustic guitar duet "Do You Want New Wave Or Do You Want The Truth." "Political Song For Michael Jackson To Sing" wraps an oblique attack on middle America in searing axework, while "History Lesson (Part II)" is a poignant piece of autobiography. Blue-collar anthem "This Ain't No Picnic" inspired a budget-priced video, which was nominated for an MTV award (they lost to Kajagoogoo).

A tour with long-time fans R.E.M. ensued, but tragedy struck on December 23, 1985, when Boon was killed in a car accident. **MA**

Lloyd Cole And The Commotions
Rattlesnakes (1984)

Label | Polydor
Producer | Paul Hardiman
Art Direction | Da Gama
Nationality | UK
Running Time | 35:29

The world conjured by Lloyd Cole and The Commotions' debut album was a rarefied one. One of the finest debuts of the 1980s, *Rattlesnakes* is at once literary and doomed, managing to sound both European and American. *Rattlesnakes* was the fantasy of an intense Glasgow University philosophy student determined to stuff as many references as possible into his songs.

It should have been ghastly, but Cole managed to imbue his lyrics with enough desire, confusion, longing, and regret to stay on this side of pretentiousness. His lyrics were funny too—a line such as "must you tell me all your secrets when it's hard enough to love you knowing nothing" is as sharp as anything by pop's other literate funnyman, Morrissey.

The album commences with debut single "Perfect Skin," with Cole singing almost twice as fast as the musicians just to cram in all his witty cinematic and literary references. The rich guitar textures provided by Neil Clark, meanwhile, gave Cole's wry asides a swirling intensity they might otherwise have lacked. "Forest Fire," "Charlotte Street," and "2CV" adroitly capture the emotions simmering beneath the surface at university dorms, while "Are You Ready To Be Heartbroken?" provides an achingly beautiful, bittersweet song of innocence soon to be lost. Producer Hardiman gently complements the music with the addition of subdued strings. For those about to graduate, we salute you. **APe**

Youssou N'Dour
Immigrés (1984)

Label | Earthworks
Producer | Youssou N'Dour
Art Direction | In Like Flynn
Nationality | Senegal
Running Time | 34:01

A teenage star in his native Senegal, N'Dour was still unknown beyond Africa when his band, Super Etoile De Dakar, arrived in Paris, the capital of the former colonial power, to entertain homesick expatriates in 1984. Within a year of recording this mini-album inspired by what he saw in France, he was on such a steep incline that he was able to tour America for the first time.

The next 12 months would see him sharing the stage and studio with Paul Simon and Peter Gabriel. It took a further two years before these debut European recordings would be officially released in English-speaking countries, by which time N'Dour was a world superstar, but the purity of these four songs still astonished those who thought they knew him.

Considerations of international status were not a priority when *Immigrés* was recorded, however. This is strictly an album for Senegalese consumption. The traditional robes and hat N'Dour wears on the sleeve were not adopted for the benefit of tourists, and the unadulterated mbalax rhythms (an Africanized form of the Cuban music that had been popular in West Africa for decades) did not come with subtitles.

Fortunately, the passion and fire that the singer and his musicians presented were simple for the uninitiated to follow: this was prime soul territory. The music might have been complex, but it was clearly designed for dancing. And that voice! **DH**

Bruce Springsteen | Born In The USA (1984)

Label | Columbia
Producer | Various
Art Direction | Andrea Klein • Annie Leibowitz
Nationality | USA
Running Time | 46:51

Gleeful giggles must have enveloped CBS in the summer of 1984. Just as *Thriller* dropped from Billboard's Top Five, *Born In The USA* (also on a CBS subsidiary) took its place, hovering near the summit for more than a year. Both have survived, with style, the hoopla of their heyday— indeed, with seven Top Ten singles apiece, they actually sound like greatest hits packages.

Springsteen's success was due in part to a new directness. The grim *Nebraska* behind him, he distilled his poppiest set from a rumored 100 songs and secured its iconographic status with Leibowitz's photograph of his denim-clad derrière.

From "Born In The USA"—which was originally an acoustic lament, and is now a Who-style thunderstorm— to the downright sexy "I'm On Fire" and warm-hearted "Glory Days," the music is deceptively commercial. "Deceptively" because the lyrics reward inspection. There is "Dancing In The Dark," about his frustration at having to write a hit. The yearningly lovely "Bobby Jean" is a homage to sidekick Steve Van Zandt. The wacky rock 'n' roll of "Working On The Highway" masks a gritty lyric, and the apparently patriotic "Born In The USA" is actually a scathing condemnation. Further confirming his brilliance, he makes the chest-beating "No Surrender" as moving as the lovesick "I'm On Fire."

The album is easily misinterpreted; then-president Ronald Reagan cited the title track as an example to follow. And its success—more than 15 million sold in the United States alone—can raise cynical hackles. Do not be fooled. In its spirit (love, home, and honesty) and its songs, the album has heart and soul to spare. **BM**

> ## "The great challenge ... is holding on to your idealism after you lose your innocence."
>
> Bruce Springsteen, c.2002

Track Listing

▶	01	**Born In The USA** (Springsteen)	4:39
	02	**Cover Me** (Springsteen)	3:29
	03	**Darlington County** (Springsteen)	4:50
	04	**Working On The Highway** (Springsteen)	3:11
	05	**Downbound Train** (Springsteen)	3:37
▶	06	**I'm On Fire** (Springsteen)	2:42
	07	**No Surrender** (Springsteen)	4:03
	08	**Bobby Jean** (Springsteen)	3:48
	09	**I'm Goin' Down** (Springsteen)	3:32
	10	**Glory Days** (Springsteen)	4:18
▶	11	**Dancing In The Dark** (Springsteen)	4:05
	12	**My Hometown** (Springsteen)	4:37

The Fall
This Nation's
Saving Grace (1985)

Label | Beggars Banquet
Producer | John Leckie
Art Direction | Michael Pollard
Nationality | UK
Running Time | 47:10

In 1985, Mark E. Smith and The Fall unleashed their tenth and most complete album to date. Producer John Leckie gave the group a far more polished sound, horrifying Smith, who insisted the finished record was mastered from his sonically inferior cassette copy. Indeed, the sweet acoustic melodies of "Paint Work" are rudely interrupted because Smith accidentally pressed "Record" on his home tape deck, creating an abstract yet effective sound collage.

The growing input of Smith's Californian wife Brix adds a melodic West Coast feel to The Fall's dissonant post-industrial rumble, allowing the group to veer from the catchy garage pop of "Barmy" and "Spoilt Victorian Child" toward more avant-garde territories—witness the pulsating electronic throb of "L.A." The raucous guitars and bludgeoning drums of "Bombast" and "What You Need" tread more familiar Fall territory, while "Gut Of The Quantifier" has Smith's usual vitriol accompanied by an attempt at rap—in a heavy Manchester, accent. The album's crowning glory is "I Am Damo Suzuki," Smith's homage to the Japanese-born former vocalist of Can. Gently lifting melodies and rhythms from Can's classic *Tago Mago*, it is both harrowing and awe-inspiring.

This Nation's Saving Grace saw The Fall gain wider acceptance, and is a great example of their ability to be pop without having to compromise their stance. **CSh**

Abdullah Ibrahim
Water From An
Ancient Well (1985)

Label | Black Hawk
Producer | Sathima Bea Benjamin
Art Direction | Zand Gee
Nationality | South Africa
Running Time | 46:42

Originally known as Dollar Brand, Abdullah Ibrahim is still Africa's greatest jazz musician, a powerful pianist deeply marked by Duke Ellington. Born and raised in Cape Town, Ibrahim started performing as a teenager, singing doo-wop, American pop tunes, and traditional South African songs. At the same time as the African National Congress was beginning to confront apartheid, Ibrahim, trumpeter Hugh Masekela, and saxophonist Kippie Moeketsi founded the Jazz Epistles, the first black jazz group to record in South Africa.

"We had to create our own voice," Ibrahim said in 1999. "It's not a question of taking bebop lines and adding it on top of our music. We had to develop a vocabulary, and we're still developing it."

No album better captures his stately, deceptively simple music than *Water From An Ancient Well*, featuring the superlative Ekaya, with flautist Carlos Ward, tenor saxophonist Ricky Ford, baritone saxophonist Charles Davis, bassist David Williams, and drummer Ben Riley. His expansive voicings give the musicians vast territory to explore, while his folk-like themes capture the poetry of daily life in South Africa.

The album contains many of his most striking tunes, such as the inexorably triumphant "Mandela," "The Wedding," and "Manenberg Revisited," which exemplifies his penchant for combining hypnotic left-hand figures with emotionally soaring melodies. **AG**

A-ha
Hunting High And Low (1985)

Label | Warner Bros.
Producer | Various
Art Direction | Jeri McManus
Nationality | Norway
Running Time | 36:39

Tears For Fears
Songs From The Big Chair (1985)

Label | Mercury
Producer | Chris Hughes
Art Direction | Tim O'Sullivan
Nationality | UK
Running Time | 56:18

This Norwegian trio were in exactly the right place at the right time to take advantage of the mid-Eighties MTV revolution. In 1985 A-ha achieved phenomenal album sales on the back of the highly innovative video for the first single from *Hunting High And Low*, "Take On Me." The state-of-the-art promo, which saw a cartoon Morten Harket leaping from the pages of a comic book to woo a surprised young woman, pushed them to the top of the Billboard charts. The song sees Harket's crooning morph effortlessly into a yearning falsetto, swept along on a frantic wave of new-romantic synths.

The sleeve art is very much of its day (artistically blurred black-and-white photography, tight T-shirts, "Lady Di" haircuts) but belies the pop genius within. The combination of guitarist and main songwriter Paul "Pal" Waaktaar with classically trained pianist Magne "Mags" Furuholmen—as well as their frontman's voice and good looks—ensured they were not just one-hit wonders.

The album threw up several gems, including the frantic, quasi-operatic pop of "The Sun Always Shines On TV"—a bona fide smash that started as a heartfelt lament and built to a Phil Spector-esque wall of chiming guitars and strings. Other standouts were the melancholic title track and the introspective "Train Of Thought." Although despised in the retro-rockist Nineties, *Hunting High And Low* remains a bright, breezy, and brilliant electro-pop classic. **JDo**

For a brief time, Tears For Fears became the biggest band on the face of the planet on the strength of this album—a release that ranks alongside *Dare* by The Human League, *Non-Stop Erotic Cabaret* by Soft Cell, and *The Lexicon of Love* by ABC as one of the best pop records of the decade. The group, who had already become regular chart fixtures in their native England, burst onto the world scene by adding a healthy dollop of glistening pop nous and organic instrumentation to their cerebral and sensitive electronic music.

Most groups would not have the nerve to open an album on such a bombastically epic and awesome track as "Shout," with its chiming guitar solos and immense drum production. But their arrogance was justified given that they had penned such an unbeatable clutch of songs. (Orbazal was to pick up the "Songwriter Of The Year" gong at the Ivor Novello Awards the following year.) "Everybody Wants To Rule The World" had lyrical ambition matched by chart success, scoring them a No. 1 hit on both sides of the Atlantic. Album tracks included the propulsive, bass-driven groove of "Mothers Talk" and the neon-drenched, soporific night-time cab ride of "The Working Hour," but it is the redemptive warmth of "Head Over Heels" that really stands out here, a song that aided their mainstream critical re-evaluation after it turned up on the soundtrack to cult movie *Donnie Darko*. **JDo**

Dire Straits | Brothers In Arms (1985)

Label | Vertigo
Producer | Neil Dorfsman • Mark Knopfler
Art Direction | Sutton Cooper • Andrew Prewett
Nationality | UK
Running Time | 55:11

This, the fifth studio album by Dire Straits, was their first to top the U.S. album chart (it stayed there for nine weeks, and was certified multiplatinum). Recorded at Air Studios, Montserrat, it also became the bestselling album of 1985 in Britain, where it was No. 1 for three months. It was also the first CD to sell one million copies.

Six years after their eponymous debut album, the group's personnel had changed considerably, with only leader Mark Knopfler and bass player John Illsley still on board. Two keyboard players, Alan Clark and Guy Fletcher, had replaced Knopfler's younger brother, rhythm guitarist David, and one Welsh drummer (Terry Williams) had supplanted another (Pick Withers).

"So Far Away," "Money For Nothing," "Walk Of Life," and "Brothers In Arms" were all hit singles on one or both sides of the Atlantic, the biggest being the riff-led "Money," which also featured co-writer Sting (like Mark Knopfler, from north-east England). Promoted by a cutting-edge animation video clip, it was tailor-made for MTV (ironic, as the station receives a dig in the lyrics) and became the group's first U.S. chart-topping single. The title track, however, is an altogether less brash—and infinitely more touching—affair, a reflective meditation on warmongering modestly accompanied by Knopfler's understated guitar.

High on atmosphere and pristinely produced, *Brothers In Arms* was arguably the peak of the group's career, and their few subsequent original albums lacked the same magic. Mark Knopfler embarked on an inevitable solo career in the 1990s, but has yet to equal the stunning success of this timeless effort. **JT**

> ## "Commercial success isn't an indication of the quality of the work ... I'd written a lot of tunes, I wanted to record 'em."
>
> Mark Knopfler, 1991

Track Listing

▶ 01	**So Far Away**	(Knopfler)	5:11
▶ 02	**Money For Nothing**	(Knopfler • Sting)	8:26
▶ 03	**Walk Of Life**	(Knopfler)	4:12
04	**Your Latest Trick**	(Knopfler)	6:33
05	**Why Worry**	(Knopfler)	8:31
06	**Ride Across The River**	(Knopfler)	6:58
07	**The Man's Too Strong**	(Knopfler)	4:40
08	**One World**	(Knopfler)	3:40
▶ 09	**Brothers In Arms**	(Knopfler)	7:00

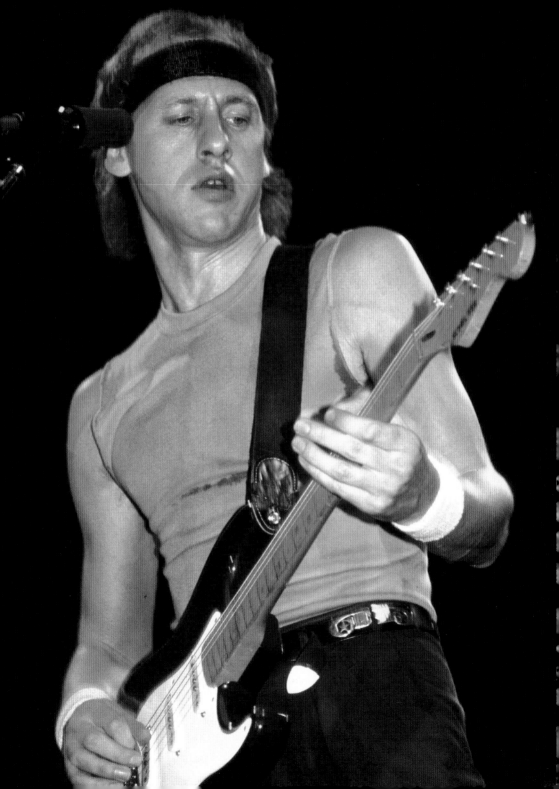

Prefab Sprout
Steve McQueen (1985)

Label | Kitchenware
Producer | Thomas Dolby • Phil Thornally
Art Direction | East Orange
Nationality | UK
Running Time | 45:22

For a short while in the mid-1980s, school was cool: you could hardly pretend to understand The Smiths, Lloyd Cole, or Scritti Politti without a degree in English literature. But the hippest name for wordsmithery was a Newcastle quartet whose run of albums meant that nobody argued when Paddy McAloon claimed he was the finest songwriter of his generation.

Debut LP *Swoon* had hinted at something perhaps too clever to connect with a wide audience. With Thomas Dolby producing, the coyness was reined in, although after "When Love Breaks Down" failed as a single, the group was generally perceived as too indie to be mainstream. Ridiculous really, for apart from the country-rockabilly swagger of "Faron Young" the songs were predominantly pop songs for a mature audience; middle of the road with edge.

But these were odd times, and the synths on "Appetite" and "When Love Breaks Down" saw some file the Sprouts in the same electropop category as the Pet Shop Boys. So they released "When Love Breaks Down" again. And again. And just when you had lost count of the number of times it had failed to chart—it charted. *Steve McQueen* capitalized on the single's success, and McAloon never looked back.

America was slower to acknowledge the band's talents, and legal action by Steve McQueen's estate held the album up (it would later be released as *Two Wheels Good Stateside*, with three extra tracks). But anybody who found it treasures it still. **DH**

Mekons
Fear And Whiskey (1985)

Label | Sin
Producer | Mekons
Art Direction | John Ingledew
Nationality | UK
Running Time | 35:17

The Mekons are one of the UK's most brilliant and undervalued groups. Formed as a loose collective in Leeds in 1977 when they started messing around with the Gang Of Four's equipment, they released a couple of chaotic LPs (plus single "Never Been In A Riot," directed at The Clash) and then took a sabbatical. Energized by the UK miners' strike of 1984 to '85, the band (with original members Jon Langford and Tom Greenhalgh) re-emerged with *Fear And Whiskey*, lauded by many as the best album of the decade.

Often—and inaccurately—considered the beginning of alt.country (a claim that forgets the work of X, Jason And The Scorchers, or The Meat Puppets), *Fear And Whiskey* is no conventional cowpunk hoedown, but rather a ferocious parcel of punk, folk, pop, dub, and country. Sure, there is Susie Honeyman's frantic fiddling, and the honky-tonk waltz of "Darkness And Doubt," but *Fear And Whiskey* is "country" as played by English punks with a fondness for Merle Haggard.

It is this conflict that lends them their jarring edge and, sounding like a collision between Gang Of Four, The Redskins, The Pogues, and Johnny Cash, the band blister through chirpy opener "Chivalry" before laying out the political backdrop on "Trouble Down South," a menacing call to arms set to a relentless military drumroll. "Hard To Be Human Again" is the brilliant, bitter highlight of side one, but the album really hits its stride in an audacious second half, culminating in the perfect pop of "Lost Dance" and the delirious cover of "Lost Highway." **PW**

Big Black
Atomizer (1986)

Label | Homestead
Producer | Big Black • Iain Burgess
Art Direction | Uncredited
Nationality | USA
Running Time | 35:44

Atomizer's iconic cartoon sleeve portrays the Earth staring down the barrel of a death ray (licensing problems nixed the original concept of Looney Tunes character Marvin The Martian toting the weapon).

Leader Steve Albini's sleeve-notes, however, eschew cartoon nihilism for gritty realism, complementing the lyric sheet's array of pedophile rape rings, small-town violence, and post-Vietnam trauma. "You can't think about it, really, because if you do then you go crazy; stark gibbering, spitting, and pissing in your pants crazy," he warned. This acrid sense of disgust was further articulated by the music's proto-industrial din.

Three men and a drum machine, Big Black surfaced in Chicago in the early 1980s. This, their debut album, crystallized the sound they developed over earlier EPs: sheets of black metal nailed to relentless drum machine pulses; a grating, claustrophobic chaos.

"Jordan, Minnesota" freezes the blood like a horror movie with a typewriter rhythm, while "Kerosene" shudders like a robo-funk Zeppelin until its harmonic guitars ignite. For "Bazooka Joe," the drumbeat includes the sampled sound of an M1 carbine being fired. Over it all, Albini barks with dispassionate repulsion; empowered by alienation, but still the enigmatic, contrary figure that would name his next band Rapeman.

A starkly moral album, *Atomizer* depicts a world ripe for destruction—and delivers that retribution in the form of scouring white noise; a cathartic purification that still burns today. **SC**

Suzanne Vega
Suzanne Vega (1985)

Label | A&M
Producer | Steve Addabbo • Lenny Kaye
Art Direction | Corey And Company
Nationality | USA
Running Time | 35:43

Born in California, and growing up in New York, Vega inhabits musical qualities of both environments. From the West Coast she derives a bohemian folksy flair, while from the urban East comes a streetwise lyricism.

An important year for the aspiring singer/ songwriter was 1979. Vega visited England to observe the explosive punk scene, and attended a Lou Reed gig back home. Both experiences pushed her lyrical approach toward realism. While Vega admits that she spoiled her early gigs with a defensive "what are you staring at?" hostility, the strength of her material, and reputation, saw her signed by A&M in 1984.

With former Patti Smith guitarist Lenny Kaye at the helm, *Suzanne Vega* was recorded in early 1985. The UK market quickly took her to heart, via the jaunty single "Marlene On The Wall." Here the observer becomes the observed, as a portrait of Marlene Dietrich watches Vega bed a procession of lovers.

Not surprisingly, given producer Lenny Kaye's credentials, the guitar sound is crisply to the fore. Vega's icy picking is warmed with subtle synthesizer and the shrewdest percussion. Her vocals veer from half-spoken caresses on "Cracking" and "Freeze Tag," to the sensual melodies of "Undertow" and "Small Blue Thing."

The album's heart is defined by a timeless fable, "The Queen And The Soldier," which recalls Sandy Denny's epic balladeering. By contrast, the adjoining "Knight Moves," has snarling stanzas not unlike those of Hüsker Dü or Kristin Hersh. **GT**

The Pogues | Rum, Sodomy, And The Lash (1985)

Label | Stiff
Producer | Philip Chevron • Elvis Costello
Art Direction | Frank Murray
Nationality | Ireland • UK
Running Time | 45:20

THE POGUES

Rum, Sodomy, And The Lash is a work of raw and raucous beauty. While the band's debut *Red Roses For Me* was overproduced and overreliant on boozy imagery, their second album bled passion, poetry, and energy.

The credit for this transition partly lies with the producer Elvis Costello, who gave the band's glorious bar-fight of a sound room to breathe. "Wild Cats Of Kilkenny" and "Sally Maclennane" roar out like Guinness-fueled brawls between The Dubliners and the Sex Pistols; a perfect fusion of Irish folk traditionalism and punk aggression.

Costello—who married bassist Cait O'Riordan the following year—later wrote that his job on the album was to sit back and capture them "in their dilapidated glory, before some more professional producer fucked them up."

But the album is more than a collection of rowdy jigs. Singer Shane MacGowan's writing had flourished since their debut, and with just a few slurred phrases he paints a captivating gallery of outsiders and lowlifes. On "The Old Main Drag," he chronicles the slow degradation of a London rent boy. The wistful ballad "A Pair Of Brown Eyes" is sung from a different perspective: one of a crippled World War I veteran.

Released the same year as the multimillion-selling *Brothers In Arms* by Dire Straits, *Rum, Sodomy, And The Lash* sounded wonderfully out of synch with the mid-1980s scene. The album's ragged majesty helped it crawl into the UK Top 20, and made a fan out of hobo king Tom Waits, who loved the group's "*Treasure Island* kind of decadence." **TB**

"I'm a bitter, twisted little shit."

Shane MacGowan, 1985

Track Listing

01	The Sick Bed Of Cúchulainn (MacGowan)		2:59
02	The Old Main Drag (MacGowan)		3:19
03	Wild Cats Of Kilkenny (Finer • MacGowan)		2:48
04	I'm A Man You Don't Meet Every Day (Trad.)		2:55
▶ 05	A Pair Of Brown Eyes (MacGowan)		4:54
▶ 06	Sally Maclennane (MacGowan)		2:43
07	A Pistol For Paddy Garcia (Finer)		2:31
08	Dirty Old Town (MacColl)		3:45
09	Jesse James (Trad.)		2:58
10	Navigator (Gaston)		4:12
11	Billy's Bones (MacGowan)		2:02
12	The Gentleman Soldier (Trad.)		2:04
▶ 13	The Band Played Waltzing Matilda (Bogle)		8:10

Kate Bush | Hounds Of Love (1985)

Label | EMI
Producer | Kate Bush • John Carder Bush
Art Direction | Bill Smith Studio
Nationality | UK
Running Time | 47:26

Kate Bush

Hounds Of Love

Bruised by the battering administered to 1982's *The Dreaming*, Kate Bush retreated to the studio. Legendarily reported to have ballooned in weight, she emerged as beautiful as ever, bearing in her arms an epic as bonkers as its predecessor but with greater songs (and much bigger sales).

The first fruit was "Running Up That Hill," a mini-epic that—shorn of Kate's hoped-for title "A Deal With God" —became her biggest international hit. Finally a star of sorts in America, she proved an inspiration to Tori Amos and Prince. The latter was smitten with "Cloudbusting," one of the charming chess pieces that make up the *Hounds* half of the album. Its extraordinary video featured Donald Sutherland—star of *Don't Look Now*, one of the "watery movies" that inspired her (in another celluloid link, the title track opens with a quote from 1957's *Night Of The Demon*).

The cinematic second half is *The Ninth Wave*. Inspired by a Tennyson poem—actually *The Coming Of Arthur*; not, as the sleeve claims, *The Holy Grail*—it veers from ballads to jigs (*Hounds* . . . has few guitars, with Killing Joke bassist Youth making the rockingest contribution on "The Big Sky"). The story finds our heroine alone in the water, lapsing into a nightmare, encountering a witchfinder, imagining a loved one at home, and being visited by her future self before being rescued.

The cover—photographed by her brother John, who also wrote the "Jig Of Life" poem—evokes both halves of the album, and completes a creation as fascinating as it is fabulous. *Hounds Of Love* is the Kate Bush album you do not have to be a fan to adore. **BM**

> "It's almost like two separate albums . . . if they're linked it's only by the theme of love."
>
> Kate Bush, 1985

Track Listing

▶ 01	**Running Up That Hill (A Deal With God)** (Bush)	5:00
02	**Hounds of Love** (Bush)	3:03
03	**The Big Sky** (Bush)	4:40
04	**Mother Stands For Comfort** (Bush)	3:08
▶ 05	**Cloudbusting** (Bush)	5:10
06	**And Dream Of Sheep** (Bush)	2:46
07	**Under Ice** (Bush)	2:22
08	**Waking The Witch** (Bush)	4:17
▶ 09	**Watching You Without Me** (Bush)	4:06
10	**Jig Of Life** (Bush)	4:17
11	**Hello Earth** (Bush)	6:00
12	**The Morning Fog** (Bush)	2:37

The Smiths | Meat Is Murder (1985)

Label | Rough Trade
Producer | John Porter • The Smiths
Art Direction | Caryn Gough • Morrissey
Nationality | UK
Running Time | 39:41

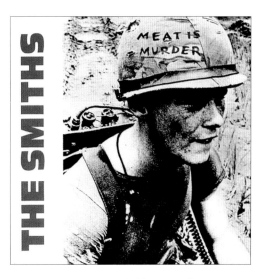

Meat Is Murder is the great lost Smiths album, in the sense that it has been obscured by their later work .

After their debut, Manchester's finest sons went into the studio with the mission statement of making a record that would better represent their live sets and BBC sessions. Not that *The Smiths* had been a total disappointment, but guitarist Johnny Marr, who is as adept at a metallic crunch ("Nowhere Fast") as a Fifties rockabilly shuffle ("Rusholme Ruffians"), would truly amaze with his guitar palette this time round.

Lyricist Morrissey was on the ball too. His attention had turned to his passions for vegetarianism, pacifism, and antiauthoritarianism—the album title, the cover (a shot of a Vietnam soldier at war), and in particular the lyrics of the title track, spoke volumes about his strong lifelong views. But elsewhere there were the first signs of real hurt in his words. "That Joke Isn't Funny Anymore" seems to beg a bully—or worse, a friend—to stop cajoling old Moz. There were also studies of a forgotten, fairground life on "Rusholme Ruffians," which drew musical "inspiration" from "His Latest Flame" by Elvis—a debt the band would later acknowledge on their live *Rank* collection.

On the CD re-release of the album, "How Soon Is Now" sits mournfully in the middle, bemoaning a youth spent being ignored in nightclubs. This admittedly great song, often used to represent The Smiths' music, stands in the way of some of their more invigorating and vibrant creations. *Meat Is Murder* is The Smiths with a point to prove. The album sounds all the sweeter when you realize they actually proved it. **JK**

> "Just as the public can be inspired they can also begin to yawn at the very notion of yet another song for a cause."
>
> Morrissey, 1989

Track Listing

▶	01	**The Headmaster Ritual** (Marr•Morrissey)	4:52
▶	02	**Rusholme Ruffians** (Marr•Morrissey)	4:19
▶	03	**I Want The One I Can't Have** (Marr•Morrissey)	3:13
	04	**What She Said** (Marr•Morrissey)	2:40
	05	**That Joke Isn't Funny Anymore** (Marr•Morrissey)	4:57
▶	06	**Nowhere Fast** (Marr•Morrissey)	2:35
	07	**Well I Wonder** (Marr•Morrissey)	4:00
	08	**Barbarism Begins At Home** (Marr•Morrissey)	7:00
	09	**Meat Is Murder** (Marr•Morrissey)	6:05

Tom Waits
Rain Dogs (1985)

Label | Island
Producer | Tom Waits
Art Direction | Anders Petersen
Nationality | USA
Running Time | 54:04

If the crash and honk of 1983's *Swordfishtrombones* upset Tom Waits fans weaned on beat poetry and piano ballads, then *Rain Dogs* had them crying into their bourbons. Musically, *Swordfishtrombones* was Waits arriving in a new town and trying to find his place; by *Rain Dogs*, he had made himself at home, albeit in a battered tin shack a long way out by the freeway.

Whether the romantic boozehound Waits played in the 1970s was born from autobiography or imagination has long been a matter for conjecture, but he is certainly in character here. *Rain Dogs* tells of a demimonde populated by Chinese barflies, blind firemen, one-armed dwarfs, a slaughterhouse boss named Uncle Vernon, a Puerto Rican mistress with a wooden leg—and that is just the first three songs. It is a song cycle about life on the fringes of society, were a society this unbalanced ever likely to exist.

The dementia of the lyrics finds echo in the music, a rag-and-bones, Weillian clatter of thumped percussion and parping horns, beer-hall pianos, and twitchy guitars (played chiefly by Marc Ribot, though Keith Richards guests), accordions, pump organs, and banjos. The fragile "Time" evokes Seventies Waits, "Blind Love" is as close to country as he has ever come, and "Downtown Train" was tamed by Rod Stewart, but *Rain Dogs* is defiantly liberated from compromise and convention. Naturally, it turned into his biggest selling record, since when it has become a staple in press surveys listing the best albums of the 1980s. **WF-J**

The Jesus & Mary Chain
Psychocandy (1985)

Label | Blanco Y Negro
Producer | The Jesus And Mary Chain
Art Direction | Uncredited
Nationality | UK
Running Time | 38:52

Having scared the hell out of everyone with their 1984 debut single on *Creation*, "Upside Down"—a relentless slab of feedback and Neanderthal drumming, Jim and William Reid spent the next year charming audiences with their novel approach to performing live. Backs to the crowd, they raised an impenetrable squall of feedback and distortion, spat at the press, and rarely played for longer than ten minutes.

Signed to Blanco Y Negro, but with Creation's Alan McGee still as their manager, the Mary Chain's debut album transpired to be a work of genius. Universally hailed in the music press, it is now routinely pointed to as one of the greatest debut albums of all time. The two Scottish brothers had pulled off the hitherto unimagined trick of welding sunny Beach Boys-style pop to the brutal feedback-drenched sonics of The Velvet Underground and a whole load of echo, with Bobby Gillespie's primitive drumming providing a masterclass in economy.

It is the three singles that are most often referred to —the leather-and-shades swagger of "You Trip Me Up," the nihilistic amphetamine rush of "Never Understand," and the bittersweet "Just Like Honey"—although the album remains electrifying in its entirety. Its influence is incalculable. Any band with a penchant for effect pedals and an ear for a jaunty melody owes them a nod. You may never again experience them live, but *Psychocandy* is as close as you will get to what one writer likened to "a chainsaw in a hurricane." **RS**

New Order
Low-Life (1985)

Label | Factory
Producer | New Order
Art Direction | Peter Saville
Nationality | UK
Running Time | 40:11

New Order's third album shone with new-found confidence. After the patchy *Movement* and the close-but-not-quite *Power, Corruption And Lies*, *Low-Life* encompassed techno pop ("Subculture"), dark gothic rock ("Sunrise"), and the first recorded incidence of country 'n' techno ("Love Vigilantes").

The album's title had been inspired by writer Jeffrey Barnard, whose line "I . . . live what's called the low life" had been sampled on "This Time Of Night." (Unimpressed, Barnard promptly sued the band.) And the record was housed in the only sleeve of their career to feature photographs of the group.

"Perfect Kiss" (simultaneously released as an extended 12-inch single) is a grandiose disco epic. Peter Hook's incomparable bass melodies and Gillian Gilbert's synthesized power chords hold everything together while drummer Stephen Morris and vocalist Bernard Sumner add cowbells, pinball machines, South American tree frogs, and a narrative of AIDS, revenge—oh, and the joys of masturbation.

The real standout, however, is the brooding and funereal instrumental "Elegia." Recorded in a marathon 24-hour session immediately after finishing a grueling UK tour, it was widely assumed to be their tribute to the late Ian Curtis, singer with New Order's former incarnation Joy Division.

Low-Life firmly established New Order as a major British act, entering the UK Top Ten and also giving the band their U.S. chart debut. **CSh**

Simply Red
Picture Book (1985)

Label | Elektra
Producer | Stewart Levine
Art Direction | Peter Barrett
Nationality | UK
Running Time | 44:22

For an album with its roots planted firmly in the Manchester soil, *Picture Book* could not have strayed further from the city's post-punk heritage. Mick Hucknall quickly tired of the restrictions of punk rock and saw Simply Red, and *Picture Book* in particular, as a vehicle to stretch his vocal ability. Released in October 1985, just one year after he formed the group with three ex-members of The Durutti Column, the album immediately found favor with the public.

Spearheaded by the blue-eyed soul of "Money's Too Tight (To Mention)"—a cover of The Valentine Brothers R&B hit—*Picture Book* made steady inroads on the British album chart, peaking at No. 2 in July 1986. Yet this was largely thanks to the Hucknall original "Holding Back The Years"—a melancholic tale of regrets and wasted time—that broke the band on both sides of the Atlantic. The singer would struggle to repeat his stunning vocal performance, which sent the song to No.1 in the U.S. Billboard chart.

This is not that *Picture Book* was all about mellow soul; "Look At You Now" and "No Direction" offer brief flirtations with and windows in on Hucknall's rockier past, while "Sad Old Red" and "Heaven" bring out the band's jazz influences.

Many now argue that the band's inconsistent lineup, with the frontman as the only concrete fixture, has prevented Simply Red from revisiting the form of their debut. But *Picture Book* at least proves the superstar red-head got to where he is for a reason. **ARo**

Dexy's Midnight Runners
Don't Stand Me Down (1985)

Label | Mercury
Producer | Various
Art Direction | Peter Barrett
Nationality | UK
Running Time | 46:28

Don't Stand Me Down is a towering achievement, one that can now be viewed as a *Pet Sounds* for the 1980s. At the time, though, it was buried by leader Kevin Rowland's stubbornness, as he sought to top the global success of 1982's *Too-Rye-Ay*, which had become a millstone around his neck; having finally gained the level of achievement he had craved, he detested it.

The painstaking sessions for the eagerly awaited follow-up took place throughout 1984. Veteran producers came and went: Jimmy Miller lasted a couple of days, as did Tom Dowd. Album centerpiece "This Is What She's Like" started as a jaunty bluebeat and ended up a mini-opera. "Knowledge Of Beauty" was originally an extensive workout based on the Irish pronunciation of the name "Dave." Acts of intransigence from Rowland, such as replacing the sound of each guitar string with separate stringed instruments and rejections of the sleeve's color, served to delay the album further.

Don't Stand Me Down was the most extreme example of Rowland's New Soul Vision, but by the time it was eventually released, in September 1985, there were few around to welcome it. Although folklore suggests that critics buried it, they did not—without a single to announce it, the album died at the hands of the paying public. At a time of routine overproduction, a record as organic and detailed as this was always going to divide a crowd. When Rowland returned to the live stage in 2003, the material from the album was the most warmly received of all. **DE**

> "We were just being incredibly meticulous and it took forever."
>
> Kevin Rowland, 2003

Track Listing

▶ 01	**The Occasional Flicker** (Rowland)	5:49
▶ 02	**This Is What She's Like** (Adams•O'Hara•Rowland)	12:24
▶ 03	**Knowledge Of Beauty** (O'Hara•Rowland•Wynne)	7:01
04	**One Of Those Things** (Marinelli•Rowland•Watchel•Zevon)	6:01
05	**Reminisce Part Two** (Rowland)	3:31
▶ 06	**Listen To This** (Adams•Rowland)	3:20
▶ 07	**The Waltz** (Rowland•Torch)	8:22

Scritti Politti
Cupid And Psyche 85 (1985)

Label | Virgin
Producer | Arif Mardin
Art Direction | Keith Breeden • Green Gartside
Nationality | UK
Running Time | 38:15

Cupid And Psyche 85 was a breakthrough for Green Gartside's Scritti Politti, spawning five UK hits and two U.S. smashes. This was the third incarnation of the band, which started in 1977 as an anarchist collective in London, cutting four experimental post-punk singles influenced, unusually, by French literary theory and Italian Marxism.

Aided by Arif Mardin's state-of-the-art production, *Cupid . . .* raised the bar for R&B. The funky "Wood Beez" and blissful lovers' rock of "The Word Girl" earned Gartside—a white art student from South Wales—the affection of Prince, Chaka Khan, Janet Jackson, Jam & Lewis, and many of his black heroes. "Perfect Way," a U.S. No. 12, was even covered by Miles Davis, who would later collaborate with the group.

Inspired by Quincy Jones' production on Michael Jackson's *Off The Wall*, Gartside decamped to Manhattan with keyboardist David Gamson and drummer Fred Maher to surround himself with session men like bassist Marcus Miller, guitarist Robert Quine, and drummer Steve Ferrone. Performing in a Jackson-influenced androgynous falsetto, Green's cryptic lyrics questioned the attainability of romance, turning the love song into a kind of lexical game.

All of this underlying value went unnoticed by most of the audience—but, with its sweet Synclaviers, Fairlight fanfares, and meticulously sequenced breakbeats, the influence of *Cupid And Psyche 85* on pop has been immeasurable. **JLe**

> **"I never listen to my own music."**
>
> Green Gartside, 2005

Track Listing

▶	01	**Word Girl (Flesh And Blood)** (Gamson•Gartside)	4:24
	02	**Small Talk** (Gamson•Gartside)	3:39
▶	03	**Absolute** (Gartside)	4:25
	04	**A Little Knowledge** (Gartside)	5:02
	05	**Don't Work That Hard** (Gartside)	3:59
▶	06	**Perfect Way** (Gamson•Gartside)	4:33
	07	**Lover To Fall** (Gartside)	3:51
▶	08	**Wood Beez (Pray Like Aretha Franklin)** (Gartside)	4:48
	09	**Hypnotize** (Gartside)	3:34

Elvis Costello And The Attractions
Blood And Chocolate (1986)

Label | Demon
Producer | Colin Fairley • Nick Lowe
Art Direction | Michael Krage
Nationality | UK
Running Time | 47:33

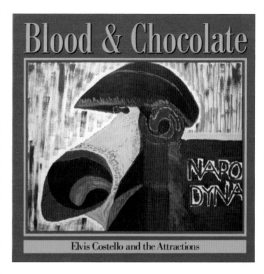

Elvis Costello began his liner notes to the reissue of *Blood And Chocolate* by informing the reader that "there is not an awful lot that needs explaining about this record." Perhaps, but those familiar only with the latter two-thirds of his career will still clock the bruising thud of appropriately titled opener "Uncomplicated" and wonder how, why, and when he got so angry.

Coming at the heels of the rootsier, Attractions-free *King Of America*, *Blood And Chocolate* is quite a shock. Cut largely live in the studio, with monitors instead of headphones and amps turned to on-stage levels, it sounds blunt, basic, muddy. This is no accident. The songs, either bilious kiss-offs or love notes wrapped in barbed wire, do not need crisp edges. Whether framed in garage rock ("I Hope You're Happy Now") or Sixties pop ("Poor Napoleon"), whether melancholic ("Home Is Anywhere You Hang Your Head") or claustrophobic ("I Want You," a career highlight), they do not get them.

The public took to the new, spite-driven Costello like a duck to gasoline; strange marketing did not help. "Tokyo Storm Warning," a furious six-minute "thug's nightmare travelog" (Costello's sleevenotes again), was chosen as the first single, a bizarre choice rendered unfathomable by the decision to split it into two clumsily faded parts, one each for sides A and B. After two further singles flopped, Costello retreated to formulate the decidedly polished pop of *Spike*. Since then, Costello has collaborated with numerous artists in a fascinating if frequently baffling career. **WF-J**

Track Listing

▶	01	**Uncomplicated** (Costello)	3:26
	02	**I Hope You're Happy Now** (Costello)	3:07
▶	03	**Tokyo Storm Warning** (Costello • O'Riordan)	6:24
	04	**Home Is Anywhere You Hang Your Head** (Costello)	5:04
▶	05	**I Want You** (Costello)	6:40
	06	**Honey Are You Straight Or Are You Blind?** (Costello)	2:08
	07	**Blue Chair** (Costello)	3:39
▶	08	**Battered Old Bird** (Costello)	5:50
	09	**Crimes Of Paris** (Costello)	4:19
	10	**Poor Napoleon** (Costello)	3:21
	11	**Next Time Round** (Costello)	3:35

Afrika Bambaataa And The Soul Sonic Force
Planet Rock—The Album (1986)

Label | Tommy Boy
Producer | Arthur Baker
Art Direction | Monica Lynch
Nationality | USA
Running Time | 42:51

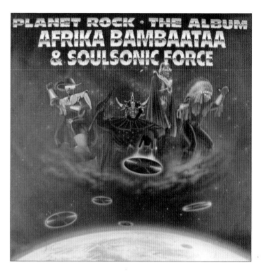

To be marked out within the innovative and forward-thinking musical sub-genre of hip hop as one of the true originals is something indeed. Afrika Bambaataa Aasim, named after a nineteenth-century Zulu chief, swapped his gang colors for record decks in the mid-1970s to become one of the triumvirate of DJs who would lay the cornerstones of hip hop, along with Kool Herc and Grandmaster Flash.

Bambaataa quickly tired of simply sourcing his beats from old funk records and created a brand new fusion, influenced by European artists such as Kraftwerk and Gary Numan as well as breakbeats. The title track from *Planet Rock—The Album* remade the former's "Trans-Europe Express" for the block-party crowd, Arthur Baker's chromium-plated production skills dovetailing neatly with Bam's irrepressible curiosity about the new science of synthesized sounds. True, the rhyming was almost added as an afterthought, but that was something the crew would rectify completely on "Looking For The Perfect Beat" which remains the greatest electro record of the 1980s.

But this compilation of 12-inch records, released on Tommy Boy before he signed a major-label contract with Capitol, also signposts something else significant: more than anyone else, Bambaataa was responsible for the genesis of the American house scene (particularly Detroit techno, Miami bass, and Chicago house), which were direct descendants of his own particular brand of electro, featured on this astounding album. **JDo**

> "This became the birth of the electro funk ... sound."

Afrika Bambaataa, 1999

Track Listing		
▶ 01 **Planet Rock**		
(Allen · Baker · Miller · Robie · Williams)		7:00
▶ 02 **Lookin' For The Perfect Beat**		
(Aasim · Allen · Baker · Miller · Robie · Williams)		7:30
03 **Renegades Of Funk**		
(Baker · Bambaataa · Miller · Robie)		6:44
04 **Frantic Situation**		
(Aasim · Allen · Baker · Evans · Halp · Henderson		
Miller · Serano · Wilfred · Williams)		3:49
05 **Who You Funkin' With?** (Bambaataa)		6:20
06 **Go Go Pop** (Bambaataa)		5:58
07 **They Made A Mistake** (Bambaataa)		5:30

Beastie Boys | Licensed To Ill (1986)

Label | Def Jam
Producer | Beastie Boys • Rick Rubin
Art Direction | Stephen Byram
Nationality | USA
Running Time | 44:20

In 1984, the Beastie Boys abandoned their punk origins to become one of the world's pioneer white rap groups.

Upon the release of this debut album, the three MCs—Mike D, MCA, and King Ad-Rock, from wealthy, Jewish backgrounds in New York—were simultaneously criticized by the hip-hop community for cultural piracy and dismissed by most critics as puerile purveyors of obnoxious party music. However *Licensed To Ill* swiftly generated a cult following that saw the album sell 750,000 copies in the first six weeks of release alone, and top the U.S. charts (the first rap album to do so). Lyrically immature it may be (the boys themselves were in their early 20s at the time), but its no-brainer hedonism was embraced by party-mad suburban teenagers everywhere (check out the gonzo humor of the plane-crash sleeve by David Gamboli, aka World B. Omes).

The Boys drop plenty of tongue-in-cheek references to hip-hop and B-Boy culture—witness "Posse In Effect" and its allusions to pistol-toting partying, and the cheesy "Girls." But the trio's DIY esthetic, postmodern referencing, and combination of strong beats and samples with heavy guitar riffs make for an intoxicating brew. "Fight For Your Right" became a party anthem, catching perfectly the crossover appeal between rock and hip hop (territory producer Rick Rubin had already visited in his work with Run DMC and L L Cool J). "Rhymin & Stealin" famously samples Zep's "When The Levee Breaks," to thunderous effect. The Motörhead-inspired "No Sleep Till Brooklyn," very funky "Brass Monkey," and "She's Crafty" proved perfect crowd pleasers.

Adolescence never sounded so much fun. **CSt**

> ## "I'm having so much fun now."
>
> MCA, 1987

Track Listing

▶	01	**Rhymin And Stealin** (Beastie Boys • Rubin)	4:08
	02	**The New Style** (Beastie Boys • Rubin)	4:36
	03	**She's Crafty** (Beastie Boys • Rubin)	3:35
	04	**Posse In Effect** (Beastie Boys • Rubin)	2:27
	05	**Slow Ride** (Beastie Boys • Rubin)	2:56
	06	**Girls** (Beastie Boys • Rubin)	2:14
▶	07	**Fight For Your Right** (Beastie Boys • Rubin)	3:28
▶	08	**No Sleep Till Brooklyn** (Beastie Boys • Rubin)	4:07
	09	**Paul Revere** (King Ad-Rock • McDaniels • Rubin • Simmons)	3:41
	10	**Hold It Now, Hit It** (Beastie Boys • Rubin)	3:26
▶	11	**Brass Monkey** (Beastie Boys • Rubin)	2:37
	12	**Slow And Low** (McDaniels • Rubin • Simmons)	3:28
	13	**Time To Get Ill** (Beastie Boys • Rubin)	3:37

Metallica | Master Of Puppets (1986)

Label | Elektra
Producer | Metallica • Flemming Rasmussen
Art Direction | Don Brautigam
Nationality | USA
Running Time | 54:00

Jostling for position with Slayer's *Reign In Blood* as the finest thrash metal album ever released, *Master Of Puppets*, Metallica's third LP, is a masterpiece on all levels. It offered the frankly astounded headbangers of the day a precisely measured and perfectly gauged combination of aggression, speed, melodic beauty, and musical intricacy. Its warm, almost delicate production and its balance of rage and depth had a colossal impact. Although Metallica have made bigger-selling albums, the band has never equaled it.

Master Of Puppets' strengths are revealed from the first track, "Battery," which tacks an acoustic-guitar intro onto a massive wall-of-sound statement before settling into a twisty, slightly over-clever riff that straddles the borders between thrash and mainstream heavy metal. The title track continues along similar lines—its mellow solo mid-section is a thing of melodic beauty—but "Disposable Heroes," along with the frantic, knowingly malevolent album closer "Damage, Inc.," reminds the listener that Metallica were, after all, a thrash metal band of enormous power. Two semi-ballad/semi-heavy workouts entitled "The Thing That Should Not Be" (the heaviest tune, in terms of sheer riff weight, that Metallica recorded until 1991's "Sad But True") and the hymn to psychosis, "Welcome Home (Sanitarium)," display the band's darker, more subtle side, while "Leper Messiah" is a slow-to-fast attack on TV evangelism.

"Orion," an instrumental epic, shows just how talented bass player Cliff Burton could be at his peak: his premature death only months after the album's release makes it an appropriate swan song. **JM**

> ## "The lyrics I write, I write pretty much for myself. I'm not telling people how to think."
>
> James Hetfield, 1986

Track Listing

▶	01	**Battery** (Hetfield·Ulrich)	5:10
▶	02	**Master Of Puppets** (Burton·Hammett·Hetfield·Ulrich)	8:38
	03	**The Thing That Should Not Be** (Hammett·Hetfield·Ulrich)	6:32
▶	04	**Welcome Home (Sanitarium)** (Hammett·Hetfield·Ulrich)	6:28
	05	**Disposable Heroes** (Hammett·Hetfield·Ulrich)	8:14
	06	**Leper Messiah** (Hetfield·Ulrich)	5:38
	07	**Orion** (Burton·Hetfield·Ulrich)	8:12
▶	08	**Damage, Inc.** (Burton·Hammett·Hetfield·Ulrich)	5:08

The The | Infected (1986)

Label | Epic
Producer | Various
Art Direction | Andy Dog
Nationality | UK
Running Time | 42:05

Explicitly political albums—for all that their heart is in the right place (depending on your political sensibilities, naturally)—have a tendency to be terribly inconsistent when it comes to their musicality. Matt Johnson's second album under the guise of The The, *Infected*, comprehensively trashed this truism.

Although Johnson had vented his anger at the state of the world on 1984's *Soul Mining*, his vision became more ambitious and coherent—and his vitriol more focused—during the two years that it took to record this sophomore effort. Released in 1986 at the apogee of the free-market Thatcher years, *Infected*—the name and title track a take on the early AIDS panic unfolding in the UK—is the sound of disillusion made music.

A large part of his ire is spent questioning the willingness with which his country was ponying up to the United States. "Sweet Bird Of Truth" was especially prescient, relating a dying U.S. airman's last words as he flies his bomber back from a Middle East raid (months after its recording, Ronald Reagan's attack on Libya from UK airbases provoked native uproar).

Johnson also rails against the destruction of a more kind and gentle England on "Heartland"—the replacement of the "Saturday morning cinema" of his childhood with "piss-stinking shopping center[s] in the new side of town"—and finds the time to set things to rights in the worlds of sexual politics and capitalism to boot. All this, set to a glorious soundtrack that features brass, strings, and backing vocals from a young Neneh Cherry ("Slow Train To Dawn"). Never before has fury sounded so funky. **SJac**

> "I've been a perfectionist in the studio, which is a neurotic condition where you just want everything to be as good as it possibly can be."
>
> Matt Johnson, 1993

Track Listing

▶	01	**Infected** (Johnson)	4:48
	02	**Out Of The Blue (Into The Fire)** (Johnson)	5:07
▶	03	**Heartland** (Johnson)	5:09
	04	**Angels Of Deception** (Johnson)	4:38
	05	**Sweet Bird Of Truth** (Johnson)	5:23
	06	**Slow Train To Dawn** (Johnson)	4:14
	07	**Twilight Of A Champion** (Johnson·Mosimann)	5:23
	08	**Mercy Beat** (Johnson)	7:23

Nanci Griffith
The Last Of The True Believers (1986)

Label | Philo
Producer | Nanci Griffith • Jim Rooney
Art Direction | Pat Alger • Nanci Griffith
Nationality | USA
Running Time | 36:34

Billy Bragg
Talking With The Taxman About Poetry (1986)

Label | Go! Discs
Producer | Kenny Jones • John Porter
Art Direction | Uncredited
Nationality | UK
Running Time | 38:20

Together with Texas contemporaries Lyle Lovett and Steve Earle, Nanci Griffith emerged like a breath of fresh air blowing through the tired mid-1980s country music scene. Her three previous albums had evidenced a growing talent, but here, on her fourth, she confirmed herself as a force to be reckoned with.

Not quite country, not quite folk, the sound is rich, rootsy, and acoustic; the songs catchy, literate, and spry. Her voice meanwhile trills, quivers, and quavers to deftly emotive and subtly empowering effect. Although Kathy Mattea had hits with two tracks off this album ("Love At The Five & Dime" and "Goin' Gone"), Griffith's distinctively sweet (but never saccharine) voice fits her own songs better.

An ex-schoolteacher, she enjoyed wearing her heart on her sleeve. Accordingly, she is pictured clutching a biography of Tennessee Williams on the front cover and Larry McMurtry's *Lonesome Dove* on the back. And yes, that is Lyle Lovett off to the right, dancing under the Woolworth's luncheonette sign.

Belying her delicate demeanor, Griffith could be a tough cookie when she had to be, both in person and in song. But when she opened her mouth to sing, it was hard not to fall a little bit in love with her. She followed this album with her major-label debut, *Lone Star State Of Mind*—twin peaks in a career that has endured more than two and a half decades. **RF**

Billy Bragg has always stood at the crossroads of the public and the private, exploring political issues and matters of the heart with equal passion. As such, the poignantly titled *Talking With The Taxman About Poetry* is perhaps the most successful synthesis of his interests, bringing together the righteous vitriol of "Ideology" with the sensitivity of "The Passion."

While Bragg's stylistic lineage can be most obviously traced to folk singers such as Pete Seeger and Woody Guthrie, he was equally influenced by the English music hall tradition, as well as classic rock 'n' roll—both are evidenced here in his cover of the obscure Count Bishops proto-punk nugget "Train Train," and the weepy "Honey I'm A Big Boy Now."

While the unabashedly strident cover and tracks such as "There Is Power In A Union" occasionally threaten to undermine the overall strength of the album, the best songs here explore the emotional consequences of politics, as in the institutional dissection of "The Marriage" and the "ideological cuddle" of "Greetings To The New Brunette."

Subtitled "The Difficult Third Album," the disc found him working more extensively with accompanists and enjoying support from the likes of Johnny Marr and Kirsty MacColl, while still retaining the sparse esthetic that showcased his sharp, reverb-heavy guitar sound. The result is a warm, direct, and still potent record. **TSh**

Talk Talk
The Colour
Of Spring (1986)

Label | EMI
Producer | Tim Friese-Greene
Art Direction | James Marsh
Nationality | UK
Running Time | 45:32

Megadeth
Peace Sells ...
But Who's Buying? (1986)

Label | Capitol
Producer | Dave Mustaine • Randy Burns
Art Direction | Ed Repka
Nationality | USA
Running Time | 39:12

It seemed like a good idea at the time, but the technological revolution of the 1980s was not kind to rock. With the gap between elevator music and Top Ten single bridged by the ubiquitous Yamaha DX7 synthesizer, a generation of drummers was being replaced by machines. The result? Really crappy drums.

A turning point of sorts came in 1986—surely the worst year for music ever—when Talk Talk, one of the main culprits of this synth-drenched rock, became the first to reject it. They lost keyboard player Simon Brenner and employed the services of producer Tim Friese-Greene—an experimental foil for the emotional songwriting of guitarist and singer Mark Hollis. Next, Hollis and Friese-Greene broke up the band's previously inflexible format, augmenting drummer Lee Harris and bassist Paul Webb with a host of guest players, including Steve Winwood, bassist Danny Thompson, and Pretenders guitarist Robbie McIntosh.

The Colour Of Spring was a revelation. Hollis' songs were finally wrapped in instrumentation sympathetic to their fragile melancholy. The haunting "April 5th" and "Chameleon Day" had a free-form, improvisational feel completely at odds with the band's past but the best examples were the sublime "Life's What You Make It" and "Living In Another World." The latter barely scraped the UK charts—a common fate of the best singles in those bleak days. **MBe**

By 1986 Megadeth singer/guitarist Dave Mustaine was on a roll. Fueled by inner rage and insecurity caused by his unceremonious ejection from Metallica three years before, battling with heroin and booze, and driven by the critical reception of his first album, 1985's *Killing Is My Business ... And Business Is Good!*, Mustaine had the world in front of him. He disappointed no one with the furious *Peace Sells ... But Who's Buying?*, the logical extension of the speedy riffing, technical guitar mastery, and political commentary that had made his first album so promising.

Although Mustaine could not really sing and his lyrics were still a bit hamfisted at this stage, the songs are unforgettable. "This is the greatest fuckin' day of my life!" he crowed at the Monsters Of Rock festival in England in 1988, as the crowd broke into the chorus ("If there's a new way/I'll be the first in line") of the title track, whose bass intro—courtesy of the long-suffering David "Dave Jr." Ellefson—is the most recognizable bass part in extreme metal. "Devil's Island," "Wake Up Dead," and an odd cover of Willie Dixon's "I Ain't Superstitious" are highlights too.

Although Megadeth's fourth album, 1990's *Rust In Peace*, was more dazzling in its arrangements and smoother in its production, it is *Peace Sells ...* that made the band into a true force to be reckoned with. Play this and hear Mustaine at his gleefully devilish peak. **JM**

Bon Jovi | Slippery When Wet (1986)

Label | Mercury
Producer | Bruce Fairbairn
Art Direction | Bill Levy
Nationality | USA
Running Time | 43:47

Critics have never been kind to Bon Jovi, frequently attributing the success of *Slippery When Wet* to the band's over-the-top sentimentality and lead singer Jon Bon Jovi's boyish good looks rather than to the band's musical abilities. No matter, though. Bon Jovi did the unthinkable with this album—they made heavy metal into a pop genre that women would be able to love. And they got themselves a multiplatinum U.S. chart-topper in the process.

Jon's ability to sing with gusto in the high registers was a great help, but so was the synth-heavy sound and infectious melodies. Moreover, Bon Jovi kept it simple, writing about everyday subjects that anyone could relate to—romantic upheavals ("You Give Love A Bad Name"—a U.S. No. 1), employment ("Livin' On A Prayer" —another No. 1), and virginity ("Never Say Goodbye"). As Chuck Klosterman wrote in his heavy metal memoir *Fargo Rock City*, Bon Jovi tugged "at heartstrings instead of brainstrings."

That is not to say metal fans had little to cheer for. The band test-marketed their songs by playing demo-versions to kids in a pizza parlor across the street from their studios to ensure their songs had a gritty integrity. Richie Sambora was the consummate lead guitarist on his blazing solos, and also repopularized the talkbox—a device first used by Peter Frampton that allows a player to simulate vocally the sound of a guitar. And for all his romantic idealism, a visceral line like "I've seen a million faces and I've rocked them all" ("Wanted Dead Or Alive") demonstrated that Jon knew how to appeal to the basest of male rock fans' desires. **JC**

> "Reaganomics had us believing that everything was cool … Everybody was having a pretty damn good time, you know?"
>
> Richie Sambora, 2002

Track Listing

01	**Let It Rock** (Bon Jovi•Sambora)		5:25
▶ 02	**You Give Love A Bad Name** (Bon Jovi•Sambora)		3:43
▶ 03	**Livin' On A Prayer** (Bon Jovi•Sambora)		4:09
04	**Social Disease** (Bon Jovi•Sambora)		4:18
▶ 05	**Wanted Dead Or Alive** (Bon Jovi•Sambora)		5:09
06	**Raise Your Hands** (Bon Jovi•Sambora)		4:17
07	**Without Love** (Bon Jovi•Sambora)		3:31
08	**I'd Die For You** (Bon Jovi•Sambora)		4:30
▶ 09	**Never Say Goodbye** (Bon Jovi•Sambora)		4:49
10	**Wild In The Streets** (Bon Jovi•Sambora)		3:56

Sonic Youth
Evol (1986)

Label | SST
Producer | Martin Bisi • Sonic Youth
Art Direction | Richard Kern • Sonic Youth
Nationality | USA
Running Time | 36:02

Sonic Youth's third album is significant for cementing the lineup with the introduction of drummer Steve Shelley and for being the first of the band's truly great, genre-defining works. Earlier records introduced them as young upstarts on the 1980s New York experimental scene, intent on wrestling new and awkward kinds of scree from their retuned guitars. But *Evol* was the point at which they really started to catch the ear.

Noisy and abrasive it may well often be, but *Evol* is laced with warped pop undertones, too. Singer/guitarist Thurston Moore has explained that the unforgiving acoustics of the tiny room *Evol* was recorded in made them lean toward melody simply to be able hear each other. Thus opener "Tom Violence": against the clang of newly discovered chords, Moore's clear, simple vocal line rises and falls in an uncomfortable harmony with the music. Similarly, Kim Gordon's ghostly, nursery rhyme-like coda on "Star Power" floats above semi-abstracted riffing, somewhere between chilling and comforting. (Is that Gordon growling and clawing at us from the cover? It looks like it could be but it is actually a still from a movie by the band's pal Richard Kern.)

Things peak with the slow-building soar of "Expressway To Yr Skull," in which all those wonderful drones, echoes, wails, pulses, and that keen melodic sense really come together. It is like an art-rock answer to "Freebird" or "Stairway To Heaven," and certainly a definitive Sonic Youth moment—rock rebuilt and retold in a strange and thrilling new language. **TH**

Slayer
Reign In Blood (1986)

Label | Def Jam
Producer | Rick Rubin • Slayer
Art Direction | Stephen Byram
Nationality | USA
Running Time | 29:00

Any album that opens with the lines, "Auschwitz, the meaning of pain. The way that I want you to die," is going to grab your attention. It certainly pricked up ears at CBS, who refused to distribute the album, possibly alerted to its extreme lyrical content by the scenes of hell and dismemberment on the cover.

Slayer formed in L.A. in 1982, gathering a cult following in a metal community that was turning away from the behemoths of the 1970s to younger, faster, and heavier bands such as Metallica and Anthrax. However, it was not until Rick Rubin signed them to his Def Jam label and gave them the clean production they had been lacking that Slayer's uncompromising vision of extreme violence, hell, and damnation was unleashed on a startled mainstream.

Musically, the album fuses the aggression and precision of thrash metal with the economy of hardcore punk—most songs clock in well under three minutes. Dave Lombardo's relentless drumming leaves the listener breathless, while Kerry King and Jeff Hanneman's solos sound more like they are disemboweling their unfortunate instruments than playing them. The album's apex is the relatively lengthy "Raining Blood"— starting with a disquieting rain effect, it launches into a galloping thrash riff, twin lead guitars eerily echoing each other throughout the track.

South Of Heaven (1988) was more accessible but, as a chilling statement of intent, *Reign In Blood* remains unsurpassed, a high-water mark for the genre. **RS**

Throwing Muses
Throwing Muses (1986)

Label | 4AD
Producer | Gil Norton
Art Direction | 23 Envelope
Nationality | USA
Running Time | 37:39

Being nuts never hurts if you want to rock. Kristin Hersh was so bonkers (okay, if you want to get technical, "bipolar") that she named her alter ego "Evil Kristen." With her half-sister Tanya Donelly on guitar, Leslie Langston on bass, and David Narcizo on drums, she became the missing link between Siouxsie and the Banshees and P.J. Harvey.

Commonly associated with labelmates and touring partners the Pixies, the band actually had more in common with acts such as X or Hüsker Dü, whose influence vastly outstripped their sales. The spiky sound and psychotic lyrics were far from user-friendly, but they conjured beauty from chaos.

Hersh's fellow Georgians R.E.M. and The B-52's are there in spirit, but the Muses' hallmarks are stop-start songs, keening vocals, and military drumming—of which "Hate My Way" is a prime example. Sliding down the scale of sanity, "Vicky's Box" opens with one of Hersh's blunter lyrics—"He won't ride in cars anymore/ It reminds him of blowjobs"—before turning into a sort of country thrash. Other standout moments include "Green"—indicative of the pop smarts that Donelly brought to the Muses, then her own band Belly—and the more conventional "Soul Soldier."

Not an easy listen, but a compelling one. Think of it as a key to a magical kingdom, whose landmarks include 1989's hook-packed *Hunkpapa*, Hersh's solo masterpiece *Hips And Makers*, and Belly's chart-busting *Star*. Fortune favors the brave: open your ears. **BM**

Paul Simon
Graceland (1986)

Label | Warner Bros.
Producer | Paul Simon
Art Direction | Jeffrey Kent Ayeroff
Nationality | USA
Running Time | 44:43

Graceland is Paul Simon's mid-life crisis. At once new and old, the album marked a crossroads not only for its creator, but for all the heavy hearts who were searching for new ways to be familiar to themselves. Some bought Ferraris; Simon went to South Africa in violation of a United Nations cultural boycott to make an album that would evoke the musical traditions of two cultures and draw a line between his own past and future.

Joining forces with esteemed local musicians like Ladysmith Black Mambazo and Tao Ea Matsekha, Simon seamlessly blended the traditional South African style known as Mbaqanga—whose three-chord structures and background harmonies reminded him of the R&B music he had loved as a child—with his own elegant pop melodies. Resounding rhythms and hopping basslines dance around Zulu shouts in "I Know What I Know"; nimble guitar lines mingle with accordion bursts on "Gumboots"; and Ladysmith Black Mambazo's haunting call-and-response moans on "Homeless" sound like a map from Africa to America and back.

At the center is Simon, a middle-aged storyteller peering forward at the prospect of becoming a "cartoon in a cartoon graveyard," crying over spilled love, and crafting some hope from the comforts and misfortunes of the past. Upon its release, *Graceland*'s unpopular political status was quickly surmounted by its captivating grace and beauty, convincing any listener that the horrors of apartheid were simply no match for the power of artistic brotherhood. **MO**

Run-DMC | Raising Hell (1986)

Label | Profile
Producer | Rick Rubin • Russell Simmons
Art Direction | Janet Perr
Nationality | USA
Running Time | 39:43

Run-DMC blasted their way through into the mainstream with this, their third album, and in so doing pulled the entire hip-hop genre along with them. In teaming up with rock-loving producer Rick Rubin, the group had forged a crossover sound that would soon make them the first global rap stars and the first hip-hop crew to appear on MTV.

This is an album crammed with classic cuts that pretty much define what these days is referred to as "old school hip hop." The partnership of the vocal duo's punchy staccato delivery with rough rock breaks culled from the likes of The Knack's "My Sharona" ("It's Tricky") and, of course, Aerosmith ("Walk This Way") created the most anthemic and catchy rap to date. Indeed, it was really "Walk This Way" that catapulted this new music into the mainstream—by teaming up with the originators of the song, Run-DMC brought the music of the ghetto to a white, middle-class audience—love at first sight for all concerned.

Countless pairs of brand new sneakers later, courtesy of the B-Boy anthem "My Adidas," *Raising Hell* went on to sell more than three million copies, at the same time catapulting the Reverend Run, Daryl Mac, and DJ Jam Master Jay to superstardom.

Almost every track on the album is a classic, but special notice should also be paid to the infectious "Peter Piper," "Hit It Run," and their re-working of James Brown on "Proud To Be Black."

The group's cross-armed stance and distinctive dress on the cover also informed the street style and attitude that prevails in hip hop to this day. **CR**

"We said it's good and bad."

Daryl McDaniels, 1998

Track Listing

▶	01	**Peter Piper** (McDaniels • Simmons)	3:25
▶	02	**It's Tricky** (McDaniels • Mizell • Rubin • Simmons)	3:03
▶	03	**My Adidas** (McDaniels • Rubin • Simmons)	2:47
▶	04	**Walk This Way** (Perry • Tyler)	5:11
	05	**Is It Live** (McDaniels • Mizell • Rubin • Sever • Simmons)	3:06
	06	**Perfection** (McDaniels • Simmons)	2:52
▶	07	**Hit It Run** (McDaniels • Mizell • Rubin • Simmons)	3:10
▶	08	**Raising Hell** (McDaniels • Rubin • Simmons)	5:31
	09	**You Be Illin'** (Mizell • Rubin • Simmons)	3:26
	10	**Dumb Girl** (McDaniels • Simmons)	3:31
	11	**Son Of Byford** (McDaniels • Simmons)	0:27
▶	12	**Proud To Be Black** (Brown • McDaniels • Simmons)	3:14

XTC
Skylarking (1986)

Label | Virgin
Producer | Todd Rundgren
Art Direction | Dave Dragon
Nationality | UK
Running Time | 45:48

Does conflict create art? The antipathy between band leader Andy Partridge and producer Todd Rundgren was so deep-seated, it is a wonder all concerned left the studio still sane. It is nothing short of miraculous that the music that emerged was so breathtaking.

The aim was modest: create a concept album that covers growing up, dawning sexuality, getting married, facing old age, and fading away, all set within the framework of a single day. Not an approach to please the record executives, who were putting pressure on the group, by now a studio-based outfit since Partridge's stage fright ruled out touring, to deliver hits.

What the group delivered was a pastoral masterpiece recognized by *Rolling Stone* as one of the decade's 50 best albums. Openers "Summer's Cauldron" and the idyllic "Grass" are all lazy heat haze and buzzing hedgerows, ironic since the demo for the former was cut during freezing January. "The Meeting Place" (with a video inspired by cult TV head-scratcher *The Prisoner*) celebrates snatched moments, while "Season Cycle" is Brian Wilson refracted through rural Britain.

Concept albums usually run aground by dint of having to chart a changing narrative, an obligation that often outstrips the artist's songwriting skills. But the move from summer into fall and on to winter is seamless, from the finger-clicking jazz of "The Man Who Sailed Around His Soul," caustic missive-to-the-Almighty "Dear God," to the rustic lament of "Sacrificial Bonfire." This is The Beatles perched on bales of hay. **CB**

Steve Earle
Guitar Town (1986)

Label | MCA
Producer | Tony Brown • Emory Gordy Jr.
Art Direction | Simon Levy
Nationality | USA
Running Time | 64:59

Steve Earle's *Guitar Town* burst into the charts in 1986, securing Earle's reputation as an outlaw troubadour. A country boy right down to his Texan boots, Earle was 30 years old and already had a string of broken marriages, addiction problems, and legal woes. He was already a successful songwriter in Nashville, but the pundits greeted *Guitar Town* with little enthusiasm.

It was then picked up by the rock press, who hailed Earle as one of the first roots rockers—a cousin to both Dwight Yoakam and Bruce Springsteen. The stories he told in his songs straddled two genres and appealed to lovers of both rock and country. He helped forge the road into alt.country that is now so well traveled by artists such as Lucinda Williams and Wilco.

Earle's frustrated songwriting years and his many personal misadventures gave him plenty of fuel for these excellent songs. "Guitar Town" is a highly effective musical expression of the thoughts of an angry young man, and an alternately joyous and cautionary depiction of life on the road.

The album also bears testament to the political shift in the United States during the Reagan 1980s, particularly on tracks such as "Someday" and "Good Ol' Boy (Gettin' Tough)." He is all dirty guitar rocker on the hilarious No. 1 title single, and expertly mines country heartbreak territory on "My Old Friend The Blues."

Earle continues to make superb records that encompass his view of the world, but this was his finest journey into the American heartland. **KC**

Bad Brains
I Against I (1986)

Label | SST
Producer | Ron St. Germain
Art Direction | Marcia Resnick
Nationality | USA
Running Time | 31:28

Blasting onto the scene in a cloud of spliff smoke and flailing dreads, Bad Brains were one of the more controversial bands to spring from Washington D.C.'s rich hardcore punk tradition. Initially branded by some as nothing more than stoned, homophobic, religious zealots, it is nevertheless hard to deny them, and their milestone I Against I, a place in U.S. hardcore history.

Though D.C.'s brand of hardcore will probably always be best known for Dischord Records, the label founded by Jeff Nelson and Ian McKaye of Minor Threat fame, Bad Brains' eponymous, tempestuous debut album (a cassette-only release in 1982) helped to define hyper-speed-thrash-punk, though dub reggae formed a major part of the mix too.

I Against I was to be the band's creative zenith. Vocalist HR's lyric could often come across as simply religious mumbo jumbo, but I Against I showed off his considerable and ferocious singing talent. Tracks such as "She's Calling You," "Sacred Love" (HR's vocals were phoned in from jail after he was busted for marijuana possession), "I Against I," and "Return To Heaven" offer some of the most angry, defiant, and politically charged lyrics of the time. Few of their peers could match the Brains' intricate rhythms, or guitarist Dr. Know's jaw-droppingly accomplished guitar solos.

The Brains helped to fuel the post-punk/metal/ funk/ reggae/soul fusion, and their role in the development of credible black rock music is acknowledged by Living Colour, among others. **TSc**

Anita Baker
Rapture (1986)

Label | Elektra
Producer | Various
Art Direction | Carol Friedman
Nationality | USA
Running Time | 37:09

There was not a lot of demand for real soul by the mid-1980s. Machines had replaced rhythm sections and the arrival of over-mannered artists such as Whitney Houston offered little in the way of sweet authenticity. Twenty-nine-year-old Detroit-dwelling Anita Baker challenged all this with her succulent album Rapture.

Already schooled in Motown and gospel, Baker joined Chapter 8 in 1975 and had enjoyed moderate success with the track "I Want To Be Your Girl." Signing to Otis Smith's Beverly Glen Music, she cut the underground hit The Songstress in 1983. A move to Elektra provided her springboard to the big time.

Utilizing an incredible array of session talent, Rapture is a highly produced diva album that still stands up perfectly. Produced mainly by ex-Chapter 8 colleague Michael J. Powell, who crafted a selection of covers and originals that suited Baker's sensual alto, the album was a compromise. Baker wanted it to be jazz out and out; Powell wanted smooth-grooving R&B. It was this give and take that truly sparked the beauty within. To dismiss this as smooth radio fodder would be to ignore the glorious spikiness in Baker's phrasing; "Sweet Love" became a huge, irresistible hit, while "Been Alone So Long" offered a slow, ruminative blues.

It was remarkable how feted Rapture was at the time—even the UK magazine The Wire suggested "The commercial sheen of Rapture cannot stop its emotional core shining through"—and, relatively, how quickly it was forgotten. **DE**

The Smiths | The Queen Is Dead (1986)

Label | Rough Trade
Producer | Johnny Marr • Morrissey
Art Direction | Caryn Gough • Morrissey
Nationality | UK
Running Time | 36:47

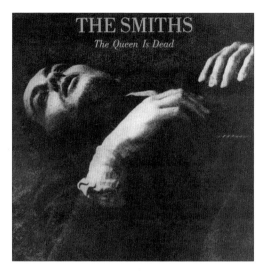

The Smiths were nothing if not prolific. *The Queen Is Dead*, recorded in December 1985 but not released until June 1986 due to legal problems, was The Smiths' third album in two years (fourth, if you include superb odds-and-ends compilation *Hatful Of Hollow*). It was also their masterpiece.

What makes the album all the more impressive is that the band were experiencing considerable difficulties at the time. They were without a consistent manager (none could contend with Morrissey and Johnny Marr's close relationship), renegotiating their contract (Rough Trade owner Geoff Travis is the Mr. Shankly of the second track), and bassist Andy Rourke was addicted to heroin (he would be sacked and reinstated between recording and release). From this conflict came an album that is by turn thrilling, beautiful, and hilarious—and all three at once in the case of the opening track, a savage, witty attack on the royal family set against a squall of overdubbed guitars (Marr's meeting of the MC5 and The Velvet Underground). There is just one duff track ("Never Had No One Ever") and even that comes as welcome respite after a breathtaking opening triple salvo.

Throughout, Marr's guitar is more abrasive and focused than ever before; Morrissey's dry wit hits every target, the self-pity perfectly phrased. The penultimate track, "There Is A Light . . . ," is one of the band's most sublime moments, the singer's melodramatic vocal chiming perfectly with Marr's relentless guitar. Their next album would prove to be almost as good. It would also be their last. **PW**

"I knew we had to deliver something great."

Johnny Marr, 2001

Track Listing		
▶ 01	The Queen Is Dead (Marr•Morrissey)	6:23
▶ 02	Frankly, Mr. Shankly (Marr•Morrissey)	2:17
▶ 03	I Know It's Over (Marr•Morrissey)	5:48
04	Never Had No One Ever (Marr•Morrissey)	3:36
05	Cemetry Gates (Marr•Morrissey)	2:39
▶ 06	Bigmouth Strikes Again (Marr•Morrissey)	3:12
07	The Boy With The Thorn In His Side (Marr•Morrissey)	3:15
08	Vicar In A Tutu (Marr•Morrissey)	2:21
▶ 09	There Is A Light That Never Goes Out (Marr•Morrissey)	4:02
10	Some Girls Are Bigger Than Others (Marr•Morrissey)	3:14

Peter Gabriel | So (1986)

Label | Virgin
Producer | Peter Gabriel • Daniel Lanois
Art Direction | Peter Saville
Nationality | UK
Running Time | 46:30

Intricate beauty or dancing chickens? Unfortunately, the latter can claim credit for elevating Peter Gabriel from arty stardom to superduperness. But though the "Sledgehammer" video's ubiquity has bludgeoned the song, its parent album is a marvel.

Not that Gabriel was a stranger to the making of great music. His first four solo albums are full of fascinating songs, but past magic moments were often buried amid lyrical and musical experimentation. *So*, in contrast, elicits a sigh of satisfaction.

Awash in delicate percussion, tasteful keyboards, and bubbling bass, "Red Rain" and "Mercy Street" (dedicated to American poet Anne Sexton) are stunning. Of the epics, the Kate Bush duet "Don't Give Up" is heartwrenching, while "In Your Eyes" achieved iconic status after its appearance in the John Cusack movie *Say Anything*.

"In Your Eyes" also heralded the international arrival of Senegalese singer Youssou N'Dour. Gabriel's commitment to world music predated *So* and continues today; no other mainstream star has done so much to introduce audiences to music they may otherwise not hear. Other collaborators on the album include Laurie "O Superman" Anderson, whose own version of "This Is The Picture" appears on her *Mister Heartbreak*.

Unhindered by a quirky title ("a nice shape but very little meaning," Gabriel told *Rolling Stone*) and a sleeve that, for once, showcased Gabriel's good looks, *So* rocketed to multimillion sales. Excellent albums followed, but the breathtaking *So* is the best introduction to a dazzling discography. **BM**

> "I tended to hide from some things, both personal and in my music... it was part of a coming-out process."

Peter Gabriel, 1987

Track Listing

01	**Red Rain** (Gabriel)		5:40
▶ 02	**Sledgehammer** (Gabriel)		5:13
▶ 03	**Don't Give Up** (Gabriel)		6:33
04	**That Voice Again** (Gabriel • Rhodes)		4:53
05	**Mercy Street** (Gabriel)		6:23
06	**Big Time** (Gabriel)		4:29
07	**We Do What We're Told (Milgram's 37)** (Gabriel)	3:22
08	**This Is The Picture (Excellent Birds)** (Anderson • Gabriel)		4:25
▶ 09	**In Your Eyes** (Gabriel)		5:30

Anthrax | Among The Living (1987)

Label | Island
Producer | Anthrax • Eddie Kramer
Art Direction | Uncredited
Nationality | USA
Running Time | 50:13

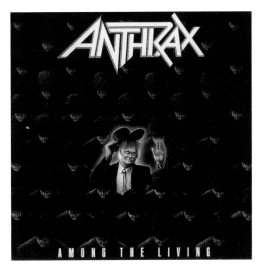

Like the other members of the big four of thrash metal —Metallica, Megadeth, and Slayer, all of whom have 1980s albums in this book—New Yorkers Anthrax hit their artistic, critical, and commercial peak early, with their third full-length album, *Among The Living*. A perfect blend of the speed that thrash fans hungered for, and which only Slayer retained by the early 1990s, crafted tunes of breathtaking unpredictability, and a unique sound, *Among The Living* hit big because it acknowledged the advent of the rap-rock movement without pandering to it. Dressed in Vision Streetwear— a hip-hop clothing label before P. Diddy ever thought of such a thing—and throwing intentionally goofy proto-Beastie Boys rap poses, the band caused a few sniggers among their ardently studs-and-leather fanbase until the songs were unleashed, silencing all criticism.

The title track is a mid-tempo display of power and a mighty album opener, but the warp-speed "Caught In A Mosh," with its no-brain, unforgettable chorus line of "Which one of these words don't you understand?/ Talkin' to you is like clapping with one hand!" and the equally mesmeric "NFL" still stand tall above most of the entire thrash canon today. The album belongs to rhythm guitarist Scott "Not" Ian, whose squeaky, supertight tone made 'Thrax instantly recognizable, and drummer Charlie Benante, a fearsomely powerful player whose speed and precision is matched among his contemporaries only by Slayer's Dave Lombardo and Pete Sandoval of Morbid Angel.

There is no forgetting the sheer joy of thrash's peak era—and this album is among the best. **JM**

> "I became a musician because I wanted to grab a guitar and play on it. It wasn't about sex!"

Scott Ian, 2005

Track Listing

01	**Among The Living** (Anthrax)		5:16
▶ 02	**Caught In A Mosh** (Anthrax)		4:59
▶ 03	**I Am The Law** (Anthrax•Lilker)		5:57
▶ 04	**Efilnikufesin (NFL)** (Anthrax)		4:54
05	**Skeleton In The Closet** (Anthrax)		5:32
06	**Indians** (Anthrax)		5:40
07	**One World** (Anthrax)		5:56
08	**ADI/Horror Of It All** (Anthrax)		7:49
09	**Imitation Of Life** (Anthrax•Lilker)		4:10

Dinosaur Jr.
You're Living All Over Me (1987)

Label | SST
Producer | Various
Art Direction | Maura Jasper
Nationality | USA
Running Time | 39:21

Named after the line which J. Mascis spat out during one of his frustrated tour bus tantrums, *You're Living All Over Me* captured the turbulent, dysfunctional beast that was Dinosaur Jr. at their flammable creative peak. Driven by intense clashes between aloof, withdrawn guitarist Mascis and emotional bassist Lou Barlow, Dinosaur Jr.'s impassioned fusion of heavy rock riffs, countrified melodies, and post-punk noise was as volatile as the lineup itself.

With opener "Little Fury Things" (featuring Lee Ranaldo of Dino-fans Sonic Youth on backing vocals), *You're Living All Over Me* stated its intentions: to pull rock into radical new shapes, until its clichés became expressive again, thanks to the new contexts Mascis placed them in. "Sludgefeast" pitches dreamy reveries against girder-heavy Sabbath riffage, while "The Lung" elevates a whimsical little ditty to an alt.rock Lynyrd Skynyrd epic, thanks to Mascis' fluid, ecstatic soloing. Elsewhere, Dinosaur explore industrial-influenced tape experiments: walls of noise swallow up the sleepy-eyed "Tarpit." Of Barlow's two songs, the stoner-folk patchwork "Poledo" was cooked up at home on his own. "I had just started smoking pot," says the bassist, "Everything sounded amazing!"

The resulting tour saw internal tensions become untenable; 1988's release *Bug* was unfortunately the lineup's swansong. But for these precious 40 minutes at least, Dinosaur Jr. contrived a beautiful—if fleeting—harmony. **SC**

> "We peaked, we'd achieved everything we'd wanted from being a band."
>
> Lou Barlow, 2005

Track Listing

▶	01	**Little Fury Things** (Mascis)	3:05
	02	**Kracked** (Mascis)	2:51
▶	03	**Sludgefeast** (Mascis)	5:14
▶	04	**The Lung** (Mascis)	3:51
	05	**Raisans** (Mascis)	3:48
	06	**Tarpit** (Mascis)	4:33
▶	07	**In A Jar** (Mascis)	3:26
	08	**Lose** (Barlow)	3:08
	09	**Poledo** (Barlow)	5:40

Dolly Parton, Linda Ronstadt, Emmylou Harris
Trio (1987)

Label | Warner Bros.
Producer | George Massenburg
Art Direction | Kosh
Nationality | USA
Running Time | 38:24

While country singers often team up on winning singles, few such all-star collaborations have produced solid full-length albums. However, the dream team of Dolly Parton, Linda Ronstadt, and Emmylou Harris achieved glorious harmony on the spellbinding *Trio*.

Artistically, *Trio* could not have come at a better time for Parton and Ronstadt. Parton had spent much of the 1980s courting the mainstream with glossy pop hits like "Islands In The Stream." Ronstadt was busy ignoring her roots in the L.A. country-folk scene in favor of recording pop standards. Commercially, both singers were doing fine—Ronstadt's *What's New* sold two million copies and Parton charted 12 Top Ten hits in five years. But something was missing—perhaps the sense of authenticity that had colored their earlier work— and both would find it when they recorded with Harris, one of the most dependable Nashville cats of all time.

Backed by a solid band that included David Lindley and Ry Cooder, the three superstars blend their voices intuitively on this sparkling collection of old-school country, hymn-like traditional numbers, and pop ballads. Although many solo highlights abound, mostly delivered by Parton, the album's best moments come with the gorgeous harmonies found on the softly soaring "Making Plans" and in the understated glory of Phil Spector's "To Know Him Is To Love Him."

Trio was a critical and commercial hit that went platinum, won a Grammy, and eventually spawned a long-awaited follow-up, 1998's *Trio II*. **JiH**

"I've made a lot of mistakes in the minds of some people."

Dolly Parton, 2002

Track Listing		
01 **The Pain Of Loving You** (Parton·Wagoner)		2:33
▶ 02 **Making Plans** (Morrison·Russell)		3:26
▶ 03 **To Know Him Is To Love Him** (Spector)		3:47
04 **Hobo's Meditation** (Rodgers)		3:16
05 **Wildflowers** (Parton)		3:35
▶ 06 **Telling Me Lies** (Cook·Thompson)		4:22
07 **My Dear Companion** (Ritchie)		2:53
▶ 08 **Those Memories Of You** (O'Bryant)		3:55
09 **I've Had Enough** (McGarrigle)		3:27
10 **Rosewood Casket** (Trad.)		3:03
11 **Farther Along** (Trad.)		4:07

Def Leppard
Hysteria (1987)

Label | Bludgeon Riffola
Producer | Robert John Lange
Art Direction | Andie Airfix
Nationality | UK
Running Time | 61:52

R.E.M.
Document (1987)

Label | IRS
Producer | Scott Litt
Art Direction | Ron Scarselli
Nationality | USA
Running Time | 39:52

Following 1983's multiplatinum *Pyromania*, singer Joe Elliott, guitarists Steve Clark and Phil Collen, bassist Rick Savage, and drummer Rick Allen decamped to Dublin with producer Robert John "Mutt" Lange, who—exhausted—dropped out. Meat Loaf mastermind Jim Steinman came aboard but proved incompatible. "I was saying how great it was to be in the city of Yeats and Joyce," recalled Steinman. "Joe Elliott said they hadn't met any local musicians yet."

On New Year's Eve, Allen lost an arm in a car crash. His colleagues continued with engineer Nigel Green, and Allen arrived in April, playing an adapted electronic kit. Coupled with the return of Lange (following his own crash), this gave a technical gleam to *Hysteria*, a title suggested by Allen. Lange scrapped the tapes and they started again. After a morale-boosting appearance at the UK's Monsters of Rock festival—"I've never seen so many hands go up in the air!" recalled Allen—*Hysteria* was completed in January 1987.

Seven U.S. hits proved the time was well spent. The grinding "Women" confirmed Leppard were as heavy as ever. The glossy "Animal" and "Hysteria" built the momentum, then the strip-club anthem "Pour Some Sugar On Me" blew it sky high. "The album started selling almost a million copies a month," marveled Elliott (U.S. sales were to hit 12 million). The bittersweet "Love Bites" topped the Hot 100, the tongue-in-cheek "Armageddon It" and "Rocket" brought up the rear—and *Hysteria* etched itself into history. **TJ**

In the early 1980s, when R.E.M. were merely a band, not a legend, their jangly guitar pop earned them a following. But it was not until their fifth album, 1987's *Document*, that Michael Stipe, Peter Buck, Bill Berry, and Mike Mills announced their plan to change the world.

That first line calls it: "The time to rise/has been engaged." "Finest Worksong," with its propulsive bass beat and stadium-ready chorus, kicks off what is arguably the last great side one of the vinyl era. It has one killer song after another, from the bouncy power pop of "Exhuming McCarthy" to the insanely catchy free-association wordplay of "It's The End Of The World As We Know It (And I Feel Fine)." True fans have that one memorized; everyone else just pretends they do.

The second half starts with R.E.M.'s first hit, "The One I Love," a song comprising a single repeated verse and a one-word chorus. It was enough to make R.E.M. a household name. From there, the album drifts into much odder territory, with the buzzing waltz of "Fireplace" and the hypnotic ballad "King Of Birds."

Document was the first of many classic albums Scott Litt would produce for R.E.M. Gone are Stipe's indecipherable murmurings. In their place, intriguing images like the chorus of "Exhuming McCarthy"— "You're sharpening stones/walking on coals/to improve your business acumen."

After *Document*, everyone was in on the R.E.M. secret. And it still sounds great today, no doubt because it influenced so much in its wake. **RM**

Prince
Sign O' The Times (1987)

The Cult
Electric (1987)

Label | Warner Bros.
Producer | Prince
Art Direction | Laura LiPuma
Nationality | USA
Running Time | 80:03

Label | Beggars Banquet
Producer | Rick Rubin
Art Direction | Keith Breeden
Nationality | UK
Running Time | 38:46

Mystery surrounds *Sign O' The Times*. Why did it sell less than the inferior *Diamonds And Pearls*? What does "Starfish And Coffee" mean? And why—after so many re-thinks—did "It" survive to the final tracklist?

The album began as *Dream Factory* in early 1986—abandoned when Prince shed both his muse Susannah Melvoin and his band The Revolution. By the year's end, he had recorded an album by his sped-up pseudonym Camille and assembled the triple set *Crystal Ball* (the full, fascinating tale is told in Per Nilsen's book *DanceMusicSexRomance*).

Unnerved by Prince's plummeting post-*Purple Rain* sales, Warner refused to release a triple album, obliging him to cherry-pick from the previous year. The result defies classification, sweeping from grinding funk to smoochy soul, with nods to idols like Joni Mitchell and Sly Stone. Imagination is abundant. The surreally jazzy "Ballad Of Dorothy Parker," the entrancingly odd "If I Was Your Girlfriend"—in 1987, none of Prince's contemporaries pushed boundaries with such rich rewards. The album is perfectly pitched, too, between serious and silly: the evangelical "The Cross" precedes Sheila E. rapping the Edward Lear poem "The Table And The Chair" in "It's Gonna Be A Beautiful Night."

"I always said," Prince told MTV in 1985, "that one day I would play all kinds of music and not be judged for the color of my skin but the quality of my work." Sales aside, this is the album that most brilliantly succeeds in realizing that ambition. **BM**

A precise, stripped-down record overflowing with riffs lifted from the shelves marked "Jimmy Page" and "Angus Young," *Electric* was the sound of The Cult abandoning their self-conscious indie-goth roots and making a memorable bid for stadium credibility. Taken firmly in hand by New York headbanger extraordinaire Rick Rubin, the band's audacious volte-face scored a bull's eye on all counts, elevating singer Ian Astbury, guitarist Billy Duffy, bassist Jamie Stewart, and drummer Les Warner to their career peak. Suburban British teenagers heard *Electric* and realized that balls-out rock was not just for Americans.

Although *Electric*'s key features—Astbury's mangling of "Yee-aah!," Duffy's searing riffage, and the outrageous artwork (a homage to Rick Griffin's Sixties Grateful Dead LP sleeves)—may seem outmoded today, the album stands tall on this list thanks to its array of shining singles. "Lil' Devil" was based on a catchy riff, while "Love Removal Machine" is the sound of the independent scene growing its hair and stealing a Les Paul. Musically, main songwriter Duffy was getting away with murder, basing both songs on a no-brain D/C/G chord progression—just as he had with the previous album's "Rain" and "She Sells Sanctuary."

"Never mind your English indie scene and its pussy jangly guitar sound," said Rubin at the time: "Let's rock!" And while that particular call to arms has been overused to the point of parody, in the case of *Electric* it was utterly appropriate. **JM**

Depeche Mode | Music For The Masses (1987)

Label | Mute
Producer | Depeche Mode • David Bascombe
Art Direction | Town And Country Planning
Nationality | UK
Running Time | 44:32

MUSIC FOR THE MASSES
DEPECHE MODE

Wimpy synth-poppers become whomping stadium-stompers! Walls crumble and Marilyn Manson is born! Oh, and did we mention they invented house music?

OK, none of that is completely true, but this is the album with which Depeche Mode bade farewell to their embryonic electro-pop and embraced the sound that inspired goth gonks and dance pioneers alike.

Its excellent predecessor *Black Celebration* came close, but a tentative production made its portentous moments sound slightly silly. In contrast, *Music For The Masses* nails you to the wall from the moment "Never Let Me Down Again" stomps from the speakers.

The power is relentless but the pace pleasingly varied. There is the lilting "The Things You Said," the chamber musical "Little 15" and—showcasing the bubbly rhythm that fed into house—the lascivious "Behind The Wheel." The CD bonus track "Pleasure, Little Treasure" goes even further, progressing from dance moves to a preview of the glam-rocking "Personal Jesus" co-opted by Marilyn Manson. Completing a collection of contrasts are the pumping "Nothing" and pomp-rocking "Pimpf" (the latter concluding with the unlisted "Mission Impossible").

Britain clung to its view of the band as peculiar pop stars. Europe and America, however, elevated them from just another (in Pet Shop Boy Neil Tennant's words) "Pretty in Pink band" to heroes (hence 1989's thunderous live set *101*), something they had never anticipated—despite the title of the album and its sleeve message, "Spreading the news around the world." **BM**

"Americans more than anyone have suffered from ten years of Toto re-runs ... we came along at the right time."

Martin Gore, 1990

Track Listing

▶	01	**Never Let Me Down Again** (Gore)	4:48
	02	**The Things You Said** (Gore)	4:03
▶	03	**Strangelove** (Gore)	4:57
	04	**Sacred** (Gore)	4:47
	05	**Little 15** (Gore)	4:19
▶	06	**Behind The Wheel** (Gore)	5:18
	07	**I Want You Now** (Gore)	3:45
	08	**To Have And To Hold** (Gore)	2:51
	09	**Nothing** (Gore)	4:18
	10	**Pimpf** (Gore)	5:26

The Sisters Of Mercy | Floodland (1987)

Label | Merciful Release / WEA
Producer | L. Alexander • A. Eldritch • J. Steinman
Art Direction | Andrew Eldritch
Nationality | UK
Running Time | 49:24

THE SISTERS OF MERCY : FLOODLAND

Strange that one of gothic rock's most iconic and influential bands has only released three studio albums in a 25-year career. *Floodland*, The Sisters of Mercy's second album, is the one where everything came together. It is a majestic work—unapologetically overblown and imbued with an irresistible charm.

Enigmatic Sisters frontman Andrew Eldritch claimed he recorded the album himself with bass player Patricia Morrison (formerly of The Gun Club) and a drum machine called Doktor Avalanche. (Eldritch later claimed that Morrison had not played a note on the record and had only picked up her guitar for the videos.) Tracks like "Dominion/Mother Russia" and "This Corrosion" are larger than life, given an extra dramatic touch by Meat Loaf producer Jim Steinman and driven by thunderous, industrial beats. (Both tracks feature the New York Choral Society.) "Flood I" plumbs gloomy depths, while in contrast to the widescreen sound on show elsewhere, the melancholic "1959" features only piano and voice.

When *Floodland* was released, gothic rock had attracted mainstream attention. Three singles were culled from the album, all of which did well in the charts. Image was always as crucial to the Sisters as the music itself, and the accompanying videos helped underline the theatrical imagery of the album.

In interviews, it is clear that Eldritch is keenly aware of a humorous side to his band, although his hordes of fans would never acknowledge such a thing. This paradox has never been as clear as on *Floodland*, which somehow manages to be tongue-in-cheek and deeply affecting at the same time. **AET**

> "It seemed like a good idea at the time to have forty people singing at once. I've no idea why."
>
> Andrew Eldritch, 1987

Track Listing

▶	01	**Dominion/Mother Russia** (Eldritch)	7:01
▶	02	**Flood I** (Eldritch)	6:22
	03	**Lucretia My Reflection** (Eldritch)	4:57
▶	04	**1959** (Eldritch)	4:09
▶	05	**This Corrosion** (Eldritch)	10:55
	06	**Flood II** (Eldritch)	6:47
	07	**Driven Like The Snow** (Eldritch)	6:27
	08	**Never Land (A Fragment)** (Eldritch)	2:46

George Michael | Faith (1987)

Label | Columbia
Producer | George Michael
Art Direction | George Michael • Stylorouge
Nationality | UK
Running Time | 57:58

By the time Wham! performed their farewell concert before 72,000 fans at Wembley Stadium in 1986, there was no leap of faith required to picture George Michael carving out a very successful solo career. He was the songwriter, lead singer, and possessed the face that millions of adoring young girls had pinned up on their bedroom walls. Yet, he surpassed all expectations with his debut solo release, *Faith*.

The landmark album sold 10 million copies worldwide (it was the first album by a white solo artist to hit the U.S. R&B No. 1 spot), spawned a staggering seven hit singles, and put Michael in the same celebrity stratosphere as Michael Jackson, Madonna, and Prince. Both gay and straight communities adopted the leather-earring-and-stubble look sported on the cover.

Faith gets off to a dramatic start as a church organ plays a snippet of the Wham! track "Freedom," coming across every bit like a funeral for a friend, and then launches forward, via a driving Bo Diddley rhythm on acoustic guitar, into the deliriously contagious title track. The mood changes on a dime as the singer caresses his way into the dreamily romantic "Father Figure" and then gets busy on the then controversial "I Want Your Sex, Pts. 1 & 2." Three songs—that is all it took for Michael to successfully frame his bubblegum past in the rearview mirror.

The album's greatness stemmed from the way it effortlessly combined pop, dance music, and R&B into an entirely individual sound. The fact that so much of it still stands tall against anything played on the radio today underlines why *Faith* remains great. **JiH**

> **"The business is built on ego, vanity, self-satisfaction, and it's total crap to pretend it's not."**
>
> George Michael, 1998

Track Listing

▶ 01	**Faith** (Michael)	3:16
▶ 02	**Father Figure** (Michael)	5:36
▶ 03	**I Want Your Sex, Pts. 1 & 2** (Michael)	9:17
04	**One More Try** (Michael)	5:50
05	**Hard Day** (Michael)	4:48
06	**Hand To Mouth** (Michael)	4:36
07	**Look At Your Hands** (Austin • Michael)	4:37
08	**Monkey** (Michael)	5:05
▶ 09	**Kissing A Fool** (Michael)	4:35
10	**Hard Day [Shep Pettibone Remix]** (Michael)	6:30
11	**A Last Request (I Want Your Sex, Pt. 3)** (Michael)	3:48

Hüsker Dü
Warehouse: Songs And Stories (1987)

Label | Warner Bros.
Producer | Grant Hart • Bob Mould
Art Direction | Daniel Corrigan
Nationality | USA
Running Time | 69:39

Critical acclaim often equals unlistenability. And so it is with Hüsker Dü's formative hardcore. But by 1985 they had replaced speed with songwriting and blueprinted a sound for future post-grungers. The sound—furious guitars, pummeling drums, Beatlesque hooks—was refined over the next two years. "It got very ritualistic," grumbled guitarist Bob Mould. "[*Warehouse*] was the same as the three albums before it."

In a sense he was right. It is distinguished from 1986's *Candy Apple Grey* mostly by its length and beautiful packaging. But *Warehouse* is a staggering testament to what can be achieved when a band's driving forces—Mould and drummer Grant Hart—loathe each other.

Mould won on numbers (11 songs to his rival's nine), having—Hart alleges—refused to allow an even split. Hart provided more diversity, thanks to the chiming "Charity, Chastity, Prudence, And Hope," the shanty-style "She Floated Away," the rock 'n' rolling "Actual Condition," and the raging "You Can Live At Home."

But Mould had his gems too; "Could You Be The One?" previews the pop sensibilities he brought to his post-Hüsker band Sugar. And best and most telling is "Friend, You've Got To Fall"—generally considered a swipe at heroin enthusiast Hart.

The band fell apart on the *Warehouse* tour and the wounds have yet to heal. But they could not have asked for a finer epitaph. **BM**

Butthole Surfers
Locust Abortion Technician (1987)

Label | Touch And Go
Producer | Paul Leary
Art Direction | The Butthole Surfers
Nationality | USA
Running Time | 32:34

In the 1980s among the post hardcore and punk community in the United States there seemed to be a headlong rush to produce the most sonically extreme record possible. No one came close to rivaling this effort.

Everything about this record is wrong. Over a lush string opening a child asks his father about regret, to which the father replies: "It's better to regret something you have done than something you haven't," before screaming "Satan! Satan!" as the band blast through a nightmarish deconstruction of the riff from Black Sabbath's "Sweet Leaf." On "22 Going On 23" a delirium tremens guitar riff and tribal drumming underpin a caller on a talk radio show discussing being sexually assaulted. Only "Human Cannonball" stands out as a "normal" song. An adrenalized three-and-a-half-minute shot of punk rock, the song impressively pointed out to naysayers that the band could "do" punk with aplomb if they chose to. It is just that they did not choose to.

The cover artwork is utterly indicative of the poly-perverse nature of the Buttholes. The fact that the band were obsessed by John Wayne Gacy (the pedocidal maniac children's entertainer and serial killer), combined with the name of the album, makes it safe to assume that this was anything but innocent.

It is a fact that there had never been a heavier and weirder record than this prior to 1987 and it is arguable that there has not been one since. **JDo**

Astor Piazzolla And Gary Burton
The New Tango (1987)

Label | Atlantic
Producer | Nesuhi Ertegun
Art Direction | Georges Braunschweig
Nationality | Argentina • USA
Running Time | 55:02

It must have been very special to be at the Montreux Festival in Switzerland, July 1986, for the summit between Astor Piazzolla—the amazing Argentine bandoneón player, and controversial composer—and Gary Burton— the acclaimed North American vibist and composer. The flashpoint was Piazzolla's composition *Suite for Vibraphone And New Tango Quintet*.

The New Tango is the live audio of this masterwork and one of their greatest performances together. Every piece is an impressionistic marvel, the drama and melancholy hues that define the work coupled with the kind of layers of improvisational interplay so important to jazz. Toss in a contemporary sensibility for dissonance and odd meter and you have got a revelatory recording, on which Piazzolla's band provide sterling backup.

The weeping violin of Fernando Suarez Paz, who lends an important sonic texture and emotion to the sextet, is one of the highlights of "Milonga Is Coming." "Vibraphonissimo" is a Piazzolla original for Burton with an angular theme and classical overtone. "Nuevo Tango" rocks upfront with an intense melody and tempo but changes time stylishly, the ensemble demonstrating an intuitive cohesion.

When Piazzolla turned the tango upside down more than 30 years previously, traditionalists were in uproar. Piazzolla passed away in 1992, but *The New Tango* stands as a monument to musical freedom. **JCV**

The Smiths
"Strangeways, Here We Come" (1987)

Label | Rough Trade
Producer | The Smiths • Stephen Street
Art Direction | Caryn Gough • Morrissey
Nationality | UK
Running Time | 35:53

After signing to EMI, *"Strangeways, Here We Come"* (named after the notorious Manchester prison), was recorded to fulfill a contractual obligation to UK indie label Rough Trade. However, disagreements concerning management and career direction were fracturing the creative partnership of Morrissey and Marr.

Morrissey's Irish roots are explored on ferocious war cry "A Rush And A Push," while Marr's crunchy glam guitar on "I Started Something" anticipates Morrissey's future solo work with Mick Ronson. Other highlights include the jolly singalong "Unhappy Birthday," the self-parodying "Stop Me If You Think You've Heard This One Before," and the dramatic "Last Night I Dreamt That Somebody Loved Me," its harrowing extended introduction underpinned by foreboding piano and rioting crowds. "Paint A Vulgar Picture," with its bitter refrain of "Re-issue! Re-package!" seems rather ironic in the light of endless Smiths and Morrissey compilations released since. The album closer "I Won't Share You" allegedly reduced drummer Mike Joyce to tears.

"Girlfriend In A Coma"—a classic example of Morrissey's abrasive wit—was released as a single in the same week that The Smiths announced their demise. Amid the drama, the parent album was rather overlooked, which is a shame. Although less highly regarded than their previous two albums, it remains a noble epitaph to one of Britain's greatest bands. **CSh**

Guns N' Roses | Appetite For Destruction (1987)

Label | Geffen
Producer | Mike Clink
Art Direction | Michael Hodgson
Nationality | USA
Running Time | 53:49

Wrapped in rags and full of drugs, Hanoi Rocks were the Stones and the Sex Pistols in one, worshipped by bandana-bearing fans and thrill-seeking critics. They made a smack-shaped splash, then vanished. Of the few who remembered them were singer Axl Rose and guitarist Izzy Stradlin, who recruited wannabe Poison string-slinger Slash, Johnny Thunders disciple Duff McKagan, and happy-go-lucky drummer Steven Adler.

Guns N' Roses outshone contemporaries like Faster Pussycat because not since Van Halen had such a charismatic cocktail of characters (notably mood-swinging Axl and Muppet riffmaster Slash) invested their clichés with such vigor; because the cover alone—Robert Williams' painting of a robo-rape—caused uproar (hence its replacement by the cross tattoo of Bill White Jr. and Andy Engell); and because MTV drip-fed "Welcome To The Jungle" and U.S. No. 1 "Sweet Child O' Mine" into Young America. Oh, and because the songs are stunning. Most, despite the group writing credit, originated with Stradlin. Believing "rock 'n' roll in general has just sucked a big fucking dick since the Pistols," he revived the raunch that distinguished GNR's ancestors Aerosmith from their contemporaries.

The punky punch of McKagan lay behind "It's So Easy," "Nightrain," and "Paradise City" (another U.S. Top Five single), while Slash and Axl spat razor-sharp lines like "Welcome To The Jungle" and "Rocket Queen."

They looked cool, they swore, they fought, they—let's bite the bullet—rocked. It was one hell of a ride, and this souvenir (15 million sold in the United States alone) will thrill forever. **BM**

> ## "Everybody wants to have that record because it's not really that safe ..."
> Slash, 1988

Track Listing

▶	01	**Welcome To The Jungle** (Guns N' Roses)	4:34
	02	**It's So Easy** (Guns N' Roses)	3:23
	03	**Nightrain** (Guns N' Roses)	4:28
	04	**Out Ta Get Me** (Guns N' Roses)	4:24
	05	**Mr. Brownstone** (Guns N' Roses)	3:49
▶	06	**Paradise City** (Guns N' Roses)	6:46
	07	**My Michelle** (Guns N' Roses)	3:40
	08	**Think About You** (Guns N' Roses)	3:52
▶	09	**Sweet Child O' Mine** (Guns N' Roses)	5:56
	10	**You're Crazy** (Guns N' Roses)	3:17
	11	**Anything Goes** (Guns N' Roses)	3:27
	12	**Rocket Queen** (Guns N' Roses)	6:13

The Jesus And Mary Chain | Darklands (1987)

Label | Blanco Y Negro
Producer | John Loder • Bill Price • William Reid
Art Direction | Helen Backhouse
Nationality | UK
Running Time | 36:03

After *Psychocandy* gave rock 'n' roll the kiss of life in 1985, Jim and William Reid got used to reading reviews advising them to split—because nothing they could do would top that barrage of feedback and misanthropy. Subconsciously, they also felt they had done it all, but now they had to prove themselves again, as musicians and songwriters.

The summer of 1986 brought their first hit single, "Some Candy Talking," which had lines forming outside record shops on the day of release. Nine months later, "April Skies," the first taste of *Darklands*, crashed into the UK Top Ten. Perfectly poised between their earlier rebel poses and a stadium air-puncher, it announced that the Mary Chain had the potential to cross over. (The not-dissimilar follow-up, "Happy When It Rains," made the same claims but fared less well.)

Now that they were a popular band with proper hits, *Darklands* was released to acclaim and a Top Five position. On the Richter scale, that is an eight. Who knows what all the new fans made of the snail-paced title track that opened the LP, or the even slower "Deep One Perfect Morning" that followed it. As far from *Psychocandy* as you could get. No feedback. Acoustic guitars. Audible lyrics. Songs apparently about love, not drugs. "Nine Million Rainy Days" echoed the Stones' "Sympathy For The Devil," and "About You" would later be covered by Sandie Shaw. Nobody rioted at their gigs.

Mission accomplished. The first half of the 1980s had seen rock sliding into middle age; now the Mary Chain had shown exactly what it was capable of, and the world was listening. **DH**

> "Everything we make sounds like a pop song, even if it's different to any other pop song."
>
> Jim Reid, 1985

Track Listing

▶ 01	**Darklands** (J. Reid • W. Reid)	5:29
02	**Deep One Perfect Morning** (J. Reid • W. Reid)	2:43
▶ 03	**Happy When It Rains** (J. Reid • W. Reid)	3:36
04	**Down On Me** (J. Reid • W. Reid)	2:36
▶ 05	**Nine Million Rainy Days** (J. Reid • W. Reid)	4:29
▶ 06	**April Skies** (J. Reid • W. Reid)	4:00
07	**Fall** (J. Reid • W. Reid)	2:28
08	**Cherry Came Too** (J. Reid • W. Reid)	3:06
▶ 09	**On The Wall** (J. Reid • W. Reid)	5:05
▶ 10	**About You** (J. Reid • W. Reid)	2:31

Ladysmith Black Mambazo | Shaka Zulu (1987)

Label | Warner Bros.
Producer | Paul Simon
Art Direction | Peter Barrett
Nationality | South Africa
Running Time | 36:41

LADYSMITH
BLACK MAMBAZO

Shaka Zulu

Recorded a year after Ladysmith Black Mambazo were catapulted into the international spotlight as the backing band on Paul Simon's groundbreaking *Graceland* (1986), *Shaka Zulu* is a cappella choir song like it has never been heard before.

The album employs the rootsy percussive rhythms of mbube (South African migrant workers' song) to revitalize a stagnant European choral tradition. Exquisite melodies built out of fluid phrasing and tranquil rhythmic textures are punctuated by almost doo-wop outbursts that give body to their celestial iscathamiya ("to walk on one's toes lightly") style.

On "Hello My Baby," this is manifested as an all-new harmonic signature that marries airy alto coos from leader Joseph Shabalala with twin tenor timbres and a septet of resonant bass beat-boxing. A truly South African sound? Maybe, but because Mambazo chose not to channel their choral interplay into overt protest song during apartheid, many critics misread courting ballads ("Yibo Labo") as exotic postcards of tribal culture. What they missed were the deeply personal psycho-geographies of apartheid buried in the songs.

As choristers, Mambazo's Christian message is less oblique, with the fervor of "King Of Kings" and "At Golgotha" tailor-made to take their gospel to a global audience. Introducing English lyrics into their Zulu songbook assured instant global success. It is a recipe that has clearly stood the test of time; 18 years after *Shaka Zulu* won the Grammy for "Best Traditional Folk Recording," *Raise Your Spirit Higher* received the award for "Best Traditional World Music Album." **MK**

> "Without hearing the lyrics, this music gets into the blood, because it comes from the blood."
>
> Joseph Shabalala, 2004

Track Listing

01	Unomathemba	(Shabalala)	3:47
▶ 02	Hello My Baby	(Shabalala)	3:09
03	At Golgotha	(Shabalala)	3:57
▶ 04	King Of Kings	(Shabalala)	4:07
05	Lomhlaba Kawunoni	(Shabalala)	2:55
06	How Long?	(Shabalala)	3:05
▶ 07	Ikhaya Lamaqhawe	(Shabalala)	3:13
▶ 08	Yibo Labo	(Shabalala)	4:39
09	Rain, Rain Beautiful Rain	(Shabalala)	2:18
10	Wawusho Kubani?	(Shabalala)	5:31

Laibach
Opus Dei (1987)

Label | Mute
Producer | Rico Conning
Art Direction | Laibach Kunst
Nationality | Slovenia
Running Time | 37:16

As the musical arm of the Neue Slowenische Kunst multimedia collective based in Ljubljana, capital of former Yugoslavia's northernmost republic of Slovenia, Laibach's adoption of the old German name for the city baited the Serb-dominated Communist authorities. A confrontational appearance on current affairs show, *TV Tednik* (*TV Weekly*) in 1983 led to the presenter demanding the political lynching of the group.

A German language remake of Queen's "One Vision" entitled "Geburt Einer Nation" ("Birth Of A Nation") went some way to explaining Laibach's view of popular culture, the group stating that "If you understand Queen, you understand totalitarianism." However their marriage of brutal industrial rhythms and Wagnerian symphonic flourishes, alongside vocalist Milan Frez's guttural (and strangely camp) delivery on "Geburt Einer Nation" and a funereal remake of Euro-Pop hit "Life Is Life" entitled "Leben Heisst Leben," suggested to some that Laibach's tongues were firmly in cheeks.

The rousing title track sinisterly sounds like a call to arms, describing the impending crisis in Yugoslavia. Indeed the foreboding "F.I.A.T." and the pummeling metal grind of "How The West Was Won" predict the political upheavals that swept Europe two years later. However, the Winston Churchill speech closing "The Great Seal" opens to question whether communist Europe would benefit from Western values. *Opus Dei*'s success ended the four-year-old ban that prevented Laibach from performing in their country. **CSh**

Napalm Death
Scum (1987)

Label | Earache
Producer | Napalm Death
Art Direction | Jeff Walker
Nationality | UK
Running Time | 33:16

Championed by the late, great BBC radio DJ John Peel, Napalm Death are the most influential name in extreme music. The Birmingham, England group pioneered an ultra-aggressive form of thrash known as grindcore, characterized by guttural vocals, distorted guitar, and hyper-speed rhythms nicknamed "blastbeats."

Although its words were incomprehensible, their landmark debut *Scum* displayed heartfelt political convictions. The sleeve depicts grotesque businessmen towering over an African family, underscored by a carpet of skulls peppered with the logos of McDonald's, Nestlé, BP, and the like. The lyric sheet reveals leftist diatribes about capitalism ("Multinational Corporations," "Instinct Of Survival"), the environment ("Point Of No Return"), and Britain's ruling elite ("CS," aka "Conservative Shithead"). "Siege Of Power" shows they were capable of verse-chorus-verse convention, but the most famous song is "You Suffer," which is literally over in a second.

The band's next album, *From Enslavement To Obliteration*, entered the UK indie chart at No. 1, and they even made the cover of *NME*. However, they were dogged by personnel changes. Original bassist/vocalist Nick Bullen and guitarist Justin Broadrick left before *Scum* was completed (they play on the first 12 tracks), the latter finding acclaim with industrial experimentalists Godflesh. Growler Lee Dorrian went on to sing intelligibly with doom rockers Cathedral. Drummer Mick Harris, the sole remnant of the original lineup, departed in 1992, rejoining Bullen in ambient dub project Scorn. **MA**

Sonic Youth
Sister (1987)

Label | SST
Producer | Sonic Youth
Art Direction | Sonic Youth
Nationality | USA
Running Time | 41:27

Although they still make gorgeous records, Sonic Youth's peak occurred in the late 1980s. *Evol* (1986) saw the New York quartet apply subtler, more melodic strokes to their atonal "no wave." Two years later, the double album *Daydream Nation* became an indie chart smash and precipitated a major label deal. *Sister* was the bridge: a concise, alluring set that balances atmospheric dissonance with breathtaking songs.

Inspired by a Philip K. Dick story, "Schizophrenia" is a mini masterpiece of sustained intrigue. As electric guitars gently thrum, Thurston Moore relates an unsettling encounter with an old friend's sister. Instead of a chorus, Moore and fellow guitarist Lee Ranaldo deftly interweave a flurry of harmonic notes. This glides into the cryptic second verse, which is spoken by bassist Kim Gordon in the voice of a disturbed girl. The band then accelerates into a euphoric climax.

Gordon sings lead for "Beauty Lies In The Eye" and "Pacific Coast Highway." The former is a haunting ambient noise ballad that alludes to abuse; the latter a scorched earth come-on that is more sinister than sexy. A cover of Crime's "Hot Wire My Heart" makes fantastic garage bubblegum, while "Cotton Crown" languidly evokes the neon-lit mystery of Manhattan before it was neutered by zero tolerance. "White Cross" finds crack drummer Steve Shelley powering a series of frenzied crescendos, like an aural tsunami.

Sister remains a classic—not just for the alternative nation, but for rock fans of every stripe. **MA**

The Triffids
Calenture (1987)

Label | Island
Producer | Gil Norton
Art Direction | Island Art
Nationality | Australia • UK
Running Time | 46:24

The son of religious parents, the young David McComb won school prizes in English literature and divinity. And nowhere are these influences more evident than on his songs for The Triffids' fourth album.

If ever a category for "gospel-indie" needed to be established, then McComb set about it with fervor. His richly sorrowful voice bears the zeal of an outback preacher. Lyrically, his poetry (for it surely is) fuels songs that burn with loss and longing. On the dazzling opener "Bury Me Deep In Love," McComb depicts "a chapel deep in a valley . . . under the shadow of a precipice." The song laments the death of a mountain climber, who plunges "to his icy mountain crypt," while an orchestra conjures joy and sorrow accordingly.

The band recorded *Calenture* in England over the spring and summer of 1987, and as he traveled between Perth and London, McComb's homesickness bore fruit with the album's slow-burning beauty "Hometown Farewell Kiss." The move also prompted the album's title—a reference to the delirium suffered by sailors after long periods away from land.

Despite wide acclaim for *Calenture*, and continued popularity on tour, The Triffids became disheartened with a relative lack of success. Their final studio album, *The Black Swan*, was a patchy affair and the band split around 1990. McComb underwent major heart surgery, and followed a brief solo career, before dying in 1999 after a car accident. The devout and harmonious *Calenture* remains a most magnificent epitaph. **GT**

Michael Jackson | Bad (1987)

Label | Epic
Producer | Quincy Jones
Art Direction | Nancy Donald • Tony Lane
Nationality | USA
Running Time | 48:10

Trying to follow any successful album is a daunting task. But no artist has ever faced greater expectations than those Michael Jackson encountered when he went into the studio to attempt to top the biggest selling album of all time, *Thriller*.

It is a credit to Jackson and producer Quincy Jones that the resulting effort did not sound like *Thriller II*. The sequel *Bad* was bigger, bolder, and "badder" than *Thriller* in just about every sense. That said, the fresh-faced kid who thrilled us with the Jackson 5 and boogied into our hearts on 1979's *Off The Wall* could still be found in *Thriller*, but by the time *Bad* hit the stores the lofty "King of Pop" title had thoroughly crushed that side. Jackson was now well on his way to becoming a chimp-loving public oddity.

The album kicks off in dizzying dancefloor fashion with a pair of songs that rank among Jackson's finest— the crotch-grabbing anthem title track and the joyful, sexy come-on "The Way You Make Me Feel." "Dirty Diana" is raunchy but forced, coming across like a direct statement to rival Prince. The disturbing "Smooth Criminal" is a genuine oddity delivered with panache and energy to spare. But Jackson has rarely sounded more believable than on the gorgeous ballad "I Just Can't Stop Loving You," while the closer "Leave Me Alone" offers a peek at the paranoia behind the facade of the successful megastar—and an expression of a plea that the world would hear repeated many times.

The album would not be a *Thriller* at the box office. But it would still sell four million copies by the year's end, which was pretty good for being *Bad*. **JiH**

> ## "I'm never pleased with anything. I'm a perfectionist. It's part of who I am."
>
> Michael Jackson, 1993

Track Listing

▶	01	**Bad** (Jackson)	4:06
▶	02	**The Way You Make Me Feel** (Jackson)	4:59
	03	**Speed Demon** (Jackson)	4:01
	04	**Liberian Girl** (Jackson)	3:53
	05	**Just Good Friends** (Britten•Lyle)	4:05
	06	**Another Part Of Me** (Jackson)	3:53
	07	**Man In The Mirror** (Ballard•Garrett)	5:18
▶	08	**I Just Can't Stop Loving You** (Jackson)	4:10
	09	**Dirty Diana** (Jackson)	4:52
▶	10	**Smooth Criminal** (Jackson)	4:16
	11	**Leave Me Alone** (Jackson)	4:37

Pet Shop Boys | Actually (1987)

Label | Parlophone
Producer | Various
Art Direction | Cindy Palmano
Nationality | UK
Running Time | 48:07

Pet Shop Boys, actually

Maybe it is no surprise that the strength of the Pet Shop Boys' second album lies in making the bleak seem beautiful. Hits like "Rent" spoke of rain-licked streets, anxiety, and prostitution—1987 was, after all, the year of "Black Monday" and the Zeebrugge ferry disaster; the Hungerford killings in the UK, growing AIDS fears, and Thatcher's re-election. And yet for all the darkness and drama *Actually* is one of the decade's most dazzling pop achievements, its urban vignettes delivered via melodic electro grooves. Even teenagers on BBC TV's weekly music program *Top Of The Pops* were happy to clap along to a song about Catholic guilt ("It's A Sin").

Following the success of debut album *Please*, the duo decided to take time out to write songs for the follow-up, calling on arranger Angelo Badalamenti, legendary composer Ennio Morricone, and a pool of different producers to make the perfect tweaks. According to vocalist and one-time *Smash Hits* editor Neil Tennant, "the idea was to make it more musically ambitious, bigger sounding."

The sound is immaculate, but somehow deeply human—much like its iconic sleeve image, which has the pair in tuxedos and bow ties, Tennant yawning. Having rejected a painting by Scottish artist Alison Watt, the pair chose the photo from a recent shoot, but then had to wrestle it from *Smash Hits*, who were about to use the image for the cover of their next issue.

Critics on both sides of the pond fell for its charms immediately, and its singles shot into the UK and U.S. Top Tens. In a traumatic year, the Pet Shop Boys seemed to soothe the pain with tenderness and wit. **SH**

> "I felt at this time that we had the secret of contemporary pop music."
>
> Neil Tennant, 2001

Track Listing

01	**One More Chance**	(Lowe·Orlando·Tennant)	5:31
▶ 02	**What Have I Done To Deserve This?** (Lowe·Tennant·Willis)		4:22
03	**Shopping**	(Lowe·Tennant)	3:37
▶ 04	**Rent**	(Lowe·Tennant)	5:07
05	**Hit Music**	(Lowe·Tennant)	4:43
06	**It Couldn't Happen Here** (Lowe·Morricone·Tennant)		5:20
▶ 07	**It's A Sin**	(Lowe·Tennant)	4:59
▶ 08	**I Want To Wake Up**	(Lowe·Tennant)	5:10
▶ 09	**Heart**	(Lowe·Tennant)	3:57
10	**King's Cross**	(Lowe·Tennant)	5:11

U2 | The Joshua Tree (1987)

Label | Island
Producer | Brian Eno • Daniel Lanois
Art Direction | Steve Averill
Nationality | Ireland • UK
Running Time | 50:11

The Joshua Tree marks the point in U2's long and gloriously inconsistent career at which they woke up to the possibilities of studio technology, expanded their sound from a post-punk chug, and found grandeur, abstraction, and finesse. Many in U2's enormous fanbase were converted to the cause by the arch wit of their post-*Achtung Baby* reawakening, but an older, possibly less sophisticated stratum of followers were grabbed by the landscaped songs of *The Joshua Tree*.

The epic nature of big-hitters such as "Where The Streets Have No Name" (whose intro is among the most spine-chilling compositions in rock, especially live), "With Or Without You" (the closest U2 had yet come to a passionate love song), and "In God's Country" (with its scintillating guitar riff) attracted most interest. But *The Joshua Tree* hooked in many more listeners, possibly those less fond of the sonic-boom pyrotechnics of Edge's guitar and more interested in subtle emotional tones, with the simple, understated beauty of "Red Hill Mining Town" and "Exit"—the latter among the darkest, most introspective songs the band has ever recorded.

If the album has a flaw, it exists in the earnest preacher-man tones of many of Bono's lyrics. While the point behind "Bullet The Blue Sky" (a criticism of U.S. activities in Central America) is salient to this day, Bono's hammy delivery of "I can see those fighter planes," coupled with his snooty frown, seems over-serious nowadays. This unfortunate tendency reached its nadir on the band's next album, *Rattle And Hum*, but it is a sign of the quality of *The Joshua Tree* that the album still richly deserves its place in this book. **JM**

Track Listing

▶	01	**Where The Streets Have No Name** (Bono • Clayton • Edge • Mullen)	5:37
▶	02	**I Still Haven't Found What I'm Looking For** (Bono • Clayton • Edge • Mullen)	4:37
▶	03	**With Or Without You** (Bono • Clayton • Edge • Mullen)	4:56
	04	**Bullet The Blue Sky** (Bono • Clayton • Edge • Mullen)	4:32
	05	**Running To Stand Still** (Bono • Clayton • Edge • Mullen)	4:18
	06	**Red Hill Mining Town** (Bono • Clayton • Edge • Mullen)	4:52
	07	**In God's Country** (Bono • Clayton • Edge • Mullen)	2:57
	08	**Trip Through Your Wires** (Bono • Clayton • Edge • Mullen)	3:32
	09	**One Tree Hill** (Bono • Clayton • Edge • Mullen)	5:23
▶	10	**Exit** (Bono • Clayton • Edge • Mullen)	4:13
	11	**Mothers Of The Disappeared** (Bono • Clayton • Edge • Mullen)	5:14

Terence Trent D'Arby | Introducing The Hardline According To Terence Trent D'Arby (1987)

Label | Columbia
Producer | Various
Art Direction | Peter Barrett
Nationality | UK
Running Time | 47:01

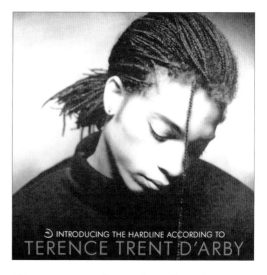

INTRODUCING THE HARDLINE ACCORDING TO
TERENCE TRENT D'ARBY

New Yorker Terence Trent D'Arby filled the R&B/soul auteur gap between Prince's mainstream success of the mid-1980s and the neo-soul movement that developed more than a decade later. The insidiously catchy "Wishing Well" (U.S. No. 1; UK No. 2) alone, with its catchy synthesizer hook, amply proved that he was an ambassador of all things soulful.

D'Arby received flak for remarking that *Introducing The Hardline . . .* was superior to The Beatles' *Sgt. Pepper's Lonely Hearts Club Band*. A singer/songwriter as well as a stylized vocalist, he makes a solid case for both aspects of his artistry here. The album still holds up well today, despite the trademark Eighties studio production sounds—such as the echoey drumbeat and period keyboards sounds on "If You All Get To Heaven," the album's opening track. The sultry "Sign Your Name"—a real showcase for the D'Arby pipes—sounds current regardless of when it is played, and the singer also demonstrates remarkable vocal strength on the a cappella "As Yet Untitled." His cover of Smokey Robinson's "Who's Lovin' You" predates the so-called smooth R&B movement that emerged in the 1990s, while the sassy "Dance Little Sister" is delivered, as the sportscasters say, with authority.

D'Arby would later go on to become as much of a personality as a musician, which rather distracted from his work. This album—a multiplatinum, Grammy award-winning bestseller, lest we forget—is a worthy reminder of his considerable talents. **YK**

"I am an artist. Absolutely."

Terence Trent D'Arby, 1993

Track Listing

01	If You All Get To Heaven (D'Arby)	5:17
▶ 02	If You Let Me Stay (D'Arby)	3:13
▶ 03	Wishing Well (D'Arby•Oliver)	3:29
04	I'll Never Turn My Back On You (Father's Words) (D'Arby)	3:36
▶ 05	Dance Little Sister (D'Arby)	3:53
06	Seven More Days (D'Arby)	4:33
07	Let's Go Forward (D'Arby)	5:31
▶ 08	Rain (D'Arby)	2:58
▶ 09	Sign Your Name (D'Arby)	4:35
10	As Yet Untitled (D'Arby)	5:33
11	Who's Lovin' You (Robinson)	4:23

The Pogues
If I Should Fall From Grace With God (1988)

Label | Stiff
Producer | Steve Lillywhite
Art Direction | Ian McKell
Nationality | Ireland • UK
Running Time | 47:34

The musical innovation and accessibility of The Pogues' third album deservedly broadened their international appeal, particularly in the United States. Pioneering the Irish folk/punk crossover, their almost rockabilly style adds musical vibrancy to Shane MacGowan's poetic lyrics, rendering it almost impossible to remain still while listening. Songs such as "Turkish Song Of The Damned," "South Australia," and the bi-lingual Spanish party vibe of "Fiesta" demonstrated their incredible musical diversity.

MacGowan's songwriting genius is captured at its best on *If I Should Fall From Grace With God*. The nine-piece band breathed energy with a distinctly Irish feel into songs that ranged from heartbreak and longing to storytelling, partying, and a whole lot of drinking. The album's strengths lie in its subject matter as much as its musicians' talent. From the show-tune-oriented "Metropolis" to the universally famous festive anthem, "Fairytale Of New York," MacGowan compensates for his lack of singing skills with charismatic lyrics that are based in a reality easily related to by listeners.

Sung as a duet with producer Steve Lillywhite's wife, the late Kirsty MacColl, "Fairytale Of New York" begins with a subdued piano intro and builds up to the swaying fast paced tempo that makes The Pogues' music so infectious. Its touchingly delivered tale of an immigrant couple falling in love, arguing, and repenting in New York became the most played Christmas song of 1988. **CSt**

THE POGUES
If I Should Fall From Grace With God

Track Listing

01	**If I Should Fall From Grace With God** (MacGowan)	2:21
▶ 02	**Turkish Song Of The Damned** (Finer • MacGowan)	3:27
03	**Bottle Of Smoke** (Finer • MacGowan)	2:47
▶ 04	**Fairytale Of New York** (Finer • MacGowan)	4:36
05	**Metropolis** (Finer)	2:50
▶ 06	**Thousands Are Sailing** (Chevron)	5:28
07	**South Australia** (Trad.)	3:28
▶ 08	**Fiesta** (Finer • MacGowan)	4:13
09	**Medley** (Trad.)	4:01
10	**Streets Of Sorrow/Birmingham Six** (MacGowan • Woods)	4:39
11	**Lullaby Of London** (MacGowan)	3:31
12	**The Battle March Medley/Sit Down By The Fire** (MacGowan)	2:16
▶ 13	**The Broad Majestic Shannon** (MacGowan)	2:52
14	**Worms** (Trad.)	1:05

Leonard Cohen | I'm Your Man (1988)

Label | Columbia
Producer | Various
Art Direction | Orchestra Paris
Nationality | Canada
Running Time | 40:41

As any fan can tell you, Leonard Cohen is one of the most gifted lyricists in the world of modern music. Hailing from Montreal, Cohen was an acclaimed poet and novelist long before he started recording his songs professionally in his mid-30s. In fact, his immortal "Suzanne" is just as likely to be found in poetry classrooms as it is in record shops.

I'm Your Man is one of the highlights in his remarkably long career. The album features more modern instrumentation than his usually sparse efforts, including synths and drum machines. For the most part, this approach successfully propels his music into the future ("First We Take Manhattan"), though a couple of tracks have dated over time (see "Jazz Police").

Still, like almost all of Cohen's albums, this one contains some true masterpieces. The woozy, shuffling title track "I'm Your Man" is a declaration of undying devotion featuring tongue-in-cheek lines ("If you want a doctor/I'll examine every inch of you"). The whole album has a streak of sly humor running through it, hinted at by the album cover photograph of Cohen in shades posing with a banana peel.

"Everybody Knows" is a droll and cynical farewell to the sexual revolution in light of the dangers of AIDS. "There's gonna be a meter on your bed that will disclose/What everybody knows." The easygoing steel guitar groove of "I Can't Forget" elevates Cohen's stunning lyrics: "The summer's almost gone/The winter's tuning up." And Jennifer Warnes' velvety smooth "doo dum dum" backing chorus is a charming highlight of the superb closer "Tower Of Song." **RM**

> **"There is an element in song that provides deep comfort and deep solace and stimulation for the imagination and courage."**
>
> Leonard Cohen, 1995

Track Listing

▶	01	**First We Take Manhattan** (Cohen)	5:59
	02	**Ain't No Cure For Love** (Cohen)	4:49
▶	03	**Everybody Knows** (Cohen • Robinson)	5:33
▶	04	**I'm Your Man** (Cohen)	4:25
	05	**Take This Waltz** (Cohen)	5:58
	06	**Jazz Police** (Cohen • Fisher)	3:51
▶	07	**I Can't Forget** (Cohen)	4:29
▶	08	**Tower Of Song** (Cohen)	5:37

The Waterboys | Fisherman's Blues (1988)

Label | Ensign
Producer | Various
Art Direction | Steve Meany
Nationality | UK
Running Time | 54:36

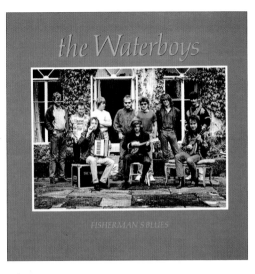

In the heyday of The Waterboys, the pundits were saying that the band could be as big as U2. "Yes," smiled Mike Scott. "But at what cost?"

After three albums, Scott had led his ever-changing charges to the top of the mountain. Their self-styled "big music" was epic and cinematic, and their star fast rising. But Scott was sick of the music business, sick of being told what to do, and sick of living in London. Enter fiddle player Steve Wickham, the group's latest recruit, who invited the band over to Ireland. That, as Scott recalls, was when "the adventure began."

Fisherman's Blues is an album that attempts to piece together the music made over what became a glorious three-year sojourn in Ireland. From the streets of Dublin to the bars of Spiddal, there were echoes of Dylan and The Band in the nature of the recordings—the musical fluency, the intuitive flow of songs and ideas, the rapport, the bonhomie, the easy switching of instruments, and the all-abiding sense of rural idyll and retreat.

Ireland—its people, its landscape, and its music—informs all, from the opening whoop of joy to the closing paean to Yeats. In between, there are waltzes and rockers and a tender reading of Van Morrison's "Sweet Thing." "And A Bang On The Ear," meantime, might have been brand new but it roars along like some traditional old favorite.

This album is a plangent work of simple joy and arrant wonder. It was drawn from hundreds of hours of tapes—highlighting both its strength and only weakness. Scott tried releasing a second volume in 2003, but the magic, like Galway mist, had gone. **RF**

"Everything changed ..."

Mike Scott, 1991

Track Listing

▶	01	**Fisherman's Blues** (Scott·Wickham)	4:27
	02	**We Will Not Be Lovers** (Scott)	7:03
▶	03	**Strange Boat** (Scott·Thistlethwaite)	3:07
	04	**World Party** (Hutchinson·Scott·Wallinger)	4:01
▶	05	**Sweet Thing** (Morrison)	7:14
	06	**Jimmy Hickey's Waltz** (Thistlethwaite)	2:06
▶	07	**And A Bang On The Ear** (Scott)	7:32
	08	**Has Anybody Here Seen Hank?** (Scott·Thistlethwaite)	3:19
	09	**When Will We Be Married?** (Trad., arr. Scott·Wickham)	3:00
	10	**When Ye Go Away** (Scott)	3:45
	11	**Dunford's Fancy** (Wickham)	1:04
▶	12	**The Stolen Child** (words W.B. Yeats adapted to music Scott)	6:55

Fishbone
Truth And Soul (1988)

Label | Columbia
Producer | Fishbone • David Kahne
Art Direction | John Guarnieri
Nationality | USA
Running Time | 41:32

Although they never became household names like their friends and Los Angeles peers the Red Hot Chili Peppers, Fishbone broke down similar musical boundaries with their exuberant fusion of ska, punk, funk, and metal. The African-American sextet formed in high school in 1979. The core lineup was singer/saxophonist Angelo Moore, guitarist Kendall Jones, bassist Norwood Fisher, trumpet player Walter Kibby, drummer Phillip "Fish" Fisher, and keyboardist/trombonist Chris Dowd (who shared a house with future solo star Jeff Buckley).

Truth And Soul, their second LP, kicks off with a heartfelt, hard rock version of Curtis Mayfield's classic junkie parable "Freddie's Dead," then moves through a kaleidoscopic array of original songs. "Ma And Pa" is a singalong skank peppered with day-glo horns, while party anthem "Bonin' In The Boneyard" rides a fantastic rubbery bassline. "Subliminal Fascism" and the sublime "Ghetto Soundwave" show different aspects of the band's ever-present social commentary. The former is a hardcore thrash protest; the latter a nuanced, poppy tale of police brutality. Acoustic ballad "Change" ends things on a note of quiet optimism.

Their most consistent record, *Truth And Soul* was Fishbone's commercial breakthrough, peaking at No. 153 on the Billboard chart. The sprawling, double album follow-up, *The Reality Of My Surroundings* (1991), cracked the Top 50, but they were unable to convert cult status into lasting mainstream success. **MA**

Everything But The Girl
Idlewild (1988)

Label | Blanco Y Negro
Producer | Ben Watt
Art Direction | Caryn Gough
Nationality | UK
Running Time | 45:07

"For your bedroom needs we sell everything but the girl," proclaimed the poster in a Hull furniture shop back in the early 1980s. Perfect inspiration for a duo whose romantic sound probably became the irresistible aphrodisiac for many a couple's copulations.

Musician Ben Watt and singer Tracey Thorn met as students in Hull, and scored individual successes on the Cherry Red label. After teaming up in earnest, they recorded a series of albums that pinched from jazz, country, torch song, and poignant pop. But a track written by the late Danny Whitten (guitarist with Crazy Horse) finally sent their career skyward. The duo gave his well-known "I Don't Want To Talk About It" the full soulful treatment. It is a classic ballad, one that almost could have been written for Thorn's aching voice. Hitting No. 3 on the UK charts, the single gave their new album major impetus.

Recorded with a small unit, featuring Ian Fraser and Peter King on saxes, there is a lounge bar, jazzy snazziness to *Idlewild*. For sure it is easy listening, but that cannot diminish the nostalgic beauty of "Oxford Street" or the boppy "These Early Days." Always keen on their poetics, they create lush acres of longing on "Blue Moon Rose" and "Shadow On A Harvest Moon."

Nearly a decade later, Thorn and Watt blended their airy artiness with trancey dance rhythms. The results were an astonishing success, especially in the United States. Everything But The Girl were suddenly among the well-heeled musical elite. **GT**

Living Colour
Vivid (1988)

Label | Epic
Producer | Ed Stasium
Art Direction | Steve Byram
Nationality | USA
Running Time | 49:13

Despite the proliferation of rap music in the late 1980s, rock 'n' roll—and certainly heavy metal—remained an almost exclusively white affair. While rock groups with black frontmen certainly existed in those days (for example, Christian rockers Kings X) the existence of a black heavy metal group was, frankly, unthinkable. New York's uncompromising Living Colour proved to be the exception to the rule.

The group was centered around its lead guitarist, the supremely talented Vernon Reid, a longstanding member of the city's underground fusion scene. (In 1985, Reid had formed the Black Rock Coalition in an effort to help musicians do away with simplistic "black" and "white" categorizations.) Add in vocalist Corey Glover, drummer Will Calhoun, and the extraordinarily gifted bassist Muzz Skillings, and *Vivid* can still rest its case as a truly original recording, one that takes in thrash, hard rock, reggae, funk, and rap.

Despite their musical excellence, it took MTV's heavy rotation of "Cult Of Personality," a Grammy award-winning critical indictment of world politicians, to garner the group the widespread praise they deserved. Elsewhere, *Vivid* is no less revolutionary—tackling suicide on "Middle Man," racism on "Funny Vibe" (featuring a Public Enemy cameo), and even celebrity stardom on "Glamour Boys." Yet while the record has aged well, the same cannot be said of the fashions—Living Colour's day-glo clothes have been consigned to the dustbins of fashion history. **BW**

Mudhoney
Superfuzz Bigmuff (1988)

Label | Sub Pop
Producer | Jack Endino
Art Direction | Charles Peterson
Nationality | USA
Running Time | 21:21

Before Nirvana's *Nevermind*—the grunge album that transcended grunge—Mudhoney's six-song *Superfuzz Bigmuff* was the recording that best expressed the sense and aesthetic of Seattle's sound in the late 1980s. All the Seattle thrill was there—a lineage comprising members of local forerunners The Melvins, Green River, and The Thrown Ups; a wall of distorted guitar; and a strong blend of garage, punk, metal, and psychedelia.

After selling more than 6,000 copies of their definitive first single, "Touch Me I'm Sick," Mudhoney's four members went into Reciprocal Studios to record this mini album under the guidance of grunge main man and producer Jack Endino. Named after guitar player Steve Turner's favorite wah-wah pedal, *Superfuzz Bigmuff* introduced the band to Europe.

The record rocks sexy and smart, humorous and hard. The blasts of noise "Mudride" and "In 'n' Out Of Grace" are two scorched monuments to the early sound of The Stooges, with Blue Cheer and Spacemen 3 thrown into the mix. The stormy but circumspect ballads "If I Think" and "Need" made a tour of the band's darker side, and "Chain That Door" is garage punk in the Billy Childish mold.

Although never serious rivals to Soundgarden, Mudhoney emerged from the underground with this mischievous workout, achieving tense and dramatic musical structures with Turner's scalping guitars, Mark Arm's angry vocals, Matt Lukin's mighty bass, and Don Peters' propulsive drums. **JG**

R.E.M. | Green (1988)

Label | Warner Bros.
Producer | Scott Litt • R.E.M.
Art Direction | Jon McCafferty
Nationality | USA
Running Time | 39:53

A frenzy of media coverage regarding freak weather conditions saw mid-1988 tagged "the greenhouse summer." In November that year, R.E.M. released their sixth studio album. Its title captured the new social concerns of the liberal left, and the music sent this Georgian quartet into stadium territory. And for all the power chords and punchy choruses, Peter Buck's deft mandolin appears on three remarkable ballads.

Green's message is first evident on the cover, where foliage, tree rings, and telegraph poles compete. The background is swathed in orange—a reference to the chemical Agent Orange employed by U.S. forces in Vietnam to raze a third of that country's forest cover. The allusion is also pursued lyrically, on the double-barreled guitar blast of "Orange Crush."

Ecological concerns feature again on the eerie "I Remember California." It is a far from predictable West Coast vision, referencing wolverines, Trident submarines, and traffic jams, before closing with the somewhat cryptic couplet "At the end of the continent/ At the edge of the continent." Then there is the kooky breakthrough single "Stand," with its wistful line "If wishes were trees, the trees would be falling."

Though R.E.M.'s next tour promoted Greenpeace and Amnesty, *Green* is far from a political manifesto in rock song. On "World Leader Pretend," Stipe's concerns are entirely first person, and "Turn You Inside Out" finds him wrestling with the dilemmas of fame.

"Are R.E.M. the best band in the world?" asked Andy Gill, reviewing *Green* in *Q*. He decided they were. And so did millions of others. **GT**

"I think public opinion can really change."

Michael Stipe, 1989

Track Listing

01	**Pop Song 89** (Berry•Buck•Mills•Stipe)	3:03
02	**Get Up** (Berry•Buck•Mills•Stipe)	2:39
▶ 03	**You Are The Everything** (Berry•Buck•Mills•Stipe)	3:41
04	**Stand** (Berry•Buck•Mills•Stipe)	3:10
▶ 05	**World Leader Pretend** (Berry•Buck•Mills•Stipe)	4:17
06	**The Wrong Child** (Berry•Buck•Mills•Stipe)	3:35
▶ 07	**Orange Crush** (Berry•Buck•Mills•Stipe)	3:50
08	**Turn You Inside Out** (Berry•Buck•Mills•Stipe)	4:15
▶ 09	**Hairshirt** (Berry•Buck•Mills•Stipe)	3:15
▶ 10	**I Remember California** (Berry•Buck•Mills•Stipe)	4:59
11	**Untitled** (Berry•Buck•Mills•Stipe)	3:09

Happy Mondays
Bummed (1988)

The Go-Betweens
16 Lovers Lane (1988)

Label | Factory
Producer | Martin Hannett
Art Direction | Central Station Design
Nationality | UK
Running Time | 37:30

Label | Beggars Banquet
Producer | Mark Wallis
Art Direction | John Willsteed
Nationality | Australia
Running Time | 37:02

The Stone Roses steal the honors in every poll, but nothing captures the maverick spirit of Britain's Manchester better than *Bummed*.

Where the Roses jingle-jangled like The Byrds, the Mondays were blacker in spirit and sound. Singer Shaun Ryder claimed the rhythms were "rip-offs of Motown," though the resultant cocktail sounds more like Talking Heads fighting The Fall.

Between the shambling "Country Song" (once titled "Some Cunt From Preston") and the "Ticket To Ride"-infringing "Lazyitis" are eight cuts of psychofunkedelia. Infamously hit and miss onstage, the Mondays are superb here: guitarist Mark Day, drummer Gaz Whelan, and Shaun's bass-playing brother Paul shine on tracks like "Performance" and "Brain Dead."

The artwork mirrored the music—the antithesis of Peter Saville's studied, refined artwork for Factory Records, it was endearingly rough and ready, not unlike the Mondays themselves (Pat and Matt Carroll, of Central Station Design, were related to the Ryders).

Star of the show, though, is Shaun, forced to write lyrics because "the rest of 'em can't be arsed." His madcap streams of consciousness are complemented by startling speech ("We've been courteous!" and "You're rendering that scaffolding dangerous!").

Bummed did not secure a foothold till "Wrote For Luck" was remixed by Paul Oakenfold and Erasure's Vince Clarke—at which point Primal Scream and The Stone Roses also discovered dance music. **BM**

The most heartbreaking album of all time? It can be. Here are ten beautiful love songs, covering the A–Z that begins with infatuation and ends in memories, but it was events behind the scenes that caused the Brisbane band's final album to be known as "the indie *Rumors*."

Returning to Australia after spending most of the decade in London, The Go-Betweens began flaking. They lost their bassist and replaced him with John Willsteed, whose history suggested he hated the band and who was about to succumb to a drink problem. Singer/songwriter Robert Forster and drummer Lindy Morrison had split up. She was about to lose her enthusiasm for band life; he, meanwhile, steeped his songs in melancholy ("Dive For Your Memory," "Clouds," "Love Is A Sign"). Grant McLennan (the other singer/songwriter) and multi-instrumentalist Amanda Brown were in love, however, and contentment flowed through McLennan's pen ("Love Goes On!," "The Devil's Eye," "Quiet Heart"). No matter what the state of your personal life, there was something here for you.

Accused of marking a softening of The Go-Betweens' post-punk spikiness, the lush *16 Lovers Lane* was a gorgeous farewell to a most cruelly overlooked band. Once you fall for the small-town dramas of "Streets Of Your Town" or "Was There Anything I Could Do?," devotion is almost always total. If Forster and McLennan's royalties do not roll in like they should, the knowledge that they created a template for literate, mature pop songs might be some compensation. **DH**

Cowboy Junkies
The Trinity Session (1988)

Tracy Chapman
Tracy Chapman (1988)

Label | RCA
Producer | Peter Moore
Art Direction | Pietro Alfieri
Nationality | Canada
Running Time | 52:00

Label | Elektra
Producer | David Kershenbaum
Art Direction | Carol Bobolts
Nationality | USA
Running Time | 35:51

Michael Timmins and his childhood friend Alan Anton had played in bands together since 1979; they recruited Michael's brother Peter Timmins in 1984, followed by Peter's sister Margo. At that time, excessive shyness prevented Margo from singing in front of the band. Instead, she turned her back to them while she crooned their fragile and beautiful tunes.

Recorded in one day around one microphone in The Holy Trinity church in downtown Toronto, Canada, at a cost of $250, *The Trinity Session* was a minimalist revelation. The sparse backing is supplemented by fiddle, mandolin, steel guitar, harmonica, and accordion—resulting in a kind of pared down, crepuscular country music, the spare but excellent production conveying an intimacy that is at times eerie.

The cover versions are sure-footed translations that revitalize the songs themselves. The understated "Sweet Jane" in particular is a gem—Lou Reed's classic never sounded so mournful—while Hank Williams' "I'm So Lonesome I Could Cry," is given a haunting reworking, with plangent steel guitar from Kim Deschamps. If this, or "To Love Is To Bury," does not break your heart, you may not have a heart.

Margo Timmins' vocals impress throughout. Her dry-eyed a cappella on the lament "Mining For Gold" makes for an arresting opener, while her sensual delivery on final track "Walking After Midnight"—a sleepwalking-paced blues accompanied by mournful harmonica—is full of sensual longing. Swoonsome. **KC**

In March 1988, London's intimate Donmar Warehouse entertained journalists with free shows by 10,000 Maniacs' Natalie Merchant. The condition was that you also stuck around for a new Warner Bros. artist to promote her stuff later. This new act was Tracy Chapman. The piercing honesty and raw soul of Chapman's guitar-vocal songs—performed without amplification—stunned most invited journalists.

The featured numbers were heard in silkier slickness on Chapman's debut, released in April. Eight weeks later, Chapman had the most extraordinary career break. A virtual newcomer, she shared the bill for Nelson Mandela's 70th birthday bash at London's Wembley Arena. The global TV audience was won over by her bluesy folk ballads and stirring statements. Within days, Tracy Chapman was a chart-topper and the yearning folk-pop of "Fast Car" a major hit.

For all their good intentions, there is a nagging naivety to several tracks. Reviewing Mandela's event, a skeptical Billy Bragg wondered if he forgave Chapman for singing "poor people gonna rise up and get their share," without explaining how. "Talkin' Bout A Revolution," which drew Bragg's comment, is a call to arms with no clear cause. And admittedly, "Across The Lines" evokes a divide between blacks and whites without much real tension. And yet the tunes are so rich in soulful simplicity, and ballads such as "Baby Can I Hold You" are so achingly tender, it is no wonder that millions were won over. **GT**

My Bloody Valentine | Isn't Anything (1988)

Label | Creation
Producer | My Bloody Valentine
Art Direction | Joe Dilworth
Nationality | Ireland · UK
Running Time | 37:55

Formed in Dublin, 1984, by guitarist Kevin Shields and drummer Colm O'Ciosoig, My Bloody Valentine moved to Holland, Berlin, and then London, losing original vocalist Dave Conway and acquiring bassist Debbie Googe and guitarist/vocalist Bilinda Butcher en route. My Bloody Valentine recorded for four different labels before moving to Creation, but their first release for the label, "You Made Me Realise," was greeted with acclaim and astonishment.

An exciting wave of U.S. underground bands such as Big Black, Dinosaur Jr., and Hüsker Dü had reopened European audiences' ears to the guitar's sonic capabilities. Inspired by this, Shields took creative control of the band and began meticulously crafting *Isn't Anything*, creating that rare thing, a guitar rock album containing no guitars—instead, they were played through endless reverb and effects, before Shields erased the instrument, leaving only the sounds generated by the effect units.

Using unconventional tunings, dislocated rhythms, sweet textured harmonies, and the predominantly sexual theme of the lyrics, the music shifts from the sensual ("Lose My Breath") to the aurally unnerving ("All I Need"). The erotically charged "Soft As Snow (But Warm Snow)" and single "Feed Me With Your Kiss" saw Shields equate his perfect pop vision with the sounds in his head.

While Shields worked obsessively in the studio, a whole host of new bands such as Ride and Lush appeared, approximating My Bloody Valentine's sound but with little of the genius and creative innovation that made *Isn't Anything* such a landmark album. **CSh**

"My version of reality . . . "

Kevin Shields 2004

Track Listing

▶	01	**Soft As Snow (But Warm Inside)** (O'Ciosoig · Shields)		2:21
	02	**Lose My Breath** (Butcher · Shields)		3:37
	03	**Cupid Come** (Butcher · Shields)		4:29
	04	**(When You Wake) You're Still In A Dream** (O'Ciosoig · Shields)		3:18
▶	05	**No More Sorry** (Butcher · Shields)		2:47
▶	06	**All I Need** (Shields)		3:07
▶	07	**Feed Me With Your Kiss** (Shields)		3:54
	08	**Sueisfine** (Shields)		2:12
	09	**Several Girls Galore** (Butcher · Shields)		2:20
	10	**You Never Should** (Shields)		3:22
	11	**Nothing Much To Lose** (Shields)		3:17
	12	**I Can See It (But I Can't Feel It)** (Shields)		3:11

Pixies | Surfer Rosa (1988)

Label | 4AD
Producer | Steve Albini
Art Direction | Vaughan Oliver
Nationality | USA
Running Time | 31:07

A bizarre collision of biblically steeped stream-of-consciousness lyrics, pidgin Spanish, roaring guitars, cranked-up drums, and deranged barking and shrieking, *Surfer Rosa* is as raw and visceral a debut as you will find in this book. For many fans of this Boston band it remains the Pixies' most powerful document.

The Pixies were formed in 1986 when Charles Michael Kirtridge Thompson IV, a.k.a. Black Francis, dropped out of college and persuaded his buddy Joey Santiago to do the same. An ad in a local paper brought on board bassist Kim Deal (credited on this record as Mrs. John Murphy) and her friend, drummer Dave Lovering. An early demo created a buzz for the nascent Pixies sound and a second was released without change on UK label 4AD as the EP *Come On Pilgrim*.

Having kicked down the door to the studio while barely trying, the band were teamed up with the uncompromising Steve Albini for the recording of their first full-length album. Notoriously antipathetic to anything human sounding, Albini gave the band only one day for vocals while spending two weeks on guitars. Any sound deemed "pussy" did not make it through the producer's filter. The results, while rough and angry, retained the melody and soaring dynamism of Thompson's original compositions.

From the stop-start stomp of "Bone Machine," the crashing guitars of "Break My Body," the vicious guitar-mediated vocal of "Something Against You" and the squealing "Broken Face," to the Deal-penned "Gigantic" and the lost-it anthem "Where Is My Mind?," a maniacal electricity courses through every song. **MBI**

"I just had a Bible upbringing."

Black Francis, 1988

Track Listing

01	**Bone Machine** (Francis)		2:58
02	**Break My Body** (Francis)		2:05
▶ 03	**Something Against You** (Francis)		1:48
04	**Broken Face** (Francis)		1:30
▶ 05	**Gigantic** (Mrs. John Murphy · Francis)		3:49
06	**River Euphrates** (Francis)		2:32
▶ 07	**Where Is My Mind** (Francis)		3:54
08	**Cactus** (Francis)		2:17
09	**Tony's Theme** (Francis)		1:52
▶ 10	**Oh My Golly!** (Francis)		1:47
11	**Vamos** (Francis)		2:53
12	**I'm Amazed** (Francis)		1:42
13	**Brick Is Red** (Francis)		2:00

Metallica | ...And Justice For All (1988)

Label | Elektra
Producer | Metallica • Flemming Rasmussen
Art Direction | Reiner Design
Nationality | USA
Running Time | 65:10

History has not been kind to Metallica's fourth album. Observers of the thrash metal genre point to its ridiculously overprocessed sound and unnecessarily complex arrangements. It is also popularly supposed to be the album on which primary songwriters James Hetfield and Lars Ulrich disappeared into a vortex of paranoia (new bassist Jason Newsted was almost mixed out, due to the pair's lack of confidence in his skills) and ambition (the spiraling riff salad of many of the songs' midsections reached almost prog-rock excess at times).

But if you can look behind the tinny sound and the overexperimentation, ...And Justice For All reveals itself as an epic, even noble concept album with many, many layers of invention to explore. The album sits between Metallica's finest hours: the melodic, aggressive beauty of 1986's *Master Of Puppets* and 1991's earth-shattering, rock club-fueling non-thrash *Metallica*—not an easy place to occupy. But if it's aggression you're after, the speedy back end of "One" needs little explanation; Kirk Hammett's twisted, never-beaten shredding on the opener "Blackened" and the title track is jaw-droppingly proficient; and the grasp of a riff that Hetfield displays on "Eye Of The Beholder" and the furious "Dyers Eve" is not to be underestimated.

Many in Metallica's fan base identify this LP as the point where the group abandoned thrash altogether ("Dyers Eve" is as close as the album gets to that vintage sound) and began looking for mainstream acceptance. But if that is the case it is a glorious farewell to the extreme sounds of *Kill 'Em All* and *Ride The Lightning*, and one that should be enjoyed to the full. **JM**

> "Sometimes I listen to *Justice ...* and think it was the blueprint for a whole musical movement."
>
> Lars Ulrich, 2005

Track Listing

▶	01	**Blackened** (Hetfield·Newsted·Ulrich)	6:40
▶	02	**...And Justice For All** (Hammett·Hetfield·Ulrich)	9:44
	03	**Eye Of The Beholder** (Hammett·Hetfield·Ulrich)	6:25
▶	04	**One** (Hetfield·Ulrich)	7:24
	05	**The Shortest Straw** (Hetfield·Ulrich)	6:35
	06	**Harvester Of Sorrow** (Hetfield·Ulrich)	5:42
	07	**The Frayed Ends Of Sanity** (Hammett·Hetfield·Ulrich)	7:40
	08	**To Live Is To Die** (Burton·Hetfield·Ulrich)	9:48
▶	09	**Dyers Eve** (Hammett·Hetfield·Ulrich)	5:12

Dinosaur Jr. | **Bug** (1988)

Label | SST
Producer | Uncredited
Art Direction | Maura Jasper
Nationality | USA
Running Time | 35:24

Few bands are as aptly named as Dinosaur Jr., a trio who fused the Jurassic influences of traditional rock elements with an impetuous, almost infantile urge for tantrum-inspired fury that saw them hailed as successors to Sonic Youth's throne of avant-garde noise supremos. That combination of old and young sounds made them trailblazers of American indie rock—loud, chaotic, and melodic all at the same time, their style would be a major influence on the slacker-generation bands who followed. *Bug* was the third and last album by the band's original incarnation. Lead guitarist and singer J. Mascis would kick out bassist Lou Barlow (who would go on to form Sebadoh) the following year.

Dinosaur Jr. was Mascis' band and he carefully scripted each song, instructing his bandmates how to play their parts. Despite this authoritarian control, each member plays like an angry virtuoso on this album, almost as if in protest, and the benefits are abundantly clear on standouts such as "Freak Scene" (a UK indie chart-topper) and "They Always Come." Mascis' crafted melodies are set against the busiest (multilayered) guitar work you will ever hear in the genre; bassist Lou Barlow's innovative basslines weave in and out of the melodies; and drummer Murph augments the aggressive sound with fast, metal-inspired fills.

Mascis knew the importance of a catchy tune. Obviously a fan of classic rock and folk, his melodies and vocal delivery recall Neil Young, especially on "Pond Song" and CD-rerelease bonus track "Keep The Glove"—in which he sings melodies as old as rock itself on top of the youthful chaos created by the rest of the band. **JC**

> "Now, looking back on it, I'm like, 'Jesus, we are so not normal! Nobody really played like that!'"
>
> Lou Barlow, 2005

Track Listing

▶ 01	**Freak Scene** (Mascis)	3:35
02	**No Bones** (Mascis)	3:42
▶ 03	**They Always Come** (Mascis)	4:25
▶ 04	**Yeah We Know** (Mascis)	5:30
05	**Let It Ride** (Mascis)	3:34
▶ 06	**Pond Song** (Mascis)	2:54
07	**Budge** (Mascis)	2:29
08	**Post** (Mascis)	3:36
09	**Don't** (Mascis)	5:39

Dagmar Krause
Tank Battles (1988)

Label | Antilles
Producer | Greg Cohen
Art Direction | Island Art
Nationality | Germany
Running Time | 39:33

K.D. Lang
Shadowland (1988)

Label | Sire
Producer | Owen Bradley
Art Direction | Jeri Heiden
Nationality | Canada
Running Time | 35:54

Born in Hamburg in 1950, the teenage Dagmar Krause sang in the city's notorious Reeperbahn nightclubs. Much later, in 1978, after starring in a London version of the Brecht/Kurt Weill musical *Mahagonny*, Krause began researching the life of Weill's compatriot, musician Hanns Eisler, who had fought with a Hungarian regiment in 1916 before teaming up with prominent poet Bertolt Brecht.

The cast of the resultant *Tank Battles* included Alexander Balanescu (viola), John Harle (saxophone), and Danny Thompson (double bass). A glossy production, and ensemble arrangments, came from Greg Cohen, who had recently worked on Tom Waits' cabaret-inspired album *Frank's Wild Years*.

Cohen's interpretations crackle with nervous tension. Staccato string and woodwind lines pulsate under Krause's metallic German vowels. Most of the tracks are rendered in English yet lose none of Brecht's bitter passions. "Song Of The Whitewash" and "Ballad Of (Bourgeois) Welfare" drip with venom, as do the militant "You Have To Pay" and "The Trenches."

Tank Battles is not without dark humor, and Krause's hushed portrayal of the prostitute "Mother Beimlein," over a simple bassoon motif, is masterly. Then there is the sweeping sorrow of "A German Mother" and "The Homecoming" to reckon with.

Robin Denselow of *The Guardian* described the album as "European soul," and no listener could surely resist Krause's heartfelt vitality. **GT**

With 1987's major label debut *Angel With A Lariat*, K. D. Lang had raised more eyebrows than she had moved units. People simply did not know what to make of lang's androgynous look and camp take on country music, which seemed better suited to college radio than airwaves dominated by George Strait and Alabama.

The most important eyebrow lifted by *Angel* . . . belonged to Owen Bradley, a producer best known for his work with major Lang influence Patsy Cline. Bradley came out of retirement to lead the Nashville sessions for *Shadowland*. The producer would take complete control in the studio, stamping out the humor and honky-tonk that filled the debut and crafting a lush mix of pop and country that perfectly suited Lang's vocals.

The album opens with a pair of gorgeous ballads, "Western Stars" and "Lock, Stock And Teardrops," and moves easily through such highlights as the sax-fueled mourner "Busy Being Blue" and the upbeat toe-tapper "Don't Let The Stars Get In Your Eyes." *Shadowland* closes with "Honky Tonk Angel's Medley," which finds Lang collaborating with the great vocal triumvirate of Brenda Lee, Loretta Lynn, and Kitty Wells. The only thing missing, Bradley said, was Patsy Cline's voice.

Shadowland proved popular with both critics and fans, although it would take three years to be certified gold. The singer would follow with one more country album, 1989's *Absolute Torch And Twang*, before fully lighting up as a torch singer with 1992's breakthrough effort *Ingénue*. **JiH**

American Music Club
California (1988)

Label | Demon
Producer | Tom Mallon
Art Direction | Bobby Neel Adams
Nationality | USA
Running Time | 41:32

Melody Maker once called American Music Club "The most criminally underrated band in the world." A pretty accurate description, as this band seems forever condemned to obscurity.

An "Americana" band long before the term was coined as a music genre, American Music Club seamlessly blend rock, punk, folk, and country on *California*, their definitive statement. Featuring the songwriting genius of Mark Eitzel, a doomed and sympathetic soul if ever there was one, it was recorded in the aftermath of their first worthwhile effort, *Engine*, released the year before. Eitzel has described *Engine* as a failed attempt at making a "big rock classic" and the members were genuinely shocked when R.E.M. took the mainstream by storm instead—a band they compared themselves to constantly. They resolved to record a quieter, more introverted album next time.

The album opens with the simple, lovelorn "Firefly," before breaking into a fierce rocker, "Somewhere," which contains the brilliant gutter poetry lines "We got a lot to lose/And maybe we can lose it all tonight." There are genuine masterpieces here, such as the soaring "Western Sky" (Eitzel breaks down in tears at the end of this song when played live on his solo live album, *Songs Of Love: Live At The Borderline*) and the heartbreaking "Blue And Grey Shirt," concerning a friend's death from AIDS. The closing track, the incredibly sad "Last Harbor," is the best thing that Eitzel has ever written. **AET**

Morrissey
"Viva Hate" (1988)

Label | Parlophone
Producer | Stephen Street
Art Direction | Morrissey
Nationality | UK
Running Time | 42:20

Without The Smiths and, more pertinently, his guitarist, songwriter, and sometime manager/nursemaid Johnny Marr, Morrissey was supposed to be a joke. Without Marr, who had signaled the end to their partnership and the greatest band of all time in 1987, a swiftly prepared Morrissey record did not bode well.

It is telling, then, that 12 years after the release of *"Viva Hate,"* Ryan Adams chose to start his debut album *Heartbreaker* with a spoken track featuring an argument about "Suedehead." A different decade, a different nationality, even a different genre—yet the impact of Morrissey and *"Viva Hate"* is still reverberating.

That Morrissey is no also-ran can be gleaned from the most cursory of looks. Breaking The Smiths' tradition of re-using vintage photos, a determined-looking Morrissey graces the album cover. By track three—"Everyday Is Like Sunday"—the singer has already delivered an anthemic ode to loneliness and despair. In short, a Morrissey classic.

With producer Stephen Street recruited as musical collaborator, there is perhaps a little too much sonic experimentation, but there is no denying the sheer quality of the likes of "Late Night, Maudlin Street," "The Ordinary Boys" (from which the new British band took their name), and the magnificent "Suedehead," as Morrissey finds a voice more direct than ever before.

With *"Viva Hate,"* Morrissey stepped out of the shadows to become—as he later said, with typical ill-modesty—perhaps the last great pop icon. **PS**

Sonic Youth | Daydream Nation (1988)

Label | Enigma
Producer | Nick Sansano • Sonic Youth
Art Direction | Slim Smith
Nationality | USA
Running Time | 70:40

Originally a double vinyl album, *Daydream Nation* marked the end of an era for Sonic Youth. Sprawling and vigorous, energetic and complex, the music refined a quest that had started in the New York underground of the early 1980s and had experimented along the way with minimalism and hardcore. Through a series of recordings, notably the fascinating *Evol* (1986) and addictive *Sister* (1987), the group were naturally heading toward this most definitive statement, the work for which they will be surely remembered—as the band that brought notions, such as alternate tunings and noise collage, to the contemporary mainstream.

Surreal and exacerbated, at the same time sharp and realistic, the album opens with a memorable street scene in the anthemic "Teen Age Riot" and ends with the convulsive beauty of three tracks that form the final suite "Trilogy." In between, the band rocks hard ("Silver Rocket,""Candle"), taking the absorbed listener through their idiosyncratic aesthetic sense ("The Sprawl," "Providence") and bravado ("Eric's Trip,""Total Trash").

Their last work for an independent label, *Daydream Nation* was engineered by Nick Sansano at Greene Street Recording, Manhattan, and took the four-piece of drummer Steve Shelley, bassist Kim Gordon, guitarists Thurston Moore, and Lee Ranaldo, to a new level of recognition as scholars of rock's past and original purveyors of a new beginning. The world was ready for another rock revolution at the dawn of the 1990s—especially that sleepwalking nation of the title, an America that now seems as remote in time as it is vividly portrayed here. **IJ**

> "Staying together so long was crucial in being taken seriously."
>
> Thurston Moore, 1987

Track Listing

▶	01	**Teen Age Riot** (Sonic Youth)	6:58
▶	02	**Silver Rocket** (Sonic Youth)	3:47
	03	**The Sprawl** (Sonic Youth)	7:42
	04	**'Cross The Breeze** (Sonic Youth)	7:00
▶	04	**Eric's Trip** (Sonic Youth)	3:48
	06	**Total Trash** (Sonic Youth)	7:32
	07	**Hey Joni** (Sonic Youth)	4:23
	08	**Providence** (Sonic Youth)	2:41
▶	09	**Candle** (Sonic Youth)	4:59
	10	**Rain King** (Sonic Youth)	4:39
▶	11	**Kissability** (Sonic Youth)	3:08
▶	12	**Trilogy (The Wonder/Hyperstation/ Eliminator Jr.)** (Sonic Youth)	14:03

The Sugarcubes | Life's Too Good (1988)

Label | One Little Indian
Producer | David Birkett • Ray Shulman
Art Direction | Me Company
Nationality | Iceland
Running Time | 33:05

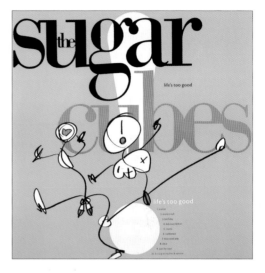

The Sugarcubes were formed in 1986, as a joke, by veterans of the Icelandic post-punk scene. The prank quickly mutated into something no one in their native country—least of all themselves—could have dreamed of. They were to become the first Icelandic band to enjoy international recognition, while also forming a launch pad for Björk's enormous solo success.

The 'Cubes had been playing the songs from *Life's Too Good* live for two years in Iceland, to no avail. All of that changed when "Birthday" was released as a single in Britain in 1987. The press in the UK went overboard in its praise and suddenly the band was at the center of a major-label bidding war. All deals were declined, however—The Sugarcubes had a strong disdain for the music business and interviews were characterized by the band's black, surreal humor.

Life's Too Good was recorded in bits and pieces over a two-year period. Reviews were ecstatic when it was finally released (in five different sleeve colors) and it certainly is an impressive debut—fresh and energetic, managing to be playfully melodic and arty at the same time. "Birthday" has an otherwordly charm to it, carried by Björk's remarkable voice, while the skewed and haunting "Deus" deceptively lures the listener in. "Coldsweat" and "Sick For Toys" show rockier, darker leanings, the latter song neatly showcasing guitarist Thor's wiry and sparkling playing. And what is Einar constantly ranting about?

A weird and wonderful watershed of a record indeed, one in which different and disparate elements combine into a strong, unique whole. **AET**

> **"Everything must be done with passion."**
>
> Björk, 1992

Track Listing

01	**Traitor** (The Sugarcubes)		3:08
▶ 02	**Motorcrash** (The Sugarcubes)		2:23
▶ 03	**Birthday** (The Sugarcubes)		3:59
04	**Delicious Demon** (The Sugarcubes)		2:43
05	**Mama** (The Sugarcubes)		2:56
▶ 06	**Coldsweat** (The Sugarcubes)		3:15
07	**Blue Eyed Pop** (The Sugarcubes)		2:38
▶ 08	**Deus** (The Sugarcubes)		4:07
▶ 09	**Sick For Toys** (The Sugarcubes)		3:15
10	**Fucking In Rhythm And Sorrow** (The Sugarcubes)		3:14
11	**Take Some Petrol Darling** (The Sugarcubes)		1:27

Dwight Yoakam
Buenas Noches From A Lonely Room (1988)

Label | Reprise
Producer | Pete Anderson
Art Direction | Kim Champagne • Dwight Yoakam
Nationality | USA
Running Time | 36:37

He looked the part right from the get-go—a long, tall drink of water in big hat, pointy boots, and impossibly tight jeans. Most of all, Dwight Yoakam sang pure honky-tonk like some lost or fallen angel. His 1986 debut *Guitars, Cadillacs Etc, Etc* had been a gem. The follow up *Hillbilly Deluxe* was even better. This, his third, was the cream of the crop.

And "Buenas Noches From A Lonely Room (She Wore Red Dresses)" was his best song. A poetic and poignant confessional of jealousy, vengeance, and murder, delivered with a tenderly wrought glint and twang. Elsewhere, "Streets Of Bakersfield" (featuring Flaco Jimenez on accordion) was an old Buck Owens favorite and somehow Yoakam managed to coax him out of retirement to sing on it (opening up a new chapter in the 58-year-old Owens' career). "I Sang Dixie," meanwhile, gently dignified the rebel South and "Hold On To God" found Yoakam embracing gospel, albeit with a little twist.

Kentucky-raised, the young Yoakam had been laughably rejected as being "too country for Nashville," so he headed for California instead, probably a more appropriate musical home anyway. Yoakam mixed country sources with influences ranging from Elvis Presley and Lefty Frizzell to The Beatles and Creedence Clearwater Revival. Dubbed a "new traditionalist," he sounded old and new at the same time. Nashville might not have approved, but he could not be denied. Critics raved and sales soared. **RF**

"I don't journal my life."

Dwight Yoakam, 2003

Track Listing

01	**I Got You** (Yoakam)	3:28
02	**One More Name** (Yoakam)	3:05
03	**What I Don't Know** (Yoakam)	3:46
04	**Home Of The Blues** (Cash•Douglas•McAlpine)	2:52
▶ 05	**Buenas Noches From A Lonely Room (She Wore Red Dresses)** (Yoakam)	4:31
06	**I Hear You Knockin'** (Miller)	3:12
▶ 07	**I Sang Dixie** (Yoakam)	3:47
▶ 08	**Streets Of Bakersfield** (Joy)	2:47
09	**Floyd County** (Yoakam)	2:55
10	**Send Me The Pillow** (Locklin)	3:00
11	**Hold On To God** (Yoakam)	3:14

Jane's Addiction
Nothing's Shocking (1988)

Label | Warner Bros.
Producer | Perry Farrell • Dave Jerden
Art Direction | Perry Farrell • Casey Niccoli
Nationality | USA
Running Time | 45:13

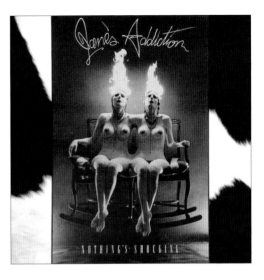

-By the late 1980s, mainstream American rock was dominated by spandex and hairspray clones who were neither heavy nor metal. Meanwhile, underground bands like Sonic Youth made little commercial impact. *Nothing's Shocking* managed to appeal to both camps, paving the way for MTV's partial embrace of "alternative" music and the success of Nirvana.

Jane's Addiction had already caught the attention of L.A. scenesters with 1987's self-titled debut, an independently released live set suggesting that psychosexual flamboyance and vaulting ambition did not die with Led Zeppelin. Their major-label follow-up catapulted singer/lyricist Perry Farrell, guitar god Dave Navarro, versatile bassist Eric Avery, and virtuoso drummer Stephen Perkins into the hearts of freaks across the nation. The aptly titled "Ocean Size" displays their superhuman prowess, its arena-ready dynamism enhanced by environmentally themed verses and a nuanced, widescreen production. "Ted, Just Admit It ..." fuses post-punk lope, funky riffage, and tribal thunder to juxtapose serial killer Ted Bundy with media coverage, while molten hard rockers "Mountain Song" and "Pigs In Zen" are instantly anthemic and energizing.

The group reveal their dreamy side with the slow-release psychedelia of "Summertime Rolls" and acoustic beauty "Jane Says"—a bittersweet portrait of drug addiction demonstrating that Farrell's nasal, echo-laden wail can handle empathy as well as outrage. Finally, rock 'n' roll was dangerous again. **MA**

Track Listing

	01	**Up The Beach** (Avery•Farrell•Navarro•Perkins)	3:00
▶	02	**Ocean Size** (Avery•Farrell•Navarro•Perkins)	4:20
	03	**Had A Dad** (Avery•Farrell•Navarro•Perkins)	3:44
▶	04	**Ted, Just Admit It ...** (Avery•Farrell•Navarro•Perkins)	7:23
	05	**Standing In The Shower ... Thinking** (Avery•Farrell•Navarro•Perkins)	3:03
▶	06	**Summertime Rolls** (Avery•Farrell•Navarro•Perkins)	6:18
▶	07	**Mountain Song** (Avery•Farrell•Navarro•Perkins)	4:03
	08	**Idiots Rule** (Avery•Farrell•Navarro•Perkins)	3:00
▶	09	**Jane Says** (Avery•Farrell•Navarro•Perkins)	4:52
	10	**Thank You Boys** (Avery•Farrell•Navarro•Perkins)	1:00
▶	11	**Pigs In Zen** (Avery•Farrell•Navarro•Perkins)	4:30

Public Enemy | It Takes A Nation Of Millions To Hold Us Back (1988)

Label | Def Jam
Producer | Various
Art Direction | Glen E. Friedman
Nationality | USA
Running Time | 57:50

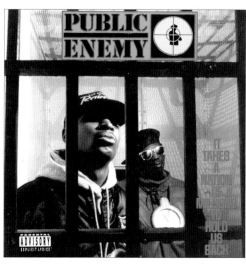

Music's worst nightmare—Public Enemy—are noise's best friend. For all *Nation's* epochal slogans, thumping funk, and political rage, the thing that impales itself in the brain is a strangled squeaky sample. Like a mouse with a trumpet, it scampers from cut to cut, but never wears thin. Chuck D. conjured up the sample at home: "My mother said, What the fuck are you doing? Is there a kettle in that record?" Inspired by hip-hop godfathers KRS-One and Eric B., he knew Public Enemy had to raise their game from 1987's bare-boned *Yo! Bum Rush the Show.*

So brilliantly did he succeed that *Nation* is still regarded as rap's finest hour. And so explosive are the songs that Public Enemy had to include instrumental interludes to provide shelter from the storm (one, "Security Of The First World," is echoed in Madonna's "Justify My Love"). Every other cut is a highlight. "Don't Believe The Hype" became an international catchphrase. "She Watch Channel Zero?!" is a landmark on the rap-rock road to Rage Against The Machine. "Night Of The Living Baseheads" and "Rebel Without A Pause" are whirlwinds of bleeps and bass and James Brown. "Cold Lampin' With Flavor" is an irrepressible showcase for Chuck's sidekick Flavor Flav. And "Black Steel," with its prison theme, is a heart-stopping epic.

Nation defies summary. In the words of the quote—originally a reference to boxer and "original gangsta" Jack Johnson—that opens "Bring The Noise," it is "too black, too strong." Its sound and fury signify so much—but you can dance to it too. **BM**

Track Listing

01	Countdown To Armageddon	(Public Enemy)	1:40
▶ 02	Bring The Noise	(Public Enemy)	3:45
▶ 03	Don't Believe The Hype	(Public Enemy)	5:19
04	Cold Lampin' With Flavor	(Public Enemy)	4:17
05	Terminator X To The Edge Of Panic (Public Enemy)		4:31
06	Mind Terrorist	(Public Enemy)	1:21
07	Louder Than A Bomb	(Public Enemy)	3:37
08	Caught, Can We Get A Witness	(Public Enemy)	4:53
09	Show 'Em Whatcha Got	(Public Enemy)	1:56
10	She Watch Channel Zero?!	(Public Enemy)	3:49
11	Night Of The Living Baseheads	(Public Enemy)	3:14
12	Black Steel In The Hour Of Chaos (Public Enemy)		6:23
13	Security Of The First World	(Public Enemy)	1:20
▶ 14	Rebel Without A Pause	(Public Enemy)	5:02
15	Prophets Of Rage	(Public Enemy)	3:18
16	Party For Your Right To Fight	(Public Enemy)	3:25

Faith No More | The Real Thing (1989)

Label | Slash
Producer | Faith No More • Matt Wallace
Art Direction | Jeff Price
Nationality | USA
Running Time | 54:58

Faith No More's third album emerged out of volatility. Formed as a post-punk outfit in 1982, the San Francisco quintet fired hard-drinking vocalist Chuck Mosley. His replacement was Mike Patton, a handsome 20-year-old from Eureka in Northern California, who possessed a multioctave range and a twisted way with words.

The new frontman proved inspirational. *The Real Thing* is diverse yet polished, ranging from mock-horror thrash attack "Surprise! You're Dead!" to queasy lounge ballad "Edge Of The World," via the title track's prog-rock convulsions and thunderous, eastern-toned instrumental "Woodpecker From Mars."

There were three memorable singles. "From Out Of Nowhere" is a driving love song garnished with a nagging riff from keyboardist Roddy Bottum, while the syncopated pop of "Falling To Pieces" showcases the funky chops of bassist Bill Gould and drummer Mike Bordin. The big hit—No. 9 in the United States—was MTV favorite "Epic": a dramatic pocket symphony featuring rapped verses, singalong chorus, Jim Martin's searing lead guitar, and a stately piano finale.

Despite their popularity with metal fans, Faith No More never liked the genre, and returned three years later with the wonderfully bizarre *Angel Dust*. Nevertheless, *The Real Thing* would be a touchstone record for nu-metal acts such as Korn and Limp Bizkit, who offered crude, humorless versions of its nuanced fusion. Patton, in particular, has been scornful of these followers. Today, he is a celebrated denizen of pop's left field, collaborating with Björk, avant-jazz icon John Zorn, and hip-hop maverick Dan The Automator. **MA**

> "We'd always been an alternative band, so it was a new place to go."
>
> Bill Gould, 1994

Track Listing

▶	01	**From Out Of Nowhere** (Faith No More)	3:20
▶	02	**Epic** (Faith No More)	4:51
▶	03	**Falling To Pieces** (Faith No More)	5:12
	04	**Surprise! You're Dead!** (Faith No More)	2:25
	05	**Zombie Eaters** (Faith No More)	5:58
▶	06	**The Real Thing** (Faith No More)	8:11
	07	**Underwater Love** (Faith No More)	3:49
	08	**The Morning After** (Faith No More)	3:41
▶	09	**Woodpecker From Mars** (Faith No More)	5:38
	10	**War Pigs** (Iommi • Ward • Butler • Osbourne)	7:43
▶	11	**Edge Of The World** (Faith No More)	4:10

Lenny Kravitz | Let Love Rule (1989)

Label | Virgin
Producer | Lenny Kravitz
Art Direction | Jeffrey Kent Ayeroff
Nationality | USA
Running Time | 55:27

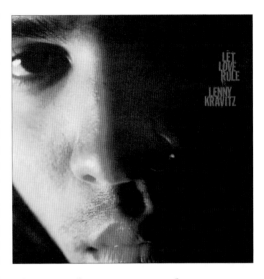

The ink was barely dry on Lenny Kravitz's first recording contract with Virgin in 1989 when he started fighting for his artistic freedom. The newcomer—who had only just abandoned his Prince-inspired act "Romeo Blue"— had a bold vision and was not willing to compromise.

When Kravitz started recording at Waterfront Studios in New Jersey, he did so using only analog equipment, without the help of a producer, without a band, and without any programmable instruments. He raised even more eyebrows by having his girlfriend, Lisa Bonet of *The Cosby Show*, co-write "Fear" and "Rosemary," as Virgin were supposedly concerned that she might become Lenny's own Yoko Ono ("in the negative sense," Kravitz bitterly stated in interviews).

But, as it turned out, there was nothing to worry about. The 13 soulful, retro-sounding funk and rock 'n' roll tunes are honest and powerful and spoke to millions, even though, with their theme of love, they do not capture the zeitgeist of the late 1980s at all.

The critics were quick to suggest that Kravitz's sound was derivative: the guitars sounded like Hendrix, the simple drum patterns brought to mind Ringo Starr, and the horn arrangements were influenced by Motown. But hardly anyone could deny that this debut is a strong and spirited statement. Kravitz's songwriting is superb, his gospel-schooled vocal delivery passionate and his courage to counter his mainstream-friendly hooks with wonderfully obscure moments of psychedelia and extended improvisation unmatched. If *Let Love Rule* had been conceived in 1969, then there would be no debating its classic status. **CL**

> ## "9 out of 10 groups that came out in '89 are gone. I'm still here."
>
> Lenny Kravitz, 1998

Track Listing

▶	01	Sittin' On Top Of The World (Kravitz)	3:16
▶	02	Let Love Rule (Kravitz)	5:42
	03	Freedom Train (Kravitz)	2:50
	04	My Precious Love (Kravitz)	5:15
	05	I Build This Garden For Us (Kravitz)	6:16
▶	06	Fear (Bonet·Kravitz)	5:25
	07	Does Anybody Out There Even Care (Kravitz)	3:42
▶	08	Mr. Cab Driver (Kravitz)	3:49
	09	Rosemary (Bonet·Kravitz)	5:27
	10	Be (Kravitz)	3:16
	11	Blues For Sister Someone (Kravitz)	2:51
	12	Empty Hands (Kravitz)	4:42
	13	Flower Child (Kravitz)	2:56

John Lee Hooker | The Healer (1989)

Label | Chameleon
Producer | Jim Gaines • Roy Rogers • Carlos Santana
Art Direction | Brandon Lively
Nationality | USA
Running Time | 41:18

John Lee Hooker was a major force in blues and R&B from the late 1940s through the 1960s, but the man who taught the public how to go "Boom Boom" did not make much noise in the 1970s and '80s. With a little help from his friends, however, John Lee Hooker instrumented a major comeback in 1989 with *The Healer*.

The album's title referred to the healing powers of the blues and it certainly healed Hooker's ailing career very quickly. It scooped a Grammy and sparked new interest in him and his work that would last through his death in 2001. Some of that should be credited to the featured guest list, which included Carlos Santana and Bonnie Raitt, but nobody boogied harder on this record than John Lee.

The Healer is built upon some truly inspired guitar work, starting with Santana's escalating leads on the Latin-flavored title track. Santana can sound pretty stale at times but his playing here is fluid and well suited to Hooker's lowly moaned lyrics. Raitt is the perfect companion on the grinding "I'm In The Mood," adding sexy slide guitar to Hooker's regular one-note rhythmic attack on hard times. Robert Cray breaks through the polish so convincingly with "Baby Lee" that one wishes he would only record with the legend in the house. Hooker reunites with Canned Heat on "Cuttin' Out." This was the formidable pairing that had produced the monster *Hooker 'n' Heat* in 1970.

Hooker alone closes shop with a trio of Mississippi-muddy numbers. The album's achingly beautiful final track, "No Substitute," serves as a fitting reminder that there was only one true Boogie Man. **JiH**

> "You look at John and you realize that there will never be another like him ... "
>
> B. B. King, 1993

Track Listing

▶ 01	**The Healer** (Hooker•Rogers•Santana•Thompson)	5:36
▶ 02	**I'm In The Mood** (Besman•Hooker)	4:30
▶ 03	**Baby Lee** (Bracken•Hooker)	3:43
04	**Cuttin' Out** (Hooker)	4:35
05	**Think Twice Before You Go** (Hooker)	2:58
06	**Sally Mae** (Hooker)	3:15
07	**That's Alright** (Hooker)	4:23
▶ 08	**Rockin' Chair** (Hooker)	4:09
09	**My Dream** (Hooker)	4:02
▶ 10	**No Substitute** (Hooker)	4:07

New Order | Technique (1989)

Label | Factory
Producer | New Order
Art Direction | Peter Saville
Nationality | UK
Running Time | 39:58

Three British rock records encapsulate the spirit of the acid house phenomenon that swept the UK at the end of the 1980s: Happy Mondays' *Bummed*; The Stone Roses' eponymous debut; and *Technique*, New Order's finest record. All three originated in Manchester.

When acid house exploded in Ibiza, New Order were already there attempting to record their fifth album. After what amounted to a hedonistic extended holiday, they returned to the UK with just 12 rhythm tracks and a guitar solo. However, after finishing the work off at Peter Gabriel's Real World studios, it soon became apparent that their time in Ibiza had not been wasted.

Technique is a masterpiece of the times. Opener "Fine Time," recorded immediately after clubbing all night, featured a surreal Barry White vocal pastiche over frenetic acid rhythms; "Round & Round" was Detroit techno, Salford style. Elsewhere, tracks such as "Love Less" and "Mr Disco" electronics perfectly complement Balearic acoustica, and while Bernard Sumner's lyrics documented his recent marriage breakup, New Order's trademark introspective gloom and dourness were replaced by beach sunsets and ecstasy.

The genre-defining *Technique* deservedly entered the UK chart at No. 1. With the rising popularity of Manchester's legendary Haçienda club—co-owned and almost entirely financed by the band—and the emergence of acid classics such as A Guy Called Gerald's "Voodoo Ray" and 808 State's "Pacific State," New Order and Madchester (as the music scene based around the city briefly became known) were at the forefront of the UK's biggest musical revolution since punk. **CSh**

> ## "We were heavily influenced by Ibiza, but not to the point we did any work."
>
> Stephen Morris, 1993

Track Listing

	#	Title		Time
▶	01	**Fine Time** (Gilbert•Hook•Morris•Sumner)		4:43
	02	**All The Way** (Gilbert•Hook•Morris•Sumner)		3:25
▶	03	**Love Less** (Gilbert•Hook•Morris•Sumner)		3:04
▶	04	**Round And Round** (Gilbert•Hook•Morris•Sumner)		4:32
	05	**Guilty Partner** (Gilbert•Hook•Morris•Sumner)		4:48
	06	**Run** (Gilbert•Hook•Morris•Sumner)		4:32
▶	07	**Mr Disco** (Gilbert•Hook•Morris•Sumner)		4:21
	08	**Vanishing Point** (Gilbert•Hook•Morris•Sumner)		5:18
	09	**Dream Attack** (Gilbert•Hook•Morris•Sumner)		5:15

Madonna | Like A Prayer (1989)

Label | Sire
Producer | Pat Leonard • Madonna
Art Direction | Margo Chase • Jeri Heiden
Nationality | USA
Running Time | 50:57

Beneath the burning crosses for which it is remembered lurks the most spectacular pop album since *Revolver*.

For sales commensurate with her fame, Madonna need only have churned out reruns of *True Blue*. Instead, she and producer Pat Leonard conceived a masterpiece that had even Peter Gabriel applauding its tunefulness.

Abdicating the dance market to Paula Abdul and Janet Jackson, Madonna restricted key collaborator Stephen "Into The Groove" Bray to two tracks. Among the casualties was the breathtaking "Supernatural," which eventually turned up on the AIDS benefit album *Red Hot And Dance*. In its place were tributes to Simon And Garfunkel ("Oh Father") and Sly And The Family Stone ("Keep It Together"), plus triumphant evocations of Sixties soul, both Staxy ("Express Yourself") and Spectorish ("Cherish").

The influence of Prince paid off not only on the duet "Love Song" (the sole product of a much-discussed musical by the pair), but also the crazed guitar on "Act Of Contrition," the psychedelia of "Dear Jessie," and the prevailing mix of sex and God (a cocktail too potent for Pepsi, who dumped a promotional tie-in).

Lyrically, the album replaced bratty avarice with humanity. "Express Yourself" is a call to arms with more on its mind than "Material Girl," while it is a family affair on "Promise To Try" (subject: the late Mrs. Ciccone), "Dear Jessie" (Pat Leonard's daughter), and "Keep It Together" ("Home Is Where The Heart Should Be"). Most startlingly, "Till Death Do Us Part" documents her alleged "night of terror" at the hands of Sean Penn.

Maturity has never sounded more fun. **BM**

> ## "This album is dedicated to my mother who taught me how to pray."
>
> Madonna, 1989

Track Listing

▶	01	**Like A Prayer** (Leonard•Madonna)	5:39
	02	**Express Yourself** (Bray•Madonna)	4:37
	03	**Love Song** (Madonna•Prince)	4:52
	04	**Till Death Do Us Part** (Leonard•Madonna)	5:16
	05	**Promise To Try** (Leonard•Madonna)	3:36
▶	06	**Cherish** (Leonard•Madonna)	5:03
	07	**Dear Jessie** (Leonard•Madonna)	4:20
▶	08	**Oh Father** (Leonard•Madonna)	4:57
	09	**Keep It Together** (Bray•Madonna)	5:03
	10	**Spanish Eyes** (Leonard•Madonna)	5:15
	11	**Act Of Contrition** (Leonard•Madonna)	2:19

Queen Latifah
All Hail The Queen (1989)

Label | Tommy Boy
Producer | Queen Latifah
Art Direction | Steven Miglio
Nationality | USA
Running Time | 63:35

Hip-hop artists often announce their arrival as something akin to the Second Coming. Following protocol, Queen Latifah certainly was not bashful with the title of her debut, *All Hail The Queen*. Yet, this album did indeed represent a pivotal moment in the rap game. Here, Latifah would help bounce the stigma surrounding female rappers and set the stage for TLC, Destiny's Child, and other independent women to follow.

Showing the type of can-do attitude that would color her entire career, the New Jersey rapper born Dana Owens shared production chores on *All Hail The Queen*—and thereby made damn sure the debut would serve as a proper introduction. Latifah's 1988 single "Wrath Of My Madness" had been a knockout, and the end product certainly proved worthy of the hype.

The album starts confidently with the funky rump-shaker "Dance For Me," which boasts some Maceo Parker-worthy saxophone. De La Soul join the party with the uproarious "Mama Gave Birth To The Soul Children" and Quasar helps extend the inviting "Come Into My House." The rapper then convincingly lays down "Latifah's Law" and returns to her first success with the irresistible "Wrath Of My Madness."

It failed to crack the Billboard Top 100—though her third album, *Black Reign*, would be the first gold record for a female rapper—but it was an awesome opener. In the years to follow, Latifah would pursue an Oprah-worthy multimedia career that peaked with her Oscar-nominated role in 2002's *Chicago*. **JiH**

Spacemen 3
Playing With Fire (1989)

Label | Fire
Producer | Peter Kember • Jason Pierce
Art Direction | Tundra
Nationality | UK
Running Time | 46:47

One of the most innovative guitar bands of the 1980s, Spacemen 3 formed in 1982. Jason Pierce and Peter "Sonic Boom" Kember met at college and were, strangely enough, born on the same day (November 19, 1965).

Early releases, including the commendable *Perfect Prescription* (1987), were influenced by Kember's fixation with The Cramps, Pierce's Stooges obsession, and a mutual love of Suicide and The Velvet Underground, but found few admirers. Then, the original rhythm section were replaced by bassist Will Carruthers (and an unnamed drummer) and things started to happen.

The repetitive Stooges-style guitar onslaught of the single "Revolution" (a call for drug legalization) saw the music media sit up and take notice. Generally, though, it was the blissed-out psychedelia on *Playing With Fire* that hooked listeners. The band's earlier psychotic guitar assaults had been replaced by Kember's hypnotic minimalism and whispered prose, particularly on the trance-like "Honey." Meanwhile Pierce's growing interest in spiritual and gospel music manifests itself on the beautiful "Lord Can You Hear Me?" The album also saw the pair beginning to write apart, their only co-composition "Suicide" was a 10-minute feedback-and-effects-ridden tribute to the band of the same name.

The album received instant critical acclaim, though it failed to chart in the UK. Pierce (and Carruthers) would go on to form Spiritualized and Kember to record as Spectrum. But as a testament to two unique talents, *Playing With Fire* is unsurpassable. **CSh**

Firehose
Fromohio (1989)

Label | SST
Producer | Ed Crawford • George Hurley • Mike Watt
Art Direction | Ed Crawford
Nationality | USA
Running Time | 31:13

By the time Firehose checked in with their third album, they had firmly established their sound. Retaining the chaotically funky rhythm work of The Minutemen, the former band of bassist Mike Watt and drummer George Hurley, Firehose opted for a more conventional approach to their muscular indie rock, tempered by guitarist/vocalist Ed Crawford's penchant for folky prettiness. That sound—raging guitar, frantic rhythm work, and acoustic beauty—found its expression in *Fromohio*.

The band tempers its rumbling, energetic attack on the lovely folk standard "Vastopol," where Crawford really shines. Opener "Riddle Of The Eighties" is the sound of writer Mike Watt taking stock of where he had been and laying out a statement of purpose for where Firehose were going. The lyrical nod to late Minutemen guitarist D. Boon in the line "Listening, whistling, missing that other dude" is set off with the reason for picking up and carrying on; "So I kept running and did the job—others counting on my clues." "Time With You" and "Mas Cajones" show the band in their best light, all passion and power. Drummer George Hurley puts in a couple of brief solo drum spots, made bearable not only by their brevity but also by the inventiveness of his ass-whupping swing. The odd waltz time of "Liberty For Our Friend," meanwhile, shows a band with a continuing restless musical spirit.

Nirvana's commercial breakthrough loomed just around the corner. This blast of punk-influenced indie rock, made with passion and conviction, was a signpost to the changes ahead. **JW**

Beastie Boys
Paul's Boutique (1989)

Label | Capitol
Producer | Various
Art Direction | Nathaniel Hornblower
Nationality | USA
Running Time | 63:03

Following the phenomenal global impact of their debut album *Licenced To Ill*, the Beasties were faced with what critics determined would be their "difficult second album." After the riotous reception their frat-house stylings and outrageous stage performances had received, not to mention the thousands of VW insignia across the globe removed by their fans, the band left their native New York for L.A. Having split with their label Def Jam, the group was now keen to move on musically from *Licensed To Ill* and chose to work with Californian production duo The Dust Brothers.

The sheer number and range of samples on this album is unrivaled, aside from De La Soul's *3 Feet High And Rising*. It was also the last "big" album to be produced with uncleared samples, and the producers were able to draw from elements as diverse as Curtis Mayfield, Led Zeppelin, The Beatles, and The Ramones.

The energy and insouciance displayed on the album, especially on tracks such as "The Sounds Of Science," "Looking Down The Barrel Of A Gun," and "Egg Man," displayed their musical and lyrical development, while "Shake Your Rump," "Hey Ladies," and "To All The Girls" left no doubt that the Beasties still knew exactly where the party was at.

The album was the perfect stepping stone from the band's punk origins to the more sophisticated output of later albums—it also captures the band at their most delicate, while still mainstream. It may be an overlooked classic, but it can still rock the party every time. **CR**

The Young Gods
L'Eau Rouge (1989)

Label | Play It Again Sam
Producer | Roli Mosimann
Art Direction | The Young Gods
Nationality | Switzerland
Running Time | 41:10

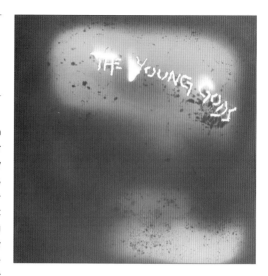

The eight-minute-long album opener "La Fille De La Mort" marks The Young Gods out as a cut above your average industrial band. For starters, it must be the only song in the genre to be recorded in waltz time, employing boulevardier-style samples of Weimar-esque accordions before building through a psychedelic whirlwind of orchestral noise into a pizzicato string loop underpinned by crashing drum patterns. (They would explore their fascination with the music of pre-war Berlin further on 1991's *The Young Gods Play Kurt Weill*.) But the more esoteric moments here are balanced out by the furious Ministry-esque bombast of "Longue Route" and "L'Amourir," the latter originally a stand-alone single and only added to later reissues of the album. On tracks such as "Crier Les Chiens," frontman Franz Treichler uses his voice as an instrument in its own right, his screeching and screaming at times resembling bird call—a technique much aped by black metal bands years later.

The band take their name from a track by The Swans, and it was by a happy piece of wish fulfillment that the Gods persuaded Michael Gira associate Roli Mosimann to take charge of the production. Instead of taking the route favored by many industrial bands of the time of turning everything up to 11, Mosimann, created acres of space for the intricate drumming and pulsing guitars to build up in layers.

The cover features the YG logo of three cave painting stickmen, against a blood-red background. **JDo**

> ## "There were a lot of question marks hanging over what we were doing."
>
> Franz Treichler, 1998

Track Listing

▶ 01	**La Fille De La Mort** (The Young Gods)	7:58
02	**Rue Des Tempêtes** (The Young Gods)	2:51
03	**L'Eau Rouge** (The Young Gods)	4:20
04	**Charlotte** (The Young Gods)	2:01
05	**Longue Route** (The Young Gods)	3:41
▶ 06	**Crier Les Chiens** (The Young Gods)	3:15
07	**Ville Notre** (The Young Gods)	4:07
08	**Les Enfants** (The Young Gods)	5:53
▶ 09	**L'Amourir** (The Young Gods)	4:18
10	**Pas Mal** (The Young Gods)	2:46

John Zorn | Spy Vs. Spy — The Music Of Ornette Coleman (1989)

Label | Nonesuch
Producer | John Zorn
Art Direction | Mark Beyer
Nationality | USA
Running Time | 40:32

More of a radical deconstruction of Ornette Coleman's songbook than an "in the tradition" homage, *Spy Vs. Spy* established John Zorn as a master of "unremittingly violent" improvisation. He, like Coleman before him, saw collective rather than autonomous improvisation as the Holy Grail. And with that mission in mind, the alto saxophonist and his crew of hip young New York City collaborators set about shattering the jazz cement to map their very own "Shape Of Jazz To Come."

This is jazz as volcanically shape-shifting game play, with saxophones trading discordant blows in separate stereo-channeled shrieks (Zorn, right, vs. Tim Berne, left) over a panoply of dueling drum (Joey Baron vs. Michael Vatcher) and bass (Mark Dresser) dissonance. Annoying tomfoolery intended to alienate sycophantic jazz purists? Maybe so, but after imploding bebop's chord-running pyrotechnics into the thrash-jazz minimalism of "Word For Bird," the collective proceeds to genre-mash blues, swing, free jazz, and Ornette's infamous harmolodic theories into something else altogether. "Rejoicing" and "Peace Warriors" shock and awe listeners into decoding tonal frequencies previously only heard in speed metal or the collage cartoon compositions of Carl Stalling.

Cartoons resurface in Mark Beyer's cover artwork, which is playfully in tune with the album's rampant anti-jazz establishment drive. Welcome to jazz for the post-punk generation. As Zorn's own liner notes broadcast: "Fucking hardcore rules." **MK**

Track Listing

01	**WRU** (Coleman)	2:38
02	**Chronology** (Coleman)	1:08
▶ 03	**Word For Bird** (Coleman)	1:14
04	**Good Old Days** (Coleman)	2:44
05	**The Disguise** (Coleman)	1:18
06	**Enfant** (Coleman)	2:37
▶ 07	**Rejoicing** (Coleman)	1:38
08	**Blues Connotation** (Coleman)	1:05
09	**C And D** (Coleman)	3:05
10	**Chippie** (Coleman)	1:08
▶ 11	**Peace Warriors** (Coleman)	1:20
12	**Ecars** (Coleman)	2:28
13	**Feet Music** (Coleman)	4:45
14	**Broadway Blues** (Coleman)	3:42
15	**Space Church** (Coleman)	2:28
16	**Zig Zag** (Coleman)	2:54
▶ 17	**Mob Job** (Coleman)	4:20

The Stone Roses | The Stone Roses (1989)

Label | Silvertone
Producer | John Leckie
Art Direction | John Squire
Nationality | UK
Running Time | 48:32

Despite their gothic moniker (and origins), The Stone Roses became synonymous with a burgeoning ecstasy scene in their hometown of Manchester, innovatively fusing dance and rock (a reflection of their influences, past and present) along with the Happy Mondays.

The sleeve artwork, inspired by both Jackson Pollock and the Paris student riots of 1968 (rioters sucked lemons to ward off the effects of tear gas), was painted by guitarist John Squire, and his masterful guitar laces the album as freely as the paint that splatters the sleeve. "Bye Bye Badman" references the 1968 riots and—along with "Elizabeth My Dear" ("Scarborough Fair" rewritten as an antimonarchy ballad)—displays the Roses' often-overlooked anti-establishment stance.

Never overstated, always essential, Squire's playing is often considered the backbone of the album. Yet special mention should also go to drummer Alan "Reni" Wren, whose smooth and accurate backing harmonies on "Bye Bye Badman" and breathtaking, spontaneous fills on the epic "I Am The Resurrection" still charm and surprise to this day.

The energy and invention of the dreamlike "Waterfall" and its cousin "Don't Stop" (the same song, played backwards, with suitably adapted lyrics) captured the sense of optimism of the era following the birth of acid house and the UK's second summer of love.

The Stone Roses managed to sum up the seemingly free spirit of their era while simultaneously recalling the creative hotbed of Sixties rock and pop. That they inadvertently produced an album more than capable of standing up to that bygone era is a marvel. **JK**

"We're just a simple beat group, simple downtrodden folk."

Ian Brown, 1989

Track Listing

▶	01	**I Wanna Be Adored** (Brown·Squire)	4:52
▶	02	**She Bangs The Drums** (Brown·Squire)	3:42
▶	03	**Waterfall** (Brown·Squire)	4:37
	04	**Don't Stop** (Brown·Squire)	5:17
	05	**Bye Bye Badman** (Brown·Squire)	4:00
	06	**Elizabeth My Dear** (Brown·Squire)	0:59
	07	**Song For My Sugar Spun Sister** (Brown·Squire)	3:25
▶	08	**Made Of Stone** (Brown·Squire)	4:10
	09	**Shoot You Down** (Brown·Squire)	4:10
	10	**This Is The One** (Brown·Squire)	4:58
▶	11	**I Am The Resurrection** (Brown·Squire)	8:12

Neneh Cherry | Raw Like Sushi (1989)

Label | Circa
Producer | Cameron McVey
Art Direction | Jean Baptiste Mondino
Nationality | Sweden
Running Time | 46:07

"It's not a feminist record," Neneh Cherry told *Face* magazine in 1988 about her debut, ". . . but it's about female strength, female power, female attitude." So runs the agenda for the Neneh Cherry manifesto. A cover of a Morgan McVey B-side, "Buffalo Stance" introduced Cherry's trademark blend of popular urban styles, street-wise sweetness, and her pride in being a woman and mother. These motifs permeate the album, co-written and produced by partner Boogie Bear (Cameron McVey, producer of Massive Attack's *Blue Lines*).

An early nomad, she traveled extensively with her mother, Swedish artist Moki and famous jazz trumpeter stepfather Don Cherry. But it was at 15 that Cherry first visited West Africa with her birth father, Sierra Leonese percussionist Amhadu Jah, and discovered the power of the maternal African woman. After spending time in New York with punk band The Slits, she moved to London in 1980 to play with jazz/funk hybrid Rip, Rig And Panic, and had her first child at 18 years old.

While tracks like "Heart" and "Phony Ladies" are scathing attacks on the fickleness of petty social and gender concerns, tracks like "Inna City Mamma" and "The Next Generation" pay homage to the independent, strong mother figure Cherry represents. She appeared on *Top Of The Pops* eight months pregnant (in skintight Lycra, no less), and featured her two month-old daughter Tyson in the clip for "Manchild." The album sold two and a half million copies, and through Cherry's charm, infectious melodies, and sweet voice it reaches a far wider audience than the individual genres she flirted with—hip hop, dance, rap, pop—usually allow. **AH-N**

"Pop...is just about making something that comes across in a simple way."

Neneh Cherry, 1992

Track Listing

▶ 01	**Buffalo Stance** (Bear·Cherry·Morgan·Ramacon)	5:42
▶ 02	**Manchild** (Bear·Cherry·Delnaja)	3:52
▶ 03	**Kisses On The Wind** (Bear·Cherry)	3:57
04	**Inna City Mamma** (Bear·Cherry·Chill)	4:51
05	**The Next Generation** (Bear·Cherry)	5:05
06	**Love Ghetto** (Bear·Cherry)	4:29
▶ 07	**Heart** (Bear·Cherry)	5:09
▶ 08	**Phoney Ladies** (Bear·Cherry)	3:54
09	**Outre Risque Locomotive** (Cherry·Malone)	5:05
10	**So Here I Come** (Bear·Cherry·Chill·New)	4:03

Baaba Maal And Mansour Seck
Djam Leelii (1989)

Label | Mango
Producer | Baaba Maal • Mansour Seck
Art Direction | Uncredited
Nationality | Senegal
Running Time | 52:50

Baaba Maal came from a family of fishermen in northern Senegal, and it was only because the family was prospering and he was doing well at school that his parents allowed him to have a part-time job singing. Change was in the air in the early 1970s, and the young Maal gained notice by singing about the frustrations of his audience. But it was only when he met Mansour Seck that being a professional musician became a real option. In West Africa, music belongs to families of griots, who use song to praise leaders and patrons and relate their histories. Seck is a griot but is also blind, and the relationship would be mutually beneficial: while he passed his knowledge on to Maal, the younger man would be his guide in many ways.

Maal and Seck left Senegal for France in the early 1980s, the former accepted into a Parisian conservatoire to study music. In 1984, along with some fellow West Africans, they recorded this informal, simple session— but it was as magical as bottled lightning. The two friends harmonizing with their yearning tenors while around them acoustic guitars mapped out simple, beguiling melodies, a solitary electric added frills, and simple percussion kept the beat. It was, said BBC Radio One's legendary DJ John Peel, like hearing Muddy Waters for the first time.

With the influences of his time in Europe providing a spur, Maal would go on to redefine African music's progressive nature, but it was with this album that he started opening doors. **DH**

> "A musician in Africa should be someone who educates. You can tell people their history."
>
> Baaba Maal, 2004

Track Listing

▶	01	Lam Tooro (Maal)	6:38
▶	02	Loodo (Maal)	6:08
	03	Muudo Hormo (Maal)	6:13
	04	Salm Inanam (Maal)	4:25
	05	Maacina Tooro (Maal)	5:47
▶	06	Djam Leelii (Maal)	6:00
▶	07	Bibbe Leydy (Maal)	6:25
	08	Sehilam (Maal)	6:21
	09	Kettodee (Maal)	4:53

Kate Bush | The Sensual World (1989)

Label | EMI
Producer | Kate Bush
Art Direction | Kindlight • Bill Smith Studio
Nationality | UK
Running Time | 42:03

THE SENSUAL WORLD · KATE BUSH

If 1985's *Hounds Of Love* saw Bush channel her adolescent high spirits for the last time, *The Sensual World* served as a coming of age. Having turned 30, she delivered her most rounded, mature album to date. She acknowledged her Irish heritage, taking inspiration both from the Celtic instrumentation, and, at least in the case of the title track, from James Joyce's most sensual of characters, Molly Bloom. There is a broader folk influence too, which is partly down to Bush's brother Paddy, a fan of ethnic music. It is he who introduced her to The Trio Bulgarka, traditional Bulgarian singers who appear throughout the album. Michael Nyman arranges strings on "Reaching Out"; Nigel Kennedy appears on "The Fog" and "Heads We're Dancing"; Dave Gilmour plays on "Love And Anger" and "Rocket's Tail." Even her father, credited as Dr. Bush, contributes spoken word dialog to "The Fog," a song nominally about a parent teaching their child to swim—symbolism that is not hard to decipher. (An additional track, "Walk Straight Down The Middle," featured on the CD.)

Although champions of her teenage spectral keening might have wished she had remained forever young, Kate breaks new ground, welcoming an era where global influences are paired with computerized proficiency. There is a distinct quality of womanly sexuality to *The Sensual World* too, as well as an attempt to address an audience outside of her Kentish back yard. Whereas once she sounded as if she was happiest playing organ in the barn behind her parents' house, here she sings as a fully accomplished recording artist ready for international success. **ARa**

> "Growing up for most people is just trying to stop escaping ...But I'm not sure if people ever grow up properly."
>
> Kate Bush, 1989

Track Listing

▶ 01	**The Sensual World** (Bush)	3:57
02	**Love And Anger** (Bush)	4:42
03	**The Fog** (Bush)	5:06
04	**Reaching Out** (Bush)	3:12
05	**Heads We're Dancing** (Bush)	5:21
▶ 06	**Deeper Understanding** (Bush)	4:46
07	**Between A Man And A Woman** (Bush)	3:30
08	**Never Be Mine** (Bush)	3:44
▶ 09	**Rocket's Tail** (Bush)	4:07
10	**This Woman's Work** (Bush)	3:38

The Cure | Disintegration (1989)

Label | Fiction
Producer | David M. Allen • Robert Smith
Art Direction | Parched Art
Nationality | UK
Running Time | 60:29

The Cure never expected to become pop stars. But pretty hits such as "Just Like Heaven" tempered their squalling diatribes and ushered them from the shadows to the charts.

Disintegration, however, aimed for a more cohesive sound. The result, said *Q* magazine, is like "being enveloped by a waterlogged and extremely capacious overcoat." Indeed, "Prayers For Rain" and "The Same Deep Water As You" are the sob-fests their titles suggest. But it is not all doom and gloom.

Just kidding. It is doom and gloom-a-go-go. Surreal ("Lullaby"), romantically ravaged ("Plainsong"), violent ("Disintegration")—but always, as *NME* enthused, "thrillingly miserable." They had hits too, the biggest being "Lovesong," a wedding gift from Smith to his fiancée Mary.

Amid the despair, bassist Simon Gallup and former Thompson Twins drummer Boris Williams rumble impressively, notably on "Fascination Street" (about Bourbon Street, the wild heart of New Orleans' French quarter). Guitarist Porl Thompson is never far away, and was later in the touring incarnation of the "Lullaby"—covering Plant and Page. Keyboardist Roger O'Donnell is a constant; Lol Tolhurst having been sidelined (a terse credit reduces him to "other instrument").

"I was worried about getting older," remembered lyricist Robert Smith, then approaching 30. Similar anxieties a decade later fueled the *Disintegration*-esque *Bloodflowers*—a lineage that was confirmed by 2003's in-concert DVD *Trilogy*, which unites the albums with their spiritual predecessor, *Pornography*. **BM**

Track Listing

01	**Plainsong** (Gallup•O'Donnell•Smith Thompson•Tolhurst•Williams)	5:16
02	**Pictures Of You** (Gallup•O'Donnell•Smith Thompson•Tolhurst•Williams)	7:28
03	**Closedown** (Gallup•O'Donnell•Smith Thompson•Tolhurst•Williams)	4:21
▶ 04	**Lovesong** (Gallup•O'Donnell•Smith Thompson•Tolhurst•Williams)	3:31
▶ 05	**Lullaby** (Gallup•O'Donnell•Smith Thompson•Tolhurst•Williams)	4:12
▶ 06	**Fascination Street** (Gallup•O'Donnell•Smith Thompson•Tolhurst•Williams)	5:17
07	**Prayers For Rain** (Gallup•O'Donnell•Smith Thompson•Tolhurst•Williams)	6:07
08	**The Same Deep Water As You** (Gallup O'Donnell•Thompson•Tolhurst•Williams)	9:23
09	**Disintegration** (Gallup•O'Donnell•Smith Thompson•Tolhurst•Williams)	8:24
10	**Untitled** (Gallup•O'Donnell•Smith Thompson•Tolhurst•Williams)	6:30

808 State | 808:90 (1989)

Label | ZTT
Producer | Uncredited
Art Direction | Ryan Art
Nationality | UK
Running Time | 39:12

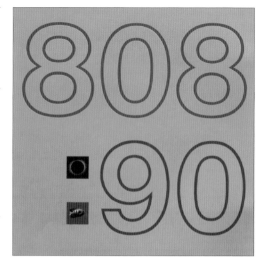

Is there something in the water in Manchester? Despite its unfounded bleak reputation, this British city has produced countless bands who have defined the pervading zeitgeist and gone on to be massively influential to other groups. In the world of dance music, 808 State (named after the Roland drum machine) rank as one of the defining and most influential groups of the early rave era. The Manchester-based trio consisted of Martin Price, Graham Massey, and Gerald Simpson (and later Andrew Barker and Darren Partington who replaced Simpson when he left to pursue a solo career as A Guy Called Gerald).

808:90, the group's third album, became one of the first pure dance albums to chart in the UK, representing a defining moment for the early UK rave scene. Combining the raw sounds of rave with a delicate, elegant sense of structure, melody, and mood, 808:90 was the sound of a unique and powerful sub-culture distilled for, arguably, the first time on a full-length LP. The album's two key songs are "Cubik" (featured only on U.S. pressings) and "Pacific"; the latter made the UK Top Ten and remains a sentimental anthem for the first rave generation today. The moving emotional content of "Pacific," with its soaring saxophone melody, is still as powerful and life-affirming as ever. "Cubik" was more of a dancefloor juggernaut, the brutal power of its instantly recognizable techno riff and rolling breakbeats still sound as potent as ever. 808 State's following album Ex:el was their biggest seller, but it was 808:90 that provided the acid house generation with the artistic validation they were previously denied. **APi**

> "It really did my head in when Guru Josh got to Spain first and got 17 weeks at number one when 'Pacific State' should've done it."
>
> Martyn Price, 1990

Track Listing

01	**Magical Dream** (808 State)		3:52
▶ 02	**Ancodia** (Uncredited)		5:47
▶ 03	**Cobra Bora** (808 State)		6:36
▶ 04	**Pacific 202** (Massey·Price·Simpson)		5:41
05	**Donkey Doctor** (808 State)		5:24
06	**80808080808** (808 State)		4:20
▶ 07	**Sunrise** (808 State)		6:33
08	**Fat Shadow** (Uncredited)		0:59

Coldcut | What's That Noise? (1989)

Label | Ahead Of Our Time
Producer | Coldcut
Art Direction | Mark Porter
Nationality | UK
Running Time | 44:54

Production duo Coldcut first came to prominence when former art teacher Jonathan More and computer programmer Matt Black unleashed "Say Kids, What Time Is It?" in 1987. Inspired by fellow sample terrorist Steinski, it was the first British sample collage record, leading to their innovative "Solid Steel" show on London's then pirate dance music station, Kiss FM. Following the equally inventive "Beats & Pieces" and DJ slots at the legendary Shoom club, they attracted widespread acclaim for their remix of Eric B & Rakim's "Paid In Full," ingeniously marrying the original to Israeli singer Ofra Haza's "Im Nin'alu."

With Amazonian vocalist Yazz, they achieved crossover success in February 1988 when the upbeat "Doctorin' The House" scaled the UK charts; it is reconstructed for the album into a sublime piece of Chicago-inspired acid house.

Other guest vocalists include the then relatively unknown Lisa Stansfield on the classy pop house of "People Hold On" and the twisted lyrical genius of Mark E. Smith on the dirge-like "(I'm) In Deep." The album's highlights include the funky "Smoke 1," later used on Queen Latifah's "Find A Way," and "Stop This Crazy Thing," which combined a dirty analog synth bassline with tribal rhythms and the impassioned vocal of Black Uhuru's Junior Reid.

Encompassing a broad cross-section of musical styles, *What's That Noise?* melds everything together with intriguing samples and effects. Its playful inventiveness paved the way for the formation of Coldcut's influential Ninja Tune label in the mid 1990s. **CSh**

"I'd like to work with The Doors, but it's a bit late now."

Matt Black, 1990

Track Listing

▶	01	People Hold On (Black•More•Stansfield)	3:58
	02	Fat (Party And Bullshit) (Black•More)	4:17
▶	03	(I'm) In Deep (Black•More•Smith)	5:08
	04	My Telephone (Black•Devaney•More Morris•Parry•Stansfield)	4:54
	05	Theme From "Reportage" (Black•More)	1:35
	06	Which Doctor? (Black•More)	4:30
▶	07	Stop This Crazy Thing (Black•More•Reid)	5:15
	08	No Connection (Black•More)	3:34
▶	09	Smoke 1 (Black•More)	4:40
▶	10	Doctorin' The House (Black•More•Yazz)	4:35
	11	What's That Noise? (Black• More)	2:28

Barry Adamson | Moss Side Story (1989)

Label | Mute
Producer | Barry Adamson
Art Direction | Barry Adamson
Nationality | UK
Running Time | 54:03

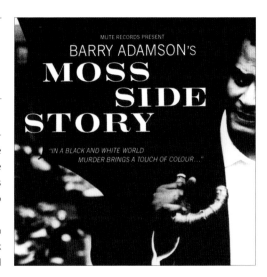

Barry Adamson made a name for himself in the UK post-punk scene as a first-rate bass player (with Magazine and the Bad Seeds). It was not until the end of the 1980s, though, that he stepped out as a solo artist. His first LP is an engaging, at times stunning, soundtrack to a movie that does not exist: *Moss Side Story*.

Named after the area of Manchester where Adamson grew up, the album is inspired by classic soundtrack composers such as John Barry—Magazine had covered Barry's Bond theme *Goldfinger*—and Ennio Morricone. A hefty dose of the post-punk sound and the avant garde also appears in the mix, recalling similar works by John Zorn.

Adamson took on the director's role for the project, conceiving the artwork, arranging the string parts, constructing sound effects, and playing most of the instruments. He also drafted in ex-colleagues Rowland S. Howard, Kid Congo Powers, and Mick Harvey, as well as avant divas Anita Lane and Diamanda Galas.

Moss Side Story's attraction lies in its well-conceived cinematic scope. Perhaps unsurprisingly, we are in the realm of film noir here, and the ambience throughout is therefore mostly dark and eerie, best sampled on tracks such as "Central Control," "Sounds From The Big House," and "The Swinging Detective." But Adamson does not constrain his vision purely to doom and gloom. "Under Wraps" is a "chase scene" piece in a peculiar lounge/bossa nova style, while "Everything Happens To Me" is a calm "love scene" piano ballad.

Adamson was to delve further into this genre, eventually providing music for genuine movies. **AET**

> ## "In a black and white world murder brings a touch of colour."
>
> Barry Adamson, 1989

Track Listing

01	**On The Wrong Side Of Relaxation** (Adamson)		5:26
▶ 02	**Under Wraps** (Adamson)		4:27
▶ 03	**Central Control** (Adamson)		2:16
04	**Round Up The Usual Suspects** (Adamson)		0:38
▶ 05	**Sounds From The Big House** (Adamson)		6:24
06	**Suck On The Honey Of Love** (Adamson)		2:13
▶ 07	**Everything Happens To Me** (Adamson)		2:42
▶ 08	**The Swinging Detective** (Adamson)		5:46
09	**Autodestruction** (Adamson)		3:49
10	**Intensive Care** (Adamson)		2:41
▶ 11	**The Most Beautiful Girl In The World** (Adamson)		4:08
12	**Free At Last** (Adamson)		1:23

Aerosmith | Pump (1989)

Label | Geffen
Producer | Bruce Fairbairn
Art Direction | Kim Champagne • Gabrielle Raumberger
Nationality | USA
Running Time | 47:39

"It is now taken for granted that Aerosmith was a great band," complained critic Dave Marsh in 1989. "Gimme a break or bring on the Nineties."

Talk about tempting fate. That November, Aerosmith unleashed a monster that mixed the vintage raunch of *Toys In The Attic* with the hook-packed eclecticism of *Pump*'s predecessor *Permanent Vacation*. And, well into 1990, they were inescapable: "Love In An Elevator," "Janie's Got A Gun," "What It Takes," and "The Other Side" stormed the Hot 100, helping the album to seven million U.S. sales.

Drug free by 1987, they had soared from the gutter with hits like "Angel." But they had leaned heavily on outside songwriters and were now determined to do things their own way.

At the time, rock was swamped with Aerosmith aficionados such as Bon Jovi, Guns N' Roses, and Mötley Crüe. Though Aerosmith collaborated with some of the same people, the results are completely different.

A more useful reference is Led Zeppelin, most obviously in the slamming riffs of " . . . Elevator" and "Voodoo Medicine Man." They also share Zeppelin's willingness to embrace elements outside hard rock, hence the delightful "Dulcimer Stomp" and sinister "Janie's Got A Gun".

Provisionally titled *Here's Looking Up Your Old Address*, the album was rechristened at Brad Whitford's behest. "*Pump*—what the fuck does that mean?" the guitarist recalled. "I don't know. It just seems very . . . Nineties." The result—clad in Norman Seeff's witty photograph—left the competition in the dust. **BM**

> "We just love to get up on stage and play."
>
> Joey Kramer, 1997

Track Listing

01	**Young Lust** (Perry • Tyler • Vallance)	4:20
02	**F.I.N.E. (Fucked Up, Insecure, Neurotic, Emotional)** (Child • Perry • Tyler)	4:06
▶ 03	**Going Down / Love In An Elevator** (Perry • Tyler)	5:41
04	**Monkey On My Back** (Perry • Tyler)	3:57
▶ 05	**Water Song / Janie's Got A Gun** (Hamilton • Tyler)	5:33
06	**Dulcimer Stomp / The Other Side** (Tyler • Vallance)	4:56
07	**My Girl** (Perry • Tyler)	3:10
08	**Don't Get Mad, Get Even** (Perry • Tyler)	4:48
09	**Hoodoo / Voodoo Medicine Man** (Tyler • Whitford)	4:39
▶ 10	**What It Takes** (Child • Perry • Tyler)	6:29

Pixies | Doolittle (1989)

Label | 4AD
Producer | Gil Norton
Art Direction | Vaughan Oliver
Nationality | USA
Running Time | 38:36

The influence of a new producer hits home from the opening bars of *Doolittle*. The clean bass notes that begin "Debaser" sing of a studio polish with which Steve Albini would hold no truck. Joey Santiago's wall of surf guitar and freakout solos are also given a cleaner sheen by Brit Gil Norton, while Kim Deal's vocal harmonies with Francis are allowed the time and space to shine. According to Santiago, Norton was a proponent of overdubbing, a process shunned by Albini on *Surfer Rosa*. The overall effect is to create a sublime pop album that launched the band from the pages of the British rock press and into the charts, spearheaded by a killer single in the form of "Monkey Gone To Heaven."

The same obsessions with old testament sin, physical destruction, and sexual deviance are filtered through Black Francis' lyrics, and in interviews at the time the songwriter acknowledged a debt to the movie director David Lynch, and particularly his keen sense of the surreal. Certainly, on *Doolittle*, the Pixies honed the technique of juxtaposing sparse bass, drums, and gentle vocal sections with buzzing, rushing swirls of guitar noise and gut-wrenching shrieks in fine surrealist style.

Indeed, it is almost impossible to separate *Doolittle* from *Surfer Rosa* in terms of quality, so sonically disparate are the two and so well have they both aged. *Doolittle* offers some sweeter numbers, in the form of "Here Comes Your Man" and "La La Love You" alongside the corrosive rock of "Wave Of Mutilation" and "Gouge Away." The only sensible answer is to listen to both again and again. **MBI**

"I'm just a college dropout …"

Black Francis, 1989

Track Listing

▶	01	**Debaser** (Francis)	2:52
	02	**Tame** (Francis)	1:55
▶	03	**Wave Of Mutilation** (Francis)	2:04
	04	**I Bleed** (Francis)	2:34
	05	**Here Comes Your Man** (Francis)	3:21
	06	**Dead** (Francis)	2:21
	07	**Monkey Gone To Heaven** (Francis)	2:56
▶	08	**Mr Grieves** (Francis)	2:05
	09	**Crackity Jones** (Francis)	1:24
▶	10	**La La Love You** (Francis)	2:43
	11	**Number 13 Baby** (Francis)	3:51
	12	**There Goes My Gun** (Francis)	1:49
	13	**Hey** (Francis)	3:31
	14	**Silver** (Deal·Francis)	2:25
▶	15	**Gouge Away** (Francis)	2:45

Bonnie Raitt | Nick Of Time (1989)

Label | Capitol
Producer | Don Was
Art Direction | Tommy Steele
Nationality | USA
Running Time | 42:31

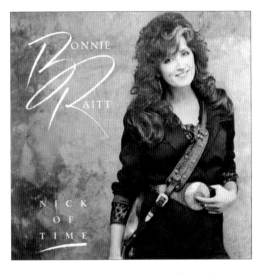

The title of Bonnie Raitt's ninth album, *Nine Lives*, seemed cruelly appropriate. A recording career that had been building slowly since 1971 indeed looked to be heading for the graveyard after that 1986 release failed to crack the Billboard Top 100 and Warner Bros. dropped her. Raitt, however, had at least one life left and she was certainly going to make it count with *Nick Of Time*.

Signing with Capitol Records, Raitt made what seemed like a curious decision to enlist producer Don Was, a man best known for crafting funky party anthems with The B-52's, to help flesh out her earthy mix of folk, blues, and rock. The gamble paid off: Was waxed Raitt's bluesy sound with an undeniably slick pop sensibility, in effect creating the template the singer is still following today.

The album opens with the cuddly title track, which smoothly sets heartache to a toe-tapping beat, and then charges ahead with "Thing Called Love," a rowdy tune that would fit easily on modern "new country" radio. Raitt honky-tonks her way through the powerful "Love Letter" and then brings it down for the mournful "Cry On My Shoulder."

Nick Of Time turned out to be Raitt's breakthrough, topping the charts, selling five million copies, and earning three Grammys in 1990 (the singer would win a fourth that year for a duet with Delbert McClinton). Raitt and Was would again collaborate on the follow-up, 1991's *Luck Of The Draw*, another blockbuster that would again win three Grammys and sell more than seven million copies. **JiH**

> ## "I'm still a bronco bull in the chute. I'm ready."
>
> Bonny Raitt, 2002

Track Listing

	#	Title	Writer	Time
▶	01	Nick Of Time	(Raitt)	3:52
▶	02	Thing Called Love	(Hiatt)	3:52
▶	03	Love Letter	(Hayes)	4:04
	04	Cry On My Shoulder	(Ruff)	3:44
	05	Real Man	(Williams)	4:27
	06	Nobody's Girl	(McNally)	3:14
▶	07	Have A Heart	(Hayes)	4:50
	08	Too Soon to Tell	(Bourke · Reid)	3:45
	09	I Will Not Be Denied	(Williams)	4:55
	10	I Ain't Gonna Let You Break My Heart Again (D. Lasley · J. Lasley)		2:38
	11	The Road's My Middle Name	(Raitt)	3:31

Fugazi | Repeater (1989)

Label | Dischord
Producer | Ted Niceley
Art Direction | Kurt Sayenga
Nationality | USA
Running Time | 35:09

If Minor Threat typified Ian McKaye's youthful rage, then Fugazi's *Repeater* balanced the idealism and sloganeering of his early suburban hardcore with an increasingly innovative and nuanced approach to anger. Sensing a move toward a more militant thug and jock mentality in the U.S. hardcore scene in the late 1980s, McKaye, the charismatic frontman of Minor Threat and co-founder of seminal Washington DC label Dischord, teamed up with former Rites Of Spring guitarist Guy Picciotto, Brendan Canty (drums), and Joe Lally (bass) to form Fugazi. *Repeater* was the document to distance them from the scene's hardliners.

Some detractors have often accused the band of "preaching," but the naive politics of early albums were absent from *Repeater*. The difference came in the tight rhythm section of Lally and Canty, which had a lot more prominence in the production. On songs such as "Sieve Fisted Find" and "Repeater," the juxtaposition of feedback and crisp basslines adds to the urgency of McKaye and Picciotto's dual vocal attack. "Greed" sounds like it could have come from a Gang Of Four record. The anger and emotion was still there, only now it was delivered in a sinewy, almost dub-like manner. The slower "Turnover," "Blueprint," and "Shut The Door" are ballad-like.

While their later work is almost art rock in comparison, the band have never ventured from their punk rock roots and staunch DIY business ethics—most of their shows are for all ages and less than $7. *Repeater* marks Fugazi's growth from angry young punks to challenging and innovative musicians. **TSc**

> "We owe you nothing. You have no control. You are not what you own."

Ian McKaye, 1989

Track Listing

01	**Turnover** (Fugazi)	4:16
▶ 02	**Repeater** (Fugazi)	3:01
03	**Brendan #1** (Fugazi)	2:32
▶ 04	**Merchandise** (Fugazi)	2:59
05	**Blueprint** (Fugazi)	3:52
▶ 06	**Sieve–Fisted Find** (Fugazi)	3:24
07	**Greed** (Fugazi)	1:47
08	**Two Beats Off** (Fugazi)	3:28
▶ 09	**Styrofoam** (Fugazi)	2:34
10	**Reprovisional** (Fugazi)	2:27
▶ 11	**Shut The Door** (Fugazi)	4:49

Soul II Soul | Club Classics Vol. One (1989)

Label | Ten Records
Producer | Nellee Hooper • Jazzie B.
Art Direction | David James
Nationality | UK
Running Time | 46:55

Soul II Soul's debut album almost single-handedly sparked an unlikely British soul revival. Fusing the laid-back vibes of reggae with hip hop's attitude and the sexy, aspirational tones of R&B and disco, the collective took British dancefloors by storm.

The original nucleus of the group consisted of Jazzie B. (rapper), Caron Wheeler (vocalist), and Nellee Hooper (producer). *Club Classics Vol. One* is best known, as are Soul II Soul themselves, for the two singles "Keep On Movin'" and "Back To Life" (the version here is a cappella). Huge hits in the UK and the United States, they remain club staples to this day. Hooper's gift for production is apparent in both; each laidback groove, melody, and vocal is given space to shine and the freedom to move. The seductive and richly produced grooves are simultaneously jazzy and dubbed out, and in the summer of 1989 they were effortlessly funkier than almost any other UK act.

Club Classics Vol. One is cleverly arranged as a club DJ set, with some tracks little more than instrumental grooves. It works brilliantly. As the first wave of acid house began to peak, Soul II Soul's positive, unifying lyrics and philosophy—"A happy face, a thumpin' bass, for a lovin' race"—perfectly captured the zeitgeist. But Hooper left the group after a solid second album, going on to work as a super-producer with stars such as Björk. Wheeler went solo, releasing two albums with mixed results. With Jazzie B. functioning without the group's core talent, Soul II Soul's constantly changing lineup has struggled to regain the high traction of the original nucleus ever since. **APi**

> "We couldn't get any more people in our parties ... because there was no one left in the streets."
>
> Jazzie B, 1992

Track Listing

	#	Title	Length
▶	01	**Keep On Movin'** (Romeo)	6:00
	02	**Fairplay** (Hooper•Romeo•Windross)	5:55
▶	03	**Holdin' On Bambeleda** (Law•Romeo)	4:13
	04	**Feeling Free** (Romeo)	4:13
	05	**African Dance** (Law•Romeo)	6:00
	06	**Dance** (Law•Romeo)	3:40
	07	**Feel Free** (Hooper•Romeo)	5:00
	08	**Happiness** (Hooper•Romeo)	5:30
▶	09	**Back To Life** (Romeo)	3:12
▶	10	**Jazzie's Groove** (Hooper•Romeo)	3:12

De La Soul
3 Feet High And Rising (1989)

Label | Tommy Boy
Producer | Prince Paul
Art Direction | Steven Miglio
Nationality | USA
Running Time | 67:25

Straight outta Long Island, accompanied by their genius producer Prince Paul, Posdnous, Trugoy the Dove, and Pasemaster Mase brought a kaleidoscopic approach to their freefalling wordage, and their sampledelic pure-pop collages. They would sire a scene and a philosophy that was initially misinterpreted as rap's echo of the hippy/psychedelic era, but was in truth a blend of Afrocentrism and the nascent buds of what would become "conscious rap."

Where contemporaries Public Enemy wrought their noise into a riotous, fearsome din, De La Soul finessed the chaos into some classic, soulful pop, the warm and summery "Eye Know" practicing beautiful alchemy with elements from Steely Dan, Otis Redding, and The Mad Lads' Volt obscurity "Make This Young Lady Mine." But while their lyrical flows mostly painted in acidic pastel shades, they did not shy away from reality: the eerie pulse of Hall And Oates' drum machine sets the tension for "Say No Go," a sober anti-drug anthem. De La's deft balance of sweet and sharp slipped this underground sound swiftly and surely into the mainstream.

Unfortunately, illicit sampling of The Turtles' version of "You Showed Me" led to a legal action that stymied hip hop's methods of production. The new laws delayed a number of albums, including the follow-up, *De La Soul Is Dead*; finally released but stripped of many samples, it struggled to repeat the success of *3 Feet High* … **SC**

Janet Jackson
Rhythm Nation 1814 (1989)

Label | A&M
Producer | Various
Art Direction | Richard Frankel
Nationality | USA
Running Time | 64:31

Funky, fabulous, and a no-filler thriller, *Rhythm Nation* … ranks beside *Off The Wall* as the Jackson family's finest.

Reluctant to play it safe, Jackson and producers Jimmy Jam and Terry Lewis refused to make a straightforward sequel to 1986's *Control*, the album with which the star had escaped underachieving obscurity. Instead, they envisaged a *What's Going On* for the looming 1990s.

In the end, social commentary was largely saved for the opening tracks, after which Jackson briskly enquires, "Get the point? Good, let's dance." Then it is into "Miss You Much," one of her record-breaking seven Top Five hits from a single album. Among the others were "Black Cat," produced by Jam and Lewis' former bandmate from The Time, Jellybean Johnson. It also features Time guitarist Jesse Johnson, on whom Jackson had an adolescent crush.

There is no trace of rock on the remaining songs. But the clattering title track—an obvious influence on the Jackson siblings' 1995 duet "Scream"—is based on Sly And The Family Stone's grinding "Thank You (Falettin Me Be Mice Elf Again)," and "Alright" is an electronic excursion that justifies its uncharacteristic length.

Of the closing trio of ballads, "Lonely" and "Come Back To Me" are achingly pretty, while "Someday Is Tonight" is an entrancingly sexy sequel to *Control*'s "Let's Wait Awhile." **BM**

Jungle Brothers
Done By The Forces Of Nature (1989)

Label | Warner Bros.
Producer | DJ Red Alert
Art Direction | A. Rahman
Nationality | USA
Running Time | 60:07

In the eyes of purists, on their sophomore effort The Jungle Brothers committed multiple sins that spanned from house rhythms to world music influences and jazz samples, meaning a sizable proportion of hip-hop fans distrusted them, finding the group dilettantish.

Nothing could be further from the truth. Early single "Girl I'll House You" sealed their fate as so-called bandwagon jumpers, but it is not representative of the playful and groove-saturated musical smorgasbord on offer here. Sure, there are house-inflected tracks such as "Tribe Vibes" but this is just part of a richer tapestry of assured, kaleidoscopic sampling, also drawing from jazz, afrobeat, and funk.

Although not as well established in the hip-hop canon, this represents the twin pinnacle of achievement of the Native Tongues collective, along with De La Soul's *3 Feet High And Rising*. The sleeve art is a pencil-rendered scene of the JBs directly between NYC and "the jungle"—a representation of their African heritage.

The Afro-centric political philosophy on this record is pronounced but tracks such as "Black Woman" and "Acknowledge Your Own History" are balanced by dancefloor killers like ""U" Make Me Sweat." *Done By . . .* was dismissed in some quarters on release because it lacked the hard edge of Public Enemy and KRS One but it still sounds playful and fresh now, and is obviously an influence on production titans The Neptunes. **JDo**

N.W.A.
Straight Outta Compton (1989)

Label | Priority
Producer | Dr. Dre • Yella
Art Direction | Helane Freeman
Nationality | USA
Running Time | 60:23

Singing raisins are often overlooked in hip-hop history. But after L.A.'s Priority Records licenced the rights to the dried grapes that performed "I Heard It Through The Grapevine" in TV commercials for California raisins—and then released an album of soul classics that sold two million copies—the label was in a position to bankroll an album that changed music forever.

Niggaz With Attitude were the fruit of Eazy E's entrepreneurship. He enlisted DJs Dr. Dre and Yella, and rappers Ice Cube and MC Ren. Early associates the DOC and Arabian Prince went on to short-lived success and obscurity, though the latter gets a fleeting namecheck on *Straight Outta Compton*, the group's first full-blown album after the showcase set *N.W.A. And The Posse* (the story is told in astonishing detail in a 2002 *L.A. Times* article by Terry McDermott; check it out online).

"Dopeman" is an early Cube gem and "Express Yourself" a popular party number—but *Compton*'s immortality rests on its opening triple threat: the brutal title track, the genre-defining "Gangsta Gangsta," and the raging "Fuck Tha Police."

When the latter earned Priority a reprimand from the FBI for encouraging "violence against and disrespect for the law enforcement officer"—and MTV banned the video for "Straight Outta Compton"—sales exploded. Once destined to languish beside Schoolly D in the anti-social rap racks, it became a cause célèbre. **BM**

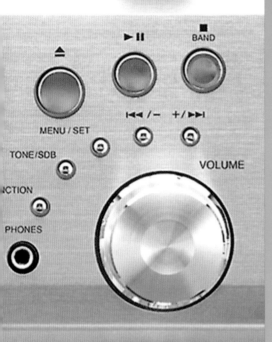

- Apartheid ends in South Africa

- Iraqi troops invade Kuwait

- Dolly the sheep born

- Google founded

- Viagra invented

1990s

Cocteau Twins | Heaven Or Las Vegas (1990)

Label | 4AD
Producer | Cocteau Twins
Art Direction | Paul West
Nationality | UK
Running Time | 36:36

While they never made much of a dent on the charts, the Cocteau Twins have always had a passionate and devoted following. There is real magic in the combination of Robin Guthrie's chiming guitar, Simon Raymonde's ominous, pulsing bass, and Elizabeth Fraser's mesmerizing vocals. With their impenetrable lyrics and intense privacy, the band quickly developed an aura of mystique. The Twins were largely responsible for defining the 4AD esthetic in the late 1980s, they have proven hugely influential over the years, and have been namechecked by artists as diverse as Prince, Madonna, and My Bloody Valentine.

For those unfamiliar with the Cocteau Twins, there is no better introduction than *Heaven Or Las Vegas*. This was the strongest and most cohesive set of songs the Twins had released since 1984's *Treasure*. Gone was the trademark ghostly, muted album artwork. Instead, the cover features a colorful swash of Vegas neon swirling against a deep blue and red sky. Similarly, the sound of *Heaven . . .* is warmer and more inviting. The melodies are catchy, the production is superb, and (gasp) you can actually make out some of the lyrics.

Songs like "Iceblink Luck" and "Heaven Or Las Vegas" are blissfully perfect Cocteau pop gems. "Fotzepolitic" starts quietly then explodes into a stunning vocal performance; Liz's angelic high notes quiver and lilt precariously above the lumbering beat. "Road, River And Rail" is mysterious and soulful. Album closer "Frou-Frou Foxes In Midsummer Fires" starts as an elegiac mood piece then erupts into a rhythmic, singsong finale. **RM**

"[Liz Fraser] was hiding behind the sounds she made."

Simon Raymonde, 2001

Track Listing

01	Cherry–Coloured Funk (Fraser・Guthrie・Raymonde)	3:12
02	Pitch The Baby (Fraser・Guthrie・Raymonde)	3:16
▶ 03	Iceblink Luck (Fraser・Guthrie・Raymonde)	3:18
04	Fifty–Fifty Clown (Fraser・Guthrie・Raymonde)	3:15
▶ 05	Heaven Or Las Vegas (Fraser・Guthrie・Raymonde)	4:56
06	I Wear Your Ring (Fraser・Guthrie・Raymonde)	3:40
▶ 07	Fotzepolitic (Fraser・Guthrie・Raymonde)	3:30
08	Wolf In The Breast (Fraser・Guthrie・Raymonde)	3:32
▶ 09	Road, River And Rail (Fraser・Guthrie・Raymonde)	3:21
▶ 10	Frou–Frou Foxes In Midsummer Fires (Fraser・Guthrie・Raymonde)	5:36

The Shamen | En-Tact (1990)

Label | One Little Indian
Producer | The Shamen
Art Direction | Uncredited
Nationality | UK
Running Time | 43:32

Formed in the mid-1980s, The Shamen began life as a psychedelic rock group formed by Colin Angus, the name coming from Angus' research into Shamanism. In the late 1980s, as rave culture began to take hold of Thatcher's Britain, Will Sinnott and "Essex boy" rapper Mr. C. joined the group, and their techno-savvy and shared interest in psychedelics soon propeled the group toward a new dance direction.

The Shamen combined underground dance culture with pop sensibility, resulting in 100,000 sales of their 1990 album *En-Tact*. After touring the UK with their cutting-edge Synergy shows, featuring live performances from The Shamen and Orbital plus DJs such as Paul Oakenfold, "Pro-Gen," reworked and released in 1991 as "Pro-Gen 91—Move Any Mountain," scaled the charts, becoming a bona-fide anthem. While filming a video for "Pro-Gen 91" in the Canary Islands, Will Sinnott tragically drowned, but fans and Will's family convinced the group to keep going. "Pro-Gen 91—Move Any Mountain" is typical of The Shamen, an uplifting song featuring positive, eco-conscious lyrics over early Nineties dance production.

The Shamen followed this with *Boss Drum*, an equally assured album that spawned the politician-baiting dance parody and UK No. 1 "Ebenezer Goode." A coded love letter to the joys of ecstasy, it led to one million album sales in the UK alone. In retrospect, time has been kinder to *En-Tact*'s more innocent, less earnest dance anthems. Its key tracks are "Pro-Gen" and the similarly positive "Make It Mine," as well as the classic Balearic acid-house of "Omega Amigo." **APi**

> "Electronic music is such a powerful way of composing ... as this album hopefully shows."
>
> Colin Angus, 1990

Track Listing

01	**Human NRG** (The Shamen)	3:22
▶ 02	**Pro-Gen (Land Of Oz Mix)** (The Shamen)	4:06
03	**Possible Worlds** (The Shamen)	3:44
▶ 04	**Omega Amigo (Steve Osbourne Mix)** (The Shamen)	4:44
05	**Evil Is Even (Edit)** (The Shamen)	4:22
▶ 06	**Hyperreal** (The Shamen)	4:31
07	**Lightspan (Will Sinnott / Irresistible Force Mix)** (The Shamen)	5:47
▶ 07	**Make It Mine (V2.5 Evil Ed)** (The Shamen)	3:57
08	**Oxygen Restriction** (The Shamen)	3:47
09	**Hear Me O My People** (The Shamen)	5:12

Deee-Lite | World Clique (1990)

Label | Elektra
Producer | Bill Coleman • Deee-Lite
Art Direction | Nick Egan
Nationality | Japan • USA • USSR
Running Time | 41:23

With the booty-shaking anthem "Groove Is In The Heart," Deee-Lite ensured that their legend would spread for years to come, thanks to various dance compilations and nostalgia shows on VH1. Recent history, however, has not been kind to this New York City-raised group that took its name from Cole Porter's "It's Delovely." The trio is commonly remembered as a one-hit wonder, but the gold-certified debut *World Clique* still stands as a convincing argument that Deee-Lite deserves to be more than just a Trivial Pursuit answer.

Starting with the spacey cover—which finds Ohio-born vocalist Kier Kirby (a.k.a. Lady Miss Kier), Russian DJ Dmitry Brill, and Japanese DJ Towa Tei adorned in gaudy club finery, set among stars and flowers—this album is full of wild psychedelia, overwhelming kitsch, and bouncing good-time club culture. In fact, a whole generation would shake hands (and hips) for the first time with club music thanks to "Groove Is In The Heart," which was a Top Ten hit more or less everywhere and ruled MTV for much of 1990.

"Good Beat" and "Power Of Love" set the dancefloor-friendly tone; Lady Miss Kier epitomizes sexy pop on "Try Me On ..." and "What Is Love?". Taken as a whole, the disc is a joyful mix of disco, rap, house, funk (aided and abetted by the Horny Horns—Maceo Parker and Fred Wesley), ambient, and techno. The party is already raging by the time the trio reaches "Groove ...," which is fueled by the talents of aforementioned saxophonist Parker, rapper Q-Tip, and superbassist Bootsy Collins (later versions of the LP featured the two bonus tracks "Deee-Lite Theme" and "Build The Bridge"). **JiH**

> ## "I don't expect you to agree with me but I will always stand up for what I believe in."
>
> Kier Kirby, 2003

Track Listing

▶	01 **Good Beat** (Deee-Lite)	4:40
▶	02 **Power Of Love** (Deee-Lite)	4:40
▶	03 **Try Me On ... I'm Very You** (Deee-Lite)	5:14
	04 **Smile On** (Deee-Lite)	3:55
	05 **What Is Love?** (Deee-Lite)	3:38
	06 **World Clique** (Deee-Lite)	3:20
▶	07 **E.S.P.** (Deee-Lite)	3:43
▶	08 **Groove Is In The Heart** (Deee-Lite)	3:51
	09 **Who Was That?** (Deee-Lite)	4:35
	10 **Deep Ending** (Deee-Lite)	3:47

The La's | The La's (1990)

Label | Go! Discs
Producer | Steve Lillywhite
Art Direction | Ryan Art
Nationality | UK
Running Time | 35:09

The La's

Any list of the best pop songs of the 1990s has to include "There She Goes" from this album, a sublime blend of chiming guitars, falsetto vocals, and a hook so catchy it will be stuck in your head for days. Even folks who have never heard of The La's are sure to recognize it from commercials and movies. Whether it is a love song to a girl or a thinly veiled ode to heroin ("Racing through my brain ... Pulsing through my vein") is debatable—a fact that must have escaped the attention of the Disney executives who used it in the soundtrack of the 1998 remake of *The Parent Trap*.

But "There She Goes" is not the only treasure buried on *The La's*. This is an album chock full of infectious two-to-three minute pop songs and ballads. "Son Of A Gun" is another highlight, with its clip-clop beat and seesawing bassline. "Timeless Melody" features a skittering rhythm and a fuzzed-out guitar solo, while "Feelin'" is a good old-fashioned gut-bucket stomp.

So with a mass of critical acclaim and strong sales in their favor, why did The La's release only one album and then fade away? Well, by most accounts, lead singer and songwriter Lee Mavers always was a surly perfectionist, and maybe a touch unstable with it. The band took four years to make *The La's* and burned through at least as many producers before the label finally lost patience and insisted they release the version piloted by Steve Lillywhite. Soon after, when Lee Mavers was asked to describe the album to *NME* he replied, "I hate it, it's the worst. A pile of shit. There is not one good thing I can find to say about it." Definitely the minority opinion, there, Lee. **RM**

> "It's like, the closer you get to perfection the closer you get to imperfection, simple as."
>
> Lee Mavers, 1995

Track Listing		
▶ 01 **Son Of A Gun** (Mavers)		1:56
02 **I Can't Sleep** (Mavers)		2:37
▶ 03 **Timeless Melody** (Mavers)		3:01
04 **Liberty Ship** (Mavers)		2:30
▶ 05 **There She Goes** (Mavers)		2:42
06 **Doledrum** (Mavers)		2:50
▶ 07 **Feelin'** (Mavers)		1:44
▶ 08 **Way Out** (Mavers)		2:32
09 **IOU** (Mavers)		2:08
10 **Freedom Song** (Mavers)		2:23
11 **Failure** (Mavers)		2:54
12 **Looking Glass** (Mavers)		7:52

The Black Crowes | Shake Your Money Maker (1990)

Label | Def American
Producer | George Drakoulias
Art Direction | Alan Forbes
Nationality | USA
Running Time | 43:42

In 1990, as this debut album from the Atlanta quintet was released, American rock was in the midst of change. Heavy metal was now well into its decline, while Seattle's alternative grunge sound was about to storm the charts. It was a difficult time for a young band to emerge who wanted to reinvigorate blues-based rock from an earlier time, via late-Sixties R&B—placing them in a tradition going back to The Allman Brothers Band and Lynyrd Skynyrd.

However, success came early to the Crowes, who sold seven million copies of their souped-up cover of Otis Redding's "Hard To Handle." As lead guitarist Rich Robinson has recognized, their story was atypical of most rock bands: "We started the other way round. There was a different process to the usual. We had a great success with our first record and later a commercial drop." The Redding cover boosted the sales of *Shake Your Money Maker*, an album of classic rock with swing and swagger in the same vein as the Stones' *Exile On Main St.* As well as the Redding cover, it featured U.S. hit single "Jealous Again" and a tender acoustic ballad about a drug addict, "She Talks To Angels," delivered by Rich's brother Chris with a maturity that belied his years.

The record stayed on the U.S. charts for 18 months. It was not groundbreaking stuff, but when the music was as funky and punchy as this, it did not need to be. The recording career of The Black Crowes has since followed a somewhat erratic trail, but then their reputation was already assured with this remarkably assured debut. **LPG**

"Some guys know how to party and some just don't."

Rich Robinson, 1996

Track Listing

01	**Twice As Hard**	(C. Robinson • R. Robinson)	4:09
▶ 02	**Jealous Again**	(C. Robinson • R. Robinson)	4:35
03	**Sister Luck**	(C. Robinson • R. Robinson)	5:13
04	**Could I've Been So Blind** (C. Robinson • R. Robinson)		3:44
05	**Seeing Things**	(C. Robinson • R. Robinson)	5:18
▶ 06	**Hard To Handle**	(Isbell • Jones • Redding)	3:08
07	**Thick 'N' Thin**	(C. Robinson • R. Robinson)	2:44
▶ 08	**She Talks To Angels** (C. Robinson • R. Robinson)		5:29
09	**Struttin' Blues**	(C. Robinson • R. Robinson)	4:09
10	**Stare It Cold**	(C. Robinson • R. Robinson)	5:13

Depeche Mode | Violator (1990)

Label | Mute
Producer | Depeche Mode • Flood
Art Direction | Anton Corbijn • Area
Nationality | UK
Running Time | 46:59

In March 1990, Depeche Mode launched a new album with what they assumed would be a low-key appearance at L.A.'s Wherehouse Records. Instead, five fans were hospitalized when, according to police, 30,000 showed up. Small wonder the band's ensuing tour was dubbed World Violation.

Oddly, the album that secured their superstardom was far more subdued than its booming predecessor, *Music For The Masses*. Only "Personal Jesus"—based on a Gary Glitter stomp—seemed suited to stadiums. The rest is writer Martin Gore's most addictive set of songs, from the techno-tinged "World In My Eyes," through the delicate "Waiting For The Night," to the ominous "Clean" (a distant descendant of Pink Floyd's "One Of These Days"). The breathing space afforded by Gore's 1989 covers set *Counterfeit* had evidently worked wonders. Four hits were the reward, of which "Enjoy The Silence" became their greatest international success.

Sophisticated but soulful, *Violator* strips the self-indulgence of oddities on *Black Celebration* and *Music For The Masses*. Unlisted instrumentals—"Crucified" after "Enjoy The Silence" and "Interlude No. 3" after "Blue Dress"—are as tricksy as it gets.

Beautifully produced by Flood—who also worked with Depeche fans Nine Inch Nails—the result is so seamless that it takes several listens to realize it is Gore, not Dave Gahan, singing "Sweetest Perfection" and "Blue Dress." Credit should also be paid to keyboardist Alan Wilder's superb arrangements throughout. *Violator* represents a group at the top of their game and still sounds effortlessly excellent today. **BM**

> **"I have a top ten list of topics …relationships, domination, lust, love, good, evil, incest, sin, religion, immorality."**
>
> Martin Gore, 1990

Track Listing

01	**World In My Eyes** (Gore)		4:26
02	**Sweetest Perfection** (Gore)		4:43
▶ 03	**Personal Jesus** (Gore)		4:56
04	**Halo** (Gore)		4:30
05	**Waiting For The Night** (Gore)		6:07
▶ 06	**Enjoy The Silence** (Gore)		6:12
▶ 07	**Policy Of Truth** (Gore)		4:55
08	**Blue Dress** (Gore)		5:42
09	**Clean** (Gore)		5:28

Pixies
Bossanova (1990)

Label | 4AD
Producer | Gil Norton
Art Direction | Vaughan Oliver
Nationality | USA
Running Time | 39:41

Megadeth
Rust In Peace (1990)

Label | Capitol
Producer | Mike Clink • Dave Mustaine
Art Direction | Shannon Ward
Nationality | USA
Running Time | 40:33

The cracks had begun to appear by the time of *Bossanova*, the Pixie dust losing a little of its magic sparkle. Following a second U.S. tour of *Doolittle* in late 1989, the Pixies took a break, having "grown tired" of each other's company. During this time Black Francis went on a solo tour and Kim Deal formed The Breeders, with whom she would go on to have a number of hits. The band hooked up again in the early summer of 1990 and returned to the studio with "fifth Pixie" Gil Norton.

The atmospheric *Bossanova* was released to mixed reviews in the fall of 1990. Tellingly, it contained no songs by Deal and had a liberal sprinkling of more gentle surf-rock tunes penned by Charles Thompson. Commercially, however, it hit the right notes, reaching No. 3 in the UK album charts and producing a couple of U.S. hits in the shape of "Velouria" and "Dig For Fire."

Lyrically, *Bossanova* represented something of a departure, too. There was less evidence of the trademark Black Francis surrealist sex and violence and an infatuation instead with UFOs: "The Happening" directly refers to the now-infamous Area 51; "Down To The Well" references the tale of alleged alien abductees Barney and Betty Hill. The savage heights of earlier Pixies material are touched by "Rock Music" and "Stormy Weather," while the use of a theremin on "Velouria" gives a nod of recognition to the surf heritage seen in the cover of The Surftones' "Cecilia Ann." Oddly enough, "Is She Weird" could have been written either for or by Deal. **MBI**

Megadeth's early career was characterized by personnel changes and unpredictability. Having been kicked out of Metallica for substance abuse, guitarist/ vocalist Dave Mustaine debuted his new thrash outfit with 1985's patchy *Killing Is My Business . . . And Business Is Good!*. Underground classic *Peace Sells . . . But Who's Buying?* came next, followed by the woeful *So Far So Good . . . So What!*. Meanwhile, Metallica had become the hippest name in metal, even winning a Grammy.

Megadeth's fourth album featured their third different lineup, with Mustaine and founding bassist Dave Ellefson being joined by guitarist Marty Friedman and drummer Nick Menza. The rejuvenated quartet played faster and tighter than before, combining a streamlined attack with stunningly precise fretwork.

However, the biggest change was their frontman's improved songwriting. All nine songs are dynamic originals, with sophisticated riffs, irresistible hooks, and lyrics that eschew both the Satanism of death/black metal and the mindless sleaze of cock rock.

The title track rails against nuclear weapons, while bipartite epic "Holy Wars . . . The Punishment Due" offers a sardonic commentary on religious intolerance. The standout single "Hangar 18" was inspired by the U.S. government's alleged UFO cover-up in Roswell.

Rust In Peace peaked at 23 on the Billboard chart, and was one of the last great records of the speed metal era. After grunge hit, Megadeth—like Metallica—switched to mid-paced hard rock. **MA**

Digital Underground
Sex Packets (1990)

Label | Tommy Boy
Producer | Digital Underground
Art Direction | Uncredited
Nationality | USA
Running Time | 64:26

Pet Shop Boys
Behaviour (1990)

Label | Parlophone
Producer | Harold Faltermeyer
Art Direction | Mark Farrow
Nationality | UK
Running Time | 49:04

Sex Packets is the brainchild of Shock G. (Greg Jacobs), a rapper and production wizard whose immense talent is matched by his eccentricity. It is a concept album built around a pill that delivers a virtual-reality sex experience set to a rich musical tapestry that borrows heavily from P-funk samples. Using live instruments and impeccable production, the music is cleverly put together, transcending P-funk and hip hop and becoming a pure expression of sex, funk, and humor.

Highlights include the sleazy slow-motion sass of the Prince-sampling title track, the hilarious crossover club hit "Humpty Dance" performed by Shock G.'s alter-ego Humpty Hump, and "Freaks Of The Industry," a hypnotic ode to freaky sex featuring some deft scratching and a sublime piano solo from the Underground's Piano Man. "Gutfest 89" features live reporting from the fictional Gutfest, a kind of X-rated sex/beauty contest set to one of the nastiest low-slung grooves of all time, while the album's closer, "Packet Man," features a dialog exchange between Shock G. (as a sex packet dealer) and his comic alter-ego Humpty Hump (as a customer).

The package is delivered with style, humor, charm, and outright absurdity and quickly becomes as irresistible as the concept itself. There are some who find the jokes sexist and the music overly reliant on sampled P-funk, but these critics are missing the point. *Sex Packets* is a uniquely eccentric hip-hop classic and conceptual album worthy of George Clinton. **APi**

Much to their frustration, Pet Shop Boys had already used the title *Introspective* on their previous studio outing. If any record of theirs ever deserved that name, it is surely this brooding and haunted affair. Neil Tennant commented that, with the world in its precarious state, he had wanted to present music that reflected personal turmoil amid global uncertainty. And, after recent collaborations with Liza Minnelli, Dusty Springfield, and Electronic, the duo were brimming with ideas.

Having vowed never to let guitars on board, it is interesting to hear the pair allow former Smiths man Johnny Marr to drip his golden plectrum over certain tracks. There is also orchestration courtesy of Angelo Badalamenti, who had made his name through movie work with David Lynch. From the outset, the mood is wistful and sober. Tennant casts a nostalgic eye back to adolescence on "Being Boring" and "This Must Be The Place I Waited Years To Leave." There is a crunching Chris Lowe synth riff on UK hit single "So Hard" and a sneer at rock's political statesmen via "How Can You Expect To Be Taken Seriously?."

But melancholia dominates, with the gorgeous "My October Symphony" and "Only The Wind" being two songs to dream with by a crackling fireside. And the heavenly "The End Of The World" finds Tennant urging us to heed prophecies of extinction. It is all cosy yet disturbing, symphonic yet somehow sparse. Maybe UK rock magazine *Sounds* got it right by proclaiming *Behaviour* "about as good as pop music gets." **GT**

Happy Mondays
Pills 'N' Thrills And Bellyaches (1990)

Label | Factory
Producer | Paul Oakenfold • Steve Osbourne
Art Direction | Central Station Design
Nationality | UK
Running Time | 43:48

Pills 'N' Thrills And Bellyaches (a reference to the Mondays' clubs 'n' drugs lifestyle) entered the UK charts at No. 1, housed in a psychedelic collage of candy wrappers. Paul Oakenfold and collaborator Steve Osbourne had previously enjoyed success with the Mondays' cover of John Kongos'"He's Gonna Step On You Again." Renamed "Step On," its chunky bassline and shuffling rhythm gave the Mondays their biggest hit.

The band's grimy industrial funk is married with subtle dance beats. Shaun Ryder's twisted lyrical genius attains new heights with his wholly unique take on modern life, crap jobs, drugs, sex, violence, and murky lowlife. "Kinky Afro"'s conversation between a self-pitying runaway father and his scornful son prompted Factory supremo Tony Wilson to pronounce it "the greatest lyrical musing on parenthood since WB Yeats' *Prayer For My Daughter*." The hook was whipped wholesale from LaBelle's "Lady Marmalade."

Latin, jazz, and hip-hop influences shape album highlights such as "Donovan"—a lyrical tribute to the Sixties folkie—and the sleazy "Bob's Your Uncle." "Loose Fit" marries dark dub textures to thinly veiled references to the flared trousers the group had brought back into fashion, while "God's Cop" takes a swipe at James Anderton, then Chief Constable of Manchester City Police, who claimed to have a hotline to God.

They never reached these astronomic heights again, but the Happy Mondays helped to bring rock music kicking and screaming into the ecstasy age. **CSh**

> ## "Our success was because of ecstasy, we started making sense to everybody."
> Bez, 2001

Track Listing

▶	01	**Kinky Afro** (Happy Mondays)	3:59
▶	02	**God's Cop** (Happy Mondays)	4:58
▶	03	**Donovan** (Happy Mondays)	4:04
	04	**Grandbag's Funeral** (Happy Mondays)	3:20
▶	05	**Loose Fit** (Happy Mondays)	5:07
	06	**Dennis and Lois** (Happy Mondays)	4:24
▶	07	**Bob's Yer Uncle** (Happy Mondays)	5:10
▶	08	**Step On** (Demetriou • Kongos)	5:17
	09	**Holiday** (Happy Mondays)	3:28
	10	**Harmony** (Happy Mondays)	4:01

George Michael
Listen Without Prejudice Vol. 1 (1990)

Label | Columbia
Producer | George Michael
Art Direction | Simon Halfon • George Michael
Nationality | UK
Running Time | 48:08

"There's something deep inside of me/there's someone I forgot to be," sang George Michael on "Freedom 90," the hit single that documented his decision to escape the restrictions of his wildly successful pop career and carve a niche as a critically acclaimed pop craftsman like Prince. Few pop stars had been quite so explicit about their agenda, yet, since his arrest for indecency in 1998, it is tempting to read in *Listen Without Prejudice* more meaning than just a spot of career repositioning.

Yet the truth is that, while being undoubtedly sincere, the lyrics reveal almost nothing about the singer's repressed sexuality. It was the music that proved how Michael had become an artist of standing. Taking in a swathe of influences—Marvin Gaye, Stevie Wonder, The Beatles, The Rolling Stones, Primal Scream ("Freedom"), and even Eighties Newcastle jazz-pop act Martin Stephenson and The Daintees ("Waiting For That Day")—he essayed a collection of thoughtful, assured songs in a variety of styles. The jazzy "Cowboys And Angels" swung confidently, while "Heal The Pain" suggested that as well as having a tight grip on songwriting, Michael was also a handy bass player, capable of McCartney-esque flourishes.

Despite being a critical triumph, the album proved calamitous for George Michael's career. When it sold relatively poorly, a hubristic Michael blamed his record company. By the time he had signed a new contract with another label, his career—and his desire for success—had lost a lot of steam. **APe**

"I just thought it was very important to explain myself."

George Michael, 2005

Track Listing

▶	01	**Praying For Time** (Michael)	4:41
▶	02	**Freedom 90** (Michael)	6:30
	03	**They Won't Go When I Go?** (Wonder • Wright)	5:06
	04	**Something To Save** (Michael)	3:18
▶	05	**Cowboys And Angels** (Michael)	7:15
▶	06	**Waiting For That Day** (Jagger • Michael • Richards)	4:49
	07	**Mothers Pride** (Michael)	3:59
▶	08	**Heal The Pain** (Michael)	4:41
	09	**Soul Free** (Michael)	5:29
	10	**Waiting (Reprise)** (Michael)	2:20

Neil Young And Crazy Horse
Ragged Glory (1990)

Label | Reprise
Producer | David Briggs • Neil Young
Art Direction | Janet Levinson
Nationality | USA
Running Time | 62:39

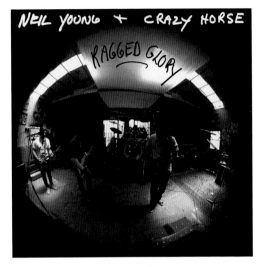

After nearly a decade of half-terrible albums, the half-brilliant *Freedom* (1989) was just about good enough to be regarded as a return to form for Neil Young. But though its enraged lyrics and acoustic/electric split echoed Young's last real triumph, 1978's *Rust Never Sleeps*, something was missing: Crazy Horse.

Simultaneously the world's worst and best band, the Horse (drummer Ralph Molina, bassist Billy Talbot, and, for Neil Young records, guitarist Frank "Poncho" Sampedro) had been Young's longest suffering sidemen. Their acrimonious split after 1987's *Life* seemed permanent but evidently *Freedom* had reminded Young how much he needed them.

Hardly the most technical of musicians, the Crazy Horse magic lay in their ham-fisted improvisation. Young had messed with their delicate chemistry too much in the past. Producer David Briggs limited Young's role to singer, songwriter, and guitarist and refused any playbacks until the recordings—made in the cavernous equipment barn pictured on the cover—were over.

Although the often nostalgic songs lack the fury of the previous album ("Country Home" and the excellent "White Line" date back to the Seventies), *Ragged Glory* is sonically everything that *Freedom* should have been. Crazy Horse's numbskull plodding and Young's frenzied, distortion-drenched solos—particularly on the livid "F*!#in' Up" and a gloriously sloppy cover of The Premiers' "Farmer John"—make this album an unlikely highlight of the then burgeoning grunge era. **MBe**

" ...it's all one big, growing, smoldering sound."

Neil Young, 1990

Track Listing		
01 Country Home (Young)		7:06
▶ 02 White Line (Young)		2:57
▶ 03 F*!#in' Up (Young)		5:55
04 Over And Over (Young)		8:28
▶ 05 Love To Burn (Young)		10:00
▶ 06 Farmer John (Harris•Terry)		4:14
07 Mansion On The Hill (Young)		4:48
▶ 08 Days That Used To Be (Young)		3:42
09 Love And Only Love (Young)		10:18
10 Mother Earth (Natural Anthem) (Young)		5:11

Ice Cube
AmeriKKKa's Most Wanted (1990)

Label | Priority
Producer | The Bomb Squad
Art Direction | Kevin Hosmann
Nationality | USA
Running Time | 49:20

Jane's Addiction
Ritual De Lo Habitual (1990)

Label | Warner Bros.
Producer | P. Farrell • D. Jerden
Art Direction | P. Farrell • C. Niccoli
Nationality | USA
Running Time | 51:38

Rotund rent-a-scowl he may now be, but as the Nineties dawned no one made more state-of-the-art rap than O'Shea "Ice Cube" Jackson. After shooting to infamy with NWA, who had the hit *Straight Outta Compton*, then splitting in a dispute over money, he hooked up with Public Enemy producers The Bomb Squad. Like their *Fear Of A Black Planet*, on which he guested, *AmeriKKKa's Most Wanted* was fragmented and fractious but funky. The P.E. connection was cemented with cameos by Chuck D. and Flavor Flav.

Cube often belies his talent as a lyricist by writing gangsta garbage and so it is here—most notoriously on "You Can't Fade Me," where he suggests kicking a pregnant girl in the stomach. Respite is offered by a witty duet with his protégé Yo-Yo ("It's A Man's World"), the incisive "Endangered Species" and "Who's The Mack?," and recurrent black comedy (the chorus of "The Nigga You Love To Hate" is a cheerful "Fuck you, Ice Cube!").

The lyrics got sharper on 1990's *Kill At Will* (added to the 2003 reissue of *AmeriKKKa ...*) and grew hypnotically unpleasant on 1991's *Death Certificate*. In 1992, he hit his zenith with Da Lench Mob's *Guerillas In Tha Mist* and the chart-topping *The Predator*.

Then he became a cuddly icon better known for movies than music. But do not let that stop you stepping back to a time when he was a vital rapper; scarier than the Sex Pistols and funky with it. **BM**

"We don't want to become like The Rolling Stones," declared Jane's Addiction when they split in 1991. Musically, they had arrived at a place all their own. *Jane's Addiction* was awash in influences (including the Stones) and *Nothing's Shocking* was Zep-heavy, but *Ritual...* is quintessential Jane's in all its vicious glory.

The introduction boasts, "We have more influence over your children than you do—but we love them." That is the last calm for 20 minutes, as punk-funk fireworks detonate one after another, culminating in the barking "Been Caught Stealing" (starring singer Perry Farrell's dog). The second half is extraordinary. "Three Days" is their "Stairway To Heaven," and the only track the daggers-drawn band recorded together. "Then She Did . . . " is an elegy for Farrell's overdosed girlfriend and suicidal mother (guitarist Dave Navarro, whose mother also met a tragic end, rated this his favorite). "Of Course" is a Middle-Eastern excursion and "Classic Girl" a lullaby for Farrell's muse, Casey Niccoli.

Before Nirvana, acts as against the grain as Pixies and Public Enemy set the agenda for danger. Equally influential, and bigger than both, Jane's Addiction battled with their paymasters and censors (the cover, illustrating the ménage-à-trois theme of "Three Days," was repackaged in a plain sleeve bearing the First Amendment), but still they launched the Lollapalooza festival. *Ritual...* is their elegant, edgy epitaph. **BM**

LL Cool J
Mama Said
Knock You Out (1990))

Label | Def Jam
Producer | LL Cool J • Marley Marl
Art Direction | The Drawing Board
Nationality | USA
Running Time | 61:42

Public Enemy
Fear Of A
Black Planet (1990)

Label | Def Jam
Producer | The Bomb Squad
Art Direction | The Drawing Board
Nationality | USA
Running Time | 63:20

In 2005, LL Cool J was able to celebrate two decades of hit albums, but he was nearly written off four years after his debut. Public Enemy's political revolution rendered his self-aggrandisement outdated; his participating in an anti-drugs campaign only earned scorn; and 1987's hit ballad "I Need Love" torpedoed his hip-hop credibility.

Bloodied but unbowed, LL got mad. *Mama Said Knock You Out* is packed with sweet delights, like the pretty "Around The Way Girl" and witty "Milky Cereal." But it is the bitter anthems that make the album not only LL's best but also a hip-hop masterpiece.

"Don't call this a comeback," he rages on the Grammy-winning title track, "I've been here for years!" Elsewhere, "To Da Break Of Dawn" tears strips off his competitors Kool Moe Dee, MC Hammer, and Ice-T. "Illegal Search" predates the thematically similar Jay-Z's "99 Problems" by 13 years, and "Mr Goodbar" sounds—musically if not lyrically—as threatening as DMX.

Producer Marley Marl keeps the bass pumping and rhythms rolling throughout. Samples on the album include Sly And The Family Stone on the title track, "All Night Long" by The Mary Jane Girls and "Impeach The President" by The Honeydrippers on "Around The Way Girl," and a snippet of Biz Markie's hip-hop classic "The Vapors" on "Cheesy Rat Blues." "Uncle L is like the future of the funk," LL Cool J rumbles on "The Boomin' System." Damn right—and damn good. **BM**

Wanna fall downstairs for an hour? No? How about while sirens scream and voices hector you about racism? Nope? *Fear Of A Black Planet*'s triumph is that it does exactly that, but is still a thrill from top to toe.

For three years, Public Enemy had ranted while the world bought Fresh Prince party jams instead. Admittedly, 1988's *It Takes A Nation Of Millions To Hold Us Back* made them hip-hop heroes, and their paramilitary trappings tantalized rock fans, but world domination was still beyond their grasp.

That changed when Spike Lee instructed them to write an anthem for his movie *Do The Right Thing.* "Fight The Power" dared to blast Elvis and John Wayne and added layers of funk where once was mostly Run DMC-style hip hop. On *Fear . . .* samples are stretched and scratched beyond recognition. The result is history's most excitingly propulsive rap album. The words woke up fans to subjects such as reparations and Malcolm X. Lyrics tackling homosexuality and anti-Semitism plumb rap's usual depths, but "Revolutionary Generation" is a rallying call on behalf of women.

Lauded by artists from Ian Brown of The Stone Roses to Björk, and shamelessly looted by The Chemical Brothers, *Fear . . .* was the most jaw-droppingly anti-commercial sound to hit the upper reaches of the chart until Radiohead's *Kid A* a decade later. But *Kid A* did not change the world. *Fear Of A Black Planet* did. **BM**

Sinéad O'Connor | I Do Not Want What I Haven't Got (1990)

Label | Ensign
Producer | Nellee Hooper • Sinéad O'Connor
Art Direction | John Maybury
Nationality | Ireland
Running Time | 51:07

Not many bald banshees ever howled out of Ireland with the impact of Sinéad O'Connor. On this, her second album, she is defiantly opinionated on anything from Catholicism to the IRA. Her own lyrics raged from the confessional, but the song that zapped her to global fame was a little-known Prince number. And more than just the track itself, the video for "Nothing Compares 2 U" was a triumph. With O'Connor's tearful face in closeup, this was pop music red in tooth and claw.

Having recently given birth, suffered miscarriages, and broken up with drummer John Reynolds, the singer has much to say. "Three Babies" finds O'Connor lamenting lost children, or lost childhoods, over an orchestral crescendo. She fuses hip hop and traditional Irish strains to render Frank O'Connor's poem "I Am Stretched On Your Grave." With ex-Adam Ant guitarist Marco Pirroni on board, there is a punk panache to "The Emperor's New Clothes" and "Jump In The River." Not everything succeeds so well, with "Black Boys On Mopeds" being as unsubtle a protest song as you can bear. But O'Connor is at her best when breaking hearts, and "The Last Day Of Our Acquaintance," with its avenging angel vocal, remains one of her finest efforts.

The coming years would see O'Connor tear up the Pope's picture on American TV, be ordained as a priest at Lourdes, and fall into devoted motherhood. It is wonderful to see her settled at last, but you cannot help missing the naked passion she dripped onto this remarkable recording. **GT**

> ## "A huge part of me is just a girl who wants to waggle her butt."
>
> Sinéad O'Connor, 2000

Track Listing

▶ 01	**Feel So Different** (O'Connor)	6:47
02	**I Am Stretched On Your Grave** (King • O'Connor)	5:33
▶ 03	**Three Babies** (O'Connor)	4:47
04	**The Emperor's New Clothes** (O'Connor)	5:16
05	**Black Boys On Mopeds** (O'Connor)	3:53
▶ 06	**Nothing Compares 2 U** (Prince)	5:10
07	**Jump In The River** (O'Connor • Pirroni)	4:12
08	**You Cause As Much Sorrow** (O'Connor)	5:04
▶ 09	**The Last Day Of Our Acquaintance** (O'Connor)	4:40
10	**I Do Not Want What I Haven't Got** (O'Connor)	5:45

A Tribe Called Quest | People's Instinctive Travels And The Paths Of Rhythm (1990)

Label | Jive
Producer | A Tribe Called Quest
Art Direction | Paije Hunyady • Bryant Peters
Nationality | USA
Running Time | 64:17

A potent blend of Afrocentric raps and unpredictable samples, *People's Instinctive Travels…* established A Tribe Called Quest as hip hop's funkiest philosophers. Q-Tip and Phife Dawg rhymed on subjects that had never registered on rap's agenda. They delivered a health sermon on "Pubic Enemy," encouraged voting on "Youthful Expression," and even recommended healthy eating in "Ham 'N' Eggs."

Although *People's Instinctive Travels…* is heavy on the message tracks, it never once sounds like a lecture. Phife and Q-Tip's lyrics are always humorous and DJ Ali Shaheed Muhammad's beat-centered mixing ensures that even the most insightful tracks can double as ass-shaking anthems. "Can I Kick It?" transforms Lou Reed's "Walk On The Wild Side" into a pure blast of hip-hop sunshine, while "I Left My Wallet In El Segundo"—a National Lampoon-style holiday adventure—joins the dots between Mariachi guitar and rolling jazz drums.

With similarly quirky albums by De La Soul and The Jungle Brothers, *People's Instinctive Travels…* marked the birth of the alt.rap scene. It inspired leftfield acts like Company Flow and Jurassic 5, and crossover stars The Fugees, to look beyond predictable James Brown samples and macho posturing.

Oddly, for such a fresh and creative album, the reaction from record buyers and critics was subdued. The album only just scraped into the Billboard chart and *Rolling Stone* labeled it one of "the least danceable rap albums ever." **TB**

Track Listing

01	**Push It Along** (Davis • Muhammad • Washington)	7:42
02	**Luck Of Lucien** (Brooks • Davis • Jackson • Muhammad)	4:32
03	**After Hours** (Davis • Muhammad)	4:39
04	**Footprints** (Davis • Muhammad • Misel • Ridgell • Wonder)	4:00
▶ 05	**I Left My Wallet In El Segundo** (Davis • Muhammad)	4:06
06	**Pubic Enemy** (Tribe Called Quest)	3:45
▶ 07	**Bonita Applebum** (Allen • Ayers • Birdsong Booker • Davis • Muhammad • Stepney)	4:11
▶ 08	**Can I Kick It?** (Davis • Muhammad • Reed)	4:52
09	**Youthful Expression** (Tribe Called Quest)	4:01
▶ 10	**Rhythm (Devoted To The Art Of Moving Butts)** (Tribe Called Quest)	3:33
11	**Mr. Muhammad** (Davis • Jones • White)	5:27
12	**Ham 'N' Eggs** (Clinton • Cordell • Davis • Muhammad • Shider)	3:54
13	**Go Ahead In The Rain** (Tribe Called Quest)	3:54
14	**Description Of A Fool** (Ayers • Birdsong • Davis • Muhammad)	5:41

Sonic Youth | Goo (1990)

Label | DGC
Producer | Nick Sansano • Sonic Youth • Ron St. Germain
Art Direction | Kevin Reagan
Nationality | USA
Running Time | 49:23

A year after *Goo*'s release, filmmaker Dave Markey traveled to Europe with Sonic Youth—the resulting documentary, *1991: The Year That Punk Broke*, is a fascinating, chaotic document of a time when they, Dinosaur Jr., and a nascent Nirvana found themselves poised on the brink of massive international success.

Originally formed in New York in 1981, Sonic Youth adapted the Velvet Underground-inspired dissonance and experimental noise of NYC no wave. Learning many of their tricks from avant-garde composer Glenn Branca's guitar ensemble, in which Sonic's Thurston Moore and Lee Ranaldo played, they refined their sound throughout the Eighties, moving from a freeform experimentalism to the more structured and critically hailed *Evol*, *Sister*, and *Daydream Nation*.

Although *Goo* was their first album on a major label, it was no sell-out. Boasting backing vocals from Dinosaur Jr.'s J. Mascis and an ahead-of-their-time crossover with Public Enemy's Chuck D. ("Kool Thing"), Goo was accessible in terms of song and structure, yet still experimental in tone and texture. Lyrics about Karen Carpenter's death from anorexia ("Tunic") and one-minute freakouts ("Scooter And Jinx") pointed to continued creative control, while ultra-cool artist Raymond Pettibon's nihilistic comic-chic sleeve paraded their continuing hipness.

While many tip the critical nod to *Daydream Nation*, *Goo* remains a masterclass in how an underground rock band can make the jump to a major label and not only survive with its soul and balls intact, but flourish and reach a wider, appreciative audience. **RS**

> "I 10'ed everything … at the end, you hear a pop where it blows up."
>
> Thurston Moore, 1991

Track Listing

▶	01	**Dirty Boots** (Sonic Youth)	5:24
▶	02	**Tunic (Song For Karen)** (Sonic Youth)	6:17
	03	**Mary–Christ** (Sonic Youth)	3:08
▶	04	**Kool Thing** (Sonic Youth)	4:04
	05	**Mote** (Sonic Youth)	7:36
	06	**My Friend Goo** (Sonic Youth)	2:18
▶	07	**Disappearer** (Sonic Youth)	5:08
	08	**Mildred Pierce** (Sonic Youth)	2:12
	09	**Cinderella's Big Score** (Sonic Youth)	5:50
	10	**Scooter And Jinx** (Sonic Youth)	1:00
▶	11	**Titanium Exposé** (Sonic Youth)	6:26

Ride | Nowhere (1990)

Label | Creation
Producer | Ride
Art Direction | Warren Bolster
Nationality | UK
Running Time | 38:50

Back in the early 1990s, there was a joke in the UK music papers that referred to an imaginary indie band, "Slowdriveride"—an amalgam of some of the groups that made up the "shoe-gazing" scene of that time. True, many were making swirly, ethereal guitar rock while idly shuffling about onstage, but the music of one band, Ride, literally soared above the rest.

After a couple of EPs for the then maverick label Creation, the teenage Oxfordshire foursome released *Nowhere* in winter 1990. It had been a year of dramatic "releases": Nelson Mandela was freed and Thatcher was booted out of government. So the mood of *Nowhere*, with its high-octane, driving guitars, and emotional sweep, hit the spot dead on.

Each song is a coruscating epic; take "Dreams Burn Down," where the crash of Loz Colbert's drums recalls the mighty pummel of John Bonham, set to a thick, almost gooey wall of sound and a syrup-sweet guitar melody. The trick on *Nowhere* is that perfect harmonies and strong basslines rise out of its tangled wash and chaos (the crowd noise in the background of "Paralysed" is actually the sound of the poll tax riots raging outside the studio).

The cover image—which has since appeared on a thousand student T-shirts—perfectly summed up the songs on the album. A fuzzy wave in a blue-green sea, as beautiful as it is forboding. Too often, Ride are compared to other artists—to their floppy-fringed contemporaries, or influences such as My Bloody Valentine and The Byrds. At last credit is being given to them for defining a sound all their own. **SH**

> ## "You have to understand, if you take any of the elements out of Ride, the sound goes completely."
>
> Loz Colbert, 1991

Track Listing

▶	01	**Seagull** (Bell·Colbert·Gardener·Queralt)	6:08
	02	**Kaleidoscope** (Bell·Colbert·Gardener·Queralt)	3:00
	03	**In A Different Place** (Bell·Colbert·Gardener·Queralt)	5:29
	04	**Polar Bear** (Bell·Colbert·Gardener·Queralt)	4:45
▶	05	**Dreams Burn Down** (Bell·Colbert·Gardener·Queralt)	6:05
	06	**Decay** (Bell·Colbert·Gardener·Queralt)	3:35
▶	07	**Paralysed** (Bell·Colbert·Gardener·Queralt)	5:32
▶	08	**Vapour Trail** (Bell·Colbert·Gardener·Queralt)	4:16

My Bloody Valentine | Loveless (1991)

Label | Creation
Producer | Colm O'Ciosoig • Kevin Shields
Art Direction | My Bloody Valentine
Nationality | UK
Running Time | 48:35

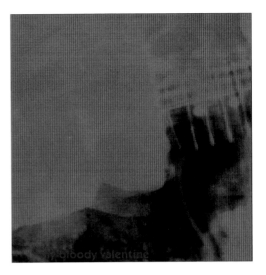

Of the small crop of bands thrown up by the short-lived British "shoe-gazing" fad of the early Nineties, My Bloody Valentine are one of the few remembered with any fondness. Their 1991 swan song *Loveless* is a near-mythic masterpiece of indie rock.

The band had initially struggled to shake The Jesus And Mary Chain comparisons invited by their distortion-saturated guitars, but by the end of the decade had created a unique sound for their 1988 Creation debut, *Isn't Anything*. That album—along with the "You Made Me Realise" single and "Glider" EP—unveiled a languid, dreamlike haze of ethereal vocals buried beneath a vast roar of distorted guitars and samples of sometimes indeterminate pitch. "The sound of God sneezing in slow motion," as *Guinness Rockopedia* described it. Shoe-gazing was born.

MBV spent the next three years, and a reported £250,000 (guitarist Kevin Shields says £140,000) on a follow-up. Made with the help of 18 engineers (despite Shields' claim that it is less sophisticated than a White Stripes record), *Loveless* filled out what now looked like the primitive sketch of *Isn't Anything*. It was another quantum leap for guitars. None of their shoe-gazing contemporaries would dare follow an album so great.

Neither would Shields, it would seem. Having helped drive the pre-Oasis Creation to the brink of bankruptcy, (and Creation boss Alan McGee to a nervous breakdown), the Valentines found themselves label-less. Nominally still in existence, despite the exit of drummer Colm O'Ciosoig and bassist Debbie Googe, MBV have yet to add to their discography. **MBI**

> ## "We started out on the wrong foot and never got back on the right one."
>
> Kevin Shields, 1991

Track Listing

▶	01	**Only Shallow** (Butcher•Shields)	4:18
	02	**Loomer** (Butcher•Shields)	2:38
▶	03	**Touched** (O'Ciosoig)	0:56
▶	04	**To Here Knows When** (Butcher•Shields)	5:31
	05	**When You Sleep** (Shields)	4:12
	06	**I Only Said** (Shields)	5:34
	07	**Come In Alone** (Shields)	3:58
▶	08	**Sometimes** (Shields)	5:19
	09	**Blown A Wish** (Butcher•Shields)	3:36
	10	**What You Want** (Shields)	5:33
▶	11	**Soon** (Shields)	7:00

Nirvana | Nevermind (1991)

Label | Geffen
Producer | Nirvana • Butch Vig
Art Direction | Robert Fisher
Nationality | USA
Running Time | 42:11

Nevermind was arguably the most important rock album of the 1990s. The warped pop songs bit with the belligerence of punk, but hit with the cranked-up power chords of metal. The album instantly established Kurt Cobain as one of rock's most distinctive singers, capable of delivering extraordinary throat-shredding vocals, but also a songwriter of genuine sensitivity and originality.

The anthemic opener, "Smells Like Teen Spirit" alternates subdued verses with howling choruses ("I was trying to write the ultimate pop song. I was basically trying to rip off the Pixies," Cobain later revealed), and kicks off with a killer riff. "Come As You Are" features another. Cobain's lyrics are teasing, contradictory, unsettling. "Territorial Pissings" is positively unhinged, a riotous helter-skelter ride driven by Dave Grohl's powerhouse drumming. But the album can shock at lower volumes too: "Polly" is a dark, acoustic-led tale of a kidnapped girl, while "Something In The Way," accompanied by a mournful cello, recalls a period Kurt spent sleeping rough.

Appropriately for such an album, the cover is both arresting and disturbing, a wry comment on humanity's materialism. Its star is five-month-old Spencer Elden; the fishhook and dollar bill were later superimposed.

A worldwide bestseller, *Nevermind* knocked Michael Jackson's *Dangerous* from the top of the Billboard Hot 200. Kurt later complained about the slickness of the album's sound—the band went out of their way to redress the balance on *In Utero,* the follow-up. But the power of *Nevermind,* and the subtlety of the songwriting, inspired a generation of musicians. **RD**

"Actually, it only took us three and a half weeks."

Dave Grohl, 1991

Track Listing

▶ 01	**Smells Like Teen Spirit** (Cobain•Grohl•Novoselic)	5:00
02	**In Bloom** (Cobain•Grohl•Novoselic)	4:13
▶ 03	**Come As You Are** (Cobain)	3:38
04	**Breed** (Cobain•Grohl•Novoselic)	3:03
05	**Lithium** (Cobain)	4:16
▶ 06	**Polly** (Cobain•Grohl•Novoselic)	2:56
▶ 07	**Territorial Pissings** (Cobain•Grohl•Novoselic)	2:22
08	**Drain You** (Cobain•Grohl•Novoselic)	3:43
09	**Lounge Act** (Cobain•Grohl•Novoselic)	2:35
10	**Stay Away** (Cobain•Grohl•Novoselic)	3:30
▶ 11	**On A Plain** (Cobain•Grohl•Novoselic)	3:12
12	**Something In The Way** (Cobain•Grohl•Novoselic)	3:43

Crowded House
Woodface (1991)

Label | Capitol
Producer | Neil Finn • Mitchell Froom
Art Direction | Nick Seymour
Nationality | Australia • New Zealand
Running Time | 47:54

When Neil Finn's initial work for *Woodface* was rejected by Capitol Records, he decided to bring his brother, Tim, into Crowded House and use material they had been working on for a movie project. This marked the first time the brothers had worked together since Split Enz.

Woodface marked a change in style and a unique sound that shied away from that of the band's previous albums. More acoustic guitar, less organ, a reluctance to use heavy production techniques, and more creative input all contributed to the change in direction.

"Weather With You" is a standout track, with its beautiful harmonies, intricate storyline, and happy, upbeat melody. "It's Only Natural" warms the heart with its romantic narrative and further established Crowded House as masters of the everyday love song. "Four Seasons In One Day," with its eerie drums and somber tones, creates a darker mood. "Fall At Your Feet" is sheer brilliance, a soulful account of the labor of love; Neil's vocals are spine-tingling, wavering effortlessly between happiness and pain.

Upon its release in 1991 the album met with considerable success in the UK. "Weather With You" was a catalyst in the album achieving platinum status and earned the group several headlining concerts at London's Wembley Stadium. That said, the band's decision to release the satirical "Chocolate Cake" as the first U.S. single proved to be their most costly mistake. However, *Woodface* will be remembered as bridging the gap between the Antipodes and the UK. **KT**

Cypress Hill
Cypress Hill (1991)

Label | Columbia
Producer | DJ Muggs
Art Direction | Stacy Drummond
Nationality | Cuba • USA
Running Time | 46:52

Stoner albums are not always a gas. For every Richard Pryor, there is a Cheech and Chong; for every David Bowie, a James Taylor. Cypress Hill are with the good guys. They stood out from the start, their Cuban roots an anomaly in a rap world that viewed anyone not from New York or California with suspicion. And, with hip hop ruled by MC Hammer at one extreme and Public Enemy at the other, no one was interested in a trio who did not dance and whose politics extended only to marijuana (good) and police (not so good).

One song secured their fortunes. It began as "Trigga Happy Nigga" on a 1990 demo, then—renamed "How I Could Just Kill A Man"—became the rap jam of the early Nineties. All the unique Cypress elements were there: B-Real's evil whine, Sen Dog's gruff rapping, and DJ Muggs' messed-up funky beats (which later fueled seminal jams such as House of Pain's "Jump Around").

The song's notoriety, sealed by an appearance on the soundtrack of the Tupac Shakur-starring *Juice*, helped *Cypress Hill* go gold. The album boasts plenty to satisfy the musical munchies, from groovy giggles like "Light Another" and the Parliament-sampling "Psychobetabuckdown" to woozy weed anthems like "Stoned Is The Way Of The Walk." Other witty touches include the "Duke Of Earl" sample that opens "Hand On The Pump," and the lasciviously Latino "Tres Equis."

While sequel *Black Sunday*, with its paranoia and painful bass, took them to the top in 1993, *Cypress Hill* is much more fun: a high that is legal but lethal. **BM**

Julian Cope
Peggy Suicide (1991)

Label | Island
Producer | Donald Ross Skinner
Art Direction | Darren Woolford
Nationality | UK
Running Time | 75:44

Gang Starr
Step In The Arena (1991)

Label | Capitol
Producer | DJ Premier
Art Direction | Marc Cozza
Nationality | USA
Running Time | 49:18

Post-punk renaissance man Julian Cope is the foremost cult artist in contemporary British music. Having piloted Liverpool's new wave chart stars The Teardrop Explodes through five turbulent years, he embarked on a multifaceted solo career in 1984 with the release of two very English psych-pop LPs: the upbeat *World Shut Your Mouth* and pastoral, Syd Barrett-influenced *Fried*. Neither record sold well, but Cope achieved a modicum of transatlantic chart success by pursuing a more arena-friendly direction in the second half of the decade. Then, dissatisfied by this compromise, he underwent a spectacular creative rebirth.

A loosely themed double album highlighting issues relating to both environmental and social justice, *Peggy Suicide* was trailed by two funky UK hits: the piano and trumpet-laden "Beautiful Love," and low-slung Hammond® groove "East Easy Rider." However, these were part of a much broader tapestry spanning gonzoid Krautrock ("Hanging Out And Hung Up On The Line"), lysergic balladry ("Pristeen"), political sound collage ("Western Front 1992 CE"), and anthemic rock 'n' roll ("Drive, She Said"). The crowning glory is "Safesurfer," a widescreen meditation on unprotected sex that boasts thrillingly vertiginous guitar features.

Cope's sprawling 1992 heathen masterpiece *Jehovahkill* marked the end of his Island contract, but he continues to explore everything from ambient Moog®-scapes to thunderous proto-metal via his own label Head Heritage. **MA**

One of hip hop's most enduring duos, arch lyricist Guru and production wizard DJ Premier failed to make an impact with 1989's debut *No More Mr. Nice Guy*, now regarding *Step In The Arena* as their debut proper.

So in today's disposable hip-hop culture, how have they managed such longevity? The key to Gang Starr is they never compromised their purist vision of what hip hop should be. Rather than chase untold riches and girls, Gang Starr reverts to hip hop's raw essence—two turntables and a microphone. Guru is an undisputed master of the latter, adept at spitting rhymes that proclaim his own brilliance, but equally capable of painting rich, high drama stories of the street. Delivered in his distinctive monotone, his hypnotic delivery is matched by DJ Premier, who was one of the first hip-hop producers to bring jazz to his sonic palette.

In "Who's Gonna Take The Weight," Guru spits knowledge against fakers and moneymakers over a bumping Premier beat and a squalling horn sample. "Just To Get A Rep" outlines the pitfalls of life as a hoodlum with scratch mixing samples over the top of a tight hip-hop groove. It sounds raw as hell.

Over their following five albums Guru and Premier have never wavered from the *Step In The Arena* formula. They continue to refine their skills, also working on solo projects such as Guru's Jazzmatazz series, but they always come back to Gang Starr. Luckily, we still have them to remind us that a back-to-basics approach is sometimes all hip hop really needs. **APi**

MC Solaar
Qui Sème Le Vent Récolte Le Tempo (1991)

Label | Polygram
Producer | Jimmy Jay
Art Direction | Alain Frappier
Nationality | France
Running Time | 52:09

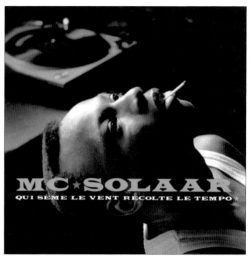

As far as American hip hop is concerned, MC Solaar is the most important thing to come out of France since the French kiss. *Qui Sème Le Vent Récolte Le Tempo* ("Who Sows The Wind Will Reap The Beat") was the breakthrough of an artist determined to prove that quality hip hop is not exclusively U.S. territory.

Solaar's strongest assets are jazzy beats and a perfectly handled sense of rhyme, supported by both state-of-the-art production skills and skillful arrangements of Jimmy Jay (that transcend those of many of Solaar's U.S. peers). On his debut, the sounds and rhythms of Solaar's rapping are musical enough be satisfying in their own right, even without translation.

Qui Sème Le Vent Récolte Le Tempo brims with beguiling accounts of lost love and social issues, enriched by great grooves to bounce to and superlative aural collages from Jay. The title track is a rollercoaster of rhymes, a tour d'honneur of the funk-rap treats to come. Tracks such as "Matière Grasse Contre Matière Grise," "Victime De La Mode," and "Armand Est Mort" are masterpieces of high-class rhyming, delivered in Solaar's trademark laid-back style. In "L'Histoire De L'Art," Solaar displays a characteristic humor, wit, and no little charisma in asserting, in an easy and nonconfrontational way, his view that the history of art should include all artists.

This album was the genesis of European and even Latin hip hop, spawned four French Top Ten singles, and set a high standard to follow. **GD**

Track Listing

01	Intro (Uncredited)		1:01
▶ 02	Qui Sème Le Vent Récolte Le Tempo (M'Barali)		4:13
▶ 03	Matière Grasse Contre Matière Grise (M'Barali)		3:30
▶ 04	Victime De La Mode (M'Barali)		3:03
▶ 05	L' Histoire De L'Art (M'Barali)		3:31
06	Armand Est Mort (M'Barali)		3:11
07	Quartier Nord (M'Barali)		3:12
08	Interlude (Uncredited)		0:29
09	A Temps Partiel (M'Barali)		3:46
10	Caroline (M'Barali)		4:43
11	La Musique Abdoucit Les Meurs (M'Barali • Payne)		5:02
12	Bouge De Là (Part 1) (M'Barali)		3:11
13	Bouge De Là (Part 2) (M'Barali)		3:05
14	Ragga Jam (M'Barali)		5:13
15	La Devise (M'Barali)		3:43
16	Funky Dreamer (Uncredited)		1:16

Jah Wobble's Invaders Of The Heart
Rising Above Bedlam (1991)

Label | EastWest
Producer | Invaders Of The Heart
Art Direction | Finn Lewis • Rich Scott
Nationality | UK
Running Time | 51:23

Prior to this, Jah Wobble's resumé was ripe with urban legend: he had been Johnny Rotten's motorbike-chain-wielding buddy/enforcer, bass player with Public Image Ltd., dub experimentalist with Holger Czukay and The Edge, bon viveur, and London Underground employee. Spiraling away from the music business, he hooked up with guitarist Justin Adams, who was interested in Middle-Eastern music. Natacha Atlas, a Spanish-Belgian singer with Arab roots, came on board early too. Their first album, *Without Judgement*, sold badly, but it was a calling card that aroused a lot of interest.

Jah Wobble's music—with its three prongs of dub bass, Latin and Maghrebi percussion, and Spanish-North African guitar lines—seemed an outrageous combination in the late 1980s, even in multicultural London. But Wobble was not alone: bands such as Transglobal Underground and Loop Guru had similar influences but were evolving from the rave scene rather than punk. Wobble's big band, however, was the force to be reckoned with. Thanks to Atlas, "Erzulie" could have been a call to prayer caught on the breeze in Damascus (and piped into a reggae disco in downtown Moscow), and "Bomba" is a trance-inducing mantra; guest vocalist Sinéad O'Connor turned the mesmeric "Visions Of You" into a hit single.

It was difficult to figure out what you were meant to do to it: dance was one option; but it also seemed to be the perfect accompaniment to a stoner's deep fug. London Underground's loss was the world's gain. **DH**

"I'm so convinced of all this that I'm giving up my day job."
Jah Wobble, 1991

Track Listing

▶ 01 **Visions Of You** (Adams•Reynolds•Wobble) 5:36
  02 **Relight The Flame** (Adams•Atlas•Wobble) 4:13
▶ 03 **Bomba**
     (Adams•Atlas•Burton•Ferda•Miller•Wobble) 5:55
  04 **Ungodly Kingdom** (Adams•Ferda•Wobble) 4:28
  05 **Rising Above Bedlam**
     (Adams•Schoots•Wobble) 3:46
▶ 06 **Erzulie** (Adams•Atlas•Wobble) 7:03
  07 **Everyman's An Island** (Adams•Ferda•Wobble) 6:28
  08 **Soledad** (Adams•Atlas•Wobble) 5:40
  09 **Sweet Divinity** (Adams•Ferda•Wobble) 4:17
  10 **Wonderful World** (Adams•Wobble) 3:57

Red Hot Chili Peppers
Blood Sugar Sex Magik (1991)

Label | Warner Bros.
Producer | Rick Rubin
Art Direction | Henky Penky
Nationality | Australia • USA
Running Time | 73:49

Bob Marley, Black Sabbath, and Bart Simpson? Mix them up and you might get Red Hot Chili Peppers. They namecheck Marley on the anthem "Give It Away," which ends with the riff from Sabbath's "Sweet Leaf" that they wound up playing on *The Simpsons*.

This cocktail is typical of the Chilis. On 1989's *Mother's Milk*, they had perfected a blend of hard rock, funk, and snappy songs. Now all they needed was a hit. Enter "Under The Bridge," Anthony Kiedis' paean to heroin brought to life by John Frusciante's heartbreaking guitar, which set the album on course for seven million U.S. sales. Frusciante is also at the heart of "I Could Have Lied," about Kiedis' non-relationship with Sinéad O'Connor, which signposts the direction they would pursue on *By The Way*. Elsewhere it is mostly sex-crazed sentiments underpinned by Flea's boingy bass and Chad Smith's relentless drums. Standouts include the vicious "Suck My Kiss" and "My Lovely Man," a tribute to Frusciante's late predecessor, Hillel Slovak.

Producer Rick Rubin—then graduating from hip hop/heavy metal to a more eclectic clientele—was perfect for a band who would mix industrial percussion and flamenco ("Breaking The Girl"), add an elegiac coda to the ultra-funky "Sir Psycho Sexy," and wind down with a wacky Robert Johnson cover. Rubin also requested just "one song about girls and cars." Keidis loathed the result—"The Greeting Song"—but today it is one of 17 incentives to board the *Blood Sugar . . .* rollercoaster. Take a ride today. **BM**

Track Listing

01	The Power Of Equality	(R.H.C.P.)	4:04
02	If You Have To Ask	(R.H.C.P.)	3:36
03	Breaking The Girl	(R.H.C.P.)	4:55
04	Funky Monks	(R.H.C.P.)	5:23
▶ 05	Suck My Kiss	(R.H.C.P.)	3:37
▶ 06	I Could Have Lied	(R.H.C.P.)	4:04
07	Mellowship Slinky In B Major	(R.H.C.P.)	3:59
08	The Righteous And The Wicked	(R.H.C.P.)	4:08
▶ 09	Give It Away	(R.H.C.P.)	4:42
10	Blood Sugar Sex Magik	(R.H.C.P.)	4:31
▶ 11	Under The Bridge	(R.H.C.P.)	4:24
12	Naked In The Rain	(R.H.C.P.)	4:25
13	Apache Rose Peacock	(R.H.C.P.)	4:42
14	The Greeting Song	(R.H.C.P.)	3:13
▶ 15	My Lovely Man	(R.H.C.P.)	4:39
16	Sir Psycho Sexy	(R.H.C.P.)	8:16
17	They're Red Hot	(Johnson)	1:11

Ice-T
OG Original Gangster (1991)

Label | Warner Bros.
Producer | The Rhyme Syndicate
Art Direction | Tim Stedman
Nationality | USA
Running Time | 72:17

OG Original Gangster is a chilling masterpiece that ruthlessly illustrates the complex forces at play within a forgotten American black underclass forced to live in urban housing projects. Unlike most gangsta rappers, alongside offering lurid tales of sex, violence, and hardcore narcotics, Ice-T (born Tracey Morrow) seeks solutions to ghetto poverty, speaks out against drug dealing and family violence, and exhorts those trapped inside the cycle to transcend it by any means necessary.

On "Ed" Ice delivers a cautionary tale about drunk driving, while on "Bitches 2" he explains the definition of a bitch, implying that it can be used to describe dishonest men, not just women—an apparent attempt to defend hip hop's overt misogyny.

OG introduces Ice's funk metal band Body Count, who would become infamous for the inflammatory song "Cop Killer." The man has a large dose of charisma, which has helped him forge a successful acting career, but it is his formidable storytelling skills that make *OG*'s lyrics and delivery so compelling. Production from Ice's Rhyme Syndicate provides stark minimal breakbeats, sharp snares, and menacing basslines perfectly suited to his chilling gangster persona. Check out "Midnight," which samples a Black Sabbath riff to create a haunting backdrop for Ice's desolate tale of South Central L.A. after dark. The end result is the aural equivalent of a perfectly paced psychological horror movie. **APi**

Mudhoney
Every Good Boy Deserves Fudge (1991)

Label | Sub Pop
Producer | Conrad Uno
Art Direction | Ed Fotheringham
Nationality | USA
Running Time | 42:29

Because of Mudhoney's lack of commercial success compared to their Seattle peers, detractors called them the guys from Green River who did not join Pearl Jam. Their fans called them pioneers of grunge, and the raw, frenetic, and confident third album *Every Good Boy Deserves Fudge* supports the fans' argument.

With its whimsical lyrics and angry sound filled out with fuzz-infused guitars and heavy drums, Mudhoney sounded like a 1950s garage band on speed. Even a cursory listen indicates that theirs was a formula copied by a host of other bands. Songs such as "Thorn" show off the surf-rock capabilities of drummer Dan Peters and Fifties-style solo riffs of guitarist Steve Turner while anticipating the angry sound of grunge just around the corner. The album's lead single, "Let It Slide," would become a minor grunge anthem with its whining lyrics and quintessential Seattle mix of distorted guitars, hummable melody, and nihilistic tendencies.

The album persists in the memory as one long, smug sneer, from the irreverent title to the vocal delivery and lyrics. ("Into The Drink," a song about dumping a girlfriend into a river, features a repetitive gang shout of the song's title during the chorus.) They even find ironic use for organ and harmonica.

Mudhoney's musical approach never led them to platinum records, but *Every Good Boy ...* is a classic album, one of the best of the genre. **JC**

Public Enemy
Apocalypse 91 …The Enemy Strikes Black (1991)

Label | Def Jam
Producer | The Imperial Grand Ministers Of Funk
Art Direction | The Drawing Board
Nationality | USA
Running Time | 52:00

With their first two groundbreaking albums, Public Enemy had established themselves as rap's most important and radical group. *Apocalypse '91 …* could not possibly be as seminal as its predecessors, yet it deserves almost as much praise.

Many record labels had suddenly developed their interest in copyright laws, something that would have made another sample-heavy Bomb Squad production unaffordable. In response, Chuck D. asked The Bomb Squad to take a back seat as executive producers and let their disciples, The Imperial Grand Ministers Of Funk, re-create the band's dense and forceful trademark sound by relying mainly on unrecognizable sources and original instrumentation.

Building songs like "Nighttrain" and "By The Time I Get To Arizona"—a masterpiece about that state's hesitation to honor Martin Luther King Jr.'s birthday as a public holiday—around a single effective sample, Public Enemy managed to save money without losing their edge. To the sounds of apocalyptic sirens and aggressive old-school beats the "Prophets Of Rage" kept on doing what they did best: educating the masses about social and racial injustice at the beginning of a decade Chuck D. had labeled "The Terrordome."

Apocalypse '91… debuted at No. 4 on the Billboard charts. More importantly, it met the high standards Public Enemy had already set for themselves. **CL**

A Tribe Called Quest
The Low End Theory (1991)

Label | Jive
Producer | Skeff Anselm
Art Direction | Zombart JK
Nationality | USA
Running Time | 48:03

With *The Low End Theory*, hip-hop innovators A Tribe Called Quest achieved a level of fusion between jazz and rap never heard before—or since. Relying on minimal programmed beats and keyboards over sampled jazz hooks (Ron Carter plays upright bass on "Verses From The Abstract"), the uncluttered production provides the perfect backdrop for MCs Q-Tip and Phife Dawg. Their separate and distinctive verbal flows combine and work off each other to the point where they sound like one artist expressing himself through two voices.

While many of their contemporaries were fixated on rapping about guns, money, and misogyny, the Tribe followed in the footsteps of Afrika Bambaataa and Erik B. & Rakim and placed social and racial problems at the forefront of their music. Playing down the irreverent lyricism of their first album, Phife and Q-Tip chose to concentrate on social issues. Their subjects ranged from sexual violence ("The Infamous Date Rape") to the shortcomings of rap and the music industry ("Rap Promoter," "Show Business"); in "Jazz (We've Got)" they produced an account of their own laid-back philosophy.

The Tribe covered a lot of ground with this record, and set a precedent that is constantly referred to and emulated today. Although the band was later to be torn apart by friction between the two MCs, this album was the best realization of their collaborative potential. **LP**

Pearl Jam | Ten (1991)

Label | Epic
Producer | Rick Parashar • Pearl Jam
Art Direction | Jeff Ament
Nationality | USA
Running Time | 50:46

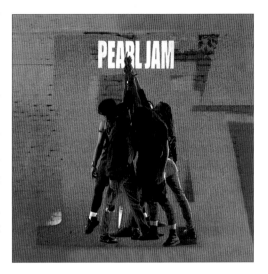

A guerilla movement is defined as an "indigenous paramilitary unit operating in small bands in occupied territory to harass and eventually overrun the enemy." In America, the last such movement of note took root in the Seattle underground of the late 1980s and early 1990s, when small bands including Nirvana, Soundgarden, Alice In Chains, and Pearl Jam had set about to waste all the deceitful hair-metal dictators.

Pearl Jam sprouted up largely intact, assembled from the hard rock remnants of pivotal local acts such as Green River and Mother Love Bone. On their debut, *Ten*, the band recalled the soaring melodic majesty and fierce integrity of original masters like Neil Young and The Doors, while at the same time sounding a battle cry for a powerful new moment in rock 'n' roll.

Ten's punishing power chords, augmented by Mike McCready's searing, bluesy licks, were immediately swallowed up by millions of teenagers starving for a new party. The anthemic first single "Alive" perfectly encapsulated the album's great strengths: a sing-along chorus, disturbingly reflective lyrics, and darkly woven guitar parts. Eddie Vedder's painfully captivating baritone pegged Pearl Jam more to the classic rock tradition than did Kurt Cobain's punky howl, which was unveiled the same year on *Nevermind*.

Put together, songs like the growling "Why Go," reverb-drenched "Oceans," and floor-stomping "Porch" oozed a river of grunge, while the hit single "Jeremy" made every shoe-gazing teenager within earshot wonder just for a moment what it would be like to blow your head off in front of your geometry class. **MO**

> "I don't know where all those songs came from ... I know he loved *Quadrophenia*."

Jeff Ament on Eddie Vedder, 1993

Track Listing

01	**Once** (Gossard•Vedder)		3:51
▶ 02	**Evenflow** (Gossard•Vedder)		4:53
▶ 03	**Alive** (Gossard•Vedder)		5:40
04	**Why Go** (Ament•Vedder)		3:19
05	**Black** (Gossard•Vedder)		5:48
06	**Jeremy** (Ament•Vedder)		5:18
07	**Oceans** (Ament•Gossard•Vedder)		2:41
▶ 08	**Porch** (Vedder)		3:30
09	**Garden** (Ament•Gossard•Vedder)		4:58
10	**Deep** (Ament•Gossard•Vedder)		4:18
▶ 11	**Release** (Ament•Gossard•Krusen•McCready•Vedder)		6:30

Saint Etienne | Foxbase Alpha (1991)

Label | Heavenly
Producer | Saint Etienne
Art Direction | Anthony Sweeney
Nationality | UK
Running Time | 48:16

When we are young, we all imagine the fantasy world we will inhabit later, the jobs we will do. Growing up in London's suburbia during the 1980s, Saint Etienne's Bob Stanley and Pete Wiggs wanted to live in Swinging Sixties London, full of groovy styles and classic pop sounds. No Austin Powers caricature; just hip young things setting the beat. And on their debut album *Foxbase Alpha*, Stanley and Wiggs—together with singer Sarah Cracknell—got their wish.

The title was taken from the pair's in-joke for a room full of attractive women (or foxes, as they would have it), while the sleeve was based on a Sixties children's book. The album itself is swathed with warm pop references: the swirling strings and girlish vocals of "Spring" invoke The Ronettes, while "Girl VII"'s stoic listing of London Underground stations recalls Peter Cook's turn in the Sixties cult classic *Bedazzled*.

Foxbase Alpha is no retro time capsule, though. While it looked to the Sixties for inspiration, the clever sampling, insistent beats, and synthesizer production (learned at home by Stanley and Wiggs) ensured Saint Etienne had one foot in the dance culture of the early Nineties. The wistful, loved-up cover of Neil Young's "Only Love Can Break Your Heart" was a club classic, paving the way for the likes of The Chemical Brothers, while "Nothing's Going To Stop Us" drove a sophisticated Rolls-Royce through clubland, proving there was more to dance than disco.

Sixties London fueled this record. Nineties London built it. But with its passport fully stamped, it was a dance classic for the whole globe. **PS**

> ## "We threw in as many of the things we loved as we could."
>
> Bob Stanley, 2001

Track Listing

	01	**This Is Radio Etienne** (Stanley·Wiggs)	0:43
▶	02	**Only Love Can Break Your Heart** (Young)	4:29
	03	**Wilson** (Stanley·Wiggs)	1:59
	04	**Carnt Sleep** (Stanley· Wiggs)	4:44
▶	05	**Girl VII** (Stanley· Wiggs)	3:46
▶	06	**Spring** (Stanley· Wiggs)	3:44
	07	**She's The One** (Stanley· Wiggs)	3:07
	08	**Stoned To Say The Least** (Stanley· Wiggs)	7:41
▶	09	**Nothing Can Stop Us** (Stanley· Wiggs)	4:19
	10	**Etienne Gonna Die** (Stanley· Wiggs)	1:29
	11	**London Belongs To Me** (Stanley· Wiggs)	3:57
	12	**Like The Swallow** (Stanley· Wiggs)	7:39
	13	**Dilworth's Theme** (Stanley· Wiggs)	0:39

Sepultura | Arise (1991)

Label | Roadrunner
Producer | Scott Burns • Sepultura
Art Direction | Michael R. Whelan
Nationality | Brazil
Running Time | 46:49

While stories of the drinking and partying that went into the making of *Arise* are rife, Sepultura's fourth album is notably more professional in its execution than any of their previous efforts. Their first recording outside Brazil, the album is markedly more polished courtesy of producer Scott Burns.

Everything about *Arise* is dark and threatening, including the distorted imagery of the cover art. Sepultura reined themselves into a more cohesive anger than pure, comparatively amateur thrash metal allows, while still maintaining a strong hold on that genre. The frantic drum pace set by Igor Cavalera almost leaps ahead of Andreas Kisser's guitar, which at times sounds like it is struggling to keep up, as it delivers intense screaming riffs. *Arise* also hints at the more experimental sounds to come on their subsequent albums, *Chaos AD* and *Roots Bloody Roots*, prior to vocalist Max Cavalera leaving the band due to management differences. His powerful vocals growl, spitting over the top of music lyrically encompassing rage and despair, most exemplified by the album's highlights "Arise" and "Desperate Cry" respectively. "Under Siege" slows down the pace momentarily, while their most rock-oriented track "Orgasmatron" (appearing as a CD bonus track) was a Motörhead cover that had long been part of Sepultra's live set.

Arise plays out as a call to arms, particularly in "Dead Embryonic Cells." It appeals to a sense of helplessness in the face of hatred and encourages the expression of anger through music, assuring sympathetic listeners that they are not alone. **CSt**

> "We could have paid ... more attention to some things, but then again, it might not sound like we had fun making it."
>
> Max Cavalera, 1997

Track Listing

▶ 01	**Arise** (Sepultura)	3.19
▶ 02	**Dead Embryonic Cells** (Sepultura)	4.52
▶ 03	**Desperate Cry** (Sepultura)	6.41
04	**Murder** (Sepultura)	3.27
05	**Subtraction** (Sepultura)	4.47
06	**Altered State** (Sepultura)	6.35
07	**Under Siege** (Sepultura)	4.54
08	**Meaningless Movements** (Sepultura)	4.41
09	**Infected Voice** (Sepultura)	3.19
▶ 10	**Orgasmatron** (Motörhead)	4.14

Slint | Spiderland (1991)

Label | Touch And Go
Producer | Brian Paulson • Slint
Art Direction | Will Oldham
Nationality | USA
Running Time | 39:32

With a status that far outweighs their scant sales, Slint, from Louisville, Kentucky, set the agenda for the Nineties post-rock field. Originally named Squirrel Bait, the band took the same influences that had propelled the American underground for years—punk and heavy metal—and twisted them into something devoid of obvious reference points.

The Steve Albini-recorded *Tweez* (1988) set out Slint's design of idiosyncratic, mostly instrumental songs that veered from sinister to relatively light-hearted. Brian McMahan's sparse vocals are sung, screamed, or spoken and rarely seem like they have anything to do with the music, as if they were left over on the tape from a previous recording. Aside from a passing resemblance to Television somewhere beneath that distortion and a jazz-like rhythmic complexity, it sounds like it comes from nowhere at all.

But it is *Spiderland* upon which Slint's mythical reputation rests. It refines *Tweez*'s rough sketches into a solid steel structure. The guitars of McMahan and David Pajo mesh into an inspired whole. Again, comparisons could be made with Television, but only because of the sheer invention. Released to critical acclaim but little commercial success, *Spiderland*'s slow-building influential status came too late for the band, which split following the album's release.

While *Nevermind*, 1991's most famous release, came from a similarly obscure background and may share this album's dynamics, its simple Black Sabbath/ Black Flag template lags way behind the inspired parallel universe in which *Spiderland* exists. **MBe**

> "Slint was unspoken. It was about subtlety, awareness ... the fraternal order of Louisville, Kentucky. Few people seem to have gotten it, but what the fuck does that matter?"
>
> David Pajo, 1993

Track Listing

▶	01	**Breadcrumb Trail** (Slint)	5:55
▶	02	**Nosferatu Man** (Slint)	5:35
	03	**Don, Aman** (Slint)	6:28
	04	**Washer** (Slint)	8:50
	05	**For Dinner** (Slint)	5:05
▶	06	**Good Morning, Captain** (Slint)	7:39

U2 | Achtung Baby (1991)

Label | Island
Producer | Brian Eno • Daniel Lanois
Art Direction | Steve Averill • Shaughn McGrath
Nationality | Ireland
Running Time | 55:22

The stupidest title for a great album could have been even worse. Before "Achtung Baby," taken from the movie *The Producers*, U2 reportedly considered "68 And I'll Owe You One."

Rattle and Hum's earnestness had painted U2 into a corner. They looked for inspiration in Berlin—where, recalled engineer Flood, "There seemed to be this dark cloud hanging over the whole session." The location did, however, yield "Zoo Station"—named after a Berlin subway stop featured in the Bowie-scored movie *Christiane F*. The connection is cemented by producer Brian Eno, who worked on Bowie's Berlin-born *"Heroes"*. Another influence was Wim Wenders—"Until The End Of The World" is named after one of his movies. He directed the video for U2's Cole Porter tribute "Night And Day," the electronic nature of which heralded their new direction.

Achtung Baby is the most successful reinvention by a group of U2's stature. The wrenching likes of "Who's Gonna Ride Your Wild Horses" would fit on *The Joshua Tree*. But others—notably the savage "The Fly" ("A phone call from hell," said Bono)—are left turns.

Heartbreakers abound, inspired by The Edge's collapsing marriage, while "One" dissected Bono's relationship with both his father and his band. "People tell me they played it at their wedding," he marveled, "Are you crazy? It's about breaking up."

Fond of contradiction, U2 planned to house the tragedy-packed album in a naked picture of Adam Clayton. They compromised on a snapshot (censored with a shamrock in some territories)—but in every other respect *Achtung Baby* is big and beautiful. **BM**

"We have to go away—and dream it all up again."

Bono, 1989

Track Listing		
01 **Zoo Station** (U2)		4:36
02 **Even Better Than The Real Thing** (U2)		3:41
▶ 03 **One** (U2)		4:36
04 **Until The End Of The World** (U2)		4:38
05 **Who's Gonna Ride Your Wild Horses** (U2)		5:16
06 **So Cruel** (U2)		5:49
▶ 07 **The Fly** (U2)		4:28
▶ 08 **Mysterious Ways** (U2)		4:03
09 **Tryin' To Throw Your Arms Around The World** (U2)		3:52
10 **Ultra Violet (Light My Way)** (U2)		5:30
11 **Acrobat** (U2)		4:30
12 **Love Is Blindness** (U2)		4:23

The KLF | The White Room (1991)

Label | KLF Communications
Producer | The KLF
Art Direction | Norbert Schoerner
Nationality | UK
Running Time | 43:48

Shrouded in mystery and occultist imagery, The KLF were the biggest selling British singles act of 1991. Formed as the Justified Ancients of Mu Mu four years previously by ex-Echo and the Bunnymen manager Bill Drummond and graphic artist James Cauty, they debuted with controversial sample collage "1987 (What The Fuck's Going On?)"—withdrawn from sale after five days following legal action by Abba. Alongside their novelty hit "Doctorin' The Tardis" (recorded under the pseudonym The Timelords), their early releases coined musical terms, such as "trance" and "chill out."

"What Time Is Love?" initially sank without trace, but its minimalist soaring synth lines stormed the European club scene in 1989 during the aftermath of the acid house revolution. A harder remix, featuring an incendiary rap from MC Bello, crashed into the UK Top Ten the following year. Its massive bass sound, accompanied by sampled crowd noise (dubbed "stadium house" by the band), was an attempt to create the atmosphere of the open air "raves" that were then springing up across the UK.

The KLF poured their profits into *The White Room* movie project, though only this so-called "soundtrack" album was to appear. Transatlantic hit "3AM Eternal" was a unique blend of Maxine Harvey's soulful vocals and the "bleep techno" popularized by LFO and Sweet Exorcist. The rest of the album utilizes then current club styles with a creative playfulness, particularly "No More Tears"' combination of dub, gospel, country slide guitars, and Latin trumpets. Result? The first truly consistent house music album. **CSh**

> "We came out of it in the black, nobody ripped us off, yet we felt absolutely awful."
>
> Bill Drummond, 1993

Track Listing

▶	01	**What Time Is Love? (LP Mix)** (Bello·Cauty·Drummond)	4:40
▶	02	**Make It Rain** (Cauty·Drummond)	4:02
▶	03	**3AM Eternal** (Cauty· Drummond·Lyte)	3:34
	04	**Church Of The KLF** (Cauty·Drummond)	1:53
	05	**Last Train To Trancentral** (Cauty·Drummond·Lyte)	5:36
	06	**Build A Fire** (Cauty·Drummond)	4:39
	07	**The White Room** (Cauty·Drummond)	5:15
▶	08	**No More Tears** (Cauty·Drummond)	9:24
	09	**Justified And Ancient** (Cauty·Drummond)	4:45

Massive Attack | Blue Lines (1991)

Label | Virgin
Producer | Johnny Dollar • Massive Attack
Art Direction | Robert "3D" Del Naja • Michael Nash
Nationality | UK
Running Time | 45:22

Massive Attack's debut album was a revelation, launching a decade-spanning movement that focused on the fusion between hip hop and coffee-table downtempo and leading to the rise of acts such as Morcheeba and Groove Armada. Massive Attack themselves have stripped down their lineup to the core trio of rappers 3-D and Daddy G. plus guest vocalist Horace Andy, which was regrettable for many fans, as the mumbling, vicious vocals of Tricky and the gorgeous, spiraling wails of Shara Nelson were the obvious high points of this fantastic album.

The two singles, "Safe From Harm"—based on a slinky Sly And Robbie sample—and the song that for thousands was the song of the decade, "Unfinished Sympathy," are high points, with the latter's rich strings anchoring Nelson's agonizingly emotional love song. But the rest of it, unusually, is almost as good, with the awesome, thundering bass groove of "Five Man Army," the sweet ambient balladeering of "Hymn Of The Big Wheel," and the funky squelch lollop of "Daydreaming" all moments to cherish. What made the record so popular was the urban chic brought to it from the dark and dangerous Bristol slums where the personnel lived and worked, and the fact that "The Wild Bunch" who produced it (among whom was future star producer Nellee Hooper) were a gang; a no-hope collective of hip hop, reggae, and weed consumers who liked their music raw and rich.

All of which makes *Blue Lines'* polished, precision-engineered sound an unexpected treasure, and certainly a perfect contender for the finest downtempo album ever made. **JM**

"You escape from yourself."

Robert Del Naja, 2003

Track Listing

▶ 01 **Safe From Harm**
(Cobham•Del Naja•Marshall•Nelson•Vowles)   5:16

02 **One Love**
(Cobham•Del Naja•Marshall•Vowles•Williams)   4:48

03 **Blue Lines** (Bennett•Brown•Carlton • Del Naja
Guerin•Marshall•Scott•Thaws•Vowles)   4:41

04 **Be Thankful For What You've Got** (DeVaughn)   4:09

▶ 05 **Five Man Army**
(Del Naja•Marshall•Thaws•Vowles•Williams)   6:04

▶ 06 **Unfinished Sympathy**
(Del Naja•Marshall•Nelson•Sharp•Vowles)   5:08

07 **Daydreaming**
(Badarou•Del Naja•Marshall•Thaws•Vowles)   4:14

08 **Lately** (Brownlee•Del Naja•Marshall
Nelson•Redmond•Simon•Vowles)   4:26

09 **Hymn Of The Big Wheel**
(Andy•Cherry•Del Naja•Marshall•Vowles)   6:36

Primal Scream | Screamadelica (1991)

Label | Creation
Producer | Various
Art Direction | Paul Cannell
Nationality | UK
Running Time | 65:02

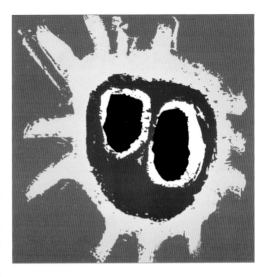

While bands such as the Happy Mondays and Stone Roses had been taking cues from club culture for a while, *Screamadelica* tore down the barriers. Bug-eyed dance fiends found merit in rock, floppy-haired indie-rockers cut loose on the dancefloor, and suddenly anyone who did not have a copy felt rather square.

Previously, Primal Scream had been an unremarkable jangly rock band with a couple of albums under their belt. However, acid house was taking off in Britain and, in 1990, they got DJ Andrew Weatherall to experiment with remixing their track "I'm Losing More Than I'll Ever Have."

The result was "Loaded." Stripped down, dubbed up, and with samples of Peter Fonda in Sixties biker movie *The Wild Angels* ("We wanna get loaded . . . we wanna have a good time"), it was a phenomenon. "Loaded" and the glorious gospel-house of "Come Together" that followed it formed the backbone of 1991's astonishing voyage into modern psychedelia (U.S./Japan pressings featured the less euphoric seven-inch version of "Come Together"). Weatherall retained the driving seat for most of its kaleidoscopic grooves, while Stones producer Jimmy Miller handled the two "rock" cuts—"Movin' On Up" and "Damaged." The Orb also crafted the mind-blowing alien dub transmission of "Higher Than The Sun," while Hypnotone helped whip 13th Floor Elevators' "Slip Inside This House" into a snarling, bass-driven beast.

A collaboration album, perhaps, but while the producers can claim much of the credit for the music, it was Primal Scream who had the vision to demonstrate that dance music could exist alongside rock. **RS**

"The best thing about 'Loaded' was that it proved we were right."

Bobby Gillespie, 1990

Track Listing		
01 Movin' On Up (Gillespie·Innes·Young)		3:50
▶ 02 Slip Inside This House (Erikson·Hall)		5:16
▶ 03 Don't Fight It, Feel it (Gillespie·Innes·Young)		6:53
▶ 04 Higher Than The Sun (Gillespie·Innes·Young)		3:38
05 Inner Flight (Gillespie·Innes·Young)		5:01
▶ 06 Come Together (Gillespie·Innes·Young)		10:21
▶ 07 Loaded (Gillespie·Innes·Young)		7:02
08 Damaged (Gillespie·Innes·Young)		5:39
▶ 09 I'm Coming Down (Gillespie·Innes·Young)		6:00
10 Higher Than The Sun — A Dub Symphony In Two Parts (Gillespie·Innes·Young)		7:38
11 Shine Like Stars (Gillespie·Innes·Young)		3:44

Teenage Fanclub | Bandwagonesque (1991)

Label | Creation
Producer | P. Chisolm • D. Fleming • Teenage Fanclub
Art Direction | Sharon Fitzgerald
Nationality | UK
Running Time | 42:51

A band for which the word "quirky" may have been invented, Teenage Fanclub had always possessed an infuriating knack of confounding expectations. They promised so much with 1990's *A Catholic Education* and the majestic "Everything Flows," but celebrated joining the prestigious Creation label with *The King*, a frankly rubbish set of instrumental covers.

Having tested the patience of a once-supportive music press, the knives were drawn for the Fannies when they released their masterpiece. A high-water mark for the British indie scene's obsession with the past, *Bandwagonesque* was steeped in rock tradition—Neil Young, Love, The Byrds, The Beach Boys, Big Star, even a half-ironic nod to Status Quo.

Yet to critics who thought it was acceptable for Primal Scream to impersonate The Rolling Stones, such unashamedly vintage influences were anathema. Little matter that *Bandwagonesque* was more consistently great than *Sweetheart Of The Rodeo* or *#1 Record*. This was a time when dance music, shoe-gazing, and the fading Madchester fad still ruled. The Fannies were labeled unimaginative—only for Suede and Oasis to be heralded as the future of British rock. Oh, the irony.

Bandwagonesque has so many highlights that you forget it is only a single album. Three indisputable classic Nineties indie singles ("The Concept," "Star Sign," "What You Do To Me"); three beautiful tear-jerkers ("December," "Guiding Star," and the instrumental, "Is This Music?"), harmonies that would make Brian Wilson blush, and a warm, overdriven edge that united Sonic Youth with The Archies. Beat that, Kurt Cobain. **MBe**

> **"The concept behind 'The Concept' is that there's no concept."**
>
> Brendan O'Hare, 1991

Track Listing

▶ 01	**The Concept**	(Blake)	6:06
02	**Satan**	(Teenage Fanclub)	1:22
▶ 03	**December**	(Love)	3:03
▶ 04	**What You Do To Me**	(Blake)	2:00
05	**I Don't Know**	(McGinley)	4:36
▶ 06	**Star Sign**	(Love)	4:56
07	**Metal Baby**	(Blake)	3:39
08	**Pet Rock**	(Love)	2:35
09	**Sidewinder**	(Love•O'Hare)	3:03
10	**Alcoholiday**	(Blake)	5:26
▶ 11	**Guiding Star**	(Love)	2:48
▶ 12	**Is This Music?**	(Love)	3:17

Metallica | Metallica (1991)

Label | Elektra
Producer | James Hetfield • Bob Rock • Lars Ulrich
Art Direction | Uncredited
Nationality | Denmark • USA
Running Time | 62:31

It is not all Garth Brooks and Eagles among the all-time bestsellers. Among them are Zeppelin, AC/DC, and Guns N' Roses too. But heaviest of all are—cue roaring crowds—Metallica.

The Bay Area brain-bashers first registered outside the metal fraternity when 1988's ... *And Justice For All* cracked Billboard's Top Ten (months before "One" gave them anything approaching a hit single); a remarkable achievement in the days before the SoundScan system made chart-toppers of Pantera and Skid Row.

But ... *And Justice For All* was a bloated beast, its songs so convoluted that the band had trouble playing them onstage. So, for *Metallica*—a.k.a. *The Black Album* —they enlisted no-nonsense hit producer Bob Rock, having been impressed by his work with Mötley Crüe.

The results—though light-years from the party-hardy Crüe—were their most concise songs, with brutally efficient riffs and attack-pattern drums, but fewer fiddly structures and much less indulgence from guitarist Kirk Hammett. Even the epics—"Whenever I May Roam,""Nothing Else Matters"—maintain interest, thanks to their sitars and strings (the latter orchestrated by Pink Floyd collaborator Michael Kamen). Hammett, drummer Lars Ulrich, and bassist Jason Newsted make key contributions (a triumph for Newsted after he had been mixed out of ... *And Justice For All*), but the star is James Hetfield. His vocals (terrifying yet tasteful), crunching guitar (see "Sad But True"), and eloquent lyrics (setting Metallica far above Zeppelin, AC/DC, and G'N'R) are a lethal cocktail that turned the likes of "Enter Sandman" into instant classics. **BM**

> "Everyone has one album when everything comes together."
>
> Lars Ulrich, 1996

Track Listing

▶	01	Enter Sandman (Hammett•Hetfield•Ulrich)	5:31
▶	02	Sad But True (Hetfield•Ulrich)	5:24
	03	Holier Than Thou (Hetfield•Ulrich)	3:47
	04	The Unforgiven (Hammett•Hetfield•Ulrich)	6:27
	05	Wherever I May Roam (Hetfield•Ulrich)	6:44
	06	Don't Tread On Me (Hetfield•Ulrich)	4:00
	07	Through The Never (Hammett•Hetfield•Ulrich)	4:04
▶	08	Nothing Else Matters (Hetfield•Ulrich)	6:28
	09	Of Wolf And Man (Hammett•Hetfield•Ulrich)	4:16
	10	The God That Failed (Hetfield•Ulrich)	5:08
	11	My Friend Of Misery (Hetfield•Newsted•Ulrich)	6:49
	12	The Struggle Within (Hetfield•Ulrich)	3:53

Pavement | Slanted And Enchanted (1992)

Label | Big Cat
Producer | Pavement
Art Direction | Stefan Sagmeister
Nationality | USA
Running Time | 39:01

If Nirvana had opened the doors for alternative bands to achieve mainstream success in 1992, Pavement seemed determined to shy away from it—to little avail. Early cassettes of their debut album *Slanted And Enchanted* did not even come with song titles, but the album still showed up in *The Village Voice* end-of-year poll in 1991. Since then, the lazy, lo-fi sound of *Slanted And Enchanted*—its very "whatever"-ness—has influenced a flock of indie rock bands.

Pavement were three friends from California: laconic singer Stephen Malkmus (credited on the sleeve as SM), guitarist Scott Kannberg (Spiral Stairs), and unruly hippy drummer Gary Young, who would hand out free cabbages at gigs before being fired from the band a year later. Having rehearsed for a week, Pavement recorded *Slanted ...* in seven days in Young's garage studio, at a cost of $800.

The tone, naturally, is scuffed and raw; Young sounds like he is drumming on a cardboard box, and there is plenty of fuzz-fried guitar. But *Slanted ...* is a hugely inventive record too, playfully weaving in elements of free jazz; and while Malkmus' lyrics are cryptic ("lies and betrayals, fruit covered nails" he muses on "Trigger Cut"), there is a real honesty and emotional charge at the heart of these songs. Take a listen to the frustration and yearning of delicious opener "Summer Babe," or the amiable I-give-up of "Zurich Is Stained," with its wobbly, clear-channeled guitars.

"We were young, naive, and we had something to believe in," reflects Kannberg. With its torn edges and messy emotions, *Slanted ...* is still a perfect record. **SH**

Track Listing

▶ 01	**Summer Babe (Winter Version)** (Kannberg·Malkmus·Young)	3:16
▶ 02	**Trigger Cut•Wounded–Kite At :17** (Kannberg·Malkmus·Young)	3:16
03	**No Life Singed Her** (Kannberg·Malkmus·Young)	2:09
▶ 04	**In The Mouth A Desert** (Kannberg·Malkmus·Young)	3:52
05	**Conduit For Sale!** (Kannberg·Malkmus·Young)	2:52
06	**Zurich Is Stained** (Kannberg·Malkmus·Young)	1:41
07	**Chesley's Little Wrists** (Kannberg·Malkmus·Young)	1:16
08	**Loretta's Scars** (Kannberg·Malkmus·Young)	2:55
▶ 09	**Here** (Kannberg·Malkmus·Young)	3:56
10	**Two States** (Kannberg·Malkmus·Young)	1:47
11	**Perfume–V** (Kannberg·Malkmus·Young)	2:09
12	**Fame Throwa** (Kannberg·Malkmus·Young)	3:22
13	**Jackals, False Grails: The Lonesome Era** (Kannberg·Malkmus·Young)	3:21
14	**Our Singer** (Kannberg·Malkmus·Young)	3:09

Aphex Twin | Selected Ambient Works 85–92 (1992)

Label | R&S
Producer | Richard D. James
Art Direction | Uncredited
Nationality | UK
Running Time | 74:20

Aphex Twin — Selected Ambient Works 85-92

Any raver worth their air-cushioned sneakers or, indeed, anyone with more than a passing interest in electronic music, should have a well-worn copy of *Selected Ambient Works 85–92* in their collection. It was a watershed for dance music, its sparse beats and haunting synth lines sounding as intoxicating and otherworldly today as they ever did.

By 1992, Richard D. James had achieved notoriety with his *Analogue Bubblebath* EPs and the acid monster that was "Didgeridoo." He had also co-formed the now legendary Rephlex records, releasing hard techno as Caustic Window. However, the dance music climate was changing, as people were beginning to explore its potential (this was at least partly down to rave's rising BPMs and increasing tendency toward novelty chart hits). In the same vein, The Orb had recently perfected their concept of "ambient house" with 1991's *Adventures Beyond The Ultraworld*. The time was right for *SAW 85–92*, a collection of ambient techno recordings created on James' homemade electronic gear (he would have been 14 in 1985).

It is a lengthy album—over 70 minutes. However, despite sounding unlike anything else, it is accessible—hypnotic, seductive, and perfectly suited to the growing army of fans of what would (annoyingly) become labeled as "intelligent dance music."

There is only one vocal sample on the entire album, from *Willy Wonka And The Chocolate Factory*—"We are the music makers, and we are the dreamers of dreams." Partly true: we can all dream, but only Richard D. James can make this music. **RS**

" ... My music's my favorite music ever."

Richard D. James, 2001

Track Listing		
▶ 01 Xtal (James)		4:51
02 Tha (James)		9:01
▶ 03 Pulsewidth (James)		3:47
04 Ageispolis (James)		5:21
05 I (James)		1:13
▶ 06 Green Calx (James)		6:02
▶ 07 Heliosphan (James)		4:51
08 We Are The Music Makers (James)		7:42
▶ 09 Schottkey 7th Path (James)		5:07
10 Ptolemy (James)		7:12
▶ 11 Hedphelym (James)		6:02
12 Delphium (James)		5:36
13 Actium (James)		7:35

Arrested Development | 3 Years, 5 Months And 2 Days In The Life Of ...(1992)

Label | Chrysalis
Producer | Speech
Art Direction | Randall Martin
Nationality | USA
Running Time | 61:08

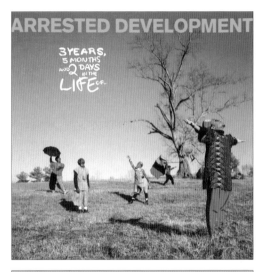

When Arrested Development's debut appeared in 1992, the Atlanta band seemed to herald a new dawn in hip hop. It seemed they had created a distinctly rural, Southern brand of the genre to blow apart the East Coast/West Coast factionalism.

Of course, it didn't happen quite like that. When Dixie did rise, it came in the form of the "Dirty South" (the source of crunk) and took its cue from the pornographic go-go of 2 Live Crew, not politically correct worthies like Arrested Development. They split in 1996 and cerebral frontman Todd Thomas, a.k.a. Speech, released pleasing but largely ignored albums.

However, it would be a crime to ignore the gentle genius of this album (titled after the time it took to land a recording contract). The centerpiece is the thumping hit "Tennessee," a half-spoken, half-sung conversation with God that beautifully articulates the painful legacy of slavery better than any other hip-hop track. Elsewhere there is a tribute to the homeless ("Mr. Wendal"), a De La Soul/Jungle Brothers-inspired reading of Sly Stone ("People Everyday"), and the vaudevillian "Mama's Always On Stage," a deep-fried Southern soul reading of Madness'"Our House."

Traces of their Southern-fried funk eventually resurfaced, particularly in the work of other Atlanta natives like TLC, Cee-Lo Green, the Goodie Mob, and notably, Andre 3000 and Outkast. It showed hip hop could draw from centuries of black musical culture while still looking into the future. **JLe**

Track Listing

01	**Man's Final Frontier** (Barnwell·Thomas)	2:38
02	**Mama's Always On Stage** (Guy·Thomas·Wells)	3:25
03	**People Everyday** (Stewart·Thomas)	3:26
04	**Blues Happy** (Barnwell·Thomas)	0:46
▶ 05	**Mr Wendal** (Stewart·Thomas)	4:06
06	**Children Play With Earth** (Barnwell·Thomas)	2:38
07	**Raining Revolution** (Thomas)	3:25
08	**Fishin' 4 Religion** (Stewart·Thomas)	4:06
09	**Give A Man A Fish** (Barnwell·Riperton·Rudolph·Thomas)	4:22
10	**U** (Clinton·Dylan·Thomas·Wynn)	4:59
11	**Eve Of Reality** (Barnwell·Thomas)	1:53
12	**Natural** (Bailey·MacKay·Thomas·White)	4:18
13	**Dawn Of The Dreads** (Thomas)	5:17
▶ 14	**Tennessee** (Jones·Thomas)	4:32
15	**Washed Away** (Thomas)	6:22
▶ 16	**People Everyday (Metamorphosis Mix)** (James·Thomas)	4:55

Koffi Olomidé | Haut De Gamme —Koweït, Rive Gauche (1992)

Label | Tamaris
Producer | Koffi Olomidé
Art Direction | Uncredited
Nationality | Democratic Republic Of Congo
Running Time | 58:12

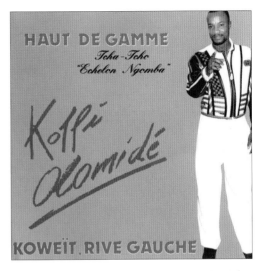

The most successful contemporary singer from Congo in Central Africa is Koffi Olomidé. He has become the biggest selling artist from the entire African continent by performing his own version of the Congolese rumba that he has dubbed "Tcha-Tcho."

Haut De Gamme—Koweït Rive Gauche was the album that led to Olomidé becoming a sensation across Africa. The songs have a typically Congolese structure—a slow and lyrical first half followed by a second half that breaks into a guitar-led dance section with repeated vocal refrains of encouragement (known as "animations") to the dancers. Olomidé has a romantic, crooning vocal style, and his lyrics, mostly in Lingala and French, are clearly the work of a poet. His music particularly appeals to a female audience; the songs are tender and often gloriously syrupy with lavish synthesized string sections and crisp programmed percussion. When the music breaks into the dance section it springs into life, with looped guitar phrases backed by snare drum and funky basslines.

The track "Papa Bonheur" has become an anthem and dancefloor favorite for Olomidé fans. More subtle and heavily arranged titles like "Qui Cherche Trouve" and "Dit Jeannot" counterpoint his gravel-edged voice with the angelic female voice of Déesse Mukangi and veteran singer Nyboma. This monumental album demonstrates that Koffi Olomidé's Congolese music is capable of balancing studio technology with the raw dancefloor energy of modern African music. **MS**

> "[Tcha-Tcho] means 'let's be true—authentic—every time.' I am different, I have class."
>
> Koffi Olomidé, 2001

Track Listing

▶ 01	**Papa Bonheur** (Olomidé)	7:10
02	**Désespoir** (Olomidé)	6:23
03	**Koweït, Rive Gauche** (Olomidé)	6:35
▶ 04	**Qui Cherche Trouve** (Olomidé)	6:46
05	**Elixir** (Olomidé)	4:52
▶ 06	**Porte-Monnaie** (Olomidé)	6:27
07	**Conte De Fées** (Olomidé)	7:15
08	**Obrigado** (Olomidé)	6:42
▶ 09	**Dit Jeannot** (Olomidé)	6:02

Morrissey | "Your Arsenal" (1992)

Label | HMV
Producer | Mick Ronson
Art Direction | E. Riff • J. Slee • Designland
Nationality | UK
Running Time | 39:32

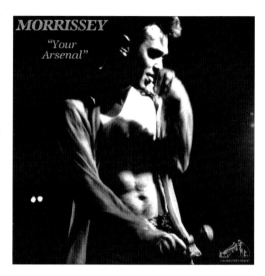

Morrissey might not have cared for controversy, but he certainly did not go out of his way to avoid it. Before *"Your Arsenal"* was even released, he had wished a variety of horrible deaths (motorway pile-ups; hotel fires) upon The Smiths' biographer, Johnny Rogan. The album itself featured a track that went by the unforgivably (in the eyes of the press) ambiguous title "The National Front Disco." And then, Morrissey appeared on stage provocatively waving a Union Jack while performing the same song at a Madness concert, in front of a backdrop featuring two skinhead girls. (The audience threw bottles at him until he left.)

"Is Morrissey Racist?" asked *NME*. Morrissey was not saying. The hoopla overshadowed an excellent album. Produced by David Bowie's ex-sideman Mick Ronson, *"Your Arsenal"* was a glam rock-infused celebration of masculinity (the album cover's homoeroticism resembles an outtake from a Robbie Williams photoshoot). Morrissey was now backed by a proper band (including Boz Boorer and Alain Whyte on guitar), and this encouraged a simulacrum of The Smiths' last-gang-in-town mentality. On Glitteresque stompathon "Glamorous Glue," Moz prophesied: "We look to Los Angeles/for the language we use/London is dead"; "We'll Let You Know" was a haunting attempt to get inside the head of football hooligans; "The National Front Disco" was thrilling and surprisingly hilarious (a disco for Nazis?). There were also missteps—particularly the kitsch single "You're The One For Me Fatty"—but *"Your Arsenal"* was certainly Morrissey's finest and most confident work for years. **PW**

> ## "I wanted to make as physical an album as I possibly could."
>
> Morrissey, 1992

Track Listing

▶ 01	**You're Gonna Need Someone On Your Side** (Morrissey • Nevin)	3:38
▶ 02	**Glamorous Glue** (Morrissey • Whyte)	4:01
▶ 03	**We'll Let You Know** (Morrissey • Whyte)	5:17
▶ 04	**The National Front Disco** (Morrissey • Whyte)	4:24
05	**Certain People I Know** (Morrissey • Whyte)	3:12
06	**We Hate It When Our Friends Become Successful** (Morrissey • Whyte)	2:30
07	**You're The One For Me, Fatty** (Morrissey • Whyte)	2:57
08	**Seasick, Yet Still Docked** (Morrissey • Whyte)	5:07
▶ 09	**I Know It's Gonna Happen Someday** (Morrissey • Nevin)	4:20
▶ 10	**Tomorrow** (Morrissey • Whyte)	4:06

Baaba Maal | Lam Toro (1992)

Label | Mango • Island
Producer | Simon Booth • Eric Clermontet • Baaba Maal
Art Direction | Uncredited
Nationality | Senegal
Running Time | 52:28

It is usually impossible to spot exact sea-change moments in music. Even the most seminal events (Elvis at Sun, the Sex Pistols' first gig) have a host of antecedents. And so it is for this album: it is not the first time an African artist had the opportunity to record with a producer who understood what a white audience —especially a young white audience wanted, but it sure felt like it.

For years, African bands had been herded into French studios and told to record their live set; then the producer would add synths so audiences at home could marvel at the new sounds. Most of those records are now hideous, but Simon Booth's work with Maal retains its freshness. The opening track, which mixes Maal's band, Daande Lenol ("Voice Of The People") with African-Jamaican toasting, should sound old hat, but it is definitely stirring stuff.

It is on the song "Daande Lenol" that Booth— previously known as a musician with Working Week, as well as a prime mover in the short-lived but influential acid jazz scene—started moving things in new directions. Or old directions: Davy Spillane's uillean pipes duet with Kaow Cissoko's kora in an atmospheric intro that sounds Irish no matter how well you get to know it. Then the tama, or "talking drum," and Maal's soaring voice join in. It builds and builds, eventually turning African seamlessly.

Inspired, Booth went on to form the Afro Celt Sound System to pursue this synthesis farther; Maal continued his pop fusion with varying degrees of success. But this was the first giant leap for both. **DH**

> "Music in Africa is communication. It's like an old man, and if it dies, it is like a library burning down."

Baaba Maal, 2005

Track Listing

▶	01	Hamady Boiro (Yelle) (Maal)	4:32
▶	02	Daande Lenol (Maal)	5:43
	03	Lem Gi (Le Miel) (Maal)	7:12
	04	Ndelorel (Maal)	4:00
▶	05	Yela (Maal)	4:37
	06	Toro (Tioulel L'Oiseau) (Maal)	2:31
	07	Daniibe (Les Exilés) (Maal)	7:58
	08	Olel (L'Echo) (Maal)	5:55
	09	Sy Sawande (Maal)	5:27
▶	10	Hamady Bogle (Maal)	4:33

Lemonheads
It's A Shame About Ray (1992)

Label | Atlantic
Producer | Evan Dando • The Robb Brothers
Art Direction | Jodi Rovin
Nationality | USA
Running Time | 33:08

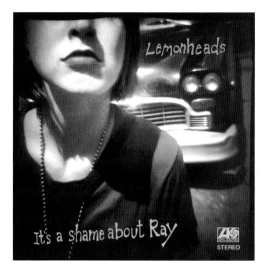

A year before *It's A Shame About Ray* came out, Evan Dando was just some guy in a poppy garage band from Boston. By 1993, he was voted one of "*People Magazine*'s Most Beautiful," and it seemed like everyone owned a copy of The Lemonheads' breakthrough fifth album.

What brought about such heady success? The meteoric impact of Nirvana's *Nevermind* (1991) had made alternative music commercially viable (The Lemonheads' mellow folk, rocking guitars, and sweet boy/girl harmonies were even tagged "bubblegrunge"). Then there was their cover of Simon and Garfunkel's "Mrs. Robinson": recorded in three hours in Berlin, after a request from a company who were re-releasing *The Graduate* and wanted to make it accessible to the new generation of slacker kids. With heavy MTV rotation and radio play, it became inescapable, and interest in *It's A Shame About Ray* (released a couple of months previously) was reignited; the track was hastily added.

But there is more to … *Ray*'s appeal than just good timing, namely Dando's golden touch with songwriting. He always had a knack for scratchy, catchy hooks, but while touring Australia—and meeting co-writer Tom Morgan—his craft developed into something magical. … *Ray* was recorded in L.A. with revered producers The Robb Brothers, and each of its 12 songs is a perfectly formed fizzing pop confection; from the crunchy strums of "Confetti"—so easy-sounding it seems Dando is making it up on the spot—to the melancholy, lost-summer wooze of "My Drug Buddy." **SH**

"I am a damn good singer."

Evan Dando, 2005

Track Listing		
01 Rockin' Stroll (Dando)		1:47
▶ 02 Confetti (Dando)		2:44
▶ 03 It's A Shame About Ray (Dando • Morgan)		3:06
04 Rudderless (Dando)		3:19
▶ 05 My Drug Buddy (Dando)		2:51
06 The Turnpike Down (Dando)		2:33
07 Bit Part (Dando, Morgan)		1:51
08 Alison's Starting To Happen (Dando)		1:59
▶ 09 Hannah And Gabi (Dando)		2:40
10 Kitchen (Dalton)		2:55
11 Ceiling Fan In My Spoon (Dando)		1:48
12 Frank Mills (Macdermot • Rado • Ragni)		1:44
13 Mrs. Robinson (Simon)		3:43

Rage Against The Machine
Rage Against The Machine (1992)

Label | Epic
Producer | Rage Against the Machine • Garth Richardson
Art Direction | Nicky Lindeman
Nationality | USA
Running Time | 52:56

Rage Against The Machine exploded into mainstream music like a musical version of *The Anarchist Cookbook*. With their original and potent mix of metal, rap, and leftist politics, Rage Against The Machine produced a debut album so powerful that it shook apathetic teenagers into an awareness of the injustices of capitalism.

Guitarist Tommy Morello's pioneering metal virtuosity added interludes of buzz-saw scratching to searing solos and Sabbath-style blood-pumping riffs—on "Know Your Enemy" he parades four successive licks ranging from funky to frenetic, plays a few bars of speed metal, and throws in some crunchy noise. Zach de la Rocha, meanwhile, belts out raised-fist rhymes with relentless energy, whether rapping the streetwise self-props of "Bombtrack," reciting the staccato history lesson of "Wake Up" (a paean to Martin Luther King, Malcolm X, and Cassius Clay), or riding the radical groove of "Township Rebellion," a tale of anti-imperialist struggle from South Central to South Africa.

De la Rocha specializes in unleashing raw rage, and his most enduring moments occur when the band's insatiable buildups leave him screaming out in repetitive defiance. "Bullet In The Head," an anti-corporate-media manifesto, climaxes in a wall of Brad Wilk's furious double-time drumming set against a devastating rapid-fire Morello lick, with de la Rocha bawling the brutal chorus until his voice gives out.

A decade later, the sound and relevancy of Rage Against The Machine's debut remains unmatched. **MW**

> ## "Fight the war, fuck the norm."
> Rage Against The Machine, "Township Rebellion," 1992

Track Listing

▶	01	**Bombtrack** (Rage Against The Machine)	4:05
▶	02	**Killing In The Name** (Rage Against The Machine)	5:14
	03	**Take The Power Back** (Rage Against The Machine)	5:37
	04	**Settle For Nothing** (Rage Against The Machine)	4:48
▶	05	**Bullet In The Head** (Rage Against The Machine)	5:10
▶	06	**Know Your Enemy** (Rage Against The Machine)	4:56
▶	07	**Wake Up** (Rage Against The Machine)	6:04
	08	**Fistful Of Steel** (Rage Against The Machine)	5:31
	09	**Township Rebellion** (Rage Against The Machine)	5:24
	10	**Freedom** (Rage Against The Machine)	6:07

The Disposable Heroes Of Hiphoprisy
Hypocrisy Is The Greatest Luxury (1992)

Label | 4th & Broadway
Producer | Jeff Mann
Art Direction | Victor Hall
Nationality | USA
Running Time | 66:26

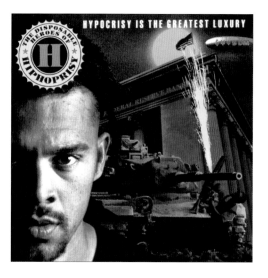

In the mid-1990s, as America continued to agonize over multiculturalism in the wake of both the Los Angeles riots and the trial of O.J. Simpson, The Disposable Heroes of Hiphoprisy—vocalist Michael Franti and musician Rono Tse—were carving out a soundtrack to the concerns of the day in a used car yard in Oakland, near San Francisco.

As logical successors to the crown of Public Enemy, The Disposable Heroes of Hiphoprisy remain unparalleled. *Hypocrisy Is The Greatest Luxury*, a deliciously sinuous and metallic collection of beats and agit-rap vocals held together by blasts of machinery, breathed life into rap music—taking in, among other issues, black-on-black violence, racism, politics, war, media manipulation, feminism, and urban despair. While their contemporaries Run-DMC and N.W.A. stuck with formulaic poses, *Hypocrisy Is The Greatest Luxury* immediately coined its own genre: dial-an-issue rap music. That is not meant to sound disparaging; the record, although ignored by urban radio at the time, is now considered a legitimate answer to the rallying cry of Sixties black poets such as The Watts Prophets and The Last Poets.

Their live show was challenging but would see the group limited to a college audience. After a subsequent collaboration with William S. Burroughs, Franti soon became bored with The Disposable Heroes Of Hiphoprisy's post-apocalyptic explorations. His current group, Spearhead, has proved to be its antithesis. **BW**

Track Listing

▶ 01	**Satanic Reverses** (Franti)	4:45
02	**Famous And Dandy (Like Amos And Andy)** (Franti)	6.34
▶ 03	**Television, The Drug Of The Nation** (Franti)	6:38
▶ 04	**Language Of Violence** (Franti)	6:15
05	**The Winter Of The Long Hot Summer** (Franti)	7:59
06	**Hypocrisy Is The Greatest Luxury** (Franti)	3:47
07	**Everyday Life Has Become A Health Risk** (Franti)	4:54
08	**Ins Greencard A-19 191 500** (Franti)	1:36
09	**Socio-Genetic Experiment** (Franti)	4:19
10	**Music And Politics** (Franti)	4:01
11	**Financial Leprosy** (Franti)	5:30
▶ 12	**California Über Alles** (Biafra·Dead Kennedys)	4:13
13	**Water Pistol Man** (Franti)	5:55

K.D. Lang | Ingénue (1992)

Label | Warner Bros.
Producer | K.D. Lang • Ben Mink • Greg Penny
Art Direction | Jeri Heiden • Glen Erler
Nationality | Canada
Running Time | 41:47

After four average if inventive country albums, K.D. Lang wanted to take a bold step. Brilliantly arranged and orchestrated by her writing partner Ben Mink, this "postnuclear cabaret," as lang called it, of category-defying pop, tango, swing, lounge, and, in a Lyle Lovett-kind-of-way, alternative country was the courageous statement of a woman coming to terms with herself.

Despite the occasional pedal-steel guitar, Lang had officially abandoned Nashville—a scene that rewarded her with Grammys but was never comfortable with her ambiguous sexuality. With *Ingénue*, the Canadian singer and songwriter chose to get personal. "Surely help will arrive soon and cure these self-induced wounds," she sang in "The Mind Of Love," revealing more about herself than on all of her previous country albums. From Glen Erler's soft and highly intimate portrait on the jacket to lines about "a great magnet" pulling "all souls towards the truth" in the hit single "Constant Craving," *Ingénue* heralded a new beginning.

The fact that, only three months after its release, Lang publicly announced her homosexuality in an interview with the Canadian newspaper *The Advocate* did not harm the album's commercial success. To Lang's great relief, people did not mind knowing that sensual songs such as "Wash Me Clean" and "Miss Chatelaine" on this emotional and entirely autobiographical record were fueled by the experience of longing for a married woman. *Ingénue* continued to be loved by millions not only for its unique and confident musical vision and superb vocal performance, but also for the honest portrayal of universal feelings. **CL**

> "*Ingénue* is based on my experiences of falling in love, and it's the most personally revealing record I've ... made."
>
> K.D. Lang, 1992

Track Listing

▶ 01	**Save Me** (lang • Mink)	4:33
02	**The Mind Of Love** (lang • Mink)	3:48
03	**Miss Chatelaine** (lang • Mink)	3:48
04	**Wash Me Clean** (lang)	3:17
▶ 05	**So It Shall Be** (lang • Penny)	4:29
06	**Still Thrives This Love** (lang • Mink)	3:33
07	**Season Of Hollow Soul** (lang • Mink)	4:56
▶ 08	**Outside Myself** (lang • Mink)	4:57
09	**Tears Of Love's Recall** (lang • Mink)	3:48
▶ 10	**Constant Craving** (lang • Mink)	4:38

Dr. Dre | The Chronic (1992)

Label | Death Row
Producer | Dr. Dre
Art Direction | Kimberly Holt
Nationality | USA
Running Time | 62:46

Rap battles are rarely dull. They can become full-blown fights and sometimes end in murder. But before the killing started, the battlefield was the Billboard chart.

In 1993, it was Eazy E. vs. Dr. Dre. They had put gangsta rap on the map with N.W.A., then fallen victim to financial feuding. Dre was rescued by rap agent Suge Knight, and the pair formed the Death Row organization. Its first offensive was *The Chronic*, which lambasts Eazy from the first to (unlisted) final track.

Eazy responded with *It's On (Dr. Dre) 187um Killa*, which accused Dre of being a "studio gangsta" and gloated that a contractual clause entitled Eazy to a slice of Dre's royalties. It went platinum but was sandbagged by sounding suspiciously like a Dre production and—unlike *The Chronic*—failing to rival *Nevermind* as the most influential album of the decade.

Dre's secret weapons were brilliant young MCs. Snoop Dogg's paw-prints cover the album, but also of note are The Lady of Rage, The D.O.C., and Kurupt. Most producers would simply have added beats to their rhymes; Dre created a whole new genre—G-funk—replacing rap's brutality with laidback, Seventies-style soul. Smashes "Let Me Ride" (source: Parliament) and "Nuthin' But A 'G' Thang" are easily matched by the Donny Hathaway-based "Lil' Ghetto Boy." Even when Dre does simply loop a beat, the results are astounding: witness the Led Zeppelin-based "Lyrical Gangbang."

Meanwhile, the Dre vs. Eazy tension simmered until the latter's death in 1995. "He can make a million records about me if he wants to," said Dre airily. "He's keeping my name out there." **BM**

Track Listing

01	**The Chronic (Intro)**	(Dogg·Dre·Wolfe)	1:58
▶ 02	**Fuck Wit Dre Day (And Everybody's Celebratin')**	(Dogg·Dre·Wolfe)	4:51
▶ 03	**Let Me Ride**	(Clinton·Collins·Dogg·Worrell)	4:21
04	**The Day The Niggaz Took Over**	(Arnaud·Colandreo·Collins·Dogg·Parker)	4:32
▶ 05	**Nuthin' But A "G" Thang**	(Dogg·Haywood·Knight)	3:58
06	**Deeez Nuuuts**	(Dogg·Dre·Wolfe)	5:06
07	**Lil' Ghetto Boy**	(Curry·Dogg)	5:27
08	**A Nigga Witta Gun**	(Curry·Snoop)	3:52
09	**Rat-Tat-Tat-Tat**	(Curry·Young)	3:48
10	**The $20 Sack Pyramid**	(Curry·Dre·Snoop)	2:53
11	**Lyrical Gangbang**	(Curry·Dogg·Dre·Kurupt·Rage·RBX·)	4:04
12	**High Powered**	(Dre·RBX·Wolfe)	2:44
13	**The Doctor's Office**	(Dre·Jewell·Lewis·Rage)	1:03
14	**Stranded On Death Row**	(Allen·Brown·Dogg Dre·Hayes·Middendorf·Nichols·Williams)	4:46
15	**The Roach (The Chronic Outro)**	(Daz·RBX·Rage)	4:36
16	**Bitches Ain't Shit**	(Curry·Daz·Dogg·Dre·Kurupt·Wolfe)	4:47

R.E.M. | Automatic For The People (1992)

Label | Warner Bros.
Producer | Scott Litt • R.E.M.
Art Direction | Anton Corbijn • Michael Stipe
Nationality | USA
Running Time | 49:31

In 1992 R.E.M. wrong-footed everyone. Previously the band had dealt in an upbeat, emotive, and hugely successful brand of folk pop on second major label album, *Out Of Time*. But the guest rappers and mandolins were soon to be replaced by something altogether more subtle, humane, and lasting.

Indeed, Anton Corbijn's sleeve photography—monochrome and moody—hinted that bleaker themes might lie within. Critics and fans alike were bowled over by the maudlin, acoustic majesty of lead single "Drive"—a transatlantic Top Five hit, yet one with no chorus and orchestration from Zep's John Paul Jones.

The title came from a restaurant in the band's hometown of Athens, Georgia. Housed beneath it were six singles (many still used as set-closers), from the lyrically obtuse yet upbeat "Sidewinder . . ." to the ever-hopeful "Everybody Hurts" (as direct and devastating a lyric as Michael Stipe ever wrote). "Man On The Moon," a crowd-pleaser about comedian Andy Kaufman, was later used in the movie of the same name.

Much here is concerned with death. The narrator of "Try Not To Breathe" is a man waiting to die. However, high point "Sweetness Follows," with spine-tingling feedback, suggests that even at the darkest moments the light is never far away. The recording took place at studios across America. "New Orleans Instrumental Number 1" wordlessly speaks of the freedom this gave them. The shortest track on the album, it portrays a band free of struggle, tugging effortlessly on a serene blanket of dark emotion that it seemed, at the time at least, only they had access to. **JK**

"For us, it feels like a real international record."

Peter Buck, 1992

Track Listing

▶	01	**Drive** (Berry•Buck•Mills•Stipe)	4:30
	02	**Try Not To Breathe** (Berry•Buck•Mills•Stipe)	3:49
▶	03	**The Sidewinder Sleeps Tonight** (Berry•Buck•Mills•Stipe)	4:06
▶	04	**Everybody Hurts** (Berry•Buck•Mills•Stipe)	5:17
	05	**New Orleans Instrumental Number 1** (Berry•Buck•Mills•Stipe)	2:12
▶	06	**Sweetness Follows** (Berry•Buck•Mills•Stipe)	4:19
	07	**Monty Got A Raw Deal** (Berry•Buck•Mills•Stipe)	4:24
	08	**Ignoreland** (Berry•Buck•Mills•Stipe)	3:15
	09	**Star Me Kitten** (Berry•Buck•Mills•Stipe)	5:12
▶	10	**Man On The Moon** (Berry•Buck•Mills•Stipe)	4:19
	11	**Nightswimming** (Berry•Buck•Mills•Stipe)	4:19
	12	**Find The River** (Berry•Buck•Mills•Stipe)	3:49

The Pharcyde | Bizarre Ride II The Pharcyde (1992)

Label | Delicious Vinyl
Producer | J-Swift
Art Direction | Mark Heimback-Nielsen
Nationality | USA
Running Time | 56:31

The Pharcyde debuted with an unforgettable album that spread the Daisy Age philosophy and musical style of the likes of De La Soul on the East Coast, to their Californian cousins. The addition of the preferred West Coast fuel of P-funk to the mix only served to create a more potent and witty brew. Tre "Slimkid" Hardson, Derrick "Fatlip" Stewart, Imani Wilcox, and Romye "Booty Brown" Robinson all emerged from the L.A. arts scene, where they had worked as dancers and choreographers on TV shows such as *In Living Color*.

Together, they created an album that was as funny as it was funky. The street-spat arguments of "Ya Mama," the hilarious "Soul Flower," and "Oh Shit," and the various skits that litter the album portray a free-spirited, fun-loving vibe, full of freaky humor, that was an instant hit with the Lollapalooza crowds they encountered on festival dates across the States.

The common belief was that the group had no idea what they were doing during the recording, but it was high school music teacher Reggie Andrews that brought them together. He oversaw the group's writing and recording and taught them the essential elements of the music industry. But while many MCs and rappers were striving to "keep it real," The Pharcyde instead went out of their way to "keep it original."

J-Swift's production, along with the core members, sacrificed the more immediately catchy hooks for greater depth and a lush, soulful sound. While this may have cost them audiences at the time, the album is now a true classic, both of its time and of hip hop. It remains an influence on the scene even today. **CR**

Track Listing

01	**4 Better Or 4 Worse (Interlude)** (Martinez)		0:36
▶ 02	**Oh Shit** (Hardson・Martinez・Stewart)		4:29
03	**It's Jigaboo Time** (Jackson・Stewart・Wilcox)		1:26
04	**4 Better Or 4 Worse** (Hardson・Martinez・Stewart)		5:03
▶ 05	**I'm That Type of Nigga** (Hardson・Jackson・Martinez)		5:16
06	**If I Were President (Skit)** (Hardson・Martinez・Robinson)		1:01
▶ 07	**Soul Flower** (Bartholomew・Harson・Kincaid)		4:23
08	**On The D.L.** (Hardson・Jackson・Martinez)		4:27
09	**Pack The Pipe** (Interlude) (Martinez)		0:21
▶ 10	**Officer** (Hardson・Martinez・Robinson)		4:00
▶ 11	**Ya Mama** (Hardson・Martinez・Robinson)		4:20
▶ 12	**Passing Me By** (Hardson・Martinez・Robinson)		5:03
13	**Otha Fish** (Barnes・Hardson・Robinson)		5:21
14	**Quinton's On The Way (Skit)** (Hardson・Howze・Martinez)		2:09
▶ 15	**Pack The Pipe** (Hardson・Howze・Martinez)		5:03
16	**Return Of The B-Boy** (Hardson・Martinez・Robinson)		3:33

Spiritualized | Lazer Guided Melodies (1992)

Label | Dedicated
Producer | Barry Clempson • Jason Pierce
Art Direction | Mr. Ugly
Nationality | UK
Running Time | 60:57

In the late 1980s, Spacemen 3 achieved a cult following in the UK, mainly down to their zonked-out live performances in which they would jam endlessly on one chord, oblivious of time and space. By 1991, however, founding members Jason "Spaceman" Pierce and Sonic Boom had fallen out so badly that their final album, *Recurring*, was split equally, with them taking one side each—Pierce's side bore the blueprint of what would become Spiritualized.

The name gave a clue as to his new direction—a combination of the drone-rock of Spacemen 3 with gospel elements. The first few tracks of *Lazer Guided ...* are a slow-building rush, scaling wild peaks and sliding back into spaced-out stupors, all driving guitars, heraldic horns, and wry lyricism—"I Want You" is about wanting to get someone out of your life. Elsewhere, music slows to a deep, cosmic pulse, frequently with drifting, phased vocals evoking the drug experience—examples are the space-gospel of "Take Your Time" or the unfathomably beautiful "Sway."

But it is the interplay between the two members that makes it all so thrilling—on "Angel Sigh," alien choirs seduce and lift the listener to the heavens, before an explosion of guitars and surging horns gut-punches them to the edges of the solar system—only for them to be slowly reeled back in, just in time for it all to happen again. Even the least suggestible listener can be left quite woozy by it all.

Later albums cemented the Spaceman's reputation as a maverick songwriting and studio genius, but this was what first truly launched him into orbit. **RS**

> "What I want to convey are the sort of feelings that I think everyone's felt in their life."
>
> Jason Pierce, 1997

Track Listing

▶	01	**You Know It's True** (Pierce)	3:38
	02	**If I Were With Her Now** (Pierce)	5:43
▶	03	**I Want You** (Pierce)	3:48
	04	**Run** (Cale • Pierce)	3:51
	05	**Smiles** (Pierce)	2:14
	06	**Step Into The Breeze** (Pierce)	2:44
	07	**Symphony Space** (Pierce)	5:55
▶	08	**Take Your Time** (Pierce)	6:52
	09	**Shine A Light** (Pierce)	7:17
▶	10	**Angel Sigh** (Pierce)	5:46
▶	11	**Sway** (Pierce • Refoy)	6:53
	12	**200 Bars** (Pierce)	6:16

Sugar | Copper Blue (1992)

Label | Rykodisc
Producer | Lou Giordano • Bob Mould
Art Direction | Mark C.
Nationality | USA
Running Time | 45:02

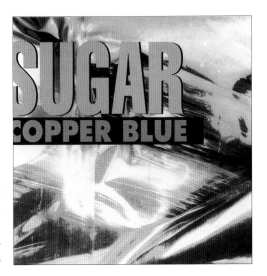

When grunge pioneers Hüsker Dü imploded, guitarist/singer Bob Mould made solo albums packed with cellos and resentment. When millions remained unmoved, he severed ties with his label and musicians, and wandered the earth alone. Then he recruited bassist David Barbe and drummer Malcolm Travis and made one of the most glorious records of the Nineties.

Mould's furious Fenders®, roaring vocals, and bitter lyrics remained. But the songs were astoundingly uplifting and, in happy contrast to Hüsker Dü's prehistoric production, sounded like avalanches.

The classics explode with barely a breath between them. At the first of several peaks, the Pixies pastiche "A Good Idea" slams into the chiming "Changes" (the most Hüskerish moment). Then it is a rollercoaster ride through what Mould described as tributes to George Martin ("Hoover Dam") and The Beatles ("If I Can't Change Your Mind") to the cinematically dramatic "Slick." "They could use it on *Beverly Hills 90210* when Luke Perry finally crashes the car," Mould told Australian fanzine *Lemon.* "See you on *Melrose Place,* Luke!"

Copper Blue was especially well received in Britain, where Sugar were signed to Creation. Mould admired noisy label-mates My Bloody Valentine, yet was dogged by questions about Nirvana, one of many groups he had inadvertently inspired. Years later he would even insist "I Hate Alternative Rock"—so give thanks that before then he gave us this masterpiece.

"There's no reason not to like it," he told *Record Collector.* "This is just a great batch of melodies and songs." Amen. **BM**

> "I certainly don't anticipate Nirvana's success opening the way for Sugar ... I fight my own fight."
>
> Bob Mould, 1992

Track Listing

	01	**The Act We Act** (Mould)	5:10
	02	**A Good Idea** (Mould)	3:47
▶	03	**Changes** (Mould)	5:01
▶	04	**Helpless** (Mould)	3:05
	05	**Hoover Dam** (Mould)	5:28
	06	**The Slim** (Mould)	5:14
▶	07	**If I Can't Change Your Mind** (Mould)	3:18
	08	**Fortune Teller** (Mould)	4:37
	09	**Slick** (Mould)	4:51
	10	**Man On The Moon** (Mould)	4:31

Tom Waits
Bone Machine (1992)

Label | Island
Producer | Tom Waits
Art Direction | Christie Rixford
Nationality | USA
Running Time | 54:14

Sonic Youth
Dirty (1992)

Label | DGC
Producer | Sonic Youth • Butch Vig
Art Direction | Kevin Reagan
Nationality | USA
Running Time | 59:00

Fueled by a love of Fifties beat poetry, high-school dropout Waits taught himself both guitar and piano and was signed in the early 1970s by manager Herb Cohen (who had worked with both Tim Buckley and Frank Zappa). But, while his character-based output as the wise vagabond informed his material throughout the 1970s, he turned to more diverse areas in the 1980s (including operas and soundtracks), and these two aspects combined in 1992's Bone Machine. (The title refers to Waits' concept of "bone music," in which music is stripped down and reduced to its minimum.)

The album includes some of Waits' most fascinating collaborations: Keith Richards co-wrote "That Feel" (also providing guitars and vocals), David Hidalgo of Los Lobos supplied violin and accordion, and Primus' Les Claypool donated electric bass. Waits also worked with Jesse Dylan on the artwork concept, the final product mirroring perfectly the shadowy delirium of the music itself.

Dark and raw, Bone Machine is no less enchanting than Waits' previous work despite its sinister edges—the coarseness of opening track "Earth Died Screaming" is balanced by the relative sweetness of "I Don't Wanna Grow Up." The hyper-distorted "Goin' Out West" typifies the album's dirty groove, and, while each track stands up on its own terms, it is doubtless the cohesion of the album's overall nightmarish tone that so deservedly won Bone Machine a Grammy in 1992 as best alternative music album. **AH-N**

Dirty was Sonic Youth's closest shot at grunge's mainstream. It is a crowning feat of sorts, a classic recording for anybody interested in the indie revolution in rock that started at the end of the Eighties. The album still resonates with undulating electricity, natural coolness, spiraling words, and a sharp world vision.

Recorded in Manhattan's Magic Shop by Butch Vig, the producer responsible for Nirvana's "Smells Like Teen Spirit," this collection shows New York's catalysts of noise-rock coming to terms with their own sonic history—traces of conceptual art, hardcore punk, and leftfield experimentation served in a cohesive, articulate fashion—while delivering a rock sound they would only occasionally recreate so vividly and efficiently.

Guitarists/singers Thurston Moore and Lee Ranaldo elaborate rich soundscapes and petrifying riffs that go from dreamy ("Theresa's Sound-World") to aggressive ("Youth Against Fascism"), while bass player Kim Gordon tries out different voices that range from feminist wrath ("Swimsuit Issue") to the rough sweetness of final scene "Créme Brûlée." Not forgetting the imaginative contributions of drummer Steve Shelley, or the fact that the strength of alternative rock hits like "100%" and "Sugar Kane" made the album a landmark.

Like all their subsequent albums, Dirty documents a band as faithful to its own multifaceted personality as to the events of its time, mixing the personal and social in stimulating layers of sound and fury. **IJ**

Stereo MCs
Connected (1992)

Label | Gee Street
Producer | Stereo MCs
Art Direction | Blue Source
Nationality | UK
Running Time | 56:10

Ministry
Psalm 69 (1992)

Label | Sire
Producer | H. Luxa • H. Pan
Art Direction | Paul Elledge
Nationality | USA
Running Time | 44:46

It was all about the hands—rapper Rob B. (a.k.a. Rob Birch) had a habit during performances of extending his at arms' length in front of his forehead, like a magician attempting to bend spoons with the power of his mind. It was an eye-catching gesture and one that seemed to sum up the Stereo MCs' message.

Anti-materialistic and positive, Birch's lyrics were a take on the righteous ire of Seventies reggae, while his image was an unlikely blend of Lavender Hill shaman and Vincent Van Gogh. Their previous album, 1990's *Supernatural*, yielded "Elevate My Mind," the first British hip-hop single ever to reach the U.S. charts, so expectations for the follow-up were high. Abandoning the samples that had served them thus far, musical supremo Nick "the Head" Hallam took a risk and drafted in live musicians as well as the talents of Welsh drummer Owen If and an expanded troupe of black female backing singers (namely Cath Coffey, Veronica Davies, and Andrea Groves, as well as a guest appearance by UK soul diva Mica Paris).

Connected reveled in gleaming bright production and robust pop hooks. The best songs—"Step It Up," "Ground Level," and "Creation"—gave Nottingham-born Rob B.'s need to commune with a beleaguered, recession-hit audience a musical setting that was equally driven and purposeful. The album was an international hit, but the effort exhausted the band, leading to their vanishing completely from the UK music scene for the next nine years. **APe**

If the earth ever opens and black skies rain fire, at least be content in the knowledge that you have the soundtrack for Armageddon in Ministry's sixth studio album *Psalm 69*. Conceived by heroin-addicted shaman Alain Jourgensen and the more enigmatic Paul Barker, the album is a teeth-grinding barrage of relentless beats borrowed from industrial music, shredding guitars, and eerie, despotic sampling of air-raid sirens, pulpit bashing, and chilling gothic choirs.

How such a jarring album infected public consciousness deeply enough to sell platinum can mostly be attributed to the lead single "Jesus Built My Hot Rod." This was virtually a novelty cut on an otherwise brutal and disturbing Doomsday concept album. The opening track, "New World Order," is a marching song for bloody revolution. The controversial video for the pounding "Just One Fix" featured a junkie in withdrawal and a truly sepulchral William S. Burroughs. The title track is a demonic juxtaposition of militaristic and evangelical chanting; Ministry's high priest Jourgensen had as much sneering contempt for power mongers as he did for the middle American culture of muscle cars and mind-numbing television.

This opus is in turns hulking and as sharp as a razor. Like a nihilistic evisceration, Ministry's music blasts away all extraneous hyperbole and leaves nothing but dread and raw synapses. Forget Marilyn Manson—nothing in U.S. music has sounded so monumental, apocalyptic, and purely wicked as *Psalm 69*. **AT**

Tori Amos | Little Earthquakes (1992)

Label | East West
Producer | Various
Art Direction | Cindy Palmano
Nationality | USA
Running Time | 57:07

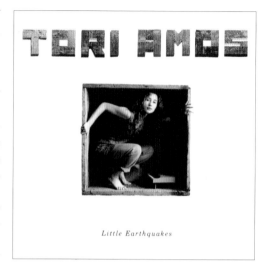

Little Earthquakes

From the disturbing lines in "Crucify" about "looking for a savior beneath these dirty sheets" to the phallic mushrooms on the back of the sleeve, *Little Earthquakes* was one of the most challenging records ever to reach a mainstream audience.

Raised, as Amos put it, with "a peace-pipe in one hand and a cross in the other," this daughter of a part-Cherokee mother and a Methodist minister redefined the role of female singer-songwriters in the 1990s by addressing persecution in religion, relationships, and sex with intriguing straightforwardness. Her solo debut contained some seriously uneasy listening, like the stirring, intimate "Me And A Gun," which concerned her real-life rape. However, the album as a whole was not entirely confrontational. For every moment of brutal directness there was a poetic and consoling metaphor; for every angry eruption of drums and guitars, a breathtakingly beautiful piano solo.

While her vocals could sound a lot like Kate Bush, anyone willing to invest time in unusually structured songs such as "Silent All These Years" and "Little Earthquakes" knew that this artist was truly an original. Being able to turn from girl to woman, from devil to goddess, and from psycho to therapist in an instant, Tori's emotional repertoire as a performer was astounding. As a singer, pianist, and composer, she had the skills and the drive to create music that was an inspiration to many. Much like Joni Mitchell, she was exploring territory off the beaten path, earning herself a devoted following as one of the richest and most courageous musical voices of her era. **CL**

"If you call me an airy-fairy, new-age hippy waif, I will cut your penis off."

Tori Amos, 1994

Track Listing

▶	01	**Crucify** (Amos)	5:00
	02	**Girl** (Amos)	4:07
▶	03	**Silent All These Years** (Amos)	4:11
	04	**Precious Things** (Amos)	4:27
	05	**Winter** (Amos)	5:42
	06	**Happy Phantom** (Amos)	3:15
▶	07	**China** (Amos)	5:00
	08	**Leather** (Amos)	3:12
	09	**Mother** (Amos)	6:59
	10	**Tear In Your Hand** (Amos)	4:38
	11	**Me And A Gun** (Amos)	3:44
▶	12	**Little Earthquakes** (Amos)	6:52

Ice Cube | The Predator (1992)

Label | Priority
Producer | Various
Art Direction | Dino Paredes
Nationality | USA
Running Time | 56:24

The most confrontational album ever to top the U.S. chart? Check. A rap masterpiece? Check.

As Christmas 1992 loomed, no rapper was bigger than Cube. Hammer and Public Enemy were slipping. Snoop was still a sidekick. Cube, however, had gone platinum with 1991's venomous *Death Certificate* and become a movie star with *Boyz N The Hood*.

No artist was better placed to articulate the rage of black America when four Los Angeles cops were acquitted of using excessive force when beating motorist Rodney King; rioters tore the city apart. Cube captures it all on an astonishing album that still thrills, years after its references have receded into history.

Emblazoned with a defiantly smoke-wreathed photo by Bruce Springsteen's sister Pamela, the album is packed with jagged chunks of funk, notably the hits "Check Yo Self" and "Wicked." Most remarkable are "We Had To Tear This Mothafucka Up"—Cube's bitterest attack on the cops, set to speaker-rattling production by Cypress Hill's DJ Muggs—and the prettily ironic "It Was A Good Day," backed by an Isley Brothers loop.

The Predator also takes pot shots at Billboard, who had slammed *Death Certificate*. Cube's revenge was complete when it became the first album to debut atop the pop and R&B charts since Stevie Wonder's *Songs In The Key Of Life*.

Remarkably, this brilliant, double-platinum album is only half the story. Released simultaneously was *Guerillas In Tha Mist* by his associates Da Lench Mob, a Cube album in all but name—and *The Predator*'s artistic equal. Both are rap's last blast as a political force. **BM**

Track Listing

01	The First Day Of School (Intro) (Uncredited)	1:19
02	When Will They Shoot? (Cube)	4:36
03	I'm Scared (Insert) (Uncredited)	1:32
▶ 04	Wicked (Cube·Jaguar)	3:55
05	Now I Gotta Wet 'Cha (Cube·Muggs)	4:03
06	The Predator (Cube)	4:03
▶ 07	It Was A Good Day (Cube)	4:19
08	We Had To Tear This Mothafucka Up (Cube·Muggs)	4:24
09	Fuck 'Em (Insert) (Uncredited)	2:02
10	Dirty Mack (Cube)	4:34
11	Don't Trust 'Em (Cube)	4:06
12	Gangsta's Fairytale 2 (Cube)	3:19
▶ 13	Check Yo Self (Cube·Muggs)	3:42
14	Who Got The Camera? (Cube)	4:37
15	Integration (Insert) (Uncredited)	2:31
16	Say Hi To The Bad Guy (Cube)	3:22

Pantera | Vulgar Display Of Power (1992)

Label | Atlantic
Producer | Terry Date • Vinnie Paul
Art Direction | Bob Defrin
Nationality | USA
Running Time | 51:45

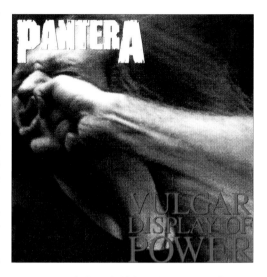

It was the buzz cut heard around the metal world. Pantera's vocalist Phil Anselmo had shorn off his locks after 1990's *Cowboys From Hell*, the first album he recorded with the band still in their poodle-metal stage. Obviously, Pantera were getting serious.

Heavy metal had often drawn its guitar histrionics from a precise, almost classical influence, but *Vulgar Display Of Power* was where Pantera guitarist Diamond (a.k.a. Dimebag) Darrell had reverted to type as a Texas bluesman. Amid the brutal chugging of their new sound was a definite sense of groove (particularly on "By Demons Be Driven") assisted by Dimebag's drumming brother Vinnie Paul and bassist Rex's rhythm work. Metal lyrics had also previously been the domain of sword and sorcery battle hymns. Anselmo's lyrics on *Vulgar Display* ... were a heady mix of self-determinism and demands for respect, at times veering a little too close to a fascistic tone than is allowed of a band comprised of whites from the South.

But this was of little concern when the playing was so taut, the death-metal double-bass drumming so ruthless, and Anselmo's voice, now rid of high-pitched wailing, so thick with furious purpose. Even their power ballads, still a standard of metal, were bludgeoning. Their tale of destructive relationships, "This Love," gave Anselmo opportunity to screech "No more head trips!" as power chords thunder into the chorus.

As long as there are angry young men, metal will survive. But every so often an album comes along that resets the course of the genre. *Vulgar Display Of Power* did just that. **AT**

> "Now with Phil in the band we've got a chance to make those riffs fully happen ... "
>
> Rex, 1988

Track Listing

▶ 01	**Mouth For War** (Pantera)	3:56
02	**New Level** (Pantera)	2:57
03	**Walk** (Pantera)	5:15
▶ 04	**Fucking Hostile** (Pantera)	2:49
▶ 05	**This Love** (Pantera)	6:32
06	**Rise** (Pantera)	4:36
07	**No Good (Attack The Radical)** (Pantera)	4:50
08	**Live In A Hole** (Pantera)	4:59
09	**Regular People (Conceit)** (Pantera)	5:27
▶ 10	**By Demons Be Driven** (Pantera)	4:39
11	**Hollow** (Pantera)	5:45

Alice In Chains | Dirt (1992)

Label | Columbia
Producer | Alice In Chains • Dave Jerden
Art Direction | Mary Maurer
Nationality | USA
Running Time | 57:30

When Seattle became identified as the epicenter of a musical movement in the early 1990s, Alice In Chains and their album *Dirt* found themselves unexpectedly in the spotlight. Until then, the band had been regarded as a rising metal band, opening for Van Halen and Poison. But their appearance in Cameron Crowe's movie *Singles*—the closest thing to a cinematic representation of grunge Seattle—immediately gave them greater prominence. The inclusion of their track "Would?" in the movie started a buzz of hype around the album *Dirt*, which was released in the fall and marked their breakthrough, entering the U.S. charts at No. 6.

The band typified the Seattle scene, with their distorted guitars, melancholic lyrics, and penchant for wearing plaid. Armed with a Black Sabbath-influenced sound and the haunting melodies of lead singer Layne Staley, *Dirt* helped to establish grunge as a genre.

The record was laden with allusions to lead singer Staley's drug addiction, a portent of his fatal overdose a decade after the album's release. There were omens enough in the drug-related and suicidal songs, such as "Junkhead" ("We are an elite race of our own/The stoners, junkies, and freaks) and "Dirt" ("I want to taste dirty, stinging pistol/In my mouth, on my tongue.")

At the time of the album's release, Staley's problems were widely denied through the music press, though it seemed everybody knew something was amiss. As *Spin* magazine wrote, "There's a brutal, though troubling, honesty in the lyrics . . . as a means of cutting yourself open and letting the listener look inside, Alice In Chains has certainly spit out a mouthful." **JC**

"When I'm writing music, I find myself in my head ..."

Layne Staley, 1995

Track Listing

▶	01	**Them Bones** (Cantrell)	2:30
	02	**Dam That River** (Cantrell)	3:09
	03	**Rain When I Die** (Cantrell • Kinney • Staley • Starr)	6:01
	04	**Sickman** (Cantrell)	5:29
▶	05	**Rooster** (Cantrell)	6:15
▶	06	**Junkhead** (Cantrell • Staley)	5:09
	07	**Dirt** (Cantrell • Staley)	5:16
	08	**God Smack** (Cantrell • Staley)	3:50
	09	**Untitled** (Uncredited)	0:43
	10	**Hate To Feel** (Staley)	5:16
	11	**Angry Chair** (Staley)	4:47
	12	**Down In A Hole** (Cantrell)	5:38
▶	13	**Would?** (Cantrell)	3:27

Nick Cave And The Bad Seeds
Henry's Dream (1992)

Label | Mute
Producer | David Briggs • Nick Cave • Mick Harvey
Art Direction | Anton Corbijn
Nationality | Australia
Running Time | 41:28

Henry's Dream, the seventh album by Nick Cave and the Bad Seeds, is vibrant and melancholy, moving and mournful. Old Testament omens are part of Cave's stock in trade and *Henry's Dream* continues the tradition; these are compelling songs of suffering and sin.

The album opens with the excellent "Papa Won't Leave You, Henry"—a chilling, cataclysmic track, and preparation for the acoustic assault to come. (Appropriately, thunder and rain accompanied the first notes of this song when it was performed at an outdoor festival in Melbourne in 1994.) Velvety acoustic guitars, and string arrangements courtesy of Mick Harvey and David Blumberg, add a further dynamic layer.

Cave's vocal delivery is dramatic and assured, whether in the solemn vocalization of the hymn-like "Christina The Astonishing," the passionate cries of "I Had A Dream, Joe," the growling screams of "Jack The Ripper," or the roaring chants of "Brother, My Cup Is Empty." His narratives of the broken and the damned make for uneasy but absorbing listening, and are frequently touched by his characteristic dark humor ("I counted up my blessings/And I counted only one").

Yet amid the chaos and tragedy are touching love songs: the devotedly delicate "Straight To You" and the romantic lament "The Loom Of The Land," though its tenderness is tempered with darker overtones—one of the young lovers carries a knife.

Vigorous, vulgar, and romantic all at once, *Henry's Dream* is an exquisite nightmare. **MBo**

> "I don't trust songs that don't have a kind of sigh within the lines somewhere."
>
> Nick Cave, 1998

Track Listing

▶	01	Papa Won't Leave You, Henry (Cave)	5:55
	02	I Had A Dream, Joe (Cave)	3:42
▶	03	Straight To You (Cave)	4:34
▶	04	Brother, My Cup Is Empty (Cave)	3:02
	05	Christina The Astonishing (Cave)	4:51
▶	06	When I First Came To Town (Cave)	5:21
▶	07	John Finns' Wife (Cave)	5:13
	08	Loom Of The Land (Cave)	5:07
▶	09	Jack The Ripper (Cave)	3:43

Nusrat Fateh Ali Khan And Party
Devotional Songs (1992)

Label | Real World
Producer | Bari Watts
Art Direction | Assorted Images
Nationality | Pakistan
Running Time | 44:51

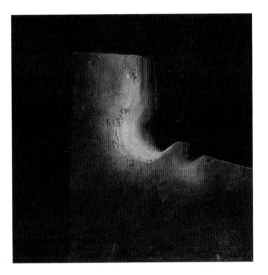

Born in 1948, Nusrat Fateh Ali Khan almost became a doctor. Instead he followed the family tradition, stretching back 20 generations, of musical performance. The Khans were steeped in the legacy of Qawwali—the devotional Sufi style in praise of God (Allah) and his prophet (Mohammed).

Khan came to a Western audience largely through Peter Gabriel's Real World label, and a stunning performance at the 1983 WOMAD festival in England. *Devotional Songs* (one of 10 Khan releases on Real World) was a critical success, being widely reviewed in the mainstream rock press. UK magazine *Vox* praised its "organic eroticism" and indeed, there is an almost sexual rhythm to these exotic hymns of praise.

Hypnotic handclaps and tabla create such tight rhythms you would swear there is electronic wizardry at work. The effect is mesmerizing and summons the feverish intensity of Khan's marathon live shows. Harmonium and mandolin provide a streetwise folksiness, with elements of Greek, Flamenco, and Celtic abounding. Behind Khan's joyous vocals, a chorus imitates in call and response fashion until a soaring trance is induced.

In the years before he died, in 1997, Khan became artist in residence at the University of Washington. He did not live to see the pain and prejudice of 9/11, and the vulgar fear it incited toward his spiritual traditions.

Listen to the glory of Khan's work and there is no trace of hatred to be found, only a profound love. **GT**

> "To travel the world, and open the hearts of those who were previously closed, is a joy."
>
> Nusrat Fateh Ali Khan, 1993

Track Listing

▶ 01	Allah Hoo Allah Hoo (Khan)	7:37
02	Yaad-E-Nabi Gulshan Mehka (Khan)	7:36
03	Haq Ali Ali Haq (Khan)	7:23
▶ 04	Ali Maula Ali Maula Ali Dam Dam (Khan)	7:44
05	Mast Nazroon Se Allah Bachhae (Khan)	6:21
▶ 06	Ni Main Jogi De Naal (Khan·Shah)	8:10

P.J. Harvey | Dry (1992)

Label | Too Pure
Producer | Robert Ellis • P. J. Harvey • Vernon
Art Direction | Uncredited
Nationality | UK
Running Time | 39:54

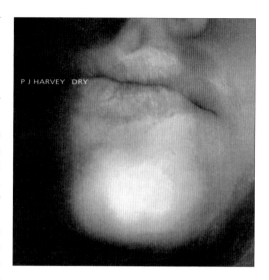

Polly Jean Harvey surfaced in 1992, a singer of pure power and raw sexuality. The eponymous trio she fronted, also including bassist Steve Vaughn and drummer Robert Ellis, performed a powerful, bluesy, post-punk guitar rock. Their debut album *Dry* integrated this style with brutally emotional songs.

In common with punk legend Patti Smith, Harvey's music and image were ambiguous and intriguing. She proved a mature and influential songwriter, at once both confrontational and vulnerable. Categorized by many as a feminist (but pilloried after she posed for explicit and controversial publicity shots), she used decadent, dark humor to attack expectations of women through her dissection of love and sex. The power of Harvey's vocals was complemented by the complexity of her lyrics. She created the captivatingly catchy "Sheela-Na-Gig," its title a reference to ancient naked female fertility symbols; the lyrics demonstrated a keen sense of independence and resolve: "Gonna wash that man right out of my hair/gonna take my hips to a man who cares." "Dress" is a sexy, seductive masterpiece that also brought into question issues of dominance and control in relationships. Both tracks were released as singles; both became indie-rock classics. But *Dry* included other greats: "Hair" and "Fountain"—slow at first, then turning furious—and "Dry," in which Harvey mixed desperate cries with bluesy riffs and punk-rock energy.

Unsurprisingly, *Rolling Stone* magazine named P. J. Harvey Best Songwriter and Best New Female Singer of 1992. *Dry* swiftly established the newcomer as a musical icon, a position that she maintains today. **MBo**

> "I am a creative artist ... but there is no way that I experience everything I write about."
>
> P. J. Harvey, 2004

Track Listing

▶ 01	**Oh My Lover** (Harvey)	4:00
02	**O Stella** (Harvey)	2:30
▶ 03	**Dress** (Ellis•Harvey)	3:16
04	**Victory** (Harvey)	3:16
05	**Happy And Bleeding** (Ellis•Harvey)	4:48
▶ 06	**Sheela–Na–Gig** (Harvey)	3:10
▶ 07	**Hair** (Harvey)	3:47
▶ 08	**Joe** (Ellis•Harvey)	2:33
09	**Plants And Rags** (Ellis•Harvey)	4:09
▶ 10	**Fountain** (Harvey)	3:53
11	**Water** (Harvey)	4:32

Suede | Suede (1993)

Label | Nude
Producer | Ed Buller
Art Direction | Peter Barrett • Andrew Biscomb
Nationality | UK
Running Time | 45:26

Suede's debut sealed the end of a media whirlwind that had began earlier in the year, with the band scoring a *Melody Maker* cover before actually releasing a note.

Very much the sum of their influences (David Bowie, The Smiths), the five-piece nevertheless successfully made an album at odds with the fast approaching grunge and slacker mores of the period. Add to this panache a flirtation with bisexuality (thanks to singer Brett Anderson, most effectively manifested through his lyrics), and you had an irresistible combination.

From the very first drum blast of "So Young," *Suede* is an arresting journey that takes in glam rock ("Animal Nitrate"'s sing-along chorus) and bleak, very urban depression (check "Breakdown" and "Sleeping Pills" for some of the most harrowing lyrics in Anderson's career).

Yet this focus on the seedier, more damaged aspects of London life also gave them great scope to make a noise. "Animal Lover," allegedly written about Damon Albarn of Blur, new boyfriend of Anderson's ex-squeeze (Elastica's Justine Frischmann), was a shrieking jolt to the senses, and "Metal Mickey" was wholly uplifting, albeit in a frustrated, satellite town way.

Anderson's anglocentric lyrics and Suede's guitar-heavy sound effectively created a blueprint for Britpop. But the group already had their sights set way above those of other debut artistes. "The Next Life," a piano ballad that tearfully dreamt of a better tomorrow, was so ridiculously dramatic, so very camp, that it rounded the album off perfectly. Just Butler and Anderson alone—the split that was to follow makes the listening experience all the more poignant. **JK**

> "The only pressure we feel is from ourselves. We've only wanted to impress each other."
>
> Brett Anderson, 1991

Track Listing

▶ 01	**So Young** (Anderson•Butler)	3:38
▶ 02	**Animal Nitrate** (Anderson•Butler)	3:27
03	**She's Not Dead** (Anderson•Butler)	4:23
04	**Moving** (Anderson•Butler)	2:50
05	**Pantomime Horse** (Anderson•Butler)	5:49
▶ 06	**The Drowners** (Anderson•Butler)	4:10
07	**Sleeping Pills** (Anderson•Butler)	3:51
08	**Breakdown** (Anderson•Butler)	6:02
▶ 09	**Metal Mickey** (Anderson•Butler)	3:27
10	**Animal Lover** (Anderson•Butler)	4:17
▶ 11	**The Next Life** (Anderson•Butler)	3:32

Paul Weller | Wild Wood (1993)

Label | Go! Discs
Producer | Brendan Lynch • Paul Weller
Art Direction | Simon Haflon • Paul Weller
Nationality | UK
Running Time | 50:09

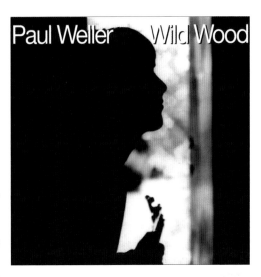

After the demise of The Style Council and a musical hiatus in the late 1980s, Paul Weller reawoke to the traditional rock influences that had originally inspired him, as well as Nick Drake's pastoral laments, Neil Young's early solo work, and the psychedelic groove of Traffic (their influence particularly noticeable in the four instrumentals on *Wild Wood*).

The chiming riffs of "Sunflower" tinge the promise of summer with a sense of loss. Two of the more powerful tracks here, "5th Season" and "The Weaver," offer perfect vehicles for Weller's gruff, impassioned voice and his underrated guitar playing. The gutsy "Can You Heal Us (Holy Man)" and "Has My Fire Really Gone Out?"—both standouts—find Weller musing on the artistic crossroads he had come to. His atavistic approach to the album is complemented by the reoccurrence of the theme of nature in his lyrics, most perfectly encapsulated in the acoustic gem of "Wild Wood," a haunting, reflective ballad capturing the record's prevailing "rustic" ambience (see also the understated, wistful "Country"). Producer Brendan Lynch added electronic textures and sweeping keyboards, and drummer Steve White's touch is masterful throughout.

Wild Wood contributed toward a general reawakening of interest in Sixties ideology, helping to inspire Britpop and earning Weller the nickname "Modfather" (figures such as Noel Gallagher were quick to cite him as an influence). The album won the Ivor Novello award for "outstanding contemporary song collection" and re-established Paul Weller as one of Britain's most gifted songwriters. **AM**

Track Listing

▶ 01	Sunflower (Weller)	4:06
02	Can You Heal Us (Holy Man) (Weller)	3:42
▶ 03	Wild Wood (Weller)	3:23
04	Instrumental One (Part 1) (Weller)	1:37
▶ 05	All The Pictures On The Wall (Weller)	3:56
▶ 06	Has My Fire Really Gone Out? (Weller)	3:50
07	Country (Weller)	3:39
08	Instrumental (Part 2) (Weller)	0:49
▶ 09	5th Season (Weller)	4:54
▶ 10	The Weaver (Weller)	3:43
11	Instrumental One (Part 2) (Weller)	0:34
▶ 12	Foot Of The Mountain (Weller)	3:38
▶ 13	Shadow Of The Sun (Weller)	7:36
14	Holy Man (reprise) (Weller)	1:51
15	Moon On Your Pyjamas (Weller)	4:01
16	Hung Up (Weller)	2:40

The Smashing Pumpkins | Siamese Dream (1993)

Label | Virgin
Producer | Billy Corgan • Butch Vig
Art Direction | Len Peltier
Nationality | USA
Running Time | 62:08

An exorcism of childhood demons? A megalomaniac's masterpiece? A full hour of hard-rock humdingers? *Siamese Dream* is all this and more.

That the album exists at all is down to the insane ambition of leader Billy Corgan. After months touring *Gish* (1991), he assumed sole responsibility for a follow-up when his bandmates failed to buy into a "weird masterplan ... to be the heaviest, meanest, rockingest ..." Ironically—given that the title refers to "living in a dream state, an organic connection between people"—the band were barely on speaking terms.

The contributions of guitarist James Iha and bassist D'Arcy Wretsky are open to conjecture; Corgan is thought to have played most of their parts himself. Powerhouse drummer Jimmy Chamberlin added to the chaos with extracurricular excess.

The "hardest, meanest, rockingest" agenda, however, is spectacularly upheld by "Cherub Rock" and "Geek U.S.A." And the monster "Silverfuck" fulfills Corgan's aim "to blend Black Sabbath power with Led Zeppelin dynamics with Pink Floyd psychedelia." But it is the melodic moments that secure *Siamese Dream's* immortality: the ringing "Today," the string-driven "Disarm," and the lullaby "Luna."

Lyrically, Corgan confronts ghosts of the past on "Disarm" (his parents) and "Spaceboy" (his handicapped brother), spins a poetic web on "Mayonaise," and picks at wounds on "Soma" (whose subject later became his ex-wife). The latter features R.E.M's Mike Mills, who declared *Siamese Dream* "a great record with or without me." Damn right. **BM**

"I don't think you have to suffer for great art."

James Iha, 1993

Track Listing

▶	01	**Cherub Rock** (Corgan)	4:57
	02	**Quiet** (Corgan)	3:42
▶	03	**Today** (Corgan)	3:19
	04	**Hummer** (Corgan)	6:57
	05	**Rocket** (Corgan)	4:06
▶	06	**Disarm** (Corgan)	3:17
	07	**Soma** (Corgan•Iha)	6:39
	08	**Geek U.S.A.** (Corgan)	5:13
	09	**Mayonaise** (Corgan•Iha)	5:49
	10	**Spaceboy** (Corgan)	4:28
	11	**Silverfuck** (Corgan)	8:43
	12	**Sweet Sweet** (Corgan)	1:38
	13	**Luna** (Corgan)	3:20

Auteurs
New Wave (1993)

Label | Hut
Producer | Luke Haines • Phil Vinall
Art Direction | P. Barrett • A. Biscomb
Nationality | UK
Running Time | 41:36

Liz Phair
Exile In Guyville (1993)

Label | Matador
Producer | Liz Phair • Brad Wood
Art Direction | Mark O. • Liz Phair
Nationality | USA
Running Time | 55:49

Formed in 1992 by arch cynic Luke Haines and girlfriend Alice Readman—both formerly of The Servants—alongside drummer Glenn Collins and cellist James Banbury, the Auteurs (named for the French movie term denoting both author and director) signed to Virgin offshoot Hut, debuting with the deceptively bright "Showgirl" that December. It scaled the UK independent charts and expectations were high for their debut album. Perhaps even more so than Blur's *Modern Life Is Rubbish* or Suede's eponymous debut, *New Wave* laid the blueprint for what would shortly become known as Britpop.

Haines' incredibly sharp, intelligent lyrics were heavily influenced by his love of theater and cinema, briefly making him the king of the studious slacker generation; the music was an exhilarating—and highly influential—mix of contemporary beats and bright guitars. The bright retro vocal stylings on "Showgirl" and "Junk Shop Clothes" betray Haines' perverse wit along with a darker, more menacing side evident on the cello-meets-glam of "How Could I Be Wrong?" and the bleak "Idiot Brother."

New Wave remains a wonderfully executed and compelling work, one that has aged more gracefully than its former rival *Suede*. Haines' subsequent erratic career has taken in a brief flirtation with retro German terrorist chic care of his Baader-Meinhof project, movie soundtrack work, and even mainstream success with the dark seedy Europop of Black Box Recorder. **CSh**

Alternative music was explosively popular in 1993, but until then had mostly been typified by grunge, a genre notable for being almost entirely devoid of women's voices. There had, of course, been some successful women in the field, notably P. J. Harvey and The Breeders' Kim Deal and Tanya Donelly, but alternative music had yet to produce a breakout female act.

That all changed with *Exile In Guyville*, the stunning debut album from 26-year-old Liz Phair, rooted in the Chicago scene that had yielded The Smashing Pumpkins. Phair channeled youthful fears and resentment into 18 taut, breathtakingly honest tracks, which were rendered more bleak by their quiet arrangements of electric guitars and keyboards. To the delight of critics and fans, Phair did not shy away from talking about sex and relationships in the most graphic terms—an exemplary track is called "Fuck And Run."

Alas, she was never to replicate *Exile In Guyville*'s artistic triumph. Two follow-ups in the 1990s generated respectful if restrained notices, but neither achieved mainstream success. Then, in 2003, Phair produced an eponymous release designed to entice younger fans—although a healthy helping of obscenities seemed calculated to reassure older listeners that the naughty Phair of *Guyville* was still lurking beneath the pop sheen. Unhappily, it did not enthrall either camp.

Whatever else happens, in *Exile In Guyville*, Phair produced a career-defining album, dense with anger and beauty. **KB**

The Afghan Whigs
Gentlemen (1993)

Label | Elektra
Producer | John Curley • Greg Dulli
Art Direction | Greg Dulli
Nationality | USA
Running Time | 48:56

Aimee Mann
"Whatever" (1993)

Label | Geffen
Producer | Jon Brion
Art Direction | Gail Marowitz
Nationality | USA
Running Time | 52:40

Although they were signed to Sub Pop for a couple of years, The Afghan Whigs stood apart from their plaid-shirted peers. Led by charismatic hedonist Greg Dulli, the besuited quartet from Cincinnati, evolved a smoldering hybrid of dynamic rock and the deepest soul. Dulli's lyrics eschewed the post-adolescent angst that dominated grunge. Instead, he explored the darkest recesses of male sexuality with an unflinching candor and bone-dry wit. The band commanded notice with 1991's insidious third LP *Congregation*, prompting a deal with Elektra. They then headed down to Memphis to cut their masterpiece.

With a detailed, neo-cinematic production, *Gentlemen* is a tour de force of velvet-glove songcraft and iron-fist expression. The title track and "Be Sweet" couch red-blooded fervor in textured, sinewy grooves. Dulli's nicotine-dusted voice opens the latter with: "Ladies let me tell you about myself/I got a dick for a brain/And my brain is gonna sell my ass to you."

The spring-loaded R&B of "Debonair" and searing, piano-patterned "What Jail Is Like" became college radio hits, but the album's emotional peak is "My Curse": a wracked, female-perspective ballad sung with gale-force devastation by Marcy Mays of folk-punkers Scrawl.

Gentlemen was a critics' favorite on both sides of the Atlantic, paving the way for brooding follow-up *Black Love* and celebratory swan song *1965* to crack the Billboard chart. The Afghan Whigs split amicably in 2001, closing out an immense cult career by opening for childhood heroes Aerosmith on a U.S. arena tour. **MA**

For musicians previously associated with successful bands, recording and releasing a debut solo album can be just like having to beat the dreaded sophomore slump all over again. In both cases, critics and listeners alike wonder if previous success could be attributed to any number of outside factors—including good timing, the input of others, and just plain luck.

Aimee Mann had success in the mid-to-late 1980s with 'Til Tuesday. As singer and bass guitarist for the Boston-based collegiate rock band, she was the voice and face behind the hit "Voices Carry" and the singles "What About Love?" and "Coming Up Close." But how well could she perform outside of a band setting?

Whatever is of particular significance in two ways. It fortified Mann's reputation as a crafty songwriter whose compositional skills matched her urbane singing style, and it established multi-instrumentalist and fellow former 'Til Tuesday member Jon Brion as a solid producer who would go on to work with the likes of ex-Talking Head David Byrne and singer/songwriter-pianists Fiona Apple and Rufus Wainwright.

Full of songs that were smartly written but never pedantic, *Whatever* presents an already developed artist with a natural instinct for harmony. The chiming guitars and levitating backing vocals on "Fifty Years After The Fair" are lightly sweetened with flourishes of Brion's glockenspiel, to perfect effect, while the somber tone of "Jacob Marley's Chain" is intriguingly offset by the militaristic percussion that marches it forward. **YK**

Grant Lee Buffalo | Fuzzy (1993)

Label | Slash
Producer | Paul Kimble
Art Direction | Liz Hale
Nationality | USA
Running Time | 46:31

When R.E.M. vocalist Michael Stipe declared *Fuzzy* "the best album of the year hands down," he was only repeating an appreciation for Grant Lee Buffalo's gothic alt.country already voiced by the critics, who had instantly warmed to the band's debut LP.

Recorded in just two weeks in Brilliant Studios, San Francisco, the album provided a refreshing alternative to America's increasingly dour grunge scene and instead took huge inspiration from the spooky century-old steel foundry where it was put to tape. What had started out as a collection of sketchy acoustic demos written by a part-time trio was transformed into booming tales of history and politics, drenched in overdriven 12-string guitars, clattering drums, and the churning of pump organs.

Like the early blues singers, Phillips' lyrics took inspiration both from the state of his nation and the mythology of the open plains. Songs like "America Snoring" and "Stars N' Stripes" were soon given the big stage they craved thanks to support slots on arena tours by acts such as Pearl Jam and The Cranberries.

With bassist Paul Kimble in production, the band was able to control the destiny of its songs, providing a haunting backing to Phillips' melodic narratives. The howl "Grace," full of grit and vitriol, sits remarkably comfortably next to soothing jazz-tinged lullabies like "You Just Have To Be Crazy." Despite never selling the millions many believed it deserved, *Fuzzy* became a staple in the diet of a new wave of troubadours hoping to carry their songs from the dustbowls of backwater America to the bright lights of the big city stage. **ARo**

> "Some music is … an intimate experience, other music is … more of a broader celebration."
>
> Grant Lee Phillips, 2000

Track Listing

▶	01	**The Shining Hour** (Phillips)	3:53
▶	02	**Jupiter and Teardrop** (Phillips)	5:57
	03	**Fuzzy** (Phillips)	4:57
	04	**Wish You Well** (Phillips)	3:28
	05	**The Hook** (Phillips)	4:10
	06	**Soft Wolf Tread** (Phillips)	2:50
▶	07	**Stars n' Stripes** (Phillips)	4:41
	08	**Dixie Drug Store** (Phillips)	3:08
▶	09	**America Snoring** (Phillips)	3:38
▶	10	**Grace** (Phillips)	6:13
	11	**You Just Have To Be Crazy** (Phillips)	3:36

Nirvana | In Utero (1993)

Label | Geffen
Producer | Steve Albini • Scott Litt
Art Direction | Kurt Cobain • Robert Fisher
Nationality | USA
Running Time | 69:05

Rock history is littered with albums crushed by the weight of expectation. *In Utero* has remained steely rigid, still a presence today despite being the follow-up to *Nevermind*, the grunge landmark of the 1990s.

Kurt Cobain was a reactionary in the truest sense. Nirvana strove to pull away from the metal sound on debut *Bleach* with the polish of *Nevermind*. With *In Utero*, they brought in "punk" producer Steve Albini. But fans and critics need not have worried—if anything, Albini's earlier work with The Breeders and the Pixies was much more chart-friendly than *In Utero*.

It is not a punk album per se. The beautiful "Dumb" is a case in point—with soft cello and an envious lyric (Kurt pines for the simple life). "Pennyroyal Tea" was similarly affecting and paced, but the band could also destroy a listener with brute force. Opener "Serve The Servants" sees Kurt forgiving his absent father atop a boisterous, off-kilter rhythm, and the explosive "Tourette's" is as good an instruction as any for the hairs on the back of your neck to stand erect.

Yet *In Utero* was not free of troubles. Geffen sniffed at an earlier version and R.E.M. producer Scott Litt was brought in to polish off some of the edges. By this point, and with Kurt's spiralling drug problem, fans began to speculate that the singer was becoming angry, that his attentions might soon lie elsewhere. With increased press intrusion into his marriage to Courtney Love, the fear was that *In Utero* might never be released.

Thankfully it was. The album remains Nirvana's most arresting, signposting the melodic direction the band would hopefully have taken, had Kurt Cobain lived. **JK**

"We wanted to pay tribute."

Kurt Cobain, 1992

Track Listing

▶	01	**Serve The Servants** (Cobain)	3:36
	02	**Scentless Apprentice** (Nirvana)	3:47
▶	03	**Heart Shaped Box** (Cobain)	4:41
	04	**Rape Me** (Cobain)	2:49
	05	**Frances Farmer Will Have Her Revenge On Seattle** (Cobain)	4:09
▶	06	**Dumb** (Cobain)	2:32
	07	**Very Ape** (Cobain)	1:55
▶	08	**Milk It** (Cobain)	3:54
	09	**Pennyroyal Tea** (Cobain)	3:37
	10	**Radio Friendly Unit Shifter** (Cobain)	4:51
	11	**Tourette's** (Cobain)	1:35
▶	12	**All Apologies** (Cobain)	3:50
	13	**Gallons Of Rubbing Alcohol Flow Through The Strip** (Nirvana)	7:33

Jamiroquai | Emergency On Planet Earth (1993)

Label | Sony
Producer | Jay Kay • Mike Nielson • Toby Smith
Art Direction | Creative Minds
Nationality | UK
Running Time | 55:18

Jamiroquai sprang out of the British acid-jazz scene of the early 1990s, blessed with both a charismatic frontman in the shape of Jay Kay—all oversized hats, energetic performances, politicized lyrics, and a voice reminiscent of Stevie Wonder—and a debut album full of irresistibly funky tunes.

The group hit the UK charts with their first single "When You Gonna Learn" in 1992, and its infectious mix of groove, didgeridoo breakdowns, and Jay Kay's and Toby Smith's arrangements and environmentally friendly lyrics impressed Sony enough for them to offer the group an eight-album deal. The album was recorded to a tight schedule, the title track being written in the studio just before it was laid down. Despite the tight turnaround, its irresistible funkiness made it an immediate chart-topper in the UK.

Emergency On Planet Earth sets the pace for most of Jamiroquai's subsequent work—from the silhouetted image of Jay Kay as "the Buffalo Man" to the 1970s-influenced funky dancefloor grooves and back-to-nature sentiment. "Too Young To Die," written in reaction to the first Gulf War, grooves hard, with soaring horns and Jay Kay's exuberant scatting sugaring the pill of the angry message. Kay stops politicizing for the funky "Whatever It Is, I Just Can't Stop," and even shows his softer side on the soulful "Blow Your Mind," while the swirling "Music Of The Mind" (a nod to Stevie, perhaps?) lets the band show their chops magnificently.

This is the joyful sound of a band out to make people think, and, just as importantly, move them onto the dancefloor. **DC**

> "I was born at the wrong time. I don't need to hear today's stuff. I don't think any of us are as good as they used to be."
>
> Jay Kay, 2001

Track Listing

	01	**When You Gonna Learn (Digeridoo)** (Kay)		3:47
▶	02	**Too Young To Die** (Kay•Smith)		6:04
	03	**Hooked Up** (Kay•Smith)		4:37
	04	**If I Like It, I Do It** (Kay•Van Gelder)		4:52
▶	05	**Music Of The Mind** (Kay•Smith)		6:22
	06	**Emergency On Planet Earth** (Kay•Smith)		4:04
▶	07	**Whatever It Is, I Just Can't Stop** (Kay)		4:07
▶	08	**Blow Your Mind** (Kay•Smith)		8:33
	09	**Revolution 1993** (Kay•Smith)		10:17
	10	**Didgin' Out** (Buchanan•Kay)		2:35

Pet Shop Boys | Very (1993)

Label | EMI
Producer | Stephen Hague • Pet Shop Boys
Art Direction | Pentagram
Nationality | UK
Running Time | 53:09

Though the Pet Shop Boys had always been really gay, *Very* was their first really, really gay album—and first UK No. 1. The epic closer—an almost Laibach-esque rendition of the Village People's "Go West" (UK No. 2)—confirms as much, but there is also the AIDS ballad "Dreaming Of The Queen," the in-the-closet "To Speak Is A Sin," and the scarily predatory "Young Offender."

Neil Tennant and Chris Lowe, who had always clearly been a bit batty in a Gilbert and George kind of way, went entirely wacky for the packaging of *Very*, particularly in the Seventies lampshade-style "take" on Devo hats and unconvincing blue and yellow space suits. (Initial pressings, in a rubbery bubble-wrap-style sleeve, included a six-track bonus instrumental album, *Relentless*.) But more importantly, they gave *Very* their all—individual singles released since arguably surpass tracks here, but this is their most coherent and delightful album. (Tennant explained that "It is called *Very* because it is very Pet Shop Boys: It's very up, it's very hi-energy, it's very romantic, it's very sad, it's very pop.")

Highest of many high points on the album is the savage "The Theatre," which Tennant apparently wrote as an answer to Phil Collins' paean to the homeless, "Another Day In Paradise," but which also serves as a critique of the societal imbalances in Prime Minister John Major's Britain. The breezy "Liberation" and the rousing "Can You Forgive Her?" are similarly magnificent pop as only the Pet Shop Boys can make it.

A colorful, bouncy offering, *Very* showed that Tennant and Lowe had the confidence to mess with their formula and still come up trumps. **DN**

"[The Pet Shop Boys] are in pop but not of it."

Neil Tennant, 1994

Track Listing

01	**Can You Forgive Her?** (Lowe • Tennant)		3:53
02	**I Wouldn't Normally Do This Kind Of Thing** (Lowe • Tennant)		3:03
03	**Liberation** (Lowe • Tennant)		4:05
04	**A Different Point Of View** (Lowe • Tennant)		3:26
05	**Dreaming Of The Queen** (Lowe • Tennant)		4:19
06	**Yesterday, When I Was Mad** (Lowe • Tennant)		3:55
▶ 07	**The Theatre** (Lowe • Tennant)		5:10
08	**One And One Make Five** (Lowe • Tennant)		3:30
▶ 09	**To Speak Is A Sin** (Lowe • Tennant)		4:45
10	**Young Offender** (Lowe • Tennant)		4:49
11	**One In A Million** (Lowe • Tennant)		3:53
▶ 12	**Go West** (Belolo • Morali • Willis)		8:21

P. J. Harvey | Rid Of Me (1993)

Label | Island
Producer | Steve Albini • Rob Ellis • Head • P.J. Harvey
Art Direction | Maria Mochnacz
Nationality | UK
Running Time | 47:59

The iconic cover photograph—sexual but unsettling, with that wild spray of black hair, those lidded eyes, and those slender shoulders—says everything about *Rid Of Me*. Stripped of all luxuries and prepared to hide nothing, this is the sound of Polly Jean Harvey tackling her sexual demons. Her British vowels and love of dirty blues riffs gave a unique twist to a rock music scene that at the time was in danger of becoming swamped by American grunge. It may have been her second album, but *Rid Of Me* marked the point at which Harvey truly set out her stall, and forms an indispensable part of her back catalog.

The album's title track brims with an acidic stomp that sounds every bit as furious as it is dominant; the screams of "Lick my legs, I'm on fire" are still as dramatic and spine tingling as they were the moment her larynx unleashed them. It is a bold opening for a record that starts out obsessed by lust, but ends breathless with concerted love on "Ecstasy."

Harvey's feral voice is matched by the blood-curdling guitar that sounds perpetually on the brink of chaos without ever actually losing control—perfectly demonstrated on the male-baiting "Man-Size" and monster boogie of "50ft Queenie."

The brutal, sometimes basic production by Steve Albini lends itself to material dripping with the stark intimacy of a cramped live performance—making it a favorite of Kurt Cobain, for one.

P. J. Harvey's primal instinct proved a major influence on *Rid Of Me*, an album that gets farther under her skin than any of her subsequent releases. **AR**

"Do I want loads of people to know who I am?"

P. J. Harvey, 1994

Track Listing

▶	01	**Rid Of Me** (Harvey)	4:28
	02	**Missed** (Harvey)	4:25
	03	**Legs** (Harvey)	3:40
▶	04	**Rub 'Til It Bleeds** (Harvey)	5:03
	05	**Hook** (Harvey)	3:56
	06	**Man-Size Sextet** (Harvey)	2:16
	07	**Highway '61 Revisited** (Dylan)	2:57
▶	08	**50ft Queenie** (Harvey)	2:23
	09	**Yuri-G** (Harvey)	3:28
▶	10	**Man-Size** (Harvey)	3:16
▶	11	**Dry** (Harvey)	3:23
	12	**Me–Jane** (Harvey)	2:42
	13	**Snake** (Harvey)	1:35
	14	**Ecstasy** (Harvey)	4:27

Blur
Modern Life Is Rubbish (1993)

Label | Food
Producer | Stephen Street
Art Direction | Stylorouge
Nationality | UK
Running Time | 55:08

Modern Life Is Rubbish might never have been made. A combination of grunge, shifting fashions, a grueling American tour, and dodgy finances left Blur positively gasping for air in the latter half of 1992. Against all odds, they produced an album many hardcore fans still consider their best.

Truly the start of Blur's Kinks-esque phase, right down to the forgotten England hinted at with the painting of the Mallard steam train on the cover, its 16 tracks (17 in the United States) offered Syd Barrett-style melancholy (the woozy "Miss America"), cheeky hooligan music hall ("Sunday Sunday"), and guitarist Graham Coxon's beloved alternative noise to boot (he is credited with playing a power drill on "Pressure On Julian"). But the album is paced and produced so beautifully that such a disparate mixture of styles gels to form a dazzling critique of a particular style of English life in the 1990s, while casting a forlorn glance back at a bygone era. Something in the swagger of instrumentals like "Intermission" and "Commercial Break," or the luscious strings on lead single "For Tomorrow," left listeners short of breath.

Could this really be the band who, just two years earlier, had been so closely identified with the much-maligned "baggy" scene? Blur's "new" image (seen on the back cover) was that of wayward mods. Further proof of their magpie cultural tendencies—and downright pop genius—was yet to come. **JK**

Sheryl Crow
Tuesday Night Music Club (1993)

Label | A&M
Producer | Bill Bottrell
Art Direction | Richard Frankel
Nationality | USA
Running Time | 49:48

It pays to hang out with the right people. Sheryl Crow did exactly that when she started palling around with an L.A.-based group of songwriters and producers who met once a week to play music and drink beer. It was collaborating with this collective, dubbed the "Tuesday Night Music Club," that would take Crow to stardom.

At the time, Crow had already recorded one album's worth of material. But this first batch was full of glossy ballads and poppy dance numbers that did not reflect the harder edged, roots-rock sound Crow wanted. The vocalist would make good on her second attempt and produce a work that perfectly captures the relaxed mood, spontaneous creativity, and drunken good times of those weekly sessions.

The album starts with the poignant power ballad "Run, Baby, Run," leading into the intriguing "Leaving Las Vegas." She then immediately issues a challenge on "Strong Enough," laying down her qualifications for a prospective lover, before wrapping up the meatiest part of the album with the defiant "Can't Cry Anymore."

The first two singles, "Run, Baby, Run" and "Leaving Las Vegas," barely dented the charts and the album was slow to catch on. Then radio grabbed hold of the unfeasibly catchy "All I Wanna Do" and made it one of the hits of 1994. The album, likewise, took off, selling nearly three million copies by the year's end and earning Crow three Grammys. **JiH**

The Fall
The Infotainment Scan (1993)

Label | Permanent
Producer | Various
Art Direction | Mark E. Smith
Nationality | UK
Running Time | 45:57

Wu-Tang Clan
Enter the Wu-Tang (36 Chambers) (1993)

Label | Loud
Producer | RZA
Art Direction | Jacqueline Murphy
Nationality | USA
Running Time | 61:35

One of the joys of Fall-loving is that each decade throws up its own indisputable Fall classic, a benchmark that their subsequent albums have to reach. *The Infotainment Scan* is the 1990s addition to this select club. Released in 1993 after their three-year sojourn with major label Phonogram, it finds the group at the peak of their game, with an incredible density of thought, tremendous invention, and deeply bleak, sideswiping humor. Mark E. Smith went back to basics, streamlining the band's sound, while developing the techno edge that had been present in The Fall's work since the mid-1980s. To this end, this is machines-man Dave Bush's album, his contributions giving the group a contemporary edge.

Smith is on sparkling form. He casts his beady, weary eye over elderly rave culture on "The League Of Baldheaded Men" and new kids on the block Suede on "Glam-Racket," while "It's A Curse" pre-empted the rise of the instant nostalgia that riddled British millennial culture. The cover of "Lost In Music" was a perfect choice for The Fall; the elegant repetition of the Sister Sledge original is here rendered abrasive.

It gets flabby around the edges of course, but the central section of *The Infotainment Scan* is some of the most brilliantly consistent music that they have ever performed. The perversity of the covers, the solidity of the groove, and the thickness of the ideas make this one of The Fall's most potent albums ever. **DE**

Rap's agenda had transformed by 1993. Political preachers like Public Enemy were swept aside by stoned gangstas like Snoop. But Wu-Tang plowed a unique furrow. Their rhymes bore scant relation to rap's drugs, guns, and bitches clichés. At heart it was traditional hip-hop braggadocio, but filtered through a fascinating martial arts lexicon.

Musically, it was light years from Public Enemy's wall of noise and Snoop's G-funk. Bite-sized chunks of piano and bass were mixed with what Wu-Tang supremo RZA described as "the kick and the snare and the horn and the boom and the bap and the scream."

Topping it off were a variety of voices: Method Man's laconic rasp, Ol' Dirty Bastard's unhinged ranting, Ghostface Killah and Raekwon's indignant ruckus-raising, and GZA's cool authority. Bringing up the rear there followed U-God (who later confessed he had no interest in martial arts) and the Rebel INS.

Likening themselves to killer bees, Wu-Tang swarmed across the industry. The (then) eight-man crew spawned a seemingly endless slew of solo albums and affiliated projects (still going strong, as evinced by Ghostface's staggering *The Pretty Toney Album* in 2004).

But even after a decade of saturation, Wu-Tang's debut still sounds like nothing on Earth. It could be genius, or just exceptionally well-done nonsense. Either way, it's energizing eccentricity par excellence. **BM**

Björk | Debut (1993)

Label | One Little Indian
Producer | Various
Art Direction | Me Company
Nationality | Iceland
Running Time | 52:12

Born in Reykjavik, Björk Gudmundsdottir showed signs in childhood of the musical maverick she would become. She started out singing alone in windy caves and by the age of 11 had recorded a hit solo album. Avant-punk groups followed, the most successful of which was The Sugarcubes. But when the band finally scored an international hit ("Hit") in 1991, Björk decided to disband the group: "I wanted danger, I wanted threats."

Clutching a tape of traditional brass band players performing her childhood compositions, Björk enlisted the help of dance music pioneer 808 State's Graham Massey, and set her course for London's underground club scene. Along with producer Nellee Hooper (Massive Attack), Björk socialized with some of the most innovative musical forces in town—Goldie, Talvin Singh—picking up ideas, sharing, cross-pollinating like a bumble bee. "Of course, there were tears and arguments from both sides," says Hooper, "but that's how you make a good record."

The result was *Debut*. While Björk describes the image of herself on the sleeve as "shy, polite," *Debut* was a revelation, a secret that demanded to be shouted, not sssh'd. At its center is Björk's extraordinary voice, which swoops from belting howls to soft, baby-like sighs. *Debut* captures the manic energy and excitement of its genesis, Björk audibly basking in such sensual hits as "Venus As A Boy." When she appeared on *MTV Unplugged* in 1992, accompanied by a troupe of monks and some perfectly pitched, singing wine glasses, it seemed Björk could charm music from sand. The world applauded, the big time beckoned: Björk had arrived. **SH**

"I've got a lot of courage, but I've also got a lot of fear."

Björk, 1995

Track Listing		
▶ 01 **Human Behaviour** (Björk•Hooper)		4:12
02 **Crying** (Björk•Hooper)		4:49
▶ 03 **Venus As A Boy** (Björk)		4:41
04 **There's More To Life Than This** (Björk•Hooper)		3:21
05 **Like Someone In Love** (Burke•Van Heusen)		4:33
▶ 06 **Big Time Sensuality** (Björk•Hooper)		3:56
07 **One Day** (Björk)		5:24
▶ 08 **Aeroplane** (Björk)		3:54
09 **Come To Me** (Björk)		4:55
10 **Violently Happy** (Björk•Hooper)		4:58
11 **The Anchor Song** (Björk)		3:32
12 **Play Dead** (Arnold•Björk•Wobble)		3:57

Orbital
Orbital II (1993)

Label | Internal
Producer | Paul Hartnoll • Phil Hartnoll
Art Direction | Fultano '93
Nationality | UK
Running Time | 65:44

Orbital sprang to life in 1989, when acid house and rave dominated music and culture in the UK. Comprising brothers Paul and Phil Hartnoll, Orbital set out to soundtrack the rave scene. While their 1991 untitled debut was very much a techno record, *Orbital II* showed a real progression both musically and creatively.

Orbital II starts with a looped sample from *Star Trek*, and even has a fake hiss of worn vinyl, added by the Hartnoll brothers as a joke. Based on long, repetitive, but always diverting samples and loops, the album is a constant flow of energy and pure dance frenzy. Sandwiched between two short samplings of artificial speech, the eight tracks build into a coherent unit and yet remain individually distinct. The slow build-up of "Lush 3-1" is the perfect preparation for follow-up, "Lush 3-2" (featuring Kirsty Hawkshaw), which, after five minutes of pure greatness, glides into "Impact," the longest track and still a live favorite. Just before the end of the record, the Hartnolls reach another height with the sublime beauty of "Halcyon + On + On," which features Kirsty Hawkshaw's vocal talents alongside a sample of Opus 3's cover of "It's A Fine Day."

Phil and Paul Hartnoll went on to captivate techno and rave audiences with their perfectly choreographed live performances around the globe (their twilight gigs at Glastonbury in 1994 and 1995 are hailed as classics). "Lush 3-1" and "Lush 3-2" are remembered fondly today as anthems for the rave movement—and, indeed, for the whole British electronic dance scene. **PN**

Snoop Doggy Dogg
Doggystyle (1993)

Label | Death Row
Producer | Dr. Dre
Art Direction | Kimberly Holt
Nationality | USA
Running Time | 52:32

Rap's cuddliest porn peddler was once a stone-cold gangsta. Such was his notoriety that *Doggystyle* became the fastest-selling debut album and the first to enter Billboard's chart at No. 1. Some success was down to the whomping "What's My Name?"—a roof-raising reworking of George Clinton's "Atomic Dog" with a hit video; some down to hype on the back of Snoop's starring on Dr. Dre's *The Chronic*. Mostly, though, it was because Snoop was embroiled in a murder case, which made him the first major rapper to (apparently) walk it like he talked it. By the time he beat the rap, *Doggystyle* had sold four million in America alone.

Conceptually, *Doggystyle* transports Curtis Mayfield's *Superfly* into the 1990s; sonically—despite samples from disco pioneer George McCrae and Japanese singer Kyu Sakamoto—it sets the seal on Dre's squelchy G-funk. The lyrics are as luridly stupid as Darryl Daniel's controversial cover cartoon, reaching an unpleasant peak on "Ain't No Fun." But overlook that and there is plenty to enjoy on this album. The guests—including crooner Nate Dogg and the afro-puffing Lady of Rage—are superb. But it is Tha Doggfather who rules; as comfortably cool with the Slick Rick remake "Lodi Dodi" as the ragga-tinged "Serial Killa" and bloodcurdling "Murder Was The Case."

There are legendary tracks: "Doggystyle," featuring George Clinton, and the original version of Dre's "The Next Episode." Even without them, *Doggystyle* is a technicolor riot. Take a bite today. **BM**

Sebadoh
Bubble And Scrape (1993)

Label | Sub Pop
Producer | Uncredited
Art Direction | Sebadoh
Nationality | USA
Running Time | 46:12

Lou Barlow originally formed Sebadoh as a side project to his bass-playing work in Dinosaur Jr., but it became a full-time concern after he was unceremoniously kicked out of that band in 1989. Thanks to personal endorsements from Kurt Cobain, associations with other alternataive rock heroes such as Pavement, Mudhoney, and Sonic Youth, and, of course, some great records, Sebadoh flourished and went on to become a byword for lo-fi, offbeat indie rock in the early 1990s.

Although there is a perception that Lou himself "is" Sebadoh, this was an entirely democratic songwriting triptych. This album belongs as much to cohorts Eric Gaffney and Jason Loewenstein as it does to Barlow. There is Gaffney's wonderful, way-leftfield art-rock ramblings, all Beefheart-like spasms and goofy eccentricities ("Emma Get Wild") while Loewenstein swings from the melancholy thrashings of "Sister" to the howling wildman stomp of "Flood." Nevertheless, it is Barlow's neurotic and forever-lovelorn amplified balladry that is perhaps most cherishable. Among the many lachrymose joys here is the magnificently morose "Two Years Two Days"—a vaguely adolescent but piercingly direct lament on love and loss, set to some forlornly desperate jangles.

Gaffney was to leave after this record. As such, it may best represent this charming band's irresistible heartbreak fetishism and strange little flights of fancy. As Barlow tells us with the album's very first line: "It's all a matter of soul and fire." **TH**

The Boo Radleys
Giant Steps (1993)

Label | Creation
Producer | BOO! Productions
Art Direction | Stephen A. Wood
Nationality | UK
Running Time | 64:04

Prior to the release of *Giant Steps*, The Boo Radleys were the runt of the Creation Records litter. The booming British indie label had yet to discover Oasis, but they had plenty of other hot bands, like Primal Scream and Teenage Fanclub. But Liverpool's Boo Radleys—named after the reclusive character in *To Kill A Mockingbird*—were mopey, Dinosaur Jr. soundalikes with unfortunate similarities to the much-derided "shoe-gazing" scene.

Then they dropped *Giant Steps*. This is a huge, kaleidoscopic record, 17 tracks that are as trippily extravagant as the acid-fried sleeve design. Sure, there are relatively straightforward strum-alongs, such as "Wish I Was Skinny" and "Barney (... And Me)." But there are also sublime "suites"—the moments where the feedback squall of "Leaves And Sand" bleeds into the zooming, stereophonic soundscapes of "Butterfly McQueen," which in turn morphs into the sunshine beats of "Rodney King." Even better is the section when the grunge-meets-Beatles rush of "Take The Time Around" slips into the cataclysmic reggae-goes-mariachi triumph of the album's lead single, "Lazarus."

It is easy to imagine that Sun Ra, Phil Spector, and Brian Wilson joined forces to write and produce a melodic, orchestral space-rock masterpiece. Instead, credit goes to the Boos' songwriter Martin Carr, while the band's own BOO! Productions dreamt up all this sonic adventurism themselves one dreary London winter. *NME* and *Select* both crowned it Album Of The Year, and it remains a cult classic to this day. **CM**

William Orbit | Strange Cargo III (1993)

Label | Virgin
Producer | William Orbit
Art Direction | Michael Freeman • Catherine McRae
Nationality | UK
Running Time | 63:47

The material for producer/remixer/composer William Orbit's techno-based third *Strange Cargo III* was recorded in 1992 but could very well have been released this morning. And that is no easy task in the electronic music field where—as is the case with hip hop—"old school" is measured in years, not decades. Orbit's beats are crisp, his orchestrations clean, and his compositions deep. His music is danceable but not dance music, per se, as it is as much for listening as grooving about.

Five different vocalists make contributions to *Strange Cargo III*. Most notable is the excellent singer-songwriter and ace Orbit musical partner Beth Orton. She co-wrote and offers up both spoken-word and sung passages on the opening track, "Water From A Vine Leaf," which is now Orbit's signature track. At more than seven minutes, it is an atmospheric micro-epic with a haunting yet grooving piano line, overlapping and hypnotic synthesizer sequences, and a satisfying climactic crescendo. The street-smart "Time To Get Wize" features a noirish dub vibe supporting Divine Washim's fluidly delivered spoken narrative. "A Touch Of The Night" has an arrangement that sounds like a gently whirling nightmare with various blips, ray-gun noises, and singer Cleo Torres' swaggering vocals seductively ganging up on the listener, though never oppressively so.

Further into his career, Orbit would become known for his production work with name artists, such as Madonna, Blur, and Melanie C. *Strange Cargo III* catches Orbit's musical star ascending mightily as he works with a cast of then unknown artists, mapping out the future as he captures his present. **YK**

> "What success does do is to give ... more self-assurance, and that's why it's useful."
>
> William Orbit, 1999

Track Listing

▶	01	**Water From A Vine Leaf** (Orbit • Orton)	7:05
	02	**Into The Paradise** (Leach • Orbit)	5:41
▶	03	**Time To Get Wize** (Orbit)	4:09
	04	**Harry Flowers** (Nitzsche)	4:31
	05	**A Touch Of The Night** (Orbit)	5:02
	06	**The Story Of Light** (Leach • Orbit)	6:21
	07	**Gringatcho Demento** (Orbit • Torres)	6:38
	08	**A Hazy Shade Of Random** (Orbit)	5:08
	09	**Best Friend, Paranoia** (Orbit • Torres)	4:35
	10	**The Monkey King** (Orbit)	5:15
	11	**Deus Ex Machina** (Orbit)	5:40
▶	12	**Water Babies** (Orbit)	3:42

Method Man | Tical (1994)

Label | Def Jam
Producer | RZA
Art Direction | The Drawing Broad
Nationality | USA
Running Time | 43:43

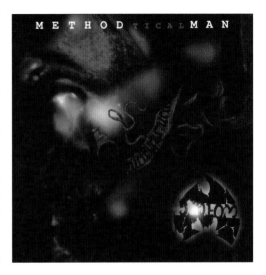

"In Staten Island we used to call weed 'method,'" Meth explained. "Then my man ... cut it down to 'metical' ... Over the course of time it got cut down to 'tical.'"

Getting wasted might be a blast. Method Man's latter-day escapades with Redman—especially 1999's brilliant *Blackout!*—certainly foster the illusion. But *Tical* evokes a scarier scenario of crack-highs, hyper-violence, and homicide.

Enter the Wu-Tang (36 Chambers) alerted the world to the rasping rhymes of Clifford "Method Man" Smith and pioneering production of Robert "RZA" Diggs. *Tical* takes that album's rawness to a new extreme: muffled beats, bass, screams, and scrapes create a horror movie of the mind. It is unsettling and, in lesser hands, might have been unlistenable.

But the rhymes provide reassurance whenever the backing teeters on the brink, much as legendary rapper Rakim had anchored his DJ Eric B's experimentation. "When Eric B and Rakim dropped 'Paid In Full,'" Meth recalled, "That's when I really became rap conscious."

Bar the humming "Bring The Pain," *Tical* was not an obvious source of hits. Def Jam pushed it to platinum by bribing Meth (with cash for a Lexus) to remake "All I Need." The result, replacing Wu-Tang with Mary J. Blige, was the beautiful "I'll Be There For You/You're All I Need To Get By." Annoyingly, it's not on *Tical*'s remastered reissue (although that does feature an extraordinary Prodigy remix of "Release Yo' Delf").

Tical 2000: Judgement Day (1998) and *Tical 0: the Prequel* (2004) curve closer to rap convention. The original—and best—is in a dark class all its own. **BM**

> ## "They gonna have their own view of what's going on."
>
> Method Man, 1995

Track Listing		
01 **Tical** (Diggs·Smith)		3:56
02 **Biscuits** (Diggs·Smith)		2:49
▶ 03 **Bring The Pain** (Diggs·Smith)		3:09
▶ 04 **All I Need** (Diggs·Smith)		3:16
05 **What The Blood Clot** (Diggs·Smith)		3:24
06 **Meth Vs. Chef** (Diggs·Smith·Woods)		3:36
07 **Sub Crazy** (Diggs·Smith)		2:15
▶ 08 **Release Yo' Delf** (Diggs·Perren·Fekaris·Smith)		4:15
09 **P.L.O. Style** (Cooney·Diggs·Smith)		2:36
10 **I Get My Thang In Action** (Diggs·Smith)		3:45
11 **Mr. Sandman** (Diggs·Hunter·Smith)		3:37
12 **Stimulation** (Diggs·Smith)		3:46
13 **Method Man (Remix)** (Diggs·Smith)		3:19

Frank Black
Teenager
Of The Year (1994)

Label | 4AD
Producer | Various
Art Direction | Uncredited
Nationality | USA
Running Time | 62:33

Girls Against Boys
Venus Luxure
No. 1 Baby (1994)

Label | Touch And Go
Producer | Ted Nicely
Art Direction | Girls Against Boys
Nationality | USA
Running Time | 46:17

Throughout the late 1980s and into the 1990s, the Pixies pioneered a sound and style that came to define alternative rock. Charles Michael Kittridge Thompson IV, a.k.a. Black Francis, had fronted this group with yowling teenage angst and an idiosyncratic line in surf punk/sci-fi songwriting. After they disbanded, he became a solo artist named Frank Black.

For years critics had attempted to categorize Black's sound—his new concept of "freedom rock" on the 22-track *Teenager Of The Year* was yet another dig at their expense. The album reveals Black revisiting his varied, American guitar-based roots, and uncovering moments of greatness and strangeness to rival any of the Pixies' best material. Without having had the outside pressure to produce a "new sound," Black moves in leisurely fashion from Spanish-influenced rock and surf guitar sounds to distorted, trashy punk, reggae, and more, all layered with his distinctive voice and wilfully abstruse lyrics. "Speedy Marie" is an off-kilter, cleverly worked love song; "Thalassocracy" and "Whatever Happened To Pong?" are exhilarating punky outbursts; and "Ole Mulholland" tells the tale of the man who designed L.A.'s water system. No, really.

The sheer weirdness of some of Black's recordings precluded mainstream acceptance—though his refusal to do press hardly helped matters. This fascinating, sprawling release deserved better. **LJ**

Underground rock, for all its merits, is not widely considered the sexiest kind of music imaginable. But even if Baltimore's Girls Against Boys are no Keith Sweat, there is an element of sleazy suggestiveness in their croaky serenades and dark-side grooves that you don't get with many of their contemporaries.

The influence of their contemporaries—Big Black, Fugazi, the Jesus Lizard—can be heard in their tendency toward noisy, unconventional rock, but they were different in a number of ways—for example, their idiosyncratic lineup. Not many punk-rock bands were using synths at the time, and even fewer had two bassists. Meanwhile, singer Scott McCloud's breathy, laconic snarl pitched somewhere between Mark E. Smith and Kurt Cobain.

They sound particularly sharp on this, their second LP. From the shuddering, black-ice riffs of opener "In Like Flynn" onward, there is something in the restraint and swing of that busy bottom-end that is just unlike any other band. They have something of the night about them, and perhaps of being talked into something against your better judgment. It's there as much in the malevolent, imploring hum of "Satin Down" as the foot-down rush of "Let Me Come Back," or "Bullet Proof Cupid"'s dirty twang. This is a record of sinister, dangerous charms, and one still proving difficult to resist over a decade later. **TH**

Jeru The Damaja
The Sun Rises
In The East (1994)

Label | Payday
Producer | Kendrick Davis • DJ Premier
Art Direction | Daniel Hastings
Nationality | USA
Running Time | 39:30

After appearing on Gang Starr's *Daily Operation*, Jeru The Damaja burst onto the East Coast scene with this, his debut album, serving up summary lyrical justice to everyone he thought was dragging hip hop down. ("Jungle Music" is a barely disguised attack on The Jungle Brothers' perceived esoteric Afro-centric stance, and "Ain't The Devil Happy" holds a mirror up to Wu-Tang Clan's money-obsessed anthem "C.R.E.A.M.") Like a lot of young hip-hop artists in the 1990s, Jeru's concise political world view is compromised by some of his more dubious rhymes ("Da Bichez"). Despite being tame compared to some of the misogyny on show at the time, this meant he fell between two significant stools—those of the "conscious" and the "street."

Jeru's lyrical bile was too much for most mainstream punters and hip-hop stars alike, but aside from lyrical concerns it is DJ Premier's outstanding production skills that mark this out as one of the best hip-hop albums of the mid-1990s.

The cover art features a crouching Jeru framed against a blood-red sunrise behind Manhattan's iconic skyline. The eagle-eyed will spot that the Statue of Liberty lies on its side, half-submerged beneath the Hudson River—and, eerily enough, that the southern tower of the World Trade Center has half collapsed and is engulfed in flames, something that Jeru references lyrically on the track "Come Clean." **JDo**

Pavement
Crooked Rain,
Crooked Rain (1994)

Label | Matador
Producer | Pavement
Art Direction | Pavement
Nationality | USA
Running Time | 42:28

Pavement became synonymous with a lifestyle and movement known as "slacker" in the early 1990s. But by 1994, and their second proper album, an audience had developed that was well in tune with the band's playful way with song structures, fusion of genres, and wayward melodic skills.

In singer and chief songwriter Stephen Malkmus, the five piece were gifted with an abstract expressionist adept at tugging on the heartstrings with the most random outbursts. On the countrified "Range Life," a song as lyrically direct as the band ever got, he lambasted the Smashing Pumpkins and The Stone Temple Pilots, much to his knowing listeners' amusement. There was a tribute to jazz legend Dave Brubeck on the instrumental 5/4 time "5-4 = Unity," and even a nod to English mods on the slow-paced closer, "Fillmore Jive." Their own brand of madness also bled through to the artwork. It featured obscured track titles and snatches of found visual items—some relevant, some not. There are lyrics scrawled in pen, yet many of them don't appear on the album.

But for all its obscurism, *Crooked Rain, Crooked Rain* remains a core classic American album, rich with hooks and melodies that could only come from a laidback generation not afraid to poke fun at itself. There is sunshine and simple fun in each and every track that cheers at every turn. It still warms the heart today. **JK**

Portishead | Dummy (1994)

Label | Go! Discs
Producer | Portishead • Adrian Utley
Art Direction | Ich And Kar
Nationality | UK
Running Time | 45:30

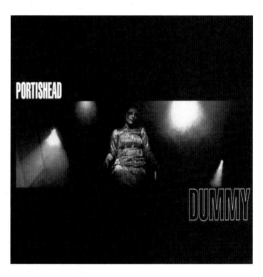

Portishead's debut, *Dummy*, is the zenith of Nineties trip-hop, a genre they did not invent, but which this haunting album redefined. The band blossomed out of the dub-oriented scene that flourished in Bristol, under the shadow of the harsh economic realities of the UK's Thatcherite legacy—Beth Gibbons first met Geoff Barrow on her job creation program, which funded her singing gigs in bars. But they took a different musical route from their kindred spirits—the dance-oriented Massive Attack or the surreal raps of Tricky.

Their darkly alluring, atmospheric sound mixed a whole new set of elements into the disjointed breakbeats: torch song, film noir, smoky jazz, Beth's exquisitely unbalanced vocals, Geoff's mastery of DJ technology, and their supreme songwriting skills. Check "Sour Times," for example, and you find a deliciously spine-tingling, torch song built on a sample from Lalo Schifrin's score for "Danube Incident" from *Mission: Impossible*. Beth's visceral vocals plead and soar over a desolate, flickering soundscape in which Adrian Utley's noir surf guitar patterns interweave with Barrow's restless turntables and samplers.

The strange seductive spell it still casts made it 1994's Album of the Year in UK magazines as diverse as *Mixmag* (dance), *The Face* (cutting-edge style), and *Melody Maker* (indie rock). By early 1995, powered by the raw intensity of its guitar and vocals, the languid, seductive "Glory Box" entered the UK pop charts at No. 13. By the end of that year Portishead had sold more than 150,000 CDs in the United States and won the UK's prestigious Mercury music prize. **MR**

> ## "I'll give Beth a backing track, and her style will change ... like a chameleon of voices."
>
> Geoff Barrow, 1995

Track Listing	
01 **Mysterons** (Barrow·Gibbons·Utley)	5:06
▶ 02 **Sour Times** (Barrow·Brooks·Gibbons Schifrin·Turner·Utley)	4:14
03 **Strangers** (Barrow·Gibbons·Shorter·Utley)	3:58
▶ 04 **It Could Be Sweet** (Barrow·Gibbons)	4:19
05 **Wandering Star** (Allen·Barrow·Brown Dickerson·Gibbons·Goldstein·Jordan Miller·Scott·Oskar)	4:56
06 **Numb** (Barrow·Gibbons·Utley)	3:57
07 **Roads** (Barrow·Gibbons·Utley)	5:09
▶ 08 **Pedestal** (Barrow·Gibbons·Utley)	3:41
▶ 09 **Biscuit** (Barrow·Gibbons·Ray)	5:04
▶ 10 **Glory Box** (Barrow·Gibbons·Hayes·Utley)	5:06

The Sabres Of Paradise | Haunted Dancehall (1994)

Label | Warp
Producer | The Sabres of Paradise
Art Direction | MadArk
Nationality | UK
Running Time | 76:49

The enigmatic Andy Weatherall was one of the original acid-house pioneers, and has produced for bands such as Primal Scream and My Bloody Valentine. While peers such as Paul Oakenfold have gone on to fame and fortune, however, Weatherall has retreated further into the techno underground, where his legendary reputation as a contrary bastard endures.

In the early 1990s, Warp Records released *Sabresonic* and *Haunted Dancehall*, both produced by Weatherall—who, with Jagz Kooner and Gary Burns, recorded as *The Sabres Of Paradise*. The former album is a classic UK techno LP most notable for the peerless "Smokebelch," an epic piece of dubby, ambient techno. The latter is an altogether darker affair. Consisting of stripped-back dub-heavy grooves, eerie strings, warped jazz, and smoky atmospheres, rarely has an album's title been so apt.

"Wilmot" begins with a brass band, of all things, constructing a big wobbly wall of noise that sounds like a carnival sideshow on acid, before unveiling itself as a supremely graceful, stoned, and elusive dub. The swaggering dub-wise funk of "Tow Truck" towers out of the speakers, propelled by a menacing guitar chord and a brooding organ."Return To Planet D" and "Theme 4" unwind into uneasy atmospheres, populated by pops, clicks, bubbles, and the ever-present Sabresonic squelch.

The CD booklet features 13 short, intriguing extracts to accompany each track on the album, credited to the novel *Haunted Dancehall* by James Woodbourne. As always, Weatherall has the last laugh: no such book exists—it is a beguiling in-joke that only further adds to the Sabres' mystique. **APi**

"You've got to ... be subversive."

Andy Weatherall, 1993

Track Listing			
01	**Bubble And Slide**	(Sabres Of Paradise)	2:39
▶ 02	**Bubble And Slide II**	(Sabres Of Paradise)	7:38
03	**Duke Of Earlsfield**	(Sabres Of Paradise)	8:42
04	**Flight Path Estate**	(Sabres Of Paradise)	3:21
05	**Planet D**	(Sabres Of Paradise)	4:41
▶ 06	**Wilmot**	(Sabres Of Paradise)	7:32
▶ 07	**Tow Truck**	(Sabres Of Paradise)	6:35
▶ 08	**Theme**	(Sabres Of Paradise)	4:48
09	**Theme 4**	(Sabres Of Paradise)	1:55
10	**Return To Planet D**	(Sabres Of Paradise)	5:04
11	**Ballad Of Nicky McGuire**	(Sabres Of Paradise)	8:30
12	**Jacob Street 7am**	(Sabres Of Paradise)	3:46
13	**Chapel Street Market 9am** (Sabres Of Paradise)			7:14
▶ 14	**Haunted Dancehall**	(Sabres Of Paradise)	4:24

Nas | Illmatic (1994)

Label | Columbia
Producer | Various
Art Direction | Jo DiDonato
Nationality | USA
Running Time | 39:44

Fusing old-school street poetry with razor-sharp production, *Illmatic* is proof that hardcore hip hop can move minds as well as feet.

The album is a brutal, yet insightful, portrait of the New York project where Nasir Jones grew up. Unlike so many of his gangsta contemporaries, Nas does not seek to glorify ghetto existence. Instead, he delivers his raps like a hardened war correspondent reporting from the front. Track "N.Y. State Of Mind" throws the listener into his Queensbridge life, a world of shootouts and drug overdoses, where even young kids wield guns. On "Life's A Bitch"—which ends with a haunting trumpet solo from his jazz-musician father, Olu Dara—the 20-year-old Nas admits that he feels "blessed" to have lived so long. It is a feeling grounded in reality. Two years earlier he had seen his brother and best friend shot on the same night. His brother survived; his friend did not.

With its high-impact rhymes alone, *Illmatic* would make it into the hip-hop hall of fame. But the crunching production work raises the album to the level of urban masterpiece. A Tribe Called Quest's Q-Tip weighs in with jazz-inflected beats on "One Love," a surprisingly touching open letter to Nas' homeboys in jail. Gang Starr's DJ Premier drops block-shaking beats on the furious battle rap of "Represent" and the nostalgic "Memory Lane," and East Coast legend Large Professor mixes rugged breaks with a sample of Jacko's "Human Nature" on album closer "It Ain't Hard To Tell."

Awarded a rare "five mics" (classic rating) by *The Source*, Nas' debut marked the beginning of street rap's renaissance. **TB**

> ## "Everything that I worry about or feel good about, I put it down musically."
>
> Nas, 1994

Track Listing

01	The Genesis	(Braithwaite·Jones)	1:45
▶ 02	N.Y. State Of Mind	(Jones·Martin)	4:54
▶ 03	Life's A Bitch	(Cruz·Dara·Jones·Scott·Wilson)	3:30
04	The World Is Yours	(Jones·Phillips)	4:50
▶ 05	Halftime	(Byrd·Jones·Mitchell)	4:20
06	Memory Lane (Sittin' In Da Park) (Barsella·Jones·Martin·Wilson)		4:08
▶ 07	One Love	(Davis·Heath·Jones)	5:25
08	One Time 4 Your Mind	(Jones·Mitchell)	3:18
▶ 09	Represent	(Martin·Nas)	4:12
10	It Ain't Hard To Tell	(Jones·Mitchell)	3:22

Beastie Boys
Ill Communication (1994)

Label | Capitol
Producer | Beastie Boys • M. Caldato Jnr.
Art Direction | Gibran Evans
Nationality | USA
Running Time | 59:55

By 1994, NYC's Beastie Boys knew precisely how to rock a party. Having honed their instrumental skills and sampling prowess on *Check Your Head* and *Paul's Boutique*, the trio went back to their studios, more than ready to experiment. They delivered a record so entrenched in their consuming passions (Buddhism, Seventies cop shows, hardcore punk), and so undeniably zeitgeist, that it was impossible to resist.

Simply put, this is an album of three parts. There are gut-wrenching, short-lived thrash-outs ("Tough Guy," "Heart Attack Man"), smooth jazz workouts or chant-infused mantras ("Flute Loop," "Shamballa") and, most effective of all, stunning sample-based loops. A song like "Root Down" is a prime example. Based around a Jimmy Smith organ loop, it builds to a crescendo (largely thanks to Mr. Smith's pioneering work) that the listener yearns for more with each play. That the track is instantly followed by "Sabotage," one of the band's most memorable performances—a live jam with the lyrics screeched over the top by all three members—makes it all the more exciting.

As a snapshot of the headspace of the three protagonists (meditation, rocking out, or being twice as cool and unique as anyone else), it is a key turning point in their career. Ultimately, *Ill Communication*, in all its kitsch, vintage burger-bar-sleeve glory, is an album about having a good time. After this, they would go on to refine their sound, but as a party record *Ill Communication* ticks all the right boxes. **JK**

Elvis Costello
Brutal Youth (1994)

Label | Warner Bros.
Producer | E. Costello • M. Froom
Art Direction | M. Krage • E. Singer
Nationality | UK
Running Time | 57:20

Elvis Costello once remarked that in his early career his record company Columbia "had always seemed to want a return to the sound that we had started out with." Eventually he gave them what they wanted, with his 1986 album *Blood And Chocolate*. Needless to say, Columbia hated it, but Costello's audience were overjoyed.

In many ways, *Brutal Youth* is another installment from the same part of Costello's dark side. Original backing band, The Attractions, and first producer Nick Lowe (sharing bass duties), reconvened for the first time in almost half a decade. Since last working with them, Costello had defied convention by doing a surf record (*Mighty Like A Rose*) and a classical album (*The Juliet Letters*). Recorded partly at Pathway Studios, London, *Brutal Youth* is spiky, venomous, and pulls no punches. "Kinder Murder" boasts razor guitars as Costello rages against ugly male bravado and rape. "My Science Fiction Twin" and "Sulky Girl" chart the emptiness of fame and power, while the warm acoustic moods "All The Rage" and "Rocking Horse Road" show a man looking back at his mistakes and losses—not with regret, but with a soulful wisdom. "13 Steps Lead Down" finds Costello letting hell rip.

It is tempting to say if this record had been recorded in the late 1970s it would already be regarded as a full classic. As it is *Brutal Youth* is unfairly underrated in Costello's canon. The "angry young man" is attractive, but the "angry wise man" is deadly. **PS**

Morrissey
Vauxhall And I (1994)

Label | Parlophone
Producer | Steve Lillywhite
Art Direction | Greg Ross
Nationality | UK
Running Time | 39:54

The deaths, one after the other in 1993, of his manager Nigel Thomas, his video director Tim Broad, and his producer Mick Ronson, who had helmed 1992's sterling *"Your Arsenal,"* affected Morrissey greatly. Moreover, after waving a Union Jack in front of a provocative backdrop while supporting Madness in Finsbury Park the same summer, he was savaged by the music press. (Britpop stole back the flag from the fascists in 1994, but few forgave Morrissey his perceived sins.) Hopes were not high for *Vauxhall And I.* They should have been.

The old nostalgic preoccupations are present and correct. "Now My Heart Is Full" name-checks four characters from Graham Greene's *Brighton Rock* along with obscure British actor Patric Doonan; "Spring-Heeled Jim" uses dialog sampled from 1958 documentary *We Are The Lambeth Boys*; "Billy Budd" refers to the character played by longtime Morrissey favorite Terence Stamp in Peter Ustinov's 1962 movie adaptation of Herman Melville's novel. And yet for all that, *Vauxhall And I* might be his most personal album. It is certainly his warmest: where Ronson turned the amps up to 11 on *"Your Arsenal,"* producer Steve Lillywhite and guitarists Alain Whyte and Boz Boorer soak *Vauxhall And I* in a dreamy melancholy. Morrissey's lyrics, too, are more reflective than ever, by turns heartbreaking ("Used To Be A Sweet Boy"), defiant ("Why Don't You Find Out For Yourself"), and helpless ("Speedway," with its ebullient, theme-shattering climax). It is his best solo record. **WF-J**

TLC
CrazySexyCool (1994)

Label | BMG
Producer | L. A. Reid
Art Direction | Christopher Stern
Nationality | USA
Running Time | 56:10

With *CrazySexyCool*, TLC stopped presenting themselves as "teenage" rebels and reintroduced themselves as an R&B act of seductive sophistication. This was in part a premeditated PR stunt to distract attention from Lisa "Left Eye" Lopes' increasingly erratic behavior, which culminated in her burning down the mansion that belonged to her boyfriend—the American football star Andre Rison—and vandalizing several of his cars. (An act that, when coupled with the fact that they did not receive fair royalties off this album, would eventually lead to the group declaring themselves bankrupt—just three months before they became history's biggest selling U.S. all-female group.)

Platinum-selling U.S. No. 1 "Creep" was a Philadelphia soul/disco-referencing slice of sweetness that was balanced out by its resigned lyrics about submission to a cheating partner. "Waterfalls" (another U.S. chart-topper) was a poppier effort with an infectious horn section that sugared the serious AIDS-awareness pill, and proved to be their biggest chart success, topping lists in the United States and Europe. But it is the cover of Prince's "If I Was Your Girlfriend" that really shines here. Removed of the neurotic and wheedling authorial voice, the song is reinvented as a practically panting ode to sexual longing. Their follow-up, 1999's *Fanmail* would go on to become their best selling album, but *CrazySexyCool* still stands as a milestone R&B release, selling 11 million copies in the United States and, deservedly, winning a Grammy. **JDo**

Oasis | Definitely Maybe (1994)

Label | Creation
Producer | Mark Coyle • Oasis
Art Direction | Brian Cannon
Nationality | UK
Running Time | 52:03

It is all too easy to forget quite how barren the musical landscape in the UK was in 1994. Britpop was yet to fully blossom, and grunge had died with Kurt Cobain. It took five of the most ordinary, working-class lads to reignite the scene, and redefine the musical landscape.

Oasis never really had an infancy. Spewed from the streets of Manchester, they seemed already fully formed. *Definitely Maybe* remains their most coherent, exciting and fresh album to date. The album cover betrayed their influences—from George Best, to Burt Bacharach, to carafes of red wine (actually blackcurrant juice). Football, music, and booze. A band of the people.

And the people loved them back. There was no pretension in their often thinly veiled reworkings of Beatles tunes. "Rock 'N' Roll Star" sets the agenda from the off, a hedonistic anthem par excellence; the exhilarating "Cigarettes And Alcohol," which references T-Rex's "Get It On," provides another. "Shakermaker," itself a New Seekers rip-off, is all the more vivid for such brazen borrowing. "Live Forever" is as classic-sounding a single as ever flowed from the pen of chief songwriter Noel Gallagher. That all five members of Oasis would actually go on to become (briefly) Nineties personifications of the true rock 'n' roll spirit makes listening to the album today much more satisfying. Even the acoustic simplicity of the closer, which fabulously determined the supposed audience's music as "Sheeee-ite," had a bite they rarely revisited.

Oasis are like a Sherman tank in the music industry. Reliable, often devastating, and something you most definitely do not want to argue with. **JK**

> ## "I care about our mum and John Lennon ... and being in a band."
> Liam Gallagher, 1994

Track Listing

▶	01	**Rock'n'Roll Star** (N. Gallagher)	5:23
	02	**Shakermaker** (N. Gallagher)	5:10
▶	03	**Live Forever** (N. Gallagher)	4:38
	04	**Up In The Sky** (N. Gallagher)	4:28
	05	**Columbia** (N. Gallagher)	6:17
	06	**Supersonic** (N. Gallagher)	4:44
	07	**Bring It On Down** (N. Gallagher)	4:17
▶	08	**Cigarettes And Alcohol** (N. Gallagher)	4:50
	09	**Digsy's Dinner** (N. Gallagher)	2:32
	10	**Slide Away** (N. Gallagher)	6:32
▶	11	**Married With Children** (N. Gallagher)	3:12

Soundgarden | Superunknown (1994)

Label | A&M
Producer | Michael Beinhorn • Soundgarden
Art Direction | Kelk
Nationality | USA
Running Time | 73:34

After Soundgarden's hometown of Seattle became the focal point for the world's music media in the early 1990s thanks to the success of Nirvana and Pearl Jam, they distinguished themselves from many of their contemporaries with the diverse experimentation of their fourth full-length album. With its moderate pace, soaring guitars, and spooky imagery, *Superunknown*'s innovative use of percussion alongside the traditional rock template, particularly on "Half"'s Middle Eastern textures, distinguished it from similar bands of the era like Stone Temple Pilots.

Their brooding Sabbath-esque atmospherics coupled with sludgy guitar riffs sat them right on the edge of the metal genre. Yet Chris Cornell's distinctive vocals and the clean delivery of his quirky lyrics was possibly what attracted rock lovers to them. "Black Hole Sun" became an anthem for the discontented, connecting with the despair of a generation on a very emotional level. Coupled with "Spoonman" it earned Soundgarden two Grammy nominations and successful sales figures.

Other gems abound throughout the record, particularly "Fell On Black Days," "Superunknown," "The Day I Tried To Live," and "4th of July." Despite each succeeding differently in their own way, they are seamed together stylistically by Michael Beinhorn's thick production, utilizing a number of overdubs and effects. Clocking in at 73 minutes, *Superunknown* could possibly have benefitted from some gentle editing. Yet it proved to be the pinnacle of Soundgarden's career— the band dispersed in 1997 after releasing just one more album, *Down On The Upside*. **CSt**

Track Listing

01	**Let Me Drown** (Cornell)	3:53
02	**My Wave** (Cornell • Thayil)	5:12
▶ 03	**Fell On Black Days** (Cornell)	4:43
04	**Mailman** (Cameron • Cornell)	4:25
▶ 05	**Superunknown** (Cornell • Thayil)	5:07
06	**Head Down** (Shepherd)	6:09
▶ 07	**Black Hole Sun** (Cornell)	5:18
▶ 08	**Spoonman** (Soundgarden)	4:06
09	**Limo Wreck** (Soundgarden)	5:47
▶ 10	**The Day I Tried To Live** (Cornell)	5:20
11	**Kickstand** (Cornell • Thayil)	1:34
12	**Fresh Tendrils** (Cameron • Cornell)	4:16
▶ 13	**4th of July** (Cornell)	5:07
14	**Half** (Shepherd)	2:16
15	**Like Suicide** (Cornell)	7:03
16	**She Likes Surprises** (Soundgarden)	3:18

The Offspring | Smash (1994)

Label | Epitaph
Producer | Thom Wilson
Art Direction | Kevin Head • Fred Hidalgo
Nationality | USA
Running Time | 46:36

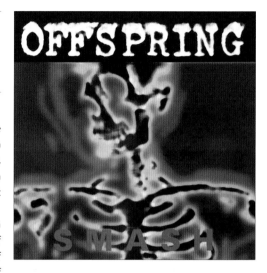

When you listen to The Offspring's *Smash* you are hearing a distillation of male adolescence, replete with petulance, idealism, bravado, insecurity, and, ultimately, juvenility. All of this impotent raging is set to a soundtrack of fevered punk and muscled rock. And that is why *Smash* has sold millions of copies worldwide.

The Offspring's third full-length album serves as a blueprint for the explosion of the most recent wave of punk music, all hinging on the phenomenal success of the first single "Come Out And Play." This fable of violent youth pivoted on an incredibly catchy Middle Eastern guitar serif. Soon afterwards punk legends Agent Orange tried to sue them for appropriating the riff but since it is a common hook known as the Phrygian scale, they could do little but watch The Offspring's coffers fill and fellow punks The Vandals write a song about the whole sorry episode entitled "Aging Orange."

This backbiting mattered little as the follow-up single "Self Esteem" caught even more ears and the album sold so much it virtually bankrolled punk label Epitaph Records and many international distributors. No matter whether the band was barreling along with the speedy punk rock in "So Alone," fist-pumping power pop in "Gotta Get Away," or even flirting with twitchy ska on "What Happened To You," addictive melodies were paramount. In the following years The Offspring became something of a novelty act, ostensibly writing pop jingles for radio. Yet back in 1994, when every ounce of their energy was directed at extending a middle finger to the world, it was difficult to ignore their sincerity. **AT**

"I think bands ... take themselves too seriously..."

Kevin "Noodles" Wasserman, 2004

Track Listing		
01 **Time To Relax** (The Offspring)	0:25
02 **Nitro (Youth Energy)** (The Offspring)	2:26
▶ 03 **Bad Habit** (The Offspring)	3:43
04 **Gotta Get Away** (The Offspring)	3:52
05 **Genocide** (The Offspring)	3:32
06 **Something To Believe In** (The Offspring)	3:17
▶ 07 **Come Out And Play** (The Offspring)	3:17
▶ 08 **Self Esteem** (The Offspring)	4:17
09 **It'll Be A Long Time** (The Offspring)	2:43
10 **Killboy Powerhead** (The Didjits)	2:02
11 **What Happened To You?** (The Offspring)	2:12
12 **So Alone** (The Offspring)	1:17
13 **Not The One** (The Offspring)	2:54
▶ 14 **Smash** (The Offspring)	10:39

Drive Like Jehu | Yank Crime (1994)

Label | Interscope
Producer | Drive Like Jehu
Art Direction | Rick Froberg
Nationality | USA
Running Time | 53:15

San Diego punk rock big chief John "Speedo" Reis has been responsible for many under-the-radar milestones over the last decade. His best-known band—trumpet-tooting punkabilly soul revue Rocket From The Crypt—did manage to peer over the mainstream barricades in the mid-1990s and still retain a fanatical, tattoo-sporting cult worldwide. Drive Like Jehu, who ran concurrent with RFTC, are not widely known outside of the punk underground but this, their second and last album, is a fearsomely abrasive and inventive fringe-rock artifact that still sets the blood rushing to this day.

Yank Crime's scratchy, monochrome cartoon cover (drawn by guitarist/lead shrieker Rick Froberg) recalls those Raymond Pettibon famously created for Black Flag, and says a great deal about the stark, foreboding music within. Fugazi's mix of boiling-point hardcore and spry, unpredictable dynamics is an obvious reference point, as are Reis' beloved Wipers, one of the great lost 1980s art punk bands, whose incredible interplay of guitar melodies really comes to bear here. This translates into the high-velocity slashes and scrapes of "Here Come The Rome Plows" and "Golden Brown" (no relation to the Stranglers song) and the drawling, wrenched repetition of "Luau."

Reis has since said that this record was far from a joy to make, largely because of the effort needed to nail its complex twists and turns. Drive Like Jehu faded away as a result. He and Froberg currently front the leaner, meaner and equally mesmerising Hot Snakes, still contributing much to punk's gradual evolution. This record is an unmissable look back at one of its biggest leaps. **TH**

> ## "I just want to be really fucking shit hot on fire."
>
> John Reis, 2000

Track Listing

▶ 01 **Here Come The Rome Plows**
(Froberg • Kennedy • Reis • Trombino)   5:44

02 **Do You Compute**
(Froberg • Kennedy • Reis • Trombino)   7:12

▶ 03 **Golden Brown**
(Froberg • Kennedy • Reis • Trombino)   3:14

▶ 04 **Luau** (Froberg • Kennedy • Reis • Trombino)   9:27

▶ 05 **Super Unison**
(Froberg • Kennedy • Reis • Trombino)   7:24

06 **New Intro** (Froberg • Kennedy • Reis • Trombino)   3:32

07 **New Math** (Froberg • Kennedy • Reis • Trombino)   4:06

08 **Human Interest**
(Froberg • Kennedy • Reis • Trombino)   3:24

09 **Sinews** (Froberg • Kennedy • Reis • Trombino)   9:12

Blur | Parklife (1994)

Label | Food
Producer | Stephen Street
Art Direction | Stylorouge
Nationality | UK
Running Time | 52:39

When Blur set about recording *Parklife* they were in serious financial trouble. Previous album *Modern Life Is Rubbish* had largely been ignored by the masses (if loved by the critics), and they desperately needed a hit. In a typically stubborn gesture, one of their ideas for the new album had been to name it "Soft Porn," with an image of Buckingham Palace on the cover.

Thankfully, what was to become the very essence of the genre known as Britpop housed an arsenal of well-crafted hits, and owed as much to the cynicism of The Kinks' Sixties as it did the emerging yob culture of the Nineties. The sleeve was consciously crafted too: an image of two toothsome greyhounds hammered the point home—this was a sharp new breed of Britishness; on the back Blur were cast as mod-ish working-class heroes, taking in the action at East London's Walthamstow greyhound stadium.

Not yet embroiled in their battle with Oasis, the four piece turned on the style with an English version of pop that could be melancholic ("End Of A Century"), thrashy ("Bank Holiday"), or downright cheeky (the title track, narrated by *Quadrophenia* actor Phil Daniels).

The sprawling, geographic "This Is A Low," which nearly ended the album, remains one of the group's greatest achievements. Lyrically based on a tea towel bassist Alex James had bought singer Damon Albarn, it slowly takes in the British coastline of the BBC's shipping forecast, backed by a mournful, outboard motor-themed musical accompaniment.

Parklife remains Blur's most focussed work, indebted to the past, yet sounding stridently modern. **JK**

Track Listing

▶ 01	**Girls And Boys** (Blur)	4:51
02	**Tracy Jacks** (Blur)	4:20
03	**End Of A Century** (Blur)	2:45
▶ 04	**Parklife** (Blur)	3:05
05	**Bank Holiday** (Blur)	1:42
▶ 06	**Badhead** (Blur)	3:25
07	**Debt Collector** (Blur)	2:10
08	**Far Out** (Blur)	1:41
▶ 09	**To The End** (Blur)	4:05
10	**London Loves** (Blur)	4:15
11	**Trouble In The Message Centre** (Blur)	4:09
▶ 12	**Clover Over Dover** (Blur)	3:22
13	**Magic America** (Blur)	3:38
14	**Jubilee** (Blur)	2:47
▶ 15	**This Is A Low** (Blur)	5:07
16	**Lot 105** (Blur)	1:17

G. Love And Special Sauce
G. Love And Special Sauce (1994)

Label | Epic
Producer | Stiff Johnson • Special Sauce
Art Direction | Karim Ek
Nationality | USA
Running Time | 58:21

Coming at a time when most people equated white rappers with the likes of Vanilla Ice, G. Love and Special Sauce's eponymous debut provided a completely new blueprint for how to make convincing, authentic, and affective hip hop. In the space of one track, "Blues Music," Love namedrops Blind Lemon Jefferson, Jimmy Smith, Woody Guthrie, Aretha Franklin, Chaka Khan, and Bob Dylan—all one needs to hear to realize the author is not interested in aping Dr. Dre—and then proceeds to touch upon all those artists with what can be best described as blues-folk hip-hop soul.

Following in the proud musical tradition of his native Philadelphia, Love sings true street-corner tunes of playing basketball ("Shooting Hoops"), boozing it up ("Cold Beverage"), and admiring the ladies ("Baby's Got Sauce"). The clattering helter-skelter instrumentation, highlighted by the trashcan-style percussion of Jeffrey "The Houseman" Clemens, is a perfect platform for what always sounds like freestyle rapping. Love tosses out lines way faster then the listener can digest them on "Fatman," "Rhyme For Summertime," and other selections moving like the traffic along Philadelphia's Interstate 76.

The highly original musical scheme first laid down on this debut, inspired such solid follow-ups as 1995's *Coast To Coast Motel* and 1997's *Yeah, It's That Easy*. The band might well go down in history for introducing vocalist-surfer Jack Johnson with the single "Rodeo Clowns," but its true legacy should be that it helped to erase the stigma of Vanilla Ice for white rappers. **JiH**

Track Listing

01	The Things That I Used To Do (G. Love)	3:35
▶ 02	Blues Music (G. Love)	4:17
03	Garbage Man (G. Love)	4:51
04	Eyes Have Miles (G. Love)	5:22
▶ 05	Baby's Got Sauce (Clemens • G. Love)	3:54
06	Rhyme For The Summertime (G. Love)	3:06
▶ 07	Cold Beverage (G. Love)	2:33
08	Fatman (G. Love)	4:16
▶ 09	This Ain't Living (G. Love • Jasper)	6:34
10	Walk To Slide (G. Love)	4:28
▶ 11	Shooting Hoops (G. Love)	3:31
12	Some Peoples Like That (G. Love)	4:49
13	Town To Town (G. Love)	3:33
14	I Love You (G. Love)	3:32

Ali Farka Touré With Ry Cooder
Talking Timbuktu (1994)

Label | World Circuit
Producer | Ry Cooder
Art Direction | Intro
Nationality | Mali • USA
Running Time | 60:01

One of the first albums to flout the rock scene's understanding of "world music," this collaboration brought a Grammy to a farm in West Africa and questioned beliefs in the "American-ness" of the blues.

Touré surfaced in Europe via recordings he had made for Radio Mali, which somehow fell into all the right hands. Musicians, DJs, and critics were shocked by this music, clearly linked to the source of the blues—so close that many still argue that the African was influenced by African-Americans; he denies it, saying this is a traditional style that had been carried across the Atlantic by slavery. The London-based World Circuit label found Touré and started recording him; Cooder got in touch and the two men met up in London in summer 1992. The next step was obvious, but took a while to get organized: Touré would rather spend his time on his farm than tour and play concerts.

Touré immediately got bad vibes from the studio. As a child he had been possessed by demons, which gave him his musical gift, and now he was being spooked. He could not play at Cooder's Santa Monica house for fear of upsetting the spirits in the ocean; in Hollywood, hungry spirits roamed the studio. "He seemed happy," explained Cooder, "But there were some deep things troubling him." The two played around with tunes and arrangements until something relaxed appeared, but the most important question was answered in their improvizations: whatever their provenance, Touré really did have the blues. **DH**

> **"For some people, Timbuktu is like the end of the world ... [but] we are right at the heart."**
>
> Ali Farka Touré, 1994

Track Listing

▶	01	**Bonde** (Touré)	5:28
▶	02	**Soukora** (Touré)	6:05
	03	**Gomni** (Touré)	7:00
	04	**Sega** (Touré)	3:10
	05	**Amandrai** (Touré)	9:23
▶	06	**Lasidan** (Touré)	6:06
▶	07	**Keito** (Touré)	5:42
	08	**Banga** (Touré)	2:32
	09	**Ai Du** (Touré)	7:09
▶	10	**Diaraby** (Trad., arr. Touré)	7:26

Hole | Live Through This (1994)

Label | Geffen
Producer | Paul Q. Kolderie • Sean Slade
Art Direction | Janet Wolsborn
Nationality | USA
Running Time | 38:19

Melody got a good beating on Hole's debut *Pretty On The Inside*; brilliant in its way, but hard work.

Live Through This, in contrast, is a shout-along sensation. Many of the songs were composed in the Courtney/Cobain cocoon—hence lines like "I don't do the dishes, I throw them in the crib"—that led to charges that Kurt wrote the songs.

Courtney conceded, in *Q*, that "Kurt's vocals are on every track, practically, but they're buried. He just came to show me some harmonies, then it was, well, keep some of mine …" Other fingerprints were left by Young Marble Giants' Stuart Moxham and Kat Bjelland of Babes In Toyland.

But it is Courtney's show. She is snarling yet assured throughout, and the lyrics yield one winner after another. "I want to be the girl with the most cake" ("Miss World") evokes the kinderwhore riot grrrl that was Courtney's media incarnation. "I fake it so real, I am beyond fake" in "Doll Parts" (named after drummer Patty Schemel's old band) even earned the approval of Joni Mitchell.

Mythology weighs heavy on *Live Through This*. It is dedicated to Joe Cole, a friend killed on the way home from a Hole show in the company of Henry Rollins. Its release fell between the deaths of Cobain and bassist Kristen Pfaff. And its lost final cut, "Rock Star" (replaced on the album but not the credits by one called "Olympia") sneers, "How'd you like to be in Nirvana? I think you'd rather die."

A lesser work would undoubtedly buckle. *Live Through This* stands tall. **BM**

"It was about trying to find ideal songs."

Courtney Love, 1994

Track Listing		
▶ 01 **Violet** (Hole)		3:24
▶ 02 **Miss World** (Hole)		3:01
03 **Plump** (Hole)		2:34
04 **Asking For It** (Hole)		3:29
05 **Jennifer's Body** (Hole)		3:42
▶ 06 **Doll Parts** (Hole)		3:32
07 **Credit In The Straight World** (Moxham)		3:12
08 **Softer, Softest** (Hole)		3:27
09 **She Walks On Me** (Hole)		3:24
10 **I Think That I Would Die** (Bjelland • Erlandson • Love)		3:37
11 **Gutless** (Hole)		2:15
12 **Rock Star** (Hole)		2:42

Massive Attack
Protection (1994)

Label | Wild Bunch
Producer | Nellee Hooper
Art Direction | Michael Nash Associates
Nationality | UK
Running Time | 43:06

Manic Street Preachers
The Holy Bible (1994)

Label | Epic
Producer | Steve Brown • Mark Freegard
Art Direction | Richey James
Nationality | UK
Running Time | 56:21

Massive Attack? More like Under Attack. Founding member Shara Nelson—the voice of their immortal "Unfinished Sympathy"—left. They confused their fan base by briefly changing their name to Massive to avoid controversy during the first Iraq war, and endured a disastrous tour of the United States.

The surviving members returned with *Protection*, which met with mixed reactions. While it proved Massive Attack could produce a fine album—and hits—without Nelson, the album took a different direction that some critics did not appreciate. The production was every bit as elaborate and interesting as their debut *Blue Lines*, but was largely instrumental.

Among the exceptions are collaborations with Tracey Thorn of Everything But The Girl. The title track is all heartbreaking vocals and densely layered beats, while "Better Things" is mournful yet otherworldly. Tricky—an original member who left for a solo career during the making of the album—contributes great vocals to "Karmacoma" and "Eurochild."

Protection helped cement Massive Attack's status as figureheads of Britain's emerging Bristol sound; paving the way for acts like Portishead, Sneaker Pimps, and Beth Orton. It was the first indicator that the style today known as trip hop was not a trend but a growing and viable genre (hence their staggering follow-up, *Mezzanine*). Massive Attack's sophomore effort's influence can be heard worldwide wherever good blunted beats are sold. **LP**

One of music's most emotionally lacerating albums, *The Holy Bible* was released just six months before Richey James disappeared near the Severn Bridge in his native Wales. The lyrics, mostly written by James, overflow with self-hate and despair. He reflects on his battle with anorexia in "4st 7lb" and declares, "I wanna be so skinny that I rot from view." This mantra for self-destruction courses through "Die In The Summertime," which opens with the chilling "Scratch my leg with a rusty nail, sadly it heals."

These bleak visions are matched by the music. Recorded at Cardiff's rundown Soundscape studio, the album is claustrophobic and abrasive. It sounds wildly different from the stadium rock of the group's earlier albums, and to every other album in 1994. While contemporaries imitated The Beatles and The Who, the Manics drew on the angular sounds of Magazine, Wire, and Gang of Four. "P.C.P." and "Revol" are raging post-punk riots, whipped up further by James Dean Bradfield's caustic riffs. Nicky Wire's off-tempo bass adds menace to "The Intense Humming Of Evil"—a brutal examination of man's capability for cruelty.

Darkness shadows the album. It was dedicated to the Manics' manager Philip Hall, who died from cancer in 1993, and wrapped in grotesque art by Jenny Saville, who let the band use her images after meeting James. *The Holy Bible* still sounds fresh—perhaps because Radiohead have since made an industry from self-loathing—but in 1994 it was a commercial disaster. **TB**

Suede
Dog Man Star (1994)

Label | Nude
Producer | Ed Buller
Art Direction | Brett Anderson
Nationality | UK
Running Time | 57:59

Suede should not have existed in 1994. They had lost Bernard Butler (chief songwriter and precociously talented guitarist) in a bitter disagreement. Then, bizarrely, they chose to audition for a new member by placing an anonymous advert in *NME*, cryptically asking for someone who was "into Suede."

But when they found 17-year-old Richard Oakes, who was more than capable of replicating the guitar wizardry Butler had created in the studio, the band played on. Everyone had expected the band to be bloodied and broken. Instead, their music took on a defiant, exciting power, from hypnotic psychedelic opener "Introducing The Band" to orchestral finale "Still Life." Audacious first single "We Are The Pigs" was rife with the kind of urban squalor often hinted at on their debut—and reflected in the androgynous nude sprawled on the still, sepia-toned album sleeve. "The Wild Ones" is full of luscious drum fills and plucked acoustic guitar—as melodic as Suede ever got. The massively grandiose "Asphalt World," stretching to nearly 10 minutes, was like a moody rock opera, set to a screenplay of ecstasy, London taxis, and rough sex. No mean feat.

That new boy Richard Oakes carried all this off without disrupting the scene speaks volumes—perhaps for his naivety, but mostly for the bloody-mindedness of singer Brett Anderson. When it seemed as if his band were on the verge of splitting, he knuckled down and focused on touring the most ambitious album of his career. **JK**

The Notorious B.I.G.
Ready To Die (1994)

Label | Bad Boy
Producer | Dominic Owen
Art Direction | The Drawing Board
Nationality | USA
Running Time | 69:03

"One of the best records ever made," declared singer-songwriter Randy Newman of *Ready To Die*. But, he continues, "It's a strange album in that the first cut says . . . 'Let's stop killing each other'—and then the rest of the record is all about people killing each other! It's the damnedest thing."

Moral ambiguity aside, *Ready To Die* is superb. With rap torn between the West Coast's glossy G-funk and the East's edgy Wu-Tanging, the Brooklyn-born Biggie's album took the best of both. The in-your-faceness is pure New York, but the production is as sumptuous as anything Dr. Dre was cooking up in California. So there are delicious helpings of funk like the Mtume-flavored "Juicy" and Isley Brothers-based "Big Poppa"—but also the woozy "The What," a Method Man duet weird enough to fit on Meth's unhinged *Tical*. Of Biggie's other collaborators, Diana "Shy Guy" King is ferocious on the jagged "Respect," and executive producer Sean "Puffy" Combs—whose Bad Boy label *Ready To Die* helped put on the map—gives the album an unparalleled sheen. Ultimately, of course, it is Biggie's show. The tongue-twisting accounts of his hustling past, the spine-chilling threats, and his visions of the future brook no argument. An element of self-mockery even redeems the "#!*@ Me" skit.

Biggie made two more fine albums before his death in 1997—Puffy's *No Way Out* and his own *Life After Death* —the posthumous *Born Again* ain't bad. But this is the true heavyweight champion. **BM**

Jeff Buckley | Grace (1994)

Label | Columbia
Producer | Jeff Buckley • Andy Wallace
Art Direction | C. Austopchuk • N. Lindeman
Nationality | USA
Running Time | 51:19

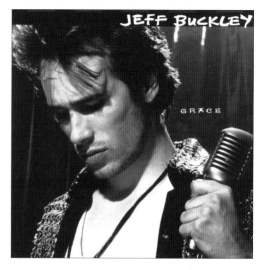

In an era when the soundtrack to angst was defined by grungey guitars and plaid shirts, Jeff Buckley's delicate melodies and aesthetic sensibilities set him a world apart. A graduate of New York's early 1990s avant-garde club scene, Buckley, whose father Tim was a folk hero of the late 1960s, recorded his first commercial four-track EP, *Live At Sin-É*, in said tiny coffeehouse in the city's bohemian East Village. Before its release by Columbia in the autumn of 1994, Buckley and his core of musicians had wasted no time in creating their first studio LP, *Grace*.

A ten-track ode to loneliness, loss, and the sheer incompetence of man in times of trouble, *Grace*'s lyrics are inescapably tinged with melancholia, but the album is saved from oversentimentality by Buckley's joyously uplifting vocals and comforting musical arrangements. The unbearably sad "Last Goodbye" is accompanied by strings that would stir the stoniest of hearts, while Benjamin Britten's "Corpus Christi Carol" gives Buckley full rein to display his astonishing multi-octave vocal range. A welcome irony of Buckley's music is that songs that had been fine-tuned in minuscule venues with primitive acoustics sound so big and glorious on this shockingly mature debut. His take on Leonard Cohen's "Hallelujah" is so confident you find yourself questioning who recorded the song first.

Grace was an instant classic, critics and musicians alike applauding Buckley's musical craftsmanship and effortless songwriting, but the glittering future predicted by all was not to be. Jeff Buckley drowned at age 30 in May 1997, leaving behind a tragically short but vitally important musical legacy. **SJac**

> ## "Sensitivity isn't being wimpy. It's about being so painfully aware that a flea landing on a dog is like a sonic boom."
>
> Jeff Buckley, 1994

Track Listing

▶	01	Mojo Pin (Buckley•Lucas)	5:41
▶	02	**Grace** (Buckley•Lucas)	5:22
	03	**Last Goodbye** (Buckley)	4:16
	04	**Lilac Wine** (Shelton)	4:31
	05	**So Real** (Buckley•Tighe)	4:41
▶	06	**Hallelujah** (Cohen)	6:52
▶	07	**Lover, You Should've Come Over** (Buckley)	6:42
	08	**Corpus Christi Carol** (Britten)	2:56
	09	**Eternal Life** (Buckley)	4:52
▶	10	**Dream Brother** (Buckley•Grondahl•Johnson)	5:26

Orbital | Snivilisation (1994)

Label | Internal
Producer | Paul Hartnoll · Phil Hartnoll
Art Direction | John Greenwood
Nationality | UK
Running Time | 75:06

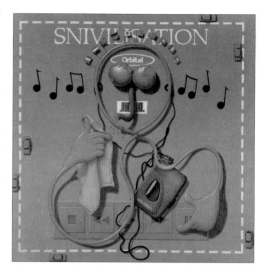

Paul and Phil Hartnoll, aka Orbital, attracted a certain amount of notoriety right from the get-go with their debut release, "Chime," which allegedly cost less than £1 to produce. With their third album, *Snivilisation*, they finally secured widespread recognition.

Marrying electronic dance music with social comment, *Snivilisation* drew on influences as diverse as Brian Eno, Philip Glass, DIY anarchist punk collective Crass, and the draconian policies brought in by the UK Conservative Party and its increasingly inept efforts to crush "rave culture." The darkly epic "Are We Here?" portrays a nightmare vision of a government intent on gagging the population into silence and austerity. Combining chilling samples and mutant drum'n'bass rhythms, it features the unique vocal talents of Alison Goldfrapp, who also contributes to the spectacular glitch-techno of "Sad But True."

"Philosophy By Numbers," satirizes our increasingly commercial environment, while the brashness of television ad breaks is parodied in "Quality Seconds," a brief interlude of atonal hardcore among the album's melodic splendor. "Crash And Carry"'s stunning rhythms evoke a dark world of car theft and society's breakdown. Orbital's satirical take on modern culture extended to the artwork, which featured a surreal hosepipe gimp listening to a Sony Walkman.

The album's compelling innovation, coupled with the duo's increasing live reputation, assured a crossover into the big league. An ambitious and passionate work, *Snivilisation* encapsulates a period when the state almost posed a serious threat to popular culture. **CSh**

> ## "All civilizations have been deluded ... conquered and died out. I can't see this one sustaining itself much longer."
>
> Phil Hartnoll, 1994

Track Listing

▶	01	**Forever** (P. Hartnoll·P. Hartnoll)	7:59
	02	**I Wish I Had Duck Feet** (P. Hartnoll·P. Hartnoll)	4:05
	03	**Sad But True** (P. Hartnoll·P. Hartnoll)	7:49
▶	04	**Crash And Carry** (P. Hartnoll·P. Hartnoll)	4:43
	05	**Science Friction** (P. Hartnoll·P. Hartnoll)	5:04
	06	**Philosophy By Numbers** (P. Hartnoll·P. Hartnoll)	6:39
	07	**Kein Trink Wasser** (P. Hartnoll·P. Hartnoll)	9:24
	08	**Quality Seconds** (P. Hartnoll·P. Hartnoll)	1:25
▶	09	**Are We Here?** (P. Hartnoll·P. Hartnoll)	15:33
▶	10	**Attached** (P. Hartnoll·P. Hartnoll)	12:25

Nirvana | MTV Unplugged In New York (1994)

Label | Geffen
Producer | Scott Litt • Nirvana
Art Direction | Robert Fisher
Nationality | USA
Running Time | 53:50

When the extended Nirvana family of Kurt Cobain, Krist Novoselic, Dave Grohl, Pat Smear, cellist Lori Goldston, and a couple of Meat Puppets walked into MTV's New York studios to make the album no one thought a grunge band ever could—an acoustic album—it was impossible to predict quite how emotional the document they would leave behind would be.

Originally transmitted for MTV's *Unplugged* show (screenshots from the performance make up the artwork), the album hints more strongly than any of their previous three at the band Nirvana could have blossomed into. Only "Come As You Are" was indebted to their heavier past; for the most part, it was the slower original tracks that saw the light of day—the likes of "Dumb," "Polly," and "Something In The Way."

An indulgent three tracks performed with and written by The Meat Puppets betrayed Cobain's desire to use his status to break respected friends' bands. Elsewhere, stunning Vaselines and Bowie covers were thoughtfully executed (at points on the latter Cobain plays Bowie's vocal line as a solo).

Lead Belly's blues standard, which closed the proceedings, has lasted the test of time as an inspired and emotional exorcism—and a chilling reminder of the great loss Kurt Cobain was to the musical world, all at once bringing America's musical heritage bang up to date with a cracked, bitter voice. When he sighs, in a moment of silence just before the climactic closing section, it seems the weight of the world is crushing him. That it eventually did makes *Unplugged*, at times, a record dangerously close to the bone. **JK**

"I ... want to change our style."

Kurt Cobain, 1994

Track Listing

▶	01	**About A Girl** (Cobain)	3:37
	02	**Come As You Are** (Cobain)	4:13
	03	**Jesus Doesn't Want Me For A Sunbeam** (Kelly•McKee)	4:37
▶	04	**The Man Who Sold The World** (Bowie)	4:20
	05	**Pennyroyal Tea** (Cobain)	3:40
▶	06	**Dumb** (Cobain)	2:52
	07	**Polly** (Cobain)	3:16
	08	**On A Plain** (Cobain)	3:44
	09	**Something In The Way** (Cobain)	4:01
	10	**Plateau** (Kirkwood)	3:38
	11	**Oh Me** (Kirkwood)	3:26
▶	12	**Lake Of Fire** (Kirkwood)	2:55
	13	**All Apologies** (Cobain)	4:23
▶	14	**Where Did You Sleep Last Night** (Ledbetter)	5:08

Nine Inch Nails | The Downward Spiral (1994)

Label | Interscope
Producer | Flood • Trent Reznor
Art Direction | Gary Talpas
Nationality | USA
Running Time | 65:02

nine inch nails: the downward spiral

Want something cheerfully glum? Take The Cure. Glossily glum? Pink Floyd, perhaps. Nastily, noisily, suicidally glum? Viva les Nails.

"The big overview," said mainman Trent Reznor, "was of somebody who throws away every aspect of his life—from relationships to religion. [It] also looks at vices as ways of trying to dull the pain. I'm talking about myself … Not that that's any great leap for me."

This paean to pain was born at the L.A. house where Charles Manson's followers murdered actress Sharon Tate. Bad vibes abounded: having failed to cook chicken for the under-nurtured Reznor, visitor Tori Amos concluded the house was cursed. Horror soaks the songs, though Reznor denies the recurrent "pigs" are related to "Piggies," the Beatles track that became a Manson anthem. Amid the industrial likes of "March Of The Pigs" are seductive moments. The danceable "Closer," its drums sampled from Iggy Pop's "Nightclubbing," boasts one of the decade's most-quoted choruses: "I want to fuck you like an animal."

Finally, there is "Hurt." "The best anti-drug song I ever heard," said Johnny Cash, whose cover version became his epitaph. Cash's heartbreaking video was by Mark Romanek, who also directed the disturbing "Closer" clip.

The Downward Spiral is as far from easy listening as multiplatinum rock has ever reached. If it "speaks" to you, and you are not Trent Reznor, be very worried. But its lacerating guitars, deafening drums, and astonishing songs are worryingly intoxicating.

And Tori's chicken? "I didn't ask," shrugged Reznor. "The ghosts ate it." **BM**

"I just didn't think it was accessible enough."

Trent Reznor, 2002

Track Listing

	01	Mr. Self Destruct (Reznor)	4:30
	02	Piggy (Reznor)	4:24
	03	Heresy (Reznor)	3:54
▶	04	March Of The Pigs (Reznor)	2:58
▶	05	Closer (Reznor)	6:13
	06	Ruiner (Reznor)	4:58
	07	The Becoming (Reznor)	5:31
	08	I Do Not Want This (Reznor)	5:41
	09	Big Man With A Gun (Reznor)	1:36
	10	A Warm Place (Reznor)	3:23
	11	Eraser (Reznor)	4:53
	12	Reptile (Reznor)	6:51
	13	The Downward Spiral (Reznor)	3:56
▶	14	Hurt (Reznor)	6:14

The Prodigy | Music For The Jilted Generation (1994)

Label | XL
Producer | Liam Howlett • Neil McLellan
Art Direction | Les Edwards • Jamie Fry • Stuart Haygarth
Nationality | UK
Running Time | 78:08

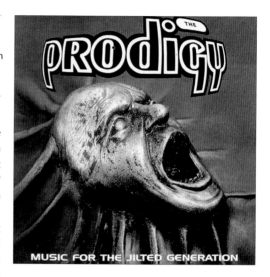

The Prodigy seemed like just more hood rats in the 1990s at a time when white Brits took so many drugs in the 1990s that they believed they could dance. But 1992's *Experience* was stronger than its hit "Charly" suggested, and touring turned The Prodigy into a true band of the people.

Along the way, however, mainman Liam Howlett became disenchanted with dance and rediscovered hip hop. . . . *Jilted Generation,* therefore, retains rave's electronica, but mixes brick-heavy beats into a synthesized symphony. Rock rears its head as well: Pop Will Eat Itself add grunge to "Their Law" and "Voodoo People" features a riff from Nirvana's "Very Ape" (these "electronic punk" experiments came to fruition on 1997's *The Fat of the Land*).

Adding color are movie clips from *The Lawnmower Man* ("Intro"), *Smokey And The Bandit* ("Their Law"), *Star Wars* ("Full Throttle"), *Poltergeist III* ("The Heat (The Energy)"), and *2001* ("Claustrophobic Sting").

Not once does this amazing album flag, though Howlett maintains "Full Throttle" and "One Love" could have been dropped. ...*Jilted Generation* was regarded at the time as a protest against governmental attempts to clamp down on raves (reinforced by Les Edward's centerfold painting). However, Howlett now derides the "stupid" title and denies any political intent (disingenuousness that was to prove useful: his next album was titled after a quote by Hermann Goering).

No matter. It paved the way for Leftfield, Underworld, and Goldie to make album-length statements and still sounds like the best head rush you will ever have. **BM**

"It could have been the death of the band ..."

Liam Howlett, 1999

Track Listing

01	**Intro** (Howlett)	0:46
02	**Break And Enter** (Howlett)	8:24
03	**Their Law** (Howlett • Pop Will Eat Itself)	6:40
04	**Full Throttle** (Howlett)	5:02
▶ 05	**Voodoo People** (Howlett • Kain)	6:27
06	**Speedway (Theme From Fastlane)** (Howlett)	8:56
07	**The Heat (The Energy)** (Howlett)	4:27
▶ 08	**Poison** (Howlett • Palmer)	6:42
▶ 09	**No Good (Start The Dance)** (Howlett)	6:17
10	**One Love (Edit)** (Howlett)	3:53
	The Narcotic Suite:	
11	**3 Kilos** (Howlett)	7:25
12	**Skylined** (Howlett)	5:58
13	**Claustrophobic Sting** (Howlett)	7:11

Green Day | Dookie (1994)

Label | Reprise
Producer | Rob Cavallo • Green Day
Art Direction | Richie Bucher
Nationality | USA
Running Time | 39:38

Punk purists still cringe at this groundbreaking record. But no one can deny that Green Day reinvigorated an old genre for a new generation with *Dookie*.

The formula was simple. Take a few power chords, a catchy tune, some tongue-in-cheek humor, and do it all fast so kids will want to jump up and down. This is hardly revolutionary: Green Day's sound and sense of irony was heavily borrowed from The Ramones and the Sex Pistols—lead singer Billie Joe Armstrong even sings with a faint attempt at an English accent. But Green Day differed from the British punk scene, by making punk a bratty ordeal free of revolutionary political pretensions, while retaining the rebellion.

In *Dookie*, Green Day had 14 furious but sweet melodies about suburban angst and ennui. The band celebrated the slacker lifestyle with lines like "I declare I don't care no more/I'm burning up and out and growing bored" ("Burnout") and songs that addressed the fading appeal of masturbation when one is bored ("Long View").

Of course, it helped the band that *Dookie* was recorded with the backing of a major label—a first for the band—and with the aid of clever videos and constant radioplay, the album produced four successful singles, including "Basket Case," which stayed on top of the U.S. charts for five weeks. But the track with the longest-lasting legacy would be "When I Come Around," a song that seemed to crystallize Woodstock '94 in less than three minutes and vault the band to superstardom. As the *New York Times* observed, "Apathy has rarely sounded so passionate." **JC**

"That's punk, playing a show, having a party."

Billie Joe Armstrong, 1994

Track Listing

▶ 01	**Burnout** (Green Day)	2:07
02	**Having A Blast** (Green Day)	2:44
03	**Chump** (Green Day)	2:54
▶ 04	**Long View** (Green Day)	3:58
05	**Welcome To Paradise** (Green Day)	3:44
06	**Pulling Teeth** (Green Day)	2:30
▶ 07	**Basket Case** (Green Day)	3:03
▶ 08	**She** (Green Day)	2:14
09	**Sassafras Roots** (Green Day)	2:37
▶ 10	**When I Come Around** (Green Day)	2:58
11	**Coming Clean** (Green Day)	1:34
12	**Emenius Sleepus** (Green Day)	1:43
13	**In The End** (Green Day)	1:46
14	**F.O.D. / All By Myself** (Green Day)	5:46

Foo Fighters | Foo Fighters (1995)

Label | Roswell
Producer | Foo Fighters • Barrett Jones
Art Direction | Tim Gabor
Nationality | USA
Running Time | 44:01

Kurt Cobain's suicide in 1994 left the rock world in shock. To his eternal credit, Nirvana drummer Dave Grohl pulled himself together smartly to create a platform for his own considerable talents: Foo Fighters—named after the U.S. military's nickname for fighter planes dispatched to investigate UFO sightings.

Although the urgent album opener, appropriately named "This Is A Call," was written after Cobain's death (along with "Oh, George" and "I'll Stick Around"; all other tracks were written by Grohl while he was still in Nirvana), the song does not hypothesize melodramatically, but its life-affirming energy does offer some consolation. The tight, powerful performance and strong vocals of the song (and of its parent album), was a tonic for forlorn fans—even though its lyrical content was predominantly nonsensical.

Foo Fighters was grunge-pop, and a splendid vehicle to display Grohl's skills. Indeed, what appears a group endeavor is actually a solo project: Grohl composed the whole album, provided vocals, guitars, bass, and drums, and recorded it in one week. The formula of soft verse/loud, dynamic chorus (a Nirvana legacy) is incorporated neatly on much of *Foo Fighters*, especially in "I'll Stick Around" and "For All The Cows." The album offers a grab-bag of delights—Beatle-esque melodies in "Big Me," atmospheric rock in "Oh, George" (a tribute to The Beatles' George Harrison), hazy guitars and lulling drums in "X-Static," and pure punk energy in "Wattershed" and "Weenie Beenie." The aptly named closer "Exhausted" leaves the listener fatigued but not bored and certainly up for more of the same. **MBo**

> " ...the band's natural instinct is to be more aggressive, louder, looser, and rawer ... "
> Dave Grohl, 2002

Track Listing

▶ 01	**This Is a Call** (Grohl)	3:53
▶ 02	**I'll Stick Around** (Grohl)	3:53
▶ 03	**Big Me** (Grohl)	2:12
▶ 04	**Alone + Easy Target** (Grohl)	4:05
05	**Good Grief** (Grohl)	4:01
06	**Floaty** (Grohl)	4:30
07	**Weenie Beenie** (Grohl)	2:45
08	**Oh, George** (Grohl)	3:00
▶ 09	**For All the Cows** (Grohl)	3:30
▶ 10	**X-Static** (Grohl)	4:13
▶ 11	**Wattershed** (Grohl)	2:15
▶ 12	**Exhausted** (Grohl)	5:44

Garbage | Garbage (1995)

Label | Mushroom
Producer | Garbage
Art Direction | Garbage • Janet Wolsborn
Nationality | UK • USA
Running Time | 50:45

One day producers Butch Vig, Steve Marker, and Duke Erikson were in a studio remixing a track for Nine Inch Nails when a visiting friend commented that what they were recording sounded like "garbage." The trashy sound they were producing became the basis for their new project and was christened after their friend's remark. Scottish vocalist Shirley Manson was recruited, and she cut a powerful figure as the frontwoman with her shock of red hair and enormous attitude. Rewriting most of the lyrics for the songs on the album, Manson articulated her battle against depression and set the tone *Garbage*'s debut.

Alternating from scathing, vicious, vengeful, wicked, longing, and vulnerable, she could sing and convey practically any mood with great aplomb: "You thought I was a little girl/you thought I was a little mouse/you thought you'd take me by surprise/Now I'm here burning down your house!" she roars in "Not My Idea." She was supported by some tremendous songwriting and musicians—lush, warm loops, tinkering, thick layers of samples, and keyboards, all cut with razor-like guitar. Tracks such as "Milk" and "A Stroke Of Luck" are darker than the deepest pits of hell; and "Vow" has to be one of the greatest ever debut singles released. Commencing with keyboards that swirl around and envelope you, it breaks into a menacing drumbeat and scorching guitar as Manson threatens to "break your little soul apart . . ."—it remains the greatest song in their repetoire. Completing the package, the sleeve came wrapped in a pink feather boa and signed with the initial "G." **KM**

> ## "I am sweet, but fuck with me and I'll mop the floor with you."
>
> Shirley Manson, 1996

Track Listing

01	**Supervixen** (Erikson•Manson•Marker•Vig)		3:56
02	**Queer** (Erikson•Manson•Marker•Vig)		4:36
▶ 03	**Only Happy When It Rains** (Erikson•Manson•Marker•Vig)		3:56
04	**As Heaven Is Wide** (Erikson•Manson•Marker•Vig)		4:44
05	**Not My Idea** (Erikson•Manson•Marker•Vig)		3:50
06	**A Stroke Of Luck** (Erikson•Manson•Marker•Vig)		4:45
▶ 07	**Vow** (Erikson•Manson•Marker•Vig)		4:30
▶ 08	**Stupid Girl** (Erikson•Manson•Marker•Vig)		4:18
09	**Dog New Tricks** (Erikson•Manson•Marker•Vig)		3:58
10	**My Lover's Box** (Erikson•Manson•Marker•Vig)		3:35
11	**Fix Me Now** (Erikson•Manson•Marker•Vig)		4:43
▶ 12	**Milk** (Erikson•Manson•Marker•Vig)		3:54

Nightmares On Wax | Smokers Delight (1995)

Label | Warp
Producer | E.A.S.E.
Art Direction | Leigh Kenny
Nationality | UK
Running Time | 73:22

Late-night chill albums do not come any better than *Smokers Delight* by Nightmares On Wax. That it also works first thing in the morning, over dinner with friends, at work, or in the bedroom, is all just icing on the cake.

Nightmares On Wax has been the name for George Evelyn's solo recordings ever since he parted ways with co-founder Kevin Harper in the early 1990s. On his own in the studio, Evelyn moved away from the darker techno of NOW's early work and developed his own groove. *Smokers Delight* features more than 70 minutes of instrumental electronica laced with down-tempo hip-hop beats and samples from classic soul and R&B artists like Quincy Jones and Smokey Robinson.

The album kicks off with a slow-building synth and bass groove called "Nights Introlude," a track Evelyn would later rework into "Les Nuits" for his excellent 1999 LP *Carboot Soul*. "Dreddoverboard" features the sound of ocean surf rolling over bongos and bass. "Pipes-Honour" sustains an echoey guitar lick, slippery bass, flute, and a yah-yah vocal sample for nine minutes of chilled-out bliss. One of the most addictive tracks on the record is "Bless My Soul," which mixes a head-nodding beat with an ear-tickling water-pan warble. "Mission Venice" starts as a catchy spy-movie theme then disappears into a wind tunnel of spacy ambience before coming out the other side.

Smokers Delight is one of those albums that everyone will ask about when they hear it playing. Then they will probably head out and buy their own copy the very next day. It is that good. **RM**

Track Listing

▶	01	**Nights Introlude** (Evelyn)	4:39
▶	02	**Dreddoverboard** (Boy Wonder•E.A.S.E.)	5:48
▶	03	**Pipes–Honour** (Evelyn)	9:05
	04	**Me + You** (Evelyn)	0:56
	05	**Stars** (Evelyn)	6:59
	06	**Wait a Minute/Prayin (For A Jeepbeat)** (Evelyn)	2:44
	07	**Groove St.** (Evelyn)	7:30
	08	**Time (To Listen)** (Evelyn)	0:25
	09	**(Man) Tha Journey** (Evelyn)	6:19
▶	10	**Bless My Soul** (Evelyn)	5:56
	11	**Cruise (Don't Stop)** (Evelyn)	7:05
▶	12	**Mission Venice** (Evelyn)	2:50
	13	**What I'm Feelin (Good)** (Evelyn)	2:26
	14	**Rise** (Evelyn)	5:14
	15	**Rise (Reprise)** (Evelyn)	1:46
	16	**Gambia Via Vagator Beach** (Evelyn)	4:41

Tricky | Maxinquaye (1995)

Label | Island
Producer | Howie B. • Kevin Petrie • Mark Saunders • Tricky
Art Direction | David Alvarez • Cally
Nationality | UK
Running Time | 57:01

He fell out of popularity so fast that it is hard now to express just how exciting a prospect a solo from Adrian "Tricky" Thaws once was. Thanks to his terrible later albums, the work of this former Massive Attack rapper has now been consigned to a nook in the dustbin of history marked "Nineties pop culture."

By the mid-1990s the iconoclastic debut album from Massive Attack, *Blue Lines*, had set the tone for tasteful contemporary music in Western Europe; any forthcoming innovation within the form (widely dubbed "trip hop") was met with heightened expectation—let alone a release from a former band member.

Tricky took the overtones of Massive Attack's "Five Man Army" and turned up the claustrophobia and menace; there are sound effects, dub inflections, and bafflingly twisted samples—West Country drum 'n' bass, no less. The music is by turns languid and violent, experimental but never self-indulgent. Yet *Maxinquaye* was also in dialog with rock's developments, turning Public Enemy's "Black Steel In The Hour Of Chaos" into an alternative rock banger. Tricky's unashamedly Bristolian rasp remains unnerving throughout (Massive Attack colleague Martine adds her velvety vocals to "Ponderosa"). Autobiographical in places, *Maxinquaye* eschews any hip-hop braggadocio, preferring instead to mine a rich seam of paranoia and hate.

Innovative, thought provoking, and intricately arranged, the album pushed spoken-word music forward in the UK. For one dizzying moment it seemed that British rap, far from being an unfortunate paradox, was very much a viable prospect. **ARa**

> ## "Technically I'm totally naive, and emotionally, I'm fucked up."
>
> Tricky, 1995

Track Listing

01	**Overcome**	(Detroit•Fahey•Tricky)	4:28
02	**Ponderosa**	(Howie B•Martine•Tricky)	3:30
▶ 03	**Black Steel**	(Ridenhour•Sadler•Shocklee)	5:39
▶ 04	**Hell Is Around The Corner**	(Hayes•Tricky)	3:46
05	**Pumpkin**	(Tricky)	4:30
▶ 06	**Aftermath**	(Tricky	7:37
07	**Abbaon Fat Track**	(Tricky)	4:26
▶ 08	**Brand New You're Retro**	(Tricky)	2:54
09	**Suffocated Love**	(Tricky)	4:52
10	**You Don't**	(Tricky)	4:39
11	**Strugglin'**	(Tricky)	6:38
12	**Feed Me**	(Tricky)	4:02

Raekwon
Only Built 4 Cuban Linx (1995)

Label | Loud
Producer | RZA
Art Direction | Miguel Rivera
Nationality | USA
Running Time | 71:51

The Smashing Pumpkins
Mellon Collie And The Infinite Sadness (1995)

Label | Virgin
Producer | B. Corgan • Flood • A. Moulder
Art Direction | B. Corgan • F. Olinsky
Nationality | USA
Running Time | 121:49

After the immense worldwide impact of the Wu-Tang Clan's 1993 debut *Enter The Wu-Tang (36 Chambers)*, solo albums from the Clan's individual members were eagerly anticipated. Alongside GZA's *Liquid Swords*, and possibly Method Man's *Tical*, Raekwon's *Only Built 4 Cuban Linx* stands out as the greatest of this first wave.

As one of the most versatile members of the Clan, Raekwon "the Chef" created a classic gangsta-rap album. Drenched in Mafia imagery and subject matter, it established the image of the MC as a Cristal-sippin', Gucci-sportin' drug baron, hustlin' pimp, and all-round player. *Cuban Linx* traces the highs and the lows of the outlaw lifestyle, from the exuberance of initial financial success, through the paranoia of ill-gotten power, to the despair and loneliness of the fallen crown as our anti-hero yearns for atonement on "Heaven And Hell."

Raekwon—along with his vocal sparring partner, fellow Wu member Ghostface Killah—delivers a moody album that groans under the weight of quality tracks—check "Ice Cream," "Criminology," "Rainy Dayz," and the fantastic "Wu-Gambinos." All of these stand out as crowning achievements in gangsta rap. The inspired production of Wu chief, RZA, weaves Latin, classical, and soul samples to form a sophisticated base for the lyrical content. The charms and tongue-in-cheek humor of *Cuban Linx* were to prove a huge influence on rising stars such as Jay-Z, Notorious B.I.G., and Nas. **CR**

Siamese Dream, The Smashing Pumpkins' first mainstream album, had enjoyed both critical acclaim and reasonable commercial success, but its sequel, *Mellon Collie And The Infinite Sadness*, more frequently ranks as the band's best. Impressively, *Mellon Collie . . .* made its mark without abandoning the emotional revelations and complexities of its predecessor. Comprising two disks, respectively named "Dawn To Dusk" and "Twilight To Starlight," the album covers the full spectrum of human emotion. *Mellon Collie . . .* is a model of contemporary alternative songwriting, from the opening self-titled track, consisting of nothing but arresting piano, to the mournful and longing symphony of strings in "Tonight, Tonight," and the raging, bitter grunge rock of "Bullet With Butterfly Wings" and "Zero."

Following its release in 1995, a tumultuous series of events propelled the album and band alike into the public eye. Within 12 months, they achieved seven Grammy nominations; touring keyboardist Jonathan Melvin died of a heroin overdose; and drummer Jimmy Chamberlin was arrested for drug possession and fired from the band. Further, in many controversial interviews singer Billy Corgan criticized his peers for failing to push musical boundaries. It is, however, undeniable that in creating *Mellon Collie . . .* Corgan effortlessly ventured into new territories and emerged with one of the most beautiful albums in rock's history. **EK**

Rocket From The Crypt
Scream, Dracula, Scream! (1995)

Label | Interscope
Producer | Rocket From The Crypt
Art Direction | Mike Nelson
Nationality | USA
Running Time | 43:41

The Chemical Brothers
Exit Planet Dust (1995)

Label | Virgin
Producer | The Chemical Brothers
Art Direction | Negativespace
Nationality | UK
Running Time | 49:27

In the mid-1990s, punk was big business. Green Day and The Offspring had turned the genre into an endless parade of Ramones riffs and Johnny Rotten sneers. *Scream, Dracula, Scream!* made punk (dis)respectable again. With its blend of Stax horns and hardcore guitars, Rocket From The Crypt's major-label debut showed punk could transcend stale Seventies nostalgia.

Recorded at Hollywood's Gold Star Studios (home of Phil Spector's Wall of Sound) *Scream, Dracula, Scream!* was conceived as a body of music, with soothing woodwind and strings replacing the silence between tracks. Nervous execs axed these flourishes, leaving a solid slab of rock 'n' roll.

"Young Livers" and "Drop Out" crash from the speakers with Gene Vincent-esque venom. The two-man horn section adds even more fire and momentum to the mix. "On A Rope" and "Born In '69" race like dragsters, driven ever faster by the punching brass. And though the album has a full tank of heaviness, it also features gentle pop delights. "Misbeaten" and "Ball Lightening" chime with sweet harmonies worthy of The Drifters.

The album inspired listeners bored with green-haired fakes to shout punk's praises once more. More importantly, the album freed up the sonic palette available to garage acts. It proved that, in the right hands, even a trumpet could sound punk. **TB**

A benchmark release for the big-beat genre, *Exit Planet Dust* features all the trademark elements of The Chemical Brothers' sound—a mouthwatering mix of pyschedelia, hip hop, breakbeats, acid house, funk, and guitar-friendly rock. Fat basslines and massive drums dominate, from opener "Leave Home," through fellow floorfiller, "In Dust We Trust," which glides beautifully into an old live version of "Song To The Siren" (sampling Meat Beat Manifesto and This Mortal Coil). The latter, the Chemicals' first ever track, was originally released in 1992 when the duo still played as The Dust Brothers. Legal action from the Beastie Boys' collaborators of the same name enforced a monicker change in 1995. The anthem "Chemical Beats," provided them with a sharper alternative, and the album's title gave a wry reference to the name change.

The strength of *Exit Planet Dust* lies in its instrumental blockbusters, but elsewhere there is evidence that the duo were already moving toward a more pop-minded approach. Standout track "Life Is Sweet" features Charlatans frontman Tim Burgess, while the closer, "Alive Alone," virtually launched Beth Orton's career.

Exit Planet Dust—appealing to both rock fans and dance music devotees alike—gave the Chemicals a Top Ten UK hit and sales of one million worldwide. Others were soon preaching the big-beat gospel, but this is where it all started.   **PN**

Tupac | Me Against The World (1995)

Label | Interscope
Producer | Sam Bostic • Tony Pizarro
Art Direction | Eric Altenburger
Nationality | USA
Running Time | 65:56

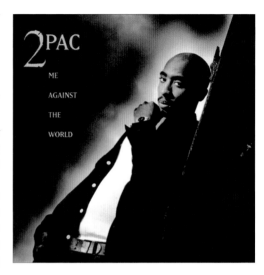

Despite its patchwork of producers, *Me Against The World* is seamlessly sophisticated—and not only Tupac's best album, but one of the most beautiful and soulful records in hip-hop history.

Embroiled in violence since graduating from funksters Digital Underground, Tupac had shot at police, scrapped with movie directors, suffered gunshots, and been accused of sexual abuse. The last charge put him behind bars for eight months, making him the first to have a U.S. No. 1 album while in jail.

This trail of destruction obscured maturing music. *2Pacalypse Now* (1991) and *Strictly For My N.I.G.G.A.Z.* (1993) are patchy mixes of Digital Underground-ish funk and hardcore rap. But the advent of G-funk (the radio-friendly genre pioneered by Dr. Dre) worked miracles: a fan of Stevie Wonder, Tupac was suited to smoother sounds.

Thug Life Vol 1 (1994) is a terrific blend of soul samples and laidback rhymes, and *Me Against The World* completes the evolution—most startlingly on "Dear Mama," a breathtaking ballad that Tupac had to be talked into including. There is also the delightful "Old School" —a tribute to New York rappers that Tupac cited in his defense when the East Coast/West Coast war blew up. The paranoia that plagues his later work is here restricted to a handful of cuts, notably the eerie "Death Around The Corner" (embellished with movie dialog from *King Of New York* and *The Untouchables*).

Freed from jail, Tupac sold his soul to Death Row and kick-started a production line of intermittently fine albums. But this is the man at his best. **BM**

"Good niggas ... die in violence."

Tupac, 1996

Track Listing

01	**Intro** (Uncredited)		1:40
02	**If I Die 2Nite** (Harvey Jr.•Shakur)		4:01
03	**Me Against The World** (Shakur)		4:40
▶ 04	**So Many Tears** (Baker•Jacobs•ShakurWalker)		3:59
▶ 05	**Temptations** (Harvey Jr.•Shakur)		5:00
06	**Young Niggaz** (Moe-Z•Shakur•Tyler)		4:53
07	**Heavy In The Game** (Bostic•Mosley•Shakur)		4:23
08	**Lord Knows** (Shakur)		4:31
▶ 09	**Dear Mama** (Pizarro•Shakur)		4:39
10	**It Ain't Easy** (Pizarro•Shakur)		4:53
11	**Can U Get Away** (Mosley•Shakur)		5:45
12	**Old School** (Shakur)		4:40
13	**Fuck The World** (Jacobs•Shakur)		4:13
14	**Death Around The Corner** (Johnny J.•Shakur)		4:07
15	**Outlaw** (Moe-Z•Shakur)		4:32

Elastica | Elastica (1995)

Label | Deceptive
Producer | Elastica • Marc Waterman
Art Direction | Anonymous
Nationality | UK
Running Time | 37:59

"Blur aren't going to make it in America," Courtney Love told British festival-goers in 1995. "It's going to be Elasticaarr." As it turned out, they went gold in the States, played Lollapalooza, and hit the Hot 100 with "Connection" and "Stutter"—gems that sparkled long after Britpop burned out.

At a time when fashionistas believed "Cool Britannia" would depose Uncle Sam, Justine Frischmann had impeccable credentials. She had been in Suede (whose Brett Anderson co-wrote her "See That Animal"), lived with Blur's Damon Albarn (who guests on *Elastica* as Dan Abnormal), and was the coolest front woman since Chrissie Hynde. Her songs, unburdened by solos or concepts, speed by. "If you want to hear the chorus again," she declared, "rewind it."

The new wavy tunes do, however, harbor quirks— seismic grinds open "Connection" (later used in a Garnier commercial), drummer Justin Welch pukes on "Line Up" (illustrating "all the shit in the music industry, the kind of stuff that makes Justine sick"), and "Car Song" is amusingly dirty (Frischmann's uncle wrote the theme for T and A-fixated comedian Benny Hill).

Journalists who celebrated Oasis' musical larceny were quick to carp at Elastica's looting of The Stranglers' "No More Heroes" for "Waking Up" and Wire's "Three Girl Rhumba" for "Connection." Elastica wound up conceding portions of the publishing to their new wave godfathers. Curiously, Blur's "Girls And Boys" has a bassline similar to "Line Up." "We don't talk about that," said Frischmann, "Those sort of things cause divorces." Nevertheless, *Elastica* still bounces brilliantly today. **BM**

"I know what we're not."

Justine Frischmann, 1995

Track Listing		
01 **Line Up** (Elastica)		3:15
02 **Annie** (Elastica)		1:13
▶ 03 **Connection** (Elastica)		2:20
04 **Car Song** (Elastica)		2:24
05 **Smile** (Elastica)		1:40
06 **Hold Me Now** (Elastica)		2:32
07 **S.O.F.T.** (Elastica)		3:58
08 **Indian Song** (Elastica)		2:46
09 **Blue** (Elastica)		2:21
10 **All Nighter** (Elastica)		1:33
▶ 11 **Waking Up** (Elastica)		3:15
12 **2:1** (Elastica)		2:31
13 **Vaseline** (Elastica)		1:22
14 **Never Here** (Elastica)		4:26
▶ 15 **Stutter** (Elastica)		2:23

Supergrass | I Should Coco (1995)

Label | Parlophone
Producer | Sam Williams
Art Direction | Supergrass
Nationality | UK
Running Time | 40:27

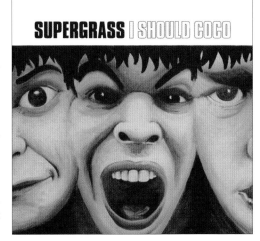

Oxford's Supergrass were still only in their late teens when they recorded their sprightly debut. Thirteen tracks bursting with the sparkle only youth can provide saw the trio instantly lauded as both accomplished songwriters and hipsters to boot.

Recorded over a week-long session in a residential countryside studio—where the boys could play pool, row boats or write masterful takes on delinquent youth—*I Should Coco* beams fun and fizz on each and every track. Even slower numbers like "Sofa (Of My Lethargy)" and "Time" could crack a smile on the face of the most hardened listener. Singles (the more upbeat tracks) such as "Lenny," "Caught By The Fuzz," and "Mansize Rooster" betrayed a youth misspent listening to glam rock, Billy Idol's Generation X, and the poppier edges of punk.

In "Alright," though, they scored their biggest goal—a surefire, summer-friendly radio smash. With lyrics revolving around cleaning teeth and staying out late, the ivory-tinkling impudence of the song was irresistible. Coupled with the endearingly childish album artwork and the mayhem of the *Prisoner*-esque promo video, Supergrass became imprinted on the nation's conscience as good-time songwriting rogues—similar, in fact, to The Monkees. Indeed, a top U.S. TV producer offered them a series, on the strength of their cool-but-likeable image. They turned him down.

As many bands do, Supergrass went on to develop a darker and more introspective side. But *I Should Coco*, wide-eyed with mischief and good vibes, remains a fun trip through British rock and pop history. **JK**

"It sounds brilliant on the radio or in a car."

Mickey Quinn, 1995

Track Listing		
01 **I'd Like To Know** (Supergrass)		4:01
▶ 02 **Caught By The Fuzz** (Supergrass)		2:16
▶ 03 **Mansize Rooster** (Supergrass)		2:34
▶ 04 **Alright** (Supergrass)		3:01
▶ 05 **Lose It** (Supergrass)		2:37
06 **Lenny** (Supergrass)		2:42
07 **Strange Ones** (Supergrass)		4:19
08 **Sitting Up Straight** (Supergrass)		2:20
09 **She's So Loose** (Supergrass)		2:59
▶ 10 **We're Not Supposed To** (Supergrass)		2:03
11 **Time** (Supergrass)		3:10
12 **Sofa (Of My Lethargy)** (Supergrass)		6:18
13 **Time To Go** (Supergrass)		1:56

Radiohead | The Bends (1995)

Label | Parlophone
Producer | John Leckie
Art Direction | Stanley Donwood
Nationality | UK
Running Time | 48:34

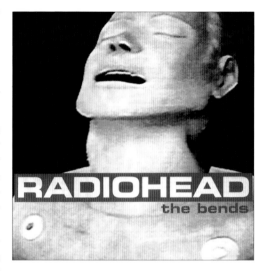

It is a well-known fact that the weight of just one hit single can destroy a band—should you duplicate your sound and be accused of selling out, or follow your artistic ideals and risk alienating your fans? Fresh from the crippling and claustrophobic success of their anthemic single "Creep," Radiohead retaliated by doing both.

The Bends is their rock masterwork. Still to explore fully their electronic fascinations, they served up a set of songs that had a defiant yet fragile identity, and more importantly, could really shake a stadium to the core. Every track commands attention, each one robust enough to be covered by buskers, sung softly on acoustic, or rocked to within an inch of its life by a full band. "Bones," "Just," and "'My Iron Lung" (a single recorded entirely live, save for the vocal track) still rouse crowds today when they are played. Then there was the quieter side—the deliciously soft sarcasm of "Nice Dream," the drowsy "Bullet Proof," or the faux-hippie sentiment of the closing track. "Immerse your soul in love," offers singer Thom Yorke, in one of his strongest performances on record to date. It is hard not to nod, dumbstruck and in awe.

Visually, *The Bends* was a mishmash, the cover featured a sprawling splattering of digital scree, topped off with Yorke's photo of a hospital resuscitation doll. It was perhaps a sign of things to come, as their later albums would be even more abstract. But in 1995 at least, Radiohead's sound was comparatively simplistic and devastatingly effective. A sound from a musical golden era. **JK**

"There's always this feeling that you're this extension of the Coca-Cola thing."

Thom Yorke, 1995

Track Listing		
▶ 01 **Planet Telex** (Radiohead)		4:19
02 **The Bends** (Radiohead)		4:06
03 **High And Dry** (Radiohead)		4:17
04 **Fake Plastic Trees** (Radiohead)		4:50
▶ 05 **Bones** (Radiohead)		3:09
06 **(Nice Dream)** (Radiohead)		3:53
▶ 07 **Just** (Radiohead)		3:54
▶ 08 **My Iron Lung** (Radiohead)		4:36
09 **Bullet Proof ... I Wish I Was** (Radiohead)		3:28
10 **Black Star** (Radiohead)		4:07
11 **Sulk** (Radiohead)		3:42
▶ 12 **Street Spirit (Fade Out)** (Radiohead)		4:13

Guided By Voices
Alien Lanes (1995)

Label | Matador
Producer | Mr. Japan
Art Direction | Bob O. • Mark O.
Nationality | USA
Running Time | 41:00

A quick read of the track listing would lead one to believe that *Alien Lanes* was recorded by a hardcore punk band—28 tracks in total, with only four longer than two minutes and one as short as 18 seconds. But in reality, this record is nothing but sweet melodic genius, a smorgasbord of lo-fi pop that distills pop hooks reminiscent of a Sixties British invasion down to the bare essentials.

Alien Lanes was the band's second release on indie label Matador, their ninth album overall, and a follow-up to their mini-breakthrough album *Bee Thousand*. Expectations were high—many expected a well-produced sound that would take the band to a greater audience. The album never broke them on the radio, but it did cement their growing cult following, who loved the band for their penchant for beer and sweet melodies: The Strokes cited GBV as a big influence and covered the first track "A Salty Salute" seven years later, while *Pitchfork Media* still ranks the album among its top from the decade.

The songs are deceptively simple—the rough hissy sound gives the impression of demo tapes from a rehearsal session in a basement rather than a polished studio album. *Rolling Stone* called it a "treasured bootleg," while frontman Robert Pollard admitted so himself in an interview in 1995: "We're just wanna-be classical rockers, really. We've just always had access to our basements and four tracks and stuff. We used to go into big studios and it never worked." **JC**

Femi Kuti
Femi Kuti (1995)

Label | Motown
Producer | Femi Kuti • Andy Lyden
Art Direction | Uncredited
Nationality | Nigeria
Running Time | 72:48

The offspring of trailblazers have it hard, and it would be easy to dismiss Femi as Fela-lite, if only his recordings did not continually prove otherwise. Furthermore, while Fela was often treated by oh-so sophisticated Westerners as a colorful eccentric, one whose politics were the result of too much herb and voodoo, Femi is a lot harder to ignore.

As a musician, he learned his chops playing sax with his dad in Egypt in the early 1980s. Although Fela's musical power was waning, this was a time of incredible political upheaval, of violence by the authoritarian Nigerian government, and barbed songs by the musician, and Femi could hardly have failed to be influenced. When he left Fela's band to start his own, Positive Force, the differences and similarities were there for all to see: this was still Afrobeat, with undisguised attacks on government corruption, but the music was geared toward listeners rather than players. For one thing, the tunes were around a third of the length of Fela's.

As Fela's health deteriorated in the 1990s, the clamor for new Kuti material increased. Eventually, Motown's Tabu label offered Femi a chance to step into his father's shoes. Fortunately, he was ready, with both a blazing band and strong material. The resulting album is a classic of jazz, funk, and rage, served in hard-hitting African rhythms, but the rough edges of Fela's mid-1970s rants have been streamlined to good effect.

In Africa, it went down a storm, though Motown's decision to close its offshoot meant Femi soon had to rethink his international career. **DH**

The Verve
A Northern Soul (1995)

Label | Hut
Producer | Owen Morris • The Verve
Art Direction | Brian Cannon
Nationality | UK
Running Time | 59:18

Genius / GZA
Liquid Swords (1995)

Label | Geffen
Producer | 4th Disciple • RZA
Art Direction | Mathematics
Nationality | USA
Running Time | 55:20

It is somewhat bizarre to praise a band for splitting up, but there are few better ways to go than this. Gritty, violent, often extreme, filled with the spirit of human suffering yet also charged with a redemptive soul.

Lyrically, The Verve's second album *A Northern Soul* is an affecting, passionate ode to chaos and ruin. Musically, having almost abandoned the shoe-gazing "sonic showers" of their debut *A Storm In Heaven*, the band serve up well-worked, heartrending songs, with frontman Richard Ashcroft's voice at its fractured best. "Cathartic" is a word bandied around music too much, but with inter-band rivalries and stolen girlfriends fueling the hurt, this record is truly self-help.

The static-laden title track feels like swimming in a choppy sea, yet leaves the listener feeling stronger. "This Is Music" is an adrenalin-pumping attack of machine-gun guitars, while "Life's An Ocean" manages to pair nightmare visions of the future with one of the most comfortingly soulful basslines ever.

Then there is "History." Issued as the band's final single (in two versions—"All farewells should be sudden," asserted the cover of one), this was a rambling epic, inspired by William Blake's poem "London," charting rejection, decline, loneliness, and fear, yet still managing to end with bright hope. It was dramatic, sudden, a shocking way to go—in short, perfect.

Of course, The Verve ruined all that by reforming several years later for *Urban Hymns*. But here they are at their uncomfortable, rewarding best. **PS**

So uncompromising that its track list bears only passing resemblance to what is in the grooves. So hardcore that its graphics owe more to graffiti than contemporary design. *Liquid Swords* is definitely one of the odder albums to crash Billboard's Top Ten.

Still, by 1995, Wu-Tang Clan had so revolutionized rap that founding cousins RZA and GZA could do whatever they wanted. RZA helmed four classics in 18 months, including *Enter The Wu-Tang Clan (36 Chambers)*. GZA was wiser following the release of *Words From The Genius* back in 1990—"The beats ain't all that," he admitted, "but, lyrically, shit was bangin'."

Liquid Swords boasts Wu hallmarks—orchestral production, hammering beats, kung fu movie steals (title from *Legend Of The Liquid Sword*, dialog from *Shogun Assassin*)—but is more musical than its predecessors, and anchored by GZA's cool delivery.

Clan members crop up throughout: Method Man nearly steals "Shadowboxin'," ODB rants on "Duel Of The Iron Mic," and "B.I.B.L.E." is a spellbinding introduction to Killah Priest. GZA reigns supreme though, notably on "Labels"—a wry tongue-twister that marries label names to a grinding groove—and "Cold World," which weds cinematic lyrics to the melody from Stevie Wonder's "Rocket Love."

He has made more solo albums—1999's excellent *Beneath The Surface* and 2002's average *Legend Of The Liquid Sword*—but this is as amazing an introduction to the weird and wonderful Wu as their own debut. **BM**

Pulp | Different Class (1995)

Label | Island
Producer | Chris Thomas
Art Direction | Pulp
Nationality | UK
Running Time | 51:54

The mid-1990s seemed a promising time for British arts and fashion. The pop music of the time heralded this new "Cool Britannia," as it was unfortunately dubbed, and the enthusiastic reinvention of the UK's glorious pop past (particularly the music of key Sixties artists such as The Beatles, The Kinks, and The Small Faces) sent ripples throughout the international music scene. At Britpop's height, a popularity war raged between Kinksian Blur and Beatlesy Oasis, but most saw the champions as being Pulp with their fifth album, *Different Class*.

Frontman Jarvis Cocker compared this feeling of exuberance to a revolution taking place for the working class. Possessing a unique gift for storytelling and a grandly theatrical style, Cocker's attention to the details that other songwriters missed—or avoided—brought his characters to vibrant life. Pulp's off-kilter take on pop swept a generation off its feet and turned the songs into anthems—witness the immortal, spiky "Common People" (there's nothing ironic about the anger in Cocker's deliver here) or the schoolday memories revisited in the glitz of "Disco 2000." "I Spy" is an arrestingly dark vignette of voyeurism, while "Sorted For E's And Wizz" is a sharply observed snapshot of the less glamorous flipside of rave culture.

The album's title came to Cocker, like an epiphany, in a club he frequented. Hence the statement on the rear of the cover: "We don't want no trouble, we just want the right to be different. That's all." Written with a superior level of style and intelligence, *Different Class* briefly elevated Pulp above all their Britpop peers. **KM**

> **"I get obsessed with girls very easily. It only ever lasts a couple of days, mind."**
>
> Jarvis Cocker, 1995

Track Listing

	01	**Mis-Shapes** (Pulp)	3:46
	02	**Pencil Skirt** (Pulp)	3:11
▶	03	**Common People** (Pulp)	5:50
	04	**I Spy** (Pulp)	5:55
▶	05	**Disco 2000** (Pulp)	4:33
	06	**Live Bed Show** (Pulp)	3:29
	07	**Something Changed** (Pulp)	3:18
	08	**Sorted For E's And Wizz** (Pulp)	3:47
▶	09	**F.E.E.L.I.N.G.C.A.L.L.E.D.L.O.V.E** (Pulp)	6:01
▶	10	**Underwear** (Pulp)	4:06
	11	**Monday Morning** (Pulp)	4:16
	12	**Bar Italia** (Pulp)	3:42

Leftfield | Leftism (1995)

Label | Hard Hands
Producer | Leftfield
Art Direction | Jonathan Cooke
Nationality | UK
Running Time | 69:39

The anticipation was simply killing us. Paul Daley and Neil Barnes had laid the solid groundwork for UK dance domination in late 1993 with the stunning "Open Up," the inflammatory collaboration with John Lydon. And then they went underground.

It was not until 15 months later that doubts about their ability to deliver were swept away. The best dance music album ever? Maybe. Certainly the most intelligent. *Leftism* is beautifully paced. "Black Flute" is the first time that the tempo is raised significantly. The previous half hour is spent delving into dark places ("Release The Pressure"), creating sounds that leave you in awe ("Melt") and ripping out your ribcage with shattering basslines ("Original"). It is a sign of intent that the album's cover is a speaker cone surrounded by a fearsome jawbone.

After seducing you, the duo decide it is time to batter you into submission. The monumental "Space Shanty" effortlessly achieves this task, seven minutes of madness that has only the Prodigy's "Voodoo People" as a rival for the genre's anthemic apex.

Having achieved this peak of intensity, lesser artists might just up the BPM. But "Inspection (Check One)" shows that invention is just as effective as acceleration. And then, after the aforementioned "Open Up," we end where we began, with things low key and socially conscious. This time it is "21st Century Poem," set to the quiet anger of Manchester wordsmith Lemn Sissay.

Leftism was Mercury Music Prize-nominated in the UK. The fact that it lost to Portishead's equally groundbreaking *Dummy* does not mask the fact that it restored faith in dance. If anyone saved a genre, it is Leftfield. **CB**

> "...your sound is influenced by the development of the machines you use."
>
> Paul Daley, 1995

Track Listing

01	**Release The Pressure** (Barnes·Daley)		7:39
02	**Afro-Left** (Barnes·Cole·Daley)		7:33
03	**Melt** (Barnes·Daley)		5:21
04	**Song Of Life** (Barnes·Daley·Rupkina)		6:55
▶ 05	**Original** (Barnes·Daley·Halliday)		6:22
06	**Black Flute** (Barnes·Daley)		3:46
▶ 07	**Space Shanty** (Barnes·Daley)		7:15
08	**Inspection (Check One)** (Barnes·Clarke·Daley)		6:30
09	**Storm 3000** (Barnes·Daley)		5:44
▶ 10	**Open Up** (Barnes·Daley·Lydon)		6:52
11	**21st Century Poem** (Barnes·Daley)		5:42

D'Angelo | Brown Sugar (1995)

Label | EMI
Producer | Kedar Massenburg
Art Direction | Henry Marquez
Nationality | USA
Running Time | 53:21

Even as it reached new heights of commercial success, urban music was clearly missing something in the early 1990s. The genre was zooming ahead on hip-hop-influenced anthems and glossy Whitney Houston-style big ballads, but it was almost entirely ignoring its past. As a pioneer of the neo-soul movement, D'Angelo would help redirect R&B back to its roots.

The singer burst onto the scene at 21, an attractively marketable readymade star with a fresh face and chiseled abs, and he would prove to be the missing link between vintage Smokey Robinson and Marvin Gaye and contemporary soul music. On his debut release, *Brown Sugar*, D'Angelo brought an unquestionably modern B-boy attitude to the party, yet one that would not have seemed out of place at the Apollo in the 1960s. The debt to Prince is also evident as the vocalist opens *Brown Sugar* with the slowly grinding title track and then slips into some purple satin sheets for "Jonz In My Bonz." There is a definite Barry White vibe going down on the bedroom jam "Alright," despite the fact that D'Angelo's high falsetto could not be more different to the soul heavyweight's canyon-deep voice. Smokey would never wear anything as racy as "Shit, Damn, Motherfucker," but D'Angelo has no trouble dressing up Robinson's "Cruisin'" in modern threads.

Brown Sugar wasn't revolutionary. It was "retro-lutionary"—a much-needed revival of R&B's past in a contemporary package. The album was a double-platinum smash that spawned four singles and set the stage for the long overdue follow-up, 2000's *Voodoo*, which debuted in the United States at No. 1. **JiH**

> "I'm making black music ... That's the only boundary to stay with."
>
> D'Angelo, 1996

Track Listing

▶	01	**Brown Sugar** (D'Angelo • Muhammad)	4:22
	02	**Alright** (D'Angelo)	5:15
	03	**Jonz In My Bonz** (D'Angelo • Stone)	5:56
	04	**Me And Those Dreamin' Eyes Of Mine** (D'Angelo)	4:46
	05	**Shit, Damn, Motherfucker** (D'Angelo)	5:14
	06	**Smooth** (L. Archer • D'Angelo)	4:18
▶	07	**Cruisin'** (Robinson • Tarplin)	6:28
	08	**When We Get By** (D'Angelo)	5:48
▶	09	**Lady** (D'Angelo • Saadiq)	5:47
	10	**Higher** (L. Archer • R. Archer • D'Angelo)	5:27

Oasis | (What's The Story) Morning Glory? (1995)

Label | Creation
Producer | Noel Gallagher • Owen Morris
Art Direction | Brian Cannon
Nationality | UK
Running Time | 50:05

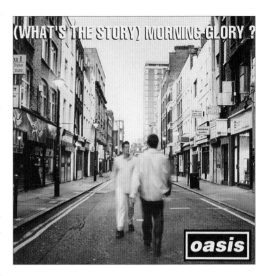

What's The Story . . . was at the epicenter of Britpop, a cultural rejuvenation that swept Britain in the 1990s, briefly reawakening a pride in home-grown music, fashion, and art not seen since the 1960s.

"Hello" is a typically arrogant opener, the chorus a cheeky nod to Gary Glitter's "Hello! Hello! I'm Back Again." The anthemic singalong "Don't Look Back In Anger" soon became a soccer stadium favorite (its lyrics had been inspired by a snippet of a John Lennon conversation). "Some Might Say" gave the band their first UK No. 1, although many felt that the album's pinnacle was the haunting, cello-accompanied "Wonderwall" (a UK No. 2)—its title taken from George Harrison's soundtrack of 1969—which Noel claimed to have written for his then girlfriend, Meg Matthews. In terms of tenderness and epic scope, however, the heartfelt "Cast No Shadow" (written about Verve singer Richard Ashcroft) tops it: the strings emote a wealth of feeling, Liam bursting out the evocative lyrics with a voice that has rarely sounded better. The title track is a combative anthem with a life-affirming chorus surrounded by apocalyptic helicopter noises. (Noel told art director Brian Cannon that the album was urban in feel—hence the sleeve photo, shot in Berwick Street, in London's Soho.) It segues into the mellifluous "Champagne Supernova," which concludes the album with histrionic guitar solos from Noel and Paul Weller.

By the summer of 1996, *What's The Story . . .* had gone platinum nine times over, defining a time and a place more absolutely than any other UK album released since. **AMa**

> "As each generation goes on they take stuff from what has gone before."
>
> Noel Gallagher, 1995

Track Listing

01	Hello (N. Gallagher)	3:23
02	Roll With It (N. Gallagher)	4:00
▶ 03	Wonderwall (N. Gallagher)	4:17
04	Don't Look Back In Anger (N. Gallagher)	4:48
05	Hey Now (N. Gallagher)	5:41
06	Instrumental (N. Gallagher)	0:44
▶ 07	Some Might Say (N. Gallagher)	5:28
▶ 08	Cast No Shadow (N. Gallagher)	4:51
09	She's Electric (N. Gallagher)	3:40
▶ 10	Morning Glory (N. Gallagher)	5:03
11	Instrumental (N. Gallagher)	0:39
▶ 12	Champagne Supernova (N. Gallagher)	7:31

Goldie
Timeless (1995)

Label | FFRR
Producer | Goldie • Rob Playford
Art Direction | Uncredited
Nationality | UK
Running Time | 113:10

Alanis Morissette
Jagged Little Pill (1995)

Label | Maverick
Producer | Glen Ballard
Art Direction | Tom Recchion
Nationality | Canada
Running Time | 57:23

Before *Timeless*, jungle or drum 'n' bass was the defiantly underground sound of the UK in the early 1990s. Jungle needed a face and a voice—enter Goldie, a larger-than-life character with a murky past and an obvious passion for the music. *Timeless* was one of the first drum 'n' bass albums produced, and the first to be embraced by the mainstream.

The album's opener and first single was the title track, an ambitious 20-minute-plus piece in three movements. "Timeless" was by turns majestic, ambient, soulful, and angry, a tour de force of complex drum rhythms and devastating basslines. "Saint Angel" featured synthesizers and crisp hi-hats building to a furious squall of razor-sharp drum rhythms. "State Of Mind" is a more gentle, reflective piece, with a poignant vocal from Lorna Harris over piano, strings, and a delicate hip-hop beat. "Angel" has dark, menacing rhythms, mutating drums interacting with a thoroughly nasty bassline. Another standout is the spellbinding epic "Sea Of Tears." Goldie said of this song, "It has its dark corners ... everybody has corners to go to. 'Sea Of Tears' is mine." "Inner City Life" is melancholic but euphoric, with the soulful vocals of Diane Charlemagne soaring over haunting strings, meticulously edited breakbeats, and deep sub-bass.

Some of *Timeless* sounds dated today, but few dance producers have come close to realizing such an ambitious artistic vision. It is the sound of future jazz from a distant planet, set to the sharpest beats. **APi**

Lazy journalists labeled *Jagged Little Pill* "therapy rock" on its appearance in 1995, due largely to Alanis Morissette's vitriolic, confessional attack on subjects such as previous lovers (famously, she hissed, "Are you thinking of me when you fuck her?" on "You Oughta Know"). But this was superficial: Morissette's first "real" record—the Canadian singer-songwriter had written naive, semi-religious pop in a younger incarnation—was a thoroughly exciting rock album with hard-hitting but never overzealous tunes and a bunch of lyrical and musical hooks to die for. The career-making single "Ironic" is an obvious high point, with Alanis' unselfconsciously clever couplets reflecting irony—or, ironically, not, as she was forced to explain over the years—but songs such as "Perfect" and "You Learn" (the latter the closest the "therapy" tag comes to hitting home) focus on subtlety rather than bombastics. And there are plenty of fireworks, with the presence of Chili Peppers Flea and Dave Navarro on "You Oughta Know" adding serious balls to the otherwise melodic sound, courtesy of Morissette's co-producer, co-writer, and emotional mentor Glen Ballard.

Jagged Little Pill sounds a little dated a decade after its release, thanks to the glut of female singer/ songwriters (Ani DiFranco, Jewel, and Avril Lavigne, for example) that followed in Alanis' footsteps. It is this aspect of *Jagged ...*'s impact—on women's rock—that marks it out for inclusion, just as much as the big, big songs it contains. **JM**

Screaming Trees
Dust (1996)

Label | Sony
Producer | George Drakoulias
Art Direction | Mark Danielson
Nationality | USA
Running Time | 44:19

When Oasis toured North America with Screaming Trees in 1996, Liam Gallagher amused himself—if no one else—by renaming them Barking Branches and Crazy Conkers. Gallagher is not noted for perspicacity, but he might have unwittingly hit the head of the nail: here was a band with a finger permanently hovering over the self-destruct button.

It was four years since *Sweet Oblivion* and the signs were not good for the four-piece's seventh release. An album's worth of material had been recorded and scrapped, and the Trees seemed about to implode at any moment. But out of the chaos emerged an album that *Rolling Stone* rightly declared to be "inspired."

Dust showed that, despite being lumped in with the Seattle scene, the band were by now grunge by association rather than actuality. It is mature and majestic, with tinges of folk ("Dying Days"—searing guitar solo from Pearl Jam's Mike McCready), psychedelia ("Traveler" and "Dime Western"), topped and tailed with Eastern influences (sitar-heavy opener "Halo Of Ashes" and percussive closer "Gospel Plow," both featuring Tom Petty stalwart Benmont Tench on mellotron). Darkening the skies above all this is Mark Lanegan's voice, a thing of abrasive beauty. "Gotta get away before I lose my mind" he growls on "All I Know".

The acclaim lavished on *Dust* only postponed the inevitable and the Screaming Trees split up in 2000. But they bowed out having finally—and magnificently—fulfilled their promise. **CB**

Super Furry Animals
Fuzzy Logic (1996)

Label | Creation
Producer | Gorwel Owen
Art Direction | B. Cannon • M. Catherall
Nationality | UK
Running Time | 37:02

The year 1996 saw much jingoistic crowing in England. For the first time in 30 years, the soccer team were doing moderately well in an international competition. Britpop was at its height, with bands such as Blur, Oasis, and Pulp dominating the day. It was pleasing, then, that one of the albums of the year belonged to a band that was resolutely, unapologetically, Welsh.

Arriving completely out of leftfield, *Fuzzy Logic* casually referenced such disparate cultural phenomena as comedian Bill Hicks, drug smuggler Howard Marks, seventeenth-century scientist Isaac Newton—and their pet hamster, Stavros. The music was an artful mish-mash of Sixties pop, punk rock, and psychedelia, with an underlying Nineties dance sensibility. Indeed, SFA had formed with the aim of making techno records and, later that summer, invaded the festival circuit in a bright blue tank with a large sound system attached and "If You Don't Want Me To Destroy You ... " painted on the gun-barrel.

Gruff Rhys' lysergic nonsense vocals were frequently hilarious yet still managed to evoke a gently parochial state of mind. The band flitted effortlessly between catchy punk-pop ("God! Show Me Magic"; "Something For The Weekend"; "Bad Behaviour") and yearning psychedelia ("Hometown Unicorn";"Gathering Moss").

SFA would go on to create more polished, rounded, "better" albums than this. But for the sheer glee and excitement of hearing a wildly inventive band just hitting their stride, *Fuzzy Logic* is hard to beat. **RS**

Fatboy Slim
Better Living Through Chemistry (1996)

Label | Skint
Producer | Fatboy Slim
Art Direction | Uncredited
Nationality | UK
Running Time | 70:59

Dr. Octagon
Dr. Octagonecologyst (1996)

Label | Bulk
Producer | Kurt Matlin • Dan Nakamura
Art Direction | Pushead
Nationality | USA
Running Time | 65:49

Norman Cook's transformation from bass guitarist-vocalist for The Housemartins to bangin' beats as DJ-producer Fatboy Slim makes for one of the more remarkable reinventions in late twentieth-century pop.

Cook had passed through several incarnations before establishing his electronic persona—Beats International (who scored a UK No. 1 with "Dub Be Good To Me"), Freakpower, Mighty Dub Katz, and Pizzaman. But it was as Fatboy Slim that he became the most recognizable name in big-beat technopop.

Better Living Through Chemistry illustrates neatly just why Cook's creations would go on to become commonplace in movies and commercials, as well as club and radio smashes. With a keen ear for hooky melodies, he incorporates esoteric samples and motifs to humorous or hip-shaking effect—and sometimes both. "Santa Cruz" has a hypnotic, xylophone-like line that grounds the blissed-out quality prevalent on the rest of the track. The power chords sampled from a cover of The Who's "I Can't Explain" mesh with shuffling drumbeats and space-age sound effects to create a groovy dance-rock hybrid in "Going Out Of My Head" (his first U.S. hit). Indeed, *Better Living Through Chemistry* prompted many listeners to start scanning the liner notes for songwriting credits, backwards-engineer the Fatboy alchemy, and root out the often obscure source material of Cook's brilliant mutations. **YK**

Pairing the most ingenious wordsmith of rap with one of the most inventive producers ever to lay down a beat, the Dr. Octagon project was destined to be a hip-hop landmark. But no one dared guess that it would be an eerie sci-fi odyssey about a time-traveling gynecologist from the year 3000.

After Kool Keith left the groundbreaking rap crew Ultramagnetic MCs he joined forces with Dan "The Automator" Nakamura (who went on to helm avant-garde hip-hop projects such as Gorillaz and Handsome Boy Modeling School). Legendary turntablist DJ Q-Bert of Invisbl Skratch Pikls, DJ Shadow, and future Keith collaborator Kutmaster Kurt were also enlisted.

Keith gave the sinister and sexually obsessed doctor a voice; in scintillating cadence he coasts through a surrealist discourse, at once transcendently articulate and audaciously crude. Nakamura created a parallel universe for the character full of subterranean beats and chilling electronic effects, in addition to the genuinely creepy medical-porn samples.

Many in the hip-hop community had trouble categorizing the album, with its confounding subject matter and revolutionary production, not to mention the unsettling artwork from early Metallica cover artist Pushead. Keith went on to complain that the only audience he gained from Dr. Octagon was white, and swiftly killed off the character on his next album. **AT**

Stereolab
Emperor Tomato Ketchup (1996)

Label | Elektra
Producer | John McEntire • Stereolab
Art Direction | Uncredited
Nationality | France • UK
Running Time | 57:14

Tortoise
Millions Now Living Will Never Die (1996)

Label | Thrill Jockey
Producer | John McEntire
Art Direction | Dan Osborn • Tortoise
Nationality | USA
Running Time | 43:02

At the heart of Stereolab are the sexy female vocals of French-born Laetitia Sadier and the Sixties-inspired kitschy pop of her native country. Then there is the influence of the minimalist Krautrock of mid-1970s Germany. And finally, there are the American elements of old-style funk and Velvet Underground simplicity.

What binds together this United Nations of sound on *Emperor Tomato Ketchup* is clever production—a unique multilayered sound that incorporates various textures (including strings, vocal harmonies, and electronica) with crystal-clear perfection.

NME called the band a "motley crew of English secondhand record dweebs, French political, er, lecturers, and instrumental boffins." But the album's broad experimental sound is an indisputably enjoyable adventure. The album opens with its strongest track, "Metronomic Underground," in which Sadier repeats the meaningless line "Crazy, sturdy, a torpedo," for most of the eight-minute track while the music underneath her vocals builds up from a simple funk groove to a loud and feverish guitar/synth ending. "Tomorrow Is Already Here" is reminiscent of Nico-era Velvet Underground, with broad spaces between the guitars and organ.

In many ways, *Emperor Tomato Ketchup* was an ambitious effort at making forgotten sounds and ideologies contemporary again. And in their own eccentric fashion, Stereolab pull it off to a tee. **JC**

Prior to Tortoise's arrival on the American college radio and indie rock scene in the mid-1990s, there was a lingering idea that electric instrumental music was the domain of folks with wide collars, flared trousers, and shag haircuts. The "kids with cred," in turn, migrated toward distressed denim, faded corduroy, and sometimes boxy spectacles. The former archetype's sound was virtuosic, clean, and perhaps overly flashy, while the latter was noisy and rebellious.

The Chicago-based modern instrumental rock collective Tortoise managed to bring together the best of both scenes. The centerpiece of this album is "Djed," a 20-minute-plus opening track. It begins with a mellow space surf rock sound that propels along effortlessly on a rock 'n' roll longboard riding synthesized, slightly spacey sonic waves. This quickly morphs into an electronic meltdown of sorts, sounding as if the CD player is breaking down. A section of repeating minimalism follows, and "Djed" ultimately concludes in a spell of subtle electro-rock. There are musical sub-plots throughout the number, and five comparatively briefer pieces finish the album out.

The simple liner notes list players' names but not their specific instruments—each member is a multi-instrumentalist, and all have other projects as musical outlets. This is an ego-free model that could serve as a template for creative rock players internationally. **YK**

Beck | Odelay (1996)

Label | Bong Load
Producer | Various
Art Direction | Robert Fisher • Beck Hansen
Nationality | USA
Running Time | 51:28

On *Odelay*, his second major-label album, Beck Hansen had something to prove. With 1994 single "Loser" he had had huge success. The song was dubbed a "slacker anthem," its chorus ("I'm a loser baby, so why don't you kill me") a global slogan, while the then 24-year-old was anointed poster boy for Generation X.

But the Los Angeleno was no dope-addled waster. "Loser" was as ironic as his indie song "MTV Makes Me Want To Smoke Crack." He was a restlessly inventive musical magpie, as enthused about folk as he was about hip hop, as adept at the moonwalk as at throwing rock-dude shapes, someone who knew his way round lo-fi recording techniques but also how to harness cutting-edge recording technology.

With *Odelay* he alchemized all these disparate ideas into one vibrant whole. Beck hooked up with The Dust Brothers, the producer-artists responsible for the vibrant buzz of the Beastie Boys' *Paul's Boutique*. It was an inspired union: first track "Devils Haircut" alone boasts a James Brown sample, big fat riffs, superfly beats, and a day-glo collage of sonic tricks and quirks. "The New Pollution" starts as cheesy easy listening before hijacking the rhythms of The Beatles' "Taxman." "Where It's At" is funkified hip hop. "Jack-Ass" is a clip-clopping country ballad, built around Them's sublime cover of Dylan's "It's All Over Now, Baby Blue."

Dazzlingly eclectic, *Odelay* is the sound of a young maverick having delirious fun and feeling his way forwards. It sold two million copies, spawned a rash of MTV hits and won two Grammies. A new kind of genius had arrived. **CM**

"'Loser' was a total fluke, a total anomaly in my music."

Beck, 2005

Track Listing

▶	01	**Devils Haircut** (Hansen•King•Simpson)	3:13
	02	**Hotwax** (Hansen•King•Simpson)	3:52
	03	**Lord Only Knows** (Hansen)	4:14
▶	04	**The New Pollution** (Hansen•King•Simpson)	3:39
	05	**Derelict** (Hansen•King•Simpson)	4:11
	06	**Novocane** (Hansen•King•Simpson)	4:38
▶	07	**Jack–Ass** (Hansen•King•Simpson)	4:00
▶	08	**Where It's At** (Hansen•King•Simpson)	5:25
	09	**Minus** (Hansen)	2:32
	10	**Sissyneck** (Hansen•King•Simpson)	4:02
	11	**Readymade** (Hansen•King•Simpson)	2:43
▶	12	**High 5 (Rock The Catskills)** (Hansen•King•Simpson)	4:10
	13	**Ramshackle** (Hansen)	4:49

Belle And Sebastian | "Tigermilk" (1996)

Label | Electric Honey
Producer | Belle And Sebastian
Art Direction | Belle And Sebastian
Nationality | UK
Running Time | 41:38

Named after French children's book *Belle Et Sébastien*, this Glasgow six-piece were wry, literate, and witty—in sharp contrast to the dominant, though rapidly declining, Britpop and dance scenes.

Like their spiritual forebears Teenage Fanclub, Belle And Sebastian were steeped in pop history. But even more so than the Fannies, principal songwriter Stuart Murdoch breathed new life into his influences. Only his beloved Felt and The Smiths had taken pop to such bittersweet extremes.

Belle And Sebastian were born during Murdoch's music business course at university. The band were mostly fellow students and *"Tigermilk"* was their final year project. Only a thousand vinyl copies were pressed and released in 1996 on the band's own Electric Honey label. By the time *"Tigermilk"* was released in remastered CD form in 1999, the band already had two more critically acclaimed albums (*If You're Feeling Sinister* and *The Boy With The Arab Strap*) to their name.

After all this, the *"Tigermilk"* re-release could hold few surprises. Belle And Sebastian seemingly arrived fully formed, with their mix of folky pop (think The Mamas And The Papas or Donovan's *A Gift From A Flower To A Garden*), baroque strings, and nods to some impeccable pop reference points, combined with an intimate knowledge of anything that had been played by John Peel during the previous 15 years ("Electronic Renaissance" is based on New Order's "Procession").

Every song is funny, sad, and warm—and guaranteed to make you feel better, no matter what is wrong. Perfect pop made by the pure of heart. **MBe**

> "In three months, we had to get a full band together and make a proper record ..."

Stuart Murdoch, 2001

Track Listing

▶	01	**The State I Am In** (Belle And Sebastian)	4:58
	02	**Expectations** (Belle And Sebastian)	3:34
	03	**She's Losing It** (Belle And Sebastian)	2:22
▶	04	**You're Just A Baby** (Belle And Sebastian)	3:41
	05	**Electronic Renaissance** (Belle And Sebastian)	4:50
	06	**I Could Be Dreaming** (Belle And Sebastian)	5:56
▶	07	**We Rule The School** (Belle And Sebastian)	3:27
	08	**My Wandering Days Are Over** (Belle And Sebastian)	5:25
	09	**I Don't Love Anyone** (Belle And Sebastian)	3:56
	10	**Mary Jo** (Belle And Sebastian)	3:29

DJ Shadow | Endtroducing ... (1996)

Label | Mo'Wax
Producer | DJ Shadow
Art Direction | Will Bunkhead • Ben Drury
Nationality | USA
Running Time | 63:03

As a teenager in California, Josh Davis listened to the classic years of hip hop and yearned to re-create the sounds of his heroes such as Public Enemy and Pete Rock. Cut off from the East and West Coast scenes of the day, he and a group of like-minded souls formed the Quannum organization, a loose collective of MCs, DJs, and producers in the San Francisco area. After producing a number of now highly collectable singles with the likes of Blackalicious, DJ Krush, and the Lifers Group (a band of maximum security prisoners), his debut for UK label Mo'Wax heralded a new era in music.

Utilizing samples from hundreds of different records, mostly forgotten releases from the 1960s and '70s, all gathered from one massive record store basement, Shadow created an unnerving but enticing soundscape. Blending prog rock with comedy recordings taken out of context, obscure folk, and layer upon layer of drums, the result was an album that sounded familiar on first hearing, but still unlike anything else. Tracks such as "The Number Song" and "Organ Donor" maintained the upbeat style of Davis' early influences while continuing the moody feel of the album. More ambient tracks such as "Midnight In A Perfect World" and "What Does Your Soul Look Like" pushed beyond the furthest reaches of what sample-based music had so far achieved.

Best enjoyed as a whole, this is a concept album without a hackneyed theme, and it paved the way for the continued success of experimentally minded artists as diverse as Massive Attack, Radiohead, and Björk, to name just a few. **CR**

> " ...an introduction to what hip hop used to represent ... "

DJ Shadow, 1997

Track Listing

	01	Best Foot Forward (Davis)	0:49
▶	02	Building Steam With A Grain of Salt (Davis)	6:41
▶	03	The Number Song (Davis)	4:38
	04	Changeling (Davis)	7:51
▶	05	What Does Your Soul Look Like, Pt. 4 (Davis)	5:08
	06	Untitled (Davis)	0:24
	07	Stem/Long Stem (Davis)	9:22
▶	08	Mutual Slump (Davis)	4:03
▶	09	Organ Donor (Davis)	1:57
	10	Why Hip Hop Sucks In '96 (Davis)	0:41
▶	11	Midnight In A Perfect World (Davis)	5:02
	12	Napalm Brain / Scatter Brain (Davis)	9:23
▶	13	What Does Your Soul Look Like (Pt1 – Blue Sky Revisit) (Davis)	7:28

Eels
Beautiful Freak (1996)

Label | Dreamworks
Producer | Various
Art Direction | Francesca Restrepo
Nationality | USA
Running Time | 43:53

Songs about sadness, loneliness, and despair have rarely sounded more quirky than *Beautiful Freak*. The debut effort for Eels is a dark treatise for the solitary-minded, and makes for headphone music par excellence.

Though officially a trio, Eels was primarily the brainchild of the melodically gifted songwriter E (a moniker short for Mark Oliver Everett), who had seen his share both of tragedy (he found his father dead when he was 19) and delayed gratification (he had a mildly successful solo career before creating Eels along with bassist Tommy Walter and drummer Butch Norton).

With titles such as "Lucky Day In Hell," lines like "Life is hard and so am I" ("Novocaine For The Soul," a surprise UK Top Ten hit), and an unsettling album cover featuring a bug-eyed prepubescent girl, *Beautiful Freak* shares many qualities with a juvenile tongue-wag. However, the music and the production of the album is anything but immature: Eels blend orchestral sounds, a church choir, fake crowd noise, guitars split between the right and left speakers, hip-hop beats, spoken word, the static sound of an old record.

Because of its wide-ranging soundscape, critics willingly accorded the album rave reviews. Music magazine *Q* tried to distill the alchemy of *Beautiful Freak*: "Imagine Beck's *Odelay* rhythms, The Beatles' songwriting maturity, Sparklehorse's simple production, Brian Wilson's visionary editing and arrangements and you have a complete musical vision, a genre-spanning soundscape that reels you in with its myriad hooks." **JC**

The Divine Comedy
Casanova (1996)

Label | Setanta
Producer | Darren Allison • Neil Hannon
Art Direction | Kevin Westenberg
Nationality | Ireland
Running Time | 51:46

It was a strange time for British music. Oasis had reduced The Beatles to a minimalist chug, Blur had revived English music hall, and many were claiming always to have had a "mod" element to their music. This lumpen revival was not without its quirks, however, as the success of Neil Hannon's Divine Comedy proved.

Hannon's finest hour, *Casanova* seemed equally inspired by Scott Walker (and thus Jacques Brel and Wally Stott) and Michael Caine's *Alfie*, though it was no pastiche but a meditation on what might have happened had the two characters thrived into the mid-1990s. The updating gave greater lyrical freedom, and it is difficult to see how even the Belgian chansonnier could have dreamed up the scenarios here: in "Something For The Weekend," the fraudulent seducer is himself mugged; in "Becoming More Like Alfie," our hero realizes, as many have, that being a gent usually equates with losing in love; and in "The Frog Princess," "Your place or mine?" becomes a refrain of regret.

Hannon played his role perfectly—to all intents he was Alfie, self-obsessed, coolly aloof, turning smoking into an art form. And the more distant he appeared, the greater his success. "Songs Of Love," one of the least imposing of the album tracks, even morphed into the theme tune for the surreal Irish priest TV comedy *Father Ted*. In early 1997, Hannon completed this stage in his career with *A Short Album About Love*, released on Valentine's Day, smartly getting out of the Sixties before his peers ended up beached by them. **DH**

Fiona Apple
Tidal (1996)

Label | Sony
Producer | Andrew Slater
Art Direction | Fred Woodward
Nationality | USA
Running Time | 51:41

Just one year after emerging from New York, ambitious 18-year-old Fiona Apple capitalized on her recent signing with Sony and released her debut album, *Tidal*. Her remarkably mature vocals and angst-ridden lyrics swiftly earned her comparisons to the empowered female heavyweights of the music world at the time—Alanis Morissette, Tori Amos, and P. J. Harvey. The album's minimalist artwork—mostly black-and-white portraits of Apple—reflects the tone of the album: self-reflective and self-indulgent perhaps, yet breathtakingly beautiful, stark, and powerful also.

Apple's sullen, heartbroken yet defiant words dictated the sound of many of the tracks. Heartache, however, had never sounded so good. The impossibly young Apple dabbled in an array of genres ranging from psychedelia, sultry jazz, and blues to confident, soulful funk. The majority of the tracks meander beyond the five-minute mark as Apple delivers her enrapturing stories, her alto pitch drifting seamlessly from the sultry, throaty vocals of standout "Criminal," to angelic heights in "Never Is A Promise"; from bitter and impassioned in "Sleep To Dream" to the longing and innocence of "The First Taste."

Along with the album's growing reputation and critical acclaim came a throng of awards and accolades. In 1997 Apple was nominated for Best New Artist and Best Rock Song ("Criminal") at the Grammys, although she would eventually accept the award for Best Rock Vocal Performance–Female for the same song. **EK**

Wilco
Being There (1996)

Label | Reprise
Producer | Wilco
Art Direction | Fireproof Design
Nationality | USA
Running Time | 76:47

Wilco's 1995 debut, *A.M.*, was a solid country-rocker that expanded naturally on the sounds Wilco frontman Jeff Tweedy had explored during four albums with his previous band, Uncle Tupelo. In that sense, *A.M.* was much like the same year's *Trace*, the debut from fellow Tupelo veteran Jay Farrar's Son Volt.

In contrast, Wilco's second release can be seen as the first mighty musical jump in a career increasingly distinguished by great artistic leaps and bounds. Having traveled the roots road for five albums, Tweedy seemed more concerned with where music was going than where it had been. He built *Being There* with walls of noise and labyrinth-like corridors of studio wizardry. The album was a shock to the system for many alt.country loyalists, but it also helped Wilco reach listeners outside the narrow *No Depression* fan base.

The look of the album is deceptively simple. A hand holding a guitar on the front and fingers playing a piano on the back do not begin to illustrate the wide range of sounds over 19 songs and 2 discs. The volley begins with "Misunderstood," a powerful hybrid that sways from tender balladry to feedback-drenched fuzz; it continues as earthy, Tupelo-friendly cuts "Far, Far Away" and "Forget The Flowers" are spliced with Stones-style rockers "Monday" and "Outtasite (Outta Mind)."

Being There, which takes its name from the 1979 Peter Sellers movie, would garner vast critical acclaim but generate only lukewarm sales, peaking at 73 on the Billboard chart and taking seven years to go gold. **JiH**

Sepultura | **Roots** (1996)

Label | Roadrunner
Producer | DJ Lethal • Ross Robinson • Sepultura
Art Direction | Bryan Thatcher
Nationality | Brazil
Running Time | 72:09

Sepultura's *Roots* was released in 1996—three years after their breakthrough, *Chaos A.D.*—and saw the Brazilian metal band boldly push its music forward into unknown territory. Drawing on Brazilian Latin and tribal music, nu-metal, and Sepultura's own thrash/death style, the results were unique—indeed, jawdropping at times. Under the direction of charismatic singer/guitarist Max Cavalera, the band delved deep into its national heritage, embracing its "roots"—as evinced by the tattooed native on the album sleeve.

The band is driven on the powerful title track. Igor Cavalera's drums are both powerful and inventive, while the drop-tuned guitars are as tight as they are brutal. The trademark sound on the album is a mid-tempo but ultra-heavy grind—put to excellent use on tracks such as "Attitude" and "Breed Apart."

The band traveled to a remote region of the Amazon to meet a tribe called the Xavantes and record the acoustic "Itsári (Live)" with them. Elsewhere, Brazilian vocalist and percussionist Carlinhos Brown guests on the brilliant "Ratamahatta," a percussion-laden tour de force. More experiments abound in "Lookaway," with contributions from DJ Lethal and Jonathan Davis.

Soon after the album Max Cavalera made his exit under dramatic circumstances. His stepson had been killed and arguments concerning management finally split the band. Cavalera formed Soulfly and the rest of the band drafted in a new singer. Sepultura have not been in a great state since *Roots*; this record shows the band at the peak of its powers. **AET**

Track Listing

▶	01	**Roots Bloody Roots** (Cavalera•Sepultura)	3:32
▶	02	**Attitude** (Cavalera•Sepultura)	4:15
	03	**Cut-Throat** (Cavalera•Sepultura)	2:44
▶	04	**Ratamahatta** (Brown•Sepultura)	4:30
	05	**Breed Apart** (Cavalera•Kisser•Sepultura)	4:01
	06	**Straighthate** (Cavalera•Sepultura)	5:21
	07	**Spit** (Cavalera•Sepultura)	2:45
▶	08	**Lookaway** (Davis•DJ Lethal•Sepultura)	5:26
	09	**Dusted** (Kisser•Sepultura)	4:03
	10	**Born Stubborn** (Cavalera•Sepultura)	4:07
	11	**Jasco** (Kisser)	1:57
▶	12	**Itsári (Live)** (Sepultura•Xavantes Tribe)	4:48
	13	**Ambush** (Cavalera•Sepultura)	4:39
	14	**Endangered Species** (Sepultura)	5:19
	15	**Dictatorshit** (Cavalera•Sepultura)	1:26
	16	**Canyon Jam** (Sepultura•Xavantes Tribe)	13:16

Barry Adamson
Oedipus Schmoedipus (1996)

Label | Mute
Producer | Barry Adamson
Art Direction | Barry Adamson
Nationality | UK
Running Time | 55:57

Fade in. Barry Adamson slumped in his studio, trying to comprehend just how Primal Scream's *Screamadelica* managed to sneak the Mercury Award away from his own *Soul Murder*. Flash forward to four years later. David Lynch's distinctive drawl blares out of Adamson's answering machine: "Barry? I've just listened to your *Oedipus Schmoedipus* album for eight hours and it's like hearing Hitch's films in your head. I need this in my next movie. It's 'cinematic soul,' kid. Patent it!" Fade out.

A year on and "Something Wicked This Way Comes" becomes the strip club swing centerpiece to Lynch's *Lost Highway*. What Lynch immediately tuned into was the ex-Magazine and Bad Seeds bassist's impeccably hip movie score vernacular. Take the way he blends Bernard Hermann's noir tapestries into the surreal supper-club jazz of "The Vibes Ain't Nothing But The Vibes" or the John Barry big-band swagger of "The Big Bamboozle." Sure, his cool jazz overhaul of Miles Davis oozes a commercial allure, yet the album deftly sidesteps the hype embedded in the mid-Nineties neo-lounge revival by inviting Pulp's Jarvis Cocker and Nick Cave to add some ironic pop panache.

It is precisely this ominously funky marriage of art rock and celluloid cheese that makes *Oedipus ...* such a compelling climax to Adamson's "unconscious trilogy" of psycho-thriller soundscapes that includes *Moss Side Story* (1989) and *Soul Murder* (1992). **MK**

Fun Lovin' Criminals
Come Find Yourself (1996)

Label | Capitol
Producer | Fun Lovin' Criminals
Art Direction | Henry Marquez
Nationality | USA
Running Time | 57:12

New York has yielded many bands capable of expressing the dark side of its hermetically sealed environment and Fun Lovin' Criminals are no exception. Huey "DiFontaine" Morgan (guitar/vox), Steve (bass/trumpet/keyboards), and Fast (drums) produced a heady mix of rock, rap, jazz, hip hop, and R&B that was coupled with streetwise stories about wannabe gangsters, drug deals, and gutter-level crime, all sung with a perennial tongue in their cheeks. Opening with the acoustic guitar chops of "Fun Lovin' Criminal" (with a nod to Hendrix's "Voodoo Chile"), the whoops and Huey's rapping conjure up smoky streets and visions of breaking and entering. Songs such as "Passive/Aggressive" and "The King Of New York" switch from mellow wah-wah guitars and caressing keyboards to power-chord choruses.

"Smoke 'Em" is a hazy, bass-ridden song championing marijuana smoking, a recreation that lends the album a certain ambience. Louis Armstrong's "We Have All The Time In The World" is given a sleazy makeover while the distorted keyboards of "Crime And Punishment" are positively menacing. It was "Scooby Snacks" that brought the trio their first chart entry (reaching No. 22 in the UK) as the group aligned themselves with director du jour Quentin Tarantino, sampling from both *Pulp Fiction* and *Reservoir Dogs*. It brought them rave reviews in both their home country and Europe, with adoring fans (and supermodels) falling for their wise-guy schtick. **AMa**

Maxwell
Maxwell's Urban Hang Suite (1996)

Label | Columbia
Producer | Stuart Matthewman • Musze
Art Direction | S. Drummond • J. Peploe
Nationality | USA
Running Time | 64:47

The Charlatans
Tellin' Stories (1996)

Label | Beggars Banquet
Producer | The Charlatans • Ric Peet
Art Direction | Tom Sheehan
Nationality | UK
Running Time | 47:01

Maxwell's Urban Hang Suite opens with the sound of a stylus hitting vinyl before the funky, chilled-out instrumental "The Urban Theme." It closes with soft vocals over "twilight in the big city" saxophone and piano. Jazz vocalists sometimes let their groups start and end sets without them: the effect here is similar.

The instrumental intro and outro set the framework for a classic album—a concept of sorts, based on the course of a brief real-life affair, and a belief in monogamy—that led the respectful, return-to-roots neo-soul movement of the 1990s. Neo-soul drew on African-American musical esthetics from the 1960s and '70s and artists such as Al Green and Marvin Gaye; "Sumthin' Sumthin'" was a collaboration with Leon Ware, who had co-written Gaye's *Let's Get It On*; guitarist Wah Wah Watson, who played on that album, is also present here. The result was an authentic yet updated sound that was as likely to employ a Fender® Rhodes keyboard as a contemporary drum machine sound.

What Maxwell brought to the table was a willingness to shed his blazer, roll up his sleeves, and get down and funky. "Ascension (Don't Ever Wonder)" struts with a loose guitar, an addictive bassline, and a taut drumbeat, with Maxwell's clear vocals soaring over the top. The seductive "Reunion" is to slow dancing what lit candles are to romantic bathtub sessions. Modern songs for the old fashioned at heart. **YK**

Known in the United States as Charlatans UK, to avoid confusion with the identically named 1960s Californian psychedelic merchants, The Charlatans were one of the few bands who bridged the gap between the Madchester scene of the early 1990s and the rise of Britpop later that decade, incorporating dance rhythms and textures into classic, Stonesy guitar rock. *Tellin' Stories*, their fifth album, finally established them as music industry heavyweights and survivors. Applauded for its diversity, poignancy, and its groove, it was by far their greatest achievement. "One To Another" will surely endure on dancefloors for years to come with its rambling, frenetic keyboards, interwoven guitar, and crashing cymbals. A tone of warmth and friendship pervades all—check out the Dylan-inspired "North Country Boy," a touching spirit-raiser that chugs along to a country-ish swagger, the tender melodies of "How Can You Leave Us," and the heartfelt title track.

On a sadder note, it is the last album they recorded with the brilliant, warm, Hammond® organ chime of keyboardist Rob Collins, who died in a car accident during recording. The final track, "Rob's Theme," is his tribute; it features a recording by his aunt of Rob talking at the age of three. His influence was so strong that the band almost split after his death. The Charlatans took on a whole new sound on successive albums, and this is what makes *Tellin' Stories* so special. **KM**

Manic Street Preachers | Everything Must Go (1996)

Label | Epic
Producer | Mike Hedges
Art Direction | Mark Farrow Design
Nationality | UK
Running Time | 45:19

On *Everything Must Go*, the Manics berated their fellow citizens for slumbering in a consumerist coma. But it was also a lament for the lost. There was the decimation of their native Wales' coal industry, but—cutting even closer—the disappearance of guitarist Richey James in 1995. His five co-writes are among the many standouts (his guitar graces "All Surface No Feeling"), from orchestral rockers to melancholic ballads.

The album was to be called *Sounds In The Grass*, after a painting by Willem de Kooning (the recipient of "Interiors"). It was renamed after a play by Patrick Jones, brother of bassist Nicky Wire, and crafted mostly in Normandy between summer 1995 and early 1996, away from a media fascinated by James' disappearance.

Where 1994's *The Holy Bible* had found favor with hardcore fans alone, the expansive *Everything . . .* earned awards, sales, and acclaim. "Sheer significance, brittle urgency, the sound of a band in bloom," enthused *NME*. The nostalgia of "Elvis Impersonator" gives way to the demonstrative title track, while "Kevin Carter" (with drummer Sean Moore doubling on brass) tackles the subject of Rwandan genocide, and "Small Black Flowers" mixes traditional Welsh harp with sweeping, desolate acoustic guitar to haunting effect. The dreamy "The Girl Who Wanted To Be God," ecstatic "Australia," and rabble-rousing Orwell homage "A Design For Life" (the first post-James cut) blend guarded optimism with despairing cynicism.

Wire wrote of his fellow Brits, "We only want to get drunk"—and drunk on the Manics they were, the album proving a triumphant, cathartic career high. **TJ**

"There was just … elation."

James Dean Bradfield, 1998

Track Listing

01	**Elvis Impersonator: Blackpool Pier** (Bradfield • James • Wire)		3:28
▶ 02	**A Design For Life** (Bradfield • Moore • Wire)		4:17
▶ 03	**Kevin Carter** (Bradfield • James • Moore • Wire)		3:25
04	**Enola/Alone** (Bradfield • Moore • Wire)		4:08
▶ 05	**Everything Must Go** (Bradfield • Moore • Wire)		3:41
▶ 06	**Small Black Flowers That Grow In The Sky** (Bradfield • James • Moore • Wire)		3:03
07	**The Girl Who Wanted To Be God** (Bradfield • James • Moore • Wire)		3:35
08	**Removables** (Bradfield • James • Moore • Wire)		3:31
09	**Australia** (Bradfield • Moore • Wire)		4:03
10	**Interiors (Song For Willem De Kooning)** (Bradfield • Moore • Wire)		4:17
11	**Further Away** (Bradfield • Moore • Wire)		3:38
12	**No Surface All Feeling** (Bradfield • Moore • Wire)	4:13	

Everything But The Girl | Walking Wounded (1996)

Label | Virgin
Producer | Various
Art Direction | Everything But The Girl • Form
Nationality | UK
Running Time | 51:55

It is rare for any artist to find their seventh album reaching a far wider public than their previous efforts. But in 1996, as Bristol trip hop proved the music of the moment, EBTG reached a commercial and artistic niche.

EBTG had pursued a varied career as purveyors of jazz-lite, indie-acoustic, electro-folk, and nouveau bossa nova among many forms, each effort characterized by Watt's melodic arrangements and Thorn's beautifully languid voice. But it was Thorn's gorgeous guest vocal on Massive Attack's acclaimed 1994 album *Protection* that showed how effectively EBTG's approach could fit contemporary chill-out sounds.

In 1995, the single "Missing" was innovatively remixed by house music DJ-producer Todd Terry and proved a U.S. and UK hit. Fusing these directions pointed the duo toward *Walking Wounded*, an album that found them employing contemporary electronic dance rhythms—trip hop, drum 'n' bass, house—although at the heart of things the duo were still writing brittle, beautiful narratives of lost love. (Marcelo Krasilcic's cover photo suggested the glamor of late-night clubbing, though Watt's angular features hinted at the near-fatal illness that had recently stricken him.)

Instrumentation is minimal: Watt plays synths and acoustic guitar and provides beats and abstract sounds. Standout track "Single" contains one of Thorn's finest ever performances, as she conveys an insecurity worthy of a bedsit Billie Holiday, while the title track serves as an elegy for clubbers who partied too hard.

Drum 'n' bass and Everything But The Girl? An unlikely combination, but it worked splendidly. **GC**

> "I'd like to think that restraint is the underlying strength of everything that we do."

Tracey Thorn, 1996

Track Listing

▶	01	**Before Today** (Thorn•Watt)	4:16
▶	02	**Wrong** (Thorn•Watt)	4:34
▶	03	**Single** (Thorn•Watt)	4:37
	04	**The Heart Remains A Child** (Thorn•Watt)	3:48
▶	05	**Walking Wounded** (Thorn•Watt)	5:59
	06	**Flipside** (Thorn•Watt)	4:31
	07	**Big Deal** (Thorn•Watt)	4:27
	08	**Mirrorball** (Thorn•Watt)	3:24
	09	**Good Cop Bad Cop** (Thorn•Watt)	4:54
	10	**Wrong (Todd Terry Remix)** (Thorn•Watt)	4:43
	11	**Walking Wounded (Omni Trio Remix)** (Thorn•Watt)	6:42

Nick Cave And The Bad Seeds
Murder Ballads (1996)

Label | Mute
Producer | Various
Art Direction | Johannes Beck • Jean-Frédéric Schnyder
Nationality | Australia
Running Time | 58:53

As rock's laureate noir, it is scarcely surprising that Nick Cave was a fan of murder ballads—a form of folk song dating back to the eighteenth century that, self-evidently, involved gruesome recounts of slaughter.

From the cover, a wintry oil as opposed to the brooding images of Cave that graced earlier releases, through to the guest vocalists (including pop siren Kylie Minogue), this is not your typical Seeds LP. The band are almost playful in their music, with the intensely personal Cave taking great pleasure in creating a darkly glittering gallery of murderous schoolgirls, distraught spouses, and psychotic serial killers.

The legendary "bad motherfucker called Stagger Lee," whose notoriety had also been celebrated by James Brown and Wilson Pickett among others, crops up in an eponymously named song, performing unspeakable acts on the drinkers of The Bucket Of Blood inn, while "The Curse Of Millhaven" sees the angelic Loretta transform into a 14-year-old banshee, reveling in the slaughter of her fellow villagers. Throughout, the Seeds build up a claustrophobic soundscape to surround Cave's damned souls.

Cave has subsequently ascribed ... *Ballads'* success to the presence of Ms. Minogue, and emphasises how the record was a "holiday" for the band, but the album, which closes with a surprisingly tender rendition of Bob Dylan's "Death Is Not The End" with guests P. J. Harvey and Shane MacGowan, is an entry in the band's discography that demands respect. **SJac**

"[The album] liberated me from writing songs about myself."

Nick Cave, 1998

Track Listing		
01 **Song Of Joy** (Cave)		6:47
▶ 02 **Stagger Lee** (Trad., arr. Cave • Bargeld • Casey • Harvey • Savage • Sclavunos • Wydler)		5:15
▶ 03 **Henry Lee** (Trad., arr. Cave)		3:58
04 **Lovely Creature** (Bargeld • Casey • Cave • Harvey • Wydler)		4:13
▶ 05 **Where The Wild Roses Grow** (Cave)		3:57
▶ 06 **The Curse Of Millhaven** (Cave)		6:55
07 **The Kindness Of Strangers** (Cave)		4:39
08 **Crow Jane** (Casey • Cave)		4:14
▶ 09 **O'Malley's Bar** (Cave)		14:28
10 **Death Is Not The End** (Dylan)		4:27

L.T.J. Bukem
Logical Progression (1996)

Label | Good Looking
Producer | Various
Art Direction | Uncredited
Nationality | UK
Running Time | 140:41

Underworld
Second Toughest In The Infants (1996)

Label | Junior Boys Own
Producer | Underworld
Art Direction | Tomato
Nationality | UK
Running Time | 73:06

It took a major blast to wake the world to the arrival of drum 'n' bass in the mid-1990s, and that blast came in the form of *Timeless*, Goldie's immortal, scene-defining album. As good as *Timeless* was, it was *Logical Progression*, released a year later in 1996, that gave the mainstream a drum 'n' bass recording it could listen to without fear of heart seizure.

Logical Progression and its label, Good Looking Records, were visions of L. T. J. Bukem (a.k.a. Danny Williamson), a champion of the soulful, jazzy, ambient side of drum 'n' bass that contrasted hyper-fast breakbeats with cosmic atmospheres, jazz riffs, and deep basslines. As well as being the leading DJ of this sound, Bukem produced several of the early records that would come to define it. With "Horizons," "Demon's Theme," and "Music," Bukem virtually invented a new, smooth, and languid style of drum 'n' bass. Also on the album are a hand-picked group of stunning drum 'n' bass tracks from producers such as Peshay, Q Project, and PFM, whose "One And Only" and "The Western Tune" (with a haunting vocal from MC Conrad) are fine examples of the emotional force of drum 'n' bass.

As an alternative to the more confrontational and dancefloor-based sounds of that period, *Logical Progression* earned strong sales and near universal acclaim, quickly becoming the preferred soundtrack in hip cafes, hair salons, and fashion stores. **APi**

Karl Hyde and Rick Smith were two seasoned journeymen with myriad haircuts behind them when Darren Emerson joined them in the late 1980s. Being 10 years younger, and a DJ, he sharpened up their dance sensibilities and the three of them began to record detailed works of baroque repetition.

Dubnobasswithmyheadman, because it came first, frequently overshadows 1996's masterly follow-up, *Second Toughest In The Infants*, a UK No. 9 hit. *Second Toughest . . .* is nothing less than the interface of prog rock and beats, representing one of the most mature and frequently surprising records of the 1990s.

Six minutes in, as the opener "Juanita" collapses into "Kiteless," comes the first piece of Underworld magic. For the real meat of the matter, the listener is directed to the polite drum 'n' bass wreckage of "Bannstyle," out of which crawls "Sappys Curry," all treated acoustic guitars and ominous beats. From "Rowla" to the closing "Stagger," Hyde is our commentator, grabbing slivers of conversation and endlessly replaying them at random.

The album was released alongside "Born Slippy (Nuxx)," the single from the movie *Trainspotting* that briefly made them top pop stars, as Hyde's ironic chant of "lager, lager, lager" was appropriated by the very people he was critiquing. "Pearls Girl" is another gem, a high-charting enigma that the group never bettered. **DE**

The Jon Spencer Blues Explosion
Now I Got Worry (1996)

Label | Matador
Producer | Jon Spencer • Jim Waters
Art Direction | Danny Clinch
Nationality | USA
Running Time | 45:10

The Cardigans
First Band
On The Moon (1996)

Label | Mercury
Producer | Tore Johansson
Art Direction | S. Fält • M. Renck
Nationality | Sweden
Running Time | 39:10

To follow his avant-garde punk project Pussy Galore, Jon Spencer celebrated the power and potency of the blues. With previous albums, critics chided Spencer for failing to make music consistent with the band's name. This time, he ensured the blues was number one.

Few albums open in such a confrontational manner. "Skunk" commences with an incandescent scream and keeps kicking with Russell Simins' resonant drums. Spencer's performance takes Elvis' sexuality and gives it a punk inflection. On "Wail," he is part Southern Baptist preacher, part bar-room blues brawler. "2Kindsa Love" seesaws between his screams and Judah Bauer's discordant rhythm guitar assault.

The attempt to live up to the Blues Explosion tag was obvious. "Chicken Dog" pays tribute to Rufus Thomas' R&B novelties "Walkin' The Dog" and "Do The Funky Chicken"—and features Thomas himself on vocals. "We offered him a hundred bucks," reported Simins, "and he came straight down … At 78 he's like the world's oldest teenager." Later, "R. L. Got Soul" continues the band's efforts to raise awareness of enigmatic bluesman R. L. Burnside, who they had backed on his *An Ass Pocket Of Whiskey*.

Jim Waters and Spencer's raw production captures the essence of the band's manic live show. While the album title might suggest Spencer has something to fear, in truth it is the listener who is forced to cower. **PE**

The Cardigans' particular brand of electronic pop on *First Band On The Moon* is not all candy sweetness and champagne fizz. Despite Tore Johansson's slick production, there is a dark cloud inside that silver lining.

"Lovefool," the album's best and most infectious song, is a perfect example of this subversive undercurrent. While guitarist Peter Svensson keeps the mood light and the beat bouncy, Nina Persson's sighing, pillow-soft vocals reveal her as a tormented victim of unrequited love. "I don't care if you really care/As long as you don't go." And the terrific tune "Step On Me" obviously fits that same damaged mold.

There is also a notable dose of heavy metal riffage coursing through this, The Cardigans' third album. Before they founded the band, Svensson and bassist Magnus Sveningsson played in a hardcore metal band, so the album's cover of Black Sabbath's "Iron Man" should come as no surprise. What is surprising is how well it works, with its trip-hop beat and processed guitars.

Other album highlights include "Your New Cuckoo," which counts among its many pleasures a cuckoo bird and a dirty little flute solo. "The Great Divide" starts out as a quiet ballad until the two-minute mark, when a guitar solo and pulsing string section turn it up a notch.

First Band On The Moon enjoyed acclaim and strong sales in America but it exploded to platinum in Japan, where The Cardigans have always hit it big. **RM**

Marilyn Manson | Antichrist Superstar (1996)

Label | Nothing
Producer | Dave "Rave" Ogilvie • Trent Reznor
Art Direction | P. R. Brown
Nationality | USA
Running Time | 77:14

"I'm an anti-hero," declared Manson in 1995. "I'll say it better on the next album." Back then he was destined to sell only to Nine Inch Nails diehards. But, nurtured for two years by Trent Reznor, the one-time protégé was now a pretender to that band's superstar throne.

Satanic imagery, references to numerology, and disturbingly distorted artwork mask a ramshackle production and a rock-star-gets-too-big-for-his-boots concept looted from Pink Floyd's movie *The Wall*. Yet while it lacks the melodic muscle and conceptual sophistication of Manson's later work, *Antichrist Superstar* is a brilliantly bloody slice of raw rock.

The punky immediacy of "1996" and "Irresponsible Hate Anthem" is balanced by the spooky "Cryptorchid" and anthemic title track, while the tribal drums of "The Beautiful People" draw on the Nine Inch Nails camp's adoration of Adam Ant.

The concept reinterprets the biblical tale of the fallen angel (hence "Little Horn"—the Anti-Christ from the book of Daniel) but was designed to elevate Manson from cult hero to icon. "Charles Manson [was] the scapegoat for a whole generation, and I see that tag being placed on me," he told *Penthouse*. The final track even boasts, "God will grovel before me." But there was humility and humor too. His biography details the pathetic nihilism of *Antichrist Superstar*'s making; hence the (backwards) message on "Tourniquet"—"This is my lowest point of vulnerability." Preparing to tour, he announced: "We're off to introduce the world to the ways of Lucifer. If the world hasn't ended by next year then we'll continue to make it end until the end of time." **BM**

Track Listing

01	**Irresponsible Hate Anthem** (Berkowitz•Gacy•Manson•Ramirez•)		4:17
▶ 02	**The Beautiful People** (Manson•Ramirez)		3:38
03	**Dried Up, Tied And Dead To The World** (Manson•Ramirez)		4:15
▶ 04	**Tourniquet** (Berkowitz•Manson•Ramirez)		4:29
05	**Little Horn** (Manson•Ramirez•Reznor)		2:43
06	**Cryptorchid** (Gacy•Manson)		2:44
07	**Deformography** (Berkowitz•Manson•Ramirez)		4:31
08	**Wormboy** (Berkowitz•Manson•Ramirez)		3:56
09	**Mister Superstar** (Manson•Ramirez)		5:04
10	**Angel With The Scabbed Wings** (Gacy•Manson•Ramirez)		3:52
11	**Kinderfeld** (Gacy•Manson•Ramirez)		4:51
▶ 12	**Antichrist Superstar** (Gacy•Manson•Ramirez)		5:14
13	**1996** (Manson•Ramirez)		4:01
14	**Minute Of Decay** (Manson)		4:44
15	**The Reflecting God** (Manson•Ramirez•Reznor)		5:36
16	**Man That You Fear** (Berkowitz•Gacy•Manson•Ramirez)		6:10
17	**Untitled** (Uncredited)		7:09

Fugees | The Score (1996)

Label | Ruffhouse
Producer | Various
Art Direction | Brain
Nationality | USA
Running Time | 73:24

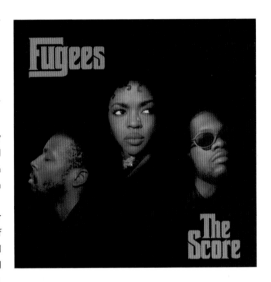

By the mid-1990s, the public were aware of socially conscious hip hop thanks to A Tribe Called Quest and De La Soul. But it would remain a mere afterthought in a genre dominated by gangsta rap—a fleabite on Snoop Dogg's tail—until the Fugees dealt *The Score*.

Dropping their initial thugg style, which never gelled on the 1994 debut *Blunted In Reality*, the trio of Lauryn Hill, Prakazrel Michel, and Wyclef Jean adopted a sunnier disposition with its second release and momentarily made speaking positive, professing hope, and respecting women seem even cooler than gangbanging. "So while you be imitating Al Capone," Hill sings on "Ready Or Not," "I be Nina Simone."

The album, which balances old-school hip hop and smooth R&B, is full of great individual performances. Hill's stunning remake of Roberta Flack's "Killing Me Softly With His Song" provided a breakthrough hit, but Jean is nearly as impressive covering Bob Marley's "No Woman, No Cry." The chemistry between the three MCs—especially between Hill and Jean, who were reportedly in the midst of a covert romance—is absolutely electric on "How Many Mics" and "Fu-Gee-La."

The Score topped the pop charts, sold six million copies and earned the group two Grammys. It also launched three solo careers, with *The Miseducation Of Lauryn Hill* even eclipsing the success, commercially and artistically, of *The Score*.

At the time of this publication, the trio still has not released a follow-up, though with each member's solo career on the downslide, it seems likely to happen. If not, *The Score* will stand as one sweet swan song. **JiH**

Track Listing

01	**Red Intro** (Uncredited)	1:51
▶ 02	**How Many Mics** (Hill•Jean•Michel)	4:28
▶ 03	**Ready Or Not** (Bell•Hart•Hill•Jean•Michel)	3:47
04	**Zealots** (Hill•Jean•Michel)	4:20
05	**The Beast** (Hill•Jean•Michel)	5:37
▶ 06	**Fu-Gee-La** (Hill•Jean•Marie•McGrier•Michel•Remi)	4:20
07	**Family Business** (Forte•Hill•Jean•Michel•Omega)	5:43
▶ 08	**Killing Me Softly With His Song** (Fox•Gimbel)	4:58
09	**The Score** (Desmond•Hill•Jean•Michel)	5:02
10	**The Mask** (Hill•Jean•Michel)	4:50
11	**Cowboys** (Forte•Hill•Jean•Pace 1•Pras Ra Digga•Young Zee)	5:23
▶ 12	**No Woman, No Cry** (Ford•Marley)	4:33
13	**Manifest/Outro** (Hill•Jean•Michel)	5:59
14	**Fu-Gee-La** (Hill•Jean•Marie•McGrier•Michel)	4:24
15	**Fu-Gee-La** (Hill•Jean•Marie•McGrier•Michel)	5:27
16	**Mista Mista** (Jean)	2:42

Ash | 1977 (1996)

Label | Infectious
Producer | Ash • Owen Morris
Art Direction | Brian Cannon • Mark Hamilton
Nationality | UK
Running Time | 62:25

It was the year punk exploded. It was the year *Star Wars* streaked across movie theater screens for the first time. And it was the year two Irish lads from Downpatrick—Tim Wheeler and Mark Hamilton—were born.

Surely one of the finest debuts of the 1990s, *1977* magically mingled the recklessness and raucousness of youthful abandon with a power-pop sensibility that belied the group's age. With drummer Rick McMurray, the Irish trio (second guitarist Charlotte Hatherley would join the following year) condensed and distilled the finest elements of pop, punk, and rock with an irresistible sense of enthusiasm.

Riding the wave of mid-Nineties Britpop on the one hand (particularly evident on string-laden tracks such as "Oh Yeah" and "Gone The Dream"), but at the same time much more individualistic than that, *1977* famously opens with the roaring crescendo of a *Star Wars* TIE Fighter. The kinetic and frantic first single, "Kung Fu"—Wheeler's homage to Jackie Chan—is surely the song every non-sports-inclined teenager dreams of writing. "Girl From Mars," the band's first UK Top Twenty hit, and "Angel Interceptor" perfectly encapsulate the amped-up, intergalactic pop vibe of this debut.

With an almost naive appetite for excess and youthful exuberance (see the almost unmentionable hidden track, the aptly named "Sick Party"), *1977* both heralded the arrival of one of the premier pop-rock groups of the coming decade and defined the musical experience of a micro-generation of youth. If you were a teenager when *1977* was released, you probably still feel like you own a small part of that story. **DZ**

> "We were only 19 ...! Most of our contemporaries ... have completely disappeared."
>
> Tim Wheeler, 2002

Track Listing

01	**Lose Control** (Hamilton • Wheeler)		3:37
▶ 02	**Goldfinger** (Wheeler)		4:31
▶ 03	**Girl From Mars** (Wheeler)		3:24
04	**I'd Give You Anything** (Wheeler)		4:37
05	**Gone The Dream** (Wheeler)		3:29
▶ 06	**Kung Fu** (Wheeler)		2:17
▶ 07	**Oh Yeah** (Wheeler)		4:45
08	**Let It Flow** (Wheeler)		4:46
09	**Innocent Smile** (Hamilton)		5:47
▶ 10	**Angel Interceptor** (McMurray • Wheeler)		4:04
11	**Lost In You** (Wheeler)		4:19
12	**Darkside Lightside** (Wheeler)		16:49

Belle And Sebastian | If You're Feeling Sinister (1996)

Label | Jeepster
Producer | Tony Doogan
Art Direction | Belle And Sebastian
Nationality | UK
Running Time | 41:07

Having recorded their debut, "*Tigermilk*," as part of a high-school, grant-funded project, Scotland's Belle And Sebastian found themselves in an enviable position. Lauded yet not deified, they maintained an air of mystery and intrigue (particularly surrounding ex-boxer Stuart Murdoch, the chief vocalist) that lent their songs an elusive charm. Even their appearance was kept under wraps—they often recruited friends to appear in press shots and on record covers (as here).

Throughout the album, their comparatively recent schooldays are in evidence—from the sporty kids in the opening track, and the people "kissing just for practice" in "Seeing Other People," to the uncertainty of youth that manifests itself in the title track.

"Seeing Other People" is a classic, with a wonky rhythm and piano line, and a narrative precisely pinpointing universal relationship themes. But to this author's ears, the star track is the whimsical and bitter "Get Me Away From Here I'm Dying," which typifies the Belle And Sebastian style of the time: a simple folk grounding, rich lyrical conceits, and a large dollop of winsome sarcasm. Also worth listening out for is the breezy summer frolicking of "Mayfly," a track so content with itself that it makes the worries expressed elsewhere all the more marked.

Belle And Sebastian were at the peak of their mythological powers. The press were keen to track them down, but they steadfastly refused to cooperate. They were a cottage industry making records for the faithful while everyone else caught up. Listening to this album today, you almost feel part of the gang. **JK**

> "I will feel a lot better when people are buying ... the songs."
>
> Stuart Murdoch, 1996

Track Listing

▶ 01	**The Stars Of Track And Field** (Belle And Sebastian)		4:48
▶ 02	**Seeing Other People** (Belle And Sebastian)		3:38
03	**Me And The Major** (Belle And Sebastian)		3:51
04	**Like Dylan In The Movies** (Belle And Sebastian)		4:14
05	**The Fox In The Snow** (Belle And Sebastian)		4:11
▶ 06	**Get Me Away From Here, I'm Dying** (Belle And Sebastian)		3:25
▶ 07	**If You're Feeling Sinister** (Belle And Sebastian)		5:21
▶ 08	**Mayfly** (Belle And Sebastian)		3:42
09	**The Boy Done Wrong Again** (Belle And Sebastian)		4:17
10	**Judy And The Dream Of Horses** (Belle And Sebastian)		3:40

Blur | **Blur** (1997)

Label | Food
Producer | Blur • Stephen Street
Art Direction | Yacht Associates
Nationality | UK
Running Time | 60:10

Blur's cover depicts a patient being rushed into the emergency ward—an admirably candid summation of the band's critical status before this album. "Country House" may have pipped Oasis' "Roll With It" to the UK No. 1 spot in the summer of 1995, but the over-thought *The Great Escape* was left in the dust by *(What's The Story) Morning Glory?*. Within a year, Britpop was dead.

Salvation came from a source they had spent most of their career railing against: America. If their previous three albums (the so-called "English trilogy") were a rejection of American rock, then what else to do but embrace it? Legend has it that this turnaround was thanks to Graham Coxon. The album certainly belongs to his noisy guitars—notably on "Song 2," which turned out to be the band's surprise breakthrough in America. Coxon also turns in the wonderful "You're So Great," his first Blur song. It is impossible to miss the influence of Pavement, Sonic Youth, Dinosaur Jr., or even Black Flag here. Damon Albarn too fell under Pavement's spell, and went on to befriend Stephen Malkmus.

Blur's music had always had its eccentricities. It is just that now these were in the foreground, thanks to producer Steven Street's uncharacteristically lo-fi recording methods. But this album also contains some of the best songs Damon Albarn has ever written. The fractured "Strange News From Another Star" and "Country Sad Ballad Man" are a universe away from the Cockney knees-up of *Parklife*. Meanwhile, the closing "Essex Dogs" proved to be the band's definitive statement on the Englishness they had spent three albums trying to capture. Truly a great escape. **MBe**

Track Listing

▶ 01	**Beetlebum** (Albarn•Coxon•James•Rowntree)	5:05
▶ 02	**Song 2** (Albarn)	2:01
03	**Country Sad Ballad Man** (Albarn•Coxon•James•Rowntree)	4:50
04	**M.O.R.** (Albarn•Coxon•James•Rowntree)	3:27
▶ 05	**On Your Own** (Albarn•Coxon•James•Rowntree)	4:26
06	**Theme From Retro** (Albarn•Coxon•James•Rowntree)	3:37
▶ 07	**You're So Great** (Coxon)	3:36
08	**Death Of A Party** (Albarn•Coxon•James•Rowntree)	4:33
09	**Chinese Bombs** (Albarn•Coxon•James•Rowntree)	1:24
10	**I'm Just A Killer For Your Love** (Albarn•Coxon•James•Rowntree)	4:11
11	**Look Inside America** (Albarn•Coxon•James•Rowntree)	3:50
▶ 12	**Strange News From Another Star** (Albarn•Coxon•James•Rowntree)	4:02
13	**Movin' On** (Albarn•Coxon•James•Rowntree)	3:44
14	**Essex Dogs** (Albarn•Coxon•James•Rowntree)	11:24

Radiohead | OK Computer (1997)

Label | Parlophone
Producer | Nigel Godrich • Radiohead
Art Direction | S. Donwood • The White Chocolate Farm
Nationality | UK
Running Time | 53:21

Synthesizing The Smiths with Queen sounds ill-advised. Happily, Radiohead's idiosyncratic influences were matched by their talent, and their third album vaulted even further than its predecessor, *The Bends*.

Success—bubbling since their early hit "Creep"—did not make 'Head head Thom Yorke a happy bunny; the cheeriest song here ("Airbag") is about "the wonderful, positive emotion you feel when you've just failed to have an accident." Elsewhere he rages against "business and bullshit" ("Electioneering"), "being trapped" ("Let Down"), and "the cupboard monster" ("Climbing Up The Walls"). Most graphic is "Paranoid Android," whose deceptively lighthearted title comes from the book *The Hitch Hiker's Guide To The Galaxy*. The words—inspired by coke-crazed socialites—are a bloodcurdling evocation of "utter fucking chaos."

Lyrical horror is mitigated by musical beauty. "Subterranean Homesick Alien" is appropriately spacey, "No Surprises" is a glockenspiel-driven delicacy, and "Let Down" is as lovely as you would expect of a song recorded in Jane Seymour's ballroom, while "Lucky" and "The Tourist" are pleasantly Pink Floydian.

Sonic surprises abound: the DJ Shadow-inspired drum loop of "Airbag," the "Happiness Is A Warm Gun"-styled epic "Paranoid Android," and the Stephen Hawking-esque "Fitter Happier" (actually an Apple Mac programmed by Yorke).

Complete with unsettlingly indistinct artwork, *OK Computer* topped transatlantic charts and was—in the band's view—overrated. But it still sounds as ambitious and ravishing as it did in 1997. **BM**

Track Listing

01	**Airbag** (C. Greenwood • J. Greenwood O'Brien • Selway • Yorke)	4:44
▶ 02	**Paranoid Android** (C. Greenwood J. Greenwood • O'Brien • Selway • Yorke)	6:23
03	**Subterranean Homesick Alien** (C. Greenwood J. Greenwood • O'Brien • Selway • Yorke)	4:27
04	**Exit Music (For A Film)** (C. Greenwood J. Greenwood • O'Brien • Selway • Yorke)	4:24
05	**Let Down** (C. Greenwood • J. Greenwood O'Brien • Selway • Yorke)	4:59
▶ 06	**Karma Police** (C. Greenwood • J. Greenwood O'Brien • Selway • Yorke)	4:21
07	**Fitter Happier** (C. Greenwood • J. Greenwood O'Brien • Selway • Yorke)	1:57
08	**Electioneering** (C. Greenwood • J. Greenwood O'Brien • Selway • Yorke)	3:50
09	**Climbing Up The Walls** (C. Greenwood J. Greenwood • O'Brien • Selway • Yorke)	4:45
▶ 10	**No Surprises** (C. Greenwood • J. Greenwood O'Brien • Selway • Yorke)	3:48
11	**Lucky** (C. Greenwood • J. Greenwood • O'Brien Selway • Yorke)	4:19
12	**The Tourist** (C. Greenwood • J. Greenwood O'Brien • Selway • Yorke)	5:24

Finley Quaye | Maverick A Strike (1997)

Label | Epic
Producer | Various
Art Direction | Uncredited
Nationality | Ghana / UK
Running Time | 51:36

Maverick A Strike provided the soundtrack to the summer of 1997, earned Finley Quaye comparisons to Bob Marley, and went on to be certified triple platinum, going Top Three in the UK.

Quaye goes some way to live up to the Marley comparison, as the album skips through a variety of styles, with his lilting voice and cool individuality keeping it all together. In the sleevenotes he namechecks everyone from Rolf Harris and naturalist David Attenborough through botanist David Bellamy and astronomer Patrick Moore to Haile Selassie and Hibernian Football Club. There is a bit of everything here—from the skanking dub of "Ultra Stimulation," "The Way Of The Explosive," and "Red Rolled And Seen," to the simple soul sounds of "Even After All" (UK No. 10) and the acid rock of "I Need A Lover."

The first single, "Sunday Shining," is an effervescent reworking of Bob Marley's "Sun Is Shining" complete with slide guitar and funky horns. "Ride On And Turn The People On," with its driving bass and Hammond® organ groove, is guaranteed to get you up and dancing, with Quaye's off-the-wall lyrics adding to the party mood. "Your Love Gets Sweeter" provides a rootsy message of pure love.

After the album's success, Quaye was criticized for living the rock star dream—long, wild nights; being "difficult" in interviews; and becoming embroiled in a feud with trip-hop god Tricky (who, it is rumored, is his nephew). But none of that dims the sheer delight of *Maverick A Strike*—the perfect album for a hazy, lazy afternoon spent chilling in the park. **DC**

> "There was a real shortage of strong songwriters around."
>
> Finley Quaye, 2005

Track Listing

01	**Ultra Stimulation** (Quaye)	3:52
02	**It's Great When We're Together** (Quaye)	3:39
▶ 03	**Sunday Shining** (Marley·Quaye)	3:42
▶ 04	**Even After All** (Quaye)	3:54
▶ 05	**Ride On And Turn The People On** (Quaye)	3:47
06	**The Way Of The Explosive** (Quaye)	4:44
▶ 07	**Your Love Gets Sweeter** (Quaye)	3:12
08	**Supreme I Preme** (Quaye)	4:59
09	**Sweet And Loving Man** (Quaye)	3:21
10	**Red Rolled And Seen** (Quaye)	4:07
11	**Falling** (Propfh·Quaye)	3:16
▶ 12	**I Need A Lover** (Quaye)	4:04
13	**Maverick A Strike** (Quaye)	4:59

Missy Misdemeanor Elliott | Supa Dupa Fly (1997)

Label | East West
Producer | Timbaland
Art Direction | Starr Foundation
Nationality | USA
Running Time | 60:06

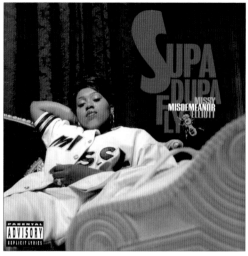

Missy Elliott is almost unquestionably the most important female hip-hop artist of the last 25 years. And this, her debut album, still stands as one of the most invigorating in the genre.

After writing a number of hits for ill-fated R&B star Aaliyah (who guests here), Elliott roped in long-time collaborator Timbaland to work on *Supa Dupa Fly*. She provided a welcome antidote to the often casually misogynist attitudes of mainstream rap, emerging as a defiantly populist artist and a consummate hit-maker without ever being anything less than ferociously forward-looking. Elliott's skill never really lay in putting down technically complex rhymes, but rather in spitting often hilarious freeform rants about sex, relationships, and smoking weed. In fact, her real talents lie in singing, which she employs on about 40 percent of this album.

"The Rain (Supa Dupa Fly)," the biggest hit featured here (aided by heavy MTV rotation of Hype Williams' accompanying video), demonstrates precisely why Timbaland's contributions are so crucial. The track marries a stone-cold millennial R&B pulse with sparse and forward-looking electronic production that upped the ante for all hip-hop producers, The Neptunes included. "Pass Da Blunt" rescues The Mighty Diamonds' "Pass The Kutchie" back from Musical Youth's faux-innocent interpretation and revives it as a stoner anthem. "Beep Me 911" and "They Don't Wanna Fuck Wit Me" amp up the clipped and futurist end of things, while "Izzy Izzy Ahh" prove she is equally at home on a ganja-infused block-party jam. **JDo**

Track Listing

01	**Busta's Intro** (Smith)	1:53
▶ 02	**Hit 'Em Wit Da Hee** (Elliott•Jones•Mosley)	4:19
▶ 03	**Sock It 2 Me** (Bell•Elliott•Harris•Hart•Mosley)	4:17
▶ 04	**The Rain (Supa Dupa Fly)** (Bryant•Elliott•Miller)	4:11
▶ 05	**Beep Me 911** (Barcliff•Elliott•Mosley)	4:57
▶ 06	**They Don't Wanna Fuck Wit Me** (Elliott•Mosley)	3:18
▶ 07	**Pass Da Blunt** (Bennett•Brown Elliott•Fergusson•Lyn•Mittoo•Mosley Sibbles•Simpson)	3:17
08	**Bite Our Style (Interlude)** (Elliott•Mosley)	0:43
09	**Friendly Skies** (Elliott•Mosley)	4:59
10	**Best Friends** (Elliott•Mosley)	4:07
▶ 11	**Don't Be Commin' (In My Face)** (Elliott•Mosley)	4:11
▶ 12	**Izzy Izzy Ahh** (Elliott•Mosley)	3:54
13	**Why You Hurt Me** (Elliott•Floyd•Mosley)	4:31
14	**I'm Talkin'** (Elliott•Mosley)	5:02
15	**Gettaway** (Elliott•Mosley•Selden•Siplin)	4:25
16	**Busta's Outro** (Mosley•Smith)	1:38
17	**Missy's Finale** (Elliott)	0:24

The Chemical Brothers | Dig Your Own Hole (1997)

Label | Virgin
Producer | The Chemical Brothers
Art Direction | Negativespace
Nationality | UK
Running Time | 63:19

In 1997, the Heavenly Social at London's Turnmills was a very exciting (and sweaty) place to be. Every Saturday, the club shook to acid house, electro, techno, hip hop, and more from the likes of Jon Carter, Richard Fearless, Dave Clarke, and Andrew Weatherall. The night's star attraction, however, was Tom Rowlands and Ed Simons—The Chemical Brothers.

Their debut *Exit Planet Dust* had caused plenty of excitement, but *Dig Your Own Hole* was where the Chemicals really got serious. The no-nonsense artwork belied the more heads-down approach within; many tracks had been road-tested in the haze of the club. "Block Rockin' Beats" explodes into life with a Schooly D sample and thunderous beats, while "Elektrobank," "Don't Stop The Rock," and "It Doesn't Matter" re-create the sensory overload of their electro-acid house DJ sets.

"Setting Sun" is all buzzsaw shrieks, Noel Gallagher's distorted drawl, and Beatles beat (wits dubbed it "Tomorrow Never Noels"); "Lost In The K-Hole," a wonky slab of horse tranquilizer dementia. "The Private Psychedelic Reel" is a jaw-dropping psychedelic techno epic, a surging series of peaks and troughs.

Along with Orbital, Prodigy, and Underworld, the Chemicals were one of the few Nineties techno acts with stadium-filling capability. Likewise, they were one of the few able to deliver a "dance" album that was not simply a series of variations on a kick-drum sound. Cross-pollinating genres as they went, and inventing a few of their own along the way, the duo's *Dig Your Own Hole* remains a monolithic testament to the transcendent power of Nineties rave culture. **RS**

> "We record it ... play it live, look at the reactions we get."
>
> Ed Simons, 1997

Track Listing

▶	01	**Block Rockin' Beats** (Rowlands·Simons·Weaver)	5:13
	02	**Dig Your Own Hole** (Rowlands·Simons)	5:27
▶	03	**Elektrobank** (Rowlands·Simons)	8:18
	04	**Piku** (Rowlands·Simons)	4:55
▶	05	**Setting Sun** (Gallagher·Rowlands·Simons)	5:28
	06	**It Doesn't Matter** (Conly·Emelin·Ford King·Rowlands·Simons·Slye)	6:14
	07	**Don't Stop The Rock** (Rowlands·Simons)	4:49
	08	**Get Up On It Like This** (Jones·Rowlands·Simons)	2:46
▶	09	**Lost In The K-Hole** (Rowlands·Simons)	3:52
	10	**Where Do I Begin?** (Rowlands·Simons)	6:56
▶	11	**The Private Psychedelic Reel** (Donahue·Rowlands·Simons)	9:21

Primal Scream | Vanishing Point (1997)

Label | Creation
Producer | B. Lynch • Primal Scream • A. Weatherall
Art Direction | Intro
Nationality | UK
Running Time | 53:31

Primal Scream remain true chameleons of rock. Latterly besotted with the dominance of electro, in their history they have been jingly indie fans, blissed-out drug-induced euphoria seekers, and then bona fide rock 'n' roll heroes. But *Vanishing Point* found them unsure of their sound—a mixture of genres and dubious darker influences that fused together for a rollercoaster ride—at times nightmarish, at others ecstatic in the truest sense.

Primal Scream made both the peaks and the troughs scintillating. Lead single "Kowalski," named after the lead character in an obscure 1970s car-chase movie (which the album was named after, and would take much influence from for its cover artwork), is a bubbling mess of bass and beats, with Bobby Gillespie's sinister whisper laced throughout. "If They Move, Kill 'Em" is a scorching two-minute stab at the senses. High pitched and beatific, and a destructive force in the live arena. Heck, they even cover Motörhead, as if to prove the point. But there are softer moments too. "Star," featuring reggae legend Augustus Pablo on melodica, is a dub plea for universal understanding much more in keeping with their *Screamadelica* ideals. "Out Of The Void" offers up a rare moment of regret—the dazed-sounding Gillespie offers "If I was a child again, I'd be holy and not insane."

If *Screamadelica* and *Give Out But Don't Give Up* were "high" albums, then *Vanishing Point* brings the listener crashing back down to earth. That it manages to do this without causing so much as a bruise is largely due to the Scream team's unbreakable sound and ethos. **JK**

> ## "*Vanishing Point* sounds like a junkyard breaking down ... It's punk rock for 1997."
>
> Bobby Gillespie, 1997

Track Listing

01	**Burning Wheel** (Duffy•Gillespie•Innes•Young)	7:06
02	**Get Duffy** (Duffy•Gillespie•Innes•Young)	4:09
▶ 03	**Kowalski** (Duffy•Gillespie•Innes•Mounfield•Young)	5:50
04	**Star** (Duffy•Gillespie•Innes•Young)	4:24
▶ 05	**If They Move, Kill 'Em** (Duffy•Gillespie•Innes•Young)	3:01
▶ 06	**Out Of The Void** (Duffy•Gillespie•Innes•Young)	3:59
07	**Stuka** (Duffy•Gillespie•Innes•Young)	5:36
08	**Medication** (Duffy•Gillespie•Innes•Young)	3:52
09	**Motörhead** (Kilmister)	3:38
▶ 10	**Trainspotting** (Duffy•Gillespie•Innes•Young)	8:07
11	**Long Life** (Duffy•Gillespie•Innes•Young)	3:49

Robert Wyatt | Shleep (1997)

Label | Hannibal
Producer | Alfreda Benge • Brian Eno • Robert Wyatt
Art Direction | Alfreda Benge • Phil Smee
Nationality | UK
Running Time | 53:38

Let's face it: in all seriousness, there are almost no performers who can make a record 30 years into their music career as full of ideas, tunes, imagination, wit, and what—for want of a better word—we could call "edginess" as Robert Wyatt's *Shleep*.

What is Wyatt's secret? Well, it might be that—like other Sixties relics who can still cut it, such as Pip Proud, Mayo Thompson, or Michael Hurley—he was a little bit outside the music business. Few veteran musicians are so beloved and admired by such a broad range of their peers. Who else could get Brian Eno and Paul Weller both working on their album at the same time—with ex-Roxy Music star Phil Manzanera, and jazz musicians Philip Catherine (guitar) and Evan Parker (saxophone)?

Wyatt's contemporary Roger Waters produced a concept album about one man's night of dreams; Wyatt commented that his lyrics "mostly struggled onto paper from endless weeks of fevered insomnia, which left me with an almost insatiable craving for the abyssal ooze of deep, deep sleep." The Dylan parody/homage "Blues In Bob Minor" would not work anywhere else in the world except right here. "Free Will And Testament," "Maryan," and "Heaps Of Shleeps" are classic Wyatt: adorable tunes, singing that is both cosily familiar and somehow slightly alienating; words that, likewise, evoke the very ordinary and the somehow unnervingly harrowing at the same time.

An often unsung (except, perhaps, in "The Duchess") hero of Wyatt's career is his wife Alfreda Benge, who contributes marvelous lyrics, stupendous cover art, and production here. **DN**

> "There are notes and intervals and chords and rhythms. Some I like, some I don't."
>
> Robert Wyatt, 1996

Track Listing

01	**Heaps Of Shleeps** (Benge • Wyatt, arr. Eno)	4:56
▶ 02	**The Duchess** (Wyatt)	4:18
03	**Maryan** (Catherine • Wyatt)	6:11
04	**Was A Friend** (Hopper • Wyatt)	6:11
05	**Free Will And Testament** (Kramer • Wyatt)	4:12
06	**September The Ninth** (Benge • Wyatt)	6:40
07	**Alien** (Benge • Wyatt)	6:47
08	**Out Of Season** (Benge • Wyatt)	2:31
▶ 09	**A Sunday In Madrid** (Benge • Wyatt)	4:41
10	**Blues In Bob Minor** (Wyatt)	5:46
11	**The Whole Point Of No Return** (Weller)	1:25

David Holmes | Let's Get Killed (1997)

Label | Go! Beat
Producer | Various
Art Direction | Glenn Leyburn
Nationality | UK
Running Time | 59:45

Winner of a 1997 *Muzik Magazine* award for his *Essential Mix* collection—an eclectic assortment of Jimi Hendrix, Northern soul, and movie scores—David Holmes' second album explored his continuing fascination with soundtrack music. Alongside co-conspirators Keith Tenniswood (Two Lone Swordsmen), Jagz Kooner, and Gary Burns (both of Sabres Of Paradise and The Aloof), Belfast's Holmes set out to document New York's seedy underbelly. By marrying snippets of conversation between tramps, hookers, pimps, and narcotics dealers to a varied selection of dub, ambient techno, jazz-funk, and Latin styles, Holmes created an intense and paranoid soundtrack to the "city that never sleeps," one even more harrowing than the twilight London underworld Sabres of Paradise achieved on 1994's *Haunted Dancehall*.

"Initially we thought it'd be a piece of piss ... "

David Holmes, 1997

   Among the album's many highlights are the jerky techno of "My Mate Paul" and the percussion-heavy "Head Rush On Lafayette." "Rodney Yates" utilizes a laid-back jazz feel married to lush strings, while "Slashers Revenge" combines a spacious dub bassline with an ominous sense of dread. Holmes also attempts to rewrite the James Bond theme among "Radio 7"'s frenetic breakbeats.

   Unsurprisingly, Holmes and co. provoked some hostility from those who they recorded. Yet it paid off: its dynamic re-creation of the fear and excitement of the big city saw the record achieve "Best Irish Album" at the Irish Rock Awards. Holmes soon found himself in demand for soundtracks, and went on to provide the scores for *Out Of Sight* and *Ocean's Eleven*. **CSh**

Track Listing

01	Listen (Holmes)	0:49
▶ 02	My Mate Paul (Holmes)	5:29
03	Let's Get Killed (Holmes)	7:28
04	Gritty Shaker (Holmes)	6:40
▶ 05	Head Rush On Lafayette (Holmes)	1:20
▶ 06	Rodney Yates (Holmes)	6:24
07	Radio 7 (Norman)	5:49
08	The Parcus & Madder Show (Holmes)	0:51
▶ 09	Slasher's Revenge (Holmes)	4:46
10	Freaknik (Holmes)	6:45
11	Caddell Returns (Holmes)	5:42
12	Don't Die Just Yet (Gainsbourg)	6:43
13	For You (Holmes)	0:59

Sleater-Kinney | Dig Me Out (1997)

Label | Kill Rock Stars
Producer | John Goodmanson
Art Direction | John Clark
Nationality | USA
Running Time | 36:24

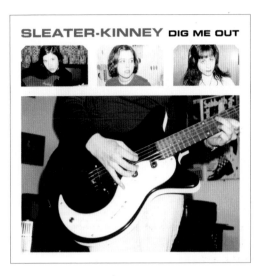

Sleater-Kinney come from a long line of punk bands from the Pacific North-West of the United States. Their gender and fondness for fem-punks Bikini Kill led them to be tagged with the riot grrrl label, but that is only part of the picture. *Sleater-Kinney* (1995) and *Call The Doctor* (1996) showed a band laden with enthusiasm, but clamoring for respect beyond a devoted cult.

Released on the proudly punk Kill Rock Stars label in 1997, *Dig Me Out* is a perfect blend of ideology, attitude, and wicked riffs. It is built around Corin Tucker and Carrie Brownstein's counterpoint vocals (particularly Tucker's captivating falsetto holler) and sparkling guitar duels (there is no bassist). Brownstein's opening guitar on the title track, punctuated by Janet Weiss' snare-drum spark, gives an immediate rush of energy.

Unlike their Kill Rock Stars antecedents—notably Bikini Kill—Sleater-Kinney are political but not confrontational. The bubblegum-sweet chorus of "Little Babies" illustrates their delicate balance of punk, politics, and pop, while the rollicking "It's Enough" juxtaposes the two-minute pop song formula with lyrics that simultaneously critique and celebrate (male) critics' and fans' fascination with girl bands.

"Not What You Want" creates an irresistible crescendo of noise; in vivid contrast, "Buy Her Candy" is a soulful ballad with subtle political commentary.

"Explosive musical chemistry that mixes infectious melodicism with innovative punk deconstruction," marveled *Rolling Stone*. Brownstein was more measured: "The excellence of *Dig Me Out* is not so bewildering to me. We've really worked hard." **PE**

> "It feels good to make a record that is a little bit more ... alive."
>
> Carrie Brownstein, 1997

Track Listing

▶	01	**Dig Me Out** (Sleater-Kinney)	2:40
	02	**One More Hour** (Sleater-Kinney)	3:19
▶	03	**Turn It On** (Sleater-Kinney)	2:47
	04	**Drama You've Been Craving** (Sleater-Kinney)	2:08
	05	**Heart Factory** (Sleater-Kinney)	3:54
	06	**Words And Guitar** (Sleater-Kinney)	2:21
	07	**It's Enough** (Sleater-Kinney)	1:46
▶	08	**Little Babies** (Sleater-Kinney)	2:22
	09	**Not What You Want** (Sleater-Kinney)	3:17
	10	**Buy Her Candy** (Sleater-Kinney)	2:02
	11	**Things You Say** (Sleater-Kinney)	2:56
	12	**Dance Song '97** (Sleater-Kinney)	2:49
	13	**Jenny** (Sleater-Kinney)	4:03

Prodigy | The Fat Of The Land (1997)

Label | XL
Producer | Liam Howlett
Art Direction | Liam Howlett • Alex Jenkins
Nationality | UK
Running Time | 56:19

Inciting arson and frightening children are not tried-and-true ways of boosting album sales. But the booming "Firestarter"—with its provocative lyric and unsettling video—kick-started *The Fat Of The Land*. Prodigy's public sent the album to No. 1 on both sides of the Atlantic; in America alone, it went double platinum before the year was out.

Prodigy penetrated popular culture with—courtesy of beat brainiac Liam Howlett—an amazing montage of guitars, samples, and electronica. There was hip hop too: "Diesel Power" showcases Kool Keith, a.k.a. Dr. Octagon, of the Ultramagnetic MCs, while "Funky Shit" takes its title from "Root Down" by the Beastie Boys. Elsewhere the album ranges from Eastern-inspired trance to a cover of L7's punk-rockin' "Fuel My Fire," featuring dynamic drumming sampled from the Cosmic Psychos' song "Lost Cause."

Courting controversy from the outset—"the fat of the land" is a quote from Nazi Hermann Goering—Prodigy upped the outrage when they released as a single the vicious "Smack My Bitch Up" (whose samples ranged from Andy Williams to Kool And The Gang). The National Organization for Women protested that it glorified violence against women, as did fellow artists Chumbawamba and Moby. A sex, drugs, and vomit-spattered video (with a neat twist) added to the furore.

These shock tactics proved short term—"Smack My Bitch Up" even sneaked onto the soundtrack of *Charlie's Angels*. But they confirmed Prodigy were, as "Firestarter" declared, "punkin' instigators." *The Fat Of The Land* complements every collection. **MBo**

> "Our outlook is: Here we are, love us or hate us. If that's punk then we're punks."

Liam Howlett, 1997

Track Listing

▶ 01	**Smack My Bitch Up** (Howlett • Miller • Randolph • Smith • Thornton)	5:42
▶ 02	**Breathe** (Flint • Howlett • Palmer)	5:34
03	**Diesel Power** (Howlett • Thornton)	4:17
04	**Funky Shit** (Diamond • Horovitz • Howlett • Yauch)	5:16
05	**Serial Thrilla** (Arran • Dyer • Flint • Howlett)	5:11
06	**Mindfields** (Howlett)	5:39
07	**Narayan** (Howlett • Mills)	9:06
▶ 08	**Firestarter** (Deal • Dudley • Flint • Horn Howlett • Jeczalik • Langan • Morley)	4:40
09	**Climbatize** (Howlett • Taylor)	6:36
10	**Fuel My Fire** (James • Knight • Sparks • Walsh)	4:18

Buena Vista Social Club
Buena Vista Social Club (1997)

Label | World Circuit
Producer | Ry Cooder
Art Direction | The Team
Nationality | Cuba • USA
Running Time | 59:43

You could not make it up: a six-million-selling Cuban album that topped the German charts and bust sanctions so the musicians could play Carnegie Hall—although you cannot buy it in Havana, where its pre-revolutionary son style is seen as old hat. Not only that, it was an accident: the plan had been to take some Malian musicians to Cuba to collaborate, but red tape meant no Africans, and studio time had already been booked. Ry Cooder asked Juan de Marcos González, credited as "A&R consultant," if he knew any musicians who might be available.

González searched Havana for survivors from Cuba's golden age, finding the singers Ibrahim Ferrer and Omara Portuondo, the pianist Rubén González, the guitarist Compay Segundo, and the bass player Cachaito López. He also put together a big band, the Afro Cuban All Stars, who recorded their own album in a burst of unhindered creativity. González was asked to suggest tunes he would like to record. He turned up the next day with them all written on a till roll. With three albums in the can, the team went their separate ways.

Although many have since decided that World Circuit knew exactly what it was doing all along, nobody could have predicted what would happen. The musicians played a handful of shows, but things snowballed without their participation. People fell for the story—retired musicians make a comeback to save music on the brink of extinction—and flocked to the stores. Was it true? Who cares? **DH**

Track Listing

▶ 01	**Chan Chan** (Repilado)	4:16
02	**De Camino A La Vereda** (Ferrer)	5:03
03	**El Cuarto De Tula** (Marquetti)	7:27
04	**Pueblo Nuevo** (González)	6:05
▶ 05	**Dos Gardenias** (Carillo)	3:02
06	**¿Y Tú Qué Has Hecho?** (Delfin)	3:13
▶ 07	**Veinte Años** (Vera)	3:29
08	**El Carretero** (Portabales)	3:28
09	**Candela** (Oramas)	5:27
10	**Amor De Loca Juventud** (Ortiz)	3:21
11	**Orgullecida** (Silveira)	3:18
12	**Murmullo** (Chepin)	3:50
▶ 13	**Buena Vista Social Club** (López)	4:50
▶ 14	**La Bayamesa** (Garay)	2:54

Nick Cave And The Bad Seeds
The Boatman's Call (1997)

Label | Mute
Producer | Nick Cave And The Bad Seeds • Flood
Art Direction | Anton Corbijn
Nationality | Australia
Running Time | 52:07

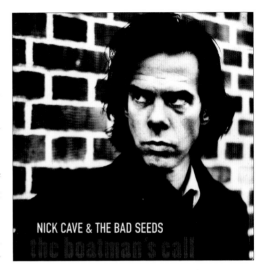

NICK CAVE & THE BAD SEEDS
the boatman's call

Although a morbidly enjoyable romp, 1996's *Murder Ballads* had been a holiday for Cave, and with *The Boatman's Call* he returned to his searingly personal approach to making music. The monochrome visage of Cave that adorns the cover lets you know this one is not going to be played for laughs, and he delivers with 12 beautifully crafted songs of heartache and doubt.

The Boatman's Call is widely feted as one of rock's great break-up albums, and said to be inspired by Cave's entanglement and subsequent split with the enchanting P. J. Harvey—whom "West Country Girl" and "Black Hair" appear to be about. Out of respect for his hurt, the Bad Seeds seem to retire to the background, their music but the most delicate soundtrack.

There is no great showboating to the lyrics of this album, just an immense sense of loss Cave articulates all too well. The world of *The Boatman's Call* is described in language that is brittle, and is a place where hope is scant—"where everybody fucks everybody else over," as Cave bemoans in "Far From Me." The titles of songs such as "People Ain't No Good" give you a fair idea where Cave's red raw heart is coming from, and it is not a pretty place. Indeed, the pain of lost love is almost conflated with that ultimate break-up, death, on "Brompton Oratory." It takes a few listens to realize Cave is mourning someone who is dead to him metaphysically—but who might as well be physically so too, for all his fine words will change things.

This is the sound of a man's heart breaking. **SJac**

> ## "Words endure, flesh does not."
> Nick Cave, 2001

Track Listing

01	**Into My Arms** (Cave)	4:15
02	**Lime-Tree Arbour** (Cave)	2:56
03	**People Ain't No Good** (Cave)	5:42
▶ 04	**Brompton Oratory** (Cave)	4:06
05	**There Is A Kingdom** (Cave)	4:52
▶ 06	**(Are You) The One That I've Been Waiting For?** (Cave)	4:05
07	**Where Do We Go Now But Nowhere?** (Cave)	5:46
08	**West Country Girl** (Cave)	2:45
09	**Black Hair** (Cave)	4:14
10	**Idiot Prayer** (Cave)	4:21
▶ 11	**Far From Me** (Cave)	5:33
12	**Green Eyes** (Cave)	3:32

The Divine Comedy
A Short Album About Love (1997)

Label | Setanta
Producer | The Divine Comedy • Jon Jacobs
Art Direction | Rob Crane
Nationality | Ireland • UK
Running Time | 31:56

SETANTA 036

The image of a super-literate, lady-chasing dandy, debuted on 1994's *Promenade* and milked on *Casanova* two years later, granted Neil Hannon a spell in the UK spotlight. On *A Short Album About Love*—released, inevitably, in Valentine's week—he played it largely straight. The record pinched its title from Polish director Krzysztof Kieslowki (substitute "Film" for "Album" for the name of his 1988 movie), but it fits.

The seven songs were recorded live with a 26-strong orchestra, post-soundcheck but pre-show, during a short run at the Shepherd's Bush Empire in late 1996 (a slightly meek Hannon admitted in a radio interview that he had later re-recorded the vocals). Aside from "If . . . ," which strings together a series of unlikely hypotheticals to affectionate though sometimes throwaway effect ("If you were a horse/I'd clean the crap out of your stable"), the record is joke-free, and much the better for it. Hannon had, literally, found his voice: rich, expressive, occasionally even Walkerian. And he had found both the arranger (Joby Talbot) and the songs to go with it, whether confident ("I'm All You Need") or beseeching ("Timewatching").

Fin De Siècle followed in 1998, a terrific record let down by two tracks that played up the group's frivolous side—inevitably, "Generation Sex" and "National Express" were two of the three chosen singles, only reinforcing Hannon's image as a singer with his tongue glued to his cheek. When the wonderful *Regeneration* emerged in 2001, fans looked elsewhere. **WF-J**

> "There are certainly no songs on this album I would recommend as a Valentine's gift to your lover."
>
> Neil Hannon, 1997

Track Listing

▶	01	**In Pursuit Of Happiness** (Hannon)	3:31
	02	**Everybody Knows (Except You)** (Hannon)	3:48
▶	03	**Someone** (Hannon)	5:58
	04	**If ...** (Hannon)	4:25
	05	**If I Were You (I'd Be Through With Me)** (Hannon)	4:41
	06	**Timewatching** (Hannon)	4:42
▶	07	**I'm All You Need** (Hannon)	4:51

Cornershop
When I Was Born For The 7th Time (1997)

Label | Wiiija Records
Producer | Various
Art Direction | Deborah Norcross
Nationality | UK
Running Time | 54:12

Fatboy Slim's remix of "Brimful Of Asha" was a worldwide No. 1 in February 1998. With its kitsch video celebrating lo-fi technology and cryptic lyric referencing the iconic Bollywood vocalist Asha Bhosle, it provided an unexpected boost for this album and introduced Cornershop to millions of new fans.

Tjinder Singh, born to Sikh parents in Preston, Lancashire, UK, formed Cornershop in the early 1990s to play angry post-punk heavily influenced by The Fall. As Singh started investigating Indian music, Cornershop later morphed into a punky world music collective, playing gigs where the assorted sitar, tabla, harmonium, and dhol drum players on stage would often outnumber the audience.

In 1997 Singh regrouped with founder member Ben Ayres to mix lo-fi guitar pop with electronica and Indian drones. The album was their most focussed and accessible to date. "Brimful Of Asha" here may sound vaguely unsatisfying to fans of the single but there are plenty of other joys on offer.

"Sleep On The Left Side" marries a qawwali harmonium drone with a loping breakbeat; "We're In Yr Corner" is a killer funk groove; "Good To Be On The Road Back Home" is a bizarre Indian take on country music; "Candyman" is a baggy groove track based on a Larry Coryell sample (and is one of three tracks co-produced with Dan The Automator). Elsewhere "Norwegian Wood" slyly subverts The Beatles' exoticization of India by reciting John Lennon's lyric in Punjabi. **JLe**

Track Listing

▶ 01	**Sleep On The Left Side** (Singh)	4:06
▶ 02	**Brimful Of Asha** (Singh)	5:17
03	**Butter The Soul** (Singh)	3:19
04	**Chocolat** (Singh)	1:24
▶ 05	**We're In Yr Corner** (Singh)	5:47
▶ 06	**Funky Days Are Back Again** (Singh)	3:41
07	**What Is Happening?** (Ayres·Singh)	2:15
08	**When The Light Appears Boy** (Ginsberg)	2:41
09	**Coming Up** (Singh)	1:03
10	**Good Shit** (Singh)	4:40
11	**Good To Be On The Road Back Home** (Singh)	5:45
12	**It's Indian Tobacco, My Friend** (Singh)	4:51
▶ 13	**Candyman** (Singh)	3:49
14	**State Troopers** (Singh)	3:07
▶ 15	**Norwegian Wood (This Bird Has Flown)** (Lennon·McCartney)	2:27

Daft Punk | Homework (1997)

Label | Virgin
Producer | Daft Punk
Art Direction | Daft Punk • Serge Nicolas
Nationality | France
Running Time | 73:31

Ravers were not ready for *Homework*. At the start of 1997, the beery charms of Britpop had seduced most of the UK's brighter young kids and electronically produced music, once so progressive, was on the back foot. But Daft Punk's hot mix of P-funk, disco, acid frequencies, and hip-hop-style sampling reinvented the form, confounding most dance practitioners of the time.

The album could have only been the work of two precocious young men who, as its title would have it, had done their homework. "It's simple, when you're a teenager, it's natural," said Guy-Manuel de Homem Christo, then only a few months into his 20s. "Any teenager goes for a living form of music, the most energetic form of music, and rock 'n' roll is not that any more. Dance music is much more young and fresh."

Having dallied with indie rock in their previous band, Darlin, Guy-Man and his charismatic production partner Thomas Bangalter went for dance music in a typically French way. Their breakthrough hit, 1995's "Da Funk," had owed as great a debt to George Clinton as to Paul Oakenfold; their follow-up single, the less energetic though more commercially successful "Around The World," also slung the most heterogeneous of influences—Kool And The Gang, Zapp, Buggles— onto one record. It was club bricolage; immediately brand new and yet utterly retro.

Homework served as a bridge between more established club styles and the burgeoning eclecticism of big beat. And it proved to many club-goers that there was more to dance music than pills and keyboard presets. **ARa**

Track Listing

	01	**Daftendirekt** (Bangalter•Homem-Christo)	2:44
	02	**WDPK 83.7 FM** (Bangalter•Homem-Christo)	0:28
▶	03	**Revolution 909** (Bangalter•Homem-Christo)	5:26
▶	04	**Da Funk** (Bangalter•Homem-Christo)	5:28
	05	**Phoenix** (Bangalter•Homem-Christo)	4:55
	06	**Fresh** (Bangalter•Homem-Christo)	4:03
▶	07	**Around The World** (Bangalter•Homem-Christo)	7:07
▶	08	**Rollin' & Scratchin'** (Bangalter•Homem-Christo)	7:26
▶	09	**Teachers** (Bangalter•Homem-Christo)	2:52
	10	**High Fidelity** (Bangalter•Homem-Christo)	6:00
	11	**Rock'N Roll** (Bangalter•Homem-Christo)	7:32
	12	**Oh Yeah** (Bangalter•Homem-Christo)	2:00
▶	13	**Burnin'** (Bangalter•Homem-Christo)	6:53
	14	**Indo Silver Club** (Bangalter•Homem-Christo)	4:32
	15	**Alive** (Bangalter•Homem-Christo)	5:15
	16	**Funk Ad** (Bangalter•Homem-Christo)	0:50

Robbie Williams | Life Thru A Lens (1997)

Label | Chrysalis
Producer | Guy Chambers • Steve Power
Art Direction | Mat Cook
Nationality | UK
Running Time | 41:44

If nothing else, *Life Thru A Lens* proved you should never turn your back on a wounded animal. Just as most people had written Robbie Williams off, confining his early attempts at solo success to the bargain bin, his debut album rose from the ashes to elevate him as arguably the biggest British pop icon for a generation.

Early singles "Lazy Days" and "South Of The Border" hit the UK Top Twenty, but it was undoubtedly "Angels" that put the world at the feet of the former "fat dancer" (quoth Noel Gallagher) from boy band Take That.

Williams' bravado sat comfortably with his new-found power-pop sound, which blended his natural cabaret showmanship with lyrics owing more than a nod to cheeky British seaside humor.

But the album would be nothing without the stellar lineup of solid populist rock arrangements co-written by Williams' accomplice, Guy Chambers, who transformed a wide-eyed debut into a hugely successful, fully fledged, stomping masterpiece.

"Let Me Entertain You" revisited the tub-thumping singalong, pyrotechnical riffs, and theatrical pomp of the glam-rock era, maintaining the singer's UK chart momentum with a No. 3 hit. That said, the contrast between autobiographical "Ego A Go Go" and the somber "One Of God's Better People" proved Williams was still torn between life in the spotlight and his working-class roots.

In retrospect, the cover shot—a pot-shot at the media circus that had engulfed Williams—was unknowingly ironic: the album sent the singer's profile stratospheric, and exacerbated that media scrum a thousandfold. **ARo**

> ## "I probably get a hundred letters that revolve around ... unstable behavior, a week."

Robbie Williams, 2004

Track Listing

01	**Lazy Days** (Chambers•Williams)		3:53
▶ 02	**Life Thru A Lens** (Chambers•Williams)		3:08
03	**Ego A Go Go** (Chambers•Williams)		3:32
▶ 04	**Angels** (Chambers•Williams)		4:24
05	**South Of The Border** (Chambers•Williams)		3:53
▶ 06	**Old Before I Die** (Bazilian•Child•Williams)		3:54
07	**One Of God's Better People** (Chambers•Williams)		3:33
▶ 08	**Let Me Entertain You** (Chambers•Williams)		4:21
09	**Killing Me** (Chambers•Williams)		3:56
10	**Clean** (Cook•Genn•Hawley•Slattery•Williams)		3:54
11	**Baby Girl Window** (Chambers•Williams)		3:16

Mariah Carey | Butterfly (1997)

Label | Columbia
Producer | Various
Art Direction | Christopher Austopchuk
Nationality | USA
Running Time | 57:12

The unhappiest chart-topping album of 1997 was easily *OK Computer*—but this runs it a close second.

Carey had envisaged *Butterfly* as a house record; the legacy of which is the David Morales-helmed "Fly Away" (based on Elton John's "Skyline Pigeon"). It evolved instead into a stunning eulogy for her failed, stifling marriage to Sony boss Tommy Mottola.

Fluffily unrepresentative, the hit "Honey" nonetheless signaled a change. Produced by Puff Daddy and based on the bass from Treacherous Three's "Body Rock," it was another rung up the hip-hop ladder—she had already worked with Ol' Dirty Bastard (on 1995's "Fantasy").

Rap weighs heaviest on *Butterfly*'s most astonishing songs. "The Roof," Carey's favorite, is based on Mobb Deep's "Shook Ones.""Breakdown," with choral hardcore by Bone Thugs-N-Harmony, proved prophetic when Carey slid off the rails in 2001.

Of the ballads, the Latino "My All" was the biggest hit, but others are more substantial. "Close My Eyes" seems to flirt with suicide. "Outside" is "about being multi-racial and feeling like I came from another planet." And there is a Dru Hill-assisted take on "my favorite Prince song ever," *Purple Rain*'s tortured "The Beautiful Ones" ("The closest to where I'm at in this stage in my life").

There are also lovely low-key moments, like the Missy Elliott co-write "Babydoll" and the evocative "Fourth Of July." Throughout, Carey reins in the excessive warbling that puts many off.

What remains is an album on which—as captured in Michael Thompson's cover photo—bitterness becomes beauty and glumness becomes gold. **BM**

"Everyone's a diva these days."

Mariah Carey, 2005

Track Listing

▶	01	**Honey** (Carey·Combs·Fareed·Hague·Jordan Larkins·McLaren·Price·Robinson)	5:01
▶	02	**Butterfly** (Afanasieff·Carey)	4:35
	03	**My All** (Afanasieff·Carey)	3:52
	04	**The Roof** (Barnes·Carey·Johnson·Muchita Olivier·Rooney)	5:14
	05	**Fourth Of July** (Afanasieff·Carey)	4:22
▶	06	**Breakdown** (Carey·Henderson·Jordan·Scruggs)	4:44
	07	**Babydoll** (Carey·Elliott·Jordan·Rooney)	5:07
	08	**Close My Eyes** (Afanasieff·Carey)	4:21
	09	**Whenever You Call** (Afanasieff·Carey)	4:21
	10	**Fly Away (Butterfly Reprise)** (Carey·John·Morales·Taupin)	3:49
	11	**The Beautiful Ones** (Prince)	6:59
	12	**Outside** (Afanasieff·Carey)	4:47

Supergrass
In It For The Money (1997)

Label | Parlophone
Producer | John Cornfield • Supergrass
Art Direction | Supergrass
Nationality | UK
Running Time | 43:11

After the rave reviews and media adulation that attended Supergrass' 1995 debut *I Should Coco*, follow-up *In It For The Money* needed to be pretty special. The trio's nonchalant, somewhat cynical acknowledgement of the high stakes was indicated by the album's title (amusingly their single in America was called "We Still Need More").

But this sense of humor belies the group's auspicious talent. The tracks on offer here (only a handful of which were written before entering the studio) are significantly more complex than those of the debut, a tribute to the trio's burgeoning musical prowess. Supergrass succeeded in composing a varied and textured album—reference points include the melodic psychedelia of The Small Faces and The Kinks, and even *Magical Mystery Tour*-era Beatles—that had critics finally acknowledging the group's substance. At the same time, it retained the pop sensibilities that had made *I Should Coco* so successful.

The boisterous, punchy "Richard III" thunders along at the breakneck speed of their debut album, while the sublime "Sun Hits The Sky" is awash with radiant wah-wah guitar. "Going Out" is highlighted by the swirling, carnival organ sounds introduced by Gaz Coombes' older brother Bob. The subtle and more introspective songs on offer—such as "Late In The Day," with its warm acoustic tones, and the harmony-laden "Its Not Me"—mark an increasingly mature level of songwriting. **KM**

Bob Dylan
Time Out Of Mind (1997)

Label | Columbia
Producer | Daniel Lanois
Art Direction | Geoff Gans
Nationality | USA
Running Time | 72:44

For album number 41, Dylan went down to Miami's Criteria Studios, and back to producer Daniel Lanois, who had been responsible for 1989's celebrated *Oh Mercy*. The sessions with assorted old troupers was a deep sound rooted in the blues but recognizably Dylan in its sting.

More an aural experience than a literary one, as its author once remarked, *Time Out Of Mind* is a serious affair, though not without humor, and one that draws together a spacious landscape of textures and drama. Listen to the raw "Million Miles"—the dense atmosphere can be cut with a knife.

At the album's heart is a gutsy, charismatic, meditative Bob Dylan, the famous nasal whine of his vocals now become a compelling rasp. The regrets of love gone wrong fuel "Standing In The Doorway" and "Love Sick"; the slightest of hopes shines through "Make You Feel My Love." "Dirt Road Blues" and "Cold Irons Bound" are clattering, metallic hillbilly and R&B, while "Trying To Get To Heaven" is prime laconic Dylan.

"Not Dark Yet" finds the elder poet facing his future with a wry grin and, as usual, offering more questions than answers. But the real vision comes at the end with "Highlands," an extended aural mirror to a world dominated by chaos and lies, a sceptic's monolog to close a dark but stimulating album.

Time Out Of Mind captured an artist who once again found himself at the crossroads—grumpy but alive; spiritually worn out but still sane. **IJ**

Roni Size/Reprazent
New Forms (1997)

Label | Talkin' Loud
Producer | Roni Size • Reprazent
Art Direction | Intro
Nationality | UK
Running Time | 133:37

The core members of Roni Size/Reprazent have worked together since the early 1990s, emerging from the Bristol music scene of that era. The four DJs and producers released a succession of singles on the now legendary V Recordings label, as well as on Full Cycle. Reprazent's evolution was completed when vocalist Onallee and a young MC called Dynamite joined the fold. Their combined sound was a neat amalgam of the musical flavors of Bristol at the time, taking in reggae, dub, break, blues, hip hop, and jungle.

The groundbreaking New Forms was released after Roni was discovered and signed by Gilles Peterson to Talkin' Loud. It includes some of the most recognizable sounds of the genre, including hits like "Watching Windows" and "Heroes," as well as "Share The Fall," all of them featuring Onallee's lush and sultry voice. Other highlights include the scorching opening track, "Railing," on which MC Dynamite shows off his amazing vocal skills, and "Brown Paper Bag," an epic drum 'n' bass anthem with a great guitar hook and a gut-wrenching bassline punctuated by heated moans from Onallee. Many tracks run for more than five minutes, but Size's skillful variation of rhythms ensures that the material never sags.

Winning the UK's Mercury Prize brought both Roni Size and drum 'n' bass into both the limelight and the mainstream. Drum 'n' bass has mutated into several sub-genres in past years, but the musical complexity of this debut album has kept it in a class of its own. **PN**

Elliott Smith
Either/Or (1997)

Label | Kill Rock Stars
Producer | Elliott Smith
Art Direction | Neil Gust • Debbie Pastor
Nationality | USA
Running Time | 36:52

Among modern singer-songwriters there are few who can match Elliott Smith for intimacy. The lo-fi, home-recording techniques of his earlier releases, documented in interviews with the magazine *Tape Op*, his fragile voice and delicate guitar playing, angry, tender, and often "fuck-you" lyrics, draw the listener inexorably into the artist's world.

Either/Or was Smith's third solo album, and possibly his richest work. Recorded over a period of almost 12 months at a number of locations, including his own apartment and that of his girlfriend, it was named after a treatise by the philosopher Søren Kierkegaard. Its production was an agonizing process: "I recorded 30 songs for the album, and I couldn't pick out any that I liked," Smith told *Rocket* in a 1997 interview. Several of these were later used on the soundtrack to *Good Will Hunting*, directed by Gus Van Sant, whom Smith had met while living in Portland. The publicity subsequently afforded to Smith revived interest in *Either/Or*.

"Ballad Of Big Nothing" is an uplifting anthem to freedom; "Between The Bars," an ode to a whiskey bottle; "Pictures Of Me," a snapshot of destructive relationships, introducing the photograph as an enduring Smith image; "No Name No. 5" was recorded in an open tuning that Smith subsequently forgot. But it is with the last two songs that the album really delivers its payload: "2.45 AM"—documenting the terrors of the wee small hours in achingly beautiful fashion—and "Say Yes"— hopelessly, wonderfully optimistic. **MBI**

The Verve | Urban Hymns (1997)

Label | Hut
Producer | Chris Potter • The Verve • Youth
Art Direction | Brian Cannon
Nationality | UK
Running Time | 75:43

Urban Hymns was released into a fervor of expectation. After a split in 1995, singer and main songwriter Richard Ashcroft re-formed the group with guitarist/keyboardist Simon Tong. Yet they lacked guitarist Nick McCabe's signature swirls. He was convinced by Ashcroft to rejoin, though trivia freaks may have noted that on the album's front cover he is looking in the opposite direction.

A fierce period of recording ensued in London's Olympic Studios, a venue Hendrix and the Stones used throughout their careers. *Urban Hymns* opens with the elegiac "Bittersweet Symphony," a song that takes 40 seconds to secure the Verve a place in British rock history. As the drums kick in, the transcendental atmosphere is manifested in Ashcroft's visionary vocals—"cos I'm a million different people from one day to the next." The looped orchestration was sampled from Andrew Loog Oldham's version of the Stones' "The Last Time." Unfortunately for the band, former Stones manager Allen Klein owned the rights—thus the royalties—to the song.

"Sonnet" and "Lucky Man" are typical of Ashcroft's anthemic songwriting, filled with raw emotion capable of connecting with the very essence of the listener's soul. The collaborative efforts are incendiary, with the lengthy space jam "Come On" and dreamlike "Catching The Butterfly," which grew out of McCabe simply fiddling with an FX pedal. Meanwhile, UK chart-topper "The Drugs Don't Work" is a heart-stirring paean about the death of Ashcroft's father.

Urban Hymns has a pioneering spirit that challenged the limitations of what British guitar bands could achieve in the 1990s. **AMa**

Track Listing

▶ 01	**Bittersweet Symphony** (Ashcroft•Jagger•Oldham•Richards)	5:50
02	**Sonnet** (Ashcroft)	4:21
▶ 03	**The Rolling People** (Ashcroft)	7:01
▶ 04	**The Drugs Don't Work** (Ashcroft)	5:05
05	**Catching The Butterfly** (Ashcroft•Jones•McCabe•Tong•Salisbury)	6:26
06	**Neon Wilderness** (Ashcroft•Jones•McCabe•Tong•Salisbury)	2:37
▶ 07	**Space And Time** (Ashcroft)	5:36
08	**Weeping Willow** (Ashcroft)	4:49
▶ 09	**Lucky Man** (Ashcroft)	4:53
10	**One Day** (Ashcroft)	5:03
▶ 11	**This Time** (Ashcroft)	3:50
12	**Velvet Morning** (Ashcroft)	4:57
13	**Come On** (Ashcroft•Jones•McCabe•Tong•Salisbury)	15:15

Spiritualized | Ladies And Gentlemen, We Are Floating In Space (1997)

Label | Dedicated
Producer | Jason Pierce
Art Direction | Mark Farrow Design • Jason Pierce
Nationality | UK
Running Time | 69:54

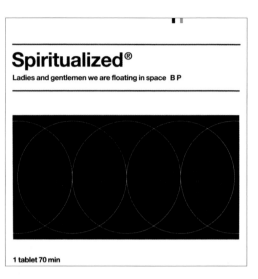

Spiritualized®
Ladies and gentlemen we are floating in space B P

1 tablet 70 min

"One tablet, for aural administration only" says the box, modeled on pharmaceutical packaging. "Play once twice daily." The disc comes sealed in a tinfoil blister pack; the sleevenotes are written in the style of medical instructions. The motto of his previous band, Spacemen 3, had been "Taking drugs to make music to take drugs to," but it was here that Jason Pierce's promises came to pass.

Or did they? Pierce is a guarded interviewee, refusing to discuss his drug consumption and preferring to let the music speak for itself. The irony is that the blank vocal delivery, masterful ambiguity, and unemotional force behind his music allows listeners to adopt for themselves the perspective of the narrator and seek out their own meanings. Beginning with the dreamy waltz of the title track, *Ladies And Gentlemen . . .* careens through a wide variety of styles. "Come Together" is gospelized heavy metal, "I Think I'm In Love" is an astonishing sickbed lament by somebody confused by symptoms that indicate either amour or imminent death. Elegiac euphoria ("Stay With Me," "Home Of The Brave," "Broken Heart") comes in waves, interspersed with white noise ("All Of My Thoughts"), and brutal punk power ("Electricity"), climaxing with the voodoo of the junkie's testimonial "Cop Shoot Cop."

Many critics pronounced it the album of the decade, but after a year on the road—including landmark shows at Glastonbury and Toronto's CN Tower—it had mutated into an even more powerful beast (see *Royal Albert Hall October 10 1997 Live*). So Pierce sacked the band. **DH**

"The songs work a capella."

Jason Pierce, 1997

Track Listing

▶	01	Ladies And Gentlemen We Are Floating In Space (Pierce)	3:40
▶	02	Come Together (Pierce)	4:40
▶	03	I Think I'm In Love (Pierce)	8:09
	04	All Of My Thoughts (Pierce)	4:36
	05	Stay With Me (Pierce)	5:08
	06	Electricity (Pierce)	3:46
▶	07	Home Of The Brave (Pierce)	2:22
	08	The Individual (Pierce)	4:15
▶	09	Broken Heart (Pierce)	6:38
	10	No God Only Religion (Pierce)	4:21
	11	Cool Waves (Pierce)	5:06
▶	12	Cop Shoot Cop (Pierce)	17:13

The Dandy Warhols | The Dandy Warhols Come Down (1997)

Label | Capitol
Producer | Tony Lash • Courtney Taylor
Art Direction | Steven Birch
Nationality | USA
Running Time | 57:01

The Dandy Warhols exploded out of Portland, Oregon, onto the U.S. scene in 1995 with their debut LP, *Dandy's Rule OK?* Employing droning riffs, layers of fuzz guitar, and raw-as-raw keyboards that recall Stereolab (and prime garage-rock), the Dandys' sophomore release *Come Down* sees frontman Courtney Taylor showcase his reincarnation as a Sixties rocker.

The quartet mock religion in "Hard-On For Jesus" and continue their exploration of drug culture in the psycho-candy pop of "Not If You Were The Last Junkie On Earth," with its memorable "heroin is so passé" quip. However, these songs, along with the hedonistic joy of hit single "Every Day Should Be A Holiday" (that cheekily references Duran Duran's "Hungry Like The Wolf") are not particularly representative of the album's muse—which seems to take greater delight in dabbling in sonic experimentation reminiscent of bands such as My Bloody Valentine (John Cale-era Velvet Underground is another tangible reference point). Following the initial adrenalin surge of "Be-In" and "Boys Better," the album's energy dissipates with the sleepwalking "Orange" and slow, sinister "I Love You."

Come Down more than delivers on the promise of the group's first record—on its release it was described by *Rolling Stone* as "the most exhilarating '60s-into-'90s excursion yet attempted by an American band." This album saw the Dandys inject a more-than-generous shot of psych-punk into a bland American musical landscape, and it promised glories to come. **SN**

Track Listing

01	**Be-In** (Taylor)	6:59
▶ 02	**Boys Better** (Taylor)	4:33
▶ 03	**Minnesoter** (Taylor)	3:02
04	**Orange** (Taylor)	4:02
05	**I Love You** (Taylor)	4:12
▶ 06	**Not If You Were The Last Junkie On Earth** (Taylor)	3:11
▶ 07	**Every Day Should Be A Holiday** (Taylor)	4:02
08	**Good Morning** (Taylor)	5:00
09	**Whipping Tree** (Taylor)	4:00
10	**Green** (Taylor)	3:10
11	**Cool As Kim Deal** (Taylor)	3:02
12	**Hard On For Jesus** (Holmstrom • Taylor)	4:36
13	**Pete International Airport** (Holmstrom • Taylor)	4:01
14	**The Creep Out** (The Dandy Warhols)	3:11

Bob Dylan
Live 1966 (1998)

Label | Columbia
Producer | Jeff Rosen
Art Direction | Barry Feinstein
Nationality | USA
Running Time | 95:19

On his tour of 1965 and 1966, Dylan had taken to opening his shows with a set of his acoustic folk hymns, followed by a set of electric rockers. The response was decidedly mixed. Young purists—many of whom had discovered folk through Dylan—felt betrayed by their hero's impulsive change of direction, and were too irate to realize that they were witnessing the birth of folk rock.

When Dylan arrived in Manchester on May 16, 1966, both he and his disciples were ready for a fight. Perhaps most distressing to the faithful—who greeted Dylan's second set with boos, hisses, and other disruptions—was that the songs bouncing off the walls of Free Trade Hall were, in fact, early Dylan favorites transformed into rollicking jaunts with the help of The Hawks, the world-class backing group who would later become The Band. Blazing renditions of "I Don't Believe You" and "One Too Many Mornings," anchored by Rick Danko's thunderous bass and Robbie Robertson's searing lead guitar, were given breathtaking new life by Dylan, who spat out the lyrics like poisoned arrows.

Most of the electric set was comprised of breakup songs, only now Dylan was aiming them at anyone who second guessed his second coming. After a soulful "Ballad Of A Thin Man," a call of "Judas!" pelted him from the crowd. Dylan retorted, "You're a liar!," before turning and ordering the Hawks to play the finale—a scintillating "Like A Rolling Stone"—"fucking loud." Dylan peered into the darkness and screamed, "How does it feeeel to be on your own?" **MO**

Manu Chao
Clandestino (1998)

Label | Virgin
Producer | Renaud Letang • Manu Chao
Art Direction | Manu Chao • F. Loriou
Nationality | France
Running Time | 45:47

After the break-up of his ethno-punk band Mano Negra in the mid-1990s, Manu Chao embarked on an expedition through Latin America, armed with his guitar, a portable eight-track, and boundless musical curiosity. Gathering a suitcase full of guerilla radio samples and an arsenal of new influences, along the way the Paris native recorded a touching collection of musical postcards that became his first solo album, *Clandestino*.

Where Mano Negra sometimes got lost in their exuberant forays from punk to ska to salsa, *Clandestino* seamlessly melds Chao's Latin-tinged stream of consciousness—subtle gestures toward reggae, rap, and techno never overwhelm the whole, each song melting into the next like entries in an intimate travel diary. Singing and rapping in French, English, Spanish, and Portuguese, the troubadour poignantly explores the heartbreak of the road in the haunting acoustic ballads "El Viento" and "La Vie," and offers glimpses into the nomad's disillusionment—in the electro-salsa romp "Luna Y Sol," he bitterly wonders if the whole world is a lie. Yet he has not lost his sense of humor— "Bongo Bong" revisits a silly Mano Negra boogie with cheeky beats and beeps—or his political militancy. Speeches by Subcommandante Marcos are sampled throughout, and Chao (*el desaparecido* to his friends) sympathizes with the continent's downtrodden peoples in songs like the dub-infused "Por El Suelo" and the driving title track, a politically charged tale of illegal migrants lost in "Babylon." **MW**

Billy Bragg And Wilco
Mermaid Avenue (1998)

Label | Elektra
Producer | Billy Bragg • Grant Showbiz • Wilco
Art Direction | Alli • Billy Bragg • Nora Guthrie
Nationality | UK • USA
Running Time | 50:08

In 1992, at Summerstage, New York, English political folk-rocker Billy Bragg performed during a concert commemorating Woodie Guthrie's birthday. In the mesmerized audience was Nora Guthrie, Woodie's daughter, who knew immediately that Bragg was the man to put music to some of her father's myriad lyrics. Bragg accepted Nora's challenge in 1995, but he found the task of searching the archive overwhelming and realized he could not do justice to the songs on his own. Two years later, he enlisted the musical expertise of American alt.country outfit Wilco.

The album *Mermaid Avenue* borrowed its name and cover art from the street in Coney Island, Brooklyn, where Guthrie had lived with his family during World War II. Recorded first in Chicago and then in Dublin, the album captured a raw earthy sound, reminiscent of early bluegrass and folk rock. It was a breakthrough for Bragg and Wilco, earning them a billing in *Rolling Stone*'s "Essential Recordings of the Nineties."

"Walt Whitman's Niece" is captivating with its joyful vocals and twangy guitar licks, while "Way Over Yonder In The Minor Key," a folk ballad backed angelically by Natalie Merchant, sees Bragg claiming "Ain't nobody who can sing like me." "California Star" was a song overlooked by Bragg, but the soothing evocation of starlit skies by Wilco's Jeff Tweedy warms the heart. "Hoodoo Voodoo" is a quirky children's tale, brought to life by Wilco; "Ingrid Bergman" professes Guthrie's secret love for the Swedish movie star. **KT**

Turbonegro
Apocalypse Dudes (1998)

Label | Bitzcore
Producer | Pal Klaastad
Art Direction | Dimitri From Oslo
Nationality | Norway
Running Time | 47:29

Shaking off the raw gutter punk atmosphere of 1996's *Ass Cobra*, Norway's sassiest rent boys birthed most righteous and majestic rock 'n' roll in their defining album. Embracing rock's true spirit: sleaze, gender bending, pouting, and preening, what separates these denim dudes from the glam metal poseurs is that they truly bring the house down with a non-stop, titanic death-punk riff-a-rama. All along it is spiced with tambourine, piano, congas, and almost constant guitar soloing from Euroboy. English may be their second language, but this only makes Hank Von Helvete's detached, contemptuous re-reading of the rock phrasebook all the more enjoyable.

Co-opting the six-headed cobra logo of the Symbionese Liberation Army for the cover adds just the right amount of comic absurdity to Turbonegro's back alley image. The homoerotic undertones in rock 'n' roll —all six members play their gay roles with Nordic solemnity—are proudly laid bare in pelvis-driven tunes like "Rendezvous With Anus" and "Prince Of the Rodeo."

Their legacy as rock stars' favorite rock stars later led to a tribute album with contributions from admirers The Supersuckers, Queens Of The Stone Age, Therapy?, The Dwarves, Zeke, and others. Upon the release of *Apocalypse Dudes*, Dead Kennedys' mouthpiece Jello Biafra posited that it was "possibly the most important European record ever." This may be true. But it is certainly the greatest example of one band's profound understanding of the meaning of rock 'n' roll. **AT**

Fatboy Slim | You've Come A Long Way, Baby (1998)

Label | Skint
Producer | Fatboy Slim
Art Direction | Red Design • Simon Thornton
Nationality | UK
Running Time | 61:37

Norman Cook was not the first bedroom DJ; nor was he the most competent. But his judicious selection of melodies, married with the juiciest of beats, made him the outrider for the resurgent club movement as the twenty-first century approached.

Although he had scored hits with The Housemartins, Beats International, and Freak Power, Fatboy Slim was the vehicle that Cook seemed to enjoy the most—just him, some cheap technology, and his record collection. The influence of The Chemical Brothers was crucial here—their work and friendship galvanized him to ape their monstrous beats and graft them to his own work.

You've Come A Long Way, Baby is a breezy blast. It is exceedingly immature, of course; "Fucking In Heaven" mentions the "f" word more than 100 times and "Acid 8000" is an affectionate, ten-years-on tribute to the Roland 303 squelching away. "Right Here, Right Now" is a perfect opener; building string swells before kicking in with stadium-sized drums. Cook's historian's-eye view ensured that he used his samples intelligently; Camille Yarborough's "Take Yo' Praise," The Chambers Brothers' "Fried Tomatoes," and The James Gang's "Ashes, The Rain & I" all feature predominately.

It made for a truly irresistible combination. The album was a multiplatinum bestseller, spawning four hit singles. It also became the signature album for "big beat," a beer-driven sloppiness that offered a counterpoint to the drug-fueled house scene. With his samples at once both humorous and poignant, Fatboy Slim had become an inarticulate poet laureate in a sense, bridging both booze and Ecstasy culture. **DE**

> ## "That was my template: make something much more soulful."
>
> Norman Cook, 2000

Track Listing

▶	01	**Right Here, Right Now** (Cook•Peters•Walsh)	6:27
▶	02	**The Rockerfeller Skank** (Barry•Cook•Terry)	6:27
	03	**Fucking In Heaven** (Cook)	3:55
	04	**Gangster Tripping** (Cook•Davis•Dust•Junkys)	5.20
	05	**Build It Up—Tear It Down** (Cook)	5:05
	06	**Kalifornia** (Cook•Mr Natural)	5:54
	07	**Soul Surfing** (Cook•Nelson•Smith)	4:57
▶	08	**You're Not From Brighton** (Cook)	5:21
▶	09	**Praise You** (Cook•Yarborough)	5:24
	10	**Love Island** (Cook)	5:19
▶	11	**Acid 8000** (Cook)	7:28

David Gray | White Ladder (1998)

Label | EastWest
Producer | David Gray • McClune • Iestyn Polson
Art Direction | Charles Cowen • Yami Matote
Nationality | UK
Running Time | 50:34

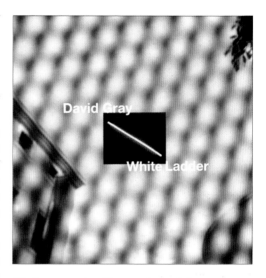

White Ladder was essentially one last roll of the dice by David Gray, a man whose promising music career appeared to be disappearing before his eyes after brief flirtations with the mainstream. But thanks to its slow-burning success, the album transformed Gray from a cult singer/songwriter cherished by few into a huge international star.

The critics who had accused him of mediocrity quickly rounded on this album of homespun simplicity. But that did not stop the record shifting 2.2 million copies in the UK, while in Ireland it became the biggest selling non-compilation album of all time. And with the British music industry still licking its wounds after the failure of big guns Blur and Oasis to crack America, *White Ladder* managed to sell two million copies Stateside without any fuss or bravado.

Standout tracks "Babylon" and "This Year's Love" are infectious acoustic tales of everyday love and loss, which bristle with an emotional honesty. But solid songwriting (Dylan an obvious influence, both in songcraft and vocal style) and the influence of multi-instrumentalist "Clune" McClune and studio boffin Iestyn Polson on rousing "Please Forgive Me" ensured the rest of *White Ladder* could break your heart while putting a smile on your face and a spring in your step.

Closing song "Say Hello Wave Goodbye"—a cover of the Soft Cell classic—was probably intended as Gray's parting thanks to those who stood by him. Instead, his beautiful rendition, full of warming strings and a passionate but dignified vocal delivery, won Gray a new army of fans that would turn his world around. **ARo**

> ## "It's generally unhealthy to be concerning yourself too much with what other people might think."
>
> David Gray, 2002

Track Listing

▶	01	**Please Forgive Me** (Gray)	5:35
▶	02	**Babylon** (Gray)	4:25
	03	**My Oh My** (Gray•McClune)	4:37
	04	**We're Not Right** (Gray•McClune•Polson)	3:03
	05	**Nightblindness** (Gray)	4:23
	06	**Silver Lining** (Gray)	5:59
	07	**White Ladder** (Gray•McClune•Polson)	4:14
▶	08	**This Year's Love** (Gray)	4:05
	09	**Sail Away** (Gray)	5:15
▶	10	**Say Hello Wave Goodbye** (Almond•Ball)	8:58

Lucinda Williams
Car Wheels On A Gravel Road (1998)

Label | Mercury
Producer | Roy Bittan • The Twangtrust • Lucinda Williams
Art Direction | Margery Greenspan
Nationality | USA
Running Time | 51:42

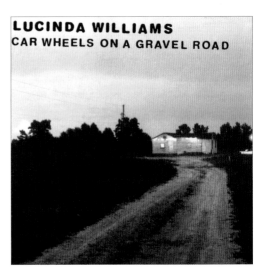

Lucinda Williams is one of those rare contemporary performers who do not compromise. That much is evident from listening to *Car Wheels On A Gravel Road*, as flawless a work of songcraft and record production as has appeared in the last ten years. But it is also evident from *Car Wheels'* copyright date—1998, six years after her previous album, *Sweet Old World*.

Suffice to say Williams takes her time, and it shows. *Car Wheels On A Gravel Road* is one of those multi-layered albums that opens up with repeated exposure, and then opens up some more. The thing to notice first is, of course, her voice, which is wistful, defiant, and wan. Then there are the remarkable arrangements in a variety of American roots idioms, from raunchy blues ("Joy") to sad country ("Concrete And Barbed Wire") and sheer power pop ("I Lost It," "Right In Time").

But most provocative are the stories Williams tells—she has a winding way of reaching climaxes that are, almost to a one, crushingly sad. To cite just one example, "2 Kool 2 Be 4-Gotten" seems at first to be a disjointed string of images from a tavern, and only in the final verses does Williams describe the moment of loss that brought her to this place.

Loss suffuses the album, the credits of which read like a "who's who" of thoughtful American songwriters—Steve Earle, Jim Lauderdale, Buddy Miller. One wishes Williams would work faster between releases, but on the other hand, with results this exquisite, one only hopes she does not rush. **KB**

"...confront your demons..."

Lucinda Williams, 1998

Track Listing		
01 **Right In Time** (Williams)		4:36
▶ 02 **Car Wheels On A Gravel Road** (Williams)		4:44
▶ 03 **2 Kool 2 Be 4-Gotten** (Williams)		4:42
▶ 04 **Drunken Angel** (Williams)		3:20
▶ 05 **Concrete And Barbed Wire** (Williams)		3:08
06 **Lake Charles** (Williams)		5:28
07 **Can't Let Go** (Weeks)		3:28
▶ 08 **I Lost It** (Williams)		3:31
▶ 09 **Metal Firecracker** (Williams)		3:30
10 **Greenville** (Williams)		3:23
11 **Still I Long For Your Kiss** (Jarvis • Williams)		4:09
12 **Joy** (Williams)		4:01
13 **Jackson** (Williams)		3:42

Pulp | This Is Hardcore (1998)

Label | Island
Producer | Chris Thomas
Art Direction | John Currin
Nationality | UK
Running Time | 69:48

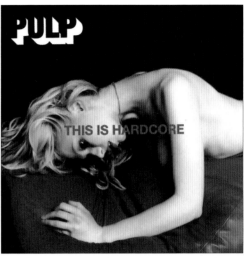

By 1997, the Britpop party had turned sour; Pulp chronicled the comedown. Those listening to *This Is Hardcore* expecting another dose of the band's trademark perky observation were in for a big surprise. If the strangely depressing single "Help The Aged" that preceded the album had not set alarm bells ringing, the message and mood of oppressive gothic-pop opener "The Fear" was unmistakable: "This is the sound of someone losing the plot/Making out they're okay when they're not/You're gonna like it, but not a lot," warned Cocker. He wasn't kidding.

Pulp had at this point overdosed on fame. "Party Hard" hinted at the excess that fostered this atmosphere with detached self-disgust.

This Is Hardcore is a profoundly unsettling piece of work (only Nirvana's *In Utero* matches it in recent times), from the celebrity-as-pornographer motif of the title track, to the nagging pessimism of the final song, which jarred so brutally with the manically upbeat mood of Blair's Britain. The album is also Pulp's most musically accomplished: "Seductive Barry" spools with relentless, mesmerizing menace; "Party Hard" is a deranged funk workout.

Although it reached No. 1, the album tanked compared to its predecessor, *Different Class*, which was probably exactly what Pulp wanted—and needed (though the cover sparked a minor furor, as the band were accused of pornographic exploitation themselves). Play it back-to-back with *Different Class* for a crash course on the perils of getting what you want, whenever you want, with whomever you want. **PW**

Track Listing

▶	01	**The Fear** (Banks·Cocker·Doyle·Mackey·Webber)	5:35
	02	**Dishes** (Banks·Cocker·Doyle·Mackey·Webber)	3:30
▶	03	**Party Hard** (Banks·Cocker·Doyle·Mackey·Webber)	4:00
	04	**Help The Aged** (Banks·Cocker·Doyle·Mackey·Webber)	4:28
▶	05	**This Is Hardcore** (Banks·Cocker·Doyle·Mackey·Thomas·Webber)	6:25
	06	**TV Movie** (Banks·Cocker·Doyle·Mackey·Webber)	3:25
	07	**A Little Soul** (Banks·Cocker·Doyle·Mackey·Webber)	3:19
	08	**I'm A Man** (Banks·Cocker·Doyle·Mackey·Webber)	4:59
▶	09	**Seductive Barry** (Banks·Cocker·Doyle·Mackey·Webber)	8:31
	10	**Sylvia** (Banks·Cocker·Doyle·Mackey·Webber)	5:44
▶	11	**Glory Days** (Banks·Cocker·Doyle·Genn·Mackey·Webber)	4:55
▶	12	**The Day After The Revolution** (Banks·Cocker·Doyle·Mackey·Webber)	14:57

Madonna | Ray Of Light (1998)

Label | Maverick
Producer | Various
Art Direction | Kevin Reagan
Nationality | USA
Running Time | 67:14

Twinkling atop Billboard's chart in the summer of Madonna's birth (1958) was "Little Star" by The Elegants. Forty years later, a song of the same name celebrated Madonna's daughter Lourdes, key to her creative rebirth.

Work began in 1997 with Babyface, her collaborator on 1994's *Bedtime Stories*. But she turned instead to songwriter Rick Nowels, techno whizkid William Orbit, and *Like A Prayer* producer Pat Leonard.

The album celebrates love over fame, most explicitly on "Drowned World/Substitute For Love." Madonna's tranquility was inspired by both Lourdes and her commitment to the Kabbala faith; hence the omission (in most territories) of the excellent "Has To Be," owing to Madonna's insistence on a lucky 13 tracks.

An extraordinary selection of sources is plundered. The storming title song is based on the obscure "Sepheryn" by Curtis & Muldoon. "Sky Fits Heaven" features (uncredited) lines by poet Max Blagg. "Candy Perfume Girl" is co-written by Prince's ex-girlfriend Susannah Melvoin. "Shanti/Ashtangi" is sung in Sanskrit. And "Drowned World" reinvents "Why I Follow The Tigers" by The San Sebastian Strings. It "follows the plot line of 'Tigers,'" said writer Rod McKuen, "which is why Anita [Kerr] and I receive co-author credit on the song and not merely sampling mention."

This variety is made cohesive by the production's electronic ebb—not unlike Massive Attack, with whom Madonna had covered Marvin Gaye's "I Want You"—and the quality of Madonna's voice, strengthened by her work on 1996's *Evita*. The album remains today, a rich, rewarding listen. **BM**

"I left off partying ... "

Madonna, 2000

Track Listing		
01	**Drowned World / Substitute For Love** (Collins·Kerr·Madonna·McKuen·Orbit)	5:08
02	**Swim** (Madonna·Orbit)	5:00
▶ 03	**Ray Of Light** (Curtis·Leach·Madonna·Muldoon·Orbit)	5:20
04	**Candy Perfume Girl** (Madonna·Melvoin·Orbit)	4:36
05	**Skin** (Leonard·Madonna)	6:21
06	**Nothing Really Matters** (Leonard·Madonna)	4:58
07	**Sky Fits Heaven** (Leonard·Madonna)	4:47
08	**Shanti / Ashtangi** (Madonna·Orbit)	4:29
▶ 09	**Frozen** (Leonard·Madonna)	6:12
▶ 10	**The Power Of Goodbye** (Madonna·Nowels)	4:12
11	**To Have And Not To Hold** (Madonna·Nowels)	5:22
12	**Little Star** (Madonna·Nowels)	5:18
13	**Mer Girl** (Madonna·Orbit)	5:31

Lauryn Hill | The Miseducation Of Lauryn Hill (1998)

Label | Ruffhouse
Producer | Lauryn Hill
Art Direction | Erwin Gorostiza • Lauryn Hill
Nationality | USA
Running Time | 77:39

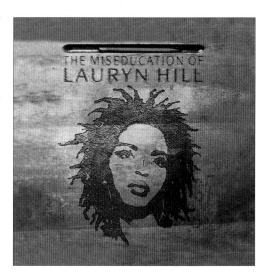

The Fugees became worldwide megastars with 1996's *The Score*, an unflinchingly positive record that rewrote the hip-hop rules. But it was a mere tune-up for what would happen when the female Fugee left the nest and released *The Miseducation Of Lauryn Hill*, which quickly became one of the most successful debut albums in pop history.

Everything about the work is striking, beginning with the cover design featuring Hill's face carved into a classroom desk. The first sound is a school bell ringing and then a teacher taking roll. Lauryn Hill, the teacher finds out, will not be attending class today. But this is not meant, at least primarily, as a statement against the system. The message, as underscored repeatedly through the lyrics, is that true education comes from being a full participant in everyday life.

Hill, just 23 at the time of the album's release, certainly does not sound like someone who needs schooling. She shows incredible vocal range and undeniable confidence during each step of the album, moving from the Fugees-style hip hop of "Lost Ones" to the sparkling pop of "Doo Wop (That Thing)." She is an impressive MC, clearly an equal in the Fugees camp, who finds her own unique mix of hardcore and hopefulness on "Final Hour." She pays tribute to her old-school influences on the bouncy "Every Ghetto, Every City" and calls upon the help of Mary J. Blige for the cleansing "I Used To Love Him."

The album was a smash hit that sold eight million copies and earned Hill five Grammys, then a single-night record for a female vocalist. **JiH**

Track Listing

01	**Intro** (Hill)		0:47
02	**Lost Ones** (Hill)		5:33
03	**Ex–Factor** (Hill)		5:26
▶ 04	**To Zion** (Hill)		6:09
▶ 05	**Doo Wop (That Thing)** (Hill)		5:20
06	**Superstar** (Hill • Newton • Poyser)		4:57
07	**Final Hour** (Hill)		4:16
▶ 08	**When It Hurts So Bad** (Hill)		5:42
▶ 09	**I Used To Love Him** (Hill)		5:39
10	**Forgive Them Father** (Hill)		5:15
▶ 11	**Every Ghetto, Every City** (Hill)		5:14
12	**Nothing Even Matters** (Hill)		5:50
▶ 13	**Everything Is Everything** (Hill • Newton)		4:53
14	**The Miseducation Of Lauryn Hill** (Hill • Newton)		4:17
15	**Can't Take My Eyes Off Of You** (Crewe • Gaudio)		3:41
16	**Sweetest Thing** (DeVorzon • Hill • Jean)		4:40

Hole | Celebrity Skin (1998)

Label | Geffen
Producer | Michael Beinhorn
Art Direction | Joe Mama-Nitzberg • Janet Wolsborn
Nationality | Canada • USA
Running Time | 50:28

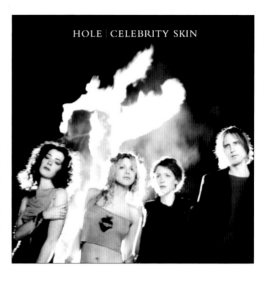

When she dies in the bathtub, who doesn't shed a tear? Courtney Love is fabulous in *The People Vs Larry Flynt*, a celluloid signal that her post-Cobain years might not be all flings and fisticuffs ("Hole is a band," huffed *Rolling Stone*, "Courtney Love is a soap opera").

The musical legacy of her mid-1990s Hollywood heyday is *Celebrity Skin*. From the whoosh that opens the title cut, it is a whirlwind ride into a post-grunge Oz. Courtney is half Dorothy, half Wicked Witch, alternately blessing and blasting those who cross her.

As the words skip between sunshine and shade, Eric Erlandson's guitar jangles and jabs, Melissa Auf Der Maur's bass rumbles and rolls, and Patty Schemel's drums smack and crash. Above it all soars the voice of Love, who roars where once she screamed. Also key are co-writers Billy Corgan of The Smashing Pumpkins, Jordan Zarorozny of Blinker The Star, and Charlotte Caffey of The Go-Go's—and producer Michael Beinhorn.

There is plenty for armchair detectives: "Boys On The Radio" is about Jeff Buckley, Brian Wilson, and the Lemonheads' Evan Dando, "Awful" is Bush's Gavin Rossdale, "Northern Star" is probably Cobain, and "Playing Your Song" fits Trent Reznor like a gothic glove.

Gossip aside, *Celebrity Skin* is a misunderstood, melodic masterpiece. "I was very disappointed for her that people didn't get behind that record," lamented Love's muse Stevie Nicks. The album takes the same sonic leap from 1994's *Live Through This* as that crunching classic did from 1991's synapse-shredding *Pretty On The Inside*—and thus completes a Hole hat trick of classic albums. **BM**

Track Listing

▶	01	**Celebrity Skin** (Corgan • Erlandson • Love)	2:42
	02	**Awful** (Auf Der Maur • Erlandson • Love • Schemel)	3:16
	03	**Hit So Hard** (Corgan • Erlandson • Love)	4:01
▶	04	**Malibu** (Corgan • Erlandson • Love)	3:50
▶	05	**Reasons To Be Beautiful** (Auf Der Maur Caffey • Erlandson • Love • Zadorozny)	5:20
	06	**Dying** (Corgan • Love)	3:45
	07	**Use Once And Destroy** (Auf Der Maur • Erlandson • Love • Schemel)	5:04
	08	**Northern Star** (Erlandson • Love)	4:58
	09	**Boys On The Radio** (Auf Der Maur • Erlandson • Love)	5:10
	10	**Heaven Tonight** (Erlandson • Love)	3:31
	11	**Playing Your Song** (Auf Der Maur • Erlandson • Love)	3:21
	12	**Petals** (Corgan • Erlandson • Love)	5:30

Mercury Rev | Deserter's Songs (1998)

Label | V2
Producer | Jonathan Donahue • Dave Fridmann
Art Direction | Kate Hyman • Kevin Salem
Nationality | USA
Running Time | 44:35

You can only make druggy pyschedelia for so long (unless you are Hawkwind). In the mid-1990s, Mercury Rev buckled down to writing songs to match their dreams and conjured a masterpiece.

"They now sound deliciously eerie," enthused *Q*, "like an experimentalist Beach Boys or Tim Burton's *The Nightmare Before Christmas*." Flugelhorns, bowed saws, and trombones might suggest medieval jazz, but it is more akin to Neil Young fronting Pink Floyd. Indeed, Jonathan Donahue's vocals are often reminiscent of Young's (and Rev have covered Young songs such as "Vampire Blues").

Beautiful as it is, the album was born from pain. The band collapsed after touring 1995's *See You On The Other Side*, and Donahue's lyrics are fueled by loss. But the results are rapturous; notably "Opus 40"—named after a sculpture in their native Catskills—which blends Donahue's poetry with quotes from Springsteen ("suicide machines") and The Doors ("alive she cried").

"Opus 40" also boasts Levon Helm of The Band, while fellow Band member Garth Hudson graces "Hudson Line." But while *Deserter's Songs* may be rooted in the 1960s, it is no dusty throwback. "Delta Sun Bottleneck Stomp" even has house-esque keyboards (and was remixed by The Chemical Brothers). A coda comes courtesy of guitarist Grasshopper's Tettix Wave Accumulator (a great name for a bunch of oscillators).

"I never feel happy," Donahue told *NME*. "I want to make a better record." With 2001's dramatic *All Is Dream* he came close—hear both and you will wonder how you managed without them. **BM**

"We were just pursuing the timeless song."

Jonathan Donahue, 1998

Track Listing

▶	01	**Holes** (Mercury Rev)	5:55
	02	**Tonite It Shows** (Mercury Rev)	3:40
	03	**Endlessly** (Mercury Rev)	4:25
	04	**I Collect Coins** (Mercury Rev)	1:27
▶	05	**Opus 40** (Mercury Rev)	5:10
	06	**Hudson Line** (Mercury Rev)	2:54
	07	**The Happy End (The Drunk Room)** (Mercury Rev)	2:06
▶	08	**Goddess On A Hiway** (Mercury Rev)	3:45
	09	**The Funny Bird** (Mercury Rev)	5:51
	10	**Pick Up If You're There** (Mercury Rev)	3:05
	11	**Delta Sun Bottleneck Stomp** (Mercury Rev)	6:17

System Of A Down
System Of A Down (1998)

Label | American
Producer | Rick Rubin • System Of A Down
Art Direction | Frank Harkins • System Of A Down
Nationality | USA
Running Time | 40:36

All members (vocalist Serj Tankian, guitarist Daron Malakian, bassist Shavo Odadjian, and drummer John Dolmayan) had played in bands prior to the formation of System Of A Down, but expectations were high after the foursome were snapped up by American Records.

This debut combines metal, blues, thrash, hardcore, rap, and rock with aspects of traditional Eastern music, but also benefits from charged, politically informed lyrics—and, refreshingly, a sense of humor. Throw in tempo changes ("Mind"), jazz passages (single "Sugar"), blinding musicianship, and a vocalist capable of death-metal screeches, melody ("Spiders"), and all in between, and the band made for a lip-smacking prospect.

System Of A Down grew up in the United States attending Armenian schools and retained strong ties to their families' ethnic heritage. This comes across in the music, but also in the socio-political nature of their lyrics—witness the fiery "P.L.U.C.K. (Politically Lying, Unholy, Cowardly Killers)" in which Serj screams about the injustice of the (internationally unrecognized) attempted genocide of the Armenian people by the Turkish government in 1915. Elsewhere, a Middle-Eastern flavor haunts the riffs in "War?" and "Peephole."

System Of A Down appealed to hard-rock fans who had become sick of modern punk and nu-metal. The band also managed to maintain their political views while making a dent in the commercial market—which grew to a multiplatinum-sized crater with the release of sophomore album, *Toxicity*. **LJ**

Track Listing

01	**Suite-Pee** (Malakian•Tankian)	2:32
02	**Know** (Malakian•Odadjian•Tankian)	2:56
▶ 03	**Sugar** (Malakian•Odadjian•Tankian)	2:33
04	**Suggestions** (Malakian•Tankian)	2:44
▶ 05	**Spiders** (Malakian•Tankian)	3:35
06	**Ddevil** (Malakian•Odadjian•Tankian)	1:43
07	**Soil** (Malakian•Tankian)	3:25
▶ 08	**War?** (Malakian•Tankian)	2:40
09	**Mind** (Malakian•Odadjian•Tankian)	6:16
10	**Peephole** (Malakian•Tankian)	4:04
11	**CUBErt** (Malakian•Tankian)	1:49
12	**Darts** (Malakian•Tankian)	2:42
▶ 13	**P.L.U.C.K. (Politically Lying, Unholy, Cowardly Killers)** (Malakian•Tankian)	3:37

Queens Of The Stone Age
Queens Of The Stone Age (1998)

Label | Loosegroove
Producer | Joe Barresi • Josh Homme
Art Direction | Kozik
Nationality | USA
Running Time | 46:27

Rising from the ashes of the band that defined that searing desert sound of stoner rock, ex-Kyuss guitarist Josh Homme stepped to the fore with Queens Of The Stone Age. Yet unlike Kyuss, Queens Of The Stone Age are as beholden to Black Sabbath as to The Beach Boys.

Homme is joined by Nick Oliveri (of splatter punks The Dwarves) and Alfredo Hernandez (also ex-Kyuss), and subsequent albums were a rock roll-call, featuring ex-Nirvana drummer and Foo Fighters head honcho Dave Grohl, former Screaming Trees vocalist Mark Lanegan, plus various blow-ins from Fu Manchu, Monster Magnet, Soundgarden, and A Perfect Circle. And this does not even begin to cover the guest spots from the likes of Shirley Manson (Garbage), Billy Gibbons (ZZ Top), and Brodie Dalle (The Distillers).

Despite this profusion of talent, from the very beginning they retained their distinctive sound probably because, even with Nick Oliveri staying for the first six years, the band has always been Homme's baby.

This, their debut, still retained the deep cosmic noodling of Kyuss but displayed much more drive and purpose, thankfully via much shorter songs than the sprawling epics his former band produced. Queens Of The Stone Age, both as an album and continuously as a band, deliver thunderous, heady, and turbulent rock.

By the time the deep throbbing piano of the final hypnotic track "I Was A Teenage Hand Model" shimmies its way into your brain, it will dawn on you that no band has fashioned sound like Queens Of The Stone Age. **AT**

Track Listing

▶	01	**Regular John** (Homme • McBain)	4:35
	02	**Avon** (Queens Of The Stone Age)	3:22
▶	03	**If Only** (Queens Of The Stone Age)	3:20
	04	**Walkin' On The Sidewalks** (Queens Of The Stone Age)	5:03
	05	**You Would Know** (Queens Of The Stone Age)	4:16
	06	**How To Handle A Rope** (Queens Of The Stone Age)	3:30
▶	07	**Mexicola** (Queens Of The Stone Age)	4:54
	08	**Hispanic Impressions** (Queens Of The Stone Age)	2:44
	09	**You Can't Quit Me Baby** (Queens Of The Stone Age)	6:33
	10	**Give The Mule What He Wants** (Queens Of The Stone Age)	3:09
▶	11	**I Was A Teenage Hand Model** (Queens Of The Stone Age)	5:01

Air | Moon Safari (1998)

Label | Virgin
Producer | Jean-Benoît Dunckel • Nicolas Godin
Art Direction | Mike Mills
Nationality | France
Running Time | 43:33

Moon Safari provides a look, a sound, and even a lifestyle, in one breezy swoop. Air's debut is kitschily retro, yet at the time of release seemed futuristic and sleek.

Much of this can be put down to the studio methodology of duo Jean-Benoît Dunckel and Nicolas Godin. Their love of analog sound—manifested most clearly through their choice of instrumentation (Moog® synths, valve amplifiers)—provided them with a trademark "chilled-out" identity that would be widely (and usually unsuccessfully) copied.

On "Sexy Boy," squelches and bass frequencies straight out of the 1970s are coupled with the weight of sultry French heritage. The album's strings, recorded at Abbey Road, were a deft touch (courtesy of David Whitaker, who had worked with Françoise Hardy and Serge Gainsbourg) that balances out the electro side of things. "Remember," the shortest track, saw French Moog® luminary Jean-Jacques Perrey coaxed into the studio—an experience he evidently enjoyed, to judge by his punchy, uplifting playing.

The result is the coffee table sound of the late 1990s. Like their *amis* Daft Punk, Air's background in the Paris club scene gave them all the encouragement they needed to make a record that would appeal to those coming home from a night out clubbing, yet most likely their parents too. Ultimately, *Moon Safari* is a beautifully human album, with cracked emotion, love, and longing aching from all ten tracks. "All I Need," may well have been a delicate nod to France's chanteuse past, but on the whole, Air were a duo very much looking to the future. **JK**

> "We are a free band. We don't care about being on the radio or having a hit."
>
> Nicolas Godin, 1999

Track Listing

▶	01	**La Femme D'Argent** (Dunckel • Godin)	7:08
▶	02	**Sexy Boy** (Dunckel • Godin)	4:57
▶	03	**All I Need** (Dunckel • Godin • Hirsch)	4:28
	04	**Kelly Watch The Stars** (Dunckel • Godin)	3:44
	05	**Talisman** (Dunckel • Godin)	4:16
▶	06	**Remember** (Dunckel • Godin • Perrey)	2:34
	07	**You Make It Easy** (Dunckel • Godin • Hirsch)	4:00
	08	**Ce Matin Là** (Dunckel • Godin • Woodcock)	3:38
	09	**New Star In The Sky (Chanson Pour Solal)** (Dunckel • Godin)	5:38
	10	**Le Voyage De Penelope** (Dunckel • Godin)	3:10

Talvin Singh | OK (1998)

Label | Island
Producer | Talvin Singh
Art Direction | Intro
Nationality | UK
Running Time | 60:42

Talvin Singh had toured the world with Sun Ra's Arkestra, guested with Madonna, Massive Attack, and Björk and formed a world beat trio with Nitin Sawhney and Keith Waithe.

He had also launched a remarkable London club night called Anokha, a thrilling showcase of Asian-influenced dub, hip hop, drum 'n' bass, and ambient music (as documented on his compilation *Soundz Of The Asian Underground*).

OK ("Go anywhere in the world and people know what OK is," he explained) was an appropriately eclectic project for such a pan-global musician. The lengthy opener "Traveller" is an epic in its own right: showcasing the vocalizing of MC Cleveland Watkiss, fluttering drum 'n' bass, slurring strings from the Madras Philharmonic Orchestra, and elegant classical flutes by Rakesh Churasia, Naveen, and Ryuichi Sakamoto. Elsewhere you will hear Japanese choirs, South Indian folk drummers, Jamaican MCs, and state-of-the-art breakbeats.

Singh displayed astonishing arrogance in interviews. He attacked Indo-jazz fusion as "exotica," lampooned those who used tablas and sitars without regard for the correct tuning, and lambasted former colleagues like Nitin Sawhney for the "ghettoized" British Asian record label Outcaste.

Many willed him to fail, but Singh pulled off a remarkable triumph with *OK*, creating audacious fusions that signaled new directions for electronica and world music alike. He was vindicated when the album beat Blur and The Chemical Brothers to win Britain's prestigious Mercury Music Award in 1999. **JLe**

> **"The industry needs to accept music that's a bit colorful. I am not a minority anymore ... "**
>
> Talvin Singh, 1999

Track Listing

▶	01	**Traveller** (Singh·Watkiss)	11:17
	02	**Butterfly** (Singh)	4:26
▶	03	**Sutrix** (Singh)	5:55
	04	**Mombasstic** (Singh)	5:45
	05	**Decca** (Singh)	1:24
	06	**Eclipse** (Singh)	5:46
▶	07	**OK** (Singh)	4:19
	08	**Light** (Singh)	6:23
	09	**Disser/Point.Mento.B** (Singh)	2:43
	10	**Soni** (Singh)	5:59
	11	**Vikram The Vampire** (Singh)	6:45

Korn | Follow The Leader (1998)

Label | Immortal
Producer | Korn • Steve Thompson • Toby Wright
Art Direction | Todd McFarlane
Nationality | USA
Running Time | 73:48

Korn's third release, *Follow The Leader*, trod the same urban/metal crossover path that saw the resounding success of the single "ADIDAS" from the Bakersfield, California band's sophomore album, *Life Is Peachy*. This move saw the band score further success in the singles charts, while *Follow The Leader* went on to set the standard for a genre that became known as nu-metal—hard rock that also drew on hip hop as an influence.

While still retaining the dark and heavy qualities that had made them so popular, Korn embrace a more sparse and groove-based sound here, allowing for greater variation in the dynamics of their sound and making them accessible to a much wider audience. Guest appearances from Pharcyde rapper Tre Hardson ("Cameltosis") and hip-hop legend Ice Cube ("Children Of The Korn") gave the group instant credibility, while Fred Durst contributes tongue-in-cheek dissing on "All In The Family" (his band, Limp Bizkit, came to be regarded as Korn's peer at nu-metal's helm). Hit single "Got The Life" (featuring disco rhythms and a slap bass) further cemented Korn's popularity.

Throughout, the lyrics are as downright nasty as hardcore fans could wish for—though frequently employed to point up intolerance and cruelty—as is Korn's trademark brutal sound (guitarists Shaffer and Welch use seven-string instruments). Todd McFarlane, creator of the comic book character Spawn, provided the cover art for the album as well as a Grammy award-winning film clip for the single, "Freak On A Leash."

So did this angry, twisted music do anything positive? It certainly made a truckload of money. **LJ**

"We've stayed underground."

Jonathan Davis, 2000

Track Listing

01–12 (silent)		
▶ 13	**It's On!** (Korn)	4:28
▶ 14	**Freak On A Leash** (Korn)	4:15
▶ 15	**Got The Life** (Korn)	3:45
16	**Dead Bodies Everywhere** (Korn)	4:44
▶ 17	**Children Of The Korn** (Korn)	3:52
18	**BBK** (Korn)	3:56
19	**Pretty** (Korn)	4:12
▶ 20	**All In The Family** (Korn)	4:48
21	**Reclaim My Place** (Korn)	4:32
22	**Justin** (Korn)	4:17
23	**Seed** (Korn)	5:54
▶ 24	**Cameltosis** (Korn)	4:38
25	**My Gift To You** (Korn)	15:40

Khaled | Kenza (1999)

Label | Barclay
Producer | Various
Art Direction | Ich And Kar
Nationality | Algeria
Running Time | 78:36

Khaled is the king of Rai, even though that music evolved from the Bedouin songs sung by "outlaw" women in 1920s Oran, Algeria. Born in 1960 in nearby Sidi-El-Houri, by the time Khaled recorded his first single, aged 16, he was a talented Rai vocalist and accordionist with a fervor for Egyptian, Spanish, and French music, along with that of The Beatles, James Brown, and Bob Marley. Adored by the young but hated by the religious establishment for his songs of passion and longing, he moved to France in 1986 and the early 1990s saw him transmuting Rai into an internationally popular music, with dancefloor smashes like the Don Was-produced "Didi" or the huge radio hit "Aicha."

In his wake, the decade saw a restless, electrifying evolution of North African music in France. Artists like Rachid Taha, Faudel, Gnawa Diffusion, and Orchestre National de Barbes all served notice on Khaled—he had no divine right to be at the cutting edge. He responded with this definitive and distinctive contribution, inspired by the new boys.

Kenza is such an epic journey that it can afford to meander up a few bland alleys, but there is no doubt about the fact that the King is here to reclaim his crown from the new pretenders. Buoyed up by the production of Rachid Taha's collaborator, Steve Hillage and, from New York's Brooklyn Funk Essential, Lati Kronlund—a kind of Gil Evans of big-band funk—the spine-tingling perfection of his mighty voice presides over a rich pan-North African vision which effortlessly shifts eastward to the Indian subcontinent or westward to Cuba and New York, taking in funk, reggae and Arabic influences. **MR**

Track Listing

▶ 01	**Aâlach Tloumouni** (Driche·Khaled)	5:02
02	**El Harba Wine** (Amar·Angar·Benamadouche·Idir·Khaled)	4:33
03	**C'est La Nuit** (Goldman)	5:04
04	**Imagine** (Lennon)	4:07
05	**Trigue Lycee** (Khaled)	4:43
06	**E'dir E'sseba** (Hamadi·Khaled·Kronlund)	5:50
07	**Ya Aâachkou** (Hamadi·Khaled·Kronlund)	3:57
08	**Melha** (Hamadi·Khaled)	6:07
▶ 09	**Raba–Raba** (H'Fit·Khaled)	5:37
▶ 10	**El Bab** (Hamadi·Khaled)	5:28
11	**El Aâdyene** (Hamadi·Khaled·Kronlund)	5:37
12	**Gouloulha–Dji** (Hamadi·Khaled·Kronlund)	5:37
▶ 13	**Mele H'bibti** (Khaled)	6:29
▶ 14	**Dewiche Tourneur** (Goldman)	6:00
15	**Leïli— "C'est La Nuit" (Arabic Version)** (Khaled·Goldman)	6:07

Kid Rock
Devil Without A Cause (1998)

Label | Lava
Producer | Kid Rock
Art Direction | Jennifer Barbato
Nationality | USA
Running Time | 71:11

After almost a decade of being snickered at, Kid Rock would have the last laugh when he embraced his inner rock 'n' roll party animal on *Devil Without A Cause*.

Rock had had plenty of close calls before, including 1990's uneven album *Grits Sandwiches For Breakfast*, but nobody, except maybe Rock himself, believed the vocalist-rapper could produce anything remotely like *Devil Without A Cause*. The timing, however, was right. Rap metal was peaking and, thus, Atlantic decided to pass Rock the mic. Immediately after signing, he rushed back to the Detroit area and began to celebrate so hard that he earned himself a night in jail. Obviously he didn't get it all out of his system before heading into the studio—the songs are filled with rowdy characters and the action swirls in hot tubs and mosh pits.

The record, which shows a cigar-smoking Rock looking suitably satanic on the cover, opens like few others. "Bawitdaba" is a monster, melding sledgehammer arena-rock riffs with chant-along lyrics. It must be played at top volume to be appreciated fully. Rock completes a potent one-two punch with the irresistible "Cowboy," an ode to sunny West Coast living. The singer then shows his range with the meticulously produced pop of "Wasting Time," which samples Fleetwood Mac, and the convincing ballad "Only God Knows Why." He also calls on fellow Detroit homeboy Eminem to help pen and rap the decadent metal-rich "F-ck Off." **JiH**

Boards Of Canada
Music Has The Right To Children (1998)

Label | Skam
Producer | M. Eoin • M. Sandison
Art Direction | Boards of Canada
Nationality | UK
Running Time | 70:57

Some artists make music so unique, they challenge not just your taste but your understanding of music. You might not like it right away, but you keep on trying. And then, somewhere around that fourth or fifth listen, there is that wonderful moment when something clicks.

Music Has The Right To Children by Boards Of Canada is one of those albums. From the moment it was released in late 1998, it caused a seismic shift in the electronica scene. A new ambient sub-genre was born, mixing pastoral melodies with darker undercurrents. This record proved to the naysayers that electronic music was not just intellectually stimulating, it could achieve real emotional depth as well.

The songs alternate between short sonic collages and longer, beat-driven tracks. The pounding beats and fragmented syllables of "Telephasic Workshop" gradually builds to a head-nodding cacophony. The only problem with the ominous bass, crispy beats, and rolling synths of "Roygbiv" is that the song is over far too soon. "Aquarius" is another standout, with its hypnotic blend of giggling children, numbers, and the word "orange."

Music Has The Right To Children also features an iconic cover. A washed-out photograph from the 1970s depicts an eerily faceless family posing at a scenic mountain overlook. It is an image that captures the essence of the music with its themes of nostalgia, the natural and the artificial, the sinister and the serene. **RM**

Suba
São Paulo
Confessions (1999)

Label | Ziriguiboom
Producer | Suba
Art Direction | Christophe Portier
Nationality | Yugoslavia
Running Time | 61:22

As a young man in Yugoslavia, Mitar Subotic studied music theory, piano and accordion playing, and composition, and created fiercely original electronic music. Shifting to Paris in 1986, his electronic piece based on Yugoslavian folk lullabies, *In The Mooncage*, received the International Fund for Promotion Of Culture award from UNESCO, which included a three-month scholarship to research indigenous music and Afro-Brazilian rhythms. The three months became three years after Suba—as he was nicknamed—fell in love with Brazil and its music, quickly learning Portuguese, and soon establishing himself as the foremost producer of new Brazilian music.

It was Suba who produced Bebel Gilberto's *Tanto Tempo* and in 1999 he released his own album, *São Paulo Confessions*, to critical acclaim. The album finds Suba creating sensual and dissonant electronic soundscapes. On "Felicidade," vocalist Cibelle croons exotic bossa nova over a shimmering rhythm. Following tune "Um Dia Comum" is spiky, abstract dance music. Suba's feel for nuances of mood and color allowed him to create fiercely expressive musical collages.

A fire broke out in Suba's apartment on November 2, 1999, and overcome by smoke, he died. His legacy may only be a handful of recordings, but for helping bring Brazilian music into the twenty-first century he will always be honored. **GC**

XTC
Apple Venus
Volume 1 (1999)

Label | TVT
Producer | Haydn Bendall • Nick Davis
Art Direction | Cactus Design
Nationality | UK
Running Time | 50:06

If some joker had handed a listener an unmarked copy of XTC's *Apple Venus Volume 1* in 1999 and claimed it was the then lost Brian Wilson masterpiece, *Smile*, it would have been easy to fall for the gag. In truth, the sunny, hopeful album turned out to be another one of XTC's mostly overlooked later masterpieces, an exquisite piece of highly orchestral pop adored by critics and basically ignored by the public. The fact that the band never toured it surely did not help sales. Plus, XTC waited seven years between releases.

Still, it is impossible to deny the potency of *Apple Venus Volume 1*, which ranks as one of the group's finest offerings. The album expands on the psychedelic Beach Boys vibe struck on *Nonsuch* with heavily layered vocal harmonies, contained experimentation, and lush passages compliments of the London Session Orchestra. Its most dramatic moment comes with the opening "River Of Orchids," as it slowly builds from a sparse string arrangement into a mesmerizing symphony of spiraling sounds and voices. Partridge then purrs alongside a skipping beat on "I'd Like That" and waltzes amid violins and trumpet on "Easter Theater."

Although the album often more closely resembles the work Partridge did with Martin Newell and Harold Budd in the mid-1990s, *Apple Venus Volume 1* was still a band affair. In fact, Colin Moulding's two quirky compositions are among the finest in this fine set. **JiH**

Skunk Anansie | Post Orgasmic Chill (1999)

Label | Virgin
Producer | Andy Wallace
Art Direction | Michael Nash Associates
Nationality | UK
Running Time | 50:51

After two warmly received albums with independent label One Little Indian, the arrival of Skunk Anansie's major-label debut was expected to see the agit-rockers breakthrough into the big-time.

Virgin forked out the cash to send the band to the plush Bearsville Studios and Clinton Studios in New York to record their highly anticipated third LP. But, despite a headlining slot at Glastonbury Festival, 1999 failed to be the year many believed the band deserved.

Vocalist Skin, with her shaved head and fearless tirades, had become the mouthpiece of British black-feminist rage; tracks like the opening "Charlie Big Potato" set the self-appointed egocentric male hierarchy firmly in its sights, and in turn the tone for the album. *Q* referred to it as "sonic warfare fed through speakers."

But the band had become accustomed to reaching the extremes of heaven and hell and proved equally at home on quieter tracks, forsaking political fury for reflection and contemplation. Skin's emotive voice soars alongside epic string arrangements on tracks "You'll Follow Me Down" and "Lately," while "Secretly" is a passionate response to infidelity.

By *Post Orgasmic Chill* the band had started to stretch their sound and new influences, such as drum 'n' bass, had burrowed into their established indie-rock. The rough edges of previous records had been worn away to pull together their vulnerability and brutish force in equal measure and with deft subtlety.

Although *Post Orgasmic Chill* proved beyond doubt to be Skunk Anansie's swan song—it remains a triumphant statement on which to bow out. **ARo**

"I don't mince words ..."

Skin, 2003

Track Listing

▶ 01	Charlie Big Potato (Ace•Lewis•Richardson•Skin)	5:30
02	On My Hotel TV (Ace•Lewis•Richardson•Skin)	3:34
03	We Don't Need Who Do You Think You Are (Ace•Lewis•Richardson•Skin)	4:21
04	Tracy's Flaw (Ace•Arran•Skin)	4.30
05	The Skank Heads (Ace•Lewis•Richardson•Skin)	3:11
▶ 06	Lately (Ace•Lewis•Richardson•Skin)	3:53
▶ 07	Secretly (Arran•Skin)	4:45
08	Good Things Don't Always Come To You (Ace•Arran•Skin)	5:25
09	Cheap Honesty (Arran•Skin)	3:47
▶ 10	You'll Follow Me Down (Arran•Skin)	4:01
11	And This Is Nothing That I Thought I Had (Ace•Lewis•Richardson•Skin)	3:04
12	I'm Not Afraid (Ace•Lewis•Richardson•Skin)	4:50

Incubus
Make Yourself (1999)

Label | Epic
Producer | Incubus • Scott Litt
Art Direction | Brandy Flower
Nationality | USA
Running Time | 48:10

The Magnetic Fields
69 Love Songs (1999)

Label | Merge
Producer | Stephin Merritt
Art Direction | Michael English
Nationality | USA
Running Time | 172:35

If nu-metal stood as one of the biggest musical genres at the turn of the millennium then *Make Yourself* was its finest hour.

Incubus fully appreciated the anger and power of the rap-rock scene, enjoying huge success without becoming a caricature of their own existence.

Make Yourself manages to bridge the tastes of a mass market without selling out to appease a single genre. For their sophomore record Incubus could have easily targeted the burgeoning teenage mosher scene, but instead they enlisted long-time R.E.M. producer Scott Litt to create a more adult and contemplative record without losing their younger fan base.

The album fuses classic riffs with Brandon Boyd's soaring vocals, and leaves listeners punching the air in triumph. The singer's natural ability to effortlessly swing from laidback cool to full-on battle cry makes "Stellar" so essential. Meanwhile, "Privilege" and "Clean" are monstrous rockers that fizz with energy.

But when they want, Incubus can change the mood without interrupting the album's flow—they turn on the funk via turntable wizardry and smooth basslines on "Battlestar Scralatchtica" and mellow out on the acoustic grunge anthem "Drive," without losing their way.

While many of its contemporaries now sound dated thanks to an over reliance on fads and gimmickry, *Make Yourself* remains a standout album thanks to the first-rate songwriting and tight musicianship that continuously throw the listener new hooks. **ARo**

Amazingly, The Magnetic Fields' triple album *69 Love Songs* actually lived up to its hubristic title, offsetting a stunning orgy of creativity with a good measure of salacious irony. The band's frontman/songwriter/ringleader, Stephin Merritt, crafted his songs out of long-forgotten pop clichés, turning them on their heads and rendering each one beautiful and timeless. Most of these poignant ditties feel disarmingly familiar, yet Merritt finds new and mischievous ways to subvert each effort, be it with schizophrenic electroclash beats, renegade ukulele lines, or lyrical insights into love's inanities.

Playing dozens of instruments and referencing sources as disparate as Abba, Tom Waits, and Kraftwerk, Merritt and three other singers adopt an array of genre-crossing and gender-bending personas: a Hibernian romantic marching off to war against a wall of reverb-drenched guitar in "Abigail, Belle Of Kilronan"; a truck-stop romantic dealing with honky-tonk wanderlust in "Papa Was A Rodeo."

Merritt slips very easily into the persona of a broken-hearted misanthrope unsure whether to shrug his shoulders—the bossa-tinged break-up song "I Think I Need A New Heart" is positively celebratory—or to despair, as in the self-deprecatory folk anthem "Grand Canyon." But his most remarkable outpourings occur when he turns his melancholic baritone to pure tenderness, as during the outrageously beautiful tear-jerker "Busby Berkeley Dreams" and the heartbreakingly honest accordion lullaby "Asleep And Dreaming." **MW**

Travis
The Man Who (1999)

Label | Independiente
Producer | Nigel Godrich • Mike Hedges
Art Direction | Blue Source
Nationality | UK
Running Time | 48:00

Slipknot
Slipknot (1999)

Label | Roadrunner
Producer | Ross Robinson
Art Direction | Slipknot
Nationality | USA
Running Time | 58:11

On May 31, 1996, four young Glaswegian musicians moved to London. They had been gigging in Scotland for five years, with little real progress. Bowing to the inevitable, they headed for the UK's music capital. Sure enough, they soon landed record and publishing deals. They released a well-received debut album of Britpop-lite tunes called *Good Feeling* and supported Oasis. But Travis had not made it yet.

In 1999, their world wobbled on its axis. Their second album, *The Man Who*, became the biggest selling album in the UK by a British band that year. By early 2000 they had won Brit Awards for Best Band and Best British Album, and there was a copy of *The Man Who* in one in eight households in Britain. Truly, this was a people's band.

Why the fuss? Because *The Man Who* is one of the most sublimely melodic, emotionally affecting, elegantly played rock records of the modern era. Just ask any member of the festival masses who stood in a field at Glastonbury, V99, or T In The Park in the summer of 1999, singing blissfully—and wetly—along to "Why Does It Always Rain On Me?" Travis were masters at crafting such perfect communal moments, with or without a helping hand from meteorology.

That is the beauty of Fran Healy's writing on *The Man Who*. His songs are deeply personal, but irresistibly inclusive. Intimate, but extrovert. "Driftwood," "Writing To Reach You," "Turn"—these are little starbursts of poetry, underpinned by soaring choruses. **CM**

Slipknot came out of nowhere (well, Des Moines, Iowa) in 1999 to unleash this concussive album on the world's metal fans. It features a vocalist who can rap, sing, scream, or growl, alongside the brutality of a thrash-metal band with extra percussion, plus the versatility of a DJ and a sampler. The music—a dense mixture of sledgehammer drums (a kit plus two sets of percussion), avalanches of guitar, turntable noise—may have been too hardcore for a mainstream audience, and the band overlooked by the masses, save for their imposing physical presence: Slipknot were nine psychopaths in jumpsuits (numbered, to distinguish them) and horror masks, who brutally assaulted their chosen sonic weaponry, and often each other, in a cacophony of measured mayhem.

Unsurprisingly, *Slipknot* took off like a rocket (platinum in the United States, gold in the UK). After a brief opening sample (an elderly woman opining, "The whole thing … I think it's sick"), "(Sic)" violently sets the tone for the album. "Eyeless" mixes a drum 'n' bass loop with merciless guitar riffage; "Surfacing" alternates piercing feedback with scratching; "Spit It Out" is speed metal meets rap. It was the softer sections of the single "Wait And Bleed" that first grabbed at an audience beyond regular metal fans, though. And the music's close association with extreme sports such as freestyle motorcross and skateboarding also gave the group an immediate avenue into a wealth of fans both young and old. **LJ**

Beth Orton | Central Reservation (1999)

Label | Heavenly
Producer | Various
Art Direction | Studio X
Nationality | UK
Running Time | 59:20

BETH ORTON CENTRAL RESERVATION

Central Reservation marked a maturation in Beth Orton's songwriting after her 1996 album *Trailer Park*, a mix of folk and subtle trip-hop beats that went gold in the UK.

Opener "Stolen Car," featuring some mesmerizing slide guitar courtesy of Ben Harper, provided a UK Top 40 hit for her. The moving "Pass In Time," which begins gently with Orton and a softly plucked guitar, develops into a powerful song that deals with a recurring theme in the artist's songwriting—her mother's death—and draws an impassioned performance from her. Jazz and folk legend Terry Callier provides backing vocals (the two had released a joint EP, "Best Bit," in 1997) which, alongside Dr. Robert's guitar arpeggios, contribute toward a wonderfully uplifting chorus.

The acoustic version of the title track is almost forgotten between "Pass In Time" and the echoed beats of "Stars All Seem To Weep," on which Orton's lightly soaring voice mixes with woven abstract noises courtesy of Ben Watt, producer, programmer, and one half of Everything But The Girl. Electronica is the exception rather than the norm here, however: in contrast to *Trailer Park*, this album's strengths lie in its stripped-down acoustic ambience and Orton's captivating vocals.

Orton has been dubbed something of a melancholy songstress, but the Dylan-like jollity of "Love Like Laughter" repudiates that charge; Ben Harper's slide guitar adds a flourish to the song. Finally, Ben Watt returns to add beats and keyboards to a more chart-friendly version of "Central Reservation."

A very strong addition to an already impressive back catalog. **AMa**

"*Central Reservation* generates a special buzz of its own."

Rolling Stone, 1999

Track Listing

▶	01	**Stolen Car** (Barnes·Blanchard·Orton·Read)	5:25
	02	**Sweetest Decline** (Orton)	5:39
	03	**Couldn't Cause Me Harm** (Barnes·Blanchard·Orton·Read)	4:48
	04	**So Much More** (Orton)	5:41
▶	05	**Pass In Time** (Orton)	7:17
	06	**Central Reservation (The Original Version)** (Orton)	4:50
▶	07	**Stars All Seem To Weep** (Orton)	4:39
	08	**Love Like Laughter** (Barnes·Orton)	3:37
▶	09	**Blood Red River** (Orton)	4:15
	10	**Devil Song** (Orton)	5:04
▶	11	**Feel To Believe** (Orton)	4:04
	12	**Central Reservation (The Then Again Version)** (Orton)	4:01

Nitin Sawhney | Beyond Skin (1999)

Label | Outcaste
Producer | Nitin Sawhney
Art Direction | Zip Design
Nationality | UK
Running Time | 58:22

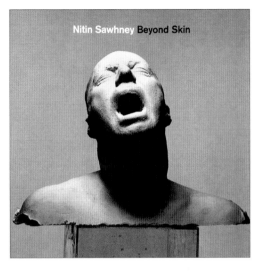

Nitin was born and raised in Rochester, Kent, the son of Hindus from the Punjab, and learned piano, guitar, and Indian percussion. From there, his resumé becomes increasingly surreal—an accountancy degree; a spell with Medway jazz-funkers The James Taylor Quartet; a worldbeat outfit with Talvin Singh called the Tihai Trio; sessions with Sinéad O'Connor, Sting, and Paul McCartney; composer in residence at the Theatre Royal Stratford; and a spell as actor and writer on the BBC comedy show *Goodness Gracious Me*.

His first solo albums *Displacing The Priest* and *Migrations* had drawn from flamenco, jazz, funk, drum 'n' bass, Indian classical taals, qawwali, bols, and Urdu verse—but the fusion process was problematic. His third album for London-based Asian imprint Outcaste, however, saw him distill this source material into something utterly unique. It is political both implicitly (investigating the links between Indian and Gypsy, between Hindu and Muslim) and explicitly (addressing the nuclear arms race between India and Pakistan and the rise of Hindu fundamentalism).

Sawhney's core band features Bombay-born bassist Shri, flamboyant U.S. percussionist Marque Gilmore, and tabla player Aref Durvesh. But, in marshaling a cast of disparate voices (Hindustani classical vocalist Devinder Singh, samba singer Nina Miranda, sighing Bengali vocalist Jayante Bose, soul diva Sanchita Farrugue, Dream Warriors rapper Spek), Sawhney works like a movie director, casting roles in his epic, beautiful, cinematic soundscapes. No wonder a career scoring movies in Hollywood beckoned. **JLe**

> ## "It's about how nationality ... and power structures take away our sense of identity."
>
> Nitin Sawhney, 1999

Track Listing

▶	01	**Broken Skin** (Farruque·Sawhney)	4:05
▶	02	**Letting Go** (Gray·Sawhney)	4:49
	03	**Homelands** (Miranda·Sawhney)	6:00
	04	**The Pilgrim** (Sawhney·Yoosuf)	4:29
	05	**Tides** (Sawhney)	5:06
	06	**Nadia** (Sawhney)	5:05
▶	07	**Immigrant** (Sawhney)	6:21
	08	**Serpents** (Sawhney)	6:17
	09	**Anthem Without Nation** (Sawhney·Singh)	5:48
	10	**Nostalgia** (Sawhney)	3:41
	11	**The Conference** (Sawhney)	2:53
▶	12	**Beyond Skin** (Sawhney)	3:48

Death In Vegas | **The Contino Sessions** (1999)

Label | Concrete
Producer | Richard Fearless • Tim Holmes
Art Direction | Richard Fearless
Nationality | UK
Running Time | 48:01

Thanks to Richard Fearless' DJ slots at London's Heavenly Social alongside The Chemical Brothers, Death In Vegas found themselves lumped in with the burgeoning "big beat" scene that was spilling lager across UK dancefloors in the late 1990s. But Fearless and David Holmes—alongside guitarist Ian Button and bassist Mat Flint—put such associations to bed with this follow-up, named after their "Contino Rooms" studio in Clerkenwell, East London.

Opening with a solitary strummed guitar and stirring minimal vocals by Fearless' girlfriend Dot Allison, "Dirge" builds gradually into an unnerving crescendo of analog synthesizer noise and walls of guitars. The dub-inspired "Soul Auctioneer," featuring Bobby Gillespie, consummates the DIV and Primal Scream mutual appreciation society, while the album's dark tone continues on "Death Threat"'s feedback and industrial electronics. "Flying" has a more spatial feel, recalling early Can, and leads to Iggy Pop's serial killer narrative "Aisha," arguably his most powerful work since The Stooges. Former Jesus And Mary Chain vocalist Jim Reid conjures up the memory of his former group on the brooding and feedback-ridden "Dance Little Sister," while "Aladdin's Story," graced by the stunning vocal talents of the London Community Gospel Choir, offers the only light relief among all the shadowy intensity.

Straddling the middle ground between modern rock music and electronic experimentalism, *Contino Sessions'* gothic eclecticism alongside records such as Massive Attack's *Mezzanine* was evidence that darker forces had replaced club culture's early optimism. **CSh**

> ## "We wanted it to be organic, like Krautrock or the psychedelic stuff, we wanted to have that raw soul."
>
> Richard Fearless, 1999

Track Listing

▶	01	**Dirge** (Fearless•Whitlock)	5:45
	02	**Soul Auctioneer** (Fearless•Gillespie•Holmes)	5:59
	03	**Death Threat** (Fearless•Holmes)	4:50
	04	**Flying** (Fearless•Holmes)	7:06
▶	05	**Aisha** (Fearless•Hellier•Holmes•Pop)	5:54
	06	**Lever Street** (Fearless•Holmes)	3:39
	07	**Aladdin's Story** (Fearless•Holmes•Unknown)	4:45
	08	**Broken Little Sister** (Button•Fearless•Flint•Holmes•Reid)	5:18
	09	**Neptune City** (Fearless•Holmes)	4:45

Moby | Play (1999)

Label | V2
Producer | Moby
Art Direction | Ysabel Zu Innhausen Un Knyphausen
Nationality | USA
Running Time | 62:43

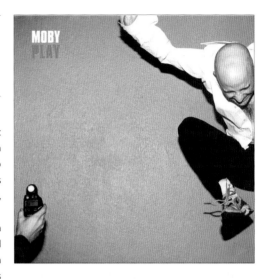

With *Play*, Moby delivered accessible electronic music that was difficult to dislike. The album coincided with the end of the genre's outsider appeal but it is unfair to hang the mainstreaming of electronica on *Play*, since its accessibility stems mainly from the inclusion of blues, gospel, and rock elements.

A direct descendant of *Moby Dick* writer Herman Melville (hence his stage name), the man born Richard Melville Hall played classical guitar, spent time in hardcore bands, and sung alt.rock before finding his place behind the turntables. His early releases were equally cheered and jeered for their user-friendly spin on club culture. By 1997's *I Like To Score*, Moby was well on his way to becoming one of the faces of electronic music, a status he would secure with *Play*.

While songs like "Honey" and "Bodyrock" could hold their own on dancefloors from Ibiza to San Francisco, *Play* is not as much a dance record as it is a pop album. Moby was magpie-like in approach, building the irresistible opener "Honey" around a short sample from Georgia blues belter Bessie Jones. He uses the Shining Light Gospel Choir for the soaring lines that fuel the intimate "Why Does My Heart Feel So Bad?" and then carefully cuts and pastes vocals from Bill Landford And The Landfordaires into the driving "Run On."

Play was an overwhelming commercial hit, scoring the top spot in Britain and selling more than two million copies. Not that everyone was so pleased: R.E.M.'s Michael Stipe complained at the time about how miffed he was to keep being mistaken for Moby on the street. **JiH**

Track Listing

▶ 01	**Honey** (Moby)	3:27
02	**Find My Baby** (Moby)	3:58
03	**Porcelain** (Moby)	4:01
▶ 04	**Why Does My Heart Feel So Bad?** (Moby)	4:23
▶ 05	**South Side** (Moby)	3:48
06	**Rushing** (Moby)	2:58
▶ 07	**Bodyrock** (Moby)	3:34
▶ 08	**Natural Blues** (Moby)	4:12
09	**Machete** (Moby)	3:36
10	**7** (Moby)	1:00
▶ 11	**Run On** (Moby)	3:43
12	**Down Slow** (Moby)	1:34
13	**If Things Were Perfect** (Moby)	4:17
14	**Everloving** (Moby)	3:24
15	**Inside** (Moby)	4:47
16	**Guitar Flute And String** (Moby)	2:07
17	**The Sky Is Broken** (Moby)	4:17
18	**My Weakness** (Moby)	3:37

The Flaming Lips
The Soft Bulletin (1999)

Label | Warner Bros.
Producer | Flaming Lips • D. Fridmann
Art Direction | George Salisbury
Nationality | USA
Running Time | 58:26

Profoundly humane. There is no better way to describe the release that finally heralded The Flaming Lips as one of the most ingenious, astonishingly honest, and downright important groups on the planet.

Still considered by many fans to be their finest piece of work, *The Soft Bulletin* saw The Flaming Lips go pop after the unashamedly ambitious (and critically polarizing) four-disc set, *Zaireeka*—all four discs designed to be played simultaneously, on four separate CD systems. With the help of producer Dave Fridmann, the Oklahoma City trio created a sound at once lush and powerful, subtle and intense, angelic and possessed. It was the album that would propel the group into the new millennium, poised to spread their message of hope for humanity, a theme developed further in follow-up *Yoshimi Battles The Pink Robots*.

A stunning symbiosis of lyrical might and musical majesty, *The Soft Bulletin* harnesses the potential power of musical expression, and converts it into a full-blown aural and cerebral assault. "Race For The Prize," with its soaring, reverb-drenched keyboard line, is a perfect opener. "Waitin' For A Superman" explores the psychological weight created by the postmodern condition, with "The Gash" acting as a kind of call to arms in this, the fight for sanity. Fridmann's influence is clear, the richer sound helps the songwriting flourish.

A conceptual masterpiece (without being a concept album), *The Soft Bulletin* steers clear of pretension by virtue of the weight and clarity of its vision. **DZ**

Les Rythmes Digitales
Darkdancer (1999)

Label | Wall of Sound
Producer | Jacques Lu Cont
Art Direction | Philip Castle
Nationality | UK
Running Time | 58:53

Released in 1999, *Darkdancer* was the second album of the Les Rythmes Digitales project. The outfit was first formed by Jacques Lu Cont (aka Stuart Price), a Francophile trapped in the body of a lad from Reading, England, who had embraced "Frenchness" as an irresistible catalyst for his energetic, hypnotic, and stylish musical output. Apparently, Lu Cont's alternative title for *Darkdancer* was "No Jacquet Required"—this allusion to Phil Collins' 1985 album would have been a neat hint of the treats to come.

Recorded at Quad Studios in New York, *Darkdancer* is Europop at its best, capturing the feel of the Eighties in a way that was actually impossible to achieve with the technology of the time. The historical resonance of the music is reinforced by the appearance of former pop idol Nik Kershaw on the beautifully crafted "Sometimes," and Boy George is rolled out for the clip to "(Hey You) What's That Sound." Les Rythmes Digitales are all about having fun—to quote one lyric, "Don't just sit there dreaming . . . dance!" From start to finish, the album casts a rhythmic spell. The driving beats and repetitive lyric of "From: Disco To: Disco" lodge firmly in the mind, making this track the definitive anthem for punters who never know when to go home after a night of clubbing. (The striking cover art was co-created by Philip Castle, the artist behind the poster for Stanley Kubrick's *A Clockwork Orange*.)

Faux French electronica at its best, *Darkdancer* is like having a discothèque on your iPod. **LA**

Le Tigre
Le Tigre (1999)

Label | Mr Lady
Producer | Chris Stamey • Le Tigre
Art Direction | Splendid Corp.
Nationality | USA
Running Time | 34:29

With the seminal riot grrl act Bikini Kill, Kathleen Hanna raged against the machine and stood up for young women. With Le Tigre, the vocalist-guitarist seems content to just groove to the beat and join the crowd on the dancefloor. But in its own way, Le Tigre is just as much about feminist issues and "girl power" as the more overtly message-driven Bikini Kill. Adopting the old adage that one "attracts more flies with honey than vinegar," Hanna has gotten out of listeners' faces and, in doing so, gotten even more into their minds.

Sugaring the pill has rarely been more effective or fun than on Le Tigre's eponymous release, an absolute smorgasbord of swirling new wave, playful electronica, softcore punk, and bubblegum pop. Le Tigre takes such a different road to the full-frontal attack found on Bikini Kill's essential Pussy Whipped, that it seems almost inconceivable that they share the same frontperson.

Originally intended as the live band behind Hanna's 1998 solo record, Julie Ruin, the trio featuring bassist Johanna Fateman and beat-master Sadie Benning gelled beautifully on Le Tigre. A driving B-52's groove drives the album's addictive opener, "Deceptacon," then buzz-saw guitar and droning vocals beg the make-or-break question "What's Yr Take On Cassavetes." The record's centerpiece is "Hot Topic," a sunny, samples-driven shout-out to pro-women activists. It is a song that will make you dance and, hopefully, inspire you to learn more about the ladies mentioned. Something for the feet and the head—and that is Le Tigre in a nutshell. **JiH**

Eminem
The Slim Shady LP (1999)

Label | Aftermath
Producer | Jeff Bass • Marky Bass • Dr. Dre
Art Direction | Mark LeRoy
Nationality | USA
Running Time | 59:48

Not since Elvis Presley shimmied on Sullivan has a white man doing black music stimulated the controversy that Marshall Mathers encountered with The Slim Shady LP. Watchdogs denounced the violent imagery and homophobic lyrics, though millions got the joke that Mathers, cloaked in the roles of street-tough Eminem and practical joker Slim Shady, was just lighting fires to watch them burn. But there was enough of a doubt in his intentions, thanks to the meticulously descriptive storylines, to make Slim Shady an intriguing soap opera.

Mathers' own soap opera began in an impoverished area of Detroit near 8 Mile Road, the thoroughfare that serves as a border between whites and blacks. He had the gift of the gab as a teen and was soon challenging the Vanilla Ice stigma as a battle rapper competing against black MCs. Despite the endorsement of Dr. Dre, who signed Mathers to his Aftermath imprint, Eminem still sounds like he is fighting for respect on Slim Shady.

The album strikes an artful balance between schoolboy shenanigans, tales from the 'hood, and horror movie plots. "My Name Is" serves as a laugh riot of an introduction, while "97' Bonnie And Clyde" is a chilling scenario in which the rapper kills his wife and takes their child along with him to dispose of the body. Other rappers have been funnier or more deadly. But no one had ever sounded both as menacing and comical as Eminem on "Guilty Conscience."

Slim Shady announced what many consider to be the voice of a generation. **JiH**

Britney Spears | ...Baby One More Time (1999)

Label | Jive
Producer | Per Magnusson • Max Martin • Eric Foster White
Art Direction | Jackie Murphy
Nationality | USA
Running Time | 42:20

There is simply no denying the huge impact that Britney Spears' debut had on popular music. With this sleek package of Euro-inspired dance numbers, heartsick love ballads, and gimmicky tunes, Spears would reignite a worldwide interest in teen-targeted acts that had not been seen on such an extreme level since David Cassidy or The Beatles. Yes, without Britney Spears, we might never have had Jessica Simpson.

Her seismic impact on popular culture spawned multiple fashion trends and generated Princess Diana-style paparazzi coverage. From as young an age as 17, she was depicted in the media as the perfect mix of seduction and innocence, and Spears quickly became a Lolita for a brand new generation of dirty old men; the number of internet searches that read "Britney Spears naked" has grown incalculable over time.

Although dismissed by most critics, ... *Baby One More Time* would quickly move more than ten million copies and become one of the biggest selling debuts of all time. Credit part of that to her million-dollar smile, but it is mainly due to the rump-shaking title track, which even haters have to admit stands as one of the era's best dance songs. Three more winners follow: the exuberant "(You Drive Me) Crazy," the anthemic ballad "Sometimes," and the gloriously empty-headed "Soda Pop." "Born To Make You Happy" is an effortlessly catchy memento from an obsessively devoted lover, in the tradition of "You Don't Have To Say You Love Me." And closing the album with a cover of Sonny Bono's "The Beat Goes On," one of the all-time hipster favorites, is a stroke of genius. **JiH**

> ## "If things slow down for me I'll definitely go to college."
>
> Britney Spears, 1999

Track Listing

	#	Title	Time
▶	01	**...Baby One More Time** (Martin)	3:30
▶	02	**(You Drive Me) Crazy** (Elofsson • Krueger • Magnusson • Martin)	3:17
▶	03	**Sometimes** (Elofsson)	4:05
▶	04	**Soda Pop** (Bassie • White)	3:20
	05	**Born To Make You Happy** (Carlsson • Lundin)	4:03
	06	**From The Bottom Of My Broken Heart** (White)	5:11
	07	**I Will Be There** (Carlsson • Martin)	3:53
	08	**I Will Still Love You** (White)	4:02
	09	**Thinkin' About You** (Bassie • White)	3:35
	10	**E-Mail My Heart** (White)	3:41
▶	11	**The Beat Goes On** (Bono)	3:43

Metallica
S&M (1999)

Label | Elektra
Producer | Various
Art Direction | Andie Airfix
Nationality | USA
Running Time | 133:01

In November 1999, Berlin celebrated the tenth anniversary of the fall of the Wall, and Metallica unleashed an orchestral ode to joy. Their ninth album captures the band in action live and playing with the San Francisco Symphony.

The rock/classical fusion dates back to horrors like *Concerto For Group And Orchestra* by Lars Ulrich's beloved Deep Purple. Metallica carried it off in style on 1991's self-titled album: "Nothing Else Matters" and "The Unforgiven" boasted orchestral backing by maestro Michael Kamen, who had worked with Eric Clapton and Pink Floyd. After years of effort, Kamen talked the metallers into a full-blown collaboration.

"He wanted to get a little more extreme," said James Hetfield. "So he chose us. I'm sure there's something more extreme—like Graveworm—but I think we were a pretty good choice. We said, Hell yeah."

This gung-ho approach works wonders on *Symphony & Metallica*. The set boasts classics from the thrilling "The Call Of Ktulu" to the crowd-pleasing "Enter Sandman," but also invigorates numbers from *Load* and *Reload* albums.

As a companion DVD illustrates, everyone revels in the collaboration, the classicists adding gothic, cinematic counterparts to the band's electric—in all senses—performance. The grandiose interplay reaches fiery heights on "Fuel," "No Leaf Clover" (one of two new songs, the other being "Human"), and the epic "One"—the audience reaction is ecstatic. Classic indeed! **TJ**

Bonnie "Prince" Billy
I See A Darkness (1999)

Label | Domino
Producer | Paul Oldham
Art Direction | Sammy Harkham
Nationality | USA
Running Time | 37:56

What with Nostradamus' end-of-the-world prophecy and the looming Millennium bug, 1999 was an uneasy year. The perfect time then, to release a record seeped in human fear, failing, and forgiveness—Will Oldham's bleak country masterpiece.

Louisville, Kentucky-born Oldham had started out as a child actor, and his ability to assume different roles spilled into his music (he recorded as Palace Brothers and Palace too). Oldham says his Bonnie "Prince" Billy moniker is a round-up of Bonnie Prince Charlie, Nat King Cole, and Billy The Kid: "It serves a lot of purposes. I feel comfortable going through a whole conversation being called Bonnie instead of Will."

Oldham being so "out" of the record makes it all the more intimate. *I See A Darkness* is full of storytelling, and like folklore, its narratives lead directly to the bigger, blacker truths. While the titles are foreboding ("Another Day Full Of Dread"), the music is soft and understated: spare piano chords, brushed drums, warm bass.

That Oldham's voice is so gentle and brittle gives potency to the dark, violent, often celebratory world he articulates. At the album's heart is its title track (memorably covered by Johnny Cash), which announces its arrival so quietly it could be death itself: "Did you ever, ever notice, the kind of thoughts I got?" asks a brave, trembling voice, an acknowledgement of the primal fears and desires that we all share.

A gothic folk touchstone. **SH**

Shack
H.M.S. Fable (1999)

Label | London
Producer | Hugh Jones • Youth
Art Direction | Stylorouge
Nationality | UK
Running Time | 46:55

Little wonder that *H.M.S. Fable* sounds so wonderful. It was made by a band drinking a final pint in the last chance saloon. These soulful songs of hardscrabble life on the streets of Liverpool were the culmination of almost two decades of musical graft, terrible misfortune, and crippling addiction. The jaunty rhythms and shouty chorus of "Lend's Some Dough" belie its subject matter— the need for cash to buy a fix of heroin. Ditto "Streets Of Kenny," a windswept folk song about a fruitless drugs search in the run-down neighborhood of Kensington.

Brothers Mick and John Head never shied away from their problems. They were open about the fact that their second album *Waterpistol* was fueled by cocaine and ecstasy; that the "side" project *The Magical World Of Michael Head And The Strands* was a heroin album. Before all that, there was Mick Head's time in The Pale Fountains, a great "lost" band revered by Echo And The Bunnymen's Ian McCulloch, but whose love of Burt Bacharach was 20 years too early. In a grim twist, Head's songwriting partner in "The Paleys," Chris McCaffrey, died of a brain tumour aged 28.

So *H.M.S. Fable* is the Heads putting all that behind them and digging deep. Their love of West Coast American pop shines through on the chiming "Since I Met You." "I Want You" is Arthur Lee's Love relocated to Merseyside. "Beautiful," "Natalie's Party," and "Comedy" are soaring pop songs, aided by Youth's lush production.

This is the sound of a fabled but troubled British songwriter making it through to the other side. **CM**

Basement Jaxx
Remedy (1999)

Label | XL
Producer | Basement Jaxx
Art Direction | Blue Source
Nationality | UK
Running Time | 57:02

Preacher's son Felix Buxton and ex-squatter Simon Ratcliffe burst out of the Brixton, South London underground club scene in the late 1990s. Longtime jazz heads and beat fanatics, this pair of DJs and producers were standard-bearers for the anti-superclub ethos that was then responsible for the more interesting noises in UK dance culture. They preferred to host rambunctious parties in the backrooms of dank pubs.

But first there was *Remedy*. Basement Jaxx's debut album is a thrilling mix of samba and Latin flavors, crunching beats, soulful vocals, and anthemic tunes precision-tooled to tear up dancefloors. It sounds like it was made in Rio, or Miami, or Paris, by a crack international squad of veteran sonic explorers. In fact, it was "homemade" in a small South London studio by two white, middle-class music fanatics-cum-geeks.

It begins with the flamenco-esque guitar strums, vocodered vocals, and pneumatic rhythms of "Rendez-Vu." And the excitement barely lets up for the following 14 tracks. Even the four get-your-breath-back interludes— "Jaxxalude," "Jazzalude," "Sneakalude," "Gemilude"—are short, sharp snippets of inventiveness, the sound of a radio dial being spun across the global groove frequencies. As heard on hit singles "Red Alert" and "Bingo Bango," this was fruity, poppy, colorful, celebratory stuff. Like a carnival on record. This is what is so exciting about *Remedy*, and why it became that rare thing: a dance album that rewarded repeated listening.

Banging, as they used to say. **CM**

Red Hot Chili Peppers | Californication (1999)

Label | Warner Bros.
Producer | Rick Rubin
Art Direction | Lawrence Azerrad • Red Hot Chili Peppers
Nationality | USA
Running Time | 56:29

With fans' expectations weighing heavily on their shoulders, the Red Hot Chili Peppers took four years to deliver *Californication*. Ousting guitarist Dave Navarro, the band reunited with John Frusciante after a drug-induced hiatus. With several members fighting their own drug addictions, many people had lost confidence in them, including their management.

The Chilis obtained new management and reinstated Rick Rubin as producer, whom they had worked with on 1989's breakthrough *Blood Sugar Sex Magik*. The result was a triumphant return to the No. 1 chart position all over the world with a new direction for the band's seventh full-length album.

While the music was rooted in their distinctive, slap-bass-oriented style, *Californication* displayed a more melodic, serious side to the band. With most of the Chilis in their late thirties, the references to marriage and children suggest a change in their maturity and priorities. The title track takes a hard look at Hollywood, and the way in which the world is consumed by the art and culture created in California. Musically the album includes more ballad-structured songs such as "Porcelain" and the strings-laden "Road Trippin'," though the band revisit their funk/punk roots on more upbeat tracks such as "I Like Dirt" and "Get On Top." *Californication* also produced new levels of vocal talent from Anthony Keidis.

In a remarkable turnaround, *Californication* saw the Red Hot Chili Peppers winning back many of their old fans, while simultaneously attracting a whole new generation of admirers. **CSt**

Track Listing

▶	01	**Around The World** (Flea·Frusciante·Kiedis·Smith)	4:00
	02	**Parallel Universe** (Flea·Frusciante·Kiedis·Smith)	4:30
▶	03	**Scar Tissue** (Flea·Frusciante·Kiedis·Smith)	3:37
	04	**Otherside** (Flea·Frusciante·Kiedis·Smith)	4:15
	05	**Get On Top** (Flea·Frusciante·Kiedis·Smith)	3:19
▶	06	**Californication** (Flea·Frusciante·Kiedis·Smith)	5:22
	07	**Easily** (Flea·Frusciante·Kiedis·Smith)	3:51
	08	**Porcelain** (Flea·Frusciante·Kiedis·Smith)	2:44
	09	**Emit Remmus** (Flea·Frusciante·Kiedis·Smith)	4:01
	10	**I Like Dirt** (Flea·Frusciante·Kiedis·Smith)	2:38
	11	**The Velvet Glove** (Flea·Frusciante·Kiedis·Smith)	3:45
	12	**Savior** (Flea·Frusciante·Kiedis·Smith)	4.54
	13	**Purple Stain** (Flea·Frusciante·Kiedis·Smith)	4:13
	14	**Right On Time** (Flea·Frusciante·Kiedis·Smith)	1:53
▶	15	**Road Trippin'** (Flea·Frusciante·Kiedis·Smith)	3:27

Sigur Rós | Ágætis Byrjun (1999)

Label | Smekkleysa
Producer | Ken Thomas
Art Direction | Sigur Rós • Gotti Bernöft
Nationality | Iceland
Running Time | 71:51

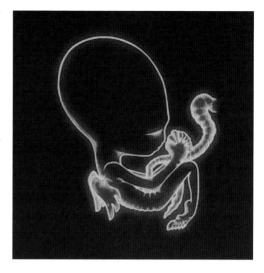

When *Ágætis Byrjun*, Sigur Rós' second studio album, was released in the summer of 1999, the head of Smekkleysa (Bad Taste) was hoping to sell 1,500 to 2,000 copies. Instead, it became a phenomenal success, both in its native country and abroad—and all purely on the strength of the beautiful, otherworldly music within.

Ágætis Byrjun (A Good Beginning) was a labor of love: the band members hand-glued the first batch of sleeves—resulting in numerous defects, as the glue spilled over on some of the CDs. Moreover, the recording process was long and painstaking, and as a consequence the release date was pushed back more than once. It was time well spent. The album fast became one of Iceland's biggest sellers ever, garnering widespread praise and shifting an estimated 500,000 copies worldwide. A remarkable feat, considering that the music is slow and ambient, textured (singer/guitarist Jonsi often uses a cello bow), with two tracks exceeding the 10-minute mark. And that the band sing in their own invented language—Hopelandic.

But make no mistake, *Ágætis Byrjun* possesses a timeless quality, a captivating ethereal presence. The opening track, the beautiful "Svefn-G-Englar," unwinds slowly and gracefully, marked by Jónsi's angelic voice. The dramatic "Vidrar Vel Til Loftárása" utilizes strings to a brilliant effect—its epic scope, breathtaking. The title track is both elegant and effortless.

Melody Maker described Sigur Rós' music as the sound of "God crying golden tears in heaven." Despite the pretentiousness of the line, this description is as close as any. Yes, *Ágætis Byrjun* is that good. **AET**

> "It's definitely fantastic that people appreciate what we're doing."
>
> Kjartan Sveinsson, 2001

Track Listing		
01	**Intro** (Sigur Rós)	1:36
▶ 02	**Svefn-G-Englar** (Sigur Rós)	10:04
03	**Starálfur** (Sigur Rós)	6:46
▶ 04	**Flugufrelsarinn** (Sigur Rós)	7:48
05	**Ný Batterí** (Sigur Rós)	8:10
06	**Hjartad Hamast (Bamm Bamm Bamm)** (Sigur Rós)	7:10
▶ 07	**Vidrar Vel Til Loftárása** (Sigur Rós)	10:17
08	**Olsen Olsen** (Sigur Rós)	8:03
▶ 09	**Ágætis Byrjun** (Sigur Rós)	7:55
10	**Avalon** (Sigur Rós)	4:02

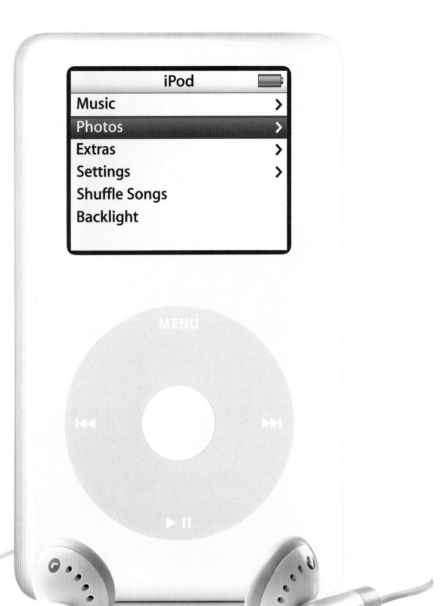

- Premiere of MTV's *The Osbournes*

- First privately funded human space flight

- Allied forces invade Iraq

- Euro introduced

- iPod launched

2000s

Doves | Lost Souls (2000)

Label | Heavenly
Producer | Doves • Steve Osborne
Art Direction | Rick Myers
Nationality | UK
Running Time | 59:08

Doves—brothers Andy and Jez Williams and school friend Jimi Goodwin—hail from Manchester and have been making music since the dawn of the 1990s. (Then known as Sub Sub, they produced the club anthem "Ain't No Love (Ain't No Use)" with house diva Melanie Williams.) Doves literally rose from the ashes of Sub Sub—in 1995, the band's studio burned down in a fire that destroyed their finished album and all their gear. The reincarnation took place in 1998 with three EP releases, after which they signed to the hip London label Heavenly.

Lost Souls bore strong links with their past, including some tracks and lots of musical references from the Sub Sub era, as well as prog-rock leanings. The mood is set by the mighty instrumental opener "Firesuite," which originated as the B-side of the final Sub Sub single. Further highlights include the epic "Sea Song," as well as a string of stunning singles—"The Man Who Told Everything," the storming "Catch The Sun," and their first release, "Cedar Room," a monumental ballad. The production is lush and intimate, a rich layering. Appropriately, Lost Souls contains reference points to much of Manchester's glorious musical heritage—notably the seductive melancholy of Joy Division and early New Order, the sparkling musicality of The Smiths, and the rhythms of early house music. (The album is dedicated to Rob Gretton, New Order's manager, who had signed Sub Sub to his label, Rob's Records.)

Nominated for the Mercury Prize, Lost Souls remains one of Doves' strongest offerings, a stellar achievement from a band who had lost everything. **PN**

"People know the words."

Jez Goodwin, 2000

Track Listing

▶	01	Firesuite (Goodwin•A. Williams•J. Williams)	4:35
▶	02	Here It Comes (Goodwin•A. Williams•J. Williams)	4:50
	03	Break Me Gently (Goodwin•A. Williams•J. Williams)	4:38
▶	04	Sea Song (Goodwin•A. Williams•J. Williams)	6:12
	05	Rise (Goodwin•A. Williams•J. Williams)	5:38
	06	Lost Souls (Goodwin•A. Williams•J. Williams)	6:09
	07	Melody Calls (Goodwin•A. Williams•J. Williams)	3:27
▶	08	Catch The Sun (Goodwin•A. Williams•J. Williams)	4:49
▶	09	The Man Who Told Everything (Goodwin•A. Williams•J. Williams)	5:47
	10	The Cedar Room (Goodwin•A. Williams•J. Williams)	7:38
	11	Reprise (Goodwin•A. Williams•J. Williams)	1:45
	12	A House (Goodwin•A. Williams•J. Williams)	3:40

Air | The Virgin Suicides (2000)

Label | Astralwerks
Producer | Air
Art Direction | Mike Mills
Nationality | France
Running Time | 40:29

Seldom has sound and vision collided so gracefully as it did on Air's soundtrack for Sofia Coppola's directorial debut. The synergy between the images, which tell the tragic tale of five sisters with nothing to live for, and the French electronica duo's mesmerizing, drama-rich score is so great that it is impossible to imagine either existing without the other.

There is a scene in the movie where a doctor asks a 13-year-old girl why she would want to commit suicide. "Obviously, doctor, you've never been a 13-year-old girl," she replies. And indeed the motivation for the girls' deaths is never explicitly explained—a mystery at the heart of the movie that Air's soundtrack takes as its atmospheric inspiration. Although several pieces hold up as individual songs, notably "Playground Love," *The Virgin Suicides* is really one gloriously sad suite. Poignant melodies appear and reappear in subtly altered form. Recalling the lushness of Angelo Badalamenti's work with David Lynch together with the leering romanticism of Serge Gainsberg, the album incorporates smoky nightclub jazz on "Playground Love" (and its even sadder twin, "Highschool Lover"), church organ and Gilmour-esque guitar on "Bathroom Girl" (indeed the influence of mid-1970s Pink Floyd pervades the album), hynotic minor-key pop with the "Cemetary Party," and retro synths everywhere.

Nicolas Godin and Jean-Benoît Dunckel expand on the work they did on debut *Moon Safari* and set the bar so high that they still have yet to reach it (2004's *Talkie Walkie* comes close). One of the most brilliant requiems in pop history. **JiH**

> "I think that we are very dreamy guys."
>
> Jean-Benoit Dunckel, 1998

Track Listing

▶	01	Playground Love (Dunckel·Godin)	3:32
	02	Clouds Up (Dunckel·Godin)	1:30
	03	Bathroom Girl (Dunckel·Godin)	2:25
	04	Cemetary Party (Dunckel·Godin)	2:36
	05	Dark Messages (Dunckel·Godin)	2:28
	06	The World "Hurricane" (Dunckel·Godin)	2:33
	07	Dirty Trip (Dunckel·Godin)	6:12
▶	08	Highschool Lover (Dunckel·Godin)	2:42
▶	09	Afternoon Sister (Dunckel·Godin)	2:24
▶	10	Ghost Song (Dunckel·Godin)	2:16
	11	Empty House (Dunckel·Godin)	2:58
	12	Dead Bodies (Dunckel·Godin)	2:59
▶	13	Suicide Underground (Dunckel·Godin)	5:54

Ryan Adams
Heartbreaker (2000)

Label | Bloodshot
Producer | Ethan Johns
Art Direction | Gina Binkley
Nationality | USA
Running Time | 52:03

Bebel Gilberto
Tanto Tempo (2000)

Label | Ziriguiboom
Producer | Suba
Art Direction | Subtle Rukus
Nationality | Brazil
Running Time | 45:07

Heartbreak and hard drink have inspired many great albums, but rarely one as tender as this, Ryan Adams' solo debut. Adams recorded *Heartbreaker*—a brutally honest chronicle of the highs and lows of love—in the wake of two scarring breakups. In 1999 his much-feted, but commercially unsuccessful, alt.country outfit Whiskeytown imploded in a mess of drink and drugs. Shortly after the collapse of the band, his relationship with long-term girlfriend Amy Lombardi also came crashing down. Adams headed south and locked himself in a Nashville studio for 14 days.

With only two rock tracks—honky-stomp opener "To Be Young (Is To Be Sad)" and the reverb-soaked "Shakedown On 9th Street"—*Heartbreaker* saw Adams cast off the teen angst and small-town fury of his earlier Whiskeytown work. With country traditionalists Gillian Welch and partner David Rawlings as his backing band, Adams developed a looser, more heartfelt style of songwriting. Slow-burning acoustic gems like "Why Do They Leave" and "Call Me On Your Way Back Home" capture Adams' sense of love betrayed with a few barely strummed chords and half-muttered phrases. His duet with alt.country royalty Emmylou Harris on the melancholic traveler's song "Oh My Sweet Carolina" sees Adams try to grasp an earlier, simpler life.

Heartbreaker transformed Adams into the critics' darling—he was called a "visionary rock troubadour" by *NME*—but failed to win over a mass audience. For that he would have to wait until his next album, *Gold*. **TB**

Contrary to popular belief, *Tanto Tempo* was not Bebel's first album. As a child she had recorded with her father (bossa nova legend João Gilberto), her mother (singer Muicha), and her uncle (the radical singer/songwriter Chico Buarque), also making an album of disco in 1986 with Brazilian rock star Cazuza. In New York she collaborated with David Byrne, Towa Tei from Deee-Lite, DJ pairing The Thievery Corporation, Beastie Boys producer Mario Castano, and even Kenny G.

Eventually returning to São Paulo, she hooked up with exiled Yugoslav producer Suba, who died just after this album was completed. His icy electronic take on the bossa nova legacy infects *Tanto Tempo*. Even the MPB classics here—including Marcos Valle's "So Nice" and Baden Powell's "Samba Da Benção"—get a delicate digital makeover, where beachside bossa nova rubs shoulders with European techno and the machine-tooled funk of New York breakbeat culture. But it is Bebel's voice—a chewy, purring, Marlboro-burnished voice that sings English in a pleasingly goofy Brazilian accent—that makes *Tanto Tempo* so compelling.

Tanto Tempo went on to become the biggest-selling Brazilian album outside of Brazil. And although Suba's innovations would be elaborated and superseded and outflanked by assorted sources—by São Paulo's drum 'n' bass jocks, by the experimental electronica boffins on Trauma Records, and by the "favela chic" of Rio's "baile funk" oddballs—*Tanto Tempo* remains a landmark in electronic music. **JLe**

M. J. Cole
Sincere (2000)

Label | Talkin' Loud
Producer | M. J. Cole
Art Direction | Michael Williams
Nationality | UK
Running Time | 58:48

Can a classically trained musician make it in the world of UK garage? In short, yes. Although Matt Coleman, a.k.a. M. J. Cole, cut his teeth in the music biz working as a sound engineer for some of drum 'n' bass' biggest names, he can certainly rinse out a tough rhythm.

Mainly it is Cole's musicality that shines on the album, which came after his debut single "Sincere" became the first UK garage tune to hit the UK charts. Cole's insistence on composing on live instruments may explain the three years it took before the album was finished. The tone is set on the introduction—a cascading piano gives way to a punishing bassline. Throughout, Cole flips between soulful excursions with lush instrumentation, and breakbeat, bass, and warped sample workouts. It is an attempt to build a bridge from his garage roots to cool clubbing—represented on the cover as an M. J. Cole boutique shopping bag.

A roster of fine collaborators really brings the album to life. Elisabeth Troy matches her soulful voice to the killer melody of "Crazy Love" and provides subtle vocals to the slower beat and swirling samples of "I See." Nova Caspar and Jay Dee add strong vocals to the strong sentiment of "Sincere," while Concept Noir take "Rough Out Here" on a Curtis Mayfield trip. And finally, MC Danny Vicious lights up "Slum King," spitting lyrics over the number's scattershot beats.

Those three years had proved worth the wait. From this album, Cole went on to become the first UK garage star to break America. **DC**

Emmylou Harris
Red Dirt Girl (2000)

Label | Nonesuch
Producer | Malcolm Burn
Art Direction | Jeri and John Heiden
Nationality | USA
Running Time | 55:57

Possessed of an achingly beautiful voice of pure, crystalline tremor, Emmylou Harris has long been one of America's finest interpreters of song. For more than 30 years she has been an omnipresent figure, hovering between genres, gliding between styles. By the early 1990s, however, she was maybe walking a little too much in the shadow of others. Her 1995 Daniel Lanois-produced album *Wrecking Ball* changed all that. A pivotal, landmark release, it reinvented her sound and redefined her art. But this, the follow-up, was better.

What distinguishes *Red Dirt Girl* from *Wrecking Ball*—and it is a significant distinction—is that here Harris has written all but one of the tracks herself. From the plangent melancholy of "Boy From Tupelo" to the poignant tribute to her father, "Bang The Drum Slowly," it is a mature and presciently crafted work of darkly poetic hurt and smolder. Harris' only other previous self-penned album had been the introspective and cathartic *The Ballad Of Sally Rose* in 1985—a record of mixed success driven and inspired by the weight of the memory of her relationship with Gram Parsons. Here, if the lyrics are less overtly personal, still they are touching and tender and ghosted with pain. Producer Malcolm Burn takes the Lanois template and runs with it. So, to a deftly skewed music that throbs and grooves, shuffles and pounds, Harris emotes songs of bruised velvet that sensitively articulate love, loss, sadness, and grief.

She has recorded more than 30 albums, but this is her most complete and fulfilled. **RF**

Limp Bizkit | Chocolate Starfish And The Hot Dog Flavored Water (2000)

Label | Interscope
Producer | Terry Date • Limp Bizkit
Art Direction | Fred Durst
Nationality | USA
Running Time | 65:13

limp bizkit
presents

chocolate st★rfish and the hot dog flavored water

Although the nu-metal movement eventually became mired in controversy, mostly on account of the lyrics, at its peak in the early 2000s it was a very powerful and commercially successful genre. At the forefront of the rap/metal charge were the notorious U.S. band Limp Bizkit, led by the confrontational vocalist (and thus quintessential frontman), Fred Durst. *Chocolate Starfish* ... was released at the height of Limp Bizkit's fame; their previous album, *Significant Other*, had already managed to grab the music world's attention—due in part to Durst's largely illiterate but effective lyrics, which largely revolved around disaffected youth (witness the frat-boy humor of the album's title).

Chocolate Starfish ... was a huge commercial success, spawning popular singles such as "My Generation," UK No. 1 "Rollin'," and "Take A Look Around" (from the *Mission: Impossible 2* soundtrack). Critics were impressed by the way the rougher sounds heard on the band's previous album had been transformed into a slickly produced combination of metal, funk, rap, and simple, effective rock. It was purchased in quantity by Limp Bizkit's many adoring fans—though with the lyric of "Hot Dog" alone boasting 36 appearances of the word "fuck," outcry from the establishment was inevitable.

The album benefited from the involvement of rappers Redman, Method Man, Xzibit, and DMX who all contributed to the album, as did actor Ben Stiller; and Stone Temple Pilots singer, Scott Weiland, who also lent his services to the production process. **EK**

Track Listing

01	**Intro** (Borland•Otto•Rivers)		1:18
02	**Hot Dog** (Borland•Otto•Rivers)		3:50
▶ 03	**My Generation** (Borland•Otto•Rivers)		3:41
04	**Full Nelson** (Borland•Otto•Rivers)		4:07
05	**My Way** (Borland•Otto•Rivers)		4:33
▶ 06	**Rollin' (Air Raid Vehicle)** (Borland•Otto•Rivers)		3:34
07	**Livin' It Up** (Borland•Otto•Rivers)		4:24
08	**The One** (Borland•Otto•Rivers)		3:42
09	**Getcha Groove On** (Borland•Otto•Rivers)		4:29
▶ 10	**Take A Look Around** (Borland•Otto•Rivers)		5:18
11	**I'll Be OK** (Borland•Otto•Rivers)		5:06
12	**Boiler** (Borland•Otto•Rivers)		7:00
13	**Hold On** (Borland•Otto•Rivers)		5:47
14	**Rollin (Urban Assault Vehicle)** (Borland•Otto•Rivers)		6:23
15	**Outro** (Borland•Otto•Rivers)		2:01

Radiohead | Kid A (2000)

Label | Parlophone
Producer | Nigel Godrich
Art Direction | Stanley Donwood • Tchocky
Nationality | UK
Running Time | 49:56

After 1997's *OK Computer*, it was generally accepted that Radiohead were one of the best bands in Britain. *Kid A*'s arrival three years later, however, was met with widespread bemusement. Critics demanded to know where the guitars were. And why Thom Yorke sounded like he was singing in a bath.

Radiohead created an album more focused on sound and texture than simple quiet/loud dynamics— let alone conventional song structures. Clicks, electronic drumbeats, and rhythmic keyboards back Yorke's lilting falsetto on "Everything In Its Right Place" and the haunting "Morning Bell." A murky bass punctuates "The National Anthem," combining with Phil Selway's drums and a horn section to create an apocalyptic finale. The beautiful acoustic guitars on "How To Disappear Completely" are layered with an atonal string section that accentuates Thom's millennial *grand-mal* "I'm not here/this isn't happening."

Guitarist Jonny Greenwood scored many of the string arrangements, making great use of the Ondes Martenot, an eerie-sounding electronic instrument dating from the 1920s (and famously used on the *Star Trek* theme music). Drum machines provide the backbone for the punching "Idioteque." "Motion Picture Soundtrack" concludes the album with a funeral-like, shuffling organ.

Kid A proved a Grammy award-winning, transatlantic chart-topper (though it had been made available, free, on the Internet weeks before the official release). It became Radiohead's breakthrough album in the United States. **AMa**

Track Listing

01	**Everything In Its Right Place** (C. Greenwood J. Greenwood • O'Brien • Selway • Yorke)	4:11
02	**Kid A** (C. Greenwood • J. Greenwood O'Brien • Selway • Yorke)	4:44
▶ 03	**The National Anthem** (C. Greenwood J. Greenwood • O'Brien • Selway • Yorke)	5:51
04	**How To Disappear Completely** (C. Greenwood J. Greenwood • O'Brien • Selway • Yorke)	5:56
05	**Treefingers** (C. Greenwood J. Greenwood • O'Brien • Selway • Yorke)	3:42
▶ 06	**Optimistic** (C. Greenwood • J. Greenwood O'Brien • Selway • Yorke)	5:16
07	**In Limbo** (C. Greenwood • J. Greenwood O'Brien • Selway • Yorke)	3:31
▶ 08	**Idioteque** (C. Greenwood • J. Greenwood O'Brien • Selway • Yorke)	5:09
▶ 09	**Morning Bell** (C. Greenwood J. Greenwood • O'Brien • Selway • Yorke)	4:35
10	**Motion Picture Soundtrack** (C. Greenwood J. Greenwood • O'Brien • Selway • Yorke)	7:01

U2 | All That You Can't Leave Behind (2000)

Label | Island
Producer | Brian Eno • Daniel Lanois
Art Direction | Steve Averill
Nationality | Ireland • UK
Running Time | 53:07

With *All That You Can't Leave Behind*, Irish stalwarts U2 cemented their place at the top of rock's pecking order. Their tenth studio album was constructed on the back of the mock-decadent *Pop* and *Zooropa* and the glam dance-rock of the unexpected *Achtung Baby*. Adopting a straightforward approach, the album sees U2 discarding their electronic experimentation in favor of stripped-back instrumentation and a lyrical content with genuinely universal appeal. It simultaneously relaunched the band as an artistic force to be reckoned with and presented frontman Bono as the most emotionally articulate of wordsmiths.

This is an album of epic proportions and no filler ("In our heads we've written 11 singles for this record," commented Bono). With a less messianic flavor than that of the quartet's more grandiose Nineties material, *All That You Can't Leave Behind* had phenomenal global success that gained great momentum after the events of 9/11—"Walk On" became an anthem of defiance for those left scarred by the World Trade Center attacks. "Beautiful Day" is an explosive song of exuberant positivity, while "Kite," written with Bono's dying father in mind, addresses the private shadow behind the public light; the song is exquisite in its simplicity.

The album picked up the 2002 Grammy award for Best Rock Album, while "Walk On," "Elevation," and the Michael Hutchence-inspired "Stuck In A Moment" earned Grammy awards in their own nominated categories. Prior to the award nominations, Bono had joked about "reapplying for the top job." It appears the boy's resumé was accepted. **SN**

> ## "You pour your life into songs, you want them to be heard."
> Bono, 2005

Track Listing

01	Beautiful Day (U2)	4:08
02	Stuck In A Moment You Can't Get Out Of (U2)	4:32
03	Elevation (U2)	3:47
04	Walk On (U2)	4:56
05	Kite (U2)	4:27
06	In A Little While (U2)	3:39
07	Wild Honey (U2)	3:47
08	Peace On Earth (U2)	4:48
09	When I Look At The World (U2)	4:18
10	New York (U2)	5:30
11	Grace (U2)	5:31
12	The Ground Beneath Her Feet (Salman Rushdie • U2)	3:44

Linkin Park | Hybrid Theory (2000)

Label | Warner Bros.
Producer | Don Gilmore
Art Direction | Frank Maddocks
Nationality | USA
Running Time | 37:44

If everything had gone according to plan, Linkin Park's onslaught of No.1 singles might have taken place years earlier. It was only after a string of rejections from various record companies that Zomba's Jeff Blue provided the then five-piece with a means to create and distribute their debut album. Hybrid Theory (titled after the group's previous name) was eventually released through Warner Bros. in 2000.

First single "One Step Closer" was an instant hit, sitting well within the nu-metal genre that had gained serious momentum by 2000. The follow-up "Closer," however, proved that Linkin Park were a band with untapped potential, their innovative mixture of old-school hip hop and rap, metal, and electronica placing them a step above their peers. The album sees them combine original, catchy beats and fierce lyrics with harder rock influences (see "A Place For My Head"), topped off with widescreen production.

Hybrid Theory's raging-yet-melodic metal vibe— witness "One Step Closer," "With You," and "Papercut"— made the band ideal candidates for the Family Values and Projekt Revolution tours in the United States. They played a staggering 324 shows in 2001. By the close of 2001 they had become one of the biggest bands of the new millennium; Hybrid Theory became the second bestselling album in the world.

January 2002's Grammy awards cemented this stellar reputation, the band receiving three nominations for Best Rock Album, Best New Artist, and Best Hard Rock Performance (for "Crawling")—the last was the one they eventually took home. **EK**

> ## "We aren't a mainstream act: the mainstream came to us."
>
> Mike Shinoda, 2003

Track Listing

01	**Papercut** (Linkin Park)	3:04
▶ 02	**One Step Closer** (Linkin Park)	2:35
03	**With You** (Dust Brothers · Linkin Park)	3:23
04	**Points Of Authority** (Linkin Park)	3:20
▶ 05	**Crawling** (Linkin Park)	3:28
06	**Runaway** (Linkin Park · Wakefield)	3:03
07	**By Myself** (Linkin Park)	3:09
▶ 08	**In The End** (Linkin Park)	3:36
09	**A Place For My Head** (Linkin Park · Wakefield)	3:04
10	**Forgotten** (Linkin Park · Wakefield)	3:14
11	**Cure For The Itch** (Linkin Park)	2:37
12	**Pushing Me Away** (Linkin Park)	3:11

Elliott Smith | Figure 8 (2000)

Label | Dreamworks
Producer | Tom Rothrock • Rob Schnapf • Elliott Smith
Art Direction | Autumn de Wilde • Dale Smith
Nationality | USA
Running Time | 52:07

The years between the recording of *Either/Or* and *Figure 8* had been turbulent ones for Elliott Smith. In 1997 friends had become concerned by his drinking and self-destructive behavior. Through their intervention he had endured a short stay at a psychiatric hospital in Arizona and the experience was an unhappy one.

The exposure of his music on the soundtrack to *Good Will Hunting* had resulted in an Oscar nomination for Best Original Song. Subsequent attention to his work brought him to a new label, Dreamworks, and with that came more lavish studio production. This is in evidence on *Figure 8*, multilayered and multitracked with strings and lusher arrangements on songs such as "Everything Means Nothing To Me."

As on earlier records, Smith's lyrical melancholy sits alongside moments of optimism, and it is tempting to imagine that this uplifted mood is more evident on *Figure 8*. Had a move to warmer climes also influenced his work? He had come to rest in L.A. after an extended period of nomadic living. The song "L.A." sums it all up, treading the edge between liberation and desolation, offering uplifting West Coast harmonies with the chorus "Last night I was about to throw it all away."

For "In The Lost And Found (Honky Bach)," Smith used the same Abbey Road piano Paul McCartney had played on "Penny Lane." As a long-time Beatles fan, this gave him genuine joy; it also prompted critics to make comparisons to the Fab Four. In the sense that this record approaches greatness they were dead right. Brilliant, broken-hearted, and far-reaching. **MBI**

Track Listing

01	Son Of Sam (Smith)	3.05
02	Somebody That I Used To Know (Smith)	2.09
▶ 03	Junk Bond Trader (Smith)	3.49
04	Everything Reminds Me Of Her (Smith)	2.37
05	Everything Means Nothing To Me (Smith)	2.24
▶ 06	L.A. (Smith)	3.14
▶ 07	In The Lost And Found (Honky Bach)/The Roost (Smith)	4.32
08	Stupidity Tries (Smith)	4.24
▶ 09	Easy Way Out (Smith)	2.44
10	Wouldn't Mama Be Proud? (Smith)	3.26
11	Color Bars (Smith)	2.18
12	Happiness/The Gondola Man (Smith)	5.04
13	Pretty Mary K (Smith)	2.36
14	I Better Be Quiet Now (Smith)	3.34
15	Can't Make A Sound (Smith)	4.18
16	Bye (Smith)	1.53

Badly Drawn Boy
The Hour Of Bewilderbeast (2000)

Label | Twisted Nerve
Producer | Various
Art Direction | Andy Votel
Nationality | UK
Running Time | 63:25

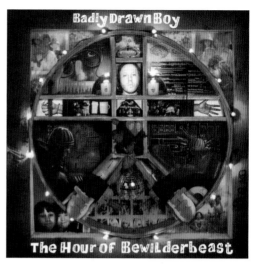

Damon Gough, a.k.a. Badly Drawn Boy, has made a habit of wrong-footing fans and critics, chiefly by following his musical heart. On his . . . *Bewilderbeast* debut, the Mancunian endeavored to make a concept album based around the course of a relationship. His rightful place at the head of the new-folk movement at the end of the millennium was nowhere better exemplified than on this 18-track epic.

Starting with the cool, finger-plucked acoustic waft of "The Shining," the mood shifts to wonky, woozy folk (on the sublime "Fall In A River"), then to riff-heavy rock ("Another Pearl") before ending up resigned and hymnal on "Epitaph." Even the near-title track, an instrumental that owes a slight debt to the *Banana Splits* theme tune, makes for a classically emotive listen.

Along the way, we hear some of his most memorable singles—check out the wah-wah intro and hook of "Once Around The Block," or the disco tinge to "Disillusion." And the whole affair is dressed in Twisted Nerve's own unique brand of visuals, with a folk-art cover detailing the components that made up Gough's creative heart (including records, music boxes, family photos, and flowers).

Around the time of recording, Gough cited Bruce Springsteen as a key influence on his work. It seemed a slightly unfashionable choice at the time, but over the years, as this album has matured, the comparison has come to seem increasingly accurate. Badly Drawn Boy really is a renegade and a folk hero. **JK**

Track Listing

▶ 01	The Shining (Gough)	5:18
02	Everybody's Stalking (Gough)	3:39
03	Bewilder (Gough)	0:48
▶ 04	Fall In A River (Gough)	2:17
05	Camping Next To Water (Gough)	3:50
06	Stone On The Water (Gough)	3:58
▶ 07	Another Pearl (Gough)	4:27
08	Body Rap (Gough)	0:45
▶ 09	Once Around The Block (Gough)	3:44
10	This Song (Gough)	1:32
▶ 11	Bewilderbeast (Gough)	3:30
12	Magic In The Air (Gough)	3:43
13	Cause A Rockslide (Gough)	5:55
14	Pissing In The Wind (Gough)	4:19
15	Blistered Heart (Gough)	1:50
16	Disillusion (Gough)	5:19
17	Say It Again (Gough)	4:41
18	Epitaph (Gough)	3:50

P.J. Harvey
Stories From The City, Stories From The Sea (2000)

Label | Island
Producer | Rob Ellis • Mick Harvey • P.J. Harvey
Art Direction | Rob Crane • Maria Mochnacz
Nationality | UK
Running Time | 50:45

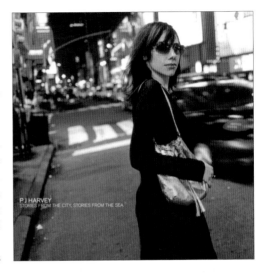

Harvey's fifth album finally brought her universal critical acclaim—it picked up the Mercury Music Prize in 2001, garnering the singer/guitarist a whole new legion of fans. The sound she embraced on *Stories* . . . was more reassuring and polished than on previous albums and suggested that she had grown up; looking at a self-confident Harvey on the cover crossing a road in New York it is difficult to disagree.

Musically still filled with fire and passion, the songs are overlaid by the jingle-jangle of Harvey's guitar, while co-conspirators Rob Ellis and Mick Harvey add layers of keyboard and piano melodies that soften the sound. Lyrically she is overtly direct and revealing. "This Is Love" positively smolders, Harvey announcing, "I can't believe life is so complex/when I just want to sit here and watch you undress" over a dirty bassline.

The work is also splashed with references to New York. Although Harvey did not want it to be referred to as her "New York album," the city's influence is clearly there. The dark, bustling resonance of "The Whores Hustle And The Hustlers Whore" echoes the danger, violence, and desperation often associated with the Big Apple—she speaks of "heroin and speed, of genocide and suicide, syphilis, and greed." During the opening track "Big Exit" she hollers, "this world's crazy, give me the gun." She has said that New York brims with an energy that London lacks, and has captured this with *Stories* . . . . Emotionally and musically, this is an album that will endure. **KM**

Track Listing

▶	01	Big Exit (Harvey)	3:51
	02	Good Fortune (Harvey)	3:20
▶	03	A Place Called Home (Harvey)	3:24
	04	One Line (Harvey)	3:14
	05	Beautiful Feeling (Harvey)	4:00
▶	06	The Whores Hustle And The Hustlers Whore (Harvey)	4:00
	07	This Mess We're In (Harvey)	3:57
	08	You Said Something (Harvey)	3:19
▶	09	Kamikaze (Harvey)	2:24
▶	10	This Is Love (Harvey)	3:48
	11	Horses In My Dreams (Harvey)	5:37
	12	We Float (Harvey)	6:09
	13	This Wicked Tongue (Harvey)	3:42

Erykah Badu | Mama's Gun (2000)

Label | Motown
Producer | Erykah Badu • James Poyser
Art Direction | Erykah Badu • Michael Whitfield
Nationality | USA
Running Time | 71:50

Baduizm, Erykah Badu's 1997 debut, introduced hip hop's own Lady Day. Its million-selling follow-up, *Mama's Gun*, telegraphed a different message. The album is a suite of songs about the darkest depths of life and love. This suited Badu, who had broken up with the father of her child, Outkast's André 3000. "Miss Jackson" was André's take on the situation; Badu's side of the story spilled out across *Mama's Gun*'s 72 minutes.

The first half boils Seventies funk down to a mean post-Missy clip. This is Badu as righteous feminized heroine, waiting for her incarcerated man (on the Stevie Wonder-sampling "Penitentiary Philosophy") and speaking up for "sagging ninnies" ("Cleva").

But the unashamedly romantic, Minnie Riperton-esque "Orange Moon" signals the second half's wounded, downcast theme. The minimal shuffle of the John Hammond-sampling "Time's A Wastin" cooks up a bleak mood, leavened only by Badu's closing moans, suffering but somehow surviving. The single "Bag Lady"—Philly soul etched with hip-hop rhythms—is bitterly sweet, a wise warning to ditch the baggage from a woman weighed low by her own.

"Green Eyes" is the album's triumph, however. An epic annotation of a broken heart, it shifts over three movements, guided by Roots bandleader ?uestlove: from scratchy Thirties jazz, through a playful but blue moment of realization, to a sweeping, mournful conclusion. Tearfully accepting that "It's too late," Badu extinguishes her last embers of hope. Naked, affecting, and exquisite, the song is a sublime closer to a most sublime album. **SC**

Track Listing

01	**Penitentiary Philosophy** (Badu•Poyser•Thompson)		6:09
▶ 02	**Didn't Cha Know** (Badu)		3:58
03	**My Life** (Badu•Poyser)		3:59
04	**...And On** (Badu•Cantero•Martin)		3:34
▶ 05	**Cleva** (Badu•Poyser)		3:45
06	**Hey Sugah** (Badu•N'dambi)		0:51
07	**Booty** (Badu)		4:04
08	**Kiss Me On My Neck (Hesi)** (Badu•DeJohnette•Poyser•Yancey)		5:34
09	**A.D. 2000** (B. Wright•E. Wright)		4:51
▶ 10	**Orange Moon** (Badu•Lacy•Martin•Young)		7:10
11	**In Love With You** (Badu•Marley)		5:21
▶ 12	**Bag Lady** (Badu•Bailey•Brown•Hale•Hayes Longmiles•Martin•Young)		5:48
13	**Time's A Wastin** (Badu•Martin)		6:42
▶ 14	**Green Eyes** (Badu•Duplaix•Poyser)		10:04

Coldplay | Parachutes (2000)

Label | Parlophone
Producer | Coldplay • Ken Nelson
Art Direction | Coldplay • Mark Tappin
Nationality | UK
Running Time | 41:44

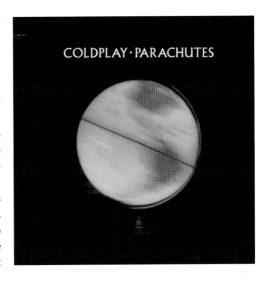

Was this part one of a skillfully conceived plan to become the first band since U2 to conquer the home market and break America and bag the beautiful Oscar-winning actress on the way?

Unlikely. Even the most cursory listen to Coldplay's debut album proves there is not a trace of cynicism. Certainly, ambition, hope, and even desire mingle with the clippy guitars and falsettos, but the charm of the band who formed at University College London, is that above all else, making music is their total passion.

In contrast to some of the stadium-sized confidence that has marked their later songs, Coldplay's debut is full of a wide-eyed wonderment as to what is possible. Like many British albums from the end of the 1990s, *Parachutes* betrays the influence of Jeff Buckley, but there is also a constant sense of innovation and invention. "Spies" is partly a delicate love song, yet with swirling strings and graceful guitar lines it is also partly a Bond theme. "Trouble" is a gentle lullaby and a deceptively vicious insight into the heart, while "Yellow" is one of the few chartbusters to trace a lineage back to My Bloody Valentine's art noise.

So, if there was no master plan, what was the blueprint for global success encoded within *Parachutes*? "I think these songs are the best in the world," suggested singer Chris Martin, before adding with typical humility, "but if I told you that you'd probably think I was really arrogant." Reflecting this spirit, *Parachutes* is flawed yet brilliant, exhilarating yet tender, confident yet shy—it is overall, a strikingly human record. No wonder it proved so popular. **PS**

Track Listing

▶ 01	Don't Panic (Berryman•Buckland•Champion•Martin)	2:17
▶ 02	Shiver (Berryman•Buckland•Champion•Martin)	4:59
▶ 03	Spies (Berryman•Buckland•Champion•Martin)	5:18
04	Sparks (Berryman•Buckland•Champion•Martin)	3:47
▶ 05	Yellow (Berryman•Buckland•Champion•Martin)	4:29
▶ 06	Trouble (Berryman•Buckland•Champion•Martin)	4:30
07	Parachutes (Berryman•Buckland•Champion•Martin)	0:46
08	High Speed (Berryman•Buckland•Champion•Martin)	4:14
09	We Never Change (Berryman•Buckland•Champion•Martin)	4:09
10	Everything's Not Lost (Berryman•Buckland•Champion•Martin)	7:15

Common
Like Water
For Chocolate (2000)

Label | MCA
Producer | The Soulquarians
Art Direction | Kenny Gravillis
Nationality | USA
Running Time | 78:00

Mike Ladd
Welcome To
The Afterfuture (2000)

Label | Ozone
Producer | Mike Ladd • Fred Ones
Art Direction | Uncredited
Nationality | USA
Running Time | 62:39

A warmth, a sense of family and community, informed *Like Water For Chocolate*, the breakthrough release from Common, balancing tales of hard reality with inspirational examples of real heroes.

Opener "Time Travelin'" traces the bloodline back to Laos, a tribute to revolutionary Afrobeat figurehead Fela Kuti that features vocals from Kuti's son, Femi. For "Heat," Common's all-star production crew, the Soulquarians (inaugurated for the album, and featuring ?uestlove, James Poysner, Jay Dee, and D'Angelo) invoked Kuti's incessant alligator-snap, one of many lethal and inventive grooves they cut for this album.

There were moments of whimsy ("The Light," which declared Common's love for Erykah Badu), moments of violence ("Payback Is A Grandmother"), proof that all life is "political." DJ Premier stepped up to the plate for "Sixth Sense," a solemn anthem to hip hop's redemptive powers, and Mos Def took the mic to cycle through life's many "Questions." And for the curtain, Common offered two respectful nods to the previous generation, a tribute to Black Panther heroine (and Tupac's mother) Assata Shakur, and a closer featuring Common's father, Lonnie "Pops" Lynn, rapping warmly of his global family, over a prime Fela vamp. Common was saying that there is a strength and a resilience to the "ghetto" that endures, and which deserves its members' nourishment and pride. **SC**

The conundrum of nature versus nurture was meaty enough to consume Shakespeare in *The Tempest*. Such puzzles of identity similarly possessed poet and rapper Mike Ladd, and it is not hard to see why. Educated in India, an acclaimed wordsmith and poet who networks furiously within the arts, Ladd is hardly the stereotypical rap MC. While he worked at New York University as a poetry lecturer, Ladd could be found speeding up the NYC freeway, mooning cops from the passenger seat.

Welcome To The Afterfuture is a grounded trip. Future-jazz instrumentals and ambient passages segue the heavy blocks of lysergic poetry, but a track like "The Animist" is as simple and direct as hip hop gets—a jazzy synth groove allied to Ladd's witty, humanist philosophizing. He is not always so approachable—within minutes the mood had changed to the fiery Sun Ra apocalypse of "Starship Nigga," itself morphing in turn to the cold chill of the alienated title track.

But Ladd's masterstroke on ...*Afterfuture* is to draw the disparate, exotic elements together. The album builds up to the astonishing "Feb 4 '99," which threads together the jarring images of Ladd's own life—frolicking in India, violence in New York, his stifling hometown of Cambridge, Massachusetts—to make a powerful statement on the concept of justice in a godless land. It is a powerfully moving blow from an artist who typically aims for the head. **SC**

Red Snapper
Our Aim
Is To Satisfy (2000)

Label | Warp
Producer | Hugo Nicholson
Art Direction | Red Design
Nationality | UK
Running Time | 57:03

The third album from instrumental trio Red Snapper, *Our Aim Is To Satisfy* introduces a wealth of musical tastes—including dub, acid jazz, phat disco beats, and a touch of hard rock—and a pioneering combination of electronica and acoustic instruments. The tracks range from smooth and melodic to dark and mysterious, not to mention one that is downright raunchy.

"Shellback" features a thumping drumbeat from Richard Thair, a pounding bassline from Ali Friend, and, to top it off, a haunting and serene vocal drip from Karime Kendra. The effortlessly driving instrumental "Don't Go Nowhere" follows, conjuring up images of a dark and smoky basement club. The band further hit their stride on "The Rough And The Quick," a funky, in-your-face number with trip-hop undertones. Kendra's sultry vocal adds extra heat to lyrics that are already simmering—"Ride a little rough and quick/cum on my tongue" (and that is the mild stuff). The song demands that a new music genre should be added to the lexicon—elec-rotica. "Belladonna" is a surreal experience, with pinging guitar and subtle double bass mixing with strings and electronic sounds.

Will Hermes neatly summed up Red Snapper's achievement in *Entertainment Weekly*: "This London crew makes a pop-jazz mural with 21st-century vision." By far the band's best release, *Our Aim Is To Satisfy* is sexy, confrontational, and mesmerizing listening. **LA**

Eminem
The Marshall
Mathers LP (2000)

Label | Interscope
Producer | Various
Art Direction | Jason Noto
Nationality | USA
Running Time | 72:05

When Eminem released his major-label debut, the scurrilous *The Slim Shady Show* (1999), the verdict of the moral guardians was unanimous: Eminem was a racist, sexist, misogynistic, homophobic outrage. Rap's cuss words and violence were hardly new, but Eminem had catapulted the music into white Middle America.

The Marshall Mathers LP exploits the furore . . . *Slim Shady* created into a Grammy-winning, meta-rap masterpiece of shock theater that blurs the distinctions between humor and horror, satire and documentary. Now Em gives us three personas to deal with—the real Marshall Mathers, cocky MC Eminem, and that whiteboy bogeyman rapper Slim Shady.

Slim and Em get the party started, spilling their vitriolic wit-stained ink on everything from censorship ("You want me to fix up lyrics while the President gets his dick sucked?"—"Who Knew"), to the celebrity phenomenon ("Stan"). Dr. Dre underscores the wild rap attacks with cheeky sound effects, sparkling liquid basslines, and stuttering pop rhythms.

But it is as his real self, Marshall Mathers, that Eminem really ruptures nerves, taking hip hop to new emotional territory in semi-autobiographical rants. What makes the murder ballad "Kim" so utterly terrifying is not all the blood, guts, and cussing ("Now Bleed! Bitch Bleed!"), but its deeply honest, deeply tragic humanity ("I swear to God, I hate you, Oh my God I love you"). **MK**

Goldfrapp | Felt Mountain (2000)

Label | Mute
Producer | Alison Goldfrapp • Will Gregory
Art Direction | Alison Goldfrapp
Nationality | UK
Running Time | 39:36

Pigeonholing is a favorite pastime for critics but here was a debut that confounded lazy attempts at categorization. Cinematic electronica, by turns glacial and decadent, seductive and threatening.

Alison Goldfrapp's strikingly singular chanteuse vocals had left several pre-*Felt Mountain* calling cards, most notably on Tricky's *Maxinquaye*, but they found their true home alongside Will Gregory's weird and wondrous orchestral compositions, drenched in strings and overtures of otherworldliness.

The album could not have got off to a more suitably strange start than "Lovely Head." A melting pot of melodrama, it had a whistled introduction, unhinged "Frankenstein would love your mind" lyrics, and inventive arrangements that belied the album's DIY roots. It all catches you off balance initially, but enough people were willing to buy into the duo's skewed viewpoint for the track to permeate the public consciousness in the UK and help the album to shift half a million copies.

The journey does not get any less compelling as it continues—Goldfrapp revels in her role as a modern version of *Cabaret*'s Sally Bowles, her voice becoming more of an instrument than a conduit for words. "Human" is a study in icy detachment, the title track is hypnotic, while "Oompa Radar" is just, well, plain weird. Throughout, Gregory's movie-music fingerprints are evident; the cap is doffed to Sergio Leone on the sleevenotes, but John Barry and Ennio Morricone could have been namechecked just as easily.

The soundtrack to a movie that has yet to be made. For once, unique is the only apt description. **CB**

> "You can't explain everything you do. No one can ... draw it out of your subconscious ... you don't always know why you've done something."
>
> Alison Goldfrapp, 2003

Track Listing

▶ 01	**Lovely Head** (Goldfrapp•Gregory)	3:49
02	**Paper Bag** (Goldfrapp•Gregory)	4:06
▶ 03	**Human** (Goldfrapp•Gregory•Locke•Norfolk)	4:37
04	**Pilots** (Goldfrapp•Gregory)	4:29
05	**Deer Stop** (Goldfrapp•Gregory)	4:07
▶ 06	**Felt Mountain** (Goldfrapp•Gregory)	4:17
07	**Oompa Radar** (Goldfrapp•Gregory)	4:42
08	**Utopia** (Goldfrapp•Gregory)	4:18
▶ 09	**Horse Tears** (Goldfrapp•Gregory)	5:11

Giant Sand | Chore Of Enchantment (2000)

Label | Thrill Jockey
Producer | Various
Art Direction | Sheila Sachs
Nationality | USA
Running Time | 59:53

After a decade in Tucson, Howe Gelb emerged with the most successful incarnation of Giant Sand: a trio with drummer John Convertino and Joey Burns on bass. The band were a musical project as unpredictable as its central figure—a singer/songwriter forever changing his route, following the freedom lessons of Bob Dylan and Neil Young and emulating the idiosyncratic weirdness of his jazz idol Thelonious Monk.

Like a faulty radio transmission, mixing country sentiment with volcanic electricity, earthiness with weirdness, Giant Sand made some of the best records of the American underground in the 1980s (*The Love Songs*, 1988) and '90s (*Center Of The Universe*, 1992), but none worked like *Chore Of Enchantment*. Recorded in Tucson, Memphis, and New York with a variety of producers, the album has a cohesive feel, the musicians losing themselves but always finding their way back.

Slide-guitar instrumental "Shrine" is played by Rainer Ptacek, who died of cancer before the album's release, and a melancholy, elegiac atmosphere permeates the record, complemented by haunting Mellotron® and organ. Lyrics are both enigmatic and colloquial; arrangements move from ethereal to punkish distortion, from silence to exuberance, with the singer always distant, whispering in your ear.

Astonishing from beginning to end, full of strange songs about women (the voluptuous "Temptation Of Egg"), midlife experiences ("Shiver," an underground hit of sorts), and the downright cryptic (the arousing guitars that fuel "Satellite"), *Chore Of Enchantment* lodges in the mind and refuses to leave. **IJ**

Track Listing

01	Overture (Gelb)	0:48
▶ 02	(Well) Dusted (For The Millennium) (Gelb)	3:47
03	Punishing Sun (Gelb)	3:13
04	X-tra Wide (Gelb)	3:27
05	1972 (Gelb)	1:03
▶ 06	Temptation Of Egg (Gelb)	3:41
▶ 07	Raw (Gelb)	3:29
08	Wolfy (Gelb)	4:25
▶ 09	Shiver (Gelb)	4:00
10	Dirty From The Rain (Gelb)	3:34
11	Astonished (In Memphis) (Gelb)	5:32
12	No Reply (Gelb)	4:34
▶ 13	Satellite (Gelb)	6:48
▶ 14	Bottom Line Man (Gelb)	4:41
15	Way To End The Day (Gelb)	4:47
16	Shrine (Ptacek)	2:04

Lambchop | Nixon (2000)

Label | Merge
Producer | Mark Nevers • Kurt Wagner
Art Direction | Eric Bailey • Wayne White
Nationality | USA
Running Time | 49:44

One of Nashville's best kept secrets, the loose and eclectic Lambchop is a collective of rotating members anchored by lead singer/songwriter Kurt Wagner. *Nixon*, their fifth album, is a lushly orchestrated, curiously timeless pleasure covering many styles, from alternative rock to country to Seventies soul.

Kurt Wagner's laid-back, intimate vocals are right on the cusp between spoken and sung, with the occasional falsetto sprinkled in for good measure—the song "You Masculine You" is sung entirely in falsetto. Wagner's lyrical content features moody and evocative images of windy porches and drunken neighbors. For a concept album supposedly about Richard Nixon, it is pretty darn hard to spot the concept, although a suggested reading list of books about Tricky Dick is included in the liner notes.

"The Old Gold Shoe" starts things off with a drowsy shuffle of bass, guitars, and lightly brushed snare drum. A lovely string section swells as Wagner offers a sly joke at his own expense with the line, "He's not even a very good singer." "Up With People," with its handclap rhythm, soaring gospel choir, and bright trumpet melody, is the album's irresistible highlight.

"What Else Could it Be?" mixes vintage disco crescendos and funky stabs of rhythm. The excellently titled "The Distance From Her To There" features a twangy pedal steel guitar and the memorable refrain, "The lights outside tonight are far from home/And I'm out drinking in the yard." *Nixon* is a low-key charmer, the perfect soundtrack for a night-time road trip or a Sunday afternoon in bed. **RM**

> **"Nashville is thought of as the country-music capital and all that crap, but it has a nice R&B history, too."**
>
> Kurt Wagner, 2000

Track Listing

▶	01	The Old Gold Shoe (Wagner)	6:21
	02	Grumpus (Wagner)	4:19
	03	You Masculine You (Wagner)	5:59
▶	04	Up With People (Wagner)	5:59
	05	Nashville Parents (Wagner)	5:38
▶	06	What Else Could It Be? (Wagner)	3:38
▶	07	The Distance From Her To There (Wagner)	4:20
	08	The Book I Haven't Read (Mayfield • Wagner)	5:44
	09	The Petrified Florist (Wagner)	4:52
	10	The Butcher Boy (Public Domain)	2:54

Ute Lemper | Punishing Kiss (2000)

Label | Polygram
Producer | Various
Art Direction | Conor Brady
Nationality | Germany
Running Time | 57:17

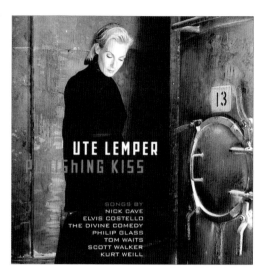

Ute Lemper is a throwback to a more glamorous age, when Greta Garbo types stalked the clubs of Weimar Germany and a woman never lit her own cigarette in public. The German-born artist would prove to be as convincingly versatile as the stars from Hollywood's Golden Age, winning praise for her performances on stage, cinema screen, and record. She was the perfect candidate to champion the Kurt Weill songbook, which she did with collections in 1992 and 1993, as well as by revitalizing *Berlin Cabaret Songs* in 1997.

Stepping out of the past, Lemper would focus mainly on modern composers for the first time with 2000's decadently beautiful *Punishing Kiss*. Of course, Lemper will only play the game if the cards are stacked in her favor. The singer does not really have to stretch to handle this newer material, given that Elvis Costello, Tom Waits, and the album's other featured songwriters are greatly influenced by Weill.

Any sense of contemporaneity really peaks with the cover, which shows the leather-clad singer vamping down a dingy back alley like Catwoman. First track "The Case Continues" is a dime-story mystery novel put to song. The three Costello-penned tunes are tailor-made for the dark, drama-rich mood. Lemper's take on Waits' "Purple Avenue" is exquisite and she delivers a big Broadway punch to Nick Cave's "Little Water Song." Neil Hannon and Joby Talbot of The Divine Comedy, who provide the backing for most tracks, also contribute three solid compositions. In the midst of all this, Lemper slips in Weill's "Tango Ballad" like the final piece of a jigsaw puzzle. **JiH**

> ## "I can be a strict authoritarian, or a little flower, or a powerful, erotic femme fatale."

Ute Lemper, 2003

Track Listing

01	The Case Continues (Hannon·Talbot)	3:51
02	Tango Ballad (Brecht·Talbot·Weill)	5:00
03	Passionate Fight (Costello·Nieve)	4:13
04	Little Water Song (Cave·Pisek)	3:58
05	Purple Avenue (Waits)	4:23
06	Streets Of Berlin (Glass·Sherman)	4:01
07	Split (Hannon·Talbot)	3:41
08	Couldn't You Keep That To Yourself (Costello)	2:49
09	Punishing Kiss (Costello·O'Riordan)	4:32
10	You Were Meant For Me (Hannon·Talbot)	5:14
11	The Part You Throw Away (Brennan·Waits)	4:44
12	Scope J (Engel)	10:51

Madonna | Music (2000)

Label | Maverick
Producer | Various
Art Direction | Kevin Reagan
Nationality | USA
Running Time | 44:38

Bestowed with the title "The Worst Actress of the Century" in 2000, Madonna redeemed herself with a renewed commitment to smart pop. Fresh from the career-revitalizing *Ray Of Light*, she enlisted Afghan-French whizkid Mirwais. His "Disco Science" looms over the opening half of the album, Madonna having been impressed by the track's dirty sound and raunchy video. The lady herself cited as influences "Afrika Bambaataa, French electronica, and Guy Ritchie"—the latter her soon-to-be husband.

Where *Ray Of Light* swirls, *Music* fizzes. "We started off with quite a lot of slow ballad songs," recalled William Orbit, "and she started to chuck them out in favor of more edgy tracks." Most startling is "Don't Tell Me," an electronic country excursion based on a song by her brother-in-law Joe Henry (with whom she sang the lovely "Guilty By Association" on the Vic Chesnutt tribute album *Sweet Relief II*). Its blend of sawdust and staccato beats fed into Jean-Baptiste Mondino's cover photograph and made sparkly Stetsons a must have.

More off-the-wall influences are alchemized in "What It Feels Like For A Girl," which opens with dialog by Charlotte Gainsbourg from the 1993 drama *The Cement Garden*, and "Gone," which marries guitar by Oasis collaborator Paul Stacey to the classical styling of composer Damian Le Gassick.

Music returned Madonna to the top of the U.S. album chart for the first time since 1989, selling more than ten million copies worldwide. *Ray Of Light* reaped the critical kudos, but *Music* is more representative of Madonna herself: fun, flashy, and fabulous. **BM**

> "What can you expect? Funky, electronic music blended with futuristic folk."
>
> Madonna, 2000

Track Listing

▶	01	**Music** (Ahmadzaï·Madonna)	3:45
	02	**Impressive Instant** (Ahmadzaï·Madonna)	3:37
	03	**Runaway Lover** (Madonna·Orbit)	4:47
	04	**I Deserve It** (Ahmadzaï·Madonna)	4:23
	05	**Amazing** (Madonna·Orbit)	3:43
	06	**Nobody's Perfect** (Ahmadzaï·Madonna)	4:58
▶	07	**Don't Tell Me** (Ahmadzaï·Henry·Madonna)	4:40
▶	08	**What It Feels Like For A Girl** (Madonna·Sigsworth)	4:43
	09	**Paradise (Not For Me)** (Ahmadzaï·Madonna)	6:33
	10	**Gone** (Le Gassick·Madonna·Young)	3:29

The Avalanches
Since I Left You (2000)

Label | Modular
Producer | Bobby C. • Darren Seltmann
Art Direction | Bobbydazzler
Nationality | Australia
Running Time | 60:00

The prospect of a six-man Australian DJ collective mixing together a set that samples The Osmonds, Kid Creole And The Coconuts, and Boney M sounds like an invitation to the world's worst party. The sonic reality, however, is a stunning and timeless pop-art mix tape, one that seems to contain the best bits of every great record ever made, while matching the urgency and bittersweet thrills of the originals.

With its lazy shuffle and sun-soaked melodies, the album's opener, title track, and first single set out the band's mission statement before slipping into Madonna's "Holiday" bassline (on "Stay Another Season"). From there it effortlessly romps through Eighties pop, Daisy Age hip hop, filtered disco, lounge music, daft movie scores, and musicals—all held together by the hiss of vinyl and flutes that drift in and out to create a hazy, dreamy soundscape. Clocking up well over 900 samples in addition to original material, the album was lovingly crafted over a two-year period by ex-Melbourne punks Robbie Chater and Darren Seltmann, Gordon McQuilten, Toni Diblasi, James De La Cruz, and Australian DJ mix champ Dexter Fabay.

Before its release the band had only a Badly Drawn Boy remix, three limited-edition EPs, and some support slots to their name. By the end of the year they had been namechecked on Aussie soap *Neighbours* and become the first act ever to be approved a Madonna sample. It was a timely reminder that two turntables and a sampler could still create pure pop joy. **MMe**

Outkast
Stankonia (2000)

Label | La Face
Producer | Various
Art Direction | Mike Rush
Nationality | USA
Running Time | 73:17

Put *Stankonia* on your stereo. Listen carefully. Hear the panting in the background? That is the sound of the rap world struggling to keep up with Atlanta's most innovative sons. Outkast's fourth album was also their most original, quite a feat as 1998's *Aquemini* had established the duo as masters of Southern soul grooves and psychedelic ghetto imagery.

Producer and keyboardist Earthtone III, who oversaw most of the album, pushed André 3000 and Big Boi away from the live instrumentation of their previous album and helped craft songs from seductively squelchy synths and clattering digital breaks. "B.O.B."—possibly the most ambitious rap track ever—crams a gospel choir, screeching Hendrix guitar, and room-shaking drum and bass into five gloriously chaotic minutes.

André and Big Boi's raps were as imaginative as the sonic backdrop. While Dr. Dre and Snoop Dogg were spitting rhymes about blunts and bitches, the Atlanta duo were writing R&B-infused letters of regret to Erykah Badu's mother ("Ms. Jackson") and chronicling teen suicide ("Toilet Tisha") over discordant bleeps.

Stankonia—its title derived from George Clinton's lexicon of funk—debuted at No. 2 on the Billboard chart and sold four million in the United States alone, elevating Outkast to rap royalty. Although Outkast were kept off the top by Jay-Z's *The Dynasty: Roc La Familia*, the album signaled the arrival of Southern hip hop as a force that could creatively and commercially challenge the giants of East and West Coast rap. **TB**

Radiohead
Amnesiac (2001)

Label | EMI
Producer | Nigel Godrich • Radiohead
Art Direction | S. Donwood • Tchocky
Nationality | UK
Running Time | 43:57

In 1999 came Blur's *13* album, with its harrowing hymns of a soul in futurist freefall, a perfect end to the musical century for pop. So how to begin the new millennium?

Radiohead had reappraised clinical technology with *OK Computer*; their next studio effort, *Kid A*, was previewed on the Internet in MP3 form. The following summer came *Amnesiac*, potentially a return to guitar-driven anxieties. But the band who had chosen their name to be nearer R.E.M. in the record racks had learned from that act's flair for constant reinvention.

Like Michael Stipe, singer Thom Yorke had twigged the value of scattered refrains and vocal enigma— "Knives out catch the mouse," "There's someone listening in," "Don't talk politics and don't throw stones," "Release me . . . where'd you park the car?" In *Amnesiac*'s electronic throbs, jazzy cacophony, and eerie loops, he creates auras of loss and isolation. Lyrical targets include world banks, the media, and Tony Blair. Elsewhere the band dabble with Egyptian mythology and redemption on the majestic "Pyramid Song." Yorke's voice is desolate, sometimes spiraling backward like a man uncertain of his message.

And yet *Amnesiac* is laden with a dark beauty that repays relistening, a treasure trove of delights—the croon-to-sneer of "You And Whose Army?"; the haunting raga-isms of "Hunting Bears"; the uneasy but beautiful "Morning Bell/Amnesiac"; and the drunken brass of closer "Life In A Glass House." Such riches are rare in this rave new world. **GT**

Silver Jews
Bright Flight (2001)

Label | Drag City
Producer | Mark Nevers
Art Direction | Uncredited
Nationality | USA
Running Time | 35:34

"People treat Silver Jews like a piece of shit," shrugged David Berman, as his fourth album was about to come out. Despite his records scoring high cred points on the indie rock scene, Silver Jews were still thought of as a Stephen Malkmus side project—Berman had been pals with the Pavement frontman since college and Malkmus appears on two Silver Jews albums. Berman had also been called a wannabe poet because, as well as making music, he had written books of poetry: "I am a poet!" he growled. With *Bright Flight*, however, he killed these concerns. Yes, there are guest musicians (including Berman's fiancée Cassie Marrett, who sings), but Malkmus does not appear, and there is no doubt that David Berman is absolutely at the helm.

Recorded in Nashville, its songs are warm, classic country-styled (a pitter-patter of drums, pedal steel, open chords), but *Bright Flight* basks in the unexpected. Berman's deep, grizzled voice wobbles like a kid on a bike, casually throwing in curveball images: "Every single thought is like a punch in the face/I'm like a rabbit freezing on a star." In a single song like "I Remember Me," there is old-fashioned romance ("they slow danced so the needle wouldn't skip") and deadpan humor (rhyming "coma" with "Oklahoma").

A poet? Yes. A solo artist whose influence creeps farther and farther outward? Undoubtedly. But perhaps it was best that Berman remained sceptical: "The minute someone would just agree with me," he said, "then I would stop." **SH**

Björk | Vespertine (2001)

Label | One Little Indian
Producer | Björk • Martin Console • Thomas Knak
Art Direction | Inez / Vinoodh • M / M
Nationality | Iceland
Running Time | 55:33

Having released three solo albums, Björk felt that she had mapped out pretty much every aspect of herself. The shy, first steps of *Debut*, the manic rush of *Post*, and the blue, potent *Homogenic*. *Vespertine*, said Björk, is "the last side of me."

Before beginning work on *Vespertine*, Björk had starred in Lars von Trier's movie, *Dancer In The Dark*, as the introverted Selma, someone living in "a locked universe." The same quiet, contemplative mood trickles through the album. According to Björk, "It's about what happens underneath my skin, the hidden place."

Vespertine buzzes with submarine activity, a sense of unseen physical or emotional twitches. In fact, Björk had been collecting microbeats since 1997, pursuing her interest in instruments like celeste, harp, and music boxes: "sounds that are short, percussive, and sweet." For *Vespertine*, she called in electronic duo Matmos, who in the past had worked with everything from a whoopee cushion to the sounds of plastic surgery.

In addition to the tiny, unnameable scratches that bubble through the album, *Vespertine* swells with orchestrations and the voices of a choir of Inuit girls from Greenland. There is a breathless freedom to songs like "It's Not Up To You," which celebrates the exhilaration of trusting the unknown ("Unthinkable surprises, about to happen," she coos), or the gently erotic "Cocoon," so intimate it is like a diary entry.

A massively successful world tour followed, and having documented everything, Björk said she felt liberated. "I could do absolutely anything right now," she said. The world held its breath. **SH**

> ## "This album is partly about creating a cocoon."
>
> Björk, 2001

Track Listing

▶	01	Hidden Place (Björk)	5:28
▶	02	Cocoon (Björk • Knak)	4:28
▶	03	It's Not Up To You (Björk)	5:08
	04	Undo (Björk • Knak)	5:38
▶	05	Pagan Poetry (Björk)	5:14
	06	Frosti (Björk)	1:41
	07	Aurora (Björk)	4:39
	08	An Echo A Stain (Björk • Sigsworth)	4:04
	09	Sun In My Mouth (Björk • Sigsworth)	2:40
	10	Heirloom (Björk • Console)	5:12
	11	Harm Of Will (Björk • Sigsworth)	4:36
	12	Unison (Björk)	6:45

Gorillaz | Gorillaz (2001)

Label | Parlophone
Producer | Various
Art Direction | Jamie Hewlett • Zombie
Nationality | Canada • UK • USA
Running Time | 64:37

Preposterous things happened to music in 2001. Tool took metal mathematics to the top of the album chart. Mariah Carey stripped on *Total Request Live*. And an oddball cartoon concept became a platinum sensation.

The brainchild of Blur's Damon Albarn and *Tank Girl* creator Jamie Hewlett, Gorillaz were cool kid 2D, snaggle-toothed bassist Murdoc, inscrutable ice maiden Noodle, and hip-hop hardman Russell. They came with a weird back story and helpings of horror iconography (hence "Dracula" on the U.S. version). Behind the imagery lay eclectic producer Dan the Automator, Tina Weymouth (whose Tom Tom Club are plausibly part of the Gorillaz family tree), Canadian DJ Kid Koala, and veteran Cuban singer Ibrahim Ferrer.

Key to their success was Del tha Funkee Homosapien (whose *I Wish My Brother George Was Here*, produced by his cousin Ice Cube, is essential for anyone who likes humor with hip hop). His lugubrious rapping helped make hits of the insanely catchy "Clint Eastwood" and "Rock The House," and led to Gorillaz hooking up with Redman and Eminem's proteges D12.

Between the ear candy numbers are flirtations with dub reggae and punk that were better realized on Blur's *Think Tank*, although "Slow Country" is one of Albarn's loveliest songs, and "M1 A1" is a powerful pastiche of Jonathan Richman's "Roadrunner."

Gorillaz are arguably best appreciated on DVD (*Gorillaz Phase One: Celebrity Take Down*) or online (www.gorillaz.com). But the album—which outsold Blur in the United States and clung to the UK chart for a year—offers entry to the musical mystery tour. **BM**

Track Listing

01	Re-Hash (Albarn•Hewlett)	3:40
02	5/4 (Albarn•Hewlett)	2:42
▶ 03	Tomorrow Comes Today (Albarn•Hewlett)	3:14
04	New Genious (Albarn•Brown•Hewlett)	3:59
▶ 05	Clint Eastwood (Albarn•Hewlett•Jones)	5:43
06	Man Research (Albarn•Hewlett)	4:32
07	Punk (Albarn•Hewlett)	1:38
08	Sound Check (Albarn•Hewlett)	4:42
09	Double Bass (Albarn•Hewlett)	4:46
▶ 10	Rock The House (Albarn•Dankworth Hewlett•Jones•Nakamura)	4:11
▶ 11	19-2000 (Albarn•Hewlett)	3:29
12	Latin Simon (¿Qué Pasa Contigo?) (Albarn•Hewlett•Villa)	3:38
13	Starshine (Albarn•Hewlett)	3:33
14	Slow Country (Albarn•Hewlett)	3:37
15	M1 A1 (Albarn•Hewlett)	4:01
16	Clint Eastwood (Ed Case•Sweetie Irie Remix) (Albarn•Case•Hewlett•Irie)	3:43
17	19-2000 (Soulchild remix) (Albarn•Hewlett)	3:29

Ryan Adams | Gold (2001)

Label | Universal
Producer | Ethan Johns
Art Direction | Ryan Adams • Karen Naff
Nationality | USA
Running Time | 69:37

If Ryan Adams were not a prolific songwriter, he would be the loudest regular at the local bar—lamenting the forces aligned against him and cracking a bottle over the head of anyone who told him to keep it to himself. Luckily, Adams is reputed to write something like nine songs a day, and they always turn out better when he really has something to complain about. In 2001, after two bad break-ups had dragged him from New York to Los Angeles, and with a fresh pile of major-label money to make his second solo album, Adams recorded 16 songs to help guide himself back home.

With a sound as diverse as its creator's changing moods and a shimmering Seventies gleam provided by producer Ethan Johns, *Gold* immediately vaulted Adams into the alt.country pantheon alongside Gillian Welch, Lucinda Williams, and Wilco.

Beginning with upbeat but bitter "New York, New York" and ending with the gorgeous, teetering "Goodnight, Hollywood Blvd," *Gold* ambles through Americana, from country to soul, blues to ballads, and all the roads in between. The album is as much a love letter to idols like Johnny Cash, Gram Parsons, and Bob Dylan as to any faded flame. The swaying, rustic chorus of "Somehow, Someday" summons Tom Petty's dustier days, while the lovely descending chords of "Answering Bell" evoke The Band.

What might normally sound clichéd, however, is instead molded into palpable heartache by Adams' lilting swoon and emotive magnetism. It takes a songwriter of considerable skill to make a world so gloomy seem so sweet. **MO**

Track Listing

01	New York, New York	(Adams)	3:47
02	Firecracker	(Adams)	2:48
▶ 03	Answering Bell	(Adams)	3:02
04	La Cienega Just Smiled	(Adams)	4:59
▶ 05	The Rescue Blues	(Adams)	3:36
06	Somehow, Someday	(Adams)	4:23
07	When The Stars Go Blue	(Adams)	3:31
08	Nobody Girl	(Adams•Johns)	9:39
09	Sylvia Plath	(Adams•Causon)	4:08
▶ 10	Enemy Fire	(Adams•Welch)	4:04
11	Gonna Make You Love Me	(Adams)	2:34
12	Wild Flowers	(Adams)	4:55
13	Harder Now That It's Over	(Adams•Stills)	4:31
14	Touch, Feel, And Lose	(Adams•Rawlings)	4:13
▶ 15	Tina Toledo's Street Walkin' Blues (Adams•Johns)		6:04
16	Goodnight, Hollywood Blvd	(Adams•Causon)	3:23

Destiny's Child | Survivor (2001)

Label | Columbia
Producer | Various
Art Direction | I.C.
Nationality | USA
Running Time | 59:45

Sony Music

Having set up the pins with 1999's *The Writing's On The Wall*, the Texas-based Destiny's Child rolled a strike with *Survivor* and firmly established themselves as the top female band of the era.

The album's title was no less than a declaration. The band were at a transitional stage, having lost three members in six months and facing lawsuits from two of the displaced. Destiny's Child were now operating as a threesome, with newcomer Michelle Williams joining Beyoncé Knowles and Kelly Rowland.

Any questions as to whether the new trio could cut it were immediately answered with "Independent Woman Part I" (which was also used as the theme to *Charlie's Angels*). The groove was the only thing that stuttered on this hip-swaying dance number as the women firmly proclaimed their emancipation. The self-assured strut continues on the killer anthem "Survivor" and then transforms into a bouncy sashay for the raucous "Bootylicious," which is built on a short sample of Stevie Nicks'"Edge Of Seventeen."

It is understandable that many would see *Survivor* as Beyoncé's first solo record, given that she co-wrote or produced all 15 tracks. Proud papa Mathew Knowles, the disc's executive producer and resident svengali, made sure that his daughter got nearly every juicy vocal lead. Beyoncé would indeed strike out on her own with 2003's *Dangerously In Love*, a blockbuster that proved nearly as good as *Survivor*, before a return to the fold for 2004's *Destiny Fulfilled*. The follow-up's title was ironic, given that the trio had already fulfilled their destiny, at least artistically, with *Survivor*. **JiH**

Track Listing

▶ 01	**Independent Women Part I** (Barnes·B. Knowles·Olivier·Rooney)	3:43
▶ 02	**Survivor** (Dent·B. Knowles·M. Knowles)	4:14
▶ 03	**Bootylicious** (Fusari·B. Knowles·Moore·Nicks)	3:27
04	**Nasty Girl** (Bassi·Dent·Hackett·B. Knowles)	4:17
05	**Fancy** (B. Knowles·Rotem·Wiggins)	4:12
06	**Apple Pie À La Mode** (Fusari·B. Knowles·Moore)	2:58
07	**Sexy Daddy** (Elliott·B. Knowles)	4:06
08	**Independent Women Part II** (Comstock Donaldson·B. Knowles·Seats·Stewart)	3:45
09	**Happy Face** (Fusari·Gaines·B. Knowles·Lee·Moore)	4:30
10	**Emotion** (B. Gibb·R. Gibb)	3:56
11	**Dangerously In Love** (B. Knowles·McCalla)	4:52
12	**Brown Eyes** (Afanasieff·B. Knowles)	4:47
13	**The Story Of Beauty** (Fambro·B. Knowles)	3:30
14	**Gospel Medley** (Franklin·B. Knowles·Smallwood)	3:26
15	**Outro (DC-3) Thank You** (Fusari·Gaines B. Knowles·Lee·Rowland·Williams)	4:02

The Strokes | Is This It (2001)

Label | Rough Trade
Producer | Gordon Raphael
Art Direction | Colin Lane
Nationality | USA
Running Time | 36:25

THE STROKES IS THIS IT

From the urgent stomp of "The Modern Age" to the melodic basslines on "Hard to Explain" and the tightly intertwined guitars on "Alone Together," *Is This It* was an exhilarating debut.

The dirty, snappy punk-pop that singer-songwriter Julian Casablancas wrote made for compulsive listening. These 11 economic bursts of energy, blessed with a positive cornucopia of sharp riffs, smartly distinguished the band from the many post-Radiohead acts of the time, more intent on creating music on an epic (for which, read: emptily bombastic) scale. (The U.S. vinyl version of the LP was released on 9/11; "New York City Cops" was pulled from the later CD version.)

The Strokes drew their influences largely from the melting pot of bands that emerged from downtown New York during the 1970s (as evinced by their thrift-store jackets, battered sneakers and drainpipe jeans). Clear reference points include The Stooges, The Cars, and Television (particularly in the interplay between the guitars of Nick Valensi and Albert Hammond Jr.).

Casablancas openly admitted his admiration of Lou Reed's Velvet Underground, and stylistically his detached, petulant drawl sounds like a lighter, younger version of his hero. At times he delivers with attitude: "I don't give a fuck," he declares on "Barely Legal," before switching to endearingly frank frustration—"I want it all, I just can't figure out ... Nothin'." The album's finale, "Take It Or Leave It", built into a euphoric crescendo—at gigs, the charismatic Casablancas frequently leapt into the audience during the song. Musical thievery has rarely sounded so much fun. **KM**

> "I got two things, my brains and my balls. And I ain't breaking them for nobody."
>
> Julian Casablancas, 2001

Track Listing

01	Is This It	(Casablancas)	2:35
▶ 02	The Modern Age	(Casablancas)	3:32
03	Soma	(Casablancas)	2:37
04	Barely Legal	(Casablancas)	3:58
05	Someday	(Casablancas)	3:07
06	Alone, Together	(Casablancas)	3:12
▶ 07	Last Nite	(Casablancas)	3:17
▶ 08	Hard To Explain	(Casablancas)	3:47
09	New York City Cops	(Casablancas)	3:37
10	Trying Your Luck	(Casablancas)	3:27
▶ 11	Take It Or Leave It	(Casablancas)	3:16

Gillian Welch | Time (The Revelator) (2001)

Label | Acony
Producer | David Rawlings
Art Direction | Frank Olinsky
Nationality | USA
Running Time | 51:14

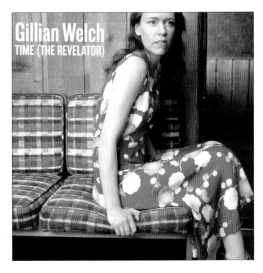

This is dark and hymnal country; rural, old-timey mountain music, haunting, plaintive, and as savagely beautiful as it gets. Does it matter that such "authentic" and "traditional" backwoods-sounding fare is actually crafted by a Los Angeles-raised and Berklee-educated musical sophisticate? Well, it does to some, though frankly it should not. Put simply, stuff this good eloquently and powerfully transcends all the petty quibbles of any dullard churl or purist. And anyway, there is a scything contemporary edge contained herein, in Welch's sluiced and aching words, and in the deftly fractured buckshot phrasing of her musical partner and guitarist extraordinaire David Rawlings. Never forget, as Welch once remarked, "Gillian Welch is a band with two members."

This is their third album and it is their best. Released at a time when the *O Brother, Where Art Thou?* phenomenon had newly piqued America's interest in its own musical roots, it confirmed their potential and cemented their reputations. Recorded on vintage equipment at Nashville's historic Studio B, the sound is crisp and clean and heavenly pure, while the sparse, flat-picked guitar and close-voiced harmonies combine once again to ghostly, plangent effect.

The album unfolds like a blood-red ribbon bleeding. From an Elvis shimmy to a president dead, song after song of subtle and slowed glimpses, poetry and fervor, twisting and trembling toward the mesmeric 15-minute closer "I Dream A Highway." An epic of passion lost or spent. This is the sound of shellac and bone, deep like a mine and dark like a bruise. **RF**

> "My God, the stuff that David is doing, it's not traditional at all."
>
> Gillian Welch, 2001

Track Listing

▶	01	Revelator (Rawlings·Welch)	6:20
	02	My First Lover (Rawlings·Welch)	3:44
	03	Dear Someone (Rawlings·Welch)	3:12
	04	Red Clay Halo (Rawlings·Welch)	3:14
▶	05	April The 14th Part 1 (Rawlings·Welch)	5:07
	06	I Want To Sing That Rock And Roll (Rawlings·Welch)	2:47
▶	07	Elvis Presley Blues (Rawlings·Welch)	4:53
▶	08	Ruination Day Part 2 (Rawlings·Welch)	2:34
	09	Everything Is Free (Rawlings·Welch)	4:43
▶	10	I Dream A Highway (Rawlings·Welch)	14:40

Gotan Project | La Revancha Del Tango (2001)

Label | ¡Ya Basta! / XL
Producer | Gotan Project
Art Direction | Uncredited
Nationality | Argentina • France
Running Time | 58:42

In its time, tango—arguably the most important music to come from Latin America—took over dancefloors and theaters all over Europe and America. Gotan Project are inspired by the same music ("gotan" is back-to-front Argentinean slang for tango) but theirs is no simple nostalgic tribute. For this album marks the revitalization of tango for the twenty-first century.

Gotan Project was the winner of the BBC3 World Music Awards for Best Newcomer in 2003, a welcome nod for Philippe Cohen Solal and his long-time friends Christoph H. Müller and Eduardo Makaroff. The project had been set up to build a bridge between traditional, mystic tango and its new Jamaican down-tempo incarnation, creating sultry, nocturnal, architectural soundscapes that combined classic tango hymns with modern beats and rhythms.

Translating as "The Revenge Of Tango", this inventive album was the most erotic return to tango since the performances of Astor Piazzolla, and DJs were quick to spread its unique, tender, fiery tracks to Europe's clubs. On "Una Musica Brutal," the melancholic range of the concertina-like bandoneon is merged with the simplicity of dub. "Triptico" features violin and a jazzy piano. Cristina Villalonga's timeless vocals on "Época" conjure up the milonga (a joyful Argentinean dance), while the political goals of Che Guevara and Evita are highlighted on "Queremos Paz" and "El Capitalismo Foráneo" respectively.

Gotan Project's mission is to bring tango back to life. *La Revancha Del Tango* is a daring, witty, and elegant declaration of intent. **GD**

> "I think it was important just to say that tango is not dead."
>
> Philippe Cohen Solal, 2003

Track Listing

▶	01	Queremos Paz [Makaroff • Müller • Solal]	5:15
	02	Época [Makaroff • Müller • Solal]	4:28
▶	03	Chunga's Revenge [Zappa]	5:02
▶	04	Triptico [Makaroff • Müller • Solal]	8:26
	05	Santa Maria (Del Buen Ayre) [Makaroff • Müller • Solal]	5:57
	06	Una Musica Brutal [Makaroff • Müller • Solal]	4:11
	07	El Capitalismo Foráneo [Buller • Flores • Solal]	6:12
▶	08	Last Tango In Paris [Barbieri]	5:50
	09	La Del Ruso [Makaroff • Müller • Solal]	6:22
▶	10	Vuelvo Al Sur [Piazzolla • Solanas]	6:59

The White Stripes | White Blood Cells (2001)

Label | Sympathy For The Record Industry
Producer | Jack White
Art Direction | Pat Pantano • Jack White
Nationality | USA
Running Time | 40:23

Beginning work on their third album, The White Stripes' mission was to make a record with no cover versions, no guitar solos, and as few overdubs as possible, as a direct reaction to the relative luxury of second album, *De Stijl*. Such Luddism reaped ironic results—*White Blood Cells* is often considered their most lavish production, spawning some of their best-known songs.

By now the integral red, white, and black identity was well in place. The artwork portrayed the duo sheltering from an ever-encroaching media, yet was also a play on the album title. But it was also full of childlike contradictions—the inner sleeve saw the pair joking around and posing for their supposed pursuers. This attitude bled through to the music. The lyrics to "Fell In Love With A Girl," a brash garage thrash guaranteed to fill any dancefloor it was played on, spoke of the contradictions between the brain of a man and a woman. "I Think I Smell A Rat" (a song Jack demoed long before The White Stripes even existed) bemoaned a youth taking advantage of their elders. Yet "I'm Finding It Harder To Be A Gentleman" begrudged ungrateful females who snubbed chivalry.

Largely though, *White Blood Cells* should be remembered for carnal blues and life-affirming thrashing. It is a petulant child that will not be taught ("Expecting"), yet also a fragile, humble school friend, ever keen to help ("We're Going To Be Friends").

Jack White was now at the peak of his songwriting powers. This excellent album remains the perfect starting point for anyone curious about white blues in the twenty-first century. **JK**

Track Listing

▶ 01	Dead Leaves And The Dirty Ground (White)	3:04
02	Hotel Yorba (White)	2:10
03	I'm Finding It Harder To Be A Gentleman (White)	2:54
▶ 04	Fell In Love With A Girl (White)	1:50
▶ 05	Expecting (White)	2:03
06	Little Room (White)	0:50
07	The Union Forever (White)	3:26
08	The Same Boy You've Always Known (White)	3:09
▶ 09	We're Going To Be Friends (White)	2:22
10	Offend In Every Way (White)	3:06
▶ 11	I Think I Smell A Rat (White)	2:04
12	Aluminum (White)	2:19
13	I Can't Wait (White)	3:38
14	Now Mary (White)	1:47
15	I Can Learn (White)	3:31
16	This Protector (White)	2:10

The Beta Band | Hot Shots II (2001)

Label | Regal
Producer | The Beta Band • Colin "C-Swing" Emmanuel
Art Direction | The Beta Band • Lizzie Finn
Nationality | UK
Running Time | 42:06

The Beta Band reveled in the fact that, media-wise at least, they never seemed to live up to their initial promise. After some stunning EPs, critics castigated their 1999 debut album so extensively that even their devoted fans turned away. The prolonged touring that the band was then forced to undertake tightened them into a sleek beast. All of which informed *Hot Shots II*, the most consistent of their three albums.

Leader Steve Mason brought in C-Swing (producer of UK stars Jamelia and Beverly Knight) to focus their eclectic sloppiness. The result? A truly original record: grooves, psychedelic folk, streaked with Who-style full-on rock. The diversity of the band's sound is best illustrated on "Quiet," its whirrs and clicks recalling Syd Barrett-era Pink Floyd, before it suddenly romps off on a dub-laden passage, culminating in a full-on rock finale. The humorous referencing of the last track "Eclipse" at once addressed and dismissed the critics who suggested the band were some kind of new Floyd. Evoking their earliest work, it displays Mason as a lyrical parodist, singing about smoking pizza pie.

Released in July 2001, *Hot Shots II* was blighted by the Betas' trademark bad luck. Lead single, "Squares," generously used a sample of "Daydream" by The Gunther Kallman Choir. The same sample was used simultaneously by I Monster, who raced up the UK charts with their own "Daydream In Blue," thus denying the Betas a hit single. The intensity of *Hot Shots II* and the band's live performances from this period, with their percussion-driven twists, will become legendary in, oh, about ten years time. Just wait and see. **DE**

> ## "*Hot Shots II* has ended up being a fair representation of the work of a good collective."
>
> Steve Mason, 2001

Track Listing

▶	01	**Squares** (Greentree•Jones•Mackay•Maclean Mason•Van Holmen•Vincent)	3:46
	02	**Al Sharp** (Greentree•Jones•Maclean•Mason)	3:35
▶	03	**Human Being** (Greentree•King•Jones• Maclean•Mason•Stern)	4:32
	04	**Gone** (Greentree•Jones•Maclean•Mason)	3:41
	05	**Dragon** (Diernhammer•Frauenberger Greentree•Jones•Maclean•Mason)	4:57
▶	06	**Broke** (Greentree•Jones•Maclean•Mason)	4:41
▶	07	**Quiet** (Greentree•Jones•Maclean•Mason)	4:49
▶	08	**Alleged** (Greentree•Jones•Maclean•Mason)	5:31
	09	**Life** (Greentree•Jones•Maclean•Mason)	3:51
	10	**Eclipse** (Greentree•Jones•Maclean•Mason)	6:34

Jay-Z | The Blueprint (2001)

Label | Roc-A-Fella
Producer | Various
Art Direction | Jason Noto
Nationality | USA
Running Time | 63:50

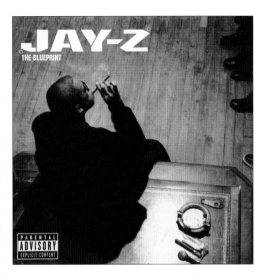

Released on September 11, 2001, *The Blueprint* was, oddly, just what New York's foremost sub-genre needed. At that time, rap in NYC was a tale of two cities. The hip-hop/soul sound, as pioneered by Sean "Puffy" Coombs, Ma$e, and boybands like 112, had been commercially successful, yet it offended purists, who championed the overly earnest, independent hip hop of Company Flow and Mos Def. Jay-Z fitted neither, yet on this, his sixth album, he managed to include tales from the city's common folk and raps about dizzying luxury, without resorting to tasteless hubris, misogyny, or displays of bad jewelry.

Building on the sentimental style pioneered by the likes of Ghostface Killah, inclusions like "Blueprint (Momma Loves Me)" underscored rap's braggadocio with a rare vulnerability. With producers like Kanye West and Just Blaze placed on *The Blueprint,* there was a warmth not heard since the Eighties soul era.

Yet it is Jay's wit that sets this album apart, as he moves between penthouse and sidewalk. If he were granted one superpower, the rapper said, he would opt for the ability to "zap all rich people and move them to the ghetto and zap the poor people to where the rich people were, so that all people could understand how each other lives. Then we figure out the rest after that." On *The Blueprint* his wish nearly comes true. "All I Need" describes a billionaire's lifestyle as succinctly as Ol' Blue Eyes himself; "Blueprint (Momma Loves Me)" renders a poverty-stricken upbringing as well as Dickens, while "Never Change" charts Jay's dizzying transition between the two. **ARa**

Track Listing

01	The Ruler's Back (Carter·Harrel·Hurtt·Sigler)	3:49
▶ 02	Takeover (Burdon·Carter·Chandler Densmore·Krieger·Lemay·Lomax·Manzarek Morrison·Parker·West)	5:13
▶ 03	Izzo (H.O.V.A.) (Carter·Gordy·Mizell·Perren·Richards·West)	4:00
▶ 04	Girls, Girls, Girls (Brock·Carter·Relf·Smith)	4:35
05	Jigga That N***a (Barnes·Carter·Olivier)	3:24
06	U Don't Know (Byrd·Carter·Smith)	3:19
07	Hola' Hovita (Carter·Mosley)	4:33
08	Heart Of The City (Ain't No Love) (Carter·Price·Walsh·West)	3:43
09	Never Change (Carter·Miller·West)	3:58
10	Song Cry (Carter·Gibbs·Johnson·Smith)	5:03
▶ 11	All I Need (Carter·Harrel)	4:28
12	Renegade (Carter·Mathers)	5:37
▶ 13	Blueprint (Momma Loves Me) (Carter·Green·Harrel)	12:08

Röyksopp | Melody A.M. (2001)

Label | Wall Of Sound
Producer | Ole J. Mjøs • Röyksopp
Art Direction | Tom Hingston Studio • Röyksopp
Nationality | Norway
Running Time | 45:58

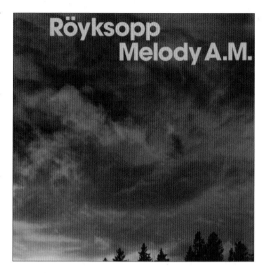

The tired old mantras—there are no great new classic tunes; dance and electronica is just repetitive noodling—were charmingly vaporized by the seductively catchy digital delight that is "Eple," the first single from *Melody A.M.*, which kicked off the twenty-first century for many of us. It spread from leftfield underground clubland to enter a more general public consciousness—apparently out of nowhere.

And what was that name all about? "You can't really call a band Röyksopp . . . ," Svein Berge admits of the electronica phenomenon he has created with his long-term musical accomplice Torbjørn Brundtland. Yet this debut album has sold more than 750,000 copies to date worldwide (400,000 in the UK) and sat high in the album charts for two consecutive years.

The two men became obsessed with making music electronically through their teenage years in Tromso—virtually on the Arctic circle—during the 1990s. Their influences include Eric Satie, Francis Lai (artporn soundtrack maestro), and Portishead. But their art lies in infectious melodies and total mastery of their electronic palette, from subtle tones and danceable grooves to the sweeping symmetry of their arrangements. Their vocal collaborators have exquisitely world-weary voices that also add to the vulnerability and humanity the duo inject into their electronica.

Well-received support slots to the likes of Moby, Pulp, and Orbital, followed by a sold-out U.S. tour in 2003, cemented Röyksopp's popularity. It remains to be seen whether this will be the first of a wondrous sequence of albums, or a brilliant one-off. **MR**

> ## "English people say 'Rouksoup' and the French say 'Rueksupé.' It's a good name ... better than ... 'Funky Bastards' or whatever."
>
> — Torbjørn Brundtland, 2002

Track Listing

▶	01	**So Easy** (Bacharach • David • Röyksopp)	3:44
▶	02	**Eple** (Röyksopp)	3:36
	03	**Sparks** (Drecker • Röyksopp)	5:23
	04	**In Space** (Röyksopp)	3:30
▶	05	**Poor Leno** (Øye • Röyksopp)	3:57
▶	06	**A Higher Place** (Röyksopp)	4:31
	07	**Röyksopp's Night Out** (Röyksopp)	7:30
▶	08	**Remind Me** (Øye • Röyksopp)	3:39
	09	**She's So** (Röyksopp • Thomas)	5:23
	10	**40 Years Back/Come** (Röyksopp)	4:45

Drive-By Truckers
Southern Rock Opera (2001)

Label | SDR
Producer | David Barbe • Drive-By Truckers
Art Direction | Lilla Hood
Nationality | USA
Running Time | 94:01

Drive-By Truckers had no business in releasing a double CD, let alone a conceptual song cycle tracing the rise and fall of a mythical guitar hero. That is the type of thing best left for mega egos like Roger Waters and Pete Townshend, not an unpretentious country-rock band that had previously recorded three mostly ignored independent records. But the aptly named *Southern Rock Opera* was championed by some as the best American rock record of 2001.

Based both on the Lynyrd Skynyrd mythology and songwriter Pattern Hood's upbringing in the American South, the twangy 90-minute epic of heartbreak and humor divides into two acts. The first addresses what it is like growing up with dreams of being a rock star; the second deals with what can happen when that vision becomes reality, ending with the death of the hero in a plane crash, à la Skynyrd's Ronnie Van Zant. The three-guitar assault on such numbers as "Ronnie And Neil" and "Let There Be Rock" further conjures the ghost of Skynyrd, while the narrative in "Days Of Graduation" and "Wallace" draws comparisons to Neil Young.

Lost Highway signed the Truckers just to release . . . *Opera*, but when the reissue failed to attract a mainstream audience the band were dropped. However, the Truckers had created a masterpiece that stands tall next to anything in the Southern rock oeuvre—including that of Lynyrd Skynyrd. **JiH**

Super Furry Animals
Rings Around The World (2001)

Label | Epic
Producer | Chris Shaw • Super Furry Animals
Art Direction | Pete Fowler • Simon Pike
Nationality | UK
Running Time | 52:54

Following the demise of their independent home, Creation Records, Super Furry Animals found themselves making their fifth album for a major label. From the first listen however, it is clear that they were never going to let this affect their fearless musical ambition and experimental bent.

The irrepressible title track,"(Drawing) Rings Around The World," replete with harmonies Brian Wilson would approve, describes a feeling of technological communication overload. It concludes with recordings of phone calls made by the band one night to random numbers around the globe. "Receptacle For The Respectable" continues the bouncy pop feel before splintering off in several different directions. Sliding effortlessly into Bacharach territory before swelling into a death metal crescendo, it also features the sound of Paul McCartney chewing celery."Run! Christian, Run!" sees country rock melt over an electronic loop to mesmerizing effect.

The group promoted *Rings Around The World* with Furrymania: a series of weekends in different cities including cinema screenings, club nights, and surround-sound gigs. Although a few critics accused the band of forcing their eccentricity a little, *Rolling Stone* captured the reaction of most listeners by describing what they had achieved as "A widescreen musical masterpiece with a knowing wink." **GSa**

Jurassic 5
Power In
Numbers (2002)

Label | Interscope
Producer | Cut Chemist • JuJu • DJ Nu-Mark
Art Direction | Soup Design Co. LA • Keith Tamashiro
Nationality | USA
Running Time | 56:19

With *Power In Numbers*, Jurassic 5 redefined their sound, driven by their own unwillingness to repeat themselves and aided by the multitalented Beatnuts.

The rich lyrics of "Freedom" take a swipe at the refusal of the world's superpowers to help the poorest nations. "Break" features relaxed rapping, a cracking snare, and a brilliant chorus echoing the guitar riff of Burt and Franklin's "Love To Hate." J5 were still on a mission to spread the message without trying to preach to the unconverted, while simultaneously distancing themselves from the self-aggrandising world of gangsta rap. JuJu from The Beatnuts presides over "One Of Them," a dark cut with sonorous repeated piano and an eerie street atmosphere. The group's verbal ingenuity and ferocity is showcased on "A Day At The Races," which features some fierce rapping from Big Daddy Kane and Percy P on a punching bass riff.

Nelly Furtado adds her angelic talents to "Thin Line." Essentially a song about the beginning of relationships and unrequited love, it represents a contemplative side of the group rarely expressed before. "What's Golden" is an infectious, bouncing track, referencing the progenitors of hip hop and using the break from Public Enemy's "Prophets Of Rage."

Power In Numbers both entertains and achieves its aim—to communicate the need for society as a whole to fight for change against the didactic few. **AMa**

Wilco
Yankee Hotel
Foxtrot (2002)

Label | Nonesuch
Producer | Jim O'Rourke • Wilco
Art Direction | Lawrence Azerrad
Nationality | USA
Running Time | 51:51

It is a classic David and Goliath story. Wilco delivered their fourth album to Warner/Reprise; the suits gave it one listen, could not see dollar signs, and made the infamously short-sighted decision to drop the band.

With that in mind, it is easy to understand why music lovers have a tendency to overstate the brilliance of *Yankee Hotel Foxtrot*. Fortunately, the album really is brilliant. From the minute-long prelude of cosmic drone, delicate piano, and scratchy static that kicks off album-opener "I Am Trying To Break Your Heart," the band is venturing into unexplored territory.

Jeff Tweedy's lyrics are intensely personal, political, and evocative. The mood of the album is ghostly and distorted, yet beautifully serene. Somber dirges like "Poor Places" and "Radio Cure" are offset by perfect pop gems such as "Heavy Metal Drummer" and "I'm The Man Who Loves You." Inspired by the short-wave radio transmissions from which the album takes its name, producer Jim O'Rourke creates a sonic texture that evokes crossed signals and vast distances.

Upon release, critics drooled and fans lined up, eager to pay for the music they had stored on their hard drives for more than a year. The album would go on to become Wilco's first gold record. Take that, Reprise.

PS: Do not miss Sam Jones' superb documentary *I Am Trying To Break Your Heart*. His cameras witnessed the whole strange saga of *Yankee Hotel Foxtrot*. **RM**

Ms. Dynamite | A Little Deeper (2002)

Label | Polydor
Producer | Various
Art Direction | Matt Hughes
Nationality | UK
Running Time | 64:10

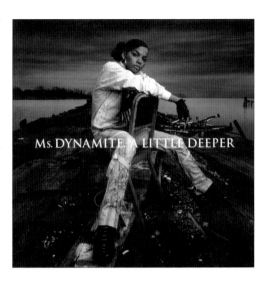

For 21 seconds in 2001, the UK was gripped by "garage," a hybrid of R&B and drum 'n' bass. It yielded a flush of hits, of which "Booo!" by Sticky showcased London teen Niomi Daley. Singing sweetly and rapping about reality not bling, she was Lady (later Ms.) Dynamite.

Having flirted with trigger-happy garage godheads So Solid Crew, she created an album that even made a splash overseas, where garage was just a place you parked your car. Though Dynamite's voice owes most to her heroine Mary J. Blige—whom she lauded as "a strong role model for young black women"—she filled a role vacated by Lauryn Hill (who had replaced R&B with acoustic miserabilism). *A Little Deeper* brilliantly fulfilled her aim to weld "soul, swing, R&B, ragga, soca, and garage" to powerful lyrics.

The sing-along "Dy-Na-Mi-Tee" and smash hit "It Takes More" (which decried "the fighting, the fucking" glamorized by her contemporaries) so entranced Coldplay's Chris Martin that he performed the songs with her in London.

But the album—unusually in a genre not noted for quality across time—harbors so many gems that it earns comparison with *The Miseducation Of Lauryn Hill*. Best is the Art Of Noise-enhanced "Afraid To Fly," whose cinematic strings make it entrancing even without the Nas rap that graced the U.S. version (America also got extra tracks—"Danger" and "Ramp"—while the original album ends with the unlisted "Get Up, Stand Up").

Plans for a follow-up, *A Little Darker*, were shelved when Dynamite became pregnant in 2003. Should that album appear, it has a truly tough act to follow. **BM**

Track Listing

01	Natural High (Interlude)	(Daley•Remi)	0:56
▶ 02	Dy-Na-Mi-Tee	(Daley•Dodd•Hibbert•Remi)	3:39
03	Anyway U Want It	(Bryce•Daley•Remi)	3:42
▶ 04	Put Him Out	(Daley•Jonback•Karlsson•Winnberg)	3:58
05	Brother	(Daley•Jonback•Karlsson•Winnberg)	3:34
▶ 06	It Takes More (Bloodshy Main Mix)	(Daley•Punch)	4:39
07	Sick 'N' Tired	(Daley•Harper)	3:34
08	Afraid 2 Fly	(Bellevue•Daley)	4:48
09	Watch Over Them	(Daley)	1:16
10	Seed Will Grow	(Daley•Marley•Remi)	3:23
11	Krazy Krush	(Daley•Karlsson•Winnberg)	3:44
12	Now U Want My Love	(Daley•Remi)	4:54
13	Too Experienced (feat. Barrington Levy)	(Andy)	2:59
14	Gotta Let U Know	(Daley•Remi)	4:09
15	All I Ever	(Daley•Dyer•Electrik•Hunte•Remi•Van Gibbs)	4:31
16	A Little Deeper	(Daley•Remi)	10:25

The Bees | Sunshine Hit Me (2002)

Label | We Love You
Producer | Paul Butler • Aaron Fletcher
Art Direction | Peter Lloyd
Nationality | UK
Running Time | 39:45

The clue may well lie in the title, but if The Bees' debut were a season, it would most definitely be summer. As the first notes of the horn-soaked "Punchbag" shimmer out, you can picture the sunlight breaking through low hanging branches. And all across these ten brief tracks, *Sunshine Hit Me* retains that lazy, sun-soaked vibe.

Part of the album's success can be attributed to the comparatively old-fashioned recording techniques. Duo Paul Butler and Aaron Fletcher (and a seemingly ever-changing cast of musicians) recorded the album in their shed on the Isle Of Wight. The worn-in, worn-out sound of their vintage equipment makes tracks like the dub-tastic "No Trophy" come alive with period fizz and sparkle. Lesser producers would have emerged from such experimentation sounding overly clever or revivalist. Yet these determined men make this fusion of their favorite music (Sixties beat, reggae, smooth jazz) modern and vital.

Single "A Minha Menina" (an Os Mutantes cover) became a summer radio smash. For a few months, culminating in a nomination for the UK's prodigious Mercury Music Prize, it seemed that every hipster owned the CD with the masked wrestler. (Peter Lloyd's visuals, based on the elaborate stage costumes of Mexican wrestlers, became instantly identified with the band—and, appropriately enough, their chaotic stage shows.) They went on to play as the backing band for Damon Albarn's Gorillaz project, and became producers of choice for many bands in England, but *Sunshine Hit Me* remains a wondrous time capsule of master producers finding their creative feet. **JK**

> "When we wrote *Sunshine Hit Me*, we had no idea we were going to be a band."
>
> Aaron Fletcher, 2004

Track Listing

▶	01 **Punchbag** (Butler•Fletcher)	3:41
	02 **Angryman** (Butler•Fletcher)	4:08
▶	03 **No Trophy** (Butler•Fletcher)	3:27
	04 **Binnel Bay** (Butler•Fletcher)	2:58
	05 **Sunshine** (Butler•Fletcher)	3:29
▶	06 **A Minha Menina** (Ben)	2:50
	07 **This Town** (Butler•Fletcher)	2:59
	08 **Sweet Like A Champion** (Butler•Fletcher)	4:28
	09 **Lying In The Snow** (Butler•Fletcher)	3:54
	10 **Zia** (Butler•Fletcher)	4:12
	11 **Sky Holds The Sun** (Butler•Fletcher)	3:39

Norah Jones | Come Away With Me (2002)

Label | Blue Note
Producer | Various
Art Direction | Jessica Novod
Nationality | USA
Running Time | 45:03

For five-foot-one females, 2002 was a jackpot year. Kylie Minogue conquered the world, while Norah Jones was on her way to ten million U.S. sales.

Both photographed beautifully—Jones' ravishing cover portrait by Joanne Savio surely prompted many impulse purchases. But there the similarities end: Minogue was poppily pyrotechnic, Jones was a cool breeze on a chart inflamed by boys in big shorts.

Though her father is sitar virtuoso Ravi Shankar, there is no trace of his Indian influence here. *Come Away With Me* is a seductive blend of folk and jazz, while Jones has a Texan twang reminiscent of Eighties star Edie Brickell. Standouts include an eyebrow-raised reading of Hank Williams' "Cold Cold Heart," a lap-dancer lyric on "I've Got To See You Again," country star J. D. Loudermilk's "Turn Me On" (also featured on her 2000 mini-album *First Sessions*), and Hoagy Carmichael's "The Nearness Of You" (the love song was previously recorded by one of Jones' favorite singers, Dinah Washington). The airy "Don't Know Why" was her breakthrough—Jones even reworked it for *Sesame Street* as "Don't Know Why I Didn't Come." But the title track is the killer: a seductive, self-penned invitation that is impossible to decline.

The Blue Note label's biggest seller and multiple Grammys were her reward. After declaring, "I listen to The Rolling Stones and I want to be in a rock band," she even earned the approval of Keith Richards. These rock tendencies have, thus far, led only to a cameo with the Foo Fighters. For now, enjoy this beautiful bubblebath of an album and await surprises to come. **BM**

"It's really mellow and quiet ..."

Norah Jones, 2003

Track Listing

▶ 01	Don't Know Why (Harris)	3:06
02	Seven Years (Alexander)	2:25
03	Cold Cold Heart (Williams)	3:38
04	Feelin' The Same Way (Alexander)	2:57
▶ 05	Come Away With Me (Jones)	3:18
06	Shoot The Moon (Harris)	3:56
▶ 07	Turn Me On (Loudermilk)	2:34
08	Lonestar (Alexander)	3:06
09	I've Got To See You Again (Harris)	4:13
10	Painter Song (Alexander·Hopkins)	2:42
11	One Flight Down (Harris)	3:05
12	Nightingale (Jones)	4:12
13	The Long Day Is Over (Harris·Jones)	2:44
14	The Nearness Of You (Carmichael·Washington)	3:07

Coldplay | A Rush Of Blood To The Head (2002)

Label | Parlophone
Producer | Coldplay • Ken Nelson
Art Direction | Solve Sundsbo
Nationality | UK
Running Time | 54:08

As the 9/11 anniversary approached, Chris Martin and his three pals unveiled their sophomore effort, penned (and designed) with a feeling of post-attack "desperation." The UK No.1 set took eight months to record in Liverpool and London, interrupted by friends who soon got "very bored," and Echo and the Bunnymen's influential Ian McCulloch. He convinced Martin the album needed "a song that goes one-two-three, one-two-three, one-two-three," resulting in the psychedelic "A Whisper."

"'A rush of blood to the head,'" Martin told yahoo.com's *LAUNCH*, "is about when you do something on impulse: when you suddenly think, 'I'm going to ask Rachel Weisz to marry me,' or 'I'm going to ring up J-Lo and ask her to do a remix album.'" In the event, Gwyneth Paltrow, not Rachel Weisz, won Martin's heart, and there is no trace of Jennifer Lopez. Instead, the pummeling piano and heartfelt vocals of "Politik" herald a manifesto of engrossing pop rock. The melodies and harmonies are gently captivating, as on the offbeat "God Put A Smile Upon Your Face" and "The Scientist" (inspired by George Harrison's "Isn't It A Pity").

Band pal Phil Harvey convinced the lads to include "Clocks"—a piano-led piece of uplifting homesickness. Contemporary hit-makers (and fans) such as Kylie Minogue also inspired the band, and the shimmering, Eastern-leaning "Daylight" is a more upbeat chop-and-loop singalong. Add in the acoustic "Green Eyes," the Floydian, stratospheric title track, and the crescendo of "Amsterdam," and you have what *NME* called "an album of outstanding natural beauty." **TJ**

Track Listing

01	**Politik** (Berryman•Buckland•Champion•Martin)	5:18
▶ 02	**In My Place** (Berryman•Buckland•Champion•Martin)	3:48
03	**God Put A Smile Upon Your Face** (Berryman•Buckland•Champion•Martin)	4:57
▶ 04	**The Scientist** (Berryman•Buckland•Champion•Martin)	5:09
▶ 05	**Clocks** (Berryman•Buckland•Champion•Martin)	5:07
06	**Daylight** (Berryman•Buckland•Champion•Martin)	5:27
07	**Green Eyes** (Berryman•Buckland•Champion•Martin)	3:43
08	**Warning Sign** (Berryman•Buckland•Champion•Martin)	5:31
09	**A Whisper** (Berryman•Buckland•Champion•Martin)	3:58
10	**A Rush Of Blood To The Head** (Berryman•Buckland•Champion•Martin)	5:51
▶ 11	**Amsterdam** (Berryman•Buckland•Champion•Martin)	5:19

The Coral | The Coral (2002)

Label | Deltasonic
Producer | Ian Broudie
Art Direction | Ian Skelly
Nationality | UK
Running Time | 33:59

The Coral were formed in 1997 in Hoylake, a small seaside town near Liverpool, by sticksman Ian Skelly and bassist Paul Duffy, but it was not until keyboardist Nick Power teamed with the aforementioned pair, plus Skelly's brother James (vocalist), Bill Ryder Jones (guitar, trumpet), and Lee Southall (guitar, vocals), four years later, that rehearsals took a serious turn.

A debut single, 2001's "Shadows Fall," set their "anything goes" manifesto with its delicious blend of Russian folk, rambunctious polka, brooding Morricone-esque soundtrack vibe, ragtime jazz, and coruscating Dick Dale-styled surf guitar. Their eponymous debut LP, produced by The Lightning Seeds' Ian Broudie, was more of the same. A sparkling mélange of snotty, snarly garage punk, catchy beat melody, and everything in between, it hit the UK Top Five in its first week of release, spawning a third single, 2002's "Skeleton Key," which pillaged homegrown influences such as Syd Barrett, Them, and The Teardrop Explodes. Fourth and fifth singles, "Goodbye" and "Dreaming Of You," proved them masters of pop, each being startlingly catchy outbursts; think The La's mixed with a heart-on-sleeve Sixties girl-group sound.

But it was not just music's past they plundered. Literature, movies, and art play a big part in the group's blueprint too—their video to "Goodbye" recreates Robin Hardy's 1973 cult flick, *The Wicker Man*, LP cut "Simon Diamond" knowingly mimics Jack Kerouac's elegy *Dr. Sax*, while their LP sleeve artwork—an eye-grabbing psychedelic collage designed by Ian Skelly—tips its hat to Cream's *Disraeli Gears* back cover. **LW**

> "If we like the sound of something then we'll explore it further."

James Skelly, 2002

Track Listing

01	Spanish Main (The Coral)	1:50
02	I Remember When (The Coral)	3:34
▶ 03	Shadows Fall (The Coral)	3:25
▶ 04	Dreaming Of You (The Coral)	2:17
05	Simon Diamond (The Coral)	2:25
▶ 06	Goodbye (The Coral)	4:02
07	Waiting For The Heartaches (The Coral)	3:58
▶ 08	Skeleton Key (The Coral)	2:58
09	Wildfire (The Coral)	2:42
10	Badman (The Coral)	2:58
11	Calendars And Clocks (The Coral)	3:50

Johnny Cash
American IV: The Man Comes Around (2002)

Label | American
Producer | Rick Rubin
Art Direction | Christine Cano
Nationality | USA
Running Time | 51:56

Johnny Cash died in September 2003, a year after *The Man Comes Around* was released, and the fourth album in the American Recordings series is shot through with inevitability, defiance, and rage. As ever, Cash is largely working with other people's songs, using his solemn timbre and empathy to make them his own. Sting (Sting!) wrote powerful murder ballad "Hung My Head," but he will know full well that Cash has now delivered the definitive performance; a repentant narrative of haunting sorrow and meaningless death. On "Hurt," Cash recasts Nine Inch Nails' bitter lament as a hymn to sincere, inexorable regret; an award-winning video lent the song unbearable pathos by switching between shots of a youthful, vigorous Cash and the present-day, frail, stubborn, elderly man.

The covers do not all hit the mark—avoid the maudlin "Danny Boy"—but many are outstanding: Depeche Mode's "Personal Jesus" becomes a dignified Jerry Lee boogie, while the full maturity of The Beatles' "In My Life" is brought out by Cash's poignant delivery. The new versions of his own back catalog are no less impressive, particularly a jaunty "Sam Hall," but the standout is probably a new composition, the opening title track. Bookended with quotes from *Revelations*, "The Man Comes Around" was inspired by a dream and the Bible, and subsequently has taken on a prophetic, surreal quality that, coupled with Cash's upbeat delivery, makes it as impressive as anything else recorded by this American colossus. **PW**

Track Listing

01	The Man Comes Around (Cash)	4:26
02	Hurt (Reznor)	3:38
03	Give My Love To Rose (Cash)	3:28
04	Bridge Over Troubled Water (Simon)	3:55
05	Hung My Head (Sting)	3:53
06	First Time Ever I Saw Your Face (MacColl)	3:52
07	Personal Jesus (Gore)	3:20
08	In My Life (Lennon·McCartney)	2:57
09	Sam Hall (Trad., arr. Cash)	2:40
10	Danny Boy (Trad., arr. Cash)	3:19
11	Desperado (Frey·Henley)	3:13
12	I'm So Lonesome I Could Cry (Williams)	3:03
13	Tear Stained Letter (Cash)	3:41
14	Streets Of Laredo (Trad., arr. Cash)	3:33
15	We'll Meet Again (Charles·Parker)	2:58

The Flaming Lips
Yoshimi Battles The Pink Robots (2002)

Label | Warner Bros.
Producer | S. Booker • The Flaming Lips • D. Fridmann
Art Direction | George Salisbury
Nationality | USA
Running Time | 47:25

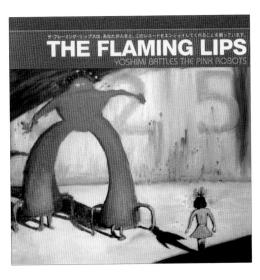

There are ways to demonstrate your commercial status and there are means to prove you are the coolest mothers currently striding the earth. Generally, these two are mutually exclusive so it is illustrative of The Flaming Lips' unique success that they managed to combine both in one gloriously irreverent moment.

Underground underachievers for much of the 1980s and 1990s, the last thing anyone expected—the band in particular—was that 2000's *Soft Bulletin* would see them become critical successes. *Yoshimi Battles The Pink Robots* confirmed that this was no fluke, and ushered in a moment of accidental genius upon the Oklahoma three-piece that symbolized their attitude.

Appearing on British chart-show institution *Top Of The Pops* in January 2003 to mark the Top Twenty showing of single "Yoshimi Battles The Pink Robots Pt. 1," The Flaming Lips recruited man-of-the-moment Justin Timberlake to play bass with them—they also convinced him to do this wearing a dolphin costume. In many ways this captures the persuasive spirit of the album. Electronic bleeps and Pink Floyd-esque prog-rock mix freely with accessible singalongs in an overall concept loosely themed around killer robots and a gutsy heroine. "Do You Realize??" delivers the most life-affirming anthem about death, while the likes of "Fight Test" blend frontman Wayne Coyne's folksy appeal with a surreal party soundtrack. Lethal machines, conceptual anthems, and the world's then hottest star dressed as a dolphin—only The Flaming Lips could do this. **PS**

Track Listing

▶ 01	Fight Test (Coyne • Drozd • Ivins)	4:14
02	One More Robot/Sympathy 3000-21 (Coyne • Drozd • Ivins)	4:59
03	Yoshimi Battles The Pink Robots Pt. 1 (Coyne • Drozd • Ivins)	4:46
▶ 04	Yoshimi Battles The Pink Robots Pt. 2 (Coyne • Drozd • Ivins)	2:57
05	In The Morning Of The Magicians (Coyne • Drozd • Ivins)	6:18
06	Ego Tripping At The Gates Of Hell (Coyne • Drozd • Ivins)	4:34
▶ 07	Are You A Hypnotist?? (Coyne • Drozd • Ivins)	4:44
08	It's Summertime (Coyne • Drozd • Ivins)	4:20
▶ 09	Do You Realize?? (Coyne • Drozd • Ivins)	3:32
▶ 10	All We Have Is Now (Coyne • Drozd • Ivins)	3:53
11	Approaching Pavonis Mons By Balloon (Utopia Planitia) (Coyne • Drozd • Ivins)	3:09

Doves | The Last Broadcast (2002)

Label | Heavenly
Producer | Doves
Art Direction | Julia Baker
Nationality | UK
Running Time | 53:55

There is a photo inside the CD booklet showing a darkening hillside at sunset, with a motorway snaking below. The image captures the essence of this Northern English act, whose windswept music offers a dramatic driving soundtrack.

Doves began life as dance outfit Sub Sub, scored a minor hit, then underwent a rethink. The trio's debut, *Lost Souls*, was a complex workout that drew comparisons with Radiohead, but this elaborate approach was somewhat distilled for *The Last Broadcast*. Also emerging from the same region were the likes of Badly Drawn Boy and Elbow. But Doves stole ahead of their rivals with a set of surging songs that took the breath away.

The band also had an unexpected boost from the British media. For incidental music on TV and radio, especially over sports montages, Jez Williams' guitar riffs were everywhere. Two UK hit singles, "There Goes The Fear" and the pulsating "Pounding," were happy recipients of this free promotion. Not that it is all dynamic anthems and chiming chords. A spooky cover of King Crimson's "Moonchild," contained within "M62 Song," and some cryptic instrumentals hark back to the trippier tracks on *Lost Souls*.

For the most part, however, this is a storming stride ahead, with Jimi Goodwin's world-weary vocals firmly to the fore. On the gospel-tinged "Satellites," he cries from a deep well of pain while, on "Friday's Dust," he sounds almost possessed above the eerie orchestration. And all this after the group's home-built studio had burned down. Thus, with a dash of pomp and a splash of pop, Doves rose from the ashes. **GT**

Track Listing

01	Intro	(Goodwin·A. Williams·J. Williams)	1:17
▶ 02	Words	(Goodwin·A. Williams·J. Williams)	5:42
▶ 03	There Goes The Fear	(Goodwin·A. Williams·J. Williams)	6:54
04	M62 Song	(Fripp·Giles·Goodwin·Lake·McDonald·Sinfield)	3:48
05	Where We're Calling From	(Goodwin·A. Williams·J. Williams)	1:24
06	N.Y.	(Goodwin·A. Williams·J. Williams)	5:46
▶ 07	Satellites	(Goodwin·A. Williams·J. Williams)	6:50
08	Friday's Dust	(Goodwin·A. Williams·J. Williams)	3:35
▶ 09	Pounding	(Goodwin·A. Williams·J. Williams)	4:45
10	Last Broadcast	(Goodwin·A. Williams·J. Williams)	3:22
▶ 11	The Sulphur Man	(Goodwin·A. Williams·J. Williams)	4:37
12	Caught By The River	(Goodwin·A. Williams·J. Williams)	5:55

Missy Elliott | Under Construction (2002)

Label | Elektra
Producer | Missy Elliott • Timbaland
Art Direction | Anita Marisa Boriboon • Lili Picou
Nationality | USA
Running Time | 59:12

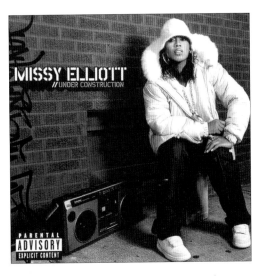

Missy Elliott opens her fourth album by explaining that she still considers herself "a work in progress." Elliott will have to pardon fans for disagreeing. From the dirty grind of the opener "Go To The Floor" to the groovy club remix of "Work It" that closes the album, *Under Construction* is the work of a hip-hop artist operating at the very top of her game.

Pairing up again with the extraordinary Timbaland—a producer who seemingly can make any noise bump like Friday night—Elliott manages to create an even stronger batch of songs than 1997's *Supa Dupa Fly*, 1999's *Da Real World*, and 2001's *Miss E . . . So Addictive*. *Under Construction* would prove to be Elliott's most commercially successful album to date, quickly selling more than two million copies when it hit the stores, and earning the singer a Grammy Award for the addictive single "Work It."

Elliott was joined by several luminaries in the studio and almost all the pairings work. Ludacris is the perfect motormouth sideman on the topsy-turvy chaos of "Gossip Folks," while Jay-Z acts as the other half of Elliott's colorful jigsaw puzzle on "Back In The Day." Beyoncé Knowles' doe-eyed hopefulness mixes surprisingly well with Elliott's street smarts on the sleek R&B dialog of "Nothing Out There For Me."

Despite the guest stars, Missy Elliott proves to be just as raunchy as any of her male peers on "Work It." But few male rappers are as clever. Instead of using one of the usual nicknames for the male genitalia, she simply lets the listener know what kind of trunk she is looking for by sampling an elephant's roar. **JiH**

"I'm not a party person."

Missy Elliott, 1999

Track Listing

▶ 01	**Go To The Floor** (Elliott•Mosley)	5:06
02	**Bring The Pain** (Elliott•Mosley•Smith)	2:59
▶ 03	**Gossip Folks** (Bridges•Elliott•Mosley)	3:54
▶ 04	**Work It** (Elliott•Mosley)	4:58
▶ 05	**Back In The Day** (Carter•Elliott•Mosley)	4:55
06	**Funky Fresh Dressed** (Elliott•Mosley)	3:56
07	**P***ycat** (Elliott•McCalla)	4:32
▶ 08	**Nothing Out There For Me** (Brockman•Elliott•Stewart)	3:05
09	**Slide** (Elliott•Mosley)	3:43
10	**Play That Beat** (Elliott•Mosley)	3:02
11	**Ain't That Funny** (Elliott•Mosley)	2:48
12	**Hot** (Elliott•Mosley)	4:09
13	**Can You Hear Me** (Brockman•Elliott•Stewart)	4:29
▶ 14	**Work It** (Elliott•Mosley)	7:36

Bruce Springsteen
The Rising (2002)

Label | Columbia
Producer | Brendan O'Brien
Art Direction | C. Austopchuk • D. Bett
Nationality | USA
Running Time | 72:50

A record born of the ashes of the 9/11 attacks? Only an artist of the caliber—and with the experience—of Bruce Springsteen could pull that off, and not create something sappy, or trite, or vaingloriously vengeful.

The Rising is Springsteen's magisterial response. He sings forcefully of waking up to an "Empty Sky," of "My City Of Ruins." Hymns the bravery of the rescuers who went "Into The Fire." Owns up to thoughts of "a little revenge" but knows "this too shall pass, I'm gonna pray . . . gonna find my way through this lonesome day" ("Lonesome Day"). Assumes the character of a traumatized survivor who feels like he is the "Nothing Man"—a ballad that aches and creaks and, ultimately, may move you to tears.

The Rising is that powerful, that impactful. For the first time since *Born In The USA,* he is reunited in the studio with the E Street Band. Eighteen years on from that huge record, these longstanding Springsteen compadres—shepherded by erstwhile "grunge" producer Brendan O'Brien—add a declamatory punch to "Lonesome Day" and the title track, and give the ballads "Nothing Man" and "You're Missing" an eerie, elegiac tone. The album is about anguish, despair, coping, moving on, coming together; it is not about any uprising. This notion of healing is inspirationally made in "Worlds Apart," which deploys the harmonium, tabla, and vocal styles used in Islamic Sufi music. In "Paradise," Springsteen even dares to sing from the perspective of a suicide bomber. Intensely moving stuff. **CM**

Beck
Sea Change (2002)

Label | Geffen
Producer | Nigel Godrich
Art Direction | Beck • Kevin Reagan
Nationality | USA
Running Time | 52:26

After a decade of grubby hip-hop beats and threadbare folk, *Sea Change* finally saw Beck grow weary of his own incessant genre hopping. And how weary he sounded. Coming hot on the heels of his split from girlfriend Leigh Limon and his becoming a Scientologist, *Sea Change* wallowed in unhappiness, which meant that—save for the odd cathartic noise blast—post-modern mischief-making was out. So while 2000's *Midnite Vultures* sounded like the soundtrack to an unmade *Banana Splits* movie, *Sea Change* sticks to simple, mournful songs with a straightforwardness that is rare for this often-obscure songwriter.

With mainstays Roger Manning, Smokey Hormel, Joey Waronker, and Justin Meldal-Johnsen sticking to an unobtrusive country-rock template (think *Harvest*), it is Beck's delicate acoustic and aching voice that propels the album. Even gadget-happy producer Nigel Godrich just gets on with the job of spilling the poor guy's heartbreak across the 12 tracks.

Some missed the experimentalism of *Odelay* or *Midnite Vultures*. Certainly the lyrics lack a little bite (he rhymes "before" with "before" on "End Of The Day"), while the vocals range from tired to clinically dead. But then, even *Sea Change*'s simple sleeve signals that the album is itself a left turn. The breathtaking orchestral arrangements on "Paper Tiger," "Lonesome Tears," and "Round The Bend" and the heartbreakingly happy/sad "Sunday Sun," and "Little One," expose a directness and sincerity that few would imagine Beck possessed. **MBe**

The Roots
Phrenology (2002)

Label | MCA
Producer | Various
Art Direction | Gravillis Inc.
Nationality | USA
Running Time | 74:26

The Roots had taken several blows throughout their career. Initially part of Philly's highbrow hip-hop set, they relocated to London in the mid-1990s to reciprocate acid jazz's flirtation with rap.

Nothing, though, could prepare for the knuckleball that was *Phrenology*. A look through the guests might suggest a backslapping pop-rap session (Nelly Furtado, Musiq Soulchild, Jill Scott, Talib Kweli) but *Phrenology* actually dips into experimental electronica, post-punk, and distortion, with a dominant rock theme. "Thought@Work" manages to make the battle-worn "Apache" loop sound original; "Rock You" is a hip-hop take on The Stooges; track three, "!!!!!!!!," is a nod to thrash metal; while lo-fi rap-rock maverick Cody ChesnuTT leads a blinding rework of his own track "The Seed." At *Phrenology*'s heart are two lengthy tracks. "Break You Off" shifts from the nu-soul stylings of Musiq to string-drenched drum 'n' bass, while the 10-minute epic "Water" starts with a stomping Timbaland shuffle before shifting into an avant-garde ambient territory, featuring squalling free-jazz guitarist James "Blood" Ulmer. The smorgasbord of inspirations is neatly mirrored in the cover art—a wealth of ideas, but all contained in the one consciousness.

Even the samples are employed with wit—"Water" samples British post-punkers The Flying Lizards, while "Quills" recontextualizes "Breakout" by the Bacharach-inspired Brit jazzers Swing Out Sister—amusingly credited on the sleeve as The Swingout Sisters. **JLe**

Yeah Yeah Yeahs
Forever To Tell (2003)

Label | Polydor
Producer | David Andrew Sitek
Art Direction | Cody Critcheloe
Nationality | USA
Running Time | 37:25

Yeah Yeah Yeahs were almost finished before they started. Their debut EP—released in spring 2002—had enjoyed staggering acclaim. There followed the familiar record company "bidding war," but the art college trio recoiled from the attention. That summer, the YYYs abandoned the first recording sessions for their album—they thought they did not have enough good songs. Having become an instant press darling on account of her unique voice, onstage animation, and singular approach to fashion, frontwoman Karen O quickly became near-phobic about publicity.

Happily, their withdrawing and starting all over again paid dividends on *Fever To Tell*. Recorded in Brooklyn and mixed in London by guitarist Nick Zinner and legendary engineer/producer Alan Moulder (My Bloody Valentine, Nine Inch Nails), it takes the arty sounds of post-millennium underground New York and shackles them to O's feline yelp.

The remarkable vocals—imagine Siouxsie Sioux, Debbie Harry, and PJ Harvey drunk on the mic in a basement bar—are only part of the frontwoman's appeal. Her mix 'n' match, punk-meets-catwalk look made her a modern pop-culture icon. See her once on a stage, lying on her back, singing and spraying beer from her mouth, and you would never forget. The band's graphic look was equally important: the flaming collage that adorns the sleeve of *Fever To Tell* speaks of a band with a rigorously independent and DIY esthetic.

The coolest and cleverest record of 2003. **CM**

The White Stripes | Elephant (2003)

Label | XL
Producer | Jack White
Art Direction | Bruce Brand • Jack White
Nationality | USA
Running Time | 49:47

When Jack and Meg White holed up in London's Toerag Studios to make their fourth album, no one knew that it would turn out so dark. Their others had been arty, simplistic, and downright loud. But *Elephant*, aside from its instantly recognizable and ecstatically dirty single ("Seven Nation Army"), was really about pushing sonic exploration as far as a duo could.

Shrouded in a symbolically heavy sleeve (Meg's foot is tied in a nod to their divorce), *Elephant* was recorded on analog equipment, with nothing employed that was produced after the mid-Seventies. The seven-minute "Ball And Biscuit," which Jack would later play live with his hero Bob Dylan, was a firm nod to his blues influences and bloody mindedness (its length could be construed as a reaction to the slapdash counter-culture the sleevenotes slated). Yet the album is also a charmingly modern beast. Dedicated to "the death of the sweetheart," *Elephant* is a visceral work that lay out of place yet completely in sync with its time. "Seven Nation Army," a single with a wordless chorus that has seen numerous dance remixes (a true sign of a rock song's crossover appeal), relayed some of Jack's concerns about his growing fame. Elsewhere lay introspection ("In The Cold, Cold Night," sung by Meg), operatic explosions ("There's No Home For You Here"), and good old nerve-tingling blues garage ("Girl, You Have No Faith In Medicine"), which the band achieve like no other. *Elephant* remains their most dynamic release and biggest seller. That it resounds with such darkness and frustration only speaks further volumes for its classic status. **JK**

Track Listing

▶	01	Seven Nation Army (White)	3:51
	02	Black Math (White)	3:03
	03	There's No Home For You Here (White)	3:43
	04	I Just Don't Know What To Do With Myself (Bacharach•David)	2:46
	05	In The Cold, Cold Night (White)	2:58
	06	I Want To Be The Boy To Warm Your Mother's Heart (White)	3:20
	07	You've Got Her In Your Pocket (White)	3:39
▶	08	Ball And Biscuit (White)	7:19
▶	09	The Hardest Button To Button (White)	3:32
	10	Little Acorns (White)	4:09
	11	Hypnotize (White)	1:48
	12	The Air Near My Fingers (White)	3:40
▶	13	Girl, You Have No Faith In Medicine (White)	3:17
	14	It's True That We Love One Another (White)	2:42

Rufus Wainwright | Want One (2003)

Label | Dreamworks
Producer | Marius De Vries
Art Direction | Rufus Wainwright • Janet Wolsborn
Nationality | USA
Running Time | 58:45

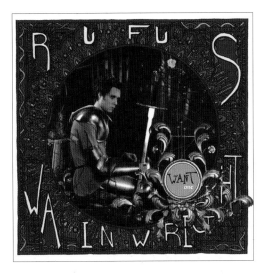

Rufus Wainwright's standing as one of the finest singer/songwriters of recent years was set with his first two solo albums. But with 2003's *Want One*, Wainwright truly arrived. His grandiose ambitions start with the cover—a self-portrait of the artist as Pre-Raphaelite knight. The music within takes in pop and rock, opera, classical, cabaret, and even Seventies adult pop. But Wainwright negotiates any danger of high-camp excess by virtue of his considerable songwriting talents and the songs' exquisitely orchestrated arrangements. The result is like a musical consisting of one showstopper after the next.

"Oh What A World" sets Wainwright's playfully arch vocal against oompah tuba, counterpoint harmonies, and a Bolero-esque outro. "Vicious World" takes swipes at self and ex-lover, to a shimmering Fender Rhodes® accompaniment. Many of the songs grow layer by layer—witness the mighty "Go Or Go Ahead," building from softly strummed intro to a strident cry in the chorus. "Vibrate" is quirkily humorous; on "Harvester Of Hearts," he is wryly lovelorn. Yet sentiment is always leavened by a deftly worked lyric or Wainwright's characteristic dry delivery.

"Dinner At Eight" provides a poignant closer, its premise a stormy meeting between father and son. The press made much of Wainwright's lineage (father, singer/songwriter Loudon Wainwright III; mother, folk singer Kate McGarrigle; sister Martha, who contributes backing vocals). But *Want One* is the work of an original artist with a healthy ego. Or, as he states in the sleevenotes: "This record is dedicated to me." **RD**

"I want the first one to at least land in Wal-Mart."

Rufus Wainwright, 2004

Track Listing

01	Oh What A World	(Wainwright)	4:23
02	I Don't Know What It Is	(Wainwright)	4:51
▶ 03	Vicious World	(Wainwright)	2:50
04	Movies Of Myself	(Wainwright)	4:31
▶ 05	Pretty Things	(Wainwright)	2:38
▶ 06	Go Or Go Ahead	(Wainwright)	6:38
▶ 07	Vibrate	(Wainwright)	2:43
▶ 08	14th Street	(Wainwright)	4:44
09	Natasha	(Wainwright)	3:28
▶ 10	Harvester Of Hearts	(Wainwright)	3:36
11	Beautiful Child	(Wainwright)	4:16
12	Want	(Wainwright)	5:11
▶ 13	11:11	(Wainwright)	4:27
▶ 14	Dinner At Eight	(Wainwright)	4:31

Outkast
Speakerboxx / The Love Below (2003)

Label | LaFace / Arista
Producer | Big Boi • André 3000
Art Direction | Jeffrey Schulz
Nationality | USA
Running Time | 134:59

After a decade making music together, André 3000 and Big Boi's response to their diverging musical interests was to effectively make an album each, but release them together under the Outkast banner. It is a good job they didn't just call it a day.

Big Boi's *Speakerboxx* is more easily categorized as hip hop, but still sounds unique. "Ghetto Musick" kicks off proceedings with wild swings in tempo as frenetic electronica alternates with slow jamming smoothness. The guest rappers lend much more than just their names with the contributions of Koncrete, Big Gipp, and Ludacris a particular highlight on the muscular "Tomb of The Bomb." Always funky, and flavored with trademark Outkast psychedelia, Big Boi puts on quite a show.

With *The Love Below*, André 3000 takes it to the next level. Singing more than rapping, he shows scant regard for musical boundaries, producing a work of the imagination that owes more than a little to Prince. The irresistible bassline and spacey vocals of "Prototype" create an impossibly lush and sexy ballad before the guitar solo takes it right into outer space. The delirious "Hey Ya" got the world to notice that Outkast were onto something special. Twisting together electro-funk, pop, and soul, it sounds like nothing else on earth.

Speakerboxx/The Love Below ultimately succeeds by virtue of both halves being united by a common, insatiable appetite for originality. **GSa**

Dizzee Rascal
Boy In Da Corner (2003)

Label | XL
Producer | Dizzee Rascal
Art Direction | Uncredited
Nationality | UK
Running Time | 57:08

By 2003, the UK garage scene had peaked and was returning to the underground. Meanwhile, Dizzee Rascal, a young, black, paranoid MC and producer, was on his way up as the unlikely champion of a new, oppressive, dense, and confronting offshoot from garage, the sub-genre now known as "grime."

Boy In Da Corner, Dizzee's 2003 debut, is an aural portrayal of life as a teenager in the housing projects of East London. Dizzee wrote and produced the album himself, describing the alienation and confusion with pinpoint accuracy. The album went gold in the UK, all the more impressive considering the harsh sonics within. Dizzee's production drew from old-school hip hop, garage, drum 'n' bass, rock, electro, and any other black music you care to name, at the same time sounding utterly alien. The sheer urban velocity of this music demanded a special MC and Dizzee was more than up to the task, spitting cockney slang and grimy battle rhymes with dexterity and style.

"I Luv U" was the album's first single—a harsh and darkly satirical account of a boy and girl failing to communicate. Like any good lyricist, Dizzee exploits different styles, from rap braggadocio ("Hold Ya Mouf," "Fix Up, Look Sharp"), to cutting social critique ("Round We Go"); and he is not afraid to reveal his sensitive side ("Brand New Day"). *Boy In Da Corner* deservedly won the prestigious Mercury Prize in 2003. **APi**

The Mars Volta
De-loused In The Comatorium (2003)

Label | Strummer
Producer | Rick Rubin
Art Direction | Storm Thorgerson
Nationality | USA
Running Time | 67:59

At The Drive-In's fêted hybrid of Fugazi's propulsive hardcore and the polish of nu-metal studio wizard Ross Robinson won them acclaim and threatened genuine mainstream crossover. But their panic-rock masked rifts within their ranks; guitarist Omar Rodriguez-Lopez and singer Cedric Bixler Zavala felt hamstrung by their bandmates' musical limitations, splitting ATD-I in early 2001 and forming The Mars Volta to pursue their love of things outside the hardcore canon.

They drew upon the Latin musics of Omar's childhood in Puerto Rico, their love of Fela Kuti, the eloquent bereftness of Miles Davis' 1970s work, and their fascination with abstract electronica. They drew upon their experimentation with drugs, and the experiences of their friend, Julio Venegas, a local artist in their hometown El Paso whose arm shriveled after he injected rat poison, and who committed suicide after surviving an overdose-induced coma.

De-loused In The Comatorium is a lucid, Dalí-esque blur of an album, painting the fevered Venegas' dying dreams through a progressive mutation of hardcore, possessed of militant groove. Beyond the music's complexity lies its emotional power, a yearning and vulnerable sense of pain articulated by epic, twisted melodies and Cedric's keening vocals. They most resemble a twenty-first century Led Zeppelin, raised on salsa and Afrobeat, funkadelia and the future. **SC**

Lightning Bolt
Wonderful Rainbow (2003)

Label | Load
Producer | Lightning Bolt
Art Direction | Brian Chippendale
Nationality | USA
Running Time | 41:38

Quite possibly the most notorious bass/drum noise rock duo to come from Rhode Island. Certainly the best known with a "singer" who barks through a contact microphone taped inside a gimp mask. Lightning Bolt does not so much play music as inflict it upon the listener in a barrage of technical noise.

The band formed in 1995, performing locally at Providence house parties as a sloppy three-piece art-school noise outfit taking their influences from Fred Frith, Derek Bailey, and Ruins; a switch to a two-piece saw a tightening of their sound. After the near-mythical status of their second album *Ride The Skies*, which inspired storms of activity on indie-rock discussion boards, Brian Chippendale (drums) and Brian Gibson (guitar) chose to turn the chaos down a notch on the follow-up *Wonderful Rainbow*. While not exactly "melodic" in the traditional sense, songs such as "Crown Of Storms," a chugging prog anthem, and "Dracula Mountain" evidenced signs of a more recognizable song structure emerging from the rumble.

While some diehard fans would say its predecessor's maelstrom of sonic violence is the key Lightning Bolt release, *Wonderful Rainbow* proves that the band are not just a one-trick pony. Although they are still tapping into the noise mother lode, they are able to create a mix of sheer abuse and welcome diversity, for a truly challenging listening experience. **TSc**

Morrissey | You Are The Quarry (2004)

Label | Attack
Producer | Jerry Finn
Art Direction | Scott King • Morrissey
Nationality | UK
Running Time | 47:13

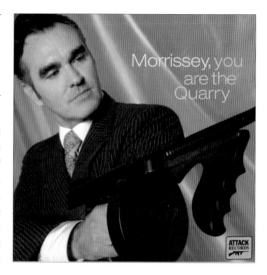

On the cover of *You Are the Quarry*, the Moz, looking dapper in a pinstriped suit, gazes down the barrel of a gangster's tommy gun. And who exactly is the quarry? Well, for starters, there is the British music press, shallow pop stars, teenage groupies, the Royal Family, President Bush, Jesus—all the usual suspects. The sideburns are gray and the pompadour sprouts from a receding hairline, but this collection of guitar anthems and ballads proves that Morrissey has not lost any of his trademark pathos and sardonic humor.

Always a flamboyant and controversial figure, Morrissey's post-Smiths solo career started out strong but grew spotty throughout the Nineties. The British music press began to turn against him as the decade wore on, so he relocated to America (Hollywood, where else?) where his fan base held strong.

Morrissey's love/hate relationship with his new home is the subject of album opener "America Is Not The World" in which he croons, "America/Your head is too big/Because America/Your belly's too big." England gets its fair share on the driving "Irish Blood, English Heart" and his swooning, bittersweet ode to slate-gray skies, "Come Back To Camden."

Over the decades, Morrissey has come up with some terrific song titles, but "I Have Forgiven Jesus" might take the crown. "First Of The Gang To Die" is a rocking, romantic ode to gang violence that boasts a lyric both wistful and drily witty.

You Are The Quarry was hailed by critics and earned Morrissey a legion of new fans. Don't call it a comeback. Just call it his best album in years. **RM**

"Somebody has to be me, so it might as well be me."

Morrissey, 2004

Track Listing

▶	01	America Is Not The World (Morrissey•Whyte)	4:03
▶	02	Irish Blood, English Heart (Morrissey•Whyte)	2:37
	03	I Have Forgiven Jesus (Morrissey•Whyte)	3:41
▶	04	Come Back To Camden (Boorer•Morrissey)	4:14
	05	I'm Not Sorry (Boorer•Morrissey)	4:41
	06	The World Is Full Of Crashing Bores (Boorer•Morrissey)	3:51
	07	How Can Anybody Possibly Know How I Feel? (Morrissey•Whyte)	3:25
▶	08	First Of The Gang To Die (Morrissey•Whyte)	3:38
	09	Let Me Kiss You (Morrissey•Whyte)	3:30
	10	All The Lazy Dykes (Morrissey•Whyte)	3:31
	11	I Like You (Boorer•Morrissey)	4:11
	12	You Know I Couldn't Last (Day•Morrissey•Whyte)	5:51

Björk | Medúlla (2004)

Label | One Little Indian
Producer | Björk
Art Direction | Inez / Vinoodh • M / M
Nationality | Iceland
Running Time | 47:12

On *Vespertine* (2001), Björk created a sound world that was obscure even for her. *Medúlla* follows a similar path: the human voice is the sole source for the music—with the exception of one gong!

Björk and fellow Icelander recording engineer Valgeir Sigurdsson had been working on the album for a year and a half before they finally decided to go all the way and use only voices. A colorful group of contributors was drafted in, among them Faith No More's Mike Patton, Robert Wyatt, Japanese voice artist Dokaka, and beatboxer Rahzel. Choirs from Iceland and the UK also make an appearance and the recording took place in various locations—Iceland, New York, the Canary Islands, Brazil, and London.

The music is an eclectic blend, consisting of ancient folk, glitch techno, contemporary classical, pop, and pure avant-garde weirdness. Björk's Icelandic roots are to the fore on the subtle and intimate "Vökuró," while "Desired Constellation" is simple and emotionally stark. Grunts, heavy breathing, and voice acrobatics pop up on several tracks—check out the amazing Inuit throat singing on "Ancestors." Elsewhere, the singer spectacularly fuses the avant garde with pop sensibilities on tracks such as "Mouth's Cradle," "Triumph Of A Heart," and "Who Is It (Carry My Joy . . .)."

In one interview, engineer Valgeir revealed that at one point he became concerned that the unusual approach might overshadow the actual music. He need not have worried: the album was greeted with universal acclaim, and hailed as yet another triumph from a consistently innovative artist. **AET**

"I just got really into yodeling."

Björk, 2004

Track Listing

01	Pleasure Is All Mine (Björk)	3.26
02	Show Me Forgiveness (Björk)	1:23
▶ 03	Where Is The Line? (Björk)	4.41
▶ 04	Vökuró (Sigurdardottir • Vidar)	3.14
05	Öll Birtan (Björk)	1.52
▶ 06	Who Is It (Carry My Joy On The Left, Carry My Pain On The Right) (Björk)	3.57
07	Submarine (Björk)	4.46
▶ 08	Desired Constellation (Alary • Björk)	4.55
09	Oceania (Björk • Sjon)	3.24
10	Sonnets/Unrealities XI (Björk • Cummings)	1.59
11	Ancestors (Björk • Tagaq)	4.08
▶ 12	Mouth's Cradle (Björk)	3.59
13	Midvikudags (Björk)	1.24
▶ 14	Triumph Of A Heart (Björk)	4.04

Mylo
Destroy Rock & Roll (2004)

Label | Breastfed
Producer | Myles MacInnes
Art Direction | Phantom
Nationality | UK
Running Time | 55:25

Scissor Sisters
Scissor Sisters (2004)

Label | Polydor
Producer | Scissor Sisters • Daniel Wise
Art Direction | Fury
Nationality | USA
Running Time | 42:55

Everybody loves Mylo. When *Destroy Rock & Roll* was released in 2004 there was not a critic who did not trumpet the skills of 24-year-old Myles (MacInnes). Doing his own production and generating all his tracks via computer, Mylo's catchy pop hooks, slick electro stabs, smooth breaks, soaring atmospherics, and pneumatic basslines put the fun back into house.

By the time *Destroy Rock & Roll* came out, the UK chart-busting "Drop The Pressure," with its catchy synth hook, had paved the way. Months before it came out it was a club anthem, played by DJs on every continent. Before that, in 2003, the album's defiant title track had been released on limited-edition seven inch. This first cut combined a heavy guitar workout with fat beats and a sample of a preacher from doomsday cult The Church Universal and Triumphant. (Mylo found the sample while he was temping at the BBC.) Elsewhere, 1980s pop, straight-up guitar rock (he admits he is a Bruce Springsteen fan), Chicago house music, and Mylo's environment all went into the album project. The atmospherics running through it were inspired by Mylo's home, the tiny Isle of Skye in Scotland where he grew up and his parents still live. The lazy, sun-drenched beats on "Sunworshipper" were dreamt up during his stint living in San Francisco.

Destroy Rock & Roll continued to supply hits long after its release: in 2005, "In My Arms" rocked dancefloors in Ibiza for an entire summer. The album is still doing it now. **CH**

New York's Scissor Sisters emerged from a brief electroclash phase that arose in their home city, to reintroduce a much-needed sense of fun to pop music. Fans eagerly embraced the group's immeasurably camp disco vibe—epitomized by frontman Jake Shears' love of sequinned Lycra. Meanwhile, feminists everywhere warmly greeted the emergence of Ana Matronic, Shears' partner in vocal adventure, who had cut her teeth on the cabaret circuit. Unsurprisingly, this plain-speaking diva became the pin-up of left-leaning movements.

Drawing inspiration from David Bowie, Roxy Music, Kurt Weill, Elton John, The Bee Gees, and an arsenal of Eighties beats, Scissor Sisters' debut album is a precious gem that sparkles with the promise of even greater things to come. Few debut albums manage to achieve the coherence of this highly polished offering. From the funky piano-based "Laura" to the infectious groove of coming-out song "Take Your Mama," via heartfelt ballad "Mary" and dancefloor call-to-arms "Filthy/Gorgeous," *Scissor Sisters* is a delightful grab-bag of a record.

Among the feast of material lies an unlikely cover of Pink Floyd's "Comfortably Numb"—the song showcases Shears' impressive falsetto range, and gave the group a first taste of chart success as their second single. "Return To Oz" paints a picture of a sad world hurtling toward its demise—a sharp contrast to the explosion of positivity that pervades the rest of the album. A magical album that should be stored close to the heart—no surprise that it became the UK's bestselling LP in 2004. **SN**

The Icarus Line
Penance Soirée (2004)

Label | V2
Producer | Mike Musmanno
Art Direction | Matt Sohl
Nationality | USA
Running Time | 53:49

From its raw declarations of musical independence, to its confrontational packaging (the track listing is hidden away in the inlay sleeve in an indecipherable scrawl), *Penance Soirée* is the perfect punk statement.

The album was a huge sonic step forward for The Icarus Line. While their 2000 debut, *Mono*, had relied on a hardcore blend of screamed vocals and stop-start guitars, *Penance Soirée* showcased a more primal, sleaze-ridden sound. Opener "Up Against The Wall Motherfuckers"—a cutting attack on commercial punk sell-outs—revolves around a brutal caveman bassline. In the four years since *Mono*, frontman Joe Cardamone's lyrics had also developed from simple declarations of punk rage into insightful tales of gutter living. Over the drunken, Stones-inspired strut of "Spike Island," the frontman snarls a story of substance abuse worthy of beat legend Charles Bukowski. Cardamone's decadent vision shines most brightly in the three-song, 20-minute odyssey that lies at the heart of *Penance Soirée*. "Kiss Like Lizards," "Getting Bright At Night," and "Big Sleep" are shackled together in a caustic tale of love gone wrong, weaving through feedback-soaked garage punk, angular noise, and dreamy space rock.

This ambition and experimentation earned *Penance Soirée* acclaim far beyond California's hardcore scene. Metal magazine *Kerrang!* called it a "stand against tedium and mediocrity," and even the conservative British newspaper *The Daily Telegraph* admitted that the album possessed a "do-or-die intensity." **TB**

Arcade Fire
Funeral (2004)

Label | Merge
Producer | Arcade Fire
Art Direction | Tracy Maurice
Nationality | Canada
Running Time | 48:00

For about 10 months in 2003, the spurious tag "emo" was a popular way to describe a peculiarly self-regarding and downbeat form of heavy rock—the etymological roots, obviously, stemming from the word "emotional." Arcade Fire's debut singlehandedly shows up this entire subgenre for the emotionally illiterate, self-indulgent, angst-ridden garbage it really is. That year, Win Butler and Regine Chassagne, partners in music and love, formed an avant-leaning indie rock outfit in Montreal to experiment in styles ranging from bossa nova to Krautrock, but their efforts were galvanized immediately by the death of Chassagne's grandmother and Butler's grandfather—Alvino Rey, the ragtime composer—within months of each other.

The resulting album is a magical-realist story of young lovers trying to escape the memories of their families, set to an ambitious, string-drenched landscape. "Neighborhood #1 (Tunnels)" sees the protagonists burrowing out of their respective family homes in order to see each other and escape the grief of their parents. Three more songs in the "Neighborhood" sequence build up a complex psycho-geographical metaphor for Butler and Chassagne's intertwined loss and love. But there is nothing postmodern about the unabashed serenade of "Crown Of Love," an epic ballad worthy of Scott Walker at his heartrending best. Despite taking in elements of The Flaming Lips, Suede, Brian Eno, and My Bloody Valentine, this album is still that oh-so-rare thing: a new album that sounds entirely original. **JDo**

Devendra Banhart
Rejoicing In The Hands (2004)

Label | Young God
Producer | Devendra Banhart • Michael Gira
Art Direction | Devendra Banhart
Nationality | USA
Running Time | 42:04

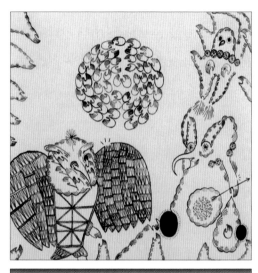

Following his delightfully lo-fi debut album *Oh Me Oh My* (2002), critics were quick to pigeonhole Devendra Banhart as the poster-boy for an indie-folk revolution. But instead of embracing his "alternative" music savant status, on *Rejoicing In The Hands* Banhart smartly sidesteps the celebrity factor by paging through an even more dog-eared singer/songwriter sketchbook of rustic string-picked things. Sure, the digest of bluegrass, country, and British folk echoes remain intact, but this time round he pushes his polymorphous perversity way beyond referential revisionism into otherworldly originality.

Basically, Banhart is impossible to decode using any of the old folk Rosetta Stones. Even attempts to decrypt the oddly tuned acoustic guitar melodies on "Poughkeepsie" as an avant-psychedelic overhaul of Harry Smith's *Anthology Of American Folk Music* (1952), or his nursery-rhyme sigh on "The Body Breaks" as a ghostly resurrection of Tyrannosaurus Rex-era Marc Bolan, end up redundant. All that the listener has recourse to are lyrical ciphers that shift from "Jabberwocky" whimsy to Rimbaud-on-acid tone poems, and even the song titles offer no semiotic relief. Just try to make sense of outrageously oblique names such as "Tit Smoking In The Temple Of Artesan Mimicry!" Hell, maybe "This Beard Is For Siobhán" is nothing more than just plain cashing in. And herein lies Banhart's masterstroke: he sounds like he doesn't give a damn if anyone is listening. **MK**

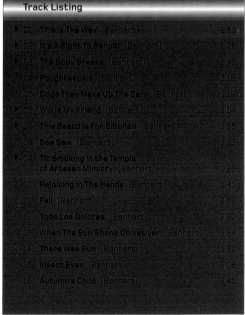

Track Listing

► 01	This Is The Way (Banhart)	2:53
► 02	It's A Sight To Behold (Banhart)	2:26
► 03	The Body Breaks (Banhart)	3:48
► 04	Poughkeepsie (Banhart)	2:18
► 05	Dogs They Make Up The Dark (Banhart)	1:19
► 06	Will Is My Friend (Banhart)	3:04
► 07	This Beard Is For Siobhán (Banhart)	2:35
08	See Saw (Banhart)	3:23
► 09	Tit Smoking In the Temple of Artesan Mimicry (Banhart)	1:25
10	Rejoicing In The Hands (Banhart)	1:41
11	Fall (Banhart)	2:53
12	Todo Los Dolores (Banhart)	2:30
13	When The Sun Shone On Vetiver (Banhart)	3:34
14	There Was Sun (Banhart)	1:31
15	Insect Eyes (Banhart)	5:08
16	Autumn's Child (Banhart)	2:41

Nick Cave And The Bad Seeds
Abattoir Blues / The Lyre Of Orpheus (2004)

Label | Mute
Producer | Nick Cave And The Bad Seeds • Nick Launay
Art Direction | Tom Hingston Studio
Nationality | Australia
Running Time | 82:24

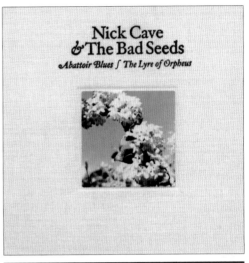

The double album usually signifies one of two things in a band's life. Most frequently it accompanies the bloated mid-career crisis, as navel-gazing sets in and 12-minute drum solos are the norm. Rarer is the instance of a band having too much killer material to shoehorn onto one album.

Produced by Nick Launay, who had helmed 2003's *Nocturama*, *AB/TLOO* sees the band—shorn of stalwart Blixa Bargeld—continue the collaborative process, with the Seeds back in the songwriting engine room. The album is positively schizophrenic, with each section dominated by a definite sound. *Abattoir Blues* contains raucous stomp-alongs that zing with Cave's humor—exhorting the listener that "If you've got a field, that won't yield, well get up and hoe it" on "There She Goes, My Beautiful World." Cave also counterbalances metaphysics with banal reality on the title track: "I went to bed last night and my moral code got jammed, I woke up this morning with a Frappucino in my hand."

The Lyre Of Orpheus sets a more contemplative tone, and contains some of the giddiest love songs Cave has yet to pen—"Breathless" coming across all Van Morrison, or the fruity "Babe, You Turn Me On" ("I put one hand on your ripe red hand heart, and the other down your panties"). There is room for a further surprise as the London Community Gospel Choir add a spiritual depth to "Carry Me" and the thrilling "O Children."

As the Seeds power on into their forties, it is clear age shall not wither them. **SJac**

Track Listing

▶	01	Get Ready For Love (Casey•Cave•Ellis•Sclavunos)	5:05
▶	02	Cannibal's Hymn (Cave)	4:54
	03	Hiding All Away (Cave)	6:31
	04	Messiah Ward (Cave)	5:15
▶	05	There She Goes, My Beautiful World (Cave)	5:17
	06	Nature Boy (Casey•Cave•Ellis•Sclavunos)	4:54
	07	Abattoir Blues (Cave•Ellis)	3:58
	08	Let The Bells Ring (Cave•Ellis)	4:26
	09	The Fable Of The Brown Ape (Cave)	2:43
▶	10	The Lyre Of Orpheus (Cave•Ellis•Casey•Sclavunos)	5:36
▶	11	Breathless (Cave)	3:13
	12	Babe, You Turn Me On (Cave)	4:21
	13	Easy Money (Cave)	6:43
▶	14	Supernaturally (Cave)	4:37
	15	Spell (Casey•Cave•Ellis•Sclavunos)	4:25
	16	Carry Me (Cave)	3:37
▶	17	O Children (Cave)	6:49

Franz Ferdinand | Franz Ferdinand (2004)

Label | Domino
Producer | Tore Johansson
Art Direction | Matt Cooper • Franz Ferdinand
Nationality | UK
Running Time | 38:45

Franz Ferdinand is the album that redefined both "indie music" and "art rock." It is distilled from defiantly left-field influences—Gang Of Four, Talking Heads, Fire Engines—and its huge hit single "Take Me Out" cockily plays fast and loose with time signatures. The sleeve design is a triumph of Soviet-style minimalism. Briskly and crisply recorded in Sweden, this is skinny New Wave as if remixed by Seventies-era David Bowie and topped off with the amphetamined rush of power pop. The energetic likes of "Jacqueline," "This Fire," and "Come On Home" sound both effortlessly modern and proudly retro.

From the off, Franz Ferdinand had a manifesto. They wanted to make music for girls to dance to. From the stage, they would maintain eye contact with the audience at all times. Having formed in the social circles surrounding Glasgow School of Art, they were intent on putting as much thought into graphic design and presentation—sleeve art, stage backdrops, videos, the clothes they wore—as into the music. They wanted, as bassist Bob Hardy wrote in an early website posting, to create emotion "on the level of Field Marshall Haig's tears that fell as he counted the statistics of the men he had sent over the top."

Franz Ferdinand could have been the most pretentious band in the world, an elitist group for music snobs. Instead, their self-titled debut was the worldwide break-out success story of 2004, selling 3.2 million copies. At one point in the United States it was selling 17,500 copies each week. Indie music and art rock had never been so popular. **CM**

> "To me The Fall is pop music as much as Duran Duran is pop music."
>
> Alex Kapranos, 2004

Track Listing

▶ 01	Jacqueline (Hardy • Kapranos • McCarthy)	3:49
02	Tell Her Tonight (Kapranos • McCarthy)	2:17
▶ 03	Take Me Out (Kapranos • McCarthy)	3:57
04	Matinee (Hardy • Kapranos • McCarthy)	4:03
▶ 05	Auf Achse (Kapranos • McCarthy)	4:19
06	Cheating On You (Kapranos • McCarthy)	2:36
▶ 07	This Fire (Kapranos • McCarthy)	4:14
▶ 08	Darts Of Pleasure (Kapranos • McCarthy)	2:59
▶ 09	Michael (Kapranos • McCarthy)	3:21
10	Come On Home (Kapranos • McCarthy)	3:46
11	40 Ft (Kapranos • McCarthy)	3:24

Kanye West
The College Dropout (2004)

Label | Roc-A-Fella Records
Producer | Kanye West
Art Direction | Native
Nationality | USA
Running Time | 72:12

The College Dropout was one of 2004's most-anticipated and best-received albums—but it almost didn't happen. Despite a reputation as a star producer, earning his name with peerless beats and chopped-off, sped-up samples, West struggled to be taken seriously as a rapper. Since the late Nineties, he had churned out hits for others—notably Jay-Z—but his own album was repeatedly pushed back. In October 2002, West suffered a car accident that almost cost him his life, and led to jaw surgery that delayed the album yet again. Fortunately, he recovered and used his misfortune to make both the heartfelt "Through The Wire"—the story of the accident looped over Chaka Khan's "Through The Fire"—and the epic "Last Call," tracing his career from his humble beginnings to being signed by Roc-A-Fella.

The College Dropout makes the best of his connections. Superstars Jay-Z and Ludacris, and street poets Talib Kweli and Mos Def, lend their skills to West's mix of innovative production and witty, insightful rhyming. He bridges the gap between conscious and radio-friendly hip hop, from the haunting spiritual chant "Jesus Walks" to the Lauryn Hill-looping "All Falls Down" and grimy anthem "The New Workout Plan."

"I feel like a lot of the soul that's in those old records that I sample is in me," declared West. "So when I hear 'em and I put 'em with the drums and I bring 'em to the new millennium, it's just like God's doing that . . ." **LP**

Cee-Lo Green
Cee-Lo Green . . . Is The Soul Machine (2004)

Label | Arista
Producer | Various
Art Direction | Jeffrey Schulz
Nationality | USA
Running Time | 65:27

In 2004, the radiant sunsplash soundclash that was going on down South was no longer news; it was a fact. Crunk was blowing up on the underground, the Dirty South movement taken to its logical conclusion, while Atlanta's psychedelic rappers Outkast had conquered the mainstream. Sensing a turnaround in their fortunes, Outkast-affiliates Goodie Mob reformed for a comeback album, though they were by now missing a member—larger-than-life crooner/MC Cee-Lo Green had gone solo, released an acclaimed debut, . . . *His Glorious Imperfections*, in 2002, and was now about to deliver his definitive statement.

Ego and charisma make for fine bedfellows, and Cee-Lo had both in abundance; the album opens with a skit, the big man imbuing his infant son with the same bountiful self-esteem he has. Within minutes, he is swirling in a carnival of summer funk, howling "God can truly work a miracle/Look at me, isn't it obvious that I'm one?" as a chorus of extras chant his hosannas.

And so Cee-Lo's sun-kissed, schizophrenic party continues—Timbaland fine-tunes the bawdy booty bash of "I'll Be Around", while Pharrell steps up for the delicious quiet storm of "Let's Stay Together." But there is never a doubt that Green himself is the real star here, though it would not be until his re-emergence as one half of the astonishing Gnarls Barkley that the public seriously took notice. **SC**

TV On The Radio
Desperate Youths, Blood Thirsty Babes (2004)

Label | Touch And Go
Producer | David Andrew Sitek
Art Direction | David Babbitt
Nationality | USA
Running Time | 47:11

Liars
They Were Wrong, So We Drowned (2004)

Label | Blast First
Producer | David Andrew Sitek • Liars
Art Direction | Beate Schlingelhoff-Gross
Nationality | Australia • USA
Running Time | 40:42

As debuts go, *Desperate Youths, Bloodthirsty Babes* is as adventurous and innovative as you could hope for. Built around soulful a cappella vocal harmonies, bumping drum patterns, and fuzzed guitar noise, an independent spirit sings from its heart and sets it apart from the riff-heavy punk and new-wave vogue into which it arrived.

TV On the Radio formed when vocalist Tunde Adebimpe and Yeah Yeah Yeahs producer David Sitek decided to pool their resources. The EP *Young Liars* was released on Touch and Go in July 2003, causing an immediate stir. A third member, Kyp Malone, was brought in to share songwriting, guitar, and vocal duties on *Desperate Youths* . . . His vocal contributions, adding high notes to Adebimpe's rich mid-range, give glorious scope to the harmonies.

"The Wrong Way" is a confrontational opener, honking sax riding on heavy one-note bass, but cedes to the two most compelling songs: "Staring At The Sun," driven and imploring, the one song carried forward from the EP; and "Dreams," both urgent and resigned, has Malone reaching impossibly high notes and Adebimpe closing on rhyming couplets: "Barracking blundering/pillaging plundering." "King Eternal" rides lurching drums to proclaim immortality, "Ambulance" offers a beautifully structured and gentle a cappella, "Poppy" gives a heartfelt account of "unselfish love." This is an album full of promise and generosity. **MBI**

Just as the heat of fashion began to boil in their adopted hometown of Williamsburg, Brooklyn, Liars took flight to New Jersey, cooking up a masterpiece of fear and alienation. An idle Google search led frontman Angus Andrew to stumble upon the Germanic legends of "Walpurgisnacht," when kidnapping witches circle the Brocken mountain on their broomsticks. The band's next batch of songs would channel the ancient tale's still-palpable ability to shock.

Having recently shed bassist Pat Noecker and drummer Ron Albertson, the Liars inducted multi-instrumentalist Julian Gross into their murky brotherhood. Along with production genius David Sitek, they hunkered down in the basement of their shared house, smoked lots of weed, and went for long walks in the forest at midnight, scaring each other with ghost stories. The fear infests the album. Liberated by their new lineup, Liars embraced a dense and doomy chaos of loops, feedback, and percussion. It echoed Sonic Youth's similarly dark *Bad Moon Rising*, recalled the spooked wooze of "Ghost Town"-era Specials, and mined the inconsolable eeriness of E.S.G.'s undead funk. Elsewhere, enigmatic musical non-sequiteurs cranked up the *Blair Witch* ambience, while the sleeve invested a very Williamsburg style with real dread. Although critics in the United States were not impressed by the album, European audiences embraced the nightmares. **SC**

The Streets | A Grand Don't Come For Free (2004)

Label | Vice
Producer | Mike Skinner
Art Direction | Alex Jenkins
Nationality | UK
Running Time | 50:36

Half of hip hop is built on bitching—not enough respect, not enough bling, too many guns, too much hate. But few have ever commiserated as cleverly as Mike Skinner about the common, everyday stuff that really gets you down. On his second full-length Streets release (after 2002's Brit- and Mercury-nominated debut, *Original Pirate Material*), the rapper is not trying to out-macho 50 Cent. He is just trying to return a DVD, make a withdrawal from a cash machine, and use his phone before the battery dies. Talk about keeping it real.

"It was supposed to be so easy," Skinner moans on the opener as he launches into perhaps the most hilarious and heartfelt hip-hop travelog through suburban existence ever laid to wax. Think *Quadrophenia* mixed with *Ulysses* in a setting of modern-day West Midlands, England, and you begin to get the picture. It is a concept album, complete with a colorful cast of boozers, gamblers, and neighborhood freaks, which follows a full story arc through minor, yet dramatic, conflicts and manages to find resolution in just under 51 minutes.

Taking a different approach to most of his genre brethren, Skinner keeps the production sparse and steady, which turns out to be the perfect living arrangement for his half-rapped, half-sung lines. His wit and love for slapstick humor are evident on the aforementioned "It Was Supposed To Be So Easy," while "Not Addicted" finds the rapper coming clean about his ineptitude as a gambler. But he is equally effective with heartbreak, displaying a tender touch on the ballads "Could Well Be In" and "Dry Your Eyes." **JiH**

> ## "It's not purely sonic pleasure: it's conflict and action and story."
> Mike Skinner, 2004

Track Listing

▶	01	It Was Supposed To Be So Easy (Skinner)	3:55
▶	02	Could Well Be In (Skinner)	4:23
▶	03	Not Addicted (Skinner)	3:40
	04	Blinded By The Lights (Skinner)	4:44
	05	Wouldn't Have It Any Other Way (Skinner)	4:36
	06	Get Out Of My House (Skinner)	3:52
▶	07	Fit But You Know It (Skinner)	4:14
	08	Such A Tw*t (Skinner)	3:47
	09	What Is He Thinking? (Skinner)	4:40
▶	10	Dry Your Eyes (Skinner)	4:31
	11	Empty Cans (Skinner)	8:14

Rufus Wainwright | Want Two (2004)

Label | Dreamworks
Producer | Marius De Vries • Rufus Wainwright
Art Direction | Rufus Wainwright • Janet Wolsborn
Nationality | USA
Running Time | 53:49

Recorded at the same sessions as 2003's *Want One*, *Want Two* confirmed that in terms of songwriting chops, old-fashioned musicianship, and sheer scale of ambition, Rufus Wainwright is out on his own.

Ambition? How about kicking off your album with the Latin mass for peace, accompanied by gypsy violin and cimbalom (dulcimer)—then swathing it in a wash of romantic strings? And ending with a Weillian Arabic-reggae offering, featuring the singular vocals of Antony and a *Smile*-esque interweaving of captivating harmony lines and grunted chants? In between there is the mock-baroque arrangement and wry humor of "Little Sister," the understated acoustic bombshell "Gay Messiah"—on which Rufus the Baptist delivers a lyric that is eyebrow-raisingly risqué—and "The Art Teacher," a poignant sketch of a schoolgirl's undying crush.

Despite the flickers of trademark sharp wit, *Want Two* has a darker side to it. There is a bittersweet elegy for Jeff Buckley ("Memphis Skyline"); "Waiting For A Dream" is angular, more worldly, with ominous percussive rushes, and *White Album*-style piano as Wainwright meditates on dark days and "an ogre in the Oval office." (Dark undertones too in his cover cameo as the Lady of Shalott; Rufus himself drew a comparison between the tragic heroine and the too-soon-gone Buckley.) But a fairytale ending is always on the cards—check out the soft-shoe shuffle "Crumb By Crumb."

Wainwright observed to *Uncut* that *Want Two* was "A kind of a yin to the other's yang." Together, they represent a major artistic statement by a singer/songwriter who has yet to make a wrong move. **RD**

"They're two separate albums ... but they form a type of suite."

Rufus Wainwright, 2005

Track Listing

▶ 01	Agnus Dei (Wainwright)	5:45
02	The One You Love (Wainwright)	3:43
03	Peach Trees (Wainwright)	5:59
04	Little Sister (Wainwright)	3:20
▶ 05	The Art Teacher (Wainwright)	3:52
06	Hometown Waltz (Wainwright)	2:31
▶ 07	This Love Affair (Wainwright)	3:13
▶ 08	Gay Messiah (Wainwright)	3:15
09	Memphis Skyline (Wainwright)	4:52
▶ 10	Waiting For A Dream (Wainwright)	4:14
11	Crumb By Crumb (Wainwright)	4:11
▶ 12	Old Whore's Diet (Featuring Antony) (Wainwright)	8:54

The Killers | Hot Fuss (2004)

Label | Lizard King Records
Producer | The Killers • Jeff Saltzman
Art Direction | Louis Marino
Nationality | USA
Running Time | 46:36

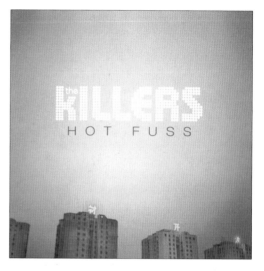

Infectious keyboards, explosive drums, sing-along choruses, swaggering riffs, a pin-up singer—wasn't that Bon Jovi? But replace bandanas with neckties and giving love a bad name with broken hearts, and you've got The Killers.

The decline of Oasis and isolation of Radiohead left a gap in the guitar market. Into the breach rushed Franz Ferdinand, hotly pursued by The Killers. But where Franz are spiky, The Killers rock. For all the British influences—Bowie, The Cure, Psychedelic Furs, Depeche Mode—their glitz and guts set them above the scene affectionately mocked in "Glamorous Indie Rock & Roll" (replaced Stateside by "Change Your Mind").

The standard is set by the arena-sized "Jenny Was A Friend Of Mine," beginning a "murder trilogy" that continues in "Midnight Show," and the then-unreleased "Leave The Bourbon On The Shelf." "It is the tale of a girl leaving her boyfriend and him killing her and then getting caught," explained singer Brandon Flowers. The onslaught continues with the chiming "Mr Brightside" —the first song written by Flowers and guitarist David Keuning after they met in Las Vegas and named themselves after a fictitious band in New Order's "Crystal" video. "Mr Brightside" and the pounding "Somebody Told Me" ensnared indie kids, then the world swooned to the stirring soul of "All These Things That I've Done." In a year on the charts, *Hot Fuss* hit No.1 in the UK and went platinum at home, yet withstood endless exposure. The cover's neon lights and Elvis-evoking logo seem entirely fitting for four of the twenty-first century's brightest stars. **BM**

"I was ... alienated as a kid."
Brandon Flowers, 2004

Track Listing

01	Jenny Was A Friend Of Mine (Flowers•Stoermer)	4:04
02	Mr Brightside (Flowers•Keuning)	3:42
03	Smile Like You Mean It (Flowers•Stoermer)	3:54
04	Somebody Told Me (Flowers•Keuning•Stoermer•Vannucci)	3:17
05	All These Things That I've Done (Flowers)	5:01
06	Andy, You're A Star (Flowers)	3:14
07	On Top (Flowers•Keuning•Stoermer•Vannucci)	4:18
08	Glamorous Indie Rock & Roll (Flowers•Keuning•Stoermer•Vannucci)	4:14
09	Believe Me Natalie (Flowers•Vannucci)	5:05
10	Midnight Show (Flowers•Stoermer)	4:02
11	Everything Will Be Alright (Flowers)	5:45

Ozomatli | Street Signs (2004)

Label | Concord
Producer | Ozomatli • T-Ray
Art Direction | Christian Lantry
Nationality | USA
Running Time | 51:40

Ozomatli street signs

Los Angelinos Ozomatli are one of the world's great bands—a twenty-first-century Los Lobos, masters of a whole range of Latin styles and rhythms, yoked to a hip-hop sensibility. Live, their good-humored virtuosity has always been compelling, but their albums had always been a little more hit and miss. Until, that is, their third full-length album to date, the Grammy gold-grabbing, unequivocal musical triumph that is *Street Signs*—a search for hope amid the destruction that is going on around us post 9/11. To create more light, they have tossed an incendiary bundle of Middle Eastern and Balkan musical idioms onto their Latin hip-hop fire.

They kick off with the triumph that is "Believe"— a hip-smacking blend of Balkan gypsy, Arabic, and indie-rock styles, featuring French gypsy fiddlers Les Yeux Noir, the Prague Symphony, and Moroccan Hassan Hakmoun on backing vocals. And the pace and stream of eclectic delights never ceases. Along with boogaloo, merengue, and tejano on this tour de force, you will find the hip-hop chaabi of "Who's To Blame" with Jurassic 5's MC Chali 2na in full flow, the Chicano rock of the love-hate song "(Who Discovered) America?," and a heart-melting Mexican beats ballad, "Santiago," with Los Lobos' David Hidalgo on guitar. You'll glimpse Hispanic heaven when revered Latin-jazz pianist Eddie Palmieri's gorgeous solo "Doña Isabelle" segues into the orgiastic salsa romp of "Nadie Te Tira."

Its release on the premier Latin-jazz label Concord Jazz (in North America) makes for a fitting stamp of approval. **MR**

"Music is . . . a language far more universal than politics."

Asdrubal Sierra, 2004

Track Listing

01	**Believe** (Mendoza • Ozomatli • Smith-Freeman)	5:02
02	**Love And Hope** (Eckl • Ozomatli • Porter)	4:24
03	**Street Signs** (Ozomatli • Smith-Freeman)	3:46
04	**(Who Discovered) America?** (Eckl • Porter • Roberts • Sierra)	4:35
▶ 05	**Who's To Blame** (Corleon • Lewis)	3:13
06	**Te Estoy Buscando** (Ozomatli)	3:50
07	**Saturday Night** (Ozomatli • Smith-Freeman)	3:59
▶ 08	**Déjame En Paz** (Ozomatli)	3:29
09	**Santiago** (Ozomatli)	5:10
▶ 10	**Ya Viene El Sol (The Beatle Bob Remix)** (Ozomatli)	3:39
11	**Doña Isabelle** (Ozomatli • Palmieri)	1:05
12	**Nadie Te Tira** (Ozomatli)	4:48
13	**Cuando Canto** (Ozomatli)	4:40

Green Day | American Idiot (2004)

Label | Reprise
Producer | Rob Cavallo • Green Day
Art Direction | Chris Bilheimer
Nationality | USA
Running Time | 57:10

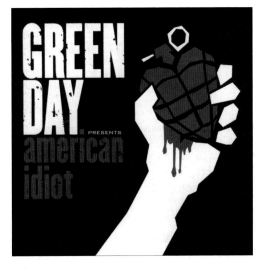

Few would have bet on Green Day making *the* hard-rock smash of the twenty-first century. Their previous album sold a "mere" half million at home, leaving singer/guitarist Billie Joe Armstrong's maturing songwriting unheralded by all but the faithful. To the public at large, they were coasting in the afterglow of 1994's dizbuster *Dookie*.

Undeterred, Armstrong, drummer Tré Cool, and bassist Mike Dirnt conceived a more-of-the-same follow-up, *Cigarettes And Valentines*... only for the tapes to go astray, obliging them to start again (allegedly, anyway; producer Rob Cavallo says the songs were simply mediocre). Perseverance paid off—to the tune of transatlantic number ones and multi-million sales—with *American Idiot*.

To the delight of furrowed-brow fans, it had a concept—albeit one indebted to The Who's *Quadrophenia*. But where *Quadrophenia* had spiritual flab, this had killer tunes. Rarely can it be said of any album containing two nine-minute epics that not a second is wasted—"Homecoming" even finds a niche for Cool's deadpan "Rock And Roll Girlfriend," one of the fruits of their post-*Cigarettes And Valentines* rebuilding.

"American Idiot," "Holiday," "Boulevard Of Broken Dreams," "Wake Me Up When September Ends," and "Jesus Of Suburbia" were the hits, but every hammering hook and soaring chorus is a winner. The album even survives a mashup (find the amusing *American Edit* online) with musicality intact. There was no need for the cover's grenade, as iconic as it is: this music was bound to explode. **BM**

"All it takes is a spark to start a riot."

Billie Joe Armstrong, 2005

Track Listing

▶ 01	American Idiot (Armstrong • Green Day)	2:54
02	Jesus Of Suburbia (Armstrong • Green Day)	9:08
03	Holiday (Armstrong • Green Day)	3:52
▶ 04	Boulevard Of Broken Dreams (Armstrong • Green Day)	4:20
05	Are We The Waiting (Armstrong • Green Day)	2:42
06	St. Jimmy (Armstrong • Green Day)	2:55
07	Give Me Novacaine (Armstrong • Green Day)	3:25
08	She's A Rebel (Armstrong • Green Day)	2:00
09	Extraordinary Girl (Armstrong • Green Day)	3:33
10	Letterbomb (Armstrong • Green Day)	4:06
▶ 11	Wake Me Up When September Ends (Armstrong • Green Day)	4:45
12	Homecoming (Armstrong • Green Day)	9:18

Common | Be (2005)

Label | GOOD/Geffen
Producer | Kanye West • J. Dilla
Art Direction | Gravillis Inc.
Nationality | USA
Running Time | 42:43

Psychedelia did rapper Common no favors. The eclectic *Electric Circus* bemused his fans ("Took it outta space and niggas thought they lost me," he admits on "Chi-City") and the end of a relationship with Erykah Badu had hardly covered him in glory.

To his rescue came a modern Midas—Kanye West. Together they crafted the spiritual successor to *The Miseducation Of Lauryn Hill* (1998); a wonderful confluence of hip hop and classic soul. *Be* soared to No. 2 in the US album chart and raised Common's profile out of the ghetto in Britain.

Stripped of Common's customary metaphors, *Be*'s lyrics are candid yet imaginative. On lead single "The Corner"—featuring rap pioneers The Last Poets—he reflects on the Chicago streets with neither sentimentality nor gun-crazed glorification. And on "Real People," he spits lines that could be Public Enemy's Chuck D, were it not for the breezy backing. The guest slots are restrained, with low-key cameos for singer-songwriter John Mayer, neo-soul man Bilal, and R&B troubadour John Legend. But in a classic slice of old-school action, Common and Kanye throw down on "The Food," ostensibly from comedian Dave Chappelle's show (source of the "Rick James, bitch" catchphrase quoted on "Chi-City").

Late producer J. Dilla helms the sweetest treats: "Love Is . . . ," even more beautiful than the Marvin Gaye song "God Is Love" that it samples, and "It's Your World," which—like Lauryn Hill's album—features kids' dreams ("I wanna be an astronaut! I wanna be a duck!") without being cloying. *Be* is simply sublime. **BM**

Richard Hawley | Coles Corner (2005)

Label | Mute
Producer | R. Hawley • C. Elliot • M. Timm
Art Direction | N. Phillips • G. James
Nationality | UK
Running Time | 46:06

Richard Hawley served in the ranks of The Longpigs and Pulp before going solo. His third album, *Lowedges*—named for an area of his hometown, Sheffield—was a low-key masterpiece of well-crafted pop, and laid the foundations for *Coles Corner*, also named after a local Sheffield landmark, where lovers met for weekend dates in the 1960s and 1970s. Appropriately, the album is firmly rooted in the past, with Hank Marvin a prime influence. Hawley's rich baritone welcomes listeners like a warm embrace, ready to shield you from the stressful sounds of grime, nu rave, and emo blasting out from teenage cellphones.

"The Ocean" ebbs, flows, and builds, with sweeping strings underpinning a subtle tale of an unfolding relationship. The countrified "Just Like The Rain" is a melancholic ode to lost love from a man who has been unlucky in matters of the heart—it is barstool philosophy at its best.

The album's highlight, "(Wading Through) The Waters of My Time," is a lush slice of heartfelt country soul—Johnny Cash playing live at a working-man's club in the North of England. Like many of the 11 tracks, the song is a brand-new 2005 Hawley original with the well-worn feel of a standard. *Coles Corner* was nominated for the 2006 Mercury Prize, and many fans had laid money on it securing the award. When fellow Sheffield tunesmiths Arctic Monkeys unexpectedly won the vote with their debut album, *Whatever People Say I Am, That's What I'm Not*, they echoed the thoughts of many in their acceptance speech: "Somebody call 999, Richard Hawley's been robbed." **JB**

"I want people to be playing it when I'm dead and gone."

Richard Hawley, 2006

Track Listing

▶ 01	Coles Corner (Hawley)	4:49
02	Just Like The Rain (Hawley)	3:17
03	Hotel Room (Hawley)	3:42
04	Darlin' Wait For Me (Hawley • Sheridan)	3:53
05	The Ocean (Hawley)	5:36
06	Born Under A Bad Sign (Hawley)	3:41
07	I Sleep Alone (Hawley)	3:44
08	Tonight (Hawley)	4:32
▶ 09	(Wading Through) The Waters Of My Time (Hawley)	3:48
10	Who's Gonna Shoe Your Pretty Little Feet? (Hawley)	4:08
11	Last Orders (Trad. Arr. Hawley)	4:59

Antony and the Johnsons | I Am A Bird Now (2005)

Label | Secretly Canadian
Producer | Antony Hegarty
Art Direction | Peter Hujar
Nationality | USA/UK
Running Time | 35:25

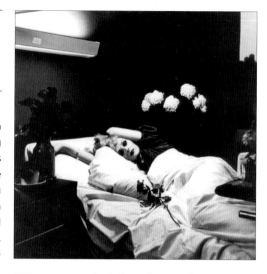

"Hope there's someone who'll take care of me when I die." One of modern music's most powerful opening lines—delivered in a truly arresting voice that echoes elements of Nina Simone and Bryan Ferry—sets the groundrules for the next half-hour: leave now if you were expecting easy listening. The second album from the band fronted by British-born, New York-based Antony Hegarty is fragile to the point of disintegration, a harrowing yet haunting experience. "Majestic while confronting mortal fears," said *The Guardian*.

Staring out blankly from the album cover is Candy Darling, a pre-op transsexual who found fleeting fame in the films of Andy Warhol. That Velvet Underground lineage continues with a poignant cameo on "Fistful Of Love" from Lou Reed (joining Boy George, Devendra Banhart, and Rufus Wainwright). More importantly, the sleeve emphasizes one of Hegarty's recurrent preoccupations: sexual identity. "One day I'll grow up, I'll know a womb within me," he sings, imagining life as a woman, on "For Today I Am A Bouy."

Hardly a recipe for mainstream acclaim, you might think. But just that awaited, with the album hitting the Top Five in the UK after winning the 2005 Mercury Prize. That surprise triumph was sandwiched between the angular indie guitars of Franz Ferdinand (2004) and Arctic Monkeys (2006). Those bands probably tell you more about the musical landscape of Britain at that moment in time, but the unexpected success of *I Am A Bird Now* was a sign that, for a while at least, there was room for something decidedly—and defiantly—different. **CB**

> ## "For me, singing has always been an opportunity to take a flight of fantasy, to dream."
>
> **Antony Hegarty, 2005**

Track Listing

▶	01	Hope There's Someone (Hegarty)	4:21
	02	My Lady Story (Hegarty)	3:33
▶	03	For Today I Am A Bouy (Hegarty)	2:36
	04	Man Is The Baby (Hegarty)	4:09
	05	You Are My Sister (Hegarty)	3:59
	06	What Can I Do? (Hegarty)	1:40
▶	07	Fistful Of Love (Hegarty)	5:52
	08	Spiralling (Hegarty)	4:25
	09	Free At Last (Hegarty)	1:36
	10	Bird Guhl (Hegarty)	3:14

Sufjan Stevens | Come On Feel The Illinoise (2005)

Label | Asthmatic Kitty
Producer | Sufjan Stevens
Art Direction | Divya Srinivasan
Nationality | USA
Running Time | 74:13

Sufjan Stevens' fifth album, and the second in his mind-boggling musical survey of the 50 American states (his home state Michigan was the first), is so grand in scope he struggled to shoehorn his ideas into one CD. In fact, he struggled so hard that an entire album of out-takes and alternate versions—*The Avalanche*—followed soon after.

The 22 tracks included here are a beguiling overview of the people, places, and history of the Prairie State, and Stevens' often dark tales of everyday folk recall the narrative songs archived by Harry Smith. The delicate "Casimir Pulaski Day" tells of stolen moments with a beloved girl, who is dying of leukemia. The elegiac "John Wayne Gacy, Jr," an ode to the Chicago-born serial killer, focuses on Gacy's childhood and is utterly haunting. And the song that perhaps received the most play on the radio, "Chicago," perfectly mixes both hope and anguish into an ultimately uplifting pop classic.

Most of the album, however, is joyously melodic and sumptuously arranged. Strings, choirs, a Wurlitzer organ, a flugelhorn, and sleighbells all make it into the final mix, with the lion's share played by Sufjan himself. His influences range from folk to Rodgers & Hammerstein, minimalism to alt-rock and beyond. If all that sounds like an unlistenable shambles, fear not—Stevens' lightness of touch makes each song as catchy and heartening as the *Waltons* theme tune.

On release, *Illinois* was showered with critical plaudits, and quite rightly too. Writing, producing, and performing a 22-track concept album featuring banjos that doesn't outstay its welcome is no mean feat. **JB**

Track Listing

	01	Concerning The UFO Sighting... (Stevens)	2:09
	02	The Black Hawk War (Stevens)	2:14
	03	Come On! Feel The Illinoise! (Stevens)	6:45
▶	04	John Wayne Gacy, Jr. (Stevens)	3:19
	05	Jacksonville (Stevens)	5:24
	06	A Short Reprise For Mary Todd... (Stevens)	0:47
▶	07	Decatur... (Stevens)	3:03
	08	One Last 'Whoo-Hoo!'... (Stevens)	0:06
▶	09	Chicago (Stevens)	6:04
▶	10	Casimir Pulaski Day (Stevens)	5:54
	11	To The Workers... (Stevens)	1:40
	12	The Man Of Metropolis... (Stevens)	6:17
	13	Prairie Fire That Wanders About (Stevens)	2:11
	14	A Conjunction Of Drones... (Stevens)	0:19
	15	The Predatory Wasp... (Stevens)	5:23
	16	They Are Night Zombies!! (Stevens)	5:09
	17	Let's Hear That String Part Again... (Stevens)	0:40
	18	In This Temple As In The Hearts... (Stevens)	0:35
	19	The Seer's Tower (Stevens)	3:54
	20	The Tallest Man... (Stevens)	7:03
	21	Riffs And Variations... (Stevens)	0:46
	22	Out Of Egypt... (Stevens)	4:21

Ali Farka Touré | Savane (2006)

Label | World Circuit
Producer | Nick Gold
Art Direction | Julian House
Nationality | Mali
Running Time | 58:37

Two-and-a-half years in the making, this masterpiece from Mali was finished mere weeks before Touré's death after a long battle with bone cancer. Now widely regarded as the finest album in a rich catalog of work, *Savane* helped garner worldwide recognition for Mali's favorite son—at home he was accorded a posthumous Commandeur de L'Ordre National du Mali (the country's highest honor) and a state funeral. Quite a send-off for an artist who considered farming his primary call in life.

With the ngoni (a traditional African lute and probable precursor to the banjo) to the fore alongside traditional percussion, the sound here is undoubtedly rooted in Malian folk, but the occasional addition of guitar, harmonica, and fiddle also evokes the early blues of Son House and Robert Johnson. Blending the two related traditions is the key to the album's unique sound.

Elsewhere, subtle country, reggae, and even flamenco influences feed into the mix, at the center of which are Touré's deep, rich vocals, sung in French and various regional dialects. "Savane" is an ode to the drought-hit grasslands of his home, telling of the journey of a man who has left the savannah for urban Europe and of his yearning to return.

At a time when the charts are populated with artists whose main gripe is the stress of dealing with their superstar lifestyles, it's no wonder this heartfelt celebration of music and roots—with its pastoral themes and contemporary reinterpretation of traditional folk—shines like a beacon. **JB**

"I know this is my best album ever."

Ali Farka Touré, 2006

Track Listing

01	Erdi (Touré)	4:42
02	Yer Bounda Fara (Touré)	4:18
03	Beto (Touré)	4:49
▶ 04	Savane (Touré)	7:43
05	Soya (Touré)	4:38
06	Penda Yoro (Touré)	5:25
07	Machengoidi (Touré)	3:35
▶ 08	Ledi Coumbe (Touré)	3:16
09	Hanana (Touré)	2:34
10	Soko Yhinka (Touré)	5:05
11	Gambari Didi (Touré)	3:49
12	Banga (Touré)	3:48
13	N'Jarou (Touré)	4:55

Muse | Black Holes & Revelations (2006)

Label | Helium 3
Producer | Rich Costey
Art Direction | Storm Thorgerson
Nationality | UK
Running Time | 45:28

Muse revel in ridiculousness. They peddle concepts and conspiracies with a stylish conviction unseen since *The X Files*. But on their fourth album, string-slinger and singer Matt Bellamy, drummer Dominic Howard, and bassist Chris Wolstenholme temper their customary hysteria with splendid songs.

Once joined by a sonic umbilical cord to Radiohead (Bellamy's vocals have an inescapably Thom Yorkish feel), Muse now pick every pomp rock cliché on the menu, and mix and match genres. Hence sci-fi silliness exhumed from *2112* by prog pioneers Rush ("Knights Of Cydonia"), robo-funk inspired by Prince and Belgian dance punks Millionaire ("Supermassive Black Hole"), and dazzling, stadium-sized singalongs ("Starlight").

Between are moments of quieter beauty, like "Soldier's Poem" and the slow-burning "Invincible." All fit loosely into a post-9/11 theme, hotly contested on fan forums, of man versus government, with the occasional excursion into outer space. "I've ousted the self-doubt that plagues you in your early years," Bellamy told *Kerrang!*. "But I seem to be much more unhappy with what's going on around us."

Appropriately for an album apparently custom-built for and by adolescent boys, *Black Holes...* became the most downloaded album of its year. Online listeners, however, were missing out on a package completed by Pink Floyd designer Storm Thorgerson, whose cover shot evokes the puppet masters of the apocalypse decried in "Assassin." But you don't have to clue up on the concept to savor the sounds. Let your inner teen out and enjoy rock at its most magnificent. **BM**

"I take music too seriously."

Matt Bellamy, 2006

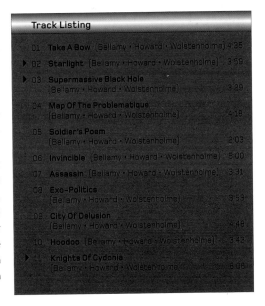

Track Listing

01	Take A Bow	(Bellamy · Howard · Wolstenholme)	4:35
▶ 02	Starlight	(Bellamy · Howard · Wolstenholme)	3:59
▶ 03	Supermassive Black Hole (Bellamy · Howard · Wolstenholme)		3:29
04	Map Of The Problematique (Bellamy · Howard · Wolstenholme)		4:18
05	Soldier's Poem (Bellamy · Howard · Wolstenholme)		2:03
06	Invincible	(Bellamy · Howard · Wolstenholme)	5:00
07	Assassin	(Bellamy · Howard · Wolstenholme)	3:31
08	Exo-Politics (Bellamy · Howard · Wolstenholme)		3:53
09	City Of Delusion (Bellamy · Howard · Wolstenholme)		4:48
10	Hoodoo	(Bellamy · Howard · Wolstenholme)	3:43
▶ 11	Knights Of Cydonia (Bellamy · Howard · Wolstenholme)		6:06

Arctic Monkeys | Whatever People Say I Am, That's What I'm Not (2006)

Label | Domino Recordings
Producer | Jim Abbiss • Alan Smyth
Art Direction | Alexandra Wolkowitz
Nationality | UK
Running Time | 55:41

Racing to the top of the charts on a wave of pure attitude and self-belief, the Arctic Monkeys had the biggest impact on British music since Oasis snarled their way to No.1 a decade previously.

Sheffield born and bred, the band referenced hometown landmarks and characters in the broadest local accents heard on the radio for ages. Building on their fierce local following, the Monkeys created a wave of online support on MySpace, offering free content to the masses across the web and harnessing the site's immense promotional power for the first time. The result was the headline-grabbing, smash-hit No.1 single "I Bet You Look Good On The Dancefloor." The wry, mocking lyrics sounded so confident that some suggested the hand of a svengali—arch pranksters the KLF were mooted—was involved.

Whatever People Say I Am . . . (its title a reference to a line from era-defining Sixties film *Billy Liar*) debuted at No.1, became the fastest-selling UK debut album ever, and won the UK's Mercury Prize. Fueled by the same taut, teenage riffing that made the Undertones minor legends decades before, this music was rooted firmly in everyday life. On "Perhaps Vampires is a Bit Strong But . . . ," the Arctic Monkeys ably critique the tabloid-fueled rock celeb-scene: "Well I ain't got no dollar signs in my eyes, that might be a surprise but it's true." As most rock stars are more likely to be seen ligging at a showbiz party than playing a guitar, what could be more rock and roll than that lyric? **JB**

Track Listing

01	The View From The Afternoon (All)	3:58
▶ 02	I Bet You Look Good On The Dancefloor (All)	2:53
▶ 03	Fake Tales Of San Francisco (All)	2:57
04	Dancing Shoes (All)	2:21
05	You Probably Couldn't See For The Lights But You Were Staring Straight At Me (All)	2:10
06	Still Take You Home (All)	2:53
07	Riot Van (All)	2:14
08	Red Light Indicates Doors Are Secured (All)	2:23
▶ 09	Mardy Bum (All)	2:55
10	Perhaps Vampires Is A Bit Strong But... (All)	4:28
▶ 11	When The Sun Goes Down (All)	3:20
▶ 12	From The Ritz To The Rubble (All)	3:13
13	A Certain Romance! (All)	5:31

Amy Winehouse
Back To Black (2006)

Label | Island
Producer | Mark Ronson • Salaam Remi
Art Direction | Alex Hutchinson
Nationality | UK
Running Time | 34:55

Jazz chameleon Amy Winehouse went to hell via Motown and 1960s girls groups to make Grammy-winning second album *Back To Black*. But for her pains she has created a sparkling masterpiece important not just in its time, but as a soul template for future generations.

Masterpiece as *Back To Black* is, it is no easy listen and the split production by Mark Ronson and Salaam Remi (who tweaked and twiddled on debut *Frank*) dilutes none of Amy's very human fallibilities.

The rousing Phil Spector-tinged lead single "Rehab" snarls and stomps its brassy foot at every "No, no, no"; the bolshy and horn-heavy "I'm No Good" teasingly brushes around your ears before sidling off into a soul sunset; "Me & Mr Jones" spits and hisses at the "fuckery" the antagonist is facing; and the title track is a relentless clank of a hook simulating the racing heartbeat that Amy feels when she glimpses her lost love with a new squeeze. La Winehouse is clearly no pop pushover.

But it is when the brass is taken away that the record becomes truly beautiful. Poignant laments "Love Is A Losing Game" and "Wake Up Alone," with their trickling gossamer production and faltering honey tones, are as refreshing as they are raw.

The cover of *Back To Black* shows our queen perched on her stool throne, face on. There are no cover-ups, no facades; this is the real Amy. And the real Amy is music's soul savior. **KBo**

Lupe Fiasco
Food & Liquor (2006)

Label | Atlantic
Producer | Various
Art Direction | NoPattern
Nationality | USA
Running Time | 72:16

Flab-free hip-hop albums are hard to find. The Grammy-nominated *Food & Liquor* is no exception, with a skippable intro and eye-glazing conclusion. But in between are 57 minutes of non-stop funtasia.

Though he idolizes rap veteran Nas, Fiasco's flow is more upbeat—closer to fellow Chicago success story Kanye West, on a remix of whose "Jesus Walks" he guested before sharing the limelight on "Touch the Sky." Leaked twice while in production, *Food & Liquor* could have been an anticlimax. Instead it emerged triumphant, its musical colors as effervescent as the cover artwork's glow.

The samples range from I Monster's "Daydream In Blue" to "Behind The Walls" by rockers UFO. Adding further light and shade are producers from Kanye to Linkin Park's Mike Shinoda, and collaborators from nu-soul sensation Jill Scott to Fiasco's first champion, Jay-Z (plus, on "I Gotcha," the inevitable spot from the Neptunes' ubiquitous Pharrell Williams).

"The title reflects on me being Muslim and being from the streets," said Fiasco. "The 'food' is the good part and the 'liquor' is the bad part."

Highlights include the irresistible hit "Kick, Push" (self-help meets skateboarding), the rocky "Real," the swirling "Daydreamin'," and the superbly spooky "The Cool." The latter bequeathed a title to Fiasco's sophomore album, on which he hoped to feature the members of Pink Floyd. That ambition failed, but Fiasco's star remains undimmed. **BM**

Ghostface Killah
Fishscale (2006)

Label | Def Jam
Producer | Various
Art Direction | Ghostface • Alli • West
Nationality | USA
Running Time | 61:48

Christina Aguilera
Back To Basics (2006)

Label | RCA
Producer | Various
Art Direction | SMOG Design, Inc.
Nationality | USA
Running Time | 78:57

The Wu-Tang Clan's star began to fade after the four or five seminal solo albums released in the wake of their devastating debut album *Enter The 36 Chambers*, but Ghostface Killah's repertoire remains the most compelling among the deluge of releases emanating from Shaolin. The slang-slinging storyteller from Staten Island has always had more street appeal than the cerebral GZA and a far more experimental edge than the weed raps of Method Man, but on *Fishscale* he finally produced an album cohesive enough to match Meth's impressive sales too.

True, some of his stream-of-consciousness rhymes are tricky to navigate, but Ghost always manages to hook the listener with his acute eye for detail. On "Whip You With a Strap," the rapper remembers his five-year-old self: "I'm trying to tie my sneaker up, I'm missing all the loops, strings going in the wrong holes . . . " Ghost meets "Beauty Jackson" and deftly describes her attractions: "When she spoke, her smoke floated when it left her throat, spelled honey when she blew it out."

Ghost's love of classic Sixties soul shines through on the beats he chose to flow on, with Pete Rock and J. Dilla (RIP) joined by underground hero MF Doom, who supplies selections from his *Special Herbs* instrumental series. The sum total is a record that blends the classic breaks of yesterday and experimental hip hop of today into something you'll still want to listen to 10 years from now—a rare claim for hip-hop albums of the past decade. **JB**

"Fun" and "funky" are terms seldom applied when artists rediscover their roots or acknowledge their influences. With a disdain for convention that makes her look like Madonna's natural heir, Christina created an ambitious album that is both.

Stripped (2002) wed grinding raunch to plangent emotion. *Back To Basics* evokes both extremes of its predecessor: "Still Dirrty" declares "I still got the nasty in me," and the staggering "Hurt" is a natural successor to "Beautiful." But where *Stripped* dynamited the barriers of bubblegum pop, this fizzes with flavors even more unpredictable.

Dominating the first half is Gang Starr's DJ Premier. Hip-hop beats meet jazzy tunes, redeeming even "Thank You," a medley of fans' voicemails to their idol. Stevie Winwood cameos, and above it all soars that remarkable voice. Building on her spectacular cover of "Carwash," Christina is in brassily bold form—notably on the irresistible "Ain't No Other Man." A world away from her peers, Christina's lyrics touch on redemption ("Hurt"), sin ("Mercy On Me"), and betrayal ("F.U.S.S.").

The exquisitely eclectic second half draws on the voices Christina emulated as a child—from Billie Holiday to Ella Fitzgerald.

With artwork that is both classic and tongue-in-cheek, *Back To Basics* is an experience to savor. Small wonder Christina bemoaned the fact that downloading was fast making such packages obsolete. But if anyone can save the form, she can. **BM**

Joanna Newsom | Ys (2006)

Label | Drag City Inc
Producer | Joanna Newsom • Van Dyke Parks
Art Direction | Benjamin A. Vierling • Richard Good
Nationality | USA
Running Time | 55:41

Californian harpist/pianist/singer-songwriter Joanna Newsom first came to prominence when she was included on the *Golden Apples Of The Sun* compilation by Devendra Banhart, head freak of the new wave of US folk, in early 2004. That scene—led by acts such as Espers, Vetiver, Banhart himself, and the reinvigorated Brit Vashti Bunyan—was duly hyped by the music press; the artists concerned quietly got on with releasing some astounding music.

Newsom's debut album, *The Milk-Eyed Mender*, was warmly received, but nothing could have prepared her for the rapturous notices earned by *Ys*. Her virtuoso harp playing is matched by rich and sensitive arrangements by Van Dyke Parks—a force behind some of The Beach Boys' best work—whose sweeping strings act as a counterpoint to the vocals.

Over the five tracks on this album, Newsom comes across like a medieval Kate Bush singing songs by Hans Christian Andersen. The UK *Guardian* newspaper's "In Praise of . . . " column—a place where rock rarely treads—drew particular attention to her lyrics: "She revels in words . . . When she sings her own words to her own music, extraordinary things happen." And what words she sings. *Ys* sees the words "inchoate" and "spelunking" make their rock debuts—and let's hear it for the neologistic "hydrocephalitic" too.

The hard-hearted listener may sniff that this album teeters on the verge of self-parody, but those of us who are happy to cast our preconceptions aside and dive into Joanna's magic kingdom are richly rewarded with a truly unique experience. **JB**

> "The goal . . . was for the harp and vocals to feel like they were developing unawares of the presence of the orchestra . . . as if the orchestra is hanging in a hallucinatory shimmer . . . "

Joanna Newsom, 2006

Track Listing

01	Emily (Newsom)	12:08
▶ 02	Monkey & Bear (Newsom)	9:28
03	Sawdust & Diamonds (Newsom)	9:55
▶ 04	Only Skin (Newsom)	16:53
05	Cosmia (Newsom)	7:17

Arcade Fire | Neon Bible (2007)

Label | Sonovox
Producer | Arcade Fire
Art Direction | Tracy Maurice
Nationality | Canada • USA
Running Time | 46:59

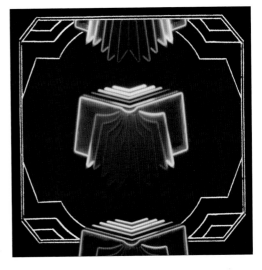

In the current musical landscape—where marketing, MySpace, celebrity gossip, and brand sponsorship overburden the pages of the rock press—it is no wonder that listeners starved of music with meaning are searching for something beyond the conveyor belt of hot new bands with dancefloor-friendly remixes and singers with a sideline in modeling. Well, French-speaking Canada probably wasn't the first place they looked, and the only clobber this lot have ever modeled could have come from an American Civil War re-enactment, but Arcade Fire make music full of significance and symbolism.

Thankfully for their fans, however, they haven't forgotten that a rock band's primary motive is to rock, and the literate bar-stool philosophy of *Neon Bible* is largely hitched to foot-on-the-monitor, fist-pumping anthems. Never predictably so, though: *Neon Bible* features strings, brass, a harp, and a gospel choir over the course of 11 songs that will ably fill stadiums for years to come. The heaviest riff here is played on a church organ rather than a Fender Stratocaster ("Intervention").

Debut album *Funeral* earned plaudits from U2—who offered the band a support slot—and David Bowie—who joined them onstage to perform "Wake Up." Doubtless Bono and Bowie will love *Neon Bible*, which could well be the best second album of the decade.

In the title track, Arcade Fire urge the listener to "take the poison of your age," like cult leaders offering a last stand against the unthinking masses. If overmarketed music lacking in substance is the poison, this album is the antidote. **JB**

"It felt sometimes like we were making a film rather than a record."

Win Butler, 2007

Track Listing

01	Black Mirror (Arcade Fire)	4:13
▶ 02	Keep The Car Running (Arcade Fire)	3:29
03	Neon Bible (Arcade Fire)	2:16
04	Intervention (Arcade Fire)	4:19
05	Black Wave / Bad Vibrations (Arcade Fire)	3:57
06	Ocean Of Noise (Arcade Fire)	4:53
▶ 07	The Well And The Lighthouse (Arcade Fire)	3:56
08	(Antichrist Television Blues) (Arcade Fire)	5:10
09	Windowsill (Arcade Fire)	4:16
10	No Cars Go (Arcade Fire)	5:43
11	My Body Is A Cage (Arcade Fire)	4:47

The Good, The Bad & The Queen
The Good, The Bad & The Queen (2007)

Label | Parlophone
Producer | Danger Mouse
Art Direction | Will Bankhead • T. Sotter Boys
Nationality | UK • Nigeria
Running Time | 47:00

Damon Albarn needs a good talking-to. The voice of Blur—and scowling alter ego 2D, of Gorillaz—made *the* brilliantly brooding soundtrack to London life in 2007 with his other new band of not-so-merry men (Clash bassist Paul Simonon, Verve strummer Simon Tong, and Afrobeat drummer Tony Allen) and is yet to crack a smile. As ever though, Damon has our full sympathy. The times are a-changing once more, you see. The Girls and Boys who playfully peppered *Parlife* are now "mixed-up people" plodding around this "stroppy little island" ("Three Changes"). Simonon's and Tong's eerie spaghetti-western guitar jars, Allen's discordant drums rattles, and Damon's world-weary whisper speaks volumes for the unspoken ennui of their "lonely homes" and sterile existence ("Green Fields").

Rent-a-genius Danger Mouse builds upon this world of dizzying claustrophobia with his slick production, creating an arresting carousel of melancholy in the album's eponymous finale, whose urgent whirl of sound will leave hungry ears wanting more.

This urgency is reflected in the cover, wherein a painted crowd appear unsure whether to gawp at the blanket of fire covering the capital's buildings or to flee—to keep up with, or keep clear from, change ("Northern Whale")—and ensures that this sometimes alien-sounding album stays human. Hell, even if the streets of London are more likely to be littered with free newspapers than gold, it is all the richer for having inspired a gem like this. **KBo**

> **"A mystery play about London."**
> Damon Albarn, 2007

Track Listing

01	History Song [All]	3:05
02	80's Life [All]	3:28
03	Northern Whale [All]	3:54
04	Kingdom Of Doom [All]	2:42
05	Herculean [All]	3:59
06	Behind The Sun [All]	2:38
07	The Bunting Song [All]	3:47
08	Nature Springs [All]	3:10
09	A Soldier's Tale [All]	2:30
10	Three Changes [All]	4:15
11	Green Fields [All]	2:26
12	The Good, The Bad & The Queen [All]	7:00

LCD Soundsystem
Sound of Silver (2007)

Label | DFA Records
Producer | The DFA
Art Direction | Michael Vadino
Nationality | USA
Running Time | 56:00

On their sparkling eponymous debut, modest dance messiahs LCD Soundsystem claimed that they were "losing their edge" to "better-looking people with more talent." Rest assured they were speaking cobblers, as follow-up *Sound Of Silver* is the epicenter of bitingly hip music.

As before, LCD cherry-pick the better bits of the 1980s—the production of Brian Eno-era Talking Heads, synth, and at times the pop sensibilities—and fold it into a foundation of glitzy glockenspiels, electro hooks, bubblegum pop, and a large sprinkling of erudite political consciousness, best showcased in magnificent single "North American Scum."

But *Sound Of Silver* is not a singles album. It is a wry dance odyssey that is more varied than their genre—riddled with the ghost of happy hardcore and ennui of new-rave trends—is credited for. In fact, the relentlessly clattering "Watch The Tapes" is perhaps the only track on the album that is straightforward "dance," if such a thing exists.

Elsewhere, "Time To Get Away" drills into the riff of "Billie Jean" before slapping on a huge Bowie stamp. "Get Innocuous!" warms the oral palette with simmering electronic patters and swooping synth stretches. "Someone Great," arguably the best track on the album, nudges at new wave with its sweetly soothing triangles, Human League-styled keyboards, and enduring themes of love and loss. The muted album cover and title are too humble. This is the sound of musical gold. **KBo**

> "My three-minute pop song is about five minutes 40."

James Murphy, 2007

Track Listing

▶	01	Get Innocuous! (Murphy - Pope)	7:11
	02	Time To Get Away (Murphy - Pope - Mahoney)	4:11
▶	03	North American Scum (Murphy)	5:25
▶	04	Someone Great (Murphy)	6:23
	05	All My Friends (Murphy - Mahoney - Pope)	7:37
	06	Us v Them (Murphy - Mahoney - Pope)	8:29
▶	07	Watch The Tapes (Murphy)	3:55
	08	Sound Of Silver (Murphy)	7:07
▶	09	New York, I Love You But You're Bringing Me Down (Murphy - Mahoney - Pope)	5:35

Radiohead | In Rainbows (2007)

Label | Self-released
Producer | Nigel Godrich
Art Direction | Stanley Donwood
Nationality | UK
Running Time | 42:34

Often, Radiohead are painted as miserable messengers of the indie world, preaching on about "the issues" and refusing to give up that grumpy bone. But after giving seventh studio album *In Rainbows* away for free—or whatever the listener deemed an appropriate price—via the internet, it is pretty hard to see them as such.

It is even harder to label them so after hearing *In Rainbows*. Closer to Thom Yorke's magnificent Mercury-nominated solo album *The Eraser* than their back catalog, *In Rainbows* is a sonic beacon of hope showing how exciting albums can be.

From the very start it's clear that this is something special: "15 Steps" pounds at your ear drums, all electro-clashing drum and bass and glimpses of the riff of "Talk Show Host," their offering for 1996's *Romeo And Juliet*. "Bodysnatchers" realizes a love of rollicking rock stylings and builds, shouts and swerves into a heavy-rock broth. "Faust Arp" is loveliness itself with a Cat Stevens guitar hook, violins, and harmonies that would put the most hard-working boy band to shame.

Elsewhere, Radiohead shed their mysterious lyrical skin of yesterday and show a new layer in "House of Cards," musing, "I don't want to be your friend, I just want to be your lover." It suggests the band are at ease with themselves and happy to reveal their true colors—appropriately enough, for an album whose cover and title refers to rainbows, biblically a peace offering.

Whether you download the album for free or pay the full whack, rest assured that *In Rainbows* is a staggeringly good listen—priceless, in fact. **KBo**

> "It's fun to make people stop for a few seconds and think about what music is worth."
>
> Jonny Greenwood, 2007

Track Listing

▶ 01	**15 Steps** (Radiohead)	3:57
02	**Bodysnatchers** (Radiohead)	4:02
03	**Nude** (Radiohead)	4:15
04	**Weird Fishes/Arpeggi** (Radiohead)	5:18
05	**All I Need** (Radiohead)	3:48
▶ 06	**Faust Arp** (Radiohead)	2:09
07	**Reckoner** (Radiohead)	4:50
▶ 08	**House Of Cards** (Radiohead)	5:28
▶ 09	**Jigsaw Falling Into Place** (Radiohead)	4:09
10	**Videotape** (Radiohead)	4:39

M.I.A. | Kala (2007)

Label | XL
Producer | Various, including Switch and Diplo
Art Direction | M.I.A.
Nationality | Sri Lanka
Running Time | 47:40

Amid pop idols and indie guitars, one maverick paints the musical town red. Make that red, yellow, purple, black, green—the riotous colors on its artwork perfectly evoke the cultural chaos in *Kala*'s songs.

With 2005's *Arular*, Maya Arulpragasam made the most sparkling debut since Madonna's first album. Its fizzing electroclash hip hop entranced fans and stars from Trent Reznor to Timbaland. For the follow-up—named after her mother—the London-based M.I.A. set her sights on America. But she was denied entry—lyrical references to the PLO probably proved unhelpful—and instead crossed the globe, recruiting Aboriginal kids and a Liberian refugee. "I put people on the map that never seen a map," she notes.

Elements of Jonathan Richman's "Roadrunner," Pixies' "Where Is My Mind," The Clash's "Straight To Hell," and Tamil and Bollywood movies added to an intoxicating cocktail.

A handful of playful moments aside, *Kala* is darker than *Arular*—compare the latter's cheeky "10 Dollar" to the terrifying "20 Dollar." "We've all watched Saddam Hussein being hanged on YouTube," she told *The List*. "What the hell have I got to add to that? I wanted to speak for everyday people." The results range from the clattering "Birdflu," through the discofied "Jimmy" and spooky "Paper Planes," to the Timbaland production "Come Around."

As with *Arular*, her sales were barely commensurate with her reviews (even staid old *Rolling Stone* rated it the best of 2007), but M.I.A. had again made a staggering album that sounded like nothing else on Earth. **BM**

Track Listing

01	**Bamboo Banga** (M.I.A. · Switch)	4:58
▶ 02	**Birdflu** (M.I.A. · Switch)	3:25
▶ 03	**Boyz** (M.I.A. · Switch)	3:27
04	**Jimmy** (M.I.A. · Switch)	3:29
05	**Hussel** (M.I.A. · Switch · Diplo)	4:25
06	**Mango Pickle Down River** (M.I.A. · Dutton · King Johnson · Ebsworth · Blair · Lewis · Adams · Wright Jarrett)	3:54
07	**20 Dollar** (M.I.A. · Switch)	4:34
08	**World Town** (M.I.A. · Switch)	3:54
09	**The Turn** (M.I.A. · Blaqstarr)	3:52
10	**XR2** (M.I.A. · Diplo · Switch)	4:21
▶ 11	**Paper Planes** (M.I.A. · Diplo)	3:25
12	**Come Around** (Mosley · Clayton · M.I.A.)	3:54

Justice | Cross (2007)

Label | Ed Banger Records
Producer | Gaspard Augé and Xavier de Rosnay
Art Direction | So-Me
Nationality | France
Running Time | 48:15

Slam that robot helmet over your ears, Thomas Bangalter, for if God is a DJ then he no longer manifests himself as Daft Punk. Today, it's French wonderboys Justice who spread his disco doctrine.

Rave-olutionary, Justice are not, but Gaspard Augé and Xavier de Rosnay—mere schoolboys when *Homework*, by obvious forefathers Daft Punk, landed in 1997—are worthy heirs to the dance throne.

Balancing a love of heavy-rock stylings, horror soundtracks, and the fantastically kitsch, *Cross* packs a thundering punch. A punch that even without 2006's glorious floorfiller "We Are Your Friends," with Simian in its throng, remains an astounding debut.

Closest musically to "We Are Your Friends" is the single "D.A.N.C.E.," which—with its lisping playground chants, funk throbs, and nod to jolly disco romper Cassius—is pure musical ambrosia. Likewise, "Tthhee Ppaarrttyy," with upcoming Ed Banger label mate Uffie—a kind of dispassionate M.I.A.—weaves crunksters Three 6 Mafia's "Stay Fly" into a fabric of paced electro threads, warming up the ears for the furious synth rush of "DVNO," which claps and soars wondrously.

Furthest from these jollities is "Stress," which forces ears down a wind tunnel where elastic Beethoven strings buzz, beats jerk, and primeval wails stab, leaving the impression that a musical revolution is being made in between your gray matter.

It is apt then, that a blaring neon crucifix should adorn the cover of *Cross*, suggesting a dance resurrection and imminent musical renaissance. Cross? Daft Punk should be livid. They are only *Human After All*. **KBo**

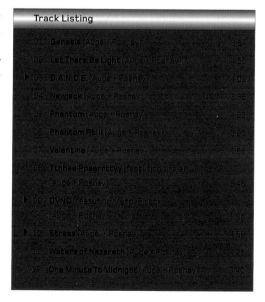

Track Listing

01. Genesis (Augé • Rosnay)   3:54
02. Let There Be Light (Augé • Rosnay)   4:58
03. D.A.N.C.E. (Augé • Rosnay)   4:02
04. Newjack (Augé • Rosnay)   3:36
05. Phantom (Augé • Rosnay)   4:22
06. Phantom Pt. II (Augé • Rosnay)   3:20
07. Valentine (Augé • Rosnay)   2:56
08. Tthhee Ppaarrttyy (featuring Uffie)
    (Augé • Rosnay)   3:46
09. DVNO (featuring Mehdi Pinson)
    (Augé • Rosnay)   3:56
10. Stress (Augé • Rosnay)   4:58
11. Waters of Nazareth (Augé • Rosnay)   5:25
12. One Minute To Midnight (Augé • Rosnay)   3:40

Klaxons | Myths Of The Near Future (2007)

Label | Polydor
Producer | James Ford
Art Direction | Klaxons
Nationality | UK
Running Time | 53:35

A union is a beautiful thing and in 2007, when indie was a stubborn shoegazer and dance an excitable whistle blower, a London three-piece saw their potential as partners and introduced them. They were not the first to do so, but this time the musical planets aligned.

That band was Klaxons. Tongue firmly in cheek and bored with ready labels, they spawned their own genre—"new rave"—which professed to be a cocktail of nu-metal guitars, indie credibility, and dance accessories.

Preceded by this reputation as self-confessed "new rave" preachers, Klaxons took listeners by surprise with their Mercury Prize-winning debut *Myths Of The Near Future*, which—bar a poorly executed Grace cover, the odd honk of a rave alarm, and a lonely yelp of "DJ!"—remained at heart a pure pop procession.

Happily this pop overshadowed the gimmicks and fourth single "Golden Skans"—all melodic hums and radio-friendly hooks—drew favorable comparisons with a happy Hard-Fi. "Magick" is a loveable mess of distorted guitars and quick key changes. "Atlantis To Interzone" is pop at its best: irreverent, fun, and infectious. And "Totem On The Timeline" and "As Above, So Below" are chorus-chanting bursts of escalating guitar heaven.

Forget the rave new world folklore surrounding the band and take no notice of the cover—a mish-mash musical mosaic hinting at their supposed splicing of genres. *Myths Of The Near Future* is just pop repackaged but, frankly, this kind of repackaging has simply never sounded better. **KBo**

"We're all into pop music."

Simon Taylor-Davis, 2007

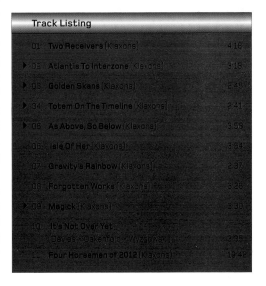

Track Listing	
01 Two Receivers (Klaxons)	4:18
▶ 02 Atlantis To Interzone (Klaxons)	3:19
▶ 03 Golden Skans (Klaxons)	2:45
▶ 04 Totem On The Timeline (Klaxons)	2:41
▶ 05 As Above, So Below (Klaxons)	3:59
06 Isle Of Her (Klaxons)	3:54
07 Gravity's Rainbow (Klaxons)	2:37
08 Forgotten Works (Klaxons)	3:26
▶ 09 Magick (Klaxons)	3:30
10 It's Not Over Yet (Daviss · Oakenfold · Wyzgowski)	3:35
11 Four Horsemen of 2012 (Klaxons)	19:42

Artist Index

General Index

Picture Credits

Album cover artwork supplied by Redferns Picture Library

Corbis
p941

Getty Images
p25, p49, p55, p67, p71, p101, p149, p211, p237, p277, p285, p309, p361, p395, p657, p687, p707, p853, p893

Redferns Picture Library p23, p29, p39, p43, p61, p65, p77, p83, p89, p95, p105, p111, p117, p123, p139, p151, p171, p175, p179, p187, p191, p203, p207, p215, p219, p225, p229, p233, p245, p253, p259, p265, p269, p273, p291, p313, p329, p341, p349, p365, p369, p379, p383, p391, p399, p403, p413, p423, p429, p433, p447, p453, p459, p465, p471, p489, p493, p507, p513, p521, p529, p533, p553, p557, p561, p571, p575, p583, p591, p605, p619, p637, p641, p645, p753, p663, p667, p677, p713, p719, p737, p741, p745, p749, p763, p767, p771, p777, p783, p793, p807, p819, p827, p831, p839, p843, p865, p877, p897, p901, p.929

Rex Features
p281, p303, p497, p501, p525, p537, p547, p611, p703, p727, p759, p789, p812, p889, p923

pp632–633
Courtesy of Denon, Japan's oldest hi-fi company, founded in 1910

pp858–859
Courtesy of Apple

Additional photography by:

Trevor Clifford
pp46–47

Chris Mattison
pp20–21

David Matson
pp448–449

Phil Wilkins
pp192–193

Acknowledgments

The publisher would like to give special thanks to Debbie Harry, to Scumeck Sabottka at Harm's Way Management, to Jason Day at Virgin Music, and to Dede Millar and Julian Ridgway at Redferns Picture Library

We would also like to express our gratitude for the assistance of the following:

Alba plc
Kenneth Burns
Terry Burrows
Tim Ferguson Hill
David Hutcheon
Elliott Jack
Ken Jones
Robert Martin
Jonathan More
Shazia Nizam
Charles Olivier
Edmund Olivier
Charlotte Walker Olivier
Rita Ray
David Roberts
Mick Rock
Charlie Rose
Sennheiser Germany/UK
Alison Taylor
Sandro Tosoni
Amy Townsend
The Vinyl Resting Place

Robert Dimery would like to give special thanks to:

Manish Agarwal
John Lewis
Bruno MacDonald
Selectadisc, London
Vinyl Vault, Cheltenham